Lecture Notes in Computer Science 16554

Founding Editors

Gerhard Goos
Juris Hartmanis

Shi Bai · Edoardo Persichetti

Editors

Public-Key Cryptography – PKC 2026

29th IACR International Conference
on Practice and Theory of Public-Key Cryptography
West Palm Beach, FL, USA, May 25–28, 2026
Proceedings, Part IV

 Springer

Editors
Shi Bai (iD)
Shanghai Jiao Tong University
Shanghai, China

Edoardo Persichetti (iD)
Florida Atlantic University
Boca Raton, FL, USA

ISSN 0302-9743 ISSN 1611-3349 (electronic)
Lecture Notes in Computer Science
ISBN 978-3-032-26739-9 ISBN 978-3-032-26740-5 (eBook)
https://doi.org/10.1007/978-3-032-26740-5

This Springer imprint is published by the registered company Springer Nature Switzerland AG
The registered company address is: Gewerbestrasse 11, 6330 Cham, Switzerland

If disposing of this product, please recycle the paper.

Preface

The 29th International Conference on Practice and Theory of Public-Key Cryptography (PKC 2026) was held in West Palm Beach, Florida, USA, from May 25 to 28, 2026. The conference was sponsored by the International Association for Cryptologic Research (IACR) and serves as the IACR's flagship conference dedicated specifically to public-key cryptography.

PKC 2026 brought together a vibrant international community of cryptography researchers, with authors representing a wide range of countries. The conference solicited original research papers on all aspects of public-key cryptography. This year, we particularly welcomed submissions on the theme "Mathematics of Public-Key Cryptography".

The conference received 259 submissions, which were reviewed by a program committee of 78 experts, including four area chairs, together with 253 external reviewers. The selection process took about two months for independent reviewing and another two months for discussion. During the discussion phase, the program chairs facilitated interactions between authors and reviewers by contacting authors to address critical questions that arose, ensuring informed decision-making. In the end, the program committee selected 65 papers for inclusion in PKC 2026. Papers were reviewed in the usual double-blind manner, with an average of about three reviews per paper. Program committee members were limited to three submissions (or four if all were coauthored with students), and their submissions were subject to additional scrutiny. The two program chairs were not permitted to submit papers.

The Best Paper Award was presented to "SQIsign with Fixed-Precision Integer Arithmetic" by Won Kim, Jeonghwan Lee, Hyeonhak Kim, and Changmin Lee.

The Test of Time Award Committee, consisting of Shi Bai, Tung Chou, Jiaxin Pan, Edoardo Persichetti, and Moti Yung, selected the recipient of the PKC 2026 Test of Time Award.

PKC is a remarkable undertaking, and it is made possible only through the hard work and significant contributions of many individuals:

- We would like to thank Veronika Kuchta and Francesco Sica (Florida Atlantic University, USA) for making the general arrangements such a success.
- We would like to express our sincere gratitude to all the authors for their trust in us, for choosing PKC 2026 as a forum for presenting their research, and for giving us the opportunity to consider their work. The quality, diversity, and creativity of their submissions were essential to shaping the program and to making PKC 2026 a vibrant and stimulating conference.
- We also thank the Program Committee, external reviewers, session chairs, invited speaker, and presenters for their tremendous work and contributions to the success of PKC 2026.

– Special thanks to the area chairs: Paulo Barreto, Mark Manulis, Pratyay Mukherjee, and Jean-Pierre Tillich. Their expertise and sound judgment were critical in helping us reach good decisions.

  We hope you enjoyed the conference and the warm welcome at PKC 2026.

May 2026   Shi Bai
                                                           Edoardo Persichetti

Organization

General Chairs

Veronika Kuchta — Florida Atlantic University, USA
Francesco Sica — Florida Atlantic University, USA

Program Committee Chairs

Shi Bai — Shanghai Jiao Tong University, China
Edoardo Persichetti — Florida Atlantic University, USA

Steering Committee

Masayuki Abe	NTT, Japan
Shi Bai	Shanghai Jiao Tong University, China
Jung Hee Cheon	Seoul National University, South Korea
Tung Chou	Academia Sinica, Taiwan
Yvo Desmedt	University of Texas at Dallas, USA
Goichiro Hanaoka (Chair)	National Institute of Advanced Industrial Science and Technology, Japan
Tibor Jager	University of Wuppertal, Germany
Aggelos Kiayias	University of Edinburgh and IOG, UK
Tanja Lange	Eindhoven University of Technology, the Netherlands
Jiaxin Pan	University of Kassel, Germany
Edoardo Persichetti	Florida Atlantic University, USA
Duong Hieu Phan	Télécom Paris, Institut Polytechnique de Paris, France
Yu Yu	Shanghai Jiao Tong University, China
Moti Yung (Secretary)	Google LLC and Columbia University, USA
Yuliang Zheng	University of Alabama at Birmingham, USA

Program Committee

Sarah Arpin	Virginia Tech, USA
Gennaro Avitabile	IMDEA Software Institute, Spain
Gustavo Banegas	Inria, France
Razvan Barbulescu	University of Bordeaux, France
Paulo Barreto	University of Washington Tacoma, USA
Andrea Basso	IBM Research Europe, Switzerland
Lubjana Beshaj	West Point Military Academy, USA
Jean-François Biasse	University of South Florida, USA
Pierre Briaud	Simula Research Lab, Norway
Daniel Cabarcas	Universidad Nacional de Colombia, Colombia
Sofía Celi	Brave, Portugal
Yanbo Chen	University of Ottawa, Canada
Jie Chen	Wuhan University, China
Mingjie Chen	KU Leuven, Belgium
Giulio Codogni	University of Rome Tor Vergata, Italy
Bernardo David	IT University of Copenhagen, Denmark
Jintai Ding	Xi'an Jiaotong-Liverpool University, China
Dung Hoang Duong	University of Wollongong, Australia
Muhammed Esgin	Monash University, Australia
Simona Etinski	Centrum Wiskunde & Informatica, the Netherlands
Luca De Feo	IBM Research Europe, Switzerland
Tako Boris Fouotsa	University of Manchester, UK
Daniele Friolo	Sapienza University of Rome, Italy
Satrajit Ghosh	Indian Institute of Technology Kharagpur, India
Valerie Gilchrist	Université Libre de Bruxelles, Belgium
Calvin Abou Haidar	NTT Social Informatics Laboratories, Japan
Lucjan Hanzlik	CISPA, Germany
Kristina Hostáková	ETH Zurich, Switzerland
Kathrin Hövelmanns	Eindhoven University of Technology, the Netherlands
Andreas Hülsing	Eindhoven University of Technology & SandboxAQ, the Netherlands
Tibor Jager	University of Wuppertal, Germany
Octavio Pérez Kempner	NTT Social Informatics Laboratories, Japan
Miran Kim	Hanyang University, South Korea
Elena Kirshanova	Technology Innovation Institute, United Arab Emirates
Chelsea Komlo	University of Waterloo, Canada

Péter Kutas	Eötvös Loránd University, Hungary & University of Birmingham, UK
Jason LeGrow	Virginia Tech, USA
Changmin Lee	Korea University, South Korea
Damien Ligier	DESILO, South Korea
Feng-Hao Liu	Washington State University, USA
Zeyu Liu	Yale University, USA
Patrick Longa	Microsoft Research, USA
Julian Loss	Ruhr University Bochum, Germany
Johanna Loyer	Inria, France
Julio López	University of Campinas, Brazil
Mark Manulis	University of the Bundeswehr, Germany
Alexander May	Ruhr University Bochum, Germany
Kirill Morozov	University of North Texas, USA
Pratyay Mukherjee	Hashgraph, India
Jiaxin Pan	University of Kassel, Germany
Yanbin Pan	Academy of Mathematics and Systems Science, China
Robi Pedersen	Technical University of Denmark, Denmark
Geovandro Pereira	LG Electronics, USA
Federico Pintore	University of Trento, Italy
Longjiang Qu	National University of Defense Technology, China
Matthieu Rivain	CryptoExperts, France
Simona Samardjiska	Radboud University, the Netherlands
Paolo Santini	Marche Polytechnic University, Italy
Santanu Sarkar	Indian Institute of Technology Madras, India
Palash Sarkar	Indian Statistical Institute, Kolkata, India
Luisa Siniscalchi	Technical University of Denmark, Denmark
Yongsoo Song	Seoul National University, South Korea
Fang Song	Portland State University, USA
Akira Takahashi	JPMorgan, USA
Jean-Pierre Tillich	Inria, France
Fernando Virdia	King's College London, UK
Zhedong Wang	Shanghai Jiao Tong University, China
Violetta Weger	Technical University of Munich, Germany
Wessel van Woerden	PQShield, UK
David Wu	University of Texas at Austin, USA
Keita Xagawa	Technology Innovation Institute, United Arab Emirates
Yu Yu	Shanghai Jiao Tong University, China
Yang Yu	Tsinghua University, China

Runzhi Zeng	University of Kassel, Germany
Fangguo Zhang	Sun Yat-sen University, China
Zhenfeng Zhang	Chinese Academy of Sciences, China
Hong-Sheng Zhou	Virginia Commonwealth University, USA
Paul Zimmermann	Inria, France

Additional Reviewers

Ittai Abraham	Clemence Chevignard
Hamza Abusalah	Jesus Chi-Domínguez
Anasuya Acharya	Ilaria Chillotti
Saed Alsayigh	Michele Ciampi
Zhiyuan An	Simone Colombo
Luong Duc Anh	Craig Costello
Daniel Augot	Geoffroy Couteau
Liljana Babinkostova	Dipayan Das
Renas Bacho	Pratish Datta
John Baena	Nicolas David
Karim Baghery	Angelo De Caro
David Balbás	Thomas Debris-Alazard
Jiawei Bao	Hugo Delavenne
Mohammed Barhoush	Giovanni Deligios
James Bartusek	Pierpaolo Della Monica
Michele Battagliola	David Dervishi
Marvin Beckmann	Julien Devevey
Nidhish Bhimrajka	Ben Dowling
Nina Bindel	Qiuyan Du
Jan Bormet	Samed Düzlü
Vincenzo Botta	Friedrich Eisenbrand
Pedro Branco	Youssef El Housni
Dung Bui	Gökberk Erdogan
Benedikt Bünz	Jonathan Eriksen
Roberto Cabral	Daniel Escudero
André Chailloux	Thomas Espitau
Suvradip Chakraborty	Sebastian Faller
Jeff Champion	Yansong Feng
Huanhuan Chen	Andrea Flamini
Qian Chen	Scott Fluhrer

Mariana Gama
Andrea Gangemi
Albert Garreta
Decio Gazzoni
Robin Geelen
Matthias Geihs
Tyler Genao
Ashrujit Ghoshal
Sara Giammusso
Emanuele Giunta
Lewis Glabush
Boru Gong
Junqing Gong
Scott Griffy
Xiaojie Guo
Guillaume Hanrot
Keitaro Hashimoto
Raphael Heitjohann
Hans Heum
Minki Hhan
Felicitas Hoermann
Clement Hoffmann
Ga Hee Hong
Annamaria Iezzi
Hansraj Jangir
Chanho Jeon
Sohyun Jeon
Mahavir Jhawar
Haoxiang Jin
Antoine Joux
Abul Kalam
Chethan Kamath
Simon Holmgaard Kamp
Jiayi Kang
Taehun Kang
Alexander Karenin
Marcel Keller
Xuan Thanh Khuc
Hyeonhak Kim
Jongmin Kim
Won Kim
Lisa Kohl
Markulf Kohlweiss
Mikhail Kudinov
Hyunji Kwag

Qiqi Lai
Yongkang Lang
Mario Larangeira
Jun Bo Lau
Abel Laval
Dania Lazzarini
Hyeonbum Lee
Mira Lee
Yesol Lee
Chen Li
Minzhang Li
Yu Li
Bei Liang
Chuanwei Lin
Kaizhan Lin
Yini Lin
Yunhao Ling
Charles Liu
Jiahui Liu
Xiangyu Liu
Zhen Liu
George Lu
Yuan Lu
Hengyi Luo
Joseph Macula
William Mahaney
Mary Maller
Lola Mallordy
Mriganka Mandal
Siva Maradana
Varun Maram
Laurane Marco
Takahiro Matsuda
Krystal Maughan
Matthias Meijers
Nikolas Melissaris
Fei Meng
Pierre Meyer
Francesco Migliaro
Omid Mir
Sara Montanari
Eduardo Morais
Tomoki Moriya
Travis Morrison
Marzio Mula

Jade Nardi
Tom Neuschulten
Tran Ngo
Ky Nguyen
Guilhem Niot
Charles Olivier-Anclin
Eli Orvis
Hussien Othman
Nikhil Pappu
Jeongeun Park
Hilder Pereira
Lam Pham
Rafael del Pino
Erik Pohle
Anmoal Porwal
Thomas Prest
Yue Qin
Tian Qiu
Rahul Rachuri
Arka Rai Choudhuri
Lars Ran
Simon Rastikian
Andrea Reale
Krijn Reijnders
Omar Renawi
Filip Richter
Doreen Riepel
Guilherme Rito
Stefan Ritterhoff
Maxime Roméas
Michael Rosenberg
Luis Ruiz-Lopez
Matteo Salvino
Swagata Sasmal
Rahul Satish
Hugo Sauerbier Couvee
Sina Schaeffler
Michael Schaller
Sven Schäge
Gabrielle Sculllard
Melvin Seitner
István András Seres
Yannick Seurin
Kecheng Shi
Shumin Si

Daniel Slamanig
Freeman Slaughter
Enrico Sorbera
Sebastian Spindler
Katherine Stange
Damien Stehlé
Shifeng Sun
Hyewon Sung
Erkan Tairi
Gang Tang
Haibo Tian
Marcel Tiepelt
Monika Trimoska
Joost van der Laan
Daan van Gent
Barry Van Leeuwen
Hernán Vanegas
Marloes Venema
Javier Verbel
Damien Vergnaud
Viktoria Villanyi
Mikhail Volkov
Benedikt Wagner
Alexandre Wallet
Xicheng Wan
Hongxiao Wang
Wei Wang
Weijie Wang
Xiao Wang
Yi Wang
Yunhao Wang
Yuntao Wang
Yuyu Wang
Weiqiang Wen
Stella Wohnig
Ivy K. Y. Woo
Han Xia
Binwu Xiang
Jun Xu
Jiahao Xuan
Anshu Yadav
Saikumar Yadugiri
Jiayun Yan
Kang Yang
Xinrui Yang

Contents

Advanced Encryption and Privacy

Homomorphic and Searchable Encryption

Protocols and Real-World Security

Advanced Encryption and Privacy

DAKE: Bandwidth-Efficient (U)AKE from Double-KEM

Hugo Beguinet[1], Céline Chevalier[2,3], Guirec Lebrun[2,5],
Thomas Legavre[1,4,5(✉)], Thomas Ricosset[1(✉)], Maxime Roméas[5],
and Éric Sageloli[1,2(✉)]

[1] Thales, Gennevilliers, France
`thomas.ricosset@thalesgroup.com`
[2] DIENS, École normale supérieure, CNRS, PSL University, Inria, Paris, France
`eric.sageloli@protonmail.com`
[3] CRED, Paris-Panthéon-Assas University, Paris, France
[4] Sorbonne Université, CNRS, LIP6, Paris, France
`thomas.legavre@lip6.fr`
[5] ANSSI, Paris, France

Abstract. Bandwidth remains a major bottleneck in post-quantum cryptography, particularly for authenticated key exchange (AKE) protocols. In this work, we present DAKE, a bandwidth-efficient AKE framework built from double-KEM constructions. DAKE comes in two main versions achieving, respectively, weak and full perfect forward secrecy, as well as explicit authentication. It further admits two variants: a unilateral version, and another where a signature scheme replaces a KEM. They are proven secure in the standard model under $\mathrm{eCK^w}$ and eCK-PFS, two strong variants of the extended Canetti–Krawczyk framework.

DAKE employs a double-KEM, a primitive that encapsulates a single key under two public keys simultaneously. Such constructions can achieve smaller encapsulation sizes than two independent KEM encapsulations, offering a significant bandwidth advantage.

To facilitate the design of double-KEMs compatible with DAKE, we introduce a chosen-key Fujisaki–Okamoto (CK-FO) transform proven in the QROM, which upgrades IND-CPA double-PKEs to IND-CCA double-KEMs while ensuring the one-sided chosen-key security required by DAKE.

As a concrete instantiation, we propose Maul, a compact double-KEM derived from ML-KEM under the Hint-MLWE assumption. Maul reuses ciphertext components to cut encapsulation size by up to 42% compared to two parallel ML-KEMs. When instantiated with Maul, DAKE achieves overall communication reductions of about 16% (mutual authentication) and 20% (unilateral), outperforming both the double-KEM AKE of Xue *et al.* (ASIACRYPT 2018) and standard ML-KEM-based AKEs.

Keywords: Post-quantum (U)AKE · Double-KEM · eCK · ML-KEM

© International Association for Cryptologic Research 2026
S. Bai and E. Persichetti (Eds.): PKC 2026, LNCS 16554, pp. 3–36, 2026.
https://doi.org/10.1007/978-3-032-26740-5_1

1   Introduction

In order to face the looming threat of large-scale quantum computers against public-key cryptography, the U.S. National Institute of Standards and Technology (NIST) launched in 2016 a standardization process to select post-quantum encryption and signature primitives resistant to quantum attacks. In particular, key encapsulation mechanisms (KEMs) were chosen to ensure the encryption functionality. KEMs serve as key exchange primitives: a sender uses an encapsulation algorithm to produce a shared secret and a ciphertext, which is then sent to the recipient. The recipient runs a decapsulation algorithm to recover the same shared secret, enabling secure communication. In mid-2022, NIST announced the first post-quantum standards: Kyber/ML-KEM [40] for key encapsulation, and Dilithium/ML-DSA [41], Falcon/FN-DSA [20], and SPHINCS$^+$/SLH-DSA [42] for digital signatures. More recently, in 2025, NIST also selected HQC [23]—a code-based KEM—as an additional standardized alternative to the lattice-based ML-KEM, in order to diversify the set of hardness assumptions.

Quantum Security Comes at a Cost. While post-quantum (PQ) primitives offer conjectured security against quantum-capable adversaries, they often impose large communication costs. For instance, ML-KEM-512 (128-bit security) has 800-byte public keys and 768-byte ciphertexts, compared to the 32-byte keys and ciphertexts of classical Curve25519 DH-KEM [3]. PQ signatures are even larger, often several kilobytes, which makes signature-based authenticated key exchange (AKE) particularly expensive.

Signature-Free AKEs. To mitigate this overhead, signature-free AKEs rely on KEMs or public-key encryptions (PKEs) for both key exchange and authentication. Early constructions stem from [8] and were later strengthened to the CK+ model in [21].[1] More recent works [26,35] improved computational efficiency by employing PKEs instead of KEMs, applying the Fujisaki–Okamoto transform at the protocol level. Yet, communication costs remain essentially unchanged. These designs have inspired practical adaptations, including post-quantum WireGuard [27] and KEMTLS [38], now under IETF standardization [43]. Related work [9] explores modular AKEs with various authentication mechanisms, including KEM-based ones, and proves their security in the CK+ model.

From Two KEMs to a Double-KEM. Even in the unilaterally authenticated setting, achieving (weak) perfect forward secrecy requires two KEMs—one for key agreement and another for authentication. Greater efficiency can be achieved through a dedicated primitive, the *double-KEM* [44], which replaces two independent KEMs with a single mechanism encapsulating under two public keys simultaneously. This design offers better compactness than parallel composition and

---

[1] [8] proved security in the CK model [10], while [21] extended this to CK+ [31], capturing weak forward secrecy (wFS) and maximal exposure attacks (MEX).

underlies the double-KEM-based AKE of [44], proven secure in the random oracle model (ROM) and in the standard model under the [IND-CK-CCA, IND-CK-CPA] assumption. The same work introduces Twin-Kyber, a size-optimized double-KEM derived from ML-KEM/Kyber [7, 40], proven [IND-CK-CCA, IND-CK-CCA]-secure in the ROM. Notably, Twin-Kyber is obtained by applying a Fujisaki–Okamoto transformation to a [IND-CK-CPA, IND-CK-CPA]-secure double-key double-message PKE.

Security notions for double-KEMs extend those of traditional KEMs. The standard notions of IND-CPA and IND-CCA are generalized to one-sided variants such as [IND-CPA, -] and [IND-CCA, -], where the adversary is given the right secret key $\mathsf{sk_R}$ during the security game. In this setting, the encapsulated key k must remain secret even if $\mathsf{sk_R}$ is known. Stronger notions, denoted [IND-CK-CPA, -] and [IND-CK-CCA, -], additionally allow the adversary to specify the right public key $\mathsf{pk_R}$ used during encapsulation.[2] Analogous notions are defined for the right side, denoted [- , IND-CK-CPA] and [- , IND-CK-CCA], where the adversary chooses the left public key $\mathsf{pk_L}$. These can also be extended to the double-key, double-message public-key encryption (2K2M-PKE) setting.

1.1   Our Contributions

We introduce DAKE, DAKE$^\sigma$, and DUAKE, three bandwidth-efficient AKE protocols built from [IND-CK-CCA, IND-CCA] double-KEMs. The underlying double-KEM can be instantiated either using two standard IND-CCA KEMs or more compact double-KEM constructions. Each protocol comes in a two-message version achieving weak perfect forward secrecy (wPFS) and a three-message version achieving full PFS, both proven secure in the standard model under the strong eCK$^\mathsf{w}$ and eCK-PFS variants [13] of the eCK model [33] respectively. These variants capture attack scenarios that are not covered by other generic post-quantum (U)AKEs analyzed in the literature [7, 22, 26, 38].

DAKE provides mutual authentication by combining a double-KEM with a standard KEM, where the double-KEM ensures initiator authentication, while the standard KEM ensures responder authentication. Responder authentication can alternatively be achieved using a signature scheme, yielding the variant DAKE$^\sigma$. We also propose DUAKE, a unilaterally authenticated variant in which only the initiator is authenticated.

Beyond key secrecy, we analyze additional properties, including *inverse match soundness*—which prevents *unknown key-share* (UKS) attacks [6]—and *explicit authentication*—which ensures that any completed session has a unique honest partner. Among the generic post-quantum (U)AKEs in the literature, the only one we are aware of that analyzes explicit authentication is [38].

To ease the construction of double-KEMs compatible with DAKE and its variants, we introduce a chosen-key Fujisaki–Okamoto (CK-FO) transform tailored to 2K2M-PKEs. Our transform is proven secure in the quantum random oracle

---

[2] These stronger notions are sometimes directly referred to as [IND-CPA, -] and [IND-CCA, -] in the literature, e.g., in [44].

model (QROM), achieving CCA security while additionally providing chosen-key security for the left encapsulation, thereby yielding a [IND-CK-CCA, IND-CCA] double-KEM, the central ingredient of DAKE. To the best of our knowledge, this is the first extension of the FO paradigm to this setting, enabling constructions of double-KEMs from a wide class of schemes that lack chosen-key security.

As a concrete instantiation, we propose Maul, a compact lattice-based double-KEM derived from Kyber/ML-KEM. Maul is obtained by applying our CK-FO transform to $\mathsf{Maul_{PKE}}$, a double-key double-message PKE built by factoring the large polynomial vector $\mathbf{u}$ from Kyber ciphertexts, reducing ciphertext size by up to 42% compared with two parallel ML-KEM instances. We prove $\mathsf{Maul_{PKE}}$ [IND-CPA, IND-CPA]-secure under MLWE and hint-MLWE [30], and its CK-FO transformation yields Maul, a compact [IND-CK-CCA, IND-CCA] double-KEM. Instantiating DAKE with Maul achieves roughly 20% global communication savings over the double-KEM-based AKE of Xue et al. [44] and over classical ML-KEM-based AKEs, highlighting the practical advantages of tightly integrated double-KEM designs.

1.2   Technical Overview

Our authenticated key exchange protocol, denoted DAKE (for <u>D</u>ouble-KEM-based <u>AKE</u>), together with its variants DAKE^σ and DUAKE, forms a versatile family of AKE constructions built upon the notion of a double-KEM.

A compact double-KEM enables, at essentially the cost of a single standard KEM encapsulation, the derivation of a shared key that depends on two distinct public keys—an operation that would otherwise require two separate encapsulations. We provide such a construction with Maul, our double-KEM variant of ML-KEM constructed via our CK-FO transform. DAKE and its variants exploit this property to achieve a substantial reduction in bandwidth compared to conventional (U)AKEs.

AKE from Double-KEM. The main protocol, DAKE, provides mutual authentication by combining a double-KEM with a standard KEM, as specified in Fig. 1, where the KEM ensures authentication of the responder. DAKE has two variants: $\mathsf{DAKE_2}$, a two-message protocol achieving weak Perfect Forward Secrecy (wPFS), and $\mathsf{DAKE_3}$, a three-message protocol achieving full PFS. The PFS ensures that a session key remains secure even if the long-term secrets used in its derivation are compromised after the session completes, wPFS is discussed below.

All our protocols achieve key secrecy in the standard model: $\mathsf{DAKE_2}$ is proven secure in the $\mathsf{eCK^w}$ model, and $\mathsf{DAKE_3}$ in the eCK-PFS model. These state-of-the-art security models refine the classical eCK model by more precisely capturing the effects of both passive and active adversarial behavior. In most other models, weak PFS requires that a session key remains secure even if the long-term secrets used in its derivation are compromised, under the additional assumptions that the adversary neither (1) modifies messages sent by the session nor

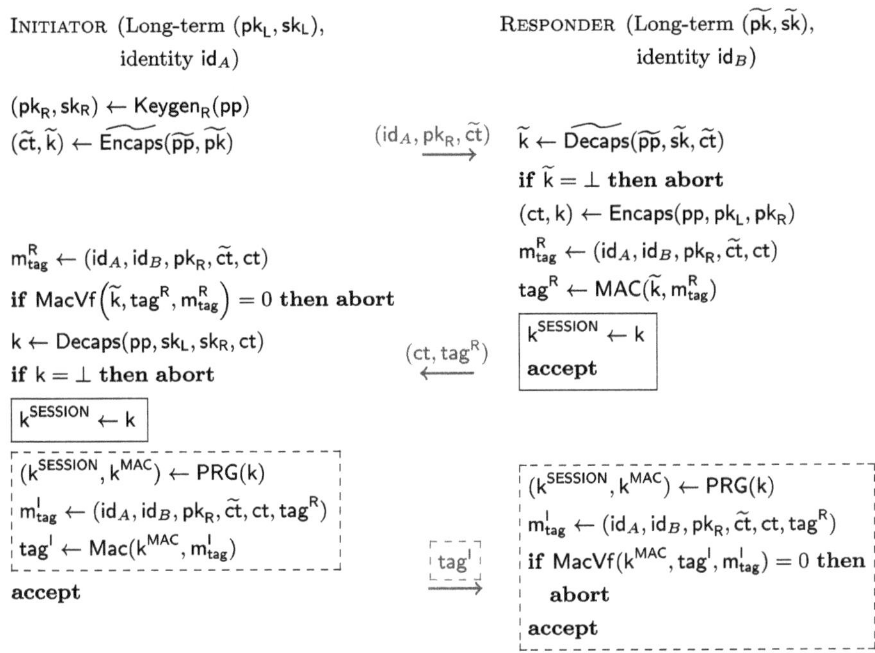

Fig. 1. The DAKE protocol. Public parameters are (1) $(\mathsf{pp}, \widetilde{\mathsf{pp}})$ with $\mathsf{pp} \leftarrow \mathsf{Setup}()$ and $\widetilde{\mathsf{pp}} \leftarrow \widetilde{\mathsf{Setup}}()$, (2) all party identities, and (3) a dictionary mapping identities to public keys. The initiator chooses its peer before sending the first message. DAKE_2 (*resp.* DAKE_3) is obtained by removing the dotted (*resp.* solid) boxes.

(2) forges or modifies messages received by the session. In contrast, $\mathsf{eCK}^{\mathsf{w}}$ and eCK-PFS ensure key secrecy even if the adversary modifies the messages sent by the session, as long as the received messages remain authentic (*i.e.*, neither forged nor modified). These refinements are enabled by the introduction of the *origin session* notion.

Responder authentication can be achieved either via an additional standard KEM—as in the baseline DAKE, which typically minimizes overall bandwidth— or via a signature scheme, yielding the variant DAKE^{σ} (see full version [5], Appendix D.1). The latter is especially relevant when the initiator's public key is unknown to the responder and therefore the initiator must attach a certificate to its first message. Although replacing a KEM ciphertext with a signature usually increases total communication, it reduces the initiator's first-message size, balancing communication costs when certificates or other extra data must be sent upfront.

Unilaterally authenticated AKEs (UAKEs), in which only one party is authenticated, have been studied in several contexts such as Tor and TLS [15, 19, 39][24, 28, 32, 38]. DUAKE, specified in Fig. 2, is our unilateral variant of DAKE, tailored for such settings. To analyze its security, we introduce the $\mathsf{u\text{-}eCK}^{\mathsf{w}}$ and

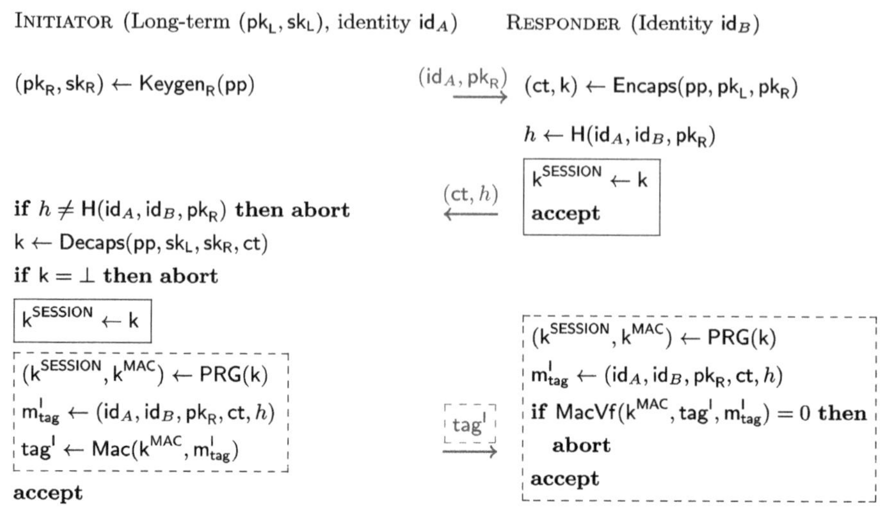

Fig. 2. The DUAKE protocol. Public parameters are (1) pp $\leftarrow$ Setup(), (2) all party identities, and (3) a dictionary mapping initiators to their public keys. The initiator chooses its peer before sending the first message. DUAKE_2 (*resp.* DUAKE_3) is obtained by removing the dotted (*resp.* solid) boxes.

u-eCK-PFS models—unilateral adaptations of the eCK^w and eCK-PFS frameworks. Essentially, $\mathsf{u\text{-}eCK}^\mathsf{w}$ and u-eCK-PFS remove from eCK^w and eCK-PFS the attack scenarios that cannot be prevented by a unilateral protocol (for instance, attacks where an active adversary impersonates a party that possesses no long-term keys). While several security models for UAKE have been proposed (*e.g.*, [24] presents a unilateral extension of the eCK model), our models strengthen these definitions by incorporating the refinements introduced in eCK^w and eCK-PFS, thereby capturing a broader range of attack scenarios. Practical use cases of DUAKE are discussed in more detail in full version, Appendix I.

The security models we consider define a protocol as secure if it satisfies two properties, called *key secrecy* and *match soundness*. The key secrecy guarantees offer resistance to *maximal exposure* (MEX), *key-compromise impersonation* (KCI) attacks, and *unknown key-share* (UKS) attacks. They also imply a form of *implicit authentication* by ensuring that the session key remains secret under active attacks whenever the peer of the session is not corrupted (in which case the peer is said to be implicitly authenticated)[3]. More precisely, both the initiator and responder are implicitly authenticated in $\mathsf{DAKE}_2, \mathsf{DAKE}_3, \mathsf{DAKE}_2^\sigma$ and DAKE_3^σ, whereas only the initiator benefits from implicit authentication in $\mathsf{DUAKE}_2, \mathsf{DUAKE}_3$. The *match soundness* property is linked to the modeling used by the security model, and is described in Sect. 3.1.

---

[3] Some additional conditions that would trivially reveal the session key to the adversary are omitted here for simplicity.

Table 1. Security properties of our AKE protocols. An asterisk ($\checkmark^*$) indicates that the corresponding property can be achieved through a minor modification that does not affect the exchanged messages. See Sect. 3.3 for details on how inverse-match soundness can be obtained using an additional KDF.

Protocol	PFS	wPFS	(Match Snd., Inv. Match)	Init-Explicit Authent.	Resp-Explicit Authent.
DAKE_2	$\times$	$\checkmark$	$(\checkmark, \checkmark^*)$	$\times$	$\checkmark$
DAKE_3	$\checkmark$	$\checkmark$	$(\checkmark, \checkmark^*)$	$\checkmark$	$\checkmark$
DAKE_2^{σ}	$\times$	$\checkmark$	$(\checkmark, \checkmark^*)$	$\times$	$\checkmark$
DAKE_3^{σ}	$\checkmark$	$\checkmark$	$(\checkmark, \checkmark^*)$	$\checkmark$	$\checkmark$
DUAKE_2	$\times$	$\checkmark$	$(\checkmark, \checkmark^*)$	$\times$	$\times$
DUAKE_3	$\checkmark$	$\checkmark$	$(\checkmark, \checkmark^*)$	$\checkmark$	$\times$

To capture security across a broad range of settings, we further study several additional properties for all our AKE protocols, with Table 1 summarizing which ones are achieved by the different variants of DAKE. Specifically, we consider *inverse match soundness* (which prevents UKS attacks under a broader range of adversarial behaviors than key secrecy alone), and *explicit authentication*. We refine the latter by distinguishing between Init-*explicit* and Resp-*explicit* authentication. In short, Init-explicit (resp. Resp-explicit) authentication ensures that if the peer of a responder session (resp. initiator session) is not corrupted (*i.e.*, its long-term secret key is unknown to the adversary) and this session has completed the protocol, then there exists an initiator (resp. responder) session that has honestly executed the protocol with it. We show that Init-explicit authentication is provided by $\mathsf{DAKE}_3, \mathsf{DAKE}_3^{\sigma}$ and DUAKE_3, while Resp-explicit authentication is ensured by $\mathsf{DAKE}_2, \mathsf{DAKE}_3, \mathsf{DAKE}_2^{\sigma}$ and DAKE_3^{σ}.

Chosen-Key FO Transform. Our Chosen-Key Fujisaki–Okamoto (CK-FO) transform enables the instantiation of DAKE and its variants from a broad class of underlying primitives by providing a generic method to transform a wide class of [IND-CPA, IND-CPA] double-key double-message PKE (2K2M-PKE) schemes into [IND-CK-CCA, IND-CCA] double-KEMs. The resulting construction guarantees chosen-key CCA security on one side and standard CCA security on the other— precisely the security properties required for instantiating DAKE and its variants. Although our concrete instantiation is lattice-based, the technique also paves the way for compact double-KEMs under other assumptions, such as code-based constructions inspired by HQC [23].

A central idea of the CK-FO transform is to restrict attention to a subclass of 2K2M-PKE constructions derived from two underlying PKEs, and to leverage not only the security of the combined scheme but also that of its constituents. The transform admits proofs of security in both the random oracle model (ROM) and the quantum random oracle model (QROM), the latter via semi-classical oracle techniques. Beyond its conceptual novelty, the CK-FO transform significantly broadens the design space: it enables double-KEMs to be instantiated from compact [IND-CPA, IND-CPA] 2K2M-PKEs that do not possess any chosen-key security.

Lattice-Based Compact Double-KEM. While DAKE, DAKE$^\sigma$, and DUAKE are generic constructions, their practical efficiency depends on the availability of compact double-KEMs. Prior work such as Twin-Kyber [44] demonstrated feasibility but left ample room for optimization. To validate our framework, we introduce Maul, a [IND-CK-CCA, IND-CCA] double-KEM derived from ML-KEM/Kyber, and use it to instantiate DAKE. By exploiting structural asymmetries in Kyber ciphertexts, Maul reduces ciphertext size by up to 42% compared to two parallel ML-KEMs, thereby minimizing message sizes in complete AKE handshakes. Table 2 compares Maul's ciphertext and public-key sizes with those of two parallel ML-KEMs and Twin-Kyber [44].

Table 2. Sizes (bytes) of the ciphers and public keys of our double-KEM Maul, compared to two parallel ML-KEM instances and to Twin-Kyber. Security levels follow the categories defined in the NIST PQC call for proposals (https://csrc.nist.gov/projects/post-quantum-cryptography/post-quantum-cryptography-standardization/call-for-proposals).

	Security Level	Maul (this work)	Twin-Kyber [44]	ML-KEM [40]
	1	896	–	1,536
Ciphertext	3	1,440	–	2,176
	5	1,856	2,464	3,136
	1	826	–	800
Public Key	3	1,240	–	1,184
	5	1,691	1,568	1,568

Maul results from applying the CK-FO transform to Maul$_{\mathsf{PKE}}$, a 2K2M-PKE that we now describe. At a high level, ML-KEM (Kyber) ciphertexts consist of two parts: a vector component $\mathbf{u}$ and a scalar component v, where $\mathbf{u}$ encodes ephemeral randomness and v encodes the message. These components are highly asymmetric in size; for instance, in ML-KEM-768, $\mathbf{u}$ occupies 950 bytes, while v is only 128 bytes. Maul$_{\mathsf{PKE}}$ exploits this imbalance by factoring the larger vector component $\mathbf{u}$, yielding ciphertexts of the form $(\mathbf{u}, v_1, v_2)$ that encrypt two messages while significantly reducing overall ciphertext size. A related construction was proposed in [29], though its security analysis was limited to a setting where the adversary is not given access to any secret key.

The security of $\mathsf{Maul}_{\mathsf{PKE}}$ is based on the Hint-MLWE assumption, a natural variant of MLWE in which the adversary receives a partial linear hint about the secret and error. To illustrate this, consider a simplified version of [IND-CPA, IND-CPA] $\mathsf{Maul}_{\mathsf{PKE}}$ encrypting two messages m_{L} and m_{R} as follows:

$$(\mathbf{u} = \mathbf{A}^{\mathsf{T}}\mathbf{s} + \mathbf{e},\ v_1 = \mathbf{t}_{\mathsf{L}}^{\mathsf{T}}\mathbf{s} + e_1 + \lceil q/2 \rceil m_{\mathsf{L}},\ v_2 = \mathbf{t}_{\mathsf{R}}^{\mathsf{T}}\mathbf{s} + e_2 + \lceil q/2 \rceil m_{\mathsf{R}}),$$

where $\mathbf{t}_{\mathsf{L}} = \mathbf{A}\mathbf{s}_{\mathsf{L}} + \mathbf{e}_{\mathsf{L}}$ and $\mathbf{t}_{\mathsf{R}} = \mathbf{A}\mathbf{s}_{\mathsf{R}} + \mathbf{e}_{\mathsf{R}}$ are public keys derived from secret keys $\mathbf{s}_{\mathsf{L}}, \mathbf{s}_{\mathsf{R}}$ and errors $\mathbf{e}_{\mathsf{L}}, \mathbf{e}_{\mathsf{R}}$. When the adversary knows the right-hand secret key $(\mathbf{s}_{\mathsf{R}}, \mathbf{e}_{\mathsf{R}})$, the component $(\mathbf{u}, v_1)$ becomes a MLWE instance with an additional known noisy linear relation: $v_2 - \mathbf{s}_{\mathsf{R}}^{\mathsf{T}}\mathbf{u} - \lceil q/2 \rceil m_{\mathsf{R}} = (\mathbf{e}_{\mathsf{R}}^{\mathsf{T}}, -\mathbf{s}_{\mathsf{R}}^{\mathsf{T}})\left(\begin{smallmatrix} \mathbf{s} \\ \mathbf{e} \end{smallmatrix}\right) + e_2$.

This precisely matches the definition of Hint-MLWE, and under this assumption, the left ciphertext $(\mathbf{u}, v_1)$ remains indistinguishable from uniform, thus ensuring the security of m_{L}.

We instantiate Maul with concrete parameters and estimate its security by adapting the heuristic framework of [16], which models non-Gaussian error distributions as Gaussians and disregards certain discrete-Gaussian-specific factors in the reduction. To support robust parameter selection, we complement this analysis with an evaluation of the best known attacks against Hint-MLWE.

The techniques underlying Maul can also be directly adapted to integer lattices, yielding a FrodoKEM-inspired [36] double-KEM with analogous security guarantees under the LWE and Hint-LWE assumptions; we leave a detailed treatment of this variant to future work. We further believe that these techniques could extend to a broader class of ElGamal-style KEMs, such as HQC [23], which has been selected for NIST standardization.

Performance of DAKE Instantiations. Beyond the security properties they guarantee, the strength of DAKE, DAKE^{σ}, and DUAKE lies in their ability to transform compact double-KEMs into bandwidth-efficient (U)AKE protocols. Instantiated with Maul, they demonstrate this potential concretely. Table 3 reports the message sizes for DAKE, DAKE^{σ}, and DUAKE instantiated with Maul, under the assumption that MAC tags, hash outputs, and identifiers have a bit-length twice the security parameter.

For comparison, existing ML-KEM-based AKE protocols (e.g., [7,22]) require transmitting at least one ephemeral public key and three ciphertexts, amounting to 6,272 bytes at NIST 5 security. The Twin-Kyber-based AKE of [44] instead transmits one ephemeral public key and two double-KEM ciphertexts, totaling 6,496 bytes at the same security level, since it employs two double-KEMs in parallel rather than combining a double-KEM with a standard KEM as in DAKE. In contrast, DAKE instantiated with Maul achieves approximately 16% overall communication savings (5,243 bytes) compared to these protocols (NIST 5), with an average reduction of 16% across NIST 1-5 security levels.

Similarly, existing ML-KEM-based UAKE protocols (e.g., [7,38]) require transmitting at least one ephemeral public key and two ciphertexts, for a total of 4,704 bytes at NIST 5 security. In comparison, DUAKE instantiated with Maul

Table 3. Message sizes (bytes) for DAKE, DAKE$^\sigma$, and DUAKE using Maul, ML-KEM, and ML-DSA. The optional third message corresponds to the full-PFS variants. Security levels follow NIST PQC categories.

Protocol	Sec. Level	Msg. 1 (Init.)	Msg. 2 (Resp.)	Msg. 3 (Init.)
	1	1,626	928	32
DAKE	3	2,376	1,488	48
	5	3,323	1,920	64
	1	858	3,316	32
DAKE$^\sigma$	3	1,288	4,749	48
	5	1,755	6,483	64
	1	858	928	32
DUAKE	3	1,288	1,488	48
	5	1,755	1,920	64

achieves about 21% overall communication savings (3,675 bytes) relative to these protocols (NIST 5), with an average reduction of 20% across NIST 1-5 levels.

1.3   Related Works

The only generic AKE we are aware of that leverages a double-KEM is the construction of Xue et al. [44], which provides weak perfect forward secrecy (wPFS) but no explicit authentication. Although it can, in principle, be instantiated with Maul (see full version, Appendix G), their protocol requires transmitting two double-KEM ciphertexts, which is essentially equivalent to four standard KEM encapsulations, whereas it is well known that wPFS AKEs can be realized with only three standard encapsulations [7]. Consequently, the construction does not fully exploit the bandwidth advantage that double-KEMs can offer over standard KEMs. Xue et al. [44] also proposed an FO transform in the ROM that upgrades any 2K2M-PKE with [IND-CK-CPA, IND-CK-CPA] security to a double-KEM with [IND-CK-CCA, IND-CK-CCA] security. Their transform, however, neither achieves one-sided chosen-key security nor extends to the QROM.

In concurrent and independent work, of which we became aware only after completing ours, Hashimoto, Katsumata, Niot, and Wiggers [25] propose a lattice-based *Reinforced*-KEM (Rebar) that also reuses the $\mathbf{u}$ component of ML-KEM ciphertexts. Unlike our double-KEM Maul, Rebar employs discrete Gaussian distributions but achieves comparable security under the same hardness assumptions. Their construction relies on an FO transform, which (when translated into the double-KEM/2K2M-PKE setting) upgrades a [IND-CK-CPA, IND-CPA] 2K2M-PKE to a [IND-CK-CCA, IND-CCA] double-KEM. This achieves CCA security on both sides, similar in spirit to the FO of [44], but without adding chosen-key security—our main novelty with the CK-FO transform. While Rebar is applied to optimize post-quantum WireGuard (with proofs in the eCK model), our focus is on designing a general family of (U)AKE protocols. This difference is also reflected in the analyzed properties: they study *identity hiding*, which we leave aside, whereas we emphasize explicit authentication, central to our framework.

Organization

The rest of the paper is organized as follows. Section 2 introduces the necessary notation and background. Section 3 presents our AKE protocols and their security properties. Section 4 describes the CK-FO transform and analyzes its security. Section 5 introduces Maul, establishing its security and parameter choices.

2 Preliminaries

We denote by $\{0, 1\}^*$ the set of binary strings. For any elements a, b from a set, we sometimes write $a = b$ to denote the Boolean predicate that evaluates to 1 if $a = b$ and 0 otherwise. We use the notation $\mathsf{Alg}(\mathsf{arg}_1, \ldots, \mathsf{arg}_n; r)$ to denote the execution of a probabilistic algorithm Alg on inputs $\mathsf{arg}_1, \ldots, \mathsf{arg}_n$ using randomness r. When the randomness is sampled internally by the algorithm, we omit r for brevity. When a tuple $(x_1, \ldots, x_n)$ is used as an argument to a function expecting a string – such as $\mathsf{H}((\mathsf{k}, m))$ or $\mathsf{Mac}(\mathsf{k}, t, (m_1, m_2))$ – we implicitly refer to an injective concatenation of $x_1, \ldots, x_n$, meaning that the original components can be unambiguously recovered from it. When the lengths of $x_1, \ldots, x_n$ are fixed and publicly known, a simple concatenation suffices. Otherwise, an appropriate encoding must be applied to ensure injectivity.

Double-KEM (2K-KEM). Introduced in [44], a double-KEM, also referred to as a double-key KEM—abbreviated as 2K-KEM in this paper—is a public-key encapsulation mechanism that operates with two pairs of public and secret keys.

Formally, a 2K-KEM $\mathsf{dKEM} = (\mathsf{Setup}, \mathsf{Keygen_L}, \mathsf{Keygen_R}, \mathsf{Encaps}, \mathsf{Decaps})$ is a tuple of five probabilistic polynomial-time (PPT) algorithms. The $\mathsf{Setup}()$ algorithm is responsible for generating public parameters pp. With these parameters, $\mathsf{Keygen_L(pp)}$ generates a left pair of public and secret keys $(\mathsf{pk_L}, \mathsf{sk_L}) \in \mathsf{PK_L} \times \mathsf{SK_L}$, while $\mathsf{Keygen_R(pp)}$ provides a right pair $(\mathsf{pk_R}, \mathsf{sk_R}) \in \mathsf{PK_R} \times \mathsf{SK_R}$. The $\mathsf{Encaps(pp, pk_L, pk_R)}$ algorithm takes the public parameters and both public keys $\mathsf{pk_L}$ and $\mathsf{pk_R}$ to produce a pair $(\mathsf{ct}, \mathsf{k}) \in \mathsf{CT} \times \mathsf{Keys}$, consisting of a ciphertext and a key. The $\mathsf{Decaps(pp, sk_L, sk_R, ct)}$ algorithm then uses the public parameters, secret keys $\mathsf{sk_L}$ and $\mathsf{sk_R}$, along with the ciphertext ct, to derive and output the key k or $\perp$ to indicate a decryption failure.

The security games we consider are defined in Fig. 3. These games are variations of the indistinguishability games for KEMs. As explained in the introduction, these variations depend on three factors: (1) which side (left or right) is considered, (2) whether we consider security with chosen-key (CK), and (3) whether a decapsulation oracle is provided to the adversary, leading to CPA or

CCA variations. We say that a 2K-KEM is $[X, Y]$ secure if it is $[X, -]$ secure and $[-, Y]$ secure. The advantage in these games, following the notations of Fig. 3, is expressed as $|\Pr[b = b'] - 1/2|$.

We also consider key-recovery games $[\text{Key-Recov}, \cdot]$ and $[\cdot, \text{Key-Recov}]$. By symmetry, we only define $[\text{Key-Recov}, \cdot]$. First, we suppose the existence of a function $\mathsf{RecovPKL}$, such that, for any $\mathsf{pp} \leftarrow \mathsf{Setup}()$ and $(\mathsf{pk_L}, \mathsf{sk_L}) \leftarrow \mathsf{Keygen_L}()$, we have $\mathsf{pk_L} = \mathsf{RecovPKL}(\mathsf{pp}, \mathsf{sk_L})$. The advantage of the game $[\text{Key-Recov}, \cdot]$ is defined as

$$\Pr\left[\mathsf{pk_L} = \mathsf{RecovPKL}(\mathsf{pp}, \mathsf{sk_L}') : \begin{array}{l} \mathsf{pp} \leftarrow \mathsf{Setup}(), (\mathsf{pk_L}, \mathsf{sk_L}) \leftarrow \mathsf{Keygen_L}(\mathsf{pp}), \\ \mathsf{sk_L}' \leftarrow \mathcal{A}(\mathsf{pp}, \mathsf{pk_L}) \end{array}\right].$$

The notions of correctness and spreadness for a 2K-KEM are defined as follows:

- For $\delta \geq 0$, a 2K-KEM is δ-correct if for $\mathsf{pp} \leftarrow \mathsf{Setup}()$, $(\mathsf{pk_L}, \mathsf{sk_L}) \leftarrow \mathsf{Keygen_L}(\mathsf{pp})$, $(\mathsf{pk_R}, \mathsf{sk_R}) \leftarrow \mathsf{Keygen_R}(\mathsf{pp})$, and $(\mathsf{ct}, \mathsf{k}) \leftarrow \mathsf{Encaps}(\mathsf{pp}, \mathsf{pk_L}, \mathsf{pk_R})$, the probability that $\mathsf{Decaps}(\mathsf{pp}, \mathsf{sk_L}, \mathsf{sk_R}, \mathsf{ct}) = \mathsf{k}$ holds is at least $1 - \delta$.
- For $\gamma > 0$, a 2K-KEM is γ-spread if, for any public parameters $\mathsf{pp} \leftarrow \mathsf{Setup}()$, any $\mathsf{pk_L}' \in \mathsf{PK_L}$, $\mathsf{pk_R}' \in \mathsf{PK_R}$, and any ciphertext $\mathsf{ct}' \in \mathsf{CT}$, we have: $\Pr\left[\mathsf{ct} = \mathsf{ct}' : (\mathsf{ct}, \mathsf{k}) \leftarrow \mathsf{Encaps}(\mathsf{pp}, \mathsf{pk_L}', \mathsf{pk_R}')\right] \leq 2^{-\gamma}$.

Double-Key Double-Message PKE (2K2M-PKE). We consider a variant of the double-key PKE of [44] that encrypts a pair of messages. A double-key double-message PKE (2K2M-PKE), functions as a PKE with two pairs of public and secret keys to encrypt two messages into a single ciphertext. Formally, a 2K2M-PKE $\mathsf{DPKE} = (\mathsf{Setup}, \mathsf{Keygen_L}, \mathsf{Keygen_R}, \mathsf{dEnc}, \mathsf{dDec})$ consists of five PPT algorithms. The $\mathsf{Setup}()$ algorithm generates and outputs the public parameters pp. With these parameters, $\mathsf{Keygen_L}(\mathsf{pp})$ generates a left pair of public and secret keys $(\mathsf{pk_L}, \mathsf{sk_L}) \in \mathsf{PK_L} \times \mathsf{SK_L}$, while $\mathsf{Keygen_R}(\mathsf{pp})$ produces a right pair $(\mathsf{pk_R}, \mathsf{sk_R}) \in \mathsf{PK_R} \times \mathsf{SK_R}$. The $\mathsf{dEnc}(\mathsf{pp}, \mathsf{pk_L}, \mathsf{pk_R}, m_L, m_R)$ algorithm takes the public parameters, the public keys $\mathsf{pk_L}$ and $\mathsf{pk_R}$, and two messages $(m_L, m_R) \in \mathcal{M}_L \times \mathcal{M}_R$ to generate a ciphertext $\mathsf{ct} \in \mathsf{CT}$. The $\mathsf{dDec}(\mathsf{pp}, \mathsf{sk_L}, \mathsf{sk_R}, \mathsf{ct})$ algorithm then uses the public parameters, secret keys $\mathsf{sk_L}$ and $\mathsf{sk_R}$, along with the ciphertext ct, to recover and output the messages $(m_L, m_R) \in \mathcal{M}_L \times \mathcal{M}_R$.

The security games for a 2K2M-PKE are outlined in Fig. 4. As for the security games of 2K-KEM, these games are variations of the indistinguishability games for PKE, adapted to the presence of two secret and public keys. For clarity, we use the following naming convention for security games: names of the form $[X, -]$ (for some text X, such as IND-CPA) denote games whose security relies on the secrecy of the left secret key, while $[-, Y]$ denotes those in which security relies on the secrecy of the right secret key. We say that a 2K2M-PKE is $[X, Y]$-secure if it is $[X, -]$-secure and $[-, Y]$-secure.

The advantage in these games, following the notations of Fig. 4, is expressed as $|\Pr[b = b'] - 1/2|$.

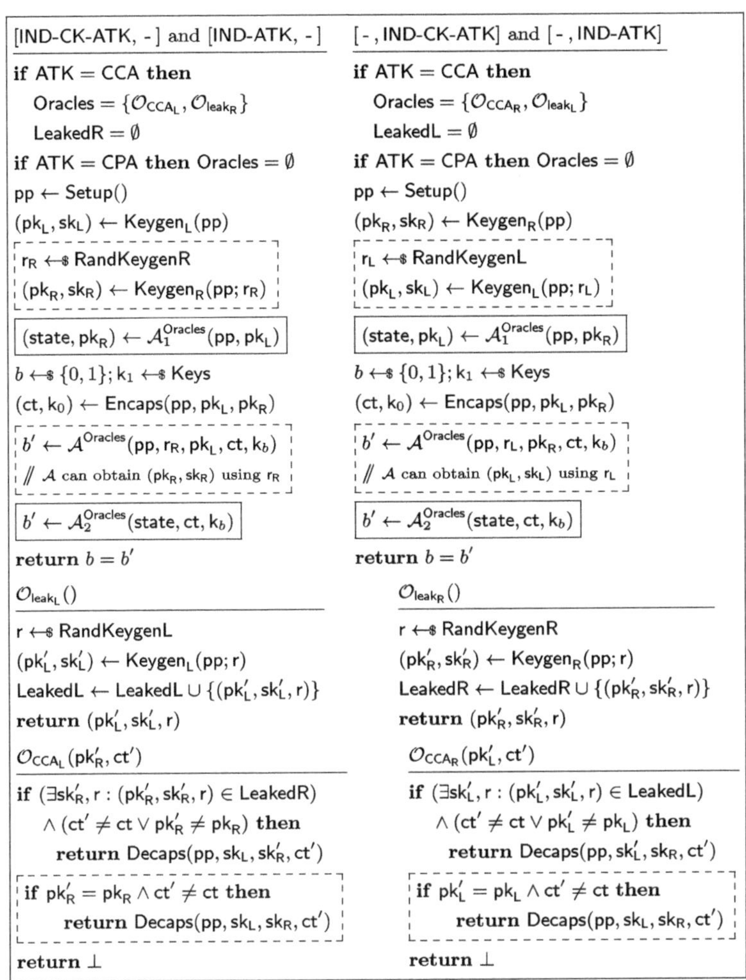

Fig. 3. 2K-KEM security games. $\mathsf{ATK} \in \{\mathsf{CPA}, \mathsf{CCA}\}$. Solid boxes are taken in account only for chosen-key security games (*i.e.* whose name contains CK) while dashed boxes are taken in account only for non-chosen-key games. $\mathsf{RandKeygenL}/\mathsf{RandKeygenR}$ denote the randomness distributions used by the $\mathsf{Keygen_L}/\mathsf{Keygen_R}$ algorithms.

Finally, for $\delta \geq 0$, a 2K2M-PKE is δ-correct if:

$$\mathbb{E}\left(\max_{\mathsf{m} \in \mathcal{M}_L \times \mathcal{M}_R} \Pr\left[\mathsf{dDec}(\mathsf{pp}, \mathsf{sk_L}, \mathsf{sk_R}, \mathsf{dEnc}(\mathsf{pp}, \mathsf{pk_L}, \mathsf{pk_R}, \mathsf{m})) = \mathsf{m})\right] \right) \geq 1 - \delta \,,$$

where expected value is taken over $\mathsf{pp} \leftarrow \mathsf{Setup}()$, $(\mathsf{pk_L}, \mathsf{sk_L}) \leftarrow \mathsf{Keygen_L}(\mathsf{pp})$, and $(\mathsf{pk_R}, \mathsf{sk_R}) \leftarrow \mathsf{Keygen_R}(\mathsf{pp})$.

[IND-CPA, -]	[- , IND-CPA]
$\mathsf{pp} \leftarrow \mathsf{Setup}()$	$\mathsf{pp} \leftarrow \mathsf{Setup}()$
$(\mathsf{pk_L}, \mathsf{sk_L}) \leftarrow \mathsf{Keygen_L}(\mathsf{pp})$	$(\mathsf{pk_R}, \mathsf{sk_R}) \leftarrow \mathsf{Keygen_R}(\mathsf{pp})$
$r_\mathsf{R} \leftarrow\!\!\$\ \mathsf{RandKeygenR}$	$r_\mathsf{L} \leftarrow\!\!\$\ \mathsf{RandKeygenL}$
$(\mathsf{pk_R}, \mathsf{sk_R}) \leftarrow \mathsf{Keygen_R}(\mathsf{pp}; r_\mathsf{R})$	$(\mathsf{pk_L}, \mathsf{sk_L}) \leftarrow \mathsf{Keygen_L}(\mathsf{pp}; r_\mathsf{L})$
$(\mathsf{state}, m_{\mathsf{L},0}, m_{\mathsf{L},1}, m_\mathsf{R})$	$(\mathsf{state}, m_{\mathsf{R},0}, m_{\mathsf{R},1}, m_\mathsf{L})$
$\quad \leftarrow \mathcal{A}_1(\mathsf{pp}, \mathsf{pk_R}, \mathsf{sk_R}, r_\mathsf{R}, \mathsf{pk_L})$	$\quad \leftarrow \mathcal{A}_1(\mathsf{pp}, \mathsf{pk_L}, \mathsf{sk_L}, r_\mathsf{L}, \mathsf{pk_R})$
$\mathsf{ct}_0 \leftarrow \mathsf{Enc}(\mathsf{pp}, \mathsf{pk_L}, \mathsf{pk_R}, (m_{\mathsf{L},0}, m_\mathsf{R}))$	$\mathsf{ct}_0 \leftarrow \mathsf{Enc}(\mathsf{pp}, \mathsf{pk_L}, \mathsf{pk_R}, (m_\mathsf{L}, m_{\mathsf{R},0}))$
$\mathsf{ct}_1 \leftarrow \mathsf{Enc}(\mathsf{pp}, \mathsf{pk_L}, \mathsf{pk_R}, (m_{\mathsf{L},1}, m_\mathsf{R}))$	$\mathsf{ct}_1 \leftarrow \mathsf{Enc}(\mathsf{pp}, \mathsf{pk_L}, \mathsf{pk_R}, (m_\mathsf{L}, m_{\mathsf{R},1}))$
$b \leftarrow\!\!\$\ \{0,1\}$	$b \leftarrow\!\!\$\ \{0,1\}$
$b' \leftarrow \mathcal{A}_2(\mathsf{state}, \mathsf{ct}_b)$	$b' \leftarrow \mathcal{A}(\mathsf{pp}, \mathsf{state}, \mathsf{ct}_b)$
return $b = b'$	**return** $b = b'$

Fig. 4. Security games of 2K2M-PKE. RandKeygenL/RandKeygenR denote the distributions of the randomness used by the $\mathsf{Keygen_L}$/$\mathsf{Keygen_R}$ algorithms.

3 Authenticated Key Exchanges from Double-KEMs

In this section, we formalize and analyze three authenticated key exchange (AKE) protocols built from $[\mathsf{IND\text{-}CK\text{-}CCA}, \mathsf{IND\text{-}CCA}]$ double-KEMs. We first recall the security models we use, then present the base protocol DAKE together with its two variants, DAKE^σ and DUAKE. In addition to the two properties required by these security models—key secrecy and match soundness—, we also consider inverse match soundness and explicit authentication.

3.1 The eCK Security Model and Its Variants

Our analysis builds on two strengthened variants of the extended Canetti–Krawczyk (eCK) model [33]: eCK^w and eCK-PFS [13].[4] The former guarantees *weak perfect forward secrecy* (wPFS), and the latter *perfect forward secrecy* (PFS). Both variants ensure key secrecy against a broader class of attack scenarios than those covered by eCK and CK^+ [31].[5]

We provide an overview of these variants; a full formalization is deferred to full version, Appendix C. In this model, the adversary can create parties (as initiators or responders), activate sessions, and interact arbitrarily with them by sending chosen messages. Each session represents a protocol execution by a party (the actor of the session). A simple protocol execution between two parties is therefore represented by two sessions. In each session, the party that the actor intends to communicate with is called its peer. Each session can be in one of these states: running, completed (the protocol finished without error), or aborted.

---

[4] As explained in Sect. 3.2, the analysis of DUAKE relies on an adaptation of these models to the unilateral setting.

[5] This strengthening is due to the use of the *origin session* notion, rather than matching sessions, in certain scenarios [13].

Multiple relations can be defined between sessions, and two are of particular importance for the security properties considered in this work:

- Informally, two sessions s, s' are said to be *matching* if they completed the protocol together. More formally, this requires that (1) they both completed, (2) they have distinct roles, (3) the peer of each session equals the actor of the other, and (4) they share the same transcript of sent and received messages.[6]
- A (not necessarily completed) session s' is said to be the *origin* of a session s if the transcript of messages received by s equals the transcript of messages sent by s'.

The eCK model and its variants consider powerful adversarial queries:

- corrupt: reveals a party's long-term secret key.
- eph-key: reveals some ephemeral elements computed by a running or completed session. Revealed elements are explicitly specified in the protocol[7].
- session-key: reveals the session key of a completed session.

Using this adversarial setting, we can now define multiple security properties. More precisely, we first define *key secrecy* and *match soundness*, which are required for a protocol to be considered secure in the eCK^w/eCK-PFS models. Then, we define two additional properties: inverse-match soundness and explicit authentication, that are also desirable for AKEs.

Key Secrecy. Key secrecy is measured by a real-or-random game: the adversary chooses a *test session* s^{Test} of its choice, receives either its true session key or a uniformly sampled one, and must distinguish between the two.

While the adversary can make adversarial queries before and after receiving the challenge key, restrictions on adversarial queries are required to prevent unavoidable attacks (*e.g.*, querying session-key on the tested session) and leads to five attack scenarios summarized in Table 4. More precisely, eCK^w—guaranteeing only weak perfect forward secrecy (wPFS)—only authorizes scenarios 1 to 4 while eCK-PFS authorizes scenarios 1 to 6—guaranteeing full perfect forward secrecy (PFS). Moreover, both models also protect against *maximal exposure* (MEX) attacks and *key-compromise impersonation* (KCI) attacks and (UKS) attacks[8].

The key secrecy game with the scenarios of eCK^w (*resp.* eCK-PFS) is called eCK^w-KeySec (*resp.* eCK-PFS-KeySec).

---

[6] When comparing the transcripts of two sessions with distinct roles, sent and received messages are inverted, since the outgoing messages of one session correspond to the incoming messages of the other. This convention is applied throughout the paper when comparing transcripts of sessions with different roles..

[7] Our definition is more general than the original eCK model and its variants, as the original model fixes this query to reveal exactly the ephemeral secret keys (i.e., the randomness coins) of session s. However, choice of which elements can be leaked is significant and may have non-trivial consequences, as illustrated in [12].

[8] Attacks where two parties derive the same session key but disagree on their peer identities.

Table 4. Summary of the attack scenarios considered. The adversary $\mathcal{A}$ is never allowed to query session-key on s^{Test} or on any session matching s^{Test}. Here, A denotes the actor of s^{Test}, P its peer, and s^{Origin} an origin session of s^{Test}. *Post-comp.* indicates that the corruption query is made after s^{Test} has completed, and *possible* means that the scenario includes both *yes* and *no* cases.

Scenario	corrupt(A)	corrupt(P)	eph-key(s^{Test})	Origin session s^{Origin} exists	eph-key(s^{Origin})
1	no	no	possible	possible	possible
2	yes	no	no	possible	possible
3	no	yes	possible	yes	no
4	yes	yes	no	yes	no
5	yes	post-comp.	no	no	–
6	no	post-comp.	possible	no	–

Match Soundness. Match soundness is defined through a game in which the adversary faces no restrictions on its queries. The adversary wins if it can produce either of the following:

- two completed sessions that are matching but derive different session keys.
- three distinct completed sessions that share the same message transcript.[9]

Informally, it ensures that the matching relation correctly captures when two sessions have executed the protocol together.

Inverse-Match Soundness. Inverse-Match Soundness is measured by a game in which the adversary faces no restrictions on its queries. The adversary wins if it produces two distinct completed sessions that output the same session key without being matching sessions.

We believe that one of the main purposes of this property is to ensure UKS security independently of the adversary's queries[10]. While we are not sure about the practical interest of this property, we explain on page 20 how to modify our protocols in a simple way to achieve it.

Explicit Authentication. Explicit Authentication ensures that whenever a session s is completed with an uncorrupted peer, it has done so with an honest partner session whose actor is s_{Peer}—we denote by s_{Actor} and s_{Peer} the actor and

---

[9] Recall that when two sessions have distinct roles, transcript equality is checked up to the inversion of sent and received messages, as explained in Footnote 6.

[10] In contrast, protocols with key secrecy already provide UKS security for all attacks that fall within the allowed key-secrecy scenarios: otherwise, the adversary could violate key secrecy by creating a non-matching session s with the same key as the test session (thus breaking UKS), and then issuing a session-key query on s.

peer of s. Care is needed in formalizing this notion: if s sends the final message of the exchange, the mere uncorruptedness of the peer cannot guarantee that this message is actually received by the honest partner.

For additional expressivity we distinguish two properties: Init-explicit authentication and Resp-explicit authentication. We take a role $X \in \{Init, Resp\}$ and denote by $\overline{X}$ the role distinct of X. In the X-explicit authentication game X-ExplicitAuth, the adversary selects a completed session s with role $\overline{X}$, under the sole restriction on adversarial queries that s_{Peer} was not corrupted before s completed. The adversary wins if there does not exist a session s' with actor s_{Peer}, peer s_{Actor} and role X, such that:

- *If the sessions with role* X *send the final message in the AKE:* s and s' share the same message transcript, except possibly for the final message sent by s and received by s'. Note that s' is not required to be completed.
- *If the sessions with role* X *do not send the final message in the AKE:* s and s' share the same message transcript, and s' is completed. Note that in this case, s and s' are matching.

3.2   Our AKE Protocols

The base protocol DAKE (Fig. 1) is a mutually authenticated key exchange that comes in two versions: $DAKE_2$, a two-message variant achieving wPFS in the eCK^w model, and $DAKE_3$, a three-message variant achieving PFS in the eCK-PFS model.

Our analysis of DAKE accounts for an eph-key query that can reveal:

- On a initiator session, the randomness used in $Keygen_R$ (which implies knowledge of sk_R). Moreover, $\tilde{k}$ can also be leaked after the session finished to compute its second message.
- On a responder session, nothing is revealed: we assume that the randomness of the encapsulation is securely erased immediately after its computation.

Two additional variants of DAKE are considered. The first, $DAKE^\sigma$, achieves responder authentication using a digital signature scheme instead of a KEM (see full version, Appendix D.1). While this typically increases overall communication bandwidth, it significantly reduces the size of the initiator's first message. The second, DUAKE, is a unilateral version providing authentication only for the initiator (Fig. 2). Its security is proven under adapted unilateral models (u-eCK^w and u-eCK-PFS), defined in full version, Appendix C.4. Further details on both variants are provided in Appendices D.1 and D.2 of full version.

3.3   Security of Our AKE Protocols

We summarize here the security properties of DAKE, $DAKE^\sigma$, and DUAKE. Note that all of them are proven in the standard model.

Key Secrecy. It is achieved for DAKE, DAKE^σ, and DUAKE, assuming the $[\mathsf{IND\text{-}CK\text{-}CCA}, \mathsf{IND\text{-}CCA}]$ security of the double-KEM and standard security assumptions on the other primitives. The 2-pass versions provide weak PFS, while the 3-pass versions achieve full PFS. The results for DAKE_3 are stated in Theorem 1, while those for DAKE_2, DAKE^σ and DUAKE are detailed in full version, Appendix E.

In addition to the definitions provided in the main body, the theorem relies on standard security properties of a KEM, a PRG, and a MAC, which are recalled in full version, Appendix A. We also use the *message–key bound* security of a MAC, which is ensured when a collision-resistant hash function is used as the underlying MAC primitive. This property is formalized by a game MacColl, in which the adversary must find two distinct pairs of keys and messages, $(\mathsf{k}, m) \neq (\mathsf{k}', m')$, and a tag tag that is valid for both pairs.

Theorem 1 (Key Secrecy of DAKE_3 in the Standard Model). *Let $\mathcal{A}$ be a PPT adversary against key secrecy of DAKE_3. Suppose it activates at most N parties and, for each party P, at most l sessions with actor or peer P. Assume that the underlying 2K-KEM is γ-spread and δ-correct while the standard KEM is δ'-correct. Let Ad^{w} denote the advantage of $\mathcal{A}$ against $\mathsf{eCK}^{\mathsf{w}}\text{-}\mathsf{KeySec}$ and $\mathsf{Ad}^{\mathsf{PFS}}$ its advantage against $\mathsf{eCK\text{-}PFS\text{-}KeySec}$. Then, in the standard model, there exist PPT adversaries $\mathcal{B}_1, \cdots, \mathcal{B}_{11}$ such that:*

$$\mathsf{Ad}^{\mathsf{w}} \leq \alpha + 4\beta + 6Nl^2\Big(\mathsf{Adv}_{\mathsf{dKEM}}^{[\mathsf{IND\text{-}CK\text{-}CCA},\, \text{-}\,]}(\mathcal{B}_6) + \mathsf{Adv}_{\mathsf{dKEM}}^{[\,\text{-}\,,\mathsf{IND\text{-}CCA}]}(\mathcal{B}_7) + 2\,\mathsf{Adv}_{\mathsf{PRG}}^{\mathsf{IND\text{-}PRG}}(\mathcal{B}_8)\Big),$$

$$\mathsf{Ad}^{\mathsf{PFS}} \leq \mathsf{Ad}^{\mathsf{w}} + \beta + 2Nl^2\Big(2\mathsf{Adv}_{\mathsf{dKEM}}^{[\mathsf{IND\text{-}CK\text{-}CCA},\, \text{-}\,]}(\mathcal{B}_9) + 2\mathsf{Adv}_{\mathsf{PRG}}^{\mathsf{IND\text{-}PRG}}(\mathcal{B}_{10}) + \mathsf{Adv}_{\mathsf{MAC}}^{\mathsf{sUnforg}}(\mathcal{B}_{11})\Big),$$

where $\alpha = \mathsf{Adv}_{\mathsf{MAC}}^{\mathsf{MacColl}}(\mathcal{B}_1) + N\mathsf{Adv}_{\widetilde{\mathsf{KEM}}}^{\mathsf{Key\text{-}Recov}}(\mathcal{B}_2) + N^2 l\Big(2\mathsf{Adv}_{\widetilde{\mathsf{KEM}}}^{\mathsf{IND\text{-}CCA}}(\mathcal{B}_3) + l\delta' + \mathsf{Adv}_{\mathsf{MAC}}^{\mathsf{sUnforg}}(\mathcal{B}_4)\Big)$ *and* $\beta = Nl\,\mathsf{Adv}_{\mathsf{dKEM}}^{[\cdot,\mathsf{Key\text{-}Recov}]}(\mathcal{B}_5) + 2Nl^2\left(\delta + 2^{-\gamma}\right)$.

Moreover, (1) $\mathcal{B}_3$ queries $\mathcal{O}_{\mathsf{CCA}}$ at most l times, (2) $\mathcal{B}_4$ queries $\mathcal{O}_{\mathsf{Mac}}$ at most l time. (3) $\mathcal{B}_6$ and $\mathcal{B}_9$ each query $\mathcal{O}_{\mathsf{leak_R}}$ and $\mathcal{O}_{\mathsf{CCA_L}}$ at most l times, (4) $\mathcal{B}_7$ does not query $\mathcal{O}_{\mathsf{leak_L}}$ and queries $\mathcal{O}_{\mathsf{CCA_R}}$ at most one time, and (5) $\mathcal{B}_{11}$ queries $\mathcal{O}_{\mathsf{Mac}}$ at most one time.

Proof. The complete proof is given in full version, Appendix E.[11] In this proof sketch, we provide the core ideas used to prove the key secrecy of DAKE_3. This explanation first covers key secrecy for Scenarios 1–4 (Table 4), and then Scenarios 5–6.

<u>Key Secrecy for Scenarios 1–4.</u> These scenarios are proven via a game sequence that progressively replaces the test session key with a uniformly random value, thereby ensuring that no adversary can win the real-or-random game.

The crucial game of this sequence is the one that replaces the key k of the test session $\mathsf{s}^{\mathsf{Test}}$, as well as the key of the unique session that also encapsulates or decapsulates this key (if such a session exists), by a uniform key.

---

[11] The complete proof is modular in order to simultaneously cover DAKE and DAKE^σ.

The change in the adversary's advantage introduced by this modification is bounded using one of the security properties of the 2K-KEM dKEM. We specify below which game is used, depending on the specific situation that can arise in Scenarios 1 to 4.

- *First possible situation:* s^{Test} *is an initiator and* eph-key *is not used on it.* We rely on $[\,\text{-}\,, \mathsf{IND\text{-}CPA}]$, which informally guarantees that k is indistinguishable from uniform, provided that $\mathsf{sk_R}$ is unknown and that $(\mathsf{pk_L}, \mathsf{sk_L})$ has been honestly generated.
- *Second possible situation:* s^{Test} *is an initiator and* corrupt *is not used on it.* We rely on $[\mathsf{IND\text{-}CCA}, \text{-}\,]$, which informally ensures that k is indistinguishable from uniform, provided that $\mathsf{sk_L}$ is unknown and that $(\mathsf{pk_R}, \mathsf{sk_R})$ has been honestly generated. Note that, unlike the previous case, CCA security is required here, since multiple sessions distinct from s^{Test} may share the same long-term key $(\mathsf{pk_L}, \mathsf{sk_L})$. The decapsulation oracle is therefore needed to simulate decapsulations for these sessions without knowing $\mathsf{sk_L}$.
- *Third possible situation:* s^{Test} *is a responder and* corrupt *is not used on its peer.* We need to rely on $[\mathsf{IND\text{-}CK\text{-}CCA}, \text{-}\,]$, which informally guarantees that k is indistinguishable from uniform provided that $\mathsf{sk_L}$ is unknown, even if $\mathsf{pk_R}$ is adversarially chosen. The chosen-key property is crucial here, since the ephemeral key $\mathsf{pk_R}$ received by s^{Test} may be chosen by the adversary. Moreover, the CCA security is required for the same reason as previous item.
- *Fourth possible situation:* s^{Test} *is a responder and* corrupt *is used on its peer.* This situation can only appear in scenario 3 or 4. Consequently, by definition of these scenarios, there exists an origin session s for s^{Test}, and eph-key has not been used on s. In particular, the ephemeral key $\mathsf{pk_R}$ received by s^{Test} was honestly generated by s. In this case, we rely on the $[\,\text{-}\,, \mathsf{IND\text{-}CCA}]$ property, which informally guarantees that k is indistinguishable from a uniform key as long as $\mathsf{sk_R}$ remains unrevealed and $(\mathsf{pk_L}, \mathsf{sk_L})$ has been honestly generated. The CCA security is required in situations where the ciphertext ct received by s differs from the ciphertext created by s^{Test}; in such cases, the decapsulation oracle must be used on ct to compute the key k of s.

Key Secrecy for Scenarios 5 and 6. We show that these scenarios can occur only with negligible probability – independently of whether the adversary won the Real-or-random game. More precisely, we first consider the execution only up to the moment when s^{Test} accepts, which implies that we can assume its peer is not corrupted. We then prove that, except with negligible probability, there exists an origin session for s^{Test}, thereby contradicting both scenarios 5 and 6. We provide more details below, depending on the role of the test session.

- *If* s^{Test} *is an initiator,* we use the security of the MAC MAC to show that $\mathsf{tag}^{\mathsf{R}}$ must have been honestly computed by a responder session s. From the content of the message authenticated by this MAC, we can then deduce that s is in fact an origin session of s^{Test}. Note that, to invoke the MAC security, we first rely on the IND-CCA security of the KEM $\widetilde{\mathsf{KEM}}$ to ensure that the key $\tilde{\mathsf{k}}$

generated by $\mathsf{s}^{\mathsf{Test}}$ is indistinguishable from a uniform key. The CCA security is necessary to compute the decapsulations performed by the responder sessions whose actor is $\mathsf{s}^{\mathsf{Test}}_{\mathsf{Peer}}$.

- *If $\mathsf{s}^{\mathsf{Test}}$ is a responder*, we use the security of the MAC to show that tag^I must have been honestly computed by an initiator session s. As in the previous case, the content of the authenticated message allows us to deduce that s is an origin session of $\mathsf{s}^{\mathsf{Test}}$. Note that to apply the MAC security, we first rely on the [IND-CK-CCA, -] security of the 2K-KEM dKEM and then on the security of PRG to ensure that the key $\mathsf{k}^{\mathsf{MAC}}$ created by $\mathsf{s}^{\mathsf{Test}}$ is indistinguishable from uniform. The use of [IND-CK-CCA, -] is justified in the same way as in the analysis of the third possible situation, in the previous paragraph explaining the proof for Scenarios 1 to 4.

Match Soundness. It is achieved for DAKE, DAKE^σ, and DUAKE. Indeed, the first condition is a direct consequence of the correctness of the used primitives. Concerning the second condition, note that:

- Two distinct initiator sessions can only derive the same key pk_R with negligible probability. The contrary would directly lead to an attack against the right-key-recovery game $[\cdot, \mathsf{Key\text{-}Recov}]$ of the 2K-KEM.
- Spreadness of the 2K-KEM implies that two responder sessions will compute the same encapsulation ct with negligible probability.

Inverse-Match Soundness. It is not guaranteed by default in DAKE, DAKE^σ, or DUAKE, but it can be enforced in a straightforward manner by deriving the session key through a collision-resistant key derivation function (KDF). Specifically, each protocol sets the session key as $\mathsf{KDF}(\mathsf{k}^{\mathsf{SESSION}}, \tau)$, where $\mathsf{k}^{\mathsf{SESSION}}$ is the initial session key, and τ is the concatenation of the message transcript and the identities of the actor and its peer.

The advantage of the collision-resistance experiment of a KDF against an adversary $\mathcal{A}$ is defined as[12] $\Pr\big[(\mathsf{k}, \mathsf{m}) \neq (\mathsf{k}', \mathsf{m}') \wedge \mathsf{KDF}(\mathsf{k}, \mathsf{m}) = \mathsf{KDF}(\mathsf{k}', \mathsf{m}') : (\mathsf{k}, \mathsf{k}', \mathsf{m}, \mathsf{m}') \leftarrow \mathcal{A}(\mathsf{pp})\big]$. We chose not to include this KDF natively, both for simplicity of the protocol description and because it is only required for this specific property.

Explicit Authentication. It is fully achieved by DAKE_3 and DAKE^σ_3, and partially achieved by our other protocols. More precisely:

- Init-explicit authentication is achieved by DAKE_3, DAKE^σ_3 and DUAKE_3.
- Resp-explicit authentication holds for DAKE_2, DAKE_3, DAKE^σ_2, and DAKE^σ_3.

---

[12] Further discussions about this notion are given in full version, Appendix A.

Theorem 2 provides precise security bounds for explicit authentication in DAKE. All remaining bounds, along with their corresponding proofs, are deferred to full version, Appendix F.

The arguments establishing explicit authentication for our protocols closely follow those used to prove key secrecy in attack scenarios 5 and 6 of Table 4.[13] The core idea is that the security of the MAC (and of the signature in the case of DAKE^σ) guarantees that the tag (or signature) received by a session s was honestly generated by another session s'. The elements authenticated by this tag (or signature) then allow concluding that s' satisfies all the requirements of the explicit authentication property. In particular, to ensure Init-explicit authentication, the message used to compute tag^I in all our three-message AKEs is defined to include both the transcript of exchanged messages and the identities of the actor and its peer. If Init-explicit authentication is not required, this message can simply be set to any fixed string.

Theorem 2 (Explicit Authentication for DAKE). *Let $\mathcal{A}$ be a PPT adversary against $\mathsf{Init\text{-}ExplicitAuth}$ for DAKE_3. Suppose it activates at most N parties and, for each party P, at most l sessions with actor or peer P. Assume that the underlying 2K-KEM is γ-spread and δ-correct. Then, in the standard model, there exist PPT adversaries $\mathcal{B}, \mathcal{C}, \mathcal{D}$ and $\mathcal{E}$ such that:*

$$\mathsf{Adv}_{\mathsf{DAKE}_3}^{\mathsf{Init\text{-}ExplicitAuth}}(\mathcal{A}) \leq Nl\,\mathsf{Adv}_{\mathsf{dKEM}}^{[\cdot,\mathsf{Key\text{-}Recov}]}(\mathcal{B}) + 2Nl^2\left(\delta + 2^{-\gamma}\right)$$

$$+ 2Nl^2\left(2\,\mathsf{Adv}_{\mathsf{dKEM}}^{[\mathsf{IND\text{-}CK\text{-}CCA},\,\text{-}\,]}(\mathcal{C}) + 2\,\mathsf{Adv}_{\mathsf{PRG}}^{\mathsf{IND\text{-}PRG}}(\mathcal{D}) + \mathsf{Adv}_{\mathsf{MAC}}^{\mathsf{sUnforg}}(\mathcal{E})\right).$$

Moreover, $\mathcal{C}$ queries $\mathcal{O}_{\mathsf{leak}_\mathsf{R}}$ and $\mathcal{O}_{\mathsf{CCA}_\mathsf{L}}$ at most l times, and $\mathcal{E}$ queries $\mathcal{O}_{\mathsf{Mac}}$ at most one time.

Now let $\Pi \in \{\mathsf{DAKE}_2, \mathsf{DAKE}_3\}$ and suppose that $\mathcal{A}$ is a PPT adversary against $\mathsf{Resp\text{-}ExplicitAuth}$ for Π. Assume the same conditions on $\mathcal{A}$ as above, and that the standard KEM is δ'-correct. Then, in the standard model, there exist PPT adversaries $\mathcal{B}, \mathcal{C}, \mathcal{D}, \mathcal{E}$ such that $\mathsf{Adv}_\Pi^{\mathsf{Resp\text{-}ExplicitAuth}}(\mathcal{A})$ is upper-bounded by:

$$\mathsf{Adv}_{\mathsf{MAC}}^{\mathsf{MacColl}}(\mathcal{B}) + N\,\mathsf{Adv}_{\widetilde{\mathsf{KEM}}}^{\mathsf{Key\text{-}Recov}}(\mathcal{C}) + N^2 l\left(2\mathsf{Adv}_{\widetilde{\mathsf{KEM}}}^{\mathsf{IND\text{-}CCA}}(\mathcal{D}) + l\delta' + \mathsf{Adv}_{\mathsf{MAC}}^{\mathsf{sUnforg}}(\mathcal{E})\right).$$

Moreover, $\mathcal{D}$ queries $\mathcal{O}_{\mathsf{CCA}}$ at most l times and $\mathcal{E}$ queries $\mathcal{O}_{\mathsf{Mac}}$ at most l times.

4   Chosen-Key Fujisaki–Okamoto Transform

In this section, we introduce and analyze a new *chosen-key* Fujisaki–Okamoto transform (CK-FO) which upgrades a double-key, double-message IND-CPA PKE into an IND-CCA double-KEM that additionally provides left chosen-key security. Concretely, in the corresponding security game the adversary may freely choose the (possibly malformed) right public key. Section 4.1 defines the class of 2K2M-PKE schemes compatible with our CK-FO, obtained by combining two PKE instances, while Sect. 4.2 presents the transform and its security proof.

---

[13] They are described in the proof sketch of Theorem 1 for the case of DAKE_3.

4.1   Combining Two **PKE** to Obtain a 2K2M-PKE

We describe a generic method for combining two PKE schemes that share common randomness into a 2K2M-PKE. This construction produces shorter ciphertexts than running the original PKEs independently, while yielding exactly the input format required by our CK-FO transform. Informally, we consider two PKE schemes whose ciphertexts share a common component c_C, and our construction keeps just one c_C instead of keeping it in both ciphertexts.

Concretely, let two PKE schemes $\mathsf{PKE_L} = (\mathsf{Setup}, \mathsf{Keygen_L}, \mathsf{Encr_L}, \mathsf{Decr_L})$ and $\mathsf{PKE_R} = (\mathsf{Setup}, \mathsf{Keygen_R}, \mathsf{Encr_R}, \mathsf{Decr_R})$ share the same setup algorithm and satisfy the following conditions:

- The randomness spaces are structured as $\mathsf{Rand_C} \times \mathsf{Rand_L}$ for $\mathsf{Encr_L}$ and $\mathsf{Rand_C} \times \mathsf{Rand_R}$ for $\mathsf{Encr_R}$, with $\mathsf{Rand_C}$ the common part.
- There exists a deterministic algorithm E_{base} that, given (pp, r_C) with public parameters pp and $r_C \in \mathsf{Rand_C}$, outputs c_C such that both $\mathsf{Encr_L}$ and $\mathsf{Encr_R}$ produce ciphertexts whose first component equals $c_C = E_{\mathsf{base}}(\mathsf{pp}, r_C)$.

Under these conditions, encryptions using the same r_C share the component c_C, which can be factored out to improve compactness. This yields the combined scheme $\mathsf{DPKE} = (\mathsf{dSetup} = \mathsf{Setup}, \mathsf{dKeygenL} = \mathsf{Keygen_L}, \mathsf{dKeygenR} = \mathsf{Keygen_R}, \mathsf{dEnc}, \mathsf{dDec})$, with algorithms dEnc and dDec given in Fig. 5.

It is important to note that IND-CPA security of $\mathsf{PKE_L}$ and $\mathsf{PKE_R}$ does not automatically imply any security for DPKE, since the two encryptions are no longer independent. The security of DPKE must therefore be established separately, on a case-by-case basis. In Sect. 5, we present $\mathsf{Maul_{PKE}}$ as an example of this transformation, whose security can be proven under lattice assumptions.

<table>
<tr><td>

$\mathsf{dEnc}(\mathsf{pp}, \mathsf{pk_L}, \mathsf{pk_R}, \mathsf{m} = (m_L, m_R))$

$r_C \leftarrow\!\!{\scriptstyle\$}\ \mathsf{Rand_C}$

$r_L \leftarrow\!\!{\scriptstyle\$}\ \mathsf{Rand_L}$

$r_R \leftarrow\!\!{\scriptstyle\$}\ \mathsf{Rand_R}$

  // Here, $c_C = E_{\mathsf{base}}(\mathsf{pp}, r_C)$

$(c_C, c_L) = \mathsf{Encr_L}(\mathsf{pp}, \mathsf{pk_L}, m_L; (r_C, r_L))$

$(c_C, c_R) = \mathsf{Encr_R}(\mathsf{pp}, \mathsf{pk_R}, m_R; (r_C, r_R))$

return (c_C, c_L, c_R)

</td><td>

$\mathsf{dDec}(\mathsf{pp}, \mathsf{sk_L}, \mathsf{sk_R}, \mathsf{ct} = (c_L, c_R))$

$m_L = \mathsf{Decr_L}(\mathsf{pp}, \mathsf{sk_L}, c_L)$

$m_R = \mathsf{Decr_R}(\mathsf{pp}, \mathsf{sk_R}, c_R)$

if $m_L = \perp \vee m_R = \perp$ **then**

   return $\perp$

return $\mathsf{m} = (m_L, m_R)$

</td></tr>
</table>

Fig. 5. Algorithms dEnc and dDec of the transformation described in Sect. 4.1.

4.2   The **CK-FO** Transform and Its Security

Our CK-FO transform takes as input a family of hash functions $(\mathsf{H_{rej}}, \mathsf{H_{key}}, \mathsf{H_{rand}}, \mathsf{H_{OTP}})$ together with a 2K2M-PKE DPKE constructed from two PKE schemes $\mathsf{PKE_L}$ and $\mathsf{PKE_R}$, as detailed in Sect. 4.1. The transform outputs a 2K-KEM, denoted $\mathsf{dKEM^{FO}}$, described in Fig. 6.

The CK-FO transform upgrades the [IND-CPA, IND-CPA] security of DPKE into the [IND-CK-CCA, IND-CCA] security of the resulting 2K-KEM.

A central difficulty in proving [IND-CK-CCA, -] security is that the adversary may choose the right public key $\mathsf{pk_R}$, which need not be well-formed. Since the 2K2M-PKE is only [IND-CPA, -]-secure, we can guarantee the security of $\mathsf{c_R}$ only when $\mathsf{pk_R}$ is generated by $\mathsf{Keygen_R}$. Otherwise, $\mathsf{c_R}$ might leak information about both its encapsulated message m_R and the common randomness r_C, potentially revealing the message m_L encapsulated in $\mathsf{c_L}$.

Our transform resolves this by concealing $\mathsf{c_R}$ using m_L (line 6 of $\mathsf{dEncaps^{FO}}$ in Fig. 6).[14] This ensures $\mathsf{c_R}$ remains hidden until m_L is recovered, allowing us to reduce the [IND-CK-CCA, -] security of $\mathsf{dKEM^{FO}}$ to the IND-CPA security of $\mathsf{PKE_L}$. The proof therefore relies fundamentally on the structure of the input 2K2M-PKE and, in particular, on the security of its left constituent PKE $\mathsf{PKE_L}$.

To obtain security in the QROM rather than only in the ROM, we must carefully select which elements are hashed. In particular, the encapsulation randomness is not derived solely from the messages m_L and m_R, but also incorporates the two public keys, as shown in the algorithm $\mathsf{dEncaps^{FO}}$ in Fig. 6. This choice is essential for the QROM proof, which uses semi-classical oracles [2], following the approach of [17].

The following theorem summarizes the security guarantees of our CK-FO transform in both the ROM and the QROM. The corresponding proofs are provided in full version, Appendix B.

Theorem 3 (CK-FO transform in ROM and QRO). *Consider random oracles* $\mathsf{H_{key}}$, $\mathsf{H_{rej}}$, $\mathsf{H_{OTP}}$, *and* $\mathsf{H_{rand}}$, *and let* DPKE *constructed from* $\mathsf{PKE_L}$ *and* $\mathsf{PKE_R}$ *be* δ-*correct. Let* $\mathcal{A}$ *be an adversary against the* [IND-CK-CCA, -] *(resp.* [- , IND-CCA]*) security of* $\mathsf{dKEM^{FO}}$, *making at most* $q_{leak}, q_{CCA}, q_{key}, q_{rej}, q_{OTP}$ *and* q_{rand} *queries to the oracles* $\mathcal{O}_{leak_R}$ *(resp.* $\mathcal{O}_{leak_L}$*),* $\mathcal{O}_{CCA_L}$ *(resp.* $\mathcal{O}_{CCA_R}$*),* $\mathsf{H_{key}}$, $\mathsf{H_{rej}}$, $\mathsf{H_{OTP}}$ *and* $\mathsf{H_{rand}}$. *Then there exists an adversary* $\mathcal{B}$ *such that:* $\mathsf{Adv}^{[\text{IND-CK-CCA, - }]}_{\mathsf{dKEM^{FO}}}(\mathcal{A})$ *and* $\mathsf{Adv}^{[\text{ - },\text{IND-CPA}]}_{\mathsf{DPKE}}(\mathcal{B})$ *are respectively upper-bounded by* $2\,\mathsf{Adv}^{\text{IND-CPA}}_{\mathsf{PKE_L}}(\mathcal{B}) + \frac{q_{rej}}{2^\nu} + q_{rand}\delta + \frac{q_{rand}+q_{key}+q_{OTP}}{|\mathcal{M}_L|}$ *and* $2\,\mathsf{Adv}^{[\text{ - },\text{IND-CPA}]}_{\mathsf{DPKE}}(\mathcal{B}) + \frac{q_{rej}}{2^\nu} + q_{rand}\delta + \frac{q_{key}}{|\mathcal{M}_R|}$. *If we operate in the quantum-accessible random oracle model with quantum-accessible oracles* $\mathsf{H_{key}}$, $\mathsf{H_{rej}}$, $\mathsf{H_{OTP}}$, *and* $\mathsf{H_{rand}}$, *and* $q_{key}, q_{rej}, q_{OTP}, q_{rand}$ *denote the respective query bounds, then there exists an adversary* $\mathcal{B}$ *such that:* $\mathsf{Adv}^{[\text{IND-CK-CCA, - }]}_{\mathsf{dKEM^{FO}}}(\mathcal{A}) \leq \beta + 2\sqrt{(\hat{q}+1)\left(2\,\mathsf{Adv}^{\text{IND-CPA}}_{\mathsf{PKE_L}}(\mathcal{B}) + 4\hat{q}/|\mathcal{M}_L|\right)}$, *and*

$\mathsf{Adv}^{[\text{ - },\text{IND-CCA}]}_{\mathsf{dKEM^{FO}}}(\mathcal{A}) \leq \tilde{\beta} + 2\sqrt{(\tilde{q}+1)}\sqrt{\left(2\,\mathsf{Adv}^{[\text{ - },\text{IND-CPA}]}_{\mathsf{DPKE}}(\mathcal{B}) + 4\tilde{q}/|\mathcal{M}_R|\right)}$. *where* $\beta = 2\,q_{rej}\,2^{-\nu/2} + 16\,q_{leak}\,\delta\,(q_{rand} + q_{CCA} + 1)^2$, $\tilde{\beta} = 2\,q_{rej}\,2^{-\nu/2} + 16\,(q_{leak} + 1)\,\delta\,(q_{rand} + q_{CCA} + 1)^2$, $\hat{q} = q_{rand} + q_{key} + q_{OTP} + q_{CCA}$ *and* $\tilde{q} = q_{rand} + q_{key} + q_{CCA}$.

---

[14] Note that the xor is well-defined: we assume that the set of right ciphertexts is contained in the binary space $\{0,1\}^\tau$ and choose $\mathsf{H_{OTP}}$ to have range $\{0,1\}^\tau$.

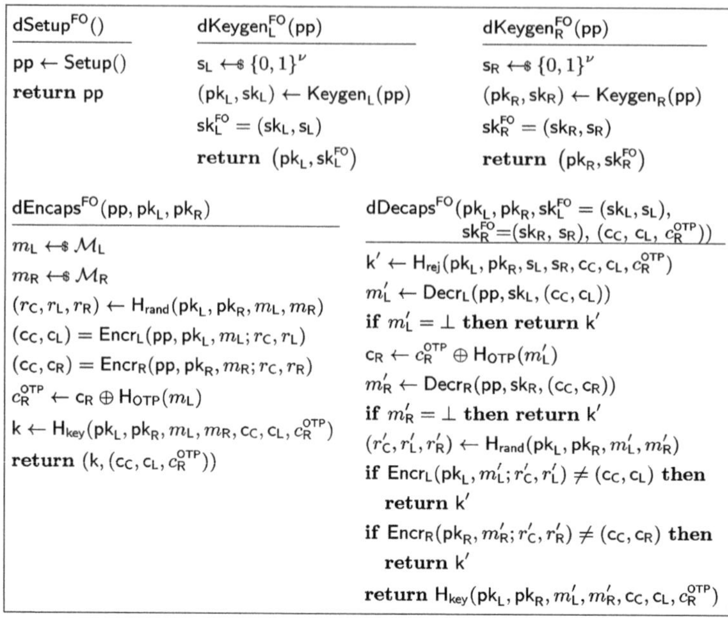

Fig. 6. Our CK-FO Transform. $(\mathsf{dSetup}, \mathsf{dKeygenL}, \mathsf{dKeygenR}, \mathsf{dEnc}, \mathsf{dDec})$ is a 2K2M-PKE built from two PKEs $\mathsf{PKE_L}$ and $\mathsf{PKE_R}$, as described in Sect. 4.1.

5   Compact Lattice-Based Double-KEM

In this section we introduce Maul, a compact 2K-KEM inspired by Kyber [37] and achieving [IND-CK-CCA, IND-CCA] security. Its security is proven in both the ROM and QROM under the MLWE and Hint-MLWE assumptions.

Maul is obtained by applying our CK-FO transform (Sect. 4) to $\mathsf{Maul_{PKE}}$, a [IND-CPA, IND-CPA]-secure 2K2M-PKE.

After introducing preliminaries in Sect. 5.1, we present the 2K2M-PKE $\mathsf{Maul_{PKE}}$ and establish its security in Sect. 5.2. Finally, the concrete parameters of Maul are provided in Sect. 5.3 and justified in Sects. 5.4 and 5.5.

5.1   Preliminaries on Lattices, MLWE, and Hint-MLWE Problems

Linear Algebra and Modular Operations. Let A be a ring. Vectors $\mathbf{u} \in A^n$ are assumed to be column vectors, and we denote by $\mathbf{u}^\mathsf{T}$ the transpose of $\mathbf{u}$. For $x \in \mathbb{R}$, we denote by $\lfloor x \rceil$ the nearest integer to x, with ties rounded up. We define the polynomial ring $\mathcal{R} := \mathbb{Z}[X]/(X^n + 1)$, where $n \in \mathbb{N}$ is called the *dimension*, to be specified as needed. For a modulus $q \in \mathbb{N}$, we define the quotient ring $\mathcal{R}_q := \mathbb{Z}_q[X]/(X^n + 1)$. For any $q > 1$, we identify $\mathcal{R}_2$ with the subset of polynomials in $\mathcal{R}_q$ whose coefficients lie in $\{0, 1\}$. For a real matrix $\mathbf{H} \in \mathbb{R}^{d \times \ell}$, we define the spectral norm $s_1(\mathbf{H})$ as $s_1(\mathbf{H}) = \max_{\mathbf{x} \neq 0} \frac{\|\mathbf{H}\mathbf{x}\|_2}{\|\mathbf{x}\|_2}$, where $\|\cdot\|_2$ denotes the euclidean norm. For $\mathbf{H} \in \mathcal{R}^{d \times \ell}$, we identify it with an associated negacyclic matrix $\bar{\mathbf{H}} \in \mathbb{Z}^{nd \times n\ell}$, and define the spectral norm of $\mathbf{H}$ as that of $\bar{\mathbf{H}}$.

Throughout this work, unless otherwise stated, all operations are performed modulo a positive integer $q \in \mathbb{N}$, which will be specified in context.

MLWE and Hint-MLWE Problems. We rely on the *module learning with errors* (MLWE) problem [34], as well as a generalized variant known as the Hint-MLWE problem [30], in which the adversary is additionally given partial information (or *hints*) about the MLWE secret and error vectors.

Definition 1 (MLWE). *Let k, m, q be positive integers, and let χ be a distribution over $\mathcal{R}^{k+m}$. The advantage of an adversary $\mathcal{A}$ against the module learning with errors problem* $\mathsf{MLWE}^{\chi}_{\mathcal{R},k,m,q}$ *is defined as:* $\big| \Pr\left[\mathcal{A}(\mathbf{A}, \mathbf{As} + \mathbf{e}) = 1\right] - \Pr\left[\mathcal{A}(\mathbf{A}, \mathbf{u}) = 1\right] \big|$, *where* $\mathbf{A} \leftarrow_{\$} \mathcal{U}\left(\mathcal{R}_q^{m \times k}\right)$, $\left(\begin{smallmatrix}\mathbf{s}\\\mathbf{e}\end{smallmatrix}\right) \leftarrow_{\$} \chi$ *and* $\mathbf{u} \leftarrow_{\$} \mathcal{U}\left(\mathcal{R}_q^m\right)$.

In the original Hint-MLWE formulation [30, Definition 7], the adversary is given noisy linear hints of the form $\gamma_i \cdot \mathbf{r} + \mathbf{y}_i$, where $\mathbf{r} = \left(\begin{smallmatrix}\mathbf{s}\\\mathbf{e}\end{smallmatrix}\right)$ is the concatenated secret-error vector, $\mathbf{y}_i$ are noise terms, and γ_i are public polynomials. This was later generalized in [18] to hints of the form $\mathbf{Hr} + \mathbf{y}$, where $\mathbf{H} \in \mathcal{R}_q^{\ell \times 2k}$ and $\mathbf{A} \in \mathcal{R}_q^{k \times k}$. We consider a slight extension of this generalization, where $\mathbf{A} \in \mathcal{R}_q^{m \times k}$ and $\mathbf{H} \in \mathcal{R}_q^{\ell \times d}$ for some $d \leq k + m$. This allows the hints to depend only on a subset of the secret-error vector.

Definition 2 (Hint-MLWE, adapted from [18]). *Let k, m, ℓ, d, q be positive integers with $d \leq k+m$, and let $J \subseteq \mathbb{Z} \cap [0, k+m-1]$ be an index set of size d. Let χ be a distribution over $\mathcal{R}^{k+m}$, χ_h a distribution over $\mathcal{R}^{\ell}$, and $\mathcal{F}$ a distribution over $\mathcal{R}_q^{\ell \times d}$.*

The advantage of an adversary $\mathcal{A}$ against the hint module learning with errors problem $\mathsf{Hint\text{-}MLWE}^{\chi, \chi_h, \mathcal{F}}_{\mathcal{R}, k, m, q, \ell, d, J}$ *is defined as* $\big| \left[\mathcal{A}(\mathbf{A}, \mathbf{As} + \mathbf{e}, \mathbf{H}, \mathbf{Hr} + \mathbf{y}) = 1\right] - \Pr\left[\mathcal{A}(\mathbf{A}, \mathbf{b}, \mathbf{H}, \mathbf{Hr} + \mathbf{y}) = 1\right] \big|$, *where* $(\mathbf{A}, \mathbf{b}, \bar{\mathbf{r}}, \mathbf{H}, \mathbf{y}) \leftarrow \mathcal{U}\left(\mathcal{R}_q^{m \times k}\right) \times \mathcal{U}\left(\mathcal{R}_q^m\right) \times \chi \times \mathcal{F} \times \chi_h$, *with* $\bar{\mathbf{r}} := \left(\begin{smallmatrix}\mathbf{s}\\\mathbf{e}\end{smallmatrix}\right) \in \mathcal{R}^{k+m}$, *and* $\mathbf{r} = (\bar{\mathbf{r}}_i)_{i \in J} \in \mathcal{R}^d$ *consists of the components of $\bar{\mathbf{r}}$ indexed by J.*

In [30], it is shown that the Hint-MLWE problem is at least as hard as the MLWE problem when the secret and error are sampled from discrete Gaussian distributions, assuming certain constraints on the width parameters. For completeness, we present an adaptation of this reduction that applies to the generalized Hint-MLWE formulation in Definition 2, under the same parameter regime. It is proven in full version, Appendix H.1.

Theorem 4 (Hardness of Hint-MLWE, adapted from [30]).
Let k, m, ℓ, d, q, J be as in Definition 2, and let $\mathcal{F}$ be a distribution over $\mathcal{S}_B :=$ $\left\{ \mathbf{H} \in \mathcal{R}_q^{\ell \times d} \mid s_1(\mathbf{H})^2 \leq B \right\}$, for $B > 0$. Let $\sigma_1, \sigma_2 > 0$, and define $\sigma > 0$ via $\frac{1}{\sigma^2} = 2\left(\frac{1}{\sigma_1^2} + \frac{B}{\sigma_2^2}\right)$. Let $\chi_h := D_{\mathbb{Z}^{\ell \cdot n}, \sigma_2}$, and let χ be a distribution over $\mathcal{R}^{k+m-d}$. Define χ_σ over $\mathcal{R}^{k+m}$ as the distribution where coordinates in J are drawn from

$D_{\mathbb{Z}^{d\cdot n},\sigma}$ and the rest from χ. If $\sigma \geq \sqrt{2} \cdot \eta_\varepsilon(\mathbb{Z}^{d\cdot n})$ for some $0 < \varepsilon \leq 1/2$, then there exists an efficient reduction from $\mathsf{MLWE}^{\chi_\sigma}_{\mathcal{R},k,m,q}$ to $\mathsf{Hint\text{-}MLWE}^{\chi_{\sigma_1},\chi_h,\mathcal{F}}_{\mathcal{R},k,m,q,\ell,d,J}$ that reduces the advantage by at most 2ε.

5.2   Maul$_\mathsf{PKE}$: A [IND-CPA, IND-CPA]-Secure 2K2M-PKE

Let $k \in \mathbb{N}$, two distributions $\mathcal{B}, \mathcal{D}$ over $\mathcal{R}$, and compression parameters $d_u, d_v \leq \log_2(q)$. For $x \in \mathbb{Q}$, we define the compression $\mathsf{Comp}_{(q,d_u)}(x) = \lfloor (2^{d_u}x)/q \rceil \bmod 2^{d_u}$, and the decompression $\mathsf{Decomp}_{(q,d_v)}(x) = \lfloor (qx)/2^{d_v} \rceil$.

Consider the Kyber-like PKE DualRegev defined in Fig. 7. Its encryption algorithm uses three sources of randomness $(\mathsf{s_C}, \mathsf{e_C}, f)$, producing ciphertexts $(\mathsf{c_C}, \mathsf{c_{scal}})$, where $\mathsf{c_C}$ depends only on $(\mathsf{s_C}, \mathsf{e_C})$. By applying the transformation from Sect. 4.1, we combine two instances of DualRegev into a 2K2M-PKE that reuses the randomness pair $(\mathsf{s_C}, \mathsf{e_C})$. The resulting scheme, Maul$_\mathsf{PKE}$, is detailed in Fig. 8. Theorem 5 analyses the security of Maul$_\mathsf{PKE}$. Its correctness is analyzed in the following lemma, proven in full version, Appendix H.2.

DualRegev.Setup ()	DualRegev.Keygen $(\mathsf{pp} = \mathbf{A})$	DualRegev.Decr$(\mathsf{pp} = \mathbf{A},$ $\mathsf{sk} = \mathbf{s}, \mathsf{ct} = (\mathsf{c_C}, \mathsf{c_{scal}}))$
$\mathbf{A} \leftarrow_\$ \mathcal{U}\left(\mathcal{R}_q^{k\times k}\right)$	$(\mathbf{s}, \mathbf{e}) \leftarrow_\$ \mathcal{B}^{2k}$	$m' \leftarrow \mathsf{Decomp}_{(q,d_v)}(\mathsf{c_{scal}})$
$\mathbf{return}\ \mathbf{A}(= \mathsf{pp})$	$\mathbf{t} \leftarrow \mathbf{As} + \mathbf{e}$	$\quad - \mathsf{Decomp}_{(q,d_u)}(\mathsf{c_C})^\mathsf{T}\mathbf{s}$
	$\mathbf{return}\ (\mathbf{t}(= \mathsf{pk}), \mathbf{s}(= \mathsf{sk}))$	$\mathbf{return}\ \lfloor 2m'/q \rceil$

DualRegev.Encr$(\mathsf{pp} = \mathbf{A}, \mathsf{pk} = \mathbf{t}, m \in \mathcal{R}_2)$		
$(\mathsf{s_C}, \mathsf{e_C}) \leftarrow_\$ \mathcal{B}^{2k}$	$\mathsf{c_C} \leftarrow \mathsf{Comp}_{(q,d_u)}(\mathbf{A}^\mathsf{T}\mathsf{s_C} + \mathsf{e_C})$	
$f \leftarrow_\$ \mathcal{D}$	$\mathsf{c_{scal}} \leftarrow \mathsf{Comp}_{(q,d_v)}(\mathsf{s_C}^\mathsf{T}\mathbf{t} + f + \lceil q/2 \rceil m)$	
	$\mathbf{return}\ \mathsf{ct} = (\mathsf{c_C}, \mathsf{c_{scal}})$	

Fig. 7. Algorithms for DualRegev.

Lemma 1 (Maul$_\mathsf{PKE}$ correctness). *Using the notation from Fig. 8, the scheme* Maul$_\mathsf{PKE}$ *is δ-correct provided that The scheme is δ-correct provided that* $\Pr\left[\|U\|_\infty \leq q/4\right] > 1 - \delta$, *where U denotes* $(f_\mathsf{L} + e_{\mathsf{c_L}} + \mathsf{s_C}^\mathsf{T}\mathbf{e_L} - (\mathbf{e_C} + \mathbf{e_{cc}})^\mathsf{T}\mathbf{s_L}, f_\mathsf{R} + e_{\mathsf{c_R}} + \mathsf{s_C}^\mathsf{T}\mathbf{e_R} - (\mathbf{e_C} + \mathbf{e_{cc}})^\mathsf{T}\mathbf{s_R})$, $\mathbf{e_{cc}} = \mathsf{Decomp}_{(q,d_u)}(\mathsf{c_C}) - \mathbf{A}^\mathsf{T}\mathsf{s_C} + \mathbf{e_C}$, $e_{\mathsf{c_L}} = \mathsf{Decomp}_{(q,d_v)}(\mathsf{c_L}) - \mathsf{s_C}^\mathsf{T}\mathbf{t_L} + f_\mathsf{L} + m_\mathsf{L}$, *and* $e_{\mathsf{c_R}} = \mathsf{Decomp}_{(q,d_v)}(\mathsf{c_R}) - \mathsf{s_C}^\mathsf{T}\mathbf{t_R} + f_\mathsf{R} + m_\mathsf{R}$.

Theorem 5 ([IND-CPA, IND-CPA] Security of Maul$_\mathsf{PKE}$). *Let consider* $\mathsf{X} \in \{[\mathsf{IND\text{-}CPA}, \text{-}], [\text{-}, \mathsf{IND\text{-}CPA}]\}$ *and $\mathcal{A}$ a PPT adversary of X security of* Maul$_\mathsf{PKE}$. *There exist PPT adversaries $\mathcal{B}, \mathcal{C}$ with same time complexity as $\mathcal{A}$ such that:* $\mathsf{Adv}^\mathsf{X}_{\mathsf{Maul_{PKE}}}(\mathcal{A}) \leq \mathsf{Adv}^{\mathsf{MLWE}_{k,k,\mathcal{B}^k,\mathcal{B}^k}}(\mathcal{B}) + \mathsf{Adv}^{\mathsf{Hint\text{-}MLWE}^{\chi,\chi_h,\mathcal{F}}_{\mathcal{R},k,k+1,q,1,2k,J}}(\mathcal{C})$. *Where* $\mathcal{F} = \mathcal{B}^k \times (-\mathcal{B}^k)$, $\chi_h = \mathcal{D}$, $\chi = \mathcal{B}^{2k} \times \mathcal{D}$ *and the subset J being the $2k$ first elements.*

$\mathsf{Maul}_{\mathsf{PKE}}.\mathsf{Setup}\,()$	$\mathsf{Maul}_{\mathsf{PKE}}.\mathsf{KeygenL}\,(\mathsf{pp}=\mathbf{A})$	$\mathsf{Maul}_{\mathsf{PKE}}.\mathsf{KeygenR}\,(\mathsf{pp}=\mathbf{A})$
$\mathbf{A}\leftarrow_{\$}\mathcal{U}\left(\mathcal{R}_q^{k\times k}\right)$	$(\mathbf{s}_\mathsf{L},\mathbf{e}_\mathsf{L})\leftarrow_{\$}\mathcal{B}^{2k}$	$(\mathbf{s}_\mathsf{R},\mathbf{e}_\mathsf{R})\leftarrow_{\$}\mathcal{B}^{2k}$
$\mathbf{return}\ \mathbf{A}(=\mathsf{pp})$	$\mathbf{t}_\mathsf{L}\leftarrow\mathbf{A}\mathbf{s}_\mathsf{L}+\mathbf{e}_\mathsf{L}$	$\mathbf{t}_\mathsf{R}\leftarrow\mathbf{A}\mathbf{s}_\mathsf{R}+\mathbf{e}_\mathsf{R}$
	$\mathbf{return}\ (\mathsf{pk}_\mathsf{L}=\mathbf{t}_\mathsf{L},\mathsf{sk}_\mathsf{L}=\mathbf{s}_\mathsf{L})$	$\mathbf{return}\ (\mathsf{pk}_\mathsf{R}=\mathbf{t}_\mathsf{R},\mathsf{sk}_\mathsf{R}=\mathbf{s}_\mathsf{R})$

$\mathsf{Maul}_{\mathsf{PKE}}.\mathsf{Encr}\big(\mathsf{pp}=\mathbf{A},\mathsf{pk}_\mathsf{L}=\mathbf{t}_\mathsf{L},$ $\mathsf{pk}_\mathsf{R}=\mathbf{t}_\mathsf{R},(m_\mathsf{L},m_\mathsf{R})\in\mathcal{R}_2^2\big)$	$\mathsf{Maul}_{\mathsf{PKE}}.\mathsf{Decr}\big(\mathsf{pp}=\mathbf{A},$ $\mathsf{sk}_\mathsf{L}=\mathbf{s}_\mathsf{L},\mathsf{sk}_\mathsf{R}=\mathbf{s}_\mathsf{R},\mathsf{ct}=(\mathsf{c}_\mathsf{C},\mathsf{c}_\mathsf{L},\mathsf{c}_\mathsf{R})\big)$
$(\mathbf{s}_\mathsf{C},\mathbf{e}_\mathsf{C})\leftarrow_{\$}\mathcal{B}^{2k}$	$m'_\mathsf{L}\leftarrow\mathsf{Decomp}_{(q,d_v)}(\mathsf{c}_\mathsf{L})$
$(f_\mathsf{L},f_\mathsf{R})\leftarrow_{\$}\mathcal{D}^{2k}$	$\quad-\mathsf{Decomp}_{(q,d_u)}(\mathsf{c}_\mathsf{C})^\mathsf{T}\mathbf{s}_\mathsf{L}$
$\mathsf{c}_\mathsf{C}\leftarrow\mathsf{Comp}_{(q,d_u)}(\mathbf{A}^\mathsf{T}\mathbf{s}_\mathsf{C}+\mathbf{e}_\mathsf{C})$	$m'_\mathsf{R}\leftarrow\mathsf{Decomp}_{(q,d_v)}(\mathsf{c}_\mathsf{R})$
$\mathsf{c}_\mathsf{L}\leftarrow\mathsf{Comp}_{(q,d_v)}(\mathbf{s}_\mathsf{C}^\mathsf{T}\mathbf{t}_\mathsf{L}+f_\mathsf{L}+\lceil q/2\rceil m_\mathsf{L})$	$\quad-\mathsf{Decomp}_{(q,d_u)}(\mathsf{c}_\mathsf{C})^\mathsf{T}\mathbf{s}_\mathsf{R}$
$\mathsf{c}_\mathsf{R}\leftarrow\mathsf{Comp}_{(q,d_v)}(\mathbf{s}_\mathsf{C}^\mathsf{T}\mathbf{t}_\mathsf{R}+f_\mathsf{R}+\lceil q/2\rceil m_\mathsf{R})$	$\mathbf{return}\ (\lfloor 2\,m'_\mathsf{L}/q\rceil,\lfloor 2\,m'_\mathsf{R}/q\rceil)$
$\mathbf{return}\ \mathsf{ct}=(\mathsf{c}_\mathsf{C},\mathsf{c}_\mathsf{L},\mathsf{c}_\mathsf{R})$	

Fig. 8. Algorithms for $\mathsf{Maul}_{\mathsf{PKE}}$.

Proof. The complete proof is provided in full version, Appendix H.2. We briefly outline here the argument for [IND-CPA, -] security; the proof for [- , IND-CPA] follows symmetrically. Moreover, it suffices to consider the variant of the scheme in which the functions Compress and Decompress are replaced by the identity.

We aim to show that the left ciphertext $\mathsf{c}_\mathsf{L}[b]$ given to the adversary $\mathcal{A}$ is indistinguishable from uniform. For this, we first introduce a game G_1 in which the vector $\mathbf{t}_\mathsf{L}$ is sampled uniformly at random, and the vectors $\mathbf{e}_\mathsf{L}$ and $\mathbf{s}_\mathsf{L}$ are no longer used. The difference in the adversary's advantage between the two games is then bounded by the MLWE advantage specified in the theorem statement.

Using the notation $\mathbf{B}^\mathsf{T}=(\mathbf{A}\mid\mathbf{t}_\mathsf{L})$, we can express the pair $(\mathsf{c}_\mathsf{C},\tilde{\mathsf{c}}_\mathsf{L})$ as $(\mathsf{c}_\mathsf{C}^\mathsf{T},\tilde{\mathsf{c}}_\mathsf{L})^\mathsf{T}=\mathbf{B}\mathbf{s}_\mathsf{C}+(\mathbf{e}_\mathsf{C}^\mathsf{T},f_\mathsf{L})^\mathsf{T}$. In G_1, we know that $\mathbf{B}$ is uniform. We would thus like to invoke the MLWE assumption to argue that $(\mathsf{c}_\mathsf{C}^\mathsf{T},\tilde{\mathsf{c}}_\mathsf{L})^\mathsf{T}$ is indistinguishable from uniform. However, the secret $\mathbf{s}_\mathsf{C}$ also appears in another term: $\mathsf{c}_\mathsf{R}=\mathbf{s}_\mathsf{C}^\mathsf{T}\mathbf{t}_\mathsf{R}+f_\mathsf{R}+\lceil q/2\rceil\,m_\mathsf{R}$, which prevents a direct application of the MLWE hypothesis. To address this, we instead rely on the Hint-MLWE hypothesis.

5.3 Parameter Selection

In this section, we propose concrete parameters for Maul, our 2K-KEM construction, targeting λ-bit [IND-CK-CCA, IND-CCA] security for $\lambda\in\{128,192,256\}$, corresponding respectively to NIST security levels 1, 3, and 5. Table 5 summarizes the parameter sets for each target security level. As shown in full version, Appendix H.3, instantiating Maul with Kyber's original parameters yielded a decapsulation failure probability δ above our design target, mainly due to the large variance of the distribution $\mathcal{D}$. To restore the intended failure probability, we slightly adjusted the parameters. For each set, we report the estimated BKZ block size (bikz) for solving the underlying Hint-MLWE problem, the ring dimension n, key dimension k, modulus q (NTT-friendly), compression parameters (d_u,d_v), and the distributions $(\mathcal{B},\mathcal{D})$ used in key generation and encap-

30   H. Beguinet et al.

sulation. Here, $\mathcal{B}_\eta$ denotes the centered binomial distribution with parameter η as defined in [40], and $\mathcal{D}_\sigma$ a *Gaussian-like* distribution of standard deviation σ, encompassing centered binomials, sums of uniforms, and discrete Gaussians. We also provide the public key and ciphertext sizes (in bytes). Estimates for bikz and δ were obtained using a modified version of the scripts[15] available at https://github.com/tlegavre/dake_estimator.

Table 5. Parameter sets for Maul, including sizes (in bytes).

	bikz	n	k	q	$\mathcal{B}$	$\mathcal{D}$	(d_u, d_v)	δ	ν	$\lvert\mathsf{pk}\rvert$	$\lvert\mathsf{ct}\rvert$	$\lvert\mathsf{pk}\rvert + \lvert\mathsf{ct}\rvert$
Maul512	337	256	2	7681	$\mathcal{B}_4$	$\mathcal{D}_{64}$	$(10, 4)$	2^{-150}	384	826	896	1722
Maul768	557	256	3	7681	$\mathcal{B}_4$	$\mathcal{D}_{64}$	$(11, 6)$	2^{-196}	512	1240	1440	2680
Maul1024	766	256	4	9473	$\mathcal{B}_4$	$\mathcal{D}_{64}$	$(12, 5)$	2^{-257}	640	1691	1856	3547

5.4 Security Estimation

Our security analysis is grounded in the assumed hardness of the MLWE problem, assessed via the *core-SVP* cost model [1]. This model estimates security levels against both classical and quantum attacks by relating them to the required BKZ block size (bikz) needed to solve the underlying MLWE instance. A conservative estimate is then derived by applying the complexity of the best known sieving algorithms—both classical and quantum [4,11]—to this block size, deliberately omitting polynomial factors in the full BKZ complexity. These omitted factors typically account for around 30 bits of security.

Transitioning from Hint-MLWE to standard MLWE for parameter estimation involves subtleties, as the distributions and parameter regimes fall outside Theorem 4 reduction. To address this, we follow the heuristic approach of Dodis et al. [16], which guides our parameter selection and hardness estimation for Hint-MLWE. Specifically, we rely on the following three heuristics:

- *Heuristic 1: Replacing Gaussian Distributions.* Although Theorem 4 formally applies to discrete Gaussians with widths above the smoothing parameter, we assume similar hardness for non-Gaussian distributions of equal variance. This is justified by their *Gaussian-like* behavior for large parameters and consistent performance in Rényi-divergence analyses.
- *Heuristic 2: Removing the Factor 2.* We omit the factor 2 in the expression $1/\sigma^2 = 2 \cdot (1/\sigma_1^2 + s_1(\mathbf{H})^2/\sigma_2^2)$ originally introduced in the Hint-MLWE reduction. As noted in [16], this factor arises from smoothing arguments specific to discrete Gaussians and is irrelevant for non-Gaussian distributions. Under this simplification, the relation between the equivalent Gaussian parameters becomes $1/\sigma^2 = 1/\sigma_1^2 + s_1(\mathbf{H})^2/\sigma_2^2$.

---

[15] https://github.com/pq-crystals/security-estimates.

– *Heuristic 3: Approximate Spectral Norm.* The security reduction involves the spectral norm $s_1(\mathbf{H})$ of the hint-related matrix $\mathbf{H} = (\mathbf{e}_L^\mathsf{T}, -\mathbf{s}_L^\mathsf{T})$. Instead of bounding this norm in the worst-case, we adopt the average-case approximation, yielding that $s_1(\mathbf{H})^2$ is replaced by $n \cdot \sigma_1^2$. This estimation gives us a baseline to assess the hardness of Hint-MLWE, with $\sigma_2 = \sqrt{n}\,\sigma_1^2$, as that of the MLWE problem, with $\sigma = \sigma_1/\sqrt{2}$.

5.5   Concrete Security Loss

We emphasise that potential security loss arising from the reduction from MLWE to Hint-MLWE is not formally captured in the above heuristic approach. In particular, it requires the standard deviation to exceed the smoothing parameter to ensure a tight reduction. Since Maul uses smaller distributions, some security loss may occur. Nevertheless, we conjecture that even under these conditions, the security of Hint-MLWE instantiated with parameters σ_1 and $\sigma_2 = \sqrt{n}\,\sigma_1^2$ remains higher than that of MLWE instantiated with parameter $\sigma_1/\sqrt{2}$. To support conjecture, we conduct empirical analyses and propose a concrete attack against Maul that explicitly exploits the hint. Details are provided in full version, Appendix H.3.

LWE with Side Information [14]. The most effective known attack against Hint-MLWE for Maul parameters relies on the framework of Ducas et al. [14], which extends the classical primal attack to incorporate auxiliary information. The standard primal attack on MLWE (typically disregarding the module structure) interprets, via a suitable embedding, the LWE instance as a *bounded distance decoding* (BDD) problem, which is then solved using lattice reduction techniques. The framework of [14] extends this approach to non-spherical (ellipsoidal) distributions and settings with side information that alters the target distribution.

Specifically, *approximate hints* arise naturally in the Maul setting when an adversary, given $(\mathbf{e}_L, \mathbf{s}_L)$, attempts to recover the encapsulated message m_R without access to $(\mathbf{e}_R, \mathbf{s}_R)$.[16] These hints take the form of noisy linear relations $\mathbf{z} = \mathbf{H}\left(\begin{smallmatrix} \mathbf{s} \\ \mathbf{e} \end{smallmatrix}\right) + \mathbf{y}$, which matches the structure of the Hint-MLWE hint in Maul, with $\mathbf{H} = (\mathbf{e}_L^\mathsf{T}, -\mathbf{s}_L^\mathsf{T})$, $(\mathbf{s}, \mathbf{e}) = (\mathbf{s}_C, \mathbf{e}_C)$, and $\mathbf{y} = f_L$.

The attack proceeds by conditioning the joint prior distribution of $(\mathbf{s}, \mathbf{e})$ on the observed hint $\mathbf{z}$. By Lemma 6 of [14], the resulting conditional distribution remains Gaussian, with covariance matrix Σ_{Hints}, but is generally no longer spherical. To compensate for this anisotropy, a linear transformation is applied to whiten the covariance, reducing the instance to an equivalent spherical BDD problem amenable to standard lattice reduction techniques.

Residual security is estimated by assuming that the vectors $\mathbf{s}$, $\mathbf{e}$, and $\mathbf{y}$ follow continuous Gaussian distributions with variances matching those of their actual distributions. This approximation enables the use of the leaky-LWE estimator from [14][17] to evaluate the impact of approximate hints.

---

[16] It is the only attack scenario where the adversary encounters a Hint-MLWE instance.
[17] https://github.com/lducas/leaky-LWE-Estimator.

Table 6. Estimated security (PrimalLWE$_{\Sigma_{\text{Hints}}}$) in bikz for Maul parameters, including upper bound (PrimalLWE$_{\sigma_1}$) and lower bound (PrimalLWE$_{\sigma_1/\sqrt{2}}$).

	PrimalLWE$_{\sigma_1}$	PrimalLWE$_{\Sigma_{\text{Hints}}}$	PrimalLWE$_{\sigma_1/\sqrt{2}}$
Maul512	373	353	338
Maul768	613	589	560
Maul1024	839	811	772

Table 6 reports the leaky-LWE estimated security (bikz) for Maul, including an upper bound, and a lower bound, under the following models:

- PrimalLWE$_{\sigma_1}$: the estimated security of a standard (M)LWE instance with secret and error distributions of standard deviation σ_1; this serves as an upper bound on the security of Hint-MLWE with parameters (σ_1, $\sigma_2 = \sqrt{n}\,\sigma_1^2$),
- PrimalLWE$_{\Sigma_{\text{Hints}}}$: the residual security after incorporating approximate hints to (M)LWE with parameter σ_1, using the leaky-LWE estimator,
- PrimalLWE$_{\sigma_1/\sqrt{2}}$: estimated (M)LWE security with parameter $\sigma_1/\sqrt{2}$.

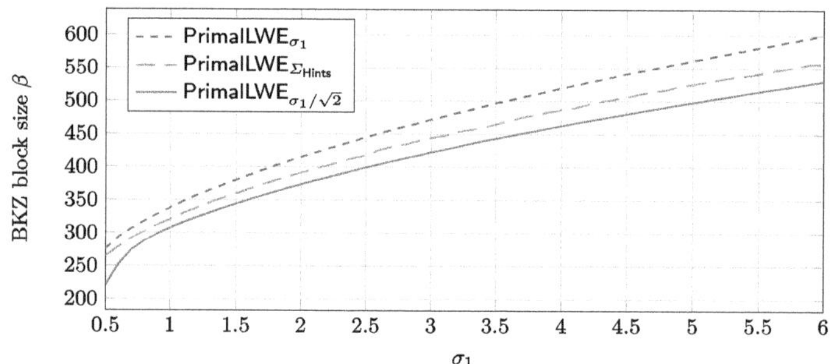

Fig. 9. Estimated security[2]4(For $k = 2$, $n = 256$, and $q = 7681$, as in the Maul512 parameter set.) (PrimalLWE$_{\Sigma_{\text{Hints}}}$) in bikz as a function of σ_1, including upper bound (PrimalLWE$_{\sigma_1}$), and lower bound (PrimalLWE$_{\sigma_1/\sqrt{2}}$).

Figure 9 shows that approximate hints weaken security, though less than the Theorem 4 reduction suggests, indicating the correctness of the Heuristics 2-3 and also that more competitive Hint-MLWE parameters may be viable.

Acknowledgements. This work has been partially supported by the European Union - Next Generation EU through the France Relance program and by the French government through the France 2030 program under the project RESQUE. This work has been further supported by the French Agence Nationale de la Recherche through the SecNISQ project (ANR-21-CE47-0014).

References

1. Alkim, E., Ducas, L., Pöppelmann, T., Schwabe, P.: Post-quantum key exchange - A new hope. In: Holz, T., Savage, S. (eds.) USENIX Security 2016: 25th USENIX Security Symposium, pp. 327–343. USENIX Association, Austin, TX, USA (2016). https://www.usenix.org/conference/usenixsecurity16/technical-sessions/presentation/alkim
2. Ambainis, A., Hamburg, M., Unruh, D.: Quantum security proofs using semi-classical oracles. In: Boldyreva, A., Micciancio, D. (eds.) CRYPTO 2019. LNCS, vol. 11693, pp. 269–295. Springer, Cham (2019). https://doi.org/10.1007/978-3-030-26951-7_10
3. Barnes, R., Bhargavan, K., Lipp, B., Wood, C.A.: Hybrid Public Key Encryption. RFC 9180 (2022). https://doi.org/10.17487/RFC9180. https://www.rfc-editor.org/info/rfc9180
4. Becker, A., Ducas, L., Gama, N., Laarhoven, T.: New directions in nearest neighbor searching with applications to lattice sieving. In: Krauthgamer, R. (ed.) 27th Annual ACM-SIAM Symposium on Discrete Algorithms, pp. 10–24. ACM-SIAM, Arlington, VA, USA (2016). https://doi.org/10.1137/1.9781611974331.ch2
5. Beguinet, H., et al.: DAKE: bandwidth-efficient (U)AKE from double-KEM. Cryptology ePrint Archive, Report 2025/1755 (2025). https://eprint.iacr.org/2025/1755
6. Blake-Wilson, S., Menezes, A.: Unknown key-share attacks on the station-to-station (STS) protocol. In: Imai, H., Zheng, Y. (eds.) PKC 1999. LNCS, vol. 1560, pp. 154–170. Springer, Heidelberg (1999). https://doi.org/10.1007/3-540-49162-7_12
7. Bos, J.W., et al.: CRYSTALS - Kyber: a CCA-secure module-lattice-based KEM. In: 2018 IEEE European Symposium on Security and Privacy, pp. 353–367. IEEE Computer Society Press, London, United Kingdom (2018). https://doi.org/10.1109/EuroSP.2018.00032
8. Boyd, C., Cliff, Y., Gonzalez Nieto, J., Paterson, K.G.: Efficient one-round key exchange in the standard model. In: Mu, Y., Susilo, W., Seberry, J. (eds.) ACISP 2008. LNCS, vol. 5107, pp. 69–83. Springer, Heidelberg (2008). https://doi.org/10.1007/978-3-540-70500-0_6
9. Boyd, C., de Kock, B., Millerjord, L.: Modular design of KEM-based authenticated key exchange. In: Simpson, L., Baee, M.A.R. (eds.) ACISP 2023. LNCS, vol. 13915, pp. 553–579. Springer, Cham (2023). https://doi.org/10.1007/978-3-031-35486-1_24
10. Canetti, R., Krawczyk, H.: Analysis of key-exchange protocols and their use for building secure channels. In: Pfitzmann, B. (ed.) EUROCRYPT 2001. LNCS, vol. 2045, pp. 453–474. Springer, Heidelberg (2001). https://doi.org/10.1007/3-540-44987-6_28
11. Chailloux, A., Loyer, J.: Lattice sieving via quantum random walks. In: Tibouchi, M., Wang, H. (eds.) ASIACRYPT 2021. LNCS, vol. 13093, pp. 63–91. Springer, Cham (2021). https://doi.org/10.1007/978-3-030-92068-5_3
12. Cremers, C.J.F.: Session-state Reveal is stronger than Ephemeral Key Reveal: attacking the NAXOS authenticated key exchange protocol. In: Abdalla, M., Pointcheval, D., Fouque, P.-A., Vergnaud, D. (eds.) ACNS 2009. LNCS, vol. 5536, pp. 20–33. Springer, Heidelberg (2009). https://doi.org/10.1007/978-3-642-01957-9_2
13. Cremers, C., Feltz, M.: Beyond eCK: perfect forward secrecy under actor compromise and ephemeral-key reveal. In: Foresti, S., Yung, M., Martinelli, F. (eds.) ESORICS 2012. LNCS, vol. 7459, pp. 734–751. Springer, Heidelberg (2012). https://doi.org/10.1007/978-3-642-33167-1_42

14. Dachman-Soled, D., Ducas, L., Gong, H., Rossi, M.: LWE with side information: attacks and concrete security estimation. In: Micciancio, D., Ristenpart, T. (eds.) CRYPTO 2020. LNCS, vol. 12171, pp. 329–358. Springer, Cham (2020). https://doi.org/10.1007/978-3-030-56880-1_12

15. Dodis, Y., Fiore, D.: Unilaterally-authenticated key exchange. In: Kiayias, A. (ed.) FC 2017. LNCS, vol. 10322, pp. 542–560. Springer, Cham (2017). https://doi.org/10.1007/978-3-319-70972-7_31

16. Dodis, Y., Jost, D., Katsumata, S., Prest, T., Schmidt, R.: Triple ratchet: a bandwidth efficient hybrid-secure signal protocol. In: Fehr, S., Fouque, P.A. (eds.) Advances in Cryptology – EUROCRYPT 2025, Part VIII. LNCS, vol. 15608, pp. 302–331. Springer, Cham (2025). https://doi.org/10.1007/978-3-031-91101-9_11

17. Duman, J., Hövelmanns, K., Kiltz, E., Lyubashevsky, V., Seiler, G.: Faster lattice-based KEMs via a generic Fujisaki-Okamoto transform using prefix hashing. In: Vigna, G., Shi, E. (eds.) ACM CCS 2021: 28th Conference on Computer and Communications Security, pp. 2722–2737. ACM Press, Virtual Event, Republic of Korea (2021). https://doi.org/10.1145/3460120.3484819

18. Esgin, M.F., Espitau, T., Niot, G., Prest, T., Sakzad, A., Steinfeld, R.: Plover: masking-friendly hash-and-sign lattice signatures. In: Joye, M., Leander, G. (eds.) Advances in Cryptology – EUROCRYPT 2024, Part VII. LNCS, vol. 14657, pp. 316–345. Springer, Cham (2024). https://doi.org/10.1007/978-3-031-58754-2_12

19. Fiore, D., Gennaro, R., Smart, N.P.: Constructing certificateless encryption and ID-based encryption from ID-based key agreement. In: Joye, M., Miyaji, A., Otsuka, A. (eds.) Pairing 2010. LNCS, vol. 6487, pp. 167–186. Springer, Heidelberg (2010). https://doi.org/10.1007/978-3-642-17455-1_11

20. Fouque, P.A., et al.: Falcon: fast-fourier lattice-based compact signatures over NTRU. Submission to the NIST's post-quantum cryptography standardization process (2020)

21. Fujioka, A., Suzuki, K., Xagawa, K., Yoneyama, K.: Strongly secure authenticated key exchange from factoring, codes, and lattices. In: Fischlin, M., Buchmann, J., Manulis, M. (eds.) PKC 2012. LNCS, vol. 7293, pp. 467–484. Springer, Heidelberg (2012). https://doi.org/10.1007/978-3-642-30057-8_28

22. Fujioka, A., Suzuki, K., Xagawa, K., Yoneyama, K.: Strongly secure authenticated key exchange from factoring, codes, and lattices. Des. Codes Crypt. **76**(3), 469–504 (2014). https://doi.org/10.1007/s10623-014-9972-2

23. Gaborit, P., et al.: Hamming Quasi-Cyclic (HQC). Submission to the NIST's post-quantum cryptography standardization process (2025)

24. Goldberg, I., Stebila, D., Ustaoglu, B.: Anonymity and one-way authentication in key exchange protocols. Des. Codes Crypt. **67**(2), 245–269 (2013). https://doi.org/10.1007/s10623-011-9604-z

25. Hashimoto, K., Katsumata, S., Niot, G., Wiggers, T.: Revisiting PQ WireGuard: a comprehensive security analysis with a new design using Reinforced KEMs p. To Appear (2026). https://eprint.iacr.org/2025/1758

26. Hövelmanns, K., Kiltz, E., Schäge, S., Unruh, D.: Generic authenticated key exchange in the quantum random oracle model. In: Kiayias, A., Kohlweiss, M., Wallden, P., Zikas, V. (eds.) PKC 2020. LNCS, vol. 12111, pp. 389–422. Springer, Cham (2020). https://doi.org/10.1007/978-3-030-45388-6_14

27. Hülsing, A., Ning, K.C., Schwabe, P., Weber, F.J., Zimmermann, P.R.: Post-quantum WireGuard. In: 2021 IEEE Symposium on Security and Privacy, pp. 304–321. IEEE Computer Society Press, San Francisco, CA, USA (2021). https://doi.org/10.1109/SP40001.2021.00030

28. Jager, T., Kohlar, F., Schäge, S., Schwenk, J.: On the security of TLS-DHE in the standard model. Cryptology ePrint Archive, Report 2011/219 (2011). https://eprint.iacr.org/2011/219

29. Katsumata, S., Kwiatkowski, K., Pintore, F., Prest, T.: Scalable ciphertext compression techniques for post-quantum KEMs and their applications. In: Moriai, S., Wang, H. (eds.) ASIACRYPT 2020. LNCS, vol. 12491, pp. 289–320. Springer, Cham (2020). https://doi.org/10.1007/978-3-030-64837-4_10

30. Kim, D., Lee, D., Seo, J., Song, Y.: Toward practical lattice-based proof of knowledge from hint-MLWE. In: Handschuh, H., Lysyanskaya, A. (eds.) Advances in Cryptology – CRYPTO 2023, Part V. LNCS, vol. 14085, pp. 549–580. Springer, Cham (2023). https://doi.org/10.1007/978-3-031-38554-4_18

31. Krawczyk, H.: HMQV: a high-performance secure Diffie-Hellman protocol. In: Shoup, V. (ed.) CRYPTO 2005. LNCS, vol. 3621, pp. 546–566. Springer, Heidelberg (2005). https://doi.org/10.1007/11535218_33

32. Krawczyk, H., Paterson, K.G., Wee, H.: On the security of the TLS protocol: a systematic analysis. In: Canetti, R., Garay, J.A. (eds.) CRYPTO 2013. LNCS, vol. 8042, pp. 429–448. Springer, Heidelberg (2013). https://doi.org/10.1007/978-3-642-40041-4_24

33. LaMacchia, B., Lauter, K., Mityagin, A.: Stronger security of authenticated key exchange. In: Susilo, W., Liu, J.K., Mu, Y. (eds.) ProvSec 2007. LNCS, vol. 4784, pp. 1–16. Springer, Heidelberg (2007). https://doi.org/10.1007/978-3-540-75670-5_1

34. Langlois, A., Stehlé, D.: Worst-case to average-case reductions for module lattices. Des. Codes Cryptogr. **75**(3), 565–599 (2015). https://doi.org/10.1007/S10623-014-9938-4

35. Lyu, Y., Liu, S.: Two-message authenticated key exchange from public-key encryption. In: Tsudik, G., Conti, M., Liang, K., Smaragdakis, G. (eds.) ESORICS 2023, Part I. LNCS, vol. 14344, pp. 414–434. Springer, Cham (2023). https://doi.org/10.1007/978-3-031-50594-2_21

36. Naehrig, M., et al.: FrodoKEM. Technical report, National Institute of Standards and Technology (2020). https://csrc.nist.gov/projects/post-quantum-cryptography/post-quantum-cryptography-standardization/round-3-submissions

37. Schwabe, P., et al.: CRYSTALS-KYBER. Technical report, National Institute of Standards and Technology (2022). https://csrc.nist.gov/Projects/post-quantum-cryptography/selected-algorithms-2022

38. Schwabe, P., Stebila, D., Wiggers, T.: Post-quantum TLS without handshake signatures. In: Ligatti, J., Ou, X., Katz, J., Vigna, G. (eds.) ACM CCS 2020: 27th Conference on Computer and Communications Security, pp. 1461–1480. ACM Press, Virtual Event, USA (2020). https://doi.org/10.1145/3372297.3423350

39. Shoup, V.: On formal models for secure key exchange. Cryptology ePrint Archive, Report 1999/012 (1999). https://eprint.iacr.org/1999/012

40. National Institute of Standards and Technology: FIPS 203: Module-lattice-based key-encapsulation mechanism standard. https://csrc.nist.gov/pubs/fips/203/final

41. National Institute of Standards and Technology: FIPS 204: Module-lattice-based digital signature standard. https://csrc.nist.gov/pubs/fips/204/final
42. National Institute of Standards and Technology: FIPS 205: Stateless hash-based digital signature standard. https://csrc.nist.gov/pubs/fips/205/final
43. Wiggers, T., Celi, S., Schwabe, P., Stebila, D., Sullivan, N.: KEM-based Authentication for TLS 1.3. Internet-Draft draft-celi-wiggers-tls-authkem-05, Internet Engineering Task Force (2025). https://datatracker.ietf.org/doc/draft-celi-wiggers-tls-authkem/05/, work in Progress
44. Xue, H., Lu, X., Li, B., Liang, B., He, J.: Understanding and constructing AKE via double-key key encapsulation mechanism. In: Peyrin, T., Galbraith, S. (eds.) ASIACRYPT 2018. LNCS, vol. 11273, pp. 158–189. Springer, Cham (2018). https://doi.org/10.1007/978-3-030-03329-3_6

Perpetual Encryption

Yevgeniy Dodis[1] and Daniel Jost[2]($\boxtimes$)

[1] New York University, New York, USA
`dodis@cs.nyu.edu`
[2] Blanqet LLC, Chicago, USA
`daniel@blanqet.net`

Abstract. Traditional public-key encryption (PKE) schemes have a static secret key. This means that the secret key owner can decrypt any old ciphertext in perpetuity. Schemes with changing secret keys, supporting so-called epochs, have been considered for a variety of reasons such as post-compromise security or more simply supporting communication among a dynamically changing group. This complicates perpetuity, especially in settings where the epoch number itself is supposed to be confidential.

We address this concern by introducing perpetual encryption (PE). The scheme leverages a trusted group manager to distribute states for each epoch such that: (1) without such a secret state, ciphertexts look pseudorandom and, hence, hide the epoch number; and (2) parties in a later epoch can still decrypt encryptions for old epochs in sublinear time (in the number of epochs). More stringently, we require that whenever a party in an earlier epoch decrypts to a message m then any party in a later epoch must arrive at the same message, even for adversarially crafted ciphertexts.

We build an efficient, unbounded-epoch PE scheme based on anonymous PKE, hashing, and other standard symmetric primitives. We also extend our scheme to protect against malicious group managers, at the expense of limiting the maximum number of epochs. All our schemes have fixed-sized states and decryption times, independent of the number of epochs.

Keywords: PKE · post-compromise security · anonymity · multi-cast

1 Introduction

Traditional public-key encryption (PKE) schemes have a static secret key sk. This means that the secret key owner can decrypt any old ciphertext c in perpetuity. Unfortunately, in some settings, one might be forced to change the secret key of the scheme. Two benign examples include: (a) various compliance regulations, demanding that one cannot use the same secret/public key for too long; or (b) *Post-Compromise Security* (PCS), where the user is trying to recover from suspected compromise of sk to ensure that future ciphertexts are secure. In this

© International Association for Cryptologic Research 2026
S. Bai and E. Persichetti (Eds.): PKC 2026, LNCS 16554, pp. 37–66, 2026.
https://doi.org/10.1007/978-3-032-26740-5_2

work, we will also be interested in another setting (c), where the secret key sk is shared by multiple users in a dynamically changing group G.

For instance, in the IETF Message Layer Security protocol [5], parties are arranged at the leaves of a binary tree with intermediate nodes having PKE key pairs assigned such that each party knows exactly the secret keys for nodes on the path from their leaf to the root. In this case, when a member U leaves the group, the secret key must change, as U should not be able to decrypt future ciphertexts. In the following, we assume the group is managed by some (semi-)trusted group manager M, which is basically the setting of *multicast encryption* [16,35,38,42,43] extensively studied in the literature (see [10] and references therein).

PERPETUITY. A natural question to consider here is whether we still want the members of group G to be able to decrypt ciphertexts encrypted using an old public key. In the traditional multicast setting, the answer is negative: the new secret key is not required to support the decryption of old ciphertexts. As we observe in this work (and describe below), there are natural applications where this answer is insufficient, and one wants any "future" secret key to still decrypt any "past" ciphertexts. This leads to the notion of *perpetual encryption* we introduce in this work. As such, perpetual encryption can be seen as the dual of the widely studied notion of forward-secure encryption.[1]

One naive way to build perpetual encryption is to never erase any of the old secrets $(sk_1, \ldots, sk_n)$, and then simply use the appropriate sk_i when decrypting a ciphertext c encrypted using pk_i. The obvious drawback of this approach is that the storage of the user grows linearly with the number of *epochs* n. Thus, as the first question, we ask:

Question 1: *Can we make users' storage sublinear in the number of epochs n?*

A simple scheme addressing this can be built from a (prefix-)delegatable PRF (DPRF) as introduced by Kiayias et al. [32]. Instead of using independent PKE secrets $(sk_1, \ldots, sk_n)$, the group manager samples sk_i using $\mathrm{DPRF}_K(i)$, i.e., uses the output of the DPRF as randomness seed for the key generation. The prefix-delegation property then allows the manager to delegate a compact key $K_{[0,n]}$ that allows users to evaluate the PRF exactly on the range $[0, n]$. A well-known DPRF is the Goldreich-Goldwasser-Micali (GGM) construction [26], which further allows each individual evaluation to be done in time sublinear in n. Thus, if each ciphertext c additionally contains the epoch i for which it was encrypted, this ciphertext can be decrypted in sublinear time using the compact key $K_{[0,n]}$, for any $n \geq i$. However, in some of our applications we will have another concern, describe below.

ANONYMITY. While PKE hides the message content, hiding metadata is becoming an increasingly important as well. For instance, while traditional secure end-to-end encrypted messaging applications protect the content of messages but

---

[1] While the notions of perpetual encryption and forward-secure encryption are inherently incompatible, one could consider hybrid notions for which, for instance, metadata enjoys the perpetuity property, while content enjoys the forward security.

rely on metadata being transmitted in the clear, Signal recently attempted to address this shortcoming by introducing "sealed-sender" [39]. In this anonymity wrapper, metadata is encrypted under a fixed key of the recipient, with the use of anonymous PKE ensuring that for two ciphertexts one cannot tell whether they are for the same or different recipients.

One might thus ask whether we can achieve metadata hiding also in our setting. To this end, Perpetual Encryption must extend the anonymity notion of PKE to also hide epoch numbers, as otherwise for two recipients in different epochs the distinguishing is trivial. For simplicity, we formalize this anonymity goal by requiring *all ciphertexts encrypted at epoch i to appear pseudorandom* over a suitably defined ciphertext space, even against users knowing some secret key sk_j for an earlier epoch $j < i$. In particular, in the naive solution, where the user U stores all keys $(sk_1, \ldots, sk_n)$, U might not immediately know which secret key sk_i to use in order to decrypt c. Meaning that it might take U linear time $\Omega(n)$ to decrypt c, by doing a trial-and-error decryption until it succeeds. Thus, if we require that all ciphertexts c look random even given some sk_j for $j < i$, we ask:

Question 2: *Can we make users' decryption time sublinear in the number of epochs n, while hiding the epoch number of the ciphertext?*

Coming back to the simple DPRF solution, we see it does not hide the epoch number. Therefore, we need a novel scheme. We describe our idea in Sect. 1.4, but first let us formalize the resulting notion, and state some of its applications.

1.1 Perpetual Encryption: Definition

We now present a brief overview of our resulting notion of Perpetual Encryption (PE). In this notion, the group manager M commits to PE parameters pub, and is in charge of updating the current public key $pk = pk_i$ for epoch i. M is also in charge of helping users U obtain the current secret key $sk = sk_i$. Using pk_i (and pub), anybody can compute a ciphertext c encrypting some message m. Moreover, c should be decryptable using any secret key sk_n for any $n \geq i$, but pseudorandom otherwise; even against attackers having some secret keys sk_j for $j < i$, accounting for dynamic groups and/or PCS.

We call these conflicting properties *perpetuity* and *pseudorandomness*, respectively. In fact, as discussed in Sect. 2, both of these properties are stronger than stated above. In particular, pseudorandomness holds in light of chosen ciphertext attack. More interestingly, perpetuity holds even against a corrupt manager M, and even when trying to decrypt potentially *malformed ciphertexts*. Intuitively, even for such malformed ciphertexts (and potentially corrupt M), the commitment pub ensures that whenever a party in an older epoch decrypts any ciphertext c to some message $m \neq \bot$, then another party in the *same or a later* epoch must decrypt c to the same message m.

As stated in Questions 1 and 2 above, the major challenge is to design PE schemes where the user's state and decryption time do not scale linearly in the number of epochs n. As our main result, we show that such PE schemes can be constructed! In fact, in our schemes both user's storage and decryption time are logarithmic in n, which means they are always (fixed) polynomial in the security parameter λ, since $\lambda \geq \log n$ anyway.

1.2   Applications

We now motivate our notion of anonymous Perpetual Encryption. First, we note that achieving either anonymity or perpetuity in isolation is relatively straightforward: First, only perpetuity is required one can use independent key pairs per epoch and send epoch numbers in the clear, making perpetuity primarily a state-management problem. Second, if one If one does not require post-compromise security or long-term key management across epochs, standard anonymous PKE with rotating keys would suffice.

Needing to decrypt old ciphertexts, however, is quite natural. Simultaneously, there is also a strong utility of anonymity. Thus, resolving the non-trivial technical tension that arises when both properties are required simultaneously is not only of theoretical interest. To illustrate this, we highlight four key scenarios:

OUT-OF-ORDER DELIVERY. Consider an asynchronous network with out-of-order delivery. For any applications where PCS is relevant, this poses the issue of being able to decrypt delayed ciphertexts. Anonymity ensures that these delayed packets do not inadvertently reveal user patterns or metadata during the transition between epochs.

PCS FOR SEALED SENDER. A further example might be an improved version of Signal's sealed-sender mechanism, where, to protect metadata (including the sender's identity), ciphertexts are additionally encrypted under the recipient's static public key, which does not have any PCS. Using PE, we can obtain post-compromise security, without having to worry that a sender is still using an old key or messages being delivered out of order. This application is a clear example of Type 2 motivation: The specific goal of Sealed Sender is to hide metadata via an outermost encryption wrapper; without strict anonymity, the protocol's purpose is defeated.

PRIVATE BLOCKCHAIN. Another application might be to design a *private* blockchain that reuses a *public* ledger—and thus avoids having its own consensus mechanism—by putting encrypted transactions onto a public blockchain. If one imagines such a private blockchain to be used by a company, then membership will however need to change with new employees being added and existing ones being removed when they leave the company. Therefore, to be practical, the encryption scheme must support PCS and, thus, rotate keys. Since the current state of a blockchain, such as the account balances, typically depends on the entire transaction history, any party newly joining such a private blockchain must be able to decrypt the entire prefix, requiring perpetuity. Finally, to maintain transaction privacy, it is essential to hide which "subchain" or sender is involved. Our construction's anonymity property is thus a necessary requirement to ensure these system-level privacy guarantees are met.

MITIGATING TRAVEL EXPOSURE. Consider a setting where a party has a set of encrypted files. They might need access to any of them during their travel, for instance because they need to get some work done. However, this party is also concerned that their device gets compromised. For example, a border agent might coerce them to hand over all their passwords to search their devices upon entering a country. To mitigate the damage, the user might want to ensure that at least future files will not be compromised. To this end, they could use PE by having some secure device they leave at home. Instead, for their travel they use a disposable "burner device." The main device can then delegate decryption access to read all existing and current files, but not future files. Anonymity ensures that the ciphertexts do not reveal travel patterns by revealing how often this delegation process has taken place or when a particular file was encrypted.

1.3 Related Primitives

Recall that PE combines the PCS, anonymity, sublinearity and perpetuity properties. We organize related work by discussing related primitive for each of these properties (some primitives will be discussed multiple times). In particular, we focus on the two most closely related primitives key-insulated encryption [20] and interval encryption [9], and show how perpetual encryption combines (the best) aspects of those two notions. We conclude with summary why none of the primitives in the literature solves our problem.

Post-compromise Security. A multitude of encryption primitives that support dynamic groups, or post-compromise security more generally, have been proposed in the past. For example, multicast encryption [16,35,38,42,43] has been extensively studied in the literature (see [10] and references therein) and assumes a semi-trusted group manager maintaining the current group membership. Continuous group key agreement (CGKA) [2] is a related primitive from the secure group messaging literature that does not rely on an explicit group manager. More broadly speaking, a line of group messaging schemes proposed schemes achieving forward secrecy and post-compromise security simultaneously (see e.g. the references in [3]).

However, most of these protocols internally rely on the naive approach of just sampling and distributing fresh key material to achieve PCS. In the following, we discuss two lines of work that bring PCS to the PKE setting and are particularly relevant to our work.

Interval Key-Encapsulation Mechanism. In recent work, Bienstock et al. [9] introduced the notion of an interval key-encapsulation mechanism (IKEM) that generalizes forward-secure KEM to also include post-compromise security. Interval PKE can then be built using the standard KEM/DEM paradigm. Analogous to forward-secure PKE, the decryptor can refresh their secret key at regular intervals called epochs. As shown by the authors, PCS however requires the public key to be updated for each epoch (instead of the encryptor just learning the correct epoch number to encrypt for). Therefore, to account for parties that do not have the latest public key, IKEM allows to derive a decryption key that works for a specific *interval* of epochs—hence the name interval KEM. A party could, for instance, derive a secret key that allows to decrypt all epochs t in an interval $[i, j]$, while later be able to update that key for epoch $j + 1$.

It is then shown that in this model the secret key must be of size linear in the interval size, i.e., linear in $j - i$. The authors provide a construction based on standard KEM which matches this lower bound while having constant sized ciphertexts and public keys, in the interval length. The construction moreover only uses a standard KEM, thus being optimal in terms of assumptions given that IKEM clearly implies standard KEM. To address the growing size of the secret key, the authors moreover propose a modified scheme that uses outsourcing to an untrusted server to store an encryption of this (still growing) key. In contrast, all of our states remain compact, at the cost of relying on a trusted group manager.

Key-Insulated Encryption. To minimize the impact of secret-key exposures, Dodis et al. [20] introduced the notion of key-insulated PKE. In their model, the secret key stored on a insecure device is refreshed regularly via interaction with a physically-secre but computationally-limited device which stores a master key. Importantly, the public key used to encrypt remains unchanged and the insecure device can decrypt without interaction with the secure device. More concretely, each refresh establishes a fresh epoch such that compromising the insecure device in epoch t does not reveal ciphertexts encrypted for any epoch other than t, yielding both FS and PCS. (Of course, PCS depends on the secure device not helping the attacker to update the key obtained during the compromise, i.e., assumes proper authentication.) The authors further considered a stronger notion in which the secure device is potentially untrusted such that compromising the secure device alone, but not the insecure device, does not affect the security of any of the encryptions. This, for example, rules out simple solutions in which the secure device samples a master key from which all epochs keys are derived.

Key insulated encryption has spurred a number of follow up work. Most notably, Cheon et al. [18] demonstrated that a notion of time-released public key encryption is equivalent to key-insulated PKE with an untrusted secure device. In [7], on the other hand, Bellare and Palacio showed that for weak key-insulated PKE—where the secure device is trusted—the notion is equivalent to IBE when further requiring random-access key updates, i.e., when key updates do not have to be applied in order. In [27], Hanaoka, Hanaoka, and Imai considered the notion of parallel key-insulated public key encryption where two (or more) secure helper devices are used in an alternating fashion, such that exposing one of the device's state does not affect security for epochs initiated by the other device. Distributing the updating process among multiple devices can moreover enable more frequent updates for schemes where the process is bounded by the computational capabilities of the helper device. In [28], Hanaoka et al. considered a hybrid notion of identity-based and key-insulated encryption where decryption keys can be refreshed without having to make update to the public keys or the user's identity. Finally, key-insulated variants of various other primitives have been considered such as symmetric key encryption [22] or signatures [21].

Anonymity. Key anonymity for public-key encryption was first formalized as anonymous PKE in [6] and is also known under different names, such as source-indistinguishable PKE and PKE with key privacy. Anonymous PKE is also a fundamental building block for various anonymity systems, such as anonymous credential systems or anonymous broadcast encryption.

Anonymity is implied by pseudorandom ciphertexts [4,8,19,36,41], i.e., for any scheme where ciphertexts appear indistinguishable from pseudorandom elements given the public key. Unlike in the symmetric-key setting, where these notions are equivalent, PKE with pseudorandom ciphertexts does not follow black-box from PKE alone. Nonetheless, in the IND-CCA2 domain, many practical schemes are naturally pseudorandom over a suitable ciphertext space.

Unfortunately, anonymity is more troublesome in the PCS setting. Neither key-insulated encryption nor IKEM offer anonymity. More concretely, both schemes [9,20] generally leak the epoch number t as part of the ciphertext. Hence, if two public keys have been updated a different number of times, then the epoch number makes it trivial to distinguish which one has been used. Of course, the weak key-insulated scheme based on IBE (where the secure device is fully trusted) can be made anonymous using an anonymous IBE scheme [11]; it is, however, an open problem to construct an anonymous key-insulated PKE scheme with strong security. Similarly, the IKEM [9] construction can be made anonymous by omitting the epoch numbers. However, this comes at the significant cost of making the decryption time linear in the interval size.

Sublinear Overhead. Key-insulated encryption has constant overhead compared to a regular PKE scheme but does not naturally support decrypting ciphertexts from older epochs. To the best of our knowledge, for all existing schemes the only way of achieving this would be to keep the secret state of all the still relevant epochs stored. Similarly, IKEM has linear overhead in terms of storage (unless outsourcing the storage). In particular, if we add anonymity both the solution based on maintaining multiple states for key-insulated encryption and the IKEM scheme from [9] require trial-decryption for every epoch in the current interval $[i, j]$. In other words, with anonymity the decryption overhead of also grows linear in the interval as well.

Perpetuity. Being able to decrypt old ciphertexts shows up in various applications (cf. Sect. 1.2). Depending on the model, various solutions might be feasible. For example, updatable encryption (UE) [12–14,23,33,34] allows updating ciphertexts that were encrypted under a key at an epoch i to become decryptable by the key at an epoch $j > i$.

In our work, however, we consider settings where the original unmodified ciphertext remains decryptable. We observe that IKEM provides this for the given interval $[i, j]$. More concretely, the derived key for such an interval can decrypt ciphertexts for any epoch $i \leq t \leq j$ and especially a key for interval $[1, j]$ roughly matches our perpetuity notion (albeit with the drawbacks regarding anonymity and state size as discussed above).

Key-insulated encryption, on the other hand, does not provide any form of perpetuity. Instead, it provides forward secrecy, which can be seen as the dual property to perpetuity. Several additional lines of work on forward-secure encryption primitives exist. Notable examples are forward-secure PKE (FS-PKE) [17]. FS-PKE can generically be built from hierarchical identity-based encryption (HIBE) [25,29]. Importantly, FS-PKE only has a single public key that is input to the encryption algorithm alongside the epoch number t, eliminating the communication overhead.

In the context of secure messaging, more recent notions emerged, such as key-evolving encryption schemes [30,37] or updatable public key encryption (UPKE) [31]. These notions trade some increased communication and coordination overhead for otherwise more efficient instantiations. For instance, in UPKE, a sender initiates an update of the keys, where the updated public key must be distributed to all other senders, and the receiver must process the updates to their secret key in order. Importantly, in the random oracle model, UPKE can be instantiated from various regular PKE schemes with minimal overhead.

Novelty of Primitive. Summarizing the discussion above, in this work, we explore the tension between three dimensions: (1) post-compromise security (PCS), (2) hiding metadata/epoch numbers, and (3) perpetuity. We abstract away the issue of (4) roster management in dynamic groups, as a likely (but possibly not only) reason for (1). To the best of our knowledge, no existing solution addresses all three aspects simultaneously. More concretely,

1. *Multicast Encryption:* addresses (1),(4), and optionally (2), but not (3). PE could likely be combined with multicast to also achieve (4), although other methods might be possible (e.g., two-factor authentication, email, physical registration).
2. *CGKA:* same as multicast, but without group manager and, hence, less efficient.
3. *Key-Insulated Encryption:* addresses (1) and optionally (2), but not (3). In fact, it cannot efficiently support (3) as it has forward secrecy.
4. *Interval-based KEM:* addresses (1),(3), but not (2).
5. *Anything Forward-Secure:* clearly contradicts (3).

We stress that even ignoring perpetuity, our formalization of metadata hiding under PCS (i.e., compromise of prior state) is stronger than most of the primitives mentioned above. For instance, multicast and CGKA completely ignore metadata, while fixed-key schemes cannot provide any level of PCS.

1.4   Overview of Our Scheme

In this section, we provide an outline of our scheme as well as discuss some of the challenges encountered. Our base scheme is built on PKE with pseudorandom ciphertexts, non-interactive commitments, a collision-resistant hash function, as well as a PRG and a PRF. We remark that PKE with pseudorandom ciphertext is clearly a minimal assumption as it is trivially implied by PE with pseudorandom ciphertexts. All operations run in time logarithmic in the maximum epoch number, and all parties' states are of logarithmic size too.

BASIC IDEA. As seen before, the naive solution of using the GGM tree as a DPRF does not work. Nevertheless, we still use binary tree of key pairs, but structure encryption differently to solve anonymity without exhaustive search in the decryption algorithm. More concretely, the group manager sets up a complete binary tree, of a given height, where epochs are consecutively assigned to leaf nodes. For each node of the tree v, the manager samples a PKE key pair $(v.sk, v.pk)$. (To have a compact representation, they use a PRF applied to the node index to derive the respective key generation randomness.)

The PE public key for epoch i then consists of the vector of PKE public keys along the path from epoch i's leaf to the root. Encrypting a message m under said public key corresponds to encrypting it under each of the PKE public keys. A decryptor in epoch j will know the secret keys for the minimal set of nodes such that exactly all the leaves from epoch 0 to j can be reached when traversing down the tree. A moment of reflection reveals that this set is the left-sibling path of the leaf of epoch $(j + 1)$, i.e., all the direct left children of nodes encountered when traversing up from that leaf. Hence, the decryptor's state is of logarithmic size in the number of epochs while one can observe that as long as $i \le j$ then the decryptor knows the secret key of exactly one node the message is encrypted to. Hence, by trial-decrypting under each of the logarithmic many secret keys they know (for each secret key trying to decrypt the component at the position in the vector corresponding to the node's height) they can recover the message.

HANDLING MALICIOUS CIPHERTEXTS. So far this obviously only handles honestly generated ciphertexts, as the different PKE encryptions are not guaranteed to be consistent. Since our notion allows for false positives, we can observe however that we only need upward consistency: if one of the component ciphertexts decrypts to m then all further up the tree must do so as well, but not necessarily the ones below. To see that this is sufficient, observe that for any two decryptors in epochs $j_1 \le j_2$ the one in epoch j_2 will decrypt the one further up the tree.

As a result, we can use the following neat trick, instead of relying on NIZKs, to ensure consistency: The encryption derives the randomness for the various encryptions using a PRG from leaf to root while including the next seed as part of the encrypted message. That is, when encrypting to the ℓ-th component of the PE public key, the party will encrypt the message (s_ℓ, m) using randomness r_ℓ and then derive $(s_{\ell+1}, r_{\ell+1}) = \mathsf{PRG}(s_\ell)$. This does not introduce any circularity. Moreover, it now allows the decryptor to verify encryptions further up the tree by re-encrypting to obtained message under the recovered randomness.

For perpetuity, there is one more subtlety: The ciphertext must only successfully decrypt with respect to one epoch, despite being generated by somebody potentially knowing all secret keys. This is closely related to the notion of *strong robustness* introduced by Abdalla et al. [1], which is observed to not hold for most common schemes. (For our insider secure scheme discussed below, we would, however, need the robustness property to extend further to maliciously generated key pairs, called complete robustness [24].) To circumvent this, we have the PE ciphertext include a non-interactive commitment to the epoch number, with the opening included as part of the PKE encryptions. Parties then validate that the epoch number is consistent with the path they are trying to decrypt for, i.e., that the path under which they try to decrypt is a suffix of the path from the epoch's corresponding leaf to the root. As a consequence, two parties in epochs j_1 and j_2 will now only both accept if one of their paths is a suffix of the other's path.

CHOSEN-CIPHERTEXT SECURITY. The scheme so far is IND-CPA secure; we want to achieve IND-CCA security. Assuming an IND-CCA secure PKE scheme does the job, except that we still need to tie the individual components together. We observe that any component already uniquely determines the consecutive components using our randomness trick. Hence it turns out to be sufficient to additionally form a hash chain over the components and the commitment, such that each component furthermore is bound to the prior components.

INSIDER SECURITY. The basic scheme achieves perpetuity provided the manager is honest. To achieve perpetuity against a malicious manager, we leverage a Merkle-Tree to ensure that parties agree on the tree of public keys. This, however, still does not necessarily ensure perpetuity, as it requires that whenever one of the parties successfully re-derives a certain ciphertext the other one who knows the secret key can actually decrypt, even if the key pair has been sampled under maliciously chosen randomness. This is addressed by requiring stronger properties on the PKE scheme to rule out such attacks. Since the manager now needs to compute the Merkle-Tree root as part of the initial setup, we have to limit the number of epochs to be polynomial in the security parameter.

1.5   Cryptographic Assumptions

Our constructions are based on standard public key encryption (PKE) and a number of symmetric primitives. Thus, while anonymous perpetual encryption is a stronger primitive than plain PKE in terms of security, we essentially establish an equivalence between PKE and PE in terms of cryptographi assumptions.

In the full version of this work, we introduce an alternative unbounded-epoch insider-secure scheme based on anonymous hierachical identity-based encryption (HIBE). This HIBE-based construction can be viewed as a more "direct" path to PE, at the cost of using stronger building blocks. It remains an open problem whether unbounded-epoch insider-secure PE can be built from plain PKE.

2   Perpetual Encryption

We now give a precise definition of (public key) Perpetual Encryption. A PE scheme is a generalization of a public-key encryption (PKE) scheme and involves three types of parties: the manager, decryptors, and encryptors. In addition, we allow for a scheme to rely on a public setup, generated by a respective algorithm.

Definition 1 (Perpetual Encryption). *A public-key perpetual encryption (PE) scheme consists of the following PPT algorithms:*

- ▷ $crs \leftarrow \mathrm{GenCRS}(1^\lambda)$
  Samples the public setup based on the security parameter.
- ▷ $(mst_0, pub, pk_0, sk_0) \leftarrow \mathrm{Setup}(1^\lambda, crs, N)$
  Takes the security parameter, CRS, and the maximum number of supported epochs N. Initiates the group manager's state mst_0 and generates additional public parameters pub (chosen for the specific instance of the scheme). It further outputs an initial public-key/secret-key pair (pk_0, sk_0).
- ▷ $(mst_{i+1}, pk_{i+1}, sk_{i+1}) \leftarrow \mathrm{Update}(mst_i)$
  Initiates a new epoch by updating the manager's state and outputting a new public-key / secret-key pair.
- ▷ $c \leftarrow \mathrm{Encrypt}(crs, pub, pk_i, m)$
  Encrypts the message m under pk_i, the public key of the i-th epoch.
- ▷ $(m, j) \leftarrow \mathrm{Decrypt}(crs, pub, sk_i, c)$
  Decrypts the ciphertext c using sk_i, the secret state of the i-th epoch. Outputs the message m and epoch $j \leq i$ under which the message was encrypted. The output can be $\bot$ to indicate a decryption error.

The group manager uses the Setup algorithm to initialize the scheme. Afterward, they can advance to the next epoch using Update. The group is maintained implicitly by distributing new secret keys to the respective parties—choosing an appropriate mechanism is left to the application. Encryption and decryption work analogously to the algorithm of a regular PKE scheme, except for also taking the public setup crs and public parameters pub, as well as the ability to decrypt under a later secret key as detailed below.

Correctness and Security. We define the correctness and security of a PE scheme. For security, we consider two properties, formalized as separate games.

Correctness. We say that a PE scheme is correct, if any key pair (pk_i, sk_i) behaves like a PKE scheme. More concretely, if a message encrypted under the public key pk_i of epoch i can be successfully decrypted under the secret key sk_i for the same epoch. (The ability to decrypt under the secret key of a later epoch will be formalized as part of security.) Moreover, we require that honestly generated public keys and secret keys successfully validate by the respective algorithms.

Definition 2. *A PE scheme is called computationally correct if, for any number of maximal epochs N, any PPT adversary $\mathcal{A}$ has negligible winning probability in the game depicted in the left of Fig. 1. It is information-theoretically correct if this holds for any $\mathcal{A}$ that makes at most polynomially many oracle queries.*

48   Y. Dodis and D. Jost

Perpetuity. Perpetuity guarantees that members in a later epoch can still decrypt. Here we consider an honest-but-curious group manager. More concretely, the game depicted on the right side of Fig. 1 generates the public parameters *pub* as well as all public keys and secret keys honestly. The adversary, however, is given the manager's state *mst* as well as all secret keys. They then try to produce a ciphertext c that successfully decrypts in an epoch i, but not in a later one $j > i$.

Observe that perpetuity does allow for false negatives: it is possible for the party j in the later epoch to decrypt while the party i in an earlier epoch rejects by outputting $\bot$. As an alternative, we also introduce *strong perpetuity* which rules out such false negatives. Whether such spurious decryptions pose a problem is application dependent—for example, in our private blockchain, one is able to tolerate false negatives at the cost of some superfluous complaints.

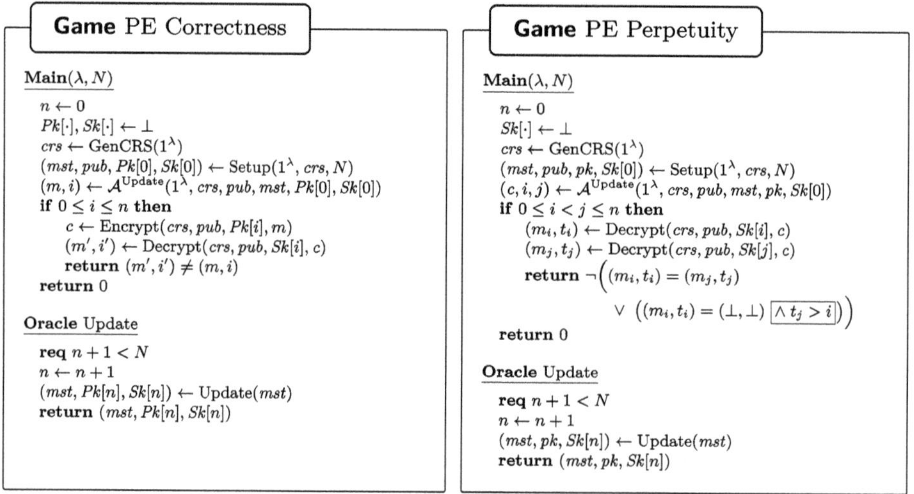

Fig. 1. The correctness and perpetuity games for a PE scheme. For the perpetuity game, the variant of strong perpetuity is obtained by adding the $\boxed{\text{boxed}}$ condition.

Definition 3. *A PE scheme satisfies* perpetuity *if any PPT adversary $\mathcal{A}$ has at most negligible probability of having the game depicted on the right in Fig. 1 returning 1. It is said to satisfy* strong perpetuity *if this holds with respect to the game omitting the $m_i \neq \bot$ check.*

Pseudorandomness. First, we consider *pseudorandomness* which prescribes both the privacy of messages towards members that are not part—or no longer part—of the group, and receiver anonymity. For this property, the manager is assumed to be honest. In a nutshell, the property corresponds to IND-CCA security with pseudorandom-looking ciphertexts: The adversary chooses a challenge message

m^* and epoch i^*. It is then given either a real encryption (if $b = 0$) or a uniform random ciphertext (if $b = 1$) to distinguish. We assume the ciphertext space $\mathrm{CSpace}_{\lambda,N}$ to be a function of the security parameter and the maximal number of epochs only.[2] The adversary is given secret keys $sk_1, \ldots, sk_{i^*-1}$, representing the state of former members of the group, as well as a decryption oracle under keys $sk_{i^*}, sk_{i^*+1}, \ldots$ for ciphertexts other than the challenge c^*. Note that this formalizes PE for some fixed-length message space. This could be relaxed by making the ciphertext space $\mathrm{CSpace}_{\lambda,N}$ depend on the message length. The game is depicted in Fig. 2. Observe that the formal game allows the adversary to choose the challenge message m^* and epoch i^* adaptively based on public and secret keys observed—subject to a non-triviality condition that $i^* > e_{\mathsf{corr}}$ where e_{corr} denotes the maximum epoch for which the adversary learned the secret key.

Definition 4. *A PE scheme with ciphertext space* $\mathrm{CSpace}_{\lambda,N}$ *is pseudorandom if for any PPT adversary* $\mathcal{A}$ *the game depicted in Fig. 2 returns 1 with at most one-half plus negligible probability.*

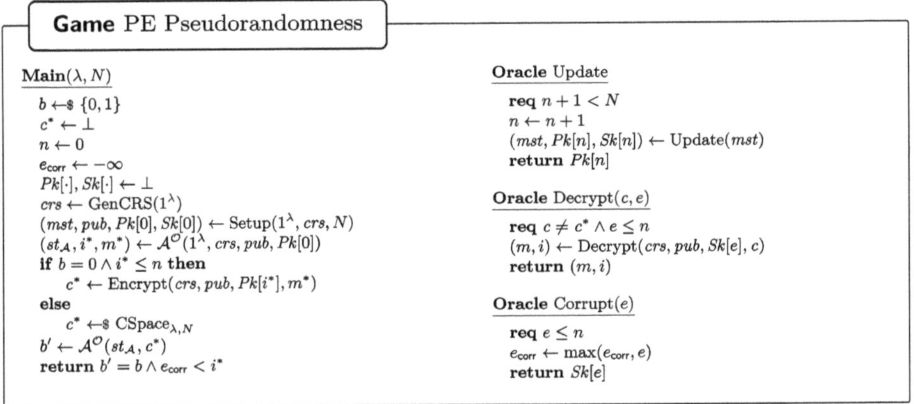

Fig. 2. The pseudorandomness game for a PE scheme. $\mathcal{O}$ denotes the set of defined oracles. The advantage of an adversary $\mathcal{A}$ is defined as the probability of the interaction between $\mathcal{A}$ and the game returning 1, minus $\frac{1}{2}$.

Unbounded Perpetual Encryption. So far, we formalized a notion of PE with a bounded number of epochs N, which is fixed during Setup. One can also consider Perpetual Encryption with no a priori bound on the number of epochs. Syntax-wise, Setup then only takes the security parameter 1^λ and the *crs* as inputs. In terms of correctness and security, the games apply when setting the bound to infinity, thereby allowing the Update oracle to be called an arbitrary (polynomial) number of times.

---

[2] For instance, for a scheme based on a cyclic group $\mathbb{G}$, the choice of $\mathbb{G}$ must not depend on *crs*. Of course, *crs* might still choose a specific generator $\langle g \rangle = \mathbb{G}$ of the group.

Interval Access. Finally, we briefly sketch an extension inspired by interval KEM [9]. Namely, while in plain PE a secret key sk_i works to decrypt ciphertexts for epochs $1 \leq t \leq i$, we can also ask for the existence of weaker keys that can only decrypt within a specific interval $[i_0, i_1]$. More specifically, following the convention of [9], we require that a party can derive a key for any suffix of their current key without the help of the group manager. Using the convention that $sk_i = sk_[0, i]$, we thus augment PE as follows:

Definition 5. *An* interval perpetual encryption *scheme is a PE scheme with the following additional algorithm:*

▷ $sk_{i_0', i_1} \leftarrow \mathrm{Delegate}(sk_{i_0, i_1}, i_0')$
  Derives a decryption key for epochs in the interval $[i_0', i_1]$, where $i_0 < i_0' < i_1$.

We only sketch the modifications to the corresponding games. For correctness, we require that sk_{i_0, i_1} can decrypt honestly generated messages for any epoch in the interval $[i_0, i_1]$. Similarly, for (strong) perpetuity we require that sk_{i_0, i_1} decrypts consistent with sk_j for epochs $i_0 \leq j \leq i_1$ (where the weak notion allows false positives if $j < i_1$. Finally, for pseudorandomness we require that a ciphertext for epoch $j < i_0$ remains pseudorandom even when given sk_{i_0, i_1}.

3 Perpetual Encryption Scheme

In this section, we first present a PE scheme for a bounded number of $N = 2^d$ epochs, input to Setup. We will, however, see that we can choose $N = 2^\lambda$ with the scheme still polynomially efficient, yielding an unbounded-epoch scheme. Of course this will come at a loss of concrete efficiency, as the key sizes as well as the efficiency of most algorithms is proportional to $\log(N)$. Therefore, there will be a trade-off between the number of epochs supported and the scheme's efficiency, making it advisable to choose N only as large as needed for the concrete use-case.

3.1 Protocol Description

We now present our (bounded-epoch) PE scheme. The scheme is primarily based on public key encryption (PKE). A pseudo-code description of the scheme is presented in Figs. 3, 4 and 5. For simplicity, the algorithms make use of a binary tree τ with N leaves as intermediate state. For example, the manager algorithms Setup and Update create such a tree and then expand the key pairs of the relevant nodes. Nodes $v \in \tau$ can have its PKE public key $v.pk$ and its secret key $v.sk$ assigned.

Common Reference String. The CRS consists of a hash key k for a collision-resistant hash function $\mathsf{H}_k(\cdot)$, as well as the public parameters $crs_,$ of the non-interactive commitment scheme $,$.

Protocol PE Manager

$\text{Setup}(1^\lambda, crs, N)$

  parse $(k, crs_{\text{COM}}) \leftarrow crs$
  $n \leftarrow 0$
  // Sample PRF seed
  $s \leftarrow\!\!\$\ \{0,1\}^\lambda$
  // Initial keys
  $\tau \leftarrow$ new tree with N leaves
  $pk \leftarrow \text{GenPk}(\tau, 0)$
  $sk \leftarrow \text{GenSk}(\tau, 0)$
  // Only keep compact state
  $mst \leftarrow s$
  $pub \leftarrow N$
  return (mst, pub, pk, sk)

$\text{Update}(mst)$

  $s \leftarrow mst$
  $n \leftarrow n + 1$
  $\tau \leftarrow$ new tree with N leaves
  $pk \leftarrow \text{GenPk}(\tau, n)$
  $sk \leftarrow \text{GenSk}(\tau, n)$
  return (mst, pk, sk)

Helper $\text{GenPk}(\tau, n)$

  $\text{pkKeys}[\cdot] \leftarrow \perp$
  for $v \in \tau.\text{RootPath}(n)$ **do**
    $r \leftarrow \text{PRF}(s, v.\text{idx})$
    $(v.sk, v.pk) \leftarrow \text{PKE.Keygen}(1^\lambda; r)$
    $\text{pkKeys}[v.\text{idx}] \leftarrow v.pk$
  return (n, pkKeys)

Helper $\text{GenSk}(\tau, n)$

  for $v \in \tau.\text{LeftSiblingPath}(n + 1) \setminus \tau.\text{RootPath}(n)$ **do**
    $r \leftarrow \text{PRF}(s, v.\text{idx})$
    $(v.sk, v.pk) \leftarrow \text{PKE.Keygen}(1^\lambda; r)$
  for $v \in \tau.\text{RootPath}(n + 1) \setminus \tau.\text{RootPath}(n)$ **do**
    $r \leftarrow \text{PRF}(s, v.\text{idx})$
    $(v.sk, v.pk) \leftarrow \text{PKE.Keygen}(1^\lambda; r)$
  // Private state
  $\text{skPriv}[\cdot] \leftarrow \perp$
  for $v \in \tau.\text{LeftSiblingPath}(n + 1)$ **do**
    $\text{skPriv}[v.\text{idx}] \leftarrow v.r$
  // Public state
  $\text{skPub}[\cdot] \leftarrow \perp$
  for $v \in \tau.\text{RootPath}(n + 1)$ **do**
    $\text{skPub}[v.\text{idx}] \leftarrow v.pk$
  return $(n, \text{skPriv}, \text{skPub})$

Fig. 3. The group manager algorithms Setup and Update.

Manager State. The manager algorithm Setup creates a binary tree with N leaves, one per epoch. For convenience, we assume nodes to be indexed by the binary string idx representing the path from the root (with an empty index) to the respective node. Each node idx has a public-key/secret-key pair (pk_{idx}, sk_{idx}) associated. To sample those keys, the manager first chooses a PRF seed s uniformly at random as part of the Setup algorithm. See Fig. 9 for a depiction of the key tree. Whenever the group manager needs any of those PKE keys for a node with index idx, it lazily generates them using the PRF: First it derives randomness $r_{idx} = \text{PRF}(s, idx)$, under a suitable encoding from the node index idx to the domain of the PRF, and then uses this to derive the key pair $(pk_{idx}, sk_{idx}) = \text{PKE.Keygen}(1^\lambda; r_{idx})$. This allows to keep only the PRF seed s as state, which remains unchanged throughout the rest of the protocol execution.

The public parameter pub simply stores the maximum number of epochs N. The initial public key pk_0 and pk_1 are computed analogously to the ones for later epochs—as described in the next section.

Public and Secret Keys. For each epoch i, the PE public key pk_i consists of:

- The epoch number i.
- For each node v on the path from the i-th leaf to the root, it contains the corresponding public key $v.pk$.

The corresponding secret key sk_i consists of the following components:

- The epoch number i.

Protocol PE Encryptor

$\text{Encrypt}(crs, pub, pk, m)$

  $(k, crs_{\mathsf{COM}}, n, \tau) \leftarrow \text{ParsePk}(crs, pub, pk)$
  // Commitment
  $r_{\mathsf{COM}} \leftarrow\!\!\$\ \{0,1\}^{\lambda}$
  $c_{\mathsf{COM}} \leftarrow \text{COM.Commit}(crs_{\mathsf{COM}}, n; r_{\mathsf{COM}})$
  // Encrypt to root path
  $C[\cdot] \leftarrow \bot$
  $\ell \leftarrow -1$
  $s_{\ell} \leftarrow\!\!\$\ \{0,1\}^{\lambda}$
  $h_{\ell+1} \leftarrow \mathsf{H}_k(c_{\mathsf{COM}})$
  for $v \in \tau.\text{RootPath}(n)$ **do**
    $\ell \leftarrow \ell + 1$
    $(s_{\ell}, r_{\ell}) \leftarrow \text{PRG}(s_{\ell-1})$
    $C[\ell] \leftarrow \text{PKE.Enc}(v.pk, (n, r_{\mathsf{COM}}, h_{\ell}, s_{\ell}, m); r_{\ell})$
    $h_{\ell+1} \leftarrow \mathsf{H}_k(h_{\ell}, C[\ell])$
  $c \leftarrow (c_{\mathsf{COM}}, C)$
  return c

Helper $\text{ParsePk}(crs, pub, pk)$

  parse $(k, crs_{\mathsf{COM}}) \leftarrow crs$
  $N \leftarrow pub$
  parse $(n, \text{pkKeys}) \leftarrow pk$
  $\tau \leftarrow$ new tree with N leaves
  for $v \in \tau.\text{RootPath}(n)$ **do**
    $v.pk \leftarrow \text{pkKeys}[v.\text{idx}]$
  return $(k, crs_{\mathsf{COM}}, n, \tau)$

Fig. 4. The encryption and the public-key verification algorithms.

- The PKE secret keys of the smallest set of nodes such that exactly the leaves from $idx_0 = \text{encode}(0, d)$ to $idx_i = \text{encode}(i, d)$ are reachable. It is easy to verify that this so-called cover consists exactly of the left-sibling path of node $idx_{i+1} = \text{encode}(i + 1, d)$—i.e., the subset of the sibling path of node idx_{i+1} which are left children of their respective parents. Let V_i denote this set of node indices for epoch i. Figure 6 illustrates the sets V_2, V_3, and V_4.
- The PKE public keys on the root path of the $(i + 1)$-th leaf.

Encryption and Decryption. Finally, let us consider encryption and decryption. In a nutshell, when encrypting a message m in epoch i one considers the path from the corresponding leaf to the root and encrypts it to all those public keys. A party knowing secret key sk_j, for $j \geq i$ knows the PKE secret keys of nodes in V_j, which contains exactly one of the nodes on the path from the leaf to the root, ensuring that each such party can decrypt. Such a scheme, however, would not achieve perpetuity as a malicious encryptor could include inconsistent, or even invalid, encryptions as part of the PE ciphertext.

We make the following observation: for two parties in epochs j_1 and j_2 with $j_1 < j_2$, respectively, the party in epoch j_1 decrypts a ciphertext further down the tree (i.e., closer to the leaf). Furthermore, recall that perpetuity requires that if the party in epoch j_1 decrypts to a valid message m so does the one in j_2, not necessarily the other way round. We leverage this as follows. In the encryption process, the encryptor generates the encryption randomness using a length-doubling PRG, by deriving the randomness from leaf to root. That is, they choose an initial seed s_{-1}, which they then expand to (s_0, r_0) and use r_0 as randomness to encrypt to the leaf's public key. The encrypted message must now not only contain m but s_0 as well. This process is then repeated up the tree, by deriving $(s_1, r_1) = \text{PRG}(s_0)$ and using r_1 to encrypt (s_1, m) under the next key and so forth. See Fig. 7 for a graphical overview of this process.

Protocol PE Decryptor

Decrypt(crs, pub, sk, c)

  $(k, crs_{\mathsf{COM}}, h_{()}, n, \tau) \leftarrow$ ParseSk(crs, pub, sk)
  parse (c_{COM}, C) $\leftarrow c$
  $m \leftarrow \bot$
  // Trial decryption on left-sibling path
  $(n', r_{\mathsf{COM}}, h, s, m) \leftarrow \bot$
  $v^* \leftarrow \bot$
  for $v \in \tau.$ LeftSiblingPath($n + 1$) **do**
    $(n', r_{\mathsf{COM}}, h, s, m) \leftarrow$ TrialDec($crs_{\mathsf{COM}}, c_{\mathsf{COM}}, n, C, v$)
    if $(n', r_{\mathsf{COM}}, h, s, m) \neq \bot$ **then**
      $v^* \leftarrow v$
      break
  req $v^* \neq \bot$
  // Check hash chain
  $h' \leftarrow \mathsf{H}_k(c_{\mathsf{COM}})$
  for $\ell = 0, \ldots, (v^*.\text{height} - 1)$ **do**
    $h' \leftarrow \mathsf{H}_k(h', C[\ell])$
  req $h = h'$
  // Check consistency up the tree
  while $v^*.$parent $\neq \bot$ **do**
    $v^* \leftarrow v^*.$parent
    $(s, r) \leftarrow$ PRG(s)
    $c' \leftarrow$ PKE.Enc($v^*.pk, (n', r_{\mathsf{COM}}, h, s, m); r$)
    req $C[v^*.\text{height}] = c'$
    $h \leftarrow \mathsf{H}_k(h, c')$
  return m

Helper TrialDec($crs_{\mathsf{COM}}, c_{\mathsf{COM}}, n, C, v$)

  $\ell \leftarrow v.$height
  try $m' \leftarrow$ PKE.Dec($v.sk, C[\ell]$)
  parse $(n', r_{\mathsf{COM}}, h, s, m) \leftarrow m'$
  req $n' \leq n$
  $c'_{\mathsf{COM}} \leftarrow$ COM.Commit($crs_{\mathsf{COM}}, n'; r_{\mathsf{COM}}$)
  req $c'_{\mathsf{COM}} = c_{\mathsf{COM}}$
  req $v \in \tau.$ RootPath(n')
  return $(n', r_{\mathsf{COM}}, h, s, m)$

Helper ParseSk(crs, pub, sk)

  parse $(k, crs_{\mathsf{COM}}) \leftarrow crs$
  $N \leftarrow pub$
  parse $(n, \text{skPriv}, \text{skPub}, \text{skHashes}) \leftarrow sk$
  $\tau \leftarrow$ new tree with N leaves
  // Store secrets
  for $v \in \tau.$ LeftSiblingPath($n + 1$) **do**
    $v.sk \leftarrow$ skPriv[$v.$idx]
  // Store public keys
  for $v \in \tau.$ RootPath($n + 1$) **do**
    $v.pk \leftarrow$ skPub[$v.$idx]
  return $(k, crs_{\mathsf{COM}}, n, \tau)$

Fig. 5. The decryption and the secret-key validation algorithms.

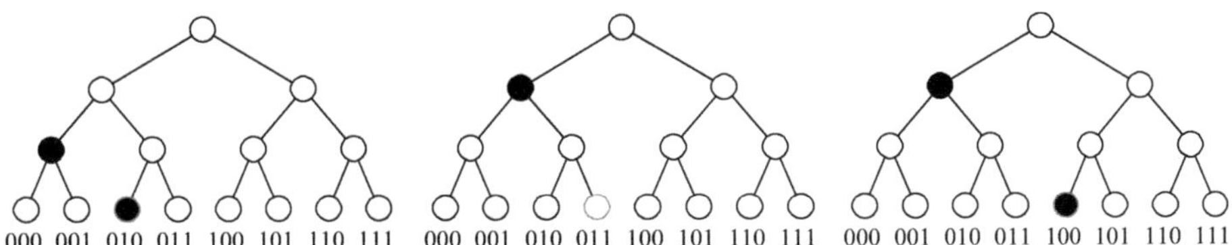

Fig. 6. An illustration of the node a party stores in epoch 2 (left), epoch 3 (middle), and epoch 4 (right). For nodes marked with black, the party's state *ust* contains the secret key *sk*, public key *pk*, as well as hash *h*.

During the decryption, a party that knows the secret key of the node at height ℓ then gets (s_ℓ, m). It then verifies the encryptions further up the tree by re-encryption of the expected message. That is, it will derive $(s_{\ell+1}, r_{\ell+1}) = \mathsf{PRG}(s_\ell)$ and check that the next ciphertext corresponds to the encryption of $(s_{\ell+1}, m)$ under $r_{\ell+1}$ and so on.

Intuitively, the decryptor should be able to perform this trial decryption using each of the secret keys they know, and output m if it succeeds. We need, however, to ensure that at most one of the trial decryptions succeeds, even if a ciphertext has been crafted by an attacker knowing all secret keys. To this end, the ciphertext must uniquely bind to the epoch number while looking pseudorandom: The PE ciphertext additionally contains a commitment $c, =, .\mathsf{Commit}(crs, , i; r,)$ to

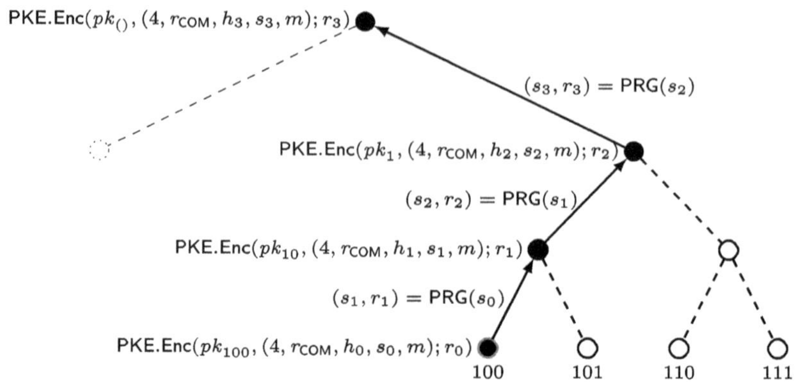

Fig. 7. An illustration of the encryption of a message m for epoch 4. The encryption randomness is generated "upwards" using a PRG, as indicated by the arrows. The term r, denotes a commitment to the epoch number 4 and h_ℓ a hash chain over the ciphertexts, and the commitment, that is computed bottom-up.

the epoch number i using randomness r,. All the PKE ciphertexts in addition then encrypt the opening r,.

Finally, to achieve IND-CCA security we need to ensure that each ciphertext component binds the prior ones (further down the tree) as well as the commitment. Let h_ℓ denote the hash over the commitment and ciphertexts 0 to $\ell - 1$. In summary, the party then encrypts $(i, r, h_\ell, s_\ell, m)$ at every height ℓ.

Efficiency. Let us briefly comment on the (asymptotic) efficiency of the scheme. Let N denote the maximal number of supported epochs and $d = \log_2(N)$. We then observe the following.

- *Manager:* The initial setup just comprises of choosing a PRF seed and producing public- and secret-keys analogous to subsequent epochs. For each epoch i, the public- and secret-keys (pk_i, sk_i) consists of $\mathcal{O}(d)$ many underlying PKE key-pairs—each of which can be efficiently derived from the PRF seed. Hence, the manager's state is of constant size and Setup and Update both take time $\mathcal{O}(d)$.
- *Encryption:* A PE public key pk_i consists of $d+1$ PKE public keys. Encryption performs one commitment, one PKE encryption per PKE public key, and $d + 1$ hash operations. Overall, Encrypt thus performs a logarithmic number of cryptographic operations.
- *Decryption:* The secret key sk_i is of size $\mathcal{O}(d)$, more concretely it consists of $d + 1$ PKE public keys and at most d PKE secret keys. Decryption performs at most d trial decryptions before verifying the output. The verification consists of first verifying the commitment and then verifying the remaining PKE ciphertexts by re-encryption. This takes at most as long as the corresponding encryption. Overall, the decryptor thus runs in time $\mathcal{O}(d)$ as well.

In summary, our scheme thus runs in logarithmic time (in the number of supported epochs). Hence, we can set, for instance, $d = \lambda$ and therefore support a virtually unbounded number of epochs.

3.2   Correctness and Security

We now state correctness, pseudorandomness, and perpetuity of our scheme. The proofs can be found in the full version of the paper.

Theorem 1. *The PE scheme depicted in Figs. 3, 4 and 5 is correct, if the underlying public-key encryption scheme is correct and the commitment scheme is binding.*

Pseudo-randomness requires both the commitment scheme and the PKE scheme to have pseudorandom-looking encryptions.[3]

Theorem 2. *The PE scheme from Figs. 3, 4 and 5 satisfies pseudorandomness (cf. Fig. 2), if the underlying public-key encryption scheme is correct and IND-CCA secure with pseudorandom ciphertexts, the commitment scheme has pseudorandomness, the hash function is collision-resistant, and the PRF and PRG satisfy their usual security notions.*

Perpetuity relies on the binding property of the commitment scheme, ensuring each ciphertext has a unique epoch associated, as well as slightly non-standard properties of the PKE scheme ensuring that decryption is deterministic and that the scheme is correct even when using adversarially chosen randomness. (Note that this is implied by perfect or information-theoretic correctness. As such, plenty of PKE schemes exist that satisfy the property.)

Theorem 3. *The PE scheme depicted in Figs. 3, 4 and 5 is perpetual, if the commitment scheme is binding, the PKE scheme has a deterministic decryption algorithm* PKE.Dec, *and is correct under maliciously chosen encryption randomness. More concretely, for any PPT adversary, $\mathcal{A}$ the following must be negligible*

$$\Pr\left[m \neq m' \;\middle|\; \begin{array}{l} (sk, pk) \leftarrow \mathsf{PKE.Keygen}(1^\lambda) \\ (m, r) \leftarrow \mathcal{A}(1^\lambda, sk, pk) \\ c \leftarrow \mathsf{PKE.Enc}(pk, m; r) \\ m' \leftarrow \mathsf{PKE.Dec}(sk, c) \end{array}\right]$$

when the probability is taken of the randomness of PKE.Keygen *and* $\mathcal{A}$.

---

[3] Unlike the symmetric-key setting, where these notions are equivalent, PKE with pseudorandom ciphertexts does not follow black-box from PKE alone. Nonetheless, in the IND-CCA2 domain, many practical schemes are naturally pseudorandom over a suitable ciphertext space.

3.3 Strong Perpetuity and Interval Access

The scheme, as introduced so far, allows for false negatives in which a ciphertext is rejected when attempting to decrypt under a secret key sk_i, but accepted under a later secret key sk_j, for $j > i$. Let us sketch a modification of the scheme that satisfies strong perpetuity. Recall that, in the base scheme, the group manager computes a PKE key-pair for every node v as $(v.pk, v.sk) = \mathsf{PKE.Keygen}(1^\lambda; v.r)$, where the randomness $v.r = \mathsf{PRF}(s, v.idx)$ is derived using a PRF from the node index $v.idx$. We make three modifications:

1. Instead of including PKE secret keys $v.sk$ in the PE secret key, the manager includes the randomness v. (Looking ahead, we will use the same modification for the scheme in Sect. 4.2.) This in itself does not affect security, as the randomness for different nodes is independent by PRF security.
2. Next, we replace the generic PRF with the Goldreich-Goldwasser-Micali (GGM) construction. Note that we *do not* apply a prefix-free coding to the node indices. As such, $v.r$ and $v.parent.r$ are no longer independent! Instead, one can derive $v.r$ from $v.parent.r$. Note however, that the randomness for any two nodes where neither one is a descendant of the other still appears independent; similarly, conditioned on $v.r$, $v.parent.r$ is still indistinguishable from uniformly at random.
3. Finally, the decryption under sk_i is modified as follows: Once the correct epoch number j has been determined via trial decryption under one of the nodes $v \in V_i$, the algorithm does not just check the path from v to the root. Instead, the algorithm derives the secret key for the j-th leaf, which is a descendant of v, and the public keys along the path from that leaf to v. (This can now be done due to using the GGM construction.) Afterward, the decryption checks the entire path from the j-th path to the root, analogous to how decryption under sk_j would do. It only outputs m if doing so yields the same message as the initial trial decryption under $v.sk$.

Those modifications only incur a constant overhead when measured in worst-time complexity; instead of decrypting a path suffix, the modified scheme now always decrypts the entire path. Furthermore, the scheme needs $\mathcal{O}(d)$ additional PRG expansions (for the GGM construction) and key derivations. It follows by inspection that the modified scheme still satisfies correctness, and now additionally satisfies strong perpetuity. (Put simply, $\mathsf{Decrypt}(crs, pub, sk_i, c)$ now only outputs a message m for epoch j after doing all the same checks as $\mathsf{Decrypt}(crs, pub, sk_j, c)$ does.) A proof of the following theorem is presented in the full version of the paper.

Theorem 4. *The modified PE scheme satisfies pseudorandomness, if the underlying public-key encryption scheme is correct and IND-CCA secure with pseudorandom ciphertexts, the commitment scheme has pseudorandomness, the hash function is collision-resistant, and the PRG satisfies the usual security notion.*

Finally, we observe that this modification naturally allows users to derive a secret key sk_{i_0, i_1} limited to a given interval $[i_0, i_1]$—as discussed in Sect. 2.

Basically, we can observe that for every such interval, there exists a minimal cover set of nodes that only allows us to reach the respective leaves. The secret keys of these nodes can then be derived to yield sk_{i_0,i_1}. Moreover, the cover set still shares exactly one node with the path from leaf $j \in [i_0, i_1]$. Thus, decryption remains essentially unchanged.

4 Insider-Secure Perpetual Encryption

In this section, we extend Perpetual Encryption to the setting of malicious group managers choosing the keys. We call this setting *insider-security* and sometimes refer to a regular PE scheme as *outsider-secure* to avoid confusion.

4.1 Syntax and Security

To achieve any kind of security against an adversarial group manager, parties must have some notion of "correct" or at least consistent keys. As a consequence, we extend our syntax to allow for validations of both public- and secret keys, against the public parameters pub and the intended epoch number i.[4]

Definition 6 (Insider-Secure Public Key PE). *An* insider-secure perpetual encryption (PE) *scheme is a PE scheme that additionally has the following two algorithms:*

▷ $\{0,1\} \leftarrow \text{ValidatePk}(crs, pub, i, pk_i)$
  Validates the public key of the i-th epoch against the public setup and the public parameters.
▷ $\{0,1\} \leftarrow \text{ValidateSk}(crs, pub, i, sk_i)$
  Validates the secret key of the i-th epoch against the public setup and the public parameters.

We extend our correctness definition analogously to ensure ValidatePk and ValidateSk to work as intended for valid keys. This rules out trivializing insider-perpetuity, which will be conditioned on parties having keys that validate.

Definition 7. *An insider-secure PE scheme is correct if it satisfies correctness of a regular PE scheme and, additionally, for any key-pair* (sk_i, pk_i) *for epoch* i *(output by* Setup *for epoch* 0 *and* Update *for later epochs) both keys validate, i.e.,* $\text{ValidatePk}(crs, pub, i, pk_i)$ *and* $\text{ValidatePk}(crs, pub, i, pk_i)$ *both return* 1.

While the above definition still considers an honest group manager, we also ask for the correctness of encryption and decryption under adversarially chosen keys as long as they validate. In other words, it must be infeasible for an adversary to come up with public parameters pub and a key pair (sk, pk), presumably for some epoch i, such that the keys validate but not constitute a correct PKE scheme. We call the respective property *robustness*.

---

[4] A slightly weaker model in which parties are assumed to have a consistent view on the public keys, e.g. by the leader posting them on a blockchain, is conceivable. We opt here for the strongest definition where parties only need to agree on crs and pub.

Definition 8. *An insider-secure PE scheme is* robust *if any PPT adversary $\mathcal{A}$ has at most negligible probability of having the game depicted on the left in Fig. 8 returning 1.*

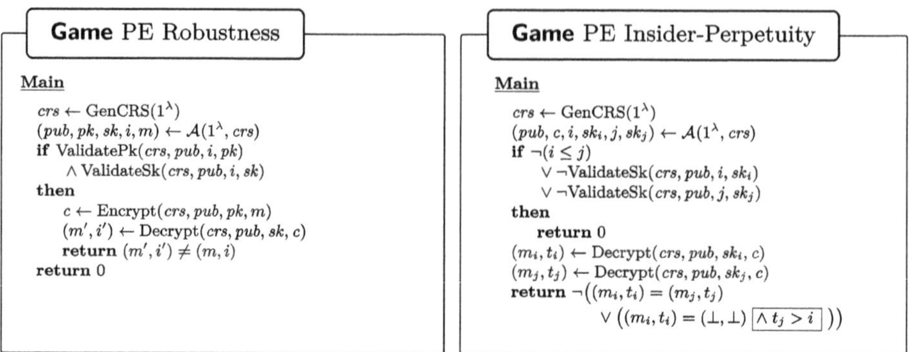

Fig. 8. Insider-security of a PE scheme. The robustness game (left) ensures validating key pairs function like a PKE scheme, while the perpetuity game (right) ensures future keys decrypt consistently. The variant of strong insider perpetuity adds the boxed condition.

Next, we consider perpetuity against an adversarial group manager choosing the keys. We call this property *insider perpetuity* or just perpetuity if clear from the context that we consider insider security. Again, we additionally consider the variant of *strong insider perpetuity*, ruling out false negatives. The respective security game is depicted on the right side of Fig. 8. When contrasted to the (outsider-)perpetuity game from Sect. 2, the group manager is replaced by the adversary, with only the public setup crs being honestly generated. In particular, the adversary freely chooses the secret keys. We say that a secret key sk_i is for epoch i if ValidateSk(crs, pub, i, sk_i) returns true. In other words, perpetuity must hold if parties are given keys that validate with respect to the public parameters pub the (malicious) group manager initially committed to.

Definition 9. *An insider-secure PE scheme satisfies (insider) perpetuity, if any PPT adversary $\mathcal{A}$ has at most negligible probability of having either of the game depicted on the right in Fig. 8 returning 1. It is said to satisfy* strong insider perpetuity *if this holds with respect to the game omitting the $m_i \neq \perp$ check.*

Finally, we note that pseudorandomness against an adversarial group manager choosing all keys is futile. We, however, still require an insider-secure PE scheme to adhere to the pseudorandomness security of an outsider-secure PE scheme. In other words, the scheme must provide pseudorandom ciphertext assuming the manager to be honest.

4.2   A Bounded Epoch Scheme

In this section, we present an insider-secure PE scheme for a bounded number of epochs. The scheme is closely based on the outsider-secure one from the previous section—however, Setup will run in time $\mathcal{O}(N)$, meaning that the scheme only works for a bounded number of epochs. A formal description of the scheme is presented in the full version of the paper.

Shortcomings of the Outsider-Secure Scheme. First, let us gain some intuition on the shortcomings of the scheme from Sect. 3 with respect to an actively malicious group manager. Most obviously, the group manager could simply produce two completely unrelated secret keys sk_i and sk_i', for presumably the same epoch. Similarly, they could produce unrelated key material across epochs, such as sk_i and sk_j for epochs $i < j$. A ciphertext that decrypts to some message m with respect to sk_i would then, with overwhelming probability, not decrypt to the same message under the other key.

A bit more subtly, malicious group members could tamper with individual PKE key pairs of the tree structure. For instance, for a node v, they could use unrelated public key pk_v and secret key sk_v'. A party that checks the ciphertext component for v by re-encrypting under pk_v and one that decrypts it under sk_v' would then yield different results. Finally, an adversary might try to reuse key material, or use related keys, for two different nodes v and v'. The last one will turn out not to be a security issue, of which we will have to convince ourselves.

Protocol Modifications. We now enhance our outsider-secure protocol to thwart those attacks. At the high level, we will force the group manager to commit to the tree of PKE key pairs as part of the public parameters pub. The common reference string crs remains unchanged, and so do the encryption Encrypt and decryption Decrypt algorithms, respectively, except for the public keys and secret keys being slightly differently formatted.

Committing to the Public Keys. Recall that in the outsider-secure scheme, the Setup algorithm created a binary tree with N leaves, one per epoch, where each node idx has an associated PKE key-pair (pk_{idx}, sk_{idx}). Those key-pairs are sampled using a PRF so that the manager's state can be compact.

For the insider-secure scheme we enhance this by computing a Merkle-Tree over all the PKE public keys and outputs the root hash $h_{()}$ as its public parameter pub. See Fig. 9 for a depiction of the (expanded) state the manager builds. Whenever the group manager hands out a PKE public key, whether as part of a PE public or secret key, they will include the respective Merkle-opening—this will then be verified by ValidatePk or ValidateSk, respectively.

Committing to the Secret Keys. The same strategy cannot be just applied to the secret keys. While one could, in principle, have the manager commit to the tree of PKE secret keys, this would not guarantee consistency between the public and

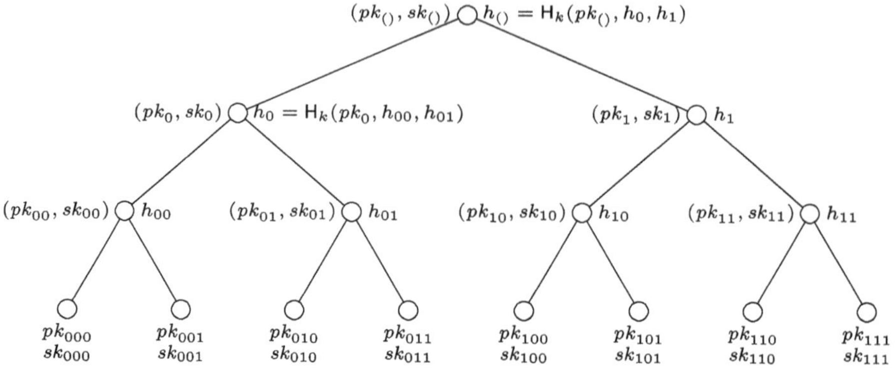

Fig. 9. The state set up by the manager for the insider-secure scheme, adding a Merkle-Tree over the public keys. The outsider-secure scheme uses the same tree of key pairs without the hashes.

secret keys of a node idx. To see why consistency is crucial, consider secret keys sk_i and sk_j, for $i < j$, and let idx be some node for which sk_i contains the PKE public key pk_{idx} whilst sk_j contains the PKE secret key sk_{idx}. Decryption using sk_i checks a ciphertext component for node idx by re-encrypting under pk_{idx}, while decrypting using sk_j will actually decrypt the component using sk_{idx}. If the former but not the latter succeeds, then this violates perpetuity. Therefore, ValidateSk(crs, pub, j, sk_j) must reject sk_j in case the key-pair is inconsistent.

To efficiently address this issue, we do not commit to the secret keys. Instead, the protocol only commits to the public keys, as described above, and requires stronger properties of the underlying PKE scheme. It validates PKE secret keys as follows:

- Instead of handing out sk_{idx}, the secret key sk_j will contain the randomness r_{idx} used to generate the key pair $(pk_{idx}, sk_{idx}) = \mathsf{PKE.Keygen}(1^\lambda; r_{idx})$;
- ValidateSk then derives (pk_{idx}, sk_{idx}) and checks pk_{idx} against the Merkle-Tree commitment.

Public- and Secret-Keys. Let us summarize the public key pk_i and secret key sk_i, respectively, for epoch i. The PE public key pk_i consists of the following components:

- The epoch number i.
- For each node v on the path from the epochs leaf idx_i to the root, it contains the corresponding public key $v.pk$.
- For each node on the sibling path, it contains the nodes' hashes, to verify the Merkle-Tree opening.

The corresponding secret key sk_i consists of the following components:

- The epoch number i.

- The *randomness* r_{idx} used to generate sk_{idx}, for each $idx \in V_i$. Recall that V_i denotes the smallest set of indices such that exactly the leaves from $idx_0 = \mathsf{encode}(0, d)$ to $idx_i = \mathsf{encode}(i, d)$ are reachable, and corresponds to the left-sibling path of the $(i + 1)$-th leaf.
- The PKE public keys on the root path of the $(i + 1)$-th leaf.
- The necessary hashes to verify the PKE public keys in V_i and on the root path of the $(i + 1)$-th leaf. In particular, the following values are included:
    - The hash for each node on the *right-sibling path* of the $(i + 1)$-th leaf;
    - The hashes of the (immediate) *children* of each node on the *left-sibling path* of the $(i + 1)$-th leaf.

Note that from the latter hashes, together with the PKE public keys, the hashes on the left-sibling path itself can be derived. Therefore, the protocol can authenticate the entire root path of the $(i + 1)$-th leaf. This in turn also authenticates its left sibling path.

Key Validation. The ValidatePk algorithm then first checks that pk_i contains the correct epoch number and all the expected PKE public keys. It then verifies those PKE public keys with respect to the Merkle-Tree root contained in *pub*. The ValidateSk algorithm works analogously. For nodes on the left-sibling path of the $(i + 1)$-th leaf, it first derives the key pair and computes its hash. Then it validates the Merkle-Tree commitments of the $(i + 1)$-th root path.

Maintaining the Manager State. Finally, let us discuss how to maintain the manager's state. In principle one could just store the PRF seed s as in the outsider-secure scheme. This would, however, require that essentially the whole Merkle-Tree is recomputed as part of each Update operation, taking $\mathcal{O}(2^d)$ time despite only needing $\mathcal{O}(d)$ hashes for each epoch. Alternatively, one could store all the hashes as part of the manager's state, making Update efficient at the cost of not having a compact state.

Fortunately, Merkle-Tree traversal [15, 40] solves this trade-off. More specifically, for epoch i, the group manager needs to be able to open the Merkle-Tree commitments for the i-th leaf (for the public key) and the $(i + 1)$-th leaf (for the secret key). A Merkle-Tree traversal exactly allows a party to open Merkle-Tree commitments for consecutive leaves in time $\mathcal{O}(d)$ while also keeping only $\mathcal{O}(d)$ state. One small caveat is that for the secret key, the manager does not just need the hashes of the left-sibling path but actually the hashes of the direct children of those nodes. Any Merkle-Tree traversal can be adjusted accordingly: Whenever the original traversal stores a hash of a node as part of its state, we can simply also keep the hashes of its two children, at a constant storage overhead. Since the only way to compute the hash of a node v is to know the hashes of its two children, this is clearly without loss of generality.

See Fig. 10 for a depiction of the state the manager expands when moving from epoch 3 to 4, to send as part of the secret key, and then keeps stored as its updated state.

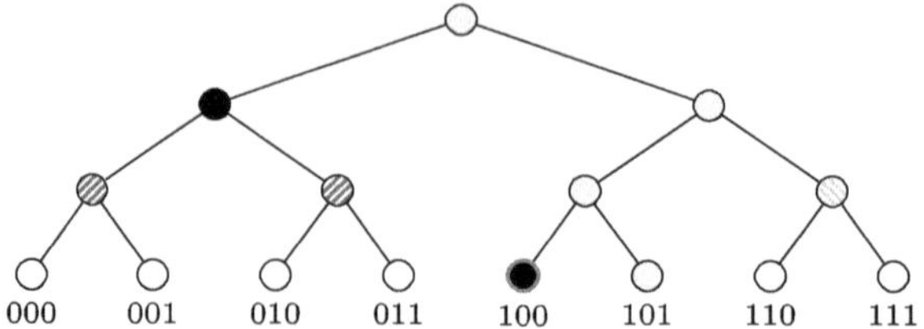

Fig. 10. An illustration of the manager's state in epoch 4. Consider the root path of the subsequent epoch 5 (nodes marked ○). The set V_4 then consists of its left-sibling path (nodes marked ●). For those nodes, the manager keeps around the randomness r_{idx}, the public key pk_{idx}, and the hash h_{idx}. For internal nodes, it additionally keeps the hash of its children as well as its sibling nodes (nodes marked ◍). Finally, it needs to be able to open the Merkle-Tree paths from the fourth and fifth leaf by having the remaining hashes for the sibling path ready (nodes marked ◎).

Efficiency. Let us briefly comment on the (asymptotic) efficiency of the scheme. Let N denote the maximal number of supported epochs and $d = \log_2(N)$. We then observe the following.

- Setup initially generates $O(N)$ PKE key-pairs and computes Merkle-Tree root over the PKE public keys. This takes $\mathcal{O}(N)$ overall time.
- A PE public key consists of $d+1$ PKE public keys and d hashes, while secret keys consists of $d+1$ PKE public keys, up to $d+1$ randomness seeds, and up to $2d$ hashes.
- Update re-computes all the PKE public keys needed for the next epoch's public and secret key, taking $\mathcal{O}(d)$ work. In addition, it generates the Merkle-Tree openings using Merkle-Tree traversal, which is known to be possible to implement in logarithmic space and time [15,40]. Hence, *mst* is of logarithmic size and Update runs in logarithmic time.
- ValidatePk and ValidateSk both run in time $\mathcal{O}(d)$, with the former simply verifying the Merkle-Tree openings and the latter doing some extra work to first derive some of the public keys.
- Encrypt and Decrypt have the same asymptotic running time as in the outsider-secure scheme.

In summary, our scheme thus runs in logarithmic time (in the number of supported epochs) except for the initial setup that runs in linear time.[5]

Cryptographic Assumptions. The scheme uses the same cryptographic building blocks as the outsider-secure one. The cryptographic assumptions also remain the same except for the Public Key Encryption (PKE) scheme, of which we need stronger properties as keys may now be adversarially generated.

---

[5] In a slightly weaker model where parties are just assumed to have a consistent view on the public keys, e.g. by having them posted on a blockchain, the scheme could thus be modified to still support an unbounded number of epochs.

In the following, we assume decryption PKE.Dec to be deterministic. In addition, we require that

$$\Pr\left[m \neq m' \;\middle|\; \begin{array}{l} (m, r_1, r_2) \leftarrow \mathcal{A}(1^\lambda) \\ (sk, pk) \leftarrow \mathsf{PKE.Keygen}(1^\lambda; r_1) \\ c \leftarrow \mathsf{PKE.Enc}(pk, m; r_2) \\ m' \leftarrow \mathsf{PKE.Dec}(sk, c) \end{array}\right] \tag{1}$$

is negligible in λ, where the randomness is taken over the adversary. Intuitively, this property will ensure that the re-encryption checks done by a party agrees with the attempted decryption performed under a later epoch's secret key. We remark that this property is implied, for example, by perfect correctness.

Finally, we require that the following probability is negligible in the security parameter:

$$\Pr\left[\begin{array}{c} m_1 \neq m_2 \\ \wedge\, pk_1 = pk_2 \end{array} \;\middle|\; \begin{array}{l} (c, r_1, r_2) \leftarrow \mathcal{A}(1^\lambda) \\ \forall i \in \{1, 2\}: \begin{array}{l} (sk_i, pk_i) \leftarrow \mathsf{PKE.Keygen}(1^\lambda; r_i) \\ m_i \leftarrow \mathsf{PKE.Dec}(sk_i, c) \end{array} \end{array}\right] \tag{2}$$

when the randomness is taken over the adversary. Intuitively this will ensure that there cannot be two secret keys, for the same epoch, that decrypt the same PKE ciphertext inconsistently. The property, for instance, is implied by schemes for which the public key uniquely determines the secret key when taken in conjunction with the previous property.

Note that the two properties are independent—one can craft a (contrived) PKE scheme that satisfies one but not the other. The former considers proper ciphertext in the range of PKE.Enc only, implying that a scheme can be made to violate the second property by adding extraneous information to each ciphertext influencing decryption depending on the secret key. (This can be done while maintaining IND-CCA security.) The former can be violated by breaking correctness for certain specific choices of randomness, that only get chosen with negligible probability in an honest execution, which can also be done for schemes with a unique secret-key to public-key mapping.

Correctness and Security. We argue the correctness and security of our enhanced scheme in the full version of the paper. The proofs mostly extend the ones from the outsider-secure scheme, making use of the Merkle-proofs (assuming collision resistance of the hash function) and the stronger correctness properties of the PKE scheme (to thwart adversarially generated keys).

Strong Perpetuity and Interval Access. The scheme can be enhanced to strong perpetuity analogous to the outsider-secure scheme (where the first modification becomes redundant). We refer to Sect. 3.3 for a description thereof.

Finally, we observe once more that the corresponding scheme naturally supports delegation of interval keys, analogous to Sect. 3.

References

1. Abdalla, M., Bellare, M., Neven, G.: Robust encryption. In: Micciancio, D. (ed.) TCC 2010. LNCS, vol. 5978, pp. 480–497. Springer, Heidelberg (2010). https://doi.org/10.1007/978-3-642-11799-2_28
2. Alwen, J., Coretti, S., Dodis, Y., Tselekounis, Y.: Security analysis and improvements for the IETF MLS standard for group messaging. In: Micciancio, D., Ristenpart, T. (eds.) CRYPTO 2020. LNCS, vol. 12170, pp. 248–277. Springer, Cham (2020). https://doi.org/10.1007/978-3-030-56784-2_9
3. Alwen, J., Hartmann, D., Kiltz, E., Mularczyk, M.: Server-aided continuous group key agreement. In: Yin, H., Stavrou, A., Cremers, C., Shi, E. (eds.) ACM CCS 2022, pp. 69–82. ACM Press (2022)
4. Aranha, D.F., Fouque, P.-A., Qian, C., Tibouchi, M., Zapalowicz, J.-C.: Binary elligator squared. In: Joux, A., Youssef, A. (eds.) SAC 2014. LNCS, vol. 8781, pp. 20–37. Springer, Cham (2014). https://doi.org/10.1007/978-3-319-13051-4_2
5. Barnes, R., Millican, J., Omara, E., Cohn-Gordon, K., Robert, R.: Message layer security (MLS) WG. https://datatracker.ietf.org/wg/mls/about/
6. Bellare, M., Boldyreva, A., Desai, A., Pointcheval, D.: Key-privacy in public-key encryption. In: Boyd, C. (ed.) ASIACRYPT 2001. LNCS, vol. 2248, pp. 566–582. Springer, Heidelberg (2001). https://doi.org/10.1007/3-540-45682-1_33
7. Bellare, M., Palacio, A.: Protecting against key exposure: strongly key-insulated encryption with optimal threshold. Appl. Algebra Eng. Commun. Comput. **16**, 06 (2002)
8. Bernstein, D.J., Hamburg, M., Krasnova, A., Lange, T.: Elligator: elliptic-curve points indistinguishable from uniform random strings. In: Sadeghi, A.-R., Gligor, V.D., Yung, M. (eds.) ACM CCS 2013, pp. 967–980. ACM Press (2013)
9. Bienstock, A., Dodis, Y., Rösler, P., Wichs, D.: Interval key-encapsulation mechanism. In: Chung, K.-M., Sasaki, Yu. (eds.) ASIACRYPT 2024, Part II. LNCS, vol. 15485, pp. 361–393. Springer, Singapore (2024)
10. Bienstock, A., Dodis, Y., Tang, Y.: Multicast key agreement, revisited. In: Galbraith, S.D. (ed.) CT-RSA 2022. LNCS, vol. 13161, pp. 1–25. Springer, Cham (2022). https://doi.org/10.1007/978-3-030-95312-6_1
11. Boneh, D., Di Crescenzo, G., Ostrovsky, R., Persiano, G.: Public key encryption with keyword search. In: Cachin, C., Camenisch, J.L. (eds.) EUROCRYPT 2004. LNCS, vol. 3027, pp. 506–522. Springer, Heidelberg (2004). https://doi.org/10.1007/978-3-540-24676-3_30
12. Boneh, D., Eskandarian, S., Kim, S., Shih, M.: Improving speed and security in updatable encryption schemes. In: Moriai, S., Wang, H. (eds.) ASIACRYPT 2020. LNCS, vol. 12493, pp. 559–589. Springer, Cham (2020). https://doi.org/10.1007/978-3-030-64840-4_19
13. Boneh, D., Lewi, K., Montgomery, H., Raghunathan, A.: Key homomorphic PRFs and their applications. In: Canetti, R., Garay, J.A. (eds.) CRYPTO 2013. LNCS, vol. 8042, pp. 410–428. Springer, Heidelberg (2013). https://doi.org/10.1007/978-3-642-40041-4_23
14. Boyd, C., Davies, G.T., Gjøsteen, K., Jiang, Y.: Fast and secure updatable encryption. In: Micciancio, D., Ristenpart, T. (eds.) CRYPTO 2020. LNCS, vol. 12170, pp. 464–493. Springer, Cham (2020). https://doi.org/10.1007/978-3-030-56784-2_16

15. Buchmann, J., Dahmen, E., Schneider, M.: Merkle tree traversal revisited. In: Buchmann, J., Ding, J. (eds.) PQCrypto 2008. LNCS, vol. 5299, pp. 63–78. Springer, Heidelberg (2008). https://doi.org/10.1007/978-3-540-88403-3_5
16. Canetti, R., Garay, J., Itkis, G., Micciancio, D., Naor, M., Pinkas, B.: Multicast security: a taxonomy and some efficient constructions. In: IEEE INFOCOM 1999, New York, NY, USA, 21–25 March 1999, pp. 708–716 (1999)
17. Canetti, R., Halevi, S., Katz, J.: A forward-secure public-key encryption scheme. In: Biham, E. (ed.) EUROCRYPT 2003. LNCS, vol. 2656, pp. 255–271. Springer, Heidelberg (2003). https://doi.org/10.1007/3-540-39200-9_16
18. Cheon, J.H., Hopper, N., Kim, Y., Osipkov, I.: Timed-release and key-insulated public key encryption. In: Di Crescenzo, G., Rubin, A. (eds.) FC 2006. LNCS, vol. 4107, pp. 191–205. Springer, Heidelberg (2006). https://doi.org/10.1007/11889663_17
19. Dodis, Y., Ganesh, C., Golovnev, A., Juels, A., Ristenpart, T.: A formal treatment of backdoored pseudorandom generators. In: Oswald, E., Fischlin, M. (eds.) EUROCRYPT 2015. LNCS, vol. 9056, pp. 101–126. Springer, Heidelberg (2015). https://doi.org/10.1007/978-3-662-46800-5_5
20. Dodis, Y., Katz, J., Xu, S., Yung, M.: Key-insulated public key cryptosystems. In: Knudsen, L.R. (ed.) EUROCRYPT 2002. LNCS, vol. 2332, pp. 65–82. Springer, Heidelberg (2002). https://doi.org/10.1007/3-540-46035-7_5
21. Dodis, Y., Katz, J., Xu, S., Yung, M.: Strong key-insulated signature schemes. In: Desmedt, Y.G. (ed.) PKC 2003. LNCS, vol. 2567, pp. 130–144. Springer, Heidelberg (2003). https://doi.org/10.1007/3-540-36288-6_10
22. Dodis, Y., Luo, W., Xu, S., Yung, M.: Key-insulated symmetric key cryptography and mitigating attacks against cryptographic cloud software. In: Youm, H.Y., Won, Y. (eds.) ASIACCS 2012, pp. 57–58. ACM Press (2012)
23. Everspaugh, A., Paterson, K., Ristenpart, T., Scott, S.: Key rotation for authenticated encryption. In: Katz, J., Shacham, H. (eds.) CRYPTO 2017. LNCS, vol. 10403, pp. 98–129. Springer, Cham (2017). https://doi.org/10.1007/978-3-319-63697-9_4
24. Farshim, P., Libert, B., Paterson, K.G., Quaglia, E.A.: Robust encryption, revisited. In: Kurosawa, K., Hanaoka, G. (eds.) PKC 2013. LNCS, vol. 7778, pp. 352–368. Springer, Heidelberg (2013). https://doi.org/10.1007/978-3-642-36362-7_22
25. Gentry, C., Silverberg, A.: Hierarchical ID-based cryptography. In: Zheng, Y. (ed.) ASIACRYPT 2002. LNCS, vol. 2501, pp. 548–566. Springer, Heidelberg (2002). https://doi.org/10.1007/3-540-36178-2_34
26. Goldreich, O., Goldwasser, S., Micali, S.: On the cryptographic applications of random functions. In: Blakley, G.R., Chaum, D. (eds.) CRYPTO 1984. LNCS, vol. 196, pp. 276–288. Springer, Heidelberg (1984)
27. Hanaoka, G., Hanaoka, Y., Imai, H.: Parallel key-insulated public key encryption. In: Yung, M., Dodis, Y., Kiayias, A., Malkin, T. (eds.) PKC 2006. LNCS, vol. 3958, pp. 105–122. Springer, Heidelberg (2006). https://doi.org/10.1007/11745853_8
28. Hanaoka, Y., Hanaoka, G., Shikata, J., Imai, H.: Identity-based hierarchical strongly key-insulated encryption and its application. In: Roy, B. (ed.) ASIACRYPT 2005. LNCS, vol. 3788, pp. 495–514. Springer, Heidelberg (2005). https://doi.org/10.1007/11593447_27
29. Horwitz, J., Lynn, B.: Toward hierarchical identity-based encryption. In: Knudsen, L.R. (ed.) EUROCRYPT 2002. LNCS, vol. 2332, pp. 466–481. Springer, Heidelberg (2002). https://doi.org/10.1007/3-540-46035-7_31

30. Jaeger, J., Stepanovs, I.: Optimal channel security against fine-grained state compromise: the safety of messaging. In: Shacham, H., Boldyreva, A. (eds.) CRYPTO 2018. LNCS, vol. 10991, pp. 33–62. Springer, Cham (2018). https://doi.org/10.1007/978-3-319-96884-1_2

31. Jost, D., Maurer, U., Mularczyk, M.: Efficient ratcheting: almost-optimal guarantees for secure messaging. In: Ishai, Y., Rijmen, V. (eds.) EUROCRYPT 2019. LNCS, vol. 11476, pp. 159–188. Springer, Cham (2019). https://doi.org/10.1007/978-3-030-17653-2_6

32. Kiayias, A., Papadopoulos, S., Triandopoulos, N., Zacharias, T.: Delegatable pseudorandom functions and applications. In: Sadeghi, A.-R., Gligor, V.D., Yung, M. (eds.) ACM CCS 2013, pp. 669–684. ACM Press (2013)

33. Klooß, M., Lehmann, A., Rupp, A.: (R)CCA secure updatable encryption with integrity protection. In: Ishai, Y., Rijmen, V. (eds.) EUROCRYPT 2019. LNCS, vol. 11476, pp. 68–99. Springer, Cham (2019). https://doi.org/10.1007/978-3-030-17653-2_3

34. Lehmann, A., Tackmann, B.: Updatable encryption with post-compromise security. In: Nielsen, J.B., Rijmen, V. (eds.) EUROCRYPT 2018. LNCS, vol. 10822, pp. 685–716. Springer, Cham (2018). https://doi.org/10.1007/978-3-319-78372-7_22

35. Mittra, S.: Iolus: a framework for scalable secure multicasting. In: Proceedings of ACM SIGCOMM, Cannes, France, 14–18 September 1997, pp. 277–288 (1997)

36. Möller, B.: A public-key encryption scheme with pseudo-random ciphertexts. In: Samarati, P., Ryan, P., Gollmann, D., Molva, R. (eds.) ESORICS 2004. LNCS, vol. 3193, pp. 335–351. Springer, Heidelberg (2004). https://doi.org/10.1007/978-3-540-30108-0_21

37. Poettering, B., Rösler, P.: Towards bidirectional ratcheted key exchange. In: Shacham, H., Boldyreva, A. (eds.) CRYPTO 2018. LNCS, vol. 10991, pp. 3–32. Springer, Cham (2018). https://doi.org/10.1007/978-3-319-96884-1_1

38. Sherman, A.T., McGrew, D.A.: Key establishment in large dynamic groups using one-way function trees. IEEE Trans. Software Eng. **29**(5), 444–458 (2003)

39. Signal. Technology preview: Sealed sender for Signal, 29 October 2018. https://signal.org/blog/sealed-sender/

40. Szydlo, M.: Merkle tree traversal in log space and time. In: Cachin, C., Camenisch, J.L. (eds.) EUROCRYPT 2004. LNCS, vol. 3027, pp. 541–554. Springer, Heidelberg (2004). https://doi.org/10.1007/978-3-540-24676-3_32

41. Tibouchi, M.: Elligator squared: uniform points on elliptic curves of prime order as uniform random strings. In: Christin, N., Safavi-Naini, R. (eds.) FC 2014. LNCS, vol. 8437, pp. 139–156. Springer, Heidelberg (2014). https://doi.org/10.1007/978-3-662-45472-5_10

42. Wallner, D.M., Harder, E.J., Agee, R.C.: Key management for multicast: issues and architectures. Internet Draft (1998). http://www.ietf.org/ID.html

43. Wong, C.K., Gouda, M., Lam, S.S.: Secure group communications using key graphs. In: Proceedings of ACM SIGCOMM, Vancouver, BC, Canada, 31 August–4 September 1998, pp. 68–79 (1998)

Post-quantum Privacy for Traceable Receipt-Free Encryption

Paola de Perthuis[1(✉)] and Thomas Peters[2]

[1] Centrum Wiskunde & Informatica (CWI), Amsterdam, The Netherlands
psamdp@cwi.nl
[2] Crypto Group, ICTEAM Institute, UCLouvain,
Ottignies-Louvain-la-Neuve, Belgium

Abstract. Traceable Receipt-free Encryption (TREnc) has recently been introduced by Devillez, Pereira and Peters (Asiacrypt'22) as a verifiable public-key encryption primitive allowing to randomize ciphertexts in order to remove any subliminal information up to a public trace which prevents the malleability of the underlying plaintexts. This unique feature generically enables the construction of voting systems by allowing voters to encrypt their votes, tracing whether a published ballot takes their choices into account, and preventing them from proving how they voted. While being a very promising primitive, the few existing TREnc mechanisms solely rely on discrete-logarithm related assumptions making them vulnerable to the well-known *harvest now, decrypt later* attack in the wait of quantum computers.

In this article, we address this limitation by building the first TREnc which can be safely used today until the advent of quantum adversaries. More precisely, based on the observation that security must hold at the time the primitive is used while only privacy should withstand in the post-quantum era, our solution relies on a mix of pre-quantum and post-quantum cryptography. As a first contribution, we generalize the original TREnc primitive that is too restrictive to be easily compatible with built-in lattice-based semantically-secure encryption. Our more flexible model keeps all the ingredients generically implying receipt-free voting. Next, we design our construction with the following essential properties for trustworthy elections: (i) it is provably-secure in the standard model; (ii) it relies on standard assumptions, namely Ring Learning With Errors (RLWE) coupled with pairing-based statistical zero-knowledge simulation-sound SXDH-based proofs; and (iii) it further enjoys a public-coin common reference string removing the need of a trusted setup.

Keywords: Traceable Receipt-Free Encryption · Post-Quantum Cryptography

1 Introduction

After the publication of its formal model in 2022 [DPP22], Traceable Receipt-free Encryption (TREnc) has recently moved from theory to practice [DPP24b] with

S. Bai and E. Persichetti (Eds.): PKC 2026, LNCS 16554, pp. 67–98, 2026.
https://doi.org/10.1007/978-3-032-26740-5_3

a Rust implementation and the removal of a trusted setup, along with tighter reductions. What makes TREnc appealing is its unique combination of security notions gathered in a single encryption primitive enabling the generic construction of receipt-free electronic voting (eVoting) with a non-interactive process. The main privacy notion of TREnc, preventing voters from proving how they vote in election applications, is the Indinstinguishability under Traceable Chosen-Ciphertext Attacks (TCCA) security. This notion differs from the classical confidentiality style of CCA security by requiring the indistinguishability of the *randomization of chosen ciphertexts* against traceable chosen-ciphertext attacks (even for maliciously generated traces) instead of the usual indistinguishability of the *encryption of chosen plaintexts*, both with access to a decryption oracle. Despite efforts to make TREnc more practical, there was until this work still no solution leading to a receipt-free voting system whose privacy would not have collapsed with the advent of quantum adversary *even if the election were already over*.

1.1   Our Contributions

A Post-Quantum Tradeoff. Although the cryptographic techniques allowing to build receipt-free voting systems with a non-interactive ballot submission process became more and more practical, the most efficient solutions solely rely on hard discrete-logarithm groups. This situation is uncomfortable since an adversary who records all the data available on the bulletin board during an election today could store this information until the advent of quantum computers would allow to break privacy. Even if [DPP22] provides a generic construction of TREnc, the state-of-the-art does not allow instantiating all of its building blocks without relying on pairing-based tools whose security requires the hardness of computing discrete logarithms.

As a first step toward designing an efficient post-quantum receipt-free election without trusted parameter generation, the current work provides the first TREnc with public-coin parameters which withstands the aforementioned *harvest now, decrypt later* attack, in the sense that the resulting election scheme would remain secure as long as the process would end before the advent of a quantum computer. Indeed, as building trustworthy post-quantum receipt-free eVoting remains very challenging, we observe that it is enough to hide the vote using a post-quantum encryption scheme (using a computational assumption since decryption must still hold) and to rely on pre-quantum tools to provide all the additional properties of the TREnc as long as the only message-related information they carry is statistically hidden.

This observation even allows us to select well-understood tools whose security relies on common standard assumptions, that we have chose to be as conservative as possible. More precisely, we can encrypt the vote message with a lattice-based scheme that has an integer modulus compatible with the size of pairing-based groups, where we can adapt the existing SXDH-based tools of previous TREnc constructions to the structure of the (R)LWE ciphertext. As usual, SXDH means that the Decisional Diffie-Hellman (DDH) assumption holds in both source groups, and RLWE refers to the Ring version of the decisional Learning With Error (LWE) assumption. This approach solves the *harvest now, decrypt later* issue because it is sufficient that the TREnc properties hold until the end of the election, after which no additional computations will occur. From that point on, the only remaining attack path for an adversary would be to break the security of the post-quantum encryption.

We stress that this solution is thus not fully post-quantum since the pre-quantum tools include zero-knowledge proofs whose soundness holds under discrete-logarithm related assumptions, and could be exploited by a quantum adversary to fake a verifiable ciphertext when a quantum computer will be available. Therefore, in the wait of new techniques to design efficient post-quantum TREnc (see *Open Problems* below), it is safer to replace pre-quantum solutions by ours. Such a priorisation of security properties has already been done in previous works (for example, in [BdPP23, BHdPP25, ETS25] for a standardized key-encapsulation mechanism).

Generalizing TREnc Security Notions. In this work, building a TREnc from lattice based assumptions has implied adapting its security definitions to a context in which the distribution of ciphertexts changes after the randomizing entity in charge of granting the Traceable Chosen-Ciphertext Attacks (TCCA) security has handled them; indeed, in previous constructions from ElGamal ciphertexts, their randomizations followed the same noise distribution as fresh encryptions, but updating the randomness in lattice-based ciphertexts without knowing their decryption key generally leads to an augmentation of their noise levels: a process which is irreversible without using the bootstrapping techniques requiring circular security that are implemented in fully-homomorphic encryption schemes. Therefore, our extended model captures two levels of ciphertexts, that are either fresh or rerandomized. Our generalization yields the previous TREnc definitions when the distributions considered are statistically close (as was the case for ElGamal ciphertexts in [DPP22, DPP24b]); nevertheless, allowing these distributions to be efficiently distinguishable in some cases require us to carefully adapt the security notions, to remain compatible with a generic transformation to receipt-free eVoting. In particular, our extension requires an additional privacy definition for fresh ciphertexts, as it is no longer implied by the TCCA notion focusing on their rerandomization.

Simpler Simulation-Sound Proofs for TREnc. Our construction makes use of a simpler simulation-sound proof technique than the one of [DPP24b] with a transparent setup, which was based on the Ràfols branching technique on Groth-Sahai (GS) proofs [Ràf15]. This latter technique relies on a GS Common Reference String (CRS) to prove relations over the exponents of source group elements in bilinear groups. To show that one of two statements is true, the prover splits the CRS into two pieces, each of which being seen as a CRS used to prove one of the branches of the OR proof. Since the prover has one degree of freedom to generate one of the pieces of the CRS, she picks one that allows simulating the proof of the statement branch for which she may not have a witness. Even if the other piece is then forced, the prover uses it as a CRS to prove the statement branch for which she knows a witness. This proof system enjoys a public-coin CRS, and the proof, *including* both CRS pieces, can be rerandomized as observed in [DPP24b], and required for TCCA security. While we also rely on OR-proof in our construction as it offers a way to create simulated proofs for an adversary that remains unable to proof false statements, we use a single GS CRS that does not require rerandomization, simplifying the design, and saving two group elements in their size when used to prove the same statements. In any case, we cannot adopt [Ràf15] as we encode the witness of the RLWE-based ciphertext into group elements so that it is easier to prove satisfiability of pairing-product equations (PPE).

Simulation-sound (extractable) proof systems with a transparent setup using OR proofs were already exhibited in [Gro06, CKLM12], but with different security notions. Only [CKLM12] supports malleability and rerandomization, but their model does not support tag-based proofs for which witnesses are always extractable: extracting a transformation is enough in their case. Difficulties also arise when proving the security of TREnc because the TCCA notion must deal with adversaries that may send as a challenge two ciphertexts associated with a tag for which she has already queried decryption, which avoids relying on programming techniques related to tags since they cannot be partitioned between those that allow simulation and those that allow extraction: all the proofs for any tags must be extractable when computed by the adversary even if these proofs must remains simulatable for the same tags. Our simulation-sound proof relies on one-time Linearly-Homomorphic Structure Preserving (LHSP) signatures, a tool we already use in the rest of the protocol for traceability, but now turned into a building-block of our OR proof. First, we rely on the Groth-Sahai proof system [GS08] for PPE to prove the knowledge of an LHSP signature when we do not have a witness for the RLWE-based ciphertext. Second, demonstrating such a knowledge is easy for null vectors, which admit degenerate signatures fulfilling the PPE. Therefore, when we have a witness for the honest branch, *i.e.*, the one related to the RLWE encryption, we manage to simulate the LHSP signature from a trivial solution of the PPE. However, when we do not have that witness, we can simulate the proof of the RLWE ciphertext by proving the other branch, *i.e.*, the knowledge of a signature-message pair depending on the tag (this tag is related to traceability as detailed later). Relying on LHSP signatures to build CCA-like encryption with (partial) randomization was already achieved in [DPP22, LPQ17], but the public key contained a structured CRS, which is avoided in the present work.

A Public-Coin CRS Generation. Finally, using GS proofs to commit to group elements using common-reference string elements drawn using public randomness, in the perfectly witness-indistinguishable mode of this proof system, allows us to remove the need for a trusted setup, consisting in a security model which may not have been realistic in real-life scenarios. As the construction presented here uses a public-coin perfectly witness-indistinguishable Groth-Sahai common reference string, it generalizes the TREnc notion of verifiability in a way in which,

though the normal key derivation does not allow the verification of ciphertexts'
(partially) belonging to the range of correct encryptions and randomizations,
there exists an indistinguishable key generation algorithm which comes with a
trapdoor allowing this partial verification; previous works exploited particular
cases in which the range could easily be verified, but this is not true in a more
general construction, even if it does not affect the overall security. Our new
notion captures this more universal definition.

1.2 Related Works and Open Problems

The motivation of TREnc comes from designing a solution to build non-interactive eVoting schemes with Receipt-Freeness in a generic way. As our work is
focused on preventing future attack on the privacy of votes in past elections,
in a long-term security perspective, we base our work on the most conservative
assumptions we could obtain: a transparent setup, lattice-based assumptions
used in post-quantum standards, and the SXDH which is for now necessary in
statistically-hiding rerandomizable zero-knowledge proofs. [DPP24c] proposed a
TREnc whose ciphertexts split into a perfectly hiding commitment part keeping
the traceability feature and an additional part which together allows decryption.
While the commitment part that is made available on the building board in the
eVoting application is post-quantum private, the remaining part seen by *any*
tallier is enough to downdrade the privacy to pre-quantum as it relies on SXDH.

Comparison with Deniable Encryption. TREnc offers a generic way to non-
interactively vote with strong Receipt Freeness (RF) with no need of any deceiving strategy (DS). The security of Deniable Encryption [CDNO96] (DE) falls
short to provide our RF which allows the adversary to provide two ballot ciphertexts with the same tracking trace to be processed (*i.e.* rerandomized) and
cast. This is achieved thanks to the TCCA notion from TREnc, but in the
d-deniability experiment the adversary only provides messages, and a random
coin is honestly drawn at random, which would not be realistic if a voter wanted
to sell their ballot. In RF, coins are maliciously chosen. Moreover, we need d to
be negligible and existing "efficient" solutions provide only an inverse of a polynomial in the security parameter. Without pre-planning (*i.e.*, DS), [SW14] has
a negligible d, but relies on indistinguishability obfuscation, which prevents this
solution to be used in elections today. Moreover, as voting systems should be
publicly verifiable, designers usually resort to additional zero-knowledge proofs
of knowledge which should then also have to be deniable in this framework.
However, to the best of our knowledge, there is no such solution available.

Open Problems for a Totally Post-quantum Solution. In the current state-of-
the-art, building a TREnc scheme requires at least two additional ingredients
to a rerandomizable semantically-secure encryption with a linear structure: tag-
based randomizable simulation-sound Zero-Knowledge (ZK) proofs to ensure
that ciphertexts have been honestly computed, and a linearly-only homomorphic signature scheme used to control the malleability of the ciphertexts, *i.e.*,

to prevent anything beyond rerandomization, except in the security proof. More precisely, the latter component leads to the traceability notion of the TREnc ciphertext, which means that no efficient adversary–even knowing the decryption key–can modify the underlying plaintext and preserve the trace of an honestly computed ciphertext while maintaining its public verifiability. This security notion ensures that even the authorities of an election cannot modify the content of ballots computed by honest voters from a TREnc.

The post-quantum literature provides solutions to linearly-only homomorphic signature for binary fields [BF11], or solutions with both additive and multiplicative homomorphism [GVW15], but it is not clear how these could be restricted to linear-only homomorphism. Even assuming restricting the homomorphism would be feasible, none of these constructions allow adapting one signature among two, and at the same time hiding which input signature has been modified. That is, while these schemes could be adapted to comply with the traceability requirement of a TREnc, they would reveal which ciphertext has been rerandomized, which prevents the TCCA notion from holding. Instead of trying to construct *ad hoc* signatures with both properties, one may rely on additional ZK proofs on top of them to confer this missing hiding property. However, it is with current knowledge unclear how one could build an appropriate efficient post-quantum proof system.

For the TCCA property, we need simulation-sound ZK proofs that also enjoy a malleability property to follow the rerandomization of ciphertexts and the hiding property explained above ensuring that one cannot infer the original proof that has been modified for a same tag. The lattice-based ZK proof systems in [LNP22,BS22] do not have all these properties. The situation is even worse if one would like the TREnc ciphertexts to ensure that plaintexts satisfy complex relations, as it is often the case in voting applications. In our case, proofs need to be: (i) adaptable to evolving statements, (ii) rerandomizable, (iii) simulation-sound, while (iv) preventing the randomizer to alter the content of the encrypted message for traceability even given the secret keys. For the first time, we show how to realize all such proofs on lattice-based ciphertexts, even though these proofs are not yet post-quantum themselves.

1.3   Technical Overview

In the generalized TREnc model presented in this paper, there are two ciphertext levels: fresh ciphertexts $C = (c, \mathsf{opk}, \Sigma, \Pi_{\mathsf{Valid}})$ are the output of the encryption algorithm, and randomized ciphertexts $\widetilde{C} = (\widetilde{c}, \mathsf{opk}, \widetilde{\Pi_{\mathsf{Trace}}}, \widetilde{\Pi_{\mathsf{Valid}}})$ are those of the randomization algorithm. Both distributions are easily recognizable in our construction, but if $\widetilde{C}$ is a randomization of C they share many things in common. First of all, $\widetilde{c}$ is a randomization of the lattice-based IND-CPA ciphertext c and they both decrypt to the same message. Second, the one-time verification key opk of the pairing-based LHSP signature used for traceability is the same. This key is generated during the computation of the fresh ciphertext along with its one-time secret key counterpart osk which itself allows producing a set Σ

of signatures on vectors related to c and the rows of a matrix $\underline{\widetilde{P}}$ encoding the public key of the lattice-based encryption scheme. These vectors are encoded in the source groups of the bilinear pairing operation, by using scalars of the lattice-based ciphertext, with integer modulus the same prime as the order of the groups, as exponents. Moreover, these signatures allows deriving a signature $\widetilde{\sigma}$ on $\widetilde{c}$, which will allow traceability. However, since in the TCCA proof we have to simulate $\widetilde{\sigma}$ (when $\widetilde{c}$ will no longer be an honest randomization of c), we turn the one-time LHSP signature scheme into a simulatable one-time LHSP signature scheme by making a non-interactive zero-knowledge (NIZK) proof of knowledge $\widetilde{\Pi_{\mathsf{Trace}}}$ of $\widetilde{\sigma}$. Eventually, Π_{Valid} and $\widetilde{\Pi_{\mathsf{Valid}}}$ complete the ciphertexts with a malleable tag-based simulation-sound extractable proof, with a hash of opk as the tag, ensuring that c and $\widetilde{c}$ are respectively well-formed, and allowing to extract the message in order to answer decryption queries. To achieve post-quantum privacy, all these proofs must statistically hide the witnesses for the actual generation of the parameters, that are also public coin. We hereafter provide more detail on how these three parts are built.

Lattice-Based IND-CPA Encryption Component. Abusing notations, a message $m = (m_1, \ldots, m_n) \in \{0;1\}^n$ is semantically encrypted into two ring elements $(\mathsf{c}, \mathsf{c}') = (\mathsf{p} \cdot \mathsf{u} + \mathsf{e}_1 + \Delta \cdot \mathsf{m}, \mathsf{p}' \cdot \mathsf{u} + \mathsf{e}_2)$ of $\mathcal{R}_p = \mathbb{Z}_p[X]/(X^n + 1)$ under RLWE, where m encodes m, $(\mathsf{p}, \mathsf{p}')$ is the public key, and random coin $(\mathsf{u}, \mathsf{e}_1, \mathsf{e}_2)$ from an appropriate distribution. The vector $c \in \mathbb{Z}_p^{2n}$ of the coefficients of $(\mathsf{c}, \mathsf{c}')$ can also be computed as $c = (m\|u)\underline{P}$ for some public matrix $\underline{P} \in \mathbb{Z}_p^{2n \times N}$ and *binary* vector $u \in \{0;1\}^{N-n}$ representing random coins. In a more compact form, $c = \underline{P}w$, denoting $w = (m\|u) \in \mathbb{Z}_p^N$ is the witness associated to the statement "c is a valid lattice-based encryption." The parameters allows rerandomizing c as $\widetilde{c} = c + \underline{\widetilde{P}}\widetilde{w}$ for a new binary witness $\widetilde{w} \in \{0;1\}^{\widetilde{N}}$ and public matrix $\underline{\widetilde{P}} \in \mathbb{Z}_p^{2n \times \widetilde{N}}$ while preserving correct decryption. We note that the fresh ciphertext c and the randomized one $\widetilde{c}$ do note have the same distribution, which is one of the reasons why this work enlarges the definition of TREnc primitives. Nevertheless, they are computationally indistinguishable since both $\underline{P}w$ and $\underline{\widetilde{P}}\widetilde{w}$ are pseudorandom under RLWE. The two remaining components of the ciphertext discussed in the next paragraphs are built in a bilinear group with the same prime order p as the lattice-based integer modulus. Any element of $v \in \mathbb{Z}_p$ that is a component of a lattice-based ciphertext carries over to the first (resp. second) source group $\mathbb{G}$ (resp. $\hat{\mathbb{G}}$) of the pairing operation by computing $vG \in \mathbb{G}$ (resp. $v\mathfrak{G} \in \hat{\mathbb{G}}$), where G (resp. $\mathfrak{G}$) is a generator of $\mathbb{G}$ (resp. $\hat{\mathbb{G}}$).

Tracing Component. Let $(\mathsf{opk}, \mathsf{osk})$ be the one-time key pair of the LHSP signature scheme. We now focus on the vector of signatures Σ in $C = (c, \mathsf{opk}, \Sigma, \Pi_{\mathsf{Valid}})$ and on the simulatable LHSP signature $\widetilde{\Pi_{\mathsf{Trace}}}$ in $\widetilde{C} = (\widetilde{c}, \mathsf{opk}, \widetilde{\Pi_{\mathsf{Trace}}}, \widetilde{\Pi_{\mathsf{Valid}}})$. Recall that the traceability notion does not only refer to finding a ciphertext thanks to opk, but to ensure that any valid ciphertext with opk decrypts to the original message m even if the adversary knows the secret decryption key (as in an election, we do not want authorities to be able to modify the ballots nor the outcome). LHSP signatures were also present in earlier constructions of TREnc, but this work moves apart from how they were previously used for two reasons. The first one is that, in our lattice setting with c and $\tilde{c}$, any linear comination of signed vectors is not a signature on a vector corresponding to an encryption of the same message. Indeed, for too large noises, correct decryption may be lost. Therefore, we focus only on binary linear combinations–subset sums–whose coefficients correspond to $\tilde{w}$. That means that the original vectors signed in Σ must come along with a way to check the validity of the linear combination. The vectors that are signed are thus simply the rows of a matrix $\underline{T}$ that encodes the extended matrix $(\underline{M}\|\underline{I}_{1+N-n})$ into $\mathbb{G}$, where $\underline{M}$ is $\underline{\widetilde{P}}^T$ with the additional row c^T at the top and $\underline{I}_{1+N-n}$ is the identity matrix in $\mathbb{Z}_p^{1+N-n}$. From that, one can derive a signature $\tilde{\sigma}$ on $(\tilde{c}^T\|1\|w^T)G$ as $(1\|w^T)\Sigma$, where the middle 1 is a testimony that we indeed keep c with coefficient 1 into $\tilde{c}$. Obviously, $\tilde{w}G$ cannot remain in the clear and we will rely on the commit-and-prove paradigm of Groth-Sahai (GS) proof system to show the satisfiability of PPE. This leads us to the second reason of our adaptation of the use of LHSP signatures: their simulatability. As explained above, we will actually prove the knowledge of $\tilde{\sigma}$ in $\widetilde{\Pi_{\mathsf{Trace}}}$, which also allows us to directly embed $\tilde{w}G$ in the same proof and guarantees its bitstring shape. In general, GS proofs do not come with a simulator for PPE statements; proofs are only statistically witness-indistinguishable from public-coin common reference strings to commit group elements. To make it statistically zero-knowledge, we will turn it into an OR proof, exactly in the same manner as required in the last verifiability component, so, we omit this discussion here. Instead, we stress that previous constructions of TREnc also embedded a way to simulate LHSP signatures, but without proofs, by signing additional vectors whose involvement in the rerandomization was related to the random-self reducibility of an SXDH instance and required random linear combinations over $\mathbb{Z}_p$, instead of the binary linear combinations we have.

Validity Component. The validity proofs Π_{Valid} and $\widetilde{\Pi_{\mathsf{Valid}}}$ have two purposes. The first one is to offer a public way to deem if a ciphertext is well-formed. This is convenient in an election, as then any observer can understand why some ballots may be discarded. The second one is to boost the confidentiality with access to a decryption oracle as required by the TCCA notion. Unlike the previous TREnc constructions, our proofs must be simulation-sound extractable, while simulation soundness was enough in [DPP22, DPP24b, DPP24c] since the reduction could keep the secret decryption key, as their schemes relied on hash proof systems, which cannot be easily handled in our lattice setting. In our case, we need to prove that $c = \underline{P}(m\|u)$, for a fresh ciphertext, and $\tilde{c} = c + \underline{\widetilde{P}}\tilde{w}$, for randomized a ciphertext, but from $\tilde{w} \in \{0; 1\}^{\tilde{N}}$ and Π_{Valid} for the fresh ciphertext c. The additional extractability feature we need comes from the bitwise decomposition. Even though we commit to bits encoded into group elements, and commitments to group elements do not always allow extracting discrete logarithms from GS proofs, the simulation soundness is enough to extract either $O = 0 \cdot G$ or $G = 1 \cdot G$, from which we can recover the exponent bit in $\mathbb{Z}_p$. Since we anyway have to prove knowledge of a bitwise representation to ensure the validity of c and $\widetilde{c}$, this extraction does not induce any asymptotical overhead.

Linear GS proofs can be aggregated to prove a statement $\widetilde{c} = \underline{P}m + \underline{\widetilde{P}}(u + \widetilde{w})$, as $\underline{\widetilde{P}}$ corresponds to the part of $\underline{P}$ that multiplies u, for a single commitment to the vector $m \| (u + \widetilde{w})$, but we will actually keep the commitments to u and $\widetilde{w}$ separate. Once again, this is due to the fact that lattice-based encryption does not support random coins of any size, and we actually need to show that both u and $\widetilde{w}$ are bitstrings, which is not the case of their sum in general. In the following explanations we do not focus on the malleability feature and randomizability of GS proofs, allowing to compute $\widetilde{\Pi}_{\mathsf{Valid}}$ from Π_{Valid} and $\widetilde{w}$, that are already described in [GS08]. Instead, we explain our malleable simulation-sound extractable proof as an OR proof with LHSP signatures and tag $\tau = \mathcal{H}(\mathsf{opk}, \mathsf{PK})$. The OR proof can be implemented by committing to a bit $\mathfrak{b}$ that indicates whether we honestly prove the statement (if $\mathfrak{b} = 0$) or whether we simulation the proof (if $\mathfrak{b} = 1$). In other words, if $\mathfrak{b} = 0$, we prove that the PPEs are satisfied for the lattice-based ciphertext component, and if $\mathfrak{b} = 1$, we prove that we know group elements corresponding to an LHSP signatures on $(G, \tau G)$ which also verify from some other PPEs. Since the public key of the one-time LHSP signature scheme consists of uniformly random group elements, the CRS may stem from a public coin generation.

For this to be compatible with GS proofs, we still need to know a witness for both branches. Fortunately, if $\boldsymbol{Q}(\boldsymbol{X}, \mathfrak{X}) = (q_1(\boldsymbol{X}, \boldsymbol{X}), \ldots, q_n(\boldsymbol{X}, \boldsymbol{X})) = (0, \ldots, 0)$ represents the PPEs for the lattice-based ciphertext component with witnesses $(\boldsymbol{X}, \boldsymbol{X})$, and $\sigma^\dagger$ a valid signature on $(G, \tau G)$, we always have a full witness as $(\mathfrak{b}(\boldsymbol{X}, \boldsymbol{X}) \| (1 - \mathfrak{b})(\sigma^\dagger \| (G, \tau G)))$ if we know a solution $(\boldsymbol{X}, \boldsymbol{X})$ or $\sigma^\dagger$. Eventually, it is easy to see that this full witness, independently of the value taken by the bit $\mathfrak{b}$, allows proving that one knows a solution $\mathfrak{b}(\boldsymbol{X}, \boldsymbol{X})$ to $\mathfrak{b} \cdot \boldsymbol{Q}(\boldsymbol{X}, \boldsymbol{X}) = (0, \ldots, 0)$ *and* a trivial signature $(1 - \mathfrak{b})\sigma^\dagger$ on the trivial vector $(1 - \mathfrak{b})(G, \tau G)$, since the verification equations of the LHSP signatures are compatible with trivial solutions. The perfect witness indistinguishable property of GS proofs perfectly hide $\mathfrak{b}$ and which branch is actually proven, hence statistical zero knowledge is granted. Finally, simulation soundness holds (as well as the extractability of group elements corresponding to the full witness used in the valid proof) since the LHSP signature is one-time unforgeable, and for any other tag $\tau^* = \mathcal{H}(\mathsf{opk}^*, \mathsf{PK})$ for $\mathsf{opk}^* \neq \mathsf{opk}$, the adversary is unable to compute a valid signature on $(G, \tau^* G)$ even if it saw a valid signature on $(G, \tau G)$ (used in our simulation), because these vectors are linearly independent.

Efficiency. Our construction incurs ciphertexts on 40 to 110 MB[1] where [DPP24b]'s would have been on 2 MB for the same parameters, which corresponds to the cost of granting post-quantum privacy, and a conservative security model with neither AGM nor GGM. Indeed, rerandomizability properties

---

[1] 47 MB for fresh ciphertexts, such as those generated by voters in an election application, and 107 MB for randomized ciphertexts published by the talliers to attest the result of the vote.

for now need to be reached through pairing techniques imposing a large lattice integer modulus, which in turn makes the lattice dimension grow, and hence the size of the witnesses on which proofs are made. Using different moduli in the lattice and order of pairing groups does not seem easily achievable for now, as relying on distinct known prime-order groups would create a soundness issue when proving smallness. Moreover, we are not aware of any efficient hidden-order (bilinear) groups enjoying rerandomizable simulation-sound proofs that would be compatible with proving statements over the integers. Hence, the sheer size of witnesses is for now an efficiency bottleneck, that will only be lifted with more developments in the rerandomizable simulation-sound zero-knowledge proof literature.

2   Preliminaries

Notations. Vectors will be denoted with bold letters, such as $\boldsymbol{v} = (v_1, \ldots, v_n)$, and be vertical unless stated otherwise. $\boldsymbol{u}\|\boldsymbol{v}$ will be used to denote the concatenation of vectors $\boldsymbol{u}$ and $\boldsymbol{v}$, and $\langle \boldsymbol{u}; \boldsymbol{v} \rangle$ their inner-product. Matrices will generally be underlined, such as with $\underline{M}$. Group elements will be denoted with capital letters. For G an element of an additive group $\mathbb{G}$ of order q, $\boldsymbol{v}G$ will denote the vector $(v_1 G, \ldots, v_n G) \in \mathbb{G}^n$, and for $\boldsymbol{G} = (G_1, \ldots, G_k)$ a vector in $\mathbb{G}^k$, $\boldsymbol{G} \cdot \boldsymbol{v}$ will denote the product matrix $(v_j G_i)_{i \in 1;k, j \in 1;n}$. A *pairing setting* $(p, \mathbb{G}, \hat{\mathbb{G}}, \mathbb{G}_T, e, G, \mathfrak{G})$ will describe two additive groups $\mathbb{G}$ and $\hat{\mathbb{G}}$ of order p, with G and $\mathfrak{G}$ two respective generators, and a bilinear pairing operation $e : \mathbb{G} \times \hat{\mathbb{G}} \to \mathbb{G}_T$ going into the multiplicative group of order p $\mathbb{G}_T$ generated by $e(G, \mathfrak{G})$.

For any quotient ring $\mathcal{R} = \mathbb{Z}_q[X]/(\mathsf{r}(X))$, with $\mathsf{r} \in \mathbb{Z}_q[X]$ of degree n, the function $\mathsf{pol}_\mathcal{R} : \mathbb{Z}_q^n \to \mathcal{R}$ will associate, to any $\boldsymbol{v} = (v_0, \ldots, v_{n-1}) \in \mathbb{Z}_q^n$, the corresponding polynomial $\sum_{i=0}^{n-1} v_i X^i \in \mathcal{R}$. For any integers $a \le b$, $[\![a; b]\!]$ will denote the set: $\{x \in \mathbb{Z} | a \le x \le b\}$. $\xleftarrow{\$} \mathcal{D}$ will denote sampling from the distribution $\mathcal{D}$. Given a finite set $\mathcal{S}$, $x \xleftarrow{\$} \mathcal{S}$ will mean that x is sampled from the uniform distribution $\mathcal{U}_\mathcal{S}$ on $\mathcal{S}$. Given two distributions $\mathcal{D}_0$ and $\mathcal{D}_1$, and a Probabilistic Polynomial Time (PPT) adversary $\mathcal{A}$, her distinguishing advantage on these distributions will be defined as: $\mathsf{Adv}_\mathcal{A}^{\mathcal{D}_0, \mathcal{D}_1} = |\mathrm{Pr}_{x \xleftarrow{\$} \mathcal{D}_0} \{\mathcal{A}(x) = 0\} - \mathrm{Pr}_{x \xleftarrow{\$} \mathcal{D}_1} \{\mathcal{A}(x) = 0\}|$.

IND-CPA security will be attained, for a public-key encryption scheme $(\mathsf{KeyGen}, \mathsf{Enc}, \mathsf{Dec})$ with message space $\mathcal{M}$, when for any PPT adversary $\mathcal{A} = (\mathcal{A}_1, \mathcal{A}_2)$, $\mathcal{A}$'s probability of winning the security game defined in Fig. 1 (*i. e.*, having it output 1), is negligibly close to one half in the security parameter λ.

$\mathsf{Exp}_\mathcal{A}^{\mathsf{CPA}}(\lambda)$:

$(\mathsf{pk}, \mathsf{sk}) \xleftarrow{\$} \mathsf{KeyGen}(1^\lambda)$
$(m_0, m_1, \mathsf{st}) \xleftarrow{\$} \mathcal{A}_1(\mathsf{pk})$
$b \xleftarrow{\$} \{0; 1\}$
if $m_0 \notin \mathcal{M}$ or $m_1 \notin \mathcal{M}$ **then** return 0
$c^* \xleftarrow{\$} \mathsf{Enc}(\mathsf{pk}, m_b)$, $b' \xleftarrow{\$} \mathcal{A}_2(c^*, \mathsf{st})$
if $b' = b$ return 1, **else** return 0

Fig. 1. IND-CPA security experiment

2.1   Hard Problems

Our construction will rely on the hardness of classical cryptographic problems; the Chosen Plaintext Attack (CPA) privacy of encrypted messages will rely on a variant of the Learning With Errors (LWE) one, stated hereafter:

Definition 1 (The Learning With Errors (LWE) Average-Case Decision Assumption). *states, with respect to $q, n \in \mathbb{N}$ and an error distribution χ, that, for $s \xleftarrow{\$} \mathbb{Z}_q^n$, the two following distributions are computationally hard to distinguish:*

$$\mathcal{D}_0 = \left\{ (a, \langle a; s \rangle + e) \in \mathbb{Z}_q^n \times \mathbb{Z}_q | a \xleftarrow{\$} \mathbb{Z}_q^n, e \xleftarrow{\$} \chi \right\}$$

$$\mathcal{D}_1 = \left\{ (a, b) \in \mathbb{Z}_q^n \times \mathbb{Z}_q | a \xleftarrow{\$} \mathbb{Z}_q^n, b \xleftarrow{\$} \mathbb{Z}_q \right\};$$

this statement is expressed with respect to any Probabilistic Polynomial Time (PPT) adversary $\mathcal{A}$ and security parameter $\lambda \in \mathbb{N}$, as: $\mathsf{Adv}_{\mathcal{A}}^{D-\mathsf{LWE}}(\lambda) = \mathsf{negl}(\lambda)$, where $\mathsf{Adv}_{\mathcal{A}}^{D-\mathsf{LWE}}(\lambda)$ denotes $\mathcal{A}$'s advantage, when provided with $\mathcal{D}_\beta$ for $\beta \xleftarrow{\$} \{0; 1\}$, in guessing the value of β.

our construction could easily be instantiated with an LWE-based Encryption scheme, though we describe an example using its polynomial ring variant:

Definition 2 (The Ring-LWE Average-Case Decision Assumption). *states, with respect to q, $n \in \mathbb{N}$, $\mathsf{r} \in \mathbb{Z}_q[X]$ an irreducible polynomial of degree n, and an error distribution χ on $\mathcal{R}$, where $\mathcal{R} \leftarrow \mathbb{Z}_q[X]/(\mathsf{r}(X))$, that, for $\mathsf{s} \xleftarrow{\$} \mathcal{R}$, the two following distributions are computationally hard to distinguish:*

$$\mathcal{D}_0 = \left\{ (\mathsf{a}, \mathsf{a} \cdot \mathsf{s} + \mathsf{e}) \in \mathcal{R}^2 | \mathsf{a} \xleftarrow{\$} \mathcal{R}, \mathsf{e} \xleftarrow{\$} \chi \right\}$$

$$\mathcal{D}_1 = \left\{ (\mathsf{a}, \mathsf{b}) \in \mathcal{R}^2 | \mathsf{a}, \mathsf{b} \xleftarrow{\$} \mathcal{R} \right\};$$

this statement is expressed with respect to any Probabilistic Polynomial Time (PPT) adversary $\mathcal{A}$ and security parameter $\lambda \in \mathbb{N}$, as: $\mathsf{Adv}_{\mathcal{A}}^{D-\mathsf{RLWE}}(\lambda) = \mathsf{negl}(\lambda)$, where $\mathsf{Adv}_{\mathcal{A}}^{D-\mathsf{RLWE}}(\lambda)$ denotes $\mathcal{A}$'s advantage, when provided with $\mathcal{D}_b$ for $b \xleftarrow{\$} \{0; 1\}$, in guessing the value of b.

The Traceability and Traceable Chosen Ciphertext Attack (TCCA) security of the scheme will rely on the SXDH assumption, presented hereafter:

Definition 3 (The Decisional Diffie-Hellman (DDH) Assumption). *states, with respect to a group $(\mathbb{G}, +)$ of prime order p, that given one of its generators, G, the two following distributions are computationally hard to distinguish:*

$$\mathcal{D}_0 = \left\{ (aG, bG, abG) | a, b \xleftarrow{\$} \mathbb{Z}_p \right\} \qquad \mathcal{D}_1 = \left\{ (aG, bG, cG) | a, b, c \xleftarrow{\$} \mathbb{Z}_p \right\};$$

this statement is expressed with respect to any PPT adversary $\mathcal{A}$ and security parameter $\lambda \in \mathbb{N}$, as: $\mathsf{Adv}_{\mathcal{A}}^{\mathsf{DDH},\mathbb{G}}(\lambda) = \mathsf{negl}(\lambda)$, where $\mathsf{Adv}_{\mathcal{A}}^{\mathsf{DDH},\mathbb{G}}(\lambda)$ denotes $\mathcal{A}$'s advantage, when receiving an element of $\mathcal{D}_b$ for $b \xleftarrow{\$} \{0; 1\}$, in guessing the value of b.

Definition 4 (The Symmetric eXternal Diffie-Hellman (SXDH) Assumption). *states, with respect to two additive groups of prime order p, $\mathbb{G}$ and $\hat{\mathbb{G}}$, and a bilinear pairing operation $e : \mathbb{G} \times \hat{\mathbb{G}} \to \mathbb{G}_T$ mapping elements into the multiplicative group $\mathbb{G}_T$ of order p, the DDH assumption is true both in $\mathbb{G}$ and in $\hat{\mathbb{G}}$; this statement is expressed with respect to any PPT adversary $\mathcal{A}$ and security parameter $\lambda \in \mathbb{N}$, as:* $\mathsf{Adv}_{\mathcal{A}}^{\mathsf{SXDH}}(\lambda) = \mathsf{negl}(\lambda)$, *where* $\mathsf{Adv}_{\mathcal{A}}^{\mathsf{SXDH}}(\lambda) = \max\{\mathsf{Adv}_{\mathcal{A}}^{\mathsf{DDH},\mathbb{G}}(\lambda), \mathsf{Adv}_{\mathcal{A}}^{\mathsf{DDH},\hat{\mathbb{G}}}(\lambda)\}$.

Finally, the TCCA security will also rely on the resistance of hash functions against collisions, a property stated here:

Definition 5 (Collision Resistance). *A family of functions $\mathcal{F}_h = \{h_k : \{0;1\}^{n(k)} \to \{0;1\}^{m(k)}\}_k$ lists collision-resistant hash functions if for any k, $n(k) \geq m(k)$, there exists a PPT algorithm Sampl outputting, on input a security parameter $\lambda \in \mathbb{N}$, h_k in the family, such that for any PPT adversary $\mathcal{A}$:*

$$\Pr\left\{\{x \neq y\} \cap \{h_k(x) = h_k(y)\} \;\middle|\; \begin{array}{c} h_k \xleftarrow{\$} \mathsf{Sampl}(1^\lambda) \\ (x,y) \xleftarrow{\$} \mathcal{A}(h_k, 1^\lambda) \end{array}\right\} \leq \mathsf{negl}(\lambda).$$

2.2   An RLWE-Based Encryption Scheme Instantiation

A simple example of such a scheme would be, starting with the FV scheme [FV12] with multiplicative depth zero, defining the plaintext space $\mathcal{R}_t = \mathbb{Z}_t[X]/(X^n+1)$, with n a power of two, and the ciphertext space $\mathcal{R}_p^2$ with $\mathcal{R}_p = \mathbb{Z}_p[X]/(X^n+1)$, $\sigma \in]0;1[$ a noise parameter, $\Delta \leftarrow \lfloor p/t \rfloor$, and $\Gamma = (p,t,n,\sigma)$ the parameter set. χ_s will denote the discrete gaussian distribution on $\mathcal{R}_p$ with standard deviation s. For any x in $\mathbb{Z}_a$, $[x]_a$ will denote its representative in $[\![-\lceil\frac{a}{2}\rceil; \lfloor\frac{a}{2}\rfloor]\!]$, when applied to a vector it will denote the operation applied to each of its components, and for any x in $\mathcal{R}_a$, $[\mathsf{x}]_a$ will denote the representative of x reduced by the quotient polynomial (X^n+1 in our case) of $\mathcal{R}_a$ with coefficients in $[\![-\lceil\frac{a}{2}\rceil; \lfloor\frac{a}{2}\rfloor]\!]$.

$\mathsf{KeyGen}(1^\lambda, \Gamma) \to (\mathsf{sk}, \mathsf{pk})$: samples $\mathsf{a} \xleftarrow{\$} \mathcal{R}_p$, and $\mathsf{s}, \mathsf{e} \xleftarrow{\$} \chi_\sigma$, sets: $(\mathsf{p}, \mathsf{p}') \leftarrow ([-(\mathsf{a} \cdot \mathsf{s} + \mathsf{e})]_p, \mathsf{a}) \in \mathcal{R}_p^2$, $\mathsf{pk} \leftarrow (\mathsf{p}, \mathsf{p}', \Delta, \sigma)$ and $\mathsf{sk} \leftarrow \mathsf{s}$, and returns $(\mathsf{sk}, \mathsf{pk})$.

$\mathsf{Enc}_{\mathsf{pk}}(\mathsf{m}) \to (\mathsf{c}, \mathsf{c}')$: samples $\mathsf{e}_1, \mathsf{e}_2 \xleftarrow{\$} \chi_\sigma$, $\boldsymbol{u} \in \{0;1\}^n$, sets $\mathsf{u} \leftarrow \mathsf{pol}_{\mathcal{R}_p}(\boldsymbol{u})$, and returns: $(\mathsf{c}, \mathsf{c}') \leftarrow ([\mathsf{p} \cdot \mathsf{u} + \mathsf{e}_1 + \Delta \cdot [\mathsf{m}]_t]_p, [\mathsf{p}' \cdot \mathsf{u} + \mathsf{e}_2]_p)$. The distribution χ_σ's standard deviation σ may also be given as an optional argument to the encryption function.

$\mathsf{Dec}_{\mathsf{sk}}((\mathsf{c}, \mathsf{c}')) \to \mathsf{m}$: computes: $\mathsf{d} \leftarrow [\mathsf{c} + \mathsf{s} \cdot \mathsf{c}']$, and returns: $\mathsf{m} \leftarrow [\lfloor \mathsf{d}/\Delta \rceil]_t$.

The ciphertexts in this scheme can be added with linear homorphism, up to a certain bound. In [FV12], the authors also show that this scheme grants semantic security from RLWE, and that the scheme is statistically correct.

A Generalized Encryption Scheme. The FV instantiation may be abstracted as a scheme $\mathsf{PQPKE} = (\mathsf{KeyGen}, \mathsf{Enc}, \mathsf{Rand}, \mathsf{Dec})$ in the following way (with appropriate choices of σ, n and $t = 2$ in the FV Γ input, and deterministic calculation of N, $\tilde{N}$), also applicable to LWE instantiations, to fit our construction.

$\mathsf{PQPKE.KeyGen}(1^\lambda, p) \to (\mathsf{pk}, \mathsf{sk})$: takes as input λ and p in $\mathbb{N}$, computes the corresponding public key lengths n, N and $\widetilde{N}$, as well as $\underline{P} = (\boldsymbol{p}_i)_{i \in [\![1;N]\!]} \in \mathbb{Z}_p^{2n \times N}$, $\underline{\widetilde{P}} = (\widetilde{\boldsymbol{p}}_i)_{i \in [\![1;\widetilde{N}]\!]} \in \mathbb{Z}_p^{2n \times \widetilde{N}}$, $\mathsf{pk} \leftarrow (\underline{P}, \underline{\widetilde{P}})$, and as a secret key sk, and outputs $(\mathsf{pk}, \mathsf{sk})$;

$\mathsf{PQPKE.Enc}_{\mathsf{pk}}(\boldsymbol{m}) \to (\boldsymbol{c}, \boldsymbol{w})$: on input a public key $\mathsf{pk} = (\underline{P}, \underline{\widetilde{P}})$ and message $\boldsymbol{m} \in \{0;1\}^n$, draws $\boldsymbol{u} \in \{0;1\}^{N-n}$ from a random distribution specified by the scheme, sets $\boldsymbol{w} \leftarrow \boldsymbol{m} \| \boldsymbol{u}$, $\boldsymbol{c} \leftarrow \underline{P}\boldsymbol{w}$, and outputs $(\boldsymbol{c}, \boldsymbol{w})$;

$\mathsf{PQPKE.Rand}_{\mathsf{pk}}(\boldsymbol{c}) \to (\widetilde{\boldsymbol{c}}, \widetilde{\boldsymbol{w}})$: on input a public key $\mathsf{pk} = (\underline{P}, \underline{\widetilde{P}})$ and $\boldsymbol{c} \in \mathbb{Z}_p^{2n}$, draws $\widetilde{\boldsymbol{s}} \in \{0;1\}^{\widetilde{N}}$ from a random distribution specified by the scheme, sets $\widetilde{\boldsymbol{c}} \leftarrow \boldsymbol{c} + \underline{\widetilde{P}}\widetilde{\boldsymbol{w}}$, and outputs $(\widetilde{\boldsymbol{c}}, \widetilde{\boldsymbol{w}})$;

$\mathsf{PQPKE.Dec}_{\mathsf{sk}}(\boldsymbol{c}) \to \boldsymbol{m}$: on input a secret key sk and $\boldsymbol{c} \in \mathbb{Z}_p^{2n}$, outputs a decrypted message $\boldsymbol{m} \in \{0;1\}^n$.

Definition 6 (Correctness). PQPKE *is correct if for any* $\lambda, p, n \in \mathbb{N}$, $\boldsymbol{m}$ *in* $\{0;1\}^n$, $\boldsymbol{u} \in \{0;1\}^{N-n}$, $\widetilde{\boldsymbol{w}} \in \{0;1\}^{\widetilde{N}}$,

$$\Pr\left[\, \mathsf{Dec}_{\mathsf{sk}}(\underline{P}(\boldsymbol{m}\|\boldsymbol{u}) + \underline{\widetilde{P}}\widetilde{\boldsymbol{w}}) \neq \boldsymbol{m} \,\middle|\, (\mathsf{pk} = (\underline{P}, \underline{\widetilde{P}}), \mathsf{sk}) \xleftarrow{\$} \mathsf{KeyGen}(1^\lambda, p) \right] \leq \mathsf{negl}(\lambda).$$

A detail of its correct and IND-CPA-secure FV instantiation is provided in the full version [dPP24a].

2.3 Linearly-Homomorphic Structure-Preserving Signatures

These signatures consist of two group elements signing a vector with components in the same group (first primitives stemming from [AFG+10, AHO10]), with the additional property (from [LPJY14]) that a linear combination of signatures will yield a signature on the corresponding linear combination of vectors. The algorithms of such an LHSP scheme are recalled hereafter:

$\mathsf{KeyGen}(\mathsf{pp}, n) \to (\mathsf{pk}, \mathsf{sk})$: on input the public parameters pp describing additive groups of primer order p, $\mathbb{G}$ and $\hat{\mathbb{G}}$, generators $\mathfrak{G}$ and $\mathfrak{H}$ of $\hat{\mathbb{G}}$, and a bilinear pairing operation $e : \mathbb{G} \times \hat{\mathbb{G}} \to \mathbb{G}_T$ mapping elements into the multiplicative group $\mathbb{G}_T$ of order p, and the vector length $n \in \mathbb{N}$ (of polynomial size), this algorithm draws $\chi_1, \ldots \chi_n, \gamma_1, \ldots, \gamma_n \xleftarrow{\$} \mathbb{Z}_p$, sets, for each index i in $[\![1;n]\!]$, $\mathfrak{G}_i \leftarrow \chi_i\mathfrak{G} + \gamma_i\mathfrak{H}$, and then the secret key to: $\mathsf{sk} \leftarrow (((\chi_i, \gamma_i))_{i \in [\![1;n]\!]}, \mathsf{pp})$, and the public key to $\mathsf{pk} \leftarrow ((\mathfrak{G}_1, \ldots, \mathfrak{G}_n), \mathsf{pp})$, finally outputting: $(\mathsf{pk}, \mathsf{sk})$.

$\mathsf{Sign}(\mathsf{sk}, (M_1, \ldots, M_n)) \to \sigma{:}]$ on input sk parsed as an output of KeyGen and $(M_1, \ldots, M_n) \in \mathbb{G}^n$, the algorithm sets and returns: $\sigma \leftarrow (\Sigma_1, \Sigma_2) \leftarrow (\sum_{i=1}^n \chi_i M_i, \sum_{i=1}^n \gamma_i M_i)$.

$\mathsf{SignDer}(\mathsf{pk}, (\omega_i)_{i=1}^m, (\sigma_i)_{i=1}^m) \to \sigma$: on input pk parsed as an output of KeyGen, $(\omega_1, \ldots, \omega_m) \in \mathbb{Z}_p^m$, for a natural m, and the σ_i's parsed as outputs of Sign, this algorithm derives a signature on the linear combination with weights ω_i of vectors they sign by outputting: $\sigma \leftarrow (\Sigma_1, \Sigma_2) \leftarrow \sum_{i=1}^m \omega_i \sigma_i$.

$\mathsf{Ver}(\mathsf{pk}, \sigma, (M_1, \ldots, M_n)) \to b$: parsing pk as a corresponding output of KeyGen, $\sigma = (\Sigma_1, \Sigma_2)$ as an output of Sign, the algorithm outputs $b \leftarrow 1$ if and only if: $e(\Sigma_1, \mathfrak{G})e(\Sigma_2, \mathfrak{H}) = \prod_{i=1}^n e(M_i, \mathfrak{G}_i)$; else, it outputs $b \leftarrow 0$.

2.4   The Groth Sahai Proof System

Provided by Groth and Sahai's seminal work in [GS08], this proof system, in a commit and prove framework, allows the randomization of commitments and proofs. Furthermore, it grants witness-indistinguishable proofs of quadratic relations (on scalars, groups elements, or a mix of both, in a pairing setting), and can be used in two indistinguishable modes, one of which leads to perfectly binding and the other to perfectly witness-indistinguishable proofs.

In this work, Groth-Sahai (GS) algorithms $\mathsf{GS} = (\mathsf{Setup}, \mathsf{BCRSGen}, \mathsf{HCRSGen}, \mathsf{Com\&Pr}, \mathsf{Rand}, \mathsf{Vf})$ will be used with a public-coin generation in the perfectly witness-indistinguishable case for the commitment of group elements. Though a full description of the algorithms in this context is provided in the full version [dPP24a], the reader will find hereafter a synthesised summary of their inputs and outputs.

$\mathsf{Setup}(1^\lambda) \to \mathsf{pp}$: on input the security parameter $\lambda \in \mathbb{N}$, returns public parameters pp providing a pairing setting with: $\mathsf{pp} \leftarrow (p, \mathbb{G}, \hat{\mathbb{G}}, \mathbb{G}_T, e, G, \mathfrak{G})$;

$\mathsf{BCRSGen}(\mathsf{pp}) \to \mathsf{crs}$: on input pp parsed as an output of Setup, generates a common reference string in the perfectly binding mode; the algorithm draws $a, t, \mathsf{a}, \mathsf{t} \overset{\$}{\leftarrow} \mathbb{Z}_p$, and sets: $\boldsymbol{U}_1 \leftarrow (G, aG), \boldsymbol{U}_2 \leftarrow (tG, taG), \boldsymbol{U}_1 \leftarrow (\mathfrak{G}, \mathsf{a}\mathfrak{G}), \boldsymbol{U}_2 \leftarrow (\mathsf{t}\mathfrak{G}, \mathsf{ta}\mathfrak{G})$, finally returning: $\mathsf{crs} \leftarrow (\boldsymbol{U}_1, \boldsymbol{U}_2, \boldsymbol{U}_1, \boldsymbol{U}_2)$.

$\mathsf{HCRSGen}(\mathsf{pp}) \to \mathsf{crs}$: on input pp parsed as an output of Setup, generates (except with negligible probability in λ) a common reference string in the perfectly witness-indistinguishable (hiding) mode, by setting and returning: $\mathsf{crs} \leftarrow (\boldsymbol{U}_1, \boldsymbol{U}_2, \boldsymbol{U}_1, \boldsymbol{U}_2) \overset{\$}{\leftarrow} \mathbb{G}^2 \times \hat{\mathbb{G}}^2$.

$\mathsf{Com\&Pr}(\mathsf{pp}, \mathsf{crs}, w, \mathcal{E}) \to \pi$: for the set of equations $\mathcal{E}$ (each one of them defined by equation-specific vectors $\boldsymbol{A}, \boldsymbol{A}$, matrices $\underline{\Gamma}$ and resulting elements T_T as defined afterwards), and a witness w listing: $\boldsymbol{X} \in \mathbb{G}^n, \boldsymbol{X} \in \hat{\mathbb{G}}^k$, that will verify all the equations at once, this algorithm will enable the proof of the set of pairing-product equations defined in $\mathcal{E}$, of the form $\langle \boldsymbol{A}; \boldsymbol{X} \rangle \langle \boldsymbol{X}; \boldsymbol{A} \rangle \boldsymbol{X}^T \underline{\Gamma} \boldsymbol{X} = T_T$, for $\boldsymbol{A} \in \mathbb{G}^k, \boldsymbol{A} \in \hat{\mathbb{G}}^n, \underline{\Gamma} \in \mathbb{Z}_p^{n \times k}, T_T \in \mathbb{G}_T$, in the variables $\boldsymbol{X} \in \hat{\mathbb{G}}^k, \boldsymbol{X} \in \mathbb{G}^n$, where the multiplication operation between an element of $\mathbb{G}$ and an element $\hat{\mathbb{G}}$ is the pairing operation e, and $\mathbb{G}_T$ is a multiplicative group: i. e., with $\boldsymbol{A} = (A_1, \ldots, A_k) \in \mathbb{G}^k, \boldsymbol{X} = (\mathfrak{X}_1, \ldots, \mathfrak{X}_k) \in \hat{\mathbb{G}}^k$, $\langle \boldsymbol{A}; \boldsymbol{X} \rangle = \prod_{i=1}^k e(A_i, X_i) \in \mathbb{G}_T$.
The algorithm outputs the proof $\pi \leftarrow (\boldsymbol{Com}_X \| \boldsymbol{Com}_X, \boldsymbol{\Pi}, \mathcal{E})$, denoting $\boldsymbol{Com}_v$ the commitment to a vector $\boldsymbol{v}$.

$\mathsf{Rand}(\mathsf{pp}, \mathsf{crs}, \pi) \to \widetilde{\pi}$: parsing π as an output of $\mathsf{Com\&Pr}$, this algorithm produces a randomized proof $\widetilde{\pi}$, also in the range of $\mathsf{Com\&Pr}(\mathsf{p}, \mathsf{crs}, \cdot, \cdot)$, and outputs it.

$\mathsf{Vf}(\mathsf{pp}, \mathsf{crs}, \pi) \to b$: parsing the proof π as $(\boldsymbol{Com}_X \| \boldsymbol{Com}_X, \boldsymbol{\Pi}, \mathcal{E})$, for each pairing-product equation in $\mathcal{E}$ of index ℓ, the algorithm checks the corresponding zero-knowledge proof of knowledge, outputting $b \leftarrow 0$ if any of these fails, and $b \leftarrow 1$ otherwise.

3   Generalizing TREnc

In our construction, the use of lattice-based ciphertexts implies that their randomized version will not have the same noise distribution as their fresh counterparts. In previous TREnc constructions, they did, and the TCCA security thus implied privacy of fresh ciphertexts with a weak CCA notion (of CCA security for ciphertexts with an adversarially-chosen tag). This is not the case for the current constructions, and as a consequence, we had to generalize previous TREnc security notions.

Moreover, we underline that the TREnc randomization notion does not need to redistribute ciphertexts' randomness in the whole randomness space, and not even in an exponentially bigger space as the one of fresh ciphertexts, as in usual noise flooding approaches that seek to mask all the noise information to a lattice ciphertext decryptor. In a TREnc scheme, randomization may be done with a simple addition of a fresh encryption of zero, under (R)LWE.

Additionally, in Traceability and Verifiability security notions, the adversary is provided with the secret-key, as these security notions should hold even against authorities in a voting system, in order to ensure the correctness of the results with respect to participants' intentions.

Definition 7 (Traceable Receipt-Free Encryption, extended from [DP-P22]). *A* Traceable Receipt-Free Encryption *scheme (TREnc) is a public key encryption scheme* $(\mathsf{Gen}, \mathsf{Enc}, \mathsf{Dec})$ *augmented with a triple of algorithms* $(\mathsf{Trace}, \mathsf{Rand}, \mathsf{Ver})$, *described hereafter, as well as a definition of a message space* $\mathcal{M}$:

$\mathsf{Gen}(1^{\lambda}) \rightarrow (\mathsf{pk}, \mathsf{sk})$: *generates and outputs a public-secret key pair* $(\mathsf{pk}, \mathsf{sk})$;

$\mathsf{Enc}(\mathsf{pk}, m) \rightarrow c$: *is split into two probabilistic sub-algorithms. First, it runs the link key generation algorithm* $\mathsf{LGen}(\mathsf{pk})$ *which outputs an ephemeral secret link key* lk. *Second, it runs the linked encryption algorithm* $\mathsf{LEnc}(\mathsf{pk}, \mathsf{lk}, m)$ *which outputs a ciphertext* c *encrypting* m, *and including a trace as defined next;*

$\mathsf{Trace}(\mathsf{pk}, c) \rightarrow t$: *returns a trace* t *on input a ciphertext* c;

$\mathsf{Rand}(\mathsf{pk}, c) \rightarrow c'$: *partially randomizes the ciphertext* c *and returns a ciphertext* c';

$\mathsf{Ver}(\mathsf{pk}, c, \ell) \rightarrow b$: *outputs* 1 *if the ciphertext* c *is deemed valid according to the context label* $\ell \in \{\mathsf{fresh}, \mathsf{rand}\}$, *and* 0 *otherwise.*

By definition, the ciphertext space $\mathcal{C}_{\mathsf{fresh}}$ *is the image of* $\mathcal{M}$ *by* $\mathsf{Enc}(\mathsf{pk}, \cdot)$, *and similarly, the ciphertext space* $\mathcal{C}_{\mathsf{rand}}$ *is the image of* $\mathcal{C}_{\mathsf{fresh}}$ *by* $\mathsf{Rand}(\mathsf{pk}, \cdot)$. *The public key* pk *can be made implicit whenever it is identifiable from the context.*

Definition 8 (Correctness.). *A TREnc must satisfy several correctness conditions: (*Link traceability*) For every* pk *in the range of* Gen, *every* lk *in the range of* $\mathsf{LGen}(\mathsf{pk})$, *the encryptions of every pair of messages* $(m_0, m_1) \in \mathcal{M}^2$ *trace to each other, that is, it always holds that* $\mathsf{Trace}(\mathsf{pk}, \mathsf{LEnc}(\mathsf{pk}, \mathsf{lk}, m_0)) = \mathsf{Trace}(\mathsf{pk}, \mathsf{LEnc}(\mathsf{pk}, \mathsf{lk}, m_1))$; *(*Publicly Traceable Randomization*) For every* pk *in the range of* Gen, *every message* $m \in \mathcal{M}$ *and every* c *in the range of* $\mathsf{Enc}(\mathsf{pk}, m)$, *we have that* $\mathsf{Dec}(\mathsf{sk}, c) = \mathsf{Dec}(\mathsf{sk}, \mathsf{Rand}(\mathsf{pk}, c))$ *and* $\mathsf{Trace}(\mathsf{pk}, c) = \mathsf{Trace}(\mathsf{pk}, \mathsf{Rand}$

$(\mathsf{pk}, c))$; (Honest verifiability) *For every* pk *in the range of* Gen, *every message* $m \in \mathcal{M}$, *and every ciphertext* $c \in \mathcal{C}_{\mathsf{fresh}}$, *it holds that* $\mathsf{Ver}(\mathsf{pk}, \mathsf{Enc}(\mathsf{pk}, m), \mathsf{fresh}) = 1$ *and* $\mathsf{Ver}(\mathsf{pk}, \mathsf{Rand}(\mathsf{pk}, c), \mathsf{rand}) = 1$.

In the original definition $\mathcal{C}_{\mathsf{fresh}}$ and $\mathcal{C}_{\mathsf{rand}}$ are equal, and Ver is independent of the context $\ell \in \{\mathsf{fresh}, \mathsf{rand}\}$. The novel general case given here also allows these spaces to be disjoint and even to easily recognize that a valid ciphertext for one context does not belong to ciphertext space of the other context, as in our new construction. The main generalization of the primitive comes to define Rand for a *one-time* execution while, in the original syntax, Rand can still be applied serially on its outputs. In [DPP22], a TREnc further comes with a strong randomization property which, while elegant, is not needed to keep the essence of the notions allowing to generically build a receipt-free voting system.

We now turn to the security model satisfied by a *general* TREnc. We start with verifiability, that we extend to the different contexts $\ell \in \{\mathsf{fresh}, \mathsf{rand}\}$. Intuitively, it should be hard given sk to produce a valid ciphertext c for one context such that c is not in the corresponding ciphertext space $\mathcal{C}_\ell$. That is, there must exist some message m, some link key lk, and some coins that can explain c as a run of the appropriate algorithms even if they are not easily computable. However, to prove the verifiability criteria, one often needs an efficient way to check if the adversary is successful or not. Unlike [DPP22], we thus explicitly require the existence of this algorithm in the definition.

Definition 9 (Verifiability, modified from [DPP22]). *A TREnc is* verifiable *if it exists efficient* SimGen *and* Check *such that:*

1. $\{(\mathsf{pk}, \mathsf{sk}) \leftarrow \mathsf{Gen}(1^\lambda)\} \approx_c \{(\mathsf{pk}, \mathsf{sk}) \mid (\mathsf{pk}, \mathsf{sk}, \mathsf{tk}) \leftarrow \mathsf{SimGen}(1^\lambda)\}$;
2. *For any* $(\mathsf{pk}, \mathsf{sk}, \mathsf{tk}) \leftarrow \mathsf{SimGen}(1^\lambda)$ *and any context* $\ell \in \{\mathsf{fresh}, \mathsf{rand}\}$, *we have* $\mathsf{Check}(\mathsf{tk}, \cdot, \ell) \in \{0, 1\}$, $\Pr[\mathsf{Check}(\mathsf{tk}, c, \ell)) = 1 \wedge \mathsf{Dec}(\mathsf{sk}, c) \notin \mathcal{M}] = \mathsf{negl}(\lambda)$, *and* $\Pr[\mathsf{Check}(\mathsf{tk}, c, \mathsf{fresh})) = 1 \wedge \mathsf{Dec}(\mathsf{sk}, \mathsf{rand}(\mathsf{pk}, c)) \notin \mathcal{M}] = \mathsf{negl}(\lambda)$;
3. *For every PPT adversary* $\mathcal{A}$, $\Pr[\mathsf{Ver}(\mathsf{pk}, c, \ell) = 1 \wedge \mathsf{Check}(\mathsf{tk}, c, \ell) = 0 \mid (\mathsf{pk}, \mathsf{sk}, \mathsf{tk}) \leftarrow \mathsf{SimGen}(1^\lambda), (c, \ell) \leftarrow \mathcal{A}(\mathsf{pk}, \mathsf{sk})] = \mathsf{negl}(\lambda)$.

The traceability notion guarantees to the orignal encryptor of a message that any ciphertext with the same trace contains the same message, even against the decryptor (as long as the encryptor uses the link key generated by LGen a single time). This notion is particularly useful in a voting system where voters keep track of their randomized ballots while being sure that the authorities cannot alter their votes. We slightly generalized the notion due to [DPP22] by granting the adversary with an oracle that produces fresh ciphertexts on input a plaintext. This allows for a more general learning phase, and the adversary is successful if it can produce a ciphertext that traces to one of the returned oracle's ciphertexts while decrypting to another message than the original. The notion from previous works reduced to a single query.

Definition 10 (Traceability, extended from [DPP22]). *A TREnc is* trace-able *if for every PPT adversary* $\mathcal{A}$, *the experiment* $\mathsf{Exp}_{\mathcal{A}}^{\mathsf{Trace}}(\lambda)$ *defined in Fig. 3 returns 1 with a negligible probability in* λ. *The traceability advantage is defined as* $\mathsf{Adv}_{\mathcal{A}}^{\mathsf{Trace}}(\lambda) = \Pr[\mathsf{Exp}_{\mathcal{A}}^{\mathsf{Trace}}(\lambda) = 1]$.

We stress that if an adversary is able to produce a ciphertext c^* such that $\mathsf{Ver}(\mathsf{pk}, c^*, \mathsf{fresh}) = 1$ in place of $\mathsf{Ver}(\mathsf{pk}, c^*, \mathsf{rand}) = 1$ in the traceablity experiment, it can simply output $c^* \leftarrow \mathsf{Rand}(\mathsf{pk}, c^*)$ to win the game.

The privacy notion of the original TREnc is the indistinguishability of the *randomization* of adversarially-chosen valid *ciphertexts* that trace to each other with access to a decryption

$\mathsf{Exp}_{\mathcal{A}}^{\mathsf{Trace}}(\lambda)$:

$(\mathsf{pk}, \mathsf{sk}) \xleftarrow{\$} \mathsf{Gen}(1^\lambda)$
$\mathcal{L} \leftarrow \varnothing$
$c^* \xleftarrow{\$} \mathcal{A}^{\mathcal{O}_{\mathsf{Enc}}}(\mathsf{sk})$
if $\exists (m, c) \in \mathcal{L} : \mathsf{Trace}(\mathsf{pk}, c) = \mathsf{Trace}(\mathsf{pk}, c^*)$
    and $\mathsf{Ver}(\mathsf{pk}, c^*, \mathsf{rand}) = 1$
    and $\mathsf{Dec}(\mathsf{sk}, c^*) \neq m$
    then return 1
else return 0.

Fig. 2. The traceability experiment. On input a message m_i, the oracle $\mathcal{O}_{\mathsf{Enc}}$ returns $c_i \leftarrow \mathsf{Enc}(\mathsf{pk}, m_i)$ and updates $\mathcal{L} \leftarrow \mathcal{L} \cup \{(m_i, c_i)\}$.

oracle. This is the TCCA notion which deviates from most of the existing game-based privacy notions whose indistinguishability is defined by *encrypting* adversarially chosen *messages*. The TCCA notion implies that any subliminal information maliciously added to an adversarially computed ciphertext does not help the adversary to distinguish which ciphertext has been processed by Rand. By encrypting a vote with a TCCA TREnc, the voter is unable to explain the content of its randomized version, hence the receipt-freeness.

Definition 11 (TCCA, adapted from [DPP22]). *A TREnc is TCCA secure if for every PPT adversary* $\mathcal{A} = (\mathcal{A}_1, \mathcal{A}_2)$, *the experiment* $\mathsf{Exp}_{\mathcal{A}}^{TCCA}(\lambda)$ *defined in Fig. 3 returns 1 with a probability negligibly close to* $\frac{1}{2}$ *in* λ, *meaning that* $\mathcal{A}$*'s advantage in distinguishing* b *is negligible in* λ.

In the TCCA and wCCA security games, the adversary is allowed to use a challenge tag which is equal to a tag of a ciphertext that was previously queried to the decryption oracle (though such a tag may not be queried to the oracle after receiving the challenge); this detail is important when transforming the TREnc construction into a voting scheme, in order to attain receipt-freeness, the notion preventing participants from selling their votes. Indeed, in the security games, the TCCA adversary will need to simulate an election result taking challenge ciphertexts into account without the decryption key, and will achieve this by querying the decryption of ciphertexts with the same tag beforehand.

This notion says nothing about the privacy of the encryption of chosen messages. Up to now, Enc could be the identity function or any function leaking its input. However, in a voting system, for instance, the ballot privacy should hold against the randomizing server that is only trusted for the receipt-freeness. In [DPP22], it has been shown that a TREnc that is also strongly randomizable when $\mathcal{C}_{\mathsf{fresh}} = \mathcal{C}_{\mathsf{rand}}$ automatically provides the privacy of the encryption. That is because the randomization fully redistribute the ciphertext among those that have the same encryted message and the same trace. Therefore, after encrypting a message we can always indistinguishably randomize it and rely on

$\mathsf{Exp}_{\mathcal{A}}^{\mathrm{TCCA}}(\lambda)$:

$(\mathsf{pk}, \mathsf{sk}) \xleftarrow{\$} \mathsf{Gen}(1^\lambda)$
$(c_0, c_1, \mathsf{st}) \xleftarrow{\$} \mathcal{A}_1^{\mathsf{Dec}(\cdot)}(\mathsf{pk})$
$b \xleftarrow{\$} \{0; 1\}$
if $\mathsf{Trace}(\mathsf{pk}, c_0) \neq \mathsf{Trace}(\mathsf{pk}, c_1)$
    or $\mathsf{Ver}(\mathsf{pk}, c_0, \mathsf{fresh}) \neq 1$
    or $\mathsf{Ver}(\mathsf{pk}, c_1, \mathsf{fresh}) \neq 1$
    then return 0
$c^* \xleftarrow{\$} \mathsf{Rand}(\mathsf{pk}, c_b)$
$b' \xleftarrow{\$} \mathcal{A}_2^{\mathsf{Dec}^*(\cdot)}(c^*, \mathsf{st})$
if $b' = b$ return 1, **else** return 0

$\mathsf{Exp}_{\mathcal{A}}^{\mathrm{wCCA}}(\lambda)$:

$(\mathsf{pk}, \mathsf{sk}) \xleftarrow{\$} \mathsf{Gen}(1^\lambda)$
$(m_0, m_1, \mathsf{lk}, \mathsf{st}) \xleftarrow{\$} \mathcal{A}_1^{\mathsf{Dec}(\cdot)}(\mathsf{pk})$
$b \xleftarrow{\$} \{0; 1\}$
if $\mathsf{lk} \notin \mathsf{LGen}(1^\lambda)$
    or $m_0 \notin \mathcal{M}$ or $m_1 \notin \mathcal{M}$
    then return 0
$c^* \xleftarrow{\$} \mathsf{LEnc}(\mathsf{pk}, \mathsf{lk}, m_b)$
$b' \xleftarrow{\$} \mathcal{A}_2^{\mathsf{Dec}^*(\cdot)}(c^*, \mathsf{st})$
if $b' = b$ return 1, **else** return 0

Fig. 3. TCCA and wCCA security experiments; $\mathcal{A}_2$ has access to a decryption oracle $\mathsf{Dec}^*(\cdot)$ which returns a decryption of any input ciphertext c such that $\mathsf{Trace}(\mathsf{pk}, c) \neq \mathsf{Trace}(\mathsf{pk}, c^*)$, and that there exists $\ell \in \{\mathsf{fresh}, \mathsf{rand}\}$ such that $\mathsf{Ver}(\mathsf{pk}, c, \ell) = 1$, and returns $\perp$ for any input ciphertext not meeting this condition, as well as to a $\mathsf{Dec}(\cdot)$ oracle doing exactly the same, but without the condition on the queries' trace.

the TCCA security. Since in general a TREnc does not necessarily satisfy this property, it must come with an additional privacy notion for the fresh ciphertexts. Here, we adopt the adaptive-tag weak CCA notion of [MRY04] defined for tag-based encryption, and naturally adapt it to our syntax as adaptive-trace weak CCA security of TREnc.

Definition 12 (wCCA, adapted from [MRY04]). *A TREnc is adaptive-trace weakly CCA secure if for every PPT adversary* $\mathcal{A} = (\mathcal{A}_1, \mathcal{A}_2)$, *the experiment* $\mathsf{Exp}_{\mathcal{A}}^{\mathrm{wCCA}}(\lambda)$ *defined in Fig. 3 returns 1 with a probability negligibly close to* $\frac{1}{2}$ *in* λ, *meaning that* $\mathcal{A}$*'s advantage in distinguishing b is negligible in* λ.

While a selective-trace notion of wCCA might be enough in some applications, the TCCA notion already requires an adaptive-trace flavor as the trace is chosen by the adversary when it sends c_0 and c_1 at the beginning of the challenge phase.

4   A Lattice-Based TREnc Scheme

This construction makes a black-box use of the Groth-Sahai scheme, denoted GS, the LHSP signature scheme, as well as the PQPKE encryption scheme described in 2.2 and instantiated from the RLWE FV scheme in the full version [dPP24a].

High-Level Description. A TREnc fresh ciphertext will consist of a lattice-based ciphertext, along with validity proofs that the noise it contains is below the required threshold, and a set of linearly-only homomorphic signatures, which are required for tracing purposes. Indeed, the randomizing algorithm taking a fresh ciphertext as input will add to the original lattice-based ciphertext a new ciphertext of zero, with a noise level that should be low enough for this operation to maintain the decryption value. This is where linearly-only homomorphic signatures play a major role: they ensure that the randomized ciphertext is equal to the fresh ciphertext plus a linear combination of public elements resulting in a ciphertext of zero. The randomizer then proves that this linear combination was done with bits, to ensure an appropriate noise level is maintained, appending these new arguments to the validity proof contained in the fresh ciphertext. Then, all these simulation-sound proofs, built using LHSP signatures and the Groth-Sahai construction, are themselves rerandomized.

Overview of the Simulation-Sound Proofs. Our proofs that linear combinations of public elements of the lattice-based encryption scheme were performed with bits, to ensure that the noise level are controlled, obtain a simulation-sound property by making use of a witness-indistinguishable OR-proof. The statement shown is that either linear combinations were made using bits, or the prover is able to solve an SXDH instance specific to the trace of the user's fresh ciphertext and the common reference string generated from public coins. In the real protocol, no user is able to generate a proof from this second statement branch, but in security proofs, it will allow simulating them without having a witness for the first branch. The way the OR-proofs are constructed is by oberving that LHSP signatures are trivial to generate for null vectors. The second branch concerning the SXDH instance consists in an LHSP signature verification. One then commits a bit $\mathfrak{b}$ that will either make it trivial, or the statement about the linear combination trivial.

Use of Groth-Sahai Zero-Knowledge Proofs. All the equations for the linear combination and signature verification equations are verified using the GS scheme. This choice allows them to be publicly rerandomizable, while allowing quadratic statements to be shown.

4.1   Initialization Algorithm **Gen**

Input: the security parameter $\lambda \in \mathbb{N}$.

Computations: picks, with public coin randomness, a pairing setting $\mathsf{pp} = (p, \mathbb{G}, \hat{\mathbb{G}}, \mathbb{G}_T, e, G, \mathfrak{G}) \xleftarrow{\$} \mathsf{GS.Setup}(1^\lambda)$, for which the SXDH assumption is assumed to hold with at least λ bits of security. The algorithm then draws $H \xleftarrow{\$} \mathbb{G}$, $\mathfrak{H} \xleftarrow{\$} \hat{\mathbb{G}}$, $\varphi = (U_1, U_2, U_1, U_2) \xleftarrow{\$} \mathsf{GS.HCRSGen}(\mathsf{pp})$, $\mathcal{H}$ a collision-free function mapping elements to $\mathbb{Z}_p$, $\mathsf{spk} \leftarrow (\mathfrak{G}_{\mathsf{spk},1}, \mathfrak{G}_{\mathsf{spk},2}) \xleftarrow{\$} \hat{\mathbb{G}}^2$, and sets: $\mathsf{crs} \leftarrow (\mathsf{pp}, \varphi, H, \mathfrak{H}, \mathsf{spk}, \mathcal{H})$. Then, it generates $(\mathsf{pk}, \mathsf{sk}) \xleftarrow{\$} \mathsf{PQPKE.KeyGen}(1^\lambda, q)$, where $\mathsf{pk} = (\underline{P}, \underline{\widetilde{P}})$, with $\underline{P} = (\boldsymbol{p}_1, \ldots, \boldsymbol{p}_N) \in \mathbb{Z}_p^{2n \times N}$ and $\underline{\widetilde{P}} = (\widetilde{\boldsymbol{p}}_1, \ldots, \widetilde{\boldsymbol{p}}_{\widetilde{N}}) \in \mathbb{Z}_p^{2n \times \widetilde{N}}$, where the dimensions n, N and $\widetilde{N}$ are defined in the key generation. The message space $\mathcal{M}$ is set to $\{0; 1\}^n$, but may easily be restrained (with according proofs on the encrypted bits) if the application requires it.

Output: the algorithm sets $\mathsf{PK} \leftarrow (\mathsf{pk}, \mathsf{crs})$ and returns: $(\mathsf{PK}, \mathsf{sk})$.

4.2   Encryption Algorithm Enc

Remark 13. Note that in the usual TREnc notation, this algorithm may be divided in LGen and LEnc phases: LGen would only correspond to the one-time signature key generation in the tracing step: $(\mathsf{osk}, \mathsf{opk}) \xleftarrow{\$} \mathsf{LHSP.KeyGen}$ $((\mathsf{pp}, \mathfrak{H}), 2n + 1 + \widetilde{N})$, outputting $(\mathsf{osk}, \mathsf{opk})$ on input PK. LEnc corresponds to all the rest of the algorithm described hereafter, outputting C on input PK, m and osk.

Input: PK, parsed as an output of Gen, and $m = (m_1, \ldots, m_n) \in \{0; 1\}^n$.

Post-quantum Ciphertext Generation. The algorithm first sets $(c, w) \xleftarrow{\$}$ $\mathsf{PQPKE.Enc_{pk}}(m)$, where $c \in \mathbb{Z}_p^{2n} = \underline{P}w$ and $w = (w_i)_i \in \{0; 1\}^N$.

Tracing. The algorithm prepares the tracing of randomizations of the fresh ciphertext, that will be computed by adding a subset of the vectors $\widetilde{p}_1, \ldots, \widetilde{p}_{\widetilde{N}}$ in $\underline{\widetilde{P}}$. The algorithm proceeds with the following steps:

1. it generates the one-time signature key pair: $(\mathsf{osk}, \mathsf{opk}) \xleftarrow{\$} \mathsf{LHSP.KeyGen}$ $((\mathsf{pp}, \mathfrak{H}), 2n + 1 + \widetilde{N})$;
2. denoting:

$$
\underline{T} \leftarrow \begin{pmatrix}
c^T & c'^T & 1 & 0 & \cdots & & 0 \\
& \widetilde{p}_1^T & 0 & 1 & \ddots & & \vdots \\
& \vdots & \vdots & & \ddots & \ddots & \ddots & \vdots \\
& \vdots & \vdots & & & \ddots & \ddots & 0 \\
& \widetilde{p}_{\widetilde{N}}^T & 0 & \cdots & & 0 & 1
\end{pmatrix} \cdot G
$$

for each i in $[\![1; 1 + \widetilde{N}]\!]$, the algorithm signs the i-th row T_i of $\underline{T}$, with:

$$
\sigma_i \leftarrow \mathsf{LHSP.Sign}(\mathsf{osk}, T_i);
$$

Validity Simulation-Sound Proof

1. the algorithm sets: $\mathfrak{b} \leftarrow 1$ (meaning that the proof will not be simulated);
2. then, in the Groth-Sahai framework, and setting the tag $\tau \leftarrow \mathcal{H}(\mathsf{opk}, \mathsf{PK})$, it generates a proof of knowledge of a solution w – colored in orange for witnesses in $\mathbb{G}$, and in cyan for witnesses in $\hat{\mathbb{G}}$, and denoting O_1 and O_2 the element O provided in two distinct commitments, to the following system of equations, denoting $p_i = (p_{i,1}, \ldots, p_{i,2n})$, $\widetilde{p}_i = (\widetilde{p}_{i,1}, \ldots, \widetilde{p}_{i,2n})$, encoded into $\mathcal{E}_{\mathsf{Valid}}$:

$$\begin{cases} \forall j \in 1; n \; : \prod_{i=1}^{N} e(w_i G, \mathfrak{b\mathfrak{G}})^{p_{i,j}} = e(c_j G, \mathfrak{b\mathfrak{G}}) & \left(\begin{smallmatrix}\text{linear}\\\text{combination}\end{smallmatrix}\right) & (1a)\\ \qquad \prod_{i=1}^{N} e(w_i G, \mathfrak{b\mathfrak{G}})^{p_{i,n+j}} = e(c_j' G, \mathfrak{b\mathfrak{G}}) & & \\[4pt] \forall i \in 1; N \; : e(w_i G, w_i \mathfrak{G}) = e(G, w_i \mathfrak{G}) & \left(\text{bits}\right) & (1b)\\ \qquad\quad e(w_i G, \mathfrak{G}) = e(G, w_i \mathfrak{G}) & & \\[4pt] e(O_1, \mathfrak{G})e(O_2, \mathfrak{H}) = e((1-\mathfrak{b})G, \mathfrak{G}_{\mathsf{spk},1})e((1-\mathfrak{b})\tau G, \mathfrak{G}_{\mathsf{spk},2}) & & \\ e(G, \mathfrak{b\mathfrak{G}})e((1-\mathfrak{b})G, \mathfrak{G}) = e(G, \mathfrak{G}) & \left(\begin{smallmatrix}\text{simulation}\\\text{soundness}\end{smallmatrix}\right) & (1c)\\ e(\tau G, \mathfrak{b\mathfrak{G}})e((1-\mathfrak{b})\tau G, \mathfrak{G}) = e(\tau G, \mathfrak{G}) & & \end{cases}$$

With:

$$\Pi_{\mathsf{Valid}} = (\mathsf{Com}, \pi, \mathcal{E}_{\mathsf{Valid}}) \xleftarrow{\$} \mathsf{GS.Com\&Pr}(\mathsf{pp}, \varphi, w, \mathcal{E}_{\mathsf{Valid}}),$$

where, denoting $[\cdot]_1$ commitments to elements of $\mathbb{G}$ and $[\cdot]_2$ to elements of $\hat{\mathbb{G}}$:

$$\mathsf{Com} \leftarrow ([\mathfrak{b\mathfrak{G}}]_2, ([w_i G]_1)_i, ([w_i G]_2)_i, [O_1]_1, [O_2]_1, [(1-\mathfrak{b})G]_1, [(1-\mathfrak{b})\tau G]_1)$$
$$\pi \leftarrow ((\pi_{1a,j})_j, (\pi_{1b,i})_i, \pi_{1c})$$

Output: the algorithm sets the whole TREnc ciphertext to: $C \leftarrow (c, \mathsf{opk}, (\sigma_i)_i, \Pi_{\mathsf{Valid}})$, and returns: (osk, C).

4.3 Tracing Algorithm **Trace**

On input a ciphertext C, parsed as an output of Enc, this algorithm returns the tracing key opk generated in the fresh ciphertext.

4.4 Randomization Algorithm **Rand**

Input: PK parsed as an output of Gen, and C parsed as an output of Enc.

Randomized Ciphertext Generation. The algorithm sets $(\widetilde{c}, \widetilde{w}) \xleftarrow{\$} \mathsf{PQPKE}$
$.\mathsf{Rand}_{\mathsf{pk}}(c)$, where $\widetilde{c} = c + \underline{\widetilde{P}}\widetilde{w} \in \mathbb{Z}_p^{2n}$ and $\widetilde{w} = (\widetilde{w}_i)_i \in \{0;1\}^{\widetilde{N}}$.

Tracing Proof. In the randomization, the tracing with signatures is made simulation-sound, building a simulation-sound zero-knowledge proof of knowledge of a signature instead of outputting one.

1. The algorithm generates a signature on $\widetilde{T} = (\widetilde{t}_1, \ldots, \widetilde{t}_{2n+1+\widetilde{N}}) \leftarrow (\widetilde{c}^T, \widetilde{c}'^T, 1, \widetilde{w}^T) = (1, \widetilde{w}^T) \cdot \underline{T}$ as

$$\sigma = (s_1, s_2) \leftarrow \sigma_1 + \sum_{i=2}^{\widetilde{N}+1} \widetilde{w}_i \sigma_i;$$

2. it sets $\widetilde{\mathfrak{b}} \leftarrow 1$, indicating that the proof is not simulated;
3. it then defines the system of equations $\widetilde{\mathcal{E}_{\mathsf{Trace}}}$ with solutions $\widetilde{w}_{\mathsf{Tr}}$ written in orange and cyan:

$$\left\{ \begin{aligned} & e(\widetilde{c_1}G, \widecheck{\mathfrak{b}}\mathfrak{G}) = e(\widetilde{\mathfrak{b}}\widetilde{t_1}G, \mathfrak{G}) \\ & \qquad\qquad \vdots \\ & e(\widetilde{c_n}'G, \widecheck{\mathfrak{b}}\mathfrak{G}) = e(\widetilde{\mathfrak{b}}\widetilde{t}_{2n}G, \mathfrak{G}) \\ & e(G, \widecheck{\mathfrak{b}}\mathfrak{G}) = e(\widetilde{\mathfrak{b}}\widetilde{t}_{2n+1}G, \mathfrak{G}) \\ & \forall k \in \left[\!\left[1; \widetilde{N}\right]\!\right] : e(\widetilde{w}_k G, \widecheck{\mathfrak{b}}\mathfrak{G}) = e(\widetilde{\mathfrak{b}}\widetilde{t}_{2n+1+k}G, \mathfrak{G}) \end{aligned} \right. \tag{2a}$$

$$e(s_1 G, \mathfrak{G})e(s_2 G, \mathfrak{H}) = \textstyle\prod_{j=1}^{2n+1+\widetilde{N}} e(\widetilde{\mathfrak{b}}\widetilde{t}_j G, \mathfrak{G}_{\mathsf{opk},j}) \tag{2b}$$

$$\begin{aligned} & e(O_3, \mathfrak{G})e(O_4, \mathfrak{H}) = e((1-\widetilde{\mathfrak{b}})G, \mathfrak{G}_{\mathsf{spk},1})e((1-\widetilde{\mathfrak{b}})\tau G, \mathfrak{G}_{\mathsf{spk},2}) \\ & e(G, \widecheck{\mathfrak{b}}\mathfrak{G})e((1-\widetilde{\mathfrak{b}})G, \mathfrak{G}) = e(G, \mathfrak{G}) \\ & e(\tau G, \widecheck{\mathfrak{b}}\mathfrak{G})e((1-\widetilde{\mathfrak{b}})\tau G, \mathfrak{G}) = e(\tau G, \mathfrak{G}) \end{aligned} \tag{2c}$$

where O_3 and O_4 are both equal to O but will be set in separate commitments. The algorithm commits to this solution and generates a Groth-Sahai proof of its fulfilment with:

$$\widetilde{\Pi_{\mathsf{Trace}}} = (\widetilde{\mathsf{Com}_{\mathsf{Tr}}}, \widetilde{\pi_{\mathsf{Tr}}}, \widetilde{\mathcal{E}_{\mathsf{Trace}}}) \xleftarrow{\$} \mathsf{GS.Com\&Pr}(\mathsf{pp}, \varphi, \widetilde{w}_{\mathsf{Tr}}, \widetilde{\mathcal{E}_{\mathsf{Trace}}}),$$

where:

$$\widetilde{\mathsf{Com}_{\mathsf{Tr}}} \leftarrow ([\widecheck{\mathfrak{b}}\mathfrak{G}]_2, ([\widetilde{w}_i G]_1)_i, ([\widetilde{\mathfrak{b}}\widetilde{t}_k G]_1)_k, ([s_j G]_1)_j, ([O_j]_1)_j, [(1-\widetilde{\mathfrak{b}})G]_1, [(1-\widetilde{\mathfrak{b}})\tau G]_1)$$
$$\widetilde{\pi_{\mathsf{Tr}}} \leftarrow ((\pi_{2a,k})_k, \pi_{2b}, \pi_{2c}).$$

Validity Proofs. Using the proof Π_{Valid} kept in C, the algorithm processes the following steps:

1. it modifies $\mathcal{E}_{\mathsf{Valid}}$ into $\widetilde{\mathcal{E}_{\mathsf{Valid}}}$ encoding the following system of equations in variables $\mathfrak{X}, (\widetilde{Z}_k)_k, (\widetilde{\mathfrak{Z}}_k)_k, (Z_i)_i, (\mathfrak{Z}_i)_i, (X_1, X_2), (Y_1, Y_2)$:

$$\left\{ \begin{aligned} & \forall j \in [\![1; n]\!] : \\ & \quad \textstyle\prod_{i=1}^{N} e(Z_i, \mathfrak{X})^{p_{i,j}} \cdot \prod_{k=1}^{\widetilde{N}} e(\widetilde{Z}_k, \mathfrak{X})^{\widetilde{p}_{i,j}} = e(\widetilde{c}_j G, \mathfrak{X}) \\ & \quad \textstyle\prod_{i=1}^{N} e(Z_i, \mathfrak{X})^{p_{i,j+n}} \cdot \prod_{k=1}^{\widetilde{N}} e(\widetilde{Z}_k, \mathfrak{X})^{\widetilde{p}_{i,j+n}} = e(\widetilde{c}_j'G, \mathfrak{X}) \end{aligned} \right. \tag{3a}$$

$$\begin{aligned} & \forall i \in [\![1; N]\!] : e(Z_i, \mathfrak{Z}_i) = e(G, \mathfrak{Z}_i) \\ & \qquad\qquad\quad e(Z_i, \mathfrak{G}) = e(G, \mathfrak{Z}_i) \end{aligned} \tag{3b}$$

$$\begin{aligned} & \forall k \in \left[\!\left[1; \widetilde{N}\right]\!\right] : e(\widetilde{Z}_i, \widetilde{\mathfrak{Z}}_i) = e(G, \widetilde{\mathfrak{Z}}_i) \\ & \qquad\qquad\quad e(\widetilde{Z}_i, \mathfrak{G}) = e(G, \widetilde{\mathfrak{Z}}_i) \end{aligned} \tag{3c}$$

$$\begin{aligned} & e(X_1, \mathfrak{G})e(X_2, \mathfrak{H}) = e(Y_1, \mathfrak{G}_{\mathsf{spk},1})e(Y_2, \mathfrak{G}_{\mathsf{spk},2}) \\ & e(G, \mathfrak{X})e(Y_1, \mathfrak{G}) = e(G, \mathfrak{G}) \\ & e(\tau G, \mathfrak{X})e(Y_2, \mathfrak{G}) = e(\tau G, \mathfrak{G}) \end{aligned} \tag{3d}$$

where the variables with a tilda are those for which it will insert new witnesses that where not in Π_{Valid};

2. it then computes of proof of knowledge of a solution in the following manner:
   - a proof for validity equations 3a is obtained using $(\pi_{1a,j})_j$, $[\mathfrak{bG}]_2$ and $[w_k G]_1$ from Π_{Valid}, along with the new $\widetilde{w}$ vector, using the homomorphism of Groth-Sahai proofs; the algorithm commits to $\widetilde{w}G$ with null randomness, computing: $[\widetilde{w}_k G]_1 \leftarrow \widetilde{w}G \cdot (0,1)$. $\left(\begin{pmatrix} \mathfrak{O} & \mathfrak{O} \\ \mathfrak{O} & \mathfrak{O} \end{pmatrix}, \begin{pmatrix} O & O \\ O & O \end{pmatrix} \right)$ is then a trivial proof of knowledge of a solution to:

$$\begin{cases} \prod_{i=1}^{\widetilde{N}} e(\widetilde{Z}_i, \mathcal{X})^{\widetilde{p}_{i,j}} & = e((\widetilde{c}_j - c_j)G, \mathcal{X}) \\ \prod_{i=1}^{\widetilde{N}} e(\widetilde{Z}_i, \mathcal{X})^{\widetilde{p}_{i,j+n}} & = e((\widetilde{c}_j{}' - c_j')G, \mathcal{X}) \end{cases}$$

   with respect to $[\mathfrak{bG}]_2$ and $([\widetilde{w}_k G]_1)_k$, and thus $(\pi_{2a,j})_j \leftarrow (\pi_{1a,j})_j$ yields a proof of equations 3a with respect to $[\mathfrak{bG}]_2$, $([w_i G]_1)_i$ and $([\widetilde{w}_j G]_1)_j$;
   - a proof of the equations 3b showing that previous witnesses are bits is already provided by $(\pi_{1b,k})_k$, which is renamed as: $(\pi_{3b,k})_k$;
   - to build a proof of Eqs. 3c that witnesses generated in the randomization are bits, the algorithm uses $([\widetilde{w}_k G]_1)_k$, along with a new commitment $([\widetilde{w}_k \mathfrak{G}]_2)_k$ to $\widetilde{w} \cdot \mathfrak{G}$, to build corresponding proofs $(\pi_{3c,k})_k$ using $([\widetilde{w}_k G]_1)_k$ and $([\widetilde{w}_k \mathfrak{G}]_2)_k$'s known randomness;
   - finally, a proof of knowledge of a solution to simulation-soundness Eqs. 3d is already provided by π_{1c}, with respect to $[\mathfrak{bG}]_2$, $[(1-\mathfrak{b})G]_1$ and $[(1-\mathfrak{b})\tau G]_1$ provided in Π_{Valid}. It is renamed as: $\pi_{3d} \leftarrow \pi_{1c}$.

3. the algorithm then randomizes all the above proofs and commitments in the Groth-Sahai framework, afterwards denoted as:

$$\widetilde{\mathsf{Com}}_{\mathsf{VI}} \leftarrow (\widetilde{[\mathfrak{bG}]}_2, (\widetilde{[w_i G]}_1)_i, (\widetilde{[w_i G]}_2)_i, (\widetilde{[\widetilde{w}_i G]}_1)_i, (\widetilde{[\widetilde{w}_i G]}_2)_i, \widetilde{[O_1]}_1, \widetilde{[O_2]}_1,$$

$$\widetilde{[(1-\mathfrak{b})G]}_1, \widetilde{[(1-\mathfrak{b})\tau G]}_1)$$

$$\widetilde{\pi}_{\mathsf{VI}} \leftarrow ((\widetilde{\pi}_{3a,j})_j, (\widetilde{\pi}_{3b,i})_i, (\widetilde{\pi}_{3c,k})_k, \widetilde{\pi}_{3d})$$

as a proof of knowledge $\widetilde{\Pi}_{\mathsf{Valid}} \leftarrow (\widetilde{\mathsf{Com}}_{\mathsf{VI}}, \widetilde{\pi}_{\mathsf{VI}}, \widetilde{\mathcal{E}}_{\mathsf{Valid}})$ with new randomness.

Output: the algorithm sets the TREnc ciphertext to: $\widetilde{C} \leftarrow (\widetilde{c}, \mathsf{opk}, \widetilde{\Pi}_{\mathsf{Trace}}, \widetilde{\Pi}_{\mathsf{Valid}})$, and returns it.

4.5 Verification Algorithm Vf

Input: PK parsed as a such-named output of Gen, C as a corresponding output of Enc or Rand, and a label $\ell \in \{\mathsf{fresh}, \mathsf{rand}\}$ indicating whether it should be validated as an output of Enc or of Rand.

Computations and Output: First, the algorithm verifies that the systems of equations described in the proofs are valid with respect to c, opk (by verifying that $\tau \leftarrow \mathcal{H}(\mathsf{opk}, \mathsf{PK})$ was correctly derived), the public vector values $p, \widetilde{p}$ derived from pk, and public parameters pp; if not, it sets and returns $b \leftarrow 0$. Then, it checks whether each proof Π is such that: $\mathsf{GS.Vf}(\mathsf{pp}, \varphi, \Pi) = 1$, and if not, sets and returns $b \leftarrow 0$. If there are signatures in the ciphertext, it checks them using opk and corresponding public vectors of the matrix $\underline{T}$, outputting $b \leftarrow 0$ if one of these tests fails. Else, it outputs $b \leftarrow 1$.

4.6   Decryption Algorithm Dec

Taking as input sk and PK parsed as corresponding outputs of Gen, and C parsed as an output of Enc or Rand, this algorithm returns: $\perp$ if $\mathsf{Vf}(C, \mathsf{PK}, \mathsf{fresh}) = \mathsf{Vf}(C, \mathsf{PK}, \mathsf{rand}) = 0$; and else: $m \leftarrow \mathsf{PQPKE.Dec}_{\mathsf{sk}}(c)$.

5   Security of the Protocol

The $\mathsf{TREnc} = (\mathsf{Gen}, \mathsf{Enc}, \mathsf{Trace}, \mathsf{Rand}, \mathsf{Dec}, \mathsf{Vf})$ scheme described in Sect. 4 is showed to verify security properties of Traceable Receipt-free Encryption (TREnc) schemes.

Theorem 14 (Correctness of TREnc). TREnc *is correct under the correctness of* PQPKE, GS *proofs, and* LHSP *signatures.*

Proof. By inspection, see the full version [dPP24a].

For the Verifiability security notion, we define the following algorithms, whose existence will allow to prove the notion is achieved:

$\mathsf{SimGen}(1^\lambda) \to (\mathsf{PK}, \mathsf{sk}, \mathsf{tk})$: does as the Gen algorithm, except that it sets $\varphi \xleftarrow{\$} \mathsf{GS.BCRSGen}(\mathsf{pp})$, generating the Groth-Sahai common reference string in an extractable mode, in which it stores the scalars a and $\mathfrak{a}$ providing the factors between φ's first and second components in each of the pairing groups. It then sets $\mathsf{tk} \leftarrow (a, \mathfrak{a}, \mathsf{PK})$ and returns $(\mathsf{PK}, \mathsf{sk}, \mathsf{tk})$;

$\mathsf{Check}(\mathsf{tk}, C, \ell) \to b$: takes as input $\ell \in \{\mathsf{fresh}, \mathsf{rand}\}$, C parsed as an output of Enc if $\ell = \mathsf{fresh}$ and of Rand if $\ell = \mathsf{rand}$, and $\mathsf{tk} = (a, \mathfrak{a}, \mathsf{PK})$. It checks that $\mathsf{Vf}(\mathsf{PK}, C, \ell) = 1$. It uses tk to extract all the witnesses committed to in Π_{Valid}, as well as in Π_{Trace} if $\ell = \mathsf{rand}$. It then checks that they verify $\mathcal{E}_{\mathsf{Valid}}$ (and $\mathcal{E}_{\mathsf{Trace}}$ if $\ell = \mathsf{rand}$). If the witnesses pass the checks, it gets in particular a bit decomposition w (and $\widetilde{w}$ if $\ell = \mathsf{rand}$) for which it verifies that: $c = \underline{P}w$ if $\ell = \mathsf{fresh}$, or that $c = \underline{P}w + \underline{\widetilde{P}}\widetilde{w}$ if $\ell = \mathsf{rand}$. If all the above checks pass, it sets $b \leftarrow 1$, else, if any step fails, $b \leftarrow 0$, and returns b.

Remark 15. The above-defined Check ensures more than the correct decryption space required by the Verifiability definition. It also guarantees that elements C with a one $\mathsf{Check}(\mathsf{tk}, C, \mathsf{fresh})$ are in $\mathcal{C}'_{\mathsf{fresh}}$ and with a one $\mathsf{Check}(\mathsf{tk}, C, \mathsf{rand})$

output are in $\mathcal{C}'_{\mathsf{rand}}$, as defined hereafter (and such that $\mathcal{C}_{\mathsf{fresh}} \subset \mathcal{C}'_{\mathsf{fresh}}$ and $\mathcal{C}_{\mathsf{rand}} \subset \mathcal{C}'_{\mathsf{rand}}$):

$$\mathcal{C}'_{\mathsf{fresh}} = \left\{ C = (\boldsymbol{c}, \mathsf{opk}, (\sigma_i)_i, \Pi_{\mathsf{Valid}}) \,\middle|\, \exists \boldsymbol{w} \in \{0;1\}^N ; \boldsymbol{c} = \underline{P}\boldsymbol{w} \right\}$$

$$\mathcal{C}'_{\mathsf{rand}} = \Big\{ C = (\boldsymbol{c}, \mathsf{opk}, \Pi_{\mathsf{Trace}}, \Pi_{\mathsf{Valid}})$$

$$\middle|\, \exists \boldsymbol{w} \in \{0;1\}^N, \widetilde{\boldsymbol{w}} \in \{0;1\}^{\widetilde{N}} ; \boldsymbol{c} = \underline{P}\boldsymbol{w} + \underline{\widetilde{P}}\widetilde{\boldsymbol{w}} \Big\}.$$

We write out this additional property as it may be useful in voting applications, as the noise level of ciphertexts will determine how many homomorphic operations may be performed on them without bootstrapping.

Theorem 16 (Verifiability of TREnc). *TREnc is verifiable under the SXDH assumption. More precisely, for any PPT adversary $\mathcal{A}$ and security parameter $\lambda \in \mathbb{N}$, $\mathsf{Adv}_{\mathcal{A}}^{\mathsf{Ver},\mathsf{TREnc}}(\lambda) \leq 3 \cdot \mathsf{Adv}_{\mathcal{A}}^{\mathsf{SXDH}}(\lambda)$.*

Proof. There are three properties to show to fit Definition 9.

The First Verifiability Property. Requires computational insdistinguishability between key pairs output by Gen and by SimGen, given a security parameter $\lambda \in \mathbb{N}$: a challenger $\mathcal{C}$ sets $(\mathsf{PK}_0, \mathsf{sk}_0) \xleftarrow{\$} \mathsf{Gen}(1^\lambda)$, and $(\mathsf{PK}_1, \mathsf{sk}_1, (a, \mathfrak{a})) \xleftarrow{\$} \mathsf{SimGen}(1^\lambda)$; $\mathcal{C}$ then draws $b \xleftarrow{\$} \{0;1\}$ and returns $(\mathsf{PK}_b, \mathsf{sk}_b)$ to a PPT adverary $\mathcal{A}$, who answers with a guess b', and winning if it is equal to b. In this game, the difference between the distributions of $(\mathsf{PK}_0, \mathsf{sk}_0)$ and $(\mathsf{PK}_1, \mathsf{sk}_1)$ is two SXDH distinguishers, hence $\mathcal{A}$'s advantage is this game is bounded by $2 \cdot \mathsf{Adv}_{\mathcal{A}}^{\mathsf{SXDH}}(\lambda)$.

The Second Property. Requires positive outputs of the Check algorithm to correspond to decryptions in the correct space. As Check outputs one only if it as extracted $\boldsymbol{w} \in \{0;1\}^N$ (and $\widetilde{\boldsymbol{w}} \in \{0;1\}^{\widetilde{N}}$ if $\ell = \mathsf{rand}$) such that $\boldsymbol{c} = \underline{P}\boldsymbol{w} + \underline{\widetilde{P}}\widetilde{\boldsymbol{w}}$, this may only happen if C is in the corresponding ciphertext space. Moreover, the noise levels of the corresponding FV ciphertexts ensure a correct decryption, and a correct decryption after randomization if the ciphertext is verified with a fresh label.

The Third Verifiability Property. Requires positive outputs of Ver to correspond to positive outputs of Check. Let us demonstrate it with a sequence of games, for a PPT adversary $\mathcal{A}$.

Game $\mathbf{G}_0$: will be the original Ver_3 game. Let $(\mathsf{pk}, \mathsf{sk}, \mathsf{tk}) \xleftarrow{\$} \mathsf{SimGen}(1^\lambda)$. The challenger sends $(\mathsf{pk}, \mathsf{sk})$ to $\mathcal{A}$. $\mathcal{A}$ then returns C, and wins the game if $\mathsf{Ver}(\mathsf{pk}, C, \ell) = 1$ but $\mathsf{Check}(\mathsf{tk}, C, \ell) = 0$.

Game $\mathbf{G}_1$: is as the previous game, but now, instead of simply running Ver in the final phase, the challenger also uses tk to extract witnesses in Π_{Valid} (and Π_{Trace} if $\ell = \mathsf{rand}$), and verifies that they fulfill the corresponding system of equations. To determine whether the adversary has won the game, it now replaces the output of Ver by one which should additionally verify this last check for one to be output. As the Groth-Sahai CRS was generated in a perfectly binding mode, the adversary's advantage has not changed with respect to the previous game: $\mathsf{Adv}_{\mathcal{A}}^{\mathbf{G}_1}(\lambda) = \mathsf{Adv}_{\mathcal{A}}^{\mathsf{Ver}_3}(\lambda)$.

Game $\mathbf{G}_2$: is as the previous game, except that now the challenger also requires the extracted $\boldsymbol{w} \in \{0;1\}^N$ (and $\widetilde{\boldsymbol{w}} \in \{0;1\}^{\widetilde{N}}$ if $\ell = \mathsf{rand}$) to be such that $\boldsymbol{c} = \underline{P}\boldsymbol{w}$ if $\ell = \mathsf{fresh}$, or that $\boldsymbol{c} = \underline{P}\boldsymbol{w} + \widetilde{\underline{P}}\widetilde{\boldsymbol{w}}$ if $\ell = \mathsf{rand}$, in order to replace the output of Ver by one. Now, both verifications correspond exactly to the deterministic execution of $\mathsf{Check}(\widetilde{C}, \ell)$, so the adversary can never win. The adversary can only distinguish this game from the previous one if the extracted $\mathfrak{b}$ is equal to zero, and this means that the challenger has extracted $S_1, S_2 \in \mathbb{G}$ such that $e(S_1, \mathfrak{G})e(S_2, \mathfrak{H}) = e(G, \mathfrak{G}_{\mathsf{spk},1})e(\tau G, \mathfrak{G}_{\mathsf{spk},2})$, which is a valid answer to the SXDH challenge given by $\mathfrak{G}, \mathfrak{H}, G, \mathfrak{G}_{\mathsf{spk},1}, \tau G, \mathfrak{G}_{\mathsf{spk},2}$, generated from random group elements. Hence: $|\mathsf{Adv}_{\mathcal{A}}^{\mathbf{G}_2}(\lambda) - \mathsf{Adv}_{\mathcal{A}}^{\mathbf{G}_1}(\lambda)| \leq \mathsf{Adv}_{\mathcal{A}}^{\mathsf{SXDH}}(\lambda)$, and $\mathsf{Adv}_{\mathcal{A}}^{\mathbf{G}_2}(\lambda) = 0$.

From the above sequence: $\mathsf{Adv}_{\mathcal{A}}^{\mathsf{Ver}_3}(\lambda) \leq \mathsf{Adv}_{\mathcal{A}}^{\mathsf{SXDH}}(\lambda)$.

Theorem 17 (Traceability of TREnc). TREnc *is traceable under the SXDH assumption. More precisely, for any security parameter $\lambda \in \mathbb{N}$ and PPT adversary $\mathcal{A}$:* $\Pr\{\mathsf{Exp}_{\mathcal{A}}^{\mathsf{Trace}}(\lambda) = 1\} \leq 2^{-2n} + \frac{1}{p} + 4 \cdot \mathsf{Adv}_{\mathcal{A}}^{\mathsf{SXDH}}(\lambda)$.

Proof. See the full version [dPP24a].

Theorem 18 (TCCA Security of TREnc). TREnc *is TCCA-secure under the SXDH and RLWE assumptions and the security of the hash function against collisions. More precisely, for any PPT adversary $\mathcal{A}$ with Q queries to the decryption oracle and security parameter $\lambda \in \mathbb{N}$:* $\mathsf{Adv}_{\mathcal{A}}^{TCCA}(\lambda) \leq \mathsf{Adv}_{\mathcal{A}}^{\mathsf{coll},\mathcal{H}}(\lambda) + \frac{Q}{p} + 3 \cdot \mathsf{Adv}_{\mathcal{A}}^{\mathsf{SXDH}}(\lambda) + \mathsf{Adv}_{\mathcal{A}}^{\mathsf{RLWE}}(\lambda)$.

Proof. See the full version [dPP24a].

Theorem 19 (wCCA Security of TREnc). TREnc *is wCCA-secure under the SXDH and RLWE assumptions and the security of the hash function against collisions. More precisely, for any PPT adversary $\mathcal{A}$ with Q queries to the decryption oracle and security parameter $\lambda \in \mathbb{N}$:* $\mathsf{Adv}_{\mathcal{A}}^{wCCA}(\lambda) \leq \mathsf{Adv}_{\mathcal{A}}^{\mathsf{coll},\mathcal{H}}(\lambda) + \frac{Q}{p} + 3 \cdot \mathsf{Adv}_{\mathcal{A}}^{\mathsf{SXDH}}(\lambda) + \mathsf{Adv}_{\mathcal{A}}^{\mathsf{RLWE}}(\lambda)$.

Proof. Obtained straighforwardly following the TCCA proof steps (the only difference being that in the challenge phase, the adversary now sends cleartexts, and gets a fresh ciphertext as an answer), as ciphertexts before and after the randomization have the same FV structure.

Theorem 20 (Post-Quantum IND-CPA Security of TREnc). TREnc *is IND-CPA-secure under the RLWE assumption; for any PPT adversary $\mathcal{A}$,* $\mathsf{Adv}_{\mathcal{A}}^{\mathsf{CPA},\mathsf{TREnc}}(\lambda) \leq \mathsf{Adv}_{\mathcal{A}}^{\mathsf{RLWE}}(\lambda)$.

Proof. See the full version [dPP24a].

6   Applications

Efficiency. Public-keys consist of 5 elements of $\mathbb{G}$, 7 elements of $\hat{\mathbb{G}}$, and a public key of the post-quantum LWE-based scheme, given by $2n$ elements of $\mathbb{Z}_p$ in the case of the FV instantiation; according to the [APS15] estimator, with p on 255 bits, binary errors and secrets, $n \leftarrow 2^{14}$ will provide an LWE security on more than 140 bits (so a reasonable RLWE security); taking $\mathbb{G}$ elements on 381 bits and $\hat{\mathbb{G}}$ elements on 762 bits (parameters obtained with a BLS12-381 instantiation) will then lead to public keys on 523 kB.

Considering messages on 40 bits (which seems realistic in a voting context), a fresh ciphertext consists of $2\widetilde{N} + 8n + 12N + 18 = 28n\lfloor \log_2(B)\rfloor + 22n + 2418$ elements of $\mathbb{G}$, $8n + 8N + 14 = 16n\lfloor \log_2(B)\rfloor + 16n + 1614$ elements of $\hat{\mathbb{G}}$, and one LWE-based ciphertext, consisting of $2n$ elements of $\mathbb{Z}_p$ in the case of the FV instantiation; for a security on more than 128 bits, this will represent, with the selected parameters and $B = 1$ (as the big p and n allow using binary errors securely), around 47 MB.

A randomized ciphertext consists of $20n + 16\widetilde{N} + 10N + 44 = 52n\lfloor \log_2(B)\rfloor + 46n + 2044$ elements of $\mathbb{G}$, $16n + 10N + 14\widetilde{N} + 28 = 48n\lfloor \log_2(B)\rfloor + 44n + 2028$ elements of $\hat{\mathbb{G}}$, and one LWE-based ciphertext, consisting of $2n$ elements of $\mathbb{Z}_p$ in the case of the FV instantiation; for a security on more than 128 bits, this will represent, with the selected parameters, around 107 MB.

Receipt-Free and Ballot-Private EVoting. The design of the TREnc primitive in [DPP22] was motivated by capturing simple yet sufficient conditions of a verifiable public-key encryption that naturally yields a voting system with a non-interactive voting process that offers ballot privacy and receipt freeness. The main definitional novelty to generically build a receipt-free voting system lied both in the ability for the users to trace their encrypted vote when their ballot ciphertext appears on a bulletin board after being processed by a randomizing server while being sure that its content has not been altered even by the authorities (from the traceability of the TREnc), and in the privacy notion defined for the first time as an indistinguishability notion achieved by randomization (TCCA). Even if the randomizing server is deemed honest to provide the receipt-freeness by honestly randomizing valid ciphertext before publishing them on a bulletin board, the server is considered malicious when it comes to proving ballot privacy. Roughly speaking, this notion is satisfied if no efficient adversary is able to distinguish whether honest ballots are compatible with the result of the election [BCG+15]. Although the trust model differs for receipt freeness and ballot privacy, a voting system based on a TCCA-secure TREnc that also enjoys a strong randomization notion [DPP22] is naturally ballot private.

In our more general definition of TREnc, it is straightforward to see that the adaptive-trace weak CCA notion given in Definition 12 is sufficient to imply the ballot privacy of a voting system that encrypts votes with a TREnc. Moreover, our TCCA definition is still equivalent of the original definition as long as the chosen ciphertexts are valid for the fresh ciphertext space $\mathcal{C}_{\mathsf{fresh}}$. Since a verifiable TREnc allows identifying those ciphertexts and since the generic voting system of [DPP22] defines the voting algorithm essentially as the encryption of the encoded-vote message, we keep the receipt freeness.

6.1 Voting System Security Notions

The generic transformation of our TREnc construction into a voting scheme follows the same recipy as the one of the original paper [DPP22]; we recall the corresponding definitions and security notions here.

Definition 21 (Voting System (from [DPP22])). *A Voting System is a tuple of probabilistic polynomial-time algorithms (*SetupElection, Vote, ProcessBallot, TraceBallot, Valid, Append, Publish, VerifyVote, Tally, VerifyResult*) associated to a result function* $\rho_m : \mathcal{V}^m \cup \{\bot\} \to \mathcal{R}$ *where* $\mathcal{V}$ *is the set of valid votes and* $\mathcal{R}$ *is the result space such that:*

SetupElection$(1^\lambda) \to$ (pk, sk)*: on input a security parameter* λ*, generates the public and secret key pair* (pk, sk) *of the election.*

Vote(id, v) $\to$ (b, aux)*: when receiving a voter* id *and a vote* v*, outputs a ballot* b *and auxiliary data* aux*. It will also be possible to call* Vote(id, v, aux) *in order to obtain a ballot (without auxiliary data this time) for the vote* v *using* aux*. This auxiliary data will be useful to define security and enables the creation of ballots that share the same* aux*.*

ProcessBallot(b) $\to \widetilde{\text{b}}$*: on input a ballot* b*, outputs an updated ballot* $\widetilde{\text{b}}$*. In our case,* $\widetilde{\text{b}}$ *will be a rerandomization of* b*.*

TraceBallot(b) $\to \tau$*: on input a ballot* b*, outputs a tag* τ*. The tag is the information that a voter can use to trace her ballot, using the* VerifyVote *algorithm.*

Valid(BB, b) $\to b$*: on input a ballot box* BB *and ballot* b*, outputs 1 if and only if the ballot is valid, and else 0.*

Append(BB, b) $\to \widetilde{\text{BB}}$*: on input a ballot box* BB *and ballot* b*, appends* ProcessBallot(b) *to* BB *iff* Valid(BB, b) $= 1$*, and then returns the updated (or identical) ballot box* $\widetilde{\text{BB}}$*.*

Publish(BB) $\to$ PBB*: on input a ballot box* BB*, outputs the public view* PBB *of* BB*, which is the one that is used to verify the election. Depending on the context, it may for instance be used to remove some voter credentials.*

VerifyVote(PBB, τ) $\to b$*: on input a public ballot box* PBB *and tag* τ*, outputs a bit b equal to 1 iff the vote corresponding to the tag* τ *(which is specific to a voter) has been processed and recorded properly.*

Tally(BB, sk) $\to$ (r, Π)*: on input a ballot box* BB *and the election secret key* sk*, outputs the tally* r *and a proof* Π *that the tally is correct with respect to the result function* ρ_m*.*

VerifyResult(PBB, r, Π) $\to b$*: on input a public ballot box* PBB*, tally result* r *and tally proof* Π*, outputs a bit b equal to 1 if and only if* Π *is a valid proof that* r *is the election result, computed with respect to* ρ_m*, corresponding to the ballots on* PBB*.*

For all of these algorithms except SetupElection*, the public key of the election* pk *is an implicit argument.*

A voting system should follow the following security notions:

Definition 22 (Tracing Correctness (from [DPP22])). *A voting system verifies tracing correctness iff for* $\lambda \in \mathbb{N}$, $(\mathsf{pk}, \mathsf{sk}) \xleftarrow{\$} \mathsf{SetupElection}(1^\lambda)$, *and every* $v, \mathsf{BB}, (\mathsf{b}, \mathsf{aux}) \xleftarrow{\$} \mathsf{Vote}(\mathsf{id}, v)$ *and* $\tau \leftarrow \mathsf{TraceBallot}(\mathsf{b})$, *for* $\widetilde{\mathsf{BB}} \leftarrow \mathsf{Append}(\mathsf{BB}, \mathsf{b})$, $\mathsf{VerifyVote}(\mathsf{Publish}(\mathsf{BB}), \tau) = 1$ *with overwhelming probability in* λ.

Definition 23 (Receipt-Freeness (from [DPP22])). *A voting system verifies receipt-freeness iff there exist algorithms* $\mathsf{SimSetupElection}$ *and* $\mathsf{SimProof}$ *such that, for* $\lambda \in \mathbb{N}$, *any PPT adversary* $\mathcal{A}$'s *advantage in distinguishing the games* $\mathsf{Exp}_{\mathcal{A},V}^{\mathsf{RF},0}(\lambda)$ *and* $\mathsf{Exp}_{\mathcal{A},V}^{\mathsf{RF},1}(\lambda)$ *defined by the oracles in Fig. 4 is negligible in* λ.

$\mathcal{O}\mathsf{init}^\beta(\lambda)$:

if $\beta = 0$ **then**
    $(\mathsf{pk}, \mathsf{sk}) \xleftarrow{\$} \mathsf{SetupElection}(1^\lambda)$
else $(\mathsf{pk}, \mathsf{sk}, \tau) \xleftarrow{\$} \mathsf{SimSetupElection}(1^\lambda)$
$\mathsf{BB}_0 \leftarrow \emptyset, \mathsf{BB}_1 \leftarrow \emptyset$
return pk.

$\mathcal{O}\mathsf{tally}^\beta$:

$(\mathsf{r}, \Pi) \xleftarrow{\$} \mathsf{Tally}(\mathsf{BB}_0, \mathsf{sk})$
if $\beta = 1$ **then** $\Pi \xleftarrow{\$} \mathsf{SimProof}(\mathsf{BB}_1, \mathsf{r}, \tau)$
return (r, Π).

$\mathcal{O}\mathsf{receiptLR}(\mathsf{b}_0, \mathsf{b}_1)$:

if $\mathsf{TraceBallot}(\mathsf{b}_0) \neq \mathsf{TraceBallot}(\mathsf{b}_1)$
    or $\mathsf{Valid}(\mathsf{BB}_0, \mathsf{b}_0) = 0$
    or $\mathsf{Valid}(\mathsf{BB}_1, \mathsf{b}_1) = 0$
    then return $\bot$
else $\mathsf{BB}_0 \leftarrow \mathsf{Append}(\mathsf{BB}_0, \mathsf{b}_0)$,
    $\mathsf{BB}_0 \leftarrow \mathsf{Append}(\mathsf{BB}_0, \mathsf{b}_0)$.

$\mathcal{O}\mathsf{board}^\beta$:

return $\mathsf{Publish}(\mathsf{BB}_\beta)$.

Fig. 4. Oracles used in the $\mathsf{Exp}_{\mathcal{A},V}^{\mathsf{RF},\beta}(\lambda)$ experiment, for $\beta \in \{0; 1\}$. The adversary first calls $\mathcal{O}\mathsf{init}^\beta(\lambda)$, and may then call the $\mathcal{O}\mathsf{board}$ and $\mathcal{O}\mathsf{receiptLR}$ oracles as much as she wants. She finally cacls $\mathcal{O}\mathsf{tally}$, receives the result of the election, and is requested to output her guess β' for the value of β, which is the output of the experiment.

Definition 24 (Ballot Traceability for Receipt-Freeness (from [DPP22])). *For every* pk *in the range of* $\mathsf{SetupElection}$, *voter identity* id, *and pair of votes* v_0, v_1, *for* $(\mathsf{b}_0, \mathsf{aux}) \xleftarrow{\$} \mathsf{Vote}(\mathsf{id}, v_0)$ *and* $\mathsf{b}_1 \xleftarrow{\$} \mathsf{Vote}(\mathsf{id}, v_1, \mathsf{aux})$, $\mathsf{TraceBallot}(\mathsf{b}_0) = \mathsf{TraceBallot}(\mathsf{b}_1)$.

6.2 Voting System Security Proofs

Deriving the voting system resulting from our TREnc as in [DPP22] also yields a secure system with the same voting system security notions, even with our more general TREnc ones. As our ciphertexts already verifiably encrypt bits, applying our modified generic TREnc-to-Vote transform inspired from [DPP22] to our TREnc immediately provides a voting scheme that can directly be used either with a homomorphic or a mixnet-based tally. Moreover, any copy of all the interactions and the adversary' view of an election using our scheme today, will remain secure against future quantum attacks (Fig. 5).

SetupElection(1^λ):

$(\mathsf{pk}, \mathsf{sk}) \xleftarrow{\$} \mathsf{Gen}(1^\lambda)$
return pk

ProcessBallot(b):

---

if $\mathsf{Ver}(\mathsf{pk}, \mathsf{b}, \mathsf{fresh}) = 0$ **then** return $\bot$
else return $\mathsf{Rand}(\mathsf{pk}, \mathsf{b})$

Valid(BB, b):

---

if $\mathsf{Ver}(\mathsf{pk}, \mathsf{b}, \mathsf{rand}) = 1 \ \wedge \ \forall \mathsf{b}' \in \mathsf{BB}$:
  $\mathsf{TraceBallot}(\mathsf{b}') \ \neq \ \mathsf{TraceBallot}(\mathsf{b})$
  then return 1
else return 0

Vote(id, $v[, \mathsf{aux}]$)

---

if aux is specified $\mathsf{lk} \leftarrow \mathsf{aux}$
else $\mathsf{lk} \leftarrow \mathsf{LGen}(\mathsf{pk})$
$\mathsf{b} \leftarrow \mathsf{LEnc}(\mathsf{pk}, \mathsf{lk}, v)$
if aux is specified return b
else return $(\mathsf{b}, \mathsf{lk})$

TraceBallot(b):

---

return $\mathsf{Trace}(\mathsf{pk}, \mathsf{b})$

VerifyVote(PBB, τ):

---

if $\exists \mathsf{b} \in \mathsf{PBB}$: $\mathsf{Ver}(\mathsf{pk}, \mathsf{b}, \mathsf{rand}) = 1 \ \wedge$
  $\tau = \mathsf{TraceBallot}(\mathsf{b})$ **then** return 1
else return 0

Fig. 5. TREnc-to-Vote compiler. Publish is simply the identity function. Tally and VerifyResult are instantiated via standard techniques.

In addition to TCCA, the receipt-freeness relies on the zero-knowledge proof that the tally of the election outputs the right result. This is captured by the SimSetupElection algorithm which indistinguishably outputs $(\mathsf{pk}, \mathsf{sk})$ as SetupElection, and by SimProof which outputs indistinguishable proofs from those of Tally given pk. $\mathsf{Adv}_{\mathcal{A}}^{\mathsf{SimSetupElection}}(\lambda)$ denotes the adversary $\mathcal{A}$'s advantage in distinguishing outputs $(\mathsf{pk}, \mathsf{sk})$ from SimSetupElection or SetupElection, and $\mathsf{Adv}_{\mathcal{A}}^{\mathsf{SimProof}}(\lambda)$ in distinguishing an output Π from SimProof or Tally, given the corresponding result r and public key pk, for a security parameter λ.

Theorem 25 (Receipt-Freeness). *If a TREnc scheme is TCCA and the tally result is proven using a zero-knowledge scheme yielding indistinguishable algorithms* SimSetupElection *and* SetupElection, *and* Tally *and* SimProof, *then the corresponding voting system is receipt-free; more precisely, for any PPT adversary $\mathcal{A}$,* $\mathsf{Adv}_{\mathcal{A}}^{\mathsf{RF}}(\lambda) \leq Q_{\mathcal{O}\mathsf{receiptLR}} \cdot \mathsf{Adv}_{\mathcal{A}}^{TCCA}(\lambda) + Q_{\mathcal{O}\mathsf{tally}} \cdot \mathsf{Adv}_{\mathcal{A}}^{\mathsf{SimProof}}(\lambda) + \mathsf{Adv}_{\mathcal{A}}^{\mathsf{SimSetupElection}}(\lambda)$, *for $Q_{\mathcal{O}\mathsf{receiptLR}}$ the number of requests $\mathcal{A}$ makes to the $\mathcal{O}$receiptLR oracle, and $\mathcal{O}$tally the number of requests she sends to $\mathcal{O}$tally.*

Proof. See the full version [dPP24a].

Traceability of TREnc yields the ballot traceability of the voting scheme. As for Ballot Privacy and Verifiability, they naturally follow as in [DPP22].

Acknowledgements. Paola de Perthuis was supported by the NWO Gravitation Project QSC. Thomas Peters is associate researcher of the Belgian Fund for Scientific Research (F.R.S.-FNRS).

References

[AFG+10] Abe, M., Fuchsbauer, G., Groth, J., Haralambiev, K., Ohkubo, M.: Structure-preserving signatures and commitments to group elements. In: Rabin, T. (ed.) CRYPTO 2010. LNCS, vol. 6223, pp. 209–236. Springer, Berlin, Heidelberg (2010)

[AHO10] Abe, M., Haralambiev, K., Ohkubo, M.: Signing on elements in bilinear groups for modular protocol design. Cryptology ePrint Archive, Report 2010/133 (2010)

[APS15] Albrecht, M.R., Player, R., Scott, S.: On the concrete hardness of learning with errors. J. Math. Cryptol. $9(3)$, 169–203 (2015)

[BCG+15] Bernhard, D., Cortier, V., Galindo, D., Pereira, O., Warinschi, B.: SoK: a comprehensive analysis of game-based ballot privacy definitions. In: 2015 IEEE Symposium on Security and Privacy, pp. 499–516 (2015)

[BdPP23] Brézot, T., de Perthuis, P., Pointcheval, D.: Covercrypt: an efficient early-abort KEM for hidden access policies with traceability from the DDH and LWE. In: Tsudik, G., Conti, M., Liang, K., Smaragdakis, G. (eds.) ESORICS 2023, Part I, volume 14344 of LNCS, pp. 372–392 (2023)

[BF11] Dan, B., Freeman, D.M.: Linearly homomorphic signatures over binary fields and new tools for lattice-based signatures. In: Catalano, D., Fazio, N., Gennaro, R., Nicolosi, A. (eds.) PKC 2011. LNCS, vol. 6571, pp. 1–16. Springer, Berlin, Heidelberg (2011)

[BHdPP25] Brézot, T., Hébant, C., de Perthuis, P., Pointcheval, D.: Security analysis of covercrypt: a quantum-safe hybrid key encapsulation mechanism for hidden access policies. Cryptology ePrint Archive, Paper 2025/544 (2025)

[BS22] Beullens, W., Seiler, G.: LaBRADOR: compact proofs for R1CS from module-SIS. Cryptology ePrint Archive, Report 2022/1341 (2022)

[CDNO96] Canetti, R., Dwork, C., Naor, M., Ostrovsky, R.: Deniable encryption. Cryptology ePrint Archive, Report 1996/002 (1996)

[CKLM12] Chase, M., Kohlweiss, M., Lysyanskaya, A., Meiklejohn, S.: Malleable proof systems and applications. In: Pointcheval, D., Johansson, T. (eds.) EUROCRYPT 2012. LNCS, vol. 7237, pp. 281–300. Springer, Berlin, Heidelberg (2012)

[DPP22] Devillez, H., Pereira, O., Peters, T.: Traceable receipt-free encryption. In: Agrawal, S., Lin, D. (eds.) ASIACRYPT 2022. Part III, volume 13793 of LNCS, pp. 273–303. Springer, Cham (2022)

[dPP24a] de Perthuis, P., Peters, T.: Post-quantum privacy for traceable receipt-free encryption. Cryptology ePrint Archive, Report 2024/2087 (2024)

[DPP24b] Devillez, H., Pereira, O., Peters, T.: Practical traceable receipt-free encryption. In: Galdi, C., Phan, D.H. (eds.) Security and Cryptography for Networks - 14th International Conference, SCN 2024, Amalfi, Italy, 11–13 September 2024, Proceedings, Part I, volume 14973 of Lecture Notes in Computer Science, pp. 367–387. Springer (2024)

[DPP24c] Van Thao, T., Doan, O.P., Peters, T.: Encryption mechanisms for receipt-free and perfectly private verifiable elections. In: Pöpper, C., Batina, L. (eds.) ACNS 24International Conference on Applied Cryptography and Network Security. Part I, volume 14583 of LNCS, pp. 257–287. Springer, Cham (2024)

[ETS25] Efficient quantum-safe hybrid key exchanges with hidden access policies. CYBER Quantum-Safe Cryptography (QSC) group, European Telecommunications Standards Institute, Sophia-Antipolis, FR (2025)

[FV12]   Fan, J., Vercauteren, F.: Somewhat practical fully homomorphic encryption. Cryptology ePrint Archive, Report 2012/144 (2012)

[Gro06] Groth, J.: Simulation-sound NIZK proofs for a practical language and constant size group signatures. In: Lai, X., Chen, K. (eds.) ASIACRYPT 2006. LNCS, vol. 4284, pp. 444–459. Springer, Berlin, Heidelberg (2006)

[GS08]   Groth, J., Sahai, A.: Efficient non-interactive proof systems for bilinear groups. In: Smart, N.P. (ed.) EUROCRYPT 2008. LNCS, vol. 4965, pp. 415–432. Springer, Berlin, Heidelberg (2008)

[GVW15] Gorbunov, S., Vaikuntanathan, V., Wichs, D.: Leveled fully homomorphic signatures from standard lattices. In: Servedio, R.A., Rubinfeld, R. (eds.) 47th ACM STOC, pp. 469–477. ACM Press (2015)

[LNP22] Lyubashevsky, V., Nguyen, N.K., Plançon, M.: Lattice-based zero-knowledge proofs and applications: shorter, simpler, and more general. In: Dodis, Y., Shrimpton, T. (eds.) CRYPTO 2022. Part II, volume 13508 of LNCS, pp. 71–101. Springer, Cham (2022)

[LPJY14] Libert, B., Peters, T., Joye, M., Yung, M.: Non-malleability from malleability: simulation-sound quasi-adaptive NIZK proofs and CCA2-secure encryption from homomorphic signatures. In: Nguyen, P.Q., Oswald, E. (eds.) EUROCRYPT 2014. LNCS, vol. 8441, pp. 514–532. Springer, Berlin, Heidelberg (2014)

[LPQ17] Libert, B., Peters, T., Qian, C.: Structure-preserving chosen-ciphertext security with shorter verifiable ciphertexts. In: Fehr, S. (ed.) PKC 2017. Part I, volume 10174 of LNCS, pp. 247–276. Springer, Berlin, Heidelberg (2017)

[MRY04] MacKenzie, P.D., Reiter, M.K., Yang, K.: Alternatives to non-malleability: definitions, constructions, and applications (extended abstract). In: Naor, M. (ed.) TCC 2004. LNCS, vol. 2951, pp. 171–190. Springer, Berlin, Heidelberg (2004)

[Ràf15] Ràfols, C.: Stretching Groth-Sahai: NIZK proofs of partial satisfiability. In: Dodis, Y., Nielsen, J.B. (eds.) TCC 2015. LNCS, vol. 9015, pp. 247–276. Springer, Heidelberg (2015). https://doi.org/10.1007/978-3-662-46497-7_10

[SW14]   Sahai, A., Waters, B.: How to use indistinguishability obfuscation: deniable encryption, and more. In: Shmoys, D.B. (ed.) 46th ACM STOC, pp. 475–484. ACM Press (2014)

Group Encryption with Oblivious Traceability

Khoa Nguyen[1] , Yanhong Xu[2,3]($\boxtimes$) , Nam Tran[1] , Willy Susilo[1] ,
and Huaxiong Wang[4]

[1] School of Computing and Information Technology, University of Wollongong,
Northfields Avenue, Wollongong, NSW 2522, Australia
[2] School of Computer Science, Shanghai Jiao Tong University, 800 Dongchuan Road,
Shanghai 200240, China
[3] Key Laboratory of Intelligent Sensing System and Security (Ministry of
Education), Hubei University, Wuhan, Hubei, China
yanhong.xu@sjtu.edu.cn
[4] School of Physical and Mathematical Sciences, Nanyang Technological University,
21 Nanyang Link, Singapore 637371, Singapore

Abstract. We revisit Group Encryption (GE)—an encryption analogue
of group signatures introduced by Kiayias et al. (Asiacrypt 2007). A GE
system simultaneously provides anonymity and traceability for receivers
who are certified group members, enabling a range of privacy-preserving
applications. While prior work has extensively addressed *how* to trace
receivers in GE, the question of *why* a ciphertext should be traceable
remains unexplored. Unlike group signatures, where opening can be justified by the signed content, tracing in GE poses a dilemma because the
underlying plaintext is confidential.

To address this gap, we introduce *Group Encryption with Oblivious
Traceability* (GEOT), an enhanced form of GE in which the traceability
of a ciphertext ψ intended for receiver id and containing message $\mathbf{w}$ is
governed by a public tracing policy $P(\mathsf{id}, \mathbf{w}) \in 0, 1$. Here, $P(\mathsf{id}, \mathbf{w}) = 0$
denotes traceability, whereas $P(\mathsf{id}, \mathbf{w}) = 1$ ensures non-traceability. The
traceability status is known to the sender but remains hidden from all
parties except the opening authority, which learns nothing about id in
the non-traceable case. GEOT further supports message filtering and
dynamic membership, following Nguyen et al. (PKC 2021). Filtering
enforces that valid ciphertexts satisfy a public policy $F(\mathbf{w}) = 1$, while
dynamicity enables users to join and leave the system over time.

We formalize GEOT with concise syntax and rigorous security notions,
and present a modular construction based on standard cryptographic
primitives: signatures, public-key encryption, and non-interactive zero-
knowledge proofs. We also give a concrete instantiation from code-based
assumptions supporting arbitrary tracing and filtering policies represented by polynomial-size Boolean circuits. In addition to expressive
filtering and tracing functionalities, our scheme achieves significant efficiency improvements over existing post-quantum GE constructions.

K. Nguyen and Y. Xu—This denotes equal contribution.

1   Introduction

Group encryption (GE), introduced by Kiayias, Tsiounis, and Yung (KTY) [33] as the encryption analogue of group signatures [18], is an appealing primitive that aims to simultaneously provide anonymity and accountability for message receivers who are registered members of a group. A GE scheme allows the sender of a message $\mathbf{w}$ to generate a verifiable ciphertext ψ such that (i) $\mathbf{w}$ can be recovered only by some anonymous receiver id who is a certified group member; (ii) an opening authority (OA) can trace ψ to id when necessary; and (iii) $\mathbf{w}$ satisfies certain message-filtering policy constraints. These properties make GE attractive from both theoretical and applied viewpoints. From a theoretical perspective, GE is considerably more intricate than group signatures because it requires proving the well-formedness of ciphertexts encrypted under hidden—but certified—public keys. Indeed, as observed by Kiayias et al. [33], GE implies hierarchical group signatures [60], a proper generalization of group signatures [9,10]. Practically, GE enables a range of privacy-preserving services [1,17,33,37,39,50,56]. Typical examples include encrypted email filtering, secure oblivious retrieval in corporate settings, and privacy-preserving financial transactions where encrypted transfers can still be traced for regulatory purposes.

Despite these advantages, GE inherits a structural weakness similar to that of group signatures: it cannot protect users' privacy against an all-powerful OA that can trace arbitrarily. Existing refinements, such as traceable GE [39], improve *how* tracing is performed but not *when* it should be invoked. In all existing schemes, the opener can freely deanonymize any ciphertext. This undermines the very privacy that GE seeks to achieve and is incompatible with modern expectations of accountability and due process.

The core conceptual gap lies in the absence of a clear rule specifying *why* a ciphertext should be traceable. In group signatures, opening a signer's identity is justified by the nature of an inappropriate or disputed message. In contrast, ciphertexts in GE conceal their contents, making it unclear under what circumstances the opening procedure ought to be triggered. For instance, if the OA suspects that some member is distributing illegal data and decides to open all ciphertexts to find the culprit, the privacy of every honest user is destroyed in the process. Such pervasive traceability is not only technically heavy-handed but also ethically questionable.

To capture a fairer balance between privacy and accountability, one may envision a tracing process that is *conditioned* on publicly verifiable criteria rather than left entirely to the discretion of the opening authority. Formally, such conditions could be represented by a *tracing policy* predicate $P(\mathsf{id}, \mathbf{w}) \in \{0,1\}$, which specifies when tracing is justified based on the receiver's certified identity id and the message content $\mathbf{w}$. Similarly, it is often desirable to restrict the kinds of messages that can be validly encrypted, according to a *filtering policy* $F(\mathbf{w}) \in \{0,1\}$ that captures format or compliance requirements. Together, these conceptual elements suggest a new direction: a group-encryption framework where the ability to trace is no longer unconditional, but instead governed by explicit, policy-driven rules that are transparent to all participants.

To better understand the need for a more balanced approach, we illustrate three representative domains where receiver privacy and accountability are required simultaneously, and where a justified and *oblivious* tracing mechanism becomes indispensable.

Healthcare Data Collaboration. In large-scale medical research, hospitals and data-trust networks routinely share sensitive datasets with certified analysts. Receiver anonymity protects analysts from profiling and ensures that their data-access patterns remain confidential, while receiver accountability guarantees that if a dataset is mishandled or leaked, regulators can identify the certified recipient responsible. This dual requirement naturally justifies the use of GE, which offers both confidentiality and traceability.

However, in standard GE, the OA can open any ciphertext, enabling mass surveillance of compliant analysts and violating privacy regulations. A more reasonable system would allow tracing only when predefined privacy or clearance policies are violated, and would otherwise hide even the *possibility* of tracing. Such an "oblivious" form of traceability can be captured by a public predicate $P(\mathsf{id}, \mathbf{w})$ that encodes oversight conditions – for example, $P(\mathsf{id}, \mathbf{w}) = 0$ if the dataset $\mathbf{w}$ contains unredacted personal identifiers or if the analyst's clearance level is below the dataset's sensitivity label. Only when P evaluates to 0 may the OA learn the receiver's identity; otherwise, even the authority remains oblivious to whom the ciphertext was intended for. The filtering policy $F(\mathbf{w})$ can further enforce that only datasets containing mandatory consent tags or schema-conformant records are accepted, while full dynamicity accommodates continual membership changes in research consortia without reinitialization.

Financial-Compliance Communication. Financial institutions must communicate sensitive alerts and transaction reports among certified compliance officers. Receiver anonymity is essential for preserving investigative independence, whereas accountability is needed to establish who handled a particular case when regulatory review occurs. This again matches the conceptual goals of GE.

Yet conventional GE permits unfettered opening, making internal communications vulnerable to privacy abuse. A fairer design would tie traceability to explicit, public rules, preventing the OA from acting outside its mandate. In this setting, a predicate $P(\mathsf{id}, \mathbf{w})$ could encode statutory triggers such as "the alert $\mathbf{w}$ describes a transaction exceeding the reportable threshold without KYC verification," or "the receiver id lacks jurisdiction over the relevant account." Only if $P(\mathsf{id}, \mathbf{w}) = 0$ can the receiver be revealed; otherwise, tracing is infeasible and its status remains hidden. Here, $F(\mathbf{w})$ may guarantee that only authenticated, well-structured alerts are encrypted, and dynamicity supports officer rotations and role changes, ensuring long-term operability.

Whistleblowing and Internal Reporting. Whistleblowing systems epitomize the tension between privacy and accountability. Employees must be able to send encrypted reports to certified investigators anonymously, yet the organization must still be able to trace a report if it contains defamatory or classified information. A GE-style design satisfies both objectives: confidentiality for reporters and conditional accountability for investigators.

However, in standard GE, pervasive traceability allows a malicious authority to open every report, compromising trust in the entire process. To prevent this, traceability should depend on an explicit policy predicate and remain hidden and unusable otherwise. For instance, $P(\mathsf{id}, \mathbf{w})$ may return 0 if the report $\mathbf{w}$ includes classified content or targets an incorrect investigative division. When P returns 0, the authority can reveal the investigator's identity; when P returns 1, even the authority learns nothing about who received the report. A filtering policy $F(\mathbf{w})$ can require that reports contain proper metadata (e.g., timestamps, case categories, or evidence references), and full dynamicity allows the investigative roster to evolve without disrupting ongoing processes.

Across these domains – healthcare collaboration, financial compliance, and whistleblowing – the need for receiver accountability justifies the use of group encryption, while the risk of privacy violations by an omnipotent opener calls for *oblivious traceability*. A tracing mechanism that is both conditional and hidden provides cryptographic fairness: tracing can occur only when justified by a public predicate, and otherwise even the authority remains ignorant of receiver identities. Message filtering and dynamic membership strengthen the model's deployability, but the essential innovation lies in ensuring that the *reason* for tracing is both explicit and privacy-preserving.

OUR CONTRIBUTIONS AND TECHNIQUES. Building upon these motivations, we formalize and realize the notion of *Group Encryption with Oblivious Traceability* (GEOT), which revolutionizes the tracing function in GE by tying it to public, verifiable conditions. In GEOT, whether a ciphertext is traceable depends on a public predicate $P(\mathsf{id}, \mathbf{w})$, and the traceability status is oblivious to all parties except the OA, which learns nothing in the non-traceable case. Our formulation provides a cryptographic setting that is fair to both users and authorities: misbehaving users cannot evade tracing, and misbehaving authorities cannot compromise the privacy of honest users. GEOT further supports message filtering and full dynamicity as suggested in [50].

We equip GEOT with concise syntax – comprising only seven algorithms compared to thirteen in [50] – and rigorous security notions, including message secrecy, several forms of anonymity, and unforgeability. We next provide a generic construction of GEOT satisfying the proposed model and relying on commonly used cryptographic building blocks. Somewhat surprisingly, we show that a secure GEOT system can be generically constructed from the same building blocks that are used for building ordinary GE systems. This generic construction is meaningful in that it isolates the essential components of GE and demonstrates that the new functionality of *oblivious traceability* can be incorporated together with previously studied features such as message filtering and full dynamicity [50], all within a single unified framework. In particular, it shows that these enhancements can be achieved without introducing additional cryptographic assumptions or complex new machinery, and can be seamlessly integrated into existing GE schemes in a modular manner. Our framework can naturally lead to concrete instantiations using existing cryptographic tools and techniques from pairings and lattices. For the sake of diversity of assumptions, we next pay attention to realizing GEOT from codes. A noticeable obstacle in the code-based setting is the current lack of a signature scheme[1] with efficient protocols [15] for proving in zero-knowledge the possession of a valid message–signature pair, which is utilized in our generic construction and which has been constructed from pairings [8,16] and lattices [14,31,36]. We nevertheless overcome this obstacle by using a code-based Merkle-tree accumulator [52], instead of a full-fledged standard-model signature. This approach is inspired by the construction of fully dynamic group encryption (FDGE) in [50]. Our code-based GEOT scheme operates smoothly with general policies and is sufficiently expressive to support arbitrary tracing and filtering policies represented by polynomial-size Boolean circuits.

Further Applications of GEOT. Beyond the classical privacy–accountability balance, GEOT also enables a new class of applications in which the traceability of ciphertexts is not merely a defensive mechanism against abuse, but a *functional feature* that parties may wish to invoke intentionally. In particular, GEOT provides a controlled environment where senders can deliberately generate ciphertexts that are traceable under specific, publicly known predicates, allowing traceability itself to become a mechanism for enforcing responsibility, eligibility, or reward.

For instance, in privacy-preserving financial systems, GEOT can protect the anonymity of ordinary low-value transfers while permitting the tracing of transactions that violate anti-money-laundering policies or exceed taxable thresholds. In other domains, receivers may have incentives or obligations to accept traceable ciphertexts. A patient may encrypt her medical records to her doctor, who is accountable for handling them responsibly; the traceability predicate ensures that, in case of dispute, the doctor's role can be verified. An elderly benefactor may send the details of his will to his lawyer, authorizing disclosure only under predefined legal conditions; here, traceability captures both timing and custodial responsibility. Similarly, a whistleblower might send evidence to a journalist who is authorized to reveal the information only if the content meets certain public-interest criteria. In all these cases, the ability to encode, in the policy predicate $P(\mathsf{id}, \mathbf{w})$, *when and why* a receiver may be traced transforms traceability from a passive safeguard into an active part of the communication semantics.

From a different angle, GEOT also supports voluntary or incentive-driven use cases. Users may intentionally produce traceable ciphertexts – e.g., when a system grants proofs, rewards, or credentials to those who send or receive verifiably traceable messages. Such flexibility is enable by the traceability condition in GEOT, which is explicit, policy-based, and cryptographically verifiable. Altogether, these examples illustrate that GEOT does not merely restrict the

---

[1] Existing code-based signatures schemes such as Stern's [59], CFS [21], WAVE [23] are not compatible with zero-knowledge proofs due to their reliance on random oracles.

authority's tracing power, but generalizes it into a programmable mechanism for modeling accountability, compliance, and incentive alignment across diverse privacy-sensitive ecosystems.

Defining GEOT. The definitions of GEOT are inspired by those of FDGE [50] and bifurcated anonymous signatures (BiAS) [38], and – to some extent – attribute-based signatures (ABS) [43]. Concretely, GEOT encompasses the full dynamicity feature of FDGE, the oblivious and predicate-based tracing feature of BiAS and the policy-based filtering feature of ABS. It is worth noting that, although GEOT is a richer and more advanced primitive than FDGE, we manage to provide a syntax that is much simpler, comprising 7 algorithms, compared to 13 algorithms of FDGE. This simplification is the result of three major changes in the definitions: (i) the key generations of the group manager (GM) and the OA are unified into the system setup algorithm; (ii) the filtering mechanism is simply defined in terms of predicates (while in GE [33], traceable GE [39] and FDGE [50], messages are associated with heavy machinery of NP-relations); (iii) the proving algorithm (used in previous systems to show the well-formedness of ciphertexts) is incorporated into the encryption algorithm.

The lifetime of a GEOT system is divided into time epochs belonging to an ordered time space $\mathcal{T} = \{\tau_1, \tau_2, \ldots\}$ of polynomial cardinality. Any GEOT system is further associated with a space $\mathcal{ID}$ of receiver identifiers, a message space $\mathcal{W}$, a collection $\mathcal{F} = \{F_\tau : \mathcal{W} \to \{0, 1\}\}$ of filtering policies and a collection $\mathcal{P} = \{P_\tau : \mathcal{ID} \times \mathcal{W} \to \{0, 1\}\}$ of tracing policies. Any ciphertext ψ in the system is bound to a time period $\tau \in \mathcal{T}$. If ψ contains message $\mathbf{w} \in \mathcal{W}$ and is intended for receiver id $\in \mathcal{ID}$, then ψ is deemed valid when $F_\tau(\mathbf{w}) = 1$, traceable when $P_\tau(\mathsf{id}, \mathbf{w}) = 0$ and non-traceable when $P_\tau(\mathsf{id}, \mathbf{w}) = 1$.

A GEOT system must satisfy the following properties: correctness, privacy and unforgeability. While **correctness** can be defined naturally, formalizing security notions for GEOT is quite non-trivial, mainly due to the introduction of tracing (and filtering) policies. In particular, there are three types of **privacy** that we should capture.

- **Message secrecy** protects the receiver from a CCA2 adversary who tries to learn information about the encrypted message and who can corrupt the whole system except for the receiver of the challenge ciphertext. Here, compared to the corresponding notion in FDGE, we have to make a restriction on the challenge tuple returned by the adversary so that to prevent it from trivially winning by outputting $(\mathsf{id}, \mathbf{w}_0, \mathbf{w}_1)$ such that $P(\mathsf{id}, \mathbf{w}_0) \neq P(\mathsf{id}, \mathbf{w}_1)$.
- **Type-1-anonymity** protects the identity of the receiver as well as whether a given ciphertext is traceable or not against a CCA2 adversary. We allow the adversary to adaptively query the opening oracle and even allow it to output a challenge tuple $(\mathsf{id}_0, \mathsf{id}_1, \mathbf{w})$ such that $P(\mathsf{id}_0, \mathbf{w}) \neq P(\mathsf{id}_1, \mathbf{w})$.
- **Type-2-anonymity** further ensures that in the non-traceable case, nothing about the receiver's identity can be learned by an adversary who can corrupt the whole system except the two challenge users.

Defining **unforgeability** for GEOT requires additional care. Intuitively, we would like to ensure that one can generate a valid ciphertext ψ if: (i) the intended receiver id is active in the system (i.e., id has joined and has not been revoked); (ii) the plaintext $\mathbf{w}$ passes the filtering policy, i.e., $F(\mathbf{w}) = 1$; (iii) id is traceable if and only if $P(\mathsf{id}, \mathbf{w}) = 0$. However, due to privacy properties, there is no efficient mechanism to determine whether a given ciphertext ψ does comply with these conditions. Hence, similar to the model of BiAS, here we also need to introduce an extractable mode for the system to determine if an adversary has produced a falsely accepted ciphertext.

Generically Constructing GEOT. Once the definitional framework has been well established, we turn our attention to designing systems satisfying the proposed security requirements, based on well-studied assumptions. To that end, we provide a generic construction of GEOT, which is essentially the first generic construction of fully dynamic group encryption, which was not given in previous works such as [50] and [56].

We first identify the cryptographic ingredients necessary for a modular construction of GEOT. Since a legitimate ciphertext must exhibit a certified group membership of the intended receiver, we would need an ordinary digital signature as a building block for GEOT. Now, the fact that only the intended receiver and the OA can potentially recover some information from a ciphertext suggests the necessity of public-key encryption (PKE) systems (with an extra requirement of key privacy for the system owned by the receiver). Finally, as a valid ciphertext must be honestly computed and must reveal no private information to the public, we would also need to employ some non-interactive zero-knowledge (NIZK) proof/argument system.

We next show that the commonly used ingredients identified above, i.e., ordinary signature, PKEs and NIZK, are indeed sufficient for designing GEOT for arbitrary tracing and filtering policies. The high-level ideas underlying the construction are as follows. Each potential user of the system is equipped with a key pair for a key-private PKE. The GM possesses a signing-verification key pair for a signature scheme, which will be used for certifying users' public keys. The OA, on the other hand, owns a key pair for another (not necessarily key-private) PKE. To send a message $\mathbf{w}$ to user id at time τ, the sender first makes sure that: (i) $\mathbf{w}$ is allowed under the filtering policy F_τ; (ii) id has been certified by the GM, and is not in the updated revocation list. Then, the sender generates two sub-ciphertexts: (i) $\mathbf{c_R}$ that encrypts $\mathbf{w}$ under the receiver's public key; and (ii) $\mathbf{c_{OA}}$ that encrypts the value $(1 - P_\tau(\mathsf{id}, \mathbf{w})) \cdot \mathsf{id}$ under the OA's public key, where $P_\tau(\cdot, \cdot)$ is the tracing predicate at time τ. Then the sender generates an NIZK argument to prove in zero-knowledge that all the steps have been done correctly. The final ciphertext ψ then is set as the triple $(\mathbf{c_R}, \mathbf{c_{OA}}, \pi)$. Verification of ψ consists of verifying π. The receiver id can recover $\mathbf{w}$ by decrypting $\mathbf{c_R}$. Meanwhile, depending on the predicate value $P_\tau(\mathsf{id}, \mathbf{w})$, the OA can learn from $\mathbf{c_{OA}}$ either id (traceable case) or $\mathbf{0}$ (non-traceable case). The correctness and security properties of the resulting GEOT system follow quite naturally from those of the employed building blocks.

Concretely Instantiating GEOT. Since the building blocks used in the above generic construction have been realized based on pairings (e.g., in the standard model via [28,34,35]) and lattices (e.g., via [31] and [57] (standard model) and [14,62] (random oracle model)), we know that the respective pairing-based and lattice-based instantiations can, in principle, be achieved. However, when it comes to designing GEOT from code-based assumptions, it is less clear how to obtain a working solution, due to the current lack of a standard-model full-fledged signature in the code-based setting – as discussed above. Nevertheless, we observe that the problem can still be overcome by slightly departing from the generic construction approach and using a Merkle tree – which can be seen as a weak form of signature – to manage the enrollments and revocations of users.

At a high level, our instantiation of GEOT is inspired by the code-based FDGE scheme of [50], and employs an updatable Merkle tree accumulator [52] for the "signature layer", anonymous CCA2 secure versions [48,54] of McEliece scheme [44] for the "encryption layers". A remarkable feature of our scheme is that it allows *arbitrary choices* of filtering and tracing policies, represented by polynomial-size Boolean circuits. To develop the supporting "zero-knowledge layer", instead of using Stern-like [59] zero-knowledge protocols as in [24,52] for proving ciphertext validity, we employ the techniques in [55] which are built upon the VOLE-in-the-Head (VOLEitH) paradigm [5,7]. By adapting these techniques to handle the algebraic relations (i.e., relations among code-based components of Merkle hash tree and McEliece encryption) and non-algebraic relations (i.e., satisfiability of Boolean circuits representing our filtering and tracing policies), we obtain significant efficiency improvements over existing GE schemes from post-quantum assumptions: the lattice-based schemes from [37,56] and the code-based scheme from [50].

Table 1. Comparison of key sizes, ciphertext size and proof size between existing post-quantum GE schemes and our code-based GEOT scheme. The data achieving 80-bit security for [37,56] are taken from [56, Table 1]. The data achieving 128-bit security for [50,51] are taken from [51, Table 1]. The data for our scheme are calculated based on parameters specified in Table 2. For filtering and tracing policies, we address relatively large Boolean circuits of size 10^5. The group size $N = 2^{10}$ is chosen for all four schemes.

	λ	GM		OA		User		Ciph.	Proof
		pk	sk	pk	sk	pk	sk		
[37]	80	68.60 GB	482.55 GB	2.37 GB	38.86 GB	2.37 GB	38.86 GB	2.36 TB	3728 TB
[56]	80	0.54 KB	1.08 KB	10.85 KB	129.50 KB	9.40 MB	112.30 MB	0.13 MB	10.32 GB
[50]	128	0.43 KB	0.85 KB	2.26 MB	6.90 MB	2.26 MB	6.90 MB	1.70 KB	46.26 GB
Ours	128	8 KB	0.25 KB	3.40 MB	6.19 MB	3.40 MB	6.19 MB	2 KB	61.43 MB

In Table 1, we give a comparison between the key sizes, ciphertext size and proof size of our GEOT scheme and the GE schemes from [37,50,56]. Our scheme not only offers much more expressive tracing and filtering functionalities but also noteworthy gains in terms of efficiency. Nevertheless, we remark that the scheme is still far from being practical, due to the need to encrypt McEliece public keys and to prove highly sophisticated relations capturing ciphertext well-formedness. We leave the question of achieving practically efficient (code-based) GEOT schemes as a fascinating open question for future investigations.

RELATED WORK. In their pioneering work that introduced GE, Kiayias et al. also provided a concrete construction based on the Decisional Composite Residuosity and the Decisional Diffie-Hellman assumptions. They used an interactive ZK proof of ciphertext well-formedness, which can be made non-interactive in the random oracle model using the Fiat-Shamir transformation [25]. Cathalo et al. [17] later suggested a non-interactive protocol based on pairings in the standard model. El Aimani and Joye [1] subsequently provided various efficiency improvements for pairing-based GE. The first post-quantum construction of GE was presented by Libert et al. [37] who put forward a lattice-based scheme.

Regarding enhanced variants of GE, Libert et al. [39] proposed a refined tracing mechanism inspired by that of traceable signatures [32]. In this setting, the OA can release a user-specific trapdoor which enables public tracing of ciphertexts sent to that user without violating the privacy of other users. However, a malicious OA can still violate the privacy of any user of its choice. Izabachène et al. [29] suggested mediated traceable anonymous encryption – a related primitive that addresses the problem of eliminating subliminal channels. Nguyen et al. [50] defined FDGE, which supports dynamic user enrollments and revocations, and described a code-based instantiation. Nguyen et al.'s construction also allows filtering of messages, based on either a "permissive policy" (that permits only messages containing certain keywords) or "prohibitive policy" (that prohibits all messages containing a substring similar to a given keyword). Subsequently, Pan et al. [56] presented a lattice-based FDGE construction that improves over [50] in several aspects.

Bifurcated anonymous signature, introduced in a recent work by Libert et al. [38], enables predicate-based oblivious tracing in the context of anonymity-oriented signatures. The novel idea underlying BiAS yields a good balance between anonymity and accountability. In [38], the authors also provided a generic construction of BiAS for arbitrary predicates in NC1, which allows standard-model instantiations from lattices and pairings. However, the technical ingredients required for their generic construction are not available in the code-based setting. In contrast, without much technical difficulty, one can design (the first) BiAS from codes based on a code-based GEOT (such as the construction discussed in the present work). Although both primitives improve group signature/encryption via the oblivious traceability feature, GEOT is more than just an encryption analogue of BiAS. As we argued earlier, oblivious traceability is not only an enhanced property but also seems to be the "right" notion for tracing in the GE context.

In a more recent work, Nguyen et al. [49] proposed the notion of Multimodal Private Signatures (MPS), which generalizes BiAS by relaxing the absolute accountability of users and categorizing users' traceable information into different levels of anonymity. We leave the problem of translating the ideas of MPS into the GE setting as an interesting question for future investigations.

The major tools for building those privacy-preserving cryptographic constructions are ZK proof [27] and argument [26] systems that allow proving the truth of a statement while revealing no additional information. Until recently, many ZK proof/argument systems used in code-based privacy-preserving cryptography followed Stern's framework [59]. Variants of Stern's protocol have been employed to design privacy-preserving constructions, such as proofs of plaintext knowledge [47], accumulators and range proofs [52], ring signatures [45,46,52], group signatures [2,24,52], proofs of valid openings for commitments and proofs for general relations [30,40], GE [50], policy-based signatures [19,61] and ABS [40].

Upon the invention of the VOLEitH techniques by Baum et al. [7], VOLEitH proof systems have gained traction in the past two years. Cui et al. [22] first constructed a standard signature scheme via the VOLEitH techniques, based on the regular syndrome decoding (SD) problems. Baum et al. [5] proposed several optimizations to further reduce the proof sizes at the cost of slightly larger computation time. Bidoux et al. [12] then constructed standard signatures based on the rank SD and minRank problems. Ouyang et al. [55] adapted the VOLEitH proof systems to handle degree-d polynomial constraints, and built efficient ring signatures, group signatures, and fully dynamic ABS. Bettaieb et al. [11] introduced VOLE-friendly modelings for SD and permuted kernel problems, and constructed efficient standard signatures and ring signatures based on these problems. Quite recently, Chiang et al. [20] proposed threshold ring signatures from AES and VOLEitH proof systems.

ORGANIZATION. The rest of the paper is organized as follows. In Sect. 2, we describe the definitions and security requirements of GEOT. In Sect. 3, we present a generic construction of GEOT from commonly used cryptographic building blocks. Our code-based instantiation of GEOT is described in Sect. 4. Due to space restrictions, the reminders on generic cryptographic primitives, backgrounds on the necessary code-based building blocks, supporting zero-knowledge protocols and security proofs can be found in the full version [53].

2   GEOT: Syntax and Security Definitions

In this section, we formalize the primitive of GEOT. A GEOT system is an enhanced group encryption system that supports conditional and oblivious tracing of ciphertexts, policy-based message filtering, as well as dynamic user enrollments and revocations.

2.1   Syntax

A GEOT system involves the following entities: a trusted authority who initializes the group parameters; senders, receivers and verifiers of ciphertexts; a group manager (GM) who is in charge of enrollments and revocations of receivers to and from the group; and an opening authority (OA) who can identify receivers of ciphertexts that are traceable.

The lifetime of a GEOT system is divided into time epochs belonging to an ordered time space $\mathcal{T} = \{\tau_1, \tau_2, \ldots\}$ of polynomial cardinality. All entities of the system have access to a group database $\mathsf{info} = (\mathsf{info}_{\tau_1}, \mathsf{info}_{\tau_2}, \ldots)$, where each entry info_τ is announced and authenticated by the GM at the beginning of time epoch τ. This entry allows the public to determine which receivers are active (i.e., those who have joined the group but have not been revoked) at time epoch τ. The GM additionally maintains a table **reg** containing registration information of all registered receivers and a regularly updated set $\mathcal{S}$ of receivers to be revoked at the next time epoch. We remark that the well-formedness of **reg** can be publicly verified by checking if there is any inconsistency with info_τ.

A GEOT system is further associated with a space $\mathcal{ID}$ (where each $\mathsf{id} \in \mathcal{ID}$ contains identifying information of the respective receiver), a message space $\mathcal{W}$, a collection $\mathcal{F} = \{F_\tau : \mathcal{W} \to \{0,1\}\}$ of message filtering policies and a collection $\mathcal{P} = \{P_\tau : \mathcal{ID} \times \mathcal{W} \to \{0,1\}\}$ of tracing policies, each of which specifies whether an intended receiver id of a message w should be traceable or not. We assume that at epoch τ, the system information info_τ uniquely defines a filtering policy F_τ and a tracing policy P_τ.

Any ciphertext ψ in the system is bound to a time epoch $\tau \in \mathcal{T}$, and can only be verified, decrypted, traced relative to the policies specified by info_τ. If ψ contains message $w \in \mathcal{W}$ and is intended for receiver $\mathsf{id} \in \mathcal{ID}$, then ψ is said to pass the filter when $F_\tau(w) = 1$, to be traceable when $P_\tau(\mathsf{id}, w) = 0$ and to be non-traceable when $P_\tau(\mathsf{id}, w) = 1$.

$\mathsf{Setup}(1^\lambda)$ On input security parameter 1^λ, this probabilistic algorithm generates public parameters pp, a secret key $\mathsf{sk_{GM}}$ for the GM and a secret key $\mathsf{sk_{OA}}$ for the OA. It also initializes the group database $\mathsf{info} := \emptyset$ and a registration table **reg** $:= \emptyset$. We assume that pp contains the specifications of $(\mathcal{T}, \mathcal{ID}, \mathcal{W}, \mathcal{F}, \mathcal{P})$ and is an implicit input of all other algorithms.

$\langle \mathsf{Join}(\mathsf{info}), \mathsf{Issue}(\mathsf{sk_{GM}}, \mathsf{info}, \mathbf{reg}) \rangle$ This is an interactive protocol between the GM and a potential group member who would like to join the group. If the protocol completes successfully, the user obtains a unique identifier $\mathsf{id} \in \mathcal{ID}$ and a membership certificate $\mathsf{cert_{id}}$ that are publicly known, together with a secret key $\mathsf{sk_{id}}$ known only to them. The GM, on the other hand, appends the registration information $(\mathsf{id}, \mathsf{cert_{id}})$ to the table **reg**.

$\mathsf{GUpdate}(\mathsf{sk_{GM}}, \mathcal{S}, \mathsf{info}, \mathbf{reg})$ Executed by the GM, this algorithm periodically updates the group information and advances the time epoch. It takes as inputs $\mathsf{sk_{GM}}$, a set of to-be-revoked users $\mathcal{S}$, the current group database info, the current registration table **reg**, and then updates the information table with the new group information $\mathsf{info} := \mathsf{info} \cup \{\mathsf{info}_{\tau_{\mathrm{new}}}\}$, where τ_{new} is the next time epoch. We remark that $\mathsf{info}_{\tau_{\mathrm{new}}}$ should be authenticated by the GM and should contain information about users who are active during epoch τ_{new}.

$\mathsf{Enc}(\tau, w, \mathsf{id}, \mathsf{cert_{id}})$ Given a time epoch τ, message w, a receiver's identifier id and its group membership certificate $\mathsf{cert_{id}}$, this probabilistic algorithm outputs a ciphertext ψ.

$\mathsf{Verify}(\tau, \psi)$ This algorithm, run by any verifier, returns 1 or 0, indicating the validity or invalidity of the ciphertext ψ.

$\mathsf{Dec}(\mathsf{sk}_{\mathsf{id}}, \tau, \psi)$ This deterministic algorithm is run by receiver id, who uses its secret key $\mathsf{sk}_{\mathsf{id}}$ to decrypt ciphertext ψ and obtain $w' \in \mathcal{W}$.

$\mathsf{Open}(\mathsf{sk}_{\mathsf{OA}}, \tau, \psi)$ This deterministic algorithm is run by the OA who possesses the key $\mathsf{sk}_{\mathsf{OA}}$. It returns a user identifier $\mathsf{id}' \in \mathcal{ID} \cup \{\bot\}$.

We also introduce the following algorithm, which will be used only in the security experiments.

$\mathsf{IsActive}(\tau, \mathsf{id})$ This algorithm returns 1 if user id is active at time epoch τ, i.e., id has been enrolled and has not been revoked, and 0 otherwise.

Remark 1. To simplify the presentation, we assume that, given pp and a time epoch τ, the descriptions of the corresponding group information info_τ, the corresponding filtering policy F_τ and the corresponding tracing policy P_τ are completely determined.

We require that a GEOT scheme must satisfy correctness, privacy (which subsumes message secrecy and receiver anonymity) and unforgeability.

CORRECTNESS. Roughly speaking, correctness requires that at any time epoch, an honestly-generated ciphertext from an active user should be successfully verified, decrypted, and opened relatively to the system policies at that epoch. More formally, for any ciphertext $\psi \leftarrow \mathsf{Enc}(\tau, w, \mathsf{id}, \mathsf{cert}_{\mathsf{id}})$, where id is active at epoch τ and $F_\tau(w) = 1$, the following conditions must hold: (i) ψ is deemed valid by the verification algorithm; (ii) decrypting ψ using secret key $\mathsf{sk}_{\mathsf{id}}$ yields w; (iii) the opening algorithm returns $\bot$ if $P_\tau(\mathsf{id}, w) = 1$, i.e., ψ is non-traceable; and (iv) the opening algorithm returns id if $P_\tau(\mathsf{id}, w) = 0$, i.e., ψ is traceable. These requirements are formally modeled in experiment $\mathbf{Exp}_{\mathcal{A}}^{\mathsf{correct}}(1^\lambda)$, which involves the following oracles.

$\mathsf{AddU}(\mathsf{sk}_{\mathsf{GM}})$ This oracle allows the adversary to add an honest user to the group at the current epoch. Upon request, it simulates an honest execution of the interactive protocol $\langle \mathsf{Join}(\mathsf{info}), \mathsf{Issue}(\mathsf{sk}_{\mathsf{GM}}, \mathsf{info}, \mathbf{reg}) \rangle$ (without the adversary's involvement). It maintains an honest-user list HUL and adds the obtained user identifier id to HUL.

$\mathsf{GUp}(\cdot)$ This oracle allows the adversary to update the group. When invoked with a set $\mathcal{S}$, it executes algorithm $\mathsf{GUpdate}(\mathsf{sk}_{\mathsf{GM}}, \mathcal{S}, \mathsf{info}, \mathbf{reg})$.

Definition 1. *Let* $\mathbf{Adv}_{\mathcal{A}}^{\mathsf{correct}}(1^\lambda) = \Pr[\mathbf{Exp}_{\mathcal{A}}^{\mathsf{correct}}(1^\lambda) = 1]$ *be the advantage of adversary* $\mathcal{A}$ *in experiment* $\mathbf{Exp}_{\mathcal{A}}^{\mathsf{correct}}(1^\lambda)$. *A* GEOT *scheme is said to be correct if the advantage of any PPT adversary* $\mathcal{A}$ *is negligible in* λ.

Experiment $\mathbf{Exp}_{\mathcal{A}}^{\mathsf{correct}}(1^\lambda)$
    $(\mathsf{pp}, \mathsf{sk}_{\mathsf{GM}}, \mathsf{sk}_{\mathsf{OA}}) \leftarrow \mathsf{Setup}(1^\lambda)$; $\mathsf{HUL} \leftarrow \emptyset$.
    $(\tau, w, \mathsf{id}) \leftarrow \mathcal{A}^{\mathsf{AddU}, \mathsf{GUp}}(\mathsf{pp})$.
    If $\mathsf{id} \notin \mathsf{HUL}$ or $\mathsf{IsActive}(\tau, \mathsf{id}) = 0$ or $F_\tau(w) = 0$, return 0.
    $\psi \leftarrow \mathsf{Enc}(\tau, w, \mathsf{id}, \mathsf{cert}_{\mathsf{id}})$. If $\mathsf{Verify}(\tau, \psi) = 0$, return 1.

$w' \leftarrow \mathsf{Dec}(\mathsf{sk}_{\mathsf{id}}, \tau, \psi)$. If $w' \neq w$, return 1.

$\mathsf{id}' \leftarrow \mathsf{Open}(\mathsf{sk}_{\mathsf{OA}}, \tau, \psi)$.

If $(P_\tau(\mathsf{id}, w) = 1$ and $\mathsf{id}' \neq \bot)$ or $(P_\tau(\mathsf{id}, w) = 0$ and $\mathsf{id}' \neq \mathsf{id})$, return 1.

Return 0.

We remark that the adversary $\mathcal{A}$ wins (i.e., the experiment returns 1) whenever it finds an epoch τ, a message w, an active, honest identifier id so that a ciphertext encrypting w at epoch τ and from user id either: (i) fails to verify, (ii) is decrypted to some other $w' \neq w$, or (iii) has an opening inconsistent with what P_τ indicates.

2.2 Privacy of GEOT

A private GEOT scheme should satisfy message secrecy, type-1-anonymity and type-2-anonymity. These notions are formalized via the following oracles.

USER() This oracle enrolls an honest user into the group. It simulates the Join algorithm and interacts with an adversary playing the role of the GM. If the interaction ends successfully, the oracle adds id to the list HUL.

RevealU($\cdot$) On input an identifier id, this oracle aborts if $\mathsf{id} \notin \mathsf{HUL}$. Otherwise, it returns the secret key $\mathsf{sk}_{\mathsf{id}}$ and adds id to a corrupted user list CUL.

DEC($\mathsf{sk}_{\mathsf{id}}, \cdot$) This oracle permits the adversary to query the decryption of a ciphertext using the secret key of user id. When queried with a pair (τ, ψ), the oracle computes $w' \leftarrow \mathsf{Dec}(\mathsf{sk}_{\mathsf{id}}, \tau, \psi)$ and returns w' to the adversary. We write $\mathsf{DEC}^{\neg(\tau, \psi)}(\mathsf{sk}_{\mathsf{id}}, \cdot)$ if the pair (τ, ψ) is prohibited from this oracle query.

OPEN($\cdot$) This oracle allows the adversary to learn the recipient of a ciphertext. When (τ, ψ) is queried, it computes $\mathsf{id}' \leftarrow \mathsf{Open}(\mathsf{sk}_{\mathsf{OA}}, \tau, \psi)$ and returns id' to the adversary. We also write $\mathsf{OPEN}^{\neg(\tau, \psi)}(\cdot)$ if the pair (τ, ψ) is precluded.

Message Secrecy. This notion protects the receiver from an adversary who tries to learn information about the underlying message. It captures the inability of an adversary to tell whether a ciphertext encrypts message w_0 or w_1, in the IND-CCA2 sense. The adversary is allowed to corrupt the GM and the OA. It can also adaptively query the decryption oracle. The formal definition is given below.

Definition 2. *A* GEOT *scheme is said to satisfy message secrecy if for any PPT adversary $\mathcal{A}$, we have* $\mathbf{Adv}_{\mathcal{A}}^{\mathsf{sec}}(1^\lambda) = |\Pr[\mathbf{Exp}_{\mathcal{A}}^{\mathsf{sec}}(1^\lambda) = 1] - \frac{1}{2}| \leq \mathsf{negl}(\lambda)$.

Experiment $\mathbf{Exp}_{\mathcal{A}}^{\mathsf{sec}}(1^\lambda)$

$(\mathsf{pp}, \mathsf{sk}_{\mathsf{GM}}, \mathsf{sk}_{\mathsf{OA}}) \leftarrow \mathsf{Setup}(1^\lambda)$; $\mathsf{HUL} \leftarrow \emptyset, \mathsf{CUL} \leftarrow \emptyset$.

$(\tau, w_0, w_1, \mathsf{id}, \mathsf{aux}) \leftarrow \mathcal{A}^{\mathsf{USER},\mathsf{RevealU},\mathsf{DEC}}(\mathsf{pp}, \mathsf{sk}_{\mathsf{GM}}, \mathsf{sk}_{\mathsf{OA}})$.

If $(\mathsf{id} \notin \mathsf{HUL} \setminus \mathsf{CUL})$ or $(\mathsf{IsActive}(\tau, \mathsf{id}) = 0)$, return 0.

If $(F_\tau(w_0) = 0)$ or $(F_\tau(w_1) = 0)$ or $(P_\tau(\mathsf{id}, w_0) \neq P_\tau(\mathsf{id}, w_1))$, return 0.

$b \xleftarrow{\$} \{0, 1\}$.

$\psi \leftarrow \mathsf{Enc}(\tau, w_b, \mathsf{id}, \mathsf{cert}_{\mathsf{id}})$.

$b' \leftarrow \mathcal{A}^{\mathsf{USER},\mathsf{RevealU},\mathsf{DEC}^{\neg(\tau, \psi)}(\mathsf{sk}_{\mathsf{id}}, \cdot)}(\mathsf{aux}, \psi)$. If $b' = b$, return 1. Else return 0.

In experiment $\mathbf{Exp}_{\mathcal{A}}^{\mathsf{sec}}(1^\lambda)$, the adversary $\mathcal{A}$ fully controls both the GM and the OA. The adversary interacts with honest users via the oracle USER and is allowed to learn secret keys of all but one honest user via the oracle RevealU. It is also allowed to make decryption queries w.r.t. decryption key $\mathsf{sk}_{\mathsf{id}'}$, for any $\mathsf{id}' \in$ HUL$\backslash$CUL. At the end of the first stage, $\mathcal{A}$ outputs a tuple $(\tau, w_0, w_1, \mathsf{id})$ satisfying the conditions specified in the experiment. Afterwards, a challenge ciphertext ψ is computed based on a random bit b and returned to $\mathcal{A}$. Upon receiving ψ, $\mathcal{A}$ continues to have access to the decryption oracle $\mathsf{DEC}(\mathsf{sk}_{\mathsf{id}}, \cdot)$, with the exception that it cannot trivially ask to decrypt ψ w.r.t. τ. Finally, $\mathcal{A}$ outputs a guess bit b' and the experiment returns 1 iff $b' = b$.

We note that the tuple $(\tau, w_0, w_1, \mathsf{id})$ outputted by $\mathcal{A}$ at the end of the first stage must satisfy $F_\tau(w_0) = F_\tau(w_1) = 1$, in order to ensure that the challenge ciphertext ψ passes the filter. We also stress that $P_\tau(\mathsf{id}, w_0) = P_\tau(\mathsf{id}, w_1)$ is a compulsory condition. Otherwise, $\mathcal{A}$ can open ψ using $\mathsf{sk}_{\mathsf{OA}}$ to tell whether ψ is traceable or non-traceable and thus can easily determine which message is encrypted. This is a notable difference compared to the formulation of message secrecy in FDGE [50], for which all the valid ciphertexts are traceable.

Type-1-Anonymity. This notion is orthogonal to message secrecy, and protects the identity of the intended receiver of a ciphertext from being extracted by a malicious adversary. It demands that the adversary $\mathcal{A}$ cannot distinguish whether a ciphertext is intended for user id_0 or user id_1 even if $\mathcal{A}$ can fully corrupt the GM. Although corruption of the OA is not permitted, $\mathcal{A}$ is allowed to adaptively query the OPEN oracle. We model this requirement in experiment $\mathbf{Exp}_{\mathcal{A}}^{\mathsf{anony}}(1^\lambda)$ and give a formal definition below.

Definition 3. *Let* $\mathbf{Adv}_{\mathcal{A}}^{\mathsf{anony}}(1^\lambda) = |\Pr[\mathbf{Exp}_{\mathcal{A}}^{\mathsf{anony}}(1^\lambda) = 1] - \frac{1}{2}|$. *A* GEOT *scheme is called type-1-anonymous if for any PPT* $\mathcal{A}$, *we have* $\mathbf{Adv}_{\mathcal{A}}^{\mathsf{anony}}(1^\lambda) \leq \mathsf{negl}(\lambda)$.

> Experiment $\mathbf{Exp}_{\mathcal{A}}^{\mathsf{anony}}(1^\lambda)$
> $(\mathsf{pp}, \mathsf{sk}_{\mathsf{GM}}, \mathsf{sk}_{\mathsf{OA}}) \leftarrow \mathsf{Setup}(1^\lambda)$; $\mathsf{HUL} \leftarrow \emptyset, \mathsf{CUL} \leftarrow \emptyset$.
> $(\tau, w, \mathsf{id}_0, \mathsf{id}_1, \mathsf{aux}) \leftarrow \mathcal{A}^{\mathsf{USER}, \mathsf{RevealU}, \mathsf{OPEN}}(\mathsf{pp}, \mathsf{sk}_{\mathsf{GM}})$.
> If $\mathsf{IsActive}(\tau, \mathsf{id}_0) = 0$ or $\mathsf{IsActive}(\tau, \mathsf{id}_1) = 0$, return 0.
> If $\mathsf{id}_0 \notin \mathsf{HUL} \setminus \mathsf{CUL}$ or $\mathsf{id}_1 \notin \mathsf{HUL} \setminus \mathsf{CUL}$, return 0.
> If $F_\tau(w) = 0$, return 0.
> $b \xleftarrow{\$} \{0, 1\}$.
> $\psi \leftarrow \mathsf{Enc}(\tau, w, \mathsf{id}_b, \mathsf{cert}_{\mathsf{id}_b})$.
> $b' \leftarrow \mathcal{A}^{\mathsf{USER}, \mathsf{RevealU}, \mathsf{OPEN}^{\neg(\tau, \psi)}, \mathsf{DEC}^{\neg(\tau, \psi)}(\mathsf{sk}_{\mathsf{id}_0}, \cdot), \mathsf{DEC}^{\neg(\tau, \psi)}(\mathsf{sk}_{\mathsf{id}_1}, \cdot)}(\mathsf{aux}, \psi)$.
> If $b' = b$, return 1. Else return 0.

In experiment $\mathbf{Exp}_{\mathcal{A}}^{\mathsf{anony}}(1^\lambda)$, the adversary $\mathcal{A}$ fully corrupts the GM and interacts with honest users and learns their secret keys via the oracles USER and RevealU, respectively. The OA remains honest, yet $\mathcal{A}$ is given CCA2 access to the opening oracle. Similar to the experiment $\mathbf{Exp}_{\mathcal{A}}^{\mathsf{sec}}(1^\lambda)$, $\mathcal{A}$ outputs a challenge tuple satisfying certain conditions and receives back a challenge ciphertext ψ based on a random bit b. The adversary is asked to determine which one of the challenge users is the intended receiver of ψ.

We remark that the adversary is allowed to choose the challenge tuple such that $P_\tau(\mathsf{id}_0, w) \neq P_\tau(\mathsf{id}_1, w)$. Thus, the definition of type-1-anonymity implies the incapability of $\mathcal{A}$ to tell apart ciphertexts that are traceable and those that are non-traceable (similar to the branch-hiding property in BiAS [38]).

It is also worth mentioning that the two challenge users must not be corrupted by $\mathcal{A}$. In fact, by the correctness of GEOT, algorithm $\mathsf{Dec}(\mathsf{sk}_{\mathsf{id}_d}, \cdot)$ can recover the underlying message w if $d = b$. Therefore, corrupting any of the challenge users would enable $\mathcal{A}$ to trivially break anonymity.

Type-2-Anonymity. This is a strengthened anonymity notion that GEOT can achieve in the non-traceable case. Here, we further allow the adversary to fully corrupt the OA if $P(\mathsf{id}_0, w) = P(\mathsf{id}_1, w) = 1$, i.e., the to-be-computed challenge ciphertext is always non-traceable. This notion requires the infeasibility of $\mathcal{A}$ possessing the opening key $\mathsf{sk}_{\mathsf{OA}}$ to learn any information about the ciphertext receiver. Type-2-anonymity is formally defined as follows.

Definition 4. *Define* $\mathbf{Adv}_{\mathcal{A}}^{\mathsf{anony-ntr}}(1^\lambda) = |\Pr[\mathbf{Exp}_{\mathcal{A}}^{\mathsf{anony-ntr}}(1^\lambda) = 1] - \frac{1}{2}|$. *A* GEOT *scheme is called type-2-anonymous if* $\mathbf{Adv}_{\mathcal{A}}^{\mathsf{anony-ntr}}(1^\lambda)$ *is negligible in* λ *for any PPT adversary* $\mathcal{A}$.

> Experiment $\mathbf{Exp}_{\mathcal{A}}^{\mathsf{anony-ntr}}(1^\lambda)$
> $(\mathsf{pp}, \mathsf{sk}_{\mathsf{GM}}, \mathsf{sk}_{\mathsf{OA}}) \leftarrow \mathsf{Setup}(1^\lambda); \mathsf{HUL} \leftarrow \emptyset, \mathsf{CUL} \leftarrow \emptyset.$
> $(\tau, w, \mathsf{id}_0, \mathsf{id}_1, \mathsf{aux}) \leftarrow \mathcal{A}^{\mathsf{USER, RevealU}}(\mathsf{pp}, \mathsf{sk}_{\mathsf{GM}}, \mathsf{sk}_{\mathsf{OA}}).$
> If $\mathsf{IsActive}(\tau, \mathsf{id}_0) = 0$ or $\mathsf{IsActive}(\tau, \mathsf{id}_1) = 0$, return 0.
> If $\mathsf{id}_0 \notin \mathsf{HUL} \setminus \mathsf{CUL}$ or $\mathsf{id}_1 \notin \mathsf{HUL} \setminus \mathsf{CUL}$, return 0.
> If $F_\tau(w) = 0$, return 0. If $\neg(P_\tau(\mathsf{id}_0, w) = P_\tau(\mathsf{id}_1, w) = 1)$, return 0.
> $b \xleftarrow{\$} \{0, 1\}.$
> $\psi \leftarrow \mathsf{Enc}(\tau, w, \mathsf{id}_b, \mathsf{cert}_{\mathsf{id}_b}).$
> $b' \leftarrow \mathcal{A}^{\mathsf{USER, RevealU}, \mathsf{DEC}^{\neg(\tau, \psi)}(\mathsf{sk}_{\mathsf{id}_0}, \cdot), \mathsf{DEC}^{\neg(\tau, \psi)}(\mathsf{sk}_{\mathsf{id}_1}, \cdot)}(\mathsf{aux}, \psi).$
> If $b' = b$, return 1. Else return 0.

2.3   Unforgeability of GEOT

Unforgeability of a GEOT system aims to prevent the system from falsely accepting inappropriate ciphertexts. It captures the infeasibility of an adversary to generate a verifiable pair (τ, ψ) such that either (i) the recipient id of ψ is not active at time epoch τ; or (ii) the encrypted message w does not satisfy the filtering policy F_τ; or (iii) the outcome of the opening algorithm is not consistent with the tracing policy P_τ, e.g., it points to a receiver id despite $P_\tau(\mathsf{id}, w) = 1$ (i.e., non-traceable case), or it declares failure despite $P_\tau(\mathsf{id}, w) = 0$ (i.e., traceable case). Formalizing this notion turns out to be a non-trivial task.

Recall that in the related contexts of traditional group signatures [9, 10, 13] and group encryption [33, 50], a violation of traceability/non-frameability can easily be detected, because the result of the opening algorithm in those systems can help determine if an adversarially produced signature/ciphertext corresponds to an honest or corrupted user. Here, in contrast, the opening algorithm of GEOT does not provide sufficient information for deciding if a ciphertext (τ, ψ) forms a forgery. If Open returns $\perp$, it is not guaranteed that the ciphertext in question is supposed to be non-traceable. Even when Open returns an identifier id, we also lack information about w (due to message secrecy) to be certain that $P_\tau(\text{id}, w) = 0$ and that user id is not framed.

To overcome the aforementioned definitional challenge, we adapt the approach of [38], by employing two auxiliary algorithms SimSetup and Extract, which allow us to extract meaningful information (such as identify id$'$ and message w') from an accepted ciphertext and to determine if a forgery has occurred.

SimSetup(1^λ) Given the security parameter 1^λ, this algorithm generates simulated (pp, sk$_{\text{GM}}$, sk$_{\text{OA}}$) together with an extraction trapdoor τ_{ext}.

Extract($\tau_{\text{ext}}, (\text{pp}, \tau, \psi)$) Given the extraction trapdoor τ_{ext}, a valid ciphertext ψ at time τ, this extraction algorithm returns a pair $(\text{id}', w') \in \mathcal{ID} \times \mathcal{W}$.

It is natural to require the indistinguishability of the outputs of Setup and SimSetup. In addition, to capture the fact that Extract outputs meaningful information, we require that the extraction result does not contradict the opening result. Formally, we define extractability as follows.

Definition 5. *A* GEOT *scheme with algorithms* (SimSetup, Extract) *is said to be extractable if the following two conditions are conformed.*

- *To any PPT adversary $\mathcal{A}$, the outputs* (pp, sk$_{\text{GM}}$, sk$_{\text{OA}}$) *from* SimSetup *and* Setup *are indistinguishable.*
- *For any PPT adversary $\mathcal{A}$ involved in experiment* $\mathbf{Exp}_{\mathcal{A}}^{\text{extract}}(1^\lambda)$, *its advantage* $\mathbf{Adv}_{\mathcal{A}}^{\text{extract}}(1^\lambda) = \Pr[\mathbf{Exp}_{\mathcal{A}}^{\text{extract}}(1^\lambda) = 1]$ *is negligible in λ.*

> Experiment $\mathbf{Exp}_{\mathcal{A}}^{\text{extract}}(1^\lambda)$
> (pp, sk$_{\text{GM}}$, sk$_{\text{OA}}$; τ_{ext}) $\leftarrow$ SimSetup(1^λ).
> $(\tau, \psi) \leftarrow \mathcal{A}(\text{pp}, \text{sk}_{\text{GM}}, \text{sk}_{\text{OA}})$.
> If info$_\tau = \perp$ or Verify$(\tau, \psi) = 0$, return 0.
> $(\text{id}', w') \leftarrow$ Extract($\tau_{\text{ext}}, \text{pp}, \tau, \psi$).
> $F_\tau(w') = 0$, return 1.
> id$^* \leftarrow$ Open(sk$_{\text{OA}}, \tau, \psi$).
> If $(P_\tau(\text{id}', w') = 1) \wedge (\text{id}^* \neq \perp)$, return 1.
> If $(P_\tau(\text{id}', w') = 0) \wedge (\text{id}^* \neq \text{id}')$, return 1.
> Else return 0.

Let us now define unforgeability of a GEOT system. We consider experiment $\mathbf{Exp}_{\mathcal{A}}^{\text{unforge}}(1^\lambda)$, which involves the following oracle.

REG() This oracle allows the adversary to introduce users to the group at the current epoch. On behalf of the GM, the oracle acts as Issue to interact with the adversary who may or may not follow the program of Join.

Definition 6. *Let* $\mathbf{Adv}_{\mathcal{A}}^{\text{unforge}}(1^\lambda) = \Pr[\mathbf{Exp}_{\mathcal{A}}^{\text{unforge}}(1^\lambda) = 1]$ *be the advantage of an adversary $\mathcal{A}$ against unforgeability. A* GEOT *scheme is unforgeable if it is extractable and the advantage of any PPT adversary $\mathcal{A}$ in experiment* $\mathbf{Exp}_{\mathcal{A}}^{\text{unforge}}(1^\lambda)$ *is negligible in λ.*

Experiment $\mathbf{Exp}_{\mathcal{A}}^{\text{unforge}}(1^\lambda)$
  $(\mathsf{pp}, \mathsf{sk}_{\mathsf{GM}}, \mathsf{sk}_{\mathsf{OA}}, \tau_{\text{ext}}) \leftarrow \mathsf{SimSetup}(1^\lambda)$.
  $(\tau, \psi) \leftarrow \mathcal{A}^{\mathsf{REG}, \mathsf{GUp}}(\mathsf{pp}, \mathsf{sk}_{\mathsf{OA}})$.
  If $\mathsf{info}_\tau = \perp$ or $\mathsf{Verify}(\tau, \psi) = 0$, return 0.
  $(\mathsf{id}', w') \leftarrow \mathsf{Extract}(\tau_{\text{ext}}, \mathsf{pp}, \tau, \psi)$.
  $\mathsf{id}^* \leftarrow \mathsf{Open}(\mathsf{sk}_{\mathsf{OA}}, \tau, \psi)$.
  If $(\mathsf{IsActive}(\tau, \mathsf{id}') = 0)$ or $F_\tau(w') = 0$, return 1.
  If $\big(P_\tau(\mathsf{id}', w') = 1\big) \wedge (\mathsf{id}^* \neq \perp)$, return 1.
  If $\big(P_\tau(\mathsf{id}', w') = 0\big) \wedge (\mathsf{id}^* \neq \mathsf{id}')$, return 1.
  Return 0.

In experiment $\mathbf{Exp}_{\mathcal{A}}^{\text{unforge}}(1^\lambda)$, adversary $\mathcal{A}$ is given simulated pp and $\mathsf{sk}_{\mathsf{OA}}$, and cannot tell if it is in an extractable mode or a real mode due to extractability. Via the oracles REG and GUp, $\mathcal{A}$ can enroll malicious users into the group and remove some users from the group, respectively. At the end of the experiment, $\mathcal{A}$ outputs (τ, ψ). The experiment then extracts (id', w') from the ciphertext using τ_{ext}. If either one of the aforementioned three cases occurs, this experiment returns 1.

3   A Generic Construction of **GEOT**

This section presents a generic construction of GEOT for arbitrary filtering and tracing policies. The construction satisfies the rigorous requirements in Sect. 2. We first provide a high-level overview of the construction in Sect. 3.1. The detailed description is then presented in Sect. 3.2 and the scheme analyses are given in Sect. 3.3. Our construction can be viewed as a feasibility result for designing GEOT based on well-studied computational assumptions and in a modular manner. In particular, it can be instantiated in the standard model from pairings and lattices, via the techniques for obtaining NIZKs for NP by Groth-Ostrovsky-Sahai [28] and by Peikert-Shiehian [57], respectively. It can also be efficiently realized in the random oracle model based on the lattice-based techniques from [14, 31, 62]. The code-based instantiation we will present in Sect. 4 is inspired by but slightly departs from this generic construction.

3.1   Technical Overview

The construction employs the following cryptographic building blocks.

- A signature scheme $\mathcal{SIG} = (\mathsf{S.Kg}, \mathsf{S.Sign}, \mathsf{S.Ver})$ that is existentially unforgeable under chosen message attacks (EUF-CMA);
- Two public-key encryption schemes $\mathcal{E}_{\mathcal{R}} = (\mathsf{E_R.Kg}, \mathsf{E_R.Enc}, \mathsf{E_R.Dec})$ and $\mathcal{E}_{\mathcal{OA}} = (\mathsf{E_{OA}.Kg}, \mathsf{E_{OA}.Enc}, \mathsf{E_{OA}.Dec})$, that satisfy IND-CCA2 security. We additionally require IK-CCA2 security (i.e., key privacy) for $\mathcal{E}_{\mathcal{R}}$;
- A dual-mode $\mathcal{NIZK}$ argument system $\mathcal{NIZK} = (\mathsf{ZK.Setup}, \mathsf{ZK.ExtSetup}, \mathsf{ZK.Prove}, \mathsf{ZK.Ver}, \mathsf{ZK.Sim}, \mathsf{ZK.Extr})$ for the NP-relation $\mathcal{R}$ defined below.

The major ideas underlying the construction are as follows. Each potential user of the system is equipped with a decryption-encryption key pair $(\mathsf{sk_{id}}, ek = \mathsf{id})$ for $\mathcal{E_R}$. The GM possesses a signing-verification key pair $(\mathsf{sk_{GM}}, \mathsf{vk_{GM}})$ for $\mathcal{SIG}$, which will be used for certifying users' public keys $ek = \mathsf{id}$. The OA, on the other hand, owns a decryption-encryption key pair $(\mathsf{sk_{OA}}, \mathsf{ek_{OA}})$ for $\mathcal{E_{OA}}$. To send a plaintext w to user id at time τ, the sender first makes sure that: (i) w is allowed under the filtering policy F_τ; (ii) id has been certified by the GM, and is not in the revocation list $\mathcal{S}$. Then, the sender generates two sub-ciphertexts:

- Ciphertext $\mathbf{c_R}$ that encrypts w under encryption key id;
- Ciphertext $\mathbf{c_{OA}}$ that encrypts the value $(1 - P_\tau(\mathsf{id}, w)) \cdot \mathsf{id}$ under the encryption key $\mathsf{ek_{OA}}$, where $P_\tau(\cdot, \cdot)$ is the tracing predicate at time τ.

Then the sender generates a NIZK argument for the relation $\mathcal{R}$, as defined in (1), to prove in ZK that all the steps have been done correctly.

$$\mathcal{R} := \Big\{ \ \big(\ x = (\mathsf{vk_{GM}}, \mathsf{ek_{OA}}, \mathbf{c_R}, \mathbf{c_{OA}}, \mathcal{S}, F_\tau, P_\tau), \xi = (w, \mathsf{id} = ek, \mathsf{cert_{id}}, s_R, s_{OA})\big) : $$
$$(\mathsf{S.Ver}(\mathsf{vk_{GM}}, \mathsf{id}, \mathsf{cert_{id}}) = 1) \wedge \big(\mathsf{id} \notin \mathcal{S}\big) \wedge \big(F_\tau(w) = 1\big)$$
$$\wedge \ \Big(\mathbf{c_R} = \mathsf{E_R.Enc}(ek, w, s_R)\Big)$$
$$\wedge \ \Big(\mathbf{c_{OA}} = \mathsf{E_{OA}.Enc}(\mathsf{ek_{OA}}, (1 - P_\tau(\mathsf{id}, w)) \cdot \mathsf{id}, s_{OA})\Big) \ \Big\}. \tag{1}$$

The ciphertext ψ then is set as the triple $(\mathbf{c_R}, \mathbf{c_{OA}}, \pi)$. Verification of ψ consists of verifying π. The receiver id can recover w by decrypting $\mathbf{c_R}$. Meanwhile, depending on the predicate value $P_\tau(\mathsf{id}, w)$, the OA can learn from $\mathbf{c_{OA}}$ either id (traceable case) or $\mathbf{0}$ (non-traceable case).

At a high level, the correctness of the obtained GEOT scheme is guaranteed by the correctness/completeness of the $\mathcal{SIG}$, $\mathcal{E_R}$, $\mathcal{E_{OA}}$ and $\mathcal{NIZK}$. The security of the scheme also relies on the security properties of these building blocks. In particular, we require key privacy for $\mathcal{E_R}$ (but not for $\mathcal{E_{OA}}$) to ensure that the ciphertext $\mathbf{c_R}$ does not leak any information about the receiver's public key.

3.2 Description of Our Generic Construction

Let $\lambda \in \mathbb{N}$ be a security parameter. Our generic construction of a GEOT system associated with $(\mathcal{T}, \mathcal{ID}, \mathcal{W}, \mathcal{F}, \mathcal{P})$ works as follows.

$\mathsf{Setup}(1^\lambda)$ This algorithm performs the following steps:
1. Run $\mathsf{S.Kg}(1^\lambda)$ to obtain a signing-verification key-pair $(\mathsf{sk_{GM}}, \mathsf{vk_{GM}})$.
2. Run $\mathsf{E_{OA}.Kg}(1^\lambda)$ to obtain a decryption-encryption key pair $(\mathsf{sk_{OA}}, \mathsf{ek_{OA}})$.
3. Run $\mathsf{ZK.Setup}(1^\lambda)$ to obtain a common reference string crs (and a simulation trapdoor τ_{sim} - which is discarded) for the NIZK system.

Return $\mathsf{pp} := (\mathsf{crs}, \mathsf{vk_{GM}}, \mathsf{ek_{OA}})$, as well as $\mathsf{sk_{GM}}$ and $\mathsf{sk_{OA}}$. The algorithm also initializes $\mathbf{reg} := \emptyset$ and $\mathsf{info} := \emptyset$.

$\langle\mathsf{Join}(\mathsf{info}), \mathsf{Issue}(\mathsf{sk_{GM}}, \mathsf{info}, \mathbf{reg})\rangle$ A user who would like to join GEOT system interacts with the GM as follows.

1. The user runs $E_R.Kg(1^\lambda)$ to obtain a decryption-encryption key pair (sk, ek). Define id $:= ek$ and send id to the GM.
2. The GM aborts if id has already been registered. Otherwise, it certifies id using sk_{GM} as $cert_{id} \leftarrow S.Sign(sk_{GM}, id)$ and sends $cert_{id}$ to the user.
3. Upon receiving $cert_{id}$, the user aborts if $S.Ver(vk_{GM}, id, cert_{id}) = 0$. Otherwise, it stores $sk_{id} := (sk, id, cert_{id})$.
4. The GM appends the registration information $(id, cert_{id})$ to the table **reg**.

$GUpdate(sk_{GM}, \mathcal{S}, info, \mathbf{reg})$ The GM updates the group information and advances the time period as follows.

1. Certify the set $\mathcal{S} = \{id_i\}_i$ of to-be-revoked users, together with the current and new time periods as $cert \leftarrow S.Sign(sk_{GM}, (\mathcal{S}, \tau_{current}, \tau_{new}))$.
2. Let $info_{\tau_{new}} = (\tau_{new}, \mathcal{S}, cert)$ and update the information table with $info := info \cup \{info_{\tau_{new}}\}$.

$Enc(\tau, w, id, cert_{id})$ This algorithm performs the following steps.

1. If $F_\tau(w) = 0$, i.e., message w does not satisfy the filtering policy F_τ, then return $\psi = \bot$.
2. If the receiver id is currently revoked, i.e., id $\in \mathcal{S}$, where $\mathcal{S}$ is fetched from $info_\tau$, then return $\psi = \bot$.
3. Encrypt the plaintext w under the receiver's public key $ek =$ id, as $\mathbf{c}_R = E_R.Enc(ek, w, s_R)$, where s_R is the encryption randomness.
4. Encrypt $(1 - P_\tau(id, w)) \cdot$ id and under the OA's public key ek_{OA} as $\mathbf{c}_{OA} = E_{OA}.Enc(ek_{OA}, (1 - P_\tau(id, w)) \cdot id, s_{OA})$, where s_{OA} is the encryption randomness.
5. Generate a non-interactive zero-knowledge argument π to prove knowledge of witness $\xi = (w, id, cert_{id}, s_R, s_{OA})$ such that:
   - id was properly certified by the GM via $cert_{id}$;
   - id is not currently revoked, i.e., id $\notin \mathcal{S}$;
   - w satisfies the filtering policy, i.e., $F_\tau(w) = 1$;
   - $\mathbf{c}_R$ and $\mathbf{c}_{OA}$ are well-formed ciphertexts of w and $(1 - P_\tau(id, w)) \cdot$ id, as described above.

   Let $x = (vk_{GM}, ek_{OA}, \mathbf{c}_R, \mathbf{c}_{OA}, \mathcal{S}, F_\tau, P_\tau)$, then we have $(x, \xi) \in \mathcal{R}$, where $\mathcal{R}$ is as defined in (1). Then, the desired NIZK argument π is generated as $\pi \leftarrow ZK.Prove(crs, x, \xi)$.
6. Let $\psi := (\mathbf{c}_R, \mathbf{c}_{OA}, \pi)$ and return ψ.

$Verify(\tau, \psi)$ This algorithm essentially consists of verifying π. It parses $\psi = (\mathbf{c}_R, \mathbf{c}_{OA}, \pi)$, then return $b' \leftarrow ZK.Ver(crs, (vk_{GM}, ek_{OA}, \mathbf{c}_R, \mathbf{c}_{OA}, \mathcal{S}, F_\tau, P_\tau), \pi)$.

$Dec(sk_{id}, \tau, \psi)$ This algorithm essentially consists of decrypting the ciphertext component $\mathbf{c}_R$. It parses $\psi = (\mathbf{c}_R, \mathbf{c}_{OA}, \pi)$, then return $w' \leftarrow E_R.Dec(sk_{id}, \mathbf{c}_R)$.

$Open(sk_{OA}, \tau, \psi)$ This algorithm basically consists of decrypting $\mathbf{c}_{OA}$. It parses $\psi = (\mathbf{c}_R, \mathbf{c}_{OA}, \pi)$, then compute $\mathbf{d} \leftarrow E_{OA}.Dec(sk_{OA}, \mathbf{c}_{OA})$. If $\mathbf{d} = \mathbf{0}$ or $\mathbf{d} \notin \mathcal{ID}$, then return $\bot$. Otherwise, return $id' = \mathbf{d}$.

AUXILIARY ALGORITHMS. We now describe the two supplementary algorithms SimSetup and Extract that are critical for analyzing the unforgeability of the proposed GEOT system.

$\mathsf{SimSetup}(1^\lambda)$ This algorithm is almost the same as the real Setup described above. The only difference is that, instead of running $\mathsf{ZK.Setup}(1^\lambda)$, it runs $\mathsf{ZK.ExtSetup}(1^\lambda)$ to obtain a crs associated with an extraction trapdoor τ_{ext}.

$\mathsf{Extract}\big(\tau_{\mathsf{ext}}, (\mathsf{pp}, \tau, \psi)\big)$ Given the extraction trapdoor τ_{ext} and a valid ciphertext $\psi = (\mathbf{c}_{\mathsf{R}}, \mathbf{c}_{\mathsf{OA}}, \pi)$ at time τ, define $x = (\mathsf{vk}_{\mathsf{GM}}, \mathsf{ek}_{\mathsf{OA}}, \mathbf{c}_{\mathsf{R}}, \mathbf{c}_{\mathsf{OA}}, \mathcal{S}, F_\tau, P_\tau)$. This algorithm computes $\xi' \leftarrow \mathsf{ZK.Extract}(\mathsf{crs}, \tau_{\mathsf{ext}}, x, \pi)$ of the form $\xi' = (w', \mathsf{id}', \mathsf{cert}'_{\mathsf{id}}, s'_{\mathsf{R}}, s'_{\mathsf{OA}})$. It then returns (id', w').

3.3 Correctness and Security Analyses

CORRECTNESS. If the employed building blocks $\mathcal{SIG}, \mathcal{E_R}, \mathcal{E_{OA}}$ are correct and $\mathcal{NIZK}$ is complete, then the proposed GEOT scheme satisfies correctness as defined in Definition 1.

First of all, during the $\langle\mathsf{Join}(\mathsf{info}), \mathsf{Issue}(\mathsf{sk}_{\mathsf{GM}}, \mathsf{info}, \mathbf{reg})\rangle$ protocol, for a newly registered user id, one has $\mathsf{S.Ver}(\mathsf{vk}_{\mathsf{GM}}, \mathsf{id}, \mathsf{cert}_{\mathsf{id}}) = 1$, thanks to the correctness of $\mathcal{SIG}$. As a result, the protocol is always successfully executed by honest parties. Next, during the encryption process, as long as $F_\tau(w) = 1$ and $\mathsf{id} \notin \mathcal{S}$, an honest ciphertext sender should be able to obtain a satisfying witness $\xi = (w, \mathsf{id}, \mathsf{cert}_{\mathsf{id}}, s_{\mathsf{R}}, s_{\mathsf{OA}})$ for the relation $\mathcal{R}$, and hence, should be able to generate a NIZK argument π. As a result, Enc should successfully output a ciphertext $\psi = (\mathbf{c}_{\mathsf{R}}, \mathbf{c}_{\mathsf{OA}}, \pi)$. Now, thanks to the completeness of $\mathcal{NIZK}$, the argument π contained in ψ should be accepted by $\mathsf{ZK.Ver}$. Therefore, the verification algorithm $\mathsf{Verify}(\tau, \psi)$ should output 1.

Moreover, the correctness of $\mathcal{E_R}$ implies that $w = w' = \mathsf{E_R.Dec}(\mathsf{sk}_{\mathsf{id}}, \mathbf{c}_{\mathsf{R}})$. Similarly, the correctness of $\mathcal{E_{OA}}$ ensures that $\mathsf{E_{OA}.Dec}(\mathsf{sk}_{\mathsf{OA}}, \mathbf{c}_{\mathsf{OA}})$ returns $\mathbf{d} = (1 - P_\tau(\mathsf{id}, w)) \cdot \mathsf{id}$. Consequently, algorithm Open returns id if $P_\tau(\mathsf{id}, w) = 0$ and it returns $\bot$ if $P_\tau(\mathsf{id}, w) = 1$.

SECURITY. The security properties of the proposed GEOT system are based on those of the employed cryptographic building blocks. In particular, **message secrecy** relies on the CCA2-security of $\mathcal{E_R}$ and the ZK property of $\mathcal{NIZK}$. The latter, together with the CCA2-security and key-privacy of $\mathcal{E_R}$ and CCA2-security of $\mathcal{E_{OA}}$, ensure **anonymity** of the system. Furthermore, **unforgeability** is based on the extractability of $\mathcal{NIZK}$ and the unforgeability of $\mathcal{SIG}$. Formally, we have the following theorem.

Theorem 1. *Assume that* $\mathcal{SIG}$ *is an EUF-CMA secure signature scheme,* $\mathcal{E_R}$ *is a key-private CCA2-secure encryption scheme,* $\mathcal{E_{OA}}$ *is a CCA2-secure encryption scheme, and* $\mathcal{NIZK}$ *is a dual-mode NIZK argument system for relation* $\mathcal{R}$. *Then the presented* GEOT *system satisfies* **message secrecy**, **Type-1 anonymity**, **Type-2 anonymity**, *and* **unforgeability**.

4   Code-Based Instantiation

In this section, using the high-level ideas of Sect. 3, we will develop a code-based GEOT scheme based on the FDGE scheme from [50]. Recall that the scheme from [50] uses an updatable code-based Merkle tree [52] (which can be seen as a weak form of signature) to manage the enrollments and revocations of users[2], CCA2-secure versions [48,54] of McEliece [44] for the encryption layers. The difference from [50] is that we employ VOLEitH-based zero-knowledge protocol [7,55] instead of Stern-like [59] zero-knowledge protocols [24,52] for proving ciphertext validity. (The details of these code-based cryptographic tools and VOLEitH-based ZK proofs are provided in the full version.)

To upgrade the scheme from [50] to a GEOT scheme, we introduce extensions with tracing and filtering policies. Our code-based GEOT scheme can work smoothly with both general policies. In particular, we model tracing policies and filtering policies as polynomial-size Boolean circuits. The supporting ZK techniques to prove correct evaluations of policies are presented in the full version.

In the random oracle model, the correctness and security properties of the scheme rely on those of the employed ingredients (i.e., code-based Merkle trees, McEliece encryption and VOLEitH-based ZK protocols) and the fact that, in the non-traceable case, even if the Type-2-anonymity adversary is given OA's secret key, it can learn no additional information about the receiver's identity.

4.1 Description of Our Code-Based Construction

In the scheme description below, we will generically use F_τ and P_τ to denote the policies without specifying their formulations.

Setup(1^λ) Given the security parameter 1^λ, this setup algorithm first generates the following public parameters, including descriptions of $\mathcal{ID}, \mathcal{W}, \mathcal{T}, \mathcal{P}, \mathcal{F}$.
   (1) Integers $n, c \in \mathbb{Z}^+$ such that $n = \mathcal{O}(\lambda)$, $c = \mathcal{O}(1)$, and $c \mid n$. Set $m = 2 \cdot 2^c \cdot n/c$. Let the user identifier space be $\mathcal{ID} = \{0,1\}^n$.
   (2) An integer $\ell = \ell(\lambda)$ that specifies the expected number $N = 2^\ell$ of users in the system.
   (3) An integer t that specifies the message space $\mathcal{W} = \{0,1\}^t$.
   (4) An ordered time space $\mathcal{T} = \{\tau_1, \tau_2, \ldots\}$.
   (5) A predicate family $\mathcal{P} = \{P_\tau : \{0,1\}^{n+t} \to \{0,1\}\}_{\tau \in \mathcal{T}}$.
   (6) A message filtering policy $\mathcal{F} = \{F_\tau : \mathcal{W} \to \{0,1\}\}_{\tau \in \mathcal{T}}$.
   (7) Two sets of parameters $(n_1, k_1, t_1, k_1 - n, n)$ and $(n_2, k_2, t_2, k_2 - t, t)$ for the McEliece encryption scheme with regular noise. (See the full version for this variant.) Thus, we also specify integers $k_{e,1}, k_{e,2}, c_{e,1}, c_{e,2}$ such that $c_{e,1} \mid k_{e,1}$, $c_{e,2} \mid k_{e,2}$ and $n_1 = k_{e,1}/c_{e,1} \cdot 2^{c_{e,1}}$, $n_2 = k_{e,2}/c_{e,2} \cdot 2^{c_{e,2}}$. We require that $n \mid n_2$ for ease of presentation. Looking ahead, the first set is used by the OA for tracing purpose while the second set is used by the users for encrypting messages.
   (8) A random matrix $\mathbf{B} \xleftarrow{\$} \{0,1\}^{n \times m}$, which specifies a code-based hash function $h_\mathbf{B}$. This hash function is then employed in the Merkle tree accumulator to accumulate user public keys and identifiers.

---

[2] Hence, compared to the construction in Sect. 3, our code-based instantiation here does not need a full-fledged signature and the revocation list $\mathcal{S}$ is handled differently.

(9) A small integer $q = 2^r$ defining the finite field $\mathbb{F}_q$ and a positive integer δ such that $\max\{c + 1, c_{e,1}, c_{e,2}\}/q^\delta = \mathsf{negl}(\lambda)$. The parameter δ defines a $[\delta, 1, \delta]$-linear code over $\mathbb{F}_q$. Looking ahead, these will serve as auxiliary parameters for the $\mathcal{F}_{\mathsf{sVOLE}}^{p,q,S_\Delta,\mathcal{C},l,\mathcal{L}}$ functionality (see the full version for details), which is called upon executing VOLEitH-based ZK proof.

(10) A hash function $\mathcal{H}_{\mathsf{FS}}$ modeled as a random oracle in the security proof.

Let

$$\mathsf{pp}' = \{n, c, m, t, \ell, N, \mathcal{T}, \mathcal{P}, \mathcal{F}, n_1, k_{e,1}, c_{e,1}, k_1, t_1, n_2, k_{e,2}, c_{e,2}, k_2, t_2, \mathbf{B}, q, \delta, \mathcal{H}_{\mathsf{FS}}\}.$$

Next, this algorithm generates secret keys for GM and OA as follows.

(i) Run the McEliece key generation $\mathsf{McKeygen}(n_1, k_1, t_1)$ twice, obtaining $(\mathbf{G}_{\mathsf{oa},0}, \mathsf{sk}_{\mathsf{Mc}}^{(\mathsf{oa},0)})$ and $(\mathbf{G}_{\mathsf{oa},1}, \mathsf{sk}_{\mathsf{Mc}}^{(\mathsf{oa},1)})$. Define $\mathsf{sk}_{\mathsf{OA}} = (\mathsf{sk}_{\mathsf{Mc}}^{(\mathsf{oa},0)}, \mathsf{sk}_{\mathsf{Mc}}^{(\mathsf{oa},1)})$.

(ii) Sample $\mathsf{sk}_{\mathsf{GM}} \xleftarrow{\$} \{0,1\}^{2n}$ and computes $\mathbf{y}_{\mathsf{GM}} = \mathbf{B} \cdot \mathsf{RE}(\mathsf{sk}_{\mathsf{GM}})$. (See the full version or [52] for the definition of the regular encoding algorithm RE.)

(iii) Initialize a registration table $\mathbf{reg} = (\mathbf{reg}[0], \ldots, \mathbf{reg}[N-1])$, where for each i, $\mathbf{reg}[i] = (\mathbf{reg}[i][0], \mathbf{reg}[i][1], \mathbf{reg}[i][2], \mathbf{reg}[i][3]) = (\mathbf{0}^n, \mathbf{0}, -1, -1)$. Here $\mathbf{reg}[i][0]$ stores a hash value, $\mathbf{reg}[i][1]$ stores the membership certificate, $\mathbf{reg}[i][2]$ and $\mathbf{reg}[i][3]$ are the epochs at which the user joins and leaves the group, respectively.

(iv) Initialize a Merkle tree MTr built from $(\mathbf{reg}[0][0], \ldots, \mathbf{reg}[N-1][0])$ using the hash function $h_{\mathbf{B}}$. Note that all nodes in MTr are zero at this stage.

(v) Initialize state $j = 0$ and group information $\mathsf{info} := \emptyset$.

Return $\mathsf{pp} = \{\mathsf{pp}', \mathbf{G}_{\mathsf{oa},0}, \mathbf{G}_{\mathsf{oa},1}, \mathbf{y}_{\mathsf{GM}}\}$, $\mathsf{sk}_{\mathsf{OA}}$, and $\mathsf{sk}_{\mathsf{GM}}$. We assume that only one with the key $\mathsf{sk}_{\mathsf{GM}}$ can edit $\mathbf{reg}$ and info, and the well-formedness of these databases can be publicly verified.

$\langle\mathsf{Join}(\mathsf{info}), \mathsf{Issue}(\mathsf{sk}_{\mathsf{GM}}, \mathsf{info}, \mathbf{reg})\rangle$ This protocol is triggered if a user requests to join the group at τ_{current}. Let the state of the GM be j and the user identifier be $\mathsf{id}_j \in \{0,1\}^n$. The user first performs the following steps.

1. Generate its encryption key by running the algorithm $\mathsf{McKeygen}(n_2, k_2, t_2)$ twice, resulting in two key pairs $(\mathbf{G}_{j,0}, \mathsf{sk}_{\mathsf{Mc}}^{(j,0)})$ and $(\mathbf{G}_{j,1}, \mathsf{sk}_{\mathsf{Mc}}^{(j,1)})$. Set $\mathsf{pk}_j = (\mathbf{G}_{j,0}, \mathbf{G}_{j,1}) \in (\{0,1\}^{n_2 \times k_2})^2$ and $\mathsf{sk}_j = (\mathsf{sk}_{\mathsf{Mc}}^{(j,0)}, \mathsf{sk}_{\mathsf{Mc}}^{(j,1)})$.

2. Next, it computes a hash $\mathbf{d}'_j$ of the key pk_j as follows:

   - For $b \in \{0,1\}$, denote $\mathbf{G}_{j,b} = [\mathbf{g}_{j,k_2 \cdot b} | \mathbf{g}_{j,k_2 \cdot b+1} | \cdots | \mathbf{g}_{j,k_2 \cdot b+k_2-1}]$.
   - For each $l = 0, \ldots, k_2 - 1$, split the column vectors $\mathbf{g}_{j,k_2 \cdot b+l} \in \{0,1\}^{n_2}$ into n_2/n column vectors $\mathbf{g}_{j,k_2 \cdot b+l,0}, \ldots, \mathbf{g}_{j,k_2 \cdot b+l,n_2/n-1} \in \{0,1\}^n$. Note that, we should have

$$\mathbf{g}_{j,k_2 \cdot b+l} = \left(\mathbf{g}_{j,k_2 \cdot b+l,0} \| \cdots \| \mathbf{g}_{j,k_2 \cdot b+l,n_2/n-1}\right)$$

   - Let $D_j = \{\mathbf{g}_{j,0,0}, \ldots, \mathbf{g}_{j,0,n_2/n-1}, \ldots, \mathbf{g}_{j,2k_2-1,0}, \ldots, \mathbf{g}_{j,2k_2-1,n_2/n-1}\}$. By "padding" zero vectors $\mathbf{0}^n$ to D_j such that $|D_j|$ is a power of 2, the sender can run the accumulating algorithm $\mathsf{TAccu}_{\mathbf{B}}(D_j)$ to obtain $\mathbf{d}'_j \in \{0,1\}^n$.

3. Let $\mathbf{B} = [\mathbf{B}_0|\mathbf{B}_1]$. Compute $\mathbf{d}_j = \mathbf{B}_0 \cdot \mathsf{RE}(\mathbf{d}'_j) \oplus \mathbf{B}_1 \cdot \mathsf{RE}(\mathsf{id}_j)$.
4. If $\mathbf{d}_j$ is non-zero, the user sends $(\mathsf{id}_j, \mathsf{pk}_j, \mathbf{d}_j)$ to the GM. Otherwise, it repeats the above steps. We remark that $\mathbf{d}_j$ is non-zero with overwhelming probability for large enough n.

Upon receiving the tuple from the user, the GM checks the following: (i) the authenticity of the user identifier id_j; (ii) both $\mathbf{G}_{j,0}$ and $\mathbf{G}_{j,1}$ are not registered by any other user; (iii) the non-zero $\mathbf{d}_j$ is computed from id_j and pk_j. If either condition is not satisfied, the GM rejects. Else, the GM sends a membership identifier $j = (j_{\ell-1}, \ldots, j_0)_2$ to the user and sets $\mathsf{cert}_{\mathsf{id}_j} = (\mathsf{bin}(j), \mathsf{id}_j, \mathsf{pk}_j, \mathbf{d}_j)$. In addition, the GM performs the following.

- Update $\mathbf{reg}[j][0] = \mathbf{d}_j$, $\mathbf{reg}[j][1] = \mathsf{cert}_{\mathsf{id}_j}$, and $\mathbf{reg}[j][2] = \tau_{\mathrm{current}}$.
- Update the Merkle tree MTr by running $\mathsf{TUpdate}_{\mathbf{B}}(j, \mathbf{d}_j)$.
- Increase the state j to $j + 1$.

$\mathsf{GUpdate}(\mathsf{sk}_{\mathsf{GM}}, \mathcal{S}, \mathsf{info}, \mathbf{reg})$ The group manager runs this algorithm to advance the time epoch to τ_{new} and update the group information to $\mathsf{info}_{\tau_{\mathrm{new}}}$. Concretely, it proceeds as follows.

1. Let $\mathcal{S} = \{i_1, i_2, \ldots, i_r\}$ be the membership identifiers of to-be-revoked users. If $\mathcal{S} = \emptyset$, go to Step 2. Else, for each $k \in [1, r]$, the GM updates MTr by running $\mathsf{TUpdate}_{\mathbf{B}}(i_k, \mathbf{0}^n)$ and sets $\mathbf{reg}[i_k][3] = \tau_{\mathrm{new}}$.
2. Let $\mathcal{D} = \{\mathbf{d}_j\}_j$ be the set of non-zero values accumulated in the updated tree MTr. For each j, let $w^{(j)} = \mathsf{TWitGen}_{\mathbf{B}}(\mathcal{D}, \mathbf{d}_j) \in \{0,1\}^{\ell} \times (\{0,1\}^n)^{\ell}$ be the witness that $\mathbf{d}_j$ is accumulated in the root $\mathbf{u}_{\tau_{\mathrm{new}}}$ of the updated tree. Then GM outputs $\mathsf{info}_{\tau_{\mathrm{new}}}$ as

$$\mathsf{info}_{\tau_{\mathrm{new}}} = (\mathbf{u}_{\tau_{\mathrm{new}}}, \{w^{(j)}\}_j).$$

We remark that the updated group information is for active users only. This is because each of the zero leaves in MTr corresponds to a user who has been revoked from the group or has not joined the group yet and thus is not allowed to receive any ciphertext at τ_{new}.

$\mathsf{Enc}(\tau, \mathbf{w}, \mathsf{id}_j, \mathsf{cert}_{\mathsf{id}_j})$ Parse $\mathsf{cert}_{\mathsf{id}_j} = ((j_{\ell-1}, \ldots, j_0)^{\top}, \mathsf{id}_j, \mathbf{G}_{j,0}, \mathbf{G}_{j,1}, \mathbf{d}_j)$, and extract $(\mathbf{G}_{\mathsf{oa},0}, \mathbf{G}_{\mathsf{oa},1})$ from pp. This algorithm is run by a sender who wishes to send a message $\mathbf{w} \in \{0,1\}^t$ to user $\mathsf{id}_j = (x_{j,0}, \ldots, x_{j,n-1})^{\top} \in \{0,1\}^n$ with respect to time epoch τ. The sender checks that $F_{\tau}(\mathbf{w}) = 1$, and id_j is active at τ. If either of the two conditions does not hold, abort. The sender then downloads from info_{τ} the associated witness $w^{(j)} = (\mathsf{bin}(j), \mathbf{w}_0, \ldots, \mathbf{w}_{\ell-1})$ and performs the following steps.

1. Encrypt $\mathbf{w}$ under the keys $\mathbf{G}_{j,0}$ and $\mathbf{G}_{j,1}$.

   - Sample vectors $\mathbf{r}_{w,0}, \mathbf{r}_{w,1} \xleftarrow{\$} \{0,1\}^{k_2-t}$ and $\mathbf{e}_{w,0}, \mathbf{e}_{w,1} \xleftarrow{\$} \mathbb{F}_2^{k_e,2}$.
   - For $i \in \{0,1\}$, compute

$$\mathbf{c}_{w,i} = \mathbf{G}_{j,i} \cdot \begin{pmatrix} \mathbf{r}_{w,i} \\ \mathbf{w} \end{pmatrix} \oplus \mathsf{RE}(\mathbf{e}_{w,i}) \in \{0,1\}^{n_2}, \tag{2}$$

where RE is the regular encoding function. Let $\mathbf{c}_w = (\mathbf{c}_{w,0}, \mathbf{c}_{w,1}) \in \{0,1\}^{n_2} \times \{0,1\}^{n_2}$.

2. Let $b = P_\tau(\mathsf{id}_j, \mathbf{w})$. Encrypt $(1-b) \cdot \mathbf{d}_j \in \{0,1\}^n$ under keys $\mathbf{G}_{\mathsf{oa},0}, \mathbf{G}_{\mathsf{oa},1}$.
   - Sample vectors $\mathbf{r}_{\mathsf{oa},0}, \mathbf{r}_{\mathsf{oa},1} \overset{\$}{\leftarrow} \{0,1\}^{k_1-n}$ and $\mathbf{e}_{\mathsf{oa},0}, \mathbf{e}_{\mathsf{oa},1} \overset{\$}{\leftarrow} \mathbb{F}_2^{k_e,1}$.
   - For $i \in \{0,1\}$, compute

$$
\mathbf{c}_{\mathsf{oa},i} = \mathbf{G}_{\mathsf{oa},i} \cdot \begin{pmatrix} \mathbf{r}_{\mathsf{oa},i} \\ (1-b) \cdot \mathbf{d}_j \end{pmatrix} \oplus \mathsf{RE}(\mathbf{e}_{\mathsf{oa},i}) \in \{0,1\}^{n_1}. \tag{3}
$$

Let $\mathbf{c}_{\mathsf{oa}} = (\mathbf{c}_{\mathsf{oa},0}, \mathbf{c}_{\mathsf{oa},1}) \in \{0,1\}^{n_1} \times \{0,1\}^{n_1}$.

3. Let ξ be of the following form

$$
\begin{aligned}
\xi = (\ & \mathbf{r}_{w,0},\ \mathbf{r}_{w,1},\ \mathbf{e}_{w,0},\ \mathbf{e}_{w,1},\ \mathbf{w},\ \mathbf{r}_{\mathsf{oa},0},\ \mathbf{r}_{\mathsf{oa},1},\ \mathbf{e}_{\mathsf{oa},0},\ \mathbf{e}_{\mathsf{oa},1}, \\
& b,\ \mathsf{bin}(j),\ \mathsf{id}_j,\ \mathbf{G}_{j,0},\ \mathbf{G}_{j,1},\ \mathbf{d}_j',\ \mathbf{d}_j,\ \mathbf{w}_0,\ \ldots,\ \mathbf{w}_{\ell-1}\ ).
\end{aligned} \tag{4}
$$

Generate an NIZK argument of knowledge of ξ such that the following conditions hold.

(a) $\mathbf{c}_{w,0}, \mathbf{c}_{w,1}$ encrypt $\mathbf{w}$ under the keys $\mathbf{G}_{j,0}, \mathbf{G}_{j,1}$, respectively. Specifically, for $i \in \{0,1\}$, the Eq. (2) holds.

(b) The plaintext $\mathbf{w}$ satisfies the filtering relation $F_\tau(\mathbf{w}) = 1$.

(c) $\mathbf{c}_{\mathsf{oa},0}, \mathbf{c}_{\mathsf{oa},1}$ encrypt $(1-b) \cdot \mathbf{d}_j$ under the keys $\mathbf{G}_{\mathsf{oa},0}, \mathbf{G}_{\mathsf{oa},1}$, i.e., the equation (3) holds for $i \in \{0,1\}$. Therefore, the non-zero $\mathbf{d}_j$ is encrypted if and only if $b = P_\tau(\mathsf{id}_j, \mathbf{w}) = 0$.

(d) The non-zero vector $\mathbf{d}_j$ is accumulated in the root $\mathbf{u}_\tau$ at epoch τ, i.e., the equation $\mathsf{TVerify}_\mathbf{B}(\mathbf{u}_\tau, \mathbf{d}_j, w^{(j)}) = 1$ holds.

(e) The keys $\mathbf{G}_{j,0}, \mathbf{G}_{j,1}$ and the user identifier id_j are hashed to a non-zero $\mathbf{d}_j$. Concretely, $\mathbf{d}_j' = \mathsf{TAccu}_\mathbf{B}(\mathbf{G}_{j,0}, \mathbf{G}_{j,1})$, $\mathbf{d}_j = \mathbf{B}_0 \cdot \mathsf{RE}(\mathbf{d}_j') \oplus \mathbf{B}_1 \cdot \mathsf{RE}(\mathsf{id}_j)$, and $\mathbf{d}_j \neq \mathbf{0}^n$. The latter two conditions are to ensure that id_j is a certified and active user at τ.

To this end, the sender converts the above conditions to a set of t_{proof} polynomial equations over $\mathbb{F}_2$, which have degrees at most $d_{\mathsf{proof}} = \max\{c+1, c_{e,1}, c_{e,2}\}$ and are satisfied by a witness in $\{0,1\}^{l_{\mathsf{proof}}}$. We specify the conversion and the values $t_{\mathsf{proof}}, d_{\mathsf{proof}}$ and l_{proof} in the full version. Then the sender executes the VOLEitH-based NIZK protocol. Let the final proof be π_ψ. Return $\psi = (\mathbf{c}_{w,0}, \mathbf{c}_{w,1}, \mathbf{c}_{\mathsf{oa},0}, \mathbf{c}_{\mathsf{oa},1}, \pi_\psi)$.

$\mathsf{Verify}(\tau, \psi)$ Let ψ be as above. This algorithm simply runs the verification algorithm of the VOLEitH proof system. Return 1 if the verification algorithm returns 1, and 0 otherwise.

$\mathsf{Dec}(\mathsf{sk}_{\mathsf{id}_j}, \tau, \psi)$ Let $\psi = (\mathbf{c}_{w,0}, \mathbf{c}_{w,1}, \mathbf{c}_{\mathsf{oa},0}, \mathbf{c}_{\mathsf{oa},1}, \pi_\psi)$ and $\mathsf{sk}_{\mathsf{id}_j} = (\mathsf{sk}_{\mathsf{Mc}}^{(j,0)}, \mathsf{sk}_{\mathsf{Mc}}^{(j,1)})$. If $\mathsf{Verify}(\tau, \psi) = 0$, return $\bot$. Otherwise, user id_j decrypts ψ by running the algorithm $\mathbf{w}' \leftarrow \mathsf{McDec}(\mathsf{sk}_{\mathsf{Mc}}^{(j,0)}, \mathbf{c}_{w,0})$.

$\mathsf{Open}(\mathsf{sk}_{\mathsf{OA}}, \tau, \psi)$ Let $\psi = (\mathbf{c}_{w,0}, \mathbf{c}_{w,1}, \mathbf{c}_{\mathsf{oa},0}, \mathbf{c}_{\mathsf{oa},1}, \pi_\psi)$ and $\mathsf{sk}_{\mathsf{OA}} = (\mathsf{sk}_{\mathsf{Mc}}^{(\mathsf{oa},0)}, \mathsf{sk}_{\mathsf{Mc}}^{(\mathsf{oa},1)})$. If $\mathsf{Verify}(\tau, \psi) = 0$, return $\bot$. Otherwise, the OA decrypts ψ by running the algorithm $\widetilde{\mathbf{d}} \leftarrow \mathsf{McDec}(\mathsf{sk}_{\mathsf{Mc}}^{(\mathsf{oa},0)}, \mathbf{c}_{\mathsf{oa},0})$.

1. If $\widetilde{\mathbf{d}} = \mathbf{0}^n$, indicating that ψ is non-traceable, return $\bot$.
2. If $\widetilde{\mathbf{d}} \neq \mathbf{0}^n$, find the index j in $\mathbf{reg}$ such that $\mathbf{reg}[j][0] = \widetilde{\mathbf{d}}$. Let $\mathbf{reg}[j][1] = (\mathsf{bin}(j), \mathsf{id}_j, \mathsf{pk}_j, \mathbf{d}_j)$, return id_j. If no such index is found, return $\bot$.

4.2   Efficiency, Correctness, and Security Analyses

Efficiency. The asymptotic efficiency of our construction is as follows.

(a) The secret key $\mathsf{sk_{GM}}$ of the GM has bit-size $\mathcal{O}(\lambda)$, while the secret key $\mathsf{sk_{OA}}$ of the OA has bit-size $\mathcal{O}(\lambda^2)$.
(b) The size of public parameters pp is dominated by that of matrices $\mathbf{G}_{\mathsf{oa},0}, \mathbf{G}_{\mathsf{oa},1}$, $\mathbf{B}$, which have bit size $\mathcal{O}(\lambda^2)$.
(c) The membership certificate and secret key of users have bit-size $\mathcal{O}(\lambda^2)$.
(d) The message sender needs to download information of bit-size $\mathcal{O}(\lambda \cdot \log \lambda)$. The verifier only needs to download $\mathbf{u}_\tau$, which has bit-size $\mathcal{O}(\lambda)$.
(e) The proof π_ψ has bit-size $\mathcal{O}(L_{\mathsf{proof}}) = \mathcal{O}(\lambda^2) + \mathcal{O}(|F_\tau|) + \mathcal{O}(|P_\tau|)$ where $|F_\tau|$ and $|P_\tau|$ denote the circuit sizes of filtering and tracing policies respectively.

We provide an example parameter set aiming to achieve 128-bit security in Table 2. These parameters are used in the comparisons provided in Table 1. We choose the McEliece parameter according to the document [3] with some modifications. One suggested parameter set (n_1, k_1, t_1) in [3] is $(3488, 2720, 64)$. Since we employ the regular noise variant of the McEliece cryptosystem, which reduces the security level by a few bits (see, e.g., [41,42, Table 1]), we thus increase n_1 to 4096. As a result, the new parameter set becomes $(4096, 3328, 64)$. It can achieve 156-bit security, according to the estimator[3] provided in [41,42]. Even when considering a new distinguishing attack [58] against binary Goppa codes, the parameter set can still achieve 128-bit security. The parameters for the VOLEitH proof systems follow the specification in [6] to ensure all proof components achieve 128-bit security. For instance, $r = 8$ and $\delta = 18$ ensure that soundness error is at most 2^{-128}. Finally, parameters for the 2-RNSD problems are chosen according to the best known attacks proposed in [4]. For the chosen parameter $(n, c, m) = (1024, 8, 2^{16})$, the GBA attack has complexity 2^{256} and the ISD attack has complexity 2^{161}, thus satisfying our requirements.

Sender's Complexity. We remark that the runtime Enc algorithm is dominated by the time for generating a VOLEitH-based NIZK proof. Using the benchmark provided in Rust library gf256, we estimate that the proof time is around 260 s.

Correctness. The correctness of the above construction relies on the following facts: (i) The VOLEitH-based NIZK argument system for generating π_ψ is perfectly complete; (ii) The employed McEliece encryption schemes are correct.

First, for an honestly generated ciphertext $\psi = (\mathbf{c}_w, \mathbf{c}_{\mathsf{oa}}, \pi_\psi)$ that encrypts $\mathbf{w}$ to id, the perfect completeness of the system that generates π_ψ ensures that the Verify algorithm returns 1. Next, the Dec algorithm outputs $\mathbf{w}' = \mathbf{w}$ with overwhelming probability due to Fact (ii). Suppose $(1 - b) \cdot \mathbf{d}$ is originally encrypted, then the outputted $\widetilde{\mathbf{d}}$ in the Open algorithm should be exactly $(1 - b) \cdot \mathbf{d}$ with all but negligible probability. Here $\mathbf{d}$ is a hash value corresponding to id. If $b = P_\tau(\mathsf{id}, \mathbf{w}) = 1$, then $\widetilde{\mathbf{d}} = \mathbf{0}^n$ and Open returns $\perp$. If $P_\tau(\mathsf{id}, \mathbf{w}) = 0$, then

---

[3] https://gist.github.com/hansliu1024/21c87609e75f6cc52decdc69981e1d5b.

Table 2. Parameters for 128-bit security level

Parameters	Description	Value
λ	Security level	128
$N = 2^{\ell}$	Expected No. of users	1024
t	Message bit length	128
n	Hash $h_{\mathbf{B}}$ output length	1024
c	$2 - \mathsf{RNSD}$ parameter	8
$m = \frac{2n}{c} \cdot 2^c$	$h_{\mathbf{B}}$ input length	2^{16}
(n_1, k_1, t_1)	McEliece parameters set 1	$(4096, 3328, 64)$
$(k_{e,1}, c_{e,1})$	Regular noise encoding	$(384, 6)$
(n_2, k_2, t_2)	McEliece parameters set 2	$(4096, 3328, 64)$
$(k_{e,2}, c_{e,2})$	Regular noise encoding	$(384, 6)$
$|P_{\tau}|$	Circuit size of P_{τ}	10^5
$|F_{\tau}|$	Circuit size of F_{τ}	10^5
$q = 2^r$	Extension field	2^8
δ	Repetition of VOLEitH	18
$s = \lambda + 16$	Universal hash parameter	144
$h = \lambda + 16$	Universal hash parameter	144
t_{proof}	Number of poly. equations	$\approx 2.72 \cdot 10^7$
l_{proof}	Number of variables	$\approx 2.73 \cdot 10^7$
d_{proof}	Max. degree of poly. equations	9

$\widetilde{\mathbf{d}} \neq \mathbf{0}^n$. In particular, $\widetilde{\mathbf{d}} = \mathbf{d}$. Therefore, the opening algorithm is able to identify the receiver id by looking up the registration table **reg**.

Security. In the following theorem, we prove that the above construction satisfies our stringent requirements in Sect. 2.2 and Sect. 2.3.

Theorem 2. *Assume that the VOLEitH-based NIZK argument system generating the proof π_{ψ} is simulation-sound extractable and ZK, the randomized McEliece cryptosystems are CPA-secure and key-private, and the AFS hash function is collision-resistant. Then in the random oracle model, the* GEOT *scheme satisfies message secrecy, type-1-anonymity, type-2-anonymity, and unforgeability.*

In the random oracle model, the above assumptions are based on the following.

1. The decisional McEliece problems and the decisional learning parity with regular noise problems are hard. This is to ensure that the randomized McEliece cryptosystems have pseudorandom ciphertexts (and hence, CPA-security and key-privacy). Via the Naor-Yung transformation [48], the obtained variant of McEliece encryption scheme is CCA2-secure.

2. The $2-\mathsf{RNSD}_{n,2n,c}$ problem is hard. Thus the used AFS hash function is collision resistant.

Acknowledgements. This work is partially supported by the National Cryptologic Science Fund of China under grant 2025NCSF02039, by the National Science Foundation of China under grants 12401693 and 12361141818, and by Singapore Ministry of Education Academic Research Fund Tier 2 Grant MOE-T2EP20223-0016, the National Research Foundation, Singapore and Infocomm Media Development Authority under its Trust Tech Funding Initiative. W. Susilo is supported by the Australian Laureate Fellowship (FL230100033). This work is also supported by the open project funding of the Key Laboratory of Intelligent Sensing System and Security (Ministry of Education), Hubei University. Any opinions, findings and conclusions or recommendations expressed in this material are those of the author(s) and do not reflect the views of National Research Foundation, Singapore and Infocomm Media Development Authority.

References

1. El Aimani, L., Joye, M.: Toward practical group encryption. In: Jacobson, M., Locasto, M., Mohassel, P., Safavi-Naini, R. (eds.) ACNS 2013. LNCS, vol. 7954, pp. 237–252. Springer, Heidelberg (2013). https://doi.org/10.1007/978-3-642-38980-1_15

2. Alamélou, Q., Blazy, O., Cauchie, S., Gaborit, P.: A code-based group signature scheme. Des. Codes Cryptogr. **82**(1–2), 469–493 (2017)

3. Albrecht, M.R., et al.: Classic McEliece: conservative code-based cryptography (2022). https://classic.mceliece.org/nist.html

4. Augot, D., Finiasz, M., Gaborit, P., Manuel, S., Sendrier, N.: SHA-3 proposal: FSB. Submission to NIST, pp. 81–85 (2008)

5. Baum, C., et al.: One tree to rule them all: optimizing GGM trees and OWFs for post-quantum signatures. In: Chung, KM., Sasaki, Y. (eds.) ASIACRYPT 2024. LNCS, vol. 15484, pp. 463–493. Springer, Cham (2024). https://doi.org/10.1007/978-981-96-0875-1_15

6. Baum, C., Braun, L., de Saint Guilhem, C.D., et al.: FAEST: algorithm specifications (2023)

7. Baum, C., et al.: Publicly verifiable zero-knowledge and post-quantum signatures from vole-in-the-head. In: Handschuh, H., Lysyanskaya, A. (eds.) CRYPTO 2023. LNCS, vol. 14085, pp. 581–615. Springer, Cham (2023). https://doi.org/10.1007/978-3-031-38554-4_19

8. Belenkiy, M., Chase, M., Kohlweiss, M., Lysyanskaya, A.: P-signatures and non-interactive anonymous credentials. In: Canetti, R. (ed.) TCC 2008. LNCS, vol. 4948, pp. 356–374. Springer, Heidelberg (2008). https://doi.org/10.1007/978-3-540-78524-8_20

9. Bellare, M., Micciancio, D., Warinschi, B.: Foundations of group signatures: formal definitions, simplified requirements, and a construction based on general assumptions. In: Biham, E. (ed.) EUROCRYPT 2003. LNCS, vol. 2656, pp. 614–629. Springer, Heidelberg (2003). https://doi.org/10.1007/3-540-39200-9_38

10. Bellare, M., Shi, H., Zhang, C.: Foundations of group signatures: the case of dynamic groups. In: Menezes, A. (ed.) CT-RSA 2005. LNCS, vol. 3376, pp. 136–153. Springer, Heidelberg (2005). https://doi.org/10.1007/978-3-540-30574-3_11

11. Bettaieb, S., Bidoux, L., Gaborit, P., Kulkarni, M.: Modelings for generic PoK and applications: shorter SD and PKP based signatures. IACR Cryptol. ePrint Arch., p. 1668 (2024)
12. Bidoux, L., Feneuil, T., Gaborit, P., Neveu, R., Rivain, M.: Dual support decomposition in the head: Shorter signatures from rank SD and minrank. In: Chung, KM., Sasaki, Y. (eds.) ASIACRYPT 2024. LNCS, vol. 15485, pp. 38–69. Springer, Singapore (2024). https://doi.org/10.1007/978-981-96-0888-1_2
13. Bootle, J., Cerulli, A., Chaidos, P., Ghadafi, E., Groth, J.: Foundations of fully dynamic group signatures. In: Manulis, M., Sadeghi, A.-R., Schneider, S. (eds.) ACNS 2016. LNCS, vol. 9696, pp. 117–136. Springer, Cham (2016). https://doi.org/10.1007/978-3-319-39555-5_7
14. Bootle, J., Lyubashevsky, V., Nguyen, N.K., Sorniotti, A.: A framework for practical anonymous credentials from lattices. In: Handschuh, H., Lysyanskaya, A. (eds.) CRYPTO 2023. LNCS, vol. 14082, pp. 384–417. Springer, Cham (2023). https://doi.org/10.1007/978-3-031-38545-2_13
15. Camenisch, J., Lysyanskaya, A.: A signature scheme with efficient protocols. In: Cimato, S., Persiano, G., Galdi, C. (eds.) SCN 2002. LNCS, vol. 2576, pp. 268–289. Springer, Heidelberg (2003). https://doi.org/10.1007/3-540-36413-7_20
16. Camenisch, J., Lysyanskaya, A.: Signature schemes and anonymous credentials from bilinear maps. In: Franklin, M. (ed.) CRYPTO 2004. LNCS, vol. 3152, pp. 56–72. Springer, Heidelberg (2004). https://doi.org/10.1007/978-3-540-28628-8_4
17. Cathalo, J., Libert, B., Yung, M.: Group encryption: non-interactive realization in the standard model. In: Matsui, M. (ed.) ASIACRYPT 2009. LNCS, vol. 5912, pp. 179–196. Springer, Heidelberg (2009). https://doi.org/10.1007/978-3-642-10366-7_11
18. Chaum, D., van Heyst, E.: Group signatures. In: Davies, D.W. (ed.) EUROCRYPT 1991. LNCS, vol. 547, pp. 257–265. Springer, Heidelberg (1991). https://doi.org/10.1007/3-540-46416-6_22
19. Cheng, S., Nguyen, K., Wang, H.: Policy-based signature scheme from lattices. Des. Codes Cryptogr. **81**(1), 43–74 (2016)
20. Chiang, J.H., Damgård, I., Duro, W.R., Engan, S., Kolby, S., Scholl, P.: Post-quantum threshold ring signature applications from vole-in-the-head. In: ACM CCS 2025, pp. 4664–4678. ACM (2025)
21. Courtois, N.T., Finiasz, M., Sendrier, N.: How to achieve a McEliece-based digital signature scheme. In: Boyd, C. (ed.) ASIACRYPT 2001. LNCS, vol. 2248, pp. 157–174. Springer, Heidelberg (2001). https://doi.org/10.1007/3-540-45682-1_10
22. Cui, H., Liu, H., Yan, D., Yang, K., Yu, Y., Zhang, K.: ReSeloveD: shorter signatures from regular syndrome decoding and VOLE-in-the-Head. In: Tang, Q., Teague, V. (eds.) PKC 2024. LNCS, vol 14601, pp. 229–258. Springer, Cham (2024). https://doi.org/10.1007/978-3-031-57718-5_8
23. Debris-Alazard, T., Sendrier, N., Tillich, J.-P.: Wave: a new family of trapdoor one-way preimage sampleable functions based on codes. In: Galbraith, S.D., Moriai, S. (eds.) ASIACRYPT 2019. LNCS, vol. 11921, pp. 21–51. Springer, Cham (2019). https://doi.org/10.1007/978-3-030-34578-5_2
24. Ezerman, M.F., Lee, H.T., Ling, S., Nguyen, K., Wang, H.: A provably secure group signature scheme from code-based assumptions. In: Iwata, T., Cheon, J.H. (eds.) ASIACRYPT 2015. LNCS, vol. 9452, pp. 260–285. Springer, Heidelberg (2015). https://doi.org/10.1007/978-3-662-48797-6_12
25. Fiat, A., Shamir, A.: How to prove yourself: practical solutions to identification and signature problems. In: Odlyzko, A.M. (ed.) CRYPTO 1986. LNCS, vol. 263, pp. 186–194. Springer, Heidelberg (1987). https://doi.org/10.1007/3-540-47721-7_12

26. Goldreich, O., Micali, S., Wigderson, A.: How to prove All NP statements in zero-knowledge and a methodology of cryptographic protocol design (extended abstract). In: Odlyzko, A.M. (ed.) CRYPTO 1986. LNCS, vol. 263, pp. 171–185. Springer, Heidelberg (1987). https://doi.org/10.1007/3-540-47721-7_11
27. Goldwasser, S., Micali, S., Rackoff, C.: The knowledge complexity of interactive proof systems. SIAM J. Comput. **18**(1), 186–208 (1989)
28. Groth, J., Ostrovsky, R., Sahai, A.: Perfect non-interactive zero knowledge for NP. In: Vaudenay, S. (ed.) EUROCRYPT 2006. LNCS, vol. 4004, pp. 339–358. Springer, Heidelberg (2006). https://doi.org/10.1007/11761679_21
29. Izabachène, M., Pointcheval, D., Vergnaud, D.: Mediated traceable anonymous encryption. In: Abdalla, M., Barreto, P.S.L.M. (eds.) LATINCRYPT 2010. LNCS, vol. 6212, pp. 40–60. Springer, Heidelberg (2010). https://doi.org/10.1007/978-3-642-14712-8_3
30. Jain, A., Krenn, S., Pietrzak, K., Tentes, A.: Commitments and efficient zero-knowledge proofs from learning parity with noise. In: Wang, X., Sako, K. (eds.) ASIACRYPT 2012. LNCS, vol. 7658, pp. 663–680. Springer, Heidelberg (2012). https://doi.org/10.1007/978-3-642-34961-4_40
31. Jeudy, C., Roux-Langlois, A., Sanders, O.: Lattice signature with efficient protocols, application to anonymous credentials. In Handschuh, H., Lysyanskaya, A. (eds.) CRYPTO 2023. LNCS, vol. 14082, pp. 351–383. Springer, Cham (2023). https://doi.org/10.1007/978-3-031-38545-2_12
32. Kiayias, A., Tsiounis, Y., Yung, M.: Traceable signatures. In: Cachin, C., Camenisch, J.L. (eds.) EUROCRYPT 2004. LNCS, vol. 3027, pp. 571–589. Springer, Heidelberg (2004). https://doi.org/10.1007/978-3-540-24676-3_34
33. Kiayias, A., Tsiounis, Y., Yung, M.: Group encryption. In: Kurosawa, K. (ed.) ASIACRYPT 2007. LNCS, vol. 4833, pp. 181–199. Springer, Heidelberg (2007). https://doi.org/10.1007/978-3-540-76900-2_11
34. Kiltz, E.: Chosen-ciphertext security from tag-based encryption. In: Halevi, S., Rabin, T. (eds.) TCC 2006. LNCS, vol. 3876, pp. 581–600. Springer, Heidelberg (2006). https://doi.org/10.1007/11681878_30
35. Kiltz, E., Pan, J., Wee, H.: Structure-preserving signatures from standard assumptions, revisited. In: Gennaro, R., Robshaw, M. (eds.) CRYPTO 2015. LNCS, vol. 9216, pp. 275–295. Springer, Heidelberg (2015). https://doi.org/10.1007/978-3-662-48000-7_14
36. Libert, B., Ling, S., Mouhartem, F., Nguyen, K., Wang, H.: Signature schemes with efficient protocols and dynamic group signatures from lattice assumptions. In: Cheon, J.H., Takagi, T. (eds.) ASIACRYPT 2016. LNCS, vol. 10032, pp. 373–403. Springer, Heidelberg (2016). https://doi.org/10.1007/978-3-662-53890-6_13
37. Libert, B., Ling, S., Mouhartem, F., Nguyen, K., Wang, H.: Zero-knowledge arguments for matrix-vector relations and lattice-based group encryption. Theor. Comput. Sci. **759**, 72–97 (2019)
38. Libert, B., Nguyen, K., Peters, T., Yung, M.: Bifurcated signatures: folding the accountability vs. anonymity dilemma into a single private signing scheme. In: Canteaut, A., Standaert, F.-X. (eds.) EUROCRYPT 2021. LNCS, vol. 12698, pp. 521–552. Springer, Cham (2021). https://doi.org/10.1007/978-3-030-77883-5_18
39. Libert, B., Yung, M., Joye, M., Peters, T.: Traceable group encryption. In: Krawczyk, H. (ed.) PKC 2014. LNCS, vol. 8383, pp. 592–610. Springer, Heidelberg (2014). https://doi.org/10.1007/978-3-642-54631-0_34
40. Ling, S., Nguyen, K., Phan, D.H., Tang, K.H., Wang, H., Xu, Y.: Fully dynamic attribute-based signatures for circuits from codes. In: Tang, Q., Teague, V. (eds.)

PKC 2024. LNCS, vol. 14601, pp. 37–73. Springer, Cham (2024). https://doi.org/10.1007/978-3-031-57718-5_2

41. Liu, H., Wang, X., Yang, K., Yu, Y.: The hardness of LPN over any integer ring and field for PCG applications. IACR Cryptol. ePrint Arch. 712 (2022)

42. Liu, H., Wang, X., Yang, K., Yu, Y.: The hardness of LPN over any integer ring and field for PCG applications. In: Joye, M., Leander, G. (eds.) EUROCRYPT 2024. LNCS, vol. 14656, pp. 149–179. Springer, Cham (2024). https://doi.org/10.1007/978-3-031-58751-1_6

43. Maji, H.K., Prabhakaran, M., Rosulek, M.: Attribute-based signatures. In: Kiayias, A. (ed.) CT-RSA 2011. LNCS, vol. 6558, pp. 376–392. Springer, Heidelberg (2011). https://doi.org/10.1007/978-3-642-19074-2_24

44. McEliece, R.J.: A public-key cryptosystem based on algebraic coding theory. Coding Thv **4244**, 114–116 (1978)

45. Aguilar Melchor, C., Cayrel, P.-L., Gaborit, P.: A new efficient threshold ring signature scheme based on coding theory. In: Buchmann, J., Ding, J. (eds.) PQCrypto 2008. LNCS, vol. 5299, pp. 1–16. Springer, Heidelberg (2008). https://doi.org/10.1007/978-3-540-88403-3_1

46. Melchor, C.A., Cayrel, P., Gaborit, P., Laguillaumie, F.: A new efficient threshold ring signature scheme based on coding theory. IEEE Trans. Inf. Theory **57**(7), 4833–4842 (2011)

47. Morozov, K., Takagi, T.: Zero-knowledge protocols for the McEliece encryption. In: Susilo, W., Mu, Y., Seberry, J. (eds.) ACISP 2012. LNCS, vol. 7372, pp. 180–193. Springer, Heidelberg (2012). https://doi.org/10.1007/978-3-642-31448-3_14

48. Naor, M., Yung, M.: Public-key cryptosystems provably secure against chosen ciphertext attacks. In: STOC 1990, pp. 427–437. ACM (1990)

49. Nguyen, K., Guo, F., Susilo, W., Yang, G.: Multimodal private signatures. In: Dodis, Y., Shrimpton, T. (eds) CRYPTO 2022. LNCS, vol. 13508, pp. 792–822. Springer, Cham (2022). https://doi.org/10.1007/978-3-031-15979-4_27

50. Nguyen, K., Safavi-Naini, R., Susilo, W., Wang, H., Xu, Y., Zeng, N.: Group encryption: full dynamicity, message filtering and code-based instantiation. In: Garay, J.A. (ed.) PKC 2021. LNCS, vol. 12711, pp. 678–708. Springer, Cham (2021). https://doi.org/10.1007/978-3-030-75248-4_24

51. Nguyen, K., Safavi-Naini, R., Susilo, W., Wang, H., Xu, Y., Zeng, N.: Group encryption: Full dynamicity, message filtering and code-based instantiation. Theor. Comput. Sci. **1007**, 114678 (2024)

52. Nguyen, K., Tang, H., Wang, H., Zeng, N.: New code-based privacy-preserving cryptographic constructions. In: Galbraith, S.D., Moriai, S. (eds.) ASIACRYPT 2019. LNCS, vol. 11922, pp. 25–55. Springer, Cham (2019). https://doi.org/10.1007/978-3-030-34621-8_2

53. Nguyen, K., Xu, Y., Tran, N., Susilo, W., Wang, H.: Group encryption with oblivious traceability. IACR Cryptol. ePrint Arch. **2026**, 405 (2026)

54. Nojima, R., Imai, H., Kobara, K., Morozov, K.: Semantic security for the McEliece cryptosystem without random oracles. Des. Codes Cryptogr. **49**(1–3), 289–305 (2008)

55. Ouyang, Y., Tang, D., Xu, Y.: Code-based zero-knowledge from vole-in-the-head and their applications: Simpler, faster, and smaller. In: Chung, K.M., Sasaki, Y. (eds.) ASIACRYPT 2024. LNCS, vol. 15488, pp. 436–470. Springer, Cham (2024). https://doi.org/10.1007/978-981-96-0935-2_14

56. Pan, J., Chen, X., Zhang, F., Susilo, W.: Lattice-based group encryption with full dynamicity and message filtering policy. In: Tibouchi, M., Wang, H. (eds.) ASI-

ACRYPT 2021. LNCS, vol. 13093, pp. 156–186. Springer, Cham (2021). https://doi.org/10.1007/978-3-030-92068-5_6

57. Peikert, C., Shiehian, S.: Noninteractive zero knowledge for np from (plain) learning with errors. In: Boldyreva, A., Micciancio, D. (eds.) CRYPTO 2019. LNCS, vol. 11692, pp. 89–114. Springer, Cham (2019). https://doi.org/10.1007/978-3-030-26948-7_4

58. Randriambololona, H.: The syzygy distinguisher. In Fehr, S., Fouque, PA. (eds.) EUROCRYPT 2025. LNCS, vol. 15606, pp. 324–354. Springer, Cham (2025). https://doi.org/10.1007/978-3-031-91095-1_12

59. Stern, J.: A new paradigm for public key identification. IEEE Trans. Inf. Theory **42**(6), 1757–1768 (1996)

60. Trolin, M., Wikström, D.: Hierarchical group signatures. In: Caires, L., Italiano, G.F., Monteiro, L., Palamidessi, C., Yung, M. (eds.) ICALP 2005. LNCS, vol. 3580, pp. 446–458. Springer, Heidelberg (2005). https://doi.org/10.1007/11523468_37

61. Xu, Y., Safavi-Naini, R., Nguyen, K., Wang, H.: Traceable policy-based signatures and instantiation from lattices. Inf. Sci. **607**, 1286–1310 (2022)

62. Yang, R., Au, M.H., Zhang, Z., Xu, Q., Yu, Z., Whyte, W.: Efficient lattice-based zero-knowledge arguments with standard soundness: construction and applications. In: Boldyreva, A., Micciancio, D. (eds.) CRYPTO 2019. LNCS, vol. 11692, pp. 147–175. Springer, Cham (2019). https://doi.org/10.1007/978-3-030-26948-7_6

Revisiting Security Definitions
of Sender-Anamorphic Encryption

Yuichi Tanishita[1,2]([✉]), Takahiro Matsuda[2], and Kanta Matsuura[1]

[1] The University of Tokyo, Tokyo, Japan
{y-tani,kanta}@iis.u-tokyo.ac.jp
[2] National Institute of Advanced Industrial Science and Technology, Tokyo, Japan
`t-matsuda@aist.go.jp`

Abstract. Sender-anamorphic encryption is a cryptographic primitive that allows a sender to covertly embed an alternative message into the ciphertext. This enables the sender to transmit the message they truly wish to send without an authority's knowledge, even if they are coerced into sending a message against their will. The concrete scenario considered here is one where the authority demands that the sender provide the public key, the plaintext, and the internal randomness used to generate the ciphertext, and then requires a proof that the coerced message was indeed encrypted correctly.

Persiano et al. (Eurocrypt 2022) formulated the security of sender-anamorphic encryption to capture this situation. Building on that, Wang et al. (Asiacrypt 2023) proposed ℓ-sender-anamorphic encryption along with its security definition. However, in the formal security definitions for sender-anamorphic encryption in these existing works, the randomness used to generate the challenge ciphertext is not given to an adversary, and thus, the potential threats are not fully accounted for.

Therefore, in this study, we redefine security for sender-anamorphic encryption so that the randomness used to generate the challenge ciphertext is provided to the adversary. We then investigate whether the existing sender-anamorphic encryption schemes by Persiano et al. and Wang et al. satisfy our refined notions of security.

Keywords: Anamorphic encryption · Public-key encryption · Randomness disclosure

1 Introduction

While encryption is a powerful tool for protecting message privacy, its security implicitly relies on two assumptions: *Receiver Privacy* that a receiver keeps the secret key confidential, and *Sender Freedom* that a sender can freely choose any message and any public key to encrypt. Persiano et al. [25] pointed out that both assumptions can be compromised by a dictator. For example, receiver privacy can be compromised if a government forces citizens to disclose their secret keys, and sender freedom can be compromised if an authority forces users to encrypt a

© International Association for Cryptologic Research 2026
S. Bai and E. Persichetti (Eds.): PKC 2026, LNCS 16554, pp. 130–161, 2026.
https://doi.org/10.1007/978-3-032-26740-5_5

designated message or implicitly restricts them from sending any messages they desire.

To address such scenarios, Persiano et al. introduced the concept of *anamorphic encryption* (AME), which enables secure communication even when either assumption is compromised. The idea of AME is embedding a hidden message (called a *duplicate message* in this context) into an ordinary ciphertext, while making the ciphertext appear legitimate to a dictator. Specifically, there are two types of anamorphic encryption: *receiver-anamorphic encryption* (RAME), which is secure against compromise of receiver privacy, and *sender-anamorphic encryption* (SAME), which is secure against compromise of sender freedom. In this work, we focus on the latter.

In the threat model underlying SAME, a dictator forces a sender to send a designated message fm (that stands for a *forced message*) to a designated receiver with its public key fpk (that stands for a *forced public key*), so the sender cannot freely choose either of the message or the receiver. Even in such a situation, SAME allows the sender to secretly embed a duplicate message dm into the ciphertext that the sender is forced to compute by the dictator by using a fake randomness generated from fpk, fm, dm, and a duplicate public key dpk, where (dpk, dsk) is the key pair of another (legitimate) receiver to whom the sender is actually trying to communicate dm. Such a ciphertext is called an *anamorphic ciphertext*. To the dictator, the anamorphic ciphertext looks like an encryption of fm under fpk, which can be decrypted to fm by the designated receiver. However, the same ciphertext can also be decrypted to the hidden duplicate message dm by the legitimate receiver with dsk.

In the original model of SAME [25], a single ciphertext of the forced message fm conveys a single duplicate message dm. Wang et al. [28] extended (relaxed) this setting by introducing *ℓ-sender anamorphic encryption* (ℓ-SAME), where a single duplicate message dm is transmitted across ℓ ciphertexts $c_1, \ldots, c_\ell$ that respectively correspond to ℓ forced messages $fm_1, \ldots, fm_\ell$. (Hence, SAME originally considered by Persiano et al. is 1-SAME in the definition of Wang et al.. Looking ahead, in this work, we will mainly treat this ℓ-sender variant.) Conceptually, an anamorphic encryption scheme extends a public-key encryption (PKE) scheme by incorporating a fake-randomness generation algorithm and an algorithm that recovers dm from anamorphic ciphertexts.

Technically speaking, in the threat model of SAME, the sender is required to produce a ciphertext using the dictator's designated fpk and fm, and to submit both the resulting ciphertext and the randomness used for encryption to prove that he has followed the order of the dictator. As long as the dictator cannot detect that the ciphertext was computed irregularly, the sender can secretly communicate dm even under the dictator's surveillance. In fact, Persiano et al. [25] describe this situation as *"the more remote adversary does select the message to be sent, lets Alice compute the ciphertext ct, and later on Alice is required to exhibit the coin tosses used to compute ct"*. This clearly indicates that Persiano et al. consider the situation in which the adversary (dictator) obtains the randomness used for encryption (of forced messages).

However, in the actual formal security definition for SAME given by Persiano et al. [25, Section 6], the randomness used in encryption is *not* given to the adversary. More specifically, in their formal security definition for SAME, the adversary receives fpk, and can access the encryption oracle that, upon receiving a pair of messages (fm, dm), returns a ciphertext of fm generated as follows, depending on the challenge bit:

- an ordinary (i.e. non-anamorphic) ciphertext of fm generated using an honestly sampled randomness, or
- an anamorphic ciphertext of fm generated using a fake randomness computed from the public parameters, fpk, fm, dpk, and dm. (This ciphertext can be decrypted to fm using fsk, while it can also be decrypted to dm using dsk.)

Security for SAME is then defined as the indistinguishability between these two cases. However, the oracle's response includes only the ciphertexts, not the corresponding randomness, which makes it impossible for the adversary to perform the intended verification. This is inconsistent with what they describe in their texts. Consequently, the dictator is not guaranteed to be able to verify whether the ciphertext was generated using the genuine randomness corresponding to (fpk, fm), and thus their formal definition fails to capture the intended threat model. The formal security definition for ℓ-SAME given by Wang et al. [28] inherits the same issue. Therefore, the existing security definitions for (ℓ-)SAME do not fully capture the threats that SAME was originally designed to address.

In this work, we revisit the formalization of SAME to provide a security definition that accurately captures the threat of compromised sender freedom.

1.1 Our Contributions

In this work, we introduce refined security notions for (ℓ-)SAME that accurately capture the threats it is originally intended to address, and then investigate whether the existing constructions satisfy our new definitions.

Refining Security Definitions. Our contributions regarding the formalization of security are as follows, which are given in Sect. 3.

1. We define the new security notion for (ℓ-)SAME that we call **SAME-R** security. In the **SAME-R** security experiment, the adversary obtains not only the ciphertexts but also the randomness used in encryption. Furthermore, we also define the stronger version of the security notion that we call **S-SAME-R** security. **S-SAME-R** security is identical to **SAME-R** security except that the adversary additionally learns fsk and dpk, in addition to fpk.
2. We introduce variants of our new notions, which we call **SAME-R'** security and **S-SAME-R'** security. In the security experiments, the adversary obtains only the randomness used in encryption (but not the ciphertext itself). **S-SAME-R'** is a stronger version of **SAME-R'**. (The difference between **SAME-R'** and **S-SAME-R'** is analogous to the one between **SAME-R** and **S-SAME-R**).

3. We show that SAME-R (resp. S-SAME-R) and SAME-R$'$ (resp. S-SAME-R$'$) are equivalent.

Our new security notions are based on the security definitions for ℓ-SAME proposed by Wang et al. [28] (which is in turn based on the one for SAME by Persiano et al. [25]). In Wang et al.'s definition for ℓ-SAME, a duplicate message dm is transmitted across ℓ ciphertexts $c_1, \ldots, c_\ell$ corresponding to forced messages $fm_1, \ldots, fm_\ell$. Their security notion captures the indistinguishability between ordinary PKE ciphertexts and anamorphic ciphertexts. Specifically, in their game, the adversary, given public parameters and the forced public key fpk, can access the encryption oracle with any pair of fm and dm. The oracle, depending on the challenge bit, either generates true randomness or fake randomness, uses it to encrypt fm, and returns the resulting ciphertext. The adversary finally outputs a guess bit, and the scheme is secure if its advantage is negligible. In our definition, the oracle's response includes not only the ciphertext but also the randomness used in its generation. This modification faithfully represents the scenario where the sender is under the surveillance of an authority that can demand both the ciphertext and the randomness, yet cannot detect whether a duplicate message is embedded. Thus, the new definition accurately models the threat.

We also introduce SAME-R$'$ and S-SAME-R$'$ security, a variant of SAME-R and S-SAME-R, respectively, in which the oracle's response consists only of the randomness, excluding the ciphertext. Although SAME-R$'$ and S-SAME-R$'$ security do not capture any new threat beyond SAME-R and S-SAME-R, it is often useful for concise proofs. Since we can prove that SAME-R (resp. S-SAME-R) is equivalent to SAME-R$'$ (resp. S-SAME-R$'$), it is sufficient to show security analysis in SAME-R$'$ or S-SAME-R$'$ in which the components of oracle responses are fewer.

For the details on our refined security notions for SAME, see Sect. 3.

Existing Constructions under New Security Notions. We investigate whether the existing SAME constructions satisfy our refined security notions. The schemes we analyzed are:

- the 1-sender anamorphic encryption scheme by Persiano et al. [25];
- the ℓ-sender PKE-based anamorphic encryption scheme by Wang et al. [28]; and
- the $(\ell + 1)$-sender hybrid-encryption-based scheme by Wang et al. [28].

Our findings are summarized as follows:

- In Sect. 4, we show that the rejection-sampling-based scheme by Persiano et al. [25, Section 6] satisfies SAME-R security. However, we show that this scheme is not S-SAME-R secure by showing an efficient attack.
- In Sect. 5, we show that the ℓ-sender PKE-based anamorphic encryption scheme by Wang et al. [28, Section 4] (which we also concisely call Wang et al.'s first scheme), satisfies SAME-R security under the same assumption as used for proving the original security notion.

- In Sect. 6, we show that the $(\ell+1)$-sender hybrid-encryption-based scheme by Wang et al. [28, Section 5] (which we also concisely call Wang et al.'s second scheme) satisfies SAME-R security, if we add some mild assumption on one of its building blocks. However, we show that this scheme is not S-SAME-R secure by showing an efficient attack.
- For Wang et al.'s first scheme, we investigate whether it satisfies S-SAME-R security. Although the original proof technique makes it difficult to directly establish this, we show that by slightly modifying the scheme, replacing the underlying PKE with hybrid encryption constructed from a key encapsulation mechanism (KEM) and a data encapsulation mechanism (DEM) with pseudorandom ciphertexts, and assuming that the hash function is a pseudorandom function (PRF), the resulting scheme achieves S-SAME-R security. (The rationale behind these modifications is discussed in Sect. 5.2).

Through these analyses, we demonstrate that the existing SAME schemes indeed satisfy the appropriate form of security that properly reflects the intended threat model. Moreover, our work realizes that while some schemes achieve the strong version of the security, others do not, clarifying the boundary between standard and strong SAME security.

1.2   Related Works

Sender-Anamorphic Encryption. The concept of SAME was first introduced by Persiano et al. [25], who formalized its security and correctness and proposed a one-bit SAME scheme based on rejection sampling. Wang et al. [28] later relaxed the original model, in which a single duplicate message dm is embedded into a single ciphertext of a forced message fm, and extended it to the ℓ-sender setting, where one duplicate message is embedded across ℓ ciphertexts of forced messages $fm_1, \ldots, fm_\ell$. They further formalized the notions of security and robustness under this extended model. Here, robustness means that the anamorphic decryption algorithm outputs a special symbol $\perp$ when given (i) a regular ciphertext with a duplicate key, or (ii) an anamorphic ciphertext with a regular secret key together. This property ensures that the anamorphic decryption algorithm produces a valid output only when it is provided with a matching anamorphic ciphertext and the corresponding secret key.

Wang et al. presented two constructions that achieve both security and robustness and established theoretical connections between SAME and other related primitives, including RAME, public stegosystems, and asymmetric algorithm-substitution attacks.[1]

Receiver-Anamorphic Encryption. The threat scenario considered in RAME concerns a compromise of receiver privacy. Specifically, the receiver's key pair (apk, ask) used for public-key communication is seized by a dictator, and all ciphertexts sent to the receiver are subject to censorship. Even in such a setting, if the sender and the receiver secretly share a duplicate key dk unknown to

---

[1] For more details of the relationships and related primitives, see [28].

the dictator, secure communication can still be achieved. The sender encrypts the forced message fm together with the duplicate message dm, the public key apk, and the duplicate key dk to produce a ciphertext. Although the dictator, using ask, can decrypt only fm and cannot detect the presence of any covert message, the legitimate receiver can use dk to decrypt the same ciphertext and recover dm. Thus, communication remains private even when receiver privacy is compromised.

The concept of RAME was first introduced by Persiano et al. [25], who formalized its syntax and security definitions. In their model, the duplicate key dk is generated together with the receiver's key pair (apk, ask). Consequently, once a dictator gains power over an already-established communication channel, it is no longer possible to retroactively create an anamorphic channel on top of it. To address this limitation, Banfi et al. [4] proposed an extended model in which dk can be generated after regular key generation. They also introduced a notion of robustness, which requires that both the regular and the anamorphic decryption algorithms output a special symbol $\perp$ when invoked with an incorrect pair of ciphertext and key, namely regular ciphertext and duplicate key, or anamorphic ciphertext and regular key. Robustness ensures that decryption succeeds only with a matching key/ciphertext pair. Several concrete constructions satisfying these properties have since been proposed [4,9,24,25].

In RAME, the sender and receiver must share a duplicate key without the dictator's recognition. This may be difficult in practice, depending on the communication setting, motivating additional research on key-exchange protocols that support such key sharing [27].

Most existing RAME schemes conceptually overlay a symmetric-key-based anamorphic channel on top of a PKE-based regular channel. To enable fine partitioning between the encryption and decryption keys, asymmetric AME was proposed by Catalano et al. [7], where distinct keys are used for the two channels. Although both asymmetric RAME and SAME appear similar in the sense that they both are PKE-based syntax for an anamorphic channel, they capture fundamentally different threats: asymmetric RAME addresses compromise of receiver privacy, whereas SAME focuses on sender freedom. Recent works of asymmetric RAME have produced a variety of results on the security and constructions [3,8,9,14,26]. A comprehensive study analyzing both symmetric and asymmetric RAME, along with their theoretical relationships, was presented in [10]. Moreover, quantum RAME has also been explored [16].

Finally, because the goal of anamorphic encryption is to conceal the existence of a covert channel from the dictator, its constructions must be built upon well-known and widely used encryption schemes. Therefore, examining some properties or constructability of RAME is important. In contrast, Dodis et al. [15] introduced the notion of anamorphic-resistant encryption (ARE), which characterizes encryption schemes that cannot be made anamorphic, and subsequent works have investigated ARE under various settings [2,5].

Other Anamorphic Primitives. The concept of anamorphic encryption has been extended to other cryptographic primitives as well. A representative example is anamorphic signatures [23], which enable a covert channel even when all signed messages must be transmitted under the surveillance of a dictator. In such settings, signatures are typically used to prove message integrity and authenticity; however, by embedding a duplicate message into the signature, the signer can establish a covert channel that remains undetectable to the dictator. Several extensions and concrete constructions of anamorphic signatures have been explored [3,11,13,20,23].

2   Preliminaries

In this section, we review the basic notation and the formal definitions for existing cryptographic primitives and their security properties used in this paper.

Basic Notation. $\mathbb{N}$ denotes the set of all natural numbers. Throughout the paper, we will use $\lambda \in \mathbb{N}$ to denote the security parameter, which will sometimes be written in its unary representation, 1^λ. Furthermore, we sometimes suppress the dependency on λ, when λ is clear from the context. If $n \in \mathbb{N}$, then we define $[n] := \{1, \ldots, n\}$. Let $\mathsf{FUNC}_{\mathcal{X} \to \mathcal{Y}}$ be the set of all functions whose domain is $\mathcal{X}$ and range is $\mathcal{Y}$. For strings x and y, $|x|$ denotes the bit length of x, $x \| y$ denotes the concatenation of x and y, and $(x \overset{?}{=} y)$ denotes the operation that returns 1 if and only if $x = y$. For a set S, $x \overset{\$}{\leftarrow} S$ denotes that an element x is chosen uniformly at random from S. $\{\mathrm{op1}, \mathrm{op2}, \cdots : x\}$ denotes the distribution of x after performing the sequence of operations op1, op2, ... For distributions $\mathcal{D}_0$ and $\mathcal{D}_1$, $\mathcal{D}_0 \equiv \mathcal{D}_1$ denotes that $\mathcal{D}_0$ is equivalent to $\mathcal{D}_1$. $y \leftarrow x$ denotes that x is deterministically assigned to the variable y. If M is a probabilistic algorithm, then $y \overset{\$}{\leftarrow} \mathsf{M}(x)$ denotes that M receives the input x and outputs y. When we need to make the randomness r used by M explicit, we denote $y \leftarrow \mathsf{M}(x; r)$ (in which case, the computation by M is deterministic on input x and r). If $\mathcal{O}$ is a probabilistic algorithm or a function, then $\mathsf{M}^{\mathcal{O}}$ denotes that M has oracle access to $\mathcal{O}$. A function $f(\lambda) : \mathbb{N} \to [0, 1]$ is called negligible if for any constants $c \in \mathbb{N}$ and all sufficiently large $\lambda \in \mathbb{N}$, we have $f(\lambda) < 1/\lambda^c$. PPT stands for probabilistic polynomial time.

Statistical Distance. Let $\mathcal{X}$ and $\mathcal{Y}$ be distributions defined over a finite set S. The statistical distance between $\mathcal{X}$ and $\mathcal{Y}$ is defined as $\mathbf{SD}(\mathcal{X}, \mathcal{Y}) := \frac{1}{2} \sum_{z \in S} \big| \Pr[\mathcal{X} = z] - \Pr[\mathcal{Y} = z] \big|$.

2.1   Properties that Generally Hold for Probability Distributions

In this paper, we will use the following simple facts that generally hold for probability distributions. For completeness, formal proofs for them are given in the full version.

Lemma 1. *Let X be a finite set, and let* $\mathsf{P} : X \to \{0,1\}$ *be an arbitrary predicate such that* $\mathsf{P}^{-1}(1) \neq \emptyset$. *Then,*

$$\left\{ h \leftarrow 0;\ do\ \{h \leftarrow h+1;\ x_h \xleftarrow{\$} X\}\ until\ \mathsf{P}(x_h) = 1 : x_h \right\} \equiv \left\{ x \xleftarrow{\$} \mathsf{P}^{-1}(1) : x \right\}.$$

Lemma 2. *Let X and Y be finite sets and $f : X \to Y$ be a function. Then,*

$$\left\{ x \xleftarrow{\$} X : x \right\} \equiv \left\{ x \xleftarrow{\$} X;\ y \leftarrow f(x);\ \widehat{x} \xleftarrow{\$} f^{-1}(y) : \widehat{x} \right\}.$$

2.2 Public-Key Encryption

Here, we review the definitions for a public-key encryption (PKE) scheme.

A PKE scheme PKE consists of the following four PPT algorithms (Setup, $\mathsf{KG}, \mathsf{Enc}, \mathsf{Dec}$).

$\mathsf{Setup}(1^\lambda) \xrightarrow{\$} \mathsf{pp}$: This is the setup algorithm that takes a security parameter 1^λ as input, and outputs a public parameter pp.

$\mathsf{KG}(\mathsf{pp}) \xrightarrow{\$} (\mathsf{pk}, \mathsf{sk})$: This is the key generation algorithm that takes a public parameter pp as input, and outputs a pair of public key and secret key $(\mathsf{pk}, \mathsf{sk})$.

$\mathsf{Enc}(\mathsf{pk}, \mathsf{m}) \xrightarrow{\$} \mathsf{c}$: This is the encryption algorithm that takes a public key pk and a plaintext m as input, and outputs a ciphertext c.

$\mathsf{Dec}(\mathsf{sk}, \mathsf{c}) \to \mathsf{m}'/\bot$: This is the decryption algorithm that takes a secret key sk and a ciphertext c as input, and outputs a decrypted plaintext m' (which could be the special symbol $\bot$ indicating a decryption error).

Correctness. We require that $\mathsf{Dec}(\mathsf{sk}, \mathsf{Enc}(\mathsf{pk}, \mathsf{m})) = \mathsf{m}$ hold for any $\lambda \in \mathbb{N}$, $\mathsf{pp} \xleftarrow{\$} \mathsf{Setup}(1^\lambda), (\mathsf{pk}, \mathsf{sk}) \xleftarrow{\$} \mathsf{KG}(\mathsf{pp})$, and plaintext m.

Security Notions. In this paper, we will treat the following two kinds of security notions for a PKE scheme.

Definition 1 (IND–CPA Security of PKE). *We say that* PKE *is* IND–CPA *secure, if for any PPT adversary* $\mathcal{A} = (\mathcal{A}_0, \mathcal{A}_1)$, $\mathsf{Adv}_{\mathsf{PKE},\mathcal{A}}^{\mathrm{IND-CPA}}(\lambda) :=$ $2 \cdot | \Pr[\mathsf{Expt}_{\mathsf{PKE},\mathcal{A}}^{\mathrm{IND-CPA}}(\lambda) = 1] - \frac{1}{2}|$ *is negligible, where the experiment* $\mathsf{Expt}_{\mathsf{PKE},\mathcal{A}}^{\mathrm{IND-CPA}}(\lambda)$ *is defined as in Fig. 1 (left).*

Definition 2 (Pseudorandomness of PKE). *We say that* PKE *satisfies pseudorandomness, if for any PPT adversary* $\mathcal{A} = (\mathcal{A}_0, \mathcal{A}_1)$, $\mathsf{Adv}_{\mathsf{PKE},\mathcal{A}}^{\mathrm{PR}}(\lambda) :=$ $2 \cdot | \Pr[\mathsf{Expt}_{\mathsf{PKE},\mathcal{A}}^{\mathrm{PR}}(\lambda) = 1] - \frac{1}{2}|$ *is negligible, where the experiment* $\mathsf{Expt}_{\mathsf{PKE},\mathcal{A}}^{\mathrm{PR}}(\lambda)$ *is defined as in Fig. 1 (right).*

$$
\begin{array}{l|l}
\mathsf{Expt}_{\mathsf{PKE},\mathcal{A}}^{\mathtt{IND\text{-}CPA}}(\lambda): & \mathsf{Expt}_{\mathsf{PKE},\mathcal{A}}^{\mathtt{PR}}(\lambda): \\
\hline
\quad b \xleftarrow{\$} \{0,1\} & \quad b \xleftarrow{\$} \{0,1\} \\
\quad \mathsf{pp} \xleftarrow{\$} \mathsf{Setup}(1^\lambda) & \quad \mathsf{pp} \xleftarrow{\$} \mathsf{Setup}(1^\lambda) \\
\quad (\mathsf{pk},\mathsf{sk}) \xleftarrow{\$} \mathsf{KG}(\mathsf{pp}) & \quad (\mathsf{pk},\mathsf{sk}) \xleftarrow{\$} \mathsf{KG}(\mathsf{pp}) \\
\quad (m_0,m_1,\mathsf{st}) \xleftarrow{\$} \mathcal{A}_0(\mathsf{pp},\mathsf{pk}) & \quad (m,\mathsf{st}) \xleftarrow{\$} \mathcal{A}_0(\mathsf{pp},\mathsf{pk}) \\
\quad c \xleftarrow{\$} \mathsf{Enc}(\mathsf{pk},m_b) & \quad c_0 \xleftarrow{\$} \mathsf{Enc}(\mathsf{pk},m) \\
\quad b' \xleftarrow{\$} \mathcal{A}_1(c,\mathsf{st}) & \quad c_1 \xleftarrow{\$} \{0,1\}^{|c_0|} \\
\quad \text{return } (b \overset{?}{=} b') & \quad b' \xleftarrow{\$} \mathcal{A}_1(c_b,\mathsf{st}) \\
& \quad \text{return } (b \overset{?}{=} b')
\end{array}
$$

Fig. 1. Security experiments for PKE: The IND-CPA experiment (left) and the experiment for pseudorandomness (right). In the IND-CPA experiment, it is required that $|m_0| = |m_1|$.

2.3   Key Encapsulation Mechanism

Here, we review the definitions for a key encapsulation mechanism (KEM).

A KEM KEM consists of the following four algorithms (KSetup, KKG, Encap, Decap).

$\mathsf{KSetup}(1^\lambda) \xrightarrow{\$} \mathsf{pp}$: This is the setup algorithm that takes a security parameter 1^λ as input, and outputs a public parameter pp.

$\mathsf{KKG}(\mathsf{pp}) \xrightarrow{\$} (\mathsf{pk},\mathsf{sk})$: This is the key generation algorithm that takes a public parameter pp as input, and outputs a pair of public key and secret key $(\mathsf{pk},\mathsf{sk})$.

$\mathsf{Encap}(\mathsf{pk}) \xrightarrow{\$} (c, K)$: This is the encapsulation algorithm that takes a public key pk as input and outputs a ciphertext c and a session-key K.

$\mathsf{Decap}(\mathsf{sk}, c) \rightarrow K'/\bot$: This is the decapsulation algorithm that takes a secret key sk and a ciphertext c as input and outputs a decapsulated session-key K', or $\bot$ to indicate a decryption failure.

Correctness. We require that for any $\lambda \in \mathbb{N}, \mathsf{pp} \xleftarrow{\$} \mathsf{KSetup}(1^\lambda)$, $(\mathsf{pk},\mathsf{sk}) \xleftarrow{\$} \mathsf{KKG}(\mathsf{pp})$, and $(c, K) \xleftarrow{\$} \mathsf{Encap}(\mathsf{pk})$, it holds that $\mathsf{Decap}(\mathsf{sk}, c) = K$.

Security Notions. In this paper, we will treat the following three kinds of security notions for a KEM.

Definition 3 (IND–CPA Security of KEM). *We say that* KEM *is* IND–CPA *secure, if for any PPT adversary* $\mathcal{A}$, $\mathsf{Adv}_{\mathsf{KEM},\mathcal{A}}^{\mathtt{IND\text{-}CPA}}(\lambda) := 2 \cdot | \Pr[\mathsf{Expt}_{\mathsf{KEM},\mathcal{A}}^{\mathtt{IND\text{-}CPA}}(\lambda) = 1] - \frac{1}{2}|$ *is negligible, where the experiment* $\mathsf{Expt}_{\mathsf{KEM},\mathcal{A}}^{\mathtt{IND\text{-}CPA}}(\lambda)$ *is defined as in Fig. 2 (left).*

Definition 4 (Pseudorandomness of KEM). *We say that* KEM *satisfies pseudorandomness, if for any PPT adversary* $\mathcal{A}$, $\mathsf{Adv}_{\mathsf{KEM},\mathcal{A}}^{\mathtt{PR}}(\lambda) :=$ $2 \cdot | \Pr[\mathsf{Expt}_{\mathsf{KEM},\mathcal{A}}^{\mathtt{PR}}(\lambda) = 1] - \frac{1}{2}|$ *is negligible, where the experiment* $\mathsf{Expt}_{\mathsf{KEM},\mathcal{A}}^{\mathtt{PR}}(\lambda)$ *is defined as in Fig. 2 (center).*

Definition 5 (Ciphertext Pseudorandomness of KEM). *We say that* KEM *satisfies* ciphertext pseudorandomness, *if for any PPT adversary* $\mathcal{A}$, $\mathsf{Adv}_{\mathsf{KEM},\mathcal{A}}^{\mathtt{CTX-PR}}(\lambda) := 2 \cdot |\Pr[\mathsf{Expt}_{\mathsf{KEM},\mathcal{A}}^{\mathtt{CTX-PR}}(\lambda) = 1] - \frac{1}{2}|$ *is negligible, where the experiment* $\mathsf{Expt}_{\mathsf{KEM},\mathcal{A}}^{\mathtt{CTX-PR}}(\lambda)$ *is defined as in Fig. 2 (right).*

It is immediate to see that pseudorandomness implies both IND-CPA security and ciphertext pseudorandomness.

$\mathsf{Expt}_{\mathsf{KEM},\mathcal{A}}^{\mathtt{IND-CPA}}(\lambda):$	$\mathsf{Expt}_{\mathsf{KEM},\mathcal{A}}^{\mathtt{PR}}(\lambda):$	$\mathsf{Expt}_{\mathsf{KEM},\mathcal{A}}^{\mathtt{CTX-PR}}(\lambda):$
$b \xleftarrow{\$} \{0,1\}$	$b \xleftarrow{\$} \{0,1\}$	$b \xleftarrow{\$} \{0,1\}$
$\mathsf{pp} \xleftarrow{\$} \mathsf{KSetup}(1^\lambda)$	$\mathsf{pp} \xleftarrow{\$} \mathsf{KSetup}(1^\lambda)$	$\mathsf{pp} \xleftarrow{\$} \mathsf{KSetup}(1^\lambda)$
$(\mathsf{pk},\mathsf{sk}) \xleftarrow{\$} \mathsf{KKG}(\mathsf{pp})$	$(\mathsf{pk},\mathsf{sk}) \xleftarrow{\$} \mathsf{KKG}(\mathsf{pp})$	$(\mathsf{pk},\mathsf{sk}) \xleftarrow{\$} \mathsf{KKG}(\mathsf{pp})$
$(\mathsf{c},\mathsf{K}_0) \xleftarrow{\$} \mathsf{Encap}(\mathsf{pk})$	$(\mathsf{c}_0,\mathsf{K}_0) \xleftarrow{\$} \mathsf{Encap}(\mathsf{pk})$	$(\mathsf{c}_0,\mathsf{K}) \xleftarrow{\$} \mathsf{Encap}(\mathsf{pk})$
$\mathsf{K}_1 \xleftarrow{\$} \{0,1\}^\lambda$	$\mathsf{c}_1 \xleftarrow{\$} \{0,1\}^{|\mathsf{c}_0|}$	$\mathsf{c}_1 \xleftarrow{\$} \{0,1\}^{|\mathsf{c}_0|}$
$b' \xleftarrow{\$} \mathcal{A}(\mathsf{pp},\mathsf{pk},\mathsf{c},\mathsf{K}_b)$	$\mathsf{K}_1 \xleftarrow{\$} \{0,1\}^\lambda$	$b' \xleftarrow{\$} \mathcal{A}(\mathsf{pp},\mathsf{pk},\mathsf{c}_b)$
return $(b \overset{?}{=} b')$	$b' \xleftarrow{\$} \mathcal{A}(\mathsf{pp},\mathsf{pk},\mathsf{c}_b,\mathsf{K}_b)$	return $(b \overset{?}{=} b')$
	return $(b \overset{?}{=} b')$	

Fig. 2. Security experiments for KEM: The IND-CPA experiment (left), the experiment for pseudorandomness (center), and the experiment for ciphertext pseudorandomness (right).

2.4 Data Encapsulation Mechanism

Here, we review the definitions for a data encapsulation mechanism (DEM). In this paper, we treat ones whose encryption algorithm is deterministic.

A DEM DEM consists of the following two algorithms $(\mathsf{DEnc}, \mathsf{DDec})$.

$\mathsf{DEnc}(\mathsf{K},\mathsf{m}) \to \mathsf{c}$: This is the encryption algorithm that takes a key K and a plaintext m as input, and outputs a ciphertext c.

$\mathsf{DDec}(\mathsf{K},\mathsf{c}) \to \mathsf{m}'/\bot$: This is the decryption algorithm that takes a key K and a ciphertext c as input, and outputs a plaintext m', or $\bot$ to indicate a decryption failure.

Correctness. We require that for any key $\mathsf{K} \in \{0,1\}^\lambda$ and a plaintext m, it holds that $\mathsf{DDec}(\mathsf{K}, \mathsf{DEnc}(\mathsf{K},\mathsf{m})) = \mathsf{m}$.

Security Notions. In this paper, we will treat the following two kinds of security notions for a DEM.

Definition 6 (IND-OT Security of DEM). *We say that* DEM *is* IND-OT *secure, if for any PPT adversary* $\mathcal{A} = (\mathcal{A}_0, \mathcal{A}_1)$, $\mathsf{Adv}_{\mathsf{DEM},\mathcal{A}}^{\mathtt{IND-OT}}(\lambda) :=$ $2 \cdot |\Pr[\mathsf{Expt}_{\mathsf{DEM},\mathcal{A}}^{\mathtt{IND-OT}}(\lambda) = 1] - \frac{1}{2}|$ *is negligible, where the experiment* $\mathsf{Expt}_{\mathsf{DEM},\mathcal{A}}^{\mathtt{IND-OT}}(\lambda)$ *is defined as in Fig. 3 (left).*

Definition 7 (Pseudorandomness of DEM). *We say that DEM satisfies pseudorandomness, if for any PPT adversary* $\mathcal{A} = (\mathcal{A}_0, \mathcal{A}_1)$, $\mathsf{Adv}^{\mathrm{PR}}_{\mathrm{DEM},\mathcal{A}}(\lambda) := 2 \cdot |\Pr[\mathsf{Expt}^{\mathrm{PR}}_{\mathrm{DEM},\mathcal{A}}(\lambda) = 1] - \frac{1}{2}|$ *is negligible, where the experiment* $\mathsf{Expt}^{\mathrm{PR}}_{\mathrm{DEM},\mathcal{A}}(\lambda)$ *is defined as in Fig. 3 (right).*

$\mathsf{Expt}^{\mathrm{IND\text{-}OT}}_{\mathrm{DEM},\mathcal{A}}(\lambda):$

$b \xleftarrow{\$} \{0,1\}$

$\mathsf{K} \xleftarrow{\$} \{0,1\}^{\lambda}$

$(\mathsf{m}_0, \mathsf{m}_1, \mathsf{st}) \xleftarrow{\$} \mathcal{A}_0(1^{\lambda})$

$\mathsf{c} \xleftarrow{\$} \mathsf{DEnc}(\mathsf{K}, \mathsf{m}_b)$

$b' \xleftarrow{\$} \mathcal{A}_1(\mathsf{c}, \mathsf{st})$

$\text{return } (b \overset{?}{=} b')$

$\mathsf{Expt}^{\mathrm{PR}}_{\mathrm{DEM},\mathcal{A}}(\lambda):$

$b \xleftarrow{\$} \{0,1\}$

$\mathsf{K} \xleftarrow{\$} \{0,1\}^{\lambda}$

$(\mathsf{m}, \mathsf{st}) \xleftarrow{\$} \mathcal{A}_0(1^{\lambda})$

$\mathsf{c}_0 \leftarrow \mathsf{DEnc}(\mathsf{K}, \mathsf{m})$

$\mathsf{c}_1 \xleftarrow{\$} \{0,1\}^{|\mathsf{c}_0|}$

$b' \xleftarrow{\$} \mathcal{A}_1(\mathsf{c}_b, \mathsf{st})$

$\text{return } (b \overset{?}{=} b')$

Fig. 3. Security experiments for DEM: The IND-OT experiment (left), and the experiment for pseudorandomness (right). In the IND-OT experiment, it is required that $|\mathsf{m}_0| = |\mathsf{m}_1|$.

2.5   Pseudorandom Function

Here, we recall the definition of a pseudorandom function (PRF).

Definition 8. *Let* $\mathsf{H} : \mathcal{K} \times \mathcal{X} \to \mathcal{Y}$ *be an efficiently computable function. We say that* H *is a* PRF *if for any PPT adversary* $\mathcal{A}$,

$$\mathsf{Adv}^{\mathrm{PRF}}_{\mathsf{H},\mathcal{A}}(\lambda) := \left| \Pr_{k \xleftarrow{\$} \mathcal{K}} [\mathcal{A}^{\mathsf{H}_k(\cdot)}(1^{\lambda}) = 1] - \Pr_{f \xleftarrow{\$} \mathrm{FUNC}_{\mathcal{X} \to \mathcal{Y}}} [\mathcal{A}^{f(\cdot)}(1^{\lambda}) = 1] \right|$$

is negligible.

2.6   Entropy-Smoothing Function

Here, we recall the definition of an entropy-smoothing function.

Definition 9. *Let* $\mathcal{K}, \mathcal{X}$, *and* $\mathcal{Y}$ *be finite sets and let* $\mathsf{H} : \mathcal{K} \times \mathcal{X} \to \mathcal{Y}$ *be an efficiently computable function. We say that* H *is* entropy-smoothing *if for any PPT adversary* $\mathcal{A}$,

$$\mathsf{Adv}^{\mathrm{ESF}}_{\mathsf{H},\mathcal{A}}(\lambda) := \left| \Pr_{\substack{k \xleftarrow{\$} \mathcal{K} \\ x \xleftarrow{\$} \mathcal{X}}} [\mathcal{A}(k, \mathsf{H}_k(x)) = 1] - \Pr_{\substack{k \xleftarrow{\$} \mathcal{K} \\ y \xleftarrow{\$} \mathcal{Y}}} [\mathcal{A}(k, y) = 1] \right|$$

is negligible.

We note that the above security definition is satisfied by a (strong) randomness extractor (where we view its seed as a key k of an entropy-smoothing function). Hence, an entropy-smoothing function exists unconditionally.

3   Refining Security Definitions of Sender-Anamorphic Encryption

In this section, we provide formal definitions of our refined security notions for SAME that we call `SAME-R` and `S-SAME-R` security. Furthermore, we introduce their variants that we call `SAME-R'` and `S-SAME-R'` security, which do not capture specific threats but are useful for security proofs.

In Sects. 3.1 and 3.2, we review the syntax and correctness, and the security definitions, respectively, for ℓ-SAME proposed by Wang et al. [28], which is a generalization of the original model proposed by Persiano et al. [25]. In ℓ-SAME, one duplicate message is transmitted through ℓ ciphertexts of forced messages, and the original definition of Persiano et al. is captured as 1-SAME. After reviewing the existing definitions, we introduce formal definitions of our refined security notions for ℓ-SAME in Sect. 3.3.

3.1   Syntax and Correctness

Let $\ell \in \mathbb{N}$. An ℓ-SAME scheme AME consists of the six algorithms (Setup, KG, Enc, Dec, fRand, dDec), among which each of (Setup, KG, Enc, Dec) is the same as the corresponding algorithm of a PKE scheme. fRand and dDec are the algorithms specific to ℓ-SAME with the following syntax:

$\mathsf{fRand}(\mathsf{pp}, (\mathsf{fpk}_i)_{i \in [\ell]}, (\mathsf{fm}_i)_{i \in [\ell]}, \mathsf{dpk}, \mathsf{dm}) \xrightarrow{\$} (r_i)_{i \in [\ell]}$: This is the fake randomness generation algorithm. It takes a public parameter pp, ℓ forced public keys $(\mathsf{fpk}_i)_{i \in [\ell]}$, ℓ forced messages $(\mathsf{fm}_i)_{i \in [\ell]}$, a duplicate public key dpk, and a duplicate message dm as input. It outputs ℓ random values $(r_i)_{i \in [\ell]} \in \mathcal{R}^\ell$, where $\mathcal{R}$ is the randomness space for Enc.

$\mathsf{dDec}(\mathsf{dsk}, (\mathsf{c}_i)_{i \in [\ell]}) \rightarrow \mathsf{dm}$: This is the decryption algorithm for anamorphic ciphertexts. It takes a duplicate secret key dsk and ℓ ciphertexts $(\mathsf{c}_i)_{i \in [\ell]}$ as input, and outputs a duplicate plaintext dm.

Correctness. We require that for any $\lambda \in \mathbb{N}$, any set of forced messages $\mathsf{fm}_1, \ldots, \mathsf{fm}_\ell$, and any duplicate message dm, the following probability is negligible:

$$
\Pr \left[
\begin{array}{l}
\mathsf{pp} \xleftarrow{\$} \mathsf{Setup}(1^\lambda); \\
\forall i \in [\ell],\ (\mathsf{fpk}_i, \mathsf{fsk}_i) \xleftarrow{\$} \mathsf{KG}(\mathsf{pp}); \\
(\mathsf{dpk}, \mathsf{dsk}) \xleftarrow{\$} \mathsf{KG}(\mathsf{pp}); \\
(r_i)_{i \in [\ell]} \xleftarrow{\$} \mathsf{fRand}(\mathsf{pp}, \mathsf{FPK}, \mathsf{FM}, \mathsf{dpk}, \mathsf{dm}); \\
\forall i \in [\ell],\ \mathsf{c}_i \leftarrow \mathsf{Enc}(\mathsf{fpk}_i,\ \mathsf{fm}_i;\ r_i)
\end{array}
\ :\ \mathsf{dDec}(\mathsf{dsk},\ (\mathsf{c}_i)_{i \in [\ell]}) \neq \mathsf{dm}
\right],
$$

where FPK denotes $(\mathsf{fpk}_i)_{i \in [\ell]}$ and FM denotes $(\mathsf{fm}_i)_{i \in [\ell]}$.

3.2   Existing Security Definitions

Here, we review the existing security definitions for ℓ-SAME introduced by Wang et al. [28], which are in turn based on the original security definition for SAME introduced by Persiano et al. [25]. To clearly distinguish these existing definitions from our refined security definitions, we call the existing security definitions "SAME security" and "S-SAME security".[2] The former is the default security notion, while the latter represents a stronger version. Both notions capture indistinguishability in the sense that an adversary holding forced public keys should be unable to determine whether given ciphertexts are normal or anamorphic. In the stronger setting, the adversary knows all the forced secret keys and a duplicate public key in addition to forced public keys, which is the only difference between SAME and S-SAME security.

Formally, the definitions of SAME security and S-SAME security are as follows.

Definition 10 ((Strong) SAME Security). *Let* $\mathsf{XXX} \in \{\mathsf{SAME}, \mathsf{S\text{-}SAME}\}$. *We say that an* ℓ-SAME *scheme* AME *is* XXX *secure if it satisfies the following conditions 1 and 2:*

1. $(\mathsf{Setup}, \mathsf{KG}, \mathsf{Enc}, \mathsf{Dec})$ *constitutes an* $\mathsf{IND\text{-}CPA}$ *secure PKE scheme.*
2. *For any PPT adversary* $\mathcal{A}$, $\mathsf{Adv}^{\mathsf{XXX}}_{\mathsf{AME},\mathcal{A}}(\lambda) := 2 \cdot |\Pr[\mathsf{Expt}^{\mathsf{XXX}}_{\mathsf{AME},\mathcal{A}}(\lambda) = 1] - \frac{1}{2}|$ *is negligible, where the experiment* $\mathsf{Expt}^{\mathsf{XXX}}_{\mathsf{AME},\mathcal{A}}(\lambda)$ *is defined as in Fig. 4.*

Although the stronger version might seem to not capture natural threats, it does capture some realistic situations, for example, when a national authority manages all citizens' keys, while the secret key of a foreign embassy within the country remains outside its control. Moreover, this stronger notion is theoretically significant due to its connections with receiver AME [28].

3.3   Our Refined Security Notions for SAME

Here, we introduce our refined security notion, SAME-R security, and its stronger version, S-SAME-R security, which are security notions for ℓ-SAME where randomness used for encryption is disclosed to an adversary. Specifically, these definitions are obtained by simply modifying the experiments for SAME security and S-SAME security so that the encryption oracle's response includes the randomness used for encryption. Receiving randomness in addition to ciphertexts, an adversary (i.e., a dictator) can verify that the ciphertexts are indeed computed from forced public keys, forced messages, and the randomness. Therefore, our formalization captures the threat that the dictator forces a sender to send ciphertexts as instructed.

We also introduce variants of our new security notions that we call SAME-R' and S-SAME-R', where the oracle's response in the experiments for these security

---

[2] Wang et al. [28] also defined the security property called robustness for ℓ-SAME. Its formal definition, as well as a discussion on the robustness of the $(\ell\text{-})$SAME schemes treated in this paper, are given in the full version.

$$\underline{\mathsf{Expt}^{\mathtt{XXX}}_{\mathsf{AME},\mathcal{A}}(\lambda):}$$

$b \xleftarrow{\$} \{0,1\}$

$\mathsf{pp} \xleftarrow{\$} \mathsf{Setup}(1^\lambda)$

for $i \in [\ell]$

   $(\mathsf{fpk}_i, \mathsf{fsk}_i) \xleftarrow{\$} \mathsf{KG}(\mathsf{pp})$

$(\mathsf{dpk}, \mathsf{dsk}) \xleftarrow{\$} \mathsf{KG}(\mathsf{pp})$

if $\mathtt{XXX} \in \{\mathtt{S\text{-}SAME}, \mathtt{S\text{-}SAME\text{-}R}, \mathtt{S\text{-}SAME\text{-}R'}\}$ then

  $\mathbf{aux} \leftarrow \big((\mathsf{fsk}_i)_{i \in [\ell]}, \mathsf{dpk}\big)$

else

  $\mathbf{aux} \leftarrow \emptyset$

$b' \xleftarrow{\$} \mathcal{A}^{\mathcal{O}^{\mathtt{XXX}}_b(\cdot,\cdot)}\big(\mathsf{pp}, (\mathsf{fpk}_i)_{i \in [\ell]}, \mathbf{aux}\big)$

return $(b \overset{?}{=} b')$

$$\underline{\mathcal{O}^{(\mathtt{S\text{-}})\mathtt{SAME}}_b(\mathsf{FM}, \mathsf{dm}):}$$

if $b = 0$ then

  $(r_i)_{i \in [\ell]} \xleftarrow{\$} \mathsf{fRand}\big(\mathsf{pp}, \mathsf{FPK}, \mathsf{FM},$

                       $\mathsf{dpk}, \mathsf{dm}\big)$

if $b = 1$ then

  $(r_i)_{i \in [\ell]} \xleftarrow{\$} \mathcal{R}^\ell$

for $i \in [\ell]$

  $\mathsf{c}_i \leftarrow \mathsf{Enc}(\mathsf{fpk}_i, \mathsf{fm}_i; r_i)$

return $(\mathsf{c}_i)_{i \in [\ell]}$

Fig. 4. The experiment for $\mathtt{XXX} \in \{\mathtt{SAME}, \mathtt{S\text{-}SAME}, \mathtt{SAME\text{-}R}, \mathtt{S\text{-}SAME\text{-}R}, \mathtt{SAME\text{-}R'},$ $\mathtt{S\text{-}SAME\text{-}R'}\}$ security for ℓ-SAME (left), and the procedure of the oracle for $\mathtt{SAME}$ and $\mathtt{S\text{-}SAME}$ security (right). $(\mathtt{S\text{-}})\mathtt{SAME}$ denotes either $\mathtt{SAME}$ or $\mathtt{S\text{-}SAME}$, FPK denotes $(\mathsf{fpk}_i)_{i \in [\ell]}$, and FM denotes $(\mathsf{fm}_i)_{i \in [\ell]}$. The oracle in the experiments for $\mathtt{SAME\text{-}R}, \mathtt{S\text{-}SAME\text{-}R}, \mathtt{SAME\text{-}R'}$, and $\mathtt{S\text{-}SAME\text{-}R'}$ security will be given in Fig 5.

notions consists only of the randomness, excluding the ciphertext. The usefulness of these variants will be explained shortly after the formal definition.

Formally, the definitions of $\mathtt{SAME\text{-}R}$, $\mathtt{S\text{-}SAME\text{-}R}$, $\mathtt{SAME\text{-}R'}$, and $\mathtt{S\text{-}SAME\text{-}R'}$ security are as follows.

Definition 11 ($\mathtt{SAME\text{-}R}$ and $\mathtt{SAME\text{-}R'}$ Security and Their Stronger Variants). *Let* $\mathtt{XXX} \in \{\mathtt{SAME\text{-}R}, \mathtt{S\text{-}SAME\text{-}R}, \mathtt{SAME\text{-}R'}, \mathtt{S\text{-}SAME\text{-}R'}\}$. *We say that an ℓ-SAME scheme* AME *is* $\mathtt{XXX}$ *secure if it satisfies the following conditions 1 and 2:*

1. *(Setup, KG, Enc, Dec) constitutes an IND–CPA secure PKE scheme.*
2. *For any PPT adversary* $\mathcal{A}$, $\mathsf{Adv}^{\mathtt{XXX}}_{\mathsf{AME},\mathcal{A}}(\lambda) := 2 \cdot |\Pr[\mathsf{Expt}^{\mathtt{XXX}}_{\mathsf{AME},\mathcal{A}}(\lambda) = 1] - \frac{1}{2}|$ *is negligible, where the experiment* $\mathsf{Expt}^{\mathtt{XXX}}_{\mathsf{AME},\mathcal{A}}(\lambda)$ *is defined as in Fig. 4 and the procedure of the oracle* $\mathcal{O}^{\mathtt{XXX}}_b$ *is defined as in Fig 5.*

It should be obvious that $\mathtt{SAME\text{-}R}$ (resp. $\mathtt{S\text{-}SAME\text{-}R}$) security implies $\mathtt{SAME}$ (resp. $\mathtt{S\text{-}SAME}$) security, since an adversary considered in the former gets more information than the latter.

Theorem 1. *If an ℓ-SAME scheme* AME *is* $\mathtt{SAME\text{-}R}$ *(resp.* $\mathtt{S\text{-}SAME\text{-}R}$*) secure, then* AME *is also* $\mathtt{SAME}$ *(resp.* $\mathtt{S\text{-}SAME}$*) secure.*

Next, we show the equivalence between $\mathtt{SAME\text{-}R}$ (resp. $\mathtt{S\text{-}SAME\text{-}R}$) and $\mathtt{SAME\text{-}R'}$ (resp. $\mathtt{S\text{-}SAME\text{-}R'}$). By this equivalence, in order to prove $\mathtt{SAME\text{-}R}$ (resp. $\mathtt{S\text{-}SAME\text{-}R}$) security, it is sufficient to prove $\mathtt{SAME\text{-}R'}$ (resp. $\mathtt{S\text{-}SAME\text{-}R'}$) security.

Theorem 2. *An ℓ-SAME scheme* AME *is* $\mathtt{SAME\text{-}R}$ *secure (resp.* $\mathtt{S\text{-}SAME\text{-}R}$*) if and only if* AME *is* $\mathtt{SAME\text{-}R'}$ *(resp.* $\mathtt{S\text{-}SAME\text{-}R'}$*).*

$$\underline{\mathcal{O}_b^{\mathtt{XXX}}(\mathsf{FM}, \mathsf{dm}):}$$

> if $b = 0$ then
>> $(r_i)_{i \in [\ell]} \xleftarrow{\$} \mathsf{fRand}(\mathsf{pp}, \mathsf{FPK}, \mathsf{FM}, \mathsf{dpk}, \mathsf{dm})$
>
> if $b = 1$ then
>> $(r_i)_{i \in [\ell]} \xleftarrow{\$} \mathcal{R}^\ell$
>
> for $i \in [\ell]$
>> $c_i \leftarrow \mathsf{Enc}(\mathsf{fpk}_i, \mathsf{fm}_i; r_i)$
>
> if $\mathtt{XXX} \in \{\mathtt{SAME\text{-}R}, \mathtt{S\text{-}SAME\text{-}R}\}$ then
>> return $(c_i, r_i)_{i \in [\ell]}$
>
> if $\mathtt{XXX} \in \{\mathtt{SAME\text{-}R}', \mathtt{S\text{-}SAME\text{-}R}'\}$ then
>> return $(r_i)_{i \in [\ell]}$

Fig. 5. Procedure of the oracle in the experiments for $\mathtt{SAME\text{-}R}$, $\mathtt{S\text{-}SAME\text{-}R}$, $\mathtt{SAME\text{-}R}'$ and $\mathtt{S\text{-}SAME\text{-}R}'$ security. FPK denotes $(\mathsf{fpk}_i)_{i \in [\ell]}$, and FM denotes $(\mathsf{fm}_i)_{i \in [\ell]}$. $\mathcal{O}_b^{\mathtt{SAME\text{-}R}}$ and $\mathcal{O}_b^{\mathtt{S\text{-}SAME\text{-}R}}$ are the encryption oracles whose output includes not only ciphertexts but also randomness used for generating the ciphertexts, and $\mathcal{O}_b^{\mathtt{SAME\text{-}R}'}$ and $\mathcal{O}_b^{\mathtt{S\text{-}SAME\text{-}R}'}$ are the randomness oracles that only output randomness used for generating the ciphertexts.

The equivalence can be established since the queried forced messages FM are chosen by an adversary itself, and thus if the adversary is given the randomness behind the randomness, then it can compute the ciphertexts by itself. For completeness, we provide the formal proof in the full version.

4   Persiano et al.'s SAME Scheme

Persiano et al. [25] showed how a PKE scheme satisfying several additional properties can be turned into a SAME scheme that can encrypt a 1-bit duplicate message. In this section, we investigate whether their scheme satisfies our refined security notions, and show that it satisfies $\mathtt{SAME\text{-}R}$ security under exactly the same assumption originally used to prove its $\mathtt{SAME}$ security, while it does not satisfy $\mathtt{S\text{-}SAME\text{-}R}$ security as there is an easy attack.

We first recall their SAME scheme. Let $\mathsf{PKE} = (\mathsf{Setup}', \mathsf{KG}', \mathsf{Enc}', \mathsf{Dec}')$ be a 1-bit PKE scheme that satisfies the following additional properties.[3]

- *(P1) Common randomness property.* For every two public keys pk_0 and pk_1 output by KG' and for every ciphertext c produced using public key pk_0 and randomness r, there exists a message m such that $c = \mathsf{Enc}'(\mathsf{pk}_1, m; r)$; that is, c is a ciphertext also for public key pk_1 with the randomness r.
- *(P2) Message recovery from randomness.* It is possible to recover the plaintext carried by a ciphertext c from the randomness r used to produce it and the public key pk.
- *(P3) Equal distribution of plaintexts.* All public keys share the same ciphertext space, and for a ciphertext c in the common ciphertext space and for a random key pair $(\mathsf{pk}, \mathsf{sk})$ as sampled by KG', c is the ciphertext of the bit 0 with a probability $1/2$.

---

[3] The description of the properties here is mostly taken verbatim from [25, Section 6.1].

Based on PKE, Persiano et al.'s SAME scheme $\mathsf{AME_{PPY}} = (\mathsf{Setup}, \mathsf{KG}, \mathsf{Enc}, \mathsf{Dec},$ $\mathsf{fRand}, \mathsf{dDec})$ is constructed as in Fig. 6.

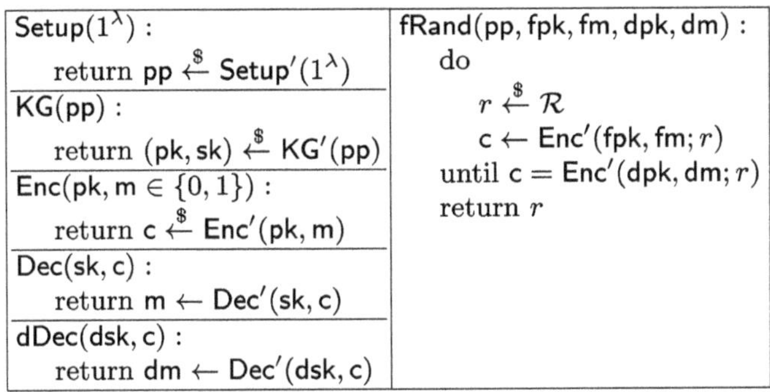

Fig. 6. Persiano et al.'s SAME scheme $\mathsf{AME_{PPY}}$ constructed from a 1-bit PKE scheme with additional properties (P1) to (P3).

Persiano et al. [25] showed the following.

Theorem 3. *If* PKE *is* $\mathsf{IND{-}CPA}$ *secure and satisfies the additional properties (P1) to (P3), then* $\mathsf{AME_{PPY}}$ *satisfies* SAME *security.*

We now state our results on Persiano et al.'s SAME scheme regarding our refined security notions for SAME.

Theorem 4. *Under exactly the same assumption as used in Theorem 3,* $\mathsf{AME_{PPY}}$ *satisfies* $\mathsf{SAME{-}R}$ *security.*

Proof. (sketch) According to the original proof for Theorem 3 in [25], the argument for showing that a genuine ciphertext is indistinguishable from an anamorphic ciphertext, namely, the indistinguishability of a ciphertext $\mathsf{c} = \mathsf{Enc}(\mathsf{fpk}, \mathsf{fm};$ $r)$ in the cases where

- r is sampled honestly from the randomness space of Enc, and
- r is generated as $r \xleftarrow{\$} \mathsf{fRand}(\mathsf{pp}, \mathsf{fpk}, \mathsf{fm}, \mathsf{dpk}, \mathsf{dm})$,

is purely statistical. Thus, the indistinguishability holds even against computationally unbounded adversaries, and giving the randomness behind the ciphertext to the adversary does no harm to the original argument, which implies that $\mathsf{AME_{PPY}}$ is $\mathsf{SAME{-}R}$ secure.   □ (**Theorem** 4)

Theorem 5. $\mathsf{AME_{PPY}}$ *is not* $\mathsf{S{-}SAME{-}R}$ *secure.*

Proof. We first describe an adversary $\mathcal{A}$ that attacks the $\mathsf{S{-}SAME{-}R}$ security of $\mathsf{AME_{PPY}}$: $\mathcal{A}$ is initially given $(\mathsf{pp}, \mathsf{fpk}, \mathsf{fsk}, \mathsf{dpk})$ as input, picks arbitrary $\mathsf{fm}, \mathsf{dm} \in \{0, 1\}$, and submits $(\mathsf{fm}, \mathsf{dm})$ to the encryption oracle $\mathcal{O}_b^{\mathsf{S{-}SAME{-}R}}$, which returns a ciphertext/randomness pair (c, r) to $\mathcal{A}$. Then, $\mathcal{A}$ sets $b' \leftarrow (\mathsf{Enc}(\mathsf{dpk}, \mathsf{dm}; r) \stackrel{?}{=} c)$, and terminates with output b'.

Let b be the challenge bit in the $\mathsf{S\text{-}SAME\text{-}R}$ experiment for $\mathcal{A}$. If $b = 0$ (i.e. r is computed using fRand), then it always holds $\mathsf{Enc}(\mathsf{dpk}, \mathsf{dm}; r) = c$, and thus it holds that $\Pr[b' = 1 | b = 0] = 1$. On the other hand, if $b = 1$ (i.e. r is sampled randomly), then $\mathsf{Enc}(\mathsf{dpk}, \mathsf{dm}; r) = c$ holds with probability $1/2$ due to the property (P3) (Equal distribution of plaintexts), and thus it holds that $\Pr[b' = 1 | b = 1] = \Pr[b' = 0 | b = 1] = 1/2$. Hence, $\mathcal{A}$'s advantage in attacking the $\mathsf{S\text{-}SAME\text{-}R}$ security of $\mathsf{AME}_{\mathsf{PPY}}$ is

$$\mathsf{Adv}^{\mathsf{S\text{-}SAME\text{-}R}}_{\mathsf{AME}_{\mathsf{PPY}}, \mathcal{A}}(\lambda) = \left| \Pr[b' = 1 | b = 0] - \Pr[b' = 1 | b = 1] \right| = \left| 1 - \frac{1}{2} \right| = \frac{1}{2},$$

which is clearly non-negligible. $\square$ (**Theorem** 5)

5 Wang et al.'s First SAME Scheme and Its Modified Scheme

In this section, we investigate whether Wang et al.'s first ℓ-SAME scheme satisfies our refined security notions. Specifically, in Sect. 5.1, we show that their first scheme satisfies $\mathsf{SAME\text{-}R}$ security. Furthermore, we consider a modified version of their scheme by slightly changing the building blocks, and show that the modified scheme satisfies $\mathsf{S\text{-}SAME\text{-}R}$ security. This result and the reason why we consider such a modified scheme will be explained in Sect. 5.2.

5.1 Wang et al.'s First Scheme and Its $\mathsf{SAME\text{-}R}$ Security

Firstly, we recall Wang et al.'s first ℓ-SAME scheme proposed in [28, Section 4], which uses a pseudorandom PKE scheme and an entropy-smoothing function as building blocks.

Formally, let $\mathsf{PKE} = (\mathsf{Setup}', \mathsf{KG}', \mathsf{Enc}', \mathsf{Dec}')$ be a PKE scheme. For simplicity, we assume that the message length encrypted by PKE is fixed to be some polynomial $n = n(\lambda)$. Let $\ell = \ell(\lambda)$ denote the ciphertext length of PKE corresponding to the fixed message length n, and let $\mathsf{H} \colon \mathcal{K} \times \{0,1\}^\ell \to \{0,1\}$ be an entropy-smoothing function where $\mathcal{K}$ denote its key space. (For better readability, we write $\mathsf{H}_k(\cdot)$ to mean $\mathsf{H}(k, \cdot)$.)

Using these building blocks, Wang et al.'s first ℓ-SAME scheme $\mathsf{AME}_{\mathsf{WCHY1}}$ $= (\mathsf{Setup}, \mathsf{KG}, \mathsf{Enc}, \mathsf{Dec}, \mathsf{fRand}, \mathsf{dDec})$ is constructed as in Fig. 7.[4]

Wang et al. showed the following theorems that guarantee the correctness and SAME security of $\mathsf{AME}_{\mathsf{WCHY1}}$.

---

[4] In Wang et al.'s original scheme, the counter `ctr` for the "do-until" loop in the description of fRand is not used, and thus is not guaranteed to terminate. Strictly speaking, therefore, fRand with the original description is an expected polynomial-time algorithm, not a PPT algorithm. In this paper, we introduce the counter so that it terminates in polynomial time.

$\mathsf{Setup}(1^\lambda):$	$\mathsf{fRand}(\mathsf{pp}, (\mathsf{fpk}_i)_{i\in[\ell]}, (\mathsf{fm}_i)_{i\in[\ell]}, \mathsf{dpk}, \mathsf{dm}):$
$\quad \mathsf{pp}' \overset{\$}{\leftarrow} \mathsf{Setup}'(1^\lambda); \ k \overset{\$}{\leftarrow} \mathcal{K}$	$\quad$ parse $\mathsf{pp} = (\mathsf{pp}', k)$
$\quad$ return $\mathsf{pp} \leftarrow (\mathsf{pp}', k)$	$\quad c' \overset{\$}{\leftarrow} \mathsf{Enc}'(\mathsf{dpk}, \mathsf{dm})$
$\mathsf{KG}(\mathsf{pp}):$	$\quad \mathsf{b}_1\|\mathsf{b}_2\|\cdots\|\mathsf{b}_\ell := c'$
$\quad$ parse $\mathsf{pp} = (\mathsf{pp}', k)$	$\quad$ for $i \in [\ell]$
$\quad$ return $(\mathsf{pk}, \mathsf{sk}) \overset{\$}{\leftarrow} \mathsf{KG}'(\mathsf{pp}')$	$\quad\quad \mathbf{ctr} \leftarrow 0$
$\mathsf{Enc}(\mathsf{pk}, \mathsf{m}):$	$\quad\quad$ do
$\quad$ return $\mathsf{c} \overset{\$}{\leftarrow} \mathsf{Enc}'(\mathsf{pk}, \mathsf{m})$	$\quad\quad\quad r^* \overset{\$}{\leftarrow} \mathcal{R}$
$\mathsf{Dec}(\mathsf{sk}, \mathsf{c}):$	$\quad\quad\quad c^* \leftarrow \mathsf{Enc}'(\mathsf{fpk}_i, \mathsf{fm}_i; r^*)$
$\quad$ return $\mathsf{m} \leftarrow \mathsf{Dec}'(\mathsf{sk}, \mathsf{c})$	$\quad\quad\quad \mathsf{b}^* \leftarrow \mathsf{H}_k(c^*)$
$\mathsf{dDec}(\mathsf{dsk}, (\mathsf{c}_i)_{i\in[\ell]}):$	$\quad\quad\quad \mathbf{ctr} \leftarrow \mathbf{ctr} + 1$
$\quad$ for $i \in [\ell]$	$\quad\quad$ until $\mathsf{b}^* = \mathsf{b}_i \vee \mathbf{ctr} \geq \lambda$
$\quad\quad \mathsf{b}_i \leftarrow \mathsf{H}_k(\mathsf{c}_i)$	$\quad\quad r_i \leftarrow r^*$
$\quad\quad c' \leftarrow \mathsf{b}_1\|\mathsf{b}_2\|\cdots\|\mathsf{b}_\ell$	$\quad$ return $(r_i)_{i\in[\ell]}$
$\quad\quad$ return $\mathsf{dm}' \leftarrow \mathsf{Dec}'(\mathsf{dsk}, c')$	

Fig. 7. Wang et al.'s first ℓ-SAME scheme $\mathsf{AME}_{\mathsf{WCHY1}}$ constructed from a pseudorandom PKE scheme and an entropy-smoothing function. In the figure, $\mathsf{b}_i \in \{0,1\}$ for every $i \in [\ell]$.

Theorem 6. *If* PKE *satisfies pseudorandomness and* H *is entropy-smoothing, then* $\mathsf{AME}_{\mathsf{WCHY1}}$ *satisfies correctness.*

Theorem 7. *If* PKE *satisfies pseudorandomness and* H *is entropy-smoothing, then* $\mathsf{AME}_{\mathsf{WCHY1}}$ *satisfies* SAME *security.*

Since the proof for the correctness of $\mathsf{AME}_{\mathsf{WCHY1}}$ is not explicitly given in [28], we provide the formal proof of Theorem 6 in the full version for completeness.

For convenience for our correctness proof (of Theorem 6), and also for our security proof below, let us introduce the following lemma, which can be used to estimate the probability that the "do-until" loop in an execution of fRand ends without finding a good fake randomness.

Lemma 3. *Let* PKE *be PKE whose plaintext (resp. ciphertext) space is* $\{0,1\}^n$ *(resp.* $\{0,1\}^\ell$) *for some polynomials* $n = n(\lambda)$ *and* $\ell = \ell(\lambda)$. *Let* $\mathsf{H}\colon \mathcal{K} \times \{0,1\}^\ell \to \{0,1\}$ *be an efficiently computable function. If* PKE *satisfies pseudorandomness and* H *satisfies entropy-smoothness, then for any PPT adversary* $\mathcal{A}$, $\mathsf{Adv}^{\mathsf{Fail}}_{\mathsf{PKE},\mathsf{H},\mathcal{A}}(\lambda) := \Pr[\mathsf{Expt}^{\mathsf{Fail}}_{\mathsf{PKE},\mathsf{H},\mathcal{A}}(\lambda) = 1]$ *is negligible, where* $\mathsf{Expt}^{\mathsf{Fail}}_{\mathsf{PKE},\mathsf{H},\mathcal{A}}(\lambda)$ *is the experiment defined as in Fig 8.*

More specifically, for any PPT adversary $\mathcal{A}$, *there exist PPT adversaries* $\mathcal{B}$ *and* $\mathcal{B}'$ *such that* $\mathsf{Adv}^{\mathsf{Fail}}_{\mathsf{PKE},\mathsf{H},\mathcal{A}}(\lambda) \leq \lambda\left(\mathsf{Adv}^{\mathsf{PR}}_{\mathsf{PKE},\mathcal{B}}(\lambda) + \mathsf{Adv}^{\mathsf{ESF}}_{\mathsf{H},\mathcal{B}'}(\lambda)\right) + 2^{-\lambda}.$

The formal proof is given in the full version. An intuition behind the proof is that if the ciphertexts $\{c_h\}$ are pseudorandom and $\{\mathsf{b}_h\}$ are computed by an entropy-smoothing function H using $\{c_h\}$ as input, then the bits $\{\mathsf{b}_h\}$ behave like uniformly random bits, and thus the probability that none of b_h hits $\mathsf{b}_{\lambda+1}$ is exponentially small in λ.

$$
\begin{aligned}
&\mathsf{Expt}^{\mathtt{Fail}}_{\mathsf{PKE,H},\mathcal{A}}(\lambda): \\
&\quad k \xleftarrow{\$} \mathcal{K} \\
&\quad \mathsf{pp} \xleftarrow{\$} \mathsf{Setup}(1^\lambda) \\
&\quad (\mathsf{pk},\mathsf{sk}) \xleftarrow{\$} \mathsf{KG}(\mathsf{pp}) \\
&\quad \mathsf{m} \xleftarrow{\$} \mathcal{A}(k,\mathsf{pp},\mathsf{pk}) \\
&\quad {}^\forall h \in [\lambda+1] : \mathsf{c}_h \xleftarrow{\$} \mathsf{Enc}(\mathsf{pk},\mathsf{m}) \\
&\quad {}^\forall h \in [\lambda+1] : \mathsf{b}_h \leftarrow \mathsf{H}_k(\mathsf{c}_h) \\
&\quad \text{if } \bigwedge_{h=1}^{\lambda}(\mathsf{b}_h \neq \mathsf{b}_{\lambda+1}) \text{ then} \\
&\qquad \text{return } 1 \\
&\quad \text{else} \\
&\qquad \text{return } 0
\end{aligned}
$$

Fig. 8. Experiment for evaluating the probability of the "failure" that could occur in an execution of fRand.

We now show that $\mathsf{AME}_{\mathtt{WCHY1}}$ satisfies SAME-R security.

Theorem 8. *If* PKE *satisfies pseudorandomness and* H *is entropy-smoothing, then* $\mathsf{AME}_{\mathtt{WCHY1}}$ *satisfies* SAME-R *security.*

Intuitions Behind the Proof. In the proof, we would like to construct a sequence of games in which the oracle's behavior is changed from using randomness generated by fRand to using uniformly sampled randomness.

In the (original) proof for SAME security of $\mathsf{AME}_{\mathtt{WCHY1}}$ in [28], such a transition is made possible by replacing all ciphertexts of forced messages and a duplicate message with random ones. As a result, the decision on whether to use sampled randomness r in oracle responses no longer depends on the queries of an adversary, and the resulting distribution of output randomness becomes identical to that of true randomness. However, in the SAME-R security model, where the randomness is revealed to the adversary, this approach no longer works. If we attempt to replace the ciphertext of forced messages with random ones using the pseudorandomness of the underlying PKE scheme, the reduction algorithm cannot return r that remains consistent with the embedded instance. Consequently, the simulation fails, and the original proof strategy cannot be applied directly in the SAME-R setting.

To prove SAME-R security, we instead modify the ciphertext of a duplicate message dm rather than the ciphertexts of the forced messages $\mathsf{fm}_1,\ldots,\mathsf{fm}_\ell$. Since the randomness used to generate the ciphertext of dm is not revealed to the adversary, we can exploit this fact together with the pseudorandomness of the underlying PKE scheme to replace the ciphertext of dm with a concatenation of $\mathsf{b}_i = \mathsf{H}_k(\mathsf{Enc}(\mathsf{fpk}_i,\mathsf{fm}_i))$ for every $i \in [\ell]$, using an additional intermediate game in which this ciphertext is sampled uniformly at random. As a result, for every $i \in [\ell]$, the generation process of b_i becomes identical to that of b^* generated in the do-until loop, and by applying the properties of rejection sampling and conditional resampling (Lemmas 1 and 2, respectively), we can show that the resulting randomness distribution is indistinguishable from that of true randomness. The full details are presented in the formal security proof below.

Proof. (Due to the space constraint, many of the details of the proof are omitted. See the full version for all the details.) Since IND–CPA security of PKE follows from the pseudorandomness of PKE, (Setup, KG, Enc, Dec) is IND–CPA secure. By Theorem 2, it is sufficient to show that $\mathsf{AME}_{\mathsf{WCHY1}}$ is SAME–R′ secure. Let $\mathcal{A}$ be a PPT adversary against the SAME–R′ security that makes q queries to the randomness oracle. We will show that for this $\mathcal{A}$, there exist PPT adversaries $\mathcal{B}, \mathcal{B}', \mathcal{B}''$, and $\mathcal{B}''''$ that satisfy

$$\mathsf{Adv}^{\mathsf{SAME-R}'}_{\mathsf{AME}_{\mathsf{WCHY1}},\mathcal{A}}(\lambda)$$
$$\leq q\mathsf{Adv}^{\mathsf{PR}}_{\mathsf{PKE},\mathcal{B}}(\lambda) + q\ell\Big(\mathsf{Adv}^{\mathsf{ESF}}_{\mathsf{H},\mathcal{B}'}(\lambda) + \mathsf{Adv}^{\mathsf{PR}}_{\mathsf{PKE},\mathcal{B}''}(\lambda) + \mathsf{Adv}^{\mathsf{Fail}}_{\mathsf{PKE},\mathsf{H},\mathcal{B}'''}(\lambda)\Big), \qquad (1)$$

which implies the theorem.

We show the above by using a sequence of games argument using eight games, described in the following. Since the only difference in $\mathsf{Expt}^{\mathsf{SAME-R}'}_{\mathsf{AME}_{\mathsf{WCHY1}},\mathcal{A}}(\lambda)$ between the cases in which the challenge bit 0 and 1 lies in the randomness oracle, we will focus on its behavior. For convenience, Figs. 9 and 10 describe the behaviors of the randomness oracle in each game. Let b be the challenge bit and b' be the guess bit output by $\mathcal{A}$ in $\mathsf{Expt}^{\mathsf{SAME-R}'}_{\mathsf{AME}_{\mathsf{WCHY1}},\mathcal{A}}(\lambda)$. Furthermore, for $N \in \{0,\ldots,7\}$, let $\mathcal{O}^{\mathsf{Rand}}_{\mathsf{Game}N}$ be the randomness oracle in Game N, and let G_N be the event that $\mathcal{A}$ returns 1 in Game $N \in \{0,1,\ldots,7\}$.

Game 0: This is exactly $\mathsf{Expt}^{\mathsf{SAME-R}'}_{\mathsf{AME}_{\mathsf{WCHY1}},\mathcal{A}}(\lambda)$ in which the challenge bit $b=0$.

By definition, we have $\Pr[b'=1 \mid b=0] = \Pr[\mathsf{G}_0]$.

Game 1: This game is the same as Game 0 except for how c is generated. Specifically, $\mathsf{c} \in \{0,1\}^\ell$ is chosen uniformly at random instead of running Enc'.

We can show that there exists a PPT adversary $\mathcal{B}$ that attacks the pseudorandomness of PKE such that

$$\Big|\Pr[\mathsf{G}_0] - \Pr[\mathsf{G}_1]\Big| = q\mathsf{Adv}^{\mathsf{PR}}_{\mathsf{PKE},\mathcal{B}}(\lambda).$$

The reduction algorithm $\mathcal{B}$ is described in the full version.

Game 2: This game is the same as Game 1 except for how $\mathsf{b}_1, \mathsf{b}_2, \ldots, \mathsf{b}_\ell$ are generated. Specifically, instead of sampling $\mathsf{b}_1\|\mathsf{b}_2\|\cdots\|\mathsf{b}_\ell$ at once, we sample it bit by bit uniformly at random inside the "for" loop.

It is straightforward to see that $\Pr[\mathsf{G}_1] = \Pr[\mathsf{G}_2]$ holds, since an ℓ-bit string chosen uniformly at random has the same distribution as an ℓ-bit string formed by concatenating random 1-bit strings.

$\mathcal{O}^{\mathsf{Rand}}_{\mathsf{Game0}}((\mathsf{fm}_i)_{i\in[\ell]}, \mathsf{dm})$:

$\quad \mathsf{c} \xleftarrow{\$} \mathsf{Enc}'(\mathsf{dpk}, \mathsf{dm}); \mathsf{b}_1\|\mathsf{b}_2\|\cdots\|\mathsf{b}_\ell := \mathsf{c}$
$\quad$ for $i \in [\ell]$
$\quad\quad \mathsf{ctr} \leftarrow 0$
$\quad\quad$ do
$\quad\quad\quad r^* \xleftarrow{\$} \mathcal{R}; \mathsf{c}^* \leftarrow \mathsf{Enc}'(\mathsf{fpk}_i, \mathsf{fm}_i; r^*)$
$\quad\quad\quad \mathsf{b}^* \leftarrow \mathsf{H}_k(\mathsf{c}^*); \mathsf{ctr} \leftarrow \mathsf{ctr} + 1$
$\quad\quad$ until $\mathsf{b}^* = \mathsf{b}_i \vee \mathsf{ctr} \geq \lambda$
$\quad\quad r_i \leftarrow r^*$
$\quad$ return $(r_i)_{i\in[\ell]}$

$\mathcal{O}^{\mathsf{Rand}}_{\mathsf{Game1}}((\mathsf{fm}_i)_{i\in[\ell]}, \mathsf{dm})$:

$\quad \mathsf{c} \xleftarrow{\$} \{0,1\}^\ell; \mathsf{b}_1\|\mathsf{b}_2\|\cdots\|\mathsf{b}_\ell := \mathsf{c}$
$\quad$ for $i \in [\ell]$
$\quad\quad \mathsf{ctr} \leftarrow 0$
$\quad\quad$ do
$\quad\quad\quad r^* \xleftarrow{\$} \mathcal{R}; \mathsf{c}^* \leftarrow \mathsf{Enc}'(\mathsf{fpk}_i, \mathsf{fm}_i; r^*)$
$\quad\quad\quad \mathsf{b}^* \leftarrow \mathsf{H}_k(\mathsf{c}^*); \mathsf{ctr} \leftarrow \mathsf{ctr} + 1$
$\quad\quad$ until $\mathsf{b}^* = \mathsf{b}_i \vee \mathsf{ctr} \geq \lambda$
$\quad\quad r_i \leftarrow r^*$
$\quad$ return $(r_i)_{i\in[\ell]}$

$\mathcal{O}^{\mathsf{Rand}}_{\mathsf{Game2}}((\mathsf{fm}_i)_{i\in[\ell]}, \mathsf{dm})$:

$\quad$ for $i \in [\ell]$
$\quad\quad \mathsf{b}_i \xleftarrow{\$} \{0,1\}$
$\quad\quad \mathsf{ctr} \leftarrow 0$
$\quad\quad$ do
$\quad\quad\quad r^* \xleftarrow{\$} \mathcal{R}; \mathsf{c}^* \leftarrow \mathsf{Enc}'(\mathsf{fpk}_i, \mathsf{fm}_i; r^*)$
$\quad\quad\quad \mathsf{b}^* \leftarrow \mathsf{H}_k(\mathsf{c}^*); \mathsf{ctr} \leftarrow \mathsf{ctr} + 1$
$\quad\quad$ until $\mathsf{b}^* = \mathsf{b}_i \vee \mathsf{ctr} \geq \lambda$
$\quad\quad r_i \leftarrow r^*$
$\quad$ return $(r_i)_{i\in[\ell]}$

$\mathcal{O}^{\mathsf{Rand}}_{\mathsf{Game3}}((\mathsf{fm}_i)_{i\in[\ell]}, \mathsf{dm})$:

$\quad$ for $i \in [\ell]$
$\quad\quad \widehat{\mathsf{c}}_i \xleftarrow{\$} \{0,1\}^\ell; \mathsf{b}_i \leftarrow \mathsf{H}_k(\widehat{\mathsf{c}}_i)$
$\quad\quad \mathsf{ctr} \leftarrow 0$
$\quad\quad$ do
$\quad\quad\quad r^* \xleftarrow{\$} \mathcal{R}; \mathsf{c}^* \leftarrow \mathsf{Enc}'(\mathsf{fpk}_i, \mathsf{fm}_i; r^*)$
$\quad\quad\quad \mathsf{b}^* \leftarrow \mathsf{H}_k(\mathsf{c}^*); \mathsf{ctr} \leftarrow \mathsf{ctr} + 1$
$\quad\quad$ until $\mathsf{b}^* = \mathsf{b}_i \vee \mathsf{ctr} \geq \lambda$
$\quad\quad r_i \leftarrow r^*$
$\quad$ return $(r_i)_{i\in[\ell]}$

Fig. 9. Behaviors of the randomness oracle $\mathcal{O}^{\mathsf{Rand}}$ in Games 0 through 3 in the proof of Theorem 8.

Game 3: This game is the same as Game 2 except for how b_i is generated inside the "for" loop for each $i \in [\ell]$. Specifically, for every $i \in [\ell]$, $\widehat{\mathsf{c}}_i \in \{0,1\}^\ell$ is chosen uniformly at random and $\mathsf{b}_i \leftarrow \mathsf{H}_k(\widehat{\mathsf{c}}_i)$ is computed, instead of randomly sampling b_i.

We can show that there exists a PPT adversary $\mathcal{B}'$ that attacks the entropy-smoothness of H such that

$$\left|\Pr[\mathsf{G}_2] - \Pr[\mathsf{G}_3]\right| = q\ell\mathsf{Adv}^{\mathsf{ESF}}_{\mathsf{H},\mathcal{B}'}(\lambda).$$

The reduction algorithm $\mathcal{B}'$ is given in the full version.

Game 4: This game is the same as Game 3 except for how $\widehat{\mathsf{c}}_i$ is computed inside the "for" loop for each $i \in [\ell]$. Specifically, for each $i \in [\ell]$, $\widehat{r}_i \in \mathcal{R}$ is chosen uniformly at random and $\widehat{\mathsf{c}}_i$ is computed by $\widehat{\mathsf{c}}_i \leftarrow \mathsf{Enc}'(\mathsf{fpk}_i, \mathsf{fm}_i; \widehat{r}_i)$, instead of sampling a random ℓ-bit string.

We can show that there exists a PPT adversary $\mathcal{B}''$ that attacks the pseudo-randomness of PKE such that

$$\left|\Pr[\mathsf{G}_3] - \Pr[\mathsf{G}_4]\right| = q\ell\mathsf{Adv}^{\mathsf{PR}}_{\mathsf{PKE},\mathcal{B}''}(\lambda).$$

The reduction algorithm $\mathcal{B}''$ is given in the full version.

$\underline{\mathcal{O}^{\mathtt{Rand}}_{\mathsf{Game4}}((\mathsf{fm}_i)_{i\in[\ell]},\mathsf{dm}):}$

  for $i \in [\ell]$

    $\widehat{r}_i \xleftarrow{\$} \mathcal{R}$; $\widehat{\mathsf{c}}_i \leftarrow \mathsf{Enc}'(\mathsf{fpk}_i, \mathsf{fm}_i;\ \widehat{r}_i)$

    $\mathsf{b}_i \leftarrow \mathsf{H}_k(\widehat{\mathsf{c}}_i)$

    $\mathtt{ctr} \leftarrow 0$

    do

      $r^* \xleftarrow{\$} \mathcal{R}$; $\mathsf{c}^* \leftarrow \mathsf{Enc}'(\mathsf{fpk}_i, \mathsf{fm}_i; r^*)$

      $\mathsf{b}^* \leftarrow \mathsf{H}_k(\mathsf{c}^*)$

      $\mathtt{ctr} \leftarrow \mathtt{ctr} + 1$

    until $\mathsf{b}^* = \mathsf{b}_i \vee \mathtt{ctr} \geq \lambda$

    $r_i \leftarrow r^*$

  return $(r_i)_{i\in[\ell]}$

$\underline{\mathcal{O}^{\mathtt{Rand}}_{\mathsf{Game5}}((\mathsf{fm}_i)_{i\in[\ell]},\mathsf{dm}):}$

  for $i \in [\ell]$

    $\widehat{r}_i \xleftarrow{\$} \mathcal{R}$; $\widehat{\mathsf{c}}_i \leftarrow \mathsf{Enc}'(\mathsf{fpk}_i, \mathsf{fm}_i;\ \widehat{r}_i)$

    $\mathsf{b}_i \leftarrow \mathsf{H}_k(\widehat{\mathsf{c}}_i)$

    do

      $r^* \xleftarrow{\$} \mathcal{R}$; $\mathsf{c}^* \xleftarrow{\$} \mathsf{Enc}'(\mathsf{fpk}_i, \mathsf{fm}_i; r^*)$

      $\mathsf{b}^* \leftarrow \mathsf{H}_k(\mathsf{c}^*)$

    until $\mathsf{b}^* = \mathsf{b}_i$

    $r_i \leftarrow r^*$

  return $(r_i)_{i\in[\ell]}$

$\underline{\mathcal{O}^{\mathtt{Rand}}_{\mathsf{Game6}}((\mathsf{fm}_i)_{i\in[\ell]},\mathsf{dm}):}$

  for $i \in [\ell]$

    $\widehat{r}_i \xleftarrow{\$} \mathcal{R}$; $\widehat{\mathsf{c}}_i \leftarrow \mathsf{Enc}'(\mathsf{fpk}_i, \mathsf{fm}_i;\ \widehat{r}_i)$

    $\mathsf{b}_i \leftarrow \mathsf{H}_k(\widehat{\mathsf{c}}_i)$

    define:

$$\mathcal{R}_i := \left\{ r \in \mathcal{R} \ \middle|\ \begin{array}{l} \mathsf{Enc}'(\mathsf{fpk}_i, \mathsf{fm}_i; r) = \mathsf{c}_i \\ \wedge\ \mathsf{H}_k(\mathsf{c}_i) = \mathsf{b}_i \end{array} \right\}$$

    $r_i \xleftarrow{\$} \mathcal{R}_i$

  return $(r_i)_{i\in[\ell]}$

$\underline{\mathcal{O}^{\mathtt{Rand}}_{\mathsf{Game7}}((\mathsf{fm}_i)_{i\in[\ell]},\mathsf{dm}):}$

  for $i \in [\ell]$

    $r_i \xleftarrow{\$} \mathcal{R}$

  return $(r_i)_{i\in[\ell]}$

Fig. 10. Behaviors of the randomness oracle $\mathcal{O}^{\mathtt{Rand}}$ in Games 4 through 7 in the proof of Theorem 8.

Game 5: This game is the same as Game 4 except for the processes and condition regarding $\mathtt{ctr}$. Specifically, in the randomness oracle, the operations $\mathtt{ctr} \leftarrow 0$ and $\mathtt{ctr} \leftarrow \mathtt{ctr} + 1$ are removed, and the loop-termination condition is changed from "until $\mathsf{b}^* = \mathsf{b}_i \vee \mathtt{ctr} \geq \lambda$" to "until $\mathsf{b}^* = \mathsf{b}_i$".

We can show that there exists a PPT adversary $\mathcal{B}'''$ that attacks the property defined in Lemma 3 such that

$$\left| \Pr[\mathsf{G}_4] - \Pr[\mathsf{G}_5] \right| \leq q\ell\mathsf{Adv}^{\mathtt{Fail}}_{\mathsf{PKE},\mathsf{H},\mathcal{B}'''}(\lambda).$$

The reduction algorithm $\mathcal{B}'''$ is given in the full version.

Game 6: This game is the same as Game 5 except for how $(r_i)_{i\in[\ell]}$ are generated. Specifically, for every $i \in [\ell]$, r_i is sampled uniformly at random from

$$\mathcal{R}_i := \left\{ r \in \mathcal{R} \mid \mathsf{Enc}'(\mathsf{fpk}_i, \mathsf{fm}_i; r) = \widehat{\mathsf{c}}_i \wedge \mathsf{H}_k(\widehat{\mathsf{c}}_i) = \mathsf{b}_i \right\}.$$

We argue that $\Pr[\mathsf{G}_5] = \Pr[\mathsf{G}_6]$ holds. To see this, fix $\mathcal{A}$'s query, $i \in [n]$, and b_i, and let us focus on the distribution of r_i. Let P be the predicate defined by $\mathsf{P}(r) := (\mathsf{H}_k(\mathsf{Enc}(\mathsf{fpk}_i, \mathsf{fm}_i; r)) \stackrel{?}{=} \mathsf{b}_i)$. Then, it is straightforward to see that the set $\mathcal{R}_i$ defined in Game 6 is exactly $\mathsf{P}^{-1}(1)$, from which r_i is chosen uniformly at random in Game 6. On the other hand, in Game 5, the distribution of r_i can be represented as follows:

$$\left\{ h \leftarrow 0; \ \text{do} \ \{h \leftarrow h+1; r_h \xleftarrow{\$} \mathcal{R}\} \ \text{until} \ \mathsf{P}(r_h) = 1 : r_h \right\}.$$

Hence, invoking Lemma 1 with the above predicate P, we can see that the distribution of r_i in Game 6 is identical to the distribution of r_i in Game 5, which implies $\Pr[\mathsf{G}_5] = \Pr[\mathsf{G}_6]$ as desired.

Game 7: In this game, for every $i \in [\ell]$, r_i is chosen uniformly at random from $\mathcal{R}$, and $(r_i)_{i \in [\ell]}$ is returned to the answer to $\mathcal{A}$'s query to the randomness oracle.

Note that Game 7 is exactly $\mathsf{Expt}^{\mathsf{SAME-R}'}_{\mathsf{AME}_{\mathsf{WCHY1}}, \mathcal{A}}(\lambda)$ in which the challenge bit $b = 1$. Hence, we have $\Pr[b' = 1 \mid b = 1] = \Pr[\mathsf{G}_7]$.

We argue that $\Pr[\mathsf{G}_6] = \Pr[\mathsf{G}_7]$ holds. To see this, let f be the function defined by $f(r) := \mathsf{H}_k(\mathsf{Enc}(\mathsf{fpk}_i, \mathsf{fm}_i; r))$. In Game 6, for every $i \in [\ell]$, the distribution of r_i is denoted as follows:

$$\left\{ \begin{array}{l} \widehat{r} \xleftarrow{\$} \mathcal{R}; \\ \mathsf{b}_i \leftarrow \mathsf{H}_k(\mathsf{Enc}(\mathsf{fpk}_i, \mathsf{fm}_i; \widehat{r})); \\ r_i \xleftarrow{\$} \left\{ r \in \mathcal{R} \mid \mathsf{H}_k(\mathsf{Enc}(\mathsf{fpk}_i, \mathsf{fm}_i; r)) = \mathsf{b}_i \right\} \end{array} \ : r_i \right\}$$

$$\equiv \left\{ \widehat{r} \xleftarrow{\$} \mathcal{R}; \mathsf{b}_i \leftarrow f(\widehat{r}); r_i \xleftarrow{\$} f^{-1}(\mathsf{b}_i) : r_i \right\}$$

Hence, by Lemma 2 with the above function f, $\{r \xleftarrow{\$} \mathcal{R} : r\} \equiv \{\widehat{r} \xleftarrow{\$} \mathcal{R}; \mathsf{b}_i \leftarrow f(\widehat{r}); r_i \xleftarrow{\$} f^{-1}(\mathsf{b}_i) : r_i\}$ holds. That is, each r_i has the same distribution between Games 6 and 7, and thus we have $\Pr[\mathsf{G}_6] = \Pr[\mathsf{G}_7]$.

Equation (1) now follows from the triangle inequality and the above established (in)equalities regarding $\Pr[\mathsf{G}_N]$. $\square$ **(Theorem** 8**)**

5.2 Modifying Wang et al.'s First Scheme for S-SAME-R Security

In this subsection, we propose a modified version of Wang et al.'s first ℓ-SAME scheme $\mathsf{AME}_{\mathsf{WCHY1}}$, and prove its S-SAME-R security.

Difficulty in the Original Scheme and Our Ideas behind the Modified Scheme. Unfortunately, we have not been able to prove or disprove that $\mathsf{AME}_{\mathsf{WCHY1}}$ satisfies the stronger notion of S-SAME-R security. Let us explain the difficulty. In the proof of SAME-R security shown in the previous subsection, the transition to the final game where true randomness is returned from the randomness oracle was made possible by ensuring that the generation process of b_i for every $i \in [\ell]$ is identical to that of b^* in the "do-until" loop in fRand. Then, the properties of the rejection sampling (Lemma 1) and conditional resampling (Lemma 2) enable us to replace the fake randomness with truly random values.

However, in the stronger security setting of S-SAME-R, the same strategy no longer works. Recall that an adversary in the S-SAME-R experiment needs to be provided the forced secret keys $\{\mathsf{fsk}_i\}_{i\in[\ell]}$ as input. However, when we attempt to make the generation method of $\mathbf{b}$ identical inside and outside the "do-until" loop by replacing $\widehat{\mathsf{c}}_i \xleftarrow{\$} \{0,1\}^\ell$ with $\widehat{\mathsf{c}}_i \leftarrow \mathsf{Enc}'(\mathsf{fpk}_i, \mathsf{fm}_i; \widehat{r}_i)$ (for a randomly chosen $\widehat{r}_i$), as in the game transition from Game 3 to Game 4 in the proof of Theorem 8, the reduction algorithm against the pseudorandomness of PKE cannot provide the $\mathsf{S\text{-}SAME\text{-}R}$ adversary with fsk_i in which the challenge instance should be embedded. Thus, the simulation cannot be carried out. Although alternative approaches might exist, we have not been able to find an effective method.

The main difficulty arises from the fact that the inputs to the entropy-smoothing function H cannot be made random, and thus it seems that the property of H cannot be properly used. To overcome the difficulty, a natural idea is to assume that H is a PRF. Then, we could expect that H behaves like a random function even when its inputs are not uniformly random. However, since the key k of H is known to the adversary in the construction of $\mathsf{AME}_{\mathsf{WCHY1}}$, it seems that we cannot also rely on the security of the PRF, since the inputs H is dependent on the adversary's queries. However, if we can guarantee that the inputs to H is independent of an adversary's queries, there is a hope that we can rely on the PRF-security of H.

To make the above ideas work, we consider a modified version of $\mathsf{AME}_{\mathsf{WCHY1}}$. Specifically, we now assume that H is a PRF, and that the underlying PKE scheme is hybrid encryption constructed from a KEM and a DEM, and we use only KEM ciphertexts as inputs to H in an execution of fRand. This modification ensures that the generation of $\{\mathbf{b}_i\}$ no longer depends on the adversary's queries, allowing the PRF-security of H and the pseudorandomness of the KEM to be invoked even when k and $\{\mathsf{fsk}_i\}_{i\in[\ell]}$ are known to the adversary. The remaining steps of the security proof can go similarly to those in the proof of Theorem 8.

Formal Description of Our Modified Scheme and Its $\mathsf{S\text{-}SAME\text{-}R}$ *Security.* Let $\mathsf{KEM} = (\mathsf{KSetup}, \mathsf{KKG}, \mathsf{Encap}, \mathsf{Decap})$ be a KEM whose ciphertext length is $\ell_{\mathsf{KEM}} = \ell_{\mathsf{KEM}}(\lambda)$. Let $\mathsf{DEM} = (\mathsf{DEnc}, \mathsf{DDec})$ be a DEM whose message length is fixed to $n = n(\lambda)$ bits, and whose ciphertext length is $\ell_{\mathsf{DEM}} = \ell_{\mathsf{DEM}}(\lambda)$. Let $\ell := \ell_{\mathsf{KEM}} + \ell_{\mathsf{DEM}}$. Furthermore, let $\mathsf{H} : \mathcal{K} \times \{0,1\}^{\ell_{\mathsf{KEM}}} \to \{0,1\}$ be a PRF. (For simplicity, we write $\mathsf{H}_k(\cdot)$ to mean $\mathsf{H}(k, \cdot)$.)

Using these building blocks, our modified version of Wang et al.'s ℓ-SAME scheme $\mathsf{AME}_{\mathsf{M\text{-}WCHY1}} = (\mathsf{Setup}, \mathsf{KG}, \mathsf{Enc}, \mathsf{Dec}, \mathsf{fRand}, \mathsf{dDec})$ is constructed as in Fig. 11.

For proving the correctness and $\mathsf{S\text{-}SAME\text{-}R}$ security of $\mathsf{AME}_{\mathsf{M\text{-}WCHY1}}$, it is useful to introduce the following lemma.

$\mathsf{Setup}(1^\lambda)$: $\quad \mathsf{pp}' \xleftarrow{\$} \mathsf{KSetup}(1^\lambda);\ k \xleftarrow{\$} \mathcal{K}$ $\quad$ return $\mathsf{pp} \leftarrow (\mathsf{pp}', k)$	$\mathsf{KG}(\mathsf{pp})$: $\quad$ parse $\mathsf{pp} = (\mathsf{pp}', k)$ $\quad (\mathsf{pk}, \mathsf{sk}) \xleftarrow{\$} \mathsf{KKG}(\mathsf{pp}')$ $\quad$ return $(\mathsf{pk}, \mathsf{sk})$
$\mathsf{Enc}(\mathsf{pk}, \mathsf{m})$: $\quad (\mathsf{c}_{\mathsf{KEM}}, \mathsf{K}) \xleftarrow{\$} \mathsf{Encap}(\mathsf{pk})$ $\quad \mathsf{c}_{\mathsf{DEM}} \leftarrow \mathsf{DEnc}(\mathsf{K}, \mathsf{m})$ $\quad$ return $(\mathsf{c}_{\mathsf{KEM}}, \mathsf{c}_{\mathsf{DEM}})$	$\mathsf{fRand}(\mathsf{pp}, (\mathsf{fpk}_i)_{i \in [\ell]}, (\mathsf{fm}_i)_{i \in [\ell]}, \mathsf{dpk}, \mathsf{dm})$: $\quad$ parse $\mathsf{pp} = (\mathsf{pp}', k)$ $\quad (\mathsf{c}_{\mathsf{KEM}}, \mathsf{K}) \xleftarrow{\$} \mathsf{Encap}(\mathsf{dpk})$ $\quad \mathsf{c}_{\mathsf{DEM}} \leftarrow \mathsf{DEnc}(\mathsf{K}, \mathsf{dm})$
$\mathsf{Dec}(\mathsf{sk}, \mathsf{c})$: $\quad$ parse $\mathsf{c} = (\mathsf{c}_{\mathsf{KEM}}, \mathsf{c}_{\mathsf{DEM}})$ $\quad \mathsf{K} \leftarrow \mathsf{Decap}(\mathsf{sk}, \mathsf{c}_{\mathsf{KEM}})$ $\quad$ if $\mathsf{K} = \bot$ then $\quad\quad$ return $\bot$ $\quad$ else $\quad\quad$ return $\mathsf{m} \leftarrow \mathsf{DDec}(\mathsf{K}, \mathsf{c}_{\mathsf{DEM}})$	$\quad \mathsf{b}_1 \| \mathsf{b}_2 \| \cdots \| \mathsf{b}_\ell \leftarrow (\mathsf{c}_{\mathsf{KEM}}, \mathsf{c}_{\mathsf{DEM}})$ $\quad$ for $i \in [\ell]$ $\quad\quad \mathbf{ctr} \leftarrow 0$ $\quad\quad$ do $\quad\quad\quad r^* \xleftarrow{\$} \mathcal{R}$ $\quad\quad\quad (\mathsf{c}^*_{\mathsf{KEM}}, \mathsf{K}^*) \leftarrow \mathsf{Encap}(\mathsf{fpk}_i; r^*)$ $\quad\quad\quad \mathsf{b}^* \leftarrow \mathsf{H}_k(\mathsf{c}^*_{\mathsf{KEM}})$ $\quad\quad\quad \mathbf{ctr} \leftarrow \mathbf{ctr} + 1$
$\mathsf{dDec}(\mathsf{dsk}, (\mathsf{c}_i)_{i \in [\ell]})$: $\quad$ for $i \in [\ell]$ $\quad\quad$ parse $\mathsf{c}_i = (\mathsf{c}_{\mathsf{KEM},i}, \mathsf{c}_{\mathsf{DEM},i})$ $\quad\quad \mathsf{b}_i \leftarrow \mathsf{H}_k(\mathsf{c}_{\mathsf{KEM},i})$ $\quad \mathsf{c}' \leftarrow \mathsf{b}_1 \| \mathsf{b}_2 \| \cdots \| \mathsf{b}_\ell$ $\quad$ parse $\mathsf{c}' = (\mathsf{c}'_{\mathsf{KEM}}, \mathsf{c}'_{\mathsf{DEM}})$ $\quad \mathsf{K}' \leftarrow \mathsf{Decap}(\mathsf{dsk}, \mathsf{c}'_{\mathsf{KEM}})$ $\quad$ if $\mathsf{K}' = \bot$ then $\quad\quad$ return $\bot$ $\quad$ else $\quad\quad$ return $\mathsf{dm}' \leftarrow \mathsf{DDec}(\mathsf{K}', \mathsf{c}'_{\mathsf{DEM}})$	$\quad\quad$ until $\mathsf{b}^* = \mathsf{b}_i \vee \mathbf{ctr} \geq \lambda$ $\quad\quad r_i \leftarrow r^*$ $\quad$ return $(r_i)_{i \in [\ell]}$

Fig. 11. Modified Version of Wang et al.'s First ℓ-SAME scheme $\mathsf{AME}_{\text{M-WCHY1}}$ constructed from a pseudorandom KEM, a pseudorandom DEM, and a PRF. In the figure, $\mathsf{b}_i \in \{0, 1\}$ for every $i \in [\ell]$.

Lemma 4. *If* KEM *satisfies ciphertext pseudorandomness and* H *is a PRF, then the following probability is negligible:*

$$\epsilon := \Pr \left[\begin{array}{l} k \xleftarrow{\$} \mathcal{K}; \\ \mathsf{pp}' \xleftarrow{\$} \mathsf{KSetup}(1^\lambda); \\ (\mathsf{pk}, \mathsf{sk}) \xleftarrow{\$} \mathsf{KKG}(\mathsf{pp}'); \\ \forall h \in [\lambda + 1], (\mathsf{c}_h, \mathsf{K}_h) \xleftarrow{\$} \mathsf{Encap}(\mathsf{pk}); \\ \forall h \in [\lambda + 1], \mathsf{b}_h \leftarrow \mathsf{H}_k(\mathsf{c}_h) \end{array} : \forall h \in [\lambda], \mathsf{b}_h \neq \mathsf{b}_{\lambda+1} \right].$$

The formal proof is given in the full version. Other than relying on the PRF-security of H (instead of entropy-smoothness), its proof is analogous to the proof for Lemma 3. (In fact, the proof is somewhat simpler in the sense that there is no adversary in this lemma.)

We now show the formal statements for its correctness and security.

Theorem 9. *If* KEM *satisfies ciphertext pseudorandomness and* H *is a PRF, then* $\mathsf{AME}_{\text{M-WCHY1}}$ *satisfies correctness.*

Theorem 10. *If* KEM *satisfies pseudorandomness,* DEM *satisfies pseudorandomness, and* H *is a PRF, then* $\mathsf{AME}_{\text{M-WCHY1}}$ *satisfies* S–SAME–R *security.*

The formal proofs of Theorems 9 and 10 are given in the full version. The proof for correctness goes similarly to the proof of Theorem 6, using Lemma 4. The proof for S–SAME–R security is based on the ideas explained at the beginning of this subsection. In its proof, the following lemma plays the key role, which allows us to overcome the difficulties that exist in the original scheme $\mathsf{AME}_{\text{WCHY1}}$. Using this lemma, we can still conduct the transitions of the games, despite in the situation where the S–SAME–R adversary is given the PRF-key k and the forced secret keys $\{\mathsf{fsk}_i\}_{i\in[\ell]}$ as input.

Lemma 5. *Define the distributions* D_{real} *and* D_{rand} *as follows:*

$$
D_{\text{real}} := \left\{
\begin{aligned}
&k \leftarrow \mathcal{K}; \\
&\mathsf{pp}' \xleftarrow{\$} \mathsf{KSetup}(1^\lambda); \\
&(\mathsf{pk},\mathsf{sk}) \xleftarrow{\$} \mathsf{KKG}(\mathsf{pp}'); \qquad : \Big(\mathsf{pp}', k, \mathsf{pk}, \mathsf{sk}, \mathsf{H}_k(c_{\mathsf{KEM}})\Big) \\
&r \xleftarrow{\$} \mathcal{R}; \\
&(c_{\mathsf{KEM}}, K) \leftarrow \mathsf{Encap}(\mathsf{pk}; r)
\end{aligned}
\right\},
$$

$$
D_{\text{rand}} := \left\{
\begin{aligned}
&k \xleftarrow{\$} \mathcal{K}; \\
&\mathsf{pp}' \leftarrow \mathsf{KSetup}(1^\lambda); \qquad : \Big(\mathsf{pp}', k, \mathsf{pk}, \mathsf{sk}, y\Big) \\
&(\mathsf{pk},\mathsf{sk}) \xleftarrow{\$} \mathsf{KKG}(\mathsf{pp}'); \\
&y \xleftarrow{\$} \{0,1\}
\end{aligned}
\right\}.
$$

Then, there exist PPT adversaries $\mathcal{B}$ *and* $\mathcal{B}'$ *such that*

$$
\mathbf{SD}(D_{\text{real}}, D_{\text{rand}}) \leq \frac{1}{\sqrt{2}}\left(\mathsf{Adv}^{\text{PR}}_{\mathsf{KEM},\mathcal{B}}(\lambda) + \mathsf{Adv}^{\text{PRF}}_{\mathsf{H},\mathcal{B}'}(\lambda) + 2^{-\ell_{\mathsf{KEM}}}\right)^{\frac{1}{2}}.
$$

In particular, if KEM *satisfies pseudorandomness and* H *is a PRF, then* $\mathbf{SD}(D_{\text{real}}, D_{\text{rand}})$ *is negligible.*

The formal proof of Lemma 5 is given in the full version. Its proof is somewhat analogous to the proof for the leftover hash lemma [18].

6   Wang Et Al.'s Second SAME Scheme

In this section, we investigate whether Wang et al.'s second scheme [28, Section 5] satisfies our refined security notions. Wang et al.'s second scheme is an $(\ell+1)$-SAME scheme where ℓ denotes the length of duplicate messages one wishes to send. Their $(\ell+1)$-SAME scheme is constructed for hybrid encryption, consisting of a so-called "module-level" KEM and a DEM. A module-level KEM is a type of KEMs that satisfy some structural properties that are satisfied by many of existing KEMs (especially the relatives of the ElGamal KEM).

Our results on Wang et al.'s second scheme are as follows: We show that their second scheme satisfies SAME-R security by assuming a special property that (a part of) the session-key generation algorithm of the underlying KEM used as a building block behaves like a PRF when the public key is not given to an adversary. (This property is called the *special PRF property*.) On the other hand, we also show that their scheme does not satisfy S-SAME-R security as there is an easy attack.

Definition of a Module-Level KEM. We first recall the definition of a module-level KEM whose definition is taken from [28, Section 5]. A module-level KEM is a KEM (KSetup, KKG, Encap, Decap) whose algorithms have the following structural properties.

KSetup(1^λ) $\xrightarrow{\$}$ pp: This is the setup algorithm.

KKG(pp) $\xrightarrow{\$}$ (pk, sk): This is the key generation algorithm that returns a public/secret key pair (pk = (ek, tk), sk = (dk, vk)) by running the following subalgorithms.

    – KEMEk(pp) $\xrightarrow{\$}$ (ek, dk) : It returns an encapsulation/decapsulation key pair (ek, dk).

    – KEMTk(pp) $\xrightarrow{\$}$ (tk, vk) : It returns a tag generation/verification key pair (tk, vk).

Encap(pk) $\xrightarrow{\$}$ (ψ, K): This is the encapsulation algorithm that returns a ciphertext $\psi = (c, \pi)$ and a session-key K by sampling a randomness $r \in \mathcal{R}_{\mathsf{KEM}}$ uniformly at random[5] and running the following subalgorithms.

    – KEMKg(ek, r) $\rightarrow$ K : It returns a session-key K.

    – KEMCg(r) $\rightarrow$ c : It returns a ciphertext c.

    – KEMTg(tk, r) $\rightarrow$ π : It returns a ciphertext tag π of c.

Decap(sk, ψ) $\rightarrow$ K'/$\perp$: This is the decapsulation algorithm by running the following subalgorithms.

    – KEMKd(dk, c) $\rightarrow$ K' : It returns a session-key K'.

    – KEMVf(vk, c) $\rightarrow$ π' : It returns a ciphertext tag π' of c.

    If $\pi' = \pi$, then Decap returns K'. Otherwise, it returns $\perp$ to indicate a decryption failure.

As explained in [28], many of the existing KEMs can be captured as a module-level KEM.

We will use a module-level KEM with the following property.

---

[5] Wang et al. [28] defined KEMRg algorithm for the randomness sampling as a subalgorithm of Encap. For simplicity and avoiding redundancy, we do not introduce KEMRg and sample the randomness directly instead.

Definition 12. *Let* KEM *be a module-level KEM. We say that* KEM *satisfies universal decryptability if the following probability is negligible:*

$$
\Pr\left[
\begin{array}{l}
\mathsf{pp}' \xleftarrow{\$} \mathsf{KSetup}(1^\lambda); \\
(\mathsf{ek}, \mathsf{dk}) \xleftarrow{\$} \mathsf{KEMEk}(\mathsf{pp}'); \\
r \xleftarrow{\$} \mathcal{R}_{\mathsf{KEM}}; \\
\mathsf{c} \leftarrow \mathsf{KEMCg}(r)
\end{array}
: \mathsf{KEMKg}(\mathsf{ek}, r) \neq \mathsf{KEMKd}(\mathsf{dk}, \mathsf{c})
\right] .
$$

Formal Description of Wang et al.'s Second Scheme and its Security. Let KEM $=$ (KSetup, KKG, Encap, Decap) be a module-level KEM, and thus it has the subalgorithms (KEMEk, KEMTk, KEMKg, KEMCg, KEMTg, KEMKd, KEMVf). We require that the randomness space of Encap, $\mathcal{R}_{\mathsf{KEM}}$, be an additive and cyclic group with a generator $1_{\mathcal{R}_{\mathsf{KEM}}}$. Let DEM $=$ (DEnc, DDec) be a DEM. Let H $: \mathcal{K} \times \{0,1\}^\ell \to \mathcal{R}_{\mathsf{KEM}}$ be an efficiently computable function, for which we write $\mathsf{H}_k(\cdot)$ to mean $\mathsf{H}(k, \cdot)$ for simplicity. Then, Wang et al.'s second $(\ell + 1)$-SAME scheme $\mathsf{AME}_{\mathrm{WCHY2}} = $ (Setup, KG, Enc, Dec, fRand, dDec) is constructed as in Fig. 12.

Wang et al. showed the following theorem that guarantees the correctness of $\mathsf{AME}_{\mathrm{WCHY2}}$.

Theorem 11. *If* KEM *satisfies correctness and universal decryptability, then* $\mathsf{AME}_{\mathrm{WCHY2}}$ *satisfies correctness.*

Regarding the S–SAME security of $\mathsf{AME}_{\mathrm{WCHY2}}$, Wang et al. showed the following theorem.

Theorem 12. *If* KEM *satisfies universal decryptability, key pseudorandomness, and the homomorphic property,* DEM *satisfies* IND–OT *security, and* H *is entropy-smoothing, then* $\mathsf{AME}_{\mathrm{WCHY2}}$ *satisfies* S–SAME *security.*

Here, the homomorphic property refers to the property that both KEMKg and KEMCg are homomorphic with respect to their randomness inputs, and the key pseudorandomness refers to the indistinguishability between a session-key K generated by $\mathsf{KEMKg}(\mathsf{ek}, r)$ and a key K sampled uniformly at random from $\mathcal{K}$ where $\mathsf{pp} \xleftarrow{\$} \mathsf{KSetup}(1^\lambda)$, $(\mathsf{ek}, \mathsf{dk}) \xleftarrow{\$} \mathsf{KEMEk}(\mathsf{pp})$, and $r \xleftarrow{\$} \mathcal{R}_{\mathsf{KEM}}$.[6]

As the main result in this section, we show that $\mathsf{AME}_{\mathrm{WCHY2}}$ satisfies SAME–R security. For showing this, we need to rely on a special property of the underlying module-level KEM that its KEMKg algorithm has a property similar to a PRF with its key ek. Thus, we introduce its formal definition below.

Definition 13. *Let* KEM *be a module-level KEM whose session-key space is* $\{0,1\}^\ell$. *We say that* KEM *satisfies the* special PRF property *if for any PPT*

---

[6] We omit the formal definitions of key pseudorandomness and the homomorphic property of a module-level KEM since we do not use them directly for our results. Note that key pseudorandomness of a module-level KEM is implied by its IND–CPA security. For the detailed definitions, please see [28].

$\mathsf{Setup}(1^\lambda)$: $\quad k \xleftarrow{\$} \mathcal{K}$ $\quad \mathsf{pp}' \xleftarrow{\$} \mathsf{KSetup}(1^\lambda)$ $\quad \text{return } \mathsf{pp} = (\mathsf{pp}', k)$	$\mathsf{fRand}(\mathsf{pp}, (\mathsf{fpk}_i)_{i \in [\ell+1]}, (\mathsf{fm}_i)_{i \in [\ell+1]}, \mathsf{dpk}, \mathsf{dm})$: $\quad \text{parse } \mathsf{pp} = (\mathsf{pp}', k)$ $\quad \text{parse } \mathsf{dpk} = (\mathsf{ek}, \mathsf{tk})$ $\quad \text{parse } \mathsf{dm} := \mathsf{b}_1 \| \mathsf{b}_2 \| \cdots \| \mathsf{b}_\ell$ $\quad \text{for } i \in [\ell+1]$ $\quad\quad \text{if } i = 1 \text{ then}$ $\quad\quad\quad r_1 \xleftarrow{\$} \mathcal{R}_{\mathsf{KEM}}$ $\quad\quad \text{else}$ $\quad\quad\quad K_i \leftarrow \mathsf{KEMKg}(\mathsf{ek}, r_{i-1})$ $\quad\quad\quad t_i \leftarrow \mathsf{H}_k(\mathsf{K}_i)$ $\quad\quad\quad r_i \leftarrow t_i + \mathsf{b}_{i-1} \cdot 1_{\mathcal{R}}$ $\quad \text{return } (r_i)_{i \in [\ell+1]}$
$\mathsf{KG}(\mathsf{pp})$: $\quad \text{parse } \mathsf{pp} = (\mathsf{pp}', k)$ $\quad (\mathsf{ek}, \mathsf{dk}) \xleftarrow{\$} \mathsf{KEMEk}(\mathsf{pp}')$ $\quad (\mathsf{tk}, \mathsf{vk}) \xleftarrow{\$} \mathsf{KEMTk}(\mathsf{pp}')$ $\quad \mathsf{pk} \leftarrow (\mathsf{ek}, \mathsf{tk})$ $\quad \mathsf{sk} \leftarrow (\mathsf{dk}, \mathsf{vk})$ $\quad \text{return } (\mathsf{pk}, \mathsf{sk})$	
$\mathsf{Enc}(\mathsf{pk}, \mathsf{m}; r)$: $\quad \text{parse } \mathsf{pk} = (\mathsf{ek}, \mathsf{tk})$ $\quad \text{parse } \mathsf{sk} = (\mathsf{dk}, \mathsf{vk})$ $\quad \mathsf{K} \leftarrow \mathsf{KEMKg}(\mathsf{ek}, r)$ $\quad \mathsf{c}_{\mathsf{KEM}} \leftarrow \mathsf{KEMCg}(r)$ $\quad \pi \leftarrow \mathsf{KEMTg}(\mathsf{tk}, r)$ $\quad \mathsf{c}_{\mathsf{DEM}} \leftarrow \mathsf{DEnc}(\mathsf{K}, \mathsf{m})$ $\quad \text{return } \mathsf{c} \leftarrow ((\mathsf{c}_{\mathsf{KEM}}, \mathsf{c}_{\mathsf{DEM}}), \pi)$	$\mathsf{dDec}(\mathsf{dsk}, (\mathsf{c}_i)_{i \in [\ell+1]})$: $\quad \text{parse } \mathsf{dsk} = (\mathsf{dk}, \mathsf{vk})$ $\quad \text{parse } (\mathsf{c}_i)_{i \in [\ell+1]} = ((\mathsf{c}_{\mathsf{KEM},i}, \mathsf{c}_{\mathsf{DEM},i}), \pi_i)_{i \in [\ell+1]}$ $\quad \text{for } i \in \{2, \ldots, \ell+1\}$ $\quad\quad K_i \leftarrow \mathsf{KEMKd}(\mathsf{dk}, \mathsf{c}_{\mathsf{KEM},i})$ $\quad\quad t_i \leftarrow \mathsf{H}_k(\mathsf{K}_i)$ $\quad\quad r_{i,0} \leftarrow t_i$ $\quad\quad C_{i,0} \leftarrow \mathsf{KEMCg}(r_{i,0})$ $\quad\quad r_{i,1} \leftarrow t_i + 1_{\mathcal{R}}$ $\quad\quad C_{i,1} \leftarrow \mathsf{KEMCg}(r_{i,1})$ $\quad\quad \text{if } \mathsf{c}_{\mathsf{KEM},i} = C_{i,0} \text{ then}$ $\quad\quad\quad \mathsf{b}_{i-1} \leftarrow 0$ $\quad\quad \text{else if } \mathsf{c}_{\mathsf{KEM},i} = C_{i,1} \text{ then}$ $\quad\quad\quad \mathsf{b}_{i-1} \leftarrow 1$ $\quad\quad \text{else}$ $\quad\quad\quad \text{return } \bot$ $\quad \text{return } \mathsf{b}_1 \| \mathsf{b}_2 \| \cdots \| \mathsf{b}_\ell$
$\mathsf{Dec}(\mathsf{sk}, \mathsf{c})$: $\quad \text{parse } \mathsf{sk} = (\mathsf{dk}, \mathsf{vk})$ $\quad \text{parse } \mathsf{c} = ((\mathsf{c}_{\mathsf{KEM}}, \mathsf{c}_{\mathsf{DEM}}), \pi)$ $\quad \mathsf{K}' \leftarrow \mathsf{KEMKd}(\mathsf{sk}, \mathsf{c}_{\mathsf{KEM}})$ $\quad \mathsf{m}' \leftarrow \mathsf{DDec}(\mathsf{K}', \mathsf{c}_{\mathsf{DEM}})$ $\quad \pi' \leftarrow \mathsf{KEMVf}(\mathsf{vk}, \mathsf{c}_{\mathsf{KEM}})$ $\quad \text{if } \pi' = \pi \text{ then}$ $\quad\quad \text{return } \mathsf{m}'$ $\quad \text{else}$ $\quad\quad \text{return } \bot$	

Fig. 12. Wang et al.'s second $(\ell+1)$-SAME scheme $\mathsf{AME}_{\mathsf{WCHY2}}$ based on a module-level KEM.

adversary $\mathcal{A}$, the following advantage is negligible:

$$\mathsf{Adv}^{\mathrm{PRF}}_{\mathsf{KEM}, \mathcal{A}}(\lambda) := \left| \Pr[\mathcal{A}^{\mathsf{KEMKg}(\mathsf{ek}, \cdot)}(\mathsf{pp}) = 1] - \Pr[\mathcal{A}^{f(\cdot)}(\mathsf{pp}) = 1] \right|,$$

where $\mathsf{pp} \xleftarrow{\$} \mathsf{KSetup}(1^\lambda)$, $(\mathsf{ek}, \mathsf{dk}) \xleftarrow{\$} \mathsf{KEMEk}(\mathsf{pp})$, *and* $f \xleftarrow{\$} \mathsf{FUNC}_{\mathcal{R}_{\mathsf{KEM}} \to \{0,1\}^\ell}$.

We stress that although ek is a part of a public key of a module-level KEM, it is treated analogously to a (secret) PRF key, i.e., it is not directly given to the adversary in the security experiment.

One might wonder whether this property is satisfied by existing module-level KEMs. We observe that the hashed ElGamal KEM (also called DHIES [1]) in which the session-key component in the original (non-hashed) ElGamal KEM is hashed by a cryptographic hash function, satisfies this property in the random oracle model. Since many of the relatives of the ElGamal KEM, e.g. [6,12,17,

19,21,22], are captured as a module-level KEM and have the ElGamal KEM as their internal structure, these KEMs also satisfy the special PRF property when (the session-key component is hashed, and) the used hash function is modeled as a random oracle. For completeness, we formally show that the hashed ElGamal KEM has the special PRF property in the full version.

We now state our results on Wang et al.'s second SAME scheme. The following theorem guarantees the SAME-R security of $\mathsf{AME}_{\mathsf{WCHY2}}$.

Theorem 13. *If* KEM *satisfies pseudorandomness and the special PRF property,* DEM *satisfies* IND-OT *security, and* H *is entropy-smoothing, then* $\mathsf{AME}_{\mathsf{WCHY2}}$ *satisfies* SAME-R *security.*

On the other hand, in the setting of S-SAME-R security, an adversary has ek and can use it to test whether the oracle response is random or not since fake randomness of this scheme is generated sequentially using KEMKg with ek. Therefore, the following holds.

Theorem 14. $\mathsf{AME}_{\mathsf{WCHY2}}$ *is not* S-SAME-R *secure.*

The formal proofs of Theorems 13 and 14 are given in the full version.

Acknowledgement. This work was partially supported by JST K Program Grant Number JPMJKP24U3, JST CREST Grant Number JPMJCR22M1, and JSPS KAKENHI Grant Number JP25KJ1176.

References

1. Abdalla, M., Bellare, M., Rogaway, P.: The oracle Diffie-Hellman assumptions and an analysis of DHIES. In: Naccache, D. (ed.) CT-RSA 2001. LNCS, vol. 2020, pp. 143–158. Springer, Heidelberg (2001). https://doi.org/10.1007/3-540-45353-9_12
2. Avitabile, G., Botta, V., Giunta, E., Mielniczuk, M., Migliaro, F.: The malice of ELFs: practical anamorphic-resistant encryption without random oracles. Cryptology ePrint Archive, Report 2025/305 (2025). https://eprint.iacr.org/2025/305
3. Banerjee, S., Pal, T., Rupp, A., Slamanig, D.: Simple public key anamorphic encryption and signature using multi-message extensions. Cryptology ePrint Archive, Report 2025/370 (2025). https://eprint.iacr.org/2025/370
4. Banfi, F., Gegier, K., Hirt, M., Maurer, U., Rito, G.: Anamorphic encryption, revisited. In: Joye, M., Leander, G. (eds.) EUROCRYPT 2024, Part II. LNCS, vol. 14652, pp. 3–32. Springer, Cham (2024). https://doi.org/10.1007/978-3-031-58723-8_1
5. Carnemolla, D., Catalano, D., Giunta, E., Migliaro, F.: Anamorphic resistant encryption: the good, the bad and the ugly. In: Kalai, Y.T., Kamara, S.F. (eds.) CRYPTO 2025, Part III. LNCS, vol. 16002, pp. 472–503. Springer, Cham (2025). https://doi.org/10.1007/978-3-032-01881-6_15
6. Cash, D., Kiltz, E., Shoup, V.: The twin Diffie-Hellman problem and applications. In: Smart, N. (ed.) EUROCRYPT 2008. LNCS, vol. 4965, pp. 127–145. Springer, Heidelberg (2008). https://doi.org/10.1007/978-3-540-78967-3_8

7. Catalano, D., Giunta, E., Migliaro, F.: Anamorphic encryption: new constructions and homomorphic realizations. In: Joye, M., Leander, G. (eds.) EUROCRYPT 2024, Part II. LNCS, vol. 14652, pp. 33–62. Springer, Cham (2024). https://doi.org/10.1007/978-3-031-58723-8_2
8. Catalano, D., Giunta, E., Migliaro, F.: Limits of black-box anamorphic encryption. In: Reyzin, L., Stebila, D. (eds.) CRYPTO 2024, Part II. LNCS, vol. 14921, pp. 352–383. Springer, Cham (2024). https://doi.org/10.1007/978-3-031-68379-4_11
9. Catalano, D., Giunta, E., Migliaro, F.: Generic anamorphic encryption, revisited: New limitations and constructions. In: Fehr, S., Fouque, P.A. (eds.) EUROCRYPT 2025, Part II. LNCS, vol. 15602, pp. 275–303. Springer, Cham (2025). https://doi.org/10.1007/978-3-031-91124-8_10
10. Choi, W., Collins, D., Liu, X., Zikas, V.: A unified treatment of anamorphic encryption. Cryptology ePrint Archive, Report 2025/309 (2025). https://eprint.iacr.org/2025/309
11. Chu, H., Do, K., Hanzlik, L., Thyagarajan, S.A.: When threshold meets anamorphic signatures: what is possible and what is not! Cryptology ePrint Archive, Report 2025/1044 (2025). https://eprint.iacr.org/2025/1044
12. Cramer, R., Shoup, V.: A practical public key cryptosystem provably secure against adaptive chosen ciphertext attack. In: Krawczyk, H. (ed.) CRYPTO 1998. LNCS, vol. 1462, pp. 13–25. Springer, Heidelberg (1998). https://doi.org/10.1007/BFb0055717
13. Deo, A., Libert, B.: Anamorphic signatures with dictator and recipient unforgeability for long messages. In: Hanaoka, G., Yang, B.Y. (eds.) ASIACRYPT 2025, Part VI. pp. 370–401. LNCS, Springer, Singapore (2025). https://doi.org/10.1007/978-981-95-5119-4_12
14. Deo, A., Libert, B.: Fully asymmetric anamorphic homomorphic encryption from LWE. Cryptology ePrint Archive, Report 2025/328 (2025). https://eprint.iacr.org/2025/328
15. Dodis, Y., Goldin, E.: Anamorphic-resistant encryption; or why the encryption debate is still alive. In: Kalai, Y.T., Kamara, S.F. (eds.) CRYPTO 2025, Part III. LNCS, vol. 16002, pp. 440–471. Springer, Cham (2025). https://doi.org/10.1007/978-3-032-01881-6_14
16. GANGULY, S., Chaudhury, S.S.: Computational quantum anamorphic encryption and anamorphic secret sharing. Cryptology ePrint Archive, Report 2025/399 (2025). https://eprint.iacr.org/2025/399
17. Hanaoka, G., Kurosawa, K.: Efficient chosen ciphertext secure public key encryption under the computational Diffie-Hellman assumption. In: Pieprzyk, J. (ed.) ASIACRYPT 2008. LNCS, vol. 5350, pp. 308–325. Springer, Heidelberg (2008). https://doi.org/10.1007/978-3-540-89255-7_19
18. Håstad, J., Impagliazzo, R., Levin, L.A., Luby, M.: A pseudorandom generator from any one-way function. SIAM J. Comput. **28**(4), 1364–1396 (1999)
19. Hofheinz, D., Kiltz, E.: Secure hybrid encryption from weakened key encapsulation. In: Menezes, A. (ed.) CRYPTO 2007. LNCS, vol. 4622, pp. 553–571. Springer, Heidelberg (2007). https://doi.org/10.1007/978-3-540-74143-5_31
20. Jaeger, J., Stracovsky, R.: Dictators? Friends? Forgers. - breaking and fixing unforgeability definitions for anamorphic signature schemes. In: Chung, K.M., Sasaki, Y. (eds.) ASIACRYPT 2024, Part II. LNCS, vol. 15485, pp. 105–137. Springer, Singapore (2024). https://doi.org/10.1007/978-981-96-0888-1_4
21. Kiltz, E.: Chosen-ciphertext secure key-encapsulation based on gap hashed Diffie-Hellman. In: Okamoto, T., Wang, X. (eds.) PKC 2007. LNCS, vol. 4450, pp. 282–297. Springer, Heidelberg (2007). https://doi.org/10.1007/978-3-540-71677-8_19

22. Kurosawa, K., Desmedt, Y.: A new paradigm of hybrid encryption scheme. In: Franklin, M. (ed.) CRYPTO 2004. LNCS, vol. 3152, pp. 426–442. Springer, Heidelberg (2004). https://doi.org/10.1007/978-3-540-28628-8_26
23. Kutylowski, M., Persiano, G., Phan, D.H., Yung, M., Zawada, M.: Anamorphic signatures: secrecy from a dictator who only permits authentication! In: Handschuh, H., Lysyanskaya, A. (eds.) CRYPTO 2023, Part II. LNCS, vol. 14082, pp. 759–790. Springer, Cham (2023). https://doi.org/10.1007/978-3-031-38545-2_25
24. Kutylowski, M., Persiano, G., Phan, D.H., Yung, M., Zawada, M.: The self-anti-censorship nature of encryption: on the prevalence of anamorphic cryptography. PoPETs **2023**(4), 170–183 (Oct 2023). https://doi.org/10.56553/popets-2023-0104
25. Persiano, G., Phan, D.H., Yung, M.: Anamorphic encryption: private communication against a dictator. In: Dunkelman, O., Dziembowski, S. (eds.) EUROCRYPT 2022, Part II. LNCS, vol. 13276, pp. 34–63. Springer, Cham (2022). https://doi.org/10.1007/978-3-031-07085-3_2
26. Persiano, G., Phan, D.H., Yung, M.: Public-key anamorphism in (CCA-secure) public-key encryption and beyond. In: Reyzin, L., Stebila, D. (eds.) CRYPTO 2024, Part II. LNCS, vol. 14921, pp. 422–455. Springer, Cham (2024). https://doi.org/10.1007/978-3-031-68379-4_13
27. Wang, W., Han, S., Liu, S.: Anamorphic authenticated key exchange: double key distribution under surveillance. In: Chung, K.M., Sasaki, Y. (eds.) ASIACRYPT 2024, Part V. LNCS, vol. 15488, pp. 168–200. Springer, Singapore (2024). https://doi.org/10.1007/978-981-96-0935-2_6
28. Wang, Y., Chen, R., Huang, X., Yung, M.: Sender-anamorphic encryption reformulated: achieving robust and generic constructions. In: Guo, J., Steinfeld, R. (eds.) ASIACRYPT 2023, Part VI. LNCS, vol. 14443, pp. 135–167. Springer, Singapore (2023). https://doi.org/10.1007/978-981-99-8736-8_5

Threshold Public-Key Encryption: Definitions, Relations, and CPA-to-CCA Transforms

Chris Brzuska[1]([✉])[iD], Michael Klooß[2,3]([✉])[iD], and Ivy K. Y. Woo[1]([✉])[iD]

[1] Aalto University, Espoo, Finland
{chris.brzuska,ivy.woo}@aalto.fi
[2] Karlsruhe Institute of Technology, Karlsruhe, Germany
klooss@mail.informatik.kit.edu
[3] KASTEL Security Research Labs, Karlsruhe, Germany

Abstract. Threshold public-key encryption (TPKE) allows t out of k parties to jointly decrypt a ciphertext, while ensuring confidentiality against any coalition of $t-1$ parties. Despite its long history and ongoing standardisation efforts, there has not been a dedicated study on its basic security notions, and a handful of variations are currently in use.

We initiate the systematic study of TPKE confidentiality and develop relations between notions contrasting indistinguishability (IND) vs. simulatability (SIM), passive (CPA) vs. active (CCA) attacks, and static vs. adaptive corruptions. One of our insights is that security under maximal corruptions does not imply security under fewer corruptions when the adversary has access to partial decryptions on challenge ciphertexts. Maximal corruption was adopted by a significant portion of prior works, and this calls for cautious interpretation when using such a notion.

We complement our study by providing two generic CPA-to-CCA transforms for TPKE. The first is effectively the Naor-Yung transform, for which we fix a gap in prior work by requiring the underlying TPKE to achieve *semi-malicious* CPA security, where the adversary can choose randomness for non-challenge ciphertexts. Our second transform applies to any CPA secure TPKE in the random oracle model. We abstract the underlying technique as a standalone novel primitive called non-interactive proof of randomness (NIPoR), and we provide a simple construction from straightline extractable non-interactive zero-knowledge proofs and commitments, which we consider of independent interest.

Keywords: threshold PKE · separations · CPA-to-CCA transforms · non-interactive proof of randomness · partial decryption queries

1 Introduction

Threshold public-key encryption (TPKE) allows decryption of a ciphertext when threshold t out of the total $k \geq t$ parties come together, and preserves confidentiality of the underlying message so long as less than t parties contribute partial

S. Bai and E. Persichetti (Eds.): PKC 2026, LNCS 16554, pp. 162–197, 2026.
https://doi.org/10.1007/978-3-032-26740-5_6

decryption shares. TPKE is a fundamental building block for multi-party computation [3], and also a classic example under the umbrella of threshold cryptography, the latter being recently recognised as a standardisation area by the National Institute of Standards and Technology (NIST) [17].

Despite the conceptual simplicity of TPKE, a handful of security notions can be considered and the relations between the different definitions are intricate. Our key contributions are two-fold: First, we clarify the impact of definitional choices on security notions and highlight aspects important to TPKE security. Second, we provide two generic CPA-to-CCA transforms of TPKE, easing the task of achieving and/or arguing CCA security for future works.

1.1   TPKE: Syntax and Security

Similar to standard public-key encryption (PKE), the key generation algorithm KGen of a TPKE outputs a public key pk for encryption, but it differs from PKE by returning a set $(sk_j)_j$ of secret key *shares*, each of which is distributed to a user j. Given a ciphertext ct and a key share sk_j, a TPKE's partial decryption algorithm ParDec derives a partial decryption pd_j.[1] Given $(pd_j)_j$ from threshold t many users, the recovery algorithm Rec returns the plaintext.

Toy Example: Threshold Signatures from TPKE. To motivate the impact of TPKE security notions in applications, we consider a simple threshold signature scheme based on a standard signature scheme with deterministic signing algorithm and a fully-homomorphic TPKE[2] [11]: The dealer encrypts the signing key ssk under TPKE to obtain ct_{ssk}, and shares the partial decryption keys. Now, every party P_j with a key share sk_j offers a partial signing service:

- A user U submits a message m to P_j and P_j decides, according to its policy, whether U should obtain a (partial) signature or not, e.g. each teacher P_j decides whether a thesis should be graded pass or fail.
- In the positive case, P_j homomorphically evaluates $\mathsf{Sign}(ssk, m)$, using ct_{ssk}, and obtains the encrypted signature ct_σ. It sends the partial decryption $pd_j = \mathsf{ParDec}(sk_j, ct_\sigma)$ back to the user U.

After obtaining sufficiently many partial decryption shares, user U reconstructs the signature σ on m via Rec. This simple protocol is *round-optimal*, since pd_j is obtained in 2 moves, and it requires *no interaction* between secret key holders.

Turning to the security of the protocol, CPA security for TPKE suffices, since an adversary can only choose the to-be-signed message, and ct_σ is computed by

---

[1] Alternatively, one can consider, e.g. interactive decryption, or decompose KGen into two algorithms which generate pk and $(sk_j)_j$ separately. See Sect. 1.3 for a discussion of syntax variations. The syntax considered in this work is one of the simplest and the most common, arguably also with the longest history.

[2] This leads to threshold fully-homomorphic encryption (TFHE), although we will only focus on TPKE security, i.e. without taking homomorphic computation into account. See Sect. 1.3 for recent results on subtleties of (non-threshold) FHE security.

honest parties. Now, intuitively, TPKE confidentiality[3] should directly imply that a signature is not forgeable for any message m which was queried to an insufficient set of parties. Surprisingly, this is *not* the case under security notions which the majority of prior works on TPKE consider, as we explain below.

Security. To see the potential (in)security of the above threshold signatures due to the underlying TPKE, we have to dive deeper into TPKE security models. Below, we restrict to *static* corruption, i.e. the adversary initially specifies the set of corrupted parties. We discuss the impact of adaptive corruption on our security notions later on.

Corruption. A main motivation of threshold primitives including TPKE and threshold signatures is to tolerate some level of corruption of the shared secrets. In a t-out-of-k TPKE, an adversary $\mathcal{A}$ may corrupt a set $\mathcal{C}$ of up to $t-1$ parties and obtain their secret key shares. Referring to Table 1, a major portion of prior works only consider $\mathcal{A}$ which corrupts a *maximal* set of $t-1$ parties. While it is common (for other cryptographic primitives) that security against maximal corruption trivially implies security against fewer corruptions, this simplification turns out to be problematic for TPKE.

In the threshold signatures example, suppose we have a $\frac{1}{2}$ recovery threshold (i.e. $\frac{t}{k} \geq \frac{1}{2}$). That is, a majority of parties P_j must decide to issue a signature on m for the user U to recovery it. If we face an adversary who can at most corrupt a fraction of $\frac{1}{4}$ users, this is not modelled by maximal corruption at all.

Partial Decryptions. In our threshold signatures example, naturally an adversary $\mathcal{A}$ will see partial decryptions of ciphertexts. This is modelled in TPKE security experiments by giving $\mathcal{A}$ gets access to a partial decryption oracle $\mathsf{ParDecO}$. One can naturally expect $\mathsf{ParDecO}$ to answer two types of partial decryption queries:

(I) queries on *non-challenge* ciphertexts (i.e. those not depending on the challenge bit), where $\mathsf{ParDecO}$ may return its partial decryptions w.r.t. all k parties;

(II) queries on *challenge* ciphertexts (i.e. whose underlying plaintexts depend on the challenge bit), for each $\mathsf{ParDecO}$ may return its partial decryptions w.r.t. some subset $S \subseteq [k] \setminus \mathcal{C}$ of parties, so that $\mathcal{A}$ cannot trivially decrypt the challenge, that is, $|S \cup \mathcal{C}| < t$.

Type I queries were commonly taken into account in prior works. However, Type II queries were rarely considered (see Table 1).

We observe that Type II queries will be crucial in our example scenario: We want the signature σ in ct_σ to be hidden until t partial decryption shares were

---

[3] and circuit privacy for FHE so that ciphertext ct_σ contains no information about ssk.

queried. Since we assume that $\mathcal{A}$ only corrupts $\frac{1}{4}$th of the parties, it is allowed to request partial signatures from less than $\frac{1}{4}$th more parties.[4]

Table 1. Prior works on TPKE (We list the works whose TPKE syntax is consistent with that considered in this work (Definition 1), which is also the most common in the literature. See Sect. 1.3 for more related works and some possible variants in syntax). [11,16,48] constructed TFHE, the above considers their schemes as TPKE. rnd: Oracle EncO releases encryption randomness. Q-stat.: Quasi-static (Remark 2). Adapt.: Adaptive. #: Implied by CCA (Remark 1). †: Implied by adaptive corruption (Theorem 1). ⋆: [26] proved CPA security and relied on our NIPoR result (Sect. 5) to achieve CCA. SIM$^-$: A version more restrictive than Definition 3. ‡: In the ring setting, also assuming known-covariance LWE.

Works	Security							Assumptions
	IND/SIM	Corr.	$|\mathcal{C}|$	ParDecO		Strength	rnd	
				Type I	Type II			
[51]	IND	Q-stat.	$t-1$	Yes	–	CCA	Yes$^\#$	CDH/DDH + RO
[8]	IND	Q-stat.	$t-1$	Yes	–	CCA	Yes$^\#$	DBDH
[2]	IND	Static	$t-1$	Yes	–	CCA	Yes$^\#$	DBDH/DLIN
[5]	SIM	Static	$t-1$	–	–	CPA	No	LWE
[11]	SIM	Q-stat.	$t-1$	–	–	CPA	No	LWE
[48]	SIM	Q-stat.	$t-1$	–	–	CPA	No	LWE
[43]	SIM	Static	$t-1$	–	–	CPA	No	LWE‡
[16]	IND	Q-stat.	$\leq t-1$	Yes	No	CPA	No	LWE
[42]	IND	Adapt.	$\leq t-1$	Yes	Yes†	CCA	Yes$^\#$	DLIN
[29]	IND	Adapt.	$\leq t-1$	Yes	Yes	CCA	Yes$^\#$	LWE(+DCR)
[26]	SIM$^-$	Static	$\leq t-1$	Yes	Yes	CPA*	Yes	LWE
Section 4	SIM	Static	$\leq t-1$	Yes	Yes	CCA	Yes$^\#$	DDH

A Separating Example. In general, security models without Type II queries seem weaker and may be insufficient for TPKE applications. As a simple example, consider a $(k/2)$-out-of-k TPKE where the encryption algorithm encrypts normally, but additionally also picks a smaller random subset S of $k/4$ parties and $(k/4)$-out-of-$(k/4)$ encrypts to them. Using Type II queries, the adversary $\mathcal{A}$ can query $k/4 < t$ partial decryptions of the challenge ciphertext on the set S of users and recover the message. Thus, such TPKE should be deemed insecure, as the chosen $k/4$ parties can jointly decrypt without meeting the threshold $t = k/2$. However, in models without Type II queries, the set S may be exploited only when all its parties are corrupt, which happens only with negligible probability $\leq (1/2)^{k/4}$ when k is sufficiently large.

---

[4] We note that, the distinction between Type I and Type II queries is obscured by *maximal* corruption, as any additional ParDec query on a challenge leads to a trivial win under maximal corruption.

The above example highlights the phenomenon that security can trivially break even for a non-corrupting adversary, although security against a maximal-corrupting adversary $\mathcal{A}$ still holds, since under maximal corruptions, allowing or disallowing Type II queries is equivalent. Therefore, for TPKE, the claim that "security under maximal corruption implies the same notion under fewer corruption" does not hold in general. Of course, the validity of this argument also depends on other aspects of the security model, e.g. adaptivity of corruption and the adversary's queries, the number of challenge queries allowed etc. This raises the question, how different TPKE security models relate and which models considered in existing works provide sufficient security guarantees.

Indistinguishability versus Simulation. Assuming that Type II queries for TPKE are at hand, we attempt to make a security reduction for our toy threshold signature. With indistinguishability-based (*IND*-CPA[5]) security for TPKE, we run into a problem: An adversary $\mathcal{A}$ against the threshold signature may request $\leq t - 1$ partial signatures for random parties on many distinct messages, e.g. 2^{30} many. Then, it may pick some, e.g. $2^{15} \gg \lambda$ out of 2^{30}, and request the t-th share. In the IND-CPA game of TPKE, the reduction cannot request the t-th partial decryption for any challenge ciphertext; it also cannot guess the 2^{15} messages and let these be the queries for non-challenge ciphertexts, since the guessing would succeed with negligible probability. Thus, we need alternative reduction strategy[6] – or better a stronger security for TPKE.

Consider a simulation-based notion for TPKE (*SIM*-CPA), where the simulator does not learn the encrypted message of a challenge ciphertext until the t-th partial decryption share is requested, which ensures confidentiality. With such notion, a reduction may then delay the request for a signature σ from the EUF-CMA game, until it needs to produce the t-th partial decryption, i.e. until $\mathcal{A}$ learns σ anyway (which does not constitute a forgery).

To sum up the learnings from the above:

- A TPKE with SIM-CPA security supporting Type II queries and allowing non-maximal corruption is convenient and ideal to instantiate our toy example.
- With an IND-CPA secure TPKE, smarter reductions are needed (see footnote 6).
- Without Type II queries, the threshold signature is completely broken.

This work focuses on TPKE and subtle details may not directly generalise to TFHE. Bridging the gap between TPKE and TFHE is a task that requires additional care (see Sect. 1.3).

---

[5] The ParDecO oracle is present for CPA and CCA. However, for CPA, ParDecO it is limited to honestly generated ciphertexts. For CCA, any ciphertext is allowed.

[6] E.g. the reduction may guess which (if any) of the 2^{30} messages will be the forgery. This works, but the reduction suffers from a 2^{30} factor reduction loss.

1.2 Our Contributions

Security Models for TPKE. We formulate two basic security notions for TPKE, one as indistinguishability games and one in simulation style, respectively. Our models are designed to take care of various natural security aspects of TPKE, including corruption and partial decryptions as discussed in Sect. 1.1. The models are formalised in Sect. 2, capturing the setting with:

- *adaptive* partial decryption queries (both Types I and II),
- *static* corruption, and
- both chosen-plaintext-attacks (CPA) and chosen-ciphertext-attacks (CCA),

By suitably restricting an adversary's ability, our models recover the majority of adversarial capabilities considered in prior works. The choice of static corruption is for two reasons: We aim to model what we believe are the minimal requirements for a reasonably secure TPKE, and we will see that adaptive corruption is impossible for simulation-based security. Our models can be both strengthened and weakened in the natural ways. To relate notions, we will also consider variants with *selective* partial decryption queries (both Types I and II) and/or *adaptive* corruption (the latter only for IND security).

Relations Between TPKE Security Notions. We prove implications and separations between different security notions, as depicted in Fig. 1. The results below highlight some aspects on CPA security under static corruption, which should be taken into account when assessing security of a TPKE.

- (Theorem 3) Under adaptive partial decryption queries, security under maximal corruption does not imply security under arbitrary number of corruptions.
- (Theorem 5) Simulation security (with mild restrictions on the simulator) against an adversary observing only a single challenge ciphertext is strictly weaker than multi-challenge security.
- (Theorem 6) Under adaptive partial decryption queries and CPA-security, learning the encryption randomness of non-challenge (honest) ciphertexts is strictly stronger than hiding it.[7]

To prove our separations, we construct (contrived) counterexample TPKE schemes. While the counterexamples for Theorem 3 and Theorem 6 are very simple, the one for Theorem 5 is quite sophisticated. It is an interesting question whether *natural* counterexamples exist. Other relations and separations include:

- (Theorem 1) Adaptive corruption automatically implies the security with Type II partial decryption queries.
- (Theorem 2) Simulation security with adaptive corruption is not achievable, assuming adaptive partial decryption queries.
- (Theorem 4) Security against selective partial decryption queries does not imply that against adaptive queries.

---

[7] Not applicable to CCA, as there is no meaningful non-challenge encryption oracle.

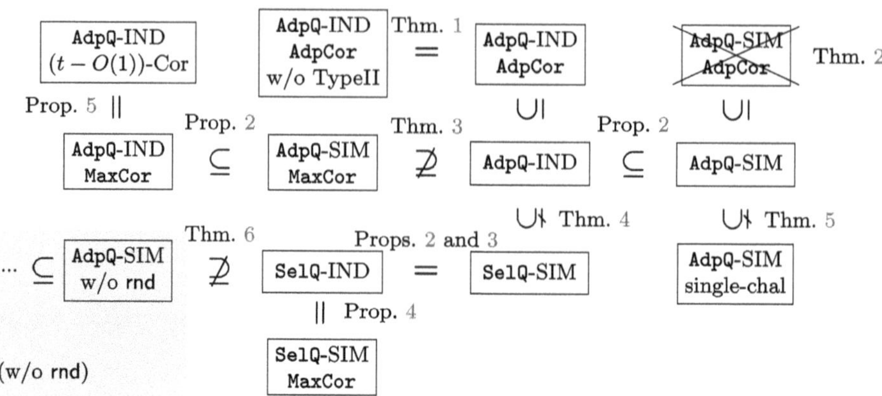

Fig. 1. Selected and simplified implication and separation results. (For a comprehensive version see the full version [18]). Setting: CPA, ParDecO answers both Types I, II queries (AdpQ for adaptive oracle answers, SelQ for selective), static corruption unless otherwise specified. Our main results are stated for the setting where the non-challenge encryption oracle EncO also outputs the encryption randomness rnd; the same set of relations again hold for the setting where EncO does not output rnd, depicted by the "w/o rnd" zone.

Theorem 2 is a simple adaptation of Nielsen's non-committing encryption impossibility result [46]. The above results raise an interesting tension between the choice of game- and simulation-based security: Game-based security with adaptive corruption and simulation-based security with static corruption are incomparable, and the suitability of either of them likely depends on applications.

Along the way, we also show other relation results which are (more) commonly expected to hold (Propositions in Fig. 1).

Beyond CPA-security, we also consider the stronger notion of CCA-security, where an adversary can issue partial decryption queries for arbitrary, maliciously generated ciphertexts [2,8,51], explained next.

CPA-to-CCA Transform I: Semi-malicious Security. We observe that the classic Naor-Yung transform [45] (and straightforward variants) to upgrade CPA to CCA security by attaching a NIZK cannot generically work for CPA secure TPKE.[8] Nevertheless, in Sect. 4 we give a result of similar spirit: When assuming *semi-malicious CPA*, where an adversary can see partial decryptions of ciphertexts generated with *adversarially chosen randomness*, CCA can be achieved by attaching a non-interactive zero-knowledge (NIZK) proof of knowledge, which proves the well-formedness of ciphertexts (Theorem 7).

---

[8] The gap in [32, Theorem 1] is, at a high level, that the Naor-Yung transform requires *perfect* correctness, but the natural analogue is not enough for TPKE when partial decryption queries are admitted. See Sect. 4.

Attaching a NIZK is a classic technique, but the subtlety lies in *when* it actually applies to a TPKE. Our message is that, to rely on this technique, a stronger baseline security of the underlying TPKE is required.

To demonstrate that our security notions are achievable, we show that the natural thresholdised ElGamal PKE (first suggested as a TPKE in [28]) achieves simulation semi-malicious CPA security[9]. Most of our proof is a direct adaption from a recent work [26] for which we claim no novelty. Applying the above NIZK-based transform, we obtain a simulation CCA-secure TPKE.

CPA-to-CCA Transform II: Non-interactive Proof of Randomness. To capture a broader class of TPKE schemes which satisfy CPA but not semi-malicious CPA security, in Sect. 5 we propose a new primitive called *non-interactive proof of randomness (NIPoR)*. A NIPoR may be seen as a variant of NIZK, whose functionality is to generate a proof that an efficient function f has been evaluated on a secret value m and secret high-entropy randomness r, resulting in some (public) value $y = f(m; r)$. By setting f as the encryption algorithm of a TPKE, one can prove that an encryption of a message m has been computed with honestly sampled and fresh randomness r.

We construct a NIPoR in the ROM, assuming the existence of straightline extractable NIZKs and commitments (Theorem 9). Using a NIPoR to attach a "randomness proof" to ciphertext, we obtain a transform which upgrades CPA to CCA security in the ROM (Theorem 10). The transform might be viewed as a "publicly verifiable Fujisaki-Okamoto (FO) transformation", and is a mix between NY and FO transforms.

Our NIPoR has already found application in the recent work [26] where it was used to upgrade a lattice-based TPKE scheme from CPA to CCA security. We believe the concept of NIPoR can find applications beyond TPKE and CPA-to-CCA transforms, and is of independent interest.

1.3   Related Works

Variations in TPKE Settings. The field of threshold encryption is vast, a variety of TPKE syntaxes (therefore also further variations in security notions) exists. For example, this work only focuses on *non-interactive* decryption, where partial decryptions are generated asynchronously without interaction between the decryption parties. The setting with interactive decryption is a natural and reasonable extension, considered in e.g. [22]. Dynamic key generation was considered in e.g. [27,49], where the trusted party can dynamically generate user secret keys (instead of all at once upfront) and encryption is w.r.t. threshold t dynamically chosen by the encryptor.

There has recently been rapid progress in TPKE constructions targeting improved efficiency and/or more advanced functionalities. A handful of models are proposed, some examples are: batch decryption [12,15,25], i.e. multiple

---

[9] Despite the decades, we are not aware of a proof showing that it meets the security we consider, in particular in presence of Type II partial decryption queries.

ciphertexts can be decrypted at once (with non-trivial efficiency constraints); silent setup [34,37,52], i.e. users can distributedly generate their own keypair; traceability [13,21], i.e. traitors who leak their decryption ability can be traced; context-dependent decryption [9], i.e. partial decryptions are bound to a context value which acts as a domain separator; server-aided decryption [47,48] (proposed for TFHE and also applies to TPKE), i.e. an additional trusted server, possibly knowing the users' secrets, may pre-process a ciphertext before it being partial-decrypted by users; and combinations of the above [14].

For each of the above, the difference in syntax inherently leads to different formal security definitions. However, we highlight that most of these variations can be seen as add-ons of the base case considered in this work, and we expect that most of our results carry over to these more advanced/complex settings.

Other Results on TPKE Security. This work focuses on *confidentiality* of TPKE, although further properties may be desired. For example, it is arguably important to model non-malleability, also called *robustness* [8,11,16,35], which guarantees that malicious partial decryptions do not allow an adversary to arbitrarily modify the message that an honest user recovers.

In a concurrent work, Boneh, Bünz, Nayak, Rotem and Shoup (BBNRS [10]) also consider the concept of Types I and II queries and refer to these as low- and high-threshold security respectively. BBNRS [9, Sec. 8, Eprint 2025-09-09] sketch how their security notions can be generalised to adaptive corruption, simulation-based security, UC-compatibility, and discuss a straightforward IND-CCA to SIM-CCA transform via non-committing encryption in the ROM. In turn, they do not consider CPA-to-CCA transforms, impossbilities, maximal corruption, and relations between various other existing security notions.

Related Notions/Primitives. Li and Micciancio (LM [41]) point out that IND-CPA security is too weak for (non-threshold) *approximately correct* FHE, since even the decryption of *honestly* generated ciphertexts might leak additional information. They suggest to strengthen IND-CPA with an additional decryption oracle D to which an adversary can query honestly generated ciphertexts. Under their CPA^D model, LM show practical attacks against approximately correct FHE schemes. This observation is analogous to the potential leakage from TPKE Type II queries that we consider. LM also study relations between variants of the definition, later expanded by [20]. Similar to our CPA notions for TPKE, CPA^D security for approximately correct FHE is fragile in that single- and multi-challenge definitions are not equivalent, and likewise, the number of decryption queries strictly increases the strength of the model. [6] study CPA^D security where (non-challenge) ciphertexts can be generated using adversarially chosen randomness, and show that such model is strictly stronger [6]; this can be seen analogous to our semi-malicious CPA security (Sect. 4). Several realistic CPA^D attacks on both approximately correct and exact FHE schemes have been implemented (cf. [23,24,36] and references therein), demonstrating that decryption of honest ciphertexts is a relevant attack angle.

For *threshold signatures*, the work of [4] introduce a fine-grained hierarchy of security notions including implications and separations, focusing on selective corruptions, similar to this work. Here, the difficulty of deciding when to consider a signature a forgery[10] is similar to the question of when to allow partial decryptions for a challenge ciphertext in TPKE. Separations between different notions for threshold signatures and encryption are conceptually related.

The question of NIZK-based variants of the Naor-Yung transform [45] in the ROM is explicitly explored in [7]. The notion of *universal samplers* [39] in the ROM bears similarities to NIPoR, but is stronger and their construction requires trusted setup to realise. Universal samplers force a party to honestly sample from a distribution (specified by a sampling circuit) such that only the output is learned. A NIPoR only asserts the correct distribution of the output, but the sampling party may be aware of the random coins; indeed, this is the case for our constructions and can be a desirable feature. The work [1] introduces the concept of an *anti-rusher* transformation for MPC in the ROM. Both works [1, 39] program random oracle queries to inject information, similar to fixing a Blum coin-toss; the technique is called *delayed backdoor programming* in [39].

2   IND and SIM Security for TPKE

Preliminaries. We let λ denote the security parameter and generally, almost all objects and families are implicitly parametrised by it and algorithms receive λ (implicitly) as input. We denote sets and tables by capital letter, e.g. S and T. For $k \in \mathbb{N}$, we write $[k]$ for $\{1, 2, ..., k\}$. As pseudocode, we write $x \leftarrow v$ to assign value v to variable x, and we write $x \leftarrow \mathsf{algo}(v)$ to run the deterministic algorithm algo on value v and assigns the result to x. Similarly, we write $x \leftarrow\!\!{\scriptstyle\$}\, S$ to sample a uniformly random value from set S and assigns the result to x, and we write $x \leftarrow\!\!{\scriptstyle\$}\, \mathsf{algo}'(v)$ to run the randomised algorithm algo' with fresh random coins on v and assigns the result to x. When an algorithm algo' has multiple outputs, we write $(x, y, z) \leftarrow\!\!{\scriptstyle\$}\, \mathsf{algo}'(v)$ and $(x, \_) \leftarrow\!\!{\scriptstyle\$}\, \mathsf{algo}'(v)$ if we ignore the values of all outputs except for the first.

An *access structure* on k parties is a set $\mathbb{A} \subseteq 2^{[k]} \setminus \emptyset$ of non-empty sets. If a set of parties $A \subseteq [k]$ satisfies $A \in \mathbb{A}$, we say that A satisfies the access structure $\mathbb{A}$. An access structure $\mathbb{A}$ is said to be monotone if the following holds for any $A, B \subseteq [k]$: If $A \in \mathbb{A}$ and $A \subseteq B$, then $B \in \mathbb{A}$. For any $t \in [k]$, a monotone access structure $\mathbb{A}_{k,t}$ is called a (t, k)-threshold access structure, if $A \in \mathbb{A}_{k,t}$ if and only if $A \subseteq [k]$ and $|A| \geq t$. Unless specified otherwise, we assume that every access structure $\mathbb{A}$ is a (t, k)-threshold structure, i.e. $\mathbb{A} = \mathbb{A}_{k,t}$. This is a simplifying assumption. Many of our results apply to general $\mathbb{A}$ with minor adaptations.

We recall definitions and security properties of pseudorandom functions (PRF), commitment schemes, and non-interactive zero-knowledge (NIZK) proofs in the full version [18].

---

[10] Important differentiations were already considered in [50].

We provide the TPKE syntax and our security definitions in Sect. 2.1, then discuss our design choices in Sect. 2.2. Moreover, we summarise the properties and their variants in Table 2.

2.1 Definitions

Definition 1 (Threshold PKE). *Let $\mathfrak{A} = (\mathfrak{A}_\lambda)_{\lambda \in \mathbb{N}}$ be a (family of) set(s) of access structures. A threshold public-key encryption (TPKE)* TPKE *for $\mathfrak{A}$ and a message space $\mathcal{M}$ consists of PPT algorithms* (KGen, Enc, ParDec, Rec) *with the following syntax:*

KGen$(1^\lambda, \mathbb{A}) \;\$\!\!\to\; (\mathsf{pk}, (\mathsf{sk}_j)_{j \in [k]})$: *The key generation algorithm, on input the security parameter 1^λ and an access structure $\mathbb{A} \in \mathfrak{A}_\lambda$ on k parties, generates the public key* pk *and a tuple of k secret keys $(\mathsf{sk}_j)_{j \in [k]}$ for each user $j \in [k]$.*

Enc$(\mathsf{pk}, \mu) \;\$\!\!\to\; \mathsf{ct}$: *The encryption algorithm encrypts a message $\mu \in \mathcal{M}$ w.r.t. the public key* pk.

ParDec$(\mathsf{sk}_j, \mathsf{ct}) \;\$\!\!\to\; \mathsf{pd}_j$: *The partial decryption algorithm receives the secret key sk_j of a user j and a ciphertext* ct, *and outputs a partial decryption pd_j.*

Rec$(\mathsf{pk}, (\mathsf{pd}_j)_{j \in T}, \mathsf{ct}) \;\$\!\!\to\; \mu'$: *The reconstruction algorithm gets a tuple of partial decryptions $(\mathsf{pd}_j)_{j \in T}$ from a set T of users and a ciphertext* ct *and outputs a message μ'. We omit* pk *as input to* Rec *whenever clear from the context.*

We require TPKE *to be correct, i.e. for any $\mathbb{A} \in \mathfrak{A}$, $(\mathsf{pk}, (\mathsf{sk}_j)_{j \in [k]}) \in$* KGen$(1^\lambda, \mathbb{A})$, *set $T \in \mathbb{A}$, and $\mu \in \mathcal{M}$, there is a negligible function ε such that*

$$
\Pr\left[\mu' = \mu \;\middle|\; \begin{array}{l} \mathsf{ct} \leftarrow \mathsf{Enc}(\mathsf{pk}, \mu) \\ \mathsf{pd}_j \leftarrow \mathsf{ParDec}(\mathsf{sk}_j, \mathsf{ct}) \;\; \forall j \in T \\ \mu' \leftarrow \mathsf{Rec}((\mathsf{pd}_j)_{j \in T}, \mathsf{ct}) \end{array} \right] \geq 1 - \varepsilon.
$$

We call ε the correctness error. *If $\varepsilon = 0$, then* TPKE *is perfectly* correct.

If any choice is valid, we often leave $\mathfrak{A}$ and $\mathcal{M}$ implicit. Below, we define TPKE game-based confidentiality (IND-CPA & IND-CCA) and simulation-based confidentiality (SIM-CPA & SIM-CCA) under *static* corruption. See the full version [18] for a definition under *adaptive* corruption.

Definition 2 (IND-CPA & IND-CCA). *A TPKE scheme* TPKE *is secure under static corruption, adaptive challenge queries and chosen plaintext attacks (*SCor-AdpQ*-IND-CPA) or chosen ciphertext attacks (*SCor-AdpQ*-IND-CCA), respectively, if for all PPT adversaries $\mathcal{A}$, the advantage* $\mathsf{Adv}^{\mathrm{IndCPA}}_{\mathsf{TPKE}, \mathcal{A}, \mathtt{AdpQ}}(\lambda) :=$

$$
\left| \Pr\left[\mathrm{IndCPA}^0_{\mathsf{TPKE}, \mathcal{A}, \mathtt{AdpQ}}(1^\lambda) = 1 \right] - \Pr\left[\mathrm{IndCPA}^1_{\mathsf{TPKE}, \mathcal{A}, \mathtt{AdpQ}}(1^\lambda) = 1 \right] \right|,
$$

or the advantage $\mathsf{Adv}^{\mathrm{IndCCA}}_{\mathsf{TPKE}, \mathcal{A}, \mathtt{AdpQ}}(\lambda) :=$

$$
\left| \Pr\left[\mathrm{IndCCA}^0_{\mathsf{TPKE}, \mathcal{A}, \mathtt{AdpQ}}(1^\lambda) = 1 \right] - \Pr\left[\mathrm{IndCCA}^1_{\mathsf{TPKE}, \mathcal{A}, \mathtt{AdpQ}}(1^\lambda) = 1 \right] \right|,
$$

is negligible, respectively, where the security experiments are defined in Fig. 2.

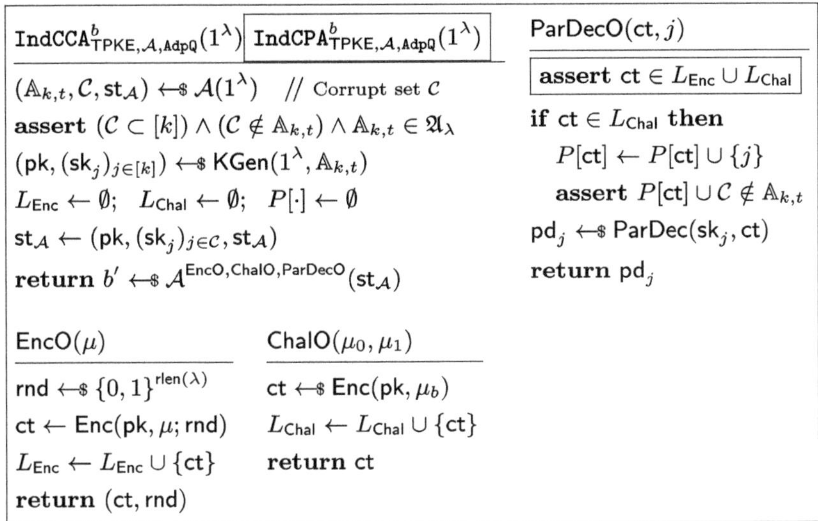

$\mathrm{IndCCA}^{b}_{\mathsf{TPKE},\mathcal{A},\mathsf{AdpQ}}(1^{\lambda})$ | $\boxed{\mathrm{IndCPA}^{b}_{\mathsf{TPKE},\mathcal{A},\mathsf{AdpQ}}(1^{\lambda})}$

$(\mathbb{A}_{k,t}, \mathcal{C}, \mathsf{st}_{\mathcal{A}}) \leftarrow\!\!\$\ \mathcal{A}(1^{\lambda})$ // Corrupt set $\mathcal{C}$

assert $(\mathcal{C} \subset [k]) \wedge (\mathcal{C} \notin \mathbb{A}_{k,t}) \wedge \mathbb{A}_{k,t} \in \mathfrak{A}_{\lambda}$

$(\mathsf{pk}, (\mathsf{sk}_{j})_{j\in[k]}) \leftarrow\!\!\$\ \mathsf{KGen}(1^{\lambda}, \mathbb{A}_{k,t})$

$L_{\mathsf{Enc}} \leftarrow \emptyset;\ \ L_{\mathsf{Chal}} \leftarrow \emptyset;\ \ P[\cdot] \leftarrow \emptyset$

$\mathsf{st}_{\mathcal{A}} \leftarrow (\mathsf{pk}, (\mathsf{sk}_{j})_{j\in\mathcal{C}}, \mathsf{st}_{\mathcal{A}})$

return $b' \leftarrow\!\!\$\ \mathcal{A}^{\mathsf{EncO},\mathsf{ChalO},\mathsf{ParDecO}}(\mathsf{st}_{\mathcal{A}})$

$\mathsf{EncO}(\mu)$

$\mathsf{rnd} \leftarrow\!\!\$\ \{0,1\}^{\mathsf{rlen}(\lambda)}$

$\mathsf{ct} \leftarrow \mathsf{Enc}(\mathsf{pk}, \mu; \mathsf{rnd})$

$L_{\mathsf{Enc}} \leftarrow L_{\mathsf{Enc}} \cup \{\mathsf{ct}\}$

return $(\mathsf{ct}, \mathsf{rnd})$

$\mathsf{ChalO}(\mu_{0}, \mu_{1})$

$\mathsf{ct} \leftarrow\!\!\$\ \mathsf{Enc}(\mathsf{pk}, \mu_{b})$

$L_{\mathsf{Chal}} \leftarrow L_{\mathsf{Chal}} \cup \{\mathsf{ct}\}$

return ct

$\mathsf{ParDecO}(\mathsf{ct}, j)$

$\boxed{\textbf{assert}\ \mathsf{ct} \in L_{\mathsf{Enc}} \cup L_{\mathsf{Chal}}}$

if $\mathsf{ct} \in L_{\mathsf{Chal}}$ **then**
  $P[\mathsf{ct}] \leftarrow P[\mathsf{ct}] \cup \{j\}$
    assert $P[\mathsf{ct}] \cup \mathcal{C} \notin \mathbb{A}_{k,t}$

$\mathsf{pd}_{j} \leftarrow\!\!\$\ \mathsf{ParDec}(\mathsf{sk}_{j}, \mathsf{ct})$

return pd_{j}

Fig. 2. $\mathrm{IndCCA}^{b}_{\mathsf{TPKE},\mathcal{A},\mathsf{AdpQ}}(1^{\lambda})$ and $\mathrm{IndCPA}^{b}_{\mathsf{TPKE},\mathcal{A},\mathsf{AdpQ}}(1^{\lambda})$ security experiments for TPKE. The $\boxed{\text{boxed code}}$ only applies to $\mathrm{IndCPA}^{b}_{\mathsf{TPKE},\mathcal{A},\mathsf{X}}(1^{\lambda})$. The oracle EncO is redundant for CCA, see Remark 1.

$\mathrm{SimCCA}^{b}_{\mathsf{TPKE},\mathcal{A},\mathcal{S},\mathsf{AdpQ}}(1^{\lambda})$ | $\boxed{\mathrm{SimCPA}^{b}_{\mathsf{TPKE},\mathcal{A},\mathcal{S},\mathsf{AdpQ}}(1^{\lambda})}$

$(\mathbb{A}_{k,t}, \mathcal{C}, \mathsf{st}_{\mathcal{A}}) \leftarrow\!\!\$\ \mathcal{A}(1^{\lambda})$ // Corrupt set $\mathcal{C}$

assert $(\mathcal{C} \subset [k]) \wedge (\mathcal{C} \notin \mathbb{A}_{k,t}) \wedge \mathbb{A}_{k,t} \in \mathfrak{A}_{\lambda}$

if $b = 0$ **then** $(\mathsf{pk}, (\mathsf{sk}_{j})_{j\in[k]}) \leftarrow\!\!\$\ \mathsf{KGen}(1^{\lambda}, \mathbb{A}_{k,t})$

if $b = 1$ **then** $(\mathsf{pk}, (\mathsf{sk}_{j})_{j\in\mathcal{C}}, \mathsf{st}_{\mathcal{S}}) \leftarrow\!\!\$\ \mathcal{S}(1^{\lambda}, \mathbb{A}_{k,t}, \mathcal{C})$

$L_{\mathsf{Enc}} \leftarrow \emptyset;\ \ L_{\mathsf{Chal}} \leftarrow \emptyset;\ \ P[\cdot] \leftarrow \emptyset;\ \ M[\cdot] \leftarrow \emptyset$

$\mathsf{st}_{\mathcal{A}} \leftarrow (\mathsf{pk}, (\mathsf{sk}_{j})_{j\in\mathcal{C}}, \mathsf{st}_{\mathcal{A}})$

return $b' \leftarrow\!\!\$\ \mathcal{A}^{\mathsf{EncO},\mathsf{ChalO},\mathsf{ParDecO}}(\mathsf{st}_{\mathcal{A}})$

$\mathsf{EncO}(\mu)$

if $b = 0$ **then**

  $\mathsf{rnd} \leftarrow\!\!\$\ \{0,1\}^{\mathsf{rlen}(\lambda)}$

  $\mathsf{ct} \leftarrow \mathsf{Enc}(\mathsf{pk}, \mu; \mathsf{rnd})$

if $b = 1$ **then** $(\mathsf{ct}, \mathsf{rnd}, \mathsf{st}_{\mathcal{S}}) \leftarrow\!\!\$\ \mathcal{S}(\mu, \mathsf{st}_{\mathcal{S}})$

$L_{\mathsf{Enc}} \leftarrow L_{\mathsf{Enc}} \cup \{\mathsf{ct}\};\ M[\mathsf{ct}] \leftarrow \mu$

return $(\mathsf{ct}, \mathsf{rnd})$

$\mathsf{ChalO}(\mu)$

if $b = 0$ **then** $\mathsf{ct} \leftarrow\!\!\$\ \mathsf{Enc}(\mathsf{pk}, \mu)$

if $b = 1$ **then** $(\mathsf{ct}, \mathsf{st}_{\mathcal{S}}) \leftarrow\!\!\$\ \mathcal{S}(\mathsf{st}_{\mathcal{S}})$

$L_{\mathsf{Chal}} \leftarrow L_{\mathsf{Chal}} \cup \{\mathsf{ct}\};\ M[\mathsf{ct}] \leftarrow \mu$

return ct

$\mathsf{ParDecO}(\mathsf{ct}, j)$

$\boxed{\textbf{assert}\ \mathsf{ct} \in L_{\mathsf{Enc}} \cup L_{\mathsf{Chal}}}$

$P[\mathsf{ct}] \leftarrow P[\mathsf{ct}] \cup \{j\}$

if $b = 0$ **then** $\mathsf{pd}_{j} \leftarrow\!\!\$\ \mathsf{ParDec}(\mathsf{sk}_{j}, \mathsf{ct})$

if $b = 1$ **then**

  if $P[\mathsf{ct}] \cup \mathcal{C} \in \mathbb{A}_{k,t} \wedge \mathsf{ct} \in L_{\mathsf{Chal}}$ **then**

    $\mu \leftarrow M[\mathsf{ct}]$

    $(\mathsf{pd}_{j}, \mathsf{st}_{\mathcal{S}}) \leftarrow\!\!\$\ \mathcal{S}(\mathsf{ct}, \mu, j, \mathsf{st}_{\mathcal{S}})$

  else $(\mathsf{pd}_{j}, \mathsf{st}_{\mathcal{S}}) \leftarrow\!\!\$\ \mathcal{S}(\mathsf{ct}, j, \mathsf{st}_{\mathcal{S}})$

return pd_{j}

Fig. 3. $\mathrm{SimCCA}^{b}_{\mathsf{TPKE},\mathcal{A},\mathcal{S},\mathsf{AdpQ}}(1^{\lambda})$ and $\mathrm{SimCPA}^{b}_{\mathsf{TPKE},\mathcal{A},\mathcal{S},\mathsf{AdpQ}}(1^{\lambda})$ security experiments for TPKE. The $\boxed{\text{boxed code}}$ only applies to $\mathrm{SimCPA}^{b}_{\mathsf{TPKE},\mathcal{A},\mathcal{S},\mathsf{AdpQ}}(1^{\lambda})$. The oracle EncO is redundant for CCA, see Remark 1.

Definition 3 (SIM-CPA & SIM-CCA). *A TPKE scheme* TPKE *is simulation-secure under static corruption, adaptive challenge queries and chosen plaintext-attacks (*SCor-AdpQ*-SIM-CPA) or chosen ciphertext attacks (*SCor-AdpQ*-SIM-CCA), respectively, if there is a PPT simulator* $\mathcal{S}$, *such that for all PPT adversaries* $\mathcal{A}$ *the advantage* $\mathsf{Adv}^{\mathrm{SimCPA}}_{\mathsf{TPKE},\mathcal{A},\mathcal{S},\mathrm{AdpQ}}(\lambda) :=$

$$\left| \Pr\left[\mathrm{SimCPA}^{0}_{\mathsf{TPKE},\mathcal{A},\mathcal{S},\mathrm{AdpQ}}(1^{\lambda}) = 1 \right] - \Pr\left[\mathrm{SimCPA}^{1}_{\mathsf{TPKE},\mathcal{A},\mathcal{S},\mathrm{AdpQ}}(1^{\lambda}) = 1 \right] \right|,$$

or the advantage $\mathsf{Adv}^{\mathrm{SimCCA}}_{\mathsf{TPKE},\mathcal{A},\mathcal{S},\mathrm{AdpQ}}(\lambda) :=$

$$\left| \Pr\left[\mathrm{SimCCA}^{0}_{\mathsf{TPKE},\mathcal{A},\mathcal{S},\mathrm{AdpQ}}(1^{\lambda}) = 1 \right] - \Pr\left[\mathrm{SimCCA}^{1}_{\mathsf{TPKE},\mathcal{A},\mathcal{S},\mathrm{AdpQ}}(1^{\lambda}) = 1 \right] \right|,$$

is negligible, respectively, where the security experiments are defined in Fig. 3.

Selective Queries. In the full version [18], we define *selective queries* security for all of the above 4 definitional variants, denoted by SCor-SelQ-Y-Z, for $\mathrm{Y} \in$ {IND, SIM} and $\mathrm{Z} \in$ {CPA, CCA}. Selective security requires the adversary to declare its queries upfront, at the same time as it chooses the corrupt parties. While selective security is too weak to be considered a reasonable target notion, it is useful to clarify in which cases the adaptivity of partial decryption queries makes one security notion stronger than another (cf. Propositions 3 and 4 and Remark 8, which are in contrast to the separations for adaptive security in Sects. 3.3 and 3.4).

Adaptive Corruption. In the full version [18], we define TPKE security under *adaptive corruption* for both the IND and SIM settings, denoted by AdpCor-X-Y-Z, for $\mathrm{X} \in$ {SelQ, AdpQ}, $\mathrm{Y} \in$ {IND, SIM} and $\mathrm{Z} \in$ {CPA, CCA}. Under adaptive corruption, an adversary $\mathcal{A}$ does not need to declare the corrupt set $\mathcal{C}$ upfront, but is given a corruption oracle CorO which it can query throughout the experiment. Upon querying on an index j, CorO returns the secret key sk_j of j. For IND, we require that $\mathcal{A}$ never corrupts an admissible set of indices; for SIM, as soon as $\mathcal{A}$ corrupts an admissible set T, the simulator $\mathcal{S}$ receives the underlying plaintext for any ct decryptable by the set T. Looking ahead, we will see that adaptive corruption is impossible in the SIM setting (Theorem 2).

Remark 1 (CCA subsumes EncO*).* For CCA security, the access to EncO in Figs. 2 and 3 is unnecessary, since an adversary $\mathcal{A}$ can query ParDecO on ciphertexts ct's generated by itself for all k parties. (In particular, $\mathcal{A}$ also knows the encryption randomness rnd for these ct's.) We keep EncO in the CCA definitions only for ease of comparison with CPA.

Remark 2 (Quasi-static Corruption). We say that TPKE is IND- resp. SIM-CPA-secure under *quasi-static* corruption and X challenge queries, if security holds w.r.t. a modified experiment $\mathrm{IndCPA}^{b}_{\mathsf{TPKE},\mathcal{A},\mathrm{X}}$ resp. $\mathrm{SimCPA}^{b}_{\mathsf{TPKE},\mathcal{A},\mathcal{S},\mathrm{X}}$, where $\mathcal{A}$ declares the corrupt set $\mathcal{C}$ after receiving pk, but still before making any oracle query to EncO, ChalO and ParDecO. For SIM-security, correspondingly, in game $b = 1$ the simulator $\mathcal{S}$ simulates pk and $(\mathsf{sk}_j)_{j \in \mathcal{C}}$ separately, the latter after $\mathcal{A}$ declaring the set $\mathcal{C}$.

The following restricted variants of security are adapted from prior works.

Definition 4 (Security under Maximal Corruption). *Let* $\mathtt{X} \in \{\mathtt{AdpQ}, \mathtt{SelQ}\}$. *A TPKE scheme* TPKE *is* $\mathtt{X}$-*IND-CPA under maximal corruption (*$\mathtt{MaxCor}$-$\mathtt{X}$-*IND-CPA), if for all PPT adversaries* $\mathcal{A}$ *which declare a corrupt set* $\mathcal{C}$ *of maximal size, i.e.* $|\mathcal{C}| = t - 1$ *for threshold* t *chosen by* $\mathcal{A}$, *the advantage* $\mathsf{Adv}^{\mathtt{IndCPA}}_{\mathsf{TPKE},\mathcal{A},\mathtt{X}}(\lambda)$ *is negligible.* $\mathtt{X}$-*SIM-CPA under maximal corruption (*$\mathtt{MaxCor}$-$\mathtt{X}$-*SIM-CPA) and CCA-variants are defined analogously.*

Note that maximal corruption only makes sense in the static (but not adaptive) corruption model.

Definition 5 (Security without Type II Queries). *Let* $\mathtt{X} \in \{\mathtt{AdpQ}, \mathtt{SelQ}\}$. *A TPKE scheme* TPKE *is* $\mathtt{X}$-*IND-CPA without Type II queries, if for all PPT adversaries* $\mathcal{A}$ *which never query* $\mathsf{ParDecO}$ *on any* $\mathsf{ct} \in L_{\mathsf{Chal}}$, *the advantage* $\mathsf{Adv}^{\mathtt{IndCPA}}_{\mathsf{TPKE},\mathcal{A},\mathtt{X}}(\lambda)$ *is negligible.* $\mathtt{X}$-*IND-CCA without Type II queries is analogous.*

Definition 6 (Single-challenge Security). *Let* $\mathtt{X} \in \{\mathtt{AdpQ}, \mathtt{SelQ}\}$. *A TPKE scheme* TPKE *is single-challenge* $\mathtt{X}$-*IND-CPA, if every PPT adversary* $\mathcal{A}$ *which makes only a single* ChalO *query has negligible advantage* $\mathsf{Adv}^{\mathtt{IndCPA}}_{\mathsf{TPKE},\mathcal{A},\mathtt{X}}(\lambda)$. *In this case, we also denote such advantage by* $\mathsf{Adv}^{\mathtt{1Ch\text{-}IndCPA}}_{\mathsf{TPKE},\mathcal{A},\mathtt{X}}(\lambda)$. *Single-challenge* $\mathtt{X}$-*SIM-CPA and CCA variants are defined analogously.*

Different mixtures of the above variants are possible. We summarise the different properties and the notations used in this work in Table 2.

2.2 Discussion

We highlight a number of security aspects in our models which are tied to TPKE, and draw connections to the models in prior works.

Corrupt Parties. Both the IND- and SIM-based (Definitions 2 and 3) models allow an adversary $\mathcal{A}$ to corrupt $|\mathcal{C}| \leq t - 1$ parties, i.e. any $\mathcal{C} \notin \mathbb{A}_{k,t}$. By restricting to the class of adversaries that corrupt a maximal set of $t - 1$ parties (Definition 4), we recover the corruption behaviour in models of a handful of prior works, including that in the seminal work of [11] which constructed TFHE and universal thresholdiser, among others, e.g. [2,8,51] (IND-based) and [5,11,43,48] (SIM-based).[11]

Looking ahead, we show that Definition 4 implies neither Definition 2 nor Definition 3 (Theorem 3). Concretely, in the case of maximal corruption, partial decryption queries on challenge ciphertexts ct returned from ChalO are disallowed in the IND setting, whereas in the SIM setting the simulator $\mathcal{S}$ always receives the plaintext μ for simulating partial decryptions. As such, maximal corruption does not capture confidentiality of messages for which the adversary

---

[11] Some with the minor difference between static and quasi-static corruption, cf. Table 1. While corruption behaviour agrees, the behaviour of oracles differs, see below.

Table 2. Summary of properties, their possible types, and notations. Default means the setting considered in Definitions 2 and 3.

Property	Type	Notation/Abbrev.	Note
Corruption	Maximal	`MaxCor`	Definition 4
	Static	`SCor`	*Default*
	Quasi-Static	–	Remark 2
	Adaptive	`AdpCor`	see full version
Type II queries	No	"without Type II queries"	Definition 5
	Yes	–	*Default*
Queries	Selective	`SelQ`	see full version
(EncO, ChalO, ParDecO)	Adaptive	`AdpQ`	*Default*
# of challenges	Single-Challenge	`1Ch`	Definition 6
	Multi-Challenge	–	*Default*
EncO oracle	Honest randomness	–	*Default*
(only applies to CPA)	Semi-malicious	`SemiMal`	Definition 7
ParDecO restriction	CPA	CPA	
	CCA	CCA	
Security Model	Indistinguishability	IND	Definition 2
	Simulation	SIM	Definition 3

obtains $< t - 1$ partial decryptions. We note that while Theorem 3 is stated for static corruption, the same holds for quasi-static corruption (Remark 2).

ParDecO *Queries for Challenges.* The IND-CPA model of [16, Def. 20] is similar to our `AdpQ`-IND-CPA model (Definition 2), but with the crucial difference that our oracle ParDecO also answers to queries on challenge ciphertexts (called Type II queries in Sect. 1.1) so long as $\mathcal{A}$ cannot trivially decrypt them. More specifically, in ParDecO in Fig. 2, if the check $\mathsf{ct} \in L_{\mathsf{Chal}}$ passes, it does not abort. If instead, ParDecO would abort for such queries, then the maximal corruption IND-CPA definition (Definition 4) implies the model in [16].

EncO *Outputs Randomness.* The IND-CPA and SIM-CPA experiments (Definitions 2 and 3) model *semi-honest* security, in that partial decryptions can only be requested for ciphertexts honestly generated by the experiment. However, even an honest-but-curious adversary $\mathcal{A}$ can observe its own randomness, so a realistic model should indeed allow $\mathcal{A}$ to observe it. Thus, for non-challenge ciphertexts (i.e. ct's output by EncO), our model also provides the encryption randomness rnd to $\mathcal{A}$. To our knowledge, this aspect has not been explicitly considered by most prior works [5, 11, 16, 43, 48] for CPA security, with the only exception being [26] (cf. Table 1).

Looking ahead, we give a positive result showing that this extra property allows a generic CPA-to-CCA transform for TPKE in the ROM (Theorem 10), and we give a separation result (Theorem 6) showing that without EncO outputting rnd leads to a strictly weaker model. All other separation results (Theorems 2 to 5) still hold when EncO does not return rnd. We note again that EncO is redundant in the CCA setting (cf. Remark 1), in which case the aspect on rnd does not matter [2,8,29,42,51].

Single vs. Multiple Challenges. Both models allow an adversary $\mathcal{A}$ to query arbitrarily many (both challenge and non-challenge) ciphertexts to model realistic applications. On the one hand, Proposition 1 confirms that IND security against a single challenge (e.g. as in [42]) implies IND security against multiple ones (e.g. as in [16]), via a straightforward hybrid argument. On the other hand, in the SIM-based setting, we show that under mild assumptions, single-challenge-SIM-CPA is strictly weaker than (multi-challenge-)SIM-CPA (Theorem 5).

Simulator Strength. Definition 3 considers a simulator $\mathcal{S}$ which can (statefully) simulate KGen, thus endowing it with additional power. In particular, $\mathcal{S}$ is allowed to simulate all secret keys sk_j, including those for the corrupt parties. We note that this suffices for guaranteeing confidentiality of a TPKE, since $\mathcal{S}$ is required to simulate both the challenge ct's and their partial decryptions pd_j without knowledge of the plaintext μ, so long as the threshold t has not been reached.

Remark 3 (Variants of Simulation Security). It is possible to consider stronger variants of Definition 3 by restricting the ability of $\mathcal{S}$, for example, disallowing $\mathcal{S}$ to simulate KGen and/or ciphertexts, forbidding $\mathcal{S}$ to know the corrupt keys $(sk_j)_{j \notin C}$, requiring $\mathcal{S}$ to be stateless (overall or between sessions), etc. For example, the variants given in the full version [18] will be used for proving Theorem 5.

Remark 4 (On Security Model of [11]). In [11] which constructed TFHE (which served as building block for the classic universal thresholdiser), the security model is split into two experiments: (1) an IND-CPA experiment forbidding any partial decryption query, and (2) a SIM-based experiment against maximally-corrupting $\mathcal{A}$, which involves a simulator $\mathcal{S}$ for partial decryptions but without guaranteeing confidentiality of ct (both under quasi-static corruption). This approach has been followed by e.g. [43]. These jointly imply MaxCor-AdpQ-SIM-CPA under quasi-static corruption (Definition 4 and Remark 2). On the other hand, the joint modelling of confidentiality and simulatability as in Definition 3 seems to enable new flexibility. For instance, a simulator $\mathcal{S}$ which simulates KGen would trivialise experiment (2) above[12], but which is not the case for Definition 3.

Remark 5 (Multiple ParDecO queries on Same Input). In both Definitions 2 and 3, when $b = 0$ and ParDecO is queried on the same (ct, j) multiple times, each time it runs ParDec honestly and obtains a (potentially) fresh partial decryption. Although not explicitly discussed, we note that this generality was not always

---

[12] This is the case of [11, Eprint, Def.5.5], as also observed by [48]. Fortunately, its security proof has not exploited this feature of their definition, and would still go through without $\mathcal{S}$ simulating KGen (which yields a meaningful notion).

achieved in prior works. For example, for the lattice-based construction of [11], where each partial decryption is an LWE sample taking the form $\mathbf{s}_j^\mathsf{T}\mathbf{A} + \mathbf{e}_j^\mathsf{T} \bmod q$ for some partial decryption key $\mathbf{s}_j$ and fresh partial decryption randomness $\mathbf{e}_j$, upon given multiple fresh partial decryptions $(\mathbf{s}_j^\mathsf{T}\mathbf{A} + \mathbf{e}_{j,i}^\mathsf{T} \bmod q)_i$ on the same query, one likely could apply an averaging attack, averaging the errors $\mathbf{e}_{j,i}$ out and recover $\mathbf{s}_j$ with decent probability. Fortunately, given a scheme that only achieves security with a restricted ParDecO answering once to each query (ct, j), one can generically compile such to one that supports "freshly generated" answers, by using a PRF to derandomise the ParDec algorithm. Specifically, let ParDec derive its randomness via $r = \mathsf{PRF}(\mathsf{ct}, \mathsf{sk}_{j,\mathsf{PRF}})$, and use this to run the original (potentially randomised) code of ParDec, see the full version [18] for a formal statement and proof.

3   Implications and Separations

We formalise the implications and separations outlined in Sect. 2.2, Fig. 1.

3.1   Preparatory Implications

First we state a few simple implications. These results are relatively standard, but they will be useful for our subsequent separations.

Proposition 1. *Let* $\mathtt{C} \in \{\mathtt{SCor}, \mathtt{AdpCor}\}$, $\mathtt{X} \in \{\mathtt{AdpQ}, \mathtt{SelQ}\}$, *and let* TPKE *be a TPKE scheme.*

(1) TPKE *is* single-challenge $\mathtt{C}$-$\mathtt{X}$-*IND-CPA.* $\Rightarrow$ TPKE *is* $\mathtt{C}$-$\mathtt{X}$-*IND-CPA.*
(2) TPKE *is* single-challenge $\mathtt{C}$-$\mathtt{X}$-*IND-CCA.* $\Rightarrow$ TPKE *is* $\mathtt{C}$-$\mathtt{X}$-*IND-CCA.*

The proof of Proposition 1 proceeds via a standard hybrid argument, where the reduction forwards the ith ChalO query as its own ChalO query and simulates answers to other ChalO queries via queries to EncO. See the full version [18] for details.

For X-SIM-CPA, it is unclear how to transform a single-challenge simulator into a multi-challenge simulator to obtain an analogue of Proposition 1. We give in Theorem 5 a separation for all simulators that do not simulate KGen.

Next we show that SIM-CPA implies IND-CPA. This implication holds for all variations of the definitions that we are aware of. We state and prove it for the variations which we use in other theorems.

Proposition 2 (SIM $\Rightarrow$ IND). *Let* $\mathtt{C} \in \{\mathtt{SCor}, \mathtt{MaxCor}\}$, $\mathtt{X} \in \{\mathtt{AdpQ}, \mathtt{SelQ}\}$, *and let* TPKE *be a TPKE scheme.*

(1) TPKE *is* $\mathtt{C}$-$\mathtt{X}$-*SIM-CPA.* $\Rightarrow$ TPKE *is* $\mathtt{C}$-$\mathtt{X}$-*IND-CPA.*
(2) TPKE *is* $\mathtt{C}$-$\mathtt{X}$-*SIM-CCA.* $\Rightarrow$ TPKE *is* $\mathtt{C}$-$\mathtt{X}$-*IND-CCA.*

The proof of Proposition 2 is standard, moving from ChalO encrypting μ_0 to simulated ChalO and then to encrypting μ_1. See the full version [18] for details. Under *selective* queries, the converse implication also holds.

Proposition 3 (SelQ-IND $\Rightarrow$ SelQ-SIM). *Let* TPKE *be a TPKE scheme.*

(1) TPKE *is* SCor-SelQ-*IND-CPA.* $\Rightarrow$ TPKE *is* SCor-SelQ-*SIM-CPA.*
(2) TPKE *is* SCor-SelQ-*IND-CCA.* $\Rightarrow$ TPKE *is* SCor-SelQ-*SIM-CCA.*

For Proposition 3, the simulator essentially runs the real game honestly, except that it encrypts zeroes whenever it does not know a challenge plaintext. The reduction to IND-CPA/CCA can forward $(\mu, 0)$ to its ChalO oracle, since $\mathcal{A}$ never makes ParDecO queries for the resulting ciphertext (as else, the simulator would know the message, since Filter does not remove those). We omit the details.

Remark 6. For Proposition 3 to hold, the simulator indeed needs to simulate KGen, else the equivalence fails for pathological schemes.[13]

3.2 Difference Between IND and SIM: (Im)possibility of Adaptive Corruption

Prior works have provided TPKE schemes that achieve adaptive corruption in the IND setting [29, 42] (cf. Table 1). Theorem 1 below shows that in the IND setting, adaptive corruption is strong enough to imply Type II queries.

Theorem 1 (IND Adaptive Corruption). *Let* X $\in$ {AdpQ, SelQ} *and let* TPKE *be a TPKE scheme.*

(1) TPKE *is single-challenge* AdpCor-X-*IND-CPA without Type II queries.* $\Rightarrow$
    TPKE *is (multi-challenge)* AdpCor-X-*IND-CPA (with Type II queries).*
(2) TPKE *is single-challenge* AdpCor-X-*IND-CCA without Type II queries.* $\Rightarrow$
    TPKE *is (multi-challenge)* AdpCor-X-*IND-CCA (with Type II queries).*

In other words, under adaptive corruption, omitting Type II queries is without loss of generality [42]. Theorem 1 relies on the observation that, in the single-challenge setting, adaptive corruption can be used by the reduction to simulate the adaptive ParDecO Type II queries. Then, by Proposition 1 single-challenge security implies multi-challenge security. We give the proof in the full version [18].

Theorem 1 does not carry over to the SIM setting. In contrast, Theorem 2 establishes that adaptive corruption in the SIM setting is impossible. Looking ahead, we will also see that in the SIM setting, even for static corruption, single-challenge security does not imply multi-challenge security (Theorem 5).

Theorem 2 (Impossibility of SIM-CPA under Adaptive Corruption). *Let* X $\in$ {AdpQ, SelQ}. *No TPKE scheme* TPKE *can be* AdpCor-X-*SIM-CPA or* AdpCor-X-*SIM-CCA.*

---

[13] If pk includes the image of a one-way function and (some) sk_j contains the preimage which is revealed by ParDecO, then simulating ParDecO is impossible, unless the simulator breaks one-wayness.

The proof of Theorem 2 is in the full version [18]. It is a simple adaptation of Nielsen's impossibility result for non-committing encryption [46]. Similar to Nielsen [46], the arguments of our impossibility also carry over to the CRS model and the *non*-programmable random oracle. However, in the *programmable* random oracle model, the impossibility does not apply.

3.3   On Static and Maximal Corruption

Having seen that adaptive corruption in the SIM setting is impossible, we turn to inspect different security notions under static corruption. In this subsection we investigate the setting of maximal corruption considered in a significant number of prior works (cf. Table 1), and show that under adaptive partial decryption queries, this restriction leads to strictly weaker and arguably inadequate security.

We construct a $TPKE'$ that is MaxCor-AdpQ-SIM-CCA and SCor-SelQ-SIM-CCA (hence also MaxCor-AdpQ-IND-CCA and SCor-SelQ-IND-CCA by Proposition 2), but neither SCor-AdpQ-SIM-CPA nor SCor-AdpQ-IND-CPA. Towards this, we first construct a $TPKE^*$ that is MaxCor-AdpQ-SIM-CPA and SCor-SelQ-SIM-CPA but not SCor-AdpQ-IND-CPA, then compile it into the desired $TPKE'$ using a generic CPA-to-CCA transform to be introduced in Sect. 4.

Let $TPKE = (KGen, Enc, ParDec, Rec)$ be a TPKE that is SCor-AdpQ-SIM-CCA. We construct $TPKE^* = (KGen^*, Enc^*, ParDec^*, Rec^*)$ in Fig. 4.

Overview. The key generation $KGen^*$ of $TPKE^*$ first checks that $k \geq \lambda$ and $t \leq \frac{k}{2} + 1$, i.e. the threshold t (and thus the number $t - 1$ of corrupted keys which the adversary can obtain) is not too high. If so, the public key pk^* consists of two public keys (pk, pk') of TPKE. The 1st pk is for all k parties and under threshold t, the 2nd pk' is only for $k' = \frac{k}{2}$ parties and under threshold $t' = k' = \frac{k}{2}$. $KGen^*$ distributes the k' secret keys w.r.t. pk to a random size-k' subset of parties $R \subseteq [k]$. Enc^* encrypts w.r.t. both pk and pk', $ParDec^*$ partial-decrypts w.r.t. both sets of secret keys, and Rec^* only decrypts the partial decryptions w.r.t. pk.

Insecurity. The scheme $TPKE^*$ in Fig. 4 does not achieve AdpQ-IND-CPA nor AdpQ-SIM-CPA under arbitrary (static) corruption. Consider $t := \frac{k}{2} + 1$. An adversary $\mathcal{A}$ can refrain from corrupting anyone, determine the set R by asking partial decryption queries, then make partial decryption queries to R for a challenge ciphertext ct. This allows $\mathcal{A}$ to distinguish challenge ciphertexts in the AdpQ-IND-CPA game. In the AdpQ-SIM-CPA game, since $|*| R = \frac{k}{2} < t$, the simulator $\mathcal{S}$ does not know the challenge message $\mu \leftarrow_\$ \mathcal{M}$. Hence it fails to emulate the partial decryption queries with high probability of $1 - 1/|\mathcal{M}|$, for $\mathcal{M}$ the message space.

CPA-Security. Under *maximal* corruption, no partial decryption query for challenge ciphertexts is allowed in the AdpQ-IND-CPA game, whereas in the AdpQ-SIM-CPA game the simulator $\mathcal{S}$ gets the challenge message μ for simulating the partial decryptions. For the SelQ-SIM-CPA and SelQ-IND-CPA games (i.e.

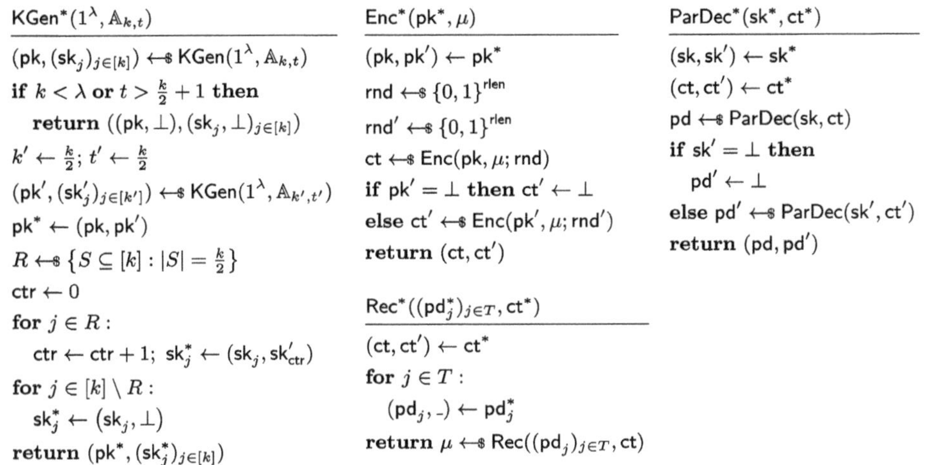

Fig. 4. Construction of pathological $\mathsf{TPKE}^* = (\mathsf{KGen}^*, \mathsf{Enc}^*, \mathsf{ParDec}^*, \mathsf{Rec}^*)$ from $\mathsf{TPKE} = (\mathsf{KGen}, \mathsf{Enc}, \mathsf{ParDec}, \mathsf{Rec})$, such that TPKE^* is secure under maximal, but not under static corruption.

arbitrary corruption but selective queries), the adversary $\mathcal{A}$ needs to guess the set R upfront, but since R is a set of size $\frac{k}{2}$ contained in $[k]$, $\mathcal{A}$ needs to guess R amongst exponentially many possibilities and is unlikely to succeed.

Upgrade to CCA-Security. To upgrade TPKE^* to TPKE' which achieves $\mathtt{MaxCor}$-$\mathtt{AdpQ}$-SIM-CCA and $\mathtt{SCor}$-$\mathtt{SelQ}$-SIM-CCA, we append a simulation-extractable NIZK certifying the computation of the encryption, which is verified before outputting a partial decryption. This can be seen as a variant of the Naor-Yung transform and is an instance of the SMT transformation to be presented in Sect. 4. The full transformed scheme TPKE' is provided in the full version [18] for completeness.

We state our formal theorems. Theorem 3 states that, in the adaptive queries setting, considering maximal corruption leads to a strictly weaker security notion, and is insecure against adversaries that can make partial decryption queries.

Theorem 3 ($\mathtt{MaxCor}$-$\mathtt{AdpQ} \not\Rightarrow \mathtt{AdpQ}$). *Let TPKE be a TPKE for access structure family $(\mathfrak{A}_\lambda)_{\lambda \in \mathbb{N}}$ such that for every λ, it holds that $\mathbb{A}_{\frac{\lambda}{2}, \frac{\lambda}{2}}, \mathbb{A}_{\lambda, \frac{\lambda}{2}+1} \in \mathfrak{A}_\lambda$.*

If TPKE is $\mathtt{SCor}$-$\mathtt{AdpQ}$-SIM-CCA, then TPKE^* in Fig. 4 is $\mathtt{MaxCor}$-$\mathtt{AdpQ}$-SIM-CPA, but not $\mathtt{SCor}$-$\mathtt{AdpQ}$-IND-CPA.

If, additionally, NIZK is a simulation-extractable NIZK, then $\mathsf{TPKE}' = \mathsf{SMT}[\mathsf{TPKE}^*, \mathsf{NIZK}]$ is $\mathtt{MaxCor}$-$\mathtt{AdpQ}$-SIM-CCA, but not $\mathtt{SCor}$-$\mathtt{AdpQ}$-IND-CPA, where the transformation SMT is defined in Fig. 8.

We stated Theorem 3 in a style where we say that TPKE' achieves the strongest possible notion (simulation-based CCA security) under maximal corruption, but does not achieve the weakest possible notion (game-based CPA security) when arbitrary (static) corruption is allowed. This separation simultaneously also establishes all immediate separations based on Proposition 2.

Next, Theorem 4 below establishes that, allowing adaptive partial decryption queries is strictly stronger than restricting to only selective partial decryption queries. We state Theorem 4 in the same style as Theorem 3.

Theorem 4 (SelQ $\not\Rightarrow$ AdpQ). *Let* TPKE *be a TPKE for access structure family* $(\mathfrak{A}_\lambda)_{\lambda \in \mathbb{N}}$ *such that for every* λ, *it holds that* $\mathbb{A}_{\frac{\lambda}{2},\frac{\lambda}{2}}, \mathbb{A}_{\lambda,\frac{\lambda}{2}+1} \in \mathfrak{A}_\lambda$.

If TPKE *is* SCor-AdpQ-*SIM-CCA, then* TPKE* *in Fig. 4 is* SCor-SelQ-*SIM-CPA, but not* SCor-AdpQ-*IND-CPA.*

If, additionally, NIZK *is a simulation-extractable NIZK, then* TPKE' = SMT[TPKE*, NIZK] *is* SCor-SelQ-*SIM-CCA, but not* SCor-AdpQ-*IND-CPA, where the transformation* SMT *is defined in Fig. 8.*

The proofs of Theorems 3 and 4 are given in the full version [18].

Remark 7. Theorems 3 and 4 require TPKE to support large thresholds $(k,t) = (\lambda, \lambda/2)$ and $(\lambda, \lambda/2+1)$. These parameters can be downscaled to $k \in \omega(1)$, since for the separations, it suffices that $k^{-k/2}$ is negligible.

For comparison, we also observe that in the much weaker setting with only selective partial decryption queries, maximal corruption is without loss of generality. This contrasts with Theorem 3 above.

Proposition 4. *Let* TPKE *be a TPKE scheme.*

(1) TPKE *is* MaxCor-SelQ-*IND-CPA.* $\Rightarrow$ TPKE *is* SCor-SelQ-*IND-CPA.*
(2) TPKE *is* MaxCor-SelQ-*IND-CCA.* $\Rightarrow$ TPKE *is* SCor-SelQ-*IND-CCA.*

By Proposition 1, it suffices to prove Proposition 4 for single-challenge SelQ-IND-CPA/CCA under static corruption. In the single-challenge, selective setting, the adversary declares its corrupt set and partial decryption queries for the single challenge ct upfront. Thus, the reduction can corrupt all these parties (which must be $< t$), as well as further parties unrelated to ct until reaching $t - 1$. The proof is given in the full version [18].

By guessing over a polynomial-size set, we have Proposition 5 which generalises to the setting with adaptive queries. Its proof is in the full version [18].

Proposition 5. *Let* $c \in \mathcal{O}(1)$ *and* TPKE *be a TPKE scheme. Let* $t' = t - c \geq 0$.

(1) TPKE *is* MaxCor-AdpQ-*IND-CPA.* $\Rightarrow$ TPKE *is* AdpQ-*IND-CPA under* t'-*corruption.*
(2) TPKE *is* MaxCor-AdpQ-*IND-CCA.* $\Rightarrow$ TPKE *is* AdpQ-*IND-CCA under* t'-*corruption.*

3.4   Single-Challenge AdpQ-SIM $\not\Rightarrow$ Multi-challenge AdpQ-SIM

We give a separation between single- and multi-challenge AdpQ-SIM-CPA under static corruption. Due to the freedom that our notion offers to a simulator, a separation is hardly straightforward. To this end, we restrict to the following:

1. We assume the existence of a TPKE scheme TPKE whose simulator $\mathcal{S}$ (I) does not simulate KGen, and (II) is *low-state* in the sense that it does not use state for simulating EncO queries and their associated ParDecO queries. We call this 1St-SIM-CPA security (see the full version [18]).
2. We achieve a separation for a strengthened SIM-CPA notion, called Hkg-SIM-CPA, where the simulator does not simulate KGen (see the full version [18]).

The notion of 1St-SIM-CPA (Item 1) is achievable whenever one can simulate partial decryptions given only ct and randomness rnd. For example, we will show that the thresholdised ElGamal PKE satisfies this notion (Theorem 8). Below we summarise how we transform a base TPKE scheme TPKE satisfying Item 1 into a scheme TPKE* in our separation. W.l.o.g. we assume that ParDec of TPKE is deterministic (cf. the full version [18]).

Our core idea is to let ParDec* of TPKE* return a NIZK which proves that the partial decryption response is computed correctly, but attaches a "one-time trapdoor" which allows the simulator $\mathcal{S}^*$ to respond arbitrarily once (while still producing a valid NIZK proof). The trapdoor is such that single-use is not noticeable, but double-use easily allows to distinguish simulated pd_j from real pd_j. Thus, $\mathcal{S}^*$ can embed one challenge response pd_j via the trapdoor, but a two-challenge simulation would require breaking either soundness of the NIZK or using the trapdoor twice (and thus be distinguishable).

Executing the above idea is problematic under Definition 3, since $\mathcal{S}^*$ may exploit its ability to simulate KGen* and program the common-reference-string (CRS) required for the NIZK, so that it may use the trapdoor repeatedly. This leads to the above restriction Item 2, i.e. forbidding $\mathcal{S}^*$ to simulate KGen*.[14] However, this also makes simulating ParDecO queries for non-challenge ciphertexts harder, as $\mathcal{S}^*$ needs to attach a valid proof to the partial decryptions without actually knowing the secret key of all parties.

To circumvent this, we rely on the restriction in Item 1 and make *non-black-box* use of the low-state simulator $\mathcal{S}$ of TPKE. Instead of proving that partial decryptions are correctly computed using ParDec*, $\mathcal{S}^*$ now only proves that they are consistently computed with the *same* deterministic, stateless program $\mathcal{S}(\cdot, \mathsf{init\text{-}st}_\mathcal{S})$ from $\mathcal{S}$, with some fixed state $\mathsf{init\text{-}st}_\mathcal{S}$ hardcoded. To fix this program, pd_j contains each time an identical commitment (computed with the same random string) to the program computing pd_j. As such, $\mathcal{S}^*$ can fix the program once to $\mathcal{S}(\cdot, \mathsf{init\text{-}st}_\mathcal{S})$.

Finally, one-time simulatability is achieved by turning the NIZK into an OR proof: pd_j additionally contains a pseudorandom value τ_j and an (fixed) commitment to a random value τ_j^* (sampled in KGen), and the OR proof establishes

---

[14] We do provide $\mathcal{S}$ with all secret key shares. But not the randomness of KGen itself. This is sufficient to embed a CRS for the NIZK.

$\underline{\mathsf{KGen}^*(1^\lambda, \mathbb{A}_{k,t})}$

$(\mathsf{pk}, (\mathsf{sk}_j)_{j\in[k]}) \leftarrow\!\!\$ \; \mathsf{KGen}(1^\lambda, \mathbb{A}_{k,t})$

$\mathsf{ck} \leftarrow\!\!\$ \; \mathsf{COM.Setup}(1^\lambda)$

$\mathsf{crs} \leftarrow\!\!\$ \; \mathsf{NIZK.Setup}(1^\lambda)$

$\mathsf{pk}^* \leftarrow (\mathsf{pk}, \mathsf{ck}, \mathsf{crs})$

for $1 \le j \le k$:

$\quad \rho_j^* \leftarrow\!\!\$ \; \{0,1\}^\lambda; \; \tau_j^* \leftarrow\!\!\$ \; \{0,1\}^\lambda$

$\quad k_{\mathsf{PRF},j}^* \leftarrow\!\!\$ \; \{0,1\}^\lambda$

$\quad \mathsf{sk}_j^* \leftarrow (\mathsf{sk}_j, \tau_j^*, \rho_j^*, k_{\mathsf{PRF},j}^*)$

return $(\mathsf{pk}^*, (\mathsf{sk}_j^*)_{j\in[k]})$

$\underline{\mathsf{Enc}^*(\mathsf{pk}^*, \mu)}$

$(\mathsf{pk}, \mathsf{ck}, \mathsf{crs}) \leftarrow \mathsf{pk}^*$

$\mathsf{ct} \leftarrow\!\!\$ \; \mathsf{Enc}(\mathsf{pk}, \mu); \; \mathsf{pad} \leftarrow\!\!\$ \; \{0,1\}^{2\lambda}$

return $(\mathsf{ct}, \mathsf{pad})$

$\underline{\mathsf{R}_{\mathsf{NIZK}}^*(\mathbb{x}, \mathbb{w} = (C_j(\cdot), \tau_j^*, \rho_j^*))}$

$(\mathsf{ck}, \mathsf{ct}, \mathsf{pd}_j, \tau_j, \mathsf{cm}_j) \leftarrow \mathbb{x}$

$b_0 \leftarrow (\mathsf{cm}_j = \mathsf{COM.Com}(\mathsf{ck}, (C_j, \tau_j^*); \rho_j^*))$

$b_1 \leftarrow (\mathsf{pd}_j = C_j(\mathsf{ct}^*))$

$b_2 \leftarrow \tau_j = \tau_j^*$

return $(b_0 \wedge b_1) \vee b_2$

$\underline{\mathsf{ParDec}^*(\mathsf{sk}_j^*, \mathsf{ct}^*)}$

$(\mathsf{sk}_j, \tau_j^*, \rho_j^*, k_{\mathsf{PRF},j}^*) \leftarrow \mathsf{sk}_j^*$

// Assign deterministic circuit

$C_j(\cdot) \leftarrow \mathsf{ParDec}(\mathsf{sk}_j, \cdot)$

// (Re)Generate commitment

$\mathsf{cm}_j \leftarrow \mathsf{Com}(\mathsf{ck}, (C_j, \tau_j^*); \rho_j^*)$

// Compute pd_j and consistency proof

$\mathsf{pd}_j \leftarrow C_j(\mathsf{ct}^*)$

$\tau_j = \mathsf{PRF}(k_{\mathsf{PRF},j}^*, \mathsf{ct}^*)$ // No trapdoor

$\mathbb{x} \leftarrow (\mathsf{ck}, \mathsf{ct}^*, \mathsf{pd}_j, \tau_j, \mathsf{cm}_j)$

$\mathbb{w} \leftarrow (C_j(\cdot), \tau_j^*, \rho_j^*)$

$\pi_j \leftarrow\!\!\$ \; \mathsf{NIZK.Prove}(\mathsf{crs}, \mathbb{x}, \mathbb{w})$

return $\mathsf{pd}_j^* \leftarrow (\mathsf{pd}_j, \tau_j, \mathsf{cm}_j, \pi_j)$

$\underline{\mathsf{Rec}^*(\mathsf{pk}^*, (\mathsf{pd}_j^*)_{j\in T}, \mathsf{ct}^*)}$

$(\mathsf{pk}, \mathsf{ck}, \mathsf{crs}) \leftarrow \mathsf{pk}^*$

$(\mathsf{ct}, \mathsf{pad}) \leftarrow \mathsf{ct}^*$

for $j \in T$:

$\quad (\mathsf{pd}_j, \tau_j, \mathsf{cm}_j, \pi_j) \leftarrow \mathsf{pd}_j^*$

$\quad \mathbb{x}_j = (\mathsf{ck}, \mathsf{ct}, \mathsf{pd}_j, \tau_j, \mathsf{cm}_j)$

$\quad$ **assert** $\mathsf{NIZK.Verify}(\mathsf{crs}, \mathbb{x}_j, \pi_j) = 1$

return $\mu \leftarrow\!\!\$ \; \mathsf{Rec}(\mathsf{pk}, (\mathsf{pd}_j)_{j\in T}, \mathsf{ct})$

Fig. 5. $\mathsf{TPKE}^* = (\mathsf{KGen}^*, \mathsf{Enc}^*, \mathsf{ParDec}^*, \mathsf{Rec}^*)$, using $\mathsf{TPKE} = (\mathsf{KGen}, \mathsf{Enc}, \mathsf{ParDec}, \mathsf{Rec})$, $\mathsf{COM} = (\mathsf{Setup}, \mathsf{Com})$, and $\mathsf{NIZK} = (\mathsf{Setup}, \mathsf{Prove}, \mathsf{Verify})$.

that either the committed circuit was executed, or that $\tau_j^* = \tau_j$. Revealing the same randomness τ_j^* twice is easily distinguishable from pseudorandomness and thus, the trapdoor τ_j^* can only be used once. Summarising, we have:

- a trapdoor (namely, the committed code) that allows $\mathcal{S}^*$ to simulate partial decryptions of all non-challenge ciphertexts, and
- a one-time trapdoor that allows $\mathcal{S}^*$ to bypass the consistent computation check in the NIZK once, to embed an answer to a challenge query.

A multi-challenge simulator would need to bypass the consistent computation check in the NIZK at least twice, which either contradicts its soundness or is easily distinguishable due to revealing τ_j^* twice. In the actual proof, the construction TPKE^* preserves simulation-security under honest key-generation, and $\mathcal{S}^*$ inherits the stateless EncO simulation from $\mathcal{S}$.

Theorem 5 (Single-challenge AdpQ-SIM-CPA). *Let* TPKE *be a TPKE which is perfectly correct and* AdpQ-1St-*SIM-CPA with deterministic* ParDec. *Let*

PRF *be a secure PRF,* COM *be a hiding and straightline extractable binding commitment scheme, and* NIZK *be a SIMEXT NIZK in the CRS model. Then* TPKE* *in Fig. 5 is single-challenge* AdpQ-1St-*SIM-CPA and single-challenge* AdpQ-Hkg-*SIM-CPA, but not (multi-challenge)* AdpQ-Hkg-*SIM-CPA.*

The adversary in the proof of Theorem 5 makes no corruption, one EncO and two ChalO queries, and has noticeable advantage. We provide the details in the full version [18]. Our simplifying assumptions of perfectness and derandomisation can easily be relaxed, we refer to the full version [18].

Remark 8. For selective queries and static corruption, single-challenge SelQ-SIM-CPA is equivalent to (multi-challenge) SelQ-SIM-CPA by Propositions 1 to 3.

3.5 On Encryption Randomness

We show that providing randomness for honest encryptions to the adversary constitutes a strictly stronger security model. Similar to Sect. 3.3, we start with TPKE = (KGen, Enc, ParDec, Rec) which is an adaptive SIM-CCA TPKE and modify it into a counterexample TPKE* = (KGen*, Enc*, ParDec*, Rec*). This time, KGen* = KGen, Enc* additionally outputs a pk$_{\mathsf{PKE}}$ for an IND-CPA public key encryption scheme, and ParDec* encrypts its own secret key under pk$_{\mathsf{PKE}}$. We provide the algorithms Enc*, ParDec* and Rec* in Fig. 6.

Enc*(pk, μ)	ParDec*(sk$_j$, (ct$'$, pk$_{\mathsf{PKE}}$))	Rec*((pd$_j$, ct$_{\mathsf{PKE},j}$)$_{j\in T}$, ct)
ct$'$ $\leftarrow\!\!\$$ Enc(pk, μ)	pd$_j$ $\leftarrow\!\!\$$ ParDec(sk$_j$, ct$'$)	(ct$'$, pk$_{\mathsf{PKE}}$) $\leftarrow$ ct
(pk$_{\mathsf{PKE}}$, sk$_{\mathsf{PKE}}$) $\leftarrow\!\!\$$ PKE.KGen(1^λ)	ct$_{\mathsf{PKE}}$ $\leftarrow\!\!\$$ PKE.Enc(pk$_{\mathsf{PKE}}$, sk$_j$)	μ $\leftarrow\!\!\$$ Rec((pd$_{k,j}$)$_{j\in T}$, ct$'$)
return (ct$'$, pk$_{\mathsf{PKE}}$)	**return** (pd$_j$, ct$_{\mathsf{PKE}}$)	**return** μ

Fig. 6. TPKE* = (KGen*, Enc*, ParDec*, Rec*), using TPKE = (KGen, Enc, ParDec, Rec) and PKE = (KGen, Enc, Dec). KGen* = KGen.

Insecurity. We observe that, if $\mathcal{A}$ knows the encryption randomness, it knows the secret key for pk$_{\mathsf{PKE}}$ and can decrypt, so that the scheme is insecure, because each partial decryption share leaks the partial decryption key. In turn, if $\mathcal{A}$ does not learn the encryption randomness, pk$_{\mathsf{PKE}}$ is a securely generated public key and thus, the TPKE scheme is as secure as without the modification. We state Theorem 6 in the same style as Theorem 3.

Theorem 6 (EncO releasing rnd). *Let* C $\in$ {SCor, AdpCor}, Y $\in$ {*IND, SIM*}. *If* TPKE *is a TPKE that is* C-AdpQ-Y-*CPA and* PKE *is a PKE that is IND-CPA, then* TPKE* *in Fig. 6 is* C-AdpQ-Y-*CPA against adversaries that do not receive* rnd *from their* EncO *queries, but is not* SCor-SelQ-*IND-CPA.*

The proof of Theorem 6 is found in the full version [18].

4   From CPA to CCA Security I: Semi-Malicious CPA

We investigate how to generalise existing CPA-to-CCA transforms for (non-threshold) PKE to TPKE. In [32], Fouque and Pointcheval discuss that the classic Naor-Yung transformation with double encryption [45] equally applies in the threshold setting, but their argument has a gap (cf. Footnote 8). Indeed, under CPA and CCA security models with partial decryption queries, we observe that such transformation cannot work generically. As an example, think of a pathological scheme where $\mathsf{ParDec}(\mathsf{sk}_i, \mathsf{ct})$ returns its secret key when decrypting a ciphertext ct which was created with some special, unlikely randomness, e.g. the all-zeroes string. For PKE, this issue can be circumvented by assuming perfect correctness [30]. However, for TPKE, perfect correctness is insufficient, since pd_j can contain additional values that are ignored by Rec.

Below, we consider a strengthened security called *semi-malicious CPA*, and show that it suffices for existing Naor-Yung-style transformations to apply.

Semi-malicious Security. Borrowing similar notions for multi-party computation (e.g. [1, 31, 40]), we define semi-malicious CPA security of TPKE, which is almost identical to CPA security, except that an adversary $\mathcal{A}$ is further allowed to query EncO for non-challenge ciphertexts generated using maliciously chosen randomness, i.e. rnd is generated by $\mathcal{A}$ itself. Other than guaranteeing stronger security and being a meaningful notion in itself, we show that a semi-malicious CPA-secure TPKE can be generically lifted to a CCA-secure TPKE by attaching a proof of knowledge of ciphertext well-formedness.

<table>
<tr><td>

$\mathsf{EncO}(\mu, \mathsf{rnd})$

——————————

$\mathsf{ct} \leftarrow \mathsf{Enc}(\mathsf{pk}, \mu; \mathsf{rnd})$

$L_{\mathsf{Enc}} \leftarrow L_{\mathsf{Enc}} \cup \{\mathsf{ct}\}$

return $(\mathsf{ct}, \mathsf{rnd})$

</td><td>

$\mathsf{EncO}(\mu, \mathsf{rnd})$

——————————

$\mathsf{ct} \leftarrow \mathsf{Enc}(\mathsf{pk}, \mu; \mathsf{rnd})$

if $b = 1$ **then** $\mathsf{st}_{\mathcal{S}} \leftarrow\!\!{}^{\$} \mathcal{S}(\mu, \mathsf{rnd}, \mathsf{st}_{\mathcal{S}})$

$L_{\mathsf{Enc}} \leftarrow L_{\mathsf{Enc}} \cup \{\mathsf{ct}\}; \quad M[\mathsf{ct}] \leftarrow \mu$

return $(\mathsf{ct}, \mathsf{rnd})$

</td></tr>
<tr><td>(a) EncO for semi-malicious IND-CPA.</td><td>(b) EncO for semi-malicious SIM-CPA.</td></tr>
</table>

Fig. 7. Semi-malicious IND- and SIM–CPA security experiments. All algorithms except EncO are identical to those in Figs. 2 and 3 respectively.

Definition 7 (Semi-malicious CPA). *Let* $\mathsf{X} \in \{\mathsf{AdpQ}, \mathsf{SelQ}\}$. *Define the experiments* $\mathsf{SemiMalIndCPA}^{b}_{\mathsf{TPKE},\mathcal{A},\mathsf{X}}$ *and* $\mathsf{SemiMalSimCPA}^{b}_{\mathsf{TPKE},\mathcal{A},\mathcal{S},\mathsf{X}}$, *which are identical to* $\mathsf{IndCPA}^{b}_{\mathsf{TPKE},\mathcal{A},\mathsf{X}}$ *and* $\mathsf{SimCPA}^{b}_{\mathsf{TPKE},\mathcal{A},\mathcal{S},\mathsf{X}}$ *in Figs. 2 and 3 respectively, except that the oracle* EncO *is replaced by that in Figs. 7a and 7b respectively. A TPKE scheme is* SCor-X-SemiMal-*IND-CPA or* SCor-X-SemiMal-*SIM-CPA, if the advantage* $\mathsf{Adv}^{\mathsf{SemiMalIndCPA}}_{\mathsf{TPKE},\mathcal{A},\mathsf{X}}(\lambda) :=$

$$\left| \Pr\left[\mathsf{SemiMalIndCPA}^{0}_{\mathsf{TPKE},\mathcal{A},\mathsf{X}}(1^{\lambda}) = 1 \right] - \Pr\left[\mathsf{SemiMalIndCPA}^{1}_{\mathsf{TPKE},\mathcal{A},\mathsf{X}}(1^{\lambda}) = 1 \right] \right|$$

is negligible, or there is a PPT simulator $\mathcal{S}$ such that $\mathsf{Adv}_{\mathsf{TPKE},\mathcal{A},\mathsf{X}}^{\mathsf{SemiMalSimCPA}}(\lambda) :=$

$$\left| \Pr\left[\mathsf{SemiMalSimCPA}_{\mathsf{TPKE},\mathcal{A},\mathcal{S},\mathsf{X}}^{0}(1^\lambda) = 1 \right] - \Pr\left[\mathsf{SemiMalSimCPA}_{\mathsf{TPKE},\mathcal{A},\mathcal{S},\mathsf{X}}^{1}(1^\lambda) = 1 \right] \right|$$

is negligible, respectively.

Remark 9. In Definition 7, oracle EncO returns (ct, rnd) to be syntactically close to other definitions. Since the adversary knows rnd and μ, the oracle could actually omit ct in its output.

Semi-malicious security under adaptive corruption (AdpCor-X-SemiMal-Y-Z) and maximal corruption (MaxCor-X-SemiMal-Y-Z) analogously (omitted).

Remark 10 (CCA $\Rightarrow$ SemiMal). It is easy to see that CCA-security implies semi-malicious CPA-security. More precisely, for C $\in$ {AdpCor, SCor, MaxCor}, X $\in$ {AdpQ, SelQ}, M $\in$ {IND, SIM}, if TPKE is C-X-M-CCA, then it is C-X-SemiMal-SIM-CPA. The reduction $\mathcal{R}$ can simply generate the responses to EncO itself (via an honest decryption), and still answer using ParDec. Since we assume CCA-security, this perfectly simulates the real C-X-M-CCA game ($b = 0$). For M = IND, $\mathcal{R}$ also simulates $b = 1$ perfectly. For M = SIM, a subtlety is that $\mathcal{S}$ for TPKE learns μ through EncO. But since $\mathcal{S}$ must also work for $\mathcal{R}$, and $\mathcal{R}$ never queries EncO, we can in fact safely "ignore" the EncO oracle for CCA-security both for M = IND and M = SIM (cf. Remark 1). Thus, the claim also holds for M = SIM.

$\mathsf{KGen}'(1^\lambda, \mathbb{A})$	$\mathsf{Enc}'(\mathsf{pk}', \mu)$
$(\mathsf{pk}, (\mathsf{sk}_j)_{j \in [k]}) \leftarrow\!\!{\scriptstyle\$}\ \mathsf{KGen}(1^\lambda, \mathbb{A})$	$(\mathsf{pk}, \mathsf{crs}) \leftarrow \mathsf{pk}'$
$\mathsf{crs} \leftarrow\!\!{\scriptstyle\$}\ \mathsf{NIZK.Setup}(1^\lambda)$	$\mathsf{rnd} \leftarrow\!\!{\scriptstyle\$}\ \{0,1\}^{\mathsf{rlen}}$
$\mathsf{pk}' \leftarrow (\mathsf{pk}, \mathsf{crs})$	$\mathsf{ct} \leftarrow\!\!{\scriptstyle\$}\ \mathsf{Enc}(\mathsf{pk}, \mu; \mathsf{rnd})$
return $(\mathsf{pk}', (\mathsf{sk}_j)_{j \in [k]})$	$\mathrm{x} \leftarrow (\mathsf{pk}, \mathsf{ct})$
	$\mathrm{w} \leftarrow (\mu, \mathsf{rnd})$
$\mathsf{ParDec}'(\mathsf{sk}_j, \mathsf{ct}')$	$\pi \leftarrow\!\!{\scriptstyle\$}\ \mathsf{NIZK.Prove}(\mathrm{x}, \mathrm{w}, \mathsf{crs})$
$(\mathsf{ct}, \pi) \leftarrow \mathsf{ct}'; \quad \mathrm{x} \leftarrow (\mathsf{pk}, \mathsf{ct})$	**return** (ct, π)
assert $\mathsf{NIZK.Verify}(\mathrm{x}, \pi, \mathsf{crs}) = 1$	
return $\mathsf{pd}_j \leftarrow\!\!{\scriptstyle\$}\ \mathsf{ParDec}(\mathsf{sk}_j, \mathsf{ct})$	

Fig. 8. Transformation TPKE$'$ = SMT[TPKE, NIZK] given NIZK for relation R = $\{((\mathsf{pk}, \mathsf{ct}), (\mu, \mathsf{rnd})) \mid \mathsf{TPKE.Enc}(\mathsf{pk}, \mu; \mathsf{rnd}) = \mathsf{ct}\}$. We set Rec$'$ = Rec.

Figure 8 shows how to transform a semi-malicious-CPA-secure TPKE into a CCA-secure TPKE$'$ = SMT[TPKE, NIZK] by appending a simulation-extractable NIZK. Theorem 7 is the security claim for TPKE$'$, its proof is in the full version [18].

Theorem 7 (Semi-Malicious CPA + NIZK ⇒ CCA). *Let* C ∈ {SCor, AdpCor, MaxCor}. *Let* NIZK *be a SIMEXT NIZK for the relation*

$$R = \{((pk, ct), (\mu, rnd)) \mid TPKE.Enc(pk, \mu; rnd) = ct\}$$

and let TPKE *be a TPKE, and* TPKE′ = SMT[TPKE, NIZK] *as in Fig. 8.*

(1) TPKE *is* C-X-SemiMal-*SIM-CPA.* ⇒ TPKE′ *is* C-X-*SIM-CCA.*
(2) TPKE *is* C-X-SemiMal-*IND-CPA.* ⇒ TPKE′ *is* C-X-*IND-CCA.*

AdpQ-*SIM-CCA-Secure TPKE.* To substantiate that our security notions are meaningful, we show that they are, despite allowing more adversarial capabilities than most prior models, achievable. Concretely, we show that the natural thresholdised ElGamal PKE achieves AdpQ-SemiMal-SIM-CPA (Definition 7). In particular, this immediately implies the CPA notions in Definitions 2 and 3.

Theorem 8. *The ElGamal TPKE (given in the full version) is* SCor-AdpQ-SemiMal-*SIM-CPA secure, if the DDH assumption holds.*

More precisely, for any PPT algorithm $\mathcal{B}$, *there is a PPT algorithm* $\mathcal{A}$ *against the DDH problem with advantage* $\mathsf{Adv}^{DDH}_{GGen,\mathcal{A}}(\lambda)$, *such that* $\mathsf{Adv}^{SemiMalSimCPA}_{ElGamal,\mathcal{B},AdpQ}(\lambda) \leq t \cdot (\mathsf{Adv}^{DDH}_{GGen,\mathcal{A}}(\lambda) + \frac{1}{q-1})$, *where* t *is the threshold and prime* q *is the group order.*

The proof of Theorem 8 is given in the full version [18]. The following is immediate by combining Theorems 7 and 8.

Corollary 1. *There exists a TPKE scheme that is* SCor-AdpQ-*SIM-CCA secure, assuming that there is a SIMEXT NIZK and that the DDH assumption holds.*

5   From CPA to CCA Security II: NIPoR

We propose a generic CPA-to-CCA transformation for TPKE, which applies also to schemes that achieve plain CPA-security but are not robust under malicious randomness. To achieve this, we present a new transformations in the ROM, which can be seen as a mix of Naor-Yung and Fujisaki-Okamoto (FO) transformation.[15]

The solution pursued in this section is based on an extension of non-interactive proofs of knowledge which we call *non-interactive proofs of randomness (NIPoR)*. At a high level, a NIPoR allows to generate a proof that an efficient function f was evaluated on a secret value m and secret high-entropy randomness r, and resulted in the (public) value $y = f(m; r)$. By setting $f := \mathsf{Enc}(pk, \cdot; \cdot)$, this allows us to prove that an encryption was computed under

---

[15] The FO transform [33] and its variants (see [38] and references therein) are well-known CPA-to-CCA transformations for PKE. However, FO-like transforms are in the ROM and generically uninstantiable [19], with few currently known exceptions [44]. The approach in this section suffers similar limitations.

pk with honestly sampled and fresh randomness. With this, we instantiate a variant of the Naor-Yung transformation in the random oracle model, which applies to any (T)PKE. We expect that NIPoRs can find applications in other settings as well.

Alternatively, our transformation may be seen as an instantiation of the FO transform, but with a *publicly verifiable* proof that the encryption randomness is truly random (in the sense of a programmable random oracle output).

5.1   Non-interactive Proof of Randomness

The NIPoR Prove algorithm generates a value y which is generated with uniform randomness r (but a malicious prover will be able to choose a random string among a polynomial number of options), together with a proof π that $y = f(m; r)$ and a tag. Conceptually, in a NIZK generated via Fiat-Shamir in the ROM, tag would be the commitment, and r would be (roughly) the output of a random oracle evaluation that also takes tag as input and thus, any change in tag induces sampling of a fresh random value.

We define NIPoRs for function families $(\mathcal{F}_\lambda)_{\lambda \in \mathbb{N}}$ with associated spaces $(\mathcal{M}_\lambda)_{\lambda \in \mathbb{N}}$ for m and $(\mathcal{R}_\lambda)_{\lambda \in \mathbb{N}}$ for r, such that for all $\lambda \in \mathbb{N}$ and all $f \in \mathcal{F}_\lambda$, the domain is $\mathcal{M}_\lambda \times \mathcal{R}_\lambda$. We require each function $f \in \mathcal{F}_\lambda$ to be identified by a function key fk and the function key spaces for different λ to be disjoint.

Definition 8 (NIPoR). *A non-interactive proof of randomness (NIPoR) for a function family $(\mathcal{F}_\lambda)_{\lambda \in \mathbb{N}}$ is a tuple* NIPoR = (Setup, Prove, Verify) *of PPT algorithms with oracle-access to a random oracle* RO, *such that*

Setup$^{\mathsf{RO}}(1^\lambda) \$\!\!\rightarrow$ crs: *The setup algorithm generates a common reference string.*
Prove$^{\mathsf{RO}}(\mathsf{crs}, f_{\mathsf{fk}}, m) \$\!\!\rightarrow (y, \mathsf{tag}, \pi)$: *The prove algorithm takes a* crs, *a function* $f_{\mathsf{fk}} \in \mathcal{F}_\lambda$ *and a value* $m \in \mathcal{M}_\lambda$ *as inputs, and returns an output* y, *a tag* tag *and proof* π.
Verify$^{\mathsf{RO}}(\mathsf{crs}, f_{\mathsf{fk}}, y, \mathsf{tag}, \pi) \$\!\!\rightarrow b$: *The verification algorithm takes as input the* crs, *a function* f_{fk}, *a value* y, *a proof* π *and a tag* tag. *It outputs a bit* $b \in \{0, 1\}$.

We require NIPoR *to be perfectly correct, that is, for all* $\lambda \in \mathbb{N}$, *any choice of random oracle,* $f_{\mathsf{fk}} \in \mathcal{F}_\lambda$ *and* $m \in \mathcal{M}_\lambda$, *it holds that*

$$\Pr\left[\mathsf{Verify}^{\mathsf{RO}}(\mathsf{crs}, f_{\mathsf{fk}}, y, \mathsf{tag}, \pi) = 1 \;\middle|\; \begin{array}{l} \mathsf{crs} \leftarrow\!\!\$\ \mathsf{Setup}^{\mathsf{RO}}(1^\lambda) \\ (y, \mathsf{tag}, \pi) \leftarrow\!\!\$\ \mathsf{Prove}^{\mathsf{RO}}(\mathsf{crs}, f_{\mathsf{fk}}, m) \end{array}\right] = 1.$$

Remark 11. As an additional property, Prove could allow the prover to recover the randomness r used to compute $y = f_{\mathsf{fk}}(m; r)$, or output r instead of y. This is useful, when the prover should get a secret output, e.g. if f_{fk} is a commitment function and the prover should learn the decommitment. However, since a NIPoR should be a proof that y was generated with honest returning y seems more natural. (A compromise is to return both y and r with a consistency requirement that $y = f_{\mathsf{fk}}(m; r)$.) Jumping ahead, we note that security could be defined w.r.t. returning r to the adversary (instead of y) in ProveO queries, which would yield a slightly *stronger* security notion than the one we define shortly. Our NIPoR construction, however, evidently satisfies this.

We define security of a NIPoR as (weak) simulation extractability, analogously to simulation extractability for NIZK for the specific relation $y = f(m; r)$. The crucial *proof of randomness property* is captured by $\mathsf{VerifyO}_1$ (cf. Figure 9), which is best viewed as an ideal functionality. Concretely, it captures that if the verify *algorithm* (which the adversary can run locally) returns 1 on a tuple $(f_{\mathsf{fk}}, y, \mathsf{tag}, \pi)$, then the value r used to generate y was actually the output of a random oracle evaluated on $(f_{\mathsf{fk}}, \mathsf{tag}, m)$ and thus uniformly random. Otherwise, the assertion in $\mathsf{VerifyO}_1$ fails and the adversary wins.

Random Oracles. The random oracle $\mathsf{TrueRand}$ is part of the ideal functionality and thus only available to the simulator, but not to the distinguisher $\mathcal{A}$. However, since NIPoRs are inherently defined in the random oracle model, the NIPoR algorithms Setup, Verify and Prove need access to a random oracle as well. This random oracle (denoted by RO_b in Fig. 9) can be programmed by the simulator (unlike the ideal functionality $\mathsf{TrueRand}$). While this gives the simulator much freedom, At first glance, this gives the simulator much freedom, but, the checks in the ideal oracle $\mathsf{VerifyO}_1$ constrain it to use the output r from $\mathsf{TrueRand}$, which is proper randomness, except that the simulator can query $\mathsf{TrueRand}$ a polynomial number of times and bias the randomness in this way.

Definition 9 ((Weak) SIMEXT). *A NIPoR for a function family $(\mathcal{F}_\lambda)_{\lambda \in \mathbb{N}}$ is* (weakly) *simulation-extractable (SIMEXT), if there exists a (stateful) PPT simulator* $\mathsf{Sim} = (\mathsf{Setup}, \mathsf{RO}, \mathsf{Sim}, \mathsf{Ext})$ *such that for all PPT adversaries $\mathcal{A}$, the advantage* $\mathsf{Adv}^{(W)\mathrm{SIMEXT}}_{\mathcal{A}, \mathsf{NIPoR}, \mathsf{Sim}}(\lambda) :=$

$$\left| \Pr[(\mathrm{W})\mathrm{SIMEXT}^0_{\mathsf{NIPoR}, \mathsf{Sim}, \mathcal{A}}(1^\lambda) = 1] - \Pr[(\mathrm{W})\mathrm{SIMEXT}^1_{\mathsf{NIPoR}, \mathsf{Sim}, \mathcal{A}}(1^\lambda) = 1] \right|$$

is negligible, where the experiments $(\mathrm{W})\mathrm{SIMEXT}^b_{\mathsf{NIPoR}, \mathsf{Sim}, \mathcal{A}}(1^\lambda)$ *are defined in Fig. 9. Moreover, we say* NIPoR *has a* tag*-only extractor, if* $\mathsf{Sim.Ext}$ *ignores* y, π *(see Fig. 9). NIPoR has a stateless extractor, if* $\mathsf{Sim.Ext}$ *does not modify its state.*

5.2 NIPoR Construction

Let $(\mathcal{R}, +)$ be an additive group whose domain is efficiently sampleable, $\mathsf{COM} = (\mathsf{COM.Setup}, \mathsf{COM.Com})$ a commitment scheme, and $(\mathcal{F}_\lambda)_\lambda$ a function family of polynomial-size circuits f_{fk} specified by function keys fk. Further, let $\mathsf{NIZK} = (\mathsf{Setup}, \mathsf{Verify}, \mathsf{Prove})$ be a NIZK for the relation

$$\mathsf{R}^* := \left\{ ((\mathsf{ck}, \mathsf{fk}, y, \mathsf{tag}, r''), (m, r', \rho)) \;\middle|\; \begin{array}{l} y = f_{\mathsf{fk}}(m; r' + r'') \\ \wedge\; \mathsf{tag} = \mathsf{COM.Com}(\mathsf{ck}, (r', m); \rho) \end{array} \right\}.$$

From these ingredients, we construct a NIPoR (cf. Fig. 10). Correctness of NIPoR follows immediately from correctness of the NIZK.

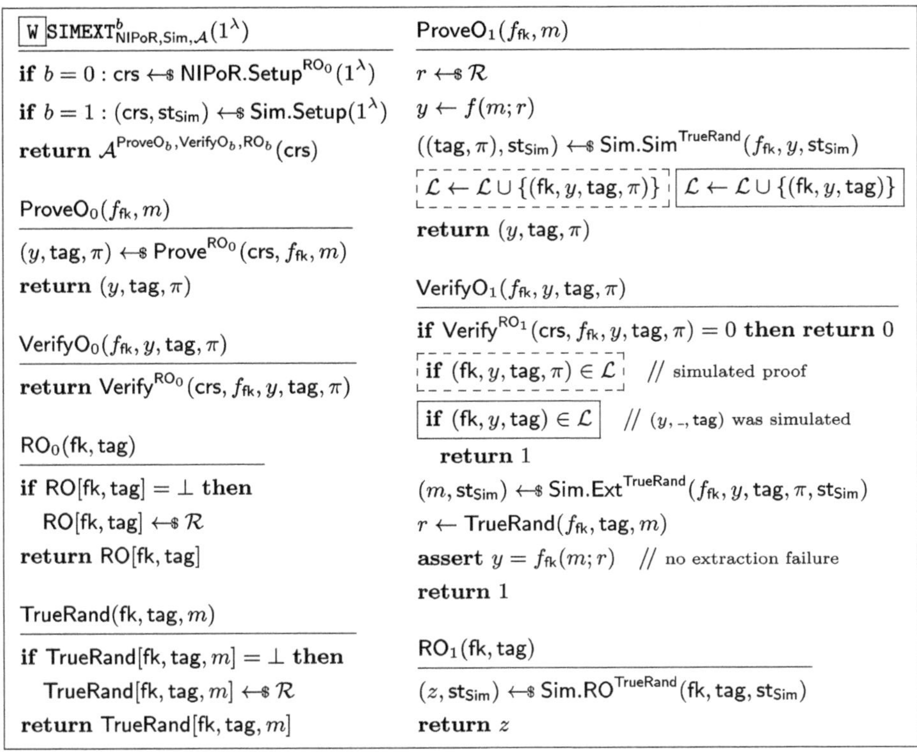

Fig. 9. Experiments for (weak) SIMEXT for NIPoR. Code in dashed and solid boxes is only executed for SIMEXT and weak SIMEXT respectively.

Theorem 9. *If* COM *is hiding and straightline extractable binding, and* NIZK *is (weakly) simulation-extractable for* R^*, *then* NIPoR *in Fig. 10 is (weakly) simulation-extractable. Moreover, it has a stateless* tag-*only extractor.*

We provide the proof of Theorem 9 in the full version [18]. Additional backgrounds on commitment schemes are found in the full version [18]. To obtain a tag-only extractor, we rely on the straightline extractable COM, which commits to both the value m and the randomness share r'. The notion of stateless tag-only extraction is convenient in security reductions, e.g. it leads to our streamlined CPA-to-CCA transformation in Theorem 10.

Remark 12 (Optimisations). The NIPoR in Fig. 10 is geared towards simplicity, its efficiency and generality can be easily improved. For example, we use a standard-model extractable binding commitment (to prove about it in R^*), but this can be relaxed, e.g. using a (succinct) standard-model commitment augmented by a (succinct) straightline extractable proof of knowledge also works.

$\mathsf{Setup}(1^\lambda)$	$\mathsf{Prove}^{\mathsf{RO}}(\mathsf{crs}, f_{\mathsf{fk}}, m)$	$\mathsf{Verify}^{\mathsf{RO}}(\mathsf{crs}, f_{\mathsf{fk}}, y, \mathsf{tag}, \pi)$
$\mathsf{ck} \leftarrow\!\!{}_{\$}\ \mathsf{COM.Setup}(1^\lambda)$	$(\mathsf{ck}, \mathsf{crs}_{\mathsf{NIZK}}) \leftarrow \mathsf{crs}$	$(\mathsf{crs}_{\mathsf{NIZK}}, \mathsf{ck}) \leftarrow \mathsf{crs}$
$\mathsf{crs}_{\mathsf{NIZK}} \leftarrow\!\!{}_{\$}\ \mathsf{NIZK.Setup}(1^\lambda)$	$r' \leftarrow\!\!{}_{\$}\ \mathcal{R}; \quad \rho \leftarrow\!\!{}_{\$}\ \{0,1\}^{\mathsf{rlen}}$	$r'' \leftarrow \mathsf{RO}(\mathsf{fk}, \mathsf{tag})$
return $\mathsf{crs} := (\mathsf{ck}, \mathsf{crs}_{\mathsf{NIZK}})$	$\mathsf{tag} \leftarrow \mathsf{COM.Com}(\mathsf{ck}, (r', m); \rho)$	$\mathbb{x} \leftarrow (\mathsf{fk}, y, \mathsf{tag}, r'')$
	$r'' \leftarrow \mathsf{RO}(\mathsf{fk}, \mathsf{tag})$	$b \leftarrow\!\!{}_{\$}\ \mathsf{NIZK.Verify}(\mathsf{crs}_{\mathsf{NIZK}}, \mathbb{x}, \pi)$
$\mathsf{RO}(\mathsf{fk}, \mathsf{tag})$	$r \leftarrow r' + r''$	**return** b
$\mathbf{if}\ \mathsf{RO}[\mathsf{fk}, \mathsf{tag}] = \bot\ \mathbf{then}$	$y \leftarrow f_{\mathsf{fk}}(m; r)$	
$\quad r'' \leftarrow\!\!{}_{\$}\ \mathcal{R}$	$\mathbb{x} \leftarrow (\mathsf{ck}, \mathsf{fk}, y, \mathsf{tag}, r'')$	
$\quad \mathsf{RO}[\mathsf{fk}, \mathsf{tag}] \leftarrow r''$	$\mathbb{w} \leftarrow (m, r', \rho)$	
return $\mathsf{RO}[\mathsf{fk}, \mathsf{tag}]$	$\pi \leftarrow\!\!{}_{\$}\ \mathsf{NIZK.Prove}(\mathsf{crs}_{\mathsf{NIZK}}, \mathbb{x}, \mathbb{w})$	
	return (y, tag, π)	

Fig. 10. $\mathsf{NIPoR} = (\mathsf{Setup}, \mathsf{Prove}, \mathsf{Verify})$ for function family $(\mathcal{F}_\lambda)_\lambda$.

5.3 CPA-To-CCA Transformation

Our CPA-to-CCA transformation is a variation of Naor-Yung double encryption: Instead of a second encryption, we use a straightline extractable binding commitment scheme — which, in turn, could be instantiated by a (perfectly correct) encryption scheme, leading to a flavour of double encryption under the hood. Instead of a NIZK, we use a NIPoR.

$\mathsf{KGen}'(1^\lambda, \mathbb{A})$	$\mathsf{Enc}'(\mathsf{pk}' = (\mathsf{crs}, \mathsf{pk}), \mu)$
$\mathsf{crs} \leftarrow\!\!{}_{\$}\ \mathsf{NIPoR.Setup}(1^\lambda)$	$\mathsf{fk} \leftarrow \mathsf{pk}; \quad m \leftarrow (\mu, r_{\mathsf{COM}})$
$(\mathsf{pk}, (\mathsf{sk}_j)_{j \in [k]}) \leftarrow\!\!{}_{\$}\ \mathsf{TPKE.KGen}(1^\lambda, \mathbb{A})$	$(\mathsf{ct}, \mathsf{tag}, \pi) \leftarrow\!\!{}_{\$}\ \mathsf{NIPoR.Prove}(\mathsf{crs}, \mathsf{fk}, m)$
$\mathsf{pk}' \leftarrow (\mathsf{crs}, \mathsf{pk})$	**return** $\mathsf{ct}' = (\mathsf{ct}, \mathsf{tag}, \pi)$
return $(\mathsf{pk}', (\mathsf{pk}', \mathsf{sk}_j)_{j \in [k]})$	
	$\mathsf{ParDec}'((\mathsf{pk}', \mathsf{sk}_j), \mathsf{ct}')$
$f_{\mathsf{fk}}(\mu; r)$	$(\mathsf{crs}, \mathsf{pk}) \leftarrow \mathsf{pk}'; \quad (\mathsf{ct}, \mathsf{tag}, \pi) \leftarrow \mathsf{ct}'$
$\mathsf{pk} \leftarrow \mathsf{fk}$	$\mathsf{fk} \leftarrow \mathsf{pk}; \quad y \leftarrow \mathsf{ct}$
$\mathsf{ct} \leftarrow \mathsf{TPKE.Enc}(\mathsf{pk}, \mu; r)$	$\mathbf{if}\ \mathsf{ct} = \bot\ \mathbf{or}\ \mathsf{NIPoR.Verify}(\mathsf{crs}, \mathsf{fk}, y, \mathsf{tag}, \pi) = 0$
return ct	$\quad$ **return** $\bot$
	return $\mathsf{pd}'_j \leftarrow\!\!{}_{\$}\ \mathsf{TPKE.ParDec}(\mathsf{sk}_j, \mathsf{ct})$

Fig. 11. Transformation $\mathsf{TPKE}' = (\mathsf{KGen}', \mathsf{Enc}', \mathsf{ParDec}', \mathsf{Rec}')$ of $\mathsf{TPKE} = (\mathsf{KGen}, \mathsf{Enc}, \mathsf{ParDec}, \mathsf{Rec})$ given COM and NIPoR for $\{f_{\mathsf{fk}}\}_{\mathsf{fk}}$. $\mathsf{Rec}' = \mathsf{Rec}$. We assume $\mathsf{TPKE.Enc}(\mathsf{pk}, \bot; r) = \bot$ for any (pk, r).

To transform a TPKE scheme $\mathsf{TPKE} = (\mathsf{KGen}, \mathsf{Enc}, \mathsf{ParDec}, \mathsf{Rec})$, we use a NIPoR for the function family in Fig. 11 (bottom left), and obtain the transformed scheme TPKE' in Fig. 11 and the following theorem.

Theorem 10. *Let* C $\in$ {SCor, AdpCor}, X $\in$ {AdpQ, SelQ}. *Let* TPKE *be a TPKE,* COM *be a hiding and straightline extractable binding commitment, and* NIPoR *be a NIPoR for the function family* $\{f_{\mathsf{fk}}\}_{\mathsf{fk}}$ *in Fig. 11 that is SIMEXT for random oracle* RO *and has a stateless* tag-*only extractor. Let* TPKE′ *be given in Fig. 11.*

(1) TPKE *is* C-X-*SIM-CPA.* $\Rightarrow$ TPKE′ *is* C-X-*SIM-CCA in the ROM.*
(2) TPKE *is* C-X-*IND-CPA.* $\Rightarrow$ TPKE′ *is* C-X-*IND-CCA in the ROM.*

The security proof works by programming the randomness in the NIPoR (through programming TrueRand in NIPoR security) to be the randomness obtained from EncO queries in the TPKE CPA-security. Thus, the NIPoR forces every valid ciphertext non-challenge to coincide with a ciphertext obtained through EncO. Here, it is crucial that EncO outputs not only the ciphertext, but also the encryption randomness. For challenge ciphertexts, the reduction simulates the NIPoR. See the full version [18] for a formal proof.

Acknowledgments. We thank the anonymous CRYPTO'25 and TCC'25 reviewers for many helpful comments on improving the content of this work and, in particular, for pointing out a flaw in an earlier version. The research of Chris Brzuska and Ivy K. Y. Woo is supported by Research Council of Finland grant 358950. This work was supported by KASTEL Security Research Labs.

References

1. Abram, D., Scholl, P., Yakoubov, S.: Distributed (correlation) samplers: how to remove a trusted dealer in one round. In: Dunkelman, O., Dziembowski, S. (eds.) EUROCRYPT 2022, Part I. LNCS, vol. 13275, pp. 790–820. Springer, Cham (2022). https://doi.org/10.1007/978-3-031-06944-4_27
2. Arita, S., Tsurudome, K.: Construction of threshold public-key encryptions through tag-based encryptions. In: Abdalla, M., Pointcheval, D., Fouque, P.-A., Vergnaud, D. (eds.) ACNS 2009. LNCS, vol. 5536, pp. 186–200. Springer, Heidelberg (2009). https://doi.org/10.1007/978-3-642-01957-9_12
3. Asharov, G., Jain, A., López-Alt, A., Tromer, E., Vaikuntanathan, V., Wichs, D.: Multiparty computation with low communication, computation and interaction via threshold FHE. In: Pointcheval, D., Johansson, T. (eds.) EUROCRYPT 2012. LNCS, vol. 7237, pp. 483–501. Springer, Heidelberg (2012). https://doi.org/10.1007/978-3-642-29011-4_29
4. Bellare, M., Crites, E.C., Komlo, C., Maller, M., Tessaro, S., Zhu, C.: Better than advertised security for non-interactive threshold signatures. In: Dodis, Y., Shrimpton, T. (eds.) CRYPTO 2022, Part IV. LNCS, vol. 13510, pp. 517–550. Springer, Cham (2022). https://doi.org/10.1007/978-3-031-15985-5_18
5. Bendlin, R., Damgård, I.: Threshold decryption and zero-knowledge proofs for lattice-based cryptosystems. In: Micciancio, D. (ed.) TCC 2010. LNCS, vol. 5978, pp. 201–218. Springer, Heidelberg (2010). https://doi.org/10.1007/978-3-642-11799-2_13

6. Bernard, O., Joye, M., Smart, N.P., Walter, M.: Drifting towards better error probabilities in fully homomorphic encryption schemes. In: Fehr, S., Fouque, P.A. (eds.) EUROCRYPT 2025, Part VIII. LNCS, vol. 15608, pp. 181–211. Springer, Cham (2025). https://doi.org/10.1007/978-3-031-91101-9_7

7. Bernhard, D., Fischlin, M., Warinschi, B.: Adaptive Proofs of Knowledge in the Random Oracle Model. In: Katz, J. (ed.) PKC 2015. LNCS, vol. 9020, pp. 629–649. Springer, Heidelberg (2015). https://doi.org/10.1007/978-3-662-46447-2_28

8. Boneh, D., Boyen, X., Halevi, S.: Chosen ciphertext secure public key threshold encryption without random oracles. In: Pointcheval, D. (ed.) CT-RSA 2006. LNCS, vol. 3860, pp. 226–243. Springer, Heidelberg (2006). https://doi.org/10.1007/11605805_15

9. Boneh, D., Bünz, B., Nayak, K., Rotem, L., Shoup, V.: Context-dependent threshold decryption and its applications. Cryptology ePrint Archive, Report 2025/279 (2025). https://eprint.iacr.org/2025/279

10. Boneh, D., Bünz, B., Nayak, K., Rotem, L., Shoup, V.: Context-dependent threshold decryption and its applications. In: Hanaoka, G., Yang, B.Y. (eds.) ASIACRYPT 2025, Part VI. LNCS, vol. 16250, pp. 506–538. Springer, Singapore (2025). https://doi.org/10.1007/978-981-95-5119-4_16

11. Boneh, D., Gennaro, R., Goldfeder, S., Jain, A., Kim, S., Rasmussen, P.M.R., Sahai, A.: Threshold cryptosystems from threshold fully homomorphic encryption. In: Shacham, H., Boldyreva, A. (eds.) CRYPTO 2018, Part I. LNCS, vol. 10991, pp. 565–596. Springer, Cham (2018). https://doi.org/10.1007/978-3-319-96884-1_19

12. Boneh, D., Laufer, E., Tas, E.N.: Batch decryption without epochs and its application to encrypted mempools. Cryptology ePrint Archive, Report 2025/1254 (2025). https://eprint.iacr.org/2025/1254

13. Boneh, D., Partap, A., Rotem, L.: Accountability for misbehavior in threshold decryption via threshold traitor tracing. In: Reyzin, L., Stebila, D. (eds.) CRYPTO 2024, Part VII. LNCS, vol. 14926, pp. 317–351. Springer, Cham (2024). https://doi.org/10.1007/978-3-031-68394-7_11

14. Bormet, J., et al.: BEAST-MEV: Batched threshold encryption with silent setup for MEV prevention. Cryptology ePrint Archive, Report 2025/1419 (2025). https://eprint.iacr.org/2025/1419

15. Bormet, J., Faust, S., Othman, H., Qu, Z.: BEAT-MEV: epochless approach to batched threshold encryption for MEV prevention. In: Bauer, L., Pellegrino, G. (eds.) USENIX Security 2025, pp. 3457–3476. USENIX Association (2025). https://www.usenix.org/conference/usenixsecurity25/presentation/bormet

16. Boudgoust, K., Scholl, P.: Simple threshold (fully homomorphic) encryption from LWE with polynomial modulus. In: Guo, J., Steinfeld, R. (eds.) ASIACRYPT 2023, Part I. LNCS, vol. 14438, pp. 371–404. Springer, Singapore (2023). https://doi.org/10.1007/978-981-99-8721-4_12

17. Brandão, L.T., Peralta, R.: NIST first call for multi-party threshold schemes (2023). https://csrc.nist.gov/publications/detail/nistir/8214c/draft

18. Brzuska, C., Klooß, M., Woo, I.K.Y.: Threshold public-key encryption: definitions, relations, and CPA-to-CCA transforms. Cryptology ePrint Archive, Report 2025/1665 (2025). https://eprint.iacr.org/2025/1665

19. Brzuska, C., Farshim, P., Mittelbach, A.: Random-oracle uninstantiability from indistinguishability obfuscation. In: Dodis, Y., Nielsen, J.B. (eds.) TCC 2015, Part II. LNCS, vol. 9015, pp. 428–455. Springer, Heidelberg (2015). https://doi.org/10.1007/978-3-662-46497-7_17

20. Canard, S., Fontaine, C., Phan, D.H., Pointcheval, D., Renard, M., Sirdey, R.: Relations among new CCA security notions for approximate FHE. Cryptology ePrint Archive, Report 2024/812 (2024). https://eprint.iacr.org/2024/812
21. Canard, S., Papon, N., Phan, D.H.: Public traceability in threshold decryption. CiC **2**(2), 21 (2025). https://doi.org/10.62056/akjb0lmol
22. Canetti, R., Goldwasser, S.: An efficient *threshold* public key cryptosystem secure against adaptive chosen ciphertext attack (extended abstract). In: Stern, J. (ed.) EUROCRYPT 1999. LNCS, vol. 1592, pp. 90–106. Springer, Heidelberg (1999). https://doi.org/10.1007/3-540-48910-X_7
23. Checri, M., Sirdey, R., Boudguiga, A., Bultel, J.P.: On the practical CPA^D security of "exact" and threshold FHE schemes and libraries. In: Reyzin, L., Stebila, D. (eds.) CRYPTO 2024, Part III. LNCS, vol. 14922, pp. 3–33. Springer, Cham (2024). https://doi.org/10.1007/978-3-031-68382-4_1
24. Cheon, J.H., Choe, H., Passelègue, A., Stehlé, D., Suvanto, E.: Attacks against the IND-CPA^D security of exact FHE schemes. In: Luo, B., Liao, X., Xu, J., Kirda, E., Lie, D. (eds.) ACM CCS 2024, pp. 2505–2519. ACM Press (2024). https://doi.org/10.1145/3658644.3690341
25. Choudhuri, A.R., Garg, S., Piet, J., Policharla, G.V.: Mempool privacy via batched threshold encryption: attacks and defenses. In: Balzarotti, D., Xu, W. (eds.) USENIX Security 2024. USENIX Association (2024). https://www.usenix.org/conference/usenixsecurity24/presentation/choudhuri
26. Cini, V., Lai, R.W.F., Woo, I.K.Y.: Pilvi: Lattice threshold PKE with small decryption shares and improved security. In: Hanaoka, G., Yang, BY. (eds.) ASIACRYPT 2025. LNCS, vol. 16250, pp. 539–569. Springer, Cham (2025). https://doi.org/10.1007/978-981-95-5119-4_17
27. Delerablée, C., Pointcheval, D.: Dynamic threshold public-key encryption. In: Wagner, D. (ed.) CRYPTO 2008. LNCS, vol. 5157, pp. 317–334. Springer, Heidelberg (2008). https://doi.org/10.1007/978-3-540-85174-5_18
28. Desmedt, Y., Frankel, Y.: Threshold cryptosystems. In: Brassard, G. (ed.) CRYPTO 1989. LNCS, vol. 435, pp. 307–315. Springer, New York (1990). https://doi.org/10.1007/0-387-34805-0_28
29. Devevey, J., Libert, B., Nguyen, K., Peters, T., Yung, M.: Non-interactive CCA2-secure threshold cryptosystems: achieving adaptive security in the standard model without pairings. In: Garay, J.A. (ed.) PKC 2021. LNCS, vol. 12710, pp. 659–690. Springer, Cham (2021). https://doi.org/10.1007/978-3-030-75245-3_24
30. Dwork, C., Naor, M., Reingold, O.: Immunizing encryption schemes from decryption errors. In: Cachin, C., Camenisch, J.L. (eds.) EUROCRYPT 2004. LNCS, vol. 3027, pp. 342–360. Springer, Heidelberg (2004). https://doi.org/10.1007/978-3-540-24676-3_21
31. Fernando, R., Jain, A., Komargodski, I.: Maliciously-secure MrNISC in the plain model. In: Hazay, C., Stam, M. (eds.) EUROCRYPT 2023, Part II. LNCS, vol. 14005, pp. 98–128. Springer, Cham (2023). https://doi.org/10.1007/978-3-031-30617-4_4
32. Fouque, P.-A., Pointcheval, D.: Threshold cryptosystems secure against chosen-ciphertext attacks. In: Boyd, C. (ed.) ASIACRYPT 2001. LNCS, vol. 2248, pp. 351–368. Springer, Heidelberg (2001). https://doi.org/10.1007/3-540-45682-1_21
33. Fujisaki, E., Okamoto, T.: Secure integration of asymmetric and symmetric encryption schemes. J. Cryptol. **26**(1), 80–101 (2011). https://doi.org/10.1007/s00145-011-9114-1

34. Garg, S., Kolonelos, D., Policharla, G.V., Wang, M.: Threshold encryption with silent setup. In: Reyzin, L., Stebila, D. (eds.) CRYPTO 2024, Part VII. LNCS, vol. 14926, pp. 352–386. Springer, Cham (2024). https://doi.org/10.1007/978-3-031-68394-7_12

35. Gennaro, R., Rabin, T., Jarecki, S., Krawczyk, H.: Robust and efficient sharing of RSA functions. J. Cryptol. **13**(2), 273–300 (2000). https://doi.org/10.1007/s001459910011

36. Guo, Q., Nabokov, D., Suvanto, E., Johansson, T.: Key recovery attacks on approximate homomorphic encryption with non-worst-case noise flooding countermeasures. In: Balzarotti, D., Xu, W. (eds.) USENIX Security 2024. USENIX Association (2024). https://www.usenix.org/conference/usenixsecurity24/presentation/guo-qian

37. Hall-Andersen, M., Simkin, M., Wagner, B.: Silent threshold encryption with one-shot adaptive security. Cryptology ePrint Archive, Report 2025/1384 (2025). https://eprint.iacr.org/2025/1384

38. Hofheinz, D., Hövelmanns, K., Kiltz, E.: A modular analysis of the Fujisaki-Okamoto transformation. In: Kalai, Y., Reyzin, L. (eds.) TCC 2017. LNCS, vol. 10677, pp. 341–371. Springer, Cham (2017). https://doi.org/10.1007/978-3-319-70500-2_12

39. Hofheinz, D., Jager, T., Khurana, D., Sahai, A., Waters, B., Zhandry, M.: How to generate and use universal samplers. In: Cheon, J.H., Takagi, T. (eds.) ASIACRYPT 2016. LNCS, vol. 10032, pp. 715–744. Springer, Heidelberg (2016). https://doi.org/10.1007/978-3-662-53890-6_24

40. Ishai, Y., Khurana, D., Sahai, A., Srinivasan, A.: Round-optimal black-box protocol compilers. In: Dunkelman, O., Dziembowski, S. (eds.) EUROCRYPT 2022, Part I. LNCS, vol. 13275, pp. 210–240. Springer, Cham (2022). https://doi.org/10.1007/978-3-031-06944-4_8

41. Li, B., Micciancio, D.: On the security of homomorphic encryption on approximate numbers. In: Canteaut, A., Standaert, F.-X. (eds.) EUROCRYPT 2021. LNCS, vol. 12696, pp. 648–677. Springer, Cham (2021). https://doi.org/10.1007/978-3-030-77870-5_23

42. Libert, B., Yung, M.: Non-interactive CCA-secure threshold cryptosystems with adaptive security: new framework and constructions. In: Cramer, R. (ed.) TCC 2012. LNCS, vol. 7194, pp. 75–93. Springer, Heidelberg (2012). https://doi.org/10.1007/978-3-642-28914-9_5

43. Micciancio, D., Suhl, A.: Simulation-secure threshold PKE from LWE with polynomial modulus. IACR Commun. Cryptol. **1**(4) (2025). https://doi.org/10.62056/a0zogy4e-

44. Murphy, A., O'Neill, A., Zaheri, M.: Instantiability of classical random-oracle-model encryption transforms. In: Agrawal, S., Lin, D. (eds.) ASIACRYPT 2022, Part IV. LNCS, vol. 13794, pp. 323–352. Springer, Cham (2022). https://doi.org/10.1007/978-3-031-22972-5_12

45. Naor, M., Yung, M.: Public-key cryptosystems provably secure against chosen ciphertext attacks. In: 22nd ACM STOC, pp. 427–437. ACM Press (1990). https://doi.org/10.1145/100216.100273

46. Nielsen, J.B.: Separating random oracle proofs from complexity theoretic proofs: the non-committing encryption case. In: Yung, M. (ed.) CRYPTO 2002. LNCS, vol. 2442, pp. 111–126. Springer, Heidelberg (2002). https://doi.org/10.1007/3-540-45708-9_8

47. Okada, H., Takagi, T.: Low communication threshold FHE from standard (module-)LWE. In: Hanaoka, G., Yang, BY. (eds.) ASIACRYPT 2025. LNCS, vol 16251, pp. 165–198. Springer, Singapore (2025). https://doi.org/10.1007/978-981-95-5122-4_6
48. Passelègue, A., Stehlé, D.: Low communication threshold fully homomorphic encryption. In: Chung, K.M., Sasaki, Y. (eds.) ASIACRYPT 2024, Part I. LNCS, vol. 15484, pp. 297–329. Springer, Singapore (2024). https://doi.org/10.1007/978-981-96-0875-1_10
49. Qin, B., Wu, Q., Zhang, L., Farras, O., Domingo-Ferrer, J.: Provably secure threshold public-key encryption with adaptive security and short ciphertexts. Inf. Sci. **210**, 67–80 (2012)
50. Shoup, V.: Practical threshold signatures. In: Preneel, B. (ed.) EUROCRYPT 2000. LNCS, vol. 1807, pp. 207–220. Springer, Heidelberg (2000). https://doi.org/10.1007/3-540-45539-6_15
51. Shoup, V., Gennaro, R.: Securing threshold cryptosystems against chosen ciphertext attack. In: Nyberg, K. (ed.) EUROCRYPT 1998. LNCS, vol. 1403, pp. 1–16. Springer, Heidelberg (1998). https://doi.org/10.1007/BFb0054113
52. Waters, B., Wu, D.J.: Silent threshold cryptography from pairings: expressive policies in the plain model. Cryptology ePrint Archive, Report 2025/1547 (2025). https://eprint.iacr.org/2025/1547

Homomorphic and Searchable Encryption

Malicious Homomorphic Secret Sharing with Applications to DV-NIZK and More

Pedro Capitão[1], Hila Dahari-Garbian[2], Lisa Kohl[1(✉)], and Zhe Li[3]

[1] CWI Amsterdam, Amsterdam, The Netherlands
{pedro.capitao,lisa.kohl}@cwi.nl
[2] Weizmann Institute of Science, Rehovot, Israel
hila.dahari@weizmann.ac.il
[3] Xidian University, Xi'an, China
lizh0048@e.ntu.edu.sg

Abstract. Homomorphic Secret Sharing (CRYPTO 2016) allows a secret to be shared among two or more parties in such a way that the parties can locally evaluate a class of functions on their shares. Homomorphic secret sharing (HSS) schemes and their underlying techniques have facilitated a wide range of applications. To account for the fact that parties generating or evaluating the shares might act maliciously, variants of HSS schemes that allow detection of such malicious behavior have been introduced. However, all prior approaches of malicious HSS that capture the class of NC1 circuits either crucially rely on a random oracle or require an non-reusable setup.

In this work, we initiate the study of malicious public-key 2-party HSS in the standard model with reusable setup, where any malicious behavior during share generation and share evaluation can be detected. Towards constructing malicious HSS, we introduce the notion of homomorphic secret sharing with *robust linear reconstruction* (RLR-HSS) and show that this notion readily implies malicious HSS. We outline challenges in instantiating RLR-HSS due to the error present in all current HSS constructions not relying on SHE/FHE, and show how to overcome these using derandomization techniques by Dwork et al. (EUROCRYPT 2004). Finally, we show applications of malicious HSS to compact designated verifier non-interactive zero knowledge arguments and maliciously secure 2-party computation in the standard model (supporting the same function class as the underlying malicious HSS).

Keywords: Homomorphic Secret Sharing · Non-Interactive Zero Knowledge · Secure 2-Party Computation

1 Introduction

Homomorphic secret sharing (HSS) [15] is a variant of secret sharing in which the parties are able to perform a supported class of computations locally on the shares. It can be viewed as a relaxation of somewhat or fully homomorphic

© International Association for Cryptologic Research 2026
S. Bai and E. Persichetti (Eds.): PKC 2026, LNCS 16554, pp. 201–234, 2026.
https://doi.org/10.1007/978-3-032-26740-5_7

encryption (FHE) to the 2- (or multi-) party setting, where the computation is distributed between non-communicating parties. HSS has proven to be a powerful tool with numerous applications, including private queries of multi-server data bases [14,16,18,29,43,58], succinct preprocessing [8,10,12], constrained pseudorandom functions [34], and more. Most noteworthy, HSS makes it possible to circumvent the circuit-size barrier of secure multi-party computation from assumptions not known to imply FHE [13,15,33,36].

Since their introduction, numerous homomorphic secret sharing (HSS) constructions have been proposed. The groundbreaking work of [15] and follow-up results [12,17] showed that based on the decisional Diffie-Hellman (DDH) assumption, it is possible to construct 2-party HSS for the class of restricted-multiplication straightline (RMS) programs.[1] Later, two-party HSS constructions for RMS programs based on the decisional composite residuosity (DCR) assumption [39,51,54], the learning with errors (LWE) assumption (without resorting to homomorphic multiplications on ciphertexts) [2,18] and class groups [1] emerged, which overcame the $1/\mathsf{poly}(\lambda)$ error present in the earlier DDH-based constructions. Building on multi-key fully homomorphic encryption, multi-party HSS for all circuits can be achieved [27,37]. Furthermore, a recent line of research introduced 2-party and multi-party HSS constructions for constant-degree polynomials, relying on variants of the learning parity with noise (LPN) assumption [10,30,33,36].

What is common to the majority of the HSS literature is that the correctness and security guarantees are in the semi-honest setting, i.e., the share generation and evaluation are assumed to be performed honestly. In fact, it is easy to see that plain HSS does not give any guarantees if the parties behave maliciously. In the setting of multi-server private information retrieval, this shortcoming has been addressed in different works on HSS with verifiable evaluation [25,26,28, 44,55,59]. In these works the shares are assumed to be generated by an honest client, while the evaluation on the shares is performed by potentially malicious servers.

In the context of secure multi-party computation with malicious security, homomorphic secret sharing schemes have been combined with generic zero knowledge proofs [15,33] or message authentication codes [1,4] to take into account malicious behavior during *share generation and evaluation*. However, all prior works either rely on random oracles (for rerandomization of the shares), or are limited to HSS for small circuit classes not capturing NC1.

The need for rerandomization stems from the fact that most HSS techniques come with a correctness error. While some constructions [12,15,17,39] involve even non-negligible correctness error that must be addressed in practical applications, all known HSS constructions for NC1 that do not rely on somewhat or fully homomorphic encryption suffer from non-perfect correctness. This issue appears to be inherent to the current techniques, and has even been demonstrated to be

---

[1] This class of programs captures branching programs and NC1 circuits [15].

so in the context of lattice-based constructions relying on the so-called rounding and lifting technique [2,5].[2]

This error constitutes an issue towards achieving malicious security of HSS in the standard model (even assuming honest generation of keys), as an adversary can choose its inputs and randomness adaptively in order to increase the error probability to non-negligible and thereby potentially learn something about the secret key of the other party or the underlying computation. In fact, common correctness definitions [15,18,51] cover only non-adaptive correctness, where correctness is guaranteed to hold only if the inputs are chosen independently of the setup parameters. This is problematic in applications such as secure computation even if relying on generic zero knowledge proofs, unless it is ensured that the parties have already committed to their inputs and randomness to be used *before* learning the HSS setup information, making the setup non-reusable across different inputs, or if additional measures are in place (e.g., if shares are re-randomized at each step of the computation using a non-predictable source of randomness such as a random oracle).

1.1 Our Contribution

In this paper, we show how to lift the non-adaptive correctness of HSS to *adaptive* correctness, which allows HSS inputs to be chosen adaptively, even after seeing the keys. To this end, we follow the derandomization techniques of Dwork et al. [38] to show that any HSS satisfying non-adaptive correctness (where the correctness error can be made sufficiently small) can be transformed into an HSS satisfying adaptive correctness. On the positive side, this allows us to lift the 3-round protocol of [1] for secure 2-party computation to the standard model (preserving the round complexity).

On the negative side, this transformation comes with a significant loss: if the original HSS scheme supports evaluation of a function class $\mathcal{F}$ which takes inputs $x \in \{0,1\}^N$, then the shares of the new scheme scale with size $|\mathcal{F}'| \cdot N \cdot \mathsf{poly}(\lambda)$, where $\mathcal{F}' \subset \mathcal{F}$ is the function class supported by the new HSS. Note that this still gives succinct secure computation, as the size of the shares only depends on the size of the function class, i.e., the number of functions in $\mathcal{F}$, and not on the size of the functions $f \in \mathcal{F}'$.[3]

Our second main contribution concerns addressing the question of whether the transformation from NIZK to rate-1 NIZK via FHE [41] can be lifted to the HSS setting. Namely, we ask if an HSS allows to transform a (DV-)NIZK into a rate-1 DV-NIZK.

---

[2] Such techniques are also what restricts most HSS constructions to the 2-party setting, primarily due to the reliance on local share conversion which is not possible with more parties.

[3] In particular, the HSS can even support a large function class $\mathcal{F}$ as long as the class of "eligible" functions is fixed to a polynomially-large set, independent of $|f|$, at the time of setup. Once this is done, the HSS parameters can be reused for arbitrary evaluations within this class.

Towards addressing this question, we observe that many HSS schemes in literature actually have a baked-in verification procedure (e.g., [1,18]) even without adding extra verification mechanisms such as message authentication codes, which we abstract as *robust linear reconstruction*. We show that this property can not only be used generically towards interactive verification of the shares (as also observed in [50]), but also to safely release "reduced" shares (where the reduction depends on the correct result of the function evaluation), while still being able to verify correctness of the evaluation. We formalize these properties as *reduced share simulatability* and *verifiability*, together capturing the notion of security against malicious adversaries, and we call a scheme with these traits malicious HSS.

We further show a transformation of NIZK to compact DV-NIZK (i.e., with proof size independent of the circuit size of the statement to be proven) which, using the transformation from non-adaptive to adaptive correctness from above, can be based on any HSS supporting robust linear reconstruction.

Since, as described above, the transformation from non-adaptive correctness to adaptive correctness is not rate-preserving, we unfortunately do not get a transformation from standard HSS to rate-1 DV-NIZK, which we leave as an interesting open question.

For completeness, we further give a direct construction of *rate*-1 malicious HSS from leveled homomorphic encryption. While this does not yield any applications that are not already known to be implied directly by leveled FHE, it appears to point out a qualitative difference of SHE/FHE-based HSS schemes and other HSS techniques for NC1 (such as "rounding and lifting" and "distributed discrete logarithm" techniques) even in a distributed setting.

In the following, we give a high-level overview of our techniques towards the transformation of NIZK to DV-NIZK via HSS with robust linear reconstruction.

1.2 Technical Overview

In this work, we focus on public-key 2-party HSS with non-interactive key aggregation. Even though HSS with non-interactive key aggregation is not formalized in prior work, we note that the HSS schemes of [1,18] can be phrased as such.[4] More precisely, an HSS with non-interactive key aggregation for a function family $\mathcal{F}$ consists of a tuple of algorithms HSS = (KeyGen, KeyComb, Enc, Eval, Comb), such that:[5]

- KeyGen on input party index b outputs a key pair $(\mathsf{pk}_b, \mathsf{sk}_b)$.
- KeyComb on input of public keys $\mathsf{pk}_0, \mathsf{pk}_1$, outputs a joint public key pk.
- Enc on input of a combined public key pk and an input x, outputs a ciphertext ct.

---

[4] HSS with non-interactive key aggregation has in fact be considered in [1] as HSS with one-round setup (see Fig. 5/Thm. 2 in the EPRINT version).

[5] Note that in the following to simplify notation we omit the Setup algorithm and public parameters and only consider function families with output in $\{0, 1\}$.

- Eval on input of a party index b, an evaluation key sk_b, a set of n ciphertexts $(\mathsf{ct}_i)_{i \in [n]}$, and a function $f \in \mathcal{F}$, computes an output share t_b.
- Comb on input of output shares t_0, t_1 returns an output value y. For now, we will consider additive reconstruction, i.e., Comb simply returns $y := t_0 + t_1$.

To satisfy correctness (with additive reconstruction), for all honestly generated parameters, all inputs x_i and all $\mathsf{ct}_i \leftarrow \mathsf{Enc}(\mathsf{pk}_i, x_i)$ it should hold:

$$\mathsf{Eval}(0, \mathsf{sk}_0, (\mathsf{ct}_i)_{i \in [n]}, f) + \mathsf{Eval}(1, \mathsf{sk}_1, (\mathsf{ct}_i)_{i \in [n]}, f) = f(x_1, \ldots, x_n).$$

Towards security, there should exist an efficient simulator such that for any input x and any party index $b \in \{0, 1\}$ it holds:

$$\{\mathsf{Sim}(\mathsf{pk}, \mathsf{sk}_b)\} \approx \{(\mathsf{Enc}(\mathsf{pk}, x), \mathsf{sk}_b)\},$$

i.e., an encryption does not reveal the underlying value even given a secret key share sk_b.

Here, one can view $(\mathsf{Enc}(\mathsf{pk}, x), \mathsf{sk}_0), (\mathsf{Enc}(\mathsf{pk}, x), \mathsf{sk}_1)$ as a 2-out-of-2 secret sharing of x.[6] Note that given a somewhat-homomorphic encryption scheme with non-interactive key aggregation one can instantiate the above homomorphic secret sharing simply by evaluating the function homomorphically on the ciphertexts and outputting the result and the secret key share.[7]

Towards Malicious HSS. However, it is easy to see that this definition is not robust against malicious behavior:

- An adversarial party might generate a public key $\hat{\mathsf{pk}}_b$ maliciously.
- An adversarial party might generate an encryption $\hat{\mathsf{ct}}_i$ maliciously.
- An adversarial party might return a wrong output share $\hat{t}_b$.

The first point is relatively straightforward to address: one can simply let the adversary prove that pk_b and ct_i were indeed generated correctly using a suitable non-interactive zero knowledge proof of knowledge.

At first glance, it might seem that the same is true to ensure correctness of the encrypted ciphertext. In fact, one can ensure that the ciphertext is well-generated with the same techniques,[8] but this does not address the fact that an adversary may adaptively choose their input and randomness in such a way that evaluation might result in a wrong share with high probability. This can be prevented by letting the adversary commit to its input and randomness ahead of time. The focus of this work, however, is to construct HSS where the adversary can choose

---

[6] For this reason we sometimes refer to the process of creating keys and ciphertexts as *share generation*.

[7] The described approach does not allow for additive reconstruction. To achieve this, one can use distributed decryption and "spooky rounding" [37]).

[8] Note that here it is crucial that ct_i is tagged with a party index b to prevent that the adversarial party "copies" an honest party's input. We will omit this in the following, but will make it explicit in the formal definition.

its input after seeing the setup, thereby making the HSS setup reusable for many inputs.

Finally, we have to address the possibility that an adversary could deviate from the protocol during evaluation. The first idea is again to add generic zero-knowledge proofs. While adding zero-knowledge to the key generation and ciphertext introduces an overhead that is independent of the circuit size, adding zero-knowledge to the evaluation algorithm would result in an overhead that scales with the circuit size of the function to be evaluated, which is not desirable.

HSS with Robust Linear Reconstruction (RLR-HSS). The starting point to overcome this issue is the observation that many HSS constructions actually have a built-in mechanism which can be exploited for the purpose of verification. Namely, the output shares (t_0, t_1) of certain 2-party HSS schemes [1,18,51,54] are vectors such that $t_0 + t_1 = f(\mathbf{x}) \cdot \mathsf{sk}$. We will refer to such a scheme in the following as HSS with *robust linear reconstruction.*[9] When first introduced, this structure was an artifact of the techniques, solely used in HSS evaluation, and disregarded at the end of the computation: namely, the evaluation key is chosen such that $\mathsf{sk}[1] = 1$, and the parties output the first entry of t_0 and t_1, respectively, to recover $f(\mathbf{x})$.

Note, however, that this structure can actually be used to check if the evaluation was performed honestly (assuming honest share generation): namely, server S_b provides the full share t_b at the end of the computation, and the client (in knowledge of sk) accepts if and only if $t_0 + t_1 = f(\mathbf{x}) \cdot \mathsf{sk}$. (This has first been observed in the context of verifiable homomorphic secret sharing [25].) Intuitively, this allows a client to check if the evaluation has been performed honestly (assuming non-colluding servers), as a malicious server S_b would need to provide $\hat{t}_b := t_b + (-1)^{f(\mathbf{x})} \cdot \mathsf{sk}$ in order to flip the output from $f(\mathbf{x}) \cdot \mathsf{sk}$ to $(1 - f(\mathbf{x})) \cdot \mathsf{sk}$, which would imply breaking security of the HSS by recovering the secret key.

Our first observation is that this technique can be extended to a distributed setting, where no party has knowledge of the secret key sk. Namely, assume that party P_b holds sk_b such that $\mathsf{sk}_0 + \mathsf{sk}_1 = \mathsf{sk}$. Then, in case $f(\mathbf{x}) = 0$ it holds $t_0 + t_1 = 0$ and in case $f(\mathbf{x}) = 1$ it holds $(t_0 - \mathsf{sk}_0) + (t_1 - \mathsf{sk}_1) = 0$. Note here that it is no longer safe to reveal the shares $(t_b, t_b - \mathsf{sk}_b)$ in the clear, as this would allow the other party to recover sk. This can be addressed in two ways. If the output of the computation is known (as will be the case in the DV-NIZK application, where the prover wants to show $f(\mathbf{x}) = 1$), the parties can safely release only the corresponding shares $t_b - f(\mathbf{x}) \cdot \mathsf{sk}_b$. If the output of the computation is not known, as is the case in applications to secure computation,

---

[9] Towards malicious security, we actually require the scheme to satisfy perfect correctness (except with negligible probability over the setup algorithm). We will come back to this issue later, and for now assume that the underlying HSS schemes satisfies perfect correctness.

the parties can instead recover the correct output using private set intersection, where party P_b inputs $\{(-1)^b \cdot t_b, (-1)^b \cdot (t_b - \mathsf{sk}_b)\}$.[10]

Formalizing Malicious Security. Towards formalizing malicious security, we extend the definition of homomorphic secret sharing by relaxing the share reconstruction algorithm Comb into two algorithms Reduce and $\mathsf{RedComb}$, where Reduce additionally gets as input the (presumably) correct function output y, and security is required to hold relative to the reduced output shares. In the above example, Reduce would get as input a bit b, share t_b, secret key share sk_b, and a function output $y = f(\mathbf{x})$ and output $u_b := (y, t_b - y \cdot \mathsf{sk}_b)$. The $\mathsf{RedComb}$ algorithm on input $(y, \tilde{u}_0), (y, \tilde{u}_1)$ would output y if and only if $\tilde{u}_0 + \tilde{u}_1 = 0$. If the output space is small (e.g. $\{0,1\}$), we no longer have to consider the share combination algorithm Comb explicitly. Instead, we can define Comb as follows: compute $u_b^y \leftarrow \mathsf{Reduce}(b, \mathsf{sk}_b, t_b, y)$ for $y \in \{0, 1\}$ and return y if and only if $\mathsf{RedComb}(u_0^y, u_1^y) = y$.[11] Defining these additional algorithms Reduce and $\mathsf{RedComb}$ lets us capture the following:

1. The reduced output share u_b relative to the correct output $y = f(\mathbf{x})$ can be released without revealing anything about the underlying inputs or computation;
2. The reduced output share u_b is sufficient to verify that the computation has in fact been performed correctly.

We will formalize these two properties as *reduced share simulatability* and *verifiability*. In a nutshell, towards reduced share simulatability we require an efficient simulator Sim such that for $b \in \{0, 1\}$ it holds

$$\{\mathsf{Sim}(\mathsf{pk}_b, f, f(\mathbf{x}))\} \approx \{\mathsf{pk}_{1-b}, (\mathsf{ct}_i)_{i\in[n]}, u_{1-b}\},$$

where $\mathsf{crs} \leftarrow \mathsf{Setup}(1^\lambda)$, $(\mathsf{pk}_{1-b}, \mathsf{sk}_{1-b}) \leftarrow \mathsf{KeyGen}(\mathsf{crs})$, $\mathsf{ct}_i \leftarrow \mathsf{Enc}(\mathsf{pk}, x_i)$, $t_b \leftarrow \mathsf{Eval}(b, \mathsf{sk}_b, f, (\mathsf{ct}_i)_{i\in[n]})$ and $u_{1-b} \leftarrow \mathsf{Reduce}(1 - b, \mathsf{sk}_{1-b}, t_{1-b}, f(\mathbf{x}))$, even for adversarially generated public key $\mathsf{pk}_b \leftarrow \mathcal{A}(\mathsf{crs}, \mathsf{pk}_{1-b})$. In other words, a reduced output share can be simulated given only knowledge of the output $f(\mathbf{x})$.

The formalization of *verifiability* (where the shares are potentially generated dishonestly) turns out a bit more involved, as we have to capture the fact that:

i. If verification passes, then the computation has been performed correctly (even if the inputs and randomness are chosen maliciously based on the setup).

---

[10] Since in the context of secure computation, the techniques of [1] allow for non-interactive reconstruction and therefore better round complexity, we do not focus on the application of this trick to secure computation in the paper.

[11] While this definition might seem limited to HSS with small output spaces $\mathcal{Y}$ on first glance, it also captures more generic HSS: namely, if the HSS support Reduce, $\mathsf{RedComb}$, where Reduce is *independent* of the output value y, the combination algorithm above is efficient even for large spaces $\mathcal{Y}$ (as the reduce algorithm yields a single output share u_b). We refer to such HSS as HSS with non-interactive share reduction in the following.

ii. If verification passes, it is safe to reveal the honest party's share u_{1-b} (even if this is derived from potentially maliciously generated shares).

Now, some or all of the ciphertexts are provided by the adversary and thus corresponding inputs must be extracted during simulation. One might think that due to the second point verifiability encompasses reduced share simulatability, but the two properties are actually incomparable, as in reduced share simulatability the adversary gets to see u_{1-b} *without* having to provide its own reduced share u_b to the simulator. While this definition of malicious security is somewhat cumbersome, we show in this paper that it is not necessary to instantiate it directly. Rather, we are able to give a generic transformation from any RLR-HSS to malicious HSS, where we use non-interactive zero knowledge proofs to enforce the correct generation of pk_b and ct_i and rely on robust linear reconstruction to achieve verifiability.

From Malicious HSS to DV-NIZK. We show that malicious HSS implies a very simple designated verifier non-interactive zero-knowledge argument, essentially lifting the construction of rate-1 NIZK from fully homomorphic encryption (FHE) [41] to HSS. Recall that in the construction of NIZK from FHE, in order to prove $f(\mathbf{w}) = 1$, the prover encrypts the witness $\mathbf{w}$ using a fully homomorphic encryption scheme and proves that the homomorphic evaluation of function f on $\mathbf{w}$ indeed results in an encryption of 1 (by opening the evaluated ciphertext). To achieve rate-1 NIZK, the paper uses hybrid encryption, i.e., encrypts the witness as $\mathbf{w} + G(s)$ for some PRG G, and then encrypts s using the FHE scheme (while also proving well-formedness of the FHE encryption). Since the verifier can check that the output ciphertext was indeed obtained via homomorphic evaluation of f on the input ciphertext and all FHE-encryptions are well-formed, soundness follows.

In this paper, we show that HSS gives rise to a similar construction resulting in DV-NIZK for languages where the evaluation of f is supported by the underlying HSS. The verifier generates $(\mathsf{pk}_1, \mathsf{sk}_1) \leftarrow \mathsf{KeyGen}(1^\lambda)$ and sends pk_1 to the prover. The prover generates its own key pair $(\mathsf{pk}_0, \mathsf{sk}_0) \leftarrow \mathsf{KeyGen}(1^\lambda)$, encrypts its witness $\mathbf{w}$ under the combined public key pk, evaluates f homomorphically on ct to obtain t_0, computes the reduced share u_0 relative to output $y = 1$ and sends $\pi := (\mathsf{pk}_0, \mathsf{ct}, u_0)$ to the verifier. The verifier then computes t_1 by evaluating f on ct using its own secret key share sk_1, computes its own reduced share u_1 relative to $y = 1$ and outputs $\mathsf{RedComb}(u_0, u_1)$. It can be seen that the resulting proof system satisfies zero knowledge because of the reduced share simulatability of the HSS and reusable soundness because of the verifiability of the HSS. Further, the transformation preserves the rate of the underlying HSS. Unfortunately, as we will explain below, dealing with the error in non-SHE/FHE-based HSS constructions does not result in rate-1 DV-NIZK. Yet, we obtain a transformation from (DV-)NIZK to *compact* (i.e., with overhead independent of the circuit size) DV-NIZK for NC1 from any HSS for NC1 satisfying non-adaptive robust linear reconstruction.

From Malicious HSS to Malicious 2PC. Finally, we give a definition of verifiability for HSS with non-interactive share reduction and show that it suffices to instantiate malicious secure 2-party computation from malicious HSS, with the property that the setup and public keys can be reused across many secure computations. The underlying HSS can be instantiated from [1]. While the MPC protocol readily follows from [1], our contribution is the generic transformation from non-adaptive to adaptive correctness (explained below), which allows to lift the result of [1] in the random oracle model to the standard model (at the cost of larger HSS parameters).

The Issue of Error. A crucial point we have not addressed so far is that the mentioned HSS constructions of [18,51,54] do not actually achieve perfect correctness. Instead, they settle for a non-adaptive version of correctness, where correctness is only guaranteed to hold with overwhelming probability over the random coins of KeyGen and Enc. If the adversary is able to choose the input x and/or the encryption randomness for Enc *after* seeing the evaluation key, this definition no longer gives any guarantees (even if the adversary follows the protocol honestly otherwise). This is not merely an artifact of the choice of a "too weak" definition but hints to an actual limitation of current techniques.

Namely, a multiplication $x \cdot y$ in HSS constructions can typically be viewed as a distributed decryption of a ciphertext $\mathsf{Enc}(\mathsf{pk}, x)$ with secret shares of $y \cdot \mathsf{sk}$. The issue is that this multiplication gives output shares over a different group than the one started from, so in order to continue the computation the parties have to perform a "share conversion" procedure. An example of share conversion is the lifting procedure of [18], where the parties lift shares $z_0 + z_1 = z \mod p$ to additive shares of z modulo q (for a larger modulus q). It turns out that if $|z| \ll p$ and z_0, z_1 are chosen at random, then with high probability it holds $z_0 + z_1 = z$ *over the integers*, and thus also modulo q as required.[12] However, there is always a non-zero chance of an error. Even more, as observed in [2], even only given access to one share, the adversary can see whether such an error potentially occurs. Namely, an error can only occur if both z_0 *and* z_1 are in the "bad area" between $-p/2 + 1$ and $-p/2 + |z|$ or both in the "bad area" between $p/2 - |z|$ and $p/2$.[13] Furthermore, the shares z_0 and z_1 are exactly $|z|$ apart modulo p, so if the adversary manages to enforce its share into the "correct" bad area (which depends on the value of z), a share conversion error will indeed occur. As the shares depend on the encryption $\mathsf{Enc}(\mathsf{pk}, x)$, an adversary can guess the value of z and choose $\mathsf{Enc}(\mathsf{pk}, x)$ such that its respective share lands in the "bad area".[14] By aiming for the interval borders $-p/2 + 1$ or $p/2$, the adversary

---

[12] Note that by choosing $p \geq |z| \cdot \lambda^{\omega(1)}$, the probability of a "lifting" error can be made negligible.

[13] For simplicity, here we assume that p is even and $\mathbb{Z}_p$ is represented as $\{-p/2 + 1, \ldots, p/2\}$.

[14] Note that enforcing z_b to land in a certain area is not trivial as the parties perform a "rounding" operation before the lifting, but the adversary can perform a similar attack on the rounding to enforce an error with high probability.

can even increase the probability of the attack to 50% (as in this case it only needs to guess correctly whether z is a positive or negative integer).

Towards Overcoming the Issue of Error. One idea to overcome the attack is to make use of the observation in [2] to our advantage: if an honest party ever observes a share in the "bad area" during evaluation, it simply aborts. There are some issues with this approach, though. First of all, whether an abort occurs or not depends on the secret key share sk_{1-b} of the honest party, and therefore only results in an HSS with "single-key" use. In the context of DV-NIZK, this observation suffices to construct a one-time DV-NIZK, where the verifier has to generate a fresh verification key for each statement to be proven. However, for applications such as secure computation this approach is not suitable, as whether an abort occurs or not depends on the intermediary values of the underlying computation (namely, the value $z = x \cdot y$ from above). In the context of secure computation this means that an adversary can learn information about the honest party's input based on whether the honest party aborts. The approach of achieving robustness via abort is therefore not productive in this setting.

Another approach is to rely on an idealized source of randomness such as a random oracle for rerandomization. If carefully implemented, this indeed yields correctness as required even in a malicious setting. This approach has been considered in the context of secure computation with malicious security in the random oracle model by [1,4]. In this work, however, we focus on achieving HSS with malicious security in the standard model.

From Negligible Error to Perfect Correctness. We show instead that one can use techniques from Dwork et al. [38] to get rid of the error, albeit unfortunately at the cost of a blow-up in parameter sizes. We start by recalling their strategy to get rid of small error in the context of public key encryption. The idea is that one can transform a public-key encryption scheme that has small correctness error (say, at most error $\epsilon = 2^{-4\lambda}$ for message space $\{0,1\}^\lambda$), into a public key encryption scheme that is perfectly correct *except on a negligible fraction of the public keys*. That is, once the public key is fixed the scheme will satisfy correctness relative to all possible messages m and encryption randomness r (except with negligible probability over the choice of the key pair). Their idea is to replace the encryption randomness $r \in \{0,1\}^{\ell(\lambda)}$ by randomness $G(s) \oplus r' \in \{0,1\}^{\ell(\lambda)}$, where $G\colon \{0,1\}^\lambda \to \{0,1\}^{\ell(\lambda)}$ is a pseudorandom generator and $r' \leftarrow_R \{0,1\}^{\ell(\lambda)}$ is a random string added to the public key. First of all, since the error probability is at most $\epsilon = 2^{-4\lambda}$, by a counting argument there must exist a fraction of at least $1 - 2^{-\lambda}$ "good key pairs", for which the probability of error is at most $2^{-3\lambda}$. For all "good key pairs" $(\mathsf{pk}, \mathsf{sk})$ we thus have

$$\Pr[\mathsf{Dec}(\mathsf{sk}, (\mathsf{Enc}(\mathsf{pk}, m; G(s) \oplus r')) \neq m] \leq 2^{-3\lambda}$$

where the probability is taken over $m \leftarrow_R \{0,1\}^\lambda$, $s \leftarrow_R \{0,1\}^\lambda$ and $r' \leftarrow_R \{0,1\}^{\ell(\lambda)}$. Finally, via a union bound over m and s we obtain that for all "good key pairs"

$$\Pr[\mathsf{Dec}(\mathsf{sk}, (\mathsf{Enc}(\mathsf{pk}, m; G(s) \oplus r')) \neq m] \leq 2^{-\lambda}$$

for all possible $m, s \in \{0,1\}^\lambda$, where the probability is taken over the random choice of $r' \leftarrow_R \{0,1\}^{\ell(\lambda)}$. Therefore, of the remaining good keys at most a fraction of $2^{-\lambda}$ of the keys lead to a correctness error on any message, resulting in a scheme with perfect correctness except with probability $2 \cdot 2^{-\lambda}$ over the choice of the key pair.

We can adapt this technique to HSS, where we want that correctness holds except with negligible probability over the setup parameters *for all possible key pairs* $(\mathsf{pk}, \mathsf{sk})$ *and for all possible encryptions of messages* $x_1, \ldots, x_n \in \{0,1\}^N$. To achieve this, we have to perform a union bound over $2^{2\lambda + n(N+\lambda)}$ values corresponding to the randomness of the choice of the key pairs $(\mathsf{pk}_b, \mathsf{sk}_b)$ and the randomness and message of all n ciphertexts, rather than only $2^{2\lambda}$ values as before. We therefore have to start with correctness error $\epsilon \leq 2^{-4\lambda - n(N+\lambda)}$. In HSS constructions with negligible correctness error such as [18,51,54], we can decrease the error probability by choosing larger parameters. For the HSS of [18], for example, the correctness error scales at least with $\max(1/p, p/q) \cdot |f|$, where $|f|$ is the number of multiplication gates when f is written as restricted multiplication straightline program, and where p is the plaintext modulus and q the ciphertext modulus of the scheme. Thus, one can choose $p = 2^{4\lambda + n(N+\lambda)} \cdot |f|$ and $q = p^2$. On the downside, this means that even sending a single field element in $\mathbb{F}_q$ requires communication $\log q = 2 \cdot (4\lambda + n(N+\lambda)) \cdot \log|f|$. We can therefore not hope to achieve constant rate (i.e., ciphertext size $N + \mathsf{poly}(\lambda)$) via this transformation, even when using additional measures such as hybrid encryption $(m \oplus G(r), \mathsf{Enc}(\mathsf{pk}, r))$ to encrypt a message $m \in \{0,1\}^N$, as the base field $\mathbb{F}_q$ is simply too large.

From Homomorphic Encryption to HSS with Perfect Correctness. To complement the above generic transformation, we give an alternative construction of HSS that achieves perfect correctness and rate-1 ciphertexts based on leveled homomorphic encryption (LHE). We note that one cannot achieve perfectly additive reconstruction even based on LHE, as this requires "spooky rounding" [37] which comes with a non-zero error. Instead, the parties can release their shares *before rounding*, so that reconstruction can performed with perfect correctness. To allow for verification, we let the parties compute $f(x) \cdot \mathsf{sk}$ instead of $f(x)$.[15] The algorithm $\mathsf{RedComb}$ then takes inputs $(t_b, t_b - \mathsf{sk}_b)$ and outputs 0 if $t_0 \approx t_1$ and 1 if $t_0 - \mathsf{sk}_0 \approx t_1 - \mathsf{sk}_1$. To avoid the error leaking anything about the underlying noise, the parties can use noise flooding (assuming a superpolynomial ciphertext modulus). Distributed reconstruction becomes a bit more difficult in this case, as the parties have to check approximate matching in a distributed setting. One way to instantiate this is to rely on structure-aware PSI [3,40,40]. Although we are not aware of any application of the obtained HSS that cannot be obtained directly from the underlying LHE scheme, we provide this trans-

---

[15] We show that this can be achieved with GSW encryption [42] without any additional circular security assumption.

formation to show a qualitative difference of homomorphic encryption and HSS techniques to our current understanding even in the distributed setting.

1.3 Related Work

In this section we give a short summary of relevant works mentioned during the introduction and further related research.

Malicious Secure Computation from HSS. Prior works achieve malicious secure computation either by relying on generic zero knowledge proofs [15,33] or random oracles [1,4]. While [33] achieves reusable setup (as they do not have to deal with error in the underlying HSS), their approach only yields secure computation that scales with $\log s/\log \log s$ in the circuit size s (due to their underlying HSS not supporting NC1). The approach of [1], on the other hand, uses message authentication codes to get the round complexity down to 3 rounds (essentially, they manage to keep the reconstruction phase non-interactive). Their approach, however, relies crucially on a random oracle to rerandomize the shares. We expect that using similar derandomization techniques as presented in our work would result in a protocol for secure computation with malicious security in 3 rounds in the standard model and leave it as an interesting open question to explore this direction further.

Verifiable HSS. The line of work on verifiable HSS [25,26,28,44,55,59] considers a server-client setting in which the shares are generated by an honest client and malicious behavior of the server is to be detected. The work of [28] gives an even stronger guarantee of public verifiability, i.e., verifiability is guaranteed to hold even if all servers are malicious. This setting is incomparable to ours: while we give guarantees even if the key generation is performed maliciously, we rely on at least one party behaving honestly throughout the computation.

Verifiable and Malicious FSS. Much work has been dedicated to achieving verifiable or even malicious secure function secret sharing [6,7,9,11,16,22,57]. This line of work crucially relies on the structure of the output for verification, and therefore is limited to FSS for simple functions such as point functions, where the parties end up with output vectors that differ at exactly one point. In the setting of HSS, however, there is typically no structure in the output itself that can be used towards verification purposes.

Multi-key HSS. Recently, [31] proposed the first multi-key HSS construction for NC1 based on DDH, serving as the secret-sharing counterpart to multi-key FHE. This differs from HSS with non-interactive key aggregation in that in multi-key HSS the parties can generate encrypted ciphertexts *before* exchanging their shares of the public key. We expect their techniques to be compatible with our transformation, which would result in a transformation from NIZK to compact NIZK based on HSS, as well as malicious secure 2-round computation in the common-reference-string model. We leave a further exploration of this direction as an interesting open question.

DV-NIZK. A series of works have focused on constructing DV-NIZKs using Σ-protocols and public-key cryptographic primitives [23,24,35,49,52,56]. However, as pointed out by [46], these works either do not provide full reusability or are limited to a specific NP language. Subsequently, in a parallel line of research [32,45,53], non-compact reusable DV-NIZKs for all NP languages were developed based on the computational Diffie-Hellman assumption. The line of work [45–47] constructed compact and reusable DV-NIZKs based on Diffie-Hellman-like assumptions in pairing-free groups. For the special class of NC1 circuits, they even provided rate-1 DV-NIZK. (DV-)NIZKs with statistical zero knowledge have been constructed in [19,48]. Here, the latter constructs NIZKs with statistical zero knowledge and proof size $|w| + |w|^\epsilon \cdot \mathsf{poly}(\lambda)$ for small constant $\epsilon < 1$. Towards generic transformations, [41] gave a transformation from (DV-)NIZK to rate-1 (DV-)NIZK based on FHE, whereas [20] recently showed a transformation from one-time DV-NIZK to reusable DV-NIZK from a public-key pseudorandom correlation function for OT (though it does not yield compact DV-NIZKs in general, due to its reliance on a Σ-protocol).

2   Preliminaries

For a natural number n, we denote by $[n]$ the set $\{1, \ldots, n\}$. We denote by λ the security parameter. We use $\mathsf{negl}(\lambda)$ to denote any negligible function and $\mathsf{poly}(\lambda)$ for any polynomially-bounded function. We allow the symbol $\perp$ to be used as a special output for any algorithm, which will typically indicate the presence of malicious behavior or improper inputs. As a convention, we define the output of any algorithm which receives $\perp$ as one of its inputs to be $\perp$. We assume stateful adversaries implicitly output some state at each invocation, to be used as additional input at their next invocation. Definitions of some standard notions such as leveled homomorphic encryption, secure computation and (DV-)NIZK used here can be found in the full version of this paper [21].

3   Homomorphic Secret Sharing

In this section, we present our definition of homomorphic secret sharing. We note that it differs from previous works in two ways. First, we require the scheme to support non-interactive key setup. As discussed in the introduction, this does not apply to all HSS schemes, but is satisfied by natural schemes such as those from the LWE and DCR assumptions. Secondly, we split up reconstruction into algorithms Reduce and RedComb, which can be viewed as a relaxation of standard HSS and which we elaborate on in more detail below.

Definition 1 (Syntax). *A 2-party homomorphic secret sharing (HSS) scheme with non-interactive key aggregation for a function family $\mathcal{F} = \{f \colon I^n \to \mathcal{Y}\}$ consists of several polynomial-time algorithms* HSS $=$ (Setup, KeyGen, KeyComb, Enc, Eval, Reduce, RedComb)*, with the following syntax:*

- crs ← Setup(1^λ): *On input the security parameter λ, the probabilistic algorithm* Setup *outputs a common reference string* crs.
- ($\mathsf{pk}_b, \mathsf{sk}_b$) ← KeyGen($b$, crs): *On input party index b and* crs, *the probabilistic algorithm* KeyGen *outputs a public key* pk_b *and secret evaluation key* sk_b.
- pk ← KeyComb(crs, pk_0, pk_1): *On input the* crs *and the distributed public key* (pk_0, pk_1), *the deterministic algorithm* KeyComb *outputs a joint public key* pk.
- ct ← Enc(b, crs, pk, x): *Given the public key* pk, *public parameter* crs, *the party index b and an input $x \in I$, the probabilistic algorithm* Enc *generates a ciphertext* ct.
- t_b ← Eval(b, crs, pk, sk_b, $(b_i, \mathsf{ct}_i)_{i \in [n]}$, f): *On input of the common reference string* crs, *a public key* pk, *a party index b, the corresponding evaluation key* sk_b, *n ciphertexts* ct_i, *each with a bit b_i indicating which party generated the ciphertext, and a function $f \in \mathcal{F}$, the deterministic algorithm* Eval *computes an output share* t_b.
- u_b ← Reduce(b, sk_b, t_b, y): *The probabilistic algorithm* Reduce *uses a secret key* sk_b *to convert a share t_b into a reduced form corresponding to an output value $y \in \mathcal{Y}$.*
- y ← RedComb(u_0, u_1): *The deterministic algorithm* RedComb *outputs an output value y or $\perp$ from two reduced shares u_0, u_1.*

We say that HSS *has* non-interactive share reduction, *if* Reduce(b, sk_b, t_b, y) *is independent of y. In this case, we write* Reduce(b, sk_b, t_b, $\perp$).

Note that this definition is a relaxation of the standard definition of HSS. In particular, we note that at first glance it seems to trivialize the definition to allow the Reduce algorithm to take the *correct* output y as input. Namely, to solely achieve correctness one could define Reduce(b, sk_b, t_b, y) as $u_b := y$ (and ignore the other inputs) and let RedComb(u_0, u_1) return $y := u_0$. If one wants to achieve verifiability, however, this does not suffice: in fact, in this work we show how to use Eval to verify that the output was indeed computed directly.

Further, if the output space $\mathcal{Y}$ is polynomial-sized (e.g., $\mathcal{Y} = \{0, 1\}$), and the HSS scheme satisfies the notion of verifiability defined below, one can derive a reconstruction algorithm which takes as input solely the shares t_0 and t_1 and returns y from Reduce and RedComb as follows: for all possible outputs $\mu \in \mathcal{Y}$, compute u_b^μ ← Reduce(b, sk_b, t_b, μ) for $b \in \{0, 1\}$; if RedComb(u_0^μ, u_1^μ) $= \mu$ for some $\mu \in \mathcal{Y}$ output $y := \mu$, else output $\perp$. While this requires interaction if executed within a larger protocol (e.g., a secure computation), in our instantiations it can be implemented by a simple PSI protocol (and, in particular, with communication that is independent of the circuit size of the function f to be evaluated).

Finally, note that if the scheme supports a Reduce algorithm that does not require taking y as input, then the resulting scheme supports a standard reconstruction algorithm even for large output space. We leave it as interesting open direction to construct malicious HSS with large output space.

The following definition asserts that, in an honest execution, the reconstruction algorithm recovers the output of the function being homomorphically evaluated. This is notably stronger than the usual (non-adaptive) definition of correctness, since we require the condition to hold with overwhelming probability over the randomness of the CRS generation, for all possible inputs and random coins of the other algorithms. In contrast, previous works (such as [18,51]) require only correctness to hold for any input with overwhelming probability over the random coins of all algorithms involved.

Definition 2 (Correctness). *We say* HSS = (Setup, KeyGen, KeyComb, Enc, Eval, Reduce, RedComb) *satisfies* correctness *relative to a function family* $\mathcal{F} = \{f \colon I^n \to \mathcal{Y}\}$ *if there exists a negligible function* negl$\colon \mathbb{N} \to \mathbb{R}_{\geq 0}$ *such that for* crs $\leftarrow$ Setup(1^λ) *the following holds, except with probability* negl(λ) *(taken over the random coins of* Setup*). For all inputs* $x_1, \ldots, x_n \in I$ *and any function* $f \in \mathcal{F}$, *for* $b \in \{0,1\}$, *for all* $(\mathsf{pk}_b, \mathsf{sk}_b)$ *in the image of* KeyGen(b, crs), pk $\leftarrow$ KeyComb$(\mathsf{crs}, \mathsf{pk}_0, \mathsf{pk}_1)$, *for all* ct_i *in the image of* Enc$(b, \mathsf{crs}, \mathsf{pk}, x_i)$ *for* $i \in [n]$, *for all* $t_b \leftarrow$ Eval$(b, \mathsf{sk}_b, (\mathsf{ct}_i)_i, f)$, *and for all* u_b *in the image of* Reduce$(b, \mathsf{sk}_b, t_b, f(x_1, \ldots, x_n))$, *it holds*

$$\mathsf{RedComb}(u_0, u_1) = f(x_1, \ldots, x_n).$$

The next definition describes a very useful property of some HSS schemes, which will be necessary for our main construction in the next section. In Sect. 5 we will look into how this property can be attained.

Definition 3 (HSS with Robust Linear Reconstruction). *We say* HSS *satisfies* robust linear reconstruction *relative to a function family* $\mathcal{F}$ *if there exists a negligible function* $\epsilon \colon \mathbb{N} \to \mathbb{R}_{\geq 0}$ *(called the* correctness error*) such that for* crs $\leftarrow$ Setup(1^λ) *the following holds, except with probability* $\epsilon(\lambda)$ *(taken over the random coins of* Setup*). For all inputs* $x_1, \ldots, x_n \in I$ *and any function* $f \in \mathcal{F}$, *for* $b \in \{0,1\}$, *for all* $(\mathsf{pk}_b, \mathsf{sk}_b)$ *in the image of* KeyGen(b, crs), pk $\leftarrow$ KeyComb$(\mathsf{crs}, \mathsf{pk}_0, \mathsf{pk}_1)$, *and for all* ct_i *in the image of* Enc$(b, \mathsf{crs}, \mathsf{pk}, x_i)$ *for* $i \in [n]$:

- *the first component* $\mathsf{sk}[1]$ *of the vector* $\mathsf{sk} := \mathsf{sk}_0 + \mathsf{sk}_1 \in \mathbb{Z}_q^k$ *is 1;*
- Eval$(0, \mathsf{crs}, \mathsf{pk}, \mathsf{sk}_0, (\mathsf{ct}_i)_i, f) +$ Eval$(1, \mathsf{crs}, \mathsf{pk}, \mathsf{sk}_1, (\mathsf{ct}_i)_i, f) = f(x_1, \ldots, x_n) \cdot \mathsf{sk}$.

We say that an HSS satisfies weakly robust linear reconstruction *relative to a function family* $\mathcal{F}$, *if the above holds with*

- Eval$(0, \mathsf{crs}, \mathsf{pk}, \mathsf{sk}_0, (\mathsf{ct}_i)_i, f) +$ Eval$(1, \mathsf{crs}, \mathsf{pk}, \mathsf{sk}_1, (\mathsf{ct}_i)_i, f) = f(x_1, \ldots, x_n)$.

Observe that robust linear reconstruction implies correctness for the combination algorithm defined in the following way: Reduce$(b, \mathsf{sk}_b, t_b, y)$ simply outputs $u_b := t_b$ and RedComb(u_0, u_1) outputs the first component of the vector $u_0 + u_1 = t_0 + t_1 = f(x_1, \ldots, x_n) \cdot (\mathsf{sk}_0 + \mathsf{sk}_1) = f(x_1, \ldots, x_n)$. We will later show that we can further use the (computational) entropy of sk to verify that the result has indeed been computed correctly.

We move on to the security notions for HSS. First we recall the traditional definition, which states that HSS encryption is semantically secure in the presence of an adversary who has access to the secret key of one (but not both) of the parties. In our setting it can be formulated as follows.

Definition 4 (Security). *We say* HSS *is* secure, *if for any (stateful) PPT adversary $\mathcal{A}$ there exists a negligible function* negl$: \mathbb{N} \to \mathbb{R}_{>0}$ *such that for any $\lambda \in \mathbb{N}$, any $b \in \{0,1\}$, for* crs $\leftarrow$ Setup(1^λ), $(\mathsf{pk}_{1-b}, \mathsf{sk}_{1-b}) \leftarrow$ KeyGen$(1-b, \mathsf{crs})$, $(\mathsf{pk}_b, x_0, x_1) \leftarrow \mathcal{A}(\mathsf{crs}, \mathsf{pk}_{1-b})$ *with* $|x_0| = |x_1|$ *and* pk $\leftarrow$ KeyComb$(\mathsf{crs}, \mathsf{pk}_0, \mathsf{pk}_1)$ *with* pk $\neq \perp$ *it holds*

$$|\Pr[\mathcal{A}(\mathsf{Enc}(1-b, \mathsf{crs}, \mathsf{pk}, x_0)) = 1] - \Pr[\mathcal{A}(\mathsf{Enc}(1-b, \mathsf{crs}, \mathsf{pk}, x_1)) = 1]| \leq \mathsf{negl}(\lambda),$$

where the probability is taken over the random coins of Setup, KeyGen, Enc *and* $\mathcal{A}$.

Next we define what we consider to be a maliciously secure HSS scheme. This notion requires the algorithms Reduce and RedComb and is split into two parts: *reduced share simulatability* and *verifiability*. In the first definition, the adversary is only given control over the key generation of one of the parties and we must be able to simulate a set of ciphertexts and a reduced share from the other party. This property will directly yield zero-knowledge for our DV-NIZK construction in Sect. 6. In the security game of the second definition, the adversary is allowed to freely create ciphertexts and reduced shares for the party it controls and can ask to see ciphertexts from the honest party. The adversary can then use a combination of these on a verification query. The real-world verification oracle returns a reduced share from the honest party only if verification succeeds; in the ideal world, the value of the evaluated function f must be correct and the reduced share is simulated (without knowledge of the honest party's secret key).

We call *malicious HSS* any scheme which satisfies the security properties of both Definitions 5 and 6, in addition to correctness (Definition 2).

<table>
<tr><td>

$\mathsf{Real}^{\mathsf{rss}}_{\mathsf{HSS},\mathcal{A},b,\mathcal{F}}(1^\lambda)$:

crs $\leftarrow$ Setup(1^λ)
$(\mathsf{pk}_{1-b}, \mathsf{sk}_{1-b}) \leftarrow$ KeyGen(crs)
$\beta \leftarrow \mathcal{A}^{\mathcal{O}^0_{\mathsf{share}}}(\mathsf{crs}, \mathsf{pk}_{1-b})$
return β

$\mathcal{O}^0_{\mathsf{share}}(\mathsf{pk}_b, (b_i, x_i)_{i \in [n]}, f)$:

pk $\leftarrow$ KeyComb$(\mathsf{crs}, \mathsf{pk}_0, \mathsf{pk}_1)$
$\mathsf{ct}_i \leftarrow$ Enc$(b_i, \mathsf{crs}, \mathsf{pk}, x_i)$ $\forall i \in [n]$
$t_{1-b} \leftarrow$ Eval$(1 - b, \mathsf{crs}, \mathsf{pk}, \mathsf{sk}_{1-b}, (b_i, \mathsf{ct}_i)_{i \in [n]}, f)$
$u_{1-b} \leftarrow$ Reduce$(1 - b, \mathsf{sk}_{1-b}, t_{1-b}, f(x_1, \ldots, x_n))$
output $((\mathsf{ct}_i)_{i \in [n]}, u_{1-b})$

</td><td>

$\mathsf{Ideal}^{\mathsf{rss}}_{\mathsf{HSS},\mathcal{A},b,\mathcal{F}}(1^\lambda)$:

$(\mathsf{td}, \widehat{\mathsf{crs}}, \widehat{\mathsf{pk}}_{1-b}) \leftarrow$ Sim$_1(1^\lambda)$
$\beta \leftarrow \mathcal{A}^{\mathcal{O}^1_{\mathsf{share}}}(\widehat{\mathsf{crs}}, \widehat{\mathsf{pk}}_{1-b})$
return β

$\mathcal{O}^1_{\mathsf{share}}(\mathsf{pk}_b, (b_i, x_i)_{i \in [n]}, f)$:

$((\mathsf{ct}_i)_{i \in [n]}, \hat{u}_{1-b}) \leftarrow$
Sim$_2(\mathsf{td}, \mathsf{pk}_b, (b_i)_{i \in [n]}, f, f(x_1, \ldots, x_n))$
output $((\mathsf{ct}_i)_{i \in [n]}, \hat{u}_{1-b})$

</td></tr>
</table>

Fig. 1. HSS Reduced share simulatability.

Definition 5 (Reduced share simulatability). *We say an HSS scheme* HSS $=$ (Setup, KeyGen, KeyComb, Enc, Eval, Reduce, RedComb) *satisfies* reduced share simulatability *relative to function class $\mathcal{F}$, if for all $b \in \{0,1\}$ there exists a PPT simulator* Sim $=$ (Sim$_1$, Sim$_2$) *such that for all PPT adversaries $\mathcal{A}$*

$$\left|\Pr\left[\mathsf{Real}^{\mathsf{rss}}_{\mathsf{HSS},\mathcal{A},b,\mathcal{F}}(1^\lambda) = 1\right] - \Pr\left[\mathsf{Ideal}^{\mathsf{rss}}_{\mathsf{HSS},\mathcal{A},b,\mathcal{F}}(1^\lambda) = 1\right]\right| \leq \mathsf{negl}(\lambda),$$

where the experiments are as defined in Fig. 1 and where the probability is taken over the random coins of Setup, KeyGen, Enc, Reduce, Sim *and* $\mathcal{A}$.

$\underline{\mathsf{Real}^{\mathsf{ver}}_{\mathsf{HSS},\mathcal{A},b,\mathcal{F}}(1^\lambda):}$

$Q := \emptyset$
$\mathsf{crs} \leftarrow \mathsf{Setup}(1^\lambda)$
$(\mathsf{pk}_{1-b}, \mathsf{sk}_{1-b}) \leftarrow \mathsf{KeyGen}(\mathsf{crs})$
$\beta \leftarrow \mathcal{A}^{\mathcal{O}^0_{\mathsf{ct}}, \mathcal{O}^0_{\mathsf{ver}}}(\mathsf{crs}, \mathsf{pk}_{1-b})$
return β

$\underline{\mathcal{O}^0_{\mathsf{ct}}(\mathsf{pk}_b, x):}$
$\mathsf{pk} \leftarrow \mathsf{KeyComb}(\mathsf{crs}, \mathsf{pk}_0, \mathsf{pk}_1)$
$\mathsf{ct} \leftarrow \mathsf{Enc}(1 - b, \mathsf{crs}, \mathsf{pk}, x)$
$Q := Q \cup \{(\mathsf{pk}_b, \mathsf{ct})\}$
return ct

$\underline{\mathcal{O}^0_{\mathsf{ver}}(\mathsf{pk}_b, (b_i, \mathsf{ct}_i)_{i \in [n]}, f, y, u_b):}$
$H := \{i \in [n] \mid b_i = 1 - b\}$
if $\exists i \in H \colon (\mathsf{pk}_b, \mathsf{ct}_i) \notin Q$ **output** $\bot$
else:
  $\mathsf{pk} \leftarrow \mathsf{KeyComb}(\mathsf{crs}, \mathsf{pk}_0, \mathsf{pk}_1)$
  $t_{1-b} \leftarrow \mathsf{Eval}(1 - b, \mathsf{crs}, \mathsf{pk}, \mathsf{sk}_{1-b}, (b_i, \mathsf{ct}_i)_{i \in [n]}, f)$
  $u_{1-b} \leftarrow \mathsf{Reduce}(1 - b, \mathsf{sk}_{1-b}, t_{1-b}, y)$
  if $\mathsf{RedComb}(u_0, u_1) \neq y$ **output** $\bot$
  else output u_{1-b}

$\underline{\mathsf{Ideal}^{\mathsf{ver}}_{\mathsf{HSS},\mathcal{A},b,\mathcal{F}}(1^\lambda):}$

$Q := \emptyset$
$(\mathsf{td}, \widehat{\mathsf{crs}}, \widehat{\mathsf{pk}}_{1-b}) \leftarrow \mathsf{Sim}_1(1^\lambda)$
$\beta \leftarrow \mathcal{A}^{\mathcal{O}^1_{\mathsf{ct}}, \mathcal{O}^1_{\mathsf{ver}}}(\widehat{\mathsf{crs}}, \widehat{\mathsf{pk}}_{1-b})$
return β

$\underline{\mathcal{O}^1_{\mathsf{ct}}(\mathsf{pk}_b, x):}$
$\mathsf{ct} \leftarrow \mathsf{Sim}_2(\widehat{\mathsf{crs}}, \widehat{\mathsf{pk}}_{1-b}, \mathsf{pk}_b)$
$Q := Q \cup \{(\mathsf{pk}_b, \mathsf{ct}, x)\}$
return ct

$\underline{\mathcal{O}^1_{\mathsf{ver}}(\mathsf{pk}_b, (b_i, \mathsf{ct}_i)_{i \in [n]}, f, y, u_b):}$
$H := \{i \in [n] \mid b_i = 1 - b\}$
if $\exists i \in H \colon (\mathsf{pk}_b, \mathsf{ct}_i, \cdot) \notin Q$ **output** $\bot$
else:
  for all $i \in H$:
    $x_i := x$ for $(\mathsf{pk}_b, \mathsf{ct}_i, x) \in Q$
  for all $i \in [n] \setminus H$:
    $x_i \leftarrow \mathsf{Sim}_3(\mathsf{td}, \mathsf{pk}_b, \mathsf{ct}_i)$
  $\hat{y} := f(x_1, \dots, x_n)$
  $\hat{u}_{1-b} \leftarrow \mathsf{Sim}_4(\mathsf{td}, \mathsf{pk}_b, (b_i, \mathsf{ct}_i)_{i \in [n]}, f, \hat{y}, u_b)$
  if $\hat{y} \neq y$ **output** $\bot$
  else output $\hat{u}_{1-b}$

Fig. 2. HSS verifiability.

Definition 6 (Verifiability). *We say an HSS scheme* HSS = (Setup, KeyGen, KeyComb, Enc, Eval, Reduce, RedComb) *satisfies* verifiability *relative to function class* $\mathcal{F}$, *if for all* $b \in \{0, 1\}$ *there exists a PPT simulator* Sim = $(\mathsf{Sim}_1, \mathsf{Sim}_2, \mathsf{Sim}_3, \mathsf{Sim}_4)$ *such that for all PPT adversaries* $\mathcal{A}$

$$\left| \Pr\left[\mathsf{Real}^{\mathsf{ver}}_{\mathsf{HSS},\mathcal{A},b,\mathcal{F}}(1^\lambda) = 1\right] - \Pr\left[\mathsf{Ideal}^{\mathsf{ver}}_{\mathsf{HSS},\mathcal{A},b,\mathcal{F}}(1^\lambda) = 1\right] \right| \leq \mathsf{negl}(\lambda),$$

where the experiments are as defined in Fig. 2 and where the probability is taken over the random coins of Setup, KeyGen, Enc, Reduce, Sim *and* $\mathcal{A}$.

We will require a slightly modified version of the verifiability definition for our application to secure 2-party computation. This variant is included in the full version [21].

4   Constructing Malicious HSS

We show how we can obtain an HSS scheme satisfying Definitions 5 and 6 from an HSS satisfying robust linear reconstruction (Definition 3), together with a NIZK proof of knowledge system and a pseudorandom generator (PRG).[16]

Construction 7. *Let $\lambda \in \mathbb{N}$ denote a security parameter. Let $G : \{0,1\}^\lambda \to \{0,1\}^N$ be a PRG, with depth d_G as a boolean circuit. Let $\overline{\mathsf{HSS}}$ be a robust linear HSS scheme, supporting the evaluation of functions computable by polynomial-sized programs of depth up to d'. Let NIZK and NIZK' be non-interactive zero-knowledge proof of knowledge systems for the language families*

$$L_{b,\overline{\mathsf{crs}}} = \{\overline{\mathsf{pk}}_b \mid \exists(\overline{\mathsf{sk}}_b, r) \ such \ that \ (\overline{\mathsf{pk}}_b, \overline{\mathsf{sk}}_b) = \overline{\mathsf{HSS}}.\mathsf{KeyGen}(b, \overline{\mathsf{crs}}; r)\},$$

$$L'_{\overline{\mathsf{crs}}} = \{(\overline{\mathsf{ct}}, \overline{\mathsf{pk}}) \mid \exists(s, r) \ such \ that \ s \in \{0,1\}^\lambda \ and \ \overline{\mathsf{ct}} = \overline{\mathsf{HSS}}.\mathsf{Enc}(\overline{\mathsf{pk}}, s; r)\},$$

respectively. Then, the following construction is an HSS supporting the evaluation of functions f computable by polynomial-sized programs of depth up to $d = d' - d_G$, with one or more inputs in $\{0,1\}^N$ and output in $\{0,1\}$.

- $\mathsf{crs} \leftarrow \mathsf{HSS}.\mathsf{Setup}(1^\lambda)$: *Generate* $\overline{\mathsf{crs}} \leftarrow \overline{\mathsf{HSS}}.\mathsf{Setup}(1^\lambda)$ *and, for* $b = 0, 1$, $\mathsf{crs}^b_{\mathsf{NIZK}} \leftarrow \mathsf{NIZK}.\mathsf{Setup}(\overline{\mathsf{crs}})$, $\mathsf{crs}^b_{\mathsf{NIZK}'} \leftarrow \mathsf{NIZK}'.\mathsf{Setup}(\overline{\mathsf{crs}})$. *Output* $\mathsf{crs} := (\overline{\mathsf{crs}}, \mathsf{crs}^0_{\mathsf{NIZK}}, \mathsf{crs}^1_{\mathsf{NIZK}}, \mathsf{crs}^0_{\mathsf{NIZK}'}, \mathsf{crs}^1_{\mathsf{NIZK}'})$.
- $(\mathsf{pk}_b, \mathsf{sk}_b) \leftarrow \mathsf{HSS}.\mathsf{KeyGen}(b, \mathsf{crs})$: *Parse* $\mathsf{crs} = (\overline{\mathsf{crs}}, \mathsf{crs}^0_{\mathsf{NIZK}}, \mathsf{crs}^1_{\mathsf{NIZK}}, \mathsf{crs}^0_{\mathsf{NIZK}'}, \mathsf{crs}^1_{\mathsf{NIZK}'})$. *Sample* $(\overline{\mathsf{pk}}_b, \overline{\mathsf{sk}}_b) \leftarrow \overline{\mathsf{HSS}}.\mathsf{KeyGen}(b, \overline{\mathsf{crs}}; r)$ *for random* r *and generate* $\pi_b \leftarrow \mathsf{NIZK}.\mathsf{Prove}(\mathsf{crs}^b_{\mathsf{NIZK}}, \overline{\mathsf{pk}}_b, (\overline{\mathsf{sk}}_b, r))$. *Set* $\mathsf{pk}_b := (\overline{\mathsf{pk}}_b, \pi_b)$ *and* $\mathsf{sk}_b := \overline{\mathsf{sk}}_b$ *and output* $(\mathsf{pk}_b, \mathsf{sk}_b)$.
- $\mathsf{pk} \leftarrow \mathsf{HSS}.\mathsf{KeyComb}(\mathsf{crs}, \mathsf{pk}_0, \mathsf{pk}_1)$: *Parse* $\mathsf{crs} = (\overline{\mathsf{crs}}, \mathsf{crs}^0_{\mathsf{NIZK}}, \mathsf{crs}^1_{\mathsf{NIZK}}, \mathsf{crs}^0_{\mathsf{NIZK}'}, \mathsf{crs}^1_{\mathsf{NIZK}'})$. *For* $b \in \{0,1\}$ *parse* $\mathsf{pk} = (\overline{\mathsf{pk}}_b, \pi_b)$ *and let* $\overline{\mathsf{pk}} \leftarrow \overline{\mathsf{HSS}}.\mathsf{KeyComb}(\overline{\mathsf{crs}}, \overline{\mathsf{pk}}_0, \overline{\mathsf{pk}}_1)$. *If* $\mathsf{NIZK}.\mathsf{Verify}(\mathsf{crs}^0_{\mathsf{NIZK}}, \overline{\mathsf{pk}}_0, \pi_0) = \mathsf{NIZK}.\mathsf{Verify}(\mathsf{crs}^1_{\mathsf{NIZK}}, \overline{\mathsf{pk}}_1, \pi_1) = 1$, *output* $\mathsf{pk} := \overline{\mathsf{pk}}$; *otherwise output* $\bot$.
- $\mathsf{ct} \leftarrow \mathsf{HSS}.\mathsf{Enc}(b, \mathsf{crs}, \mathsf{pk}, x)$: *For* $x \in \{0,1\}^N$ *proceed as follows. Parse* $\mathsf{crs} = (\overline{\mathsf{crs}}, \mathsf{crs}^0_{\mathsf{NIZK}}, \mathsf{crs}^1_{\mathsf{NIZK}}, \mathsf{crs}^0_{\mathsf{NIZK}'}, \mathsf{crs}^1_{\mathsf{NIZK}'})$. *Generate a seed* $s \leftarrow_R \{0,1\}^\lambda$, *an HSS encryption* $\overline{\mathsf{ct}} \leftarrow \overline{\mathsf{HSS}}.\mathsf{Enc}(\mathsf{pk}, s; r)$, *and a proof* $\pi \leftarrow \mathsf{NIZK}'.\mathsf{Prove}(\mathsf{crs}^b_{\mathsf{NIZK}'}, (\overline{\mathsf{ct}}, \mathsf{pk}), (s, r))$. *Set a one-time pad encryption* $\mathsf{OTP} := G(s) \oplus x$. *Output* $\mathsf{ct} = (\overline{\mathsf{ct}}, \pi, \mathsf{OTP})$.

- $t_b \leftarrow \mathsf{HSS}.\mathsf{Eval}(b, \mathsf{crs}, \mathsf{pk}, \mathsf{sk}_b, (b_i, \mathsf{ct}_i)_{i \in [n]}, f)$: *Parse* $\mathsf{crs} = (\overline{\mathsf{crs}}, \mathsf{crs}^0_{\mathsf{NIZK}}, \mathsf{crs}^1_{\mathsf{NIZK}}, \mathsf{crs}^0_{\mathsf{NIZK}'}, \mathsf{crs}^1_{\mathsf{NIZK}'})$. *Parse* $\mathsf{ct}_i = (\overline{\mathsf{ct}}_i, \pi_i, \mathsf{OTP}_i)$. *Compute* $t_b \leftarrow \overline{\mathsf{HSS}}.\mathsf{Eval}(b, \overline{\mathsf{crs}}, \overline{\mathsf{pk}}, \overline{\mathsf{sk}}_b, (\overline{\mathsf{ct}}_i)_{i \in [n]}, f')$, *where*

$$f'(s_1, \ldots, s_n) := f(G(s_1) \oplus \mathsf{OTP}_1, \ldots, G(s_n) \oplus \mathsf{OTP}_n).$$

If $\mathsf{NIZK}'.\mathsf{Verify}(\mathsf{crs}^{b_i}_{\mathsf{NIZK}'}, (\overline{\mathsf{ct}}_i, \mathsf{pk}), \pi_i) = 1$ *for all* $i \in [n]$, *output* t_b; *otherwise output* $\bot$.

---

[16] The use of a PRG in this construction is only necessary if we are interested in obtaining compactness; otherwise, it can be simplified by doing away with the "hybrid encryption" technique.

- $u_b \leftarrow \mathsf{HSS.Reduce}(b, \mathsf{sk}_b, t_b, y)$: *Output* $u_b := (y, t_b - y \cdot \mathsf{sk}_b)$.
- $y \leftarrow \mathsf{HSS.RedComb}(u_0, u_1)$: *Parse* $u_b =: (\tilde{y}_b, \tilde{u}_b)$. *If* $y_0 = y_1$ *and* $\tilde{u}_0 + \tilde{u}_1 = 0$, *output* $y := y_0$; *otherwise output* $\perp$.

Correctness. It can easily be checked that this scheme satisfies correctness, as per Definition 2. In fact, letting $y := f'(s_1, \ldots, s_n) = f(x_1, \ldots, x_n)$, for honestly generated shares $u_b := (y, \tilde{u}_b)$ we have $\tilde{u}_b = t_b - y \cdot \mathsf{sk}_b$ for $b \in \{0, 1\}$ and, by the robust linear reconstruction of $\overline{\mathsf{HSS}}$, $t_0 + t_1 = y \cdot (\mathsf{sk}_0 + \mathsf{sk}_1)$. It follows that $\tilde{u}_0 + \tilde{u}_1 = t_0 - y \cdot \mathsf{sk}_0 + t_1 - y \cdot \mathsf{sk}_1 = t_0 + t_1 - y \cdot (\mathsf{sk}_0 + \mathsf{sk}_1) = 0$. Note also that all the intermediate proofs are accepted, by the completeness of NIZK and NIZK'.

Ciphertext Size. HSS has rate-1 ciphertexts, as the size of an encryption of an input x is $|\mathsf{ct}| = |x| + \mathsf{poly}(\lambda)$, independently of the function to be evaluated.

Theorem 8 (Malicious HSS security). *Let $\lambda \in \mathbb{N}$ denote a security parameter. Let $G : \{0, 1\}^\lambda \to \{0, 1\}^N$ be a PRG, with depth d_G as a boolean circuit. Let $\overline{\mathsf{HSS}}$ be a robust linear HSS scheme, supporting the evaluation of functions computable by polynomial-sized programs of depth up to d'. Let NIZK and NIZK' be non-interactive zero-knowledge proof of knowledge systems for the families of languages $L_{b,\overline{\mathsf{crs}}}$ and $L'_{\overline{\mathsf{crs}}}$, respectively, as in Construction 7.*

Then HSS, defined in Construction 7, satisfies reduced share simulatability and verifiability, as per Definitions 5 and 6, while supporting the evaluation of functions f computable by polynomial-sized programs of depth up to $d = d' - d_G$, with one or more inputs in $\{0, 1\}^N$ and output in $\{0, 1\}$.

Proof. We define the simulators required by the security definition of reduced share simulatability.

- $\mathsf{Sim}_1(1^\lambda)$:
  1. Generate $\overline{\mathsf{crs}} \leftarrow \overline{\mathsf{HSS}}.\mathsf{Setup}(1^\lambda)$
  2. $(\mathsf{crs}^\beta_{\mathsf{NIZK}}, \mathsf{td}^\beta_{\mathsf{NIZK}}) \leftarrow \mathsf{NIZK.TSetup}(\overline{\mathsf{crs}})$, $\beta \in \{0, 1\}$
  3. $(\mathsf{crs}^\beta_{\mathsf{NIZK}'}, \mathsf{td}^\beta_{\mathsf{NIZK}'}) \leftarrow \mathsf{NIZK}'.\mathsf{TSetup}(\overline{\mathsf{crs}})$, $\beta \in \{0, 1\}$
  4. $\mathsf{crs} := (\overline{\mathsf{crs}}, \mathsf{crs}^0_{\mathsf{NIZK}}, \mathsf{crs}^1_{\mathsf{NIZK}}, \mathsf{crs}^0_{\mathsf{NIZK}'}, \mathsf{crs}^1_{\mathsf{NIZK}'})$, $\mathsf{td} := (\mathsf{crs}, \mathsf{td}^0_{\mathsf{NIZK}}, \mathsf{td}^1_{\mathsf{NIZK}}, \mathsf{td}^0_{\mathsf{NIZK}'}, \mathsf{td}^1_{\mathsf{NIZK}'})$
  5. $(\overline{\mathsf{pk}}_{1-b}, \overline{\mathsf{sk}}_{1-b}) \leftarrow \overline{\mathsf{HSS}}.\mathsf{KeyGen}(\overline{\mathsf{crs}})$
  6. $\pi_{1-b} \leftarrow \mathsf{NIZK.Sim}(\mathsf{crs}^{1-b}_{\mathsf{NIZK}}, \overline{\mathsf{pk}}_{1-b})$
  7. $\mathsf{pk}_{1-b} := (\overline{\mathsf{pk}}_{1-b}, \pi_{1-b})$
  8. Output $(\mathsf{td}, \mathsf{crs}, \mathsf{pk}_{1-b})$.
- $\mathsf{Sim}_2(\mathsf{td}, \mathsf{pk}_b, (b_i)_{i \in [n]}, f, y)$:
  1. Parse $\mathsf{crs} = (\overline{\mathsf{crs}}, \mathsf{crs}^0_{\mathsf{NIZK}}, \mathsf{crs}^1_{\mathsf{NIZK}}, \mathsf{crs}^0_{\mathsf{NIZK}'}, \mathsf{crs}^1_{\mathsf{NIZK}'})$, $\mathsf{td} = (\mathsf{crs}, \mathsf{td}^0_{\mathsf{NIZK}}, \mathsf{td}^1_{\mathsf{NIZK}}, \mathsf{td}^0_{\mathsf{NIZK}'}, \mathsf{td}^1_{\mathsf{NIZK}'})$
  2. Parse $\mathsf{pk}_b = (\overline{\mathsf{pk}}_b, \pi_b)$
  3. $(\mathsf{sk}_b, r) \leftarrow \mathsf{NIZK.Ext}(\mathsf{crs}^b_{\mathsf{NIZK}}, \mathsf{td}^b_{\mathsf{NIZK}}, \overline{\mathsf{pk}}_b, \pi_b)$
  4. $\mathsf{pk} \leftarrow \mathsf{HSS.KeyComb}(\mathsf{crs}, \mathsf{pk}_{1-b}, \mathsf{pk}_b)$
  5. For $i \in [n]$:

     i. $\overline{\mathsf{ct}}_i \leftarrow \overline{\mathsf{HSS}}.\mathsf{Enc}(\mathsf{pk}, 0^\lambda)$

     ii. $\pi_i \leftarrow \mathsf{NIZK'}.\mathsf{Sim}(\mathsf{crs}_{\mathsf{NIZK'}}^{b_i}, (\overline{\mathsf{ct}}_i, \mathsf{pk}))$

     iii. $\mathsf{ct}_i := (\overline{\mathsf{ct}}_i, \pi_i, \mathsf{OTP}_i)$, where $\mathsf{OTP}_i \leftarrow \{0,1\}^N$

6. $t_b \leftarrow \mathsf{HSS}.\mathsf{Eval}(b, \mathsf{crs}, \mathsf{pk}, \mathsf{sk}_b, (b_i, \mathsf{ct}_i)_{i \in [n]}, f)$

7. $u_{1-b} := (y, y \cdot \mathsf{sk}_b - t_b)$

8. Output $((\mathsf{ct}_i)_{i \in [n]}, u_{1-b})$.

Now we define a sequence of indistinguishable hybrid games.

- **$\mathbf{H}_0$** : This is the real game described in Definition 5, with output as generated by $\beta \leftarrow \mathcal{A}^{\mathcal{O}_{\mathsf{share}}^0(\cdot,\cdot,\cdot)}(\mathsf{crs}, \mathsf{pk}_{1-b})$, where $\mathsf{crs} \leftarrow \mathsf{HSS}.\mathsf{Setup}(1^\lambda)$ and $(\mathsf{pk}_{1-b}, \mathsf{sk}_{1-b}) \leftarrow \mathsf{HSS}.\mathsf{KeyGen}(\mathsf{crs})$.

- **$\mathbf{H}_1$** : In this hybrid we generate the crs as in Sim_1, with $(\mathsf{crs}_{\mathsf{NIZK}}^\beta, \mathsf{td}_{\mathsf{NIZK}}^\beta) \leftarrow \mathsf{NIZK}.\mathsf{TSetup}(\overline{\mathsf{crs}})$ and $(\mathsf{crs}_{\mathsf{NIZK'}}^\beta, \mathsf{td}_{\mathsf{NIZK'}}^\beta) \leftarrow \mathsf{NIZK'}.\mathsf{TSetup}(\overline{\mathsf{crs}})$ for $\beta \in \{0,1\}$. Additionally, we include a simulated proof $\pi_{1-b} \leftarrow \mathsf{NIZK}.\mathsf{Sim}(\mathsf{crs}_{\mathsf{NIZK}}^{1-b}, \overline{\mathsf{pk}}_{1-b})$ in the public key pk, and in the oracle $\mathcal{O}_{\mathsf{share}}(\cdot,\cdot,\cdot)$ we change the proof in the ciphertexts $\mathsf{ct}_i = (\overline{\mathsf{ct}}_i, \pi_i, \mathsf{OTP}_i)$ to be $\pi_i \leftarrow \mathsf{NIZK'}.\mathsf{Sim}(\mathsf{crs}_{\mathsf{NIZK'}}^{b_i}, (\overline{\mathsf{ct}}_i, \mathsf{pk}))$.

- **$\mathbf{H}_2$** : We now change the way in which the reduced share is computed, in the oracle $\mathcal{O}_{\mathsf{share}}^0(\cdot,\cdot,\cdot)$: it is now $u_{1-b} := (y, y \cdot \mathsf{sk}_b - t_b)$, where $t_b \leftarrow \mathsf{HSS}.\mathsf{Eval}(b, \mathsf{crs}, \mathsf{pk}, \mathsf{sk}_b, (b_i, \mathsf{ct}_i)_{i \in [n]}, f)$, $(\mathsf{sk}_b, r) \leftarrow \mathsf{NIZK}.\mathsf{Ext}(\mathsf{crs}_{\mathsf{NIZK}}^b, \mathsf{td}_{\mathsf{NIZK}}^b, \overline{\mathsf{pk}}_b, \pi_b)$ and $y = f(x_1, \ldots, x_n)$.

- For every $0 \le q \le q_{\mathsf{max}}$ and $0 \le i \le n_{\mathsf{max}}$, we define $\mathbf{H}_3^{q,i}$ (where q_{max} and n_{max} are upper bounds on the number of queries to $\mathcal{O}_{\mathsf{share}}$ and the number of inputs x_i in a query, respectively): In this hybrid, all ciphertexts in the first $q-1$ queries and the first i ciphertexts in the q-th query to $\mathcal{O}_{\mathsf{share}}$ are changed. Specifically, they are of the form $c_j = (\overline{c}_j, \pi_j, \mathsf{OTP}_j)$, where we change the components $\overline{c}_j$ and OTP_j to $\overline{c}_j \leftarrow \overline{\mathsf{HSS}}.\mathsf{Enc}(\overline{\mathsf{pk}}, 0^\lambda)$ and $\mathsf{OTP}_j \leftarrow \{0,1\}^N$. We remark that $\mathbf{H}_3^{0,0}$ is identical to $\mathbf{H}_2$ and $\mathbf{H}_3^{q_{\mathsf{max}}, n_{\mathsf{max}}}$ is the ideal-world game of Definition 5.

We show that each hybrid is computationally indistinguishable from the next.

$\mathbf{H}_0 \approx \mathbf{H}_1$: By the mode-indistinguishability property of NIZK and NIZK', the two methods of creating the crs are indistinguishable. Moreover, $\pi_{1-b} \leftarrow \mathsf{NIZK}.\mathsf{Sim}(\mathsf{crs}_{\mathsf{NIZK}}^{1-b}, \overline{\mathsf{pk}}_{1-b})$ is indistinguishable from $\pi_{1-b} \leftarrow \mathsf{NIZK}.\mathsf{Prove}(\mathsf{crs}_{\mathsf{NIZK}}^{1-b}, \overline{\mathsf{pk}}_{1-b}, (\overline{\mathsf{sk}}_{1-b}, r))$ and $\pi_i \leftarrow \mathsf{NIZK'}.\mathsf{Sim}(\mathsf{crs}_{\mathsf{NIZK'}}^{b_i}, (\overline{\mathsf{ct}}_i, \mathsf{pk}))$ is indistinguishable from $\pi_i \leftarrow \mathsf{NIZK'}.\mathsf{Prove}(\mathsf{crs}_{\mathsf{NIZK'}}^{b_i}, (\overline{\mathsf{ct}}_i, \mathsf{pk}), (s_i, r_i))$.

$\mathbf{H}_1 \approx \mathbf{H}_2$: Consider a query $(\mathsf{pk}_b, (b_i, x_i)_{i \in [n]}, f)$ to $\mathcal{O}_{\mathsf{share}}$ and let $y = f(x_1, \ldots, x_n)$. By knowledge soundness of NIZK, the extracted key sk_b is valid: $(\overline{\mathsf{pk}}_b, \mathsf{sk}_b) = \overline{\mathsf{HSS}}.\mathsf{KeyGen}(\mathsf{pp}; r)$ for some randomness r. Therefore, by the robust linear reconstruction property of $\overline{\mathsf{HSS}}$, we have

$$t_b + t_{1-b} = f'(s_1, \ldots, s_n) \cdot (\mathsf{sk}_b + \mathsf{sk}_{1-b}).$$

Since $f'(s_1, \ldots, s_n) = y$, we can rewrite this as

$$t_{1-b} - y \cdot \mathsf{sk}_{1-b} = y \cdot \mathsf{sk}_b - t_b,$$

which shows that $\tilde{u}_{1-b} := t_{1-b} - y \cdot \mathsf{sk}_{1-b}$ (as defined in $\mathbf{H}_1$) and $\tilde{u}_{1-b} := y \cdot \mathsf{sk}_b - t_b$ (as defined in $\mathbf{H}_2$) are identical.

$\mathbf{H}_3^{q,i-1} \approx \mathbf{H}_3^{q,i}$ for all $0 \leq q \leq q_{\mathsf{max}}$, $0 < i \leq n_{\mathsf{max}}$: We introduce an intermediate hybrid $\mathbf{H}'$ in which (for the q-th query) the i-th ciphertext $\mathsf{ct}_i = (\overline{\mathsf{ct}}_i, \pi_i, \mathsf{OTP}_i)$ has its first component changed to $\overline{\mathsf{ct}}_i \leftarrow \overline{\mathsf{HSS}}.\mathsf{Enc}(\overline{\mathsf{pk}}, 0^\lambda)$, this being its only difference from $\mathbf{H}_3^{q,i-1}$, but the last component remains as $\mathsf{OTP}_i = G(s_i) \oplus x_i$ (its only difference from $\mathbf{H}_3^{q,i}$).

We first show that $\mathbf{H}_3^{q,i-1}$ and $\mathbf{H}'$ are indistinguishable through a reduction to the security of $\overline{\mathsf{HSS}}$. Consider a PPT adversary $\mathcal{B}_{q,i}$ which, on input $(\overline{\mathsf{crs}}, \overline{\mathsf{pk}}_{1-b})$, generates $(\mathsf{crs}_{\mathsf{NIZK}}^\beta, \mathsf{td}_{\mathsf{NIZK}}^\beta) \leftarrow \mathsf{NIZK}.\mathsf{TSetup}(\overline{\mathsf{crs}})$ as well as $(\mathsf{crs}_{\mathsf{NIZK}'}^\beta, \mathsf{td}_{\mathsf{NIZK}'}^\beta) \leftarrow \mathsf{NIZK}'.\mathsf{TSetup}(\overline{\mathsf{crs}})$ for $\beta \in \{0,1\}$ and sets $\mathsf{crs} := (\overline{\mathsf{crs}}, \mathsf{crs}_{\mathsf{NIZK}}^0, \mathsf{crs}_{\mathsf{NIZK}}^1, \mathsf{crs}_{\mathsf{NIZK}'}^0, \mathsf{crs}_{\mathsf{NIZK}'}^1)$. Then $\mathcal{B}_{q,i}$ lets $\mathsf{pk}_{1-b} = (\overline{\mathsf{pk}}_{1-b}, \pi_{1-b})$, where $\pi_{1-b} \leftarrow \mathsf{NIZK}.\mathsf{Sim}(\mathsf{crs}_{\mathsf{NIZK}}^{1-b}, \overline{\mathsf{pk}}_{1-b})$, and runs $\beta \leftarrow \mathcal{A}(\mathsf{crs}, \mathsf{pk}_{1-b})$. When $\mathcal{A}$ queries $\mathcal{O}_{\mathsf{share}}$ on some input $(\mathsf{pk}_b, (b_i, x_i)_{i \in [n]}, f)$, $\mathcal{B}_{q,i}$ returns $((c_j)_{j \in [n]}, u_{1-b})$, where u_{1-b} is computed as in $\mathbf{H}_2$ and the ciphertexts $c_j = (\overline{c}_j, \pi_j, \mathsf{OTP}_j)$ are generated as follows.

- If fewer than q queries have been made, or if it is the q-th query and $j < i$, then $\overline{c}_j \leftarrow \mathsf{HSS}.\mathsf{Enc}(\overline{\mathsf{pk}}, 0^\lambda)$; if it is the q-th query and $j = i$, then $\overline{c}_j$ is obtained from the $\overline{\mathsf{HSS}}$ challenger when $\mathcal{B}$ sends the public key and pair of messages $(\overline{\mathsf{pk}}_b, s_i, 0^\lambda)$; otherwise $\overline{c}_j \leftarrow \mathsf{HSS}.\mathsf{Enc}(\overline{\mathsf{pk}}, s_j)$.
- For all queries, $\pi_j \leftarrow \mathsf{NIZK}'.\mathsf{Sim}(\mathsf{crs}_{\mathsf{NIZK}'}^{b_j}, (\overline{c}_j, \mathsf{pk}))$ for all j.
- If fewer than q queries have been made, or if it is the q-th query and $j < i$, then $\mathsf{OTP}_j \leftarrow \{0,1\}^N$; otherwise $\mathsf{OTP}_j := G(s_j) \oplus x_j$.

We define the output of $\mathcal{B}_{q,i}$ as the output of $\mathcal{A}$. Since the view of $\mathcal{A}$ corresponds to $\mathbf{H}_3^{q,i-1}$ if ct_i is an encryption of s_i and to $\mathbf{H}'$ if ct_i is an encryption of 0^λ, the distinguishing advantage of $\mathcal{B}$ is identical to that of $\mathcal{A}$.

We now show that $\mathbf{H}'$ and $\mathbf{H}_3^{q,i}$ are indistinguishable through a reduction to the pseudorandomness of G. We define a PPT adversary $\hat{\mathcal{B}}_{q,i}$, which needs to decide whether its input $\gamma \in \{0,1\}^N$ is the output of G (on a random seed) or a random string. $\hat{\mathcal{B}}_{q,i}$ generates $(\mathsf{td}, \mathsf{crs}, \mathsf{pk}_{1-b})$ (and all variables therein) as specified in Sim_1. Then it runs $\beta \leftarrow \mathcal{A}(\mathsf{crs}, \mathsf{pk}_{1-b})$, simulating $\mathcal{O}_{\mathsf{share}}$ as described next, and outputs β. If $\mathcal{A}$ queries $\mathcal{O}_{\mathsf{share}}(\mathsf{pk}_b, (b_i, x_i)_{i \in [n]}, f)$, then $\hat{\mathcal{B}}_{q,i}$ returns $((c_j)_{j \in [n]}, u_{1-b})$, where u_{1-b} is computed as in $\mathbf{H}_2$ and the ciphertexts $c_j = (\overline{c}_j, \pi_j, \mathsf{OTP}_j)$ are generated as follows.

- If fewer than q queries have been made, or if it is the q-th query and $j \leq i$, then $\overline{c}_j \leftarrow \mathsf{HSS}.\mathsf{Enc}(\overline{\mathsf{pk}}, 0^\lambda)$; otherwise $\overline{c}_j \leftarrow \mathsf{HSS}.\mathsf{Enc}(\overline{\mathsf{pk}}, s_j)$.
- For all queries, $\pi_j \leftarrow \mathsf{NIZK}'.\mathsf{Sim}(\mathsf{crs}_{\mathsf{NIZK}'}^{b_j}, (\overline{c}_j, \mathsf{pk}))$ for all j.
- If fewer than q queries have been made, or if it is the q-th query and $j < i$, then $\mathsf{OTP}_j \leftarrow \{0,1\}^N$; if it is the q-th query and $j = i$, then $\mathsf{OTP}_i := \gamma \oplus x_i$; otherwise $\mathsf{OTP}_j := G(s_j) \oplus x_j$.

Clearly, the output of $\mathcal{A}$ is distributed as in $\mathbf{H}'$ if $\gamma = G(s_i)$ for some $s_i \leftarrow \{0,1\}^\lambda$, and as in $\mathbf{H}_3^{q,i}$ if $\gamma \leftarrow \{0,1\}^N$. Therefore $\hat{\mathcal{B}}_{q,i}$ and $\mathcal{A}$ have the same distinguishing advantage.

The argument above can also be used to show that $\mathbf{H}_3^{q-1,n_{\mathsf{max}}} \approx \mathbf{H}_3^{q,0}$ for all $0 < q \leq q_{\mathsf{max}}$. Overall we have that the distinguishing advantage of $\mathcal{A}$ between $\mathbf{H}_3^{0,0}$ and $\mathbf{H}_3^{q_{\mathsf{max}}, n_{\mathsf{max}}}$ is bounded by

$$q_{\mathsf{max}} \cdot n_{\mathsf{max}} \cdot \max_{q,i} \left\{ \mathsf{Adv}_{\overline{\mathsf{HSS}}, \mathcal{B}_{q,i}}^{\mathsf{hss}}(\lambda) + \mathsf{Adv}_{G, \hat{\mathcal{B}}_{q,i}}^{\mathsf{prg}}(\lambda) \right\},$$

which concludes the proof of reduced share simulatability. We can use a generally similar approach to show that our construction satisfies verifiability. The proof is included in the full version [21].

Remark 9. A verifiable HSS with non-interactive share reduction, as necessary for the secure 2-party computation application, can be obtained by combining the techniques of [1] with the transformation from Sect. 5. We give an outline of the construction in the following. Let $\mathbb{F}$ be a large field and $\mathcal{F} = \{f\colon \mathbb{F}\times\mathbb{F}\to\mathbb{F}\}$ be a function class. Let further HSS have *weakly robust linear reconstruction* (this can be obtained from a standard HSS via NIZKs as above and using the transformation of Sect. 5) for function family $\mathcal{F}' = \{f'_b\colon ((\alpha_0, x_0), (\alpha_1, x_1)) \mapsto (f(x_0, x_1), \alpha_b \cdot f(x_0, x_1)) \mid f \in \mathcal{F}, b \in \{0,1\}\}$. Then, we can obtain a verifiable HSS with non-interactive share reduction for function family $\mathcal{F}$ as follows:

- *Encryption.* Party P_b chooses $\alpha_b \leftarrow \mathbb{F}$ and encrypts (α_b, x_b).
- *Evaluation.* For $\beta \in \{0, 1\}$, party P_b computes shares $t_b^\beta \leftarrow$ HSS.Eval$(b, \mathsf{crs}, \mathsf{pk}, \mathsf{sk}_b, (b, \mathsf{ct}_b)_{b\in\{0,1\}}, f'_\beta)$.
- *Share reduction.* For $\beta \in \{0, 1\}$, party P_b parses $t_b^\beta = (y_b^\beta, z_b^\beta, \hat{t}_b^\beta)$, where $(y_b^\beta, z_b^\beta) \in \mathbb{F}^2$ are the additive output shares, and sends the share (y_b^{1-b}, z_b^{1-b}) to P_{1-b}.[17]
- *Reconstruction.* Party P_b, given $(\alpha_b, (y_0^b, z_0^b), (y_1^b, z_1^b))$, outputs $y := y_0^b + y_1^b$ if $z_0^b + z_1^b = \alpha_b \cdot y$ and $\perp$ otherwise.

5   Towards Robust Linear HSS

The starting point for our construction of a malicious HSS scheme in the previous section was a notion we called robust linear reconstruction (Definition 3). In this section we will show how this property can be obtained, namely from standard HSS or from homomorphic encryption.

5.1   From Standard HSS

We start by giving an intermediary definition of HSS with *non-adaptive robust linear reconstruction*, which more closely captures the standard non-adaptive notion of correctness (except that the reconstruction is required to have a specific structure). [18]

Definition 10 (HSS with Non-Adaptive Robust Linear Reconstruction). *We say a scheme* HSS $=$ (Setup, KeyGen, KeyComb, Enc, Eval) *satisfies* non-adaptive robust linear reconstruction *relative to a function family $\mathcal{F}$ if there*

---

[17] This step does not require knowledge of the output and can thus be written in the form Reduce$(b, \mathsf{sk}_b, t_b, \perp)$.

[18] See the full version [21] for a look at how some HSS schemes in the literature fit into this framework.

exists a negligible function $\epsilon \colon \mathbb{N} \to \mathbb{R}_{\geq 0}$ *(called the* correctness error*) such that for any (fixed) inputs* $x_1, \ldots, x_n \in I$ *and function* $f \in \mathcal{F}$, *for* $b \in \{0, 1\}$, *for* $\mathsf{crs} \leftarrow \mathsf{Setup}(1^\lambda)$, $(\mathsf{pk}_b, \mathsf{sk}_b) \leftarrow \mathsf{KeyGen}(b, \mathsf{crs})$, $\mathsf{pk} \leftarrow \mathsf{KeyComb}(\mathsf{crs}, \mathsf{pk}_0, \mathsf{pk}_1)$, *and for* $\mathsf{ct}_i \leftarrow \mathsf{Enc}(\mathsf{pk}, x_i)$ *for* $i \in [n]$:

- *the first component* $\mathsf{sk}[1]$ *of the vector* $\mathsf{sk} := \mathsf{sk}_0 + \mathsf{sk}_1 \in \mathbb{Z}_q^k$ *is 1;*
- $\mathsf{Eval}(0, \mathsf{crs}, \mathsf{pk}, \mathsf{sk}_0, (\mathsf{ct}_i)_i, f) + \mathsf{Eval}(1, \mathsf{crs}, \mathsf{pk}, \mathsf{sk}_1, (\mathsf{ct}_i)_i, f) = f(x_1, \ldots, x_n) \cdot \mathsf{sk}$,

except with probability $\epsilon(\lambda)$ *taken over the random coins of* Setup, KeyGen *and* Enc.

We say that an HSS *satisfies* weakly non-adaptive robust linear reconstruction *relative to a function family* $\mathcal{F}$, *if the above holds with*

- $\mathsf{Eval}(0, \mathsf{crs}, \mathsf{pk}, \mathsf{sk}_0, (\mathsf{ct}_i)_i, f) + \mathsf{Eval}(1, \mathsf{crs}, \mathsf{pk}, \mathsf{sk}_1, (\mathsf{ct}_i)_i, f) = f(x_1, \ldots, x_n).$

We now present our transformation from non-adaptive to adaptive correctness, based on techniques from [38]. Note that we impose a strong requirement on the correctness error of the HSS from which we start. To achieve this, the HSS parameters will typically scale (logarithmically) with the size of the input and function spaces. This is a problem as, by the compactness requirement of HSS, shares should be independent of the size $|f|$ (measured in number of operations) of the function to be evaluated and for typical function classes we have $|f| \approx \log |\mathcal{F}|$. One way to mitigate this drawback is to restrict the function class; at best, one can remove the dependency on $|\mathcal{F}|$ by considering evaluation of a polynomially-large class of functions, independent of $|f|$, which is typically not an issue in applications, as in many settings the computation to be performed is fixed or agreed upon before the parties set up the parameters. The below transformation therefore only gives an HSS with compactness for *small* function classes $\mathcal{F}$.

Theorem 11. *Let* HSS *be a scheme that satisfies (weakly) non-adaptive linear reconstruction relative to function family* $\mathcal{F}$ *and input space* I *with correctness error* $\epsilon(\lambda) \leq 2^{-4\lambda - \log|\mathcal{F}| - n(\log|I| + \lambda)}$, *and where* KeyGen *and* Enc *take at most* $\ell(\lambda)$ *random coins as input. Let* $G \colon \{0,1\}^\lambda \to \{0,1\}^{\ell(\lambda)}$ *be a secure pseudorandom generator. Then, there exists a (stateful)* HSS *scheme* HSS' *with (weakly) robust linear reconstruction relative to* $\mathcal{F}$ *(as per Definition 3).*

Proof. Without loss of generality we can assume that the algorithms KeyGen and Enc take exactly $\ell(\lambda)$ random coins (as they can ignore any additional ones). We construct HSS as follows (where we only state changed algorithms):

- $\mathsf{Setup}'(1^\lambda)$: Run $\mathsf{crs} \leftarrow \mathsf{Setup}(1^\lambda)$. Generate $R_0, R_1, r_1, \ldots, r_n \leftarrow \{0,1\}^{\ell(\lambda)}$. Output $\mathsf{crs}' := (\mathsf{crs}, R_0, R_1, r_1, \ldots, r_n)$.
- $\mathsf{KeyGen}'(b, \mathsf{crs})$: Parse $\mathsf{crs}' =: (\mathsf{crs}, R_0, R_1, r_1, \ldots, r_n)$. Sample $S_b \leftarrow \{0,1\}^\lambda$. Generate $(\mathsf{pk}, \mathsf{sk}) \leftarrow \mathsf{KeyGen}(\mathsf{crs}; G(S_b) \oplus R_b)$.
- $\mathsf{Enc}'(b, \mathsf{crs}, \mathsf{pk}, x_i)$: Parse $\mathsf{crs}' =: (\mathsf{crs}, R_0, R_1, r_1, \ldots, r_n)$. Sample $s_i \leftarrow \{0,1\}^\lambda$. Generate $\mathsf{ct} \leftarrow \mathsf{Enc}(b, \mathsf{crs}, \mathsf{pk}, x_i; G(s_i) \oplus r_i)$.

It is straightforward to see this transformation does not affect security guarantees of the HSS, as an attacker on the security of HSS' could be transformed into either an attacker on the pseudorandomness of G or the security of HSS. It is left to show that HSS' indeed satisfies robust linear reconstruction as required. First, note that, for any fixed function $f \in \mathcal{F}$ and inputs $x_1, \ldots, x_n \in I$, a correctness error in HSS with probability more than $2^\lambda \cdot \epsilon(\lambda)$ can occur for at most a $2^{-\lambda}$ fraction of the setup parameters crs (as otherwise the scheme would have a higher correctness error overall). For the remaining "good" setup parameters crs the error probability is at most $2^\lambda \cdot \epsilon(\lambda)$, where the probability is taken over the randomness of KeyGen and Enc. Now, taking a union bound over all random strings $S_0, S_1, s_1, \ldots, s_n \in \{0,1\}^\lambda$ and all possible inputs $x_1, \ldots, x_n \in I$ and functions $f \in \mathcal{F}$ (this is necessary since which random strings cause an error may depend on the inputs and function being evaluated), we obtain that a correctness error on *any* input for *any* randomness occurs in HSS' at most with probability $2^\lambda \cdot \epsilon(\lambda) \cdot 2^{2\lambda + \log |\mathcal{F}| + n \cdot (\log |I| + \lambda)} \leq 2^{-\lambda}$. We thus obtain that HSS' satisfies robust linear reconstruction (with error probability $2^{-\lambda+1}$ over the choice of the setup).

5.2   From Homomorphic Encryption

In this section we will explain how we can use a (leveled) homomorphic encryption scheme to obtain malicious HSS. To that end, we define the *special nearly linear decryption property* of LHE. For instance, the GSW scheme [42] can be adapted to fit into our framework and satisfy this property. We describe in more detail how that can be done in the full version [21].

Definition 12 (Special nearly linear decryption). *We say* $\mathsf{HE} = ($Setup, KeyGen, KeyComb, Enc, Eval, Dec$)$ *has* (d, k, p, q, B)*-special nearly linear decryption if for all* $\lambda \in \mathbb{N}$*, for all public parameters* $\mathsf{pp} \leftarrow \mathsf{Setup}(1^\lambda, 1^d)$*, for all key pairs* $(\mathsf{pk}_b, \mathsf{sk}_b) \leftarrow \mathsf{KeyGen}(b, \mathsf{pp})$*, for all public keys* $\mathsf{pk} \leftarrow \mathsf{KeyComb}(\mathsf{pp}, \mathsf{pk}_0, \mathsf{pk}_1)$*, for all inputs* $x_1, \ldots, x_\ell \in \{0,1\}$*, for all encryptions* $\mathsf{ct}_i \leftarrow \mathsf{Enc}(\mathsf{pk}, x_i)$ *of* x_i*, for arbitrary polynomial-sized circuits* $C \colon \{0,1\}^\ell \to \{0,1\}$ *of depth at most* d*, and all ciphertexts* $\mathsf{ct}' \leftarrow \mathsf{Eval}(\mathsf{pk}, \mathsf{ct}_1, \ldots, \mathsf{ct}_\ell, C)$ *it holds that:*

- *the first component of the vector* $\mathsf{sk} := \mathsf{sk}_0 + \mathsf{sk}_1 \in \mathbb{Z}_q^k$ *is 1;*
- $\mathsf{ct}' \in \mathbb{Z}_q^{k \times k}$*;*
- $\mathsf{sk}^\top \cdot \mathsf{ct}' = \frac{q}{p} \cdot C(x_1, \ldots, x_\ell) \cdot \mathsf{sk} + e \mod q$ *for some error vector* $e \in \mathbb{Z}_q^k$ *which is bounded by* $\|e\|_\infty \leq B$*.*

Note that if the scheme satisfies (d, k, p, q, B)-special nearly linear decryption for small enough B (namely, $B < \frac{q}{2p}$), then it satisfies perfect correctness for all circuits C of depth at most d, as one can obtain $C(x)$ by rounding the first entry of the vector $\mathsf{ct}' \cdot \mathsf{sk}$ to the closest multiple of q/p.

Since we have at our disposal LHE schemes with perfect correctness, we do not need to use the techniques of the previous section to prevent a malicious adversary from exploiting correctness errors. On the other hand, due to the small noise present when decrypting an LHE ciphertext we cannot achieve robust linear reconstruction exactly as stated in Definition 3 – we get only an approximate equality in the last equation of the definition – and for that reason we cannot apply the results from Sect. 4 directly. The transformation from LHE with special nearly linear decryption into HSS with this "approximate" robust linear reconstruction is actually very straightforward: the HSS algorithms Setup, KeyGen, KeyComb, Enc are identical to those of LHE, and the evaluation algorithm is defined as follows.

- Eval$(b, \mathsf{crs}, \mathsf{pk}, \mathsf{sk}_b, (b_i, \mathsf{ct}_i)_{i \in [n]}, C)$: Compute $\overline{\mathsf{ct}}' \leftarrow$ HE.Eval$((\overline{\mathsf{ct}}_1, \ldots, \overline{\mathsf{ct}}_\ell), C)$ and output $t_b := \overline{\mathsf{ct}}' \cdot \mathsf{sk}_b$.

Using similar techniques as described in Sect. 4, this can be converted into a malicious HSS scheme. We leave the construction to the full version of this paper [21].

6 Applications

In this section, we outline applications of malicious HSS to DV-NIZK and malicious secure computation.

6.1 Designated-Verifier NIZK

In this section we show how the HSS properties can be leveraged to create a designated-verifier NIZK scheme. Given that our construction of malicious HSS in this work employs itself a proof system (specifically, a NIZK proof of knowledge), it may seem odd to use such an HSS to construct a DV-NIZK. The main benefit of this approach is that we are able to obtain a *compact* DV-NIZK, even if the underlying NIZK proof of knowledge is not compact. We note also that for this application the aforementioned NIZK proof of knowledge in the preprocessing (CRS) model can be replaced by one in the designated-verifier model in a straightforward manner, though this requires weakening our definition of malicious zero-knowledge (which allows the verifier to generate a public key) to one where the public key is honestly generated during setup (as part of the CRS).[19] We thus obtain a transformation from DV-NIZK to compact DV-NIZK. We present below our DV-NIZK scheme, built directly from malicious HSS.

Construction 13. *Fix a security parameter λ and consider the following.*

- *Let $\mathcal{R} : \{0,1\}^n \times \{0,1\}^m \to \{0,1\}$ be an NP relation.*
- *Given $\mathcal{R}$, define the function f_x as $f_x(w) := \mathcal{R}(x, w)$ for $x \in \{0,1\}^n$.*
- *Let* HSS $=$ (Setup, KeyGen, KeyComb, Enc, Eval, Reduce, RedComb) *be a homomorphic secret sharing scheme for the function class $\mathcal{F}_\mathcal{R} := \{f_x : x \in \{0,1\}^n\}$.*

---

[19] In this setting, only party P_0 (the prover) needs to provide proofs of proper key and ciphertext generation; the other party can be a designated verifier for these proofs.

The dvNIZK *is constructed as follows.*

- crs $\leftarrow$ dvNIZK.Setup(1^λ): *Generate* crs$_{\mathsf{HSS}}$ $\leftarrow$ HSS.Setup(1^λ) *and output* crs := crs$_{\mathsf{HSS}}$.
- (pk, sk) $\leftarrow$ dvNIZK.KeyGen(crs): *Output* (pk$_1$, sk$_1$) $\leftarrow$ HSS.KeyGen(1, crs$_{\mathsf{HSS}}$).
- π $\leftarrow$ dvNIZK.Prove(crs, pk, x, w): *Let* pk$_1$:= pk. *Sample* (sk$_0$, pk$_0$) $\leftarrow$ HSS.KeyGen(0, crs$_{\mathsf{HSS}}$) *and let* pk$_{\mathsf{HSS}}$ $\leftarrow$ HSS.KeyComb(crs$_{\mathsf{HSS}}$, pk$_0$, pk$_1$). *Next, encrypt the witness as* ct $\leftarrow$ HSS.Enc(0, crs$_{\mathsf{HSS}}$, pk$_{\mathsf{HSS}}$, w). *Evaluate* t_0 $\leftarrow$ HSS.Eval(0, crs$_{\mathsf{HSS}}$, pk$_{\mathsf{HSS}}$, sk$_0$, (0, ct), f_x) *and let* u_0 $\leftarrow$ HSS.Reduce(0, sk$_0$, t_0, 1). *Output the proof*

$$\pi := (\mathsf{pk}_0, \mathsf{ct}, u_0).$$

- dvNIZK.Verify(crs, sk, x, π): *Parse* pk =: pk$_1$, sk =: sk$_1$, π =: (pk$_0$, ct, u_0) *and set the public key* pk$_{\mathsf{HSS}}$ $\leftarrow$ HSS.KeyComb(crs$_{\mathsf{HSS}}$, pk$_0$, pk$_1$). *Compute* t_1 $\leftarrow$ HSS.Eval(1, crs$_{\mathsf{HSS}}$, pk$_{\mathsf{HSS}}$, sk$_1$, (0, ct), f_x) *and* u_1 $\leftarrow$ HSS.Reduce(1, sk$_1$, t_1, 1). *Finally, output* 1 *if* HSS.RedComb(u_0, u_1) = 1 *and* 0 *otherwise.*

Proof Length. If HSS has rate 1, then so does dvNIZK. Indeed, for a proof $\pi = (\mathsf{pk}_0, \mathsf{ct}, u_0)$, we have $|\mathsf{pk}_0| = \mathsf{poly}(\lambda)$, $|u_0| = \mathsf{poly}(\lambda)$ and $|\mathsf{ct}| = |w| + \mathsf{poly}(\lambda)$. Hence the total proof length is $|w| + \mathsf{poly}(\lambda)$.

Theorem 14. *Let $\mathcal{R}$ be an NP relation and* HSS *a malicious homomorphic secret sharing scheme (as per Definitions 2, 5 and 6) for the function family $\mathcal{F}_{\mathcal{R}}$. Then* dvNIZK *is a secure designated-verifier non-interactive zero-knowledge proof system for $\mathcal{R}$.*

Proof (Completeness). Assume $(\mathsf{pk}_0, \mathsf{ct}, u_0)$ is an honest proof for $(x, w) \in \mathcal{R}$. Then an honest verifier will always accept, since both shares are reduced with respect to the value $1 = f_x(w)$ and thus, by the correctness of HSS, we have HSS.RedComb(u_0, u_1) = 1.

Proof (Soundness). In order to prove (restricted) soundness, we consider the following games. Let $x \notin \mathcal{L}$ and suppose an adversary $\mathcal{A}$ breaks the soundness of dvNIZK.

- $\mathbf{H}_0$: This is the real game of the soundness definition, which can be described as follows.
    1. Sample crs$_{\mathsf{HSS}}$ $\leftarrow$ HSS.Setup(1^λ) and (sk$_1$, pk$_1$) $\leftarrow$ HSS.KeyGen(1, crs$_{\mathsf{HSS}}$), let crs := crs$_{\mathsf{HSS}}$, sk := sk$_1$, and send (crs$_{\mathsf{HSS}}$, pk$_1$) to $\mathcal{A}$.
    2. $\mathcal{A}$ makes a polynomial number of verification queries. Given a query (x, π), the challenger answers the query with dvNIZK.Verify(crs, sk, x, π). In particular, for a proof $\pi = (\mathsf{pk}_0, \mathsf{ct}, u_0)$, the challenger computes t_1 $\leftarrow$ HSS.Eval(1, sk$_1$, ct, f_x), u_1 $\leftarrow$ HSS.Reduce(1, sk$_1$, t_1, 1) and outputs 1 if HSS.RedComb(u_0, u_1) = 1 and 0 otherwise.
    3. After the queries, $\mathcal{A}$ outputs π^* and $\mathcal{A}$ wins if Verify(crs, sk, x, π^*) = 1.
- $\mathbf{H}_1$: In this game we use some of the simulators from Definition 6.

1. First, generate $(\mathsf{td}_{\mathsf{HSS}}, \mathsf{crs}_{\mathsf{HSS}}) \leftarrow \mathsf{Sim}_{\mathsf{HSS},1}(1^\lambda)$ and $(\mathsf{sk}_1, \mathsf{pk}_1) \leftarrow \mathsf{HSS.KeyGen}(1, \mathsf{crs}_{\mathsf{HSS}})$, $\mathsf{crs} := \mathsf{crs}_{\mathsf{HSS}}$, $\mathsf{sk} := \mathsf{sk}_1$, and send $(\mathsf{crs}_{\mathsf{HSS}}, \mathsf{pk}_1)$ to $\mathcal{A}$.
2. $\mathcal{A}$ makes a polynomial number of verification queries. Given a query (x, π), the challenger answers the query with $\overline{\mathsf{Verify}}(\mathsf{crs}, \mathsf{sk}, x, \pi)$, where $\overline{\mathsf{Verify}}$ is defined as follows: compute $w \leftarrow \mathsf{Sim}_{\mathsf{HSS},4}(\mathsf{td}_{\mathsf{HSS}}, \mathsf{pk}_0, \mathsf{ct})$ and accept if and only if $f_x(w) = 1$.
3. After the queries, $\mathcal{A}$ outputs π^*. We say $\mathcal{A}$ wins if $\overline{\mathsf{Verify}}(\mathsf{crs}, \mathsf{sk}, x, \pi^*) = 1$.

We will use the verifiability property of HSS to show that the difference in the success probability of $\mathcal{A}$ from $\mathbf{H}_0$ to $\mathbf{H}_1$ is negligible. Consider the following HSS adversary $\mathcal{B}$, which attempts to distinguish $\mathsf{Real}^{\mathsf{ver}}_{\mathsf{HSS},\mathcal{B},0,f_x}(1^\lambda)$ from $\mathsf{Ideal}^{\mathsf{ver}}_{\mathsf{HSS},\mathcal{B},0,f_x}(1^\lambda)$. $\mathcal{B}$ is given input $(\mathsf{crs}_{\mathsf{HSS}}, \mathsf{pk}_1)$ and access to oracles $\mathcal{O}_{\mathsf{ct}}$, $\mathcal{O}_{\mathsf{eval}}$. $\mathcal{B}$ runs $\mathcal{A}$ on input $\mathsf{crs}_{\mathsf{HSS}}$, answering the verification queries of $\mathcal{A}$ as follows: on query (x, π), where $\pi = (\mathsf{pk}_0, \mathsf{ct}, u_0)$, query $u_1 \leftarrow \mathcal{O}_{\mathsf{eval}}(\mathsf{pk}_0, (0, \mathsf{ct}), 1, u_0)$ and output 1 if $u_1 \neq \perp$. When $\mathcal{A}$ outputs π^*, $\mathcal{B}$ similarly queries $u_1 \leftarrow \mathcal{O}_{\mathsf{eval}}(\mathsf{pk}_0, (0, \mathsf{ct}), 1, u_0)$ and outputs 1 if $u_1 \neq \perp$ and 0 otherwise.

Observe that in the real-world HSS experiment $\mathcal{B}$ simulates the view of $\mathcal{A}$ in $\mathbf{H}_0$, while in the ideal-world experiment it simulates the view of $\mathcal{A}$ in $\mathbf{H}_1$. Moreover, in both experiments $\mathcal{B}$ outputs 1 if and only if $\mathcal{A}$ wins its respective game. It follows that the difference in success probability between $\mathbf{H}_0$ and $\mathbf{H}_1$ is negligible.

Now, to complete the proof, we show that $\mathcal{A}$ has success probability 0 in $\mathbf{H}_1$. Suppose, by contradiction, that $\mathcal{A}$ outputs π^* such that $\overline{\mathsf{Verify}}(\mathsf{crs}, \mathsf{sk}, x, \pi^*) = 1$. Let $\pi^* = (\mathsf{pk}_0, \mathsf{ct}, u_0)$ and $w^* \leftarrow \mathsf{Sim}_{\mathsf{HSS},4}(\mathsf{td}_{\mathsf{HSS}}, \mathsf{pk}_0, \mathsf{ct})$. Then $1 = f_x(w^*) = \mathcal{R}(x, w^*)$, contradicting the assumption that $x \notin \mathcal{L}$.

Proof (Zero knowledge). From the reduced share simulatability of HSS, there exist simulators $\mathsf{Sim}_{\mathsf{HSS},1}$, $\mathsf{Sim}_{\mathsf{HSS},2}$ as in Definition 5. We construct the two dvNIZK simulators as follows.

- $\mathsf{Sim}_{\mathsf{dvNIZK},1}(1^\lambda)$: Run $(\mathsf{td}_{\mathsf{HSS}}, \mathsf{crs}_{\mathsf{HSS}}, \mathsf{pk}_0) \leftarrow \mathsf{Sim}_{\mathsf{HSS},1}(1^\lambda)$ and output

$$\mathsf{td} := (\mathsf{td}_{\mathsf{HSS}}, \mathsf{pk}_0), \quad \mathsf{crs} := \mathsf{crs}_{\mathsf{HSS}}.$$

- $\mathsf{Sim}_{\mathsf{dvNIZK},2}(\mathsf{td}, \mathsf{crs}, \mathsf{pk}, x)$: Parse $\mathsf{td} = (\mathsf{td}_{\mathsf{HSS}}, \mathsf{pk}_0)$ and let $\mathsf{pk}_1 := \mathsf{pk}$. Compute $(\mathsf{ct}, u_0) \leftarrow \mathsf{Sim}_{\mathsf{HSS},2}(\mathsf{td}_{\mathsf{HSS}}, \mathsf{pk}_1, 0, f_x, 1)$. Output $\pi := (\mathsf{pk}_0, \mathsf{ct}, u_0)$.

The result now follows from Definition 5, through the following reduction. Let $\mathcal{A}$ be an adversary on the malicious zero-knowledge property of dvNIZK. We define an adversary $\mathcal{B}$ which distinguishes the distributions $\mathsf{Real}^{\mathsf{rss}}_{\mathsf{HSS},\mathcal{A},1,\mathcal{F}}(1^\lambda)$ and $\mathsf{Ideal}^{\mathsf{rss}}_{\mathsf{HSS},\mathcal{A},1,\mathcal{F}}(1^\lambda)$. On input $(\mathsf{crs}, \mathsf{pk}_0)$, $\mathcal{B}$ runs $\mathcal{A}(\mathsf{crs})$, simulating its oracle as follows. On a query (pk, x, w), $\mathcal{B}$ lets $\mathsf{pk}_1 := \mathsf{pk}$ and queries its own oracle on $(\mathsf{pk}_1, (0, w), f_x)$. The oracle outputs (ct, u_0) and $\mathcal{B}$ returns $\pi := (\mathsf{pk}_0, \mathsf{ct}, u_0)$ to $\mathcal{A}$. The output of $\mathcal{B}$ is the output bit of $\mathcal{A}$. Since $\mathcal{B}$ perfectly simulates either the oracle $\mathcal{O}_0$ (in the real experiment) or $\mathcal{O}_1$ (in the ideal experiment), the distinguishing advantage of $\mathcal{A}$ is equal to that of $\mathcal{B}$ and therefore negligible.

The above result gives a rate-1 DV-NIZK from rate-1 malicious HSS. Unfortunately, this is not something we are able to achieve from standard assumptions since, as discussed before, our transformation from HSS with non-adaptive to adaptive linear reconstruction has an overhead which scales with the size of the function and input spaces. What we do achieve by putting together our results from Sects. 4, 5, and 6 is the following theorem. Note that here we do not require any compactness properties from the underlying HSS and NIZK and that an HSS scheme with the properties mentioned below can be constructed from the LWE or DCR assumptions if the function class is contained in NC1 (see Appendix D in the full version [21]).[20]

Theorem 15. *Let $\mathcal{R}$ be an NP relation. If there exist an HSS with non-adaptive robust linear reconstruction for $\mathcal{F}_{\mathcal{R}}$ and NIZK proof-of-knowledge systems for the language families L, L' (cf. Construction 7), then there exists a compact DV-NIZK proof system for $\mathcal{R}$.*

6.2   Secure 2-Party Computation

In this section, we construct a maliciously secure two-party computation (2PC) protocol from malicious HSS. Our protocol requires a total of 3 rounds of communication in the standard model (using a CRS).

We consider an adversary who is computationally bounded, malicious (it may instruct a corrupted party to deviate from the protocol) and who may corrupt one of the two parties. We prove that our protocol securely realizes the 2-party function evaluation functionality $\mathcal{F}_{2PC}$. We formalize it with the assumption that both parties should learn the output of the function evaluation, but the adversary has the ability to selectively abort the protocol, preventing the honest party from receiving the output.[21]

Instantiating with an HSS scheme for NC1 programs with compact shares, the communication complexity of our protocol is $\mathsf{poly}(\lambda) \cdot \log |\mathbb{F}|$, independently of the program size (Fig. 3).

This protocol has *reusable setup*, in the sense that the first step of the protocol (key generation) is independent of the private inputs x_0, x_1 and the same setup can be reused for multiple different inputs (and multiple functions f, if this is supported by the HSS). We note that HSS with interactive share reduction can also used for the purpose of constructing 2-party computation, at the cost of an extra round in the end (as exchanging shares is only safe if the result indeed verifies, and has therefore to be performed within a secure computation).

Theorem 16. *Let $\mathbb{F}$ be a field, $\mathcal{F} = \{f\colon \mathbb{F} \times \mathbb{F} \to \mathbb{F}\}$ a family of functions, and $\mathsf{HSS} = (\mathsf{Setup}, \mathsf{KeyGen}, \mathsf{KeyComb}, \mathsf{Enc}, \mathsf{Eval}, \mathsf{Reduce}, \mathsf{RedComb})$ a malicious homomorphic secret sharing scheme* with simulatable non-interactive share

---

[20] We simplify the result by removing the hybrid encryption step (i.e. the use of a PRG) from the malicious HSS construction from Sect. 4, which is no longer necessary.

[21] We describe the functionalities $\mathcal{F}_{2PC}$ in the case of one corruption. If no party is corrupted, then $\mathcal{F}_{2PC}$ outputs y to both parties.

Parameters: A security parameter $\lambda \in \mathbb{N}$, a function $f \colon \mathbb{F} \times \mathbb{F} \to \mathbb{F}$.

Input phase: The uncorrupted party P_{1-b} provides input $x_{1-b} \in \mathbb{F}$, while the adversary chooses the input $x_b \in \mathbb{F}$ of the corrupted party P_b.

Computation phase: The functionality computes $y := f(x_0, x_1)$.

Selective abort: The adversary receives y and returns either 'continue' or 'abort'.

Output phase: In the case of 'continue', the uncorrupted party P_{1-b} receives and outputs y; in the case of 'abort', P_{1-b} outputs $\perp$. The corrupted party P_b outputs $\perp$ and the adversary has some arbitrary output.

Fig. 3. Functionality $\mathcal{F}_{2\mathsf{PC}}$

The common reference string is $\mathsf{crs} \leftarrow \mathsf{HSS.Setup}(1^\lambda)$.

- Party P_b generates $(\mathsf{pk}_b, \mathsf{sk}_b) \leftarrow \mathsf{HSS.KeyGen}(b, \mathsf{crs})$ and sends pk_b to the other party. Both parties set $\mathsf{pk} \leftarrow \mathsf{KeyComb}(\mathsf{crs}, \mathsf{pk}_0, \mathsf{pk}_1)$ as the joint public key.
- Party P_b encrypts their input x_b as $\mathsf{ct}_b \leftarrow \mathsf{HSS.Enc}(b, \mathsf{crs}, \mathsf{pk}, x_b)$ and sends ct_b to the other party.
- Party P_b locally evaluates $t_b \leftarrow \mathsf{HSS.Eval}(b, \mathsf{crs}, \mathsf{pk}, \mathsf{sk}_b, (b, \mathsf{ct}_b)_{b \in \{0,1\}}, f)$, computes $u_b \leftarrow \mathsf{HSS.Reduce}(b, \mathsf{sk}_b, t_b, \perp)$ and sends u_b to party P_{1-b}.
- Party P_b on receiving u_{1-b} computes $y \leftarrow \mathsf{RedComb}(u_0, u_1)$ and outputs y.

Fig. 4. Protocol for maliciously secure 2-party computation

reduction *relative to $\mathcal{F}$.*[22] *Then, the protocol from Fig. 4 securely realizes functionality $\mathcal{F}_{2\mathsf{PC}}$ against a malicious PPT adversary who corrupts at most one party. Further, the setup can be reused for an arbitrary number of evaluations.*

Proof. Let $\mathcal{A}$ be a (stateful, rushing) real-world adversary which corrupts party P_b for some $b \in \{0, 1\}$. Let $(\mathsf{Sim}_1, \mathsf{Sim}_2, \mathsf{Sim}_3, \mathsf{Sim}_4)$ be the simulator from the HSS security definition. We define an ideal-world adversary $\mathcal{S}$ as follows.

1. $\mathcal{S}$ runs $(\mathsf{td}, \mathsf{crs}, \mathsf{pk}_{1-b}) \leftarrow \mathsf{Sim}_1(1^\lambda)$, and sends crs, pk_{1-b} to $\mathcal{A}$, who returns pk_b.
2. $\mathcal{S}$ computes $\mathsf{ct}_{1-b} \leftarrow \mathsf{Sim}_2(\mathsf{crs}, \mathsf{pk}_0, \mathsf{pk}_1)$ and sends ct_{1-b} to $\mathcal{A}$, who returns ct_b.
3. $\mathcal{S}$ extracts $x_b \leftarrow \mathsf{Sim}_3(\mathsf{td}, \mathsf{pk}_b, \mathsf{ct}_b)$ and sends x_b to $\mathcal{F}_{2\mathsf{PC}}$, which returns $y := f(x_0, x_1)$.
4. $\mathcal{S}$ computes $u_{1-b} \leftarrow \mathsf{Sim}_4(\mathsf{td}, \mathsf{pk}_b, \{(b, \mathsf{ct}_b)\}_{b \in \{0,1\}}, f, y)$. and sends u_{1-b} to $\mathcal{A}$.
5. $\mathcal{S}$ receives u_b from $\mathcal{A}$ and computes $y' \leftarrow \mathsf{RedComb}(u_0, u_1)$. If $y \neq y'$, $\mathcal{S}$ sends 'abort' to $\mathcal{F}_{2\mathsf{PC}}$, otherwise 'continue'.

---

[22] See the full version [21] for a formal definition.

It is straightforward to see that a distinguisher between the real and simulated view of the adversary in this protocol can be transformed into an adversary on the verifiability of HSS with non-interactive share reduction.

Similarly, reusability is a straightforward consequence of the security of HSS (where the definition allows the adversary to make an arbitrary number of encryption, simulated share and verification queries). This concludes the proof.

Acknowledgements. Pedro Capitão has been supported by the NWO Gravitation Project QSC. Most of this research was carried out while Hila Dahari-Garbian was enrolled as a student at the Weizmann Institute of Science. Hila Dahari-Garbian is supported in part by grants from the Israel Science Foundation (no. 1834/23, and 2337/22), and supported in part by AFOSR Award FA9550-21-1-0046. The work of Lisa Kohl is funded by NWO Talent Programme Veni (VI.Veni.222.348) and by NWO Gravitation project QSC. Part of this work was conducted while the author was visiting the Simons Institute for the Theory of Computing. The work of Zhe Li is supported in part by the Xiaomi Young Scholars Program. Part of this work was carried out while Zhe Li was a postdoctoral researcher at CWI.

References

1. Abram, D., Damgård, I., Orlandi, C., Scholl, P.: An algebraic framework for silent preprocessing with trustless setup and active security. In: Dodis, Y., Shrimpton, T. (eds.) CRYPTO 2022, Part IV. LNCS, vol. 13510, pp. 421–452 (2022). https://doi.org/10.1007/978-3-031-15985-5_15
2. Attema, T., Capitão, P., Kohl, L.: On homomorphic secret sharing from polynomial-modulus LWE. In: PKC 2023, Part II. LNCS, pp. 3–32 (2023). https://doi.org/10.1007/978-3-031-31371-4_1
3. van Baarsen, A., Pu, S.: Fuzzy private set intersection with large hyperballs, pp. 340–369. LNCS (2024). https://doi.org/10.1007/978-3-031-58740-5_12
4. Baum, C., Escudero, D., Pedrouzo-Ulloa, A., Scholl, P., Troncoso-Pastoriza, J.R.: Efficient protocols for oblivious linear function evaluation from ring-LWE. J. Comput. Secur. **30**(1), 39–78 (2022)
5. Benhamouda, F., Degwekar, A., Ishai, Y., Rabin, T.: On the local leakage resilience of linear secret sharing schemes. In: Shacham, H., Boldyreva, A. (eds.) CRYPTO 2018. LNCS, vol. 10991, pp. 531–561. Springer, Cham (2018). https://doi.org/10.1007/978-3-319-96884-1_18
6. Boneh, D., Boyle, E., Corrigan-Gibbs, H., Gilboa, N., Ishai, Y.: Lightweight techniques for private heavy hitters. In: 2021 IEEE Symposium on Security and Privacy, pp. 762–776. IEEE Computer Society Press (2021). https://doi.org/10.1109/SP40001.2021.00048
7. Boneh, D., Boyle, E., Corrigan-Gibbs, H., Gilboa, N., Ishai, Y.: Arithmetic sketching. In: CRYPTO 2023, Part I. LNCS, pp. 171–202 (2023). https://doi.org/10.1007/978-3-031-38557-5_6
8. Boyle, E., Couteau, G., Gilboa, N., Ishai, Y.: Compressing vector OLE. In: Lie, D., Mannan, M., Backes, M., Wang, X. (eds.) ACM CCS 2018, pp. 896–912. ACM Press (2018). https://doi.org/10.1145/3243734.3243868

9. Boyle, E., Couteau, G., Gilboa, N., Ishai, Y., Kohl, L., Rindal, P., Scholl, P.: Efficient two-round OT extension and silent non-interactive secure computation. In: Cavallaro, L., Kinder, J., Wang, X., Katz, J. (eds.) ACM CCS 2019, pp. 291–308. ACM Press (2019). https://doi.org/10.1145/3319535.3354255

10. Boyle, E., Couteau, G., Gilboa, N., Ishai, Y., Kohl, L., Scholl, P.: Efficient pseudorandom correlation generators: silent OT extension and more. In: Boldyreva, A., Micciancio, D. (eds.) CRYPTO 2019. LNCS, vol. 11694, pp. 489–518. Springer, Cham (2019). https://doi.org/10.1007/978-3-030-26954-8_16

11. Boyle, E., Couteau, G., Gilboa, N., Ishai, Y., Kohl, L., Scholl, P.: Efficient pseudorandom correlation generators from ring-LPN. In: Micciancio, D., Ristenpart, T. (eds.) CRYPTO 2020. LNCS, vol. 12171, pp. 387–416. Springer, Cham (2020). https://doi.org/10.1007/978-3-030-56880-1_14

12. Boyle, E., Couteau, G., Gilboa, N., Ishai, Y., Orrù, M.: Homomorphic secret sharing: optimizations and applications. In: Thuraisingham, B.M., Evans, D., Malkin, T., Xu, D. (eds.) ACM CCS 2017, pp. 2105–2122. ACM Press (2017). https://doi.org/10.1145/3133956.3134107

13. Boyle, E., Couteau, G., Meyer, P.: Sublinear-communication secure multiparty computation does not require FHE. In: EUROCRYPT 2023, Part II. LNCS, pp. 159–189 (2023). https://doi.org/10.1007/978-3-031-30617-4_6

14. Boyle, E., Gilboa, N., Ishai, Y.: Function secret sharing. In: Oswald, E., Fischlin, M. (eds.) EUROCRYPT 2015. LNCS, vol. 9057, pp. 337–367. Springer, Heidelberg (2015). https://doi.org/10.1007/978-3-662-46803-6_12

15. Boyle, E., Gilboa, N., Ishai, Y.: Breaking the circuit size barrier for secure computation under DDH. In: Robshaw, M., Katz, J. (eds.) CRYPTO 2016. LNCS, vol. 9814, pp. 509–539. Springer, Heidelberg (2016). https://doi.org/10.1007/978-3-662-53018-4_19

16. Boyle, E., Gilboa, N., Ishai, Y.: Function secret sharing: improvements and extensions. In: Weippl, E.R., Katzenbeisser, S., Kruegel, C., Myers, A.C., Halevi, S. (eds.) ACM CCS 2016, pp. 1292–1303. ACM Press (2016). https://doi.org/10.1145/2976749.2978429

17. Boyle, E., Gilboa, N., Ishai, Y.: Group-based secure computation: optimizing rounds, communication, and computation. In: Coron, J.-S., Nielsen, J.B. (eds.) EUROCRYPT 2017. LNCS, vol. 10211, pp. 163–193. Springer, Cham (2017). https://doi.org/10.1007/978-3-319-56614-6_6

18. Boyle, E., Kohl, L., Scholl, P.: Homomorphic secret sharing from lattices without FHE. In: Ishai, Y., Rijmen, V. (eds.) EUROCRYPT 2019. LNCS, vol. 11477, pp. 3–33. Springer, Cham (2019). https://doi.org/10.1007/978-3-030-17656-3_1

19. Branco, P., Döttling, N., Srinivasan, A.: Rate-1 statistical non-interactive zero-knowledge. Cryptology ePrint Archive (2024)

20. Bui, D., Couteau, G., Meyer, P., Passelègue, A., Riahinia, M.: Fast public-key silent OT and more from constrained Naor-Reingold. LNCS, pp. 88–118 (2024). https://doi.org/10.1007/978-3-031-58751-1_4

21. Capitão, P., Dahari-Garbian, H., Kohl, L., Li, Z.: Malicious homomorphic secret sharing with applications to DV-NIZK and more. Cryptology ePrint Archive, Paper 2025/2077 (2025). https://eprint.iacr.org/2025/2077

22. de Castro, L., Polychroniadou, A.: Lightweight, maliciously secure verifiable function secret sharing. In: Dunkelman, O., Dziembowski, S. (eds.) EUROCRYPT 2022, Part I. LNCS, vol. 13275, pp. 150–179 (2022). https://doi.org/10.1007/978-3-031-06944-4_6

23. Chaidos, P., Couteau, G.: Efficient designated-verifier non-interactive zero-knowledge proofs of knowledge. In: Nielsen, J.B., Rijmen, V. (eds.) EUROCRYPT 2018. LNCS, vol. 10822, pp. 193–221. Springer, Cham (2018). https://doi.org/10.1007/978-3-319-78372-7_7

24. Chaidos, P., Groth, J.: Making sigma-protocols non-interactive without random oracles. In: Katz, J. (ed.) PKC 2015. LNCS, vol. 9020, pp. 650–670. Springer, Heidelberg (2015). https://doi.org/10.1007/978-3-662-46447-2_29

25. Chen, X.: Verifiable homomorphic secret sharing for machine learning classifiers. IEEE Access **11**, 43639–43647 (2023)

26. Chen, X., Zhang, L.F.: Two-server verifiable homomorphic secret sharing for high-degree polynomials. In: Susilo, W., Deng, R.H., Guo, F., Li, Y., Intan, R. (eds.) ISC 2020. LNCS, vol. 12472, pp. 75–91. Springer, Cham (2020). https://doi.org/10.1007/978-3-030-62974-8_5

27. Chillotti, I., Orsini, E., Scholl, P., Smart, N.P., Van Leeuwen, B.: Scooby: improved multi-party homomorphic secret sharing based on FHE. In: International Conference on Security and Cryptography for Networks, pp. 540–563. Springer (2022)

28. Choudhuri, A.R., Goel, A., Hegde, A., Jain, A.: Homomorphic secret sharing with verifiable evaluation. LNCS, pp. 614–650 (2024). https://doi.org/10.1007/978-3-031-78023-3_20

29. Corrigan-Gibbs, H., Boneh, D., Mazières, D.: Riposte: an anonymous messaging system handling millions of users. In: 2015 IEEE Symposium on Security and Privacy, pp. 321–338. IEEE Computer Society Press (2015). https://doi.org/10.1109/SP.2015.27

30. Couteau, G.: A note on the communication complexity of multiparty computation in the correlated randomness model. In: Ishai, Y., Rijmen, V. (eds.) EUROCRYPT 2019. LNCS, vol. 11477, pp. 473–503. Springer, Cham (2019). https://doi.org/10.1007/978-3-030-17656-3_17

31. Couteau, G., Devadas, L., Hegde, A., Jain, A., Servan-Schreiber, S.: Multi-key homomorphic secret sharing. IACR Cryptol. ePrint Arch. 094 (2025). http://eprint.iacr.org/2025/094

32. Couteau, G., Hofheinz, D.: Designated-verifier pseudorandom generators, and their applications. In: Ishai, Y., Rijmen, V. (eds.) EUROCRYPT 2019. LNCS, vol. 11477, pp. 562–592. Springer, Cham (2019). https://doi.org/10.1007/978-3-030-17656-3_20

33. Couteau, G., Meyer, P.: Breaking the circuit size barrier for secure computation under quasi-polynomial LPN. In: Canteaut, A., Standaert, F.-X. (eds.) EURO-CRYPT 2021. LNCS, vol. 12697, pp. 842–870. Springer, Cham (2021). https://doi.org/10.1007/978-3-030-77886-6_29

34. Couteau, G., Meyer, P., Passelègue, A., Riahinia, M.: Constrained pseudorandom functions from homomorphic secret sharing. In: EUROCRYPT 2023, Part III. LNCS, pp. 194–224 (2023). https://doi.org/10.1007/978-3-031-30620-4_7

35. Damgård, I., Fazio, N., Nicolosi, A.: Non-interactive zero-knowledge from homomorphic encryption. In: Halevi, S., Rabin, T. (eds.) TCC 2006. LNCS, vol. 3876, pp. 41–59. Springer, Heidelberg (2006). https://doi.org/10.1007/11681878_3

36. Dao, Q., Ishai, Y., Jain, A., Lin, H.: Multi-party homomorphic secret sharing and sublinear MPC from sparse LPN. In: CRYPTO 2023, Part II. LNCS, pp. 315–348 (2023). https://doi.org/10.1007/978-3-031-38545-2_11

37. Dodis, Y., Halevi, S., Rothblum, R.D., Wichs, D.: Spooky encryption and its applications. In: Robshaw, M., Katz, J. (eds.) CRYPTO 2016. LNCS, vol. 9816, pp. 93–122. Springer, Heidelberg (2016). https://doi.org/10.1007/978-3-662-53015-3_4

38. Dwork, C., Naor, M., Reingold, O.: Immunizing encryption schemes from decryption errors. In: Cachin, C., Camenisch, J.L. (eds.) EUROCRYPT 2004. LNCS, vol. 3027, pp. 342–360. Springer, Heidelberg (2004). https://doi.org/10.1007/978-3-540-24676-3_21

39. Fazio, N., Gennaro, R., Jafarikhah, T., Skeith, W.E.: Homomorphic secret sharing from paillier encryption. In: Okamoto, T., Yu, Y., Au, M.H., Li, Y. (eds.) ProvSec 2017. LNCS, vol. 10592, pp. 381–399. Springer, Cham (2017). https://doi.org/10.1007/978-3-319-68637-0_23

40. Garimella, G., Rosulek, M., Singh, J.: Structure-aware private set intersection, with applications to fuzzy matching. In: Dodis, Y., Shrimpton, T. (eds.) CRYPTO 2022, Part I. LNCS, vol. 13507, pp. 323–352 (2022). https://doi.org/10.1007/978-3-031-15802-5_12

41. Gentry, C., Groth, J., Ishai, Y., Peikert, C., Sahai, A., Smith, A.: Using fully homomorphic hybrid encryption to minimize non-interative zero-knowledge proofs. J. Cryptol. **28**(4), 820–843 (2014). https://doi.org/10.1007/s00145-014-9184-y

42. Gentry, C., Sahai, A., Waters, B.: Homomorphic encryption from learning with errors: conceptually-simpler, asymptotically-faster, attribute-based. In: Canetti, R., Garay, J.A. (eds.) CRYPTO 2013. LNCS, vol. 8042, pp. 75–92. Springer, Heidelberg (2013). https://doi.org/10.1007/978-3-642-40041-4_5

43. Gilboa, N., Ishai, Y.: Distributed point functions and their applications. In: Nguyen, P.Q., Oswald, E. (eds.) EUROCRYPT 2014. LNCS, vol. 8441, pp. 640–658. Springer, Heidelberg (2014). https://doi.org/10.1007/978-3-642-55220-5_35

44. He, Y., Zhang, L.F.: Cheater-identifiable homomorphic secret sharing for outsourcing computations. J. Ambient. Intell. Humaniz. Comput. **11**(11), 5103–5113 (2020). https://doi.org/10.1007/s12652-020-01814-5

45. Katsumata, S., Nishimaki, R., Yamada, S., Yamakawa, T.: Designated verifier/prover and preprocessing NIZKs from Diffie-Hellman assumptions. In: Ishai, Y., Rijmen, V. (eds.) EUROCRYPT 2019. LNCS, vol. 11477, pp. 622–651. Springer, Cham (2019). https://doi.org/10.1007/978-3-030-17656-3_22

46. Katsumata, S., Nishimaki, R., Yamada, S., Yamakawa, T.: Exploring constructions of compact NIZKs from various assumptions. In: Boldyreva, A., Micciancio, D. (eds.) CRYPTO 2019. LNCS, vol. 11694, pp. 639–669. Springer, Cham (2019). https://doi.org/10.1007/978-3-030-26954-8_21

47. Katsumata, S., Nishimaki, R., Yamada, S., Yamakawa, T.: Compact NIZKs from standard assumptions on bilinear maps. In: Canteaut, A., Ishai, Y. (eds.) EUROCRYPT 2020. LNCS, vol. 12107, pp. 379–409. Springer, Cham (2020). https://doi.org/10.1007/978-3-030-45727-3_13

48. Libert, B., Passelègue, A., Wee, H., Wu, D.J.: New constructions of statistical NIZKs: dual-mode DV-NIZKs and more. In: Canteaut, A., Ishai, Y. (eds.) EUROCRYPT 2020. LNCS, vol. 12107, pp. 410–441. Springer, Cham (2020). https://doi.org/10.1007/978-3-030-45727-3_14

49. Lipmaa, H.: Optimally sound sigma protocols under DCRA. In: Kiayias, A. (ed.) FC 2017. LNCS, vol. 10322, pp. 182–203. Springer, Cham (2017). https://doi.org/10.1007/978-3-319-70972-7_10

50. Meyer, P., Orlandi, C., Roy, L., Scholl, P.: Silent circuit relinearisation: sublinear-size (boolean and arithmetic) garbled circuits from DCR. Cryptology ePrint Archive, Report 2025/245 (2025). https://eprint.iacr.org/2025/245

51. Orlandi, C., Scholl, P., Yakoubov, S.: The rise of paillier: homomorphic secret sharing and public-key silent OT. In: Canteaut, A., Standaert, F.-X. (eds.) EUROCRYPT 2021. LNCS, vol. 12696, pp. 678–708. Springer, Cham (2021). https://doi.org/10.1007/978-3-030-77870-5_24

52. Pass, R., Shelat, A., Vaikuntanathan, V.: Construction of a non-malleable encryption scheme from any semantically secure one. In: Dwork, C. (ed.) CRYPTO 2006. LNCS, vol. 4117, pp. 271–289. Springer, Heidelberg (2006). https://doi.org/10.1007/11818175_16
53. Quach, W., Rothblum, R.D., Wichs, D.: Reusable designated-verifier NIZKs for all NP from CDH. In: Ishai, Y., Rijmen, V. (eds.) EUROCRYPT 2019. LNCS, vol. 11477, pp. 593–621. Springer, Cham (2019). https://doi.org/10.1007/978-3-030-17656-3_21
54. Roy, L., Singh, J.: Large message homomorphic secret sharing from DCR and applications. In: Malkin, T., Peikert, C. (eds.) CRYPTO 2021. LNCS, vol. 12827, pp. 687–717. Springer, Cham (2021). https://doi.org/10.1007/978-3-030-84252-9_23
55. Tsaloli, G., Liang, B., Mitrokotsa, A.: Verifiable homomorphic secret sharing. In: Baek, J., Susilo, W., Kim, J. (eds.) ProvSec 2018. LNCS, vol. 11192, pp. 40–55. Springer, Cham (2018). https://doi.org/10.1007/978-3-030-01446-9_3
56. Ventre, C., Visconti, I.: Co-sound zero-knowledge with public keys. In: Preneel, B. (ed.) AFRICACRYPT 2009. LNCS, vol. 5580, pp. 287–304. Springer, Heidelberg (2009). https://doi.org/10.1007/978-3-642-02384-2_18
57. Wagh, S.: Pika: secure computation using function secret sharing over rings. Proc. Priv. Enhancing Technol. (2022)
58. Wang, F., Yun, C., Goldwasser, S., Vaikuntanathan, V., Zaharia, M.: Splinter: practical private queries on public data. In: 14th USENIX Symposium on Networked Systems Design and Implementation (NSDI 2017), pp. 299–313 (2017)
59. Yoshida, M., Obana, S.: Verifiably multiplicative secret sharing. IEEE Trans. Inf. Theory 65(5), 3233–3245 (2018)

Succinctly Verifiable Computation over Additively-Homomorphically Encrypted Data: Making Privacy-Preserving Blueprints Practical

Scott Griffy[1]([✉]), Markulf Kohlweiss[2], Anna Lysyanskaya[1], and Meghna Sengupta[3]

[1] Brown University, Providence, USA
{scott_griffy,anna_lysyanskaya}@brown.edu
[2] University of Edinburgh and Input Output, Edinburgh, UK
markulf.kohlweiss@ed.ac.uk
[3] University of Edinburgh, Edinburgh, UK
M.Sengupta-1@sms.ed.ac.uk

Abstract. Introduced by Kohlweiss, Lysyanskaya, and Nguyen (Eurocrypt'23), a privacy-preserving blueprint (PPB) allows an auditor of a privacy system, on input x, to create a public encoding pk of the function $f(x, \cdot)$ that reveals nothing about x. Yet, a user who knows pk and a y that corresponds to a commitment to y, C_y, can compute an escrow Z of the value $f(x, y)$; Z will verifiably correspond to pk and C_y. The auditor will be able to recover $f(x, y)$ from Z, but will learn no other information about y. For example, let $f(x, y)$ be the "watchlist" function that outputs y iff y is on the list x; a PPB for such a function (which we call an f-PPB) allows the auditor to trace watchlisted users in an otherwise anonymous system.

PPBs are a—socially important and potentially controversial—instance of the actively secure non-interactive secure computation (NISC) problem. As such, they can be naturally constructed from homomorphic encryption and efficient proof systems. In this work, we present a framework for additively homomorphic encryption (AHE) with efficient proof systems that yields a dramatically improved PPB both in efficiency and security. In our setting, AHE allows one to compute an encryption, c_f, of a polynomial $f(x_1, \ldots, x_n, y_1, \ldots, y_k)$ on input the values: $y_1, \ldots, y_k$ and only the (additively homomorphic) encryptions of $x_1, \ldots, x_n$. For AHE that satisfies a set of natural requirements, we give a NIZK proof system for showing the correct computation of c_f and proves that the $y_1, \ldots, y_k$ values used in the computation of c_f correspond to public commitments $C_1, \ldots, C_k$. The resulting proof's size is $O(k \log d)$ (independent of n) where d is the maximum degree of any variable in f. Critically, the proof can be computed without knowledge of $x_1, \ldots, x_n$ only requiring the encryptions of these values. We show how our proof system can be instantiated both with ElGamal-based encryption (under DDH) and with a variant of the Camenisch-Shoup cryptosystem (under DCR and Strong RSA). Applying our proof system to Camenisch-Shoup

© International Association for Cryptologic Research 2026
S. Bai and E. Persichetti (Eds.): PKC 2026, LNCS 16554, pp. 235–269, 2026.
https://doi.org/10.1007/978-3-032-26740-5_8

ciphertexts is novel and extends previous work to apply to more general polynomials.

Using our NIZK proof system for additively homomorphic computation we achieve the following results: (1) We provide efficient schemes for a useful class of functions f; for example, we show how to realize f that would allow the auditor to trace all private payment transactions of a suspect user in a central bank digital currency (CBDC). (2) For the watchlist and related functions, we reduce the size of the escrow Z from linear in the size of the auditor's input x, to logarithmic. Additionally, (3) we define and satisfy a stronger notion of security for f-PPBs, where a malicious auditor cannot frame a user in a transaction in which the user was not involved in.

1   Introduction

The Need for Privacy Preserving Blueprints. Not all citizens are lawful and not all governments democratic, thus cryptographers have developed powerful tools to trade off our fundamental need to protect our personal privacy with the legitimate needs of systems and governments to enforce rules and laws and to regulate finance. Among these tools, anonymous credentials [19,25,41], [4,5,20,21,24,34,35,40,43,47] and related technologies such as e-cash [26] are prominent examples. Such systems allow a user with a cryptographic commitment C_y to his data y to prove that y is somehow certified by some authority or authorities; in the case of anonymous payments, they further allow to prove that a payment transaction based on the user's private data y was executed correctly.

In a recent paper, Kohlweiss, Lysyanskaya and Nguyen (KLN) [37] added *privacy-preserving blueprints* (PPBs) to the repertoire of cryptographic algorithms to depolarise the issue of privacy and accountability. In an f-PPB system, the goal is to allow an authorized party called an "auditor" to learn $f(x, y)$ where x is the auditor's secret input that's fixed once and for all, and y is a user's secret input to a transaction; if a PPB system is used in tandem with an anonymous credential system, y can include meaningful information about the user's identity. Via an appropriate choice of f, an f-PPB system makes it possible to perform audits of the anonymous system while leaking no information other than the output of the chosen function, f. For example, x could be a watchlist of suspected criminals which allows us to define $f_{watchlist}$ as follows: $f_{watchlist}(x, y) = y$ if y is on the list x, and $\perp$ otherwise. An $f_{watchlist}$-PPB would allow the auditor to trace all of the suspects' transactions, but none of the transactions of other people. A PPB further requires that the secret x corresponds to a publicly known commitment C_x that can be further certified by an external party, so that a malicious auditor cannot make up x at will.

While citizens cannot see the full watchlist, they can still see the size of the list and the fact that there was a lawfully obtained warrant for placing a person on it. The existence of a practical cryptographic system that can provide this tracing capability in a way that is transparent would strike a reasonable balance, and, as a result, may sway the policy conversation (in which law enforcement voices are often louder than those of privacy advocates) in favor of using more anonymous systems for central bank digital currencies (CBDCs).

In a PPB system, first, the auditor sets up his public key pk and secret key sk on input the secret x and a commitment C_x to x for which the auditor knows the opening (C_x may be signed by an external validator). A PPB includes a public verification procedure VerPK(pk, C_x) for ensuring that pk corresponds to the commitment C_x. Now the system is ready for blueprinting transactions; there is no limit on the number of such transactions. In a transaction, a user with secret input y and a commitment C_y to y to which the user knows the opening r computes the escrow $Z = $ Escrow(pk, y, r) of y under pk (where y meaningfully corresponds to some information about this user, for example: their identity in an anonymous credential system). A PPB includes a public verification procedure VerEscrow(pk, C_y, Z) for ensuring that Z corresponds to pk and C_y. Finally, using sk, the auditor runs the decryption algorithm to recover $z = f(x, y)$ from Z. The reason that it is called a privacy-preserving *blueprint* is that we can think of pk as a "blueprint" of the function $f(x, \cdot)$ such that a user can use the blueprint to verifiably evaluate $f(x, \cdot)$ on their y.

An f-PPB is realizable for any efficiently computable function f from general NIZK and either fully homomorphic encryption (FHE) or non-interactive secure computation (NISC) [37] by representing the function as a circuit. However, this general approach is not suitable for practical use. KLN additionally gave a more practical construction of $f_{watchlist}$-PPB from the ElGamal cryptosystem and proof systems about discrete logarithm relations in the random-oracle model, though even with this more practical construction, the size of their escrow is linear in the size of the watchlist.

We argue that this linear size is not sufficient to be useful in practice. To bridge this gap, we develop a commit-and-prove framework for working with additively-homomorphically encrypted data that is also relevant for other actively secure non-interactive secure computation (NISC) problems.

Additively homomorphic encryption (Definition 4) allows one to compute, on input ciphertexts $c_1, \ldots, c_n$ that encrypt $x_1, \ldots, x_n$, and other inputs $y_1, \ldots, y_k$, the value $f(x_1, \ldots, x_n, y_1, \ldots, y_k)$ for any polynomial f in which each monomial has total degree at most 1 in the x-variables (but can be arbitrary in the y-variables).

Our First Contribution: A Modular Framework for Succinct Verifiable Secure Computation on Additively-Homomorphically Encrypted Data. In this paper, we give a non-interactive zero-knowledge proof system (in the random-oracle model) for showing that a ciphertext c_f is the result of homomorphically evaluating f on $c_1, \ldots, c_n$ and private inputs $y_1, \ldots, y_k$ that correspond to commitments $C_1, \ldots, C_k$. Our proof system, described in Sect. 3 outputs *succinct* proofs, i.e. their size is $O(k \log d)$ where k is the number of private inputs, and d is an upper bound on the degree of any variable in f; note that the size of the proof is independent of the number n of the x-variables. Our technique is similar to [13] though we do not use pairings and our technique is general enough to apply to composite-order groups. Similar to [13], we need to reduce the degree of the polynomial f by half with each recursion to achieve a succinct proof. To ensure information is not leaked by these half-degree polynomials, we must include "intermediate" ciphertexts in the proof. To protect these intermediate ciphertexts from being decrypted by the auditor, we introduce *commitments to ciphertexts* which are additionally useful to prove correctness of our blueprints scheme in the "commit-and-prove" paradigm allowing our proofs to be very modular. We give two different practical instantiations of this framework: one under the DDH assumption (using the ElGamal cryptosystem) and the other under the Strong RSA and Decisional Composite Residuosity assumptions (using the Camenisch-Shoup cryptosystem): Sect. 4.1 is dedicated to the description of these additively homomorphic cryptosystems, while Sect. 4.2 constructs commitments to Camenisch-Shoup ciphertexts and the proof systems that serve as building blocks for the framework. Our framework is definitionally similar to [8]. We present our construction of commitments to ElGamal ciphertexts to the full version of this paper [33] since they are less technical than commitments to Camenisch-Shoup ciphertexts.

Our Second Contribution: Realizing PPBs for Central Bank Digital Currencies (CBDCs). Since the KLN paper first appeared, privacy-preserving blueprints received some attention in the civil liberties discourse [46] because of (among other things) the following application to CBDCs: suppose that the auditor's input x is a list of suspected criminals' unique identifiers. Suppose a user's input y contains this user's unique identifier y_{id} as well as seed y_{seed} from which all of this user's e-coins' serial numbers are generated. This is consistent with, e.g., compact e-cash [17] and related schemes [16, 18, 36, 48], including those proposed specifically for the CBDC application [36, 48]. In this case, we want an f_{CBDC}-PPB scheme where the function f_{CBDC} is as follows: $f_{CBDC}(x, y) = y$ if $y_{id} \in x$, and $\perp$ otherwise. A PPB with these properties will allow the auditor to not only identify that a transaction was carried out by a suspect, but also to recover the seed y_{seed} and trace all of the user's transactions, even as the rest of the users' privacy is protected. This application to anonymous payments is attractive to those who advocate that a CBDC can be privacy-preserving even while enabling lawful investigations. Unfortunately, the alternative to yielding ground on this to law enforcement is that central banks throughout the world would adopt a CBDC that provides no privacy—even from third-party observers—to individuals, in the name of compliance with law enforcement.

KLN give a practical construction that works for $f_{watchlist}$ but their techniques are not sufficient for f_{CBDC}. This is due to their use of ElGamal encryption which recovers g^y from the escrow where g is a generator of the group used for ElGamal (where the discrete logarithm problem is hard). From g^y it is possible to recover y by brute-force search if only a small number of bits of y are still unknown; but it wouldn't be possible to recover y_{seed}, since the size of a pseudorandom seed must be too large to allow brute-force search. We give a practical instantiation of a f_{CBDC}-PPB construction (Sect. 5.2). By "practical", we mean that it can be instantiated efficiently using proof systems for discrete logarithm relations in the random-oracle model.

Our Third Contribution: Logarithmic Size of Escrows (Z). The KLN approach is also not good enough for either f_{CBDC}-PPBs or even $f_{watchlist}$-PPBs because we expect the watchlist x to be quite large. In the KLN construction, the size of the escrow Z was linear in the size of the watchlist x. Using the fact that our framework produces succinct proofs, we give a substantial improvement: a construction of a f_{CBDC}-PPB and a $f_{watchlist}$-PPB where the size of the escrow, Z (including the proof of correct computation), is logarithmic in the size of x; this is achieved because the proof system we use in the construction (in Sect. 5.3) uses our succinct approach (i.e. our first contribution described above).

Our Fourth Contribution: Stronger Security. The KLN definition of security [37] does not rule out that a malicious auditor would be able to produce pk, sk, C_y and Z such that the decryption algorithm will output $z \neq f(x, y)$. In Sect. 1.2, we discuss how the KLN construction of $f_{watchlist}$-PPB allowed for a "framing" attack: a malicious auditor causing an escrow to decrypt to the identity of an honest user y who is not a party to the transaction. Addressing these security issues using our new proof framework from our first contribution and the reworked functionality is our fourth and final contribution.

We improve the definition of security of PPB to that of *non-frameable* PPB: we add the requirement that the decryption algorithm's output be publicly verifiable. In Sect. 5.1, we present this improved definition. Our constructions (which are also presented in Sect. 5.1) achieve non-frameability.

Summary of How this Paper is Organized. In Sect. 1.1 below we give a more detailed overview of our techniques for achieving verifiable computation over additively homorphically encrypted data, and why they lead to an efficient construction of f_{CBDC}-PPBs. In Sect. 1.2 we explain why and how we improved the definition of privacy-preserving blueprints to incorporate non-frameability. To conclude the introduction, in Sect. 1.3, we review related work and provide efficiency analysis and comparison with KLN.

After going over the preliminaries in Sect. 2, we dive into our commit-and-prove framework in Sect. 3: In Sect. 3.1, we go over the "commit" part, and in Sects. 3.2 and 3.3, over the "prove" part. Section 4 explains how to adapt the ElGamal and the Camenisch-Shoup cryptosystems; the (adapted) additively homomorphic encryption schemes are given in Sect. 4.1; while the a commitment scheme for committing to ciphertexts and related proof systems that fit the requirements of our framework is given in Sect. 4.2 for Camenisch-Shoup ciphertexts (a second construction of these commitments for ElGamal ciphertexts is available in the full version of this paper [33]). Armed with these tools, in Sect. 5 we define and realize non-frameable privacy-preserving blueprints.

1.1 Our Framework for Verifiable Computation

Let us focus on a concrete example. At a high level, a f_{CBDC}-PPB scheme will work as follows: The auditor will first find the coefficients of the polynomial $P(\chi) = a_0 + a_1\chi + \ldots + a_n\chi^n$ of degree n whose roots are values on the list x, and it will output a public key pk of an encryption scheme, as well as the encryptions of the coefficients of P; i.e. $X = (\mathsf{pk}, \boxed{a_0}_{\mathsf{pk}}, \ldots \boxed{a_n}_{\mathsf{pk}})$, where $\boxed{m}_{\mathsf{pk}}$ denotes an encryption of a message m under the public key pk (and we drop the subscript when clear from the context). Let $f(a_0, \ldots, a_n, y_{id}, y, s) = \left(s \sum_{i=0}^{n} a_i y_{id}^i\right) + y$. Note that if $f_{CBDC}(x, y_{id}, y) \neq \perp$, then $f(\mathbf{a}, y_{id}, y, s) = y$; else, if the user picks s uniformly at random, then $f(\mathbf{a}, y_{id}, y, s)$ is also random. Thus, the goal is for the user to compute c_f, an encryption of $f(a_0, \ldots, a_n, y_{id}, y, s)$, from X.

If the underlying encryption scheme is additively homomorphic, then $c_f = \boxed{f(a_0, \ldots, a_n, y_{id}, y, s)}$ can be computed using homomorphic addition: Let the symbol '$\oplus$' denote the homomorphic operation on ciphertexts, and let $\odot$ denote multiplying a ciphertext by a scalar. Then $c_f = \left(\bigoplus_{i=0}^{n}(sy_{id}^i) \odot \boxed{a_i}\right) \oplus \boxed{y}$. For actively secure NISC, the user needs to compute a zero-knowledge proof that c_f was computed correctly from X and the user's secret inputs s, y and y_{id} that correspond to commitments C_s, C_y and $C_{y_{id}}$. While general-purpose ZK proof systems can be used here, a proof system designed hand-in-hand with the underlying encryption scheme can take advantage of efficient discrete logarithm representation proofs and impose only a minimal overhead over encryption; the classical results on efficient multi-party computation of Cramer, Damgård and Nielsen [28] serve as the inspiration for this approach.

We suggest a modular, commit-and-prove [7] approach for constructing a proof that a given ciphertext is the result of a computation on additively-homomorphically encrypted data. For example, here the output ciphertext c_f is the result of applying a series of homomorphic operations, starting with the input ciphertexts $\{\boxed{a_i}\}$ and the user's inputs. In order to prove correctness of c_f in our framework, one forms commitments to the intermediate steps of this computation (for example, the intermediate ciphertexts $\boxed{a_i} \odot y_{id}^i$) and proves that each of these intermediate steps was carried out correctly. These intermediate steps include the evaluations of different "folds" of the succinct proof which can leak information since an adversarial verifier knows the polynomial and secret key for the encryption scheme. In contrast, previous work [8,13] operates in a more restrictive setting in which the verifier does not know the decryption key.

Thus, our main new building block is an additively homomorphic encryption scheme equipped with (1) a cryptographic commitment scheme for committing to ciphertexts; and (2) proof systems for proving properties of committed ciphertexts, such as the property that a committed ciphertext c was obtained from committed ciphertexts c_1 and c_2, along with a committed scalar a, as follows: $c = c_1 \oplus (c_2 \odot a)$. (See Sect. 3.1 for the more formal treatment.)

Next, let us explain how to instantiate this framework with the ElGamal cryptosystem. Let G be a group of prime order q with generator g_1; an ElGamal public key is a group element g_2; an encryption of $M \in G$ is $(g_1^r, g_2^r M)$ for random $r \in \mathbb{Z}_q$. ElGamal is not, strictly speaking, an additively homomorphic encryption scheme, but a multiplicatively homomorphic one: $(g_1^r, g_2^r M) \oplus (g_1^{r'}, g_2^{r'} M') = (g_1^{r+r'}, g_2^{r+r'} MM')$. However, we can define a "lifted" ElGamal cryptosystem: to encrypt the message m, use the ElGamal cryptosystem to encrypt g_1^m; i.e. $\boxed{m} = (g_1^r, g_2^r g_1^m)$. The problem is that, instead of outputting m, the decryption algorithm outputs g_1^m; converting it to m requires that m come from a small space, so that it can be found via brute-force search; we call this flavor of encryption "semi"-encryption. Still, for some applications (such as realizing $f_{watchlist}$-PPBs), this is good enough.

Our Techniques for Achieving Succinct Proofs. The naïve way for computing a proof π of correctness of c_f is to form a commitment to the ciphertext that is the result of each intermediate step in the computation (for example, the values $\boxed{a_i} \odot y_{id}^i$ in the example above), meaning that the size of the proof will need to be linear in the degree d of the polynomial f (and in the description of the polynomial altogether). To reduce the dependence on the degree from d to $O(\log d)$, we adapt the ingenious technique of Lund, Fortnow, Karloff and Nisan [39], also employed by [30, 42, 50], for recursively simplifying statements about polynomials by halving the degree of uni-variate polynomials and eliminating variables of multi-variate polynomials to commit-and-prove-style computations on encrypted data. We compare our technique to more works in Sect. 1.3 and the full version of this paper [33].

The overall idea, described in Sect. 3.2 (and generalized to the multivariate case in Sect. 3.3), is to recursively halve the degree of the polynomial. Suppose that we need to prove that a ciphertext $c_f = \boxed{f(x_1, \ldots, x_n, y_1, \ldots, y_k)}$; the prover and verifier both know $\{\boxed{x_i}\}_{i \in [n]}$; further, the prover knows $y_1, \ldots, y_k$ (and thus can compute c_f) while the verifier knows just the corresponding commitments $\{C_{y_i} = \mathsf{Com}(y_i; r_i)\}$. Suppose the degree of y_1 in f is d. The recursive step is to reduce the proof of this statement to the proof that another ciphertext $c_{f'}$ is an encryption of $f'(x_1, \ldots, x_n, y_1, \ldots, y_k)$, where in f' the degree of y_1 is $d/2$. This is accomplished by taking the upper half of the polynomial (terms including $y^{i+d/2}$ for some $i \geq 0$) and dividing it by $y^{d/2}$. The first and (reduced) upper half are then combined using a random linear combination, reducing the goal to be proving correctness of a polynomial of degree $d/2$. The Schwartz-Zippel lemma then ensures that proving the reduced degree polynomial ensures correctness of the larger degree polynomial. It is important that the ciphertext $c_{f'}$ used in the recursive step not be given to the verifier in the clear; otherwise, it will leak information to the adversary who knows the decryption key. Instead, our proof system works for *committed* ciphertexts.

To obtain a commitment to an ElGamal ciphertext $\boxed{a} = (A, A')$, we first extend Pedersen commitments (with generators g and h) to commit to group elements. To commit to A, we sample $s_A, r_A \leftarrow \mathbb{Z}_q$ and the commitment is $C_A = (C_{A,1}, C_{A,2}) = (Ag^{s_A}, g^{s_A} h^{r_A})$; similarly, we can form a commitment $C_{A'} = (C_{A',1}, C_{A',2})$. Thus, a commitment to $\boxed{a}$ is $C_{\boxed{a}} = (C_A, C_{A'})$. It is easy to see that this commitment scheme has convenient homomorphic properties: if '$*$' denotes applying the group operation componentwise, then $C_{\boxed{a}} * C_{\boxed{b}} = C_{\boxed{a+b}}$. As shown in Sect. 4, this allows for efficient proof systems for properties of committed ciphertexts needed for our framework. Additionally, we show in Sect. 4 that our framework can also be instantiated, under the Paillier assumption, with a semantically secure variant of the Camenisch-Shoup cryptosystem [22].

Why f_{CBDC}-PPB was not Achievable in KLN. KLN's limitation was that it used lifted ElGamal, and thus, in the event that the user was on the watchlist, the decryption algorithm was only able to recover g^y from the escrow, rather than y in the clear. As explained earlier, this is not good enough if y comes from a large enough domain (for example if it contains a seed for a PRF) and cannot be brute-force-searched. The Camenisch-Shoup based instantiation of our framework allows the decryption algorithm to recover y, which yields f_{CBDC}-blueprints. While the ElGamal-based instantiation can work as well if we split the payment tracing seed into sufficiently small chunks, this comes at the cost of efficiency (see the full version of this paper [33]).

1.2 Non-frameability and Why It Matters

A further contribution to privacy-preserving blueprints is an additional property: *non-frameability*, which our constructions satisfy. The concept of non-frameability was first introduced in the work of Camenisch [15]. The paper introduced it for the group signature scheme setting as the property that the manager (even if they collude with a group member) cannot falsely accuse group members. Subsequently, Bellare, Shi and Zhang [6] formalized the property for group signature schemes.

At a high-level there are similarities with the property of non-frameability as we define it and as defined by [6]. Both properties require that if some authority (the opener in the case of [6] and the auditor in our case) wants to prove that a user took some action (signing a message in the case of [6] and showing an anonymous credential in the case of blueprints) they must provide verifiable proof. One difference between the schemes is that in [6] the opener traces any user indiscriminately. In our case, the auditor's functionality is not "trace" but the function f. (In the case of watchlists, that means the auditor can trace iff the user is on the watchlist.) Also, a group signature scheme provides tracing for group members who are signing messages, whereas in blueprints, the functionality is to trace users who are using an anonymous credential scheme, which does not imply that these traceable users sign any messages. Thus, it is not trivial to construct blueprints from the group signature scheme in [6].

The watchlist PPB scheme of [37] is frameable, i.e., a malicious auditor can collude with a malicious user to produce Z that will decrypt to the identity of an honest user who was not a party to the transaction (and who may or may not be on the watchlist). The gist of their scheme is that pk includes encrypted coefficients of a polynomial P such that $P(y) = 0$ if and only if y is on the watchlist x. The escrow $Z = (\hat{Z}, \pi)$ produced by the user whose identity is y consists of the encryption $\hat{Z}$ of $rP(y) + y$ for a random r chosen by the user, as well as a proof π that indeed $\hat{Z}$ was computed correctly. In order to frame the user with identity y^*, a malicious user whose identity is y and to whom the coefficients of the polynomial P are known (as would be the case if the auditor is malicious) needs to solve for r^* in the $r^*P(y) + y = y^*$, and will produce an escrow $Z = (\hat{Z}, \pi)$ by following the original algorithm, but just using $r = r^*$.

This attack is outside the KLN security model, and therefore does not contradict their security analysis (which is correct). One could also argue that frameability, also known as deniability, can be a feature and not a bug. We discuss this at greater length in the full version of this paper [33].

In Sect. 5.1, we improve the KLN definition of privacy-preserving blueprints by incorporating non-frameability. The decryption algorithm must now produce a proof π_z of correct decryption, and a new algorithm Judge verifies this proof. The proof π_z is important when the auditor's output is used as evidence in legal proceedings[1] or as input in a smart contract, e.g., an Ethereum Eigenlayer slashing operation or crime restitution.

In order to obtain a practical non-frameable f-PPB for the watchlist function, we modify the KLN construction as follows: our Escrow algorithm will output $(\hat{Z}, \hat{Z}', \pi)$, where $\hat{Z}$ is an encryption of $rP(y) + y$ (just as before), and the additional value $\hat{Z}'$ is an encryption of $r'P(y)$, while, as before, the proof π is to ensure that $\hat{Z}$ and $\hat{Z}'$ were computed correctly. If π verifies, the decryption algorithm will decrypt $\hat{Z}$ iff $\hat{Z}'$ decrypts to 0; it will output $\perp$ otherwise. Our succinct proofs are compatible with this non-framing construction.

1.3   Related Work and Efficiency Analysis

Recent years have seen an explosion of techniques for zero-knowledge proof systems [9,14,27,32,49]. Many of these are for general circuits, but particularly related to our work are those that, like us, make use of efficient Σ-protocols for algebraic relations over committed values and also achieve succinctness [2,3,12]. Broadly speaking, while these approaches have significantly advanced the state of the art, there remains ongoing interest in adapting such frameworks to settings like verifiable computation over encrypted data—a scenario that these works do not directly address. We discuss how our approach connects to and extends this line of work in the full version of this paper [33].

To summarize, there is a long and active line of work on "bulletproofs" (BPs) [10,12–14,38], which efficiently prove relations between group elements in a succinct way. Many of these protocols—contrary to the initial BPs—rely on pairings, whereas our construction explores an alternative approach that avoids them. Among these, our solution is technically closest to [38], though our framework is designed to operate in composite order groups such as $\mathbb{Z}_n$, a choice that enables constructions of particular relevance to our setting.

When compared with [37], our escrows consist of 58 group elements and 52 scalar elements per recursion, leading to ElGamal escrows of size 2.6kB $\times \log(n)$ (for a watch list of size n) and Camenischâ ĂŞShoup escrows roughly ten times larger at 28kB $\times \log(n)$ for a 2048-bit modulus. This implies that our ElGamal escrow achieves better asymptotic efficiency beyond roughly 60 suspects

---

[1] Interestingly, this is currently rarely the case for existing investigations employing mass or targeted surveillance. Instead, law enforcement follow a complicated process of parallel construction where not always lawfully attained evidence is used to inform a lawful investigation [11].

on the watchlist, with comparable computation time per recursion. For example, when the watchlist has 16,000 suspects, an escrow in our new system only requires 8KB compared to the previous work which would require 500KB. These comparisons illustrate how the broader research community continues to refine efficiencyâĂŞsecurity trade-offs across related constructions, and our framework contributes another point in this rich and still-evolving design space.

As an application, PPBs are also closely related to client side scanning (CSS)—a mostly non-cryptographic solution that might at best achieve something akin to blueprint hiding. However, we imagine blueprints to have a more restrictive mandate than CSS thereby mitigating several of the well-known concerns raised against CSS [1]. That is, PPBs should only scan very high-value information y (from a criminal perspective). The still relatively high costs of the secure computation enforces the need for this requirement. Still, sufficiently powerful PPBs could, in principle, also be used to perform client-side scanning on images. This should be subject to further work, covering both the technical and ethical/political aspects of the problem. PPBs can also achieve non-frameability while this is inherently challenging in CSS, as adversaries or authorities could potentially manipulate detection systems to falsely implicate individuals.

2   Preliminaries

2.1   Zero-Knowledge Proofs of Knowledge

Black-Box Partially Straight-Line (BB-PSL) NIZK. Non-interactive zero-knowledge (NIZK) proofs are an important building block for us. We follow the KLN notation and definitions (Sec. 2.1 of [37]) of the completeness and ZK properties of NIZK proof system, provided in abbreviated form in Definition 1 below.

Definition 1 (Completeness and ZK of NIZK [37]]). *Let $\mathcal{R}$ be a relation. Let S be a setup model (e.g., the CRS model or the random oracle model). Let P^S and V^S be (non-interactive) algorithms for the prover and the verifier in the S-setup model. $(\mathsf{P}^\mathsf{S}, \mathsf{V}^\mathsf{S})$ constitute a complete proof system if for all $(\mathrm{x}, \mathrm{w}) \in \mathcal{R}$, $\Pr\left[\pi \leftarrow \mathsf{P}^\mathsf{S}(\mathrm{x}, \mathrm{w}) : \mathsf{V}^\mathsf{S}(\mathrm{x}, \pi) = 0\right] = 0$.*

They satisfy the zero-knowledge property if for any PPT adversary Adv in the experiment of Fig. 1, the advantage function $\nu(\lambda)$ defined below is negligible:
$$\mathsf{Adv}_\mathsf{Adv}^\mathsf{NIZK} = |\Pr[\mathsf{NIZK}^{\mathsf{Adv},0}(1^\lambda) = 0] - \Pr[\mathsf{NIZK}^{\mathsf{Adv},1}(1^\lambda) = 0]| = \nu(\lambda)$$

Let us review BB-PSL simulation extractable proof systems [37] (Definition 2). The straight-line extractor here does not extract the entire witness, but just some function of it; simultaneously, a black-box extractor (that's allowed to rewind the adversary) can extract the entire witness. In the full version of this paper [33], we motivate this definition further.

Definition 2 (Black-box partial straight-line simulation extractability). *A proof system (as defined in Definition 1) is BB-PSL simulation extractable if $\exists$ PPT Ext, ExtSL s.t. the advantage (defined below) of any PPT*

$\mathsf{NIZK}^{\mathsf{Adv},0}(1^\lambda)$	$\mathcal{O}_\mathsf{S}(m)$	$\mathcal{O}_\mathsf{P}(\mathbb{x}, \mathbb{w})$
return $\mathsf{Adv}^{\mathsf{S}(\cdot),\mathsf{P}^\mathsf{S}(\cdot,\cdot)}(1^\lambda)$	$\mathsf{st}, h, \tau_{\mathsf{Ext}} \leftarrow \mathsf{SimS}(\mathsf{st}, m)$	**if** $(\mathbb{x}, \mathbb{w}) \notin \mathcal{R}$: **return** $\perp$
$\mathsf{NIZK}^{\mathsf{Adv},1}(1^\lambda)$	**return** h	$\mathsf{st}, \pi \leftarrow \mathsf{Sim}(\mathsf{st}, \mathbb{x})$
return $\mathsf{Adv}^{\mathcal{O}_\mathsf{S}(\cdot),\mathcal{O}_\mathsf{P}(\cdot,\cdot)}(1^\lambda)$		**return** π

Fig. 1. NIZK game

adversary is negligible: $\mathsf{Adv}^{\mathsf{NISimBBPSLExt}}_{\mathsf{Adv},f} = \Pr[f\text{-}\mathsf{NISimBBPSLExt}^{\mathsf{Adv}}(1^\lambda) = 1] = \nu(\lambda)$ *for some negligible function* ν *(Fig. 2).*

$f\text{-}\mathsf{NISimBBPSLExt}^{\mathsf{Adv}}(1^\lambda)$

1 : $\mathcal{Q}, \mathcal{Q}_\mathsf{S} \leftarrow [\ ]; (\mathbb{x}, \pi) \leftarrow \mathsf{Adv}^{\tilde{\mathcal{O}}_\mathsf{S}(\cdot),\mathcal{O}_\mathsf{Sim}(\cdot)}(1^\lambda)$

2 : $\mathbb{w} \leftarrow \mathsf{Ext}^{\mathsf{BB(Adv)}}(\mathcal{Q}_\mathsf{S}, \mathbb{x}, \pi); \mathbb{w}' \leftarrow \mathsf{ExtSL}(\mathcal{Q}_\mathsf{S}, \mathbb{x}, \pi)$

3 : **return** $\mathsf{V}^{\mathcal{O}_\mathsf{S}}(\mathbb{x}, \pi) \wedge (\mathbb{x}, \pi) \notin \mathcal{Q} \wedge ((\mathbb{x}, \mathbb{w}) \notin \mathcal{R} \vee \mathbb{w}' \neq f(\mathbb{w}))$

$\mathcal{O}_\mathsf{S}(m)\ \underline{\tilde{\mathcal{O}}_\mathsf{S}(m)}$	$\mathcal{O}_\mathsf{Sim}(\mathbb{x})$
1 : $\mathsf{st}, h, \tau_{\mathsf{Ext}} \leftarrow \mathsf{SimS}(\mathsf{st}, m)$	1 : $\mathsf{st}, \pi \leftarrow \mathsf{Sim}(\mathsf{st}, \mathbb{x})$
2 : $\mathcal{Q}_\mathsf{S}.\mathsf{add}((m, h, \tau_{\mathsf{Ext}}))$	2 : $\mathcal{Q}.\mathsf{add}((\mathbb{x}, \pi))$
3 : **return** $h, \underline{\tau_{\mathsf{Ext}}}$	3 : **return** π

Fig. 2. $f\text{-}\mathsf{NISimBBPSLExt}$ game—note that the trapdoor τ_{Ext} is hidden from V.

Proofs of Equivalent Representations of Discrete Logarithms. (*eqrep*). Using known techniques, we can construct a Σ-protocol that proves the relation in Definition 3 in both cyclic groups of prime order where the DDH and CDH problems are hard as well as $\mathbb{Z}_{n^2}$. We describe such a protocol in the full version of this paper [33]. When using this protocol, we employ Camenisch-Stadler notation to denote witnesses and relations [23], e.g. $\mathsf{NIZK}[witness : statement]$.

Definition 3 (Relation for proof of multiplication of witnesses over bases in cryptographic groups). *Let* $R_{eqrep\text{-}\mathcal{G}^*}(\mathbb{x}, \mathbb{w})$ *be the relation that accepts if the following two conditions hold:*
(1) $\mathbb{x} = (\mu, \{x_i, \{g_{i,1}, \ldots, g_{i,m}\}\}_{i=1}^k)$, *all the* x_i's *and* $g_{i,j}$'s *are elements of* $\mathcal{G}$, *and witness* $\mathbb{w} = (\{b_i\}_{i=0}^k, \{w_j\}_{j=1}^m)$ *is such that* $x_i = b_i \prod_{j=1}^m g_{i,j}^{w_j}$ *where* $b_i \in \mathcal{B}$.
(2) If $\forall i \in [m], w_i = \prod_{j \in \mu(i)} w_j$ *where* μ *is a map* $\mu : [m] \to \mathcal{P}([m])$ *and* $\mathcal{P}([m])$ *is the set of all subsets of* $[m]$.

We instantiate this definition in the full version of this paper [33] with $\mathcal{G} = \mathbb{G}_p$, a cyclic group of order p, and with $\mathcal{G} = \mathbb{Z}_{n^2}$. In the former case, $\mathcal{B} = \{1\}$, yielding exact equality of representation. In the latter, $\mathcal{B} = \{-1, 1\}$, so the relation only holds for the absolute values.

2.2 Additively Homomorphic Encryption

Additively Homomorphic $\mathfrak{g}$-Semi-encryption Scheme. We need an appropriate additively homomorphic (AH) semantically secure public-key encryption scheme. Our application can tolerate a relaxed version of encryption, in which the decryption algorithm need not recover the original plaintext m, but just some function $\mathfrak{g}(m)$, where $\mathfrak{g}$ is a (not necessarily efficiently) invertible function. This relaxation allows us to view the ElGamal cryptosystem as additively homomorphic. Let us define it formally.

Definition 4 (Additively homomorphic $\mathfrak{g}$-semi-encryption scheme). *A set of three polynomial-time algorithms $AH = (\mathsf{KeyGen}_{AH}, \mathsf{Enc}_{AH}, \mathsf{Dec}_{AH})$ constitutes a semantically secure homomorphic $\mathfrak{g}$-semi-encryption scheme if it satisfies the following input-output specification as well as correctness, security, and homomorphic properties:*

> **Input-output specification** KeyGen_{AH} *and* Enc_{AH} *have the same input-output specifications as those for key generation and encryption algorithms, respectively, for a public-key encryption scheme.* $\mathsf{Dec}_{AH}(\mathsf{sk}_{AH}, c)$ *takes as input a secret key* sk_{AH} *and a ciphertext, and outputs a value* $m' = \mathfrak{g}(m)$ *for some* $m \in \mathcal{M}$ *where* $\mathcal{M}$ *is the message space of the encryption scheme[2].*
>
> **Correctness** *For all* $(\mathsf{pk}, \mathsf{sk}) \in \mathsf{KeyGen}_{AH}$, *for all* $m \in \mathcal{M}$, *for all* $c \in \mathsf{Enc}_{AH}(\mathsf{pk}, m)$, $\mathsf{Dec}_{AH}(\mathsf{sk}, c) = \mathfrak{g}(m)$. *I.e., the decryption algorithm correctly recovers* $\mathfrak{g}(m)$ *from an encryption of* m.
>
> **Security** *The definition of semantic security for a* $\mathfrak{g}$-semi-encryption *is the same definition as the semantic security of a regular encryption scheme [31].*
>
> **Additively homomorphic properties** *(1)* $\mathcal{M}$ *is an algebraic ring and (2) there is an efficient deterministic algorithm* Op_{AH} *that takes as input the public key* pk_{AH} *and two ciphertexts,* c_1 *and* c_2 *and outputs a ciphertext* c' *such that for all* $\mathsf{pk}_{AH} \in \mathsf{KeyGen}_{AH}$, *for all* $m_1, m_2 \in \mathcal{M}$, *for all ciphertexts* $c_1 \in \mathsf{Enc}(\mathsf{pk}_{AH}, m_1)$ *and* $c_2 \in \mathsf{Enc}(\mathsf{pk}_{AH}, m_2)$, *if* $c' = \mathsf{Op}_{AH}(\mathsf{pk}_{AH}, c_1, c_2)$, *then* $c' \in \mathsf{Enc}(\mathsf{pk}_{AH}, m_1 + m_2)$.

For our constructions in Sect. 4.1 we define $\mathcal{M}$ as $\mathbb{Z}_p$ for a prime p for ElGamal or $\mathbb{Z}_N$ for an RSA modulus N for Camenisch-Shoup.

Further (inspired by Cramer, Damgård and Nielsen's [28] formalization of an additively homomorphic cryptosystem), we also need a way to sample new encryptions of messages, i.e., compute $c' \leftarrow \mathsf{Enc}(\mathsf{pk}_{AH}, m)$ given any $c \in \mathsf{Enc}(\mathsf{pk}_{AH}, m)$. That is, we require that this be achieved by forming a fresh encryption of 0, $c_0 \leftarrow \mathsf{Enc}(\mathsf{pk}_{AH}, 0)$ and then adding c_0 to c, resulting in $c' = c \oplus c_0$. Further, we need AH to include efficient algorithms for obtaining $c' \in \mathsf{Enc}(\mathsf{pk}_{AH}, am)$ from $c \in \mathsf{Enc}(\mathsf{pk}_{AH}, m)$ and $a \in \mathcal{M}$.

---

[2] In general, $\mathcal{M}$ and $\mathfrak{g}$ may depend on the public key, pk_{AH}, but in our constructions, this is not the case. Our scalar commitments share this same message space.

Notation for Additively-Homomorphic Encryption. We will generally use the lowercase c label to refer to ciphertexts (while uppercase C refers to commitments). If c_1 and c_2 are ciphertexts, will use $c_1 \oplus c_2$ to denote the output of $\mathsf{Op}(\mathsf{pk}, c_1, c_2)$. We use $\boxed{a}_{\mathsf{pk}}$ to represent an encryption of a under the public key pk using the scheme AH; we will drop the subscript and denote it $\boxed{a}$ when pk is clear from the context. By $\boxed{a} = \boxed{c} \oplus \boxed{d}$ we denote that the ciphertext $\boxed{a}$ was generated by running the algorithm $\mathsf{Op}(\mathsf{pk}, \boxed{c}, \boxed{d})$; thus $\boxed{a} = \boxed{c+d}$; $y \odot \boxed{a}$ denotes applying this operation y times; in our instantiations this will yield $\boxed{ya}$ and is efficient for large y with repeated squaring; $\bigoplus_{i=0}^{n} \boxed{a_i}$ denotes applying Op n times on the set $\{\boxed{a_i} : i \in [0...n]\}$. We will write the set of integers from 1 to m as $[m]$.

2.3 Privacy Preserving f-Blueprint Schemes (PPBs)

[37] defines a blueprint scheme as in Definition 3. We will modify their definition to serve our new use-case of non-frameable privacy preserving blueprints in Sect. 5.1. A blueprint scheme has three parties - an auditor, a set of users and a set of recipients.

$\mathsf{Setup}(1^\lambda, cpar) \to \Lambda$: Outputs public parameters Λ.
$\mathsf{KeyGen}(\Lambda, x, r_x) \to (\mathsf{pk_A}, \mathsf{sk_A})$: The key generation algorithm for auditor A.
$\mathsf{VerPK}(\Lambda, \mathsf{pk_A}, C_x) \to 1$ or 0: Takes the auditor's public key $\mathsf{pk_A}$ and a commitment C_x
    as input, verifies that the auditor's public key was computed correctly w.r.t. C_x.
$\mathsf{Escrow}(\Lambda, \mathsf{pk_A}, y, r_y) \to Z$: Takes Λ, $\mathsf{pk_A}$, and commitment value and opening (y, r_y) as
    input and outputs an escrow Z for commitment $C = \mathsf{Com}(y; r_y)$.
$\mathsf{VerEscrow}(\Lambda, \mathsf{pk_A}, C_y, Z) \to 1$ or 0: Takes the auditor's public key $\mathsf{pk_A}$, commitment
    C_y, and escrow Z as input and verifies that Z was computed correctly w.r.t. C_y.
$\mathsf{Dec}(\Lambda, \mathsf{sk_A}, C_y, Z) \to f(x, y)$ or $\perp$: Takes the auditor's secret key $\mathsf{sk_A}$, a commitment
    C_y and an escrow Z as input. It decrypts the escrow and returns the output $f(x, y)$
    if C_y is a commitment to y and $\mathsf{VerEscrow}(\Lambda, \mathsf{pk_A}, C_y, Z) = 1$.

Fig. 3. An f-blueprint scheme.

KLN define a *secure* f-blueprint scheme as one that possesses the following properties - (a) Correctness of VerPK and $\mathsf{VerEscrow}$, (b) Correctness of Dec (c) Soundness (d) Blueprint Hiding (e) Privacy against Dishonest Auditor and (f) Privacy with Honest Auditor. We recall these definitions in the full version of this paper [33].

3 Succinct Proofs for Verifiable Secure Computation on Additively-Homomorphic Ciphertexts

In this section, we describe our new succinct proof system for verifiable secure computation, as introduced on page 3 in our first contribution. Suppose that we have an additively homomorphic $\mathfrak{g}$-semi cryptosystem $\Gamma^{\mathsf{Enc}} = (\mathsf{Setup}, \mathsf{Enc},$

Dec, $\oplus, \odot$) as discussed in Definition 4. Let pk be a public key for this cryptosystem given a set of ciphertexts $c_1, \ldots, c_n$ whose plaintexts are $x_1, \ldots, x_n$, and a set of scalars $y_1, \ldots, y_k$, the additively homomorphic property of the cryptosystem allows anyone to compute a ciphertext c_f which is the encryption of $f(x_1, \ldots, x_n, y_1 \ldots, y_k)$, where f is a polynomial. This polynomial is of max degree 1 in any x_i, or, in other words: the polynomial is made up of n monomials, $\{f_i\}_{i \in [n]}$, where $f_i = a_i x_i^{b_i} \prod_{j=1}^{k} y_j^{d_{i,j}}$, b_i is a bit ($\{0,1\}$), a_i is a coefficient of f, and $d_{i,j}$ is an integer. In this section, we provide a framework for efficiently obtaining a proof system, in the random-oracle model, for the following relation, parameterized[3] by the polynomial f:

$$R_f((r_1, \ldots, r_k, y_1, \ldots, y_k), (C_1, \ldots, C_k, c_1, \ldots, c_n, c_f)) = 1 \text{ iff}$$
$$\exists x_1, \ldots, x_n \text{ such that } C_j = \mathsf{Com}(y_j, r_j) \ \forall 1 \leq j \leq k$$
$$\wedge \, c_i \in \mathsf{Enc}(\mathsf{pk}, x_i) \ \forall 1 \leq i \leq n \wedge c_f \in \mathsf{Enc}(\mathsf{pk}, f(x_1, \ldots, x_n, y_1, \ldots, y_k))$$

Our proof system is complete, zero-knowledge and satisfies the definition of a (not straight-line extractable) proof of knowledge in the random-oracle model. To compile it into a partially straight-line extractable (g-BB-PSL) proof system, it will be sufficient to combine it with a g-BB-PSL proof of knowledge of the opening of the commitments $C_1, \ldots, C_k$ which we do in Sect. 5.3.

Construction of a Proof System for R_f. Proving R_f directly using standard discrete logarithm representation proofs would yield a proof of size $\Omega(k d_{\mathsf{max}})$ where d_{max} is the largest degree among any $y_i, i \in [k]$. To make this more succinct, our proof system halves the degree with each step. This reduces the size of the proof from linear in d_{max} to $O(k \log(d_{\mathsf{max}}))$. The proof size is independent of the number of monomials in f and ciphertexts, and depends only on k (the number of variables $y_1, \ldots, y_k$) and the degree d_{max}.

Each step of this proof will reduce the task of proving the correct evaluation of a polynomial f to that of another polynomial f'. To achieve succinctness, at each step we will pick a variable and ensure that the degree of f' in that variable is at most half that of f. For example, proving that $c_f = \boxed{f(x_1, x_2, y_1, y_2)}$ where $f = x_1 y_1^8 y_2 + x_2 y_1^7 y_2$ will be reduced to proving that $c_{f'} = \boxed{f'(x_1', x_2', y_1, y_2)}$ where $f' = x_1' y_1^4 y_2 + x_2' y_1^3 y_2$. We can see that the degree of f' in y_1 has been reduced by 4 here compared to f.[4] In this section, we will explain how the ciphertexts $\boxed{x_1'}$ and $\boxed{x_2'}$ can be computed from $\boxed{x_1}$ and $\boxed{x_2}$ by both the prover and verifier in a way that ensures that proving the correctness of f' implies the correctness of f. Because we want to achieve zero knowledge even when the adversary knows the secret key of the encryption scheme, a zero-knowledge simulator cannot simply make up an arbitrary value for $c_{f'}$: the adversary would be able to decrypt it and detect simulation. Thus, we need to instead commit

---

[3] This relation is also parameterized by the parameters of the associated commitment and encryption schemes (for Com and Enc) along with the public key, pk. We omit this for readability since it is clear from context.

[4] As noted in Sect. 1.1 and related work, these techniques resemble [39] and Bulletproofs but present unique challenges when applied to committed ciphertexts.

to this value and perform the proof that the committed value was computed correctly. We call these *commitments to additively homomorphic ciphertexts* and we define them in Sect. 3.1 and construct them in Sect. 4.

3.1   Basic Building Blocks

Commitment to $\{y_1, \ldots, y_k\}$. Our relation R_f is defined relative to a non-interactive commitment scheme for scalars (CSetup, Com). Com takes as input an element y from the message space $\mathcal{M}$ and a random value r sampled uniformly at random from $[R]$ for some integer R.

Proofs of Correct Modular Addition and Multiplication of Committed Values. In order to construct this proof system, we need to add and multiply the values in our scalar commitments together (using ring arithmetic in the message space $\mathcal{M}$). This will be used to realize *eqrep* (Definition 3) and thus realize our commitments to ciphertexts. We often call these "commitments to scalars" since their committed values will be multiplied with encrypted values. Let us define the following relations:[5]

- $R_{\mathsf{add}}((x_1, r_1, x_2, r_2, x_3, r_3), (C_1, C_2, C_3)) = 1$ iff $\forall i \in [3] : C_i = \mathsf{Com}(x_i; r_i)$, and $x_3 = x_1 + x_2 \in \mathcal{M}$. Let $(\mathsf{Prove}^{\mathsf{add}}, \mathsf{Verify}^{\mathsf{add}})$ be a BB NIZK proof system for R_{add}.
- $R_{\mathsf{mult}}((x_1, r_1, x_2, r_2, x_3, r_3), (C_1, C_2, C_3)) = 1$ iff $\forall i \in [3] : C_i = \mathsf{Com}(x_i; r_i)$, and $x_3 = x_1 x_2 \in \mathcal{M}$. Let $(\mathsf{Prove}^{\mathsf{mult}}, \mathsf{Verify}^{\mathsf{mult}})$ be a BB NIZK proof system for R_{mult}.

We also need this commitment scheme to have a zero-knowledge proof of knowledge $(\mathsf{Prove}^{\mathsf{Com}}, \mathsf{Verify}^{\mathsf{Com}})$ of opening, i.e. a BB NIZK for the relation $R_{\mathsf{Com}} = ((m, r), (C))$ iff $\mathsf{Com}(m; r) = C$.

Commitment to Ciphertexts. In order to prove correctness of an intermediate step in a longer computation over (semi-)encrypted data without revealing the ciphertext obtained in that step itself (which would leak data), we need to be able to commit to ciphertexts and prove properties of committed ciphertexts. Thus, we need a non-interactive statistically hiding, computationally binding commitment scheme Com_{AH} (parameterized by public parameters *params* generated by Setup_{AH}) for committing to ciphertexts $c \in \mathsf{Enc}_{AH}(\mathsf{pk}, \cdot)$ and we need protocols for proving statements about committed ciphertexts, as described below. We use a subscript notation (i.e. Com_{AH}) to distinguish this scheme from our commitments to scalars which do not have a subscript (the commitment function for scalars is Com). If randomness is not supplied to Com_{AH}, it will sample randomness and output it, e.g.: $(C, r) = \mathsf{Com}_{AH}(\boxed{a})$ implies that $C = \mathsf{Com}_{AH}(\boxed{a}; r)$.

Proofs of Relations Between Committed Ciphertexts. We need BB NIZK proof systems for (1) proving knowledge of a committed ciphertext; (2) proving

---

[5] R_{add} is trivial with additively homomorphic commitments, but we present this function for generality.

that a committed ciphertext is the result of applying Op_{AH} to other committed ciphertexts; (3) proving that a committed ciphertext is the result of applying Op_{AH} to another committed ciphertext α times, where α is the opening of a commitment (under the scalar commitment scheme Com) to an element of $\mathcal{M}$; and (4) proving that a committed ciphertext is an encryption of a committed scalar. (4) is often called "verifiable encryption" (VE). More precisely, let us define the following relations:[6]:

- $R_{\mathsf{Com}_{AH}}((c,r),C) = 1$ iff $C = \mathsf{Com}_{AH}(c;r)$;
- $R_{\oplus}((c_1,r_1,c_2,r_2,c_3,r_3),(C_1,C_2,C_3)) = 1$ iff $\forall i \in [3] : C_i = \mathsf{Com}_{AH}(c_i;r_i)$ and $c_3 = \mathsf{Op}_{AH}(c_1,c_2)$;
- $R_{\odot}((c_1,r_1,c_2,r_2,x,r_3),(C_1,C_2,C_3)) = 1$ iff $\forall i \in [2] : C_i = \mathsf{Com}_{AH}(c_i;r_i)$, $C_3 = \mathsf{Com}(x;r_3)$ and $c_2 = c_1 \odot x$.
- $R_{VE}((c_1,r_1,r_{c_1},y,r_2),(C_1,C_2)) = 1$ iff $C_1 = \mathsf{Com}_{AH}(c_1;r_1)$, $C_2 = \mathsf{Com}(y;r_2)$ and $c_1 = \mathsf{Enc}_{AH}(\mathsf{pk}_{AH},y;r_{c_1})$.

Our construction will use the BB NIZKs ($\mathsf{Prove}^{\mathsf{Com}_{AH}}$, $\mathsf{Verify}^{\mathsf{Com}_{AH}}$) for the relation $R_{\mathsf{Com}_{AH}}$, ($\mathsf{Prove}^{\oplus}$, $\mathsf{Verify}^{\oplus}$) for the relation $R_{\oplus}$, ($\mathsf{Prove}^{\odot}$, $\mathsf{Verify}^{\odot}$) for the relation $R_{\odot}$, and ($\mathsf{Prove}^{\mathsf{enc}}$, $\mathsf{Verify}^{\mathsf{enc}}$) for the relation R_{VE} as building blocks. As before, we omit the parameters and public keys from these relations when it is clear. These proof systems exist generically for any cryptosystem and any set of commitment schemes by representing the Com function as a circuit; however, for the specific instantiations of semi-encryption and commitment schemes we consider, we also show how to construct them efficiently in Sect. 4.

Notation. We will use the Camenisch-Stadler notation described in Sect. 2.1 to describe proofs over committed ciphertexts. For example, if we have $A = \mathsf{Com}_{AH}(\boxed{a};r_a)$, $B = \mathsf{Com}_{AH}(\boxed{b};r_b)$, and $C = \mathsf{Com}(c;r_c)$ and want to prove that $a = bc$, we'll denote the output of the prover's computation as $\pi = \mathsf{NIZK}[\boxed{a},\boxed{b},c,r_a,r_b,r_c : A = \mathsf{Com}_{AH}(\boxed{a},r_a) \wedge B = \mathsf{Com}_{AH}(\boxed{b},r_b) \wedge C = \mathsf{Com}(c;r_C,a_C) \wedge \boxed{a} = \boxed{b} \odot c]$. This π is computed by calling $\mathsf{Prove}^{\odot}(A,B,C,\boxed{a},r_a,\boxed{b},r_b,c,r_c)$. If π is accepted by the verification algorithm (i.e. $\mathsf{Verify}^{\odot}(A,B,C,\pi) = 1$) we can extract openings for A, B and C to ciphertexts $\boxed{a}$, $\boxed{b}$ and scalar c respectively, such that $\boxed{a} = \boxed{b} \odot c$.

3.2   Efficient Proof System for R_f for $k = 1$

In this section we show how to efficiently instantiate a NIZK proof for the relation R_f when $k = 1$, i.e. there is a single variable y. This will help the reader understand our construction for multi-variate polynomials in Sect. 3.3.

---

[6] Similar to our commitments to scalars, $R_{\oplus}$ is not necessary if the commitments are additively homomorphic but we present this here for generality.

Observe that it is sufficient[7] to provide a proof system for the polynomial $P = \sum_{i=0}^{n-1} x_i y^i$. Thus we give a proof system for the relation R_P. In our proof system for R_P, we will also construct a proof system for R_P^* in which the statement contains not the ciphertext c_P but a commitment $C_P = \mathsf{Com}_{AH}(c_P, r_P)$ which will help with recursion. Assume WLOG[8] that n (the number of ciphertexts) is a power of two. More formally,

$$R_P^*((r, y, c_P, r_P), (C_y, c_0, \ldots, c_{n-1}, C_P)) = 1 \text{ iff}$$
$$R_P(r, y, C_y, c_0, \ldots, c_{n-1}, c_P) = 1 \wedge C_P = \mathsf{Com}_{AH}(c_P, r_P).$$

Input to the Recursive Step. Our PoK_P^* algorithm in Algorithm 2 recursively computes a proof until R_P^* is satisfied, i.e., C_P is a commitment to $c_P = \boxed{e} = \boxed{P(x_0, \ldots, x_{n-1}, y)}$. The input to PoK_P^* includes an auxiliary input aux, in addition to the statement and witness for the relation R_P^*. aux consists of commitments to a logarithmic number of powers of y, i.e. commitments $\{C_{y^{2^i}}\}$ to $\{y^{2^i}\} = \{y^2, y^4, y^8, \ldots, y^{n/2}\}$ and NIZK proofs that for $i > 1$, each $C_{y^{2^i}}$ is computed correctly from $C_{y^{2^{i-1}}}$ (using the proof system for commitments to scalars described above). aux is of size that is logarithmic in n and the verifier need not verify any proofs in it more than once. We assume that the prover remembers how it computed aux (so we won't explicitly pass the openings of the commitments in aux to the recursive step). Algorithm 1 is a "wrapper" algorithm that, on input the statement-witness pair for relation R_P transforms it into the statement-witness pair for relation R_P^*, initializes aux with $\{C_{y^{2^i}}\}$ and their proofs of correctness, initializes the transcript τ and calls PoK_P^* .

Ensuring Soundness for the Recursive Proof. The prover and verifier can both compute encrypted evaluations of the polynomial $P(x_0, \ldots, x_{n-1}, \gamma)$ on any input γ using the ciphertexts $\{c_i\}$. They can further break P into two parts such that $P(x_0, \ldots, x_{n-1}, \gamma) = P_1(x_0, \ldots, x_{n/2-1}, \gamma) + P_2(x_{n/2}, \ldots, x_{n-1}, \gamma)$ where P_1 contains the monomials $x_i \gamma^i$ for $i < n/2$, and P_2 contains monomials of higher degree in γ. We can represent P as $P(x_0, \ldots, x_{n-1}, \gamma) = P_1(x_0, \ldots, x_{n/2-1}, \gamma) + \gamma^{n/2} P_3(x_{n/2}, \ldots, x_{n-1}, \gamma)$ where $P_3(\gamma) = P_2(\gamma)/\gamma^{n/2}$.

To recurse, the prover commits to ciphertexts $\boxed{e_1} = \boxed{P_1(x_0, \ldots, x_{n/2-1}, y)}$, $\boxed{e_2} = \boxed{P_2(x_{n/2}, \ldots, x_{n-1}, y)}$, $\boxed{e_3} = \boxed{P_3(x_{n/2}, \ldots, x_{n-1}, y)}$, and then proves (using the proof systems for proving properties of committed ciphertexts) that

---

[7] From here, to obtain the proof system for any $f = a_{00} + \sum_{i=0}^{n-1} \sum_{j=0}^{n-1} a_{i,j} x_j y^i$, we use the homomorphic properties of the cryptosystem to compute $c_i' = \boxed{\sum_{j=0}^{n-1} a_{i,j} x_j}$ for $0 \leq i < n$, (deterministically, using the all-0 string for encryption) incorporate the term a_{00} by letting $c_0'' = c_0' \oplus \boxed{a_{00}}$ and then invoke the proof system for P on input ciphertexts $c_0'', c_1', \ldots, c_{n-1}'$. Here we assume that the degree of y is n, but this is WLOG as the complexity of the proof system is not dependant on the number of ciphertexts.

[8] This is without loss of generality: to reduce to this case, prover and verifier can both compute the extra ciphertexts $c_n, \ldots, c_{2^a-1}$ (so that the total number is a power of two) by encrypting 0 with fixed randomness.

$\boxed{e} = \boxed{e_1} \oplus \boxed{e_2}$ and $\boxed{e_2} = y^{n/2} \odot \boxed{e_3}$ using the commitment $C_{y^{n/2}}$ found in aux. Thus, the prover has reduced the task of proving that C_P is a commitment to $\boxed{e} = \boxed{P(x_0, \ldots, x_{n-1}, y)}$ for a polynomial P of degree $n-1$ to the task of proving that C_{P_1} is a commitment to $\boxed{e_1} = \boxed{P_1(x_0, \ldots, x_{n/2-1}, y)}$ and C_{P_3} is a commitment to $\boxed{e_3} = \boxed{P_3(x_0, \ldots, x_{n/2-1}, y)}$, where P_1 and P_3 are both polynomials of degree $n/2 - 1$.

To take advantage of recursion, we need to use just one recursive call in order to prove that the openings of C_{P_1} and C_{P_3} (i.e., $\boxed{e_1}$ and $\boxed{e_3}$ respectively) are encrypted evaluations of P_1 and P_3. To do so, prover and verifier define a new polynomial P' of degree $(n-1)/2$ by taking a random linear combination of P_1 and P_3: let α be the output of the random oracle on input the elements of the proof that have been computed so far. Let $P'(x_0, \ldots, x_{n-1}, y) = P_1(x_0, \ldots, x_{n-1}, y) + \alpha P_3(x_0, \ldots, x_{n-1}, y)$. By the Schwartz-Zippel Lemma ([44,45]), if committed $\boxed{e_1} \neq \boxed{P_1(y)}$ or committed $\boxed{e_3} \neq \boxed{P_3(y)}$, then with overwhelming probability over the choice of α, $\boxed{e_1} \oplus (\alpha \odot \boxed{e_3}) \neq \boxed{P'(x_0, \ldots, x_{n-1}, y)}$. Let $C_{P'}$ be a commitment to the ciphertext $\boxed{e'} = \boxed{e_1} \oplus (\alpha \odot \boxed{e_3})$; the prover can provide a proof that indeed $C_{P'}$ is a commitment to $\boxed{e'}$ computed this way based on C_{P_1} and C_{P_3} and α using the proof systems for committed ciphertexts.

Next, we use recursion to prove that $C_{P'}$ corresponds to correctly evaluating the polynomial P', i.e. it is a commitment to $\boxed{P'(x_0, \ldots, x_{n-1}, y)}$. To do so, we call PoK_P^* on input ciphertexts $(c_0', \ldots, c_{n/2-1}')$ where $c_i' = \boxed{x_i} \oplus (\alpha \odot \boxed{x_{n/2} + i})$.

Algorithm 1. $\mathsf{PoK}_P(r, y, \underline{C_y, c_0, \ldots, c_{n-1}, c_P}) \to \pi$

 Let $c_i = \{\boxed{x_i}\}_{i \in [0 \ldots n-1]})$;
 Prover needs to prove that $c_P = \boxed{e} = \bigoplus_{i=0}^{n}(\boxed{x_i} \odot y^i)$
 To format c_P for the recursion, we commit to it with known randomness e.g. 0
1: $C_P \leftarrow \mathsf{Com}_{AH}(c_P; 0)$
2: For $i = 1$ to $\log n$, let $(C_{y^{2^i}}, r_i) = \mathsf{Com}(y^{2^i})$
   and let $\pi_{y^{2^i}} \leftarrow \mathsf{NIZK}[(z, r_{i-1}, r_i) : C_{y^{2^{i-1}}} = \mathsf{Com}(z; r_{i-1}) \wedge C_{y^{2^i}} = \mathsf{Com}(z^2; r_i)]$.
3: Initialize $\mathsf{aux} = (\{C_{y^{2^i}}, \pi_{y^{2^i}}\}_{i \in [\log(n)]})$, $\tau = (C_y, c_0, \ldots, c_{n-1}, c_P)$.
4: **return** $\mathsf{aux}, \mathsf{PoK}_P^*(r_y, y, c_P, r_P, C_y, c_0, \ldots, c_{n-1}, C_P, \mathsf{aux}, \tau)$

Theorem 1. *Our scheme in Algorithms 1 and 2 are complete and ZK (Definition 1).*

Theorem 2. *The PoK_P^* function in Algorithm 2 is black-box (BB) simulation extractable with respect to Definition 2 for the relation R_P^*.*

For compactness, here we only present the prover's algorithms; the verifier's algorithms (provided in the full version of this paper [33]) should follow from the prover's algorithms. For readability, in the list of inputs to the prover, we underline those inputs that are also given to the verifier. We prove Theorems 1 and 2 in the full version of this paper [33] where we also show how to instantiate our NIZK proofs from *eqrep* (*eqrep* is described in Definition 3).

Algorithm 2. $\mathsf{PoK}_P^*(r_y, y, c_P, r_P, \underline{C_y, c_0, \ldots, c_{n-1}, C_P, \mathsf{aux}, \tau}) \rightarrow \pi'$

Let $c_i = \{\boxed{x_i}\}_{i \in [0 \ldots n-1]}; c_P = \boxed{e}$

    Prover needs to prove that $C_P = \mathsf{Com}_{AH}(\boxed{e}; r_P)$ where $\boxed{e} = \bigoplus_{i=0}^{n-1} \boxed{x_i} \odot y^i = \boxed{\sum_{i=0}^{n-1} y^i x_i}$ and $C_y = \mathsf{Com}(y; r_y)$

If the degree of the polynomial is low enough, prove its computation directly:

1: **if** $n = 1$, **return** (π_1) where $\pi_1 \leftarrow \mathsf{NIZK}[r : \mathsf{Com}_{AH}(\boxed{x_0}, r) = C_P]$

    If not, we will need to reduce the degree needed to prove C and recurse.

    To do so, first, commit to the lower half of the polynomial:

2: $(C_1, \rho_1) = \mathsf{Com}_{AH}(\boxed{e_1})$ where $\boxed{e_1} = \bigoplus_{i=0}^{n/2-1} \boxed{x_i} \cdot y^i = \boxed{\sum_{i=0}^{n/2-1} y^i x_i}$

    Next, commit to the upper half of the polynomial

3: $(C_2, \rho_2) = \mathsf{Com}_{AH}(\boxed{e_2})$

    where $\boxed{e_2} = \bigoplus_{i=0}^{n/2-1} \boxed{x_{i+n/2}} \odot y^{i+n/2} = \boxed{\sum_{i=0}^{n/2-1} y^{i+n/2} x_{i+n/2}}$

    Lastly, commit to the upper half of the polynomial with the degree lowered by half

4: $(C_3, \rho_3) = \mathsf{Com}_{AH}(\boxed{e_3})$ where $\boxed{e_3} = \bigoplus_{i=0}^{n/2-1} \boxed{x_{i+n/2}} \odot y^i = \boxed{\sum_{i=0}^{n/2-1} y^i x_{i+n/2}}$

    Query the random oracle on the current transcript of the proof so far, (C_1, C_2, C_3, τ)

5: $\alpha \leftarrow H(C_1, C_2, C_3, \tau)$

    Compute the encryptions of the new coefficients for a reduced degree polynomial

6: $\forall i \in [n/2 - 1], c_i' = \boxed{x_i'} = \boxed{x_i} \oplus (\boxed{x_{i+n/2}} \odot \alpha)$

    Compute a new evaluation over this reduced degree polynomial:

7: $(C_P', r') = \mathsf{Com}_{AH}(\boxed{e'})$ where $\boxed{e'} = \bigoplus_{i=0}^{n/2-1} \boxed{x_i'} \odot y^i$

    Prove that this new commitment C_P' is consistent with C_P, C_1, C_2, and C_3.

8: $\pi_\alpha \leftarrow \mathsf{NIZK}[r, \rho_1, \rho_2, \rho_3, r', r_y, y, \boxed{e}, \boxed{e_1}, \boxed{e_2}, \boxed{e_3}, \boxed{e'} :$

9:     $\mathsf{Com}_{AH}(\boxed{e}, r) = C_P \wedge \mathsf{Com}_{AH}(\boxed{e'}, r') = C_P' \wedge \forall 1 \le i \le 3 : \mathsf{Com}_{AH}(\boxed{e_i}, \rho_i) = C_i$

10:     $\wedge \boxed{e} = \boxed{e_1} \oplus \boxed{e_2}$

11:     $\wedge \boxed{e_2} = y^{n/2} \odot \boxed{e_3}$ ▷ proven relative to $C_{y^{n/2}}$ in aux

12:     $\wedge \boxed{e'} = \boxed{e_1} \oplus (\alpha \odot \boxed{e_3})]$

13: $\pi = (C_1, C_2, C_3, C_P', \pi_\alpha)$

14: $\tau' = (\pi, \tau)$ ▷ Append this proof to the transcript

15: **return** $(\pi, \mathsf{PoK}_P^*(r_y, y, \boxed{e'}, r', C_y, c_0', \ldots, c_{n/2-1}', C_P', \mathsf{aux}, \tau'))$

3.3   Proof System for Multivariate Polynomials

We present our algorithm for polynomials with multiple y_i values in the full version of this paper [33]. This algorithm proves the relation R_y described at the start of this section. In essence, the algorithm will perform the same recursive step as Algorithm 2 until it has reduced the degree of a y_i variable to 0. The algorithm then recurses on the remaining $k - 1$ y_i variables until none are left. At this point, the evaluation has been fully proven.

For intuition, we describe how our protocol would prove the correct computation of an example polynomial: $f(x_1, x_2, y_1, y_2) = a_1 x_1 y_1 y_2 + a_2 x_2 y_1^2 y_2$. Our proof function will first focus on y_1, finding that the maximum degree of this variable, $d_{\mathsf{max}} = 2$. It will then compute $f_1(x_1, x_2, y_1, y_2) = a_1 x_1 y_1 y_2$ and $f_2(x_1, x_2, y_1, y_2) = a_2 x_2 y_1^2 y_2$ as well as $f_3(x_1, x_2, y_1, y_2) = (a_2 x_2 y_1^2 y_2)/y_1 = a_2 x_2 y_1 y_2$. The proof function will then commit to encryptions of these polynomials, and hash the transcript to receive the challenge, α. It will then prove the relation[9] $f(\ldots) = f_1(\ldots) + f_2(\ldots)$ and $f_2(\ldots) = y_1 * f_3(\ldots)$. It will then compute $f'(\ldots) = f_1(\ldots) + \alpha f_3(\ldots) = a_1 x_1 y_1 y_2 + a_2' x_2 y_1 y_2$ where $a_2' = a_2 * \alpha$. This process will repeat for f', with the prover recomputing $d_{\max}$ for y_1 to be 1. The prover will then compute $f_1', f_2',$ and f_3' (similar to how they computed $f_1, f_2,$ and f_3) but this time, the prover will find that $f_1'(\ldots) = 0$ (since no monomial has degree of y_1 less than $d_{\max}/2 = 1/2$) and $f_3'(\ldots) = (a_1 x_1 y_1 y_2 + a_2' x_2 y_1 y_2)/y_1 = a_1 x_1 y_2 + a_2' x_2 y_2$. Thus, $f''(\ldots) = f_1'(\ldots) + \alpha f_3'(\ldots) = 0 + \alpha'(a_1 x_1 y_2 + a_2' x_2 y_2)$ (for the challenge, α'). Thus, the prover has removed y_1 from the polynomial to be proven. Once this repeats to remove y_2, the prover is left with $f^*(\ldots) = a_1^* x_1 + a_2^* x_2$ where a_1^* and a_2^* are some combination of the coefficients of f and the challenges from the previous recursive steps. This is a linear function in the x_i's where the α's are known by the verifier so the verifier can simply compute the encryption of $f^*(\ldots)$ at this point and the prover can prove that they've committed to this encryption. We give our results for this relation in Theorems 4 and 3 which we prove in the full version of this paper [33].

Theorem 3. *The multi-variate version of our scheme in Algorithm 1 and Algorithm 2 (described in the full version of this paper [33]) is complete and ZK (Definition 1).*

Theorem 4. *The multi-variate version of our scheme in Algorithm 1 and Algorithm 2 (described in the full version of this paper [33]) is black-box (BB) simulation extractable with respect to Definition 2 for the relation R_f defined in Sect. 3.*

4   Instantiations of Commitments to Additively-Homomorphic Ciphertexts

As explained on page 3 in our first contribution, for our proof system from Sect. 3 to be efficient, we require schemes to compute over commitments to additively homomorphic ciphertexts that we define in Sect. 3.1. In this section, we introduce some efficient instantiations of these schemes.

We first define variants of ElGamal and Camenisch-Shoup encryption, in Sect. 4.1. Specifically, we define "lifted" ElGamal and Camenisch-Shoup in a "commitment-friendly" group. We then construct commitments to ciphertexts and associated proof systems for adding and multiplying ElGamal ciphertexts and Camenisch-Shoup ciphertexts. We use (Lifted) ElGamal which is a $\mathfrak{g}$-semi-encryption as defined in Sect. 3 with message space $\mathcal{M} = \mathbb{Z}_p$ and $\mathfrak{g}(x) = h^x \bmod p$. Camenisch-Shoup encryption has the advantage that it allows for the efficient computation of discrete logarithms in a subgroup of size n where n is an RSA modulus. Thus, with Camenisch-Shoup encryption, we can efficiently decrypt ciphertexts when the message space has exponential size. Thus, our Camenisch-Shoup construction is a $\mathfrak{g}$-semi-encryption where $\mathfrak{g}$ is the identity

---

[9] For compactness, we've replaced the input to functions, x_1, x_2, y_1, y_2, with ellipses.

function (i.e. a standard encryption scheme). In our Camenisch-Shoup construction, the message space is $\mathcal{M} = \mathbb{Z}_n$. In Sect. 4.2 we construct commitments to Camenisch-Shoup ciphertexts. As the setting of ElGamal is simpler, we only include it in the full version of this paper [33] though we review some elements of ElGamal encryption which explain why it is similar to Camenisch-Shoup.

4.1 Encryption Schemes

We review (Lifted) ElGamal encryption in Fig. 4a and a modified Camenisch-Shoup encryption in Fig. 4b. We include an extra generator (h) for lifting to exponents in ElGamal so that we can draw parallels between ElGamal and Camenisch-Shoup (ElGamal encryption generally uses the default generator, $h = g$). We see that both ElGamal and Camenisch-Shoup have similar homomorphic properties. Specifically for two encryptions, $(g^r, k^r h^m)$ and $(g^{r'}, k^{r'} h^{m'})$, $(g^r \cdot g^{r'}, k^r h^m \cdot k^{r'} h^{m'})$ is a valid encryption of $\mathfrak{g}(m + m')$ in both encryption schemes where k is the public key. Also, exponentiation is similar, *i.e.*, $((g^r)^y, (k^r h^m)^y)$ is a valid encryption of $\mathfrak{g}(ym)$ in both encryption schemes.

Our modification to Camenisch-Shoup encryption includes replacing some values (parameter $g \in \mathbb{Z}_n$ and ciphertext c) with their absolute values. Modifying Camenisch-Shoup in this way ensures that the elements of honest Camenisch-Shoup ciphertexts lie in a "commitment-friendly" sub-group $|QR_{n^2}|$ where $|QR_{n^2}| = \{|x| : x \in QR_{n^2}\}$, QR_{n^2} is the quadratic residues in $\mathbb{Z}_{n^2}$ (elements that have a square root in $\mathbb{Z}_{n^2}$), and $|\cdot|$ is the absolute value function such that $|x|$ of an element $x \in \mathbb{Z}_{n^2}$ is $n^2 - x$ if $x > \lfloor n^2/2 \rfloor$ and x otherwise. One nice property of $|QR_{n^2}|$ is that it is cyclic (which helps with our hiding and ZK proofs) and also $|QR_{n^2}|$ is efficiently sampleable by sampling a random element of $\mathbb{Z}_{n^2}$, squaring it, and taking its absolute value.

Critically, elements of $|QR_{n^2}|$ are always equal to their absolute value i.e. $|x| = x$ for elements in $|QR_{n^2}|$. This is important because it means that using *eqrep*-$\mathbb{Z}_{n^2}$ (as defined in Sect. 2.1) to prove relations between $|QR_{n^2}|$ elements works perfectly, where-as for $\mathbb{Z}_{n^2}$ it only holds for the absolute values of these elements. As an example, if we wanted to prove that we know a such that $c = g^a$ in $\mathbb{Z}_{n^2}^*$, we could only prove that $c = bg^a$ for some $b \in \{-1, 1\}$. Ultimately, we use $|QR_{n^2}|$ since we want to ensure that after performing exponentiation and multiplication proofs over commitments to ciphertexts, the ciphertext decrypts to the expected value. We can see in Fig. 4b that the encryption scheme decrypts the absolute value of a ciphertext exactly the same as the original ciphertext. This is clear from rewriting the decryption process as $m = (((c_1^2/(c_0^2)^x)^t \bmod n^2) - 1)/n$. The first operation the decryptor does is square both elements of the ciphertext, and our claim follows from the fact that $|x|^2 = x^2 \in \mathbb{Z}_{n^2}$. The proofs of our ElGamal commitments use the *eqrep*-$\mathbb{G}_p$ protocol (in Sect. 2.1) which does not have the same limitations as *eqrep*-$\mathbb{Z}_{n^2}$. Unfortunately, $|QR_{n^2}|$ is not efficiently recognizable, but if every ciphertext comes with a proof of correct encryption (starting from honest parameters) we can be assured that the resulting ciphertext lives in $|QR_{n^2}|$. We show in the full version of this paper [33] that in our modified Camenisch-Shoup scheme, g and h are both in the group

$|QR_{n^2}|$. Thus, if we can create commitments to elements of $|QR_{n^2}|$, we can use them to commit to our modified Camenisch-Shoup ciphertexts and construct the associated protocols for multiplication and exponentiation.

<table>
<tr><td colspan="2">

$\mathsf{Setup}(1^\lambda) \to params_{ElG}$

1:    Generate cyclic group of prime order p, $\mathbb{G}_p$

2:    $g, h \leftarrow\!\!\$ \; \mathbb{G}_p$

3:    **return** $(g, h, \mathbb{G}_p)$

</td></tr>
</table>

$\mathsf{Setup}(1^\lambda) \to params_{ElG}$	$\mathsf{Setup}(1^\lambda) \to params_{CS}$
1: Generate cyclic group of prime order p, $\mathbb{G}_p$	1: Sample a safe RSA modulus, $n = pq = (2p' + 1)(2q' + 1)$
2: $g, h \leftarrow\!\!\$ \; \mathbb{G}_p$	2: $g' \leftarrow\!\!\$ \; |QR_{n^2}|, g = |(g')^n|, h = (1 + n)$,
3: **return** $(g, h, \mathbb{G}_p)$	3: **return** $params_{CS} = (n, g, h)$
$\mathsf{KeyGen}(params_{ElG}) \to (\mathsf{pk}, \mathsf{sk})$	$\mathsf{KeyGen}(params_{CS}) \to (\mathsf{pk}, \mathsf{sk})$
1: $x \leftarrow\!\!\$ \; \mathbb{Z}_p$;	1: $\mathsf{sk} = x \leftarrow\!\!\$ \; [n^2/4], \mathsf{pk} = k = |g^x| \quad /\!\!/ \text{ in } |QR_{n^2}|$
2: **return** $\mathsf{pk} \leftarrow g^x, \mathsf{sk} \leftarrow x$;	2: **return** pk, sk
$\mathsf{Enc}(\mathsf{pk} = k, m) \to c$	$\mathsf{Enc}(\mathsf{pk}, m \in [n]) \to c$
1: $r \leftarrow\!\!\$ \; \mathbb{Z}_p$;	1: $r \leftarrow\!\!\$ \; [n/4]$,
2: **return** $c = (g^r, k^r h^m)$	2: **return** $c = (|g^r|, |k^r h^m|) \quad /\!\!/ \text{ in } |QR_{n^2}|$
$\mathsf{Dec}(\mathsf{sk}, c = (c_0, c_1)) \to M$	$\mathsf{Dec}(\mathsf{sk}, c = (c_0, c_1)) \to m$
1: $z = c_0^{\mathsf{sk}} = k^r$	1: $t = 2^{-1} \mod n$
2: **return** $c_1/z = M = h^m$	2: $M = c_1/c_0^x \quad /\!\!/ \text{ in } \mathbb{Z}_{n^2}$
	3: **return** $m = ((M^{2t} \mod n^2) - 1)/n$
(a) Lifted ElGamal	(b) Simplified Camenisch-Shoup

Fig. 4. Encryption schemes.

4.2 Commitments to $|QR_{n^2}|$ and Camenisch-Shoup Ciphertexts

To construct commitments to Camenisch-Shoup ciphertexts, we need to construct commitments to the elements of the group in which components of a Camenisch-Shoup ciphertexts lie. We accomplish this by using Damgård-Fujisaki integer commitments [29] that are similar to Pedersen commitments. We adapt Damgård-Fujisaki commitments to "live" in $\mathbb{Z}_{n^2}$ in Fig. 5 in functions Setup_{DF} and Com_{DF}. We prove them secure in the full version of this paper [33]. To give intuition, these commitments appear very similar to Pedersen commitments, using two generators of a group as the public parameters and exponentiating them in a similar way to commit to integers. In this scheme, B is such that 2^B is larger than the order of $|QR_{n^2}|$ (i.e. $2^B = n^2/4$).

Using Damgård-Fujisaki commitments that live in $\mathbb{Z}_{n^2}$ will allow us to use the *eqrep*-$\mathbb{Z}_{n^2}$ protocol from Definition 3 to complete proofs of multiplication and exponentiation of our $|QR_{n^2}|$ commitments[10].

---

[10] We could use Damgård-Fujisaki commitments as-is (such that they live in $\mathbb{Z}_n$), but our $|QR_{n^2}|$ commitments would then consist of elements in $\mathbb{Z}_{n^2}$ and $\mathbb{Z}_n$, requiring a new *eqrep* protocol that spans both groups. It is not clear if this alternative approach would be more efficient or simpler.

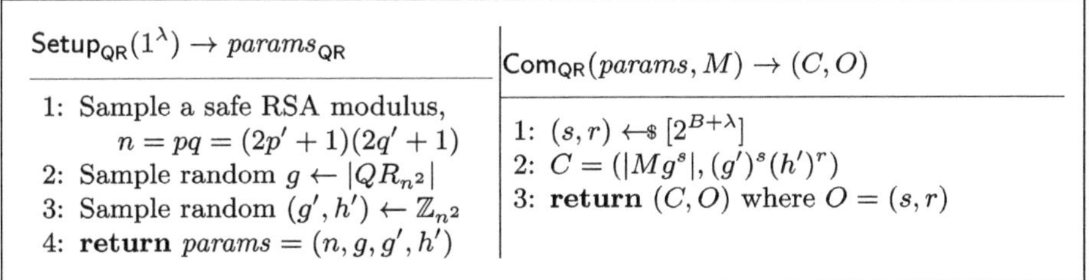

$$\begin{array}{l|l}
\mathsf{Setup}_{\mathsf{DF}}(1^\lambda) \to params_{\mathsf{DF}} : & \mathsf{Commit}_{\mathsf{DF}}(params, m) \to (C, O) : \\
\hline
\text{1: Sample a safe RSA modulus,} & \text{1: To commit to integer, } m, \text{ com-} \\
\quad\quad n = pq = (2p' + 1)(2q' + 1) & \quad\quad \text{pute: } C = g^m h^r \text{ where } r \leftarrow_\$ \\
\text{2: Sample random } g, h \in \mathbb{Z}_{n^2}. & \quad\quad [2^{B+\lambda}] \\
\text{3: } \mathbf{return}\ params = (g, h) & \text{2: } \mathbf{return}\ (C, O) \text{ where } O = r
\end{array}$$

Fig. 5. Simplified Damgård-Fujisaki commitments in $\mathbb{Z}_{n^2}$.

Next, by employing Damgård-Fujisaki commitments that live in $\mathbb{Z}_{n^2}$, we can construct a scheme for committing to elements of $|QR_{n^2}|$ (and then we can use $|QR_{n^2}|$ commitments to construct commits to Camenisch-Shoup ciphertexts). We show this scheme in Fig. 6 in functions $\mathsf{Setup}_{\mathsf{QR}}$ and $\mathsf{Com}_{\mathsf{QR}}$. Similar to in the Damgård-Fujisaki commitments, B is such that 2^B is larger than the order of $|QR_{n^2}|$. We show that such commitments are hiding and binding in the full version of this paper [33]. We can see that these $|QR_{n^2}|$ commitments are multiplicatively homomorphic, i.e. if you take two $|QR_{n^2}|$ commitments $c = (c_1, c_2)$ committing to element M and $d = (d_1, d_2)$ committing to element N, then if you compute their pair-wise multiplication: $e = (c_1 * d_1, c_2 * d_2)$, this results in a commitment to $M * N$ with opening information $s_c + s_d, r_c + r_d$, computed pair-wise, where s_c, r_c is the opening information for c and s_d, r_d is the opening information for d.

$$\begin{array}{l|l}
\mathsf{Setup}_{\mathsf{QR}}(1^\lambda) \to params_{\mathsf{QR}} & \mathsf{Com}_{\mathsf{QR}}(params, M) \to (C, O) \\
\hline
\text{1: Sample a safe RSA modulus,} & \text{1: } (s, r) \leftarrow_\$ [2^{B+\lambda}] \\
\quad\quad n = pq = (2p' + 1)(2q' + 1) & \text{2: } C = (|Mg^s|, (g')^s (h')^r) \\
\text{2: Sample random } g \leftarrow |QR_{n^2}| & \text{3: } \mathbf{return}\ (C, O) \text{ where } O = (s, r) \\
\text{3: Sample random } (g', h') \leftarrow \mathbb{Z}_{n^2} & \\
\text{4: } \mathbf{return}\ params = (n, g, g', h') &
\end{array}$$

Fig. 6. $|QR_{n^2}|$-Commitments.

Auxiliary Proofs for Commitments to $|QR_{n^2}|$. We now describe protocols that we can use to create proofs of opening, multiplication, and exponentiation of elements in $|QR_{n^2}|$ which can be verified using only their commitments. To proof of knowledge of an **opening** for a $|QR_{n^2}|$-commitment, we note that the second part of a $|QR_{n^2}|$ commitment (in Fig. 6) is simply a Damgård-Fujisaki commitment (from Fig. 5) that lives in $\mathbb{Z}_{n^2}$. Thus, we can use the Damgård-Fujisaki commitment opening proof protocol [29], to create a proof of opening of the second part of the commitment which suffices as a proof of opening for a $|QR_{n^2}|$ commitment. To prove the **multiplication** of $|QR_{n^2}|$-commitments (*i.e.*, given three $|QR_{n^2}|$-commitments, C_1, C_2, and C_3, committed to $|QR_{n^2}|$ elements, E_1, E_2, and E_3 prove that $E_1 = E_2 * E_3$), we can utilize the homomorphic property of the commitments. Each commitment consists of two elements of $|QR_{n^2}|$, $C_i = (C_{i,1}, C_{i,2})$. To perform this proof, we compute a fourth commitment, $C_4 = (C_{4,1}, C_{4,2}) = (C_{1,1}/(C_{2,1}C_{3,1}), C_{1,2}/(C_{2,2}C_{3,2})$ and prove that it is a commitment to $1 \in |QR_{n^2}|$. This is equivalent to proving multiplication because of the homomorphic properties of the commitments and can be proven using *eqrep-$\mathbb{Z}_{n^2}$* from Sect. 2.1. To prove the **exponentiation** of $|QR_{n^2}|$-commitments, we can similarly use *eqrep-$\mathbb{Z}_{n^2}$* from Sect. 2.1. This proof operates over two commitments $C_1 = (C_{1,1}, C_{1,2})$ and $C_2 = (C_{2,1}, C_{2,2})$ to $|QR_{n^2}|$ elements E_1, E_2 (resp.) and one commitment C_y to scalar y and proves that $E_1 = E_2^y$. We describe the exact relations used with *eqrep-$\mathbb{Z}_{n^2}$* in the full version of this paper [33].

Commitments to Camenisch-Shoup Encryptions. Since we constructed commitments to elements of $|QR_{n^2}|$ along with their associated proof protocols, we can use these commitments with Camenisch-Shoup ciphertexts. We present the full construction in the full version of this paper [33] and describe it in Fig. 7. The Prove functions in Fig. 7 satisfy the relations between committed ciphertexts described in Sect. 3.1. Similar to Sect. 3.2, we underline elements known to the verifier so that the reader can intuit how the proof is verified.

We prove Theorem 5 in the full version of this paper [33].

Theorem 5 (Security of Camenisch-Shoup commitments). *Our construction of Camenisch-Shoup commitments in the full version of this paper [33] (partially described in Fig. 7) satisfies four properties: (1) statistically hiding; (2) computationally binding; (3) our protocols ($\mathsf{Prove}_{CS}^{\mathsf{Com}_{AH}}$, $\mathsf{Prove}_{CS}^{\mathsf{enc}}$, $\mathsf{Prove}_{CS}^{\odot}$, and $\mathsf{Prove}_{CS}^{\oplus}$) are computationally zero-knowledge; and (4) computationally black-box knowledge extractable assuming that the Strong RSA and Decisional Composite Residuosity assumptions hold.*

5   Applications of Our Framework to Privacy-Preserving Blueprints

Given this new efficient framework for verifiable computation on ciphertexts, we are now equipped to build a PPB scheme that supports the f_{CBDC} functionality, has more succinct escrow proofs, and can withstand the framing attack in Sect. 1.2. We present the non-frameability result first as this allows us to recall the generic construction of PPB from homomorphic-enough encryption (HEC), which one can think of as a passively secure PPB. In Sect. 5.2 we instantiate HEC using additively homomorphic encryption in such a way that Camenisch-Shoup gives us a HEC for f_{CBDC}, and in Sect. 5.3 we show a succinct proof system which ensures escrows are created honestly.

- $\mathsf{Setup}_{CS}(1^\lambda) \to params$: Generates the parameters for a Camenisch-Shoup encryption scheme, $params_{CS}$ from Fig. 4.1b, the parameters for a $|QR_{n^2}|$ commitment scheme, $params_{\mathsf{QR}}$ from Fig. 4.3, and for a scalar commitment scheme, $params_{\mathsf{DF}}$.
- $\mathsf{Com}_{CS}(params, c) \to (C, O)$: Takes in a Camenisch-Shoup encryption, $c = (c_1, c_2)$ and uses the $|QR_{n^2}|$ commitment scheme to commit to each element, $(C_1, O_1) = \mathsf{Com}_{\mathsf{QR}}(c_1)$, $(C_2, O_2) = \mathsf{Com}_{\mathsf{QR}}(c_2)$ with the opening being $O = (O_1, O_2)$.
- $\mathsf{Prove}_{CS}^{\mathsf{Com}_{AH}}(params, c, M, O, \underline{C}) \to \pi$: Parse the encryption into two $|QR_{n^2}|$ elements, $c = (c_1, c_2)$. Perform a proof of opening of both $|QR_{n^2}|$ commitments (C_1 and C_2) to c_1 and c_2.
- $\mathsf{Prove}_{CS}^{\oplus}(params, c_a, c_b, c_c, O_a, O_b, O_c, \underline{C_a, C_b, C_c}) \to \pi$: Parse the encryption, $c_a = (c_{a,1}, c_{a,2})$ and similarly parse c_b and c_c. Compute two $|QR_{n^2}|$ multiplication proofs over C_a, C_b, and C_b proving that $c_{a,1} * c_{b,1} = c_{c,1}$ and $c_{a,2} * c_{b,2} = c_{c,2}$. Output these proofs as π.
- $\mathsf{Prove}_{CS}^{\odot}(params, c_a, c_b, O_a, O_b, r_y, y, \underline{C_a, C_b, C_y}) \to \pi$: Let $C_y = \mathsf{Com}(y; r_y)$. Similar to the $\mathsf{Prove}_{CS}^{\oplus}$ function, parse c_a and c_b into their $|QR_{n^2}|$ elements. Perform two proofs of exponentiation of $|QR_{n^2}|$ commitments for $c_{b,1}^y = c_{a,1}$ and $c_{b,2}^y = c_{a,2}$. Output these proofs as π.
- $\mathsf{Prove}_{CS}^{\mathsf{enc}}(params, \mathsf{pk}_{AH}, c_a, r_a, O_a, y, r_y, \underline{C_a, C_y}) \to \pi$: Parse the encryption as $c_a = (g^y h^{r_a}, g^{r_a})$ where g, h are the parameters for the encryption scheme. Parse the commitments similar to previous functions. Commit to the generator (g) and public key (h) of the Camenisch-Shoup scheme, yielding C_g and C_h. Use these $|QR_{n^2}|$ commitments to prove that $c_{a,1} = g^y h^{r_a}$ and that $c_{a,2} = g^{r_a}$. Output these proofs as π.

Fig. 7. Summary of Camenisch-Shoup commitments.

5.1 Non-frameable Privacy-Preserving Blueprints

To systematically prevent framing attacks and formally define and prove non-frameability, we extend the formal definition of a blueprint scheme of [37], see Sect. 2.3. We change the Dec algorithm to additionally output a proof of correct decryption and introduce a Judge algorithm for verifying this proof.

Definition 5 (A non-frameable f-blueprint scheme). *For a non-interactive commitment scheme* ($\mathsf{CSetup}, \mathsf{Com}$), *a non-frameable f-blueprint scheme consists of all the algorithms of a basic f-blueprint scheme with an adapted Dec algorithm and an additional Judge algorithm:*

$\mathsf{Dec}(\Lambda, \mathsf{sk}_A, C_y, Z) \to (f(x, y), \pi_z)$ or $\perp$: Takes the auditor's secret key sk_A, commitment C_y and escrow Z such that $\mathsf{VerEscrow}(\Lambda, \mathsf{pk}_A, C_y, Z) = 1$ as input. Decrypts the escrow and returns the output $f(x, y)$ if C_y is a commitment to y. Additionally it returns a proof, π_z, that proves to the Judge algorithm that $f(x, y)$ was decrypted correctly from Z.

$\mathsf{Judge}(\Lambda, \mathsf{pk}_A, C_x, C_y, Z, z, \pi_z) \to 0$ or 1: Takes as input the public key of the auditor, pk_A, the commitment to the watchlist and user data, C_x and C_y, the escrow, Z, the decrypted value, z, a proof of correct decryption, π_z and verifies that z was obtained correctly from escrow Z.

Intuitively, non-frameability requires that Judge only accept valid results.

Definition 6 (Non-Frameability). *Let C_x and C_y be commitments computed from (x, r_x) and (y, r_y) respectively. Non-frameability guarantees that any pk_A, Z, z, π_z that passes $\mathsf{Judge}(\Lambda, \mathsf{pk}_A, C_x, C_y, Z, z, \pi_z)$ will imply that $f(x, y) = z$ with overwhelming probability. More formally, for all PPT adversaries $\mathcal{A}$, there exists a negligible function ν such that: $Pr[\mathsf{NonFraming}^{\mathcal{A}}_{\mathsf{Blu}}(\lambda) = 1] < \nu(\lambda)$ (Fig. 8).*

$\mathsf{NonFraming}^{\mathcal{A}}_{\mathsf{Blu}}(\lambda)$

1 :　$cpar \leftarrow \mathsf{CSetup}(1^\lambda)$

2 :　$\Lambda \leftarrow \mathsf{Setup}(1^\lambda, cpar)$

3 :　$(\mathsf{pk}_A, x, r_x, y, r_y, Z, z, \pi_z) \leftarrow \mathcal{A}(1^\lambda, \Lambda)$

4 :　$C_x = \mathsf{Com}_{cpar}(x, r_x); C_y = \mathsf{Com}_{cpar}(y, r_y)$

5 :　**return** $[(\mathsf{Judge}(\Lambda, \mathsf{pk}_A, C_x, C_y, Z, z, \pi_z) = 1) \wedge (f(x, y) \neq z)]$

Fig. 8. Experiments $\mathsf{NonFraming}^{\mathsf{Adv}}_{\mathsf{Blu}}(\lambda)$.

KLN uses a "homomorphic-enough" encryption (HEC) scheme to generically construct their PPB scheme. We extend their construction by adapting Dec and adding Judge in Fig. 11. The KLN HEC scheme is parameterized by a function family and is correct if it is possible to compute any function from that family using only the ciphertexts. Existing HEC schemes that are only correct as defined by KLN will not be sufficient to construct non-frameable blueprint schemes. Our main insight for adapting the generic construction of blueprints from a HEC scheme is that the adversary now controls the randomness r to the HEC encryption algorithm, in addition to the randomness r_Z, and can thus exercise additional control over the output of HECEnc. Thus, we need to create a definition that is stronger than correctness that we refer to as *HEC consistency*. We will construct such HEC schemes using AHE in Sect. 5.2.

Definition 7 (Consistent homomorphic-enough cryptosystem (HEC) for a function family). *Let $F = \{f \mid f : domain_{f,x} \times domain_{f,y} \mapsto range_f\}$ be a set of polynomial-time computable functions. We say that algorithms $HEC = (HEC_{SETUP}, HEC_{ENC}, HEC_{EVAL}, HEC_{DEC}, HEC_{DIRECT})$ constitute a HEC for F if they satisfy the input-output, consistency, and security requirements below (Fig. 9):*

HEC Consistency. For an adversary $\mathcal{A}$ and scheme HEC, let $\mathsf{Adv}_{\mathrm{HEC},\mathcal{A}}$ be the probability that the experiment HECCONSISTENT in Fig. 10 accepts. HEC is *consistent* if $\mathsf{Adv}_{\mathrm{HEC},\mathcal{A}}$ is negligible for all PPT algorithms $\mathcal{A}$. In the HEC consistency game, the adversary outputs x, y, and the randomness for the HEC scheme (r, r_Z), and the encryption and evaluation algorithms cannot produce a ciphertext that decrypts to a plaintext other than $f(x, y)$.

- HECSETUP(1^λ) → *hecpar* takes the security parameter as input, outputs the parameters *hecpar*.
- HECENC(*hecpar*, f, x) → (X, d) takes parameters *hecpar*, a function $f \in F$, and a value $x \in domain_{f,x}$ as input, outputs an encrypted representation X of the function $f(x, \cdot)$, and a decryption key d.
- HECEVAL(*hecpar*, f, X, y) → Z takes as input the parameters *hecpar*, a function $f \in F$, an encrypted representation of $f(x, \cdot)$, and a value $y \in domain_{f,y}$ and outputs a ciphertext Z, an encryption of $f(x, y)$.
- HECDEC(*hecpar*, d, Z) → z takes as input the parameters *hecpar*, the decryption key d, and a ciphertext Z, decrypts Z to obtain a value z.
- HECDIRECT(*hecpar*, X, z) → Z on input *hecpar*, an encrypted representation X of some function, and a value z, outputs a ciphertext Z.

Fig. 9. Algorithms of HEC scheme for F.

HECCONSISTENT$^{\mathcal{A}}(\lambda)$	HECCORRECT$^{\mathcal{A}}(\lambda)$
1 : $hecpar \leftarrow$ HECSETUP(λ)	1 : $hecpar \leftarrow$ HECSETUP(λ)
2 : $(f, x, r, y, r_Z) \leftarrow \mathcal{A}(1^\lambda, hecpar)$	2 : $(f, x, \mathsf{st}) \leftarrow \mathcal{A}(1^\lambda, hecpar)$
3 : **if** $f \notin F \vee x \notin domain_{f,x} \vee y \notin domain_{f,y}$	3 : **if** $f \in F, x \in domain_{f,x}$
4 : **return** 0	4 : $(X, d) \leftarrow$ HECENC($hecpar$, f, x)
5 : $(X, d) \leftarrow$ HECENC($hecpar$, f, x; r)	5 : $(y, r_Z) \leftarrow \mathcal{A}(\mathsf{st}, X)$
6 : $Z \leftarrow$ HECEVAL($hecpar$, f, X, y; r_Z)	6 : **if** $y \in domain_{f,y}$
7 : **if** HECDEC($hecpar$, d, Z) $\neq f(x, y)$	7 : $Z \leftarrow$ HECEVAL($hecpar$, f, X, y; r_Z)
8 : **return** 1	8 : **if** HECDEC($hecpar$, d, Z) $\neq f(x, y)$
9 : **return** 0	9 : **return** 1
	10 : **return** 0

Fig. 10. Our HEC consistency game and the original correctness game of KLN for comparison.

HEC Security. We provide the formal definitions for the Security of x, security of x and y from third parties, and security of DIRECTZ in the full version of this paper [33].

Relying on HEC consistency we reprove Theorem 2 of [37].

Theorem 6. *If HEC is a consistent and secure homomorphic-enough cryptosystem, the commitment scheme is binding, and the NIZK PoKs Ψ_1, Ψ_2 and Ψ_3 are zero-knowledge and BB-PSL simulation extractable then our generic blueprint scheme is a secure, non-frameable f-blueprint scheme.*

The full proof of Theorem 6 can be found in the full version of this paper [33], but we provide some intuition here. The correctness of the Judge algorithm follows from the completeness of the NIZK PoKs Ψ_1, Ψ_2 and Ψ_3. To show non-frameability of the f-blueprint scheme, we argue that any successful adversary must violate one of the three underlying assumptions: (a) the BB-extractability of the NIZK Ψ_2 or Ψ_3, (b) the consistency of the HEC scheme or (c) the computa-

$\underline{\mathsf{Setup}(\lambda, cpar, \mathsf{S}_1, \mathsf{S}_2, \mathsf{S}_3)}$

1 : $hecpar \leftarrow \mathrm{HECSETUP}(1^\lambda)$

2 :   **return** $\Lambda = (\lambda, cpar, hecpar, \mathsf{S}_1, \mathsf{S}_2, \mathsf{S}_3)$

$\underline{\mathsf{KeyGen}(\Lambda, x, r_x)}$

1 :   **parse** $\Lambda = (\lambda, cpar, hecpar, \mathsf{S}_1, \mathsf{S}_2, \mathsf{S}_3)$

2 : $(X, d) \xleftarrow{r} \mathrm{HECENC}(hecpar, f, x)$

3 : $C_x \leftarrow \mathsf{Com}_{cpar}(x; r_x); C_d \xleftarrow{r_d} \mathsf{Com}_{cpar}(d)$

4 : $\pi_\mathsf{A} \leftarrow \mathsf{PoK}^{\mathsf{S}_1}_{\Psi_1}\big\{(x, d, r, r_x, r_d) :$

5 : $(X, d) = \mathrm{HECENC}(hecpar, f, x; r)$

6 : $\wedge\, C_x = \mathsf{Com}_{cpar}(x; r_x)$

7 : $\wedge\, C_d = \mathsf{Com}_{cpar}(d; r_d)\big\}$

8 : $\mathsf{pk}_\mathsf{A} \leftarrow (X, C_x, C_d, \pi_\mathsf{A}); \mathsf{sk}_\mathsf{A} \leftarrow (\mathsf{pk}_\mathsf{A}, d, r_d)$

9 :   **return** $(\mathsf{pk}_\mathsf{A}, \mathsf{sk}_\mathsf{A})$

$\underline{\mathsf{VerPK}(\Lambda, \mathsf{pk}_\mathsf{A}, C_x)}$

1 :   **parse** $\Lambda = (\lambda, cpar, hecpar, \mathsf{S}_1, \mathsf{S}_2, \mathsf{S}_3)$

2 :   **parse** $\mathsf{pk}_\mathsf{A} = (X, C'_x, \pi_\mathsf{A})$

3 :   **return** $\mathsf{V}^{\mathsf{S}_1}_1((X, hecpar, f, C_x, cpar), \pi_\mathsf{A})$

4 : $\wedge\, (C'_x = C_x)$

$\underline{\mathsf{Judge}(\Lambda, \mathsf{pk}_\mathsf{A}, C_x, C_y, Z = (\hat{Z}, \pi_\mathsf{U}), z, \pi_Z)}$

1 :   **parse** $\Lambda = (\lambda, cpar, hecpar, \mathsf{S}_1, \mathsf{S}_2, \mathsf{S}_3)$

2 :   **parse** $\mathsf{pk}_\mathsf{A} = (\_, \_, C_d, \_)$

3 :   **return** $\mathsf{V}^{\mathsf{S}_3}_3((z, hecpar, \hat{Z}, C_d), \pi_Z)$

4 : $\wedge\, \mathsf{VerPK}(\Lambda, \mathsf{pk}_\mathsf{A}, C_x)$

5 : $\wedge\, \mathsf{VerEscrow}(\Lambda, \mathsf{pk}_\mathsf{A}, C_y, Z)$

$\underline{\mathsf{Escrow}(\Lambda, \mathsf{pk}_\mathsf{A}, y, r_y)}$

1 :   **parse** $\Lambda = (\lambda, cpar, hecpar, \mathsf{S}_1, \mathsf{S}_2, \mathsf{S}_3)$

2 :   **parse** $\mathsf{pk}_\mathsf{A} = (X, C_x, \_)$

3 :   **if** $\mathsf{VerPK}(\Lambda, \mathsf{pk}_\mathsf{A}, C_x) = 0$

4 :   **return** 0

5 : $\hat{Z} \xleftarrow{r_{\hat{Z}}} \mathrm{HECEVAL}(hecpar, f, X, y)$

6 : $C_y \leftarrow \mathsf{Com}_{cpar}(y; r_y)$

7 : $\pi_\mathsf{U} \leftarrow \mathsf{PoK}^{\mathsf{S}_2}_{\Psi_2}\big\{(y, r_y, r_{\hat{Z}}) :$

8 : $\hat{Z} = \mathrm{HECEVAL}(hecpar, f, X, y; r_{\hat{Z}})$

9 : $\wedge\, C_y = \mathsf{Com}_{cpar}(y; r_y)\big\}$

10 :   **return** $(\hat{Z}, \pi_\mathsf{U})$

$\underline{\mathsf{VerEscrow}(\Lambda, \mathsf{pk}_\mathsf{A}, C_y, Z = (\hat{Z}, \pi_\mathsf{U}))}$

1 :   **parse** $\Lambda = (\lambda, cpar, hecpar, \mathsf{S}_1, \mathsf{S}_2, \mathsf{S}_3)$

2 :   **parse** $\mathsf{pk}_\mathsf{A} = (\_, C_x, \_, \_)$

3 :   **return** $\mathsf{VerPK}(\Lambda, \mathsf{pk}_\mathsf{A}, C_x)$

4 : $\wedge\, \mathsf{V}^{\mathsf{S}_2}_2((\hat{Z}, hecpar, f, X, C_y, cpar), \pi_\mathsf{U})$

$\underline{\mathsf{Dec}(\Lambda, \mathsf{sk}_\mathsf{A}, C_y, Z = (\hat{Z}, \pi_\mathsf{U}))}$

1 :   **parse** $\Lambda = (\lambda, cpar, hecpar, \mathsf{S}_1, \mathsf{S}_2, \mathsf{S}_3)$

2 :   **parse** $\mathsf{sk}_\mathsf{A} = (\mathsf{pk}_\mathsf{A}, d, r_d)$

3 :   **parse** $\mathsf{pk}_\mathsf{A} = (\_, \_, C_d, \_)$

4 :   **if** $\mathsf{VerEscrow}(\Lambda, \mathsf{pk}_\mathsf{A}, C_y, Z) = 0$

5 :   **return** $\bot$

6 : $z \leftarrow \mathrm{HECDEC}(hecpar, d, \hat{Z})$

7 : $\pi_Z \leftarrow \mathsf{PoK}^{\mathsf{S}_3}_{\Psi_3}\big\{d, r_d :$

8 : $z = \mathrm{HECDEC}(hecpar, d, \hat{Z})$

9 : $\wedge\, C_d = \mathsf{Com}_{cpar}(d; r_d)\big\}$

10 :   **return** (z, π_Z)

Fig. 11. Construction of generic f-blueprint scheme from HEC and NIZK PoKs Ψ_1, Ψ_2 and Ψ_3 with setup $\mathsf{S}_1, \mathsf{S}_2,$ and S_3 respectively.

tional binding property of the commitment scheme. Hence, under these standard assumptions, the f-blueprint scheme is non-frameable.

5.2   Instantiation of Consistent HEC Schemes

It turns out that the FHE based HEC scheme of [37] is already consistent, as can be seen in the full version of this paper [33].

In this section, we provide a consistent HEC scheme for realizing a non-frameable CBDC and watchlist PPB scheme. In Fig. 12 we construct the algo-

$\mathrm{HECEVAL}(hecpar, f_{n,k}, X, y; r_{\hat{Z}})$	$\mathrm{HECDEC}(hecpar, d, Z)$
1: **parse** $X = (\mathsf{pk}_{AH}, A_0, ..., A_n)$,	1: **parse** $d = (\mathsf{sk}_E, f_{n,k}, x)$,
$y = (y_{id}, y_{at})$, $/\!/\ \lvert y_{at} \rvert = k$	$Z = (Z_{id}, Z_{at}, Z_{nf})$
$r_{\hat{Z}} = (r_{id}, r_{at}, r_1, r_2, r_3)$	2: $y'_{id} \leftarrow \mathsf{Dec}(\mathsf{sk}_E, Z_{id})$
2: $E \leftarrow \bigoplus_{i=0}^{n} (A_i \odot y_{id}^{i})$	3: $y'_{at} \leftarrow \mathsf{Dec}(\mathsf{sk}_E, Z_{at})$
3: $Y_{id} \leftarrow \mathsf{Enc}(\mathsf{pk}_{AH}, y_{id}; r_{id})$	4: $y' \leftarrow \mathsf{Dec}(\mathsf{sk}_E, Z_{nf})$
4: $Y_{at} \leftarrow \mathsf{Enc}(\mathsf{pk}_{AH}, y_{at}; r_{at})$	5: **if** $y' \neq \mathfrak{g}(0)$, **return** $\emptyset$
5: $Z_{id} \leftarrow (r_1 \odot E) \oplus Y_{id}$	6: **return** (y_{id}, y_{at})
6: $Z_{at} \leftarrow (r_2 \odot E) \oplus Y_{at}; Z_{nf} = r_3 \odot E$	where $\mathfrak{g}(y_{at}) = y'_{at} \wedge \mathfrak{g}(y_{id}) = y'_{id}$
7: **return** $Z = (Z_{id}, Z_{at}, Z_{nf})$	$\wedge\ y_{id} \in x \wedge y_{at} \in domain_{f, y_{at}}$

Fig. 12. HEC algorithms: we omit the functions HECENC and HECDIRECT as they are unchanged from KLN and instead present them in the full version of this paper [33].

rithms HECEVAL and HECDEC for the function family $\{f_{n,k}\}_{n,k \in \mathbb{Z}}$, where n is the length of the auditor's list $x = \{x_1, \ldots, x_n\}$ and k is the bit length of the user's attribute y_{at}, where the user's input consists of the user's identifier y_{id} and an attribute: $y = (y_{id}, y_{at})$. $f_{n,k}$ is defined as $f_{n,k}(x, y) = y$ if $y_{id} \in x$ and $f_{n,k} = \emptyset$ otherwise. We discuss why this watchlist function is useful for the watchlist/CBDC application in Sect. 1. y_{id} uniquely identifies a user and y_{at} could be any useful data about the user such as a seed for tracing the user's anonymous payments. We construct a HECEVAL algorithm for multiple attributes in the full construction of our HEC scheme in the full version of this paper [33].

The HECENC algorithm (Fig. 12) takes as input the list x of n watchlisted identities, and computes a polynomial $P(\chi) = \sum_{i \in [n]} a_i \chi^i$ such that $P(y_{id}) = 0$ if and only if $y_{id} \in x$. Then, it samples a key pair $(\mathsf{pk}_{AH}, \mathsf{sk}_{AH})$ for a semantically secure $\mathfrak{g}$-semi-encryption scheme (Definition 4), and outputs the public key $X = (\mathsf{pk}_{AH}, \{A_i = \mathsf{Enc}(\mathsf{pk}_{AH}, a_i)\}_{i \in [0...n]})$ where the a_i's are coefficients of P, and the decryption key $d = (\mathsf{sk}_{AH}, x)$.

On input the public key X and the value $y = (y_{id}, y_{at})$, HECEVAL will output the escrow $Z = (Z_{id}, Z_{at}, Z_{nf})$ which consists of three ciphertexts under the key pk_{AH}; these will decrypt to the values $(y_{id}, y_{at}, 0)$ if and only if $y_{id} \in x$; otherwise they will decrypt to uniformly random elements of the message space, independent of y. As we show in more detail in Fig. 12, additively homomorphic properties of the underlying (semi-)encryption scheme allow the evaluator to form the ciphertext E so that it will be an encryption of $P(y_{id})$. The evaluator also encrypts the identity y_{id} and attribute y_{at}, yielding ciphertexts Y_{id} and Y_{at}. The escrow of y_{id} is then formed as $Z_{id} = (r_1 \odot E) \oplus Y_{id} = ((r_1 \odot \boxed{P(y_{id})}) \oplus \boxed{y_{id}} = \boxed{r_1 P(y_{id}) + y_{id}}$, which is an encryption of y_{id} if E is an encryption of 0 (i.e. whenever $y_{id} \in x$), and an encryption of a random value otherwise, thanks to the randomizer r_1. Similarly, the escrow of y_{at} is $Z_{at} = (r_2 \odot E) \oplus$

$Y_{at} = \boxed{r_2 P(y_{id}) + y_{at}}$. To make the HEC consistent, we include $Z_{nf} = r_3 \odot E = \boxed{r_3 P(y_{id})}$, which will decrypt to 0 if and only if $y_{id} \in x$.

HECDEC takes as input the HEC decryption key $d = (\mathsf{sk}_{AH}, x)$ and the escrow Z. It recovers y'_{id}, y'_{at}, and y' by decrypting the escrows (Z_{id}, Z_{at}, Z_{nf}) using the secret key, sk_{AH}. By the correctness property of the decryption algorithm for $\mathfrak{g}$-semi-encryption, we know that for $Z \in \mathrm{HECENC}(X, y)$, $y' = \mathfrak{g}(r_3 P(y_{id})) = \mathfrak{g}(0)$ if and only if $y_{id} \in x$; so if $y' \neq \mathfrak{g}(0)$, HECDEC outputs $\perp$. Else, we know that $y_{id} \in x$, so HECDEC must somehow determine (1) y_{id} from $y'_{id} = \mathfrak{g}(y_{id})$, and (2) y_{at} from $y'_{attr} = \mathfrak{g}(y_{at})$. Let us explain how HECDEC can do so.

If $\mathfrak{g}$ is the identity function then this step is trivial; we show in Sect. 4 that we can achieve an additively homomorphic $\mathfrak{g}$-semi-encryption scheme where $\mathfrak{g}$ is the identity function under the decisional composite residuosity assumption using the Camenisch-Shoup cryptosystem. If, however, $\mathfrak{g}$ is a one-way injective function, then (1) can be done by looking for $\mathfrak{g}(y_{id})$ on the list $\mathfrak{g}(x_1), \ldots, \mathfrak{g}(x_n)$ where $x_i \in x$ and (2) can only be done by exhaustive search, which is only possible if y_{at} comes from a small space. This is the approach that was (implicitly) taken by the original PPB paper of Kohlweiss et al.: since the ElGamal cryptosystem is only additively homomorphic when viewed as a $\mathfrak{g}$-semi-encryption scheme, and $\mathfrak{g}$ is a one-way function, they could only accept attributes from a small space.

Theorem 7 (Security of the construction in Fig. 12). *Assuming our AHE scheme is secure, our construction of HEC in the full version of this paper [33] (partially described in Fig. 12) achieves HEC consistency as defined in Definition 10; and security of y, security of x and y from third parties, and security of* DIRECTZ, *as discussed in Sect. 5.1 and defined in the full version of this paper [33].*

Proof of Theorem 7. We focus on consistency and prove the remaining properties in the full version of this paper [33]. Because we include $Z_{nf} = E \odot r_3$ in the escrow, an auditor can prove that this is an encryption of 0. This ensures that the y_{id} is actually on the watchlist as the polynomial has roots at each entry of the watchlist. Formally, if an adversary were to be able to produce a $(f, x, \mathsf{st}, r, y, r_Z)$ such that $Z \leftarrow \mathrm{HECEVAL}(hecpar, f, X, y; r_Z)$ but $\mathrm{HECDEC}(hecpar, d, Z) \neq f(x, y)$, we see that $E \odot r_3 = 0$ in this case, which implies that $r_3 P(y) = 0$. This is only true if $y \in x$ since $r_3 > 0$. In this case, because HECEVAL is proven to be correctly computed, $E \odot r_1$ decrypts to 0. Thus, $y' = \mathsf{Dec}(Y)$. Thus, this decrypts to the correct value.

5.3 Efficient Instantiation of HEC Evaluation Proof Ψ_2

In this section we show how to use the techniques introduced in Sect. 3.2 to efficiently instantiate a NIZK proof used in the Escrow algorithm in Fig. 11 to compute π_U. This proof is for the following relation:
$$R_{\Psi_2}((y, r_y, r_{\hat{Z}}), (\hat{Z}, X, f_{n,k}, C_y)) = 1 \text{ iff } \hat{Z} = \mathrm{HECEVAL}(hecpar, f_{n,k}, X, y; r_{\hat{Z}})$$

$\wedge C_y = \mathsf{Com}(y; r_y)$ where $f_{n,k}$ is the watchlist blueprinting function described at the start of this section. We can use similar techniques to that of Ψ_2 to construct proofs for Ψ_1 and Ψ_3.

In Algorithm 3, we give the construction of Ψ_2 for HECEVAL. This function calls the proof function for R_f from Sect. 3 on lines 11, 12, and 13 in order to prove correct computation of Z_{id}, Z_{at}, and Z_{nf}. Because of the succinctness of our proof for R_f, the complexity of our proof will be $O(\log(n))$ since we evaluate with a constant number of variables.

Our proof system must have the zero-knowledge and extractability properties needed for the proofs of both blueprint hiding and user privacy (discussed in Sect. 5.1 and reviewed in the full version of this paper [33]) for our construction in Fig. 11. The zero-knowledge property is standard; for extractability, recall that we require both the usual black-box proof of knowledge property, as well as partial straight-line extraction of $\mathfrak{g}(y)$; $\mathfrak{g}$ is some function such that $\mathfrak{g}(y)$, jointly with x is sufficient to compute $f(x, y)$ because there is some efficiently computable function f^* such that $f^*(x, \mathfrak{g}(y)) = f(x, y)$. In order to achieve straight-line extractability of $\mathfrak{g}(y)$, our proof system requires that the prover $\mathfrak{g}$-semi-encrypt y under a public key "in the sky", i.e. a public key that's part of the parameters generated during setup; the knowledge extractor's trapdoor will be the decryption key. To that end, we use a public-key $\mathfrak{g}$-semi-encryption scheme ($\Gamma_{sky} = \{\mathsf{KeyGen}_{sky}, \mathsf{Enc}_{sky}, \mathsf{Dec}_{sky}\}$). (Using our notation from Definition 2, the prover retrieves the public key in the sky by querying setup S_2).

Algorithm 3. $\mathsf{PoK}^{S_2}_{\Psi_2}(hecpar, f, X, y, r_y, r_{\hat{Z}}) \to \pi$

---

    parse $X = (\mathsf{pk}_{AH}, \{\boxed{a_i}\}_{i \in [0...n]}); r_{\hat{Z}} = (r_1, r_2, r_3, r_{id}, r_{attr})$

1: $(y_{id}, y_{at}) \leftarrow y; (C_{id}, r_{id}) = \mathsf{Com}(y_{id}); (C_{at}, r_{at}) = \mathsf{Com}(y_{at}); C_y \leftarrow \mathsf{Com}(y; r_y)$

2: $Z_{id} = \mathsf{Enc}_{AH}(\mathsf{pk}_{AH}, y_{id}; r_{id}) \oplus (r_1 \odot \boxed{e}); Z_{at} = \mathsf{Enc}_{AH}(\mathsf{pk}_{AH}, y_{at}; r_{attr}) \oplus (r_2 \odot \boxed{e})$

3: $Z_{nf} = r_3 \odot \boxed{e}; Z = (Z_{id}, Z_{at}, Z_{nf})$

4: $\mathsf{pk}_{sky} \leftarrow S_2(1^\lambda); C_{sky} = \mathsf{Enc}_{sky}(\mathsf{pk}_{sky}, y; r_{sky});$

5: $\pi_{sky} = \mathsf{NIZK}[y, r_y, r_{sky} : C_{sky} = \mathsf{Enc}(\mathsf{pk}_{sky}, y; r_{sky}) \wedge C_y = \mathsf{Com}(y; r_y)]$

6: $\forall i \in [3], (C_{r_i}, \rho_i) = \mathsf{Com}(r_i)$

7: $f_{id}(a_0, \ldots, a_n, y_{id}, r_1) = y_{id} + a_0 r_1 y_{id}^0 + a_1 r_1 y_{id}^1 + \ldots + a_n r_1 y_{id}^n$

8: $f_{at}(a_0, \ldots, a_n, y_{id}, y_{at}, r_2) = y_{at} + a_0 r_2 y_{id}^0 + a_1 r_2 y_{id}^1 + \ldots + a_n r_2 y_{id}^n$

9: $f_{nf}(a_0, \ldots, a_n, y_{id}, r_3) = a_0 r_3 y_{id}^0 + a_1 r_3 y_{id}^1 + \ldots + a_n r_3 y_{id}^n$

10: $\pi_y = \mathsf{NIZK}[y_{id}, r_{id}, y_{at}, r_{at} : C_{id} = \mathsf{Com}(y_{id}; r_{id}) \wedge C_{at} = \mathsf{Com}(y_{at}; r_{at}) \wedge (y_{id}, y_{at}) = y \wedge C_y = \mathsf{Com}(y; r_y)]$

11: $\pi_{id} = \mathsf{NIZK}[y_{id}, r_{id}, r_1, \rho_{id} : Z_{id} = \mathsf{Enc}_{AH}(f_{id}(a_0, \ldots, a_n, y_{id}, r_1)) \wedge C_{id} = \mathsf{Com}(y_{id}; r_{id}) \wedge C_{r_1} = \mathsf{Com}(r_1; \rho_1)]$

12: $\pi_{at} = \mathsf{NIZK}[y_{id}, r_{id}, y_{at}, r_{at}, r_2, \rho_2 : Z_{at} = \mathsf{Enc}_{AH}(f_{at}(a_0, \ldots, a_n, y_{id}, y_{at}, r_2)) \wedge C_{id} = \mathsf{Com}(y_{id}; r_{id}) \wedge C_{at} = \mathsf{Com}(y_{at}; r_{at}) \wedge C_{r_2} = \mathsf{Com}(r_2; \rho_2)]$

13: $\pi_{nf} = \mathsf{NIZK}[y_{id}, r_3 : Z_{nf} = \mathsf{Enc}_{AH}(f_{nf}(a_0, \ldots, a_n, y_{id}, r_3)) \wedge C_{id} = \mathsf{Com}(y_{id}; r_{id}) \wedge C_{r_3} = \mathsf{Com}(r_3; \rho_3)]$

14: **return** $(\pi_{id}, \pi_{at}, \pi_{nf}, \pi_{sky}, C_{sky}, \{C_{r_i}\}_{i \in [3]}, \pi_y)$

We present the verification functions for PoK_{Ψ_2} and PoK_P^* in the full version of this paper [33]. We prove Theorems 8 and 9 in the full version of this paper [33].

Theorem 8. *Our scheme in Algorithm 3 is complete and ZK (Definition 1).*

Theorem 9 (g^*-BB-PSL for Ψ_2). *If PoK_P^* is a BB NIZK for the relation R_P (where R_P is defined as $R_P((C, C_{y_{id}}, X, n), (O, O_{y_{id}}, y_{id})) = 1$ iff $C = \mathsf{Com}_{AH}(\mathsf{Enc}_{AH}(\mathsf{pk}_{AH}, \bigoplus_{i=0}^{n}(\boxed{a_i} \odot y_{id}^i); O)) \wedge C_{y_{id}} = \mathsf{Com}(y, O_{y_{id}}))$ and if $\Gamma_{sky} = \{\mathsf{KeyGen}_{sky}, \mathsf{Enc}_{sky}, \mathsf{Dec}_{sky}\}$ is a semantically secure $\mathfrak{g}$-semi-encryption scheme, our Ψ_2 proof is a g^*-BB-PSL protocol, where $g^*(y, r_{\hat{Z}}) = \mathfrak{g}(y)$.*

Acknowledgements. Anna Lysyanskaya and Scott Griffy were supported by NSF Grants 2312241, 2154170, and 2247305 as well as the Peter G. Peterson Foundation and the Ethereum Foundation. Markulf Kohlweiss and Meghna Sengupta were supported by Input Output (iohk.io) through their funding of the University of Edinburgh ZK Lab. We'd also like to acknowledge Victor Youdom Kemmoe and Eileen Nolan for their helpful discussions.

References

1. Abelson, H., et al.: Bugs in our pockets: the risks of client-side scanning. J. Cybersecur. **10**(1), tyad020 (2024). https://doi.org/10.1093/cybsec/tyad020
2. Attema, T., Cascudo, I., Cramer, R., Damgård, I., Escudero, D.: Vector commitments over rings and compressed Σ-protocols. In: Kiltz, E., Vaikuntanathan, V. (eds.) TCC 2022, Part I. LNCS, vol. 13747, pp. 173–202. Springer, Cham (2022). https://doi.org/10.1007/978-3-031-22318-1_7
3. Attema, T., Cramer, R.: Compressed Σ-protocol theory and practical application to plug & play secure algorithmics. In: Micciancio, D., Ristenpart, T. (eds.) CRYPTO 2020. LNCS, vol. 12172, pp. 513–543. Springer, Cham (2020). https://doi.org/10.1007/978-3-030-56877-1_18
4. Baldimtsi, F., Lysyanskaya, A.: Anonymous credentials light. In: Sadeghi, A.R., Gligor, V.D., Yung, M. (eds.) ACM CCS 2013, pp. 1087–1098. ACM Press (2013). https://doi.org/10.1145/2508859.2516687
5. Bangerter, E., Camenisch, J., Lysyanskaya, A.: A cryptographic framework for the controlled release of certified data. In: Christianson, B., Crispo, B., Malcolm, J.A., Roe, M. (eds.) Security Protocols 2004. LNCS, vol. 3957, pp. 20–42. Springer, Heidelberg (2006). https://doi.org/10.1007/11861386_4
6. Bellare, M., Shi, H., Zhang, C.: Foundations of group signatures: the case of dynamic groups. In: Menezes, A. (ed.) CT-RSA 2005. LNCS, vol. 3376, pp. 136–153. Springer, Heidelberg (2005). https://doi.org/10.1007/978-3-540-30574-3_11
7. Benarroch, D., et al.: Proposal: commit-and-prove zero-knowledge proof systems and extensions. https://docs.zkproof.org/pages/standards/accepted-workshop4/proposal-commit.pdf
8. Bhadauria, R., Hazay, C., Venkitasubramaniam, M., Wu, W., Zhang, Y.: Private polynomial commitments and applications to MPC. In: Boldyreva, A., Kolesnikov, V. (eds.) PKC 2023, Part II. LNCS, vol. 13941, pp. 127–158. Springer, Cham (2023). https://doi.org/10.1007/978-3-031-31371-4_5

9. Block, A.R., Fang, Z., Katz, J., Thaler, J., Waldner, H., Zhang, Y.: Field-agnostic SNARKs from expand-accumulate codes. In: Reyzin, L., Stebila, D. (eds.) CRYPTO 2024, Part X. LNCS, vol. 14929, pp. 276–307. Springer, Cham (2024). https://doi.org/10.1007/978-3-031-68403-6_9

10. Bootle, J., Cerulli, A., Chaidos, P., Groth, J., Petit, C.: Efficient zero-knowledge arguments for arithmetic circuits in the discrete log setting. In: Fischlin, M., Coron, J.-S. (eds.) EUROCRYPT 2016. LNCS, vol. 9666, pp. 327–357. Springer, Heidelberg (2016). https://doi.org/10.1007/978-3-662-49896-5_12

11. Boyle, D.: The problem of "parallel construction" in criminal investigations. https://www.boylejasari.com/the-problem-of-parallel-construction-in-criminal-investigations/. Accessed 13 Feb 2024

12. Bünz, B., Bootle, J., Boneh, D., Poelstra, A., Wuille, P., Maxwell, G.: Bulletproofs: short proofs for confidential transactions and more. In: 2018 IEEE Symposium on Security and Privacy, pp. 315–334. IEEE Computer Society Press (2018). https://doi.org/10.1109/SP.2018.00020

13. Bünz, B., Fisch, B., Szepieniec, A.: Transparent SNARKs from DARK compilers. In: Canteaut, A., Ishai, Y. (eds.) EUROCRYPT 2020. LNCS, vol. 12105, pp. 677–706. Springer, Cham (2020). https://doi.org/10.1007/978-3-030-45721-1_24

14. Bünz, B., Maller, M., Mishra, P., Tyagi, N., Vesely, P.: Proofs for inner pairing products and applications. In: Tibouchi, M., Wang, H. (eds.) ASIACRYPT 2021. LNCS, vol. 13092, pp. 65–97. Springer, Cham (2021). https://doi.org/10.1007/978-3-030-92078-4_3

15. Camenisch, J.: Efficient and generalized group signatures. In: Fumy, W. (ed.) EUROCRYPT 1997. LNCS, vol. 1233, pp. 465–479. Springer, Heidelberg (1997). https://doi.org/10.1007/3-540-69053-0_32

16. Camenisch, J., Hohenberger, S., Kohlweiss, M., Lysyanskaya, A., Meyerovich, M.: How to win the clonewars: efficient periodic n-times anonymous authentication. In: Juels, A., Wright, R.N., De Capitani di Vimercati, S. (eds.) ACM CCS 2006, pp. 201–210. ACM Press (2006). https://doi.org/10.1145/1180405.1180431

17. Camenisch, J., Hohenberger, S., Lysyanskaya, A.: Compact E-cash. In: Cramer, R. (ed.) EUROCRYPT 2005. LNCS, vol. 3494, pp. 302–321. Springer, Heidelberg (2005). https://doi.org/10.1007/11426639_18

18. Camenisch, J., Hohenberger, S., Lysyanskaya, A.: Balancing accountability and privacy using E-cash (extended abstract). In: De Prisco, R., Yung, M. (eds.) SCN 2006. LNCS, vol. 4116, pp. 141–155. Springer, Heidelberg (2006). https://doi.org/10.1007/11832072_10

19. Camenisch, J., Lysyanskaya, A.: An identity escrow scheme with appointed verifiers. In: Kilian, J. (ed.) CRYPTO 2001. LNCS, vol. 2139, pp. 388–407. Springer, Heidelberg (2001). https://doi.org/10.1007/3-540-44647-8_23

20. Camenisch, J., Lysyanskaya, A.: Dynamic accumulators and application to efficient revocation of anonymous credentials. In: Yung, M. (ed.) CRYPTO 2002. LNCS, vol. 2442, pp. 61–76. Springer, Heidelberg (2002). https://doi.org/10.1007/3-540-45708-9_5

21. Camenisch, J., Lysyanskaya, A.: Signature schemes and anonymous credentials from bilinear maps. In: Franklin, M. (ed.) CRYPTO 2004. LNCS, vol. 3152, pp. 56–72. Springer, Heidelberg (2004). https://doi.org/10.1007/978-3-540-28628-8_4

22. Camenisch, J., Shoup, V.: Practical verifiable encryption and decryption of discrete logarithms. In: Boneh, D. (ed.) CRYPTO 2003. LNCS, vol. 2729, pp. 126–144. Springer, Heidelberg (2003). https://doi.org/10.1007/978-3-540-45146-4_8

23. Camenisch, J., Stadler, M.: Proof systems for general statements about discrete logarithms. Technical Report TR 260, Institute for Theoretical Computer Science, ETH Zürich (1997)
24. Camenisch, J., Van Herreweghen, E.: Design and implementation of the idemix anonymous credential system. In: Atluri, V. (ed.) ACM CCS 2002, pp. 21–30. ACM Press (2002). https://doi.org/10.1145/586110.586114
25. Chaum, D.: Showing credentials without identification transferring signatures between unconditionally unlinkable pseudonyms. In: Seberry, J., Pieprzyk, J. (eds.) AUSCRYPT 1990. LNCS, vol. 453, pp. 245–264. Springer, Heidelberg (1990). https://doi.org/10.1007/BFb0030366
26. Chaum, D., Fiat, A., Naor, M.: Untraceable electronic cash. In: Goldwasser, S. (ed.) CRYPTO 1988. LNCS, vol. 403, pp. 319–327. Springer, New York (1990). https://doi.org/10.1007/0-387-34799-2_25
27. Chen, B., Bünz, B., Boneh, D., Zhang, Z.: HyperPlonk: plonk with linear-time prover and high-degree custom gates. In: Hazay, C., Stam, M. (eds.) EURO-CRYPT 2023, Part II. LNCS, vol. 14005, pp. 499–530. Springer, Cham (2023). https://doi.org/10.1007/978-3-031-30617-4_17
28. Cramer, R., Damgård, I., Nielsen, J.B.: Multiparty computation from threshold homomorphic encryption. In: Pfitzmann, B. (ed.) EUROCRYPT 2001. LNCS, vol. 2045, pp. 280–300. Springer, Heidelberg (2001). https://doi.org/10.1007/3-540-44987-6_18
29. Damgård, I., Fujisaki, E.: An integer commitment scheme based on groups with hidden order. In: ASIACRYPT 2002. LNCS, vol. 2501 (2002)
30. Goldwasser, S., Kalai, Y.T., Rothblum, G.N.: Delegating computation: interactive proofs for muggles. In: Ladner, R.E., Dwork, C. (eds.) 40th ACM STOC, pp. 113–122. ACM Press (2008). https://doi.org/10.1145/1374376.1374396
31. Goldwasser, S., Micali, S.: Probabilistic encryption and how to play mental poker keeping secret all partial information. In: 14th ACM STOC, pp. 365–377. ACM Press (1982). https://doi.org/10.1145/800070.802212
32. Golovnev, A., Lee, J., Setty, S.T.V., Thaler, J., Wahby, R.S.: Brakedown: linear-time and field-agnostic SNARKs for R1CS. In: Handschuh, H., Lysyanskaya, A. (eds.) CRYPTO 2023, Part II. LNCS, vol. 14082, pp. 193–226. Springer, Cham (2023). https://doi.org/10.1007/978-3-031-38545-2_7
33. Griffy, S., Kohlweiss, M., Lysyanskaya, A., Sengupta, M.: Succinctly verifiable computation over additively-homomorphically encrypted data: making privacy-preserving blueprints practical. Cryptology ePrint Archive, Paper 2024/675 (2024). https://eprint.iacr.org/2024/675
34. Hanzlik, L., Slamanig, D.: With a little help from my friends: constructing practical anonymous credentials. In: Vigna, G., Shi, E. (eds.) ACM CCS 2021, pp. 2004–2023. ACM Press (2021). https://doi.org/10.1145/3460120.3484582
35. Hesse, J., Singh, N., Sorniotti, A.: How to bind anonymous credentials to humans. In: Calandrino, J.A., Troncoso, C. (eds.) 32nd USENIX Security Symposium, USENIX Security 2023, Anaheim, CA, USA, 9–11 August 2023, pp. 3047–3064. USENIX Association (2023). https://www.usenix.org/conference/usenixsecurity23/presentation/hesse
36. Kiayias, A., Kohlweiss, M., Sarencheh, A.: PEReDi: privacy-enhanced, regulated and distributed central bank digital currencies. In: Yin, H., Stavrou, A., Cremers, C., Shi, E. (eds.) ACM CCS 2022, pp. 1739–1752. ACM Press (2022). https://doi.org/10.1145/3548606.3560707

37. Kohlweiss, M., Lysyanskaya, A., Nguyen, A.: Privacy-preserving blueprints. In: Hazay, C., Stam, M. (eds.) EUROCRYPT 2023, Part II. LNCS, vol. 14005, pp. 594–625. Springer, Cham (2023). https://doi.org/10.1007/978-3-031-30617-4_20
38. Lai, R.W.F., Malavolta, G., Ronge, V.: Succinct arguments for bilinear group arithmetic: practical structure-preserving cryptography. In: Cavallaro, L., Kinder, J., Wang, X., Katz, J. (eds.) ACM CCS 2019, pp. 2057–2074. ACM Press (2019). https://doi.org/10.1145/3319535.3354262
39. Lund, C., Fortnow, L., Karloff, H.J., Nisan, N.: Algebraic methods for interactive proof systems. J. ACM **39**(4), 859–868 (1992)
40. Lysyanskaya, A.: Signature schemes and applications to cryptographic protocol design. Ph.D. thesis, Massachusetts Institute of Technology, Cambridge, Massachusetts (2002)
41. Lysyanskaya, A., Rivest, R., Sahai, A., Wolf, S.: Pseudonym systems. In: Heys, H., Adams, C. (eds.) Selected Areas in Cryptography. LNCS, vol. 1758 (1999)
42. Pietrzak, K.: Simple verifiable delay functions. In: Blum, A. (ed.) ITCS 2019, vol. 124, pp. 60:1–60:15. LIPIcs (2019). https://doi.org/10.4230/LIPIcs.ITCS.2019.60
43. Rosenberg, M., White, J.D., Garman, C., Miers, I.: zk-creds: flexible anonymous credentials from zkSNARKs and existing identity infrastructure. In: 2023 IEEE Symposium on Security and Privacy, pp. 790–808. IEEE Computer Society Press (2023). https://doi.org/10.1109/SP46215.2023.10179430
44. Schwartz, J.T.: Fast probabilistic algorithms for verification of polynomial identities. J. ACM **27**(4), 701–717 (1980). https://doi.org/10.1145/322217.322225
45. Shoup, V.: Lower bounds for discrete logarithms and related problems. In: Fumy, W. (ed.) EUROCRYPT 1997. LNCS, vol. 1233, pp. 256–266. Springer, Heidelberg (1997). https://doi.org/10.1007/3-540-69053-0_18
46. Stanley, J.: Paths toward an acceptable public digital currency. ACLU White Paper (2023). https://www.aclu.org/wp-content/uploads/legal-documents/cbdc_white_paper_-_0882_0.pdf
47. Tessaro, S., Zhu, C.: Revisiting BBS signatures. In: Hazay, C., Stam, M. (eds.) EUROCRYPT 2023, Part V. LNCS, vol. 14008, pp. 691–721. Springer, Cham (2023). https://doi.org/10.1007/978-3-031-30589-4_24
48. Tomescu, A., et al.: UTT: decentralized ecash with accountable privacy. Cryptology ePrint Archive, Report 2022/452 (2022). https://eprint.iacr.org/2022/452
49. Wang, R., Hazay, C., Venkitasubramaniam, M.: Ligetron: lightweight scalable end-to-end zero-knowledge proofs post-quantum zk-snarks on a browser. In: IEEE Symposium on Security and Privacy, SP 2024, San Francisco, CA, USA, 19–23 May 2024, pp. 1760–1776. IEEE (2024)
50. Xie, T., Zhang, J., Zhang, Y., Papamanthou, C., Song, D.: Libra: succinct zero-knowledge proofs with optimal prover computation. In: Boldyreva, A., Micciancio, D. (eds.) CRYPTO 2019. LNCS, vol. 11694, pp. 733–764. Springer, Cham (2019). https://doi.org/10.1007/978-3-030-26954-8_24

Multi-hop Multi-key Homomorphic Signatures with Context Hiding from Standard Assumptions

Abtin Afshar[(⊠)], Jiaqi Cheng, and Rishab Goyal[iD]

University of Wisconsin-Madison, Madison, WI, USA
{abtin,jiaqicheng,rishab}@cs.wisc.edu

Abstract. We design homomorphic signatures that support arbitrary homomorphic computations from a wide variety of standard falsifiable assumptions (such as decision-linear, or DDH, or learning with errors). Unlike known folklore solutions, we do not put any artificial restrictions on the evaluator, and support homomorphic evaluation on any combination of evaluated signatures. The size of evaluated signatures and verification key grows polynomially in the circuit depth, but is otherwise independent of the circuit/data size. Our designs naturally generalize to multi-key homomorphism. This gives the first multi-key homomorphic signature system with full succinctness under the same set of assumptions. We also achieve full context hiding without sacrificing homomorphism, under the hardness of learning with errors. All our constructions satisfy full (adaptive) security.

1 Introduction

Homomorphic signatures [1,13,14,51,58] enable computations on *secretly* signed data. They represent a significant advancement in cryptography, akin to homomorphic encryption [19,21,44,46,72], and have proven to be quite useful for numerous applications. E.g., computing statistics on signed data [14], network coding [1,2], proofs of retrievability [74], trustworthy delegation [41,51,69], attribute-based signatures [64,75], and verifying image transformations [31]. Using homomorphic signatures, for any computable circuit C, we can derive a new signature $\sigma_{C,y}$ from a signature σ_M for data M. In words, $\sigma_{C,y}$ is an unforgeable token validating possession of a signature σ_M on some data M such that $C(M) = y$.

In most applications, we want the ability to homomorphically evaluate signatures in a continuous step-by-step fashion. That is, we want homomorphic computations to be supported over an evaluated signature. To further illustrate the point, let us recall the original motivating application of network coding [1,13,14]. Each router: (i) receives a sequence of signed messages from its preceding routers, (ii) homomorphically creates a random linear combination of

---

R. Goyal—Support for this research was provided by OVCRGE at UW–Madison with funding from the Wisconsin Alumni Research Foundation.

S. Bai and E. Persichetti (Eds.): PKC 2026, LNCS 16554, pp. 270–301, 2026.
https://doi.org/10.1007/978-3-032-26740-5_9

incoming signatures, and (iii) sends the homomorphically evaluated signature to the next router. Such an operation is carried out iteratively by every router in the network. Thus, this needs continuous homomorphism over evaluated signatures, each independently computed by a different router. Similar requirements are enforced by many classic applications such as certified data analysis, computation on outsourced data, certified redaction, and more [1,13,14,51,58].

More generally, it might be that a user cannot access the entire dataset, or its signature, or the full circuit description, at the time evaluation starts. This could be due to resource unavailability, or lack of authorization, or scalability/performance issues, etc. For example, consider a cloud provider (say Apple) storing petabytes of user data (e.g., images, documents) across a large group of independent servers. To counter storage of illicit material (e.g., copyrighted data, deepfake images), each server could store digital signatures proving user data provenance [31]. Suppose an auditor (say FBI) wants the cloud provider to prove that none of its servers are storing any illicit material. Homomorphic signatures can be a powerful tool to assist such secure audits very efficiently. However, this is only possible as long as they support (distributed) evaluation where the entire signed data is not available at one place. Moreover, due to the sheer volume of data stored by even a single server, it could be impractical to run homomorphic evaluation in one-shot.

Capturing General Homomorphism. To ensure maximum applicability and flexibility, the most general approach for defining homomorphic signatures is to define every cryptographic operation atomically. Thus, consider that each bit of dataset $M = (m_1, \ldots)$ can be signed independently and asynchronously, i.e. $\mathsf{Sign}(\mathsf{sk}, i, m_i) \to \sigma_i$. And, an evaluator can run homomorphic computation on any subset S of the signed dataset $\{\sigma_i\}_{i \in S}$, or any sequence of evaluated signatures $\{\sigma_{C_i, y_i}\}_i$ where $y_i = C_i(M)$. This gives a very general abstraction for homomorphic signatures, and is sometimes referred to as multi-hop evaluation. It enables all known applications including those discussed above. It provides fully parallelizable data signing and signature evaluation, thereby resolving the challenges due to scalability, availability, and authorization.

The two most desirable properties for homomorphic signatures are *succinctness* and *unforgeability*. Succinctness states that the size of a derived signature $\sigma_{C,y}$ must not grow with the original data or computation size. Unforgeability states that an attacker cannot create an accepting signature σ^* for any circuit C^* and output y^*, s.t. $y^* \neq C^*(M)$ where M is the data that was signed.

Beyond succinctness and unforgeability, a variety of additional desirable features have been studied in the literature such as context hiding, fast verification, and multi-key evaluation (refer to [37,51] for a detailed discussion.) Context hiding states that a malicious user should not learn anything about dataset M from $\sigma_{C,y}$, beyond what is revealed by C and y. The fast verification property states that a verifier can pre-process the circuit C to compute a short digest h_C, where an *online* verifier can verify signature $\sigma_{C,y}$, given y and h_C, in time independent of $|C|$. Finally, multi-key homomorphic signatures generalize regular homomorphic signatures to the multi-signer setting, where homomorphic evaluation can be performed on data signed by many different signers.

A Folklore Approach to Designing (Multi-key) Homomorphic Signatures. There is a popular folklore approach for designing (mult-key) homomorphic signatures from RAM delegation systems. The idea is to convert any (vanilla) signature scheme into a homomorphic signature. Rather than signing the dataset directly, a signer first hashes it and then signs it. Now, to evaluate a circuit C on signature σ for dataset M, a user creates a RAM proof π that certifies $C(M) = y$, and includes it as part of the evaluated signature (in addition to σ, digest of M). To verify an evaluated signature, one can first check σ is a valid signature for (digest of) M, and next it can validate the RAM proof π given the digest of M. For subsequent evaluation hops, this approach can be easily extended to create a chain of evaluated signatures. While this approach is incredibly powerful in designing (multi-key) homomorphic signatures, it has a serious limitation! We **cannot** take two evaluated signatures (say $\widehat{\sigma}_1$ and $\widehat{\sigma}_2$) computed on the same original dataset M, and homomorphically evaluate a circuit on them *jointly*. The reason is the folklore chaining idea would require us to keep both signatures, $\widehat{\sigma}_1$ and $\widehat{\sigma}_2$, as part of the evaluated signature. This is because we cannot verify the computation without explicit knowledge of both signatures. Thus, the size of signature is no longer succinct, but grows linearly with the number of signatures that are combined in each homomorphic operation. We elaborate on this folklore approach in the full version, and summarize that the folklore solution is insufficient for many applications (e.g., network coding), and does not fully solve the homomorphic signature problem.

In this work, our focus is on designing (multi-key) homomorphic signatures that achieve full succinctness, even if an evaluator wants to jointly evaluate any arbitrary number of evaluated signatures. We add that one could compare the above notion of "chained" homomorphism and general multi-hop homomorphism with incrementally verifiable computation (IVC) [77] and proof carrying data [28], respectively. IVCs are a specialization of PCDs, and it is well known that PCDs are much stronger than IVCs. Similarly, general multi-hop homomorphism is much more powerful than "chained" homomorphism for homomorphic signatures. This is because chained-homomorphism allows only a straight-line chain of evaluation (like IVCs), while general multi-hop evaluation allows for arbitrary graph structures of evaluation (like PCDs).

Our Results. We design homomorphic signatures for arbitrary polynomial-sized circuits satisfying all aforementioned properties from a variety of standard assumptions such as DDH [33,34], decision-linear (DLIN) [12], and learning with errors (LWE) [70]. Our signatures are (a) *fully-succinct*, support (b) *general multi-hop* and (c) *multi-key evaluation*, and satisfy (d) *fast verification*, and (e) *full (adaptive) unforgeability*. The sizes of signatures as well as the verification keys grow as $\mathsf{poly}(\lambda, d)$, where d is the maximum depth of the circuits that can be evaluated. Thus, the efficiency does not scale with the dataset size $|M|$, circuit size $|C|$, or the total number of signers n (in case of multi-key evaluation). Moreover, our LWE-based homomorphic signatures satisfy (f) *full context hiding*. While under DLIN, or DDH, we can make evaluated signatures (g) *context hiding at the cost of sacrificing homomorphism* (similar to [51]).

Additionally, we show an interesting trade-off, where we can further reduce our signature size to not grow polynomially with the circuit depth/width as long as we restrict to a single evaluation over signed data. That is, for single-hop homomorphic signatures, we can obtain signature size of $\mathsf{poly}(\lambda, \log|C|)$, with only polynomial security loss. The central toolkit that we rely on is the recent exciting work on non-interactive batch arguments (BARGs) and its extensions [18,20,29,30,32,59,60,68,71]. In the main body, we state our main theorems more generally.

Comparing our Results. We provide the *first* homomorphic signature system that supports *general homomorphic computations* from *(falsifiable) non-lattice assumptions such as* DLIN and DDH. All other homomorphic signatures, from standard falsifiable assumptions [66], either rely on lattices [17,37,51], or only support 'chained' homomorphic evaluation [11,25,59,78], or constant number of evaluations [36,52,75]. Chained homomorphic evaluation corresponds to sequential (straight-line) evaluation, where two or more evaluated signatures **cannot** be homomorphically evaluated. And, by constant number of hops, we mean that the total number of evaluations that can be performed on signed data is at most $O(1)$. Such restrictions prohibit using homomorphic signatures in many applications, including network coding and secure data auditing.

Moreover, our LWE-based construction is the *first* homomorphic signature system *with context hiding*. In the original construction by Gorbunov et al. [51], one had to *turn off homomorphism to make evaluated signatures context hiding*. In our construction, we do not have such restrictions, and even our intermediate evaluated signatures are context hiding.

Finally, we give the *first* homomorphic signature system that satisfies *full-succinctness in the multi-key model from standard falsifiable assumptions* [37]. In prior works [37,38,73], the signature size grew polynomially with the number of signers, n. Whereas the size of our signatures does not grow with n, thereby achieving fully-succinctness from standard falsifiable assumptions. Moreover, our LWE-based multi-key homomorphic signature scheme also achieves *context hiding*.

Related Work. Since early 2000s, homomorphic signatures with varying functionalities have been designed [1,5,8–10,13–15,24,26,35,39,42,43,58,74]. All of these had one or more restrictions (private verifiability, limited homomorphism). The only exception was the folklore approach based on succinct non-interactive arguments of knowledge (SNARKs) [61,65]. Basically, each homomorphic evaluation can be proved succinctly by a SNARK, and unforgeability follows from knowledge soundness of SNARKs. SNARKs are known to have strong implausibility results from falsifiable assumptions [23,47]. In 2015, Gorbunov et al. [51] designed the first fully-homomorphic signature scheme under standard lattice assumptions [6]. This was a major achievement in the study of homomorphic signatures. Since then, there has been a large body of exciting work [11,17,25,36,37,40,52,59,62,75,78] leading to many new designs and extensions.

State-of-the-Art. Currently, there are four major approaches to design fully homomorphic signatures – algebraic constructions from lattices [17,36,37,51,75], generic constructions from functional commitments and mutable batch arguments [11,25,52,59,78], from indistinguishability obfuscation [40], and from SNARKs [43,51,61,62,65]. The first approach behind lattice-based schemes does not generalize to other cryptographic assumptions. And, as discussed earlier, they also do not satisfy context hiding or full succinctness in the multi-key model. The second approach from functional commitments and mutable batch arguments only support 'chained' or constant-hop homomorphism, thus do not achieve general multi-hop homomorphism. The other two approaches, from obfuscation and SNARKs, rely on non-falsifiable assumptions [23,47,49]. Although indistinguishability obfuscation can be constructed from a careful combination of sub-exponential-hardness of well-founded assumptions [56,57], our goal is to come up with direct constructions and *not* rely on combinations of multiple cryptographic assumptions[1].

Concurrent Work. In a concurrent work, Anthoine, Balbás, and Fiore [7] designed fully-succinct multi-key homomorphic signatures [37] by combining batch arguments and functional commitments [63]. Both works achieve signature size to be independent of the number of signers. The main differences are their scheme [7] is inspired by the folklore approach (see full version for explanation), thus can only support 'chained' (multi-hop) homomorphic evaluation. While we can support general (multi-hop) homomorphic evaluation. We highlight that in the original version of our paper (concurrent to [7]) we only proved selective security of our design, and just briefly sketched how our approach easily extends to the multi-key setting. Later on (and this should be treated as non-concurrent to [7]), we realized that our scheme was already adaptively secure, thus updated our security proof. Our current version has identical results as to our original version, except the adaptive security portion. Other than that, the only difference between our original and current version is that we have re-organized different sections of the paper, and made editorial improvements.

In a subsequent work [55] built attribute-based signatures where the public parameters and the signature size grow with $\mathsf{poly}(\lambda, \log |x|, \log C)$. Note that using Tsabary's transformation [75], our (single-hop) homomorphic signature implies an attribute-based signature with similar efficiency, except that it only satisfies a weaker hiding/privacy notion.

2   Technical Overview

Our starting point is the recent template for designing homomorphic signatures by Goyal [52]. Their idea was to combine monotone-policy SNARGs for

---

[1] While combining cryptographic assumptions is a very successful research strategy [3, 4,53,56,57] to break new ground in cryptography, it is always desirable to reduce the strength of computational assumptions needed for a particular cryptographic task. We study the problem of homomorphic signatures with the same motivation.

batchNP (henceforth monotone SNARGs) [18,67] with vanilla signatures[2]. Below we briefly review BARGs and monotone SNARGs, as they will be essential tools throughout the sequel. Any reader familiar with these concepts can skip the next two paragraphs, and move to the simplified template for designing homomorphic signatures from monotone SNARGs.

Reviewing BARGs and Monotone SNARGs. BARGs allow a prover to generate a succinct proof π for a batch of statements that $\{x_i \in \mathcal{L}\}_{i \leq k}$ for some NP language $\mathcal{L}$, where k denotes the batch size. Succinctness is defined as the size of proof π being independent of batch size k. Soundness states that an attacker cannot create an accepting proof for a batch of instances containing at least one invalid instance $x_i \notin \mathcal{L}$. Somewhere extractable BARGs (seBARGs) [29,30] are a mild strengthening of BARGs, which enable extraction of a witness for a single statement at some trapdoor index $i^* \in [k]$ (secretly embedded in the crs). This extraction is enabled by a trapdoor key, associated with crs.

In a recent beautiful work, Brakerski et al. [18] introduced the concept of monotone SNARGs. These SNARGs enable computation of general *monotone circuits* over the validity of a batch of statements. That is, for any monotone circuit C, and any batch of statements $(x_1, \ldots, x_k)$, a prover can create a succinct proof to prove there exist witnesses $(\omega_1, \ldots, \omega_k)$ such that $C(b_1, \ldots, b_k) = 1$, where $b_i = \mathcal{R}(x_i, w_i)$ (i.e., b_i denotes satisfiability of instance-witness pair as per $\mathcal{L}$). Succinctness is defined as the proof size being independent of k as well as circuit size, $|C|$. Soundness states that an attacker cannot create an accepting proof, for a batch of instances $\{x_i\}_i$ and monotone circuit C, for which there does not exist a sequence of witnesses $\{\omega_i\}_i$ that satisfies the monotone circuit.

Monotone SNARGs to Homomorphic Signatures. To sign the i-th bit of the dataset $M = (m_1, \ldots)$, the signer uses any vanilla signature scheme. That is, it signs the message (i, m_i) to compute σ_i. In order to compute a circuit C on the signed dataset M, the plan is for the evaluator to compute a monotone SNARG proof for C using $\{\sigma_i\}_i$ as witnesses. However, C could be non-monotonic, thus their [52] idea was to deterministically encode C into a monotone circuit $\tilde{C}$ of similar size. At a high level, this works by encoding the input x to circuit C into a string $\tilde{x} = (x, x \oplus 1^{|x|})$, and ensuring that $C(x) = \tilde{C}(\tilde{x})$ for every x. Such translations are well known in the literature [54,76], and for completeness, we provide it in the full version.

Once we can encode C into a monotone circuit $\tilde{C}$, then homomorphic evaluation is relatively straightforward. The evaluator computes a monotone SNARG for $\tilde{C}$, where it uses σ_i as a witness for the i-th statement if $m_i = 1$, otherwise it uses it for the $(|m|+i)$-th statement. (The underlying NP relation $\mathcal{R}$ for the batch language portion corresponds to the signature verification circuit.) The resulting proof is viewed as an evaluated signature. To argue unforgeability, Goyal relied on the *full extraction* property of monotone SNARGs [18]. The intuition was to

---

[2] Although [52] uses a more general template, described via a new primitive called *mutable* batch arguments [52], it is possible to summarize the ideas using only monotone SNARGs.

extract a sequence of satisfying witnesses for the monotone circuit $\tilde{C}$ from an evaluated signature/proof, and one of those witnesses will serve as a forgery on the vanilla signature scheme.

Does this Handle General Homomorphic Evaluation? Recall that an evaluator could want to evaluate any sequence of evaluated signatures $\{\sigma_{C_i, y_i}\}_i$ as well, and not just plain (non-evaluated) signatures. A natural approach would be to use a monotone SNARG proof as a witness during future homomorphic evaluations. Namely, given a set of circuit-output values and *evaluated* signatures, generate a fresh monotone SNARG proof for the next hop of homomorphic evaluation, while using the *evaluated* signatures as the witnesses. At first glance, it might appear that this approach will be sufficient for handling all homomorphic computations. Unfortunately, this is not the case!

Why is Composing Monotone SNARGs Insufficient? The naive approach of composing monotone SNARGs is quite limiting. In a few words, the issue is the large blow-up in the signature size due to composition of monotone SNARGs. This was noted in [52], and this is why their construction only supports $O(1)$ evaluation hops. Simply put, the issue is that the size of a monotone SNARG proof polynomially grows with the size of a single witness, and thus a recursive composition of such SNARG proofs will lead to cascading polynomials (i.e., $\mathsf{poly}(\mathsf{poly}(\ldots\mathsf{poly}(\cdot))))$. Therefore, monotone SNARGs can only be composed constant number of times, which is not ideal.

Similar issues were recently faced [32] in the context of composing BARGs to design (unbounded) aggregate signatures [16] and incrementally verifiable computation protocols [77]. Their main insight was to design optimal-rate BARG proofs [32,68]. An optimal-rate BARG proof, also commonly referred to as rate-1 BARGs, have a special succinctness property which states $|\pi| = |\omega| + \mathsf{poly}(\lambda, \log k)$. That is, the size of the proof is equal to the size of a single witness, plus fixed additive polynomial terms.

First Idea and Why it Fails! Our intuition is that using rate-1 BARGs should be enough to improve the efficiency of existing monotone SNARGs [18,67], and this will help us get around the above recursive composition issue. Unfortunately, even if we are able to design such composable monotone SNARGs, this will not be enough! The issue is that for our homomorphic signature scheme to be unforgeable, we really need our monotone SNARGs to be composable as well as *fully extractable*. Moreover, to prove full (adaptive) unforgeability, we need the underlying monotone SNARGs to be adaptively-knowledge-sound. It is well-known that adaptively-knowledge-sound BARGs are as challenging to design as SNARKs [20, Section 6.1]. Since monotone SNARGs with knowledge soundness are clearly more powerful than BARGs, thus this suggests that we will face well-known black-box barriers [48] in designing *fully extractable* monotone SNARGs. We did not face this issue in single/constant-hop, since composability was not an issue.

Opening up Monotone SNARGs: Using Somewhere Extractable BARGs. As we explained above, using monotone SNARGs as a black box is not good enough. To get around the barrier of inability to prove security while just relying on non-extractable monotone SNARGs, our approach is to open up the existing designs for monotone SNARGs [18,67]. It turns out all existing constructions for monotone SNARGs follow a similar template, which is to use seBARGs as a core primitive and create the SNARG proof as a batch proof. Therefore, intrinsically, a monotone SNARG construction does enjoy a 'somewhere-extraction-style' feature that we plan to exploit to get around the *full* extraction barrier.

In more detail, let us recall the canonical template for designing monotone SNARGs [18]. Consider a batch of instances $(x_1, \ldots, x_k)$, witnesses $(w_1, \ldots, w_k)$, an NP relation $\mathcal{R}$, and a monotone circuit $\tilde{C}$. The canonical template to create a monotone SNARG for these elements is the following two-step method:

1. Create a short (digested) commitment dig of all wire values, as computed during the evaluation of $\tilde{C}(\mathcal{R}(x_1, w_1), \ldots, \mathcal{R}(x_k, w_k))$.
2. Create a BARG to prove a batch of two types of statements:
   (a) Each *input* wire is correctly computed and committed. That is, the input wire i is set to be $\mathcal{R}(x_i, w_i)$, and $\mathcal{R}(x_i, w_i)$ is correctly committed inside dig w.r.t. input wire i.
   (b) Each *internal* wire is correctly computed and committed. That is, if an internal wire j is the output wire of some gate g, where wires j_0, j_1 are its input wires, then the wire values committed inside dig are consistent w.r.t. gate g.

The monotone SNARG simply contains the digest dig and a batch proof π, proving validity of all aforementioned statements. Since the size of the batch proof does not scale with the batch size (which is almost the number of wires in circuit $\tilde{C}$), thus the resulting monotone SNARG proof is succinct.

Brakerski et al. [18] instantiated the above template with a hash function with short local openings to create the wire commitments (e.g., Merkle tree) and a somewhere extractable BARG. They proved the above monotone SNARG proof system to be computationally sound. At a very high level, the soundness proof follows the folklore global-to-local style of reduction [50]. By this we mean, that suppose a cheating prover creates an accepting proof for an invalid statement, then one could identify at least one gate/wire in the claimed evaluation dig of the monotone circuit $\tilde{C}$ such that it proves an incorrect statement.

A bit more concretely, we can visualize this as a *guessing-based* 'top-down reduction'. Here the reduction starts from the top (i.e., the output wire) and traces a path down the monotone circuit. Its goal is to find either a gate, such that the internal wire was not correctly evaluated and/or committed, or an input wire was not correctly set and/or committed. Since the circuit under consideration is a monotone circuit, thus starting from the output layer one can argue that if, for any layer, there is an internal wire j whose value claimed in the proof is greater than its actual value in the correct computation, then the invariant of wire's actual value being greater than the claimed value will also hold for at least one of the input wires of the corresponding gate with output wire j. This way a reduction can guess a path from the output wire to the input wire catching the adversary at least one layer along this path.

Building Multi-hop Directly from seBARGs. Our strategy for designing multi-hop homomorphic signatures, without using *full extractability* of monotone SNARGs, is to carefully instantiate the above template for multi-hop evaluations. Basically, our plan is to use seBARGs as the underlying technical tool instead, and execute a similar top-down reduction where we will view a multi-hop signature as an seBARG proof along with a (short) digest of all internal wires of all evaluated circuits. Thus, we do not need to worry about full extractability, and just by exploiting somewhere extractability of seBARGs, we plan to reduce unforgeability to soundness of seBARGs, collision resistance of hash functions, and unforgeability of underlying signatures.

While the above strategy carries the right ideas, there are still two important caveats that we would like to point out. First, in such a top-down reduction approach, one cannot deterministically figure out which wire at any layer in the proof is greater than its actual value, thus the reduction must guess this at each layer. This implies that there is a factor-of-two security loss per layer in the reduction as we go down the monotone circuit. Therefore, if the circuit has depth d, then we have to rely on 2^d hardness of the underlying seBARG. By using standard complexity leveraging techniques, we can execute the proof strategy while reducing to sub-exponential security of the underlying assumptions[3].

The second (and bigger) caveat with this strategy is that we need the seBARG to be *'extractable for two instances'*. That is, we need witness extractability for two instances from the batch of, say k, instances. This is essential because, to argue the soundness, we need to extract two seBARG witnesses (i.e., wire values and their openings) from two consecutive layers of the monotone circuit. If we do not extract at two locations, then the iterative top-down proof strategy does not work.

Why is Extracting at Two Places an Issue for Multi-hop? Recall that to get around the large blow-up issue in the signature size due to proof composition, we are considering relying on composable/rate-1 BARGs to ensure the blow-up is controlled. This is because by using rate-1 seBARGs we might just have to pay an additive polynomial cost each time we homomorphically evaluate a set of evaluated signatures.

Unfortunately, the current security proof strategy heavily relies on the layer-by-layer argument and, hence requires at least one extraction on each layer. This suggests that the seBARGs must be extractable on two indices. Note that any seBARGs that is extractable on N witnesses can be generically built using N seBARGs that are extractable on a single witness. However, this brings down

---

[3] Brakerski et al. [18] and Nasser et al. [67] also considered alternate proof strategies to prove soundness without incurring this sub-exponential loss, but those do not seem to be compatible with our multi-hop homomorphic signature construction. We leave proving unforgeability of our multi-hop homomorphic signatures from polynomial hardness as an interesting open problem.

the proof-rate from 1 to $1/N$. Because, for each (single-witness-extractable) seBARG, the proof size grows as $|\omega| + \mathsf{poly}(\lambda)$. This means that even if we start with rate-1 seBARGs (which is the optimal rate possible for straightline-extraction[4]), for the above construction we will have to use two rate-1 seBARGs (or one rate-$\frac{1}{2}$ seBARG extractable on two indices). Thus, $\pi = 2|\omega_i| + \mathsf{poly}$ which would mean that by recursively composing such proofs, the resulting seBARG proofs (in turn, the multi-hop signatures) will grow as 2^t, where t is the number of hops.

While this is already interesting as it enables logarithmic number of evaluation hops, our end goal is to enable general multi-hop homomorphic evaluation. Thus, plugging in a rate-1 seBARG directly into the above construction is not sufficient for handling an arbitrary polynomial number of hops.

Our Core Technique: Width-2 chained composition of rate-1 and poor-rate seBARGs. One of our main insights is the fact that there is an implicit structure in the language used for seBARGs while designing homomorphic signatures. Recall that the BARG proof, in the multi-hop signature candidate construction, checks the consistency of the internal gates in addition to the correctness of the input wires. While the witnesses proving validity of the 'input wires' could potentially be large (since the witness could be an already evaluated signature), the witnesses for the 'internal wires' (i.e., for checking gate consistency) are always *a fixed short polynomial regardless of the number of evaluation hops performed.*

This core observation drives our main modification to the current multi-hop construction. Our idea is that an evaluator now will generate *two separate* seBARG proofs. Instead of generating a single seBARG proof that is extractable on two indices (i.e., say a rate-$\frac{1}{2}$ proof) for the "composed" language (i.e., validity of input wires and gate consistency), we generate *two* seBARG proofs—(1) for proving validity of the input wires, we use an seBARG proof system that is *extractable on just a single index (i.e., a rate-1 proof)*, while (2) for proving gate consistency, for the entire evaluated circuit, we use an seBARG proof system that is extractable on two indices (i.e., say a rate-$\frac{1}{2}$ proof).

Now one might wonder that this actually is increasing the size of an evaluated signature! Quite clearly, now the evaluated signature contains two seBARG proofs instead of one. Moreover, one seBARG is extractable on two indices, while the other on just one. Thus, in summation, one can potentially extract three witnesses from the proofs jointly. This is unlike the original design, where there is just one seBARG extractable on two indices. *While at first, this seems counterproductive, we have made great progress and this proof splitting operation enables arbitrary polynomial composition of evaluated signatures.*

To understand further, let us look more carefully at our modified multi-hop signature design. By splitting the seBARG proofs into two separate proofs, we are really composing the underlying seBARG proofs in an "atypical" fashion.

---

[4] A recent work by Cheng and Goyal [27] proves a stronger result about optimality of rate-1 BARGs, wherein they show any improvement would lead to a fully-succinct SNARK thereby facing Gentry-Wichs black-box barriers [48].

Note that the invariant is that there are two seBARG proofs that are part of any evaluated signature. Now whenever an evaluated signature is used as a witness for the next level of homomorphic evaluation, then the evaluated signature is **never** used as a witness by an seBARG prover whose rate is lower than 1. In words, the invariant that we maintain is that output of a poor-rate seBARG proof (which is extractable at two indices) is never used as a witness in another poor-rate seBARG proof computation, but only in some rate-1 seBARG proof computation. Thus, the blow-up due to seBARG proof composition is still capped at an additive growth each time, where the factor-of-2 (due to poor-rate) never gets cascaded.

It is crucial to note that the above guarantees that the recursive composition of seBARG proofs only happens on the first seBARG, which is rate-1. Note that any evaluated signature size is simply $|\pi_{\mathsf{BARG}}^{(1)}| + |\pi_{\mathsf{BARG}}^{(2)}| + |\mathsf{com}|$. Here the commitment com is just a Merkle tree hash, hence its size is $\mathsf{poly}(\lambda)$. Suppose that the signatures that we get as inputs for homomorphic evaluation are of size $\leq \ell_\sigma$. The first BARG proof, $\pi_{\mathsf{BARG}}^{(1)}$, is a rate-1 seBARG on the input signatures, thus its size is $|\ell_\sigma| + \mathsf{poly}(\lambda)$. While the second seBARG (extractable at two places) only checks for the gate consistency w.r.t. the commitment openings, thus its size is $\mathsf{poly}(\lambda)$. Therefore the output signature/proof size will be $\ell_{\sigma'} = |\ell_\sigma| + \mathsf{poly}(\lambda)$, as desired.

Despite this modification, we observe that a similar guessing-based top-down reduction strategy is sufficient. Except, at some points in the security reduction, we will extract from the rate-1 seBARG, while at other points we extract from the poor-rate seBARG. Namely, we perform a layer-by-layer analysis using the second seBARG to extract two witnesses, while at the input layer, we will use the first seBARG to extract a single witness. Here the single witness at the input layer could itself be an evaluated signature, thus it is recursively extracted by following the same strategy. Below we provide a more detailed sketch of our multi-hop signature construction.

Our Multi-hop Homomorphic Signatures. We use vanilla signatures, hash functions with local openings, and seBARGs as follows:

- The signing algorithm is a regular signature Sig that sign (i, m_i) using $\mathsf{sig.sk}$ to get σ_i. We let y^t be the evaluated message at the t-th hop and y^0 is simply the messages $(m_1, \ldots, m_\ell)$ signed by regular digital signature.
- At the t-th hop, the evaluation algorithm does the following:
  1. Given C and y^{t-1}, compute $y = C(y^{t-1})$ and construct the corresponding monotone circuit $\tilde{C}_y$ (similarly to single-hop setting), and compute all the wire values $(b_1, \ldots, b_N)$ in the evaluation of $\tilde{C}_y(y^{t-1}, y^{t-1} \oplus 1^\ell)$.
  2. Compute digest h of $(b_1, \ldots, b_N)$ and opening ρ_i using a Merkle tree hash.
  3. Compute a rate-1 seBARG proof on the statements $(1, \ldots, 2\ell)$ and the witnesses $((b_1, \rho_1, \sigma_1^{t-1}), \ldots, (b_\ell, \rho_\ell, \sigma_\ell^{t-1}), (b_{\ell+1}, \rho_{\ell+1}, \sigma_1^{t-1}), \ldots, (b_{2\ell}, \rho_{2\ell}, \sigma_\ell^{t-1}))$ for the NP relation:

$$\mathcal{R}^{(1)} :- \mathbb{1} \left(\begin{array}{l} \rho_i \text{ is a valid opening for } b_i \text{ w.r.t. dig} \wedge \\ b_i = \mathbb{1} \left(\begin{array}{l} (i \leq \ell \ \wedge \ \sigma_i^{t-1} \text{ is a valid signature for 1)} \vee \\ (i > \ell \ \wedge \ \sigma_{i-\ell}^{t-1} \text{ is a valid signature for 0)} \end{array} \right) \end{array} \right) .$$

4. Compute a poor-rate (extractable on two indices) seBARG proof on the statements $(2\ell + 1, \ldots, N)$ and the witnesses $\omega_i = (b_i, b_{i_0}, b_{i_1}, \rho_i, \rho_{i_0}, \rho_{i_1})$ (where i is the output and i_0, i_1 are the inputs of gate i) for the NP relation:

$$\mathcal{R}^{(2)} :\!- \mathbb{1} \begin{pmatrix} \rho_i, \rho_{i_0}, \rho_{i_1} \text{ are valid openings for } b_i, b_{i_0}, b_{i_1} \text{ w.r.t. } h \ \wedge \\ b_i, b_{i_0}, b_{i_1} \text{ are consistent with gate } i \ \wedge \\ \text{if } i = N \text{ then } b_i = 1 \end{pmatrix}.$$

To argue the soundness, we will proceed with a layer-by-layer analysis, similar to [18]. Let the correct evaluation of the circuit $\tilde{C}$ where $b_i = R(x_i, w_i)$ for $i \in [2k]$ be $(b_1^*, \ldots, b_N^*)$. Define the hybrid for wire i at layer L to be the following:

When $\mathsf{crs}_{\mathsf{BARG}}^{(2)}$ is extractable on the statement corresponding to some gate g in layer L, then for the committed value b_i in the digest dig, where wire i is the output of gate g, it holds that $b_i > b_i^*$.

Now the claim is that if an efficient adversary can forge a signature, that is to generate an accepting proof for a message y^* such that $y^* \neq C(y^{t-1})$, then in every layer L, there is a gate g for which the hybrid invariant holds. We will prove our claim inductively starting from the last (output) layer. Note that if $y^* \neq C(y^{t-1})$ then $\tilde{C}_y(y^{t-1}, y^{t-1} \oplus 1^\ell) = 0$. Therefore if the proof is accepted, the invariant holds for the output layer and value b_N (Note that at the beginning we let the seBARG be extractable on the output gate). Now suppose the invariant holds for some gate g in layer L, our goal is to show that it also holds for layer $L - 1$.

First, using seBARG extraction, we extract a witness for the corresponding statement to gate g in $\pi_{\mathsf{BARG}}^{(2)}$. Let i_0 and i_1 be the input wires to gate g and b_{i_0} and b_{i_1} be the committed values in the digest dig. Since $b_i > b_i^*$ and gate g is monotone, by the gate consistency it holds that for some bit e, $b_{i_e} > b_{i_e}^*$. Now using the CRS indistinguishability of seBARGs, we let $\mathsf{crs}_{\mathsf{BARG}}^{(2)}$ to be extractable on gate g' whose output is wire i_e (while keeping $\mathsf{crs}_{\mathsf{BARG}}^{(2)}$ extractable on gate g). By the collision resistance property of the Merkle tree hash, overlapping parts (the openings of wire i_e) of the extracted witnesses on gate g and g' should be consistent. Thus for the extracted witness of gate g' it holds that $b_{i_e} > b_{i_e}^*$, which means that the invariant holds for level $L - 1$. Therefore by the induction, the invariant should hold for some wire value in the inputs. Now we let $\mathsf{crs}_{\mathsf{BARG}}^{(1)}$ be extractable on that wire, and then extract a witness for the input layer which by the construction implies a forgery σ_i^{t-1} for a message y_i^{t-1}.

Hence, by following the same argument hop-by-hop, we can extract a forgery σ_i at the input layer on a message m_i. Finally, we will use the unforgeability of the regular signature to conclude the soundness argument. We prove the following, and provide more details later in Sect. 3.

Context-Hiding and Fast Verification. Next, we show that the above template can be easily extended to enable context-hiding, and fast verification.

Context hiding for homomorphic signatures states that an evaluated signature does not reveal anything about the dataset m, beyond what can be learnt given circuit C and output y. Gorbunov et al. [51] proposed a simple generic template to obtain context-hiding property by applying NIZKAoKs as long as the homomorphic signatures were 'pre-processable'. Their core idea was that if one could preprocess the circuit C to a short digest, such that a verification algorithm only needs the short digest and not the circuit C, then one could generate a NIZK proof using the actual (non-context-hiding) evaluated signature as a witness. In words, the verification first pre-processes the circuit C to compute the digest, and then runs the NIZK verification. Now the security (unforgeability) of the system can be argued by combining NIZK extraction with the unforgeability of underlying homomorphic signatures, while context-hiding can be reduced to the zero-knowledge property of the NIZK scheme.

We follow a similar strategy for context hiding. Our approach is to rely on the fairly standardized online/offline verification features of BARGs [29], that is the verification algorithm of a BARG scheme can be split into a (slow) pre-verification and a (fast) online verification, and then use NIZKs to make our signatures context-hiding. We point out that rate-1 seBARGs [32,68] also satisfy such a online/offline verification property. Thus, our starting observation is that since our template also uses seBARGs, thus it satisfies a desired online/offline verification property.

Next, to make it context-hiding, we again employ a similar strategy. Namely, we use NIZKs to hide any non-trivial information about the input dataset as well as the intermediate values during the homomorphic evaluation. However, since we want to achieve context-hiding for any evaluated signature after any number of hops, thus must use a NIZK during every homomorphic evaluation. A straightforward application of NIZKs will not work since the NIZKs are *not succinct*. A NIZK proof can be as large as the underlying NP verification circuit, thus we cannot compose NIZKs as we were able to compose seBARGs.

To get around this issue, we additionally rely on rate-1 NIZKs. Gentry et al. [45] provided a generic template to build such composable (rate-1) NIZKAoK by combining fully homomorphic encryption and regular NIZKs. By using their compiler and plugging it in our multi-hop signature scheme, the composition issue is almost fixed. However, there is one last issue: the CRS size and verification time still grow in this recursive NIZK composition. Even for rate-1 NIZKs, the CRS size could grow with the statement and witness size, thus recursive composition leads to a blow-up in the verification circuit size. To handle this, we use another layer of RAM delegation to make composition of NIZK verification efficient. As in prior works [29], the RAM delegation verifier computes the digest of the input, and assesses whether the transformation from the input hash is valid. To optimize the verifier's efficiency, we split the hash digest, and generate a short digest of the NIZK CRS in the setup stage. Thus, the verifier is no longer required to generate the hash digest of the NIZK CRS during verification. Instead, the verifier only generates the digest of variable inputs, thereby ensuring verifier succinctness. For more details, we refer the reader to Sect. 4.

Multi-key Homomorphism. Finally, we show that the above construction template can be easily extended to support multi-key homomorphism. Recall that in multi-key model, the dataset can be signed using multiple different authorities. Namely, the setup algorithm now generates a set of public parameter pp, and a tuple of (sk, vk) for ℓ different users in the system. The signing algorithm uses sk_i to sign m_i, namely $\mathsf{Sign}(sk_i, (i, m_i)) \to \sigma_i$. For simplicity, we are assuming that authority i signs message i. The construction is nearly identical to our current construction, except we need to define homomorphic evaluation w.r.t. multiple signers. This can be easily handled by switching the NP statements at every input wire. While evaluating the signature for the first time, we will use vk_i corresponding to the appropriate user to check the validity of the associated signature. Now for evaluating an evaluated signature, we will use $\{vk_i\}_i$ corresponding to the appropriate user(s) to check the validity of the associated evaluated signature. The security proof would stay the same, as by a hop-by-hop extraction we will extract a forgery on some m_i w.r.t. vk_i of some honest signer. For more details, we refer the reader to Sect. 5.

Additional Results. The above concludes a high level overview of our main results. Additionally, we also provide another homomorphic signature scheme where the signature size is even shorter (i.e., it grows only logarithmically with circuit size, instead of polynomially with circuit depth). However, we can only enable such an optimization at the cost of giving up multi-hop evaluation. That is, our homomorphic signature with shorter signatures can only support one single homomorphic evaluation, but cannot be further composed. We provide an in-depth technical overview of our single-hop homomorphic signature scheme with shorter signatures, and provide the full construction and proof in the full version. Lastly, we also show an interesting connection between a recently introduced generalization of aggregate signatures, called monotone-policy aggregate signatures [22,67], and single-hop homomorphic signatures. In the full version, we also show that single-hop homomorphic signatures can also be designed from monotone-policy aggregate signatures.

3   Multi-hop Homomorphic Signature

Before we proceed with the definition of multi-hop homomorphic signatures we need to define structured circuits[5] that is our way of denoting evaluation of different circuits in different hops over different inputs.

Structured Circuit C. Let $\mathcal{C}_{\ell,d,s_C}$ be a class of single-bit output circuits where ℓ is the maximum input size, d is the maximum depth, and s_C is the maximum size of any circuit $C \in \mathcal{C}_{\ell,d,s_C}$. We define structured circuit $C = (G, (C_v)_{v \in V})$ where $G = (V, E)$ is a tree[6] and a circuit $C_v \in \mathcal{C}_{\ell,d,s_C}$ is associated to each node $v \in V$. Moreover the inputs to any circuit C_v are the outputs of circuits associated to

---

[5] A similar concept is often called labelled circuits in the homomorphic evaluation literature.

[6] More on this on the structure of G in Sect. 3.4.

v's child nodes. Furthermore, any input wire i to any circuit C_v such that v is a leaf in graph G, is labelled with id_i. Hence any circuit C_v with n_{in} inputs such that v is a leaf in graph G is associated with $(\mathsf{id}_i)_{i \in [n_{\mathsf{in}}]}$.

By **composing** $(\mathsf{C}_i)_{i \in [\ell]}$ and some $C \in \mathcal{C}_{\ell,d,\mathsf{s}_C}$ we mean the following operation – if C_i is empty then let C be a graph G with a single node v^* where C is associated to v^*, (i.e. let $C_{v^*} = C$) and output C. Otherwise, do the following:

1. Let $\mathsf{C}_i = ((G_i = (V_i, E_i), (C_v)_{v \in V_i}))$ and v_i be the root of G_i.
2. Construct $G = (V, E)$ where $V = \bigcup_{i=1}^{\ell} V_i \cup \{v^*\}$ and $E = \bigcup_{i=1}^{\ell} E_i \cup \{(v_1, v^*), \dots, (v_\ell, v^*)\}$.
3. Associate C to v^*, i.e. let $C_{v^*} = C$. Output $\mathsf{C} = (G, (C_v)_{v \in V})$.

By **decomposing** C to its children and a circuit C we mean finding all $(\mathsf{C}_i)_{i \in [\ell]}$ and a circuit C s.t. $(v_i, v) \in E$ where v_i is the root of G_i and v is the root of G and C is associated to v.

3.1 Definition

Syntax. A homomorphic signature scheme consists of the following polynomial time algorithms:

$\mathsf{Setup}(1^\lambda, 1^K, \ell, d, \mathsf{s}_C) \to (\mathsf{pk}, \mathsf{sk})$. The setup algorithm takes as input a security parameter λ, number of maximum hops K, a max number of circuit inputs ℓ, a max circuit depth d, and a max circuit size s_C, and outputs verification/secret key $(\mathsf{pk}, \mathsf{sk})$.

$\mathsf{Sign}(\mathsf{sk}, \mathsf{id}, b) \to \sigma$. This is a probabilistic signing algorithm that takes as input signing key sk, index id, and a single bit message b. It outputs signature σ.

$\mathsf{Eval}(\mathsf{pk}, t, (b_i, \sigma_i, \mathsf{C}_i)_{i \in [\ell']}, C) \to \sigma$. The evaluator algorithm takes as input a public verification key pk, a number of hops t, and a set of ℓ bits b_i with their corresponding signatures σ_i, and structured evaluation circuits C_i where $\ell' \le \ell$. Additionally, it takes a circuit $C \in \mathcal{C}_{\ell,d,\mathsf{s}_C}$ s.t. C takes ℓ-bits inputs. The algorithm outputs a newly generated signature σ.

$\mathsf{Verify}(\mathsf{pk}, y, \sigma, \mathsf{C}) \to 0/1$. The verification algorithm takes as input a verification key pk, a message y, a signature σ, and a structured circuit C. It outputs a bit $0/1$ to signal whether σ is a valid signature.

Definition 1 (Multi-Hop Homomorphic Signature). *A multi-hop homomorphic signature scheme* $\mathsf{HSig} = (\mathsf{Setup}, \mathsf{Sign}, \mathsf{Eval}, \mathsf{Verify})$ *is required to satisfy the following properties:*

Completeness. *For any* $\lambda, K, \ell, d, \mathsf{s}_C \in \mathbb{N}$*, and* $(b_i, \sigma_i, \mathsf{C}_i)_{i \in [\ell']}$ *and circuit* $C \in \mathcal{C}_{\ell,d,\mathsf{s}_C}$ *there exists a negligible function* $\mathsf{negl}(\cdot)$ *such that the following probability is greater than or equal to* $1 - \mathsf{negl}(\lambda)$*:*

$$\Pr\left[\mathsf{Verify}(\mathsf{pk}, y, \sigma, \mathsf{C}) = 1 : \begin{array}{l} (\mathsf{pk}, \mathsf{sk}) \leftarrow \mathsf{Setup}(1^\lambda, 1^K, \ell, d, \mathsf{s}_C), \\ \forall i \in [\ell'], \mathsf{Verify}(\mathsf{pk}, b_i, \sigma_i, \mathsf{C}_i) = 1, \\ \sigma = \mathsf{Eval}(\mathsf{pk}, t, (b_i, \sigma_i, \mathsf{C}_i)_{i \in [\ell']}, C), \\ y = C(b_1, \dots, b_\ell) \end{array}\right],$$

where C *is the output of composing* $(\mathsf{C}_i)_{i\in[\ell']}$ *with* C.

Efficiency. *For the completeness experiment above the following hold:*

- $|\mathsf{pk}|, |\sigma| \leq \mathsf{poly}(\lambda, d, K)$.
- *Setup runs in time* $\mathsf{poly}(\lambda, d, K)$, *and evaluation and verification run in time* $\mathsf{poly}(\lambda, |V|, \mathsf{s}_C)$ *where* $|V|$ *denote the number of nodes in* G *where* $G \in \mathsf{C}$.

Adaptive Unforgeability. *A multi-hop homomorphic signature scheme satisfies unforgeability if for every stateful PPT attacker* $\mathcal{A}$, *there exists a negligible function* $\mathsf{negl}(\cdot)$ *such that for all* $\lambda, \ell, d, \mathsf{s}_C \in \mathbb{N}$, *the following probability is at most* $\mathsf{negl}(\lambda)$:

$$\Pr\left[\begin{array}{l} y^* \neq y \\ \wedge \; \mathsf{Verify}(\mathsf{pk}, y^*, \sigma^*, \mathsf{C}^*) = 1 \end{array} : \begin{array}{l} (\mathsf{pk}, \mathsf{sk}) \leftarrow \mathsf{Setup}(1^\lambda, 1^K, \ell, d, \mathsf{s}_C) \\ (\mathcal{I}, (b_{\mathsf{id}})_{\mathsf{id}\in\mathcal{I}}) \leftarrow \mathcal{A}(\mathsf{pk}) \\ \forall \mathsf{id} \in \mathcal{I}, \sigma_{\mathsf{id}} \leftarrow \mathsf{Sign}(\mathsf{sk}, \mathsf{id}, b_i) \\ (\mathsf{C}^*, y^*, \sigma^*) \leftarrow \mathcal{A}((\sigma_{\mathsf{id}})_{\mathsf{id}\in\mathcal{I}}) \end{array} \right],$$

where y *is the actual output of the structured circuit* C *given* $(b_{\mathsf{id}})_{\mathsf{id}\in\mathcal{I}}$.

3.2   Construction

Notation and Parameters. For ease of exposition (and w.l.o.g.) we assume that any $C_v \in \mathcal{C}_{\ell,d,\mathsf{s}_C}$ has exactly ℓ inputs, namely, $\ell' = \ell$. Throughout our construction, we set the security parameter for all underlying primitives to be $\lambda' = (\lambda + 4dK)^{O(1)}$. This ensures that we rely on their sub-exponential security: We define a "strong" negligible function $\mathsf{negl}'(\cdot)$, such that $\mathsf{negl}'(\lambda) \leq 2^{-\lambda^c}$ for some $0 < c < 1$. We assume that subexponentially-secure cryptographic primitives under security parameter λ' in our work to be secure against PPT adversaries, and every PPT adversary has at most $\mathsf{negl}'(\lambda') \leq \frac{1}{2^{\lambda+4dK}}$ advantage.

Let N denote the maximum number of wires and 2ℓ denote the number of input wires in any monotone circuit $\tilde{C}_y$ where $\tilde{C}_y = \mathcal{T}(C, y)$, $C \in \mathcal{C}_{\ell,d,\mathsf{s}_C}$, and y is C's output. Thus, the circuit $\tilde{C}_y$ has $N - 2\ell$ internal wires and $N - 2\ell$ gates.

Throughout this paper we will not explicitly give out the length for setup of BAGRs (and in the following sections for setup of NIZKs) as they're clear from the context. We emphasize that for simplicity of presentation we are assuming that all circuits have exactly ℓ inputs, thus an arbitrary tree G of such structure could be of large (exponential in depth) size. Hence the exact input size would depend up on the structure of $G \in \mathsf{C}$ which directly depends upon the actual value of ℓ' for every node in G.

Let $\mathsf{BARG} = (\mathsf{BARG.Setup}, \mathsf{BARG.Prove}, \mathsf{BARG.Verify}, \mathsf{BARG.Extract})$ be a rate-1 somewhere extractable batch argument , $\mathsf{H} = (\mathsf{H.Setup}, \mathsf{H.Hash}, \mathsf{H.Open}, \mathsf{H.Verify})$ be a hash Tree, $\mathsf{Sig} = (\mathsf{Sig.Setup}, \mathsf{Sig.Verify})$ be a digital signature scheme, and $\mathsf{Del} = (\mathsf{Del.Setup}, \mathsf{Del.Prove}, \mathsf{Del.Digest}, \mathsf{Del.Verify})$ be a RAM delegation scheme. We present our multi-hop homomorphic signature as follows:

$\mathsf{Setup}(1^\lambda, 1^K, \ell, d, \mathsf{s}_C) \rightarrow (\mathsf{pk}, \mathsf{sk})$. The setup algorithm first samples a hash key $\mathsf{hk} \leftarrow \mathsf{H.Setup}(1^{\lambda'})$, and generates signature secret key and verification key

$(\mathsf{sk}_0, \mathsf{vk}_0) \leftarrow \mathsf{Sig.Setup}(1^{\lambda'})$, and let $\mathsf{pk}_0 = \mathsf{vk}_0$ and for all $i \in [K]$, it does the following

1. Generates seBARG parameters as follows for languages $\mathcal{L}_i^0, \mathcal{L}_i^1$: $(\mathsf{barg.crs}_i^0, \mathsf{barg.td}_i^0) \leftarrow \mathsf{BARG.Setup}(1^{\lambda'}, N - 2\ell, (N - 2\ell, N - 2\ell))$ for $\mathcal{L}_i^0$ (Fig. 1) $(\mathsf{barg.crs}_i^1, \mathsf{barg.td}_i^1) \leftarrow \mathsf{BARG.Setup}(1^{\lambda'}, 2\ell, 1)$ for $\mathcal{L}_i^1$ (Fig. 2).
2. Samples RAM delegation CRS with respect to machine $\mathcal{R}_i$ (Fig. 3) as $\mathsf{del.crs}_i \leftarrow \mathsf{Del.Setup}(1^{\lambda'}, 2^\lambda)$.
3. Computes hash of implicit input of $\mathcal{R}_i$ as $h_i^{\mathsf{imp}} = \mathsf{Del.Digest}(\mathsf{hk}, (\mathsf{barg.crs}_i^0, \mathsf{barg.crs}_i^1, (\mathsf{pk}_j)_{j \in [i-1]}))$.
4. Sets $\mathsf{pk}_i = (\mathsf{barg.crs}_i^0, \mathsf{barg.crs}_i^1, \mathsf{del.crs}_i, h_i^{\mathsf{imp}}, \mathsf{hk})$.

Finally it outputs $\mathsf{pk} = (\mathsf{pk}_0, \ldots, \mathsf{pk}_K), \mathsf{sk} = \mathsf{sk}_0$.

$\mathsf{Sign}(\mathsf{sk}, \mathsf{id}, b) \rightarrow \sigma$. It outputs the signature for message bit b at index id as $\sigma \leftarrow \mathsf{Sig.Sign}(\mathsf{sk}, (\mathsf{id}, b))$.

Language $\mathcal{L}_i^0$

Hardwired: hk.
Instance: $x = (j, h, \tilde{C}_y)$.
Witness: $\omega = (b_j, b_{j_0}, b_{j_1}, \rho_j, \rho_{j_0}, \rho_{j_1})$.
Membership: Let gate c in monotone circuit $\tilde{C}_y$ be the gate that takes as input the j_0-th and the j_1-th wire, and outputs the j-th wire (where $2\ell + 1 \le j \le N$). ω is a valid witness for $x \in \mathcal{L}_i^0$ if all of the followings are satisfied:

- For all $\alpha \in \{j, j_0, j_1\}$, $\mathsf{H.Verify}(\mathsf{hk}, h, \alpha, b_\alpha, \rho_\alpha) = 1$.
- $c(b_{j_0}, b_{j_1}) = b_j$.
- If $j = N$, then $b_j = 1$.

Fig. 1. Description of language $\mathcal{L}_i^0$.

$\mathsf{Eval}(\mathsf{pk}, t, (b_i, \sigma_i, \mathsf{C}_i)_{i \in [\ell]}, C) \rightarrow \sigma$. The evaluation algorithm for the t-th hop follows these steps:

1. If C_i is empty for all i, then we assume that the circuit C is a labelled circuit where C' is the circuit and $(\mathsf{id}_i)_{i \in [\ell]}$ are labels for the input wires. It computes $y = C'(b_1, \ldots, b_\ell)$ and generates the monotone circuit $\tilde{C}_y = \mathcal{T}(C', y)$ using the transformation algorithm defined in the full version, where $\tilde{C}_y$ has a total number of N wires. It sets $b_i = 1 - b_{i-\ell}$ for all $i \in \{\ell + 1, \ldots, 2\ell\}$. It then computes $\tilde{C}_y$ gate by gate, to find b_i (for all $i \in \{2\ell + 1, \ldots, N\}$) as the value of the i-th wire of circuit $\tilde{C}_y$, and computes $h = \mathsf{H.Hash}(\mathsf{hk}, (b_1, \ldots, b_N))$.
2. For all $i \in [N]$, it computes the hash openings as $\rho_i = \mathsf{H.Open}(\mathsf{hk}, (b_1, \ldots, b_N), i)$.
3. It assigns an instance and a witness to each input wire. For all $i \in [\ell]$, if C_i is empty, then
    - $x_i = (i, \mathsf{id}_i, h)$, $\omega_i = (\sigma_i, b_i, \rho_i)$, and $x_{i+\ell} = (i + \ell, \mathsf{id}_i, h)$, $\omega_{i+\ell} = (\sigma_i, 1 - b_i, \rho_{i+\ell})$.

Language $\mathcal{L}_i^1$

Hardwired: pk_{i-1}.

Instance: x.

Witness: ω.

Membership: ω is a valid witness for $x \in \mathcal{L}_i^1$ if all of the following are satisfied:

If $i = 1$ let $x = (j, \mathsf{id}, h)$, $\omega = (\sigma, b, \rho)$, and check:

- $\mathsf{H.Verify}(\mathsf{hk}, h, j, b, \rho) = 1$,
- $\mathsf{Sig.Verify}(\mathsf{pk}_{i-1}, (\mathsf{id}, b), \sigma) = 1$ for $1 \le j \le \ell$,
- $\mathsf{Sig.Verify}(\mathsf{pk}_{i-1}, (\mathsf{id}, 1 - b), \sigma) = 1$ for $\ell + 1 \le j \le 2\ell$.

If $i \ge 2$, let $x = (j, h, \mathsf{C})$, $\omega = (\sigma, b, \rho)$, and $\sigma = (h, \mathsf{del}.\pi, \mathsf{barg}.\pi^0, \mathsf{barg}.\pi^1)$. Additionally parse pk_{i-1} to find $(\mathsf{del.crs}_{i-1}, h_{i-1}^{\mathsf{imp}})$. Then check:

- $\mathsf{H.Verify}(\mathsf{hk}, h, j, b, \rho) = 1$,
- $\mathsf{Del.Verify}(\mathsf{del.crs}_{i-1}, h_{i-1}^{\mathsf{imp}}, (\mathsf{barg}.\pi^0, \mathsf{barg}.\pi^1, b, h, \mathsf{C}), \mathsf{del}.\pi) = 1$, for $1 \le j \le \ell$.
- $\mathsf{Del.Verify}(\mathsf{del.crs}_{i-1}, h_{i-1}^{\mathsf{imp}}, (\mathsf{barg}.\pi^0, \mathsf{barg}.\pi^1, 1 - b, h, \mathsf{C}), \mathsf{del}.\pi) = 1$ for $\ell + 1 \le j \le 2\ell$.

Fig. 2. Description of the language $\mathcal{L}_i^1$.

Otherwise,

- $x_i = (i, h, \mathsf{C}_i)$, $\omega_i = (\sigma_i, b_i, \rho_i)$, and $x_{i+\ell} = (i + \ell, h, \mathsf{C}_i)$, $\omega_{i+\ell} = (\sigma_i, 1 - b_i, \rho_{i+\ell})$.

4. It assigns an instance and a witness for each internal wire. For every $i \in \{2\ell + 1, \ldots, N\}$, find a gate s.t. its output is wire i and let wires i_0 and i_1 be the inputs to such a gate. Then let
   - $x_i = (i, h, \tilde{C}_y)$, and $\omega_i = (b_i, b_{i_0}, b_{i_1}, \rho_j, \rho_{i_0}, \rho_{i_1})$.
5. It computes BARG proofs for $\mathcal{L}_i^1$ and $\mathcal{L}_i^2$ as follows:
   - $\mathsf{barg}.\pi^0 \leftarrow \mathsf{BARG.Prove}(\mathsf{barg.crs}_t^0, (x_i)_{i \in \{2\ell+1,\ldots,N\}}, (\omega_i)_{i \in \{2\ell+1,\ldots,N\}})$.
   - $\mathsf{barg}.\pi^1 \leftarrow \mathsf{BARG.Prove}(\mathsf{barg.crs}_t^1, (x_i)_{i \in [2\ell]}, (\omega_i)_{i \in [2\ell]})$.
6. Compute C by composing $(\mathsf{C}_i)_{i \in [\ell]}$ and C.
7. It generates a RAM delegation proof:
   - $\mathsf{del}.\pi \leftarrow \mathsf{Del.Prove}(\mathsf{del.crs}_t, (\mathsf{barg}.\pi^0, \mathsf{barg}.\pi^1, y, h, \mathsf{C}),$
     $(\mathsf{barg.crs}_t^0, \mathsf{barg.crs}_t^1, (\mathsf{pk}_j)_{j \in [t-1]}))$.
8. It outputs signature σ as $(h, \mathsf{del}.\pi, \mathsf{barg}.\pi^0, \mathsf{barg}.\pi^1)$.

$\mathsf{Verify}(\mathsf{pk}, y, \sigma, \mathsf{C}) \to \{0, 1\}$. If C is empty then it outputs whatever $\mathsf{Sig.Verify}(\mathsf{pk}_0, (\mathsf{id}, y), \sigma)$ outputs. Otherwise it parses $\sigma = (h, \mathsf{del}.\pi, \mathsf{barg}.\pi^0, \mathsf{barg}.\pi^1)$ and $\mathsf{pk}_t = (\mathsf{barg.crs}_t^0, \mathsf{barg.crs}_t^1, \mathsf{del.crs}_t, h_t^{\mathsf{imp}}, \mathsf{hk})$ and outputs $\mathsf{Del.Verify}(\mathsf{del.crs}_t, h_t^{\mathsf{imp}}, (\mathsf{barg}.\pi^0, \mathsf{barg}.\pi^1, y, h, \mathsf{C}), \mathsf{del}.\pi)$.

Remark 1. We apply a universal security parameter $\lambda' = (\lambda + 4dK)^{O(1)}$ for the design of the setup algorithm above. In fact for the above design where $\mathsf{pk} = (\mathsf{pk}_0, \ldots, \mathsf{pk}_K)$ and one may apply a tighter security parameter as $\lambda' = (\lambda + 4d \cdot (K - i))^{O(1)}$ when generating pk_i for $i \in [K]$.

RAM Machine $\mathcal{R}_i$

Explicit Input:: $\mathsf{barg}.\pi^0, \mathsf{barg}.\pi^1, y, h, \mathsf{C}$.

Implicit Input: $\mathsf{barg}.\mathsf{crs}_i^0, \mathsf{barg}.\mathsf{crs}_i^1, (\mathsf{pk}_j)_{j \in [i-1]}$.

Output: $\mathcal{R}_i$ follows these steps:

1. Decomposes C to its children $(\mathsf{C}_j)_{j \in [\ell]}$ and a circuit C.
2. Sets monotone circuit $\tilde{C}_y = \mathcal{T}(C, y)$.
3. For $j \in [\ell]$, sets $x_j = (j, h, \mathsf{C}_j)$, and $x_{j+\ell} = (j + \ell, h, \mathsf{C}_j)$.
4. For $j \in \{2\ell + 1, \ldots, N\}$, sets x_j as $(j, h, \tilde{C}_y)$.
5. Accepts if and only if
   - $\mathsf{BARG.Verify}(\mathsf{barg}.\mathsf{crs}_i^0, (x_j)_{j \in \{2\ell+1,\ldots,N\}}, \mathsf{barg}.\pi^0) = 1$,
   - $\mathsf{BARG.Verify}(\mathsf{barg}.\mathsf{crs}_i^1, (x_j)_{j \in [2\ell]}, \mathsf{barg}.\pi^1) = 1$.

Fig. 3. Description of RAM Machine $\mathcal{R}_i$.

Completeness. The completeness of our scheme directly follows from the completeness of public key signature scheme sig, somewhere extractable batch argument barg, RAM delegation del, and the monotone circuit transformation.

Efficiency. Next, we analyze the efficiency of the above design.

Lemma 1. *Assume that* $\mathsf{BARG} = (\mathsf{BARG.Setup}, \mathsf{BARG.Prove}, \mathsf{BARG.Verify}, \mathsf{BARG.Extract})$ *is a rate-1 somewhere extractable batch argument. Then our design satisfies the efficiency definition.*

Proof. We analyze the signature size using an inductive proof. Let σ_t be the signature at the t-th hop, such that $\sigma_t \leftarrow \mathsf{Eval}(\mathsf{vk}, t, (b_i, \sigma_i, \mathsf{C}_i)_{i \in [\ell]}, C)$.

Claim 1. *For all $t \in [K]$, there exists a universal polynomial $\mathsf{poly}(\cdot)$ such that $|\sigma_t| \leq t \cdot \mathsf{poly}(\lambda')$.*

Proof. We prove the claim through induction.

Base Case ($t = 1$). By our design, $\sigma_t = (h, \mathsf{del}.\pi, \mathsf{barg}.\pi^0, \mathsf{barg}.\pi^1)$. Hash value h and delegated proof $\mathsf{del}.\pi$ are local parameters such that $|h| + |\mathsf{del}.\pi| \leq \mathsf{poly}(\lambda')$. Next we analyze the size of $\mathsf{barg}.\pi^0$, since the witness of language $\mathcal{L}_i^0$ only contains local hash parameters for all $i \in [K]$ and barg is rate-1, $|\mathsf{barg}.\pi^0| \leq \mathsf{poly}(\lambda')$. For the first hop evaluation where $t = 1$, witness of language $\mathcal{L}_1^1$ consists of local hash parameters and basic public key signatures. Due to rate-1 seBARG, $|\mathsf{barg}.\pi^1| \leq \mathsf{poly}(\lambda')$ for some universal polynomial $\mathsf{poly}(\cdot)$. Thus the claim holds for $t = 1$.

Inductive Step ($2 \leq t \leq K$). For $\sigma_t = (h, \mathsf{del}.\pi, \mathsf{barg}.\pi^0, \mathsf{barg}.\pi^1)$, given the locality properties of Hash Tree and rate-1 seBARG, the overall size $|h| + |\mathsf{del}.\pi| + |\mathsf{barg}.\pi^0| \leq \mathsf{poly}(\lambda')$. Additionally, it follows that $|\mathsf{barg}.\pi^1| \leq |\sigma_{t-1}| + \mathsf{poly}(\lambda')$. Thus, $|\sigma_t| \leq |\sigma_{t-1}| + \mathsf{poly}(\lambda')$ for some universal polynomial $\mathsf{poly}(\cdot)$. By our inductive hypothesis, $|\sigma_{t-1}| \leq (t - 1) \cdot \mathsf{poly}(\lambda')$. Putting the above together completes the proof for the claim.

The above claim implies that $|\sigma| \leq \mathsf{poly}(\lambda', K) \leq \mathsf{poly}(\lambda, d, K)$. Next, we analyze the verification key size and verifier running time. For $t \in [K]$, $\mathsf{pk}_t = (\mathsf{barg.crs}_t^0, \mathsf{barg.crs}_t^1, \mathsf{del.crs}_i, h_i^{\mathsf{imp}}, \mathsf{hk})$. By succinctness of rate-1 BARG barg, RAM delegation del, $|\mathsf{pk}_t|$ and setup running time for the t-th hop is bounded by $\mathsf{poly}(\lambda')$. Overall verification key size and setup running time is at most $\mathsf{poly}(\lambda', K) = \mathsf{poly}(\lambda, d, K)$.

For all $t \in [K]$, the verifier for the t-th hop runs a RAM delegation verifier for the RAM machine $\mathcal{R}_t$. $\mathcal{R}_t$ takes $(\mathsf{barg}.\pi^0, \mathsf{barg}.\pi^1, y, h, \mathsf{C})$ as its variable input. By the succinctness of RAM delegation, verifier's running time depends polynomially on the size of the variable input and the security parameter λ'. By Theorem 1, we have $|\sigma| \leq \mathsf{poly}(\lambda', K)$, which implies $|\mathsf{barg}.\pi^0| + |\mathsf{barg}.\pi^1| + |h| \leq \mathsf{poly}(\lambda', K)$. Size of the graph $G = (V, E)$ at circuits $\{C_v\}_{v \in V}$ is at most $\mathsf{poly}(n, |\mathcal{C}_{\ell,d,\mathsf{s}_C}|)$. Thus, verifier's running time is $\mathsf{poly}(\lambda', K, |V|, |\mathcal{C}_{\ell,d,\mathsf{s}_C}|)$.

3.3 Unforgeability

Theorem 2. *Assume that* BARG *satisfies sub-exponential index hiding and somewhere argument of knowledge,* Del *satisfies sub-exponential soundness, digital signature* Sig *satisfies sub-exponential unforgeability, and* H *satisfies sub-exponentially secure collision-resistance property, then our construction satisfies adaptive unforgeability.*

Proof. We provide an overview of proof and refer the reader to the full version for the complete proof. The way the proof goes is similar as the proof for low-depth circuit monotone snarg [18]. Consider a PPT adversary $\mathcal{A}$ that breaks the adaptive unforgeability of our multi-hop homomorphic signature scheme: $\mathcal{A}$ outputs a sequence of messages $\{\beta_{\mathsf{id}}\}_{\mathsf{id} \in \mathcal{I}}$ and receives $\sigma_{\mathsf{id}} \leftarrow \mathsf{sig.Sign}(\mathsf{sk}, (\mathsf{id}, \beta_{\mathsf{id}}))$ for all $\mathsf{id} \in \mathcal{I}$. It then outputs a tree $G = (V, E)$, a set of circuits $\{C_v\}_{v \in V}$, a message y^*, and the corresponding labels $\{\mathsf{id}_i\}_{i \in [M]}$ (structured circuit takes M input bits). For all $\mathsf{id} \in \mathcal{I}$, the challenger computes and outputs $\sigma_{\mathsf{id}} \leftarrow \mathsf{sig.Sign}(\mathsf{sk}, (\mathsf{id}, \beta_{\mathsf{id}}))$. Let root denote the root node of G. Let y be the actual output of the structured circuits $\{C_v\}_{v \in V}$ taking $\{\beta_{\mathsf{id}_i}\}_{i \in [M]}$ as input. $\mathcal{A}$ wins if and only if $\mathsf{Verify}(\mathsf{pk}, y^*, \sigma^*, \mathsf{C}) = 1$ for $\mathsf{C} = (G, \{C_v\}_{v \in V})$ and $y^* \neq y$ by unforgeability definition.

Let root denote the root node of G and assume that C_{root} takes ℓ bits of input without loss of generality. Set circuit $\tilde{C}_{y^*}$ as the monotone circuit of circuit C_{root}. Assume without loss of generality that $\tilde{C}_{y^*}$ has a total of N bits of input. For $i \in [N]$, define b_i^* as the "true" value of each wire $\tilde{C}_{y^*}$: For $i \in [\ell]$, set b_i^* as the output by the structured circuit $\{C_v\}_{v \in V_i}$ over the signed inputs $\{\beta_{\mathsf{id}}\}_{\mathsf{id} \in \mathcal{I}}$, and set $b_{i+\ell}^*$ as $1 - b_i^*$. The wires $(b_{2\ell+1}^*, \ldots, b_N^*)$ are set to be the value of internal wires correspondingly. To break unforgeability, $\mathcal{A}$ produces a proof proving that $b_N > b_N^*$ (the output wire) in the hash-and-barg proof for the monotone circuit $\tilde{C}_{y^*}$. Let $\mathsf{Adv}_{\mathcal{A}}$ denote $\mathcal{A}$'s advantage. If the trapdoor indices are properly set at the next level of the circuit, it implies that a reduction algorithm could extract some internal wire $b_j > b_j^*$ with an advantage of approximately $\frac{\mathsf{Adv}_{\mathcal{A}}}{2}$ (and at least $\frac{\mathsf{Adv}_{\mathcal{A}}}{3}$), where j is one of the two input wires to the output gate and the trapdoor is exactly set at index j. By applying a series of inductive hybrid proofs, we know that at least one input wire at the base layer which contains digital signatures allows a reduction algorithm to break unforgeability of digital signature scheme sig with advantage more than $\frac{\mathsf{Adv}_{\mathcal{A}}}{3d \cdot K}$, given that the trapdoors indexes are correctly set so that the reduction algorithm could perform an extraction at such input wire. Here, the total depth of the structured circuit is capped at $d \cdot k$. Finally, we conclude that such PPT adversary $\mathcal{A}$ cannot exist under the assumption of sub-exponential security.

3.4   Further Optimization

Fast Verification. As mentioned in the technical overview one can consider the verification with pre-processing where the verifier algorithm is split to a PreVerify and an OnlineVerify such that the pre-verification computes a short digest of the large input C and the fast online verification algorithm only takes the short digest as input and verifies the signature. This implies an online verification algorithm that only grows with the depth of the computation instead of the entire size of the computation, namely the online verifier grows with $\mathsf{poly}(\lambda, d, K)$. More on how offline and online verification works can be found in the full version where we show how to make our construction of single-hop homomorphic signature to be context hiding by taking advantage of the fast verification.

Remark 2. The verification first transforms C that is the circuit associated with the root of $G \in \mathsf{C}$ to a monotone circuit $\tilde{C}_y$ and then verifies the statement. Thus the online verification would require a digest of the statements where the circuit C is transformed to a monotone one. However, our monotone circuit transformation $\tilde{C}_y = \mathcal{T}(C, y)$ takes the output $C(m) = y$ as input. Hence this seems to cause an issue because the input m (and hence the output y) is not available when one is digesting C in the offline/pre-verification.

We observe that one can get around this issue by taking advantage of the structure of transformation $\mathcal{T}$. Namely, the transformation from C to C_y using output y, only affects the last layer of C_y. Moreover, the transformation from C_y to a monotone circuit $\tilde{C}_y$ works layer by layer (transforms each layer independently). Therefore, the offline verification can compute a partial digest of $\tilde{C}_y$ and let the online verification compute the complementary digest given a short partial circuit (i.e. the last layer of C_y) which would be a fast operation.

More General Computation. In our construction we assume the graph G is a tree, which already covers a large class of computation especially because circuit C_v can be any general circuit, namely it can copy its inputs. However, one might wonder about a more general case in which G is a DAG. More specifically, consider a real world scenario that a user homomorphically evaluates a signature σ for some b and several other users later on want to compute signatures σ_i for b_i using b as their input. Moreover, another user wants to compute a signature σ^* on some b^* that is computed over b_i values as input. In this case the tree representation of G leads to large (even of exponential size in the depth if it happen in several hops) C. Hence, by considering G to be a DAG one can capture more real world applications.

While at a first glance this seems to be a more convoluted task as one has to prove the consistency of the reused wires across different users, we observe that our construction indeed captures this more general problem if we consider that every intermediate circuit is also a labelled circuit. This is due to the fact that our proof is based on an inductive guessing strategy over the layers (depth/hops), hence one does not need to explicitly enforce the consistency of such values across the structured circuit. For ease of exposition, we provide our construction where the computation graph is viewed as a tree.

4   Towards Context Hiding Homomorphic Signatures

The efficiency, completeness, and unforgeability definition of multi-hop homomorphic signature with context hiding is exactly the same as the general multi-hop homomorphic signature scheme. Hence below we only define the context hiding property.

Definition 2 (Context Hiding). *A multi-hop homomorphic signature scheme satisfies context-hiding if there exist a stateful PPT simulator $\mathcal{S}$ such that for every stateful PPT attacker $\mathcal{A}$, there exists a negligible function $\mathsf{negl}(\cdot)$ such that for all $\lambda, \ell, d, \mathsf{s}_C \in \mathbb{N}$, the following probability is at most $1/2 + \mathsf{negl}(\lambda)$:*

$$
\Pr\left[
\begin{array}{l}
\mathcal{A}(\sigma_b) = b \;\wedge \\
C \in \mathcal{C}_{\ell, d, \mathsf{s}_C} \;\wedge \\
\forall\, v \in V_i : \; C_v \in \mathcal{C}_{\ell, d, \mathsf{s}_C} \;\wedge \\
\mathsf{Verify}(\mathsf{pk}_0, y, \sigma_0, \mathsf{C}) = 1 \;\wedge \\
\mathsf{Verify}(\mathsf{pk}_1, y, \sigma_1, \mathsf{C}) = 1
\end{array}
\;:\;
\begin{array}{l}
(\mathsf{pk}_0, \mathsf{sk}_0) \leftarrow \mathsf{Setup}(1^\lambda, 1^K, \ell, d, \mathsf{s}_C) \\
(\mathsf{pk}_1, \mathsf{sk}_1) \leftarrow \mathcal{S}(1^\lambda, 1^K, \ell, d, \mathsf{s}_C), b \leftarrow \{0,1\} \\
((b_i, \sigma_i, \mathsf{C}_i)_{i \in [\ell]}, C) \leftarrow \mathcal{A}^{\mathsf{Sign}(\mathsf{sk}_b, \cdot, \cdot)}(\mathsf{pk}_b) \\
\sigma_0 \leftarrow \mathsf{Eval}(\mathsf{pk}_b, t, (b_i, \sigma_i, \mathsf{C}_i)_{i \in [\ell]}, C) \\
\sigma_1 \leftarrow \mathcal{S}(t, (\mathsf{C}_i)_{i \in [\ell]}, C) \\
y = C((b_i)_{i \in [\ell]})
\end{array}
\right],
$$

where C is the composition of $(\mathsf{C}_i)_{i \in [\ell]}$ and C.

Construction. In addition to the notations and parameters described in Construction 3.2, we let $\mathsf{NIZK} = (\mathsf{NIZK.Setup}, \mathsf{NIZK.Prove}, \mathsf{NIZK.Verify})$ be a rate-1 NIZK and $\mathsf{PKE} = (\mathsf{PKE.Gen}, \mathsf{PKE.Enc}, \mathsf{PKE.Dec})$ be a PKE system. We present our construction of multi-hop homomorphic signature with context hiding as follows:

$\mathsf{Setup}(1^\lambda, 1^K, \ell, d, \mathsf{s}_C) \to (\mathsf{pk}, \mathsf{sk})$. The setup algorithm is identical to the setup algorithm of the design without context hiding in Construction 3.2, except that it samples $\mathsf{pke.pk} \leftarrow \mathsf{PKE.Gen}(1^{\lambda'})$ and include $\mathsf{pke.pk}$ in every pk_i, and for every $i \in [K]$:

    1. samples a NIZK CRS as $(\mathsf{nizk.crs}_i, \mathsf{nizk.td}_i) \leftarrow \mathsf{NIZK.Setup}(1^{\lambda'})$ for language $\mathcal{L}_i^2$ (Fig. 4),

    2. includes each $\mathsf{nizk.crs}_i$ as part of verification key pk_i,

3. sets hash value as $h_i^{\mathsf{imp}} = \mathsf{del.Digest}(\mathsf{hk}, (\mathsf{barg.crs}_i^0, \mathsf{barg.crs}_i^1, (\mathsf{pk}_j)_{j \in [t-1]},$ $\mathsf{pke.pk}, \mathsf{nizk.crs}_i))$, and

4. slightly modifies the description of RAM machine $\mathcal{R}_i$.

$\mathsf{Sign}(\mathsf{sk}, \mathsf{id}, b) \to \sigma$. Same in Construction 3.2.

$\mathsf{Eval}(\mathsf{pk}, t, (b_i, \sigma_i, \mathsf{C}_i)_{i \in [\ell]}, C) \to \sigma$. The evaluation algorithm is the same as Eval in Sect. 3, except for Items 7 and 8 where the evaluator additionally generates and computes the RAM proof for the NIZK verification as follows:

7. It samples randomness r, encrypts h as $\mathsf{ct}_h = \mathsf{PKE.Enc}(\mathsf{pke.pk}, h; r)$, and computes a NIZK proof
   - $\mathsf{nizk.\pi} \leftarrow \mathsf{NIZK.Prove}(\mathsf{nizk.crs}_t, (\mathsf{barg.crs}_t^0, \mathsf{barg.crs}_t^1, \mathsf{pke.pk}, y, \mathsf{ct}_h, C),$ $(\mathsf{barg.\pi}^0, \mathsf{barg.\pi}^1, r, h))$.

   Then, it generates a RAM delegation proof
   - $\mathsf{del.\pi} \leftarrow \mathsf{Del.Prove}(\mathsf{del.crs}_t, (\mathsf{nizk.\pi}, y, \mathsf{ct}_h, C), (\mathsf{barg.crs}_t^0, \mathsf{barg.crs}_t^1,$ $(\mathsf{pk}_j)_{j \in [t-1]}, \mathsf{pke.pk}, \mathsf{nizk.crs}_t))$.

8. It outputs signature σ as $(\mathsf{ct}_h, \mathsf{del.\pi}, \mathsf{nizk.\pi})$.

$\mathsf{Verify}(\mathsf{pk}, y, \sigma, C) \to \{0, 1\}$. The verification algorithm is similar to Construction 3.2, except that the RAM delegation verifier takes as input $\mathsf{nizk.\pi}, \mathsf{ct}_h$ instead of $\mathsf{barg.\pi}^0, \mathsf{barg.\pi}^1, h$. It outputs

$$\mathsf{del.Verify}(\mathsf{del.crs}_t, h_t^{\mathsf{imp}}, (\mathsf{nizk.\pi}, y, \mathsf{ct}_h, C), \mathsf{del.\pi}).$$

Language $\mathcal{L}_i^2$

Hardwired: $\mathsf{barg.crs}_i^0, \mathsf{barg.crs}_i^1, (\mathsf{pk}_j)_{j \in [i-1]}, \mathsf{pke.pk}$

Instance: $x = (y, \mathsf{ct}_h, C)$.

Witness: $\omega = (\mathsf{barg.\pi}^0, \mathsf{barg.\pi}^1, r, h)$.

Membership: ω is a valid witness for $x \in \mathcal{L}_i^2$ if all of the following are satisfied:

1. $\mathsf{PKE.Enc}(\mathsf{pke.pk}, r, h) = \mathsf{ct}_h$.
2. $\mathsf{BARG.Verify}(\mathsf{barg.crs}_i^0, (x_j)_{j \in \{2\ell+1,\dots,N\}}, \mathsf{barg.\pi}^0) = 1$,
3. $\mathsf{BARG.Verify}(\mathsf{barg.crs}_i^1, (x_j)_{j \in [2\ell]}, \mathsf{barg.\pi}^1) = 1$.

where $(x_j)_{j \in [N]}$ is defined as follows — Decompose C to its children $(\mathsf{C}_j)_{j \in [\ell]}$ and a circuit C, and Set $\tilde{C}_y$ as $\tilde{C}_y = \mathcal{T}(C, y)$. Then,

- For $j \in [\ell]$, let $x_j = (j, h, \mathsf{C}_j)$, and $x_{j+\ell} = (j + \ell, h, \mathsf{C}_j)$.
- For $j \in \{2\ell + 1, \dots, N\}$, let $x_j = (j, h, \tilde{C}_y)$.

Fig. 4. Description of language $\mathcal{L}_i^2$.

RAM Machine $\mathcal{R}_i$

Explicit Input:: $\mathsf{nizk}.\pi, y, \mathsf{ct}_h, \mathsf{C}$.

Implicit Input: $\mathsf{barg.crs}_i^0, \mathsf{barg.crs}_i^1, (\mathsf{pk}_j)_{j \in [i-1]}, \mathsf{pke.pk}, \mathsf{nizk.crs}_i$.

Output: If $\mathsf{NIZK.Verify}(\mathsf{nizk.crs}_i, (y, \mathsf{ct}_h, \mathsf{C}), \mathsf{nizk}.\pi) = 1$, then $\mathcal{R}_i$ accepts. Otherwise, it rejects.

Fig. 5. Description of RAM Machine $\mathcal{R}_i$.

Completeness. The completeness of our scheme directly follows from the completeness of public key encryption scheme PKE, NIZK scheme NIZK, public key signature scheme Sig, somewhere extractable batch argument BARG, RAM delegation Del, and the monotone circuit transformation (Fig. 5).

Efficiency. The only difference between this design and the design of Sect. 3 is that we replace some inputs of RAM Machine $\mathcal{R}_i$ with a NIZK proof $\mathsf{nizk}.\pi$. Since the NIZK we applied is of rate-1, we conclude that the efficiency of the above design satisfies the requirement as it directly follows from the proof of Lemma 1.

Unforgeability. The proof of unforgeability is a direct extension of the proof of Theorem 2, except we need additional hybrids to rely on NIZK extractability. Formally, we show the following:

Theorem 3. *Assume that* BARG *satisfies sub-exponentially secure index hiding and somewhere argument of knowledge,* NIZK *satisfies sub-exponential argument of knowledge,* Del *satisfies sub-exponential soundness, digital signature* Sig *satisfies sub-exponential unforgeability, and* H *satisfies sub-exponentially secure collision-resistance property, then our construction satisfies adaptive unforgeability.*

The formal unforgeability proof follows a similar inductive approach to Theorem 2. The detailed analysis and the hybrid arguments can be found in the full version.

Context Hiding. Finally, we prove context hiding of our construction. Formally, we show the following:

Theorem 4. *Assume that* NIZK *satisfies zero knowledge property and* PKE *satisfies semantic security then our construction satisfies context hiding.*

Next we provide an overview of the context hiding proof and refer the reader to the full version for a complete analysis.

Context hiding proof overview. Intuitively, in our construction, the verifier verifies the evaluated proof by checking the NIZK proof nizk.π using RAM Machine $\mathcal{R}_t$ (for signature at hop $t \leq K$). Thus, the simulator of our design simply simulates a NIZK proof as signature using the NIZK simulator. However, this is not enough to guarantee context hiding, since we also use pke to encrypt hash value h (hash of the root circuit wires). Thus, to make it context hiding, we need to change the encryption of hash value as well. The idea simply is once we simulate the NIZK proofs, then we can rely on semantic security of pke to hide the digest of the wires as well.

Corollary 1. *Assuming sub-exponential* LWE, *there exists a multi-hop homomorphic signature scheme satisfying context hiding.*

Proof. [45] proposed a design of rate-1 NIZK of argument of knowledge using homomorphic encryption scheme which is only known to be built from the learning with error assumption. [32] proposed a design of rate-1 somewhere extractable BARGs from learning with error. Thus by Theorem 3 and Theorem 4, our corollary follows.

5   Extending to Multi-key Homomorphism

Structured circuit C. We use similar structured circuits as in Sect. 3 except that we additionally require any circuit C_v with n_{in} inputs such that v is a leaf in graph G is associated with $(\mathsf{vk}_i)_{i \in [n_{\mathsf{in}}]}$.

Definition. Here we define multi-hop multi-key homomorphic signature scheme by describing what changes compared to the single-key setting.

Syntax. The syntax is similar to that of Sect. 3.1 except that there is an additional KeyGen algorithm as follows:

KeyGen(1^λ) $\to$ (vk, sk). The key generation algorithm takes as input security parameter λ, and outputs verification/secret key (vk, sk).

Definition 3 (Multi-Hop Multi-Key Homomorphic Signature). *A multi-hop multi-key homomorphic signature scheme* MKHSig = (Setup, KeyGen, Sign, Eval, Verify) *is required to satisfy the following properties:*

> **Completeness.** *The completeness is defined similar to Definition 1 except that we require every verification key* vk *in any structured circuit* C_i *for* $i \in [\ell']$ *is honestly generated.*
> **Efficiency.** *The efficiency is defined similar to Definition 1.*

Adaptive Unforgeability. *A multi-hop homomorphic signature scheme satisfies unforgeability if for every admissible stateful PPT attacker $\mathcal{A}$, there exists a negligible function $\mathsf{negl}(\cdot)$ such that for all $\lambda, \ell, d, \mathsf{s}_C \in \mathbb{N}$, the following probability is at most $\mathsf{negl}(\lambda)$:*

$$
\Pr\left[
\begin{array}{l}
y^* \neq y \\
\wedge\, \mathsf{Verify}(\mathsf{vk}, y^*, \sigma^*, \mathsf{C}^*) = 1
\end{array}
:
\begin{array}{l}
\mathsf{pk} \leftarrow \mathsf{Setup}(1^\lambda, 1^K, \ell, d, \mathsf{s}_C) \\
\mathcal{J} \leftarrow \mathcal{A}(\mathsf{pk}) \\
\forall \hat{\mathsf{id}} \in \mathcal{J}, (\mathsf{sk}_{\hat{\mathsf{id}}}, \mathsf{vk}_{\hat{\mathsf{id}}}) \leftarrow \mathsf{KeyGen}(1^\lambda) \\
(\mathcal{I}, (b_{\mathsf{id}^*})_{\mathsf{id}^* \in \mathcal{I}}) \leftarrow \mathcal{A}((\mathsf{vk}_{\hat{\mathsf{id}}})_{\hat{\mathsf{id}} \in \mathcal{J}}) \\
\forall \mathsf{id}^* = (\hat{\mathsf{id}}, \mathsf{id}) \in \mathcal{I}, \sigma_{\mathsf{id}^*} \leftarrow \mathsf{Sign}(\mathsf{sk}_{\hat{\mathsf{id}}}, \mathsf{id}, b_i) \\
(\mathcal{J}') \leftarrow \mathcal{A}((\sigma_{\mathsf{id}^*})_{\mathsf{id}^* \in \mathcal{I}}), \mathcal{J}' \subseteq \mathcal{J}, \\
(\mathsf{C}^*, y^*, \sigma^*) \leftarrow \mathcal{A}((\mathsf{sk}_{\hat{\mathsf{id}}})_{\hat{\mathsf{id}} \in \mathcal{J}'})
\end{array}
\right]
$$

where y is the actual output of the structured circuit C^* given $(b_{\mathsf{id}^*})_{\mathsf{id}^* \in \mathcal{I}}$ and $\mathcal{A}$ is admissible if for every label $\mathsf{vk}_{\hat{\mathsf{id}}}$ in the structured circuit C^* it holds that $\hat{\mathsf{id}} \notin \mathcal{J}'$.

NOTE. *We remark that in the above security experiment, we consider a slightly simplified experiment where the attacker indicates all keys it wants to corrupt at once. However, one could consider more general attackers which make signature queries as well as signing key corruption queries adaptively in an arbitrarily interleaved order. Our construction is secure under such a more general security experiment as well, but for simplicity, we consider all corruptions happen at once.*

Construction. We slightly modify $\mathcal{L}_i^1$ as follows—If $i = 1$ then it parses $x = (j, \underline{\mathsf{vk}}, \mathsf{id}, h)$ and to run the signature verification it uses vk instead of pk_0. Now since $\mathcal{L}_i^1$ is slightly modified, we let $n_{\mathsf{bp},1,1} = \log 2\ell + 2\lambda + |\mathsf{vk}|$.

$\mathsf{Setup}(1^\lambda, 1^K, \ell, d, \mathsf{s}_C) \to \mathsf{pk}$. Similar to that of Construction 3.2, except that it doesn't sample the $(\mathsf{sk}', \mathsf{vk}')$.

$\mathsf{KeyGen}(1^\lambda) \to (\mathsf{vk}, \mathsf{sk})$. It simply samples a signing-verification key pair as $(\mathsf{sk}, \mathsf{vk}) \leftarrow \mathsf{Sig.Setup}(1^{\lambda'})$.

$\mathsf{Sign}(\mathsf{sk}, \mathsf{id}, b) \to \sigma$. Similar to that of Construction 3.2.

$\mathsf{Eval}(\mathsf{pk}, t, (b_i, \sigma_i, \mathsf{C}_i)_{i \in [\ell]}, C) \to \sigma$. Similar to that of Construction 3.2, except that in Item 1 if C_i is empty then in addition to $(\mathsf{id}_i)_{i \in [\ell]}$ it finds $(\mathsf{vk}_i)_{i \in [\ell]}$ in the labelled circuit C, and in Item 3 if C_i is empty for $i \in [\ell]$ it lets $x_i = (i, \mathsf{vk}_i, \mathsf{id}_i, h)$ and $x_{i+\ell} = (i + \ell, \mathsf{vk}_i, \mathsf{id}_i, h)$

$\mathsf{Verify}(\mathsf{pk}, y, \sigma, \mathsf{C}) \to \{0, 1\}$. If C is empty then the verification outputs whatever $\mathsf{Sig.Verify}(\mathsf{pk}, (\mathsf{id}, y), \sigma)$ outputs, otherwise it is similar to the verifier in Construction 3.2.

Remark 3 (Multi-hop multi-key homomorphic signature with context hiding). Similarly our construction of multi-hop homomorphic signature with context hiding (see Sect. 4) extends to the multi-key setting with a few minor modifications.

Theorem 5. *If* BARG *is a sub-exponentially secure seBARG,* Del *is a sub-exponentially secure delegation scheme,* Sig *is a sub-exponentially secure digital signature scheme, and* H *is a sub-exponentially secure hash tree, then the above construction is a multi-hop multi-key-homomorphic signature scheme.*

Corollary 2. *Assuming sub-exponential security of either* LWE, *k-*LIN *over pairing groups, or* DDH, *there exists a multi-hop multi-key homomorphic signature scheme.*

Proof (Proof of Theorem 5). The completeness and efficiency proof are similar to those of Construction 3.2. For Adaptive unforgeability, recall that the proof of Construction 3.2 follows an inductive approach by propagating $\mathcal{A}$'s advantage in forging a homomorphically evaluated signature to a forgery on a digital signature at the bottom level. The proof of the multi-key setting is very similar except that the reduction algorithm has to additionally simulate the corruption queries for $\mathcal{A}$. Hence we let the reduction algorithm guess a $\hat{\mathsf{id}}$ and then simulate the experiment for the adversary as follows—for the guesses $\hat{\mathsf{id}}$ the reduction algorithm queries the digital signature scheme for the verification key, and it generates the rest of the verification keys itself. Our reduction algorithm succeeds only if the guessing from root to leaf leads to a forgery on $\mathsf{vk}_{\hat{\mathsf{id}}}$ hence there is a $1/|\mathcal{J}|$ loss in the security of the scheme. The rest of the proof is similar to that of Construction 3.2.

References

1. Agrawal, S., Boneh, D.: Homomorphic MACs: MAC-based integrity for network coding. In: Abdalla, M., Pointcheval, D., Fouque, P.-A., Vergnaud, D. (eds.) ACNS 2009. LNCS, vol. 5536, pp. 292–305. Springer, Heidelberg (2009). https://doi.org/10.1007/978-3-642-01957-9_18
2. Agrawal, S., Boneh, D., Boyen, X., Freeman, D.M.: Preventing pollution attacks in multi-source network coding. In: Nguyen, P.Q., Pointcheval, D. (eds.) PKC 2010. LNCS, vol. 6056, pp. 161–176. Springer, Heidelberg (2010). https://doi.org/10.1007/978-3-642-13013-7_10
3. Agrawal, S., Wichs, D., Yamada, S.: Optimal broadcast encryption from LWE and pairings in the standard model. In: Pass, R., Pietrzak, K. (eds.) TCC 2020, Part I. LNCS, vol. 12550, pp. 149–178. Springer, Cham (2020). https://doi.org/10.1007/978-3-030-64375-1_6
4. Agrawal, S., Yamada, S.: Optimal broadcast encryption from pairings and LWE. In: Canteaut, A., Ishai, Y. (eds.) EUROCRYPT 2020, Part I. LNCS, vol. 12105, pp. 13–43. Springer, Cham (2020). https://doi.org/10.1007/978-3-030-45721-1_2
5. Ahn, J.H., Boneh, D., Camenisch, J., Hohenberger, S., Shelat, A., Waters, B.: Computing on authenticated data. In: Theory of Cryptography: 9th Theory of Cryptography Conference, TCC 2012, Taormina, Sicily, Italy, 19–21 May 2012, Proceedings 9, pp. 1–20. Springer (2012)
6. Ajtai, M.: Generating hard instances of lattice problems. In: Proceedings of the Twenty-Eighth Annual ACM Symposium on Theory of Computing, pp. 99–108 (1996)

7. Anthoine, G., Balbás, D., Fiore, D.: Fully-succinct multi-key homomorphic signatures from standard assumptions. In: Reyzin, L., Stebila, D. (eds.) CRYPTO 2024. LNCS, vol. 14922, pp. 317–351. Springer, Cham (2024). https://doi.org/10.1007/978-3-031-68382-4_10

8. Ateniese, G., et al.: Provable data possession at untrusted stores. In: Proceedings of the 14th ACM Conference on Computer and Communications Security, pp. 598–609 (2007)

9. Ateniese, G., Kamara, S., Katz, J.: Proofs of storage from homomorphic identification protocols. In: Matsui, M. (ed.) ASIACRYPT 2009. LNCS, vol. 5912, pp. 319–333. Springer, Heidelberg (2009). https://doi.org/10.1007/978-3-642-10366-7_19

10. Attrapadung, N., Libert, B.: homomorphic network coding signatures in the standard model. In: Catalano, D., Fazio, N., Gennaro, R., Nicolosi, A. (eds.) PKC 2011. LNCS, vol. 6571, pp. 17–34. Springer, Heidelberg (2011). https://doi.org/10.1007/978-3-642-19379-8_2

11. Balbás, D., Catalano, D., Fiore, D., Lai, R.W.: Chainable functional commitments for unbounded-depth circuits. In: In: Rothblum, G., Wee, H. (eds.) TCC 2023. LNCS, vol. 14371, pp. 363–393. Springer, Cham (2023). https://doi.org/10.1007/978-3-031-48621-0_13

12. Boneh, D., Boyen, X., Shacham, H.: Short group signatures. In: Franklin, M. (ed.) CRYPTO 2004. LNCS, vol. 3152, pp. 41–55. Springer, Heidelberg (2004). https://doi.org/10.1007/978-3-540-28628-8_3

13. Boneh, D., Freeman, D., Katz, J., Waters, B.: Signing a linear subspace: signature schemes for network coding. In: Jarecki, S., Tsudik, G. (eds.) PKC 2009. LNCS, vol. 5443, pp. 68–87. Springer, Heidelberg (2009). https://doi.org/10.1007/978-3-642-00468-1_5

14. Boneh, D., Freeman, D.M.: Homomorphic signatures for polynomial functions. In: Paterson, K.G. (ed.) EUROCRYPT 2011. LNCS, vol. 6632, pp. 149–168. Springer, Heidelberg (2011). https://doi.org/10.1007/978-3-642-20465-4_10

15. Boneh, D., Freeman, D.M.: Linearly homomorphic signatures over binary fields and new tools for lattice-based signatures. In: Catalano, D., Fazio, N., Gennaro, R., Nicolosi, A. (eds.) PKC 2011. LNCS, vol. 6571, pp. 1–16. Springer, Heidelberg (2011). https://doi.org/10.1007/978-3-642-19379-8_1

16. Boneh, D., Gentry, C., Lynn, B., Shacham, H.: Aggregate and verifiably encrypted signatures from bilinear maps. In: Biham, E. (ed.) EUROCRYPT 2003. LNCS, vol. 2656, pp. 416–432. Springer, Heidelberg (2003). https://doi.org/10.1007/3-540-39200-9_26

17. Boyen, X., Fan, X., Shi, E.: Adaptively secure fully homomorphic signatures based on lattices. Cryptology ePrint Archive (2014)

18. Brakerski, Z., Brodsky, M.F., Kalai, Y.T., Lombardi, A., Paneth, O.: SNARGs for monotone policy batch NP. In: Handschuh, H., Lysyanskaya, A. (eds) CRYPTO 2023. LNCS, vol. 14082, pp. 252–283. Springer, Cham (2023). https://doi.org/10.1007/978-3-031-38545-2_9

19. Brakerski, Z., Gentry, C., Vaikuntanathan, V.: (leveled) fully homomorphic encryption without bootstrapping. ACM Trans. Comput. Theory (TOCT) $6(3)$, 1–36 (2014)

20. Brakerski, Z., Holmgren, J., Kalai, Y.: Non-interactive delegation and batch np verification from standard computational assumptions. In: Proceedings of the 49th Annual ACM SIGACT Symposium on Theory of Computing, pp. 474–482 (2017)

21. Brakerski, Z., Vaikuntanathan, V.: Efficient fully homomorphic encryption from (standard) LWE. SIAM J. Comput. $43(2)$, 831–871 (2014)

22. Brodsky, M.F., Choudhuri, A.R., Jain, A., Paneth, O.: Monotone-policy aggregate signatures. In: Joye, M., Leander, G. (eds) EUROCRYPT 2024. LNCS, vol. 14654, pp. 168–195. Springer, Cham (2024). https://doi.org/10.1007/978-3-031-58737-5_7
23. Campanelli, M., Ganesh, C., Khoshakhlagh, H., Siim, J.: Impossibilities in succinct arguments: Black-box extraction and more. In: El Mrabet, N., De Feo, L., Duquesne, S. (eds.) AFRICACRYPT 2023. LNCS, vol. 14064, pp. 465–489. Springer, Cham (2023). https://doi.org/10.1007/978-3-031-37679-5_20
24. Catalano, D., Fiore, D.: Practical homomorphic MACs for arithmetic circuits. In: Johansson, T., Nguyen, P.Q. (eds.) EUROCRYPT 2013. LNCS, vol. 7881, pp. 336–352. Springer, Heidelberg (2013). https://doi.org/10.1007/978-3-642-38348-9_21
25. Catalano, D., Fiore, D., Tucker, I.: Additive-homomorphic functional commitments and applications to homomorphic signatures. In: Agrawal, S., Lin, D. (eds.) ASIACRYPT 2022. LNCS, vol. 13794, pp. 159–188. Springer, Cham (2022). https://doi.org/10.1007/978-3-031-22972-5_6
26. Catalano, D., Fiore, D., Warinschi, B.: Efficient network coding signatures in the standard model. In: Fischlin, M., Buchmann, J., Manulis, M. (eds.) PKC 2012. LNCS, vol. 7293, pp. 680–696. Springer, Heidelberg (2012). https://doi.org/10.1007/978-3-642-30057-8_40
27. Cheng, J., Goyal, R.: Boosting snarks and rate-1 barrier in arguments of knowledge. Unpublished manuscript (personal communication) (2024)
28. Chiesa, A., Tromer, E.: Proof-carrying data and hearsay arguments from signature cards. In: ICS, vol. 10, pp. 310–331 (2010)
29. Choudhuri, A.R., Jain, A., Jin, Z.: Non-interactive batch arguments for np from standard assumptions. In: Malkin, T., Peikert, C. (eds.) CRYPTO 2021. LNCS, vol. 12828, pp. 394–423. Springer, Cham (2021). https://doi.org/10.1007/978-3-030-84259-8_14
30. Choudhuri, A.R., Jain, A., Jin, Z.: SNARGs for $\mathcal{P}$ from LWE. Cryptology ePrint Archive, Paper 2021/808 (2021). https://eprint.iacr.org/2021/808
31. Datta, T., Chen, B., Boneh, D.: VerITAS: verifying image transformations at scale. Cryptology ePrint Archive (2024)
32. Devadas, L., Goyal, R., Kalai, Y., Vaikuntanathan, V.: Rate-1 non-interactive arguments for batch-NP and applications. In: 63rd Annual Symposium on Foundations of Computer Science, pp. 1057–1068. IEEE Computer Society Press (2022). https://doi.org/10.1109/FOCS54457.2022.00103
33. Diffie, W., Hellman, M.E.: Multiuser cryptographic techniques. In: AFIPS National Computer Conference, pp. 109–112 (1976)
34. Diffie, W., Hellman, M.E.: New directions in cryptography (1976)
35. Dodis, Y., Vadhan, S., Wichs, D.: Proofs of retrievability via hardness amplification. In: Reingold, O. (ed.) TCC 2009. LNCS, vol. 5444, pp. 109–127. Springer, Heidelberg (2009). https://doi.org/10.1007/978-3-642-00457-5_8
36. El Kaafarani, A., Katsumata, S.: Attribute-based signatures for unbounded circuits in the ROM and efficient instantiations from lattices. In: Abdalla, M., Dahab, R. (eds.) PKC 2018. LNCS, vol. 10770, pp. 89–119. Springer, Cham (2018). https://doi.org/10.1007/978-3-319-76581-5_4
37. Fiore, D., Mitrokotsa, A., Nizzardo, L., Pagnin, E.: Multi-key homomorphic authenticators. In: Cheon, J.H., Takagi, T. (eds.) ASIACRYPT 2016. LNCS, vol. 10032, pp. 499–530. Springer, Heidelberg (2016). https://doi.org/10.1007/978-3-662-53890-6_17
38. Fiore, D., Pagnin, E.: Matrioska: a compiler for multi-key homomorphic signatures. In: Catalano, D., De Prisco, R. (eds.) SCN 2018. LNCS, vol. 11035, pp. 43–62. Springer, Cham (2018). https://doi.org/10.1007/978-3-319-98113-0_3

39. Freeman, D.M.: Improved security for linearly homomorphic signatures: a generic framework. In: Fischlin, M., Buchmann, J., Manulis, M. (eds.) PKC 2012. LNCS, vol. 7293, pp. 697–714. Springer, Heidelberg (2012). https://doi.org/10.1007/978-3-642-30057-8_41

40. Gay, R., Ursu, B.: On instantiating unleveled fully-homomorphic signatures from falsifiable assumptions. In: Tang, Q., Teague, V. (eds.) PKC 2024. LNCS, vol. 14601, pp. 74–104. Springer, Cham (2024). https://doi.org/10.1007/978-3-031-57718-5_3

41. Gennaro, R., Gentry, C., Parno, B.: Non-interactive verifiable computing: outsourcing computation to untrusted workers. In: Rabin, T. (ed.) CRYPTO 2010. LNCS, vol. 6223, pp. 465–482. Springer, Heidelberg (2010). https://doi.org/10.1007/978-3-642-14623-7_25

42. Gennaro, R., Katz, J., Krawczyk, H., Rabin, T.: Secure network coding over the integers. In: Nguyen, P.Q., Pointcheval, D. (eds.) PKC 2010. LNCS, vol. 6056, pp. 142–160. Springer, Heidelberg (2010). https://doi.org/10.1007/978-3-642-13013-7_9

43. Gennaro, R., Wichs, D.: Fully homomorphic message authenticators. In: Sako, K., Sarkar, P. (eds.) ASIACRYPT 2013. LNCS, vol. 8270, pp. 301–320. Springer, Heidelberg (2013). https://doi.org/10.1007/978-3-642-42045-0_16

44. Gentry, C.: A fully homomorphic encryption scheme. Stanford university (2009)

45. Gentry, C., Groth, J., Ishai, Y., Peikert, C., Sahai, A., Smith, A.: Using fully homomorphic hybrid encryption to minimize non-interative zero-knowledge proofs. J. Cryptol. **28**(4), 820–843 (2015)

46. Gentry, C., Sahai, A., Waters, B.: Homomorphic encryption from learning with errors: conceptually-simpler, asymptotically-faster, attribute-based. In: Canetti, R., Garay, J.A. (eds.) CRYPTO 2013. LNCS, vol. 8042, pp. 75–92. Springer, Heidelberg (2013). https://doi.org/10.1007/978-3-642-40041-4_5

47. Gentry, C., Wichs, D.: Separating succinct non-interactive arguments from all falsifiable assumptions. In: Proceedings of the Forty-Third Annual ACM Symposium on Theory of Computing, pp. 99–108 (2011)

48. Gentry, C., Wichs, D.: Separating succinct non-interactive arguments from all falsifiable assumptions. In: Fortnow, L., Vadhan, S.P. (eds.) 43rd Annual ACM Symposium on Theory of Computing, pp. 99–108. ACM Press (2011). https://doi.org/10.1145/1993636.1993651

49. Goldwasser, S., Tauman Kalai, Y.: Cryptographic assumptions: a position paper. In: Kushilevitz, E., Malkin, T. (eds.) TCC 2016. LNCS, vol. 9562, pp. 505–522. Springer, Heidelberg (2016). https://doi.org/10.1007/978-3-662-49096-9_21

50. Goldwasser, S., Kalai, Y.T., Rothblum, G.N.: Delegating computation: interactive proofs for muggles. J. ACM (JACM) **62**(4), 1–64 (2015)

51. Gorbunov, S., Vaikuntanathan, V., Wichs, D.: Leveled fully homomorphic signatures from standard lattices. In: Proceedings of the Forty-Seventh Annual ACM Symposium on Theory of Computing, pp. 469–477 (2015)

52. Goyal, R.: Mutable batch arguments and applications. Cryptology ePrint Archive, Paper 2024/737 (2024). https://eprint.iacr.org/2024/737

53. Goyal, R., Quach, W., Waters, B., Wichs, D.: Broadcast and trace with N^ε ciphertext size from standard assumptions. In: Boldyreva, A., Micciancio, D. (eds.) CRYPTO 2019. LNCS, vol. 11694, pp. 826–855. Springer, Cham (2019). https://doi.org/10.1007/978-3-030-26954-8_27

54. Goyal, V., Pandey, O., Sahai, A., Waters, B.: Attribute-based encryption for fine-grained access control of encrypted data. In: CCS 2006 (2006)

55. Hayashi, R., Sakai, Y., Yamada, S.: Attribute-based signatures for circuits with optimal parameter size from standard assumptions. Cryptology ePrint Archive (2024)
56. Jain, A., Lin, H., Sahai, A.: Indistinguishability obfuscation from well-founded assumptions. In: Proceedings of the 53rd Annual ACM SIGACT Symposium on Theory of Computing, pp. 60–73 (2021)
57. Jain, A., Lin, H., Sahai, A.: Indistinguishability obfuscation from LPN over $\mathbb{F}_p$, DLIN, and PRGs in NC^0. In: Dunkelman, O., Dziembowski, S. (eds) EUROCRYPT 2022LNCS, vol. 13275, pp. 670–699. Springer, Cham (2022). https://doi.org/10.1007/978-3-031-06944-4_23
58. Johnson, R., Molnar, D., Song, D., Wagner, D.: Homomorphic signature schemes. In: Preneel, B. (ed.) CT-RSA 2002. LNCS, vol. 2271, pp. 244–262. Springer, Heidelberg (2002). https://doi.org/10.1007/3-540-45760-7_17
59. Kalai, Y., Lombardi, A., Vaikuntanathan, V., Wichs, D.: Boosting batch arguments and ram delegation. In: Proceedings of the 55th Annual ACM Symposium on Theory of Computing, pp. 1545–1552 (2023)
60. Kalai, Y.T., Paneth, O., Yang, L.: How to delegate computations publicly. In: Proceedings of the 51st Annual ACM SIGACT Symposium on Theory of Computing, pp. 1115–1124 (2019)
61. Kilian, J.: A note on efficient zero-knowledge proofs and arguments. In: Proceedings of the Twenty-Fourth Annual ACM Symposium on Theory of Computing, pp. 723–732 (1992)
62. Lai, R.W.F., Tai, R.K.H., Wong, H.W.H., Chow, S.S.M.: Multi-key homomorphic signatures unforgeable under insider corruption. In: Peyrin, T., Galbraith, S. (eds.) ASIACRYPT 2018. LNCS, vol. 11273, pp. 465–492. Springer, Cham (2018). https://doi.org/10.1007/978-3-030-03329-3_16
63. Libert, B., Ramanna, S.C., Yung, M.: Functional commitment schemes: from polynomial commitments to pairing-based accumulators from simple assumptions. In: 43rd International Colloquium on Automata, Languages and Programming (ICALP 2016) (2016)
64. Maji, H.K., Prabhakaran, M., Rosulek, M.: Attribute-based signatures. In: Kiayias, A. (ed.) CT-RSA 2011. LNCS, vol. 6558, pp. 376–392. Springer, Heidelberg (2011). https://doi.org/10.1007/978-3-642-19074-2_24
65. Micali, S.: CS proofs. In: Proceedings 35th Annual Symposium on Foundations of Computer Science, pp. 436–453 (1994). https://doi.org/10.1109/SFCS.1994.365746
66. Naor, M.: On cryptographic assumptions and challenges. In: Boneh, D. (ed.) CRYPTO 2003. LNCS, vol. 2729, pp. 96–109. Springer, Heidelberg (2003). https://doi.org/10.1007/978-3-540-45146-4_6
67. Nassar, S., Waters, B., Wu, D.J.: Monotone policy BARGs from BARGs and additively homomorphic encryption. Cryptology ePrint Archive (2023)
68. Paneth, O., Pass, R.: Incrementally verifiable computation via rate-1 batch arguments. In: 63rd Annual Symposium on Foundations of Computer Science, pp. 1045–1056. IEEE Computer Society Press (2022). https://doi.org/10.1109/FOCS54457.2022.00102
69. Parno, B., Howell, J., Gentry, C., Raykova, M.: Pinocchio: nearly practical verifiable computation. Commun. ACM **59**(2), 103–112 (2016)
70. Regev, O.: On lattices, learning with errors, random linear codes, and cryptography. In: 37th Annual ACM Symposium on Theory of Computing (2005). https://doi.org/10.1145/1060590.1060603

71. Reingold, O., Rothblum, G.N., Rothblum, R.D.: Constant-round interactive proofs for delegating computation. In: Proceedings of the Forty-Eighth Annual ACM Symposium on Theory of Computing, pp. 49–62 (2016)
72. Rivest, R.L., Adleman, L., Dertouzos, M.L., et al.: On data banks and privacy homomorphisms. Found. Secure Comput. 4(11), 169–180 (1978)
73. Samarin, S.D., Fiore, D., Venturi, D., Amini, M.: A compiler for multi-key homomorphic signatures for turing machines. Theoret. Comput. Sci. **889**, 145–170 (2021)
74. Shacham, H., Waters, B.: Compact proofs of retrievability. J. Cryptol. **26**(3), 442–483 (2013)
75. Tsabary, R.: An equivalence between attribute-based signatures and homomorphic signatures, and new constructions for both. In: Kalai, Y., Reyzin, L. (eds.) TCC 2017. LNCS, vol. 10678, pp. 489–518. Springer, Cham (2017). https://doi.org/10.1007/978-3-319-70503-3_16
76. Vadhan, S.P.: An unconditional study of computational zero knowledge. SIAM J. Comput. **36**(4), 1160–1214 (2006)
77. Valiant, P.: Incrementally verifiable computation or proofs of knowledge imply time/space efficiency. In: Canetti, R. (ed.) TCC 2008. LNCS, vol. 4948, pp. 1–18. Springer, Heidelberg (2008). https://doi.org/10.1007/978-3-540-78524-8_1
78. Wee, H., Wu, D.J.: Succinct functional commitments for circuits from k-lin. In: Joye, M., Leander, G. (eds.) EUROCRYPT 2024. LNCS, vol. 14652, pp. 280–310. Springer, Cham (2024). https://doi.org/10.1007/978-3-031-58723-8_10

Efficient and Post-quantum Conjunctive Dynamic SSE with Strong Privacy Guarantees

Bibhas Chandra Das[1,2], Nilanjan Datta[1,3], Avijit Dutta[1,3],
Avishek Majumder[4], Debdeep Mukhopadhyay[5], Sikhar Patranabis[6(✉)],
Subhabrata Samajder[1,3], and Laltu Sardar[7]

[1] Institute for Advancing Intelligence, TCG CREST, Kolkata, India
{bibhaschandra.das,nilanjan.datta,avijit.dutta,
subhabrata.samajder}@tcgcrest.org
[2] Chennai Mathematical Institute, Chennai, India
[3] Academy of Scientific and Innovative Research, Ghaziabad, India
[4] Krea University, Sri City, India
avishek.majumder@krea.edu.in
[5] Indian Institute of Technology, Kharagpur, Kharagpur, India
debdeep@cse.iitkgp.ac.in
[6] IBM Research, Bengaluru, India
sikhar.patranabis@ibm.com
[7] Indian Institute of Science Education and Research Thiruvananthapuram,
Thiruvananthapuram, India
laltu.sardar@iisertvm.ac.in

Abstract. Designing dynamic searchable symmetric encryption (DSSE) supporting conjunctive keyword queries over encrypted document collections is an important research area. Unfortunately, state-of-the-art conjunctive DSSE schemes such as **ODXT** (Patranabis et al., NDSS '21), and **SDSSE-CQ** and its variants (Zuo et al., PoPETS '25) either fail to achieve the desired levels of security (in particular, forward and/or backward privacy), or incur prohibitively large communication requirements and client-side computational overheads, which is undesirable for practical applications. In addition, all known conjunctive DSSE schemes that are both forward and backward private are quantum-broken due to their inherent reliance on discrete log-hard, prime-order cyclic groups.

In this paper, we address the open question of designing practically efficient, low-leakage, forward and backward private conjunctive DSSE with small communication requirements and small client-side overheads. Towards this goal, we introduce the first systematic and rigorously formal notions of backward privacy for conjunctive queries that naturally extend the corresponding notions of backward privacy for single-keyword DSSE. Next, as our main contribution, we propose a new framework for conjunctive DSSE called **fp-GA-ODXT** that improves upon both **ODXT** and **SDSSE-CQ**-variants by achieving full-fledged forward privacy and strong backward privacy guarantees, while incurring small client-side computation and low communication overheads. We then demonstrate two instantiations of our **fp-GA-ODXT** framework:

S. Bai and E. Persichetti (Eds.): PKC 2026, LNCS 16554, pp. 302–334, 2026.
https://doi.org/10.1007/978-3-032-26740-5_10

- A concretely efficient, classically secure instance based on discrete log-hard groups and an RSA-based trapdoor permutation, which we implement and benchmark. Our experiments demonstrate that we achieve smaller communication overheads and client-side computation for both updates and conjunctive searches as compared to both **ODXT** and **SDSSE-CQ**-variants. These come at the cost of a mild increase in server computation (which we view as an acceptable tradeoff in practice).

- A post-quantum instantiation based on lattices and isogenies of supersingular elliptic curves, thus solving the longstanding open question of designing asymptotically efficient, forward and backward private conjunctive DSSE schemes with post-quantum security.

Keywords: Dynamic SSE · Forward Privacy · Backward Privacy · Post Quantum Security

1   Introduction

Searchable Symmetric Encryption (SSE) allows a client to outsource a symmetrically encrypted document collection (where each document/file in the collection is tagged with a set of keywords) to an (untrusted) server, while retaining the ability to directly execute keyword queries [17,38]. Other cryptographic primitives supporting encrypted search such as fully homomorphic encryption (FHE) [8] and oblivious RAM [23,39], minimize information leakage to the server, but incur high computational/communication overheads in the process. On the other hand, SSE achieves a reasonable trade-off between security and efficiency by minimizing the computational and communication overheads, while adhering to a rigorously formalized leakage function. Security analysis of SSE typically involves two steps: (i) a simulation-based proof that establishes that an SSE scheme leaks no information to the server beyond what is captured by the leakage function, and (ii) a cryptanalysis-based argument to establish that the leakage function is benign, i.e., does not leak sensitive information about the client's data/queries.

Static SSE. Initial studies of SSE were restricted to the very simple functionality of *single keyword* search over *static* databases (e.g., [17,22,38]). A more recent line of works has extended the study of SSE over static databases to richer functionalities beyond single keyword search, including conjunctive, disjunctive, and more general Boolean queries [11,21,26,28]. However, to be truly practical, an SSE scheme should ideally support both keyword searches and *dynamic updates* to the database, simultaneously.

Dynamic SSE. The study of SSE for dynamic databases (abbreviated as DSSE throughout) was initiated in [10,15,27]. However, these schemes were found to be vulnerable to data/query recovery attacks [9,46]. Subsequently, a line of works [6, 7] introduced two security notions for DSSE, which have been adopted widely in several subsequent DSSE schemes [14,16,40,41,48]:

- *Forward privacy:* informally ensures that the update operation cannot be linked to any previous search operations.
- *Backward privacy:* informally ensures that during identical search queries, the server should not be able to learn about documents/files that were previously added and later deleted.

The authors of [7] further described three categories of backward privacy that leak progressively more information to the server about a queried keyword w: (i) Type-I backward privacy leaks the documents currently matching w, the time of their insertion, and the total number of updates on w; (ii) Type-II backward privacy leaks, in addition to Type-I, when all updates on w happened without leaking their specific content; (iii) Type-III backward privacy, in addition to Type-II leakages, leaks the information about which deletion cancels which insertion. By definition, Type-I is the strongest, and Type-III is the weakest notion of backward privacy.

Several works [7, 14, 16, 40, 41, 48] have subsequently proposed DSSE schemes supporting single keyword queries while achieving both forward privacy and (any one of the aforementioned notions of) backward privacy. While many of these schemes are extremely efficient, they are unfortunately too limited in terms of query expressiveness. Many practical applications require the client to query the *conjunction* of two or more keywords, i.e., identify the documents that contain *all* keywords in a given set. This motivates the need for DSSE schemes satisfying suitable notions of forward and backward privacy while supporting conjunctive keyword queries, which is the focus of this work.

Conjunctive DSSE. A conjunctive search query $q = w_1 \land w_2 \land \cdots \land w_n$ requires the server to return documents containing all the keywords $w_1, w_2, \ldots, w_n$. Note that one can achieve conjunctive DSSE from single-keyword DSSE in a black-box manner by simply invoking the single-keyword DSSE to query each w_i, and then computing the intersection locally at the client. Besides incurring additional undesirable leakage (e.g., the frequency of each keyword), this approach incurs computational and communication overheads that scale with the frequency of the *most frequent keyword,* As noted in [11], this is highly undesirable in practice. Certain early works on conjunctive DSSE [24, 44, 45] proposed more sophisticated schemes for conjunctive SSE, but these schemes only achieve forward privacy, and not backward privacy.

Conjunctive DSSE from the OXT Template. In the setting of static SSE, a template for designing practically efficient conjunctive SSE was introduced in the widely studied OXT protocol of [11]. In particular, OXT supports highly efficient, single-round, low-leakage conjunctive keyword searches, where the computational and communication complexity only scales with the frequency of the *least* frequent keyword. The first work to translate the template of OXT into the setting of dynamic databases was ODXT [33]. ODXT supports efficient, single-round conjunctive keyword queries with the same asymptotic computational and communication overheads as OXT, while also supporting efficient, non-interactive updates. Unfortunately, as noted in [47], ODXT *does not* achieve the desired level of forward privacy.

Alternatives to ODXT. Concurrent to [33], the authors of [49] proposed FBDSSE-CQ and SFBDSSE-CQ – two conjunctive DSSE schemes achieving both forward privacy and (a weaker notion of) backward privacy. However, both constructions incur computational and communication overheads that scale with the frequency of the *most frequent keyword* (same as the naïve solution). In practice, for moderately sized databases, both constructions incur query communication in the range of gigabytes, which is prohibitively large. As a result, these schemes do not scale to large databases in practice.

A follow-up work [47] proposed two new conjunctive DSSE schemes based on the same OXT framework, called SDSSE-CQ and SDSSE-CQ-S. Both constructions use Aura [40], a forward and backward private DSSE scheme for single keyword search, as their underlying protocol. While these schemes fix the forward privacy issues of ODXT [33], they incur additional search leakage, resulting in significantly weaker backward privacy guarantees. One can easily observe that for a conjunction of n keywords, the search protocol of both these schemes additionally invokes n instances of the search protocol of the underlying single keyword SSE. Furthermore, both of these schemes incur substantial communication and computation overhead on the client side. This is highly undesirable, in particular, in many practical applications of SSE, where the client could be resource-constrained. For such applications, high client computation represents a major bottleneck for practical scalability. Alongside this, in a very recent work [19], Das has identified an inconsistency in the stronger backward privacy claim of SDSSE-CQ-S and has shown that both SDSSE-CQ and SDSSE-CQ-S guarantee a very weak level of backward privacy.

A possible approach towards fixing this state of affairs would be to design a conjunctive DSSE scheme that achieves both forward and backward privacy *and* reduces the computational and communication overheads for the client, while potentially incurring larger server-side computation. Since the server (e.g., a cloud service provider) is typically equipped with stronger computational capabilities, this would be a much more reasonable tradeoff. To the best of our knowledge, no existing conjunctive DSSE scheme achieves this property. This motivates us to ask the following question:

> *Can we design efficient, low-leakage, forward and backward private conjunctive DSSE with small communication and client-side overheads?*

Ad-hoc nature of Backward Privacy Definitions. A closer look reveals another issue with existing forward and backward private conjunctive DSSE schemes [33,47,49], namely, all of these works introduce ad-hoc notions of backward privacy that are only satisfied by their specific scheme. Such definitions are fundamentally incompatible with the systematic categorizations of backward privacy leakage introduced in [7] for single-keyword DSSE and used consistently in several subsequent works [14,16,40,41,48]. The lack of formal, uniformly applicable notions of backward privacy for conjunctive DSSE not only makes it difficult to compare the existing schemes [33, 47, 49] in terms of their leakage, but also fails to provide future efforts to design conjunctive DSSE with a reasonable baseline/framework for evaluating their leakage functions.

Lack of Post-Quantum Conjunctive DSSE. Finally, we note that all of the conjunctive DSSE schemes today with forward and backward privacy [33, 47, 49] fundamentally rely on the hardness of the discrete logarithm problem over cyclic, prime-order groups (this is, in fact, inherited from the original design of OXT in [11]). As a result, they would be fundamentally broken by a quantum computer capable of running Shor's algorithm. We note here that a recent line of works [42, 43] have proposed post-quantum conjunctive *static* SSE schemes from lattice-based assumptions. However, these schemes have no dynamic counterparts today. This leads to the following question:

Can we design a post-quantum conjunctive DSSE scheme?

1.1   Our Contributions

We answer both of the above questions in the affirmative. Our contributions are summarized below.

Systematizing Backward Privacy of Conjunctive DSSE. As a first contribution, we propose a new formal framework for systematizing backward privacy of conjunctive DSSE. We extend and formalize the existing backward privacy notions - Type-I, Type-II, and Type-III - originally designed for single-keyword DSSE, adapting them for conjunctive queries. We categorize backward privacy for conjunctive DSSE into three classes, C1, C2, and C3, which naturally build upon the existing backward privacy notions while capturing the possible information leakage in conjunctive searches. Additionally, we introduced a refined notion of backward privacy, dubbed C2$^-$, which is particularly relevant for OXT-based DSSE protocols, and offers stronger backward privacy guarantees than C2. To the best of our knowledge, this represents the first attempt to systematically formalize backward privacy notions for DSSE schemes that support conjunctive queries. In particular, by unifying previous definitions, our model provides a clearer understanding of the security of existing schemes. Notably, our analysis confirms that ODXT achieves the strongest backward privacy among all known conjunctive DSSE schemes.

fp-GA-ODXT. As our main contribution, we design fp-GA-ODXT – a variant of ODXT that achieves full-fledged forward privacy while retaining strong backward privacy, low client-side computation, and small communication overhead. To this end, we first introduce an intermediate, cryptographic group action [3] based generalization of ODXT, that we call GA-ODXT. More specifically, unlike ODXT which relies explicitly on the classical hardness of discrete log over cyclic, prime-order groups, GA-ODXT relies on the hardness of the group action-based

Table 1. Comparison of state-of-the-art conjunctive DSSE schemes that achieve both forward and backward privacy. Here, W and D denote the number of keywords and file identifiers in the database, respectively. For a conjunctive search query of the form $(w_1 \wedge w_2 \wedge \cdots \wedge w_n)$, where w_1 is the least frequent keyword, c_{w_i} for each $i \in [n]$ denotes the number of update operations involving the keyword w_i.

Construction	Forward Privacy	Backward Privacy	Communication		Client Computation		Storage
			Update	Search	Update	Search	
ODXT [33]	$\times$	C2$^-$	$O(1)$	$O(n.c_{w_1})$	$O(1)$	$O(1)$	$O(W)$
FBDSSE-CQ [49]	$\checkmark$	C2	$O(D)$	$O(n + D)$	$O(D)$	$O(D.\Sigma_{i=1}^n c_{w_i})$	$O(W)$
SFBDSSE-CQ [49]	$\checkmark$	C2	$O(D)$	$O(n + D)$	$O(s.D)$	$O(s.D)$	$O(1)$
SDSSE-CQ [47]	$\checkmark$	C2-II	$O(1)$	$O(n.c_{w_1})$	$O(1)$	$O(n.c_{w_1})$	$O(W)$
SDSSE-CQ-S [47]	$\checkmark$	C2-I	$O(1)$	$O(n.c_{w_1} + \Sigma_{i=2}^n c_{w_i})$	$O(1)$	$O(n.c_{w_1} + \Sigma_{i=2}^n c_{w_i})$	$O(W)$
fp-GA-ODXT [Sec.4.3]	$\checkmark$	C2$^-$	$O(1)$	$O(n + c_{w_1})$	$O(1)$	$O(n + c_{w_1})$	$O(W)$

analogue of the discrete log hardness assumption. However, similar to ODXT, GA-ODXT also does not achieve full-fledged forward privacy. Nonetheless, we leverage this generic abstraction to identify and patch the fundamental source of this issue with forward privacy to propose fp-GA-ODXT. Beyond fixing the forward privacy issues with ODXT, another novel design feature of fp-GA-ODXT is its usage of *backward*-chaining to (asymptotically) retain the same overall communication overhead, the same client-side overhead during update, and a smaller client-side overhead during search compared to ODXT.

We summarize and compare the security and efficiency of state-of-the-art conjunctive DSSE schemes (that achieve both forward and backward privacy) with fp-GA-ODXT in Table 1. We note that, asymptotically, fp-GA-ODXT provides the highest level of privacy guarantees (forward privacy and strong C2$^-$ backward privacy) among all efficient conjunctive DSSE schemes and also achieves small client-side computation and low communication overhead. In particular, fp-GA-ODXT avoids the pitfalls of prior approaches [47, 49] towards fixing the forward privacy issues of ODXT, which result in substantially larger client-side overheads and communication requirements, as well as weaker backward privacy guarantees. As a tradeoff, fp-GA-ODXT incurs mildly larger computational overheads at the server. As explained earlier, in most practical realizations of SSE, the client is expected to be resource-constrained, while the server is typically equipped with stronger compute capabilities (which is the fundamental motivation for outsourcing data in the first place). Hence, we view this as a much more acceptable tradeoff in practice.

Concretely Efficient Instantiation of fp-GA-ODXT. We present a classically secure and concretely efficient instantiation of fp-GA-ODXT based on a combination of discrete log-hard prime order groups (same as ODXT) and RSA-based trapdoor permutations (for backward-chaining). We implement and benchmark this instantiation, and compare it with both ODXT and SDSSE-CQ/SDSSE-CQ-S [47]. Our results show that: (i) our average update time and communication overheads are similar to ODXT and 1.4$\times$ smaller than SDSSE-CQ/SDSSE-CQ-S, (ii) as the number of *xterm* in the conjunction increases, the search communication cost of our scheme remains constant and minimal, whereas it increases linearly for both ODXT and SDSSE-CQ/SDSSE-CQ-S, and finally (iii) our average client-side search time is about 1.2× smaller than ODXT, 1.6× smaller than SDSSE-CQ, and 3× smaller than SDSSE-CQ-S. As a tradeoff, from the construction presented in Sect. 4.3, it is clear that our scheme has an increased server computation overhead. As explained earlier, we view this as a reasonable trade-off, especially in practical scenarios where the SSE client is significantly resource-constrained.

Post-quantum Instantiation of fp-GA-ODXT . We next present a post-quantum instantiation of fp-GA-ODXT based on the combined (worst-case) hardness of lattice problems *and* the hardness of computing isogeny maps between supersingular elliptic curves. Concretely, we use known instantiations of effective group actions from well-studied isogeny-based hardness assumptions (in particular, assumptions over CSIDH [13], CSI-FiSh [4], Scallop [20], and PEGASIS [18]) to instantiate the GA-ODXT component of fp-GA-ODXT. A core technical novelty of this construction is that we replace the use of the RSA-based trapdoor permutation for backward-chaining in our classical instantiation with an *injective trapdoor function* based on the hardness of the short integer solutions (SIS) problem [2]. This yields the *first* (to the best of our knowledge) post-quantum candidate for forward and backward private conjunctive DSSE with desirable asymptotic efficiency guarantees and strong levels of security.

We remark that the post-quantum instantiation is likely to be less efficient than the quantum-broken counterpart (this is a natural and somewhat inherent tradeoff that also applies to other cryptographic primitives being standardized, such as KEMs/signatures), and a fair comparison would require one to also benchmark the natural CSIDH-based analogues of ODXT [33] and SDSSE-CQ/SDSSE-CQ-S [47], for which there are also no implementations at the moment. We leave achieving an optimized implementation of the post-quantum solution as an important but independent future work.

2   Preliminaries

Notations. For any natural number $n \in \mathbb{N}$, we write $[n]$ to denote the set $\{1, \ldots, n\}$. Similarly, for $i, j \in \mathbb{N}$ with $i < j$, we write $[i, j]$ to denote the set $\{i, i + 1, \ldots, j\}$. For a random variable X, we write $x \xleftarrow{\$} \mathcal{X}$ to denote that x is sampled uniformly at random from $\mathcal{X}$. The output x of a deterministic algorithm $\mathcal{A}$ is denoted by $x \leftarrow \mathcal{A}$ and the output x of a randomized algorithm $\mathcal{A}^{\$}$ is denoted by $x \xleftarrow{\#} \mathcal{A}^{\$}$. For two variables x, y, we write $x \leftarrow y$ to denote the assignment of the value in y to the variable x. We refer to $\lambda \in \mathbb{N}$ as the security parameter and denote by $\mathsf{poly}(\lambda)$ and $\mathsf{negl}(\lambda)$ as a generic polynomial function and negligible function in λ, respectively.

Databases. We write $\mathcal{W}$ to denote a set of distinct keywords, which we call a *dictionary*. Let $\mathcal{F}$ be a collection of files such that each file $f \in \mathcal{F}$ is associated with an identifier $id \in \mathcal{ID}$, and contains keywords from a set $\mathcal{W}$. A database DB refers to the set of all keyword-identifier pairs across the files in $\mathcal{F}$. More formally, we have $DB = \{(w, id) : w \in \mathcal{W}, id \in \mathcal{ID}\}$ such that a given pair $(w, id) \in DB$ if and only if the keyword w is in a file $f \in \mathcal{F}$ with the identifier id. For a given keyword $w \in \mathcal{W}$, $DB(w)$ denotes the set of all file identifiers containing w as a keyword. W denotes the number of keywords present in the database DB, i.e.,

$$W = |\{w : (w, id) \in DB \text{ for some } id \in \mathcal{ID}\}|$$

Similarly, D denotes the total number of files in the database DB, i.e.

$$D = |\{id : (w, id) \in DB \text{ for some } w \in \mathcal{W}\}|$$

Clearly, $W \leq |\mathcal{W}|$ and $D \leq |\mathcal{ID}|$.

Conjunctive Queries. We represent a conjunctive search query over n distinct keywords as $q = w_1 \wedge w_2 \wedge \cdots \wedge w_n$ and define the set $DB(q) = \cap_{i=1}^{n} DB(w_i)$ to be the result of the conjunctive search query. We typically assume (without loss of generality) that the keyword w_1 is the least frequently updated keyword in the conjunction q. We refer to w_1 as the *s-term*, and all the other keywords in the conjunction as *x-terms*.

2.1   Cryptographic Primitives

Pseudo-Random Function: Let $\mathsf{Func}(\{0,1\}^n)$ be the set of all functions from $\{0,1\}^n$ to $\{0,1\}^n$ and $\mathsf{F} : \{0,1\}^k \times \{0,1\}^n \to \{0,1\}^n$ be a family of keyed functions from $\{0,1\}^n$ to $\{0,1\}^n$. The PRF advantage $\mathbf{Adv}_{\mathsf{F},\mathcal{A}}^{\mathrm{PRF}}(\lambda)$ of F with respect to a distinguisher $\mathcal{A}$ is defined as the absolute difference between the probability that $\mathcal{A}$ interacting with $\mathsf{F}_K = \mathsf{F}(K, \cdot)$ for a randomly sampled secret key K outputs 1, and the probability that $\mathcal{A}$ interacting with a function R chosen uniformly at random from $\mathsf{Func}(\{0,1\}^n)$ outputs 1. That is,

$$\mathbf{Adv}_{\mathsf{F},\mathcal{A}}^{\mathrm{PRF}}(\lambda) \overset{\Delta}{=} \left| \Pr_K[\mathcal{A}^{\mathsf{F}_K} = 1] - \Pr_R[\mathcal{A}^R = 1] \right|.$$

We say that F is a PRF if the maximum pseudorandom function advantage of F is $negl(\lambda)$ where the maximum is taken over all distinguishers $\mathcal{A}$ that make polynomial many queries to its oracle.

Hash Function: A hash function $\mathsf{H} : \{0,1\}^* \to \{0,1\}^n$ is a function that takes a message of arbitrary length and produces a fixed-length string. In this paper, we assume that a hash function behaves like a random oracle.

2.2   Cryptographic Group Actions

We recall the formal definition of cryptographic group actions from [3].

Group Action. Let G be a group and U be a set. Then G is said to *act on U* if there is a function $\star : G \times U \to U$ that satisfies the following two properties:

1. Identity: For any $u \in U$, we have $e \star u = u$, where e is the identity element of G.
2. Compatibility: $(gh) \star u = g \star (h \star u)$ for any $g, h \in G$ and any $u \in U$.

We use the notation $(G, U, \star)$ to denote such a group action throughout. We consider group actions that satisfy one or more of the following properties:

1. *Abelian:* The group G is abelian.
2. *Transitive:* For every $u_1, u_2 \in U$, there exists a group element $g \in G$ such that $u_2 = g \star u_1$. For such a transitive group action, the set U is called a *homogeneous space* for G.
3. *Faithful:* For each group element $g \in G$, either g is the identity element of G or there exists an element $u \in U$ such that $u \neq g \star u$.
4. *Free:* For each group element $g \in G$, g is the identity element of G if and only if there exists some element $u \in U$ such that $u = g \star u$.
5. *Regular:* Both free and transitive, i.e., the map $f_u : g \mapsto g \star u$ defines a bijection between G and U, or any $u \in U$. Consequently, if G (or U) is finite, then we must have $|G| = |U|$.

Effective Group Action (EGA). An abelian and regular group action $(G, U, \star)$ is *effective* if the following properties are satisfied:

1. The group G is finite and there exist probabilistic polynomial time (PPT) algorithms for:
   (a) *Membership testing,* i.e., to decide if a given bit string represents a valid group element in G.
   (b) *Equality testing,* i.e., to decide if two bit strings represent the same group element in G.
   (c) *Sampling,* i.e., to sample an element g according to some distribution on G. In this paper, we consider distributions that are (statistically close to) uniform.
   (d) *Operation,* i.e., to compute gh for any $g, h \in G$.
   (e) *Inversion,* i.e., to compute g^{-1} for any $g \in G$.
2. The set U is finite, and there exist efficient algorithms for:
   (a) *Membership testing,* i.e., to decide if a bit string represents a valid element of the set U.
   (b) *Unique representation,* i.e., given any arbitrary set element $u \in U$, compute a string $\hat{u}$ that canonically represents u.
3. There exists a distinguished element $u_0 \in U$, called the *origin*, such that its bit-string representation is known.
4. There exists an efficient algorithm that, given (some bit-string representations of) any $g \in G$ and any $u \in U$, outputs $g \star u$.

2.3 Cryptographic Hardness Assumptions

The security proofs of our constructions depend on the following two cryptographic hard problems. The first one is the well-known Decisional Diffie-Hellman (DDH) problem. Security of the classical instantiation of our construction is based on it. The second is a generalization of the DDH problem in the group action setting. Security of the post-quantum instantiation of our construction is based on it.

Definition 1 (DDH Assumption). *Let $\mathbb{G}$ be a finite cyclic group of prime order p and let g be a generator of the cyclic group which is uniformly sampled from $\mathbb{G}$. We say that the DDH problem is hard for the group $\mathbb{G}$, if for any probabilistic polynomial time algorithm $\mathcal{A}$,*

$$\mathbf{Adv}_{\mathcal{A}}^{\mathrm{DDH}}(\lambda) \triangleq \; |\Pr[\mathcal{A}(g, g^{\alpha}, g^{\beta}, g^{\alpha\beta}) = 1] - \Pr[\mathcal{A}(g, g^{\alpha}, g^{\beta}, g^{\gamma}) = 1] \; | \; \leq \; \mathsf{negl}(\lambda),$$

where $\alpha, \beta, \gamma \xleftarrow{\$} \mathbb{Z}_p^*$ and the group $\mathbb{G}$ (and consequently, its order p and it's generator) depend on the security parameter λ.

Definition 2 (Group Action DDH (GA-DDH) Assumption). *Let $(G, U, \star)$ be an EGA as defined above. We say that the DDH assumption holds with respect to a group action $(G, U, \star)$ if for any security parameter λ such that $|G| = \omega(\lambda^c)$ for any $c = O(1)$, for any $g, h, k \leftarrow G$, for any $u \leftarrow U$, and any PPT adversary $\mathbf{Adv}$, we have*

$$\mathbf{Adv}_{\mathcal{A}}^{\mathrm{GA\text{-}DDH}}(\lambda) \triangleq |\Pr[\mathcal{A}(u, g \star u, h \star u, (g \cdot h) \star u) = 1] - $$
$$\Pr[\mathcal{A}(u, g \star u, h \star u, k \star u) = 1]| \leq \mathsf{negl}(\lambda).$$

2.4 Dynamic Searchable Symmetric Encryption Schemes

A dynamic searchable symmetric encryption (DSSE) scheme consists of three interactive algorithms: Setup, Update, and Search. We adopted the following definition of DSSE from Chamani et al. [14].

- The Setup algorithm takes as input the security parameter λ and the database DB and outputs a state σ, which is kept secret, and an encrypted database EDB, which is made public.
- The Update algorithm is interactive. First, the client takes as input the current state σ, the operation $op \in \{add, del\}$, and a keyword-identifier pair (w, id) and outputs an update token UT, which is sent to the server. On input UT, the server updates the encrypted database EDB and the client state σ also gets updated.
- The Search algorithm is also an interactive one. Here, the client first takes as input the current state σ and a query q and outputs a search token ST, which is sent to the server. The server uses the search token ST and the encrypted database EDB to retrieve the desired encrypted identifiers and send the identifiers to the client. The client finally outputs the list of file identifiers.

2.5   Security of DSSE

To understand the security of a DSSE scheme, we first define the notion of a leakage function. Formally, the leakage function for any DSSE scheme is given by

$$\mathcal{L} \triangleq \left(\mathcal{L}^{\mathsf{SetUp}}, \mathcal{L}^{\mathsf{Update}}, \mathcal{L}^{\mathsf{Search}}\right),$$

where $\mathcal{L}^{\mathsf{SetUp}}$, $\mathcal{L}^{\mathsf{Update}}$ and $\mathcal{L}^{\mathsf{Search}}$ denotes the leakage to a semi-honest adversarial server $\mathcal{A}$ during the Setup, Update and Search algorithms respectively. With this, the security model of a DSSE scheme is given by two experiments, namely Real and Ideal. The experiments are defined as follows:

Real World: On input the security parameter λ and a database DB, the real challenger first returns an encrypted database EDB following the SetUp algorithm of the scheme. Then $\mathcal{A}$ interacts with the real challenger with update or search queries. The challenger responds to each of these queries following the Update and Search algorithms of the scheme. Finally, $\mathcal{A}$ outputs a single bit b.

Ideal World: Here the encrypted database EDB is simulated by a stateful probabilistic polynomial time simulator $\mathcal{S}$ in spite of the real challenger following the setup leakage $\mathcal{L}^{\mathsf{SetUp}}$ of the scheme. To respond to the update or search queries of the adversary $\mathcal{A}$, the simulator $\mathcal{S}$ uses the update leakage $\mathcal{L}^{\mathsf{Update}}$ or the search leakage $\mathcal{L}^{\mathsf{Search}}$, respectively. Finally, $\mathcal{A}$ outputs a single bit b.

Definition 3 (DSSE Security). *A DSSE scheme is said to be adaptively secure with respect to a leakage function $\mathcal{L}$ if for any security parameter $\lambda \in \mathbb{N}$ and for any probabilistic polynomial time adversary $\mathcal{A}$, there exists a probabilistic polynomial-time simulator $\mathcal{S}$ such that*

$$\left|\Pr[\mathsf{Real}_{\mathcal{A}}(\lambda) = 1] - \Pr[\mathsf{Ideal}_{\mathcal{A},\mathcal{S}}(\lambda) = 1]\right| \leq \mathsf{negl}(\lambda).$$

3   Forward and Backward Privacy of Conjunctive DSSE

In this section, we revisit the security definition of forward and backward privacy for single-keyword DSSE from [6, 7, 16]. We then introduce a new notion of backward privacy for conjunctive DSSE.

3.1   Forward and Backward Privacy of Single-Keyword DSSE

Let $\mathcal{Q}$ list all queries the adversarial server issues. Note that queries can be of the following two types: (i) an update query at timestamp t, involving keyword w on file identifier id, denoted as $(t, op, (w, id))$, where $op \in \{add, del\}$, (ii) a search query for a keyword w at timestamp t, denoted as (t, w). The following are different leakage functions associated with search and update queries.

$\mathsf{sp}(w)$: The search pattern leaks the repetition of search queries on keyword w.

$$\mathsf{sp}(w) \triangleq \{t : (t, w) \in \mathcal{Q}.\}$$

TimeDB(w): TimeDB(w) leaks the (t, id) pairs such that the keyword w has been added to the file identifier id at timestamp t, and has further not been removed.

$$\mathsf{TimeDB}(w) \triangleq \left\{ (t, id) : (t, add, (w, id)) \in \mathcal{Q} \wedge \forall\, t' > t, (t', del, (w, id)) \notin \mathcal{Q} \right\}.$$

Updates(w): At any instance, Updates(w) contains the timestamps at which all the updates on w has occurred.

$$\mathsf{Updates}(w) \triangleq \left\{ t : (t, op, (w, id)) \in \mathcal{Q} \right\}.$$

DelHist(w): At any instance, DelHist(w) contains the pair (t^+, t^-) such that w has been added in some file at timestamp t^+ and later has been deleted from it at timestamp t^-.

$$\mathsf{DelHist}(w) \triangleq \{ (t^+, t^-) : \exists\, id \text{ such that } (t^+, add, (w, id)) \in \mathcal{Q} \wedge$$
$$(t^-, del, (w, id)) \in \mathcal{Q} \}.$$

With these definitions of leakage functions, we now discuss forward privacy and three types of backward privacy for single-keyword DSSE. For the rest of the section, $\mathcal{L}'$ and $\mathcal{L}''$ are stateless functions, and update queries are restricted to adding or deleting a single keyword-identifier pair.

Forward Privacy: An adaptively secure DSSE scheme Σ with corresponding leakage function $\mathcal{L}_\Sigma$ is forward private iff $\mathcal{L}_\Sigma^{\mathsf{Update}}$ can be written as:

$$\mathcal{L}_\Sigma^{\mathsf{Update}}(t, op, (w, id)) = \mathcal{L}'(op, id),$$

Type-I Backward Privacy: An adaptively secure DSSE scheme Σ with corresponding leakage function $\mathcal{L}_\Sigma$ is insertion pattern revealing backward private (or Type-I backward private) iff $\mathcal{L}_\Sigma^{\mathsf{Update}}$ and $\mathcal{L}_\Sigma^{\mathsf{Search}}$ can be written as:

$$\mathcal{L}_\Sigma^{\mathsf{Update}}(t, op, (w, id)) = \mathcal{L}'(op),$$
$$\mathcal{L}_\Sigma^{\mathsf{Search}}(t, w) = \mathcal{L}''(\mathsf{sp}(w), \mathsf{TimeDB}(w), c_w),$$

where c_w is the number of updates on keyword w.

Type-II Backward Privacy: An adaptively secure DSSE scheme with corresponding leakage function $\mathcal{L}$ is update pattern revealing backward private (or Type-II backward private) iff $\mathcal{L}_\Sigma^{\mathsf{Update}}$ and $\mathcal{L}_\Sigma^{\mathsf{Search}}$ can be written as:

$$\mathcal{L}_\Sigma^{\mathsf{Update}}(t, op, (w, id)) = \mathcal{L}'(op, w),$$
$$\mathcal{L}_\Sigma^{\mathsf{Search}}(t, w) = \mathcal{L}''(\mathsf{sp}(w), \mathsf{TimeDB}(w), \mathsf{Updates}(w)).$$

Type-III Backward Privacy: A adaptively secure DSSE scheme with corresponding leakage function $\mathcal{L}$ is weakly backward private (or Type-III backward private) iff $\mathcal{L}_\Sigma^{\mathsf{Update}}$ and $\mathcal{L}_\Sigma^{\mathsf{Search}}$ can be written as:

$$\mathcal{L}_\Sigma^{\mathsf{Update}}(t, op, (w, id)) = \mathcal{L}'(op, w),$$
$$\mathcal{L}_\Sigma^{\mathsf{Search}}(t, w) = \mathcal{L}''(\mathsf{sp}(w), \mathsf{TimeDB}(w), \mathsf{Updates}(w), \mathsf{DelHist}(w)).$$

It is obvious that in terms of privacy, a construction achieving Type-I backward privacy is the strongest one, while a construction achieving Type-III is the weakest one. Now assume for two notions of privacy A and B, $A \prec B$ represents A is a weaker notion than B. In other words, a scheme achieving security A leaks more information as compared to a scheme achieving security B. Thus, we can write the following relation with respect to backward privacy:

$$\text{Type-III} \prec \text{Type-II} \prec \text{Type-I}.$$

3.2   Understanding the Leakage from Conjunctive Queries

Having defined the backward privacy of the single keyword DSSE schemes, our target now is to extend the definitions to the general backward privacy notion for conjunctive DSSE schemes. For that, let us consider that at any instance $\mathcal{Q}$ is the list of all queries issued by an adversarial server executing any conjunctive DSSE scheme with a client. The update query is the same as the single-keyword case above. In place of a single keyword search, a search query for the conjunction of keywords $w_1, w_2, \cdots, w_n$ at timestamp t is denoted by (t, q) where $q = w_1 \wedge w_2 \wedge \cdots \wedge w_n$. By convention, we always consider w_1 as the keyword with the least number of updates. Also for a conjunctive query q, we denote $W^q = \{w_1, w_2, \ldots, w_n\}$ as the set of keywords involved in the query. Before defining the formal notion of backward privacy for conjunction, we introduce the following leakage functions. Each of these functions is the most intuitive extension of the leakage functions from single-keyword settings and captures a wide range of leakage components related to conjunctive DSSE schemes, except the SizeC leakage. The SizeC leakage is independent of the other leakage functions and comes into consideration only for conjunctive DSSE schemes.

Search Patterns: We consider the following two notations for search patterns.

(i) $\mathsf{sp}(q)$: This search pattern leaks the repetition on each keyword $w \in q$. Formally, we have:
$$\mathsf{sp}(q) \; = \; \bigcup_{w \in W^q} \mathsf{sp}(w).$$

(ii) $\mathsf{sp}^-(q)$: This restricted search pattern only leaks the search pattern of the previous searches that have the same s-term as q. Formally,
$$\mathsf{sp}^-(q) \; = \; \{t : \exists (t, q') \in \mathcal{Q} \wedge sterm(q') = w_1\}$$

Note that $\mathsf{sp}^-(q)$ leakage is strictly less than $\mathsf{sp}(w_1)$ since it only leaks the timestamps of those search queries whose s-term is w_1. Thus, if there is a search query at some timestamp t' with w_1 as x-term, then $t' \in \mathsf{sp}(w_1)$ but $t' \notin \mathsf{sp}^-(q)$.

Output Leakage: During any conjunctive query q, the output leakage function $\mathsf{TimeDB}(q)$ is defined to be the list of all file identifiers in the conjunction along with the corresponding $\{t_i\}_{i=1}^{n}$ containing insertion timestamps for each keyword in the conjunction. Here, t_i indicates the timestamp when keyword w_i was inserted into the file with identifier id_i.

$$\mathsf{TimeDB}(q) \overset{\Delta}{=} \Big\{ \Big(\{t_i\}_{i=1}^{n} , id \Big) : \forall\, i\, \Big[(t_i, add, (w_i, id)) \in \mathcal{Q} \,\wedge$$
$$\forall\, t' > t_i, (t', del, (w_i, id)) \notin \mathcal{Q} \Big] \Big\}.$$

Note that an adversary only learns the set of all timestamps, but not the exact mapping of keywords to those timestamps. This definition is adapted from [33].

Update Leakage: We consider two types of update leakage components as described below:

(i) $\mathsf{UpdatesC}(q)$: During any conjunctive search query q, $\mathsf{UpdatesC}(q)$ leaks all the timestamps of all the updates involving each searched keyword w_i.

$$\mathsf{UpdatesC}(q) \overset{\Delta}{=} \bigcup_{i=1}^{n} \mathsf{Updates}(w_i).$$

This definition is equivalent to the definition of $\mathsf{Time}(q)$ leakage from [49] and extends the $\mathsf{Updates}(w)$ leakage of the single-keyword case. We believe that $\mathsf{UpdatesC}$ is a more intuitive name for this leakage function as it motivates the trivial extension from the single keyword case.

(ii) $\mathsf{UpdatesC}^{-}(q)$: The leakage function $\mathsf{UpdatesC}^{-}(q)$ reveals (i) the timestamps of all updates associated with the search term w_1, and (ii) all pairs of timestamps corresponding to updates of the *sterm* w_1 and the associated *xterms* that occur in the same file identifier id and involve the same update operation op. To formally define this leakage, let us define the following leakage

$$\mathsf{Updates}(w_1, w_i) = \{(t_1, t_i) \mid \exists(op,\ id) \,:\, (t_1, op, (id, w_1)) \,\wedge\, (t_i, op, (id, w_i)) \in \mathcal{Q}\}.$$

Now we define the $\mathsf{UpdatesC}^{-}(q)$ leakage as follows:

$$\mathsf{UpdatesC}^{-}(q) \overset{\Delta}{=} \mathsf{Updates}(w_1) \cup \left(\bigcup_{i=1}^{n} \mathsf{Updates}(w_1, w_i) \right).$$

It is easy to see that, by definition, $\mathsf{UpdatesC}^{-}(q)$ leaks less than what $\mathsf{UpdatesC}(q)$ leaks.

Deletion Leakage: During any conjunctive search query q, the deletion leakage is captured by the leakage function $\mathsf{DelHistC}(q)$ that leaks the pair of timestamps

(t_i^+, t_i^-) such that there exists some $w_i \in W^q$ such that w_i is inserted to some file at timestamp t_i^+ and later deleted from it at timestamp t_i^-. Formally,

$$\mathsf{DelHistC}(q) \triangleq \Big\{ (t_i^+, t_i^-) : \exists\, w_i, id \text{ such that } (t_i^+, add, (w_i, id)) \in \mathcal{Q} \,\wedge$$

$$(t_i^-, del, (w_i, id)) \in \mathcal{Q} \Big\}.$$

This is a completely new leakage function, a trivial extension to $\mathsf{DelHist}(w)$ leakage of the single keyword case.

Size Leakage: During a conjunctive search query q, a protocol can leak information about the number of matching files for some of the conjunctive sub-queries. Depending on the amount of information leak, we define the following three types of SizeC leakage.

$$\mathsf{SizeC\text{-}I}(q) \triangleq \{ \, |\mathsf{DB}(w_1) \cap \mathsf{DB}(w_j)| \ : \ j \in [2, n]\}$$

where w_1 is the current least frequent search keyword.

Now consider for some $q^* \in \mathcal{Q}$, w^* denotes the corresponding least frequent search keyword. Then we define,

$$\mathsf{SizeC\text{-}II}(q) \triangleq \{|\mathsf{DB}(w^*) \cap \mathsf{DB}(w_j)| \mid \exists q^* \in \mathcal{Q} : w_j \in W^q \cap W^{q^*} \}.$$

Finally, we define the weakest notion for SizeC leakage, which leaks the number of matching files for any possible sub-conjunction.

$$\mathsf{SizeC\text{-}III}(q) \triangleq \{ \, |\mathsf{DB}(w_i) \cap \mathsf{DB}(w_j)| \ : \ i, j \in [2, n] \ \& \ i \neq j\}.$$

These new definitions formalize and generalize the definition of size leakage components provided in [47], which were specific to the SDSSE-CQ and SDSSE-CQ-S constructions.

3.3   New Backward Privacy Notion for Conjunctive DSSE

We now introduce three security notions of backward privacy for conjunctive search queries. It is worth mentioning that the definition is a very intuitive extension of the same notion for single-keyword DSSE and efficiently captures all the leakage components corresponding to any conjunctive DSSE scheme defined to date. As previous $\mathcal{L}'$ and $\mathcal{L}''$ are stateless functions.

C1 (Conjunctive Type-I) Backward Privacy: An adaptively secure DSSE scheme Σ with corresponding leakage function $\mathcal{L}_\Sigma$ is combined insertion time revealing backward private (or C1 backward private) iff $\mathcal{L}_\Sigma^{\mathsf{Update}}$ and $\mathcal{L}_\Sigma^{\mathsf{Search}}$ can be written as:

$$\mathcal{L}_\Sigma^{\mathsf{Update}}(t, op, (w, id)) = \mathcal{L}'(op),$$

$$\mathcal{L}_\Sigma^{\mathsf{Search}}(t, q) = \mathcal{L}''\Big(\mathsf{sp}(q), \mathsf{TimeDB}(q), \sum_{i=1}^{n} c_{w_i}\Big).$$

Here c_{w_i} denotes the number of updates corresponding to keyword w_i. In a nutshell, during any search operation for a query q, the notion C1 leaks the list of all file identifiers matching the conjunction, corresponding insertion times, and the total number of updates across all searched keywords, but not all c_{w_i} individually. Note that, $\mathsf{TimeDB}(q)$ boils down to $\mathsf{TimeDB}(w)$ when $q = w$. Hence, our definition of C1 backward privacy naturally extends the notion of Type-I backward privacy.

C2 (Conjunctive Type-II) Backward Privacy. An adaptively secure DSSE scheme Σ with corresponding leakage function $\mathcal{L}_\Sigma$ is combined update time revealing backward private (or C2 backward private) iff $\mathcal{L}_\Sigma^{\mathsf{Update}}$ and $\mathcal{L}_\Sigma^{\mathsf{Search}}$ can be written as:

$$\mathcal{L}_\Sigma^{\mathsf{Update}}(t, op, (w, id)) = \mathcal{L}'(op),$$
$$\mathcal{L}_\Sigma^{\mathsf{Search}}(t, q) = \mathcal{L}''\big(\mathsf{sp}(q), \mathsf{TimeDB}(q), \mathsf{UpdatesC}(q)\big).$$

Informally, during any search query q, along with the leakage components of C1, C2 additionally leaks the timestamps of all the update operations corresponding to each w_i.

Note that, for $q = w$, $\mathsf{UpdatesC}(q) = \mathsf{Updates}(w)$. Hence, our definition of C2 backward privacy naturally extends the notion of Type-II backward privacy for single-keyword DSSE.

C3 (Conjunctive Type-III) Backward Privacy: An adaptively secure DSSE scheme with corresponding leakage function $\mathcal{L}_\Sigma$ is C3 combined weak backward private iff $\mathcal{L}_\Sigma^{\mathsf{Update}}$ and $\mathcal{L}_\Sigma^{\mathsf{Search}}$ can be written as:

$$\mathcal{L}_\Sigma^{\mathsf{Update}}(t, op, (w, id)) = \mathcal{L}'(op),$$
$$\mathcal{L}_\Sigma^{\mathsf{Search}}(t, q) = \mathcal{L}''\big(\mathsf{sp}(q), \mathsf{TimeDB}(q), \mathsf{UpdatesC}(q), \mathsf{DelHistC}(q)\big).$$

Along with the leakage components corresponding to C2, C3 also leaks the information *which deletion cancels out which addition* for any searched keyword w_i. Since for $q = w$, $\mathsf{DelHistC}(q) = \mathsf{DelHist}(w)$. Hence, our definition of C3 backward privacy naturally extends the notion of Type-III backward privacy.

The above definitions cover all common leakage components for any conjunctive DSSE scheme. However, certain conjunctive DSSE schemes additionally leak information about the number of matching files for some sub-conjunctions. To capture this additional leakage, we define three additional types of SizeC leakage functions in Sect. 3.2, which are independent of the other leakage components. To measure the level of backward privacy for any conjunctive DSSE scheme, we first identify where its leakage profile sits in our new backward privacy notion, and whenever there is any SizeC leakage, we explicitly add the corresponding level of SizeC leakage to the common backward privacy guarantee. For example, if some conjunctive DSSE scheme Σ guarantees C2 backward privacy and its size leakage is subsumed by SizeC-II, then we say Σ is C1-II backward private.

Next, we introduce another notion of backward privacy, which is particularly relevant for OXT based constructions. This notion is a similar but slightly stronger variant of C2 backward privacy as described below:

C2⁻ (Conjunctive Strong Type-II) Backward Privacy: This notion is close to C2 backward privacy; however, it has a reduced search pattern and update leakage components. To be precise, for a conjunctive query q, the search pattern only leaks the search pattern of the previous searches that have the same s-term as q, and the update function leaks (i) all the update operations corresponding to the s-term, and (ii) a restricted number of update operations corresponding to the x-terms. Formally, an adaptively secure DSSE scheme Σ with corresponding leakage function $\mathcal{L}_\Sigma$ is combined update time revealing backward private (or strong C2 backward private) iff $\mathcal{L}_\Sigma^{\mathsf{Update}}$ and $\mathcal{L}_\Sigma^{\mathsf{Search}}$ can be written as:

$$\mathcal{L}_\Sigma^{\mathsf{Update}}(t, op, (w, id)) = \mathcal{L}'(op),$$
$$\mathcal{L}_\Sigma^{\mathsf{Search}}(t, q) = \mathcal{L}''\left(\mathsf{sp}^-(q), \mathsf{TimeDB}(q), \mathsf{UpdatesC}^-(q)\right).$$

Note that, for $q = w$, $\mathsf{sp}^-(q) = \mathsf{sp}(w)$, $\mathsf{UpdatesC}^-(q) = \mathsf{Updates}(w)$, and hence, this notion can also be considered as an extension of the notion of Type-II backward privacy for single-keyword DSSE.

3.4 Analyzing Prior Schemes

It is evident that, for conjunctive DSSE, C1 and C3 represent the strongest and weakest notions of backward privacy, respectively. In other words, we have a privacy *ranking* of the form

$$\mathsf{C3} \prec \mathsf{C2} \prec \mathsf{C2}^- \prec \mathsf{C1}.$$

Analyzing prior conjunctive DSSE schemes with respect to the above notions of backward privacy yields the following observations:

- ODXT [33], achieves C2⁻ backward privacy.
- Both FBDSSE-CQ and SFBDSSE-CQ from [49] achieve C2 backward privacy.
- SDSSE-CQ and SDSSE-CQ-S from [47] achieve C2-II and C2-I backward privacy, respectively.

Overall, ODXT satisfies the strongest notion of backward privacy. This motivates us to build a *conjunctive* DSSE scheme that simultaneously achieves forward privacy (unlike ODXT) and a notion of backward privacy that is similar to ODXT (i.e., stronger than the notions of backward privacy achieved by FBDSSE-CQ, SFBDSSE-CQ, SDSSE-CQ, and SDSSE-CQ-S).

4 A Framework for Forward and Strongly Backward Private Conjunctive DSSE

In this section, we present fp-GA-ODXT – a new framework for designing conjunctive DSSE schemes that simultaneously achieve forward privacy and a notion of backward privacy that is similar to ODXT. Our framework is based on effective group actions and injective trapdoor functions.

Algorithm 1 : GA-ODXT.Update $(op, (w, id))$

1: **function** CLIENT
2:      $\mathsf{addr} \leftarrow F(K_T, w\|c_w\|0)$
3:      $\mathsf{val} \leftarrow F(K_T, w\|c_w\|1) \oplus id\|op$
4:      $\alpha \leftarrow F_G(K_Y, id\|op) \cdot (F_G(K_Z, w\|c_w))^{-1}$
5:      $\mathsf{xtag} \leftarrow (F_G(K_X, w) \cdot F_G(K_Y, id\|op)) \star u$
6:      Send $(\mathsf{addr}, \mathsf{val}, \alpha, \mathsf{xtag})$ to Server

1: **function** SERVER
2:      $\mathsf{TSet}[\mathsf{addr}] = (\mathsf{val}, \alpha)$
3:      $\mathsf{XSet}[\mathsf{xtag}] = 1$

4.1 GA-ODXT: An Adaptation of ODXT to Group Actions

We first adapt the construction ODXT to the group action setting. Note that ODXT is based on $\mathbb{G}$, a cyclic group of prime order p, a generator g where the DDH assumption holds. Here we consider the group action adaptation of ODXT, dubbed GA-ODXT, that works on an EGA $(G, U, \star)$ as defined in Sect. 2.2. We consider $|G| = |U| = O(2^\lambda)$, where λ is the security parameter. Let u be an element uniformly sampled from the set U. We assume u to be public. The construction is built on two PRFs $F : \{0,1\}^\lambda \times \{0,1\}^* \to \{0,1\}^\lambda$ and $F_G : \{0,1\}^\lambda \times \{0,1\}^* \to G$. One may wonder if there exists such a PRF F_G with the above-mentioned domain and range. In practice, one can always construct F_G by simply taking the output of the PRF F and hashing it into the group G. This is possible because of its dense representation. To keep things simple, we leave out these technical details. The construction is based on the GA-DDH assumption (Definition 2). The update and search operations of the GA-ODXT construction are described in Algorithm 1 and 2, respectively.

4.2 Issues with Forward Privacy in GA-ODXT

Similar to ODXT, GA-ODXT is not forward private. Intuitively, failing to provide forward privacy means that the series of computations does not guarantee that the search operation cannot link to any future update operation on the x-terms of that search. Let us consider the following example that depicts that GA-ODXT does not preserve forward privacy. Consider a database where the keyword w_1 is present in the file id_1, and the keyword w_2 is present in the files id_2 and id_3, but not in id_1. Suppose the client performs a search operation $w_1 \wedge w_2$, where w_1 is the least frequent keyword, i.e., the s-term. Of course, the search result will return an empty set. However, during this search operation, the server gets to learn

$$\mathsf{xtag} = (F_G(K_X, w) \cdot F_G(K_Y, id\|op)) \star u \ ,$$

which is currently not a valid one. Later, at some point, if w_2 is added to the file id_1, then during the update operation, the client will generate the same xtag and send it to the server. Upon receiving this xtag from the client, the server

---

Algorithm 2 : GA-ODXT.Search $(w_1 \wedge w_2 \wedge \cdots \wedge w_n)$

1: **function** CLIENT (ROUND 1)
2:     **for** $c = 1, 2, \ldots, c_{w_1}$ **do**
3:         $\mathsf{saddr}_c \leftarrow F(K_T, w\|c\|0)$
4:         **for** $i = 2, 3, \ldots, n$ **do**
5:             $\mathsf{xtoken}_{i,c} \leftarrow (F_G(K_X, w_i) \cdot F_G(K_Z, w\|c)) \star u$
6:     Send $(\{\mathsf{saddr}_c\}_{c=1}^{c_{w_1}}, \ \{\{\mathsf{xtoken}_{i,c}\}_{i=2}^{n}\}_{c=1}^{c_{w_1}})$ to Server

7: **function** SERVER
8:     **for** $c = 1, 2, \ldots, c_{w_1}$ **do**
9:         $\mathsf{cnt}_c \leftarrow 1$
10:        $(\mathsf{val}_c, \alpha_c) \leftarrow \mathsf{TSet}[\mathsf{saddr}_c]$
11:        **for** $i = 2, 3, \ldots, n$ **do**
12:            $\mathsf{xtag}_{i,c} = \alpha_c \star \mathsf{xtoken}_{i,c}$
13:            **if** $\mathsf{XSet}[\mathsf{xtag}_{i,c}] = 1$ **then**
14:                $\mathsf{cnt}_c \leftarrow \mathsf{cnt}_c + 1$
15:    Send $(\{c, \mathsf{val}_c, \mathsf{cnt}_c\}_{c=1}^{c_{w_1}})$ to Client

16: **function** CLIENT (ROUND 2)
17:     **for** $c = 1, 2, \ldots, c_{w_1}$ **do**
18:        $(id_c, op) \leftarrow F(K_T, w_1\|c\|1) \oplus \mathsf{val}_c$
19:        **if** $op = add \wedge \mathsf{cnt}_c = n$ **then** Res $\leftarrow$ Res $\cup \{id_c\}$
20:        **else** Res $\leftarrow$ Res $\setminus \{id_c\}$
21:     Output Res

---

can check that this has already been computed in a previous search operation. Hence, it can deduce the information that *"the keyword that is updated in a file was a part of the previous conjunctive search operation"*, which is not expected in a forward private DSSE scheme. The core problem for this attack lies in the fact that the xtag values do not depend on the update operation's timestamp of occurrence. In other words, what we expect is that the server should not be able to recompute a valid xtag until the client has previously computed that during some update.

A Naïve Solution. It is clear from the above discussion that we need to consider the update counter or update timestamp while generating xtag values during updates. A naive approach to do so would be to add the current update count c_w of the keyword w in the $xtag$ values as follows:

$$\mathsf{xtag} \leftarrow (F_G(K_X, w\|c_w) \cdot F_G(K_Y, id\|op)) \star u.$$

Consequently, we would require the generation of xtoken to be modified as:

$$\mathsf{xtoken}_{i,c} \leftarrow (F_G(K_X, w_i\|c_i) \cdot F_G(K_Z, w_1\|c)) \star u, \ \forall \ c_i \in [c_{w_i}], \ c \in [c_{w_1}].$$

This should solve the forward privacy issue as the xtag values corresponding to a keyword now depend on the update count of the keyword. So, for the server reconstruction of xtag value, it now largely depends on whether the update has occurred before the search or not. However, this doesn't come for free - as evident from the above modification, the client now needs to send c_{w_i} many xtoken values for each x-term w_i and each update on s-term w_1. This essentially amplifies the client-side search communication cost to $O\big(c_{w_1} \cdot \sum_{i=2}^{n} c_{w_i}\big)$, which is identical to the cost of performing a single keyword query for each keyword in the conjunction.

4.3   The fp-GA-ODXT Framework

The above discussion motivates us to extend GA-ODXT to achieve forward privacy without increasing the overhead of the client computation and communication. To be specific, our primary target is to include the current update count for any keyword during updates to that keyword, but do so in a feasible, practical way. That is, we want the client-side computational cost not to blow up during conjunctive search queries as a result of the modification to the update. We generically address this problem and consider a function f_{ow} that satisfies the following properties.

(i) For each keyword w, client should be able to efficiently compute $f_{ow}(w, \cdot)$
(ii) For each keyword w, the server should be able to efficiently compute $f_{ow}(w, c)$ from the knowledge of $f_{ow}(w, c + 1)$. That is, backward computation should be easy for the server.
(iii) For each keyword w, the server should not be able to efficiently compute $f_{ow}(w, c + 1)$ from $f_{ow}(w, c)$, i.e., forward computation should be hard for the server.

Now, given such a function, we define the cross tag during an update operation as follows:

$$\mathsf{xtag} \leftarrow \big(F_G(K_X, w) \cdot F_G(K_Y, id\|op) \cdot f_{ow}(w, j)\big) \star u\,,$$

where j is the number of update on the keyword w. Now, during the conjunctive search for $(w_1 \wedge w_2 \wedge \cdots \wedge w_n)$, the xtoken values corresponding to x-term w_i are computed as:

$$\mathsf{xtoken}_{i,c} \leftarrow F_G(K_X, w_i) \cdot F_G(K_Z, w_1\|c) \star u\,,$$

where $i \in \{2, 3, \ldots, n\}$ and $c \in [c_{w_1}]$. The server computes all the possible xtag values as:

$$(\alpha_c \cdot f_{ow}(w_i, c)) \star \mathsf{xtoken}_{i,c}\,,$$

for each $i \in \{2, 3, \ldots, n\}$ and $c \in [c_{w_i}]$ and checks whether any of these reconstructed values are valid or not. This is easy for the server with the knowledge of $\mathsf{xtoken}_{i,c}$ and previously stored α_c values. Note that property (P1) and (P2) of f_{ow} ensures that the server can compute all of $f_{ow}(w_i, c_{w_i}), f_{ow}(w_i, c_{w_i} - 1), \ldots, f_{ow}(w_i, 1)$ from the knowledge of $f_{ow}(w_i, c_{w_i})$. However, since the server can not compute $f_{ow}(w_i, c_{w_i} + \ell)$ from $f_{ow}(w_i, c_{w_i})$ for any $i \in \{2, 3, \ldots, n\}$ and

---

Algorithm 3 : fp-GA-ODXT.Update $(op, (w, id))$

1: **function** CLIENT
2:     $\mathsf{addr} \leftarrow F(K_T, w\|c_w\|0)$
3:     $\mathsf{val} \leftarrow F(K_T, w\|c_w\|1) \oplus id\|op$
4:     $\alpha \leftarrow F_G(K_Y, id\|op) \cdot F_G(K_Z, w\|c_w)^{-1}$
5:     $\mathsf{xtag} \leftarrow (F_G(K_X, w) \cdot F_G(K_Y, id\|op) \cdot \mathsf{f_{ow}}(w, c_w)) \star u$
6:     Send $(\mathsf{addr}, \mathsf{val}, \alpha, \mathsf{xtag})$ to Server

1: **function** SERVER
2:     $\mathsf{TSet}[\mathsf{addr}] \leftarrow (\mathsf{val}, \alpha)$
3:     $\mathsf{XSet}[\mathsf{xtag}] \leftarrow 1$

$\ell \geq 1$, by property (P3), it fails to link this search operation to any future update operation on w_i. Now, let us see the correctness of the construction. Suppose the keyword w_1 and w_i were added to the identifier id at their c^{th} and j^{th} update operation, respectively. Then, during the search operation, the server computes the jth xtag corresponding to w_i as:

$$
\begin{aligned}
\mathsf{xtag}'_{i,j} &= (\alpha_c \cdot \mathsf{f_{ow}}(w_i, j)) \star \mathsf{xtoken}_{i,c} \\
&= ((F_G(K_Y, id\|op) \cdot F_G(K_Z, w_1\|c)^{-1}) \cdot \mathsf{f_{ow}}(w_i, j)) \star \\
&\quad (F_G(K_X, w_i) \cdot F_G(K_Z, w_1\|c) \star u) \\
&= (F_G(K_X, w_i) \cdot F_G(K_Y, id\|op) \cdot \mathsf{f_{ow}}(w_i, j)) \star u.
\end{aligned}
$$

where the last equality follows from the compatibility of the group action.

Improving the Communication Complexity. Next, we observe that during any search operation of the form $(w_1 \wedge \cdots \wedge w_n)$, the client computes and sends c_{w_1} many x-tokens corresponding to each x-term (i.e., w_2 to w_n), essentially making the communication complexity during a search operation $n.c_{w_1}$. So, we investigate whether it is possible to reduce the communication complexity by sending a single x-token for each x-term, along with auxiliary information, so that the remaining x-token generation is delegated to the server. We answer this affirmatively by using the concept of s-tokens that essentially helps the server to generate x-token $\mathsf{xtoken}_{i,j}$ from $\mathsf{xtoken}_{i,j-1}$ and stoken_j, for every x-term i and any $j \in [c_{w_1}]$. We present the update and search operations of GA-ODXT in Algorithms 3 and 4, respectively. Note that, in Algorithm 4, the public computation of $\mathsf{f_{ow}}(w_i, j-1)$ from $\mathsf{f_{ow}}(w_i, j)$ is denoted as $\mathsf{f_{ow}}(w_i, j-1) = \phi(\mathsf{f_{ow}}(w_i, j))$.

It is easy to see the client's computation and communication overhead for an update and a search operation for some conjunction of n keywords is $O(1)$ and $O(n + c_{w_1})$, respectively.

4.4   Security of fp-GA-ODXT

The leakage profile of fp-GA-ODXT is given by

$$
\mathcal{L}_{\mathsf{fp\text{-}GA\text{-}ODXT}} = \left(\mathcal{L}^{\mathsf{Setup}}_{\mathsf{fp\text{-}GA\text{-}ODXT}}, \mathcal{L}^{\mathsf{Update}}_{\mathsf{fp\text{-}GA\text{-}ODXT}}, \mathcal{L}^{\mathsf{Search}}_{\mathsf{fp\text{-}GA\text{-}ODXT}} \right),
$$

Algorithm 4 : fp-GA-ODXT.Search $(w_1 \wedge w_2 \wedge \cdots \wedge w_n)$

1: **function** CLIENT (ROUND 1)
2:     **for** $c = c_{w_1}, (c_{w_1} - 1), \ldots, 1$ **do**
3:         $\mathsf{saddr}_c \leftarrow F(K_T, w_1 \| c \| 0)$
4:         $\mathsf{stoken}_c \leftarrow F_G(K_Z, w_1 \| c)^{-1} \cdot F_G(K_Z, w_1 \| c - 1)$

5:     **for** $i = 2, 3, \ldots, n$ **do**
6:         $\mathsf{xtoken}_{i, c_{w_i}} \leftarrow (F_G(K_X, w_i) \cdot F_G(K_Z, w_1 \| c_{w_1})) \star u$

7:     Send $\left(\{\mathsf{saddr}_c\}_{c=1}^{c_{w_1}}, \left\{\mathsf{xtoken}_{i, c_{w_i}}\right\}_{i=2}^{n}, \{\mathsf{stoken}_i\}_{i=1}^{c_{w_1}}, \{\mathsf{f}_{\mathsf{ow}}(w_i, c_{w_i})\}_{i=2}^{n} \right)$ to Server

1: **function** SERVER
2:     **for** $c = c_{w_1}, (c_{w_1} - 1), \ldots, 1$ **do**
3:         $\mathsf{cnt}_c \leftarrow 1$
4:         $(\mathsf{val}_c, \alpha_c) \leftarrow \mathsf{TSet}[\mathsf{saddr}_c]$
5:         **for** $i = 2, 3, \ldots, n$ **do**
6:             **for** $j = c_{w_i}, (c_{w_i} - 1), \ldots, 1$ **do**
7:                 $\mathsf{xtag}' = (\alpha_c \cdot \mathsf{f}_{\mathsf{ow}}(w_i, j)) \star \mathsf{xtoken}_{i, c}$
8:                 **if** $\mathsf{XSet}[\mathsf{xtag}'] = 1$ **then**
9:                     $\mathsf{cnt}_c \leftarrow \mathsf{cnt}_c + 1$
10:                    **break**
11:                $\mathsf{f}_{\mathsf{ow}}(w_i, j - 1) \leftarrow \phi(\mathsf{f}_{\mathsf{ow}}(w_i, j))$
12:            $\mathsf{xtoken}_{i, c-1} \leftarrow (\mathsf{stoken}_c) \star \mathsf{xtoken}_{i, c}$
13:    Send $\left(\{c, \mathsf{val}_c, \mathsf{cnt}_c\}_{c=1}^{c_{w_1}} \right)$ to Client

1: **function** CLIENT (ROUND 2)
2:     **for** $c = 1, 2, \ldots, c_{w_1}$ **do**
3:         $id_c \| op \leftarrow F(K_T, w \| c \| 1) \oplus \mathsf{val}_c$
4:         **if** $op = add \wedge \mathsf{cnt}_c = n$ **then** $\mathsf{Res} \leftarrow \mathsf{Res} \cup \{id_c\}$
5:         **else** $\mathsf{Res} \leftarrow \mathsf{Res} \setminus \{id_c\}$
6:     Output Res

---

where each leakage is described below.

$$\mathcal{L}^{\mathsf{Setup}}_{\mathsf{fp\text{-}GA\text{-}ODXT}}(\mathcal{Q}) = \mathcal{L}^{\mathsf{Update}}_{\mathsf{fp\text{-}GA\text{-}ODXT}}(\mathcal{Q}) = \emptyset,$$

$$\mathcal{L}^{\mathsf{Search}}_{\mathsf{fp\text{-}GA\text{-}ODXT}}(\mathcal{Q}) = \left(\mathsf{sp}^-(q), \mathsf{TimeDB}(q), \mathsf{Updates}^-(q)\right).$$

Observe that the leakage profile defined above satisfies the definition of $C2^-$-backward privacy from Sect. 3. We now state the main security theorem for fp-GA-ODXT.

Theorem 1. *Let F and F_G be two independent secure PRFs, and let f_{ow} be a one-way trapdoor function. Then, our proposed construction fp-GA-ODXT is adaptively secure, forward private, and $C2^-$ backward private for the leakage function $\mathcal{L}_{\text{fp-GA-ODXT}}$:*

$$|\Pr[\text{fp-GA-ODXT}_{\mathcal{A}}(\lambda) = 1] - \Pr[\mathsf{Ideal}_{\mathcal{A}, \mathcal{S}}(\lambda) = 1]|$$

$$\leq 4 \cdot \mathbf{Adv}^{\mathrm{PRF}}_{F_G, \mathcal{B}_1}(\lambda) + 2 \cdot \mathbf{Adv}^{\mathrm{PRF}}_{F, \mathcal{B}_2}(\lambda) + \mathbf{Adv}^{\mathrm{GA\text{-}DDH}}_{\mathcal{B}_3}(\lambda) + \frac{6poly(\lambda)}{2^{\lambda-1}}.$$

We defer the detailed proof of this theorem to the full version of the paper.

5   Concrete Instantiations of fp-GA-ODXT

This section provides two concrete instantiations of fp-GA-ODXT. The first, classical instantiation is a close variant of ODXT that makes minimal changes to ODXT to guarantee forward-privacy. Similar to ODXT, this instantiation of fp-GA-ODXT is based on the DDH assumption, with some additional techniques based on RSA groups. Next, we provide an instantiation of fp-GA-ODXT based on a combination of lattices and isogenies of elliptic curves that can be conjectured to be post-quantum secure. To our knowledge, this yields the first plausibly post-quantum conjunctive DSSE scheme.

5.1   Classical Instantiation from DDH and RSA

We choose a large prime p and work on $\mathbb{G}$, a cyclic group of order p where the DDH problem is assumed to be hard. INSTANTIATION OF f_{ow}: We instantiate f_{ow} using a trapdoor one-way permutation Π and a PRF F as follows:

$$f_{ow}(w, i) :- \Pi_{\mathsf{PK}}^{(\ell-j)}(F_K(w)),$$

where ℓ is the parameter that denotes the maximum number of updates on any keyword. We use the RSA one-way trapdoor permutation, a popular choice for instantiating the trapdoor one-way permutation. Let p and q be two large primes of the same size and $N = pq$. We choose (e, d) such that $ed = 1 \mod \phi(N)$, and define (N, e) to be the public key and (N, d) to be the trapdoor. Define the trapdoor one-way permutation as follows:

$$\Pi_{\mathsf{PK}}(x) = x^e \mod N, \quad \Pi_{\mathsf{SK}}^{-1}(x) = x^d \mod N.$$

Since, Π is a permutation, it holds that for all x, $\Pi_{\mathsf{PK}}(x) = \Pi_{\mathsf{SK}}^{-1}(x)$. Now it is easy to see that all three desired properties of f_{ow} hold:

- For each keyword, the client can efficiently compute $f_{ow}(w, i) :=$ $\Pi_{\mathsf{PK}}^{(\ell-j)}(F_K(w))$.
- For each keyword w, the server can compute $f_{ow}(w, i-1)$ from the knowledge of $f_{ow}(w, i)$ by simply applying Π_{PK}:

$$f_{ow}(w, i-1) := \Pi_{\mathsf{PK}}(f_{ow}(w, i)).$$

- For each keyword w, it is difficult for the server to efficiently compute $f_{ow}(w, i+1)$ from $f_{ow}(w, i)$, as computing $\Pi_{\mathsf{PK}}^{(\ell-i-1)}(F_K(w))$ from $\Pi_{\mathsf{PK}}^{(\ell-i)}(F_K(w))$ is essentially computing Π_{SK}^{-1} on $\Pi_{\mathsf{PK}}^{(\ell-i-1)}(F_K(w))$, which is difficult.

Thus, the above instantiation satisfies all of the desired properties of f_{ow}, while relying on the hardness of the RSA one-way trapdoor permutations.

5.2   Post-quantum Instantiation from Lattices and Isogenies

We present a second, post-quantum instantiation of our fp-GA-ODXT framework based on the (worst-case) hardness of lattice problems *and* the (average-case) hardness of computing isogeny maps between supersingular elliptic curves.

ISOGENY BASED INSTANTIATION OF EFFECTIVE GROUP ACTION: The group action layer of our framework fp-GA-ODXT can be instantiated using *any* effective group action instance satisfying the GA-DDH assumption 2. As noted in [3], the GA-DDH assumption plausibly holds over the group-action implied by isogenies of supersingular "oriented" elliptic curves over F_p. This group action underlies CSIDH [13] and several of its follow-ups, such as CSI-FiSh [4], Scallop [20], and PEGASIS [18].

The only known cryptanalytic studies of GA-DDH over any of these group action instances follow from cryptanalytic studies of CSIDH and its variants. Such studies suggest that using the same set of parameters as CSIDH-2048 would allow our GA-DDH-based instantiation of fp-GA-ODXT to achieve the same level of security as NIST's level-1 security for post-quantum standards/candidates for key-encapsulation and digital signatures.

Remark. We remark here that the recent attacks on SIKE/SIDH [12,31,37] do not impact our proposed instantiation of fp-GA-ODXT. This is because SIKE and SIDH are based on an entirely different family of isogenies of supersingular "non-oriented" elliptic curves over F_{p^2}, which do not yield effective group actions. The aforementioned attacks on SIDH/SIKE *do not* impact the hardness of GA-DDH over isogenies of supersingular "oriented" elliptic curves over F_p, which CSIDH and its variants are based on.

SISBASED INSTANTIATION OF f_{ow}: Let $m, n, N, \beta \in \mathbb{N}$ be parameters such that $\ell = \lceil \log_\beta N \rceil$, $m = n\ell$. If $N < \beta^\ell$, we write $N = \sum_{i \in [0, \ell-1]} N_i \cdot \beta^i$ in the β-ary expansion. If $N = \beta^\ell$, we write $N_0 = \ldots = N_{\ell-2} = 0$ and $N_{\ell-1} = \beta$. For any matrix $\mathbf{A} \in \mathbb{Z}_N^{n \times m}$, we define the function $\mathsf{SIS}_{\mathbf{A},\beta} : \mathbb{Z}_N^n \to \mathbb{Z}_\beta^m$ that takes as input a vector $\mathbf{v} \in \mathbb{Z}_N^n$ and outputs a vector $\mathbf{z} \in \mathbb{Z}_\beta^m$ such that

$$\mathbf{A}\mathbf{z} = \mathbf{v} \ (mod \ N).$$

Now recall from Sect. 4.3 and Theorem 1 that for correctness and security of our framework, we require the following properties from f_{ow} and f_{ow}^{-1}:

(a) f_{ow} has the same input and output space,
(b) f_{ow} is hard to compute publicly, but is efficiently computable given a trapdoor.
(c) f_{ow}^{-1} is publicly and efficiently computable, and
(d) f_{ow} and f_{ow}^{-1} are universal.

So, the natural starting point for a SIS-based realization of f_{ow} is the function $\mathsf{SIS}_{\mathbf{A},\beta}$ for an appropriate choice of parameters (m, n, N, β) for SIS hardness. The corresponding inverse function then becomes

$$\mathsf{SIS}^{-1}_{\mathbf{A},\beta}(\mathbf{z}) = \mathbf{A}\mathbf{z} \; (mod \; N).$$

For this choice of f_{ow}, property (b) follows from SIS-hardness and the availability of SIS trapdoors, (c) follows from inspection, and (d) holds by the leftover hash lemma [25]. But the problem remains with property (a). For this purpose, we define the generalized gadget vector $\mathbf{g}$ and the generalized gadget matrix $\mathbf{G}$ as follows:

$$\mathbf{g}^{\mathrm{T}} = \begin{pmatrix} 1 & \beta & \cdots & \beta^{\ell} \end{pmatrix}, \quad \mathbf{G} = \mathbf{I}_n \otimes \mathbf{g}^{\mathrm{T}},$$

where $\mathbf{I}_n$ is the identity matrix of dimension n and $\otimes$ denotes the matrix-vector tensor operator. We additionally define the operator $\mathbf{G}^{-1} : \mathbb{Z}_N^n \to \mathbb{Z}_\beta^m$ as the β-ary expansion operator that maps any vector $\mathbf{v} \in \mathbf{Z}_N^n$ to the concatenation of the β-ary representation of its components, i.e.

$$\mathbf{G}^{-1}\left(\mathbf{v} = (v_1, \ldots, v_n)\right) = \left((v_{1,i})_{i \in [0,\ell-1]}, \ldots, (v_{n,i})_{i \in [0,\ell-1]}\right),$$

such that for each $j \in [1,n]$, $v_j = \sum_{i \in [0,\ell-1]} v_{j,i} \cdot \beta^i$. Note that $\mathbf{G}^{-1}$ is efficiently computable. Now, we define the functions $h_{\mathbf{A},\beta} : \mathbb{Z}_N^n \to \mathbb{Z}_N^n$ and $h^{-1}_{\mathbf{A},\beta} : \mathbb{Z}_N^n \to \mathbb{Z}_N^n$ as follows:

$$h_{\mathbf{A},\beta} = \mathbf{G} \cdot \mathsf{SIS}_{\mathbf{A},\beta}, \quad h^{-1}_{\mathbf{A},\beta} = \mathbf{A}\mathbf{G}^{-1}.$$

With these definitions in hand, we observe that:

- For any $\mathbf{v} \in \mathbb{Z}_N^n$, we have

$$h^{-1}_{\mathbf{A},\beta}\left(h_{\mathbf{A},\beta}(\mathbf{v})\right) = \mathbf{v}.$$

- For any $\mathbf{v} \in \mathbb{Z}_N^n$, $h^{-1}_{\mathbf{A},\beta}(\mathbf{v})$ is publicly and efficiently computable.
- Given only $\mathbf{A}$, computing $h_{\mathbf{A},\beta}(\mathbf{v})$ is computationally hard assuming the hardness of the SIS problem for parameters (m, n, N, β).
- Given a SIS trapdoor for $\mathbf{A}$ [32], one can efficiently compute $h_{\mathbf{A},\beta}(\mathbf{v})$ for any (pseudo)random $\mathbf{v} \in \mathbb{Z}_N^n$ (by the leftover hash lemma [25]).

Now we will describe our concrete SIS based instantiation of f_{ow}. For this purpose, let us first $F : \mathcal{K} \times \{0,1\}^* \to \mathbb{Z}_N^n$ be a PRF family, and let $K \in \mathcal{K}$ be a PRF key. We note that such a PRF can be easily instantiated in practice. Now, for any keyword w, we set $\mathsf{f}_{\mathsf{ow}}(w,0) = F(K,w)$ and for each $i \geq 1$, we set

$$\mathsf{f}_{\mathsf{ow}}(w, i+1) = \mathbf{G}(\mathsf{SIS}_{\mathbf{A},\beta}(\mathbf{v})) = h_{\mathbf{A},\beta}(\mathsf{f}_{\mathsf{ow}}(w,i)).$$

With this definition of f_{ow}, property (a) follows immediately. Moreover, since $\mathbf{G}$ and $\mathbf{G}^{-1}$ are both bijective operators and efficiently computable, the properties (b), (c), and (d) remain unaffected.

Formally, we have the following:

- Given a SIS trapdoor for $\mathbf{A}$ (stored privately by the client), the client can compute $\mathsf{f}_{\mathsf{ow}}(w, i+1) = h_{\mathbf{A},\beta}(\mathsf{f}_{\mathsf{ow}}(w,i))$ for any keyword w.

- The server can compute $f_{ow}(w, i) = h_{\mathbf{A},\beta}^{-1}(f_{ow}(w, i+1))$ publicly and efficiently.
- Given only $\mathbf{A}$, it is computationally hard for the server to compute $f_{ow}(w, i+1)$ given $f_{ow}(w, i)$.

Thus, the above instantiation satisfies all of the desired properties of f_{ow}, while relying on the post-quantum hardness of the SIS problem. Putting this together with known isogeny-based instantiations of GA-DDH-hard effective group actions [4,13,20] yields a post-quantum instantiation of fp-GA-ODXT.

Parameter Choices: The above construction can be instantiated in practice using any state-of-the-art implementation of isogeny-based group actions, such as CSIDH-512/1024 [13], or variants of CSIDH such as CSI-FiSh [4] and Scallop [20]. For the lattice-based implementation of f_{ow}, one would typically set parameters $n = 1024$, a suitable prime q (e.g., $q = 3329$ as in ML-KEM [1,5]), $m > 3n \log q$ for the leftover hash lemma [25] to hold, and β is set to an arbitrary (small) constant. The parameters n, N, and β (where N is the same as the prime q) are determined by standard choices for SIS-hardness [2,29,30,34,35]. The parameter m needs to simultaneously satisfy the hardness of SIS and the leftover hash lemma [25]. From [36], the above-mentioned condition on m satisfies both requirements simultaneously.

INTERACTION BETWEEN GROUP ACTIONS AND SIS-BASED OWF: In Algorithms 3 and 4, the interfacing between the effective group action and f_{ow} requires that the output space of f_{ow} is the same as the group $\mathcal{G}$. Note that: For an instantiation of effective group action based on CSIDH-2048, the group $\mathcal{G}$ is isomorphic to $\mathbb{Z}_M$ for a 1024-bit prime M. On the other hand, the input and output spaces of the SIS-based instantiation of f_{ow} are $\mathbb{Z}_N^n$, where n is the dimension parameter for LWE and N is the underlying prime. For $N = 3329$ and $n = 1024$ (which gives us the desired SIS hardness), $\mathbb{Z}_N^n$ is (almost) isomorphic to $\mathbb{Z}_L$ for 1035-bit L. For aligning these two spaces, we need a universal and collision-resistant encoding map from $\mathbb{Z}_M$ to $\mathbb{Z}_L$. This can be instantiated in practice using, say, SHA-512 (modeled as a universal and collision-resistant hash function). Since Algorithms 3 and 4 never use the reverse decoding from the group $\mathcal{G}$ to the output space of f_{ow}, we do not actually require a corresponding decoding function.

6   Implementation and Performance Evaluation

We implement the classical instantiation of the fp-GA-ODXT based on DDH and RSA from Sect. 5.1, and compare its performance with state-of-the-art conjunctive DSSE schemes: ODXT, SDSSE-CQ, and SDSSE-CQ-S. To ensure a fair comparison, we follow an experimental setup similar to that used in [47]. We choose a synthetic dataset with 1 *million* documents. To ensure reliable results, we performed each operation 100 times and reported the average to eliminate any outlier effects. In the update phase, each document has been considered at least once with no faulty updates[1].

---

[1] faulty updates mean adding a keyword to a file which already contains it or deleting a keyword from a file which does not contain it.

Table 2. Client-side update communication cost for each keyword-identifier pair (in bytes)

Operation Type	fp-GA-ODXT	SDSSE-CQ	SDSSE-CQ-S	ODXT
Addition	192	2 Aura update *id* size 116 & 64	2 Aura update *id* size 116 & 68	192
Deletion	192	0	0	192

Table 3. Client-side update time per keyword-identifier pair (in milliseconds)

# of Updates	fp-GA-ODXT	SDSSE-CQ	SDSSE-CQ-S	ODXT
1000	0.57	0.81	0.83	0.55
10000	0.58	0.68	0.74	0.43
100000	0.58	0.77	0.77	0.49
1000000	0.55	0.86	0.91	0.50

We compare the performance of our proposed framework fp-GA-ODXT with ODXT, SDSSE-CQ, and SDSSE-CQ-S across two key aspects: (i) average update time and communication cost, and (ii) average search time and communication cost. Following [47], while calculating the average search time, search queries were performed on two conjunctions only, as queries with more keywords can be parallelized. Here, we summarize our experimental findings. For the system setup, all other detailed descriptions and the justification of the experimental results, please refer to the full version of this paper.

6.1   Average Update Time and Communication Cost

Due to similar design choices, the average update communication cost of our instantiation is almost the same as the ODXT protocol of [33]. Regarding SDSSE-CQ and SDSSE-CQ-S [47], both these schemes additionally use two separate instances of an underlying single-keyword DSSE scheme, as example Aura [40] in our experiments, during any update query. Following the construction of Aura, if the corresponding update operation is *add* then the update communication cost of both these schemes is much higher than ODXT and consequently fp-GA-ODXT. But if the update operation is *del*, then the update communication cost becomes zero. A summary of our findings is presented in Table 2.

Regarding the average update time, our scheme exhibits performance very similar to ODXT, as expected. In contrast, SDSSE-CQ and SDSSE-CQ-S incur higher update times due to the use of advanced cryptographic primitives such as Compressed Symmetric Revocable Encryption (CSRE). Our findings are summarized in Table 3.

Table 4. Client-side search communication cost (in megabytes)

$|DB(w_1)| = 10^3$	fp-GA-ODXT	SDSSE-CQ	SDSSE-CQ-S	ODXT
$w_1 \wedge w_2$	0.112	0.104	0.20	0.080
$w_1 \wedge w_2 \wedge w_3$	0.112	0.188	0.38	0.144
$w_1 \wedge w_2 \wedge w_3 \wedge w_4$	0.112	0.272	0.56	0.208

6.2   Average Search Time and Communication Cost

Recall, search queries in all the schemes under consideration are performed in three stages: the client generates the search tokens and sends them to the server, the server calculates the encrypted search result and sends it back to the client, and finally, the client decrypts the encrypted result set and outputs the final result. Clearly communication overhead for the latter two stages will be almost equivalent for all the schemes. So we will only report the communication overhead for the client while sending the search tokens to the server. Our findings are summarized in Table 4. The table clearly shows that fp-GA-ODXT has the least average search communication overhead among all these schemes. Moreover, as the number of *xterm* in the conjunction increases, the communication cost for ODXT, SDSSE-CQ, and SDSSE-CQ-S increases linearly. Whereas, due to our novel technique of offloading the computational burden from the client to the server, our scheme fp-GA-ODXT has a constant communication overhead across a varying number of *xterm*.

Similar to the communication cost, while reporting the average search time, we only consider the time required for generating the search tokens on the client-side. This is because a server is typically equipped with more powerful hardware resources, and the other client computation, i.e., decrypting encrypted search results, takes almost the same time across all schemes.

We report average search times for two distinct query types, which are also quite familiar in the literature of conjunctive DSSE [33,47]. In the first query type, the frequency of *sterm* is fixed at 10, and the frequency of *xterm* is set to 10, 100, 1000, and 10000. In the second query type, the frequency of *xterm* is fixed at 10000, and the frequency of *sterm* is set to 10, 100, 1000, and 10000. We present the experimental results for the two query types in Table 5 and Table 6, respectively. It is clearly visible that, for the first type of queries, the performance of our scheme is similar to ODXT and SDSSE-CQ and is much better than SDSSE-CQ-S. On the other hand, for the second type of queries, our scheme has a clear advantage over any of the other three schemes. Note that, for SDSSE-CQ and SDSSE-CQ-S, during any conjunction of n keywords, two types of search tokens are generated by the client: (i) search token for the n instances of the underlying single keyword SSE scheme Aura and (ii) search token for checking the conjunction. We only report the time that is required to generate the second type of search tokens, although their performance is not better than ours. Obviously enough, once we additionally consider the time to generate the other type of search tokens, their performances become even worse.

Table 5. Client-side average search time (in milliseconds) for fixed $|DB(w_1)| = 10$

$|DB(w_2)|$	fp-GA-ODXT	SDSSE-CQ	SDSSE-CQ-S	ODXT
10^1	1.525	0.227	0.277	1.548
10^2	1.552	0.207	0.637	1.532
10^3	1.425	0.206	3.763	1.489
10^4	1.52	0.208	32.111	1.541

Table 6. Client-side average search time (in milliseconds) for fixed $|DB(w_2)| = 10000$

$|DB(w_1)|$	fp-GA-ODXT	SDSSE-CQ	SDSSE-CQ-S	ODXT
10^1	1.52	0.208	32.111	1.541
10^2	5.151	2.067	38.724	5.14
10^3	14.481	21.213	58.515	15.219
10^4	108.724	184.809	261.458	115.129

7   Conclusion

In this paper, we addressed the open question of designing a practically efficient, low-leakage, full-fledged forward and backward private conjunctive DSSE scheme with small communication requirements and small client-side overheads. As a first contribution, we introduced the first systematic and rigorous formal notions of backward privacy for conjunctive queries, namely Type C1, C2, and C3, naturally extending the notion of Type-I, Type-II, and Type-III backward privacy for single-keyword DSSE schemes. We additionally defined a backward privacy notion specific to the OXT framework, dubbed $C2^-$, which is similar to but a stronger notion than C2.

Next, as our main contribution, we proposed a new generic conjunctive DSSE framework called fp-GA-ODXT that improves upon both ODXT and SDSSE-CQ-variants by achieving full-fledged forward privacy and strong backward privacy guarantees, while incurring lower client-side computation and smaller communication overheads. We demonstrated and analyzed two instantiations of our fp-GA-ODXT framework:

- A concretely efficient, classically secure instance based on discrete log-hard groups and an RSA-based trapdoor permutation, which we implemented and benchmarked. We implement and benchmark this instantiation, and compare it with both ODXT and SDSSE-CQ/SDSSE-CQ-S [47]. Our experiments demonstrate that we achieve smaller communication overheads and client-side computation for both updates and conjunctive searches as compared to both ODXT and SDSSE-CQ-variants. These come at the cost of an increase in server computation, which we view as a reasonable trade-off, especially in practical scenarios where the SSE client is significantly resource-constrained.

- A post-quantum instantiation based on (worst-case) hardness of lattice problems *and* the (average-case) hardness of computing isogeny maps between supersingular elliptic curves. This solves the longstanding open question of designing asymptotically efficient, forward and backward private conjunctive DSSE schemes with post-quantum security.

We leave it as an interesting open question to extend the fp-GA-ODXT framework to support other query types such as substring/range queries, as well as to support multi-client scenarios.

References

1. Module-lattice-based key-encapsulation mechanism standard. https://doi.org/10.6028/NIST.FIPS.203
2. Ajtai, M.: Generating hard instances of lattice problems (extended abstract). In: 28th ACM STOC, pp. 99–108. ACM Press (1996). https://doi.org/10.1145/237814.237838
3. Alamati, N., De Feo, L., Montgomery, H., Patranabis, S.: Cryptographic group actions and applications. In: Moriai, S., Wang, H. (eds.) ASIACRYPT 2020, Part II. LNCS, vol. 12492, pp. 411–439. Springer, Cham (2020). https://doi.org/10.1007/978-3-030-64834-3_14
4. Beullens, W., Kleinjung, T., Vercauteren, F.: CSI-FiSh: efficient isogeny based signatures through class group computations. In: Galbraith, S.D., Moriai, S. (eds.) ASIACRYPT 2019, Part I. LNCS, vol. 11921, pp. 227–247. Springer, Cham (2019). https://doi.org/10.1007/978-3-030-34578-5_9
5. Bos, J., et al.: Crystals-kyber: a CCA-secure module-lattice-based KEM. In: 2018 IEEE European symposium on security and privacy (EuroS&P), pp. 353–367. IEEE (2018)
6. Bost, R.: $\sum o\varphi o\varsigma$: Forward secure searchable encryption. In: Weippl, E.R., Katzenbeisser, S., Kruegel, C., Myers, A.C., Halevi, S. (eds.) Proceedings of the 2016 ACM SIGSAC Conference on Computer and Communications Security, Vienna, Austria, 24–28 October 2016, pp. 1143–1154. ACM (2016). https://doi.org/10.1145/2976749.2978303
7. Bost, R., Minaud, B., Ohrimenko, O.: Forward and backward private searchable encryption from constrained cryptographic primitives. In: Thuraisingham, B., Evans, D., Malkin, T., Xu, D. (eds.) Proceedings of the 2017 ACM SIGSAC Conference on Computer and Communications Security, CCS 2017, Dallas, TX, USA, 30 October–03 November 2017, pp. 1465–1482. ACM (2017). https://doi.org/10.1145/3133956.3133980
8. Brakerski, Z., Gentry, C., Vaikuntanathan, V.: Fully homomorphic encryption without bootstrapping. Electron. Colloquium Comput. Complex. **TR11-111** (2011). https://eccc.weizmann.ac.il/report/2011/111
9. Cash, D., Grubbs, P., Perry, J., Ristenpart, T.: Leakage-abuse attacks against searchable encryption. In: Ray, I., Li, N., Kruegel, C. (eds.) Proceedings of the 22nd ACM SIGSAC Conference on Computer and Communications Security, Denver, CO, USA, 12–16 October 2015, pp. 668–679. ACM (2015). https://doi.org/10.1145/2810103.2813700

10. Cash, D., et al.: Dynamic searchable encryption in very-large databases: data structures and implementation. In: 21st Annual Network and Distributed System Security Symposium, NDSS 2014, San Diego, California, USA, 23–26 February 2014. The Internet Society (2014)
11. Cash, D., Jarecki, S., Jutla, C., Krawczyk, H., Roşu, M.-C., Steiner, M.: Highly-scalable searchable symmetric encryption with support for Boolean queries. In: Canetti, R., Garay, J.A. (eds.) CRYPTO 2013, Part I. LNCS, vol. 8042, pp. 353–373. Springer, Heidelberg (2013). https://doi.org/10.1007/978-3-642-40041-4_20
12. Castryck, W., Decru, T.: An efficient key recovery attack on SIDH. In: Hazay, C., Stam, M. (eds) EUROCRYPT 2023. LNCS, vol. 14008, pp. 423–447. Springer, Cham (2023). https://doi.org/10.1007/978-3-031-30589-4_15
13. Castryck, W., Lange, T., Martindale, C., Panny, L., Renes, J.: CSIDH: an efficient post-quantum commutative group action. In: Peyrin, T., Galbraith, S. (eds.) ASIACRYPT 2018, Part III. LNCS, vol. 11274, pp. 395–427. Springer, Cham (2018). https://doi.org/10.1007/978-3-030-03332-3_15
14. Chamani, J.G., Papadopoulos, D., Papamanthou, C., Jalili, R.: New constructions for forward and backward private symmetric searchable encryption. In: Lie, D., Mannan, M., Backes, M., Wang, X. (eds.) Proceedings of the 2018 ACM SIGSAC Conference on Computer and Communications Security, CCS 2018, Toronto, ON, Canada, 15–19 October 2018, pp. 1038–1055. ACM (2018). https://doi.org/10.1145/3243734.3243833
15. Chang, Y.-C., Mitzenmacher, M.: Privacy preserving keyword searches on remote encrypted data. In: Ioannidis, J., Keromytis, A., Yung, M. (eds.) ACNS 2005. LNCS, vol. 3531, pp. 442–455. Springer, Heidelberg (2005). https://doi.org/10.1007/11496137_30
16. Chatterjee, S., Puria, S.K.P., Shah, A.: Efficient backward private searchable encryption. J. Comput. Secur. **28**(2), 229–267 (2020). https://doi.org/10.3233/JCS-191322
17. Curtmola, R., Garay, J.A., Kamara, S., Ostrovsky, R.: Searchable symmetric encryption: improved definitions and efficient constructions. In: Juels, A., Wright, R.N., di Vimercati, S.D.C. (eds.) Proceedings of the 13th ACM Conference on Computer and Communications Security, CCS 2006, Alexandria, VA, USA, 30 October–3 November 2006, pp. 79–88. ACM (2006). https://doi.org/10.1145/1180405.1180417
18. Dartois, P., et al.: PEGASIS: practical effective class group action using 4-dimensional isogenies. In: Tauman Kalai, Y., Kamara, S.F. (eds.) CRYPTO 2025. LNCS, vol. 16000, pp. 67–99. Springer, Cham (2025). https://doi.org/10.1007/978-3-032-01855-7_3
19. Das, B.C.: Conjunctive dynamic SSE schemes under scrutiny: Exposing privacy issues in SDSSE-CQ-S and VCDSSE. In: Nitaj, A., Petkova-Nikova, S., Rijmen, V. (eds.) AFRICACRYPT 2025. LNCS, vol. 15651, pp. 417–440. Springer, Cham (2025). https://doi.org/10.1007/978-3-031-97260-7_19
20. De Feo, L., et al.: SCALLOP: scaling the CSI-FiSh. In: Boldyreva, A., Kolesnikov, V. (eds.) PKC 2023, Part I. LNCS, vol. 13940, pp. 345–375. Springer, Heidelberg (2023). https://doi.org/10.1007/978-3-031-31368-4_13
21. Faber, S., Jarecki, S., Krawczyk, H., Nguyen, Q., Rosu, M., Steiner, M.: Rich queries on encrypted data: beyond exact matches. In: Pernul, G., Ryan, P.Y.A., Weippl, E. (eds.) ESORICS 2015. LNCS, vol. 9327, pp. 123–145. Springer, Cham (2015). https://doi.org/10.1007/978-3-319-24177-7_7
22. Goh, E.: Secure indexes. IACR Cryptol. ePrint Arch. p. 216 (2003). http://eprint.iacr.org/2003/216

23. Goldreich, O., Ostrovsky, R.: Software protection and simulation on oblivious rams. J. ACM **43**(3), 431–473 (1996). https://doi.org/10.1145/233551.233553
24. Hu, C., Song, X., Liu, P., Xin, Y., Xu, Y., Duan, Y., Hao, R.: Forward secure conjunctive-keyword searchable encryption. IEEE Access **7**, 35035–35048 (2019). https://doi.org/10.1109/ACCESS.2019.2902855
25. Impagliazzo, R., Levin, L.A., Luby, M.: Pseudo-random generation from one-way functions (extended abstracts). In: 21st ACM STOC, pp. 12–24. ACM Press (1989). https://doi.org/10.1145/73007.73009
26. Kamara, S., Moataz, T.: Boolean searchable symmetric encryption with worst-case sub-linear complexity. In: Coron, J.-S., Nielsen, J.B. (eds.) EUROCRYPT 2017, Part III. LNCS, vol. 10212, pp. 94–124. Springer, Cham (2017). https://doi.org/10.1007/978-3-319-56617-7_4
27. Kamara, S., Papamanthou, C., Roeder, T.: Dynamic searchable symmetric encryption. In: Yu, T., Danezis, G., Gligor, V.D. (eds.) the ACM Conference on Computer and Communications Security, CCS 2012, Raleigh, NC, USA, 16–18 October 2012, pp. 965–976. ACM (2012). https://doi.org/10.1145/2382196.2382298
28. Lai, S., Patranabis, S., Sakzad, A., Liu, J.K., Mukhopadhyay, D., Steinfeld, R., Sun, S., Liu, D., Zuo, C.: Result pattern hiding searchable encryption for conjunctive queries. In: Lie, D., Mannan, M., Backes, M., Wang, X. (eds.) Proceedings of the 2018 ACM SIGSAC Conference on Computer and Communications Security, CCS 2018, Toronto, ON, Canada, 15–19 October 2018, pp. 745–762. ACM (2018). https://doi.org/10.1145/3243734.3243753
29. Lyubashevsky, V., Peikert, C., Regev, O.: On ideal lattices and learning with errors over rings. In: Gilbert, H. (ed.) EUROCRYPT 2010. LNCS, vol. 6110, pp. 1–23. Springer, Heidelberg (2010). https://doi.org/10.1007/978-3-642-13190-5_1
30. Lyubashevsky, V., Peikert, C., Regev, O.: A toolkit for ring-LWE cryptography. In: Johansson, T., Nguyen, P.Q. (eds.) EUROCRYPT 2013. LNCS, vol. 7881, pp. 35–54. Springer, Heidelberg (2013). https://doi.org/10.1007/978-3-642-38348-9_3
31. Maino, L., Martindale, C., Panny, L., Pope, G., Wesolowski, B.: A direct key recovery attack on SIDH. In: Hazay, C., Stam, M. (eds.) EUROCRYPT 2023. LNCS, vol. 14008, pp. 448–471. Springer, Cham (2023). https://doi.org/10.1007/978-3-031-30589-4_16
32. Micciancio, D., Peikert, C.: Trapdoors for lattices: simpler, tighter, faster, smaller. In: Pointcheval, D., Johansson, T. (eds.) EUROCRYPT 2012. LNCS, vol. 7237, pp. 700–718. Springer, Heidelberg (2012). https://doi.org/10.1007/978-3-642-29011-4_41
33. Patranabis, S., Mukhopadhyay, D.: Forward and backward private conjunctive searchable symmetric encryption. In: 28th Annual Network and Distributed System Security Symposium, NDSS 2021, virtually, 21–25 February 2021. The Internet Society (2021). https://www.ndss-symposium.org/ndss-paper/forward-and-backward-private-conjunctive-searchable-symmetric-encryption/
34. Regev, O.: New lattice-based cryptographic constructions. J. ACM **51**(6), 899–942 (2004)
35. Regev, O.: On lattices, learning with errors, random linear codes, and cryptography. J. ACM **56**(6), 34:1–34:40 (2009)
36. Regev, O.: The learning with errors problem (invited survey). In: Proceedings of the 25th Annual IEEE Conference on Computational Complexity, CCC 2010, pp. 191–204. IEEE Computer Society (2010)
37. Robert, D.: Breaking SIDH in polynomial time. In: Hazay, C., Stam, M. (eds.) EUROCRYPT 2023, Part V. LNCS, vol. 14008, pp. 472–503. Springer, Heidelberg (2023). https://doi.org/10.1007/978-3-031-30589-4_17

38. Song, D.X., Wagner, D.A., Perrig, A.: Practical techniques for searches on encrypted data. In: 2000 IEEE Symposium on Security and Privacy, Berkeley, California, USA, 14–17 May 2000, pp. 44–55. IEEE Computer Society (2000). https://doi.org/10.1109/SECPRI.2000.848445

39. Stefanov, E., et al.: Path ORAM: an extremely simple oblivious RAM protocol. In: Sadeghi, A., Gligor, V.D., Yung, M. (eds.) 2013 ACM SIGSAC Conference on Computer and Communications Security, CCS 2013, Berlin, Germany, 4–8 November 2013, pp. 299–310. ACM (2013). https://doi.org/10.1145/2508859.2516660

40. Sun, S., et al.: Practical non-interactive searchable encryption with forward and backward privacy. In: 28th Annual Network and Distributed System Security Symposium, NDSS 2021, virtually, 21–25 February 2021. The Internet Society (2021)

41. Sun, S., et al.: Practical backward-secure searchable encryption from symmetric puncturable encryption. In: Lie, D., Mannan, M., Backes, M., Wang, X. (eds.) Proceedings of the 2018 ACM SIGSAC Conference on Computer and Communications Security, CCS 2018, Toronto, ON, Canada, 15–19 October 2018, pp. 763–780. ACM (2018). https://doi.org/10.1145/3243734.3243782

42. Talapatra, D., Patranabis, S., Mukhopadhyay, D.: Conjunctive searchable symmetric encryption from hard lattices. In: 8th IEEE European Symposium on Security and Privacy, EuroS&P 2023, Delft, Netherlands, 3–7 July 2023, pp. 958–978. IEEE (2023). https://doi.org/10.1109/EUROSP57164.2023.00061

43. Talapatra, D., Patranabis, S., Mukhopadhyay, D.: Highly scalable searchable symmetric encryption for Boolean queries from NTRU lattice trapdoors. IACR Commun. Cryptol. 2(2), 6 (2025). https://doi.org/10.62056/AE89N59P1

44. Wang, Y., Wang, J., Sun, S., Miao, M., Chen, X.: Toward forward secure SSE supporting conjunctive keyword search. IEEE Access 7, 142762–142772 (2019). https://doi.org/10.1109/ACCESS.2019.2944246

45. Wu, Z., Li, K.: VBTree: forward secure conjunctive queries over encrypted data for cloud computing. VLDB J. 28(1), 25–46 (2019). https://doi.org/10.1007/s00778-018-0517-6

46. Zhang, Y., Katz, J., Papamanthou, C.: All your queries are belong to us: the power of file-injection attacks on searchable encryption. In: Holz, T., Savage, S. (eds.) 25th USENIX Security Symposium, USENIX Security 16, Austin, TX, USA, 10–12 August 2016, pp. 707–720. USENIX Association (2016). https://www.usenix.org/conference/usenixsecurity16/technical-sessions/presentation/zhang

47. Zuo, C., et al.: Searchable encryption for conjunctive queries with extended forward and backward privacy. Proc. Priv. Enhancing Technol. 2025(1), 440–455 (2025). https://doi.org/10.56553/POPETS-2025-0024

48. Zuo, C., Sun, S.-F., Liu, J.K., Shao, J., Pieprzyk, J.: Dynamic searchable symmetric encryption schemes supporting range queries with forward (and backward) security. In: Lopez, J., Zhou, J., Soriano, M. (eds.) ESORICS 2018, Part II. LNCS, vol. 11099, pp. 228–246. Springer, Cham (2018). https://doi.org/10.1007/978-3-319-98989-1_12

49. Zuo, C., Sun, S., Liu, J.K., Shao, J., Pieprzyk, J., Wei, G.: Forward and backward private dynamic searchable symmetric encryption for conjunctive queries. IACR Cryptol. ePrint Arch. 1357 (2020). https://eprint.iacr.org/2020/1357

Faster Bootstrapping for CKKS with Less Modulus Consumption

Lianglin Yan[1,2], Pengfei Zeng[1,2], Heyang Cao[1,2], Peizhe Song[1,2],
and Mingsheng Wang[1(✉)]

[1] State Key Laboratory of Cyberspace Security Defense, Institute of Information
Engineering, CAS, Beijing, China
`{caoheyang,songpeizhe,wangmingsheng}@iie.ac.cn`
[2] School of Cyber Security, University of Chinese Academy of Sciences, Beijing,
China
`{yanlianglin20,zengpengfei20}@mails.ucas.ac.cn`

Abstract. In fully homomorphic encryption, bootstrapping serves as a
key component while also remaining the performance bottleneck of the
scheme. Specifically, for CKKS bootstrapping, this bottleneck is reflected
in significant computational overhead and modulus consumption.

In this work, we improve the CKKS bootstrapping with lower
time complexity and less modulus consumption. We first propose a
novel rescaling operation, called level-conserving rescaling, that acts on
CoeffsToSlots for saving moduli. Secondly, we reconstruct the rotation
keys and merge the plaintext-ciphertext multiplication and rescaling
operations into the key-switching procedure, which reduces the time complexity of matrix-vector multiplication for matrices with ≤ 64 non-zero
diagonals, albeit with increased space overhead. By combining the two
methods in CoeffsToSlots in a non-trivial manner, we not only further
accelerate the homomorphic linear transformations and save one level of
moduli, but also reduce the total size of rotation keys.

Experiments demonstrate the practicability of our techniques. Compared to the state of the art, our approaches save one level of moduli,
achieving a $20\% \sim 35\%$ improvement in bootstrapping throughput and
an $11.9\% \sim 15.2\%$ reduction of rotation key size in CoeffsToSlots. Furthermore, with sufficient storage, our technology achieves up to 40%
higher bootstrapping throughput than before, at the cost of doubling
the rotation key size in CoeffsToSlots. The bootstrapping precision and
failure probability remain identical to the previous method.

Keywords: Homomorphic encryption · CKKS bootstrapping · Linear
transformation · Key-switching · Rescaling

1 Introduction

Homomorphic encryption (HE) is an encryption scheme that enables one to
compute on encrypted data without knowing secrets. The research in this area

S. Bai and E. Persichetti (Eds.): PKC 2026, LNCS 16554, pp. 335–366, 2026.
https://doi.org/10.1007/978-3-032-26740-5_11

has made great progress since Gentry's lattice-based construction [21] of the first fully homomorphic encryption (FHE) scheme in 2009. Due to the powerful ability to perform computations on encrypted data, FHE gradually becomes a popular solution for processing private information in an untrusted environment.

As a leveled HE (LHE) scheme relying on the Ring Learning with Errors (RLWE) problem [40], the Cheon–Kim–Kim–Song (CKKS) scheme is the only scheme supporting approximate homomorphic evaluation of algorithms over complex (or real) vectors, which is important in many applications like machine learning [34,35,39]. In recent years, CKKS has been improved in both algorithm and implementation [2,15,26,31,33,42] to achieve an efficient evaluation of complicated circuits (e.g., deep neural networks). Moreover, bootstrapping is required when evaluating the extremely deep circuits.

Bootstrapping is a technique that makes an LHE scheme become an FHE scheme. It takes a zero-level ciphertext as input and outputs the ciphertext of the same message at a high level. CKKS bootstrapping was first proposed by Cheon et al. [14]. Their core idea is raising the ciphertext level first and then eliminating the extra term in the plaintext via homomorphic modular reduction and linear transformations[1] (see Sect. 2.2 for details). The modular reduction was initially approximated by a sine function, and transformed into a Taylor polynomial for evaluation. To achieve a high performance, a series of subsequent works improved the evaluation method of the modular reduction function, such as Chebyshev interpolation [11,26], inverse sine function [36] and so on [6,27,37]. On the other hand, several works [11,32] focused on reducing the modulus consumption of bootstrapping, thus promoting the homomorphic evaluation ability of the bootstrapped scheme.

In addition, optimizing linear transformations also benefits bootstrapping. In CKKS bootstrapping, homomorphic linear transformations are essentially homomorphic matrix-vector multiplications [11,14,25], and the state-of-the-art linear transformations were introduced in [6]. The work in [6] adopted the matrix factorization algorithm [11,25], and introduced the double-hoisting BSGS algorithm for matrix-vector multiplications (detailed in Sect. 4.1). In this work, we aim to improve the performance of CKKS bootstrapping beyond the state of the art by optimizing the homomorphic linear transformations, especially the CoeffsToSlots procedure (introduced in Sect. 2.2).

1.1   Our Contributions

We introduce two new technologies, one of which saves the modulus level and the other accelerates the matrix-vector multiplications in CoeffsToSlots. They can be combined to achieve better results.

- We propose a novel *level-conserving rescaling* (LCR) technique that acts on CoeffsToSlots for saving moduli. It should be performed after ModRaise and before key-switching (Sect. 3).

---

[1] In CKKS bootstrapping, homomorphic linear transformations represent the CoeffsToSlots and SlotsToCoeffs procedures.

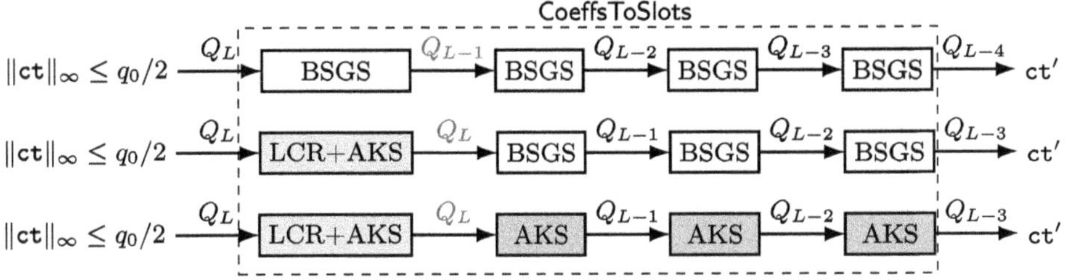

Fig. 1. Flowchart of the CoeffsToSlots procedure in prior works [6,7] (above), lossless strategy (middle) and time-memory trade-of strategy (below). As an example illustration, we assume that the CoeffsToSlots is factorized into 4 sparse diagonal matrices (i.e., 4-step decomposition). We omit the conjugation operations for simplicity.

- We present an innovative *aggregated key-switching* (AKS) technique, which speeds up the homomorphic matrix-vector multiplication when BSGS approach is discarded. Technically, we first observe that, in matrix-vector multiplication, the conventional Baby-Step Giant-Step (BSGS) approach can be removed without noticeable efficiency loss when the number of non-zero diagonals $r \le 32$. Then, we replace the BSGS approach with AKS method. The new key-switching operation substantially reduces the time complexity, and even compensates for the lost efficiency of discarding BSGS when $r = 64$. Complexity analysis shows that the improved matrix-vector multiplication algorithm is up to $2.5\times$ (theoretical) faster than the previous BSGS method, while requiring more rotation keys in pre-computations. The idea of AKS may be of independent interest to the FHE community (Sect. 4).

- We devise a new combination method for LCR and AKS by using the GHS-type key-switching[2] *non-trivially*. Applying to the first matrix-vector multiplication of CoeffsToSlots, LCR + AKS saves one level of moduli and reduces the time complexity. Notably, the use of GHS-type key-switching *further* decreases the time complexity and *reduces* the total size of the rotation keys, such that the combined algorithm is a *lossless improvement* (Sect. 5).

- To demonstrate the practical improvements, we implement the proposed techniques in bootstrapping via two strategies: a lossless strategy and a time-memory trade-off strategy (illustrated in Fig. 1). The experimental results show that, compared to prior methods [6,7]: (1) Our methods save one level of moduli in bootstrapping and increase the remaining homomorphic capacity. (2) The lossless strategy achieves a $20\%\times \sim 35\%\times$ throughput speedup and reduces the rotation key size in CoeffsToSlots by 11.9% to 15.2%. (3) The time-memory trade-off strategy achieves up to 40% speedup in bootstrapping throughput under similar parameters, and doubles the rotation key size in CoeffsToSlots, it would be useful when storage space is sufficient (Sect. 6).

---

[2] GHS-type key-switching refers to the key-switching that employs an auxiliary modulus P to control the noise [22]. See Sect. 2.3.

1.2 Technical Overview

We fist recap some necessary background concepts. Let $\mathcal{R}_Q = \mathbb{Z}[X]/(X^N+1, Q)$ and $\left\{ Q_\ell = \prod_{i=0}^{\ell} q_i \right\}_{0 \leq \ell \leq L}$ is the modulus chain for ciphertexts. To evaluate the decryption circuit homomorphically, standard CKKS bootstrapping executes four steps: ModRaise, CoeffsToSlots, EvalMod, and SlotsToCoeffs. The first operation, ModRaise, raises the ciphertext from the base level q_0 to the maximum level Q_L. Then, CoeffsToSlots packs the plaintext coefficients into slots. This can be done by homomorphically evaluating iDFT (i.e., a homomorphic matrix-vector multiplication). The subsequent EvalMod operation enables homomorphic modular reduction, and the final ciphertext is obtained following the SlotsToCoeffs operation, which retrieves messages from the slot side to the coefficient side.

This work mainly focuses on the ModRaise and CoeffsToSlots, especially the homomorphic matrix-vector multiplications. A widely used optimization for homomorphic matrix-vector multiplication is the Baby-Step Giant-Step (BSGS) approach. It divides the algorithm into two loops, each of which contains rotation and key-switching operations. Additionally, we also need to perform Rescale operation after each homomorphic multiplication. It multiples the ciphertext by a rescaling factor to reduce the ciphertext noise, consuming one level of moduli in the process.

The First Idea. Our first idea stems from an observation on the Rescale operation and the ModRaise procedure. We find that the ModRaise operation raises the modulus from q_0 to Q_L while preserving the ciphertext values, which implies that the output ciphertext $\mathtt{ct} \in \mathcal{R}_{Q_L}^2$ has coefficients bounded by $\|\mathtt{ct}\|)_\infty \leq q_0/2$. These coefficients are significantly smaller than the ring modulus Q_L. Therefore, we have $[\langle \mathtt{ct}, \mathtt{sk} \rangle]_{Q_L} = \langle \mathtt{ct}, \mathtt{sk} \rangle$ where $\mathtt{sk}$ is the secret key. After rescaling by q_L, $\mathtt{ct}$ becomes $\mathtt{ct}' = \lfloor \frac{1}{q_L} \cdot \mathtt{ct} \rceil$ and

$$[\langle \mathtt{ct}', \mathtt{sk} \rangle]_{Q_{L-1}} = \langle \mathtt{ct}', \mathtt{sk} \rangle = [\langle \mathtt{ct}', \mathtt{sk} \rangle]_{Q_L},$$

which means the modulus of $\mathtt{ct}'$ can be set to Q_L instead of Q_{L-1} without impacting the validity of the encryption. In other words, we can perform a *level-conserving* rescaling (LCR) operation on such a *small coefficient ciphertext* $\mathtt{ct}$ to preserve its level. However, using the level-conserving rescaling after ModRaise remains a challenge: rescaling is typically performed after the key-switching operation, as in CoeffsToSlots. Since the ciphertext coefficients after key-switching become uniformly distributed over $\mathbb{Z}_{Q_L}$, the level-conserving rescaling technique can no longer be applied.

An Attempt. To enable the LCR in CoeffsToSlots, we try to delay the key-switching and move the scalar multiplication and rescaling operations forward, which undermines the structure of BSGS (see Sect. 3.2). As a result, this attempt preserves the modulus level but incurs unacceptable time and space overhead. To address this, we aim to reduce the algorithmic overhead in two steps: (1)

The large overhead is because we break the BSGS approach. So, can we discard BSGS without causing significant efficiency losses? (2) We need to introduce additional techniques to enhance overall efficiency without BSGS.

Efforts in the Two Steps. Now, we temporarily forget about LCR and focus on the homomorphic matrix-vector multiplication algorithm. Let r be the number of non-zero diagonals of the matrix and r_1, r_2 be the number of loops in Baby-Step and Giant-Step, respectively. Then, it requires that $r = r_1 \cdot r_2$.

In step 1, we notice two facts: (1) The time complexity of the double-hoisting BSGS algorithm is minimized when the ratio r_1/r_2 is optimally set to 8 or 16 [6]. (2) Discarding BSGS approach in matrix-vector multiplication is equivalent to applying BSGS with $r_1 = r, r_2 = 1$ (i.e., $r_1/r_2 = r$). This implies that for $r \leq 16$, discarding BSGS inherently achieves the optimal ratio, incurring no efficiency loss theoretically. For $r = 32$, discarding BSGS results in only a slight loss of efficiency (30.4021 vs. 30.4018, see Table 1). In summary, we find that *for matrices with $r \leq 32$, discarding BSGS incurs a small efficiency loss* for double-hoisting matrix-vector multiplication.

In step 2, we introduce an *aggregated key-switching* (AKS) technique that accelerates the double-hoisting matrix-vector multiplication algorithm when the BSGS approach is not used. The main idea of AKS is merging the scalar multiplication and rescaling operations into key-switching procedure. Let s_1, s_2 be secret keys, P be the auxiliary modulus for key-switching and $\mathsf{ct} = (c_0, c_1) \in \mathcal{R}^2_{Q_\ell}$ be a ciphertext. We know that the switching key of key-switching from s_1 to s_2 is the ciphertext evk, an encryption of Ps_1 with respect to secret s_2, and during key-switching, the term Ps_1 is multiplied by c_1. Based on this observation, we modify the switching key to the encryption of $\frac{Pms_1}{q_\ell}$, where m is a plaintext from DFT/iDFT matrix, and $1/q_\ell$ is the rescaling factor. Consequently, after key-switching (including ModDown), the term $\frac{ms_1}{q_\ell} \cdot c_1$ is generated, whereas the original key-switching produces $s_1 \cdot c_1$. This modification enables the scalar multiplication and rescaling on c_1 to be completed within the key-switching operation itself. As a result, only scalar multiplication and rescaling operations on c_0 need to be evaluated separately, reducing the overall time complexity.

Compared to the BSGS method, the improved matrix-vector multiplication algorithm with AKS *reduces the overall time complexity when $r \leq 64$*. This is because the efficiency loss from discarding BSGS is fully compensated by the aggregated key-switching approach when $32 \leq r \leq 64$ (see Table 2). We also note that this method introduces a time-space trade-off as it requires more rotation keys than the BSGS method.

The Combination. We now combine the LCR into the improved matrix-vector multiplication algorithm with the AKS approach. A key challenge arises because the CRT composition step in the hybrid key-switching causes the rescaling operation to rely on the modulus $Q_{\ell-1}$ instead of Q_ℓ. This reliance critically obstructs the level preservation in key-switching (see Sect. 5.1). To resolve this, we employ

the GHS-type key-switching while keeping the auxiliary modulus P unchanged—
a non-trivial modification. This approach not only *preserves the modulus level*,
but also *further lowers* the time complexity and *decreases* the total size of the
rotation keys. Consequently, we obtain a *losslessly improved* matrix-vector multiplication algorithm for the first matrix in CoeffsToSlots with $r \le 64$.

Up to now, we have three kinds of methods for matrix-vector multiplication
algorithms in bootstrapping:

- The BSGS method, which is the state of the art prior to our work.
- The AKS method, which achieves a better efficiency than BSGS method when
  $r \le 64$, at the cost of space overhead.
- The LCR+AKS method, which preserves the modulus level and outperforms
  the above two methods in both time and space overhead, but only applicable
  to the first matrix in CoeffsToSlots with $r \le 64$ and only be used once.

Applying to Bootstrapping. In the state-of-the-art CKKS bootstrapping,
the DFT/iDFT matrix is factorized into sparse diagonal matrices by utilizing
the matrix factorization method from [11,25], typically with $r \approx 16$ or 32 (resp.
32 or 64) for 4-step (resp. 3-step) decomposition. Thus, our proposed algorithms
(AKS and LCR+AKS) are applicable in real-world bootstrapping. We provide
different bootstrapping strategies in application (refer to Fig. 1).

Lossless Improvement (for Limited Storage). For the lossless strategy, since
the LCR+AKS method outperforms BSGS in both time and space overhead,
our improved bootstrapping saves one level of moduli, achieving a throughput
$1.20 \sim 1.35$ times that of the previous method under similar parameters, and
the rotation key size in CoeffsToSlots is $11.9\% \sim 15.2\%$ smaller than before
(illustrated in Table 4).

Higher Throughput with Increased Key Materials (for Sufficient Storage). The
LCR+AKS and AKS methods can be jointly applied to bootstrapping for better
efficiency, at the cost of an increased rotation key size. In experiments, our time-
memory trade-off strategy achieves up to 40% higher throughput while doubling
the rotation key size in CoeffsToSlots, compared to prior bootstrapping methods
[6,7]. We also propose more optimization techniques (including reusing AKS
keys in circuit evaluation) to enhance the applicability of AKS method (refer to
Appendix H in the full version).

1.3   Compatibility with Other Technologies

The only limitation of our technique is that we have not yet considered sparsely
packed ciphertexts, as noted in Remark 1, and we believe this will be addressed
in the near future. In fact, our method is compatible with most mainstream
techniques for fully-packed ciphertext bootstrapping, including the sparse-secret
encapsulation [7] and the subring secret encapsulation [41]. We provide a detailed
discussion in Sect. 6.3.

1.4   Related Works

According to the suggestion of Cheon et al. [14], it is essential to perform homomorphic Encode and Decode algorithms before and after EvalMod, by using CoeffsToSlots and SlotsToCoeffs, respectively. Homomorphic encoding/decoding involves homomorphic iDFT/DFT, which is a homomorphic matrix-vector multiplication, optimized by the Baby-Step Giant-Step (BSGS) approach in $\mathcal{O}\left(\sqrt{n}\right)$ rotations and 1 depth. Later, Cheon et al. [11] and Han et al. [25] exploited the structure of DFT algorithm and factorized the DFT/iDFT matrix into several sparse block diagonal matrices to achieve a faster linear transform in $\mathcal{O}\left(\sqrt{\gamma}\log_\gamma n\right)$ rotations with $\mathcal{O}\left(\log_\gamma n\right)$ depth, where γ is a radix specified by users.

Several works improved the homomorphic rotations of matrix-vector multiplication. The hoisting technique, from Halevi and Shoup [24], preposes the Decomp step before the loop due to the property $[\phi_k(a)]_{q_i} = \phi_k\left([a]_{q_i}\right)$ for $a \in \mathcal{R}_Q$ with $\phi_k : X \mapsto X^{5^k} \mod (X^N + 1)$, which reduces the number of Number Theoretic Transforms (NTTs) and CRT reconstructions. Bossuat et al. [6] optimized this hoisting technique by applying ϕ_k^{-1} to rotation keys and commuting Permute and MultSum steps. They also constructed a double-hoisting BSGS matrix-vector multiplication by delaying the ModDown step outside the loop, which significantly reduces the complexity of linear transformation. They analyzed the ratio of n_1/n_2 for the best performance. However, the high modulus consumption is still the weakness of bootstrapping. For a 25-level CKKS scheme, as shown in [6], only 10 levels are left after bootstrapping for continuing homomorphic computations.

To reduce the modulus consumption of bootstrapping, Kim et al. [32] replaced EvalMod by EvalRound, which is defined as EvalRound: $x \mapsto x - \mathsf{EvalMod}(x)$. For previous bootstrapping algorithms, smaller scaling factors for encoding iDFT matrices allow less modulus consumption in the rescaling of CoeffsToSlots, but yields a relative large noise. Such a noise would be further enlarged in subsequent procedures and finally impact the output precision. The subtraction operation in EvalRound gets rid of the relative large error, therefore allowing smaller scaling factors and saving moduli in CoeffsToSlots. The subsequent work EvalRound$^+$ [43] resolved some problems of EvalRound and further reduced the modulus consumption. Additionally, Cheon et al. proposed the Tuple-CKKS [13] for homomorphic multiplication with lower modulus consumption in the CKKS scheme. A recent work, OverModRaise [30], also aimed to save bootstrapping modulus by exploring CoeffsToSlots, and the ideas can be combined with our work.

1.5   Road-Map

Section 2 introduces some preliminaries. In Sect. 3, we show the level-conserving rescaling technique and present the initial attempt to use it. Section 4 contains the analysis of discarding BSGS and our improved matrix-vector multiplication algorithm with aggregated key-switching. We combine the proposed two approaches in Sect. 5 and provide the evaluation results in Sect. 6. Finally, we conclude our work in Sect. 7.

2   Preliminaries

Notations. In this paper, we let N be a power-of-two integer, $q_0, q_1, \cdots, q_L, p_0, p_1, \cdots, p_{k-1}$ be $L + k + 1$ distinct primes, and $Q_\ell = \prod_{i=0}^{\ell} q_i$, $P_j = \prod_{i=0}^{j} p_i$ for $0 \leq \ell \leq L$ and $0 \leq j < k$. For simplicity, we write $Q = Q_L$ and $P = P_{k-1}$. We define $\mathcal{R}_Q = \mathbb{Z}_Q[X]/(X^N + 1)$, the cyclotomic polynomial ring over the integers modulo Q. We also enforce $q_i \equiv 1 \pmod{2N}$ (as well as p_i) so that $\mathcal{R}_{PQ}$ is NTT-friendly. We write lower-case letters as integers or elements in $\mathcal{R}_Q$, while bold-faced lower-case letters represent (column) vectors, e.g., $\boldsymbol{v} = (v_0, v_1, \cdots, v_{m-1})^T$ where $v_i \in \mathbb{Z}$ or $\mathcal{R}_Q$ and $\boldsymbol{v}^T$ is the transpose vector of $\boldsymbol{v}$. Matrices over integers or polynomials are represented in bold-faced upper-case letters such as $\boldsymbol{M}$. The inner product of $\boldsymbol{a} = (a_0, a_1, \cdots, a_{n-1})$ and $\boldsymbol{b} = (b_0, b_1, \cdots, b_{n-1})$ is defined as $\langle \boldsymbol{a}, \boldsymbol{b} \rangle = \sum_{i=0}^{n-1} a_i \cdot b_i$. We denote $\|a\|_\infty$ the infinity norm of the coefficients vector of the polynomial a. $U(\cdot)$ denotes the uniform distribution over some set. Without causing ambiguity, we simplify $c_1 + c_2 \bmod (Q, X^N + 1)$ (resp. $c_1 \cdot c_2 \bmod (Q, X^N + 1)$) as $c_1 + c_2$ (resp. $c_1 \cdot c_2$) for $c_1, c_2 \in \mathcal{R}_Q$.

For reduction, $[x]_Q \in (-Q/2, Q/2]$ denotes the reduction of x modulo Q, and $\lfloor x \rfloor, \lceil x \rceil, \lfloor x \rceil$ represent rounding x to the floor, ceiling and nearest integer, respectively (if x is a polynomial, the operation is applied coefficient-wise).

For RNS-CKKS, we let $\mathcal{B} = \{q_0, q_1, \cdots, q_L\}$, $\mathcal{C} = \{p_0, p_1, \cdots, p_{k-1}\}$ and $\mathcal{D} = \mathcal{B} \cup \mathcal{C}$. Moreover, we assume that $L + 1 = \alpha \cdot \mathbf{dnum}$ and split the set $\mathcal{B}$ into $\mathbf{dnum}$ segments, each with α numbers, i.e., $D_j = \prod_{i=j\alpha}^{(j+1)\alpha-1} q_i$ for $0 \leq j < \mathbf{dnum}$. For a polynomial $a \in \mathcal{R}_Q$, there are two RNS representations: one is the coefficient form, denoted as $[a]_\mathcal{B} = (a_0, \cdots, a_L) \in \mathcal{R}_{q_0} \times \cdots \times \mathcal{R}_{q_L}$, where $a_i = [a]_{q_i}$; the other one is NTT form, denoted as $\hat{a} = (\hat{a}_0, \cdots, \hat{a}_L) \in \mathbb{Z}_{q_0}^N \times \mathbb{Z}_{q_1}^N \times \cdots \times \mathbb{Z}_{q_L}^N$, where $\hat{a}_i = \mathtt{NTT}(a_i)$. Unless otherwise noted, a denotes its representation in coefficient form and $\hat{a}$ denotes its representation in NTT form.

2.1   The Full-RNS CKKS Scheme

We review the CKKS scheme [16] and its homomorphic operations in a generalized perspective. The RNS representation of these operations are presented in Appendix A. Recall that RNS representation is just for better efficiency, rationale and correctness still depend on the original scheme.

Encoding and Decoding. Encoding and decoding algorithms are designed to perform transformation between *complex vector* and *plaintext polynomial* over $\mathcal{R} = \mathbb{Z}[X]/(X^N + 1)$. The vector is called *message* with $N/2$ components, and each component corresponds to a *slot*. To describe the encoding/decoding procedures, we show the canonical embedding first.

Let $\zeta = e^{i\pi/N} \in \mathbb{C}$ be a primary $2N$-th root of unity, and define $\zeta_j = \zeta^{5^j}$ for $j = 0, 1, \cdots, N/2 - 1$. Let $\mathcal{P} = \mathbb{R}[X]/(X^N + 1)$. A modified canonical embedding is defined as $\tau : \mathcal{P} \to \mathbb{C}^{N/2}, m(X) \mapsto \left(m(\zeta_0), m(\zeta_1), \cdots, m(\zeta_{N/2-1})\right)$. If we present $m(X)$ by its coefficient vector $(m_0, m_1, \cdots, m_{N-1})$, then this mapping can be rewritten as

$$\begin{bmatrix} 1 & \zeta_0 & \zeta_0^2 & \cdots & \zeta_0^{N-1} \\ 1 & \zeta_1 & \zeta_1^2 & \cdots & \zeta_1^{N-1} \\ \vdots & \vdots & \vdots & \ddots & \vdots \\ 1 & \zeta_{\frac{N}{2}-1} & \zeta_{\frac{N}{2}-1}^2 & \cdots & \zeta_{\frac{N}{2}-1}^{N-1} \end{bmatrix} \begin{bmatrix} m_0 \\ m_1 \\ \vdots \\ m_{N-1} \end{bmatrix} = \begin{bmatrix} m(\zeta_0) \\ m(\zeta_1) \\ \vdots \\ m(\zeta_{N/2-1}) \end{bmatrix}, \tag{1}$$

which is essentially related to the Discrete Fourier Transformation (DFT). Similarly, the mapping $\tau^{-1} : \mathbb{C}^{N/2} \to \mathcal{P}$ involves an inverse DFT (iDFT). With DFT/iDFT, we can encode a complex vector $z \in \mathbb{C}^{N/2}$ to a plaintext polynomial $\mathtt{pt} \in \mathcal{R}$ and decode $\mathtt{pt}$ back to z.

- Encode(z, Δ). For message $z \in \mathbb{C}^{N/2}$ and scaling factor Δ, output the plaintext polynomial

$$\mathtt{pt} = \lfloor \Delta \cdot \mathtt{iDFT}(z; \bar{z}) \rceil \in \mathcal{R},$$

  where $\bar{z}$ is the complex conjugation of z and $\lfloor \cdot \rceil$ discretizes elements from $\mathcal{P}$ to $\mathcal{R}$.
- Decode$(\mathtt{pt}, \Delta)$. For plaintext polynomial $\mathtt{pt}$ and scaling factor Δ, compute

$$(z; \bar{z}) = \frac{1}{\Delta} \cdot \mathtt{DFT}(\mathtt{pt}),$$

  and output the message $z \in \mathbb{C}^{N/2}$.

Basic Operations. Let χ_{key} be the uniform distribution over the set of polynomials with coefficient vector in $\{0, \pm 1\}^N$ and Hamming weight h, χ_{enc} be the distribution over $\mathcal{R}$ with coefficients distributed over $\{-1, 0, 1\}$ with respective probabilities $\{1/4, 1/2, 1/4\}$, and χ_{err} be the distribution over $\mathcal{R}$ with coefficients following a Gaussian distribution with standard deviation σ. Let $\phi_k : m(X) \mapsto m(X^k) \pmod{(X^N + 1)}$ be the Galois mapping over $\mathcal{P}$. ℓ is an integer satisfying $0 \leq \ell \leq L$ and $\beta = \lceil (\ell+1)/\alpha \rceil$.

- CKKS.Setup(1^λ): Given the security parameter λ, generate parameters N, small moduli $\{q_0, \cdots q_L\}$, $\{p_0, \cdots p_{k-1}\}$ and big moduli $Q, P, \{D_j\}_{0 \leq j < \mathsf{dnum}}$, as required in notations. Generate Hamming weight h, Gaussian standard deviation σ to instantiate distributions χ_{key} and χ_{err}.
- CKKS.SwitchKeyGen(s_1, s_2): To generate the switching key for key-switching from s_1 to s_2, we sample $a_j \leftarrow U(\mathcal{R}_{PQ})$ and $e_j \leftarrow \chi_{\mathsf{err}}$, then return $\mathsf{evk}_{s_1 \to s_2} = (\mathsf{evk}_0, \mathsf{evk}_1, \cdots, \mathsf{evk}_{\mathsf{dnum}-1})$, where $\mathsf{evk}_j = \left(-a_j s_2 + P s_1 \cdot D_j^* \cdot \hat{D}_j + e_j, a_j\right) \in \mathcal{R}_{PQ}^2$ for $\hat{D}_j = Q/D_j$, $D_j^* = \left[\hat{D}_j^{-1}\right]_{D_j}$ and $0 \leq j < \mathsf{dnum}^3$.

---

[3] Here we use the hybrid key-switching method with RNS-decomposition and move the D_j^* to evk [23] for optimization.

- CKKS.KeyGen($\cdot$): This procedure generates the secret key $\texttt{sk}$, the public key $\texttt{pk}$, the relinearization key $\texttt{rlk}$, the rotation key $\texttt{rtk}$ and the complex conjugation key $\texttt{conjk}$. Specifically, we sample $s \leftarrow \chi_{\mathsf{key}}$ and $\texttt{sk} = (1, s)$. $\texttt{pk} = (-as + e, a) \in \mathcal{R}_Q^2$ by sampling $a \leftarrow U(\mathcal{R}_Q)$ and $e \leftarrow \chi_{\mathsf{err}}$. $\texttt{rlk} = \mathsf{CKKS.SwitchKeyGen}(s^2, s), \texttt{rtk}_k = \mathsf{CKKS.SwitchKeyGen}(\phi_{5^k}(s), s)$, and $\texttt{conjk} = \mathsf{CKKS.SwitchKeyGen}(\phi_{-1}(s), s)$.
- CKKS.Enc$_{\texttt{pk}}$(pt): For $\texttt{pt} \in \mathcal{R}$, sample $v \leftarrow \chi_{\mathsf{enc}}$ and $e_0, e_1 \leftarrow \chi_{\mathsf{err}}$, compute $\texttt{ct} = v \cdot \texttt{pk} + (\texttt{pt} + e_0, e_1) \in \mathcal{R}_Q^2$.
- CKKS.Dec$_{\texttt{sk}}$(ct): For $\texttt{ct} = (c_0, c_1) \in \mathcal{R}_{Q_\ell}^2$, compute $\texttt{pt} = [\langle \texttt{ct}, \texttt{sk} \rangle]_{Q_0} = [c_0 + c_1 s]_{Q_0} \in \mathcal{R}$.
- CKKS.Add(ct, ct$'$): For $\texttt{ct}, \texttt{ct}' \in \mathcal{R}_{Q_\ell}^2$, compute $\texttt{ct}_{\mathsf{Add}} = \texttt{ct} + \texttt{ct}' \in \mathcal{R}_{Q_\ell}^2$.
- CKKS.KeySwitch(d, evk): For $d \in \mathcal{R}_{Q_\ell}$ a polynomial, decompose d into $\boldsymbol{d} = \left([d]_{D_0}, [d]_{D_1}, \cdots, [d]_{D_{\beta-1}}\right) \in \mathcal{R}^\beta$, and return $(d_0', d_1') = \lfloor \frac{1}{P} \cdot \sum_{j=0}^{\beta-1} [d]_{D_j} \cdot \texttt{evk}_j \rceil \in \mathcal{R}_{Q_\ell}^2$.
- CKKS.Mult(ct, ct$'$, rlk): For $\texttt{ct} = (c_0, c_1) \in \mathcal{R}_{Q_\ell}^2$, $\texttt{ct}' = (c_0', c_1') \in \mathcal{R}_{Q_\ell}^2$, first compute $(d_0, d_1, d_2) = (c_0 c_0', c_0 c_1' + c_1 c_0', c_1 c_1') \in \mathcal{R}_{Q_\ell}^3$, then $\texttt{ct}_{\mathsf{Mult}} = (d_0, d_1) + \mathsf{CKKS.KeySwitch}(d_2, \texttt{rlk}) \in \mathcal{R}_{Q_\ell}^2$.
- CKKS.Rescale(ct): For $\texttt{ct} \in \mathcal{R}_{Q_\ell}^2$, output $\texttt{ct}' = \lfloor \frac{1}{q_\ell} \cdot \texttt{ct} \rceil \in \mathcal{R}_{Q_{\ell-1}}^2$.
- CKKS.Rotate(ct, k, rtk$_k$): For $\texttt{ct} = (c_0, c_1) \in \mathcal{R}_{Q_\ell}^2$, return $\texttt{ct}_{\mathsf{rot}_k} = (\phi_{5^k}(c_0), 0) + \mathsf{CKKS.KeySwitch}(\phi_{5^k}(c_1), \texttt{rtk}) \in \mathcal{R}_{Q_\ell}^2$.
- CKKS.Conjugate(ct, conjk): For $\texttt{ct} = (c_0, c_1) \in \mathcal{R}_{Q_\ell}^2$, return $\texttt{ct}_{\mathsf{conj}} = (\phi_{-1}(c_0), 0) + \mathsf{CKKS.KeySwitch}(\phi_{-1}(c_1), \texttt{conjk}) \in \mathcal{R}_{Q_\ell}^2$.

2.2 Overview of Bootstrapping Circuit

For LHE schemes, the level of ciphertexts decreases as the homomorphic multiplication is performed, thus the homomorphic operation must terminate after evaluating a certain depth circuit. In order to compute arbitrary deep circuits, bootstrapping is performed when the level is exhausted. Following Gentry's [21] blueprint, bootstrapping algorithm is essentially a "recryption", it evaluates the decryption circuit homomorphically to transfer the ciphertexts that no longer support homomorphic multiplication, to the relatively *fresher* ciphertexts for supporting further homomorphic computations. For a CKKS ciphertext, the level determines how fresh it is, therefore the first step of CKKS bootstrapping is raising modulus. However, raising a ciphertext $\texttt{ct} \in \mathcal{R}_{q_0}$ to $\texttt{ct}' \in \mathcal{R}_{Q_L}$ will introduce an extra term $q_0 I$ into the plaintext. Bootstrapping solves this problem by developing the homomorphic modular function.

Recall the CKKS scheme, a message (complex vector) becomes a plaintext (polynomial) after encoding, and a plaintext becomes a ciphertext (polynomial vector) after encrypting. A homomorphic operation over ciphertexts corresponds to a similar operation over messages (*slot side*) rather than the plaintexts (*coefficient side*), so the design of homomorphic circuits should be oriented to the operations required by messages over slot side. Unfortunately, the extra term $q_0 I$ appears on the coefficient side. Thus, we need to move the plaintext (coefficient side), including $q_0 I$, to the slot side before evaluating the modular function, and move back after that for recovery. These can be done by homomorphic encoding and homomorphic decoding.

Let $\mathtt{ct}$ be a ciphertext encrypting a plaintext $\mathtt{pt}$ (message z on slot side) at level 0, we can perform bootstrapping on $\mathtt{ct}$ as follows[4].

- ModRaise: For $\mathtt{ct} \in \mathcal{R}_{q_0}^2$, it satisfies $[\langle \mathtt{ct}, \mathtt{sk} \rangle]_{q_0} = \mathtt{pt} + e$. We view it as $\mathtt{ct} \in \mathcal{R}_{Q_L}^2$ (In RNS, this step involves the fast basis conversion). One can see that the decryption becomes $[\langle \mathtt{ct}, sk \rangle]_{Q_L} = q_0 I + \mathtt{pt} + e$ for a polynomial $I(X)$ with integer coefficients.
- CoeffsToSlots: From the perspective of the slot, we let $A_{(k,j)} = \left(\zeta^{j \cdot 5^k} \right)_{0 \leq k,j < N/2}$, then $\mathtt{iDFT}(z; \bar{z}) = \frac{1}{2} \left(A^{-1} z + \overline{A^{-1} z}; -i \cdot A^{-1} z + i \cdot \overline{A^{-1} z} \right) \in \mathbb{R}^N$ [6]. To evaluate encoding, we need two ciphertexts to store the homomorphic iDFT result since each ciphertext only provides $N/2$ slots. Homomorphically, compute $\mathtt{ct}' = \mathsf{MatMult}\left(\frac{1}{2} A^{-1}, \mathtt{ct} \right)$ (see Subsect. 3.2), then $\mathtt{ct}_1 = \mathtt{ct}' + \mathsf{Conjugate}(\mathtt{ct}')$, $\mathtt{ct}_2 = -X^{N/2} \cdot \mathtt{ct}' + X^{N/2} \cdot \mathsf{Conjugate}(\mathtt{ct}')$. Note that the messages on the slot side of $\mathtt{ct}_1$ and $\mathtt{ct}_2$, denoted as z_1 and z_2, are the coefficients of $(q_0 I + \mathtt{pt} + e)/\Delta$ where Δ is the scaling factor[5].
- EvalMod: Modular function cannot be evaluated directly in CKKS, thus we approximate it by $f(x) = \frac{q_0}{\Delta \cdot 2\pi} \sin\left(2\pi x \frac{\Delta}{q_0} \right)$ and use some polynomials to approximate this trigonometric function [6] in a fixed interval. Therefore, EvalMod can be done by evaluating these polynomials homomorphically. As a result, we have ciphertexts $\mathtt{ct}_3 = \mathsf{EvalMod}(\mathtt{ct}_1)$ and $\mathtt{ct}_4 = \mathsf{EvalMod}(\mathtt{ct}_2)$ with the messages z_3 and z_4 on slot side, respectively. The encrypting messages are the coefficients of $(\mathtt{pt} + e)/\Delta$.
- SlotsToCoeffs: On the slot side, $\mathsf{DFT}(\mathtt{pt} + e) = A z_3 + i \cdot A z_4 = A (z_3 + i \cdot z_4)$. For homomorphic evaluation, compute $\mathtt{ct}' = \mathtt{ct}_3 + X^{N/2} \cdot \mathtt{ct}_4$, then $\mathtt{ct}_{\mathsf{out}} = \mathsf{MatMult}(A, \mathtt{ct}')$. Note that the message on the slot side has been recovered to the original z (approximately), thus $\mathtt{pt} + e$ is back to the coefficient side.

It is worth stating that $\mathtt{ct}_{\mathsf{out}} \in \mathcal{R}_{Q_\ell}^2$ for some $0 < \ell < L$ since all the homomorphic multiplications in bootstrapping need to consume levels.

2.3   Key-Switching

There are three types of key-switching techniques so far. The first one is BV-type key-switching, proposed by Brakerski and Vaikuntanathan [10]. They use a basis w to decompose the ciphertext and encode the power-part of w into the switching keys. This method reduces the noise of key-switching but require more computations. The second one is GHS-type key-switching, proposed by Gentry, Halevi, and Smart in [22]. Their idea is to temporarily extend the size of modulus Q with another modulus P, then reduce modulus to control the noise. However, this lowers the multiplicative depth supported by the scheme. Another one is the hybrid method of BV-type and GHS-type key-switching techniques [22,28]. It is a trade-off between efficiency and the number of levels of the scheme. In this

---

[4] For the reasons in Remark 1, we don't consider the sparsely packed ciphertext and SubSum operation throughout this paper.

[5] The error term changes during the homomorphic computation, but we still use e to denote it for simplicity.

paper, we mainly focus on the hybrid method, and the GHS-type key-switching will be used in the algorithm from Sect. 5.

Note that our proposed aggregated key-switching in Sect. 4 differs from these three methods. While the aforementioned methods focus on noise control during key-switching, we redesign the switching keys to achieve higher efficiency. In practice, our approach is implemented in conjunction with one of the three methods mentioned above.

3 Level-Conserving Rescaling

In this section, we first propose a new rescaling technique and show the challenge of applying it to CoeffsToSlots. To overcome the challenge, we make an attempt. Although the result is not satisfactory, it is crucial for subsequent improvements in the later sections.

Let $\mathcal{P} = \mathbb{R}[X]/(X^N + 1)$. Throughout this paper, we sometimes use non-integer polynomials (in $\mathcal{P}$) as plaintexts for the sake of analysis, as in [16].

3.1 The Rationales

Existing Rescaling. So far, for leveled homomorphic encryption schemes, the only way to reduce the error of a ciphertext is performing modulus switching, which is called *rescaling* in CKKS. While reducing errors, the ciphertext modulus should be reduced accordingly to maintain the validity of the ciphertext.

Specifically, for a ciphertext $\mathtt{ct} \in \mathcal{R}^2_{Q_\ell}$ encrypting plaintext $\mathtt{pt}$ with respect to secret key $\mathtt{sk}$, it is well-known that $[\langle \mathtt{ct}, \mathtt{sk} \rangle]_{Q_\ell} = \mathtt{pt} + e$ where e is the error and $\|\mathtt{pt} + e|)_\infty < Q_\ell/2$. We reformulate it as $\langle \mathtt{ct}, \mathtt{sk} \rangle = \mathtt{pt} + e + kQ_\ell$ for a polynomial k with integer coefficients. After rescaling by q_ℓ, we have ciphertext $\mathtt{ct}' = \lfloor \frac{1}{q_\ell} \cdot \mathtt{ct} \rceil$ that satisfies $\langle \mathtt{ct}', \mathtt{sk} \rangle \approx (\mathtt{pt} + e)/q_\ell + kQ_{\ell-1}$. To eliminate the term $kQ_{\ell-1}$, the modulus of $\mathtt{ct}'$ should be $Q_{\ell-1}$ rather than Q_ℓ. Moreover, if $\|(\mathtt{pt} + e)/q_\ell|)_\infty < Q_0/2$, Lemma 1 states that the modulus of $\mathtt{ct}'$ can be any element of $\{Q_i\}_{0 \leq i \leq \ell-1}$ (via the application of DropLevel), but cannot be Q_ℓ or any other larger modulus.

Lemma 1. *Let* $\left\{ Q_i = \prod_{j=0}^{i} q_j \right\}_{0 \leq i \leq L}$ *be the moduli of CKKS. For any ciphertext* $\mathtt{ct} \in \mathcal{R}^2_{Q_\ell}$ *encrypting* $\mathtt{pt}$ *with error* e, *it can be (approximately) decrypted to* $\mathtt{pt}$ *with any modulus* Q_i *if* $\|\mathtt{pt} + e|)_\infty < Q_i/2$ *and* $Q_i|Q_\ell$.

Proof. Let $\mathtt{ct}$ encrypt the plaintext $\mathtt{pt}$ with respect to the secret key $\mathtt{sk}$, we know that $[\langle \mathtt{ct}, \mathtt{sk} \rangle]_{Q_\ell} = \mathtt{pt} + e$ where e is the error term. Then $\langle \mathtt{ct}, \mathtt{sk} \rangle = \mathtt{pt} + e + kQ_\ell$ for k a polynomial with integer coefficients, it is obvious that for any $Q_i|Q_\ell$ and $\|\mathtt{pt} + e|)_\infty < Q_i/2$, $[\langle \mathtt{ct}, \mathtt{sk} \rangle]_{Q_i} = \mathtt{pt} + e$ holds. $\qquad\square$

To save modulus consumption of homomorphic operation, we would like to know whether there exists a rescaling operation that does not reduce modulus while maintaining the correct plaintext. That is, under what conditions can Q_ℓ be the modulus of the rescaled ciphertext $\mathtt{ct}'$? The above analysis implies that $\|\langle \mathtt{ct}, \mathtt{sk} \rangle|)_\infty < Q_\ell/2$ seems like an answer, but it is almost impossible since the coefficients of $\mathtt{ct}$ are usually uniform over $\mathbb{Z}_{Q_\ell}$ due to the RLWE assumption.

Our Rescaling. Fortunately, an in-depth observation into ModRaise makes *rescaling without modulus consumption* possible. Recall the process of ModRaise, the output ciphertext ct is at level L, but is not uniformly distributed over $\mathcal{R}_{Q_L}^2$. More specifically, it comes from the same $\mathtt{ct} \in \mathcal{R}_{q_0}^2$ and satisfies that $\langle \mathtt{ct}, \mathtt{sk} \rangle = q_0 I + \mathtt{pt} + e \ll Q_L/2$. After rescaling by q_L, ct becomes ct$'$ and $[\langle \mathtt{ct}', \mathtt{sk} \rangle]_{Q_{L-1}} = [\langle \mathtt{ct}', \mathtt{sk} \rangle]_{Q_L} \approx (q_0 I + \mathtt{pt} + e)/q_L$, which means that the modulus of ct$'$ stays at Q_L after rescaling. We call this new rescaling operation *level-conserving rescaling* (LCR).

Next, we show the concrete algorithm of level-conserving rescaling, and propose Theorem 1 that provides the correctness and the conditions for applying this new rescaling operation.

The algorithm of level-conserving rescaling is the same as CKKS.Rescale, except that the output ct$'$ is treated as a ciphertext in level ℓ. Alternatively, it can also be viewed as a combination of an ordinary rescaling from Q_ℓ to $Q_{\ell-1}$ and a modraise from $Q_{\ell-1}$ to Q_ℓ. The operation is presented as follow (see Appendix B.1 for the RNS version).

- LCRescale(ct): For $\mathtt{ct} \in \mathcal{R}_{Q_\ell}^2$, output $\mathtt{ct}' = \lfloor \frac{1}{q_\ell} \cdot \mathtt{ct} \rceil \in \mathcal{R}_{Q_\ell}^2$.

Theorem 1. *For ciphertext* ct *regarding to plaintext* pt, *secret key* sk *and modulus* Q_ℓ, *if* $\|\langle \mathtt{ct}, \mathtt{sk} \rangle|\|_\infty < Q_\ell/2$, *then* $\mathtt{ct}' = \mathsf{LCRescale}(\mathtt{ct})$ *is the ciphertext of* pt$/q_\ell$ *with respect to the same secret* sk *and modulus* Q_ℓ.

Proof. According to the decryption, we know $\langle \mathtt{ct}, \mathtt{sk} \rangle = \mathtt{pt} + e + kQ_\ell$ with $\|\mathtt{pt} + e|\|_\infty < Q_\ell/2$ for an error e and a polynomial k with integer coefficients. If $\|\langle \mathtt{ct}, \mathtt{sk} \rangle|\|_\infty < Q_\ell/2$, then $k = 0$, i.e., $\langle \mathtt{ct}, \mathtt{sk} \rangle = \mathtt{pt} + e$. After level-conserving rescaling, $\mathtt{ct}' = \lfloor \frac{1}{q_\ell} \cdot \mathtt{ct} \rceil = \frac{1}{q_\ell} \cdot \mathtt{ct} + \mathbf{r}$ where $\mathbf{r}$ is the rounding term with $\|\mathbf{r}|\|_\infty \leq 1/2$. We have

$$[\langle \mathtt{ct}', \mathtt{sk} \rangle]_{Q_\ell} = \left[\frac{1}{q_\ell} \cdot \langle \mathtt{ct}, \mathtt{sk} \rangle + \langle \mathbf{r}, \mathtt{sk} \rangle \right]_{Q_\ell} = \frac{\mathtt{pt}}{q_\ell} + e'$$

where $e' = \frac{e}{q_\ell} + \langle \mathbf{r}, \mathtt{sk} \rangle$ and $\|\langle \mathbf{r}, \mathtt{sk} \rangle|\|_\infty \leq \frac{h+1}{2}$.   □

The Challenge. Theorem 1 claims that such level-conserving rescaling can only be applied to those ciphertexts that have relatively small coefficients, i.e., $\|\langle \mathtt{ct}, \mathtt{sk} \rangle|\|_\infty < Q_\ell/2$. We also find that the ciphertext after ModRaise exactly satisfies this requirement. However, rescaling is usually performed after homomorphic multiplication, and homomorphic multiplication requires the key-switching operation, which involves an inner-product between the ciphertext and evk. This product would make the coefficients of the ciphertext uniform over $\mathbb{Z}_{Q_\ell}$, and then level-conserving rescaling becomes useless. Therefore, the application of the level-conserving rescaling technique is still significantly challenging. In the next subsection, we try to apply it to CoeffsToSlots.

348   L. Yan et al.

Remark 1. In sparsely packed ciphertexts, the SubSum algorithm is performed after ModRaise [6,14], which contains the rotations and key-switching operations. As mentioned before, key-switching would break the small coefficient property of the ciphertexts and make level-conserving rescaling useless. Therefore, in this paper, we assume that all ciphertexts are fully packed.

3.2 An Attempt: Level-Conserving Matrix×Vector

As the procedure immediately following ModRaise, CoeffsToSlots should be explored for applying the level-conserving rescaling. In CoeffsToSlots, rescaling is performed at the end of the homomorphic matrix-vector multiplication. So we try to modify the matrix-vector multiplication algorithm by moving rescaling forward and see what will happen.

Original Algorithm. In CKKS bootstrapping [14], homomorphic matrix-vector multiplication involves plaintext-ciphertext multiplications and rotations. More formally, let $n = N/2$, for a matrix $\boldsymbol{M} = (M_{i,j})_{0 \leq i,j < n} \in \mathbb{C}^{n \times n}$ and a ciphertext ct with message $\boldsymbol{z} \in \mathbb{C}^n$ on slots, the goal of linear transformation is to compute a ciphertext ct' with message $\boldsymbol{Mz}$ on slots. Let $\rho_j(\cdot)$ denote the cyclic shift of j positions to the left ($j < 0$ means cyclic shift to right), $\boldsymbol{u}_j = (M_{0,j}, M_{1,j+1}, \cdots, M_{n-j-1,n-1}, M_{n-j,0}, \cdots, M_{n-1,j-1}) \in \mathbb{C}^n$ denote the shifted diagonal vector of $\boldsymbol{M}$ for $0 \leq j < n$, as presented in [14,24], then the matrix-vector multiplication can be represented as

$$\boldsymbol{M} \cdot \boldsymbol{z} = \sum_{j=0}^{n-1} (\boldsymbol{u}_j \odot \rho_j(\boldsymbol{z})) \tag{2}$$

where $\odot$ is the Hadamard product of vectors. Using the idea of Baby-Step Giant-Step (BSGS) algorithm, it can be optimized to

$$\boldsymbol{M} \cdot \boldsymbol{z} = \sum_{j=0}^{n_2-1} \rho_{n_1 \cdot j} \left(\sum_{i=0}^{n_1-1} \rho_{-n_1 \cdot j}(\boldsymbol{u}_{n_1 \cdot j + i}) \odot \rho_i(\boldsymbol{z}) \right) \tag{3}$$

where $n_1 = \mathcal{O}(\sqrt{n})$ and $n_2 = n/n_1$ are both integers. Homomorphically, the matrix-vector multiplication is described as follows, which requires $\mathcal{O}(n_1 + n_2)$ rotations and $\mathcal{O}(n)$ scalar multiplications (plaintext-ciphertext multiplications).

MatMult($\boldsymbol{M}$, ct): BSGS algorithm of matrix-vector multiplication in [14].

Input: A matrix $\boldsymbol{M} \in \mathbb{C}^{n \times n}$, a ciphertext $\text{ct} \in \mathcal{R}^2_{Q_\ell}$, $n = n_1 n_2$, a scaling factor Δ and the required rotation keys $\{\text{rtk}_k\}_{0 \leq k < n}$.

Output: A ciphertext $\text{ct}' \in \mathcal{R}^2_{Q_{\ell-1}}$.

Step 1 (Precomputation): $\text{pt}_{n_1 \cdot j + i} = \text{Encode}(\rho_{-n_1 \cdot j}(\boldsymbol{u}_{n_1 \cdot j + i}), \Delta) \in \mathcal{R}$ for $0 \leq i < n_1, 0 \leq j < n_2$.

Step 2 (Baby-Step): Compute $\text{ct}_j = \sum_{i=0}^{n_1-1} (\text{pt}_{n_1 \cdot j + i} \cdot \text{CKKS.Rotate}(\text{ct}, i, \text{rtk}_i))$ $\in \mathcal{R}^2_{Q_\ell}$ for $0 \leq j < n_2$.

Step 3 (Giant-Step): Compute $\text{ct} = \sum_{j=0}^{n_2-1} \text{CKKS.Rotate}(\text{ct}_j, n_1 \cdot j, \text{rtk}_{n_1 \cdot j})$.

Step 4 (Rescaling): Compute $\text{ct}' = \text{CKKS.Rescale}(\text{ct}) \in \mathcal{R}^2_{Q_{\ell-1}}$.

Tentative Modification. In the BSGS algorithm of matrix-vector multiplication, the rescaling operation is after rotations, and the key-switching operation in rotations breaks the small coefficient property of ciphertext. Therefore, to use the level-conserving rescaling, we need to discard the BSGS algorithm and delay the rotations.

We rewrite Eq. (2) as

$$M \cdot z = \sum_{j=0}^{n-1} \rho_j \left(\rho_{-j}(u_j) \odot z \right), \tag{4}$$

and put the rescaling before homomorphic rotations. Moreover, we replace the rescaling operation by the level-conserving rescaling, to obtain a *level-conserving matrix-vector multiplication* that does not consume any modulus. The correctness of the proposed algorithm relies on the Theorem 1 that has been proven.

---

level-conserving matrix-vector multiplication algorithm.

Input: A matrix $M \in \mathbb{C}^{n \times n}$ with $\{u_j\}_{0 \leq j < n}$ its shifted diagonal vectors, ciphertext $\mathsf{ct} \in \mathcal{R}_{Q_L}^2$ is the output of ModRaise, a scaling factor Δ and the required rotation keys $\{\mathtt{rtk}_j\}_{0 \leq j < n}$.

Output: A ciphertext $\mathsf{ct}' \in \mathcal{R}_{Q_L}^2$.

Step 1 (Precomputation): $\mathsf{pt}_j = \mathsf{Encode}(\rho_{-j}(u_j), \Delta) \in \mathcal{R}$ for $0 \leq j < n$.

Step 2 (Multiplication and rescaling): Compute $\mathsf{ct}_j = \mathsf{LCRescale}(\mathsf{pt}_j \cdot \mathsf{ct}) \in \mathcal{R}_{Q_L}^2$ for $0 \leq j < n$.

Step 3 (Rotations): Compute $\mathsf{ct}' = \sum_{j=0}^{n-1} \mathsf{CKKS.Rotate}(\mathsf{ct}_j, j, \mathtt{rtk}_j) \in \mathcal{R}_{Q_L}^2$.

Results of the Attempt. It is easy to see that the level-conserving matrix-vector multiplication consumes no modulus, thus saving one level of moduli in bootstrapping. However, without the BSGS algorithm, the algorithmic overhead (both time and space) is worse than before. The modified algorithm requires $n - 1$ rotations while the original method requires $n_1 + n_2 - 2 \approx \mathcal{O}(\sqrt{n})$ rotations, which also means more memory is needed to store the rotation keys. The modified algorithm also repeats rescaling operation n times while the BSGS method only needs 1 rescaling. Overall, this result is not satisfactory. Despite saving the modulus, it seems that the overhead loss is not worth it.

Next Directions. We believe that the modification in the attempt for saving modulus is on the right path, but we need to reduce the algorithmic overhead. A high-level analysis does not seem to provide solutions, we will conduct a deeper analysis of the matrix-vector multiplication algorithm. Note that the complexity increased because we discard the idea of BSGS. So we consider, is there a case where discarding BSGS does not bring efficiency loss? (We find the case in Subsect. 4.1). Additionally, We can introduce more techniques to further reduce the complexity, which is exactly what we will do in Subsect. 4.2.

4   Improved Matrix-Vector Multiplication with Aggregated Key-Switching

In this section, we temporarily forget about the level-conserving rescaling proposed in Sect. 3 and focus on improving matrix-vector multiplication without BSGS. In Subsect. 4.1, we recall the existing double-hoisting BSGS matrix-vector multiplication in [6] and provide a theoretical complexity analysis. We notice that when using the matrix factorization approach [11,25] in linear transformations of bootstrapping, the number of non-zero diagonals of the factorized matrices is small. In this case, discarding BSGS seems to incur no (or very small) efficiency loss, especially with non-zero diagonals ≤ 32. Furthermore, in Subsect. 4.2, we introduce the aggregated key-switching approach to further reduce the computational overhead of matrix-vector multiplication without BSGS for matrices with non-zero diagonals ≤ 64.

For a detailed complexity analysis, we consider the full-RNS CKKS in this section. The basic homomorphic operations of the RNS-CKKS are presented in Appendix A. Unless otherwise stated, notations in this section are consistent with those in Sect. 2 and Appendix A. In RNS representation, we assume that all polynomials are presented in the NTT form by default, and would be converted into the coefficient form when required. Additionally, let $n = N/2$, $n_1 n_2 = n$, $\mathcal{B}_\ell = \{q_0, q_1, \cdots, q_\ell\}$, $\mathcal{D}_\ell = \mathcal{B}_\ell \cup \mathcal{C}$ for $0 \leq \ell \leq L$, and the number of separated segments $\beta = \lceil (\ell + 1)/\alpha \rceil$. Let $\hat{D}_j = Q/D_j$, and $D_j^* = \left[\hat{D}_j^{-1}\right]_{D_j}$ denoting the inverse of $\hat{D}_j$ modulo D_j for $0 \leq j < \beta$.

4.1   Existing Double-Hoisting BSGS Matrix-Vector Multiplication

We discuss the double-hoisting BSGS matrix-vector multiplication algorithm in [6] since it contains most of the existing optimizations related to linear transformations, such as the hybrid key-switching approach, the improved key-switching keys (including both $\hat{D}_j$ and D_j^*), the optimized hoisting-rotations and the double-hoisting BSGS algorithm by delaying the ModDown step. For simplicity, we let φ_k denote the automorphism ϕ_{5^k} (defined in Subsect. 2.1). In precomputations, we need to compute the modified rotation keys

$$\widetilde{\mathsf{rtk}}_{k,j} = \left(\widetilde{\mathsf{rtk}}^0_{k,j}, \widetilde{\mathsf{rtk}}^1_{k,j}\right) = \left(\left[-a_j\varphi_k^{-1}(s) + Ps \cdot \hat{D}_j \cdot D_j^* + e_j\right]_{PQ_L}, [a_j]_{PQ_L}\right)$$

where $0 \leq j < \mathsf{dnum}$ and k is the rotation position number. For matrix $\boldsymbol{M} \in \mathbb{C}^{n \times n}$, we encode its shifted diagonal vector into

$$\mathsf{pt}_{n_1 \cdot t + i} = \mathsf{Encode}(\rho_{-n_1 \cdot t}(\boldsymbol{u}_{n_1 \cdot t + i}), \Delta) \in \mathcal{R}$$

for $0 \leq i < n_1, 0 \leq t < n_2$, according to Eq. (3).

The double-hoisting BSGS algorithm of matrix-vector multiplication in [6].

Input: Ciphertext $\hat{ct} = (\hat{c}_0, \hat{c}_1) \in \left(\prod_{j'=0}^{\ell} \mathbb{Z}_{q_{j'}}^N\right)^2$, plaintexts $\{\hat{pt}_{n_1 \cdot t + i}\}$ and the rotation keys $\left\{\widehat{rtk}_{i,j}, \widehat{rtk}_{n_1 \cdot t, j}\right\}$ for $0 \le i < n_1, 0 \le t < n_2, 0 \le j < \beta$.

Output: $\hat{ct}' \in \left(\prod_{j'=0}^{\ell-1} \mathbb{Z}_{q_{j'}}^N\right)^2$, the evaluation of $M \times \hat{ct}$.

Step 1 (Decompose): (1) iNTT: $c_1 = \text{iNTT}(\hat{c}_1) \in \prod_{j'=0}^{\ell} \mathcal{R}_{q_{j'}}$. (2) Decompose: $d_j = \text{Decomp}(c_1) \in \prod_{j'=0}^{\ell} \mathcal{R}_{q_{j'}} \times \prod_{i'=0}^{k-1} \mathcal{R}_{p_{i'}}$ for $0 \le j < \beta$. (3) NTT: Let $\hat{d} = \left(\hat{d}_j\right)_{0 \le j < \beta}$ where $\hat{d}_j = \text{NTT}(d_j) \in \prod_{j'=0}^{\ell} \mathbb{Z}_{q_{j'}}^N \times \prod_{i'=0}^{k-1} \mathbb{Z}_{p_{i'}}^N$.

Step 2 (MultSum): (1) Compute $P \cdot \hat{c}_0$: $\hat{c}_0' = ([P \cdot \hat{c}_0^{(0)}]_{q_0}, \cdots, [P \cdot \hat{c}_0^{(\ell)}]_{q_\ell}, 0, \cdots, 0) \in \prod_{j'=0}^{\ell} \mathbb{Z}_{q_{j'}}^N \times \prod_{i'=0}^{k-1} \mathbb{Z}_{p_{i'}}^N$. (2) MultSum: For $0 \le i < n_1$, compute $\left(\hat{a}_i, \hat{b}_i\right) = \text{MultSum}(\hat{d}, \widehat{rtk}_i)$, then let $\left(\hat{a}_i, \hat{b}_i\right) = \left(\hat{a}_i, \hat{b}_i\right) + (\hat{c}_0', 0)$.

Step 3 (Permute): For $0 \le i < n_1$, $\left(\hat{a}_i, \hat{b}_i\right) = \left(\varphi_i(\hat{a}_i), \varphi_i(\hat{b}_i)\right)$.

Step 4 (ScalarMult+Add): For $0 \le t < n_2$, compute $\hat{u}_t = (\hat{u}_{t,0}, \hat{u}_{t,1}) = \sum_{i=0}^{n_1-1} \text{PlainMult}\left(\hat{pt}_{n_1 \cdot t + i}, \left(\hat{a}_i, \hat{b}_i\right)\right) \in \left(\prod_{j'=0}^{\ell} \mathbb{Z}_{q_{j'}}^N \times \prod_{i'=0}^{k-1} \mathbb{Z}_{p_{i'}}^N\right)^2$.

Step 5 (ModDown): (1) iNTT: For $0 \le t < n_2$, $u_t = \text{iNTT}(\hat{u}_t)$. (2) ModDown: For $0 \le t < n_2$, $(u_{t,0}, u_{t,1}) = \text{ModDown}(u_t) \in \left(\prod_{j'=0}^{\ell} \mathcal{R}_{q_{j'}}\right)^2$.

Step 6 (Decompose): (1) Decompose: For $0 \le t < n_2$, $w_{t,j} = \text{Decomp}(u_{t,1}) \in \prod_{j'=0}^{\ell} \mathcal{R}_{q_{j'}} \times \prod_{i'=0}^{k-1} \mathcal{R}_{p_{i'}}$ where $0 \le j < \beta$. (2) NTT: For $0 \le t < n_2$, let $\hat{w}_t = (\hat{w}_{t,j})_{0 \le j < \beta}$ where $\hat{w}_{t,j} = \text{NTT}(w_{t,j})$.

Step 7 (MultSum): For $0 \le t < n_2$, compute $(\hat{r}_{t,0}, \hat{r}_{t,1}) = \text{MultSum}(\hat{w}_t, \widehat{rtk}_{n_1 \cdot t}) \in \left(\prod_{j'=0}^{\ell} \mathbb{Z}_{q_{j'}}^N \times \prod_{i'=0}^{k-1} \mathbb{Z}_{p_{i'}}^N\right)^2$.

Step 8 (Permute+Add): $\hat{r} = (\hat{r}_0, \hat{r}_1) = \left(\sum_{t=0}^{n_2-1} \varphi_{n_1 \cdot t}(\hat{r}_{t,0}), \sum_{t=0}^{n_2-1} \varphi_{n_1 \cdot t}(\hat{r}_{t,1})\right) \in \left(\prod_{j'=0}^{\ell} \mathbb{Z}_{q_{j'}}^N \times \prod_{i'=0}^{k-1} \mathbb{Z}_{p_{i'}}^N\right)^2$. $r_2 = \sum_{t=0}^{n_2-1} \varphi_{n_1 \cdot t}(u_{t,0}) \in \prod_{j'=0}^{\ell} \mathcal{R}_{q_{j'}}$.

Step 9 (ModDown): (1) iNTT: $r = \text{iNTT}(\hat{r})$. (2) ModDown: $(r_0, r_1) = \text{ModDown}(r)$. (3) $(r_0, r_1) = (r_0, r_1) + (r_2, 0)$.

Step 10 (Rescaling): (1) Rescale: $r' = \text{Rescale}((r_0, r_1)) \in \left(\prod_{j'=0}^{\ell-1} \mathcal{R}_{q_{j'}}\right)^2$. (2) NTT: $\hat{ct}' = \text{NTT}(r')$.

We show the algorithm above in RNS representation to facilitate the analysis of the time complexity (provided in Appendix E). We use $\widehat{rtk}$ to represent the NTT form of $\widehat{rtk}$. The basic operations, including Decomp, MultSum, PlainMult, ModDown and Rescale, are listed in Appendix A.1 and A.2.

Roughly speaking, the time complexity of the double-hoisting BSGS algorithm can be divided into two parts: n ScalarMult and rotations, where rotations comprise four steps (Decompose, MultSum, ModDown and Permute). Also refer to [6], the complexity of these rotations can be described as

$$n_2 \cdot (Decompose + MultSum + ModDown + Permute)$$
$$+ n_1 \cdot (MultSum + Permute) + Decompose + ModDown.$$

Thus the total complexity can be minimized when the ratio n_1/n_2 reaches to an optimal value.

Table 1. Time complexity of the double-hoisting BSGS algorithm in [6] for different r_1/r_2 and different r. The used parameters are $N = 2^{16}, \ell = 24, k = 5, \alpha = 5$. Mult represents the integer multiplication in $\mathbb{Z}_{q_{j'}}$ or $\mathbb{Z}_{p_{i'}}$, whose values are calculated according to the complexity analysis from Appendix E. "-" means the ratio is impossible since $r_1 \cdot r_2 = r$ and r_1, r_2 must be integers.

	$r=8$ r_1/r_2	log(#Mult)	$r=16$ r_1/r_2	log(#Mult)	$r=32$ r_1/r_2	log(#Mult)
	1	-	1	30.703	1	-
	2	30.019	2	-	2	30.816
	4	-	4	30.158	4	-
	8	**29.667**	8	-	8	**30.4018**
	16	-	16	**29.956**	16	-
	32	-	32	-	32	30.4021

	$r=64$ r_1/r_2	log(#Mult)	$r=128$ r_1/r_2	log(#Mult)	$r=256$ r_1/r_2	log(#Mult)
	1	31.608	1	-	1	32.641
	2	-	2	31.778	2	-
	4	31.017	4	-	4	32.067
	8	-	8	**31.3511**	8	-
	16	**30.792**	16	-	16	**31.850**
	32	-	32	31.3514	32	-
	64	31.018	64	-	64	32.068

If we discard the BSGS method in linear transformations, it is equivalent to setting $n_1/n_2 = n$ with $n_1 = n$ and $n_2 = 1$. At first glance, this is a terrible idea. However, when we apply the matrix factorization approach [11,25], which is widely utilized in practice, to bootstrapping, the number of non-zero diagonals of the factorized matrices becomes a constant r instead of n (also with r_1, r_2 instead of n_1, n_2). Typically, the number of non-zero diagonals is around 16 or 32 (resp. 32 or 64) for 4-depth (resp. 3-depth) factorization in CoeffsToSlots[6] with $N = 2^{16}$. In this case, discarding BSGS means setting r_1/r_2 to 16, 32 or 64.

Moreover, Bossuat et al. show that the best ratio of the double-hoisting BSGS is usually 8 or 16 (Table 2 in [6]), our results in Table 1 also support it. If $r = 16$, discarding BSGS implies setting the ratio optimal, which has no efficiency loss (even has efficiency gain if the original BSGS doesn't use the optimal ratio). If $r = 32$, discarding BSGS has only a slight efficiency loss (see Table 1, 30.4021 vs. 30.4018), which can be compensated by the aggregated key-switching proposed in Sect. 4.2. For larger r, discarding BSGS will produce a worse efficiency, which

---

[6] "4-depth factorization in CoeffsToSlots" means factorizing the iDFT-related matrix into 4 sparse diagonal matrices, thus the depth of CoeffsToSlots is 4.

is consistent with the common consensus. We point out that when $r = 64$, the efficiency loss of discarding BSGS is non-negligible; however, this can be compensated by adopting the improved algorithm in Sect. 4.2 (See Table 2 for details).

Overall, in the case of matrices with ≤ 32 non-zero diagonals, discarding BSGS seems to incur no (or small) efficiency loss for double-hoisting matrix-vector multiplication.

Remark 2. Note that while the above argument may be logically rigorous, its conclusion is relatively theoretical. In fact, counting the number of multiplications modulo $q_{j'}$ or $p_{i'}$ is not a reliable indicator of actual efficiency. Real-world efficiency is dependent on parameters, implementation, and hardware environment. Therefore, in practice, even when matrices have only a small number of non-zero diagonals, directly discarding BSGS may still incur a minor efficiency loss. We stress that discarding BSGS is not an optimization in itself; rather, it can serve as a trade-off tool to enable other optimization techniques (e.g., the proposed LCR).

4.2 Faster Matrix-Vector Multiplication for Sparse Diagonal Matrix

In this subsection, we continue to consider the sparse diagonal matrices (i.e., ≤ 64 non-zero diagonals). We propose a new key-switching technique that can reduce the time complexity of matrix-vector multiplications without BSGS method. We first show the new key-switching method (called aggregated key-switching), then provide the improved matrix-vector multiplication algorithm and the complexity analysis. We also compare the improved algorithm with the double-hoisting BSGS algorithm in [6].

Aggregated Key-Switching (AKS). To reduce the number of scalar multiplications and rescaling operations, we merge them into the key-switching procedure. Specifically, for the plaintext-ciphertext multiplication $m \times \mathtt{ct}$ with modulus Q_ℓ, and the key-switching from s_1 to s_2, we redefine the key-switching keys $\{\mathtt{evk}_j\}_{0 \leq j < \mathtt{dnum}}$ as

$$\mathtt{evk}_j = \left(\mathtt{evk}_j^0, \mathtt{evk}_j^1\right) = \left(\left[-a_j \cdot s_2 + \left\lfloor \frac{\left[Pms_1 \cdot \hat{D}_j \cdot D_j^*\right]_{PQ_L}}{q_\ell} \right\rceil + e_j\right]_{PQ_L} , [a_j]_{PQ_L}\right)$$

where $a_j \leftarrow U\left(\mathcal{R}_{PQ_L}\right)$ and $e_j \leftarrow \chi_{\mathsf{err}}$ for $0 \leq j < \mathtt{dnum}$[7]. In homomorphic evaluations, for $\mathtt{ct} = (c_0, c_1) \in \mathcal{R}_{Q_\ell}^2$, we perform the following procedure.

---

[7] See Appendix B.2 for the RNS version.

(1)**Key-Switching:** $(d_0, d_1) = \lfloor \frac{1}{P} \cdot \left(\sum_{j=0}^{\beta-1} [c_1]_{D_j} \cdot \mathbf{evk}_j \pmod{PQ_{\ell-1}} \right) \rceil \in \mathcal{R}^2_{Q_{\ell-1}}$.

(2)**ScalarMult+Rescale:** $c'_0 = \mathsf{CKKS.Rescale}(m \cdot c_0) = \lfloor \frac{1}{q_\ell} \cdot m \cdot c_0 \rceil \in \mathcal{R}_{Q_{\ell-1}}$.

(3)**Addition:** $\mathbf{ct}' = (d_0, d_1) + (c'_0, 0) \in \mathcal{R}^2_{Q_{\ell-1}}$.

Then, we have Theorem 2 stating that this procedure completes the key-switching, plaintext-ciphertext product and rescaling operations. The proof of Theorem 2 including the noise analysis is provided in Appendix C.

Theorem 2. *Let m be a plaintext, $\mathbf{ct}$ be a ciphertext encrypting $\mathbf{pt}$ with respect to secret s_1 and modulus Q_ℓ. Then the output of the above procedure is a valid encryption of $\frac{1}{q_\ell} \cdot m \cdot \mathbf{pt}$ with respect to s_2 and $Q_{\ell-1}$.*

Improved Matrix-Vector Multiplication. We now discuss our improved matrix-vector multiplication algorithm. As mentioned before, when using the matrix factorization method of [11,25] in bootstrapping, the DFT/iDFT matrices are decomposed into several sparse matrices with typically 16/32 non-zero diagonals, and discarding BSGS will bring no (or small) efficiency loss in this case. On this basis, we use the AKS technique for less multiplications.

For matrix $M \in \mathbb{C}^{n \times n}$, according to Eq. (4), we encode its shifted diagonal vector into $m_i = \mathsf{Encode}(\rho_{-i}(\boldsymbol{u}_i), \Delta) \in \mathcal{R}$ for $0 \leq i < n$[8]. Moreover, we write

$$\widetilde{\mathbf{rtk}}_{i,j} = \left(\widetilde{\mathbf{rtk}}^0_{i,j}, \widetilde{\mathbf{rtk}}^1_{i,j} \right) = \left(\left[-a_j \varphi_i^{-1}(s) + \lfloor \frac{\left[Pm_i s \cdot \hat{D}_j \cdot D_j^* \right]_{PQ_L}}{q_\ell} \rceil + e_j \right]_{PQ_L}, [a_j]_{PQ_L} \right)$$

where $0 \leq j < \mathsf{dnum}$ and i is the rotation position number. Then, we show our improved algorithm in RNS representation on the next page.

Complexity Analysis. As in Appendix E, we count the number of integer multiplications in $\mathbb{Z}_{q_{j'}}$ or $\mathbb{Z}_{p_{i'}}$ for time complexity.

- Step 1: This step is the same as the Step 1 of the algorithm in Subsect. 4.1, thus the complexity is $(\ell+1)N \log N + (\alpha + (\ell + k + 1 - \alpha)(\alpha + 1)) \beta N + (\ell + k + 1 - \alpha)\beta N \log N$ (see Appendix E).
- Step 2: Complexity of n MultSum operations over $\ell + k$ small moduli is $2(\ell + k)\beta n N$ (see Appendix D.4). DropLevel has no integer multiplication.
- Step 3: Complexity of n PlainMult operations for $\hat{c}_0$ over $\ell + 1$ small moduli is $(\ell + 1)nN$ (see Appendix D.5).
- Step 4: There is no integer multiplications in Permute and additions.

---

[8] For easy description, we still use n to denote the number of rotations. When comparing complexity, we set n to the number of non-zero diagonals r.

- Step 5: (1) u has $2(\ell + k)$ polynomials, thus the iNTT complexity is $2(\ell + k)N \log N$. (2) The ModDown procedure from $\mathcal{D}_{\ell-1}$ to $\mathcal{B}_{\ell-1}$ has complexity of $2(k\ell + 2\ell + k)N$ (similar to Appendix D.3).
- Step 6: (1) The iNTT complexity is $(\ell + 1)N \log N$ since r has $\ell + 1$ polynomials. (2) The complexity of rescaling on r is ℓN (see Appendix D.6).
- Step 7: u' has 2ℓ polynomials, thus the NTT complexity is $2\ell N \log N$.

Our improved (sparse) matrix$\times$vector algorithm with AKS.

Input: Ciphertext $\hat{ct} = (\hat{c}_0, \hat{c}_1) \in \left(\prod_{j'=0}^{\ell} \mathbb{Z}_{q_{j'}}^N\right)^2$, plaintexts $\{\hat{m}_i\}$ and the rotation keys $\left\{\widehat{\text{rtk}}_{i,j}\right\}$ for $0 \leq i < n$, $0 \leq j < \beta$.

Output: $\hat{ct}' \in \left(\prod_{j'=0}^{\ell-1} \mathbb{Z}_{q_{j'}}^N\right)^2$, the evaluation of $M \times \hat{ct}$.

Step 1 (Decompose): (1) iNTT: $c_1 = \text{iNTT}(\hat{c}_1)$. (2) Decompose: $d_j = \text{Decomp}(c_1) \in \prod_{j'=0}^{\ell} \mathcal{R}_{q_{j'}} \times \prod_{i'=0}^{k-1} \mathcal{R}_{p_{i'}}$ for $0 \leq j < \beta$. (3) NTT: Let $\hat{d} = \left(\hat{d}_j\right)_{0 \leq j < \beta}$ where $\hat{d}_j = \text{NTT}(d_j)$.

Step 2 (MultSum): For $0 \leq i < n$, compute $\left(\hat{a}_i, \hat{b}_i\right) = \text{MultSum}(\hat{d}, \widehat{\text{rtk}}_i) \in \left(\prod_{j'=0}^{\ell-1} \mathbb{Z}_{q_{j'}}^N \times \prod_{i'=0}^{k-1} \mathbb{Z}_{p_{i'}}^N\right)^2$ (This is done with an RNS.DropLevel).

Step 3 (ScalarMult): For $0 \leq i < n$, $\hat{w}_i = \text{PlainMult}\left(\hat{m}_i, \hat{c}_0\right) \in \prod_{j'=0}^{\ell} \mathbb{Z}_{q_{j'}}^N$.

Step 4 (Permute+Add): Compute $\hat{u} = (\hat{u}_0, \hat{u}_1) = \left(\sum_{i=0}^{n-1} \varphi_i(\hat{a}_i), \sum_{i=0}^{n-1} \varphi_i(\hat{b}_i)\right)$, $\hat{r} = \sum_{i=0}^{n-1} \varphi_i(\hat{w}_i)$.

Step 5 (ModDown): (1) iNTT: $u = \text{iNTT}(\hat{u})$. (2) ModDown: $(u'_0, u'_1) = \text{ModDown}(u) \in \left(\prod_{j'=0}^{\ell-1} \mathcal{R}_{q_{j'}}\right)^2$.

Step 6 (Rescaling): (1) iNTT: $r = \text{iNTT}(\hat{r}) \in \prod_{j'=0}^{\ell} \mathcal{R}_{q_{j'}}$. (2) Rescale: $r' = \text{Rescale}(r) \in \prod_{j'=0}^{\ell-1} \mathcal{R}_{q_{j'}}$.

Step 7 (NTT): $u' = (r', 0) + (u'_0, u'_1)$, then $\hat{ct}' = \text{NTT}(u') \in \left(\prod_{j'=0}^{\ell-1} \mathbb{Z}_{q_{j'}}^N\right)^2$.

Complexity Comparison. Here we compare the complexity of our improved matrix$\times$vector algorithm and the double-hoisting BSGS algorithm in [6] when focusing on the sparse diagonal matrix. We assume that the number of non-zero diagonals in matrix M is r, then for the complexity, $n = r$ and $n_1 = r_1, n_2 = r_2$ with $r_1 \cdot r_2 = r$. According to the complexity analysis in Appendix E and this subsection, we compute the value of the time complexity for various values of r when N, ℓ, k and α are fixed. The results in Table 2 show that our improved algorithm without BSGS is faster than the double-hoisting BSGS algorithm when $r \leq 64$, especially achieves at most $2.497\times$ speedup when $r = 16$. For matrices with $r \geq 128$, discarding BSGS significantly increases the time complexity that even cannot be compensated by the AKS technique.

For space complexity, our algorithm needs $r - 1$ rotation keys while previous BSGS algorithm requires the number of $r_1 + r_2 - 2$, which means that the improved algorithm in this section is a time-memory trade-off. In Subsect. 5.1, we further modify it and obtain a lossless improvement.

Table 2. Time complexity comparison of the double-hoisting BSGS algorithm from [6] and our algorithm from Sect. 4.2 in the case of sparse diagonal matrix. The used parameters are $N = 2^{16}, \ell = 24, k = 5, \alpha = 5$. Mult represents the integer multiplication in $\mathbb{Z}_{q_{j'}}$ or $\mathbb{Z}_{p_{i'}}$. Values are calculated from "Complexity Analysis" of Appendix E and Sect. 4.2. "-" means the ratio is impossible since r_1, r_2 must be integers.

		BSGS in [6]	Ours				BSGS in [6]	Ours	
r	r_1/r_2	$\log(\#\text{Mult})$	$\log(\#\text{Mult})$	Speedup	r	r_1/r_2	$\log(\#\text{Mult})$	$\log(\#\text{Mult})$	Speedup
16	1	30.703	29.383	2.497×	32	1	-	29.940	-
	2	-		-		2	30.816		1.835×
	4	30.158		1.711×		4	-		-
	8	-		-		8	**30.4018**		1.377×
	16	**29.956**		1.488×		16	-		-
	32	-		-		32	30.4021		1.378×
64	1	31.608	30.655	1.936×	128	1	-	31.488	-
	2	-		-		2	31.778		1.223×
	4	31.017		1.285×		4	-		-
	8	-		-		8	**31.3511**		0.909×
	16	**30.792**		1.100×		16	-		-
	32	-		-		32	31.3514		0.910×
	64	31.018		1.286×		64	-		-

5   Combining Them in Bootstrapping

Now, we recall the level-conserving rescaling in Sect. 3. In CKKS bootstrapping, the DFT/iDFT matrix is factorized into several sparse diagonal matrices by using the matrix factorization approach [11,25] (assuming that the number of non-zero diagonals ≤ 64). It is easy to see that, LCR can save the modulus in the first matrix-vector multiplication of CoeffsToSlots, and the idea of AKS can reduce the time complexity of all the matrix-vector multiplications but requiring more rotation keys. Therefore, for the first matrix-vector multiplication of CoeffsToSlots, one can combine the two ideas since BSGS is discarded; for other matrix-vector multiplications (including those in SlotsToCoeffs), one can use the improved algorithm with AKS (or not if the memory space is insufficient).

5.1   The Combined Algorithm for the First Matrix-Vector Multiplication of **CoeffsToSlots**

Next, we discuss the combined algorithm (LCR+AKS) for matrix-vector multiplication (detailed in Appendix F), which contains both LCR and AKS techniques. Compared to the algorithm with AKS alone, there are *three differences*.

- Level is not reduced in the aggregated key-switching procedure.
- Rescaling is replaced by the level-conserving rescaling operation.
- Use the GHS-type key-switching instead of the hybrid method.

The first two differences are easy to understand. In the third point, we adopt the GHS-type key-switching because: the hybrid key-switching involves the CRT composition $\sum_{j=0}^{\beta-1} [c_1]_{D_j} \cdot \hat{D}_j D_j^* = c_1 + k_2 Q_\ell$ where k_2 a polynomial with integer coefficients (see Eq. (6) of Appendix C). After rescaling by q_ℓ, the term $k_2 Q_\ell$ becomes $k_2 Q_{\ell-1}$ and cannot be eliminated by modulo Q_ℓ. So we cannot maintain the modulus level after key-switching. To overcome this, we utilize the GHS-type key-switching. Normally, changing hybrid key-switching to GHS-type requires increasing the auxiliary module P. However, we do not need to increase P, we use the same auxiliary modulus P as in the hybrid key-switching, so the number of the total levels of the scheme is maintained. This can be done due to the small coefficient property of the ciphertext, which leads to a small noise (see the noise analysis below).

Concretely, in the combined algorithm for matrix-vector multiplication, we write the rotation keys (with the same notations as before) as

$$\widetilde{\mathbf{rtk}}_i = \left(\widetilde{\mathbf{rtk}}_i^0, \widetilde{\mathbf{rtk}}_i^1\right) = \left(\left[-a\varphi_i^{-1}(s) + \lfloor \frac{[Pm_is]_{PQ_L}}{q_L} \rceil + e\right]_{PQ_L}, [a]_{PQ_L}\right) \quad (5)$$

where i is the rotation position number, $a \leftarrow U(\mathcal{R}_{PQ_L})$ and $e \leftarrow \chi_{\text{err}}$. In the key-switching procedure, for $\mathtt{ct} = (c_0, c_1) \in \mathcal{R}_{Q_L}^2$ the output of ModRaise with $\|c_0|)_\infty, \|c_1|)_\infty \leq q_0/2$, we perform

$$(d_0, d_1) = \lfloor \frac{1}{P} \cdot \left(c_1 \cdot \widetilde{\mathbf{rtk}}_i \quad (\text{mod } PQ_L)\right) \rceil \in \mathcal{R}_{Q_L}^2.$$

In the noise analysis, one can prove that

$$\frac{1}{P} \cdot c_1 \cdot \lfloor \frac{[Pm_is]_{PQ_L}}{q_L} \rceil = \frac{c_1}{P} \cdot \left(\frac{Pm_is}{q_L} + r\right) = \frac{m_i \cdot c_1 s}{q_L} + \frac{c_1 r}{P}$$

since $\|Pm_is|)_\infty \ll PQ_L/2$, where r is the rounding term with $\|r|)_\infty \leq 1/2$. Let $c_0 + c_1 s = q_0 I + \mathtt{pt} + e'$. Then, following the derivation similar to the end of Appendix C, we obtain the final error formed as $\frac{m_i e'}{q_L} + \frac{c_1 r + c_1 e}{P} + e_r$, where e_r is the small noise generated by rounding operations. The c_1-related noise satisfies $\|\frac{c_1 r + c_1 e}{P}|)_\infty \leq \frac{q_0 N}{4P} + \frac{q_0 N \cdot \|e|)_\infty}{2P} \ll 1$ since $q_0 \ll P$.

Two other advantages of GHS-type key-switching are: (1) it lowers the time complexity of Decomp and MultSum steps by a factor of about $\mathtt{dnum}$ because the ciphertext c_1 no longer needs to be decomposed; (2) it reduces the size of each $\mathtt{rtk}$ by a factor of $\mathtt{dnum}$.

Table 3. Parameter sets used in our experiments. "Left" represents the remaining moduli after bootstrapping. ($\cdot$) in CtS means the saved moduli by LCR. For all sets, security $\lambda \approx 128$ bits, the number of non-zero diagonals ≤ 64, $h = N/2$ and $\tilde{h} = 32$ (density of the ephemeral secret).

| | Scheme Parameters | | | | | | | Bootstrapping Parameters | | | |
| | | | | | | | | $\log(q_{j'})$ | | | |
Set	$\log(PQ)$	N	Δ	L	α	dnum	$\log(p_{i'})$	Left	StC	Sine	CtS
I	1767	2^{16}	2^{40}	28	6	5	$6 \cdot 61$	$60 + 13 \cdot 40$	$3 \cdot 39$	$8 \cdot 60$	$4 \cdot 56$
I$'$	**1751**		2^{40}	28	6	5	$6 \cdot 61$	$60 + \mathbf{14} \cdot \mathbf{40}$	$3 \cdot 39$	$8 \cdot 60$	$(\mathbf{56}) + \mathbf{3} \cdot \mathbf{56}$
II	1788	2^{16}	2^{45}	27	5	6	$5 \cdot 61$	$60 + 9 \cdot 45$	$3 \cdot 42$	$11 \cdot 60$	$4 \cdot 58$
II$'$	**1775**		2^{45}	27	5	6	$5 \cdot 61$	$60 + \mathbf{10} \cdot \mathbf{45}$	$3 \cdot 42$	$11 \cdot 60$	$(\mathbf{58}) + \mathbf{3} \cdot \mathbf{58}$
III	1793	2^{16}	2^{30}	25	5	6	$5 \cdot 61$	$55 + 11.5 \cdot 60$	$1.5 \cdot 60$	$8 \cdot 55$	$4 \cdot 53$
III$'$	1799		2^{30}	25	5	6	$5 \cdot 61$	$55 + \mathbf{12.5} \cdot \mathbf{60}$	$1.5 \cdot 60$	$8 \cdot 55$	$(\mathbf{53}) + \mathbf{3} \cdot \mathbf{53}$

As results, compared with the algorithms in Sect. 4.1 (BSGS) and 4.2 (AKS), the combined algorithm (LCR+AKS) not only saves one level of moduli, but also further improves efficiency and reduces the total size of the rotation keys (this is shown in Subsect. 6.2). This makes the combined algorithm a lossless improvement. For completeness, we present the detailed operations and complexity analysis of this combined algorithm in Appendix F.

6   Experiments

We conducted experiments on the proof-of-concept implementation of the proposed techniques. Our code is developed upon the Lattigo library [33][9]. All experiments in our paper were performed with a single thread on a machine equipped with Intel(R) Core(TM) i7-9700 3.00GHz CPU and 256GB memory, running on Windows 10 Pro Version 2H22. The environment information includes Go version 1.22.1 and GOARCH amd64. We benchmark against [7] as it included the state-of-the-art linear transformation [6] and introduced the sparse-secret encapsulation technology that is mandatory in conventional dense key bootstrapping. To demonstrate the improvements, we implemented our methods based on [7]. The details of applying our methods to the sparse-secret encapsulation are presented in Sect. 6.3. For a relatively fair comparison, we utilized Lattigo to re-run the experiments of prior work [7] on our machine instead of using their reported values directly.

6.1   Parameter Sets and Bootstrapping Metrics

Table 3 describes the parameters used in our experiments. I, II, III are from [7] and I$'$, II$'$, III$'$ are the corresponding modified parameter sets designed for our

---

[9] https://github.com/Fainabi/Lattigo-LCR-AKS.

LCR method. Unlike the related work [32] that requires carefully constructing their parameters, for an existing parameter set, we directly allocate the saved moduli to the "Left" part for a stronger remaining homomorphic capacity. Moreover, our bootstrapping remains the same precision and failure probability as before since the proposed techniques have no impact on these metrics. For our modified parameter sets I' and II', the maximum of modulus (PQ) is smaller than previous, which might yield some benefits on security.

We also use the bootstrapping utility metric *bootstrapping throughput* in our experiments (introduced in Subsect. 5.3 of [11] and defined in Subsect. 7.1 of [6]). It is formulated as

$$throughput = \frac{n \cdot \log(\epsilon^{-1}) \cdot \log(Q_{\text{Left}})}{time},$$

where $n = N/2$ is the number of slots, $\log(\epsilon^{-1})$ is the output precision, $\log(Q_{\text{Left}})$ represents the remaining homomorphic capacity and time is the CPU time of bootstrapping.

6.2   Results

Now we discuss how to use the proposed techniques to achieve *higher throughput* bootstrapping with *reduced* **rtk** *size*. As illustrated in Fig. 1, we employ the *lossless strategy* based on the sparse-secret encapsulation bootstrapping in [7], i.e., use the combined algorithm (LCR+AKS) for the first matrix-vector multiplication in CoeffsToSlots and use the previous BSGS algorithm (from [6]) for the other matrix-vector multiplications. Experimental results are summarized in Table 4.

In Table 4, we can see that our technology lowers the running time of ModRaise and the first matrix-vector multiplication (Mat 1) in CoeffsToSlots, and saves one level of moduli, resulting in a higher bootstrapping throughput and reduced **rtk** size in CoeffsToSlots. Specifically, our ModRaise runs $9.4\times \sim 9.8\times$ faster than [7] as the second key-switching operation in the sparse-secret encapsulation is merged into the AKS procedure (refer to Sect. 6.3). In the first level of CoeffsToSlots (Mat 1), our LCR + AKS method accelerates the matrix-vector multiplication by a factor of $3.0 \sim 3.5$. The running time of the other matrix-vector multiplications (Mat 2, Mat 3 and Mat 4) in CoeffsToSlots of set I' (resp. II' and III') is sometimes slightly longer than that of set I (resp. II and III), this is because our bootstrapping strategy performs the same (BSGS) algorithm at a higher level due to the level-conserving rescaling technique. Consequently, our advanced bootstrapping throughput reaches $1.20\times \sim 1.35\times$ that of [7] over similar parameters. Note that the bootstrapping precision and failure probability remain identical to the previous method.

Table 4. The bootstrapping performance improvements of applying our lossless strategy (I′, II′, III′) to [7] (I, II, III). Our proposal was implemented based on [7] with sparse-secret encapsulation. Mat 1, Mat 2, Mat 3 and Mat 4 denote the four-level matrix-vector multiplications of CtS, respectively, and the numbers below them denote the number of non-zero diagonals. log(bits/s) is the logarithm value of throughput. $\log(\epsilon^{-1})$ is the output precision. rtk size only contains the rotation keys in CtS. We sample the complex messages from the square of $-1-i$ and $1+i$ uniformly.

		Bootstrapping Performance								
	ModRaise time(s)	CoeffsToSlots time(s)				BTS time(s)	$\log(Q_{\text{Left}})$	$\log(\epsilon^{-1})$	$\log(\text{bits/s})$	rtk size (GB)
Set		Mat 1 (32)	Mat 2 (15)	Mat 3 (15)	Mat 4 (31)					
I-[7]	1.14	3.62	1.85	1.79	3.34	25.98	580	27.8	24.28	5.47
I′-our	**0.12**	**1.19**	1.88	1.81	3.29	23.20	**620**	27.8	**24.54**	**4.82**
II-[7]	1.18	3.87	1.98	1.98	3.13	27.99	465	32.9	24.09	6.19
II′-our	**0.12**	**1.10**	1.81	1.73	3.24	22.91	**510**	32.9	**24.52**	**5.25**
III-[7]	1.03	3.45	1.82	1.52	2.78	23.37	745	19.7	24.29	5.81
III′-our	**0.11**	**1.03**	1.73	1.74	2.69	20.21	**805**	19.7	**24.62**	**4.93**

For space cost, LCR + AKS requires more rotation keys than [7], but the size of each rtk is smaller on account of the GHS-type key-switching. In the experimental results, the total size of rotation keys in CoeffsToSlots under I′-our (resp. II′-our and III′-our) is 11.9% (resp. 15.2% and 15.1%) smaller than that under I- [7] (resp. II- [7] and III- [7]).

6.3   More Discussions

Other Bootstrapping Strategies. Assume that there are d_{CtS} and d_{StC} (sparse) matrix-vector multiplications in CoeffsToSlots and SlotsToCoeffs, respectively. The above experiments show an improvement of employing LCR+AKS in the first level of CoeffsToSlots while using the BSGS approach for the other levels. In practice, if there is sufficient storage space, one can apply the algorithm with AKS to the other $d_{\text{CtS}} + d_{\text{StC}} - 1$ matrices to obtain a higher throughput. This is because the AKS method is faster than the BSGS algorithm but requires more rtk size. The more times the AKS method is utilized, the greater the efficiency gains achieved, but also the higher the memory overhead incurred. We need to decide which matrices use the AKS method according to the storage resources. It is essentially an optimization problem.

In Appendix G of the full version, we discuss how to find an appropriate time-memory trade-off strategy based on the available storage space. We also present a bootstrapping strategy as an example (i.e., the time-memory trade-of strategy in Fig. 1), and implement it using the parameters from Table 3 and sparse-secret encapsulation from [7]. Results in Table 9 (see the full version paper) demonstrate that, the example strategy has a bootstrapping throughput 25% ∼ 40% higher than [7] while doubling the rtk size in CoeffsToSlots.

The state-of-the-art CKKS bootstrapping includes several noticeable technologies, and different technologies focus on different procedures. Our proposals mainly focus on the ModRaise and CoeffsToSlots procedures. More specifically, we care about two requirements:

- The LCR+AKS requires that the ciphertext coefficients remain small enough.
- The LCR+AKS and AKS methods both need to merge the plaintext-ciphertext multiplication and rescaling operations into the key-switching, thus requiring to put the scalar multiplication and rescaling forward in matrix-vector multiplication.

Therefore, the technologies that focus on EvalMod [6,11,26,27,36–38], or focus on linear transformations but don't conflict with the two requirements [30,32,43] (including the StC-first bootstrapping [12]), are all compatible with our methods, as well as those using CKKS as a subroutine (e.g., iterative CKKS bootstrapping [3,29], CKKS-style TFHE functional bootstrapping [1,5], and so on [4,18]). The combination of these technologies and LCR + AKS is straightforward without additional modifications.

Sparse-Secret Encapsulation. The sparse-secret encapsulation technique proposed in [7] is also compatible with our methods. We have incorporated it with our methods in the above experiments. Here we discuss how this integration is implemented. In the sparse-secret encapsulation, the authors introduced two key-switching operations, one key-switching from dense key s to sparse key $\tilde{s}$ is performed before ModRaise, while the other key-switching from sparse key $\tilde{s}$ to dense key s is performed after ModRaise. The second key-switching would make the ciphertext coefficients uniformly distributed over $\mathbb{Z}_{Q_L}$, which seems to prevent the utility of the subsequent LCR. In fact, we can directly merge the second key-switching (from $\tilde{s}$ to s) with the aggregated key-switching (from s to $\varphi_i^{-1}(s)$) into one aggregated key-switching from $\tilde{s}$ to $\varphi_i^{-1}(s)$, because they are two consecutive key-switching operations in bootstrapping (no trace computation in fully packed ciphertexts). Thus, the LCR component is still applied. This merging also reduces one switching key.

EvalRound$^+$. Most recently, Sung et al. proposed EvalRound$^+$ algorithm [43] that also saves the modulus consumption in CKKS bootstrapping. We can apply the LCR+AKS to the CtS* of EvalRound$^+$ to further save one level of moduli (along with better efficiency). Moreover, applying LCR+AKS to the additional CtS in EvalRound$^+$ can reduce its efficiency loss. As an illustration, we provided the experimental results of incorporating LCR+AKS into EvalRound$^+$, as shown in Table 6.

Table 5. Parameter set "EvalRound$^+$" is from [43] and "LCR+EvalRound$^+$" is the variant.

Set	Scheme Parameters								Bootstrapping Parameters			
									$\log(q_{j'})$			
	$\log(PQ)$	N	h	Δ	L	α	k	$\log(p_{i'})$	Left	StC	Sine	CtS
[43]	1438	2^{16}	192	2^{40}	24	5	5	$5 \cdot 61$	$60 + 9 \cdot 40$	$3 \cdot 39$	$8 \cdot 60$	$4 \cdot 29$
LCR+AKS+[43]	**1409**			2^{40}	23	5	5	$5 \cdot 61$	$60 + 9 \cdot 40$	$3 \cdot 39$	$8 \cdot 60$	$(\mathbf{29}) + \mathbf{3} \cdot \mathbf{29}$

Table 6. The bootstrapping performance improvements of applying LCR and AKS to EvalRound$^+$ [43]. We use the parameters in Table 5. "CtS time" means the running time of the additional CtS in EvalRound$^+$. $\log(\epsilon^{-1})$ is the output precision. rtk size only contains the rotation keys in CtS and CtS*.

Set	Bootstrapping Performance					
	ModRaise time(s)	CtS* time(s)	CtS time(s)	BTS time(s)	$\log(\epsilon^{-1})$	rtk size (GB)
[43]	0.26	5.43	3.50	16.99	27.30	4.69
LCR+AKS+[43]	**0.09**	**4.54**	**3.24**	**15.54**	27.30	3.99

7   Conclusion and Future Work

In this paper, we improved the RNS-CKKS bootstrapping algorithm with faster speed and less modulus consumption by exploring several techniques for the homomorphic linear transformations. We first introduced the level-conserving rescaling, which can be performed in CoeffsToSlots and saves the modulus. The second proposed technique aggregated key-switching works well in the matrix-vector multiplications for sparse diagonal ($\#$(non-zero diagonals)≤ 64) matrices with lower time complexity. Prior to this work, the matrix-vector multiplication in CKKS bootstrapping is evaluated by the double-hoisting BSGS algorithm [6]. Based on the matrix factorization approach [11,25] and the GHS-type key-switching, we discarded the BSGS method and applied the two novel techniques to bootstrapping successfully for better efficiency and less modulus consumption. The implementation results demonstrate that our method increases the remaining homomorphic capacity and improves the homomorphic linear transformations significantly in CKKS bootstrapping.

One potential future research line is to explore how to apply the proposed approaches to BGV/BFV [8,9,20] or FHEW/TFHE [17,19] schemes. Additionally, taking into account the hardware-based optimizations is beneficial for implementation and realistic applications.

Acknowledgments. We thank Dr. Ming Luo for helpful discussions. We would like to thank the anonymous reviewers for their helpful suggestions. This work is supported by the Strategic Priority Research Program of the Chinese Academy of Sciences under Grant XDB0690200, and the "Climbing Program" Special Project for Basic and Frontier Research of the Institute of Information Engineering, Chinese Academy of Sciences (No. 2024000051).

Appendix

All the appendices can be found in the full version of this paper, see the latest version at https://eprint.iacr.org/2025/1403.

References

1. Alexandru, A., Kim, A., Polyakov, Y.: General functional bootstrapping using CKKS. In: Tauman Kalai, Y., Kamara, S.F. (eds.) Advances in Cryptology – CRYPTO 2025, pp. 304–337. Springer, Cham (2025). https://doi.org/10.1007/978-3-032-01881-6_10

2. Badawi, A.A., et al.: OpenFHE: open-source fully homomorphic encryption library. Cryptology ePrint Archive, Paper 2022/915 (2022). https://eprint.iacr.org/2022/915

3. Bae, Y., Cheon, J.H., Cho, W., Kim, J., Kim, T.: META-BTS: bootstrapping precision beyond the limit. In: Yin, H., Stavrou, A., Cremers, C., Shi, E. (eds.) ACM CCS 2022, pp. 223–234. ACM Press (2022). https://doi.org/10.1145/3548606.3560696

4. Bae, Y., Cheon, J.H., Kim, J., Stehlé, D.: Bootstrapping bits with CKKS. In: Joye, M., Leander, G. (eds.) Advances in Cryptology – EUROCRYPT 2024, pp. 94–123 (2024). https://doi.org/10.1007/978-3-031-58723-8_4

5. Bae, Y., Kim, J., Stehlé, D., Suvanto, E.: Bootstrapping small integers with CKKS. In: Chung, K.M., Sasaki, Y. (eds.) Advances in Cryptology – ASIACRYPT 2024, pp. 330–360 (2025). https://doi.org/10.1007/978-981-96-0875-1_11

6. Bossuat, J.-P., Mouchet, C., Troncoso-Pastoriza, J., Hubaux, J.-P.: Efficient bootstrapping for approximate homomorphic encryption with non-sparse keys. In: Canteaut, A., Standaert, F.-X. (eds.) EUROCRYPT 2021. LNCS, vol. 12696, pp. 587–617. Springer, Cham (2021). https://doi.org/10.1007/978-3-030-77870-5_21

7. Bossuat, J.P., Troncoso-Pastoriza, J.R., Hubaux, J.P.: Bootstrapping for approximate homomorphic encryption with negligible failure-probability by using sparse-secret encapsulation. In: Ateniese, G., Venturi, D. (eds.) ACNS 22. LNCS, vol. 13269, pp. 521–541. Springer, Heidelberg (2022). https://doi.org/10.1007/978-3-031-09234-3_26

8. Brakerski, Z.: Fully homomorphic encryption without modulus switching from classical GapSVP. In: Safavi-Naini, R., Canetti, R. (eds.) CRYPTO 2012. LNCS, vol. 7417, pp. 868–886. Springer, Heidelberg (2012). https://doi.org/10.1007/978-3-642-32009-5_50

9. Brakerski, Z., Gentry, C., Vaikuntanathan, V.: (Leveled) fully homomorphic encryption without bootstrapping. In: Goldwasser, S. (ed.) ITCS 2012, pp. 309–325. ACM (2012). https://doi.org/10.1145/2090236.2090262

10. Brakerski, Z., Vaikuntanathan, V.: Efficient fully homomorphic encryption from (standard) LWE. In: Ostrovsky, R. (ed.) 52nd FOCS, pp. 97–106. IEEE Computer Society Press (2011). https://doi.org/10.1109/FOCS.2011.12

11. Chen, H., Chillotti, I., Song, Y.: Improved bootstrapping for approximate homomorphic encryption. In: Ishai, Y., Rijmen, V. (eds.) EUROCRYPT 2019. LNCS, vol. 11477, pp. 34–54. Springer, Cham (2019). https://doi.org/10.1007/978-3-030-17656-3_2

12. Chen, H., Han, K.: Homomorphic lower digits removal and improved FHE bootstrapping. In: Nielsen, J.B., Rijmen, V. (eds.) EUROCRYPT 2018. LNCS, vol. 10820, pp. 315–337. Springer, Cham (2018). https://doi.org/10.1007/978-3-319-78381-9_12

13. Cheon, J.H., Cho, W., Kim, J., Stehlé, D.: Homomorphic multiple precision multiplication for CKKS and reduced modulus consumption. In: ACM CCS 2023, pp. 696–710 (2023). https://doi.org/10.1145/3576915.3623086

14. Cheon, J.H., Han, K., Kim, A., Kim, M., Song, Y.: Bootstrapping for approximate homomorphic encryption. In: Nielsen, J.B., Rijmen, V. (eds.) EUROCRYPT 2018. LNCS, vol. 10820, pp. 360–384. Springer, Cham (2018). https://doi.org/10.1007/978-3-319-78381-9_14

15. Cheon, J.H., Han, K., Kim, A., Kim, M., Song, Y.: A full RNS variant of approximate homomorphic encryption. In: Cid, C., Jacobson Jr., M.J. (eds.) Selected Areas in Cryptography – SAC 2018, pp. 347–368. Springer, Cham (2019). https://doi.org/10.1007/978-3-030-10970-7_16

16. Cheon, J.H., Kim, A., Kim, M., Song, Y.: Homomorphic encryption for arithmetic of approximate numbers. In: Takagi, T., Peyrin, T. (eds.) ASIACRYPT 2017. LNCS, vol. 10624, pp. 409–437. Springer, Cham (2017). https://doi.org/10.1007/978-3-319-70694-8_15

17. Chillotti, I., Gama, N., Georgieva, M., Izabachène, M.: TFHE: fast fully homomorphic encryption over the torus. J. Cryptol. **33**(1), 34–91 (2019). https://doi.org/10.1007/s00145-019-09319-x

18. Drucker, N., Moshkowich, G., Pelleg, T., Shaul, H.: BLEACH: cleaning errors in discrete computations over CKKS. J. Cryptol. **37** (2023). https://doi.org/10.1007/s00145-023-09483-1

19. Ducas, L., Micciancio, D.: FHEW: bootstrapping homomorphic encryption in less than a second. In: Oswald, E., Fischlin, M. (eds.) EUROCRYPT 2015. LNCS, vol. 9056, pp. 617–640. Springer, Heidelberg (2015). https://doi.org/10.1007/978-3-662-46800-5_24

20. Fan, J., Vercauteren, F.: Somewhat practical fully homomorphic encryption. Cryptology ePrint Archive, Report 2012/144 (2012). https://eprint.iacr.org/2012/144

21. Gentry, C.: Fully homomorphic encryption using ideal lattices. In: Mitzenmacher, M. (ed.) 41st ACM STOC, pp. 169–178. ACM Press (2009). https://doi.org/10.1145/1536414.1536440

22. Gentry, C., Halevi, S., Smart, N.P.: Homomorphic evaluation of the AES circuit. In: Safavi-Naini, R., Canetti, R. (eds.) CRYPTO 2012. LNCS, vol. 7417, pp. 850–867. Springer, Heidelberg (2012). https://doi.org/10.1007/978-3-642-32009-5_49

23. Halevi, S., Polyakov, Y., Shoup, V.: An improved RNS variant of the BFV homomorphic encryption scheme. In: Matsui, M. (ed.) CT-RSA 2019. LNCS, vol. 11405, pp. 83–105. Springer, Cham (2019). https://doi.org/10.1007/978-3-030-12612-4_5

24. Halevi, S., Shoup, V.: Faster homomorphic linear transformations in HElib. In: Shacham, H., Boldyreva, A. (eds.) CRYPTO 2018. LNCS, vol. 10991, pp. 93–120. Springer, Cham (2018). https://doi.org/10.1007/978-3-319-96884-1_4

25. Han, K., Hhan, M., Cheon, J.H.: Improved homomorphic discrete fourier transforms and FHE bootstrapping. IEEE Access **7**, 57361–57370 (2019). https://doi.org/10.1109/ACCESS.2019.2913850

26. Han, K., Ki, D.: Better bootstrapping for approximate homomorphic encryption. In: Jarecki, S. (ed.) CT-RSA 2020. LNCS, vol. 12006, pp. 364–390. Springer, Cham (2020). https://doi.org/10.1007/978-3-030-40186-3_16

27. Jutla, C.S., Manohar, N.: Sine series approximation of the mod function for bootstrapping of approximate HE. In: Dunkelman, O., Dziembowski, S. (eds.) Advances in Cryptology – EUROCRYPT 2022, pp. 491–520 (2022). https://doi.org/10.1007/978-3-031-06944-4_17

28. Kim, A., Polyakov, Y., Zucca, V.: Revisiting homomorphic encryption schemes for finite fields. In: Tibouchi, M., Wang, H. (eds.) ASIACRYPT 2021. LNCS, vol. 13092, pp. 608–639. Springer, Cham (2021). https://doi.org/10.1007/978-3-030-92078-4_21

29. Kim, J., Seo, J., Song, Y.: Simpler and faster BFV bootstrapping for arbitrary plaintext modulus from CKKS. In: ACM CCS 2024, pp. 2535–2546 (2024). https://doi.org/10.1145/3658644.3670302

30. Kim, J., Cheon, J.H., Yeo, Y.: Overmodraise: reducing modulus consumption of CKKS bootstrapping. IACR Commun. Cryptol. **2**(3) (2025). https://doi.org/10.62056/a3n5qjp10

31. Kim, M., Lee, D., Seo, J., Song, Y.: Accelerating HE operations from key decomposition technique. In: Handschuh, H., Lysyanskaya, A. (eds.) CRYPTO 2023, Part IV. LNCS, vol. 14084, pp. 70–92. Springer, Heidelberg (2023). https://doi.org/10.1007/978-3-031-38551-3_3

32. Kim, S., Park, M., Kim, J., Kim, T., Min, C.: EvalRound algorithm in CKKS bootstrapping. In: Agrawal, S., Lin, D. (eds.) ASIACRYPT 2022, Part II. LNCS, vol. 13792, pp. 161–187. Springer, Heidelberg (2022). https://doi.org/10.1007/978-3-031-22966-4_6

33. Lattigo v6 (2024). https://github.com/tuneinsight/lattig, ePFL-LDS, Tune Insight SA

34. Lee, E., et al.: Low-complexity deep convolutional neural networks on fully homomorphic encryption using multiplexed parallel convolutions. In: Chaudhuri, K., Jegelka, S., Song, L., Szepesvari, C., Niu, G., Sabato, S. (eds.) Proceedings of the 39th International Conference on Machine Learning, vol. 162, pp. 12403–12422 (2022). https://proceedings.mlr.press/v162/lee22e.html

35. Lee, J.W., et al.: Privacy-preserving machine learning with fully homomorphic encryption for deep neural network. IEEE Access **10**, 30039–30054 (2022). https://doi.org/10.1109/ACCESS.2022.3159694

36. Lee, J.-W., Lee, E., Lee, Y., Kim, Y.-S., No, J.-S.: High-precision bootstrapping of RNS-CKKS homomorphic encryption using optimal minimax polynomial approximation and inverse sine function. In: Canteaut, A., Standaert, F.-X. (eds.) EUROCRYPT 2021. LNCS, vol. 12696, pp. 618–647. Springer, Cham (2021). https://doi.org/10.1007/978-3-030-77870-5_22

37. Lee, Y., Lee, J.W., Kim, Y.S., Kim, Y., No, J.S., Kang, H.: High-precision bootstrapping for approximate homomorphic encryption by error variance minimization. In: Dunkelman, O., Dziembowski, S. (eds.) Advances in Cryptology – EUROCRYPT 2022, pp. 551–580 (2022). https://doi.org/10.1007/978-3-031-06944-4_19

38. Li, H., Mo, W., Shen, C., Pang, L.: EvalComp: bootstrapping based on homomorphic comparison function for CKKS. IEEE Trans. Inf. Forensics Secur. **20**, 1349–1361 (2025). https://doi.org/10.1109/TIFS.2024.3516553
39. Lou, Q., Jiang, L.: HEMET: a homomorphic-encryption-friendly privacy-preserving mobile neural network architecture. In: Meila, M., Zhang, T. (eds.) Proceedings of the 38th International Conference on Machine Learning, vol. 139, pp. 7102–7110 (2021). https://proceedings.mlr.press/v139/lou21a.html
40. Lyubashevsky, V., Peikert, C., Regev, O.: On ideal lattices and learning with errors over rings. In: Gilbert, H. (ed.) EUROCRYPT 2010. LNCS, vol. 6110, pp. 1–23. Springer, Heidelberg (2010). https://doi.org/10.1007/978-3-642-13190-5_1
41. Ma, S., Huang, T., Wang, A., Wang, X.: Practical dense-key bootstrapping with subring secret encapsulation. In: Hanaoka, G., Yang, B.Y. (eds.) Advances in Cryptology – ASIACRYPT 2025, pp. 101–130. Springer, Singapore (2026). https://doi.org/10.1007/978-981-95-5122-4_4
42. Microsoft SEAL (release 4.1) (2023). https://github.com/Microsoft/SEAL, Microsoft Research, Redmond, WA
43. Sung, H., Seo, S., Kim, T., Min, C.: EvalRound+ bootstrapping and its rigorous analysis for CKKS scheme. IEEE Access **13**, 140847–140866 (2025). https://doi.org/10.1109/ACCESS.2025.3595177

Protocols and Real-World Security

Beyond the 1/2 Bound: On the Theory and Practice of Biprimality Tests

ChihYun Chuang[1]([✉]), IHung Hsu[1], and TingFang Lee[2]

[1] AMIS, Taipei, Taiwan
`{chihyun,glen}@am.is`
[2] Division of Biostatistics, NYU Langone Health, New York, USA
`Ting-Fang.Lee@nyulangone.org`

Abstract. The Boneh-Franklin (BF) biprimality test, a cornerstone of distributed RSA key generation, has a universally accepted worst-case soundness error of 1/2. We show that this two-decade-old bound is not tight and present a collection of results that refine and generalize this fundamental test. Our contributions are threefold: **(1) A Tight Soundness Bound for the BF Test:** Our primary contribution is a rigorous proof that the worst-case acceptance probability of the BF test for a non-RSA modulus is at most 1/4, not the long-accepted 1/2. By constructing cases that meet this bound, we establish that it is tight. This fundamental result allows existing protocols to halve the required iterations, thereby improving the efficiency of verifying valid moduli while maintaining the same security level. **(2) A Generalized Test for Universal Applicability and a Nuanced Verdict:** We introduce a versatile Lucas-sequence-based test that resolves the long-standing limitation of the BF test to Blum integers. While we prove its soundness error is theoretically and empirically superior in the vast majority of cases, our analysis, based on a performance model parameterized by simulation, indicates a critical trade-off. For the specific task of generating Blum integers, the exceptional local computation speed of the BF test suggests it maintains a practical advantage in latency-sensitive environments. This nuanced finding underscores the critical interplay between theoretical soundness error and real-world performance. **(3) New Protocols for an Expanded Design Space:** We construct new distributed verification protocols that realize our foundational insights. Our Lucas-based protocol provides the first efficient, provably secure solution for generating arbitrary standard RSA moduli in the semi-honest model, alongside a maliciously secure variant for Blum integers. This fills a critical gap for applications requiring generality and, combined with our comparative analysis, provides a clearer and more complete toolkit for protocol designers. Overall, our work refines the theoretical bounds of biprimality testing and provides a more efficient and versatile foundation for distributed RSA key generation.

Keywords: Biprimality Test · RSA Modulus · Distributed Cryptography · Multi-Party Computation

A full version of this paper is available at IACR ePrint 2024/2072.

S. Bai and E. Persichetti (Eds.): PKC 2026, LNCS 16554, pp. 369–400, 2026.
https://doi.org/10.1007/978-3-032-26740-5_12

1   Introduction

The security of foundational public-key cryptosystems like RSA [28] rests on the elegant complexities of number theory. A central challenge within this paradigm is generating the required secret primes, p and q, without a single point of failure. Multi-Party Computation (MPC) offers a robust solution by allowing multiple parties to collectively compute the public modulus $N = pq$ from their private inputs while preserving confidentiality. This technique has become a critical building block for numerous advanced cryptographic primitives, such as threshold homomorphic encryption [19,20], time-lock puzzles [1,25,29], accumulators [4,6,24], and verifiable delay functions [5,13,17,21,26,31]. However, this distributed approach introduces a fundamental mathematical problem: how to efficiently verify number-theoretic properties, such as the biprimality of N, when the underlying factors must remain secret.

The primary objective in distributed RSA modulus generation is to design a secure protocol for n parties, resilient against up to $t < n$ colluding adversaries. The protocol should output a random and valid RSA modulus $N = pq$, where p, q are distinct primes of a specified size, such that an adversary learns nothing beyond N, ensuring the privacy of p and q. Such protocols typically involve two phases: **(a) Prime Candidate Sieving**: participants generate a potential RSA modulus N that does not divide by a prime less than a predetermined integer $p_{\min}$; and **(b) Biprimality test**: the candidate N is repeatedly tested by a biprimality test. If N is rejected by the biprimality test, then the process starts over. Current state-of-the-art sieving techniques often employ the Chinese Remainder Theorem (CRT) to efficiently generate candidates N free of small prime factors [11,30]. For biprimality testing, variants of the Miller-Rabin primality test (cf. [10, Section 3.2]) and Boneh-Franklin (BF) biprimality test (cf. Theorem 1) have been commonly used.

Among these, the BF test [7] has become a foundational building block in numerous state-of-the-art protocols for distributed RSA generation [7,12,18,30], largely due to its conceptual simplicity and efficiency per iteration in an MPC setting. However, its widespread adoption has been blocked by a critical efficiency bottleneck rooted in its theoretical understanding. The worst-case soundness error of the test is universally accepted to be $1/2$, forcing protocols to perform a large number of costly iterations (e.g., 80 iterations for 2^{-80} security) to ensure soundness. This raises a fundamental question: is this $1/2$ bound the true theoretical limit of the test, making such a high iteration count an unavoidable cost for verifying an RSA modulus?

This inefficiency becomes more apparent when compared to the Miller-Rabin primality test. The Miller-Rabin test exhibits a strictly lower worst-case soundness error of $1/4$ [9,27]. Furthermore, subsequent studies [10,15] have formally derived its average-case properties, utilizing these bounds to propose a significantly reduced iteration count for achieving a target security level. However, for applications requiring provable security guarantees, relying on average-case results can be problematic. A critical, yet often unstated, issue is that the average-case soundness of Miller-Rabin tests is proven under the assumption that primes are chosen uniformly at random. This assumption is not met by many efficient distributed RSA generation algorithms [7,11,12,14,18,30], which produce primes from non-uniform distributions (e.g., sums of uniform variables) to achieve MPC efficiency. Therefore, with provable security as the foremost priority, utilizing the worst-case soundness error to establish the number of verification rounds remains an essential requirement.

In light of these challenges, although the Miller-Rabin test exhibits a lower worst-case soundness error compared to the BF test, its distributed protocols are significantly more complex. This inherent complexity is precisely why prior works have relied on average-case results to boost its practical efficiency. Furthermore, in the realm of biprimality testing, the standard BF test is strictly confined to generating Blum integers; determining whether this limitation can be removed remains a compelling open question. Motivated by these observations, our work sets out to explore the true theoretical limits of the BF test and to investigate whether the strict limitation to Blum integers can be overcome.

Related Work. The paradigm of distributed RSA moduli generation was established in the seminal work of Boneh and Franklin [7]. They presented an efficient protocol for verifying if a modulus $N = pq$ is biprime without disclosing the factors p and q. Their construction is secure against semi-honest adversaries, assuming an honest majority. The test guarantees perfect completeness, always accepting a valid RSA modulus, while ensuring a soundness error of at most $1/2$. The paper detailed two distinct biprimality tests, primarily differing in their core algebraic checks: one verifies that $\gcd(pq, (p-1)(q-1)) = 1$, whereas the other relies on exponentiation within the quotient group $\left(\mathbb{Z}_N[x]/(x^2 + 1)\right)^\times / \mathbb{Z}_N^\times$.

The mainstream approach in subsequent literature has largely centered on the variant that checks the condition $\gcd(pq, p+q-1) = 1$. A pivotal contribution came from Algesheimer et al. [2], who developed a distributed Miller-Rabin test secure against a dishonest majority. This direction, leveraging the Miller-Rabin framework for biprimality testing, has since been advanced by several other studies [10,14].

Separately, another body of work has investigated the average-case error probability of these tests. Assuming a uniformly random input, Damgård et al. [15] derived an upper bound on this error for the Miller-Rabin test, and Einsele et al. [16] did so for Lucas-based tests. More recently, Burkhardt et al. [10] provided a comprehensive survey of the state-of-the-art, while also proposing improvements in RSA candidate sieving and enhanced security models.

1.1 Our Contributions

Our work provides a precise analysis of the worst-case soundness error bound for the existing BF test using a precise counting formula, introduces a novel testing method applicable to more general RSA moduli, and conducts a rigorous comparative evaluation that clarifies the practical trade-offs between these methods. Consequently, similar to the Miller-Rabin test, the BF test now only requires $s/2$

iterations to achieve a security level of 2^{-s}. Furthermore, our analysis reveals that in the specific scenario of generating Blum integers, the BF test remains the superior choice. Our primary contributions are:

1. A Precise Counting Formula for Biprimality Tests. Our foundational contribution is a precise characterization of the algebraic structure of false witnesses for biprimality tests proposed by Boneh-Franklin. This counting formula yields two immediate and significant consequences:

A Tighter Bound for the Boneh-Franklin Test. We prove that the worst-case soundness error for the BF test is $1/4$, not the long-accepted $1/2$. This theoretical result directly enhances the efficiency of numerous existing protocols. For instance, the protocol against malicious adversaries of Chen et al. [11], our tighter bound reduces the required number of iterations from approximately $2.5s$ to $\lceil 1.475s \rceil$ to achieve a failure probability of less than 2^{-s}.

The First Direct, Quantitative Comparison of Biprimality Tests. Our framework facilitates the first direct, quantitative comparison of the soundness of different biprimality tests, including the BF test, the variant Miller-Rabin test, and our proposed Lucas test. This enables the deep performance analysis presented in Sect. 5, which was previously not possible.

2. A Novel, Generalized Test with Widespread Soundness Superiority. Inspired by our counting strategy, we introduce a versatile biprimality test based on Lucas sequences. This test has two key advantages:

A Provable and Empirically Widespread Soundness Advantage. Enabled by our framework, we formally prove that for a significant class of non-RSA moduli, our Lucas test has a strictly lower soundness error. Our empirical results (cf. Table 3) strongly confirm that this theoretical advantage holds in over 99.99% of tested cases, establishing the compelling hypothesis that the Lucas test, by requiring fewer average rejection rounds, could overcome its marginal local computation cost.

Relaxed Prime Constraints. A crucial advantage is that our test operates without the common $p \equiv q \equiv 3 \pmod 4$ restriction. This broadens its applicability to all standard RSA moduli, including those required for advanced schemes such as the Joye-Libert cryptosystem [23] and KMOV cryptosystem [8], filling a critical gap in the literature.

3. A Rigorous Performance Verdict and Secure Protocols. To definitively test the aforementioned hypothesis, a key contribution of our work is the development of a holistic performance model that precisely characterizes the performance trade-offs (cf. Sect. 5.3). This model indicates a crucial insight: when instantiated with conservative, empirically-grounded parameters, the extreme local efficiency of the BF test suggests it maintains a practical advantage in most realistic scenarios for generating Blum integers.

Finally, we construct secure and practical protocols for our Lucas test. We provide both an efficient controllable method and a general MPC-based approach to securely generate the required parameter D. Building on these solutions, we construct a Lucas-based protocol for the semi-honest model that ensures privacy for all standard RSA moduli (cf. Theorem 3), and adapt it to the malicious model for Blum integers (cf. Theorem 4). To validate our claims, our implementation is publicly available for reproducibility[1].

1.2 Technical Overview

We now provide a high-level roadmap of the technical framework underlying our results. Fundamentally, establishing the worst-case soundness of a biprimality test reduces to computing the exact ratio of passing witnesses to all valid candidates. To tackle this algebraic counting problem within specific multiplicative groups associated with $\mathbb{Z}_N$ and its quadratic algebras, we develop a unified framework that systematically reduces the problem scale. Specifically, we utilize the CRT to decompose the global counting problem into local prime-power components, resolve the base cases, and subsequently apply Hensel lifting to obtain the exact solutions. By applying this approach to the BF test's Sylow 2-subgroup structure, we reveal that its theoretical worst-case configuration is structurally impossible, tightening the bound to 1/4 (Sect. 3.1). We then deploy this exact machinery to rigorously quantify the false witnesses of our proposed Lucas test (Sect. 3.2).

Translating the Lucas test into a secure protocol (Sect. 4) introduces a unique challenge: jointly sampling a public parameter D that satisfies the hidden constraint $(\frac{-D}{p}) = -1$ without leaking the secret prime p. To overcome this, we design two distinct parameter-generation strategies. For arbitrary RSA moduli, we propose an interactive rejection-sampling approach that guarantees a negligible abort probability while strictly bounding the adversarial factoring advantage by a constant factor $2^{\mathsf{LeakBound}}$. Alternatively, we construct a perfectly leakage-free variant that shifts this burden to the MPC prime generation phase. By embedding specific quadratic non-residue constraints (e.g., $p \equiv a \pmod{4D}$) directly into the distributed sieving process, the Legendre symbol condition is satisfied implicitly by construction.

In the proof against semi-honest adversaries, a novel trapdoor mechanism (Sect. 4.1) within the quadratic algebra is introduced: the simulator predetermines the exponentiation outcome and reverse-engineers the public Lucas parameters (P, Q) to match, ensuring indistinguishability. As for the model against malicious adversaries, we adapt the commit-and-prove framework of Chen et al. [11]. It (Sect. 4.2) combines semi-honest execution with a Schnorr-like zero-knowledge proof to enforce honest behavior, achieving a provable soundness bound of $\gamma := \frac{5}{8} + \frac{0.625}{p_{\min}-3}$ per round.

---

2 Preliminaries

Basic notations. *Let $\mathbb{N}$ denote the set of natural numbers, and let $\mathbb{Z}$ be the ring of integers. For a finite set S, $|S|$ denotes its cardinality. Let $\mathbb{Z}_N$ denote the additive group of integers modulo N, and let $\mathbb{Z}_N^\times$ be its multiplicative group of units. The order of this multiplicative group is $|\mathbb{Z}_N^\times| = \phi(N)$, where ϕ is Euler's totient function. The greatest common divisor of two positive integers $x, y \in \mathbb{N}$ is denoted by $\gcd(x, y)$. Let $[a]_m$ denote the additive sharing of a value a over the domain $\mathbb{Z}_m$. In this scheme, each participant $\mathcal{P}_i$ (for $i \in \{1, \ldots, n\}$) holds a secret share $\mathfrak{a}_i \in \mathbb{Z}_m$ such that $\sum_{i=1}^n \mathfrak{a}_i \equiv a \pmod{m}$. Similarly, $[a]_\mathbb{Z}$ denotes the secure additive sharing of a over the integers $\mathbb{Z}$, where each participant holds a share $\mathfrak{a}_i \in \mathbb{Z}$ satisfying $\sum_{i=1}^n \mathfrak{a}_i = a$. For a finite set S, the notation $a \leftarrow S$ indicates that a is sampled uniformly at random from S.*

To formally evaluate the biprimality tests, we define the following key parameters and sets. Given two odd positive integers p, q, set $e_4(= e_4(p, q)) := \frac{1}{4}\left(p + \left(\frac{-1}{p}\right)\right)\left(q + \left(\frac{-1}{q}\right)\right)$. In particular, if $p \equiv q \equiv 3 \pmod 4$, then $e_4 = (p-1)(q-1)/4$. Here $\left(\frac{\cdot}{\cdot}\right)$ is the Jacobi symbol. For odd integers p, q, we set

$$\mathrm{BF}(N, e_4) := \left\{ g \in \mathbb{Z}_N^\times \mid g^{e_4} \equiv \pm 1 \pmod N \right\}, \quad G(N) := \left\{ g \in \mathbb{Z}_N^\times \ \middle|\ \left(\frac{g}{N}\right) = 1 \right\},$$

$$\mathcal{Z}^\epsilon(D, N) := \left\{ (P, Q) \ \middle|\ \begin{array}{l} P^2 - 4Q = D \pmod N, \\ \left(\frac{Q}{N}\right) = \epsilon, \gcd(Q, N) = 1, \\ 0 \le P, Q < N \end{array} \right\},$$

$$\mathrm{LPBP}(D, N, e_4) := \left\{ (P, Q) \ \middle|\ \begin{array}{l} 0 \le P, Q < N, \\ \gcd(Q, N) = 1, \\ P^2 - 4Q = D \pmod N, \\ (\alpha\beta^{-1})^{e_4} \equiv \pm 1 \pmod{N\mathcal{O}_D} \end{array} \right\}.$$

For $\epsilon \in \{\pm 1\}$, we define the union $\mathcal{Z}(D, N) = \mathcal{Z}^{+1}(D, N) \cup \mathcal{Z}^{-1}(D, N)$. In the definitions above, α and β are the two distinct roots of the quadratic polynomial $x^2 - Px + Q$, and $\mathcal{O}_D := \mathbb{Z}[x]/\langle x^2 - Px + Q \rangle$ denotes the quadratic algebra. When $p \equiv q \equiv 3 \pmod 4$, the set $\mathrm{BF}(N, e_4)$ forms a subgroup of $G(N)$. Under the same conditions, $\mathrm{LPBP}(D, N, e_4)$ is a subset of $\mathcal{Z}^{+1}(D, N)$ (see Proposition 2). Assuming $p \equiv q \equiv 3 \pmod 4$ and D is a perfect square, we are primarily interested in evaluating two quantities: $\beta_{\mathrm{Lucas}}(D, N, e_4) := \frac{|\mathrm{LPBP}(D,N,e_4)|}{|\mathcal{Z}^{+1}(D,N)|}$ and $\beta_{\mathrm{BF}}(N, e_4) := \frac{|\mathrm{BF}(N,e_4)|}{|G(N)|}$. These two ratios represent the soundness errors of their respective biprimality tests; they quantify the probability that a randomly selected candidate passes the test when $N = pq$ is a composite, non-RSA modulus. Note that Propositions 1 and 2 imply that $\beta_{\mathrm{Lucas}}(D, N, e_4)$ is independent of the specific choice of the perfect square D, provided $p \equiv q \equiv 3 \pmod 4$. For simplicity, we adopt the shorthand notation $\beta_{\mathrm{Lucas}}(N, e_4) := \beta_{\mathrm{Lucas}}(1, N, e_4)$.

2.1   Boneh-Franklin Biprimality Test

A core component of distributed RSA key generation is the Boneh-Franklin (BF) biprimality test [7]. It provides an efficient method for parties to verify that a shared candidate modulus N is the product of two distinct primes, p and q, without revealing these secret factors. The core logic of a single, idealized round of the test is captured in Algorithm 1.

Algorithm 1: Boneh-Franklin Biprimality Test (Single Round)

Input: Odd integer $N = pq$, where $p, q \equiv 3 \pmod 4$ and
$\gcd(N, p + q - 1) = 1$.

1 Select an integer $g \in \mathbb{Z}_N^\times$ with $\left(\frac{g}{N}\right) = 1$;
2 **if** $g^{e_4} \equiv \pm 1 \pmod N$ **then**
  | **return true;**
  end
3 **return false;**

---

3   Soundness Analysis of Biprimality Tests

Before delving into the specific counting formulas for the Boneh-Franklin and Lucas tests, we provide a unified intuition for our proofs. Determining the worst-case upper bound, specifically maximizing the possible ratio $|H|/|G|$, for a composite, non-RSA modulus N is fundamentally equivalent to studying the behavior of the Sylow 2-subgroups within the underlying algebraic structures of these tests.

By decomposing the relevant set via the CRT, one might naively assume that the absolute worst-case scenario occurs when N is square-free and composed of exactly three distinct prime factors, seemingly yielding a soundness error of $1/2$. However, our proofs reveal a fundamental algebraic barrier: the specific input conditions of both tests strictly force this worst-case $1/2$ to be unattainable.

- **In the Boneh-Franklin Test:** The condition $N \equiv 1 \pmod 4$ strictly implies that any false modulus composed of three prime factors must contain at least one factor $p_i \equiv 1 \pmod 4$. This inevitably expands the Sylow 2-subgroup of $p_i - 1$, strictly depressing the upper bound to $1/4$.
- **In the Lucas Test:** The analysis is remarkably parallel, despite operating in a quadratic algebra. Driven by the constraint $\left(\frac{-D}{p}\right) = \left(\frac{-D}{q}\right) = -1$, a similar algebraic contradiction prevents all prime factors from taking the minimal Sylow 2-subgroup size.

This shared algebraic phenomenon, where structural congruences force an expanded Sylow 2-subgroup, elegantly unifies both proofs and explains why the worst-case soundness error is strictly bounded at $1/4$ rather than $1/2$.

3.1 Refined Analysis of the Boneh-Franklin Test

In this context, the set of all potential witnesses, G, is the set $G(N) = \{g \in \mathbb{Z}_N^\times \mid \left(\frac{g}{N}\right) = 1\}$, while the set of passing witnesses, H, is $\mathrm{BF}(N, e_4) = \{g \in \mathbb{Z}_N^\times \mid g^{e_4} \equiv \pm 1 \pmod{N}\}$. We demonstrate that, contrary to the long-held belief of a $1/2$ worst-case soundness, a belief based on analyses that went no further than proving $\mathrm{BF}(N, e_4) \subset G(N)$, the tightest bound is in fact $1/4$. We adapt this general counting framework to refine the long-standing soundness bound of the BF test, and then apply this canonical approach to rigorously establish the soundness of our proposed Lucas test.

The Precise Counting Formula. The precise counting formulas of $\mathrm{BF}(N, e_4)$ and $G(N)$ are given below. First, to derive the formula for $|\mathrm{BF}(N, e_4)|$, our proof relies on a fundamental result for counting roots of unity in cyclic groups.

Lemma 1. [3, Lemma 2.1] *Let G be a cyclic group and d an integer. There are exactly $\gcd(d, |G|)$ dth-roots of 1 in G.*

By applying this result to the cyclic subgroups of $\mathbb{Z}_N^\times$ that arise from the CRT, we obtain the following precise formula.

Lemma 2. *Let $p \equiv q \equiv 3 \pmod{4}$ with $\gcd\left(pq, e_4\right) = 1$. Assume that $N := pq = \prod_{i=1}^{s} p_i^{r_i}$, where p_i is prime for all i, then we have*

$$|\mathrm{BF}(N, e_4)| = 2 \cdot \prod_{i=1}^{s} \gcd(e_4, d_i).$$

Here $p_i - 1 = 2^{k_i} d_i$ with $2 \nmid d_i$ for all $1 \leq i \leq s$.

Proof. Since e_4 is odd, we have

$$|\{g \in \mathbb{Z}_N^\times \mid g^{e_4} \equiv 1 \pmod{N}\}| = |\{g \in \mathbb{Z}_N^\times \mid g^{e_4} \equiv -1 \pmod{N}\}|$$

by the bijective map $g \mapsto -g$, which implies that

$$|\mathrm{BF}(N, e_4)| = 2 \cdot |\{g \in \mathbb{Z}_N^\times \mid g^{e_4} \equiv 1 \pmod{N}\}|.$$

By the Chinese Remainder Theorem (CRT), we can reduce the problem to counting the e_4-th roots of 1 in each local group $(\mathbb{Z}/p_i^{r_i}\mathbb{Z})^\times$. Since N is odd, these local groups are cyclic [22, Theorem 3, Chap. 4]. Combining this fact with Lemma 1, the number of e_4-th roots of 1 in the group $(\mathbb{Z}/p_i^{r_i}\mathbb{Z})^\times$ is

$$\gcd(e_4, \phi(p_i^{r_i})) = \gcd(e_4, p_i - 1), \text{ since } \gcd(e_4, N) = 1,$$
$$= \gcd(e_4, d_i), \text{ since } e_4 \text{ is odd}.$$

The result follows from the multiplicativity property of the CRT. $\qquad\square$

Lemma 3. *Let* $N = \prod_{i=1}^{s} p_i^{r_i}$ *be a positive odd integer. Then, the cardinality of* $G(N)$ *is given by:*

$$|G(N)| = \begin{cases} \phi(N), & \text{if } N \text{ is a perfect square;} \\ \phi(N)/2, & \text{if } N \text{ is not a perfect square.} \end{cases}$$

Proof. When N is a perfect square, $\left(\frac{x}{N}\right) = 1$ for all $x \in \mathbb{Z}_N^{\times}$, yielding $|G(N)| = \phi(N)$. When N is not a perfect square, there exists an element $a \in \mathbb{Z}_N^{\times}$ such that $\left(\frac{a}{N}\right) = -1$. Since the map $x \mapsto ax$ is a bijection on $\mathbb{Z}_N^{\times}$, we have $\sum_{x \in \mathbb{Z}_N^{\times}} \left(\frac{x}{N}\right) = \sum_{x \in \mathbb{Z}_N^{\times}} \left(\frac{ax}{N}\right) = -\sum_{x \in \mathbb{Z}_N^{\times}} \left(\frac{x}{N}\right)$. This implies the character sum is 0. Consequently, exactly half of the elements evaluate to 1, yielding $|G(N)| = \phi(N)/2$. $\qquad\square$

A Tighter Worst-Case Bound of 1/4. Our proof of a tighter bound for non-RSA moduli relies on a case-by-case analysis based on the number of prime factors and their exponents.

Theorem 1 (Boneh-Franklin biprimality test). *Let N be an odd integer given as the product of two integers $p, q \equiv 3 \pmod 4$, and let $e_4 = (p-1)(q-1)/4$ be the test exponent, with $\gcd(N, e_4) = 1$. Then we have*

Completeness: *If N is an RSA modulus, then $\mathrm{BF}(N, e_4) = G(N)$.*
Soundness: *If $N \neq 9$ is a non-RSA modulus, then $|\mathrm{BF}(N, e_4)| \leq |G(N)|/4$.*

Proof. We now apply the counting strategy outlined in our introduction. The proof hinges on a structural analysis of the non-RSA modulus N, particularly when it has three or more prime factors.

Case 1: N is a valid RSA modulus (p, q are distinct primes). Recall that $p_i - 1 = 2^{k_i} d_i$ with odd d_i for all i using the same notation as in Lemma 2. First, consider the case p, q are distinct primes, which implies $e_4 = d_1 d_2$ and $k_1 = k_2 = 1$. From Lemma 3, the proof of this case is completed by $\mathrm{BF}(N, e_4) \subset G(N)$, and the following equality:

$$|\mathrm{BF}(N, e_4)| = 2\gcd(e_4, d_1) \cdot \gcd(e_4, d_2) = 2d_1 d_2 = \phi(N)/2 = |G(N)|.$$

Case 2: N is not an RSA modulus. Before analyzing each case, we first emphasize that by Lemma 2 and Lemma 3, for all $N = \prod_{i=1}^{s} p_i^{r_i}$, the soundness error β_{BF} is given by

$$\beta_{\mathrm{BF}}(N, e_4) = \begin{cases} \dfrac{2\prod_{i=1}^{s} \gcd(e_4, d_i)}{\prod_{i=1}^{s} p_i^{r_i-1}(p_i - 1)} \leq \dfrac{2^{1-\sum k_i}}{\prod_{i=1}^{s} p_i^{r_i-1}}, & \text{if } N \text{ is a square;} \\[4ex] \dfrac{2\prod_{i=1}^{s} \gcd(e_4, d_i)}{(\prod_{i=1}^{s} p_i^{r_i-1}(p_i - 1))/2} \leq \dfrac{2^{2-\sum k_i}}{\prod_{i=1}^{s} p_i^{r_i-1}}, & \text{otherwise.} \end{cases} \tag{1}$$

Subcase 2.1: N is a perfect square. A perfect square N implies that its prime factorization $N = \prod p_i^{r_i}$ has $r_i \geq 2$ for all $1 \leq i \leq s$. The upper bound for this expression occurs when the number of prime factors s is minimized (i.e., $s = 1$), and the values of p_i and r_i in the denominator are as small as possible (i.e., $r_1 = 2, p_1 = 7$ or $r_1 = 4, p_1 = 3$). Hence, we have an upper bound is $1/p_1 < 1/7$, since the theorem explicitly excludes the case $p = q = 3$.

Subcase 2.2: N is square-free (with $s \geq 3$ distinct prime factors). Consider the case $s = 3$. We first establish the modular properties of the prime factors $\{p_1, p_2, p_3\}$. From the condition of this theorem, $N = pq$ with $p, q \equiv 3 \pmod 4$, which implies $N = p_1 p_2 p_3 \equiv 1 \pmod 4$, so there exists at least one p_i of them to be congruent to 1 (mod 4) for some $1 \leq i \leq 3$. For such p_i with $p_i \equiv 1$ (mod 4), its corresponding exponent k_i is at least 2. Thus, for our set of three prime factors, the sum of the exponents is bounded by $\sum_{i=1}^{3} k_i \geq 1 + 1 + 2 = 4$, which gives the desired result for $s = 3$:

$$\beta_{\mathrm{BF}}(N, e_4) \leq 2^{2-\sum k_i} \leq 2^{2-4} = 1/4.$$

For cases where $s = 4$, the argument is more direct. Since $k_i \geq 1$ for any odd prime p_i, the sum of exponents is bounded by $\sum_{i=1}^{s} k_i \geq s$. Therefore, the general bound is:

$$\beta_{\mathrm{BF}}(N, e_4) \leq 2^{2-\sum k_i} \leq 2^{2-s} \leq 1/4.$$

For any $s \geq 5$, the bound becomes strictly tighter (e.g., $2^{2-5} = 1/8$ or smaller). Thus, the worst-case probability for any $s \geq 3$ is $1/4$.

Subcase 2.3: N is neither a perfect square nor square-free. This case is defined by two conditions: (1) at least one exponent r_i is odd (non-perfect-square), and (2) at least one exponent $r_j \geq 2$ (non-square-free). First, consider the case $s = 1$, then the formula of β_{BF} gives us

$$\beta_{\mathrm{BF}}(N, e_4) \leq 2^{2-1} \cdot p_1^{1-r_1} \leq 2 \cdot 3^{1-3} = 2/9.$$

Next, if $s \geq 2$, then without loss of generality, we may assume $N = p_1^2 \prod_{i=2}^{s} p_i^{r_i}$. Recall the estimate of β_{BF} is given in the inequality (1). Therefore, the worst-case soundness error β_{BF} is attained by choosing the smallest possible parameters: $s = 2$ and $p_1 = 3$. For the resulting case where $N = 3^2 p_2^{r_2}$, this maximum possible error is exactly $1/6$, which occurs when $r_2 = 1, p_2 = 5$.

Having analyzed all possible structures for a non-RSA modulus N, we have shown that the soundness error is at most $1/4$ in every case (excluding $N = 9$). This completes the proof. $\qquad\qquad\square$

Conditions for the Worst-Case Scenario. Based on the proof of Theorem 1, we establish the necessary and sufficient conditions for the worst-case scenario to occur.

Corollary 1. *Assume that the assumption of Theorem 1 holds. The equality $|\mathrm{BF}(N, e_4)| = |G(N)|/4$ is true if and only if $N = \prod_{i=1}^{s} p_i^{r_i}$ has one of the two structures described in Table 1, up to the symmetry of the inputs p and q.*

Table 1. Necessary and Sufficient Conditions for the Worst-Case Soundness Error

Case	Structure	Prime Factor Conditions	GCD Conditions
$s = 3$	$p = p_1 p_2$ $q = p_3$	$p_1 \equiv 5 \ (\mathrm{mod}\ 8)$ $p_2, p_3 \equiv 3 \ (\mathrm{mod}\ 4)$	$\gcd(e_4, p_1 - 1) = \frac{p_1 - 1}{4}$ $\gcd(e_4, p_i - 1) = \frac{p_i - 1}{2}$ for $i \in \{2, 3\}$
$s = 4$	$p = p_1 p_2 p_3$ $q = p_4$	$p_i \equiv 3 \ (\mathrm{mod}\ 4)$ for all $i \in \{1, \ldots, 4\}$	$\gcd(e_4, p_i - 1) = \frac{p_i - 1}{2}$ for all $i \in \{1, \ldots, 4\}$

Proof. From the proof of Theorem 1, the maximum value can occur only if N is square-free with $s = 3$ or 4, and the equality holds throughout the estimate (1).
$\square$

Tightness of the Bound. To explain that the $1/4$ soundness bound is tight, we construct infinitely many pairs (p, q) that satisfies the conditions of the first worst-case scenario ($s = 3$) from Table 1. Note that Dirichlet's theorem on arithmetic progressions ensures that there are infinitely many primes p' such that $p' \equiv 23 \ (\mathrm{mod}\ 420)$. We set $p = p_1 p_2$ with $p_1 = 5, p_2 = 3$, and $q = p_3 = p'$. These satisfy the prime factor conditions in Table 1. We now verify the GCD conditions. The term $e_4 = (p - 1)(q - 1)/4 = 7(p' - 1)/2$. For example, to check the condition for $p_1 = 5$, we compute $\gcd(e_4, p_1 - 1) = \gcd(7(p' - 1)/2, 4)$. Since $p' \equiv 23 \ (\mathrm{mod}\ 420)$, $p' - 1 = 22 + 420k$, which means $(p' - 1)/2 = 11 + 210k$ is odd. Therefore, $\gcd(7(p' - 1)/2, 4) = 1$, which equals $(p_1 - 1)/4$. A similar check confirms the other conditions.

3.2 Soundness Analysis of the Lucas Test

We first present the standard Lucas test for prime numbers, and also provide an algorithmic representation to give the reader a clearer understanding of the verification method in our proposed test.

Let P and Q be integers, $D := P^2 - 4Q$, and $\mathcal{O}_D$ be the quadratic algebra. If a prime p with $p \nmid 2QD$, then we have

$$(\alpha \beta^{-1})^{p - \left(\frac{D}{p}\right)} \equiv 1 \quad (\mathrm{mod}\ p\mathcal{O}_D).$$

Here α, β are two distinct roots of the polynomial $x^2 - Px + Q$ (cf. [3]). This thus provides a primality test. Inspired by this property, we have designed a novel biprimality test.

Before detailing the algorithm, we provide the intuition behind its construction. To transition from a single-prime test to a biprimality test for an RSA modulus $N = pq$, we naturally look for an exponent that simultaneously annihilates the underlying algebraic groups for both prime factors. By constructing the index $e_4 = \left[p - \left(\frac{D}{p}\right)\right]\left[q - \left(\frac{D}{q}\right)\right]/4$, we guarantee that it relates to a common multiple of the respective group orders modulo p and modulo q. Consequently, by CRT, the congruence naturally holds modulo $N = pq$.

Algorithm 2: The Proposed Lucas Biprimality Test

Input: Odd integers p, q where $N = pq$ and $\gcd(N, e_4) = 1$, with
$e_4 = [p + (\frac{-1}{p})][q + (\frac{-1}{q})]/4$.

1 Select an integer D such that $(\frac{-D}{p}) = (\frac{-D}{q}) = -1$;

2 Randomly select $P \in \mathbb{Z}_N$ such that $(\frac{Q}{N}) = 1$, where $Q = (P^2 - D)/4$;

3 **if** $(\alpha\beta^{-1})^{e_4} \equiv \pm 1 \pmod{N\mathcal{O}_D}$ **then**
  | **return** true;
  end

4 **return** false;

In the BF test, verification relies solely on the multiplicative group $\mathbb{Z}_N^\times$, where false witnesses only need to align with a static period $p_i - 1$. The Lucas test, however, evaluates the roots of a quadratic polynomial $x^2 - Px + Q$, inextricably linking addition (trace P) and multiplication (norm Q). Consequently, the underlying test period shifts to $p_i - (\frac{D}{p_i})$. Because the Legendre symbol $(\frac{D}{p_i}) \in \{\pm 1\}$ introduces a dynamic sign fluctuation, satisfying this quadratic period imposes strictly tighter arithmetic constraints than the static $p_i - 1$. This drastically reduces the chance of coincidental alignment by prime factors, giving the Lucas test a much stronger restrictive power against false witnesses.

By analogy with the study of the BF test, we investigate sets $\mathcal{Z}^{+1}(D, N)$ and $\mathrm{LPBP}(D, N, e_4)$ comprising the elements that fulfill Steps (1) and (2) of Algorithm 2, respectively. In the following propositions, we determine their cardinalities to evaluate the soundness of the proposed Lucas test.

Proposition 1. *Let D be an integer and $N := \prod_{i=1}^{s} p_i^{r_i}$ be a positive integer with* $\gcd(N, 2D) = 1$. *For each prime factor p_i, let $A_i := p_i - (\frac{D}{p_i}) - 1$. Further, let $S_1 := \{i \mid r_i \text{ is odd}\}$. Then:*

$$|\mathcal{Z}^{+1}(D, N)| = \begin{cases} \prod_{i=1}^{s} p_i^{r_i-1}\left(p_i - \left(\frac{D}{p_i}\right) - 1\right), & \text{if } N \text{ is square;} \\ \frac{1}{2}\left(\prod_{i=1}^{s} p_i^{r_i-1}\right)\left(\prod_{i=1}^{s} A_i + (-1)^{|S_1|}\prod_{i \in S_1^c} A_i\right), & \text{otherwise.} \end{cases}$$

where S_1^c is the complement of S_1, i.e., the set of indices i for which r_i is even.

Proof (Proof Sketch). We only sketch the proof for a non-square N, as the case of a square N is simpler. By the CRT, it suffices to count the cardinality over prime power moduli $N = p^r$.

For the base case $r = 1$, we introduce two auxiliary subsets, S^{+1} and S^{-1}, defined for $\epsilon \in \{\pm 1\}$ as:

$$S^\epsilon = \left\{1 \le i \le \frac{p-1}{2} \;\middle|\; \left(\frac{i^2 + D/4}{p}\right) = \epsilon, \text{ and } i^2 \not\equiv \frac{-D}{4} \pmod{p}\right\}.$$

To evaluate these sets, we compute the sum $|S^{+1}| + |S^{-1}|$ (which represents the total number of valid elements) and the difference $|S^{+1}| - |S^{-1}|$ (which can be evaluated exactly using classical character sums over quadratic polynomials). Solving this linear system of two equations yields the exact cardinalities for $|S^{+1}|$ and $|S^{-1}|$, directly providing the size of $\mathcal{Z}^\epsilon(D, p)$.

For higher prime powers $r \geq 2$, we lift the base-case solutions from $\mathbb{Z}_p$ to $\mathbb{Z}_{p^r}$ via a standard application of Hensel's Lemma. Finally, combining these local counts across all prime factors via the CRT, and applying mathematical induction, the resulting algebraic product simplifies to the overall closed-form formula. The complete, rigorous derivation is deferred to the full version of this paper. $\qquad\square$

Next, we study the cardinality of the set LPBP and then prove it is a subset of $\mathcal{Z}^{+1}$.

Proposition 2. *Let p, q be positive odd integers, $N = pq = \prod_{i=1}^{s} p_i^{r_i}$, and D be an integer in $\mathbb{Z}$ with $\gcd(2D, N) = 1$, and $\left(\frac{-D}{p}\right) = \left(\frac{-D}{q}\right) = -1$. Then we have the following:*

1. *The set $\mathrm{LPBP}(D, N, e_4)$ is a subset of $\mathcal{Z}^{+1}(D, N)$.*
2. *Furthermore, assuming $\gcd(N, e_4) = 1$, its cardinality is given by*

$$|\mathrm{LPBP}(D, N, e_4)| = \prod_{i=1}^{s} \big(\gcd(e_4, d_i') - 1 \big) + \prod_{i=1}^{s} \gcd(e_4, d_i'),$$

where the decomposition is now $p_i - \left(\frac{D}{p_i}\right) = 2^{k_i'} d_i'$ with $2 \nmid d_i'$ for all $1 \leq i \leq s$.

Proof. We establish Claim 1 only for non-square D by leveraging the properties of conjugation and the norm map in the quadratic extension $\mathcal{O}_D/N\mathcal{O}_D$.

Let $(P, Q) \in \mathrm{LPBP}(D, N, e_4)$, which implies $(\alpha\beta^{-1})^{e_4} \equiv \pm 1 \pmod{N\mathcal{O}_D}$. We must show that $\left(\frac{Q}{N}\right) = 1$. Since e_4 is odd and $Q = \alpha\beta$, we have $\left(\frac{Q}{N}\right) = \left(\frac{Q^{e_4}}{N}\right) = \left(\frac{(\alpha\beta)^{e_4}}{N}\right)$.

Case A: $(\alpha\beta^{-1})^{e_4} \equiv 1 \pmod{N\mathcal{O}_D}$.
This implies $\alpha^{e_4} \equiv \beta^{e_4} \pmod{N\mathcal{O}_D}$. Since β is the conjugate of α, α^{e_4} is invariant under conjugation and thus belongs to the base ring, i.e., $\alpha^{e_4} \equiv A \in \mathbb{Z}_N$. Its norm satisfies $Q^{e_4} \equiv \alpha^{e_4}\beta^{e_4} \equiv A^2 \pmod{N}$. Therefore, $\left(\frac{Q^{e_4}}{N}\right) = \left(\frac{A^2}{N}\right) = 1$.

Case B: $(\alpha\beta^{-1})^{e_4} \equiv -1 \pmod{N\mathcal{O}_D}$.
This implies $\alpha^{e_4} \equiv -\beta^{e_4} \pmod{N\mathcal{O}_D}$. Thus, α^{e_4} is a purely quadratic element, meaning $\alpha^{e_4} \equiv B\sqrt{D} \pmod{N\mathcal{O}_D}$ for some $B \in \mathbb{Z}_N$. Its norm is $Q^{e_4} \equiv (B\sqrt{D})(-B\sqrt{D}) \equiv -B^2 D \pmod{N}$. Evaluating the Jacobi symbol yields:

$$\left(\frac{Q^{e_4}}{N}\right) = \left(\frac{-B^2 D}{N}\right) = \left(\frac{-D}{N}\right).$$

By the premise $\left(\frac{-D}{p}\right) = \left(\frac{-D}{q}\right) = -1$, we have $\left(\frac{-D}{N}\right) = (-1)(-1) = 1$. Thus, $\left(\frac{Q^{e_4}}{N}\right) = 1$. In both cases, $\left(\frac{Q}{N}\right) = 1$, which completes the proof of Claim 1.

Proof of Claim 2. To determine the cardinality of LPBP, we follow the methodology detailed in [3, Section 1.4]. By the CRT, the global counting problem reduces to evaluating the local sets $\mathrm{LPBP}(D, p_i^{r_i}, e_4)$. These local sets are partitioned into two disjoint cases based on the value of $(\alpha\beta^{-1})^{e_4}$ (mod $p_i^{r_i}\mathcal{O}_D$).

Case 1: $(\alpha\beta^{-1})^{e_4} \equiv 1$ (mod $p_i^{r_i}\mathcal{O}_D$).

Since the order of the norm-1 group $(\widehat{\mathcal{O}_D/p_i^{r_i}})$ is known to be $p_i^{r_i-1}(p_i - (\frac{D}{p_i}))$, the number of its e_4-th roots of unity is given by:

$$d = \gcd\left(e_4, p_i^{r_i-1}(p_i - (\tfrac{D}{p_i}))\right)$$
$$= \gcd(e_4, p_i - (\tfrac{D}{p_i})) \qquad\qquad (\text{since } \gcd(e_4, N) = 1)$$
$$= \gcd(e_4, d_i'). \qquad\qquad (\text{since } e_4 \text{ is odd})$$

Excluding roots where $\alpha\beta^{-1} - 1$ is not invertible modulo p_i, the local cardinality for this case is exactly $\gcd(e_4, d_i') - 1$.

Case 2: $(\alpha\beta^{-1})^{e_4} \equiv -1$ (mod $p_i^{r_i}\mathcal{O}_D$).
In this case, the condition for the invertibility of $1 - (\alpha\beta^{-1})$ (mod p_i) is always satisfied. Thus, the local cardinality for this case is simply $\gcd(e_4, d_i')$.

Aggregating these local results via the CRT requires observing that the global congruence $(\alpha\beta^{-1})^{e_4} \equiv \pm 1$ (mod $N\mathcal{O}_D$) forces the local congruences to be either $+1$ for all prime factors or -1 for all prime factors simultaneously. Summing the products of these two strictly disjoint global scenarios yields the closed-form expression in the proposition. $\qquad\square$

Finally, the soundness error, denoted β_{Lucas}, is estimated as follows.

Theorem 2. *Let N be an odd integer given as a product of two odd integers p, q. Let e_4 be the test exponent with $\gcd(N, e_4) = 1$. Let D be an integer such that $\gcd(2D, N) = 1$ and $\left(\frac{-D}{p}\right) = \left(\frac{-D}{q}\right) = -1$. The proposed Lucas test has the following properties:*

Completeness: *If N is an RSA modulus, then $\mathrm{LPBP}(D, N, e_4) = \mathcal{Z}^{+1}(D, N)$.*
Soundness: *If N is non-RSA and its minimal prime factor $p_{\min} \geq 11$, the soundness error is bounded by:* $\beta_{\mathrm{Lucas}}(D, N, e_4) < \frac{1}{4} + \frac{1.25}{p_{\min}-3}.$

Proof. Follow the same methodology of Theorem 1.
Case 1: N is a valid RSA modulus (p and q are distinct primes). Our goal is to prove that $\mathrm{LPBP}(D, N, e_4) = \mathcal{Z}^{+1}(D, N)$. Since Proposition 2 already establishes that $\mathrm{LPBP}(D, N, e_4) \subseteq \mathcal{Z}^{+1}(D, N)$, it suffices to show that their cardinalities are equal.

We use the notation $p_1 = p, p_2 = q$ and the decomposition $p_i - (\frac{D}{p_i}) = 2^{k_i'}d_i'$. The condition of the theorem premises $\left(\frac{-D}{p_i}\right) = -1$ implies the identity

$p_i - \left(\frac{D}{p_i}\right) = p_i + \left(\frac{-1}{p_i}\right)$. Notice that $p_i + \left(\frac{-1}{p_i}\right) = 2d_i'$. Substituting this directly into the definition of e_4 gives $e_4 = \frac{1}{4}\left[p + \left(\frac{-1}{p}\right)\right]\left[q + \left(\frac{-1}{q}\right)\right] = d_1' d_2'$. This identity immediately implies that $\gcd(e_4, d_1') = d_1'$ and $\gcd(e_4, d_2') = d_2'$. Now, we have

$$|\mathrm{LPBP}(D, N, e_4)| = \left(\gcd(e_4, d_1') - 1\right)\left(\gcd(e_4, d_2') - 1\right) + \gcd(e_4, d_1')\gcd(e_4, d_2')$$
$$= (d_1' - 1)(d_2' - 1) + d_1' d_2' = 2d_1' d_2' - d_1' - d_2' + 1.$$

Next, Proposition 1 says that

$$|\mathcal{Z}^{+1}(D, N)| = \left((2d_1' - 1)(2d_2' - 1) + 1\right)/2 = 2d_1' d_2' - d_1' - d_2' + 1.$$

Case 2: Non-RSA Moduli. For the remaining cases, considering $N = \prod_i p_i^{r_i}$, applying Proposition 1 and Proposition 2 yields the following upper bound for the soundness error β_{Lucas}:

$$\beta_{\mathrm{Lucas}}(N, e_4) \qquad\qquad\qquad\qquad\qquad\qquad\qquad\qquad\qquad (2)$$

$$\leq \begin{cases} \dfrac{2^{1-\sum k_i}\prod_{i=1}^{s}(p_i - 1)}{\prod_{i=1}^{s} p_i^{r_i - 1}(p_i - 2)}, & \text{if } N \text{ is a square;} \\[4ex] \dfrac{2^{2-\sum k_i}\prod_{i=1}^{s}(p_i - 1)}{\left(\prod_{i=1}^{s} p_i^{r_i - 1}\right)\left(\prod_{i=1}^{s}(p_i - 2) - \prod_{i \in S_1^c}(p_i - 2)\right)}, & \text{otherwise.} \end{cases}$$

Here, we recall that $S_1^c = \{i \mid r_i \text{ is even}\}$ is the set of indices corresponding to even exponents in the prime factorization of N.

Subcase 2.1: N is a perfect square. The Eq. (2) implies that for all $p_i \geq 11$,

$$\beta_{\mathrm{Lucas}}(D, N, e_4) \leq \left(\frac{2}{\prod_{i=1}^{s} p_i^{r_i - 1}}\right)\left(\frac{\prod_{i=1}^{s} 2^{-k_i}(p_i - 1)}{\prod_{i=1}^{s}(p_i - 2)}\right)$$

$$\leq \left(\frac{2}{\prod_{i=1}^{s} p_i^{r_i - 1}}\right)\left(\prod_{i=1}^{s}\left(\frac{1}{2} + \frac{1}{2(p_i - 2)}\right)\right) \leq \left(\frac{2}{11}\right)\left(\frac{1}{2} + \frac{1}{18}\right) = \frac{10}{99}.$$

Subcase 2.2: N is square-free. When N is square-free. Consider the case $s = 3$. Then there exists one of $\{p_1, p_2, p_3\}$ is $4 \mid p_i - \left(\frac{D}{p_i}\right)$. If not, for all $1 \leq i \leq 3$, $p_i - \left(\frac{D}{p_i}\right) = 2d_i'$ with odd d_i' hold (i.e. $k_i' = 1$), which is equivalent to $p_i \equiv -\left(\frac{D}{p_i}\right)$ (mod 4). Let's assume, without loss of generality, that the inputs are $p = p_1$ and $q = p_2 p_3$. The condition of the theorem implies that $\left(\frac{-D}{p}\right) = \left(\frac{-D}{q}\right) = -1$. From $\left(\frac{-D}{q}\right) = -1$, we have $\left(\frac{D}{q}\right) = -\left(\frac{-1}{q}\right)$. Our contradiction assumption for p_2, p_3 means $p_2 \equiv -\left(\frac{D}{p_2}\right)$ (mod 4) and $p_3 \equiv -\left(\frac{D}{p_3}\right)$ (mod 4). Multiplying these congruences gives $q = p_2 p_3 \equiv \left(\frac{D}{p_2}\right)\left(\frac{D}{p_3}\right) = \left(\frac{D}{q}\right)$ (mod 4). So we have derived $q \equiv \left(\frac{D}{q}\right)$ (mod 4). Substituting in the identity $\left(\frac{D}{q}\right) = -\left(\frac{-1}{q}\right)$, we get:

$$q + \left(\frac{-1}{q}\right) \equiv 0 \pmod 4,$$

which gives us a contradiction, because $q + \left(\frac{-1}{q}\right) \equiv 2 \pmod{4}$ for any odd integers $q > 1$. Hence, our initial assumption that all $k_i' = 1$ must be false. Therefore, at least one $k_i' \geq 2$, which implies $\sum_{i=1}^{3} k_i' \geq 4$. Therefore, applying Eq. (2), we obtain that

$$\beta_{\text{Lucas}}(D, N, e_4) < \frac{1}{4}\left[\frac{\prod_{i=1}^{3}(p_i - 1)}{\prod_{i=1}^{3}(p_i - 2) - 1}\right] < \frac{1}{4}\left[\frac{(p_{\min} - 1)^3}{(p_{\min} - 2)^3 - 1}\right]$$

$$\leq \frac{1}{4}\left[\frac{(p_{\min} - 1)^4}{(p_{\min} - 2)^4 - 1}\right], \quad \text{for all } p_{\min} \geq 5.$$

Similarly, as $s = 4$, we also have

$$\beta_{\text{Lucas}}(D, N, e_4) < \frac{1}{4}\left[\frac{(p_{\min} - 1)^4}{(p_{\min} - 2)^4 - 1}\right].$$

When $s \geq 5$, applying the following fact

$$\frac{\prod_{i=1}^{s}(p_i - 1)}{\prod_{i=1}^{s}(p_i - 2) - 1} < \left[\frac{\prod_{i=1}^{4}(p_i - 1)}{\prod_{i=1}^{4}(p_i - 2) - 1}\right]\left[\frac{\prod_{i=5}^{s}(p_i - 1)}{\prod_{i=5}^{s}(p_i - 2) - 1}\right],$$

we arrive that, for $s \geq 5$,

$$\beta_{\text{Lucas}}(D, N, e_4) \leq 2^{2-k_1-\ldots-k_s}\frac{\prod_{i=1}^{s}(p_i - 1)}{\prod_{i=1}^{s}(p_i - 2) - 1} < \frac{1}{4}\left[\frac{(p_{\min} - 1)^4}{(p_{\min} - 2)^4 - 1}\right].$$

Thus, for any $s \geq 3$, the soundness error is bounded by:

$$\beta_{\text{Lucas}}(D, N, e_4) < \frac{1}{4}\left[\frac{(p_{\min} - 1)^4}{(p_{\min} - 2)^4 - 1}\right] < \frac{1}{4} + \frac{1.25}{p_{\min} - 3},$$

where the last inequality follows from a standard algebraic expansion.

Subcase 2.3: N is neither a perfect square nor square-free. This case is defined by two conditions: (1) at least one exponent r_i is odd, which means $|S_1| \geq 1$ and (2) at least one exponent $r_j \geq 2$. Note that

$$\prod_{i \in S_1^c}\left(p_i - \left(\frac{D}{p_i}\right) - 1\right)\left(\prod_{i \in S_1}\left(p_i - \left(\frac{D}{p_i}\right) - 1\right) + (-1)^{|S_1|}\right)$$

$$\geq \prod_{i \in S_1^c}(p_i - 2)\left(\prod_{i \in S_1}(p_i - 2) - 1\right).$$

Equation 2 shows that for all $p_i \geq 11$,

$$\beta_{\text{Lucas}}(D, N, e_4) \leq \left[\frac{4}{\prod_{i=1}^{s} p_i^{r_i-1}}\right]\left[\frac{\prod_{i=1}^{s} 2^{-k_i}(p_i - 1)}{\prod_{i=1}^{s}(p_i - 2) - \prod_{i \in S_1^c}(p_i - 2)}\right]$$

$$\leq \left[\frac{4}{\prod_{i=1}^{s} p_i^{r_i-1}}\right]\left[\frac{\prod_{i=1}^{s}\left(\frac{1}{2} + \frac{1}{2(p_i-2)}\right)}{1 - \left(\prod_{i \in S_1}(p_i - 2)\right)^{-1}}\right] \leq \left[\frac{4}{11}\right]\left[\frac{\frac{1}{2} + \frac{1}{18}}{1 - 9^{-1}}\right] = \frac{5}{22}.$$

Having analyzed all possible structures for a non-RSA modulus N, we have shown that the soundness error is bounded as claimed. $\qquad\square$

Remark 1. A final point regarding the premise $\left(\frac{-D}{p}\right) = -1$: this condition is not met if the input p is a perfect square. This poses no issue for our protocol for two key reasons. First, from a practical standpoint, the probability of a large integer chosen from the sum of uniform distributions being a perfect square is negligible. Second, and more importantly, if the input p is a perfect square, it cannot be a prime number, which means the resulting modulus $N = pq$ is an invalid RSA modulus. The failure to satisfy this premise is thus a feature, not a bug, as it is one way the protocol can reject invalid inputs.

4   The Proposed Lucas Biprimality Protocols

Distributed biprimality tests are essential components of distributed RSA key generation. The joint generation of an RSA modulus can be simplified into two main steps: 1) candidate modulus generation, where potential prime factors p and q are sampled in secret-shared form and their product $N = p \cdot q$ is securely computed using multi-party computation algorithms; and 2) RSA modulus verification, where participants verify that N is an RSA modulus without disclosing the underlying secret factors. In such distributed environments, sensitive values are maintained in secret-shared form among n participants $\mathcal{P}_1, \ldots, \mathcal{P}_n$, and to facilitate the description of our protocols, we recall that $[a]_m$ denotes the additive sharing of a value a over the finite group $\mathbb{Z}_m$, where each participant $\mathcal{P}_i$ holds a secret share $\mathfrak{a}_i \in \mathbb{Z}_m$ such that $\sum_{i=1}^{n} \mathfrak{a}_i \equiv a \pmod{m}$, and similarly, $[a]_{\mathbb{Z}}$ represents additive sharing over the integers satisfying $\sum_{i=1}^{n} \mathfrak{a}_i = a$ in $\mathbb{Z}$.

We propose two protocols based on Theorem 2. The first achieves security against semi-honest adversaries for all standard RSA moduli, while the second provides security with abort against malicious adversaries for the case of Blum integers. Both protocols are proven secure in the standard stand-alone model.

4.1   The Semi-honest Setting

To translate our Lucas test into a secure protocol, we must address a critical challenge that does not exist in the original Boneh-Franklin setting: the selection of the parameter D. For non-Blum integers, the protocol must securely find a D satisfying both $\left(\frac{-D}{N}\right) = 1$ and $\left(\frac{-D}{p}\right) = -1$. A naive interactive search for D would leak information about the secret prime p with each tested candidate. This challenge exposes a fundamental trade-off between generality, efficiency, and perfect (leakage-free) security. Consequently, this section explores the two viable pathways that navigate this trade-off: one offering perfect security in controlled environments, and another providing a broadly applicable solution that accepts bounded leakage as a deliberate engineering compromise. We then present our main protocol, π_{RSA}^{S}, which formalizes the latter approach.

Navigating the Security-Generality Trade-Off

A Leakage-Free but Constrained Approach. Our primary and most efficient solution mirrors the elegant approach for Blum integers where $D = 1$ is pre-selected. The core idea is to pre-fix a public value for D and impose congruence constraints on p and q during their generation. This guarantees that the conditions are met automatically, circumventing any interactive and potentially leaky search. For instance, by choosing a small prime D (e.g., $D = 3$) and ensuring primes are generated such that $p \equiv a \pmod{4D}$ and $q \equiv b \pmod{4D}$ for appropriate non-residues a, b, this leakage problem is entirely bypassed. This design principle ensures that the biprimality test remains as leakage-resilient as the original Boneh-Franklin test.

A General Approach with Bounded Leakage. For applications requiring full generality where pre-constraining primes is infeasible, a direct trade-off emerges between achieving perfect security and maintaining practical efficiency. Guided by the principle of practical viability, our work focuses on a strategy that deliberately navigates this compromise. We propose capping the interactive search for a suitable prime D at a constant number of trials, LeakBound (e.g., 7). Under the standard heuristic that the Legendre symbol behaves like a random coin flip, the probability of failing to find a suitable D for a valid prime after LeakBound independent trials is approximately $(1/2)^{\mathsf{LeakBound}}$. This design offers a twofold benefit: it guarantees a strictly bounded and tolerable abort probability ($< 2^{-\mathsf{LeakBound}}$) for valid moduli while retaining universal applicability. The explicit cost of this generality is a bounded information leakage of LeakBound bits about the secret p. This quantifiable leakage is reflected directly in the security analysis, where the reduction to the factoring problem incurs a concrete loss factor of $2^{\mathsf{LeakBound}}$. This bounds the adversarial advantage by $2^{\mathsf{LeakBound}}\epsilon$, where ϵ denotes the advantage of factoring N, a standard consequence of the simulation's need to correctly guess the Legendre symbols of the sampled candidates.

The Protocol and Its Security. We now present our main semi-honest protocol, $\pi_{\mathrm{RSA}}^{\mathcal{S}}$, which formalizes the generally applicable, bounded-leakage approach. We first define its target functionality, which captures the protocol's behavior, including the bounded leakage. To facilitate the secure computation of the exponent, we assume the input shares $[p]_{\mathbb{Z}}$ and $[q]_{\mathbb{Z}}$ possess a specific structure modulo 4, a standard technique first introduced by Boneh and Franklin [7].

Functionality 1 $\mathcal{F}_{\mathrm{RSA}}^{\mathcal{S}}(n, \mathsf{LeakBound})$

Inputs: Each party $\mathcal{P}_i$ has a public number $N = pq$, $p \pmod 4$, $q \pmod 4$, shares $[p]_{\mathbb{Z}}$ and $[q]_{\mathbb{Z}}$, where each share satisfies $\mathfrak{p}_1 \equiv p \pmod 4$, $\mathfrak{q}_1 \equiv q \pmod 4$, and $\mathfrak{p}_i \equiv \mathfrak{q}_i \equiv 0 \pmod 4$ for all $2 \le i \le n$.

Outputs:
If $p \equiv q \equiv 3 \pmod 4$:

- If $p \neq q$ are both primes and $\gcd(N, e_4) = 1$, then each party receives (RSAModulus, $\emptyset$).
- Otherwise, each party receives (NonRSAModulus, $\{\mathfrak{p}_i, \mathfrak{q}_i\}_{i=1}^n$).

Else:

Let $S_{\mathrm{Leak}} := \{D_k \in [3, D_{\min}] \mid (\frac{-D_k}{N}) = 1 \text{ and } D_k \text{ is prime}\}$, where $D_{\min}$ is the minimal odd prime satisfying $(\frac{-D_{\min}}{p}) = -1$ and $(\frac{-D_{\min}}{N}) = 1$.

- If $|S_{\mathrm{Leak}}| > \mathsf{LeakBound}$, then each party receives (AbortLeakBound, $\{\mathfrak{p}_i, \mathfrak{q}_i\}_{i=1}^n$).
- If $|S_{\mathrm{Leak}}| \leq \mathsf{LeakBound}$, and $p \neq q$ are both primes such that $\gcd(N, e_4) = 1$, then each party receives (RSAModulus, $\{(\frac{D_k}{p})\}_{D_k \in S_{\mathrm{Leak}}}$).
- Otherwise, each party receives (NonRSAModulus, $\{\mathfrak{p}_i, \mathfrak{q}_i\}_{i=1}^n$).

The realization of this functionality, Protocol 1, consists of the bounded search for D followed by κ iterations of the core exponentiation test. To compute the necessary Legendre symbols, it relies on an ideal functionality $\mathcal{F}_{\mathrm{Leg}}$, the formal construction and security proof of which are provided in the full version of this paper.

Protocol 1   Lucas Biprimality Test $\pi_{\mathrm{RSA}}^{\mathcal{S}}(n, \kappa, \mathsf{LeakBound})$

Inputs: Each party $\mathcal{P}_i$ has $p \pmod 4$, $q \pmod 4$, N and $[p]_{\mathbb{Z}}, [q]_{\mathbb{Z}}$ with the structure defined in Functionality 1.

Outputs: $\left(\text{RSAModulus}, \left\{ \left(\frac{D_k}{p} \right) \right\}_{D_k \in S_{\mathrm{Leak}}} \right)$, (NonRSAModulus, $\{\mathfrak{p}_i, \mathfrak{q}_i\}_{i=1}^n$), or (AbortLeakBound, $\{\mathfrak{p}_i, \mathfrak{q}_i\}_{i=1}^n$).

Select an appropriate positive integer D:

1. If $p \equiv q \equiv 3 \pmod 4$, parties set $D = 1$, $S_{\mathrm{Leak}} := \emptyset$, and proceed to Step 5.
2. Let D_k be the k-th odd prime in the sequence $(3, 5, 7, \dots)$. If $\left(\frac{-D_k}{N} \right) \neq 1$, increment k and repeat Step 2. Otherwise, proceed to Step 3.
3. Party $\mathcal{P}_i$ adds D_k to S_{Leak}. If $|S_{\mathrm{Leak}}| > \mathsf{LeakBound}$, the party broadcasts its shares and returns (AbortLeakBound, $\{\mathfrak{p}_i, \mathfrak{q}_i\}_{i=1}^n$). Otherwise, it sends $([p]_{\mathbb{Z}}, p \pmod 4, D_k)$ to the functionality $\mathcal{F}_{\mathrm{Leg}}$ to obtain $\left(\frac{-D_k}{p} \right)$.
4. If $\left(\frac{-D_k}{p} \right) = -1$, parties set $D = D_k$ and proceed to Step 5. Else, parties increment k and return to Step 2.

Exponential verification: For $j = 1, \dots, \kappa$:

5. Sample $P_j \leftarrow \mathbb{Z}_N$ and set $Q_j := (P_j^2 - D) \cdot 4^{-1}$. If $\gcd(N, Q_j) \neq 1$, abort by broadcasting shares.
6. If $\left(\frac{Q_j}{N} \right) \neq 1$, they restart from Step 5 (via rejection sampling).

7. The parties securely compute $u_j = (\alpha_j \beta_j^{-1})^{e_4}$ using $\mathcal{F}_{\text{Shuffle}}$, an ideal functionality that securely aggregates their local multiplicative shares into a public product, where α_j, β_j are roots of $x^2 - P_j x + Q_j$.
8. All parties check $u_j \equiv \pm 1 \pmod{N\mathcal{O}_D}$. If the check fails, they abort by broadcasting shares.

GCD Test:

9. Parties securely compute a randomized multiple of e_4, denoted z, using $\mathcal{F}_{\text{ModMul}}$, an ideal functionality that facilitates secure modular multiplication over $\mathbb{Z}_N$ on secret-shared values.
10. Parties open z and check if $\gcd(N, z) = 1$. If the check fails, they abort by broadcasting shares.

If all verifications pass, the protocol outputs $\left(\texttt{RSAModulus}, \left\{ \left(\frac{D_k}{p} \right) \right\}_{D_k \in S_{\text{Leak}}} \right)$.

Theorem 3. *Let p and q be odd integers, $N = pq$, and let $p_{\min}$ be the minimal prime factor of N. Let $\kappa, \mathsf{LeakBound} > 0$ be security parameters. The inputs to $\mathcal{P}_i$ are given as $(N, [p]_{\mathbb{Z}}, [q]_{\mathbb{Z}})$, where each share satisfies $\mathfrak{p}_1 \equiv p \pmod 4$, $\mathfrak{q}_1 \equiv q \pmod 4$, and $\mathfrak{p}_i \equiv \mathfrak{q}_i \equiv 0 \pmod 4$ for all $2 \leq i \leq n$. If $p_{\min} \geq 11$, then Protocol $\pi_{\text{RSA}}^{\mathcal{S}}$ $(n-1)$-privately computes the functionality $\mathcal{F}_{\text{RSA}}^{\mathcal{S}}$ in the $\mathcal{F}_{\text{Leg}}, \mathcal{F}_{\text{Shuffle}}, \mathcal{F}_{\text{ModMul}}$-hybrid model.*

Proof (Sketch). We prove the theorem for the case of a semi-honest adversary, as the protocol essentially implements a secure MPC version of Algorithm 2. The privacy of this protocol is established via the standard simulation paradigm. The core intuition relies on a novel trapdoor mechanism: because the Lucas test operates in the quadratic algebra $\mathcal{O}_D/N\mathcal{O}_D$, the simulator can pre-determine the test's outcome (i.e., fixing $(\alpha\beta^{-1})^{e_4}$) and subsequently reverse-engineer the public parameters (P, Q) to match. This allows the simulator to generate an indistinguishable transcript without knowing the underlying secret factors.

Correctness. The correctness of the protocol follows directly from the properties of the underlying Lucas biprimality test, as established in Theorem 2. Specifically:

1. $|S_{Leak}| > \mathsf{LeakBound}$. The protocol aborts during the parameter search phase and directly outputs $\texttt{AbortLeakBound}$.
2. $|S_{Leak}| \leq \mathsf{LeakBound}$, $p \neq q$ **are primes, and** $\gcd(N, e_4) = 1$. These inputs satisfy the completeness conditions of the Lucas and GCD tests. Consequently, the protocol passes all verifications and outputs $\texttt{RSAModulus}$ with overwhelming probability.
3. $|S_{Leak}| \leq \mathsf{LeakBound}$, **and either N is not biprime or** $\gcd(N, e_4) \neq 1$. By Theorem 2, the protocol falsely passes the κ verification rounds to output $\texttt{RSAModulus}$ with a negligible probability bounded by $\left(\frac{1}{4} + \frac{1.25}{p_{\min} - 3} \right)^{\kappa}$. Thus, it successfully rejects the candidate and outputs $\texttt{NonRSAModulus}$ with overwhelming probability.

Privacy. For privacy, we sketch the construction of a simulator $\mathcal{S}$. When the functionality's output is `NonRSAModulus` or `AbortLeakBound`, the simulation is straightforward, since the output includes all honest parties' shares $\{\mathfrak{p}_i, \mathfrak{q}_i\}_{i=1}^n$. We thus focus on the challenging case where the output is `RSAModulus`. The core task for the simulator is to generate a valid transcript, particularly the values $\{u_j\}_{j=1}^\kappa$, without knowledge of the honest parties' secret shares.

The simulation hinges on a trapdoor mechanism to construct the public Lucas parameters P_j, Q_j. The goal is to fix the value of $u_j \equiv (\alpha_j \beta_j^{-1})^{e_4} \pmod{N\mathcal{O}_D}$, which can be either 1 or -1, before determining P_j and Q_j.

To achieve this, the simulator proceeds as follows:

1. It randomly samples $v_j, w_j \in \mathbb{Z}_N$ (with $\gcd(v_j^2 - w_j^2 D, N) = 1$) and a bit $b_j \in \{0, 1\}$.
2. Let $a_j = (v_j + w_j\sqrt{D})/(v_j - w_j\sqrt{D})$. Since a_j has norm 1 and e_4 is odd, we have $(a_j^2)^{e_4} \equiv 1 \pmod{N\mathcal{O}_D}$. By setting $\alpha_j\beta_j^{-1} := a_j^2(-1)^{b_j}$, it follows that $(\alpha_j\beta_j^{-1})^{e_4} \equiv (-1)^{b_j} \pmod{N\mathcal{O}_D}$. This allows the simulator to know the value of u_j (which will be $(-1)^{b_j}$) in advance.
3. With the value of $\alpha_j\beta_j^{-1}$ fixed, the simulator can uniquely determine the corresponding public parameters (P_j, Q_j) by solving the relations $\alpha_j\beta_j^{-1} = \alpha_j^2 Q_j^{-1}$ and $P_j^2 - 4Q_j \equiv D \pmod{N}$. These relations provide the trapdoor to generate the public transcript values.

Finally, the indistinguishability of the simulated transcript follows from the fact that the mapping between the sampled elements (v_j, w_j, b_j) and the resulting public parameters (P_j, Q_j) is a bijection onto the set of valid protocol messages. This ensures that the distribution of P_j values generated by the simulator is identical to that in a real-world execution. Since the simulator produces a statistically indistinguishable transcript without access to any secret information, the protocol satisfies strict privacy against semi-honest adversaries. □

4.2   The Malicious Setting

This section addresses the challenge of securing it against malicious adversaries. Transitioning from the semi-honest setting requires significant strengthening. We adopt the established commit-and-prove paradigm of Chen et al. [11], which is directly applicable because the core algebraic structure of the Lucas test, a single multiplicative group exponentiation, is readily amenable to the Schnorr-like zero-knowledge proofs used to enforce honest execution.

Our goal here is not to present a fully optimized or universal protocol, but rather to provide a crucial proof-of-concept. We aim to demonstrate that the core algebraic structure of the Lucas test is compatible with such malicious-security transformations. To this end, we focus our analysis on the foundational case of Blum integers, for which $D = 1$. By constructing a secure variant for this domain, we establish that the Lucas test is not inherently limited to the semi-honest model. The generalization of this protocol to all RSA moduli and its concrete performance optimization are left as important directions for future work.

Our formal analysis will employ the biprimality test functionality $\mathcal{F}_{\mathrm{BI}}^{\mathcal{M}}$, as introduced by Chen et al. [11, Functionality 4.2].

Functionality 2 $\mathcal{F}_{\mathrm{BI}}^{\mathcal{M}}(n)$

Inputs: Each party $\mathcal{P}_i$ has a public number N, shares $[p]_{\mathbb{Z}}$ and $[q]_{\mathbb{Z}}$ with $\mathfrak{p}_i, \mathfrak{q}_i \geq 0$.

Outputs:
If all the following conditions are satisfied, then $\mathcal{F}_{\mathrm{BI}}^{\mathcal{M}}$ sends the message BlumInteger to the adversary $\mathcal{S}$:

1. All parties agree on the value of N;
2. $N = p \cdot q$;
3. $p \neq q$ are both primes;
4. $p \equiv q \equiv 3 \pmod 4$;
5. $\gcd(N, e_4) = 1$;
6. $\mathfrak{p}_i \geq 0$ and $\mathfrak{q}_i \geq 0$ for all i.

If $\mathcal{S}$ responds with proceed, then output BlumInteger to all parties. If $\mathcal{S}$ responds with cheat, or if any of the previous conditions are false, then output $\{(\mathfrak{p}_i, \mathfrak{q}_i)\}_{i=1}^{n}$ directly to $\mathcal{S}$, and output NonBlumInteger to all parties.

Compared to the protocol by Chen et al., our approach incorporates an explicit check for $p \equiv q \equiv 3 \pmod 4$. Furthermore, we relax the requirement for p and q; instead of needing them to be confined by a fixed upper bound M (i.e., $0 < \mathfrak{p}_i, \mathfrak{q}_i < M$), our analysis only assumes $\mathfrak{p}_i, \mathfrak{q}_i > 0$. While this broader condition on p, q might theoretically include small primes if $p_{\min}$ is not enforced, this is not a concern in our setting as the target functionality is assumed to output p, q forming a Blum integer. Thus, an explicit upper bound M is unnecessary for the security of our protocol. In addition, we provide several technical recommendations to further optimize the protocol by Chen et al. in the full version of this paper.

The overall single-round soundness error of the proposed Lucas test, which we denote by $\beta_{\mathrm{Lucas}}^{\mathcal{M}}$, combines two factors: the soundness of the underlying Lucas test, bounded by $\beta_{\mathrm{Lucas}} := \frac{1}{4} + \frac{1.25}{p_{\min}-3}$ (Theorem 2), and the 1/2 soundness of the Schnorr-like zero-knowledge verification. This yields a total error of: $\beta_{\mathrm{Lucas}}^{\mathcal{M}} \leq \beta_{\mathrm{Lucas}} + (1 - \beta_{\mathrm{Lucas}}) \cdot \frac{1}{2} = \frac{5}{8} + \frac{0.625}{p_{\min}-3}$. Consequently, to achieve an overall soundness error of $2^{-\kappa}$, the protocol must be iterated $\lceil \kappa / \log_2(\beta_{\mathrm{Lucas}}^{\mathcal{M}}{}^{-1}) \rceil = \left\lceil \left(\log_2 \frac{8p_{\min}-24}{5p_{\min}-10}\right)^{-1} \kappa \right\rceil$ times. For instance, setting $p_{\min} = 233$ requires $\lceil 1.489\kappa \rceil$ iterations to achieve the target security of $2^{-\kappa}$.

Our protocol is constructed in the hybrid model, relying on several standard ideal functionalities to perform fundamental cryptographic tasks. For general-purpose secure computation, we utilize $\mathcal{F}_{\mathrm{ComCompute}}$ [11], which allows parties to first commit to their private inputs and later securely evaluate an agreed-upon public function on these committed values. To generate shared secrets that sum to zero, a common requirement for masking, we employ $\mathcal{F}_{\mathrm{Zero}}$ [11]. Finally, our protocol also makes use of standard functionalities for commitment ($\mathcal{F}_{\mathrm{Com}}$) and coin-tossing ($\mathcal{F}_{\mathrm{CT}}$) to, respectively, ensure parties are bound to their choices and to generate public randomness [11].

Protocol 2 Malicious Lucas Biprimality Test $\pi_{\mathrm{BI}}^{\mathcal{M}}(n, \kappa, p_{\min})$

Inputs: Each party $\mathcal{P}_i$ has N and $[p]_{\mathbb{Z}}, [q]_{\mathbb{Z}}$ with $0 \leq \mathfrak{p}_i, \mathfrak{q}_i$, where each share satisfies $\mathfrak{p}_1 \equiv \mathfrak{q}_1 \equiv 3 \pmod 4$, and $\mathfrak{p}_i \equiv \mathfrak{q}_i \equiv 0 \pmod 4$ for all $2 \leq i \leq n$.

Outputs: `BlumInteger` or `NonBlumInteger`.

Commitment Phase:

1. Let $\kappa_{\min} := \left\lceil \left(\log_2 \frac{8 p_{\min} - 24}{5 p_{\min} - 10} \right)^{-1} \kappa \right\rceil$. Party $\mathcal{P}_i$ samples $\tau_{i,j} \leftarrow \mathbb{Z}_{2^{2\kappa - 1} n^3 N \kappa_{\min}}$
   for $1 \leq j \leq \kappa_{\min}$, and sends $\left(\texttt{commit}, i, (\mathfrak{p}_i, \mathfrak{q}_i, \{\tau_{i,j}\}_{j=1}^{\kappa_{\min}}) \right)$ to the commit-and-compute functionality $\mathcal{F}_{\mathrm{ComCompute}}$.
2. Each party $\mathcal{P}_i$ sends `sample` to the zero-share generation functionality $\mathcal{F}_{\mathrm{Zero}}(2^{\kappa - 3} nN)$ and receives r_i in response.

Lucas Test Phase:

3. Parties invoke the coin-tossing functionality $\mathcal{F}_{\mathrm{CT}}(\mathcal{Z}^{+1}(1, N))$ to obtain $\{(P_j, Q_j)\}_{j=1}^{\kappa_{\min}}$.
4. Party $\mathcal{P}_1$ sets $y_{1,j} := (\alpha_j \beta_j^{-1})^{r_1 + (\mathfrak{p}_1(\frac{-1}{q}) + \mathfrak{q}_1(\frac{-1}{p}) + 6)/4}$, and the other parties set $y_{i,j} := (\alpha_j \beta_j^{-1})^{r_i + (\mathfrak{p}_i(\frac{-1}{q}) + \mathfrak{q}_i(\frac{-1}{p}))/4}$ for all $2 \leq i \leq n$ and $1 \leq j \leq \kappa_{\min}$. Here α_j and β_j are the two roots of $x^2 - P_j x + Q_j = 0$. Party $\mathcal{P}_i$ then sends $(\texttt{commit}, i, \{y_{i,j}\}_{j=1}^{\kappa_{\min}})$ to the commitment functionality $\mathcal{F}_{\mathrm{Com}}$.
5. Party $\mathcal{P}_i$ sends $(\texttt{decommit}, i)$ to $\mathcal{F}_{\mathrm{Com}}$ and receives $\{y_{i',j}\}_{j=1}^{\kappa_{\min}}$ for $i' \neq i$.
6. The parties output `NonBlumInteger` and halt if there exists $1 \leq j \leq \kappa_{\min}$ such that
$$(\alpha_j \beta_j^{-1})^{(N-5)/4} \cdot \prod_{i=1}^{n} y_{i,j} \not\equiv \pm 1 \pmod N.$$

Zero-Knowledge Verification Phase :

7. For $1 \leq j \leq \kappa_{\min}$, each party $\mathcal{P}_i$ computes $\gamma_{i,j} = (\alpha_j \beta_j^{-1})^{\tau_{i,j}} \pmod N$, and broadcasts $\{\gamma_{i,j}\}_{j=1}^{\kappa_{\min}}$.
8. All parties send `flip` to $\mathcal{F}_{\mathrm{CT}}(\{0,1\}^{\kappa_{\min}})$ and then obtain an agreed-upon random bit vector $\boldsymbol{c} = (c_j)$ of length $\kappa_{\min}$.

9. For $1 \leq j \leq \kappa_{\min}$, the party $\mathcal{P}_1$ computes

$$\zeta_{1,j} = \tau_{1,j} + c_j \cdot \left(r_1 - (\mathfrak{p}_1 + \mathfrak{q}_1 - 6)/4\right),$$

   and every other party $\mathcal{P}_i$ for $2 \leq i \leq n$ computes

$$\zeta_{i,j} = \tau_{i,j} + c_j \cdot \left(r_i - (\mathfrak{p}_i + \mathfrak{q}_i)/4\right).$$

   They all broadcast the values they have computed to one another.
10. The parties halt and output `NonBlumInteger` if there exists any $1 \leq j \leq \kappa_{\min}$ such that

$$\prod_{i=1}^{n}(\alpha_j \beta_j^{-1})^{\zeta_{i,j}} \not\equiv \prod_{i=1}^{n} \gamma_{i,j} \cdot y_{i,j}^{c_j} \pmod{N}.$$

11. Let C be a monolithic circuit verifying the aforementioned modulus properties and Schnorr-like relations with the public values N, $\boldsymbol{c}$, and ζ hard-coded. The parties send $(\texttt{compute}, 1, \{1, \ldots, n\}, C)$ to $\mathcal{F}_{\text{ComCompute}}$, and in response they all receive z or `VerifyFail`. If they receive `VerifyFail`, or if $\mathcal{F}_{\text{ComCompute}}$ aborts, then the parties halt and output `NonBlumInteger`.
12. The parties halt and output `BlumInteger` if $\gcd(z, N) = 1$, or halt and output `NonBlumInteger` otherwise.

While a full implementation and concrete benchmarking of the malicious protocol are beyond the scope of this work, we briefly analyze its performance characteristics. The dominant overhead stems from the generic secure computation within the $\mathcal{F}_{\text{ComCompute}}$ functionality, which validates all relationships between secret shares and the public transcript via a monolithic verification circuit.

This verification component, executed via secure computation, performs three main tasks:

1. **Modulus Validation:** Confirms that the secret shares $(\mathfrak{p}_i, \mathfrak{q}_i)$ correctly reconstruct the public modulus $N = (\sum \mathfrak{p}_i)(\sum \mathfrak{q}_i)$ as a Blum integer.
2. **Transcript Validation:** Validates the consistency of the zero-knowledge proof transcript by verifying Schnorr-like relations between the parties' commitments, challenges, and responses.
3. **GCD Output:** If all checks pass, it computes $z = r \cdot (p + q - 1) \pmod{N}$, which is used in a final GCD test to verify the coprimality of the exponent e_4 and N.

The circuit's complexity is primarily driven by large integer arithmetic. For n parties and $\kappa_{\min}$ iterations, the main computational components are two large multiplications and approximately $O(n \cdot \kappa_{\min} \cdot \ell)$ arithmetic operations to validate the zero-knowledge responses, where ℓ is the bit-length of N. Given that these computations are realized using a generic MPC framework, the concrete costs, particularly in terms of communication rounds and total data transferred, are expected to be substantial. A detailed estimation of the circuit size and its corresponding gate complexity is provided in the full version of this paper.

We posit that these costs could be dramatically reduced by designing a dedicated, more efficient zero-knowledge proof system for these specific algebraic relations, rather than relying on generic MPC. We leave such concrete optimizations as a significant direction for future work.

Theorem 4. *Let $\kappa > 0$ be a security parameter. The inputs to all participants $\{\mathcal{P}_i\}_{i=1}^n$ are given as $(N, [p]_\mathbb{Z}, [q]_\mathbb{Z})$. If $p_{\min} \geq 11$, then Protocol $\pi_{\mathrm{BI}}^\mathcal{M}$ $(n-1)$-securely computes the functionality $\mathcal{F}_{\mathrm{BI}}^\mathcal{M}$ with abort in the $(\mathcal{F}_{\mathrm{ComCompute}}, \mathcal{F}_{\mathrm{Zero}}, \mathcal{F}_{\mathrm{CT}}, \mathcal{F}_{\mathrm{Com}})$-hybrid model.*

Proof (Sketch). The proof demonstrates that Protocol $\pi_{\mathrm{BI}}^\mathcal{M}$ securely computes the functionality $\mathcal{F}_{\mathrm{BI}}^\mathcal{M}$ against a malicious adversary, $\mathcal{A}$, in the hybrid model. To achieve malicious security, we rely on the established commit-and-prove paradigm via a Schnorr-like zero-knowledge proof. The core intuition for the simulation is that the simulator $\mathcal{S}$ works backwards: it simulates the zero-knowledge responses prior to receiving the random challenges. This seamlessly forces the transcript to evaluate as a valid Blum integer check without requiring the underlying secret shares.

Case 1: The functionality's output is `BlumInteger` (Success Case). In this case, $\mathcal{S}$ must generate a full, consistent protocol transcript without knowing the honest parties' secret shares. $\mathcal{S}$ programs the ideal coin-tossing functionality $\mathcal{F}_{\mathrm{CT}}$ to output the public Lucas parameters P_j using the same trapdoor technique as in the semi-honest case (cf. Theorem 3), which allows it to know the outcome of each test in advance.

To complete the transcript, $\mathcal{S}$ simulates the values $y_{i,j}$ for the honest parties. For all but one designated honest party $\mathcal{P}_{i'}$, it samples their values $y_{i,j}$ by raising the base $(\alpha_j \beta_j^{-1})$ to fresh, large random exponents. The value for the final party, $y_{i',j}$, is then uniquely determined by solving the global verification equation to match the predetermined outcome $(-1)^{b_j}$. For the zero-knowledge proof, the tuple $(\zeta_{i,j}, c_j, \gamma_{i,j})$ is simulated using a standard backward-simulating technique. $\mathcal{S}$ first samples the challenges $\{c_j\}$ and the responses $\{\zeta_{i,j}\}$ for the honest parties, defines the commitments as $\gamma_{i,j} := (\alpha_j \beta_j^{-1})^{\zeta_{i,j}} \cdot y_{i,j}^{-c_j}$, and then programs the ideal functionality $\mathcal{F}_{\mathrm{CT}}$ to output these exact challenges $\{c_j\}$. This ensures that the simulated transcript is statistically indistinguishable from a real execution due to the large sampling range and the standard properties of the underlying zero-knowledge proof system.

Case 2: The functionality's output is `NonBlumInteger` (Abort Case). We argue for correctness: if the inputs provided by the adversary do not form a valid Blum integer, the protocol will abort with overwhelming probability. The Lucas test, as per Theorem 2, ensures that a non-Blum integer N passes the core test with probability at most $\left(\frac{1}{4} + \frac{1.25}{p_{\min}-3}\right)^{\kappa_{\min}}$. Furthermore, the zero-knowledge proof ensures that any malicious deviation (i.e., introducing a non-zero offset) will be detected with probability at least $1/2$ per iteration, as the adversary must commit to their values before receiving the random challenge c_j. The overall probability of an adversary successfully deceiving the protocol is thus negligible.

$\square$

5   Performance Modeling and Simulation-Based Analysis

Having established the broader applicability of our Lucas-based test, this section aims to illuminate the factors governing practical performance in the common scenario of generating Blum integers. Our goal is not to declare a universal winner, but to explore the nuanced trade-offs between theoretical soundness and computational efficiency. To this end, our evaluation unfolds in three stages: we first establish the soundness landscape (Sect. 5.1), then filter out the variant Miller-Rabin (vMR) test, which, despite a comparable worst-case soundness, is shown to be non-competitive due to its significant protocol overhead (Sect. 5.2), and finally resolve the subtle trade-off between the BF and Lucas tests using a holistic performance model (Sect. 5.3).

5.1   Theoretical and Empirical Comparison of Soundness Errors

To substantiate the soundness advantage outlined in Sect. 3, this section provides a detailed theoretical and empirical analysis. We begin our theoretical analysis by formalizing the comparison between the Boneh-Franklin and Lucas tests. We analyze the ratio of the two soundness errors, $\beta_{\text{Lucas}}/\beta_{\text{BF}}$, for a given modulus N. Let $\mathbf{1}_{\mathbb{P}}(\cdot)$ be the indicator function of positive integers. Based on the counting formulas established in Proposition 1 and Lemma 2, this ratio can be expressed as:

$$\frac{\beta_{\text{Lucas}}(N, e_4)}{\beta_{\text{BF}}(N, e_4)} = \left(\frac{\prod_{i=1}^{s}(\gcd(e_4, d_i) - 1) + \prod_{i=1}^{s} \gcd(e_4, d_i)}{2 \prod_{i=1}^{s} \gcd(e_4, d_i)} \right) \cdot \left(\frac{\prod_{i=1}^{s}(p_i - 1)}{\prod_{i \in S_1^c}(p_i - 2) \left(\prod_{i \in S_1}(p_i - 2) + \mathbf{1}_{\mathbb{P}}(|S_1|)(-1)^{|S_1|} \right)} \right) . \tag{3}$$

The first term in (3), involving the GCDs, is always less than or equal to $1/2$ if any $\gcd(e_4, d_i) = 1$, and approaches 1 only when all $\gcd(e_4, d_i)$ are large. The second term, involving the prime factors, is typically slightly greater than 1. Our theoretical findings regarding this ratio are summarized in Table 2.

Table 2. Theoretical Comparison of Soundness Errors

Case Analysis	GCD Conditions	Other Conditions	Conclusion
Typical Case (Non-maximal GCD)	$\exists i$ s.t. $\gcd(d_i, e_4) = 1$	$p_{\min} \geq 467, \log_2(N) \leq 2048$	$\beta_{\text{Lucas}} < \beta_{\text{BF}}$
Worst Case (Maximal GCD)	$\forall i, d_i \mid e_4$	$\forall i, p_i \equiv 3 \pmod 4, p_i > 3$	$\beta_{\text{Lucas}} \geq \beta_{\text{BF}}$

To empirically validate our theoretical analysis, we conducted an extensive search over all non-RSA moduli $N = pq$ with p, q up to $1,440,003$. The results are summarized in Table 3.

Table 3. Pairwise comparison of soundness errors across three tests.

Method	$\beta = \frac{\beta_{\mathrm{BF}}}{\beta_{\mathrm{MR}}}$	$\beta = \frac{\beta_{\mathrm{BF}}}{\beta_{\mathrm{Lucas}}}$	$\beta = \frac{\beta_{\mathrm{Lucas}}}{\beta_{\mathrm{MR}}}$
$\beta < 1$	0.08%	< 0.01%	54.26%
$\beta = 1$	54.18%	0%	0%
$\beta > 1$	45.74%	> 99.99%	45.74%

Count of non-RSA moduli $N = pq$ (with $3 \le p < q \le 1440003$, $p \equiv q \equiv 3 \pmod 4$, etc.) satisfying the ratio conditions. See main text for full details.

As predicted by our theoretical analysis, the data show that in over 99.99% of cases, the Lucas test offers a strictly lower soundness error than the BF test ($\beta_{\mathrm{BF}}/\beta_{\mathrm{Lucas}} > 1$). The absence of observed cases where $\beta = 1$ is also consistent with our theory; since our experiment enforces $p_{\min} \ge 541$, any boundary case would require an extremely large and specifically structured modulus $N > p_{\min}^3 \approx 1.58 \times 10^8$, which was not encountered in our search space. This empirical result provides overwhelming evidence that the "Favorable Case" identified in our theory is not a mere special condition, but the prevailing reality.

5.2   Computational Cost Comparison of Three Tests

To evaluate the efficiency of our protocol, we compare its per-iteration cost against the BF protocol as presented in [18] and the vMR test from [10], focusing on the common case of generating Blum integers. In this setting, our Lucas test is nearly identical in cost to the BF test; both operate in the same group ($\mathbb{Z}_N^{\times}$ since $D = 1$) and rely on a single, lightweight MPC shuffle protocol.

Both tests, however, are demonstrably more efficient than the vMR. As detailed in Table 4, the vMR protocol is substantially more complex. A detailed analysis of local computation reveals that the two $|N|/2$-bit exponentiations required by vMR are, in aggregate, theoretically faster than the single $|N|$-bit exponentiation in our test and the BF test. However, this local performance gain is rendered insignificant by the protocol's overall cost. The vMR test's reliance on multiple heavyweight MPC subroutines, including the expensive "Divisible" macro, creates a communication and computation bottleneck that far outweighs any local efficiency advantage. While the worst-case soundness errors of our Lucas test and the vMR test are practically indistinguishable for realistic parameters (both converging to $1/4$), the deciding factor becomes protocol efficiency. Here, our test's simplicity and lower overhead make it the unequivocal alternative to the vMR for applications requiring provable security. This result allows us to focus the final, most nuanced performance analysis on the head-to-head competition between our Lucas test and the BF test.

Table 4. Single Execution Comparison for Three Tests

Method	BF test	vMR test	Proposed test
Basis selection	$g \leftarrow \mathbb{Z}_N$ s.t. $\left(\frac{g}{N}\right) = 1$	$v \leftarrow \mathbb{Z}_N$	$P \leftarrow \mathbb{Z}_N$ s.t. $\left(\frac{P^2-1}{N}\right) = 1$
Exponential test (local)	$\mathcal{P}_1 : g^{\frac{N-(\mathsf{p}_i+\mathsf{q}_i)+1}{4}}$ $\mathcal{P}_i : g^{\frac{-\mathsf{p}_i-\mathsf{q}_i}{4}}$	$\mathcal{P}_1 : v^{\frac{f_i-1}{2}}$ $\mathcal{P}_i : v^{\frac{f_i}{2}}$	$\mathcal{P}_1 :$ $\left(\frac{p+1}{p-1}\right)^{\frac{N-(\mathsf{p}_i+\mathsf{q}_i)+1}{4}}$ $\mathcal{P}_i : \left(\frac{p+1}{p-1}\right)^{\frac{-\mathsf{p}_i-\mathsf{q}_i}{4}}$
Exponential test (MPC)	$g^{e_4} \leftarrow$ Shuffle	Mul-to-Add $[v^{\frac{f-1}{2}}] \leftarrow$ Divisible $[y_{+1}y_{-1}] \leftarrow$ Mult	$(\alpha\beta^{-1})^{e_4} \leftarrow$ Shuffle
GCD test (MPC)	$[r] \leftarrow$ Sample $[r(p+q-1)] \leftarrow$ Mult	*None*[1]	$[r] \leftarrow$ Sample $[r(p+q-1)] \leftarrow$ Mult

Note: The calculations of the vMR test need to be executed for both $f = p$ and $f = q$. **Basis selection** refers to the conditions of the basis for exponential calculations. In **Exponential test (MPC)**, the Shuffle protocol outputs the product of shares. Mul-to-Add is the conversion of multiplicative to additive shares. The output of Divisible $y_{\pm 1}$ indicates if $v^{(f\pm 1)/2} \equiv 0 \pmod{f}$. Mult denotes MPC multiplication. Sample outputs a random element.
[1] The Variant Miller-Rabin test needs to confirm that $p \neq q$.

5.3 Performance Modeling and Evaluation

Now, we resolve the subtle performance trade-off between our Lucas test and the BF test. We employ a holistic performance model to evaluate these methods, clarifying that this constitutes a heuristic analysis rather than a definitive benchmark. The model is parameterized by local computation costs obtained from single-machine simulations to provide a conservative estimate of performance trends.

A Holistic Performance Model. To deliver a conclusive verdict, our evaluation distinguishes between provable security (the iterations required for worst-case soundness) and practical efficiency (the average time to reject invalid candidates, which dominates key generation). Our tighter 1/4 bound for the BF test significantly closes the gap in the former, making iteration counts far more comparable and shifting the focus to the latter: practical rejection speed.

The critical metric is the expected time to reject an invalid modulus N, denoted $E[T(N)]$. This integrates theoretical soundness with per-iteration cost as follows:

$$E[T(N)] = (1 - \beta(N))^{-1} \times (T_{\text{local}} + T_{\text{net}}). \tag{4}$$

Here $\beta(N)$ is the single-round soundness error, T_{local} is the local computation time, and T_{net} is the network latency. This model provides a key insight: since T_{net} often constitutes the dominant overhead in MPC, even a small, consistent advantage in T_{local} can decisively impact the overall rejection speed.

Benchmarking Local Computation Cost. To obtain a noise-free parameterization of T_{local}, we isolate computational costs from variable network latency using a laptop. Our SageMath implementation simulated 2, 3, and 4-party protocols for 2048-bit and 3072-bit moduli on a MacBook Pro (Apple M2, 16 GB RAM). The resulting average execution times are presented in Table 5.

Table 5. Execution time (mean ± std, in ms) for the proposed and competing methods.

| | N : 2048 bits | | N : 3072 bits | |
	Proposed test	Boneh-Franklin	Proposed test	Boneh-Franklin
$n = 2$	3.199 ± 0.251	3.145 ± 0.124	12.320 ± 0.462	12.253 ± 0.574
$n = 3$	4.550 ± 0.350	4.367 ± 0.253	17.310 ± 0.906	16.907 ± 0.588
$n = 4$	6.151 ± 0.329	5.992 ± 0.404	21.386 ± 1.006	21.300 ± 1.146

Evaluation and Verdict. By rearranging (4), we find that the Lucas test outperforms the BF test if and only if:

$$\beta_{\text{BF}}(N) > \frac{T_{\text{local,Lucas}} - T_{\text{local,BF}}}{(T_{\text{net}} + T_{\text{local,Lucas}}) - (T_{\text{net}} + T_{\text{local,BF}}) \left(\frac{\beta_{\text{Lucas}}(N)}{\beta_{\text{BF}}(N)} \right)}.$$

To parameterize this condition, we adopt a standard WAN latency of $T_{\text{net}} = 100$ ms and a conservative soundness ratio $\beta_{\text{Lucas}}/\beta_{\text{BF}} = 0.5$. Substituting our empirical values from Table 5 (specifically the minimal observed difference $\Delta T_{\text{local}} = 0.054$ ms from the $n = 2$ case), the theoretical threshold is $\beta_{\text{BF}} > 0.00105$.

To ensure a rigorous stress-test, we adopt a threshold of 0.0002, which is nearly an order of magnitude more favorable to the Lucas test. Under this biased condition, the BF test is slower only if $\beta_{\text{BF}} > 0.0002$. However, our extensive numerical analysis, referenced in the full version of this paper, reveals that over 87% of non-RSA moduli within the testable range fail to meet this threshold. Hence, we conclude with high confidence that the practical superiority of the BF test is decisive. Although the Lucas test offers better soundness, its advantage is too infrequent to offset its higher per-round local computation cost, particularly in low-latency environments where the T_{local} gap is further amplified.

Table 6. A Comparative Overview of Three Biprimality Tests

Feature	Boneh-Franklin	Miller-Rabin	Proposed Test
Worst-Case Soundness[a]	$1/2 \to 1/4$	$1/4$	$1/4 + \frac{1.25}{p_{\min} - 3}$
Exceptional Cases	$p = q = 3$	$p, q \le 9$	$p_{\min} < 11$
Extra Assumption	$\gcd(pq, e_4) = 1$	p, q equal-length	$\gcd(pq, e_4) = 1$
Empirical Soundness	_3_	_2_	_1_
MPC Efficiency*	_1_	_3_	_1_
Local Computation*	_1_	_3_	_2_
Leakage	No	No	None / Bounded[b]
RSA Moduli Type	Blum only	Blum only	Arbitrary

* Rankings where 1 is best. Comparisons are in the semi-honest model.
[a] The worst-case soundness error, excluding the exceptional cases listed below.
[b] The protocol is completely leak-free for Blum integers, while for non-Blum integers, it offers both leak-free and bounded-leakage variants (see Sect. 4.1).

6 Conclusion

In this work, we have fundamentally revisited the Boneh-Franklin (BF) biprimality test. A key contribution of this work was a rigorous proof tightening its worst-case soundness bound from $1/2$ to a tight $1/4$, a result of immediate practical significance that halves the required iterations for many existing protocols (as summarized in Table 6). We also introduced a more versatile test based on Lucas sequences, which provides the first efficient and provably secure solution for generating all standard RSA moduli in a distributed setting, not just Blum integers.

Our comparative analysis, however, reveals a key and subtle insight. Through a holistic performance model, we demonstrated that for the common case of generating Blum integers, the extreme local computation efficiency of the BF test often outweighs the superior empirical soundness of the Lucas test. This provides a data-driven verdict for practitioners: while our Lucas test expands the design space, the newly-fortified BF test remains the superior practical choice in its original domain. This work thus provides a clearer toolkit for designers and opens avenues for future research. A particularly compelling direction is the potential creation of a distributed analogue to the highly robust Baillie-PSW test. By pairing our Lucas protocol with the BF test within an MPC framework, it is possible to construct a composite biprimality test of exceptional strength and efficiency. Verifying this possibility remains an interesting question.

Acknowledgements. We thank the anonymous reviewers for their valuable feedback and Yu-Te Lin (AMIS) for supporting this research. We also thank Gemini 2.5 Pro for its assistance in refining the language and enhancing the fluency of the manuscript.

References

1. Abadi, A., Ristea, D., Murdoch, S.J.: Delegated time-lock puzzle. arXiv preprint arXiv:2308.01280 (2023)
2. Algesheimer, J., Camenisch, J., Shoup, V.: Efficient computation modulo a shared secret with application to the generation of shared safe-prime products. In: Yung, M. (ed.) CRYPTO 2002. LNCS, vol. 2442, pp. 417–432. Springer, Heidelberg (2002). https://doi.org/10.1007/3-540-45708-9_27
3. Arnault, F.: The Rabin-Monier theorem for Lucas pseudoprimes. Math. Comput. **66**, 869–881 (1997). https://doi.org/10.1090/S0025-5718-97-00836-3
4. Benaloh, J., de Mare, M., Accumulators, O.W.: A decentralized alternative to digital signatures. In: Advances in Cryptology-Proceedings of Eurocrypt, vol. 93 (1994)
5. Boneh, D., Bonneau, J., Bünz, B., Fisch, B.: Verifiable delay functions. In: Shacham, H., Boldyreva, A. (eds.) CRYPTO 2018. LNCS, vol. 10991, pp. 757–788. Springer, Cham (2018). https://doi.org/10.1007/978-3-319-96884-1_25
6. Boneh, D., Bünz, B., Fisch, B.: Batching techniques for accumulators with applications to IOPs and stateless blockchains. In: Boldyreva, A., Micciancio, D. (eds.) CRYPTO 2019. LNCS, vol. 11692, pp. 561–586. Springer, Cham (2019). https://doi.org/10.1007/978-3-030-26948-7_20
7. Boneh, D., Franklin, M.: Efficient generation of shared RSA keys. J. ACM **48** (2001). https://doi.org/10.1145/502090.502094
8. Boudabra, M., Nitaj, A.: A new RSA variant based on elliptic curves. Cryptography (2023). https://doi.org/10.3390/cryptography7030037
9. Buhler, J., Stevenhagen, P.: Algorithmic number theory. Lattices, number fields, curves and cryptography. Reprint of the 2008 hardback ed. Cambridge University Press (2011)
10. Burkhardt, J., Damgård, I., Frederiksen, T., Ghosh, S., Orlandi, C.: Improved distributed RSA key generation using the Miller-Rabin test. In: CCS 2023: Proceedings of the 2023 ACM SIGSAC Conference on Computer and Communications Security, pp. 2501–2515 (2023). https://doi.org/10.1145/3576915.3623163
11. Chen, M., et al.: Multiparty generation of an RSA modulus. J. Cryptol. **35** (2022). https://doi.org/10.1007/s00145-021-09395-y
12. Chen, M., et al.: Diogenes: lightweight scalable RSA modulus generation with a dishonest majority. In: 2021 IEEE Symposium on Security and Privacy (SP), pp. 590–607. IEEE (2021)
13. Chvojka, P.: Private coin verifiable delay function. Cryptology ePrint Archive (2023)
14. Damgård, I., Mikkelsen, G.L.: Efficient, robust and constant-round distributed RSA key generation. In: Micciancio, D. (ed.) TCC 2010. LNCS, vol. 5978, pp. 183–200. Springer, Heidelberg (2010). https://doi.org/10.1007/978-3-642-11799-2_12
15. Damgård, I., Landrock, P., Pomerance, C.: Average case error estimates for the strong probable prime test. Math. Comput. **61**, 177 (1993). https://doi.org/10.2307/2152945

16. Einsele, S., Paterson, K.: Average case error estimates of the strong Lucas test. Designs, Codes and Cryptography, pp. 1–38 (2024). https://doi.org/10.1007/s10623-023-01347-w

17. Ephraim, N., Freitag, C., Komargodski, I., Pass, R.: Continuous verifiable delay functions. In: Canteaut, A., Ishai, Y. (eds.) EUROCRYPT 2020. LNCS, vol. 12107, pp. 125–154. Springer, Cham (2020). https://doi.org/10.1007/978-3-030-45727-3_5

18. Frederiksen, T.K., Lindell, Y., Osheter, V., Pinkas, B.: Fast distributed RSA key generation for semi-honest and malicious adversaries. In: Shacham, H., Boldyreva, A. (eds.) CRYPTO 2018. LNCS, vol. 10992, pp. 331–361. Springer, Cham (2018). https://doi.org/10.1007/978-3-319-96881-0_12

19. Friedman, O., Marmor, A., Mutzari, D., Scaly, Y.C., Spiizer, Y., Yanai, A.: Tiresias: large scale, maliciously secure threshold Paillier. Cryptology ePrint Archive (2023)

20. Hazay, C., Mikkelsen, G.L., Rabin, T., Toft, T., Nicolosi, A.A.: Efficient RSA key generation and threshold Paillier in the two-party setting. J. Cryptol. **32**, 265–323 (2019)

21. Hoffmann, C., Hubáček, P., Kamath, C., Krňák, T.: (verifiable) delay functions from Lucas sequences. Cryptology ePrint Archive (2023)

22. Ireland, K., Rosen, M.I.: A Classical Introduction to Modern Number Theory, vol. 84. Springer (1990)

23. Joye, M., Libert, B.: Efficient cryptosystems from 2^k-th power residue symbols. In: Johansson, T., Nguyen, P.Q. (eds.) EUROCRYPT 2013. LNCS, vol. 7881, pp. 76–92. Springer, Heidelberg (2013). https://doi.org/10.1007/978-3-642-38348-9_5

24. Khedr, W.I., Khater, H.M., Mohamed, E.R.: Cryptographic accumulator-based scheme for critical data integrity verification in cloud storage. IEEE Access **7**, 65635–65651 (2019)

25. Malavolta, G., Thyagarajan, S.A.K.: Homomorphic time-lock puzzles and applications. In: Boldyreva, A., Micciancio, D. (eds.) CRYPTO 2019. LNCS, vol. 11692, pp. 620–649. Springer, Cham (2019). https://doi.org/10.1007/978-3-030-26948-7_22

26. Pietrzak, K.: Simple verifiable delay functions. In: 10th Innovations in Theoretical Computer Science Conference (ITCS 2019). Schloss Dagstuhl-Leibniz-Zentrum fuer Informatik (2018)

27. Rabin, M.: Probabilistic algorithm for testing primality. J. Number Theory **12**, 128–138 (1980). https://doi.org/10.1016/0022-314X(80)90084-0

28. Rivest, R., Shamir, A., Adleman, L.: A method for obtaining digital signatures and public-key cryptosystems. Commun. ACM **26**, 96–99 (1983). https://doi.org/10.1145/359340.359342

29. Rivest, R.L., Shamir, A., Wagner, D.A.: Time-lock puzzles and timed-release crypto. 1996 Technical Report (1996)

30. Delpech de Saint Guilhem, C., Makri, E., Rotaru, D., Tanguy, T.: The return of Eratosthenes: secure generation of RSA moduli using distributed sieving. In: ACM CCS 2021, pp. 594–609 (2021)

31. Wesolowski, B.: Efficient verifiable delay functions. In: Ishai, Y., Rijmen, V. (eds.) EUROCRYPT 2019. LNCS, vol. 11478, pp. 379–407. Springer, Cham (2019). https://doi.org/10.1007/978-3-030-17659-4_13

On the Preimage Leakage
of Property-Preserving Hash

Yangzhou Cao[1], Min Luo[1(✉)] (iD), Cong Peng[1(✉)] (iD), Yi Wang[2] (iD),
Rongmao Chen[2] (iD), and Debiao He[1] (iD)

[1] Key Laboratory of Aerospace Information Security and Trusted Computing,
Ministry of Education, School of Cyber Science and Engineering,
Wuhan University, Wuhan, China
{yangzhoucao,mluo,cpeng,hedebiao}@whu.edu.cn
[2] School of Computer, National University of Defense Technology, Changsha, China
{wangyi14,chromao}@nudt.edu.cn

Abstract. Property-Preserving Hash (PPH) achieves compression of
large-scale data while providing predicate evaluation functionality on
hash digests. PPH can be used to construct new cryptographic primitives
or directly applied to privacy-sensitive data scenarios. These constructions or applications impose privacy requirements on the information
leakage of PPH. The property definition of PPH follows the Direct-Access
Robustness. However, the information leakage of PPH hash values concerning the preimage has not been formally analyzed or defined. In this
work, we first propose $\mathcal{L}$-Simulation, a simulation-based definition to formalize the information disclosure of PPH hash values with respect to the
preimage. We introduce a leakage profile in the simulation to quantify the
level of preimage leakage. Subsequently, based on this formal definition,
we analyze and evaluate the PPH scheme in Order-Revealing Encryption
(ORE) and all PPH schemes for the Hamming distance predicate. Our
formal proofs demonstrate that the PPH in ORE achieves an ideal leakage bound. However, the PPH schemes by Fleischhacker and Simkin at
Eurocrypt 2021 and Fleischhacker et al. at Eurocrypt 2022 suffer from
partial preimage leakage. To address this issue, we propose a new PPH
construction for the Hamming distance predicate. Our scheme reduces
leakage while supporting additive homomorphism and scalar multiplicative homomorphism, enhancing security and broadening its applicability.

Keywords: Property-Preserving · Leakage Profile · Hash Preimage

1 Introduction

Traditional cryptographic primitives provide adequate support for data privacy
protection [11]. However, perfect obfuscation of plaintext completely disrupts the
relationships between messages. In emerging fields such as Structured Encryption
[12], Functional Encryption [13], Private Information Retrieval [14], and Privacy-
Preserving Computation [15], there is a growing need to obfuscate plaintext while

S. Bai and E. Persichetti (Eds.): PKC 2026, LNCS 16554, pp. 401–430, 2026.
https://doi.org/10.1007/978-3-032-26740-5_13

preserving computational and matching functionalities over ciphertexts. With the advent of the big data era, the demand for storage, retrieval, and sharing of high-dimensional data has surged.

Traditional hash schemes often disregard the inherent properties of data during dimensionality reduction [11], resulting in hash digests that fail to retain critical features of the original data. Property-Preserving Hash (PPH) enables the compression of large-scale data while maintaining predicate evaluation capabilities on hash values. Specifically, given PPH digests $H_{PPH}(A)$ and $H_{PPH}(B)$ corresponding to data A and B, the evaluation algorithm $\mathsf{Eval}(H_{PPH}(A), H_{PPH}(B))$ can determine the predicate relationship $P(A, B)$ between the two datasets. Depending on the predicate supported by the PPH, it can be utilized to construct novel cryptographic primitives or be applied in practical scenarios. However, we note that throughout the evolution of PPH, the information leakage of the preimage via the hash value has been neglected.

The information leakage of PPH is intrinsically linked to the security of cryptographic primitives constructed from it. In the construction of cryptographic primitives, PPH can be employed to design certain Order-Revealing Encryption (ORE) schemes. ORE allows comparison over ciphertexts to reveal the order of the underlying plaintexts. The comparison functionality in ORE can be realized using PPH. For instance, the order of plaintext strings can be reduced to bitwise comparisons from the most significant bit (MSB) to the least significant bit (LSB) [9]. Thus, a PPH supporting bitwise comparison predicates can be leveraged to construct ORE schemes. It is worth noting that ORE must carefully control the information leakage from the comparison algorithm [17]. Ideally, ORE should reveal nothing beyond the relative order of plaintexts. Therefore, in PPH-based ORE constructions, it is crucial to rigorously manage the leakage of the PPH scheme.

The information leakage of PPH needs to be evaluated and controlled in privacy-sensitive data compression applications [18]. In practical applications, PPH that supports Hamming distance predicates can be utilized for geolocation matching [1] and biometric information matching [2]. Hamming distance can be used to measure the proximity between two locations as well as the similarity between equal-length strings (e.g., text or genomic data). Thus, after sensitive data—such as geographic coordinates, text, or genetic sequences—are compressed via PPH, their relative distance relationships can still be efficiently and publicly evaluated using the Hamming distance predicate supported by the PPH scheme. However, if the PPH compression or evaluation process introduces additional leakage beyond the intended distance comparison, such additional leakage could lead to severe privacy breaches in these applications. For example, a PPH without information leakage consideration might allow an adversary to infer partial information about the original data (e.g., reconstructing approximate locations or revealing patterns in genomic sequences). Therefore, when applying PPH in privacy-sensitive scenarios, it is critical to rigorously analyze and minimize potential information leakage to ensure that only the necessary relation is revealed.

Therefore, information leakage about the preimages in PPH should be carefully analyzed and evaluated.

The property definition of PPH was first introduced in the work [7], which formalized the notion of Direct-Access Robustness. Specifically, an adversary with access to a hash function h sampled from the PPH algorithm should only succeed with negligible probability in outputting messages A and B such that $\mathsf{Eval}(H_{PPH}(A), H_{PPH}(B)) \neq P(A, B)$. Subsequent works [4,6,8] proposed PPH schemes for the Hamming distance predicate, with improvements primarily focusing on lower bounds and weaker security assumptions.

However, Direct-Access Robustness only ensures the correctness of PPH, while existing works largely overlook privacy-related security properties in practical applications. We observe that directly applying the PPH schemes by [6] and [8] to privacy-sensitive evaluation scenarios may lead to partial preimage leakage, as detailed in Sect. 4.2 and 4.3.

The current research on PPH has not adequately addressed the issue of preimage information leakage. This motivates us to systematically enhance PPH security through three key dimensions: (1) formalizing appropriate security notions of leakage, (2) conducting security analyses of existing schemes, and (3) developing novel constructions with minimized leakage. More specifically, our investigation focuses on addressing the following questions:

Is it possible to define a novel security property to assess the preimage information leakage of PPH? What are the existing bounds and potential risks of information leakage in current PPH schemes? How can we construct a PPH scheme with minimal leakage for the Hamming distance predicate?

Motivations. First, we argue that PPH holds significant promise for privacy-sensitive applications. Therefore, in addition to ensuring robustness, it is crucial to formally define the information leakage property for PPH. The property aims to quantify the information leakage of the evaluation algorithm with respect to the original input data. The ideal leakage profile would reveal only the predicate evaluation result without disclosing any additional information about the preimages. By defining different levels of leakage, we can systematically classify the privacy-security strength of PPH schemes.

Second, based on our preceding discussion regarding the newly defined security property and preimage information leakage in PPH, our objective is to conduct a security analysis of existing PPH schemes. We aim to examine whether these schemes can be formally proven to satisfy the security property or whether they exhibit potential privacy leakage vulnerabilities under the given security definition.

Third, we aim to construct a better PPH to minimize information leakage while preserving message homomorphism to ensure both security and functionality in privacy-preserving computations.

1.1　Our Contributions

In this work, we introduce a novel information leakage security property $\mathcal{L}$-Simulation for PPH by drawing inspiration from the Oracle Simulation concept in Relational Hash and the leakage profile in ORE. This security property formally defines an upper bound on the leakage of PPH evaluation algorithms, enabling systematic classification of PPH schemes based on their privacy protection levels.

Under this new information leakage security definition, we conduct a security analysis of existing PPH schemes and obtain several positive and negative results. The positive result demonstrates that the PPH in ORE can be proven to achieve ideal leakage under the new security definition, meaning that it reveals nothing beyond the predicate relation and leaks no additional information about the preimages. The negative result is that the PPH schemes [6] and [8] suffer from partial preimage leakage attacks under public evaluation and these two PPH constructions do not satisfy $\mathcal{L}$-Simulation we proposed. Furthermore, we identify that the leakage of a single hash pair can be amplified through repeated public evaluations, which exacerbates privacy risks.

Building upon Fleischhacker and Simkin's framework, we propose a new randomized Homomorphic Robust Property-Preserving Hash (HRPPH) scheme for the Hamming distance predicate. Our HRPPH supports additive homomorphism and scalar multiplicative homomorphism, while provably satisfying our strengthened information leakage security model—$\mathcal{L}$-Simulation. We also construct a multi-input HRPPH extension supporting more complex predicate evaluations.

1.2　Technical Overview

Our work stems from the analysis of the PPH in the work by Fleischhacker and Simkin [6]. Therefore, we briefly review the core ideas of their work [6].

The PPH scheme in [6] focuses on a Hamming distance predicate between sets. For two sets $A = \{a_1, ..., a_n\}$ and $B = \{b_1, ..., b_n\}$, where n is the size of sets, and assume both sets have the same size, the Hamming distance between sets A and B is defined as the half size of their symmetric difference

$$D_H(A, B) = \frac{|A \triangle B|}{2} = \frac{|(A \backslash B) \cup (B \backslash A)|}{2}.$$

They encode the elements of the set as the roots of a polynomial $f_A(x) = \prod_{i=1}^{n}(x - a_i)$. The ratio of $f_A(x)$ and $f_B(x)$ eliminates the common factors in $f_A(x)$ and $f_B(x)$. The degree of the rational function $f_{A \triangle B}(x)$ is defined as

$$\deg(f_{A \triangle B}(x)) = \deg(f_{A \backslash B}(x)) + \deg(f_{B \backslash A}(x)) = 2 \cdot D_H(A, B).$$

For a Hamming distance predicate

$$P_H(A, B) = \begin{cases} 1, & D_H(A, B) \leq t \\ 0, & D_H(A, B) > t \end{cases},$$

where t is an artificially set Hamming distance threshold, their PPH scheme outputs $2t$ distinct points of $f_A(x_1), ..., f_A(x_{2t})$ and $f_B(x_1), ..., f_B(x_{2t})$. If the rational function $\frac{f'_{A\setminus B}(x)}{f'_{B\setminus A}(x)}$ reconstructed from $\frac{f_A(x_1)}{f_B(x_1)}, ..., \frac{f_A(x_{2t})}{f_B(x_{2t})}$ by the rational interpolation algorithm is equal to $\frac{f_A(x)}{f_B(x)}$, that means the Hamming distance of A and B is no more than t. Their scheme uses polynomial evaluations at random points to verify polynomial equality.

Leakage of PPH. Regarding the PPH scheme proposed by Fleischhacker and Simkin, it is found that when $P_H(A, B) = 1$, the adversary can fully recover all coefficients of the rational function $\frac{f'_{A\setminus B}(x)}{f'_{B\setminus A}(x)}$ via the rational interpolation algorithm. It is easy to observe that the zeros of $f'_{A\setminus B}(x)$ are exactly the elements in the set $A\setminus B$. Through the algorithm for calculating polynomial zeros, the adversary can completely recover the $A\setminus B$ subset of set A and the $B\setminus A$ subset of set B. Therefore, the PPH scheme by Fleischhacker and Simkin leaks additional information about the preimages—beyond the result of the Hamming distance predicate—during predicate evaluation.

Definition of Leakage. Defining the information leakage of PPH hash values concerning their preimages is our primary consideration. Existing provable security frameworks—including game-based and simulation-based security—can effectively characterize such leakage. In the game-based security definition, the requirement that the hash value reveals no information about the preimage can be formalized as the computational indistinguishability between: (1)a hash value generated by the PPH algorithm, and (2) a hash value sampled uniformly at random from the output space. Furthermore, the security model treats the PPH as an oracle $\mathcal{O}_{PPH}$, where the adversary cannot compute hash values independently—instead, it must query $\mathcal{O}_{PPH}$ to obtain the hash value $h(M)$ for a message M. It is evident that predicate evaluation in PPH inherently compromises the indistinguishability of hash values. Consequently, in existing security proofs for PPH within ORE, the adversary is restricted to querying the hash oracle only on message pairs (A, B) where $P(A, B) = 0$.

Nevertheless, the game-based security definition of PPH exhibits two critical limitations. First, the requirement for hash values to be uniformly random is overly stringent and unnecessarily restrictive. Second, the definition fails to account for potential information leakage when the predicate evaluation yields $P(A, B) = 1$.

In the simulation-based security definition, the requirement that the hash value reveals no information about the preimage can be formalized as the existence of a simulator capable of simulating all possible hash outputs while maintaining an identical distribution to that of the real PPH scheme. Building upon the leakage assessment methodology employed in ORE and Searchable Encryption (SE) [21], we incorporate a leakage function $\mathcal{L}$ within our simulator to establish an upper bound on the information leakage about PPH preimages.

This leakage function is explicitly defined to account for all possible cases of predicate evaluations $P(A, B)$.

Construction Improvement. In our work, we propose a novel construction for PPH based on [6]. Specifically, we introduce a homomorphic PPH scheme for the Hamming distance predicate between tuples. Given two tuples $A = \{a_1, ..., a_n\}$ and $B = \{b_1, ..., b_n\}$, where n is the length of tuples, and assume both tuples have the same length, the Hamming distance predicate is formally defined as $D_H(A, B) = \sum_{i=1}^{n} 1(a_i \neq b_i)$, where $1(a_i \neq b_i)$ is a indicator function. If $a_i \neq b_i$ it outputs 1; otherwise, it outputs 0. We encode the tuple A into a polynomial $f_A(x)$ from $(x_1, a_1), ..., (x_n, a_n)$ by the interpolation algorithm. Following the same encoding method, we construct the polynomial $f_B(x)$ for tuple B. For the polynomial $f_A(x) - f_B(x)$, if $a_i = b_i, i \in [n]$, then by the Polynomial Factor Theorem, there exists a polynomial $g(x)$ such that $f_A(x) - f_B(x) = (x - x_i) \cdot g(x)$. Therefore, we define a public polynomial $f_P(x) = \prod_{i=1}^{n}(x - x_i)$. By dividing the polynomial $f_A(x) - f_B(x)$ by the public polynomial $f_P(x)$, identical elements at the same positions in the tuple are "eliminated". The degree of the rational function $\frac{f_A(x) - f_B(x)}{f_P(x)}$ will decrease. Subsequent steps are similar to those in work [6]. When the degree of the rational function does not exceed the number of points in the hash value, the rational function can be recovered via the rational interpolation algorithm. Similarly, we use polynomial evaluations at random points to verify polynomial equality.

In our new scheme, the reconstructed rational polynomial does not direct preimage information. This critical modification introduces an additional degree of freedom in our security simulation framework. Furthermore, we preserve the homomorphism of the polynomial at the tuple level. Specifically, for polynomials $f_A(x)$ and $f_B(x)$ encoded by tuples A and B, it holds that

$$f_A(x) + f_B(x) = f_{A+B}(x), A + B = (a_1 + b_1, ..., a_n + b_n),$$

$$\alpha \cdot f_A(x) = f_{\alpha \cdot A}(x), \alpha \cdot A = (\alpha \cdot a_1, ..., \alpha \cdot a_n).$$

1.3   Related Works

In this section, we survey the literature on PPH and summarize the conclusions of existing works.

The concept of PPH originates from sketching [19] and locality-sensitive hashing [20], with the core idea being the evaluation of predicates on compressed digests of large messages. In the work of Boyle et al. [7], the notion of Direct-Access Robust PPH was first formally defined. Direct-Access Robustness stands as the strongest correctness definition for PPH to date. Their work presented two PPH constructions for the Gap-Hamming predicate, based on generic collision-resistant hash functions and low-density parity-check codes, respectively. This paper laid the foundation for subsequent research on robust property-preserving hash (RPPH).

In the work of Fleischhacker and Simkin at Eurocrypt 2021 [6], a Robust Property-Preserving Hash (RPPH) for the exact Hamming distance predicate was proposed based on bilinear pairing groups. The Direct-Access Robustness of this RPPH relies on the non-standard assumption n-Strong Bilinear Discrete Logarithm (n-SBDL). In a subsequent work by Fleischhacker et al. at Eurocrypt 2022 [8], a PPH for Hamming distance was constructed based on the standard Short Integer Solution (SIS) assumption. This scheme demonstrates advantages over the previous work in terms of security, computational performance, and a lower bound.

In the work of Holmgren et al. at CRYPTO 2022 [4], a PPH with improved lower bound and compression ratios was built using error-correcting codes and collision-resistant hash functions. In the final section of this work, the authors studied randomized robust PPH (R2P2H) for Hamming distance, where the hash computation is a probabilistic algorithm, and the same message can be compressed into different digests. From the perspective of the Direct-Access Robustness definition, the security of R2P2H is weaker than that of RPPH.

In the work by Liu et al. [5], a Homomorphic Robust Property-Preserving Hash (HRPPH) was proposed for single-input Hamming weight and Gap-k Greater-Than predicates. In machine learning scenarios, the PPH hash value of a linear regression model $H(f(x) = a \cdot x + b)$ can be represented as $a \cdot H(x) + H(b)$ using HRPPH. We argue that homomorphism is a powerful functional property for applications requiring data privacy guarantees. However, this work similarly lacks a formal definition and proof of privacy-related security properties, leaving open critical questions about the extent of information leakage in homomorphic PPH schemes.

The aforementioned improvements to PPH primarily focus on lower bounds and compression ratios, without considering the privacy attributes of PPH. In earlier research preceding PPH, Mandal and Arnab Roy [3] introduced the cryptographic primitive Relational Hash. The distinction between Relational Hash and PPH lies in the fact that the hash computations for messages A and B in Relational Hash are performed using different algorithms, $h_1(A)$ and $h_2(B)$. This work defines security properties for Relational Hash, including one-wayness, twin one-wayness, unforgeability, and oracle simulatibility. Among these, Oracle Simulation ensures that h_1 and h_2 do not leak any information beyond the predicate relationship of the messages. We adapt this privacy property and incorporate it into PPH.

2   Preliminaries

In this section, we introduce notations, definitions, and lemmas. Let λ denote the security parameter. The notation $poly(\lambda)$ represents functions computable by PPT algorithms, while $negl(\lambda)$ denotes negligible functions. A function is considered negligible if, for any exponent e, there exists some N such that for all $\lambda > N, negl(\lambda) < \frac{1}{\lambda^e}$. For a degree-$n$ polynomial $f_A(x) = \sum_{i=0}^{n} c_{A,i} \cdot x^i$, we refer to $c_{A,i}$ as the i-th coefficient of $f_A(x)$. The notation $[n]$ represents the set of integers $\{1, ..., n\}$. An n-length tuple is denoted as $A = (a_1, ..., a_n)$, where $a_1 \in X_1, ..., a_n \in X_n$, and X_i represents the element space for the i-th position of the tuple. Note that the element spaces may vary across different positions. For tuples A, B and a scalar k, let $A + B + k = (a_1 + b_1 + k, ..., a_n + b_n + k)$. Let $\|A\|_0$ denote the L_0 Norm of the tuple A. The L_0 Norm is defined as the number of non-zero elements in the tuple.

Hamming Distance Between Two Tuples. For two given tuples $A := (a_1, ..., a_n)$ and $B := (b_1, ..., b_n)$ with tuple length n, the Hamming Distance $D_H(A, B)$ between tuples A and B is defined as follows

$$D_H(A, B) = |\Phi| \ , \ \Phi = \{i \in [n] | a_i \neq b_i\}.$$

Hamming Distance Between Multiple Tuples. For l given tuples $A_1 := (a_{1,1}, ..., a_{1,n}), ..., A_l := (a_{l,1}, ..., a_{l,n})$ with tuple length n, the Hamming Distance $D_H(A_1, ..., A_l)$ between tuples $A_1, ..., A_l$ is defined as follows

$$D_H(A_1, ..., A_l) = |\Phi| \ , \ \Phi = \{i \in [l] | \exists j \in [n], a_{i,j} \neq a_{i,j}\}.$$

Hamming Distance Between Sets. For two given sets $A := \{a_1, ..., a_n\}$ and $B := \{b_1, ..., b_n\}$ with set length n, the Hamming Distance $D_H(A, B)$ between sets A and B is defined as follows

$$D_H(A, B) = \frac{|(A \backslash B) \cup (B \backslash A)|}{2}.$$

Definition 1 ((The n-Strong Bilinear Discrete Logarithm (n-SBDL) Assumption)). *For the generators g_1, g_2 of $\mathbb{G}_1$, $\mathbb{G}_2$ with group order p and bilinear map $e : \mathbb{G}_1 \times \mathbb{G}_2 \rightarrow \mathbb{G}_T$, n-SBDL problem is hard for any PPT adversary $\mathcal{A}$:*

$$\Pr \left[r = r' \left| \begin{array}{c} (\mathbb{G}_1, \mathbb{G}_2, \mathbb{G}_T, e, p, g_1, g_2) \leftarrow \mathsf{GGen}(1^\lambda), \\ r \xleftarrow{\$} \mathbb{Z}_p, \\ \boldsymbol{R_1} := \left(g_1 \ g_1^r \ \cdots \ g_1^{r^n}\right), \\ \boldsymbol{R_2} := \left(g_2 \ g_2^r \ \cdots \ g_2^{r^n}\right), \\ r' \leftarrow \mathcal{A}(\mathbb{G}_1, \mathbb{G}_2, \mathbb{G}_T, e, p, \boldsymbol{R_1}, \boldsymbol{R_2}) \end{array} \right. \right] \leqslant negl(\lambda).$$

2.1   Property-Preserving Hash

Definition 2 (Deterministic Property-Preserving Hash). *A property-preserving hash scheme $\mathcal{H} = \{h : X \rightarrow Y\}$ for a two-input predicate is a tuple of polynomial-time algorithms* (Sample, Hash, Eval) *defined as follows:*

- Sample$(1^\lambda) \rightarrow H$: *The hash sample algorithm is a deterministic algorithm that takes as input a security parameter λ and outputs the hash function public parameters H.*

- $\mathsf{Hash}(H, M) \to h(H, M)$: *The hash algorithm is a randomized algorithm that takes as input a hash function H and a message M, then outputs a hash value $h(H, M)$.*
- $\mathsf{Eval}(H, h(H, M_1), h(H, M_2)) \to 0/1$: *The hash evaluation algorithm is a deterministic and public algorithm that takes as input two hash values $h(M_1), h(M_2)$ and the hash function h, then outputs a evaluation result 1 or 0. For the Public Property-Preserving Hash, Eval can be executed by anyone without any private keys.*

Definition 3 (Randomized Property-Preserving Hash). *A property-preserving hash scheme $\mathcal{H} = \{h : X \to Y\}$ for a two-input predicate is a tuple of polynomial-time algorithms* ($\mathsf{Sample}, \mathsf{Hash}, \mathsf{Eval}$) *defined as follows:*

- $\mathsf{Sample}(1^\lambda) \to H$: *The hash sample algorithm is a deterministic algorithm that takes as input a security parameter λ and outputs the hash function public parameters H.*
- $\mathsf{Hash}(H, M, r) \to h(H, M)$: *The hash algorithm is a randomized algorithm that takes as input a hash function H, a message M and random value r, then outputs a hash value $h(H, M)$.*
- $\mathsf{Eval}(H, h(H, M_1), h(H, M_2)) \to 0/1$: *The hash evaluation algorithm is a deterministic and public algorithm that takes as input two hash values $h(M_1), h(M_2)$ and the hash function h, then outputs a evaluation result 1 or 0.*

Definition 4 (Homomorphic Property). *For a class of predicates P and a family of PPH functions $\mathcal{H} = \{h : X \to Y\}$, a homomorphic PPH scheme requires the following properties:*

- ***Additively Homomorphic:*** $\forall M_1, M_2 \in \mathcal{M}, h(M_1+M_2) = h(M_1)\oplus h(M_2)$.
- ***Scalar Multiplicatively Homomorphic:*** $\forall M \in \mathcal{M}$ *and* $\alpha \in \mathbb{Z}_q^*, h(\alpha \cdot M) = \alpha \otimes h(M)$.

Definition 5 (Direct-Access Robustness). *For a class of predicates P and a family of PPH functions h, a PPH scheme is direct-access robust if for any PPT adversary $\mathcal{A}$:*

$$\Pr\left[\mathsf{Eval}(h, h(A), h(B)) \neq P(A, B) \;\middle|\; \begin{array}{l} h \leftarrow \mathsf{Sample}(1^\lambda), \\ (A, B) \leftarrow \mathcal{A}(h) \end{array}\right] \leqslant negl(\lambda).$$

Definition 6 (One-way). *For a class of predicates P, a PPH function family $\mathcal{H}$ is one-way if for any PPT adversary $\mathcal{A}$*

$$\Pr\left[M = M' \;\middle|\; \begin{array}{l} h \leftarrow \mathsf{Sample}(1^\lambda), \\ h(M) \leftarrow \mathsf{Hash}(h, M), \\ M' \leftarrow \mathcal{A}(h, h(M)) \end{array}\right] \leqslant negl(\lambda).$$

2.2 Polynomial Preliminaries

Rational Functions. A rational function is the quotient of two polynomials. For a rational function $r(x) = \frac{f(x)}{g(x)}$ composed of two polynomials $f(x)$ and $g(x)$, there may exist a polynomial $p(x)$ such that

$$r(x) = \frac{f(x)}{g(x)} = \frac{f'(x) \cdot p(x)}{g'(x) \cdot p(x)} = \frac{f'(x)}{g'(x)}$$

Definition 7 (Degree of Rational Functions.). *A degree of Rational Function $r(x) = \frac{f(x)}{g(x)}$ is defined as follows*

$$\deg(r(x)) = \deg(f'(x)) + \deg(g'(x)),$$

where $f'(x)$ and $g'(x)$ are defined as above.

Rational Polynomial Interpolation (RPI): For a rational polynomial $r(x) = \frac{f(x)}{g(x)}$, no less than $\deg(r(x)) + 1$ distinct pairs $(y_i, \frac{f(y_i)}{g(y_i)})$ can recover the complete coefficients of polynomials $f'(x)$ and $g'(x)$, where $f'(x)$ and $(g'(x)$ are defined as above.

$$\Pr\left[\begin{array}{c} f_1(x) = f'(x), \\ f_2(x) = g'(x) \end{array}\middle| \begin{array}{c} f_1(x), f_2(x) \leftarrow \mathsf{RPIA}\big((y_1, \frac{f(y_1)}{g(y_1)}), ..., (y_n, \frac{f(y_n)}{g(y_n)})\big), \\ n > \deg(r(x)), y_1 \neq y_2... \neq y_n \end{array}\right] = 1.$$

Random Encoding Tuples as Polynomials. For a given tuple $T := (t_1, ..., t_n)$ where $t_i \in \mathcal{T}_i$, we define the polynomial encoding of the tuple T as $f_T(x)$ by polynomial interpolation algorithm from $t + 1$ points $\big((0, t_0), (1, t_1), ..., (n, t_n)\big)$, where $t_0 \xleftarrow{\$} \mathbb{Z}_q^*$. We provide below the construction of the polynomial $f_T(x)$ via the Lagrange polynomial interpolation algorithm

$$f_T(x) = \sum_{i=0}^{n} \Big(\prod_{j=0, j\neq i}^{n} \frac{x - j}{i - j} \Big) \cdot t_i.$$

Lemma 1. *For two given polynomials $f_A(x)$ and $f_B(x)$ randomly encoded from tuples $A := (a_1, ..., a_n)$ and $B := (b_1, ..., b_n)$, it holds that*

$$D_H(A, B) = \frac{1}{2}\deg\Big(\frac{f_A(x) - f_B(x)}{\prod_{i=1}^{n}(x - i)}\Big).$$

Proof. Observe that $f_A(x)$ and $f_B(x)$ are polynomials with highest degree n and each polynomial has $n + 1$ polynomial coefficients to be determined. Hence $\deg(f_A(x)) = \deg(f_B(x)) = n$. We define a set $\Phi := \{i \in [n] | a_i = b_i\}$ where $d(A, B) = n - |\Phi|$ and we have

$$\frac{f_A(x) - f_B(x)}{\prod\limits_{i=1}^{n}(x-i)} = \frac{\prod\limits_{i\in\Phi}(x-i)\cdot f_1'(x)}{\prod\limits_{i\in\Phi}(x-i)\cdot\prod\limits_{i\in\{[n]-\Phi\}}(x-i)} = \frac{f_1'(x)}{\prod\limits_{i\in\{[n]-\Phi\}}(x-i)}.$$

Then, we have

$$\deg(f_1'(x)) = n - |\Phi| = \deg(\prod_{i\in\{[n]-\Phi\}}(x-i)),$$

$$\deg(\frac{f_A(x) - f_B(x)}{\prod\limits_{i=1}^{n}(x-i)}) = \deg(f_1'(x)) + \deg(\prod_{i\in\{[n]-\Phi\}}(x-i)).$$

Finally, combining the above equations and we thus have $D_H(A,B) = \frac{1}{2}\deg(\frac{f_A(x)-f_B(x)}{\prod\limits_{i=1}^{n}(x-i)})$.

Encoding Sets as Polynomials. Consider a set $A = \{a_1, ..., a_l\}$ and a set $B = \{b_1, ..., b_l\}$ with elements from the universe U, where l is the number of elements in the set. Encoding the set A as a polynomial $f_A(x) = \prod\limits_{i=1}^{l}(x - a_i) = \sum_{i=0}^{l} c_{f_A,i}\cdot x^i$, where $c_{f_A,i}$ the ith coefficient of the polynomial $f_A(x)$ and $c_{f_A,l} = 1$. Encoding the set B as a polynomial $f_B(x) = \prod\limits_{i=1}^{l}(x - b_i) = \sum_{i=0}^{l} c_{f_B,i}\cdot x^i$ similarly. The rational function $f_{A\triangle B}(x)$ is defined as

$$f_{A\triangle B}(x) := \frac{f_A(x)}{f_B(x)} = \frac{f_{A\backslash B}(x)}{f_{B\backslash A}(x)}$$

where $A\triangle B = (A\backslash B) \cup (B\backslash A)$. The ratio of $f_A(x)$ and $f_B(x)$ eliminates the same elemental factors in $f_A(x)$ and $f_B(x)$. The set $A\triangle B$ retains all the distinct elements in set A and set B. So the corresponding coding polynomial $f_{A\triangle B}(x)$ of the set $A\triangle B$ can be represented by the ratio of $f_A(x)$ and $f_B(x)$. The polynomial $f_{A\backslash B}$ denotes the encoding polynomial for $A\backslash B$, where the set $A\backslash B$ is the set A minus the set B. Further we can get the equation $f_{A\triangle B}(x) = \frac{f_{A\backslash B}(x)}{f_{B\backslash A}(x)}$.

The Hamming distance $D_H(A,B)$ between two sets A and B is denoted as

$$D_H(A,B) = \frac{|D|}{2}, D = \{x | (x \in A \wedge x \notin B) \vee (x \in B \wedge x \notin A)\}$$

The Hamming distance predicate P_H between two sets A and B is defined as

$$P_H(A,B) = \begin{cases} 1, & |A \cap B| \le t \\ 0, & else \end{cases}$$

where t is an artificially set Hamming distance threshold. Based on the above polynomial encoding of sets, we can convert the Hamming distance predicate P_H to

$$P_H(A, B) = \begin{cases} 1, & \deg(f_{A \triangle B}(x)) \leq 2t \\ 0, & \deg(f_{A \triangle B}(x)) > 2t \end{cases}$$

where $\deg(f(x))$ denotes the degree of the polynomial $f(x)$.

2.3 PPH Scheme by Fleischhacker and Simkin [6] from Polynomial

For a two-input Hamming distance predicate P_H, the property-preserving hash function family $\mathcal{H} = \{h : X \to Y\}$ consists of the following three algorithms:

- $\mathsf{Sample}(1^\lambda) \to h$: The hash function h is randomly generated by the security parameter λ. Select bilinear group $\mathbb{G}_1, \mathbb{G}_2$ with group order p and bilinear map $e : \mathbb{G}_1 \times \mathbb{G}_2 \to \mathbb{G}_T$. Randomly select group generator $g_1 \xleftarrow{R} \mathbb{G}_1, g_2 \xleftarrow{R} \mathbb{G}_2$. Randomly choose $r \xleftarrow{R} \mathbb{Z}_p$ and generate a matrix

$$\boldsymbol{R_1} := (g_1, g_1^r, ..., g_1^{r^n}) \quad , \quad \boldsymbol{R_2} := (g_2, g_2^r, ..., g_2^{r^n})$$

  Then return $h := (e, \mathbb{G}_1, \mathbb{G}_2, \mathbb{G}_T, \boldsymbol{R_1}, \boldsymbol{R_2})$.
- $\mathsf{Hash}(h, A) \to h(A)$: Generate a deterministic hash value $h(A)$ on the set $A = \{a_1, ..., a_n\}$ of user attributes by hash function h. First encode the set A as a polynomial $f_A(x) = \prod_{i=1}^{n} (x - a_i)$ and generate t pairs

$$\boldsymbol{P_A} := \big((N + 1, f_A(N + 1)), ..., (N + t, f_A(N + 2t))\big)$$

  Compute $P'_A = \prod_{i=0}^{n} \boldsymbol{R}_{1,i}^{c_{f_A,i}} = \prod_{i=0}^{n} (g_1^{r^i})^{c_{f_A,i}} = g_1^{\sum_{i=0}^{n} c_{f_A,i} \cdot r^i} = g_1^{f_A(r)}$ and then return $h(A) := (\boldsymbol{P_A}, P'_A)$.
- $\mathsf{Eval}(h, h(A), h(B)) \to 0/1$: For the hash values $h(A)$ and $h(B)$ generated by the hash function h for set A and set B, the result of the Hamming distance predicate evaluation between set A and set B can be publicly accessed via Eval. Parse $h(B)$ as $(\boldsymbol{P_B}, P'_B)$ and compute

$$\boldsymbol{s} := \Big((N + 1, \tfrac{f_A(N+1)}{f_B(N+1)}), ..., (N + 2t, \tfrac{f_A(N+2t)}{f_B(N+2t)})\Big)$$

It can get $(f_1, f_2) \leftarrow \mathsf{RPIA}(\boldsymbol{s})$ from Rational Polynomial Interpolation Algorithm(RPIA). If

$$e(P'_A, \prod_{i=0}^{n} \boldsymbol{R}_{2,i}^{c_{f_2,i}}) \stackrel{?}{=} e(P'_B, \prod_{i=0}^{n} \boldsymbol{R}_{2,i}^{c_{f_1,i}})$$

then output 1, otherwise output 0.

3   Defining Information Leakage of PPH

In this section, we formally define the privacy property of PPH and introduce the notion of PPH leakage profile. We analyze the Restricted Chosen Input Security of PPH in the context of ORE. To enhance the applicability of its security definition and introduce smooth leakage levels, we propose a simulation definition with a leakage function.

3.1 $\mathcal{L}$-Simulation

Inspired by Relational Hash, we formalize the notion of $\mathcal{L}$-Simulation for PPH. We model PPH as an oracle that the adversary must query to obtain message digests. $\mathcal{L}$-Simulation is a simulation-based security property. In the real-world execution, denoted as Oracle-Real, the protocol operates as follows. Correspondingly, in the ideal world, we construct Oracle-Ideal$_{\mathcal{S},\mathcal{L}}^{\mathsf{PPH}}$ using a PPT simulator $\mathcal{S}$ and a leakage function $\mathcal{L}$. The security requirement stipulates that the adversary cannot distinguish between its interactions with the PPH oracle in the real world versus the ideal world, thereby ensuring that the PPH scheme reveals no information about the preimage beyond what is explicitly permitted by the leakage function $\mathcal{L}$.

Definition 8. *A PPH scheme is $\mathcal{L}$-Simulation with leakage $\mathcal{L}$, if there exists a PPT simulator $\mathcal{S}$ that constructs an ideal-world PPH oracle Oracle-Ideal$_{\mathcal{S},\mathcal{L}}^{\mathsf{PPH}}$ based on the leakage function $\mathcal{L}$ for all possible outputs, such that for any PPT adversary $\mathcal{A}$, the real-world oracle Oracle-Real^{PPH} and Oracle-Ideal$_{\mathcal{S},\mathcal{L}}^{\mathsf{PPH}}$ are computationally indistinguishable.*

<table>
<tr><td>

Adaptive type:

- Oracle-Real$^{\mathsf{PPH}}(h, M)$:
  1:$\overline{h(M) \leftarrow \mathsf{Hash}(h, M)};$
  2:**return** $h(M)$

- Oracle-Ideal$_{\mathcal{S},\mathcal{L}}^{\mathsf{PPH}}(h, M)$:
  1:$\overline{h(M) \leftarrow \mathcal{S}(h, \mathcal{Q}, \mathcal{L}(M, \mathcal{Q}))};$
  2:$\mathcal{Q} = \mathcal{Q} \cup \{(h, M, h(M))\};$
  3:**return** $h(M)$

</td><td>

Non-adaptive type:

- Oracle-Real$^{\mathsf{PPH}}(h, M_1, ..., M_q)$:
  1:$\overline{\textbf{for } i \in [1, q]}$
  2:   $h(M_i) \leftarrow \mathsf{Hash}(h, M_i);$
  3:**return** $h(M_1), ..., h(M_q)$

- Oracle-Ideal$_{\mathcal{S},\mathcal{L}}^{\mathsf{PPH}}(h, M_1, ..., M_q)$:
  1:$\overline{h(M_1), ..., h(M_q) \leftarrow}$
  $\mathcal{S}(h, \mathcal{L}(M_1, ..., M_q));$
  2:**return** $h(M_1), ..., h(M_q)$

</td></tr>
</table>

There are two types of $\mathcal{L}$-Simulation: the Adaptive type and the Non-adaptive type. In the Adaptive type, the adversary is allowed to query the Oracle up to q times. The i-th Oracle query made by the adversary is based on the returned results of the previous $(i - 1)$ queries. Moreover, when the simulator returns the result of the i-th query, it is unable to predict the content of the adversary's $(i + 1)$-th query. In the Non-adaptive type, the adversary is only permitted to query the Oracle once. Specifically, the adversary queries the hash values $h(M_1), ..., h(M_q)$ corresponding to q messages $M_1, ..., M_q$. It is evident that the Adaptive type features weaker assumption and stronger security. So all subsequent $\mathcal{L}$-Simulation of PPH are conducted under the Adaptive type.

Perfect Leakage Profile of PPH. Theoretically, the optimal leakage for a PPH scheme should reveal nothing beyond the predicate relations between messages. The ideal leakage, denoted as $\mathcal{L}_0$, is formally defined as follows:

$$\mathcal{L}_0(M_1, ..., M_n) := (\forall i, j \in [n], i \neq j, P(M_i, M_j)).$$

$\mathcal{L}$-Simulation of Randomized PPH. For a deterministic PPH, the same hash function h and message M will yield the same hash digest $h(M)$. In Randomized PPH, the probabilistic computation of the hash digest requires the introduction of a random value r. Therefore, in $\mathcal{L}$-Simulation definition of Randomized PPH, the real-world oracle is modified to $h(M) \leftarrow \mathsf{Hash}(h, M, r)$, where $r \xleftarrow{\$} \mathcal{R}$. The ideal-world oracle is modified to $h(M) \leftarrow \mathcal{S}(h, r, \mathcal{Q}, \mathcal{L}(M, \mathcal{Q}))$, where $r \xleftarrow{\$} \mathcal{R}$.

3.2   Comparison with Restricted Chosen Input Security of PPH Schemes in ORE

In ORE schemes, the PPH introduces additional privacy guarantees. The Restricted Chosen Input Security (RCIS) ensures the randomness of the PPH output. By restricting the conditions under which the adversary $\mathcal{A}$ can query the PPH hash oracle, it constrains $\mathcal{A}$ to only inquire about message digests that do not satisfy the predicate relation P with respect to the target message M^*. The definition of this security model implies that the PPH output does not leak any additional information beyond the predicate evaluation result. The definition of the advantage on Restricted Chosen Input Security and the description of the hash oracle for PPH are specified as follows.

Definition 9. *For a predicate P, the PPH scheme is restricted chosen input secure for any PPT adversary $\mathcal{A}$ with PPH oracle* $\mathsf{Oracle\text{-}Hash_{PPH}}$ *if the following advantage* $\mathsf{Adv}^{\mathsf{RCIS}} \leq negl(\lambda)$

$$\mathsf{Adv}^{\mathsf{RCIS}} := \left| \Pr \left[b = b' \,\middle|\, \begin{array}{c} h \leftarrow \mathsf{Sample}(1^\lambda), \\ M^* \leftarrow \mathcal{A}(h), b \xleftarrow{\$} \{0,1\}, \\ H_0 \leftarrow \mathsf{Hash}(h, M^*), \\ H_1 \xleftarrow{\$} \mathcal{H}, \\ b' \leftarrow \mathcal{A}^{\mathsf{Hash_{PPH}}(h,\cdot)}(h, H_b) \end{array} \right] - \frac{1}{2} \right|.$$

```
-  Oracle-Hash_PPH(h, M) :
  1: If P(M, M*) = 1 ∨ P(M*, M) = 1, return ⊥;
  2: Else h(M) ← PPH.Hash(h, M);
  3:     return h(M)
```

The security model of RCIS has two defined deficiencies. First, the property that the PPH output is indistinguishable from a random value in the output space is overly strong. The reason for introducing the PPH of RCIS into the ORE scheme is that the ciphertext output of the encryption scheme must satisfy indistinguishability. Therefore, the PPH output of the plaintext in ORE must satisfy the indistinguishability. While the RCIS security model characterizes the protection of preimage information by the hash digest, it additionally imposes an extra requirement on output indistinguishability. However, in traditional PPH, the indistinguishability of hash outputs is not necessary. Thus, we need a more adaptable security model to precisely characterize the protection of preimage information.

Second, the restriction on the hash oracle in the RCIS security model is overly direct. This restriction prohibits any query involving a message M that satisfies $P(M, M^*) = 1$ with respect to the target message M^*. The indistinguishability property of RCIS's PPH output only holds for messages that do not satisfy the predicate relation. This is because, for the adversary, the output of PPH.Eval is always 0. Consequently, the adversary cannot obtain any meaningful information that satisfies the predicate relation through PPH.Eval. For messages that do satisfy the predicate relation, whether information beyond the predicate itself is leaked remains uncharacterized. Therefore, our $\mathcal{L}$-Simulation provides a smooth definition of information leakage for arbitrary message digests.

4   Analysing Information Leakage of PPH

In this section, we formalize and prove the security of PPH for ORE under the newly proposed $\mathcal{L}$-Simulation model, analyzing its leakage profile. Finally, we examine all existing PPH schemes for Hamming distance predicate under $\mathcal{L}$-Simulation framework and evaluate its leakage. Our findings reveal that two schemes [6,8] do not satisfy $\mathcal{L}$-Simulation security. Specifically, these two PPH constructions [6,8] lead to partial preimage leakage, and this leakage is further amplified in certain scenarios.

4.1   Analysing PPH in ORE

Before analyzing the leakage of PPH in ORE, we first review the PPH scheme from the work [9]. The predicate of this PPH is defined as follows

$$P_{ORE}(A, B) = \begin{cases} 1, & A = B + 1 \\ 0, & else \end{cases}.$$

For a two-input predicate P_{ORE}, the property-preserving hash function family $\mathcal{H} = \{h : X \to Y\}$ consists of the following three algorithms:

- Sample$(1^\lambda) \to h$: The hash function h is randomly generated by the security parameter λ. Select bilinear group $\mathbb{G}_1, \mathbb{G}_2$ with group order p and bilinear map

$e : \mathbb{G}_1 \times \mathbb{G}_2 \rightarrow \mathbb{G}_T$. Randomly select group generator $g_1 \xleftarrow{R} \mathbb{G}_1, g_2 \xleftarrow{R} \mathbb{G}_2$. Let $F : \{0,1\}^\lambda \times \{0,1\}^\lambda \rightarrow \mathbb{Z}_p$ be a secure Pseudorandom Function (PRF). Randomly choose $k \xleftarrow{R} \{0,1\}^\lambda$. Then return $h := (e, \mathbb{G}_1, \mathbb{G}_2, \mathbb{G}_T, g_1, g_2, F, k)$.

- Hash$(h, A) \rightarrow h(A)$: Generate the randomized hash value $h(A)$ on message A by hash function h. Randomly choose $r_1, r_2 \xleftarrow{R} \mathbb{Z}_p$ and compute

$$h(A) = (g_1^{r_1}, g_1^{r_1 \cdot F(k,A)}, g_2^{r_2}, g_2^{r_2 \cdot F(k,A+1)})$$

and then return $h(A) := (H_1, H_2, H_3, H_4)$.

- Eval$(h, h(A), h(B)) \rightarrow 0/1$: For the hash values $h(A)$ and $h(B)$ generated by the hash function h for A and B, the result of the predicate evaluation can be publicly accessed via Eval. Parse $h(B)$ as (H_1', H_2', H_3', H_4'). If $e(H_1, H_4') = e(H_2, H_1')$ output 1, otherwise output 0.

Theorem 1. *The PPH in [9] for the predicate P_{ORE} is $\mathcal{L}$-Simulation with the leakage function $\mathcal{L}(M_1, ..., M_n) = (\forall i, j \in [n], i \neq j, P(M_i, M_j))$, if F is a secure PRF.*

Proof. We construct a series of hybrid experiments for the PPH oracle in the ideal world. In G_1, prior to the commencement of the game, we replaced the PRF in the simulator's execution with a uniformly random function $F^* \xleftarrow{R}$ Funs$[\{0,1\}^\lambda, \{0,1\}^\lambda]$. The remaining procedures in the simulator remain unaltered. It is evident that if the PRF is secure, then G_0 and G_1 are computationally indistinguishable. The construction of the simulator in G_1 is as follows.

1: **if** $\mathcal{Q} = \varnothing$ **then**
2:　　$M^* \xleftarrow{\$} \mathcal{M}$;
3:　　$r_1, r_2 \xleftarrow{\$} \mathbb{Z}_p$;
4:　　$h(M) = (g_1^{r_1}, g_1^{r_1 \cdot F^*(M^*)}, g_2^{r_2}, g_2^{r_2 \cdot F^*(M^*+1)})$;
5:　　$\mathcal{Q} = \mathcal{Q} \cup \{h, h(M)\}$;
6:　　**return** $h(M)$.
7: **else**
8:　　for query (h, M_i);
9:　　$M_i^* = M^* - M + M_i$;
10:　　$r_{1,i}, r_{2,i} \xleftarrow{R} \mathbb{Z}_p$;
11:　　$h(M_i) = (g_1^{r_{1,i}}, g_1^{r_{1,i} \cdot F^*(M_i^*)}, g_2^{r_{2,i}}, g_2^{r_{2,i} \cdot F^*(M_i^*+1)})$;
12:　　$\mathcal{Q} = \mathcal{Q} \cup \{h, h(M_i)\}$
13:　　**return** $h(M_i)$.
14: **end if**

In the construction of the simulator, we note that line 9 appears inconsistent with the leakage function

$$\mathcal{L}_0(M_1, ..., M_n) = (\forall i, j \in [n], i \neq j, P(M_i, M_j), P(M_j, M_i)).$$

Firstly, since the predicate of the PPH is asymmetric and the evaluation of the PPH is public, the ideal leakage function includes two components $P(M_i, M_j)$ and $P(M_j, M_i)$. The ideal leakage of this PPH is $m \pm 1$ for the message m. In the Non-adaptive type of $\mathcal{L}$-Simulation, the simulator can simulate the query responses of Oracle-Ideal$_{S,\mathcal{L}}^{\mathsf{PPH}}$ based on the ideal leakage function $\mathcal{L}_0$.

Secondly, under adaptive type, because the adversary queries the PPH oracle one message at a time, and the simulator has no information about the adversary's subsequent queries. Consequently, the simulator can only simulate based on the worst-case scenario of the ideal leakage function $\mathcal{L}_0$, which is defined as follows

$$\mathcal{L}_{worst}(M_1, ..., M_n) = (\forall i, j \in [n], i \neq j, M_i - M_j).$$

The expansion of the leakage function from $\mathcal{L}_0$ to $\mathcal{L}_{worst}$ is caused by the inherent properties of the predicate. This does not affect the evaluation of the leakage level of the PPH.

We can observe that in the ideal world, the responses from the PPH oracle are identically distributed to those in the real world. Moreover, in the ideal world, the adversary's evaluation of the oracle's responses through Eval remains consistent. The simulator can successfully simulate any possible massage within the message space. Therefore, the adversary cannot distinguish between the real-world and ideal-world PPH oracles with more than a negligible advantage.

Furthermore, since the leakage function is defined to be equivalent to the predicate relation, this PPH achieves $\mathcal{L}_0$-Simulation under the ideal leakage bound.

4.2 Partial Preimage Leakage of PPH Scheme by Fleischhacker and Simkin [6]

The hash preimage in the Fleischhacker-Simkin scheme is a set of l elements. We next explain in detail that the Eval algorithm in Fleischhacker-Simkin scheme leaks some of the elements in the preimage set.

The Eval algorithm in the Fleischhacker-Simkin scheme allows us to completely recover the polynomials $f_{A \setminus B}(x)$ and $f_{B \setminus A}(x)$ by the RPI algorithm for sets A and B satisfying the condition $P_H(A, B) = 1$. The zeros of the polynomials $f_{A \setminus B}(x)$ and $f_{B \setminus A}(x)$ are some of the elements in set A and set B. Knowing all the coefficients of the polynomials $f_{A \setminus B}(x)$ and $f_{B \setminus A}$, the partial preimage elements of the sets A and B can be obtained by an algorithm with computational complexity less than $O(n^3)$, where n is the degree of the polynomial $f_{A \setminus B}(x)$.

Correctness of the Leakage. When the degree $\deg(f_{A \triangle B}(x))$ is less than t, the polynomials $f_1(x)$ and $f_2(x)$ derived by the RPIA satisfy

$$f_1(x) = f_{A \setminus B}(x), f_2(x) = f_{B \setminus A}(x)$$

So, the equation $\frac{f_A(r)}{f_B(r)} = \frac{f_1(r)}{f_2(r)}$ holds and $\mathsf{Eval}(h, h(A), h(B)) = 1$.

Algorithm 1 Partial Preimage Leakage

Input: h, $h(A)$ and $h(B)$;
Output: L_A and L_B;
 1: **if** $\mathsf{Eval}(h, h(A), h(B)) = 0$ **then**
 2:     Abort this leakage;
 3: **else**
 4:     Compute s from $h(A)$ and $h(B)$;
 5:     $\dfrac{f_{A\backslash B}(x)}{f_{B\backslash A}(x)} \leftarrow \mathsf{RPIA}(s)$;
 6:     **for** the set A **do**
 7:        Construct the companion matrix $C_{A\backslash B}$ of polynomial $f_{A\backslash B}(x) = \sum_{i=0}^{n} c_{f_{A\backslash B},i} \cdot x^i$;

$$
C_{A\backslash B} = \begin{bmatrix}
-c_{f_{A\backslash B},n-1} & 1 & 0 & \cdots & 0 & 0 \\
-c_{f_{A\backslash B},n-2} & 0 & 1 & \cdots & 0 & 0 \\
\vdots & & \vdots & \ddots & \vdots & \vdots \\
-c_{f_{A\backslash B},2} & 0 & 0 & \cdots & 1 & 0 \\
-c_{f_{A\backslash B},1} & 0 & 0 & \cdots & 0 & 1 \\
-c_{f_{A\backslash B},0} & 0 & 0 & \cdots & 0 & 0
\end{bmatrix}
$$

 8:        Compute $\lambda_{A\backslash B}$ by matrix eigenvalue decomposition of $C_{A\backslash B}$;
 9:        $L_A = L_A \cup \lambda_{A\backslash B}$;
10:     **end for**
11:     Run the same for the set B to $f_{B\backslash A}(x)$;
12: **end if**
13: **return** L_A and L_B;

And if degree $\deg(f_{A\triangle B}(x))$ does not exceed t, $f_1(x)$ and $f_2(x)$ recovered by RPIA have passed verification with negligible probability. So in the first step of Algorithm 1, $f_1(x) \neq f_{A\backslash B}(x)$ and $f_2(x) \neq f_{B\backslash A}(x)$ hold with $1 - neg(\lambda)$ probability when $\mathsf{Eval}(h, h(A), h(B)) = 0$.

Parse $f_{A\backslash B}(x)$ as $\prod_{i=1}^{n}(x - a_i') = \sum_{i=0}^{n} c_{f_{A\backslash B},i} \cdot x^i = x^n + c_{f_{A\backslash B},n-1} \cdot x^{n-1} + \ldots + c_{f_{A\backslash B},1} \cdot x + c_{f_{A\backslash B},0}$ where $a_i' \in A\backslash B$. The eigenvalues $\lambda_{A\backslash B}$ of the matrix $C_{A\backslash B}$ are the zeros of the polynomial $f_{A\backslash B}(x)$. E is a $n \times n$ unit matrix.

$$|\lambda_{A\backslash B} E - C_{A\backslash B}| = \begin{vmatrix} \lambda_{A\backslash B} + c_{f_{A\backslash B},n-1} & -1 & 0 & \cdots & 0 & 0 \\ c_{f_{A\backslash B},n-2} & \lambda_{A\backslash B} & -1 & \cdots & 0 & 0 \\ \vdots & \vdots & \vdots & \ddots & \vdots & \vdots \\ c_{f_{A\backslash B},2} & 0 & 0 & \cdots & -1 & 0 \\ c_{f_{A\backslash B},1} & 0 & 0 & \cdots & \lambda_{A\backslash B} & -1 \\ c_{f_{A\backslash B},0} & 0 & 0 & \cdots & 0 & \lambda_{A\backslash B} \end{vmatrix}$$

$$= (\lambda_{A\backslash B} + c_{f_{A\backslash B},n-1}) \begin{vmatrix} \lambda_{A\backslash B} & -1 & \cdots & 0 & 0 \\ \vdots & \ddots & \ddots & \vdots & \vdots \\ 0 & 0 & \ddots & \ddots & 0 \\ 0 & 0 & \cdots & \ddots & -1 \\ 0 & 0 & \cdots & 0 & \lambda_{A\backslash B} \end{vmatrix} + (-c_{f_{A\backslash B},n-2}) \begin{vmatrix} -1 & 0 & \cdots & 0 & 0 \\ \vdots & \lambda_{A\backslash B} & -1 & \vdots & \vdots \\ 0 & 0 & \ddots & \ddots & 0 \\ 0 & 0 & \cdots & \ddots & -1 \\ 0 & 0 & \cdots & 0 & \lambda_{A\backslash B} \end{vmatrix} + \cdots$$

$$= (\lambda_{A\backslash B} + c_{f_{A\backslash B},n-1})\lambda_{A\backslash B}^{n-1} + c_{f_{A\backslash B},n-2}\lambda_{A\backslash B}^{n-2} + \ldots + c_{f_{A\backslash B},0} = \sum_{i=0}^{n} c_{f_{A\backslash B},i} \cdot \lambda_{A\backslash B}^{i}$$

The computational complexity of the eigenvalue decomposition algorithm for an $n \times n$ matrix $C_{A\backslash B}$ is $O(n^3)$. The upper bound of n is the number of attribute set elements l. So there exists an effective PPT leakage algorithm causing partial preimage disclosure of the PPH scheme.

The above leakage method can cause the leakage of the preimages of the partial set $A\backslash B$ in the user's attribute set A. Further research is needed to expand the scope of preimage leakage or even leak all the preimages of the attribute set.

Expanding the Scope of Leakage. For leaking the target set A, since PPH's Hash and Eval algorithms are publicly available, anyone leaks the $A\backslash B$ portion of the set A via the Partial Preimage Leakage method. With increasing number of uses of PPH on the h sampled by the set A, the adversary leaks the preimage $A\backslash B_1, A\backslash B_2, \ldots$ of the set A part in parallel. With the method above, the original image leakage range can be extended to $(A\backslash B_1) \cup (A\backslash B_2) \cup \ldots$.

The Leakage Profile of PPH scheme by Fleischhacker and Simkin [6]. We now proceed to formalize the PPH scheme in [6] within our $\mathcal{L}$-Simulation framework. Building upon the notion of Partial Preimage Leakage introduced earlier, we define the leakage function for the PPH scheme as follows

$$\mathcal{L}(M_1, \ldots, M_n) := (\forall i, j \in [n], i \neq j, P(M_i, M_j), M_i\backslash M_j, M_j\backslash M_i).$$

Under the Adaptive-type L-Simulation model, the simulator cannot predict the sequence of messages queried by the adversary. Therefore, the simulator has to simulate the hash responses according to the worst-case leakage profile. The worst-case leakage function is defined as follows.

$$\mathcal{L}_{worst}(M_1, \ldots, M_n) := (\forall i, j \in [n], i \neq j, P(M_i, M_j), M_i, M_j).$$

According to the leakage function $\mathcal{L}$, the adversary can construct a specific sequence of message queries that fully exposes the preimages of the messages.

It is straightforward to observe that the adversary can distinguish between the responses from the real-world and ideal-world oracle, which results in the nonexistence of a simulator that can simulate all possible outputs. The conclusion is that the PPH scheme in [6] is not secure under Adaptive-type $\mathcal{L}$-Simulation model.

4.3 Analysing Leakage of Other PPH Schemes

In this subsection, we conduct a leakage analysis of existing PPH schemes for Hamming distance predicate. The existing works on PPH for Hamming distance predicate include [6,8], and [4]. We have already presented a detailed leakage analysis of the scheme by Fleischhacker et al. [6] in Sect. 4.2. The works [8] and [4] are both constructed based on coding techniques, and their leakage will be analyzed in detail below.

Leakage of Fleischhacker et al. Scheme [8]. The similarity between this work and the construction in [6] lies in that both convert the Hamming distance predicate into a symmetric set difference. This PPH scheme is based on the Robust Set Encodings proposed in that work. The robustness of Robust Set Encodings is defined as follows:

$$\Pr\left[\begin{array}{c} m' \notin \{m_1 \triangle m_2, \bot\} \vee \\ (|m_1 \triangle m_2| < t \wedge m' = \bot) \end{array} \left| \begin{array}{l} f \leftarrow \mathsf{Sample}(1^\lambda, t), \\ m_1, m_2 \leftarrow \mathcal{A}(f, t), \\ e_1 \leftarrow \mathsf{Encode}(f, m_1), \\ e_2 \leftarrow \mathsf{Encode}(f, m_2), \\ m' \leftarrow \mathsf{Decode}(f, e_1, e_2) \end{array}\right.\right] \leqslant negl(\lambda).$$

This robustness implies that if the Hamming distance between messages m_1 and m_2 is less than $2t$, the Decode function of Robust Set Encodings can fully recover the symmetric set difference $m_1 \triangle m_2$. The construction of the PPH scheme in this work is almost entirely derived from Robust Set Encodings. Thus, the leakage of this PPH scheme is consistent with that in the work [6].

$$\mathcal{L}_{[8]}(M_1, ..., M_n) := (\forall i, j \in [n], i \neq j, P(M_i, M_j), M_i \backslash M_j, M_j \backslash M_i).$$

Leakage of Holmgren et al. Scheme [4]. Before analyzing the leakage of this work, we first review its construction idea. The PPH schemes in this work is constructed based on Syndrome Decoding. For a code C that supports list-decoding of up to t errors, there exists a parity-check matrix $\boldsymbol{P} \in \mathbb{F}^{(n-k) \times n}$ such that for any error vector $\boldsymbol{e} \in \mathbb{F}^n$ with Hamming weight no more than t, $\boldsymbol{e}$ can be recovered from the syndrome $\boldsymbol{P} \cdot \boldsymbol{e}$.

Specifically, the hash function h generated by the sampling algorithm of the PPH scheme consists of a parity-check matrix $\boldsymbol{P}$ and a random matrix $\boldsymbol{A} \xleftarrow{\$} \mathbb{F}_2^{\lambda \times n}$. For messages $\boldsymbol{m_1}$ and $\boldsymbol{m_2}$, the hash computation algorithm of the PPH scheme generates hash digests as follows:

$$H_{PPH}(\boldsymbol{m_1}) = (\boldsymbol{P} \cdot \boldsymbol{m_1}, \boldsymbol{A} \cdot \boldsymbol{m_1}) \ , \ H_{PPH}(\boldsymbol{m_2}) = (\boldsymbol{P} \cdot \boldsymbol{m_2}, \boldsymbol{A} \cdot \boldsymbol{m_2}).$$

The evaluation algorithm of the PPH scheme obtains potential error vectors e' through $P \cdot m_1 - P \cdot m_2$ and the decoding algorithm of code C. If e' satisfies $A \cdot e' = A \cdot m_1 - A \cdot m_2$, this indicates that the Hamming distance between messages m_1 and m_2 is at most t.

It is not difficult to observe that when the Hamming distance between messages m_1 and m_2 is at most t, the e' returned by the successful decoding of $P \cdot m_1 - P \cdot m_2$ equals $m_1 - m_2$. Beyond knowing the decision result of the Hamming distance predicate, the adversary also obtains the subtraction of the two hash preimages.

The aforementioned Non-robust PPH is one of the schemes in work [4]. The RPPH from Homomorphic Collision Resistance and the RPPH from Standard Collision Resistance are improvements constructed based on the Non-robust PPH. All PPH constructions in this work rely on the error-correcting capability of codes. Thus, the leakage present in the Non-robust PPH also exists in other schemes within work [4].

$$\mathcal{L}_{[4]}(M_1, ..., M_n) := (\forall i, j \in [n], i \neq j, P(M_i, M_j), M_i - M_j).$$

The security of Relational Hash (RH) for Hamming Proximity in [3] relies on SXDH assumption. Since SXDH doesn't hold in symmetric pairing groups, we haven't found a way to adapt RH construction to symmetry. Furthermore, we think there exist fundamental differences between RH and PPH. So we do not include [3] in the comparison scope.

Below is a comparison of leakages in existing PPH schemes for the Hamming distance predicate. It turns out that our optimized scheme, which is built upon the construction from [6], exhibits the minimal leakage to date. Constructions based on bilinear groups and polynomials offer greater potential for richer functional relations (we provide homomorphism and multi-input predicates in Sect. 5 compared to those based on coding) (Table 1).

Table 1. Comparison with the leakage of existing PPH schemes for Hamming distance predicate.

PPH Scheme	Construction Method	Leakage Profile
Fleischhacker et al. [6]	Bilinear pairing	Partial preimages
Fleischhacker et al. [8]	Robust set encodings	Partial preimages
Holmgren et al. [4]	Linear error-correcting codes	Subtraction of preimages
Our scheme	Bilinear pairings	Subtraction of preimages

5 Our Privacy-Preserving HRPPH Scheme for Hamming Distance Predicate

In this section, we propose a new PPH construction based on polynomial techniques and formally proof the security of the scheme. After introducing the definition of leakage of Eval to PPH, we reduce the leakage of Eval of the PPH scheme in [6] from the leakage of partial preimages to the leakage of a functional relationship between preimages. The reduction of the leakage of Eval can effectively resist the hash one-way attack caused by the Preimage Leakage Problem. While reducing the leakage of Eval, this PPH scheme supports additive homomorphism and scalar multiplicative homomorphism.

5.1   Randomized Privacy-Preserving HRPPH Scheme

Compared to the PPH scheme in [6], the input form of this scheme is more general. The scheme in [6] is for predicate comparison between the sets $A = \{a_1, ..., a_n\}$ and $B = \{b_1, ..., b_n\}$. The scheme proposed in this paper supports predicate comparison between tuples $A = (a_1, ..., a_n)$ and $B = (b_1, ..., b_n)$. Compared to set inputs, tuple inputs provide the advantages of ordering and repeatability of elements.

For two n-tuples $A = (a_1, ..., a_n)$ and $B = (b_1, ..., b_n)$, let $a_i, b_i \in [N_i] \cup \{0\}$ for $i \in [1, n]$. We can define 0 elements in a tuple to indicate that this tuple is the empty at that position. So for tuples with different lengths can be made up 0 to symmetric tuples with the same length.

For a two-input Hamming distance predicate P_H,

$$P_H(A, B) = \begin{cases} 1, & D_H(A, B) \leq t \\ 0, & D_H(A, B) > t \end{cases},$$

the property-preserving hash function family $\mathcal{H} = \{h : X \to Y\}$ consists of the following three algorithms:

- $\underline{\mathsf{Sample}(1^\lambda) \to h}$

  The hash function h is randomly generated by the security parameter λ. Select bilinear group $\mathbb{G}_1, \mathbb{G}_2$ with group order p and bilinear map $e : \mathbb{G}_1 \times \mathbb{G}_2 \to \mathbb{G}_T$. Randomly select group generators $g_1 \xleftarrow{\$} \mathbb{G}_1, g_2 \xleftarrow{\$} \mathbb{G}_2$. Randomly choose $r \xleftarrow{\$} \mathbb{Z}_p \backslash \{[n] \cup \{0\}\}$ and generate two vectors

  $$\boldsymbol{R_1} := \left(g_1\ g_1^r\ ...\ g_1^{r^n}\right), \boldsymbol{R_2} := \left(g_2\ g_2^r\ ...\ g_2^{r^n}\right).$$

  Return $h := (\mathbb{G}_1, \mathbb{G}_2, \mathbb{G}_T, e, \boldsymbol{R_1}, \boldsymbol{R_2})$.

- $\underline{\mathsf{Hash}(h, A) \to h(A)}$

  Generate a probabilistic hash value $h(A)$ on the tuple $A = (a_1, ..., a_n)$ by hash function h. First randomly select $\beta_A \xleftarrow{\$} \mathbb{Z}_q^*$ and encode the tuple A as a polynomial

  $$f_A(x) = \sum_{i=0}^{n} c_{A,i} \cdot x^i \longleftarrow \mathsf{PIA}\big((0, \beta_A), (1, a_1), ..., (n, a_n)\big).$$

by the Polynomial Interpolation Algorithm(PIA). Then generate t points

$$\boldsymbol{X_A} := \left((n+1, f_A(n+1)), ..., (n+t, f_A(n+2t+1))\right).$$

Compute $Y_A := \prod_{i=0}^{n} (g_1^{r^i})^{c_{A,i}} = g_1^{f_A(r)}$.
Return $h(A) := (\boldsymbol{X_A}, Y_A)$.

- $\mathsf{Eval}(h, h(A), h(B)) \to 0/1$

For the hash values $h(A)$ and $h(B) := (\boldsymbol{X_B}, Y_B)$ generated by the hash function h for tuples A and $B := (b_1, ..., b_n)$, construct the public polynomial $f_P(x) = \prod_{i=1}^{n}(x-i) = \sum_{i=0}^{n} c_{P,i} \cdot x^i$, and generate t points $\boldsymbol{P} := (n+1, f_P(n+1)), ..., (n+t, f_P(n+2t+1))$. Compute $Y_P = \prod_{i=0}^{n} (g_1^{r^i})^{c_{P,i}} = g_1^{f_P(r)}$ for Eval.

For $i \in [1, 2t+1]$, compute

$$s_i := \frac{f_A(n+i) - f_B(n+i)}{f_P(n+i)}.$$

It can get two proportional polynomials $f_1(x)$ and $f_2(x)$

$$\left(f_1(x) = \sum_{i=0}^{n} c_{1,i} \cdot x^i \quad , \quad f_2(x) = \sum_{i=0}^{n} c_{2,i} \cdot x^i\right) \longleftarrow \mathsf{RPIA}\left((n+1, s_1), ..., (n+t, s_{2t+1})\right)$$

from Rational Polynomial Interpolation Algorithm(RPIA).
Return $e(\frac{Y_A}{Y_B}, \prod_{i=0}^{n} (g_2^{r^i})^{c_{2,i}}) \stackrel{?}{=} e(Y_P, \prod_{i=0}^{n} (g_2^{r^i})^{c_{1,i}})$.

Additively Homomorphic: $\forall M_1, M_2 \in \mathcal{M}$,

$$\begin{aligned}
h(M_1 + M_2) &= (\boldsymbol{X_{M_1+M_2}}, Y_{M_1+M_2}) \\
&= ((f_{M_1}(n+1) + f_{M_2}(n+1), ..., f_{M_1}(n+t) + f_{M_2}(n+t)), g_1^{f_{M_1}(r)+f_{M_2}(r)}) \\
&= (\boldsymbol{X_{M_1}} + \boldsymbol{X_{M_2}}, Y_{M_1} \cdot Y_{M_2}).
\end{aligned}$$

Scalar Multiplicatively Homomorphic: $\forall M \in \mathcal{M}$ and $\alpha \in \mathbb{Z}_q^*$,

$$\begin{aligned}
h(\alpha \cdot M) &= (\boldsymbol{X_{\alpha \cdot M}}, Y_{\alpha \cdot M}) \\
&= ((\alpha \cdot f_M(n+1), ..., \alpha \cdot f_M(n+t)), g_1^{\alpha \cdot f_M(r)}) \\
&= (\alpha \cdot \boldsymbol{X_M}, Y_M^\alpha).
\end{aligned}$$

Theorem 2. *The PPH is direct-access robust for the two-input Hamming distance predicate, if the n-SBDL assumption holds.*

Proof. Assume $\mathcal{A}$ is a arbitrary PPT adversary who can break direct-access robust of this PPH scheme with a non-negligible advantage. For the hash values

$h(A) := (\boldsymbol{X}_A, Y_A)$ and $h(B) := (\boldsymbol{X}_B, Y_B)$ generated by the hash function h for two tuples $A := (a_1, ..., a_n)$ and $B := (b_1, ..., b_n)$, we can have

$$\Pr[\mathsf{Eval}(h, h(A), h(B)) \neq P_H(A, B)]$$
$$= \Pr[\mathsf{Eval}(h, h(A), h(B)) = 0 \wedge P_H(A, B) = 1]$$
$$+ \Pr[\mathsf{Eval}(h, h(A), h(B)) = 1 \wedge P_H(A, B) = 0].$$

So the advantage of adversary $\mathcal{A}$ in breaking direct-access robust consists of the probabilities under **Case 1** and **Case 2**, respectively.

Case 1: $\mathsf{Eval}(h, h(A), h(B)) = 0 \wedge P_H(A, B) = 1$.

According to the predicate relation, we can get

$$P_H(A, B) = 1 \Leftrightarrow \|A - B\|_0 \leq t.$$

We define a set $\varPhi := \{i \in [n] \,|\, a_i - b_i = 0\}$ and have

$$\|A - B\|_0 \leq t \Leftrightarrow n \geq |\varPhi| \geq n - t.$$

For polynomials $f_A(x)$ and $f_B(x)$ encoded by tuples A and B, we have

$$\frac{f_A(x) - f_B(x)}{f_P(x)} = \frac{\prod\limits_{i \in \varPhi} (x - i) \cdot f_1'(x)}{\prod\limits_{i \in \varPhi} (x - i) \cdot \prod\limits_{i \in \{[n] - \varPhi\}} (x - i)} = \frac{f_1'(x)}{f_2'(x)}.$$

That means

$$n \geq |\varPhi| \geq n - t \Leftrightarrow \deg\left(\frac{f_1'(x)}{f_2'(x)}\right) \leq 2t + 1.$$

Since our hash computation introduces random values, the probability that two random values are equal is $\frac{1}{p}$. Therefore, $\deg(f_1'(x)) \leq t + 1$ holds with a probability of $1 - \frac{1}{p}$. According to RPIA, Eval recovers the polynomials $f_1(x)$ and $f_2(x)$ through $2t + 1$ points $(s_1, ..., s_{2t+1})$, where $f_1(x) = f_1'(x)$, $f_2(x) = f_2'(x)$. For all r, we have

$$\frac{f_A(r) - f_B(r)}{f_P(r)} = \frac{f_1(r)}{f_2(r)} = \frac{\sum_{i=0}^{n} c_{1,i} \cdot r^i}{\sum_{i=0}^{n} c_{2,i} \cdot r^i}.$$

Finally, we observe that

$$e\left(\frac{Y_A}{Y_B} \cdot g_1 \,, \prod_{i=0}^{n} (g_2^{r^i})^{c_{2,i}}\right) \stackrel{?}{=} e\left(Y_P \,, \prod_{i=0}^{n} (g_2^{r^i})^{c_{1,i}}\right)$$
$$\Leftrightarrow e\left(g_1^{f_A(r) - f_B(r)} \,, \prod_{i=0}^{n} (g_2^{r^i})^{c_{2,i}}\right) \stackrel{?}{=} e\left(g_1^{f_P(r)} \,, \prod_{i=0}^{n} (g_2^{r^i})^{c_{1,i}}\right).$$

So the above determination of the equation must pass and we proof that

$$\Pr[\mathsf{Eval}(h, h(A), h(B)) = 0 \,|\, P_H(A, B) = 1] = 0.$$

Case 2: $\mathsf{Eval}(h, h(A), h(B)) = 1 \wedge P_H(A, B) = 0$.

Assume $\mathcal{A}$ is an arbitrary PPT adversary who can break direct-access robust of this PPH scheme in **Case 2** with a non-negligible advantage. We can construct an adversary $\mathcal{B}$ to break the n-Strong Bilinear Discrete Logarithm (n-SBDL) hard problem.

After adversary $\mathcal{B}$ gets $(\mathbb{G}_1, \mathbb{G}_2, \mathbb{G}_T, e, p, \boldsymbol{R_1}, \boldsymbol{R_2})$ from the n-SBDL instance, $\mathcal{B}$ send $h := (\mathbb{G}_1, \mathbb{G}_2, \mathbb{G}_T, e, \boldsymbol{R_1}, \boldsymbol{R_2})$ to the adversary $\mathcal{A}$.

Adversary $\mathcal{A}$ outputs two tuples (A, B) and sends to adversary $\mathcal{B}$, if $P_H(A, B) = 1$, adversary $\mathcal{B}$ aborts. Otherwise randomly choose $\beta_1, \beta_2 \xleftarrow{\$} \mathbb{Z}_q^*$ and generate hash values $h(A), h(B)$. Assume that the two tuples (A, B) produced by $\mathcal{A}$ satisfies $\mathsf{Eval}(h, h(A), h(B)) = 1 \wedge P_H(A, B) = 0$, it means

$$P_H(A, B) = 0 \Leftrightarrow \deg(\frac{f_1'(x)}{f_2'(x)}) > 2t + 1,$$

Since the PPH evaluation $\mathsf{Eval}(h, h(A), h(B)) = 1$, the following transformation holds

$$e(\frac{Y_A}{Y_B} \, , \, \prod_{i=0}^{n}(g_2^{r^i})^{c_{2,i}}) = e(Y_P \, , \, \prod_{i=0}^{n}(g_2^{r^i})^{c_{1,i}})$$

$$\Leftrightarrow \frac{f_A(x) - f_B(x)}{f_P(x)} = \frac{f_1(x)}{f_2(x)}$$

$$\Leftrightarrow \frac{(f_A(x) - f_B(x)) \cdot f_2(x) - f_P(x) \cdot f_1(x)}{f_P(x) \cdot f_2(x)} = 0.$$

$\mathcal{B}$ computes the polynomials $f_1(x)$ and $f_2(x)$ through $2t + 1$ points $(s_1, ..., s_{2t+1})$ but $\frac{f_1(x)}{f_2(x)} \neq \frac{f_1'(x)}{f_2'(x)}$. Then, $\mathcal{B}$ constructs the polynomial $F(x) = (f_A(x) - f_B(x)) \cdot f_2(x) - f_P(x) \cdot f_1(x)$. By using the matrix eigenvalue decomposition mentioned in **3.1** to find the roots of the polynomial, $\mathcal{B}$ can obtain the set Φ_{root} containing all the roots of $F(x)$. We observe that r is one of the roots in the set Φ_{root}. For each $\phi_i \in \Phi_{root}$, $\mathcal{B}$ tests whether $g_1^{\phi_i} \stackrel{?}{=} g_1^r$ from $\boldsymbol{R_1}$. If $r \in [n]$, $\mathcal{B}$ aborts. Since r is randomly generated from the n-SBDL instance, $\Pr[\mathcal{B} \text{ aborts}] = \Pr[r \in [n]] = \frac{n}{p}$.

Now, we observe that the reduction $\mathcal{B}$ is successful.

$$\Pr[\mathsf{Eval}(h, h(A), h(B)) = 1 \wedge P(A, B) = 0] \leq (1 - \frac{n}{p}) \cdot \mathsf{Adv}_{\mathsf{nSBDL}}$$

Combining the conclusions of **Case 1** and **Case 2**, we conclude that

$$\Pr[\mathsf{Eval}(h, h(A), h(B)) \neq P_H(A, B)] \leq (1 - \frac{n}{p}) \cdot \mathsf{Adv}_{\mathsf{nSBDL}}.$$

Theorem 3. *Our PPH in for the predicate P_H is $\mathcal{L}$-Simulation with the leakage function $\mathcal{L}(M_1, ..., M_n) = (\forall i, j \in [n], i \neq j, P(M_i, M_j), M_i - M_j)$.*

Proof. We construct the PPH oracle in the ideal world. The construction of the simulator $\mathcal{S}$ is as follows.

For adversaries in both the real world and the ideal world, their views are consistent regarding the oracle response hash values evaluated by the Eval. The

---

1: **if** $\mathcal{Q} = \varnothing$ **then**
2:     $m_1^* \xleftarrow{\$} \mathcal{M}_1, ..., m_n^* \xleftarrow{\$} \mathcal{M}_n$;
3:     $M^* := (m_1^*, ..., m_n^*)$;
4:     $\beta_{M^*} \xleftarrow{\$} \mathbb{Z}_q^*$;
5:     $f_{M^*}(x) \longleftarrow \mathsf{PIA}((0, \beta_{M^*}), (1, m_1^*), ..., (n, m_n^*))$;
6:     $\boldsymbol{X}_{M^*} := (f_{M^*}(n+1), ..., f_{M^*}(n+2t+1))$;
7:     $Y_{M^*} = \prod_{i=0}^{n} (g_1^{r^i})^{c_{M^*,i}} = g_1^{f_{M^*}(r)}$;
8:     $h(M) = (\boldsymbol{X}_{M^*}, Y_{M^*})$;
9:     $\mathcal{Q} = \mathcal{Q} \cup \{h, h(M)\}$
10:     **return** $h(M)$.
11: **else**
12:     for query (h, M_i);
13:     $M_i^* = M^* - M + M_i = (m_1^* - m_1 + m_{1,i}, ..., m_n^* - m_n + m_{n,i})$;
14:     $\beta_{M_i} \xleftarrow{\$} \mathbb{Z}_q^*$;
15:     $f_{M_i^*}(x) \longleftarrow \mathsf{PIA}((0, \beta_{M_i^*}), (1, m_{1,i}^*), ..., (n, m_{n,i}^*))$;
16:     $\boldsymbol{X}_{M_i^*} := (f_{M_i^*}(n+1), ..., f_{M_i^*}(n+2t+1))$;
17:     $Y_{M_i^*} = \prod_{i=0}^{n} (g_1^{r^i})^{c_{M_i^*,i}} = g_1^{f_{M_i^*}(r)}$;
18:     $h(M_i) = (\boldsymbol{X}_{M_i^*}, Y_{M_i^*})$;
19:     $\mathcal{Q} = \mathcal{Q} \cup \{h, h(M_i)\}$
20:     **return** $h(M_i)$.
21: **end if**

---

query list $\mathcal{Q}$ in the ideal world is identically distributed to that in the real world. In the ideal world, the simulator's first oracle query is randomly selected from the message space, ensuring that the simulation in the ideal world is applicable to all possibility. Therefore, we construct an efficient simulator that proves our scheme achieves $\mathcal{L}$-Simulation.

5.2   Multi-input Privacy-Preserving HRPPH Scheme

Utilizing the homomorphic property of the PPH construction from Sect. 5.1, we can extend the two-input Hamming distance predicate of PPH to a multi-input Hamming distance predicate. The multi-input Hamming distance predicate is defined as follows.

$$P_H(A_1, ..., A_l) = \begin{cases} 1, & D_H(A_1, ..., A_l) \leq t \\ 0, & D_H(A_1, ..., A_l) > t \end{cases}$$

The specific construction of the multi-input PPH is as follows.

- $\mathsf{Sample}(1^\lambda) \rightarrow h$
  Same as two-input PPH scheme from Sect. 5.1.
- $\mathsf{Hash}(h, A) \rightarrow h(A)$
  Same as two-input PPH scheme from Sect. 5.1.

- $\mathsf{Eval}(h, h(A_1), ..., h(A_l)) \to 0/1$

  For l hash values $h(A_1) := (\boldsymbol{X}_{A_1}, Y_{A_1}), ..., h(A_l) := (\boldsymbol{X}_{A_l}, Y_{A_l})$ generated by the hash function h for tuples $A_1 := (a_{1,1}, ..., a_{1,n}), ..., A_l := (a_{l,1}, ..., a_{l,n})$, construct the public polynomial $f_P(x) = \prod_{i=1}^{n}(x - i) = \sum_{i=0}^{n} c_{P,i} \cdot x^i$, and generate $2t + 1$ points $\boldsymbol{P} := (n+1, f_P(n+1)), ..., (n+t, f_P(n+2t+1))$. Compute $Y_P = \prod_{i=0}^{n}(g_1^{r^i})^{c_{P,i}} = g_1^{f_P(r)}$ for Eval. Randomly select $k_1, ..., k_{l-1} \xleftarrow{\$} \mathbb{Z}_q^*$ For $i \in [1, 2t + 1]$, compute

$$s_i := \frac{k_1 \cdot (f_{A_1}(n+i) - f_{A_2}(n+i)) + ... + k_{l-1} \cdot (f_{A_1}(n+i) - f_{A_l}(n+i))}{f_P(n+i)}.$$

It can get two proportional polynomials $f_1(x)$ and $f_2(x)$

$$(f_1(x) = \sum_{i=0}^{n} c_{1,i} \cdot x^i \ , \ f_2(x) = \sum_{i=0}^{n} c_{2,i} \cdot x^i) \longleftarrow \mathsf{RPIA}((n+1, s_1), ..., (n+t, s_{2t+1}))$$

from Rational Polynomial Interpolation Algorithm(RPIA).

Return $e\big(\big(\prod_{i=1}^{l-1}(\frac{Y_{A_1}}{Y_{A_{i+1}}})^{k_i} \ , \ \prod_{i=0}^{n}(g_2^{r^i})^{c_{2,i}}\big) \stackrel{?}{=} e(Y_P \ , \ \prod_{i=0}^{n}(g_2^{r^i})^{c_{1,i}}).$

Theorem 4. *The PPH is direct-access robust for the multi-input Hamming distance predicate, if the n-SBDL assumption holds.*

Proof. Assume $\mathcal{A}$ is a arbitrary PPT adversary who can break direct-access robust of this PPH scheme with a non-negligible advantage. For the hash values $h(A_1) := (\boldsymbol{X}_{A_1}, Y_{A_1}), ..., h(A_l) := (\boldsymbol{X}_{A_l}, Y_{A_l})$ generated by the hash function h for two tuples $A_1 := (a_{1,1}, ..., a_{1,n}), ..., A_l := (a_{l,1}, ..., a_{l,n})$, we can have

$$\Pr[\mathsf{Eval}(h, h(A_1), ..., h(A_l)) \neq P_H(A_1, ..., A_l)]$$
$$= \Pr[\mathsf{Eval}(h, h(A_1), ..., h(A_l)) = 0 \wedge P_H(A_1, ..., A_l) = 1]$$
$$+ \Pr[\mathsf{Eval}(h, h(A_1), ..., h(A_l)) = 1 \wedge P_H(A_1, ..., A_l) = 0].$$

So the advantage of adversary $\mathcal{A}$ in breaking direct-access robust consists of the probabilities under **Case 1** and **Case 2**, respectively.

Case 1: $\mathsf{Eval}(h, h(A_1), ..., h(A_l)) = 0 \wedge P_H(A_1, ..., A_l) = 1.$

According to the predicate relation, we can get

$$P_H(A_1, ..., A_l) = 1 \Leftrightarrow \forall k_1, ..., k_{l-1}, \|k_1 \cdot (A_1 - A_2) + ... + k_{l-1} \cdot (A_1 - A_l)\|_0 \leq t.$$

For polynomials $f_{A_1}(x), ..., f_{A_l}(x)$ encoded by tuples $A_1, ..., A_l$, we have

$$\frac{k_1 \cdot (f_{A_1}(x) - f_{A_2}(x)) + ... + k_{l-1} \cdot (f_{A_1}(x) - f_{A_l}(x))}{f_P(x)} = \frac{\prod_{i \in \Phi}(x - i) \cdot f_1'(x)}{\prod_{i \in \Phi}(x - i) \cdot \prod_{i \in \{[n] - \Phi\}}(x - i)},$$

428   Y. Cao et al.

where the set Φ is defined as $\Phi := \{i \in [n] | a_{1,i} = a_{2,i} = ... = a_{l,i}\}$. The degree of the rational polynomials such that

$$\deg(\frac{k_1 \cdot (f_{A_1}(x) - f_{A_2}(x)) + ... + k_{l-1} \cdot (f_{A_1}(x) - f_{A_l}(x))}{f_P(x)}) \le 2t + 1.$$

Similar to the proof for the two-input Hamming distance predicate PPH, we can have

$$\Pr[\mathsf{Eval}(h, h(A), h(B)) = 0 | P_H(A, B) = 1] = 0.$$

Case 2: $\mathsf{Eval}(h, h(A_1), ..., h(A_l)) = 1 \wedge P_H(A_1, ..., A_l) = 0.$

Assume $\mathcal{A}$ is an arbitrary PPT adversary who can break direct-access robust of this PPH scheme in **Case 2** with a non-negligible advantage. We can construct an adversary $\mathcal{B}$ to break the (n-SBDL) hard problem.

After adversary $\mathcal{B}$ gets $(\mathbb{G}_1, \mathbb{G}_2, \mathbb{G}_T, e, p, \boldsymbol{R_1}, \boldsymbol{R_2})$ from the n-SBDL instance, $\mathcal{B}$ send $h := (\mathbb{G}_1, \mathbb{G}_2, \mathbb{G}_T, e, \boldsymbol{R_1}, \boldsymbol{R_2})$ to the adversary $\mathcal{A}$.

Adversary $\mathcal{A}$ outputs l tuples $A_1, ..., A_l$ and sends to adversary $\mathcal{B}$, if $P_H(A_1, ..., A_l) = 1$, adversary $\mathcal{B}$ aborts. Otherwise randomly choose $\beta_1, ..., \beta_l \xleftarrow{\$} \mathbb{Z}_q^*$ and generate hash values $h(A_1), ..., h(A_l)$. Assume that the two tuples (A, B) produced by $\mathcal{A}$ satisfies $\mathsf{Eval}(h, h(A_1), ..., h(A_l)) = 1 \wedge P_H(A_1, ..., A_l) = 0.$

For $k_1, ..., k_{l-1} \xleftarrow{\$} \mathbb{Z}_q^*$, it holds that

$$\Pr[k_i \cdot (a_1 - a_2) + ... + k_{l-1} \cdot (a_1 - a_l) | \exists i, j \in [n], i \ne j, a_i \ne a_j] \le \frac{1}{q}.$$

So, because of $P_H(A_1, ..., A_l) = 0$, it holds that

$$\Pr[\deg(\frac{k_1 \cdot (f_{A_1}(x) - f_{A_2}(x)) + ... + k_{l-1} \cdot (f_{A_1}(x) - f_{A_l}(x))}{f_P(x)}) > 2t + 1] > 1 - \frac{1}{q}.$$

Then $\frac{f_1(x)}{f_2(x)} \ne \frac{f_1'(x)}{f_2'(x)}$ holds with probability $1 - \frac{1}{q}$.

Since the PPH evaluation $\mathsf{Eval}(h, h(A_1), ..., h(A_l)) = 1$, the following transformation holds

$$e((\prod_{i=1}^{l-1}(\frac{Y_{A_1}}{Y_{A_{i+1}}})^{k_i} , \prod_{i=0}^{n}(g_2^{r^i})^{c_{2,i}}) = e(Y_P , \prod_{i=0}^{n}(g_2^{r^i})^{c_{1,i}})$$

$$\Leftrightarrow \frac{k_1 \cdot (f_{A_1}(x) - f_{A_2}(x)) + ... + k_{l-1} \cdot (f_{A_1}(x) - f_{A_l}(x))}{f_P(x)} = \frac{f_1(x)}{f_2(x)}$$

$$\Leftrightarrow \frac{(k_1 \cdot (f_{A_1}(x) - f_{A_2}(x)) + ... + k_{l-1} \cdot (f_{A_1}(x) - f_{A_l}(x))) \cdot f_2(x) - f_P(x) \cdot f_1(x)}{f_P(x) \cdot f_2(x)} = 0.$$

Finally, $\mathcal{B}$ constructs the polynomial $F(x) = (k_1 \cdot (f_{A_1}(x) - f_{A_2}(x)) + ... + k_{l-1} \cdot (f_{A_1}(x) - f_{A_l}(x))) \cdot f_2(x) - f_P(x) \cdot f_1(x)$ and successfully extract r to break the n-SBDL with probability $(1 - \frac{n}{q})(1 - \frac{1}{q})$. It is similar to the proof for the two-input Hamming distance predicate PPH.

$$\Pr[\mathsf{Eval}(h, h(A_1), ..., h(A_l)) = 1 \wedge P_H(A_1, ..., A_l) = 0] \le (1 - \frac{n}{p}) \cdot \mathsf{Adv_{nSBDL}}$$

Combining the conclusions of **Case 1** and **Case 2**, we conclude that

$$\Pr[\mathsf{Eval}(h, h(A_1), ..., h(A_l)) \neq P_H(A_1, ..., A_l)] \leq (1 - \frac{n}{p})(1 - \frac{1}{q}) \cdot \mathsf{Adv}_{\mathsf{nSBDL}}.$$

6 Conclusion

In this work, we focused on the privacy security of PPH, systematically conducting research on its leakage property definition, existing scheme analysis, and improved scheme construction. First, we proposed a novel security notion for PPH, termed $\mathcal{L}$-Simulation. This notion introduces the leakage profile to quantitatively assess the preimage information leakage incurred by the public evaluation algorithm. Second, grounded in the formal definition of the $\mathcal{L}$-Simulation security model, we performed a rigorous leakage bound analysis on all existing PPH schemes for Hamming distance predicate. Our analysis leads to a negative finding: two schemes [6] and [8] do not satisfy adaptive-type $\mathcal{L}$-Simulation security, rendering them vulnerable to partial preimage leakage. Finally, we presented a new HRPPH for Hamming distance predicate. Notably, our proposed scheme achieves lower leakage while supporting both additive homomorphism and scalar multiplicative homomorphism, which not only enhances the security but also expands its applicability to a broader range of cryptographic scenarios requiring homomorphic operations.

Acknowledgments. This work was supported by the National Key Research and Development Program of China (No. 2022YFB3102400), the National Natural Science Foundation of China (Nos. U23A20302, 62325209, 62272350, 62122092, 62202485), the Science and Technology Innovation Program of Hunan Province (No. 2025RC1040), Young Elite Scientists Sponsorship Program by China Association for Science and Technology (No. YESS20230028), Foundation of National State Key Laboratory (No. 2024-KJWPDL-13).

References

1. Xie, H., Guo, Y., Jia, X.: A privacy-preserving online ride-hailing system without involving a third trusted server. IEEE Trans. Inf. Forensics Secur. **16**, 3068–3081 (2021)
2. Jiang, M., Liu, S., Han, S., Gu, D.: Biometric-based two-factor authentication scheme under database leakage. Theoret. Comput. Sci. **1000**, 114552 (2024)
3. Mandal, A., Roy, A.: Relational hash: probabilistic hash for verifying relations, secure against forgery and more. In: Gennaro, R., Robshaw, M. (eds.) CRYPTO 2015. LNCS, vol. 9215, pp. 518–537. Springer, Heidelberg (2015). https://doi.org/10.1007/978-3-662-47989-6_25
4. Holmgren, J., Liu, M., Tyner, L., Wichs, D.: Nearly optimal property preserving hashing. In: Annual International Cryptology Conference, pp. 473–502. Springer (2022)

5. Liu, K., Li, X., Takagi, T.: Robust property-preserving hash meets homomorphism. In: International Conference on Information Security, pp. 537–556. Springer (2023)

6. Fleischhacker, N., Simkin, M.: Robust property-preserving hash functions for hamming distance and more. In: Canteaut, A., Standaert, F.-X. (eds.) EUROCRYPT 2021. LNCS, vol. 12698, pp. 311–337. Springer, Cham (2021). https://doi.org/10.1007/978-3-030-77883-5_11

7. Boyle, E., LaVigne, R., Vaikuntanathan, V.: Adversarially robust property preserving hash functions. Cryptology ePrint Archive (2018)

8. Fleischhacker, N., Larsen, K.G., Simkin, M.: Property-preserving hash functions for hamming distance from standard assumptions. In: Annual International Conference on the Theory and Applications of Cryptographic Techniques, pp. 764–781. Springer (2022)

9. Cash, D., Liu, F.-H., O'Neill, A., Zhandry, M., Zhang, C.: Parameter-hiding order revealing encryption. In: Peyrin, T., Galbraith, S. (eds.) ASIACRYPT 2018. LNCS, vol. 11272, pp. 181–210. Springer, Cham (2018). https://doi.org/10.1007/978-3-030-03326-2_7

10. Peng, C., Chen, R., Wang, Y., He, D., Huang, X.: Parameter-hiding order-revealing encryption without pairings. In: IACR International Conference on Public-Key Cryptography, pp. 227–256. Springer (2024)

11. Acar, A., Aksu, H., Uluagac, A.S., Conti, M.: A survey on homomorphic encryption schemes: theory and implementation. ACM Comput. Surv. (CSUR) **51**(4), 1–35 (2018)

12. Chase, M., Kamara, S.: Structured encryption and controlled disclosure. In: Abe, M. (ed.) ASIACRYPT 2010. LNCS, vol. 6477, pp. 577–594. Springer, Heidelberg (2010). https://doi.org/10.1007/978-3-642-17373-8_33

13. Boneh, D., Sahai, A., Waters, B.: Functional encryption: definitions and challenges. In: Ishai, Y. (ed.) TCC 2011. LNCS, vol. 6597, pp. 253–273. Springer, Heidelberg (2011). https://doi.org/10.1007/978-3-642-19571-6_16

14. Chor, B., Kushilevitz, E., Goldreich, O., Sudan, M.: Private information retrieval. J. ACM (JACM) **45**(6), 965–981 (1998)

15. Bogdanov, D., Laur, S., Willemson, J.: Sharemind: a framework for fast privacy-preserving computations. In: Jajodia, S., Lopez, J. (eds.) ESORICS 2008. LNCS, vol. 5283, pp. 192–206. Springer, Heidelberg (2008). https://doi.org/10.1007/978-3-540-88313-5_13

16. Carter, J.L., Wegman, M.N.: Universal classes of hash functions. In: Proceedings of the Ninth Annual ACM Symposium on Theory of Computing, pp. 106–112 (1977)

17. Jurado, M., Palamidessi, C., Smith, G.: A formal information-theoretic leakage analysis of order-revealing encryption. In: 2021 IEEE 34th Computer Security Foundations Symposium (CSF), pp. 1–16. IEEE (2021)

18. Turati, F., Cotrini, C., Kubicek, K., Basin, D.: Locality-sensitive hashing does not guarantee privacy! attacks on Google's floc and the minhash hierarchy system. arXiv preprint arXiv:2302.13635 (2023)

19. Kockan, C., et al.: Sketching algorithms for genomic data analysis and querying in a secure enclave. Nat. Methods **17**(3), 295–301 (2020)

20. Datar, M., Immorlica, N., Indyk, P., Mirrokni, V.S.: Locality-sensitive hashing scheme based on p-stable distributions. In: Proceedings of the Twentieth Annual Symposium on Computational Geometry, pp. 253–262 (2004)

21. Cash, D., Grubbs, P., Perry, J., Ristenpart, T.: Leakage-abuse attacks against searchable encryption. In: Proceedings of the 22nd ACM SIGSAC Conference on Computer and Communications Security, pp. 668–679 (2015)

Anonymity of X-Wing and Its Variants

Jiawei Bao$^{(\boxtimes)}$ and Jiaxin Pan

University of Kassel, Kassel, Germany
`{jiawei.bao,jiaxin.pan}@uni-kassel.de`

Abstract. X-Wing (Barbosa et al., CiC Volume 1, Issue 1) is a hybrid key encapsulation mechanism (KEM) currently considered for standardization by IETF and deployed by major companies such as Google to ensure a secure transition to post-quantum cryptography. It combines a classical X25519 KEM with the post-quantum ML-KEM-768.

In this paper, we propose the first analysis of the anonymity of X-Wing. We are interested in tight and memory-tight reductions that offer stronger security guarantees. We first establish in the standard model that for any IND-CCA secure KEM, weak anonymity implies full anonymity, and our reduction is tight not only in success probability and time but also in memory consumption. We then prove in the random oracle model that X-Wing achieves weak anonymity if both X25519 and ML-KEM-768 are weakly anonymous. The former can even be proven without a hardness assumption.

Our proof on the weak anonymity of X-Wing does not preserve the memory-tightness of the underlying KEMs. To improve it, we propose a slight variant of X-Wing that preserves memory-tightness. Finally, we improve the existing IND-CCA proof of the original X-Wing by Barbosa et al. using our new memory-tight analysis.

Keywords: Anonymity · hybrid key encapsulation mechanism · post-quantum cryptography · memory tightness

1 Introduction

Key encapsulation mechanisms (KEMs) are arguably the most important primitive in public-key cryptography. They can be used to construct public-key encryption schemes [29], authenticated key exchange protocols (AKEs) [28,36], password-based key exchange protocols [7,37], and many more. Hence, their security is crucial.

HYBRID KEM. The development of large-scale quantum computers poses a fundamental threat to classical KEM or public-key cryptography in general. This is because schemes based on RSA and (elliptic-curve) Diffie–Hellman can be efficiently broken by Shor's algorithm with a capable quantum computer. To address this risk, post-quantum cryptography (PQC) is constructing new algorithms [31,39] based on problems (such as lattice-based ones) that are assumed to be hard even to a quantum adversary.

© International Association for Cryptologic Research 2026
S. Bai and E. Persichetti (Eds.): PKC 2026, LNCS 16554, pp. 431–460, 2026.
https://doi.org/10.1007/978-3-032-26740-5_14

However, relying solely on PQC schemes in critical systems is rather risky, since they are new and come with a lack of extensive cryptanalysis or mature implementation. For instance, several previous implementations of Kyber [39] (which was recently used to derive the ML-KEM standard [34]) have been found to have timing vulnerabilities [12] and FPGA bitstream attacks [33]. Hence, the hybrid approach is recommended by many national security agencies, such as those from 18 EU member states[1] and the UK[2].

We are interested in hybrid KEMs in this paper. A hybrid KEM is essentially combining a classically deployed KEM with a post-quantum one in such a way that the combination is at least as secure as the deployed one, and the deployed KEM (e.g. the ElGamal KEM) has a long history of cryptanalysis and mature implementations. This design mitigates the uncertain security risks surrounding newly standardized PQC algorithms and ensures a smooth and secure transition toward quantum-safe cryptography in real-world applications such as TLS, SSH, and IKE. X-Wing [5] is among the well-known hybrid KEMs, which combines the ElGamal KEM on Curve25519 [30] and ML-KEM. It is very plausible that IETF will standardize X-Wing [16], and major companies like Google have already integrated X-Wing into their products[3]. This shows the pragmatic value of X-Wing during the post-quantum transitional period. Hence, it motivates us to better understand the security of X-Wing.

SECURITY OF X-WING. Standard security notion of a KEM is indistinguishability against chosen-ciphertext attacks (IND-CCA), where an adversary is asked to distinguish an honestly encapsulated key from random, given the ability to ask for decryption on adaptively chosen ciphertexts. Beyond IND-CCA, anonymity (or key privacy) is another important security guarantee for KEM. In particular, it is required when it is used to construct password-based key exchange protocols [7,37]. Other well-known applications of anonymous KEM (or anonymous PKE) schemes include the deployed Zcash system [11], anonymous credential systems [14], auction protocols [38], and anonymous key exchange protocols [35].

We are interested in the anonymity of X-Wing, since it will lead to new hybrid constructions of the aforementioned applications and safeguard the post-quantum transition. In an anonymous KEM, we require that the ciphertexts and the encapsulated keys leak no information about the corresponding public key. A weaker form of anonymity requires only the ciphertexts are (computationally) independent of the public key. As in the IND security, we allow an anonymity adversary to perform CCA attacks. We denote the (weak) anonymity against CCA as ANO-CCA and wANO-CCA respectively. Our goal is to achieve ANO-CCA.

---

[1] https://www.bsi.bund.de/SharedDocs/Downloads/EN/BSI/Crypto/PQC-joint-statement.pdf.

[2] https://www.ncsc.gov.uk/whitepaper/next-steps-preparing-for-post-quantum-cryptography#section_5.

[3] https://bughunters.google.com/blog/5266882047639552/why-hybrid-deployments-are-key-to-secure-pqc-migration.

1.1   Our Contributions

This work has two major contributions, formally proving the anonymity of X-Wing in the random oracle model and proposing a slight variant of X-Wing whose security proof preserves not only (probability-time) tightness of the underlying KEMs, but also their memory-tightness [3]. Our results show that X-Wing (or our new variant) can serve as a drop-in replacement for the previously mentioned anonymous-KEM-based protocol, enabling a hybrid implementation that ensures a secure PQC transition. We detail our contributions here.

INTERLUDE: TIGHT SECURITY AND MEMORY TIGHTNESS. Reductions with tightness on success probability, running time, and memory are preferable, since they provide stronger security guarantees. A classical understanding of tight security [8–10] is that a reduction $\mathcal{R}$ between a cryptographic problem P and a scheme S preserves the *success probability* and *running time* of the adversary $\mathcal{A}$ against S. Concretely, imagine that $\mathcal{A}$ breaks S with probability $\varepsilon_{\mathcal{A}}$ and running time $t_{\mathcal{A}}$ and using $\mathcal{A}$, $\mathcal{R}$ can break P with probability $\varepsilon_{\mathcal{R}}$ and running time $t_{\mathcal{R}}$. We say the reduction $\mathcal{R}$ is tight if $t_{\mathcal{A}} \approx t_{\mathcal{R}}$ and $\varepsilon_{\mathcal{A}} \leq L \cdot \varepsilon_{\mathcal{R}}$ with a small constant L (e.g., $L = 1$ or 2). With a tight reduction, a practitioner does not need to adjust the parameters of the underlying instance of P, giving us more efficient implementation.

Recently, it has been discovered that some cryptographic problems are memory-sensitive, namely, with more memory these problems become easier to solve. The lattice problem underlying the ML-KEM-768 is one of such problems [2,6,15,25,26]. Hence, a reduction that consumes large memory does not make much sense, since in this case the underlying memory-sensitive problem may not be hard. In our analysis of X-Wing we also focus on the memory consumption of our reductions and in many cases we can construct memory-tight reductions. The study of memory-tight reductions was initiated by Auerbach et al. [3], and a reduction is memory-tight if $m_{\mathcal{R}} \approx m_{\mathcal{A}}$ where $m_{\mathcal{A}}$ and $m_{\mathcal{R}}$ are the amount of memory used by $\mathcal{A}$ and $\mathcal{R}$. We refer [3] for more discussion on the motivation of memory-tightness.

FORMAL ANALYSIS OF X-WING. We formally prove the anonymity of X-Wing. We first establish a general lemma that, for any IND-CCA secure KEM, its wANO-CCA implies ANO-CCA. This lemma is proven in the standard model. After that, we consider the anonymity of X-Wing. More precisely, we prove that

(1) If the ML-KEM-768 is IND-CCA secure, then the ANO-CCA security of X-Wing is implied by the wANO-CCA and WCPR-CCA security of ML-KEM-768 and wANO-PCA security of X25519. Here 'WCPR' stands for weak chosen-preimage resistance, which states that if we use a different secret key to decapsulate a challenge ciphertext then we get a pseudorandom outcome. And 'PCA' stands for plaintext-checking attacks, where adversaries can submit plaintext-ciphertext pairs to check if they correspond to each other. The security proof here is *memory-tight.*

(2) If the ML-KEM-768 is not IND-CCA secure, then the wANO-CCA security of X-Wing is implied by the wANO-PCA security of both X25519 and ML-KEM-768. By the general lemma, this yields ANO-CCA security of X-Wing.

In fact, this second implication achieves a stronger wANO-CCA security of X-Wing, namely, an anonymity adversary is allowed to decapsulate a challenge ciphertext, but it is not memory-tight.

Both implications are proven in the random oracle model. Our proofs require both X25519 and ML-KEM-768 to be weakly anonymous, otherwise the anonymity of X-Wing will be trivially broken. Previously, a similar observation was made in [24], but we relax it to weak anonymity.

MEMORY-TIGHT ANONYMOUS KEM. We now turn to the discussion of the (memory) tightness of our reductions. The generic "wANO-CCA-to-ANO-CCA" implication is tight in terms of success probability, time and memory. However, the existing IND-CCA security proof of X-Wing is not memory-tight [5]. In addition, we prove the IND-CCA security of X-Wing with a memory-tight reduction in the full version [4], which improves the work of Barbosa [5]. But the reduction in the above Item (2) is not memory-tight.

Motivated by this, we make one modification to X-Wing, namely, we include ciphertexts and keys from both X25519 and ML-KEM-768 into the hash function that derives the final encapsulation key. By doing so, we can simulate the random oracle without keeping its history, and thus it yields a memory-tight proof.

OPEN PROBLEMS. We leave proving the security of X-Wing in the quantum random oracle model (QROM) as an interesting open problem. This seems technically challenging, since our anonymity proof must abort if the adversary queries the random oracle at the challenge key, which the proof does not know. Even in the classical random oracle model, it is already non-trivial. In the QROM, one cannot apply standard reprogramming techniques, such as the One-Way-to-Hiding lemma [40], to reprogram the challenge point without knowledge of its position.

1.2 Related Work

Very recently, Günther et al.[24] proposed a new KEM combiner that can achieve strong pseudorandomness under chosen-ciphertext attacks (SPR-CCA) (as defined in [41]), which implies ANO-CCA. Interestingly, the anonymity of their combiner does not requires both their underlying KEMs to be anonymous, but rather the outer one to have statistically uniform ciphertexts (which can be satisfied by the ElGamal KEM). This improves over X-Wing. Moreover, we note that the underlying KEMs have to be SPR-CCA secure in [24], which is stronger than the weak anonymity required in our proofs, since the SPR-CCA security additional allows adversaries to possess the encapsulated key to the challenge ciphertext. To achieve the combination, their construction relies on less standard symmetric primitives, including a length-preserving symmetric encryption scheme, a split-key PRF, and a PRG.

Grubbs et al. [23] initiated the analysis of post-quantum KEM (excluding hybrid KEMs). They proved the anonymity of Fujisaki-Okamato (FO) transformations and its variants [18–20,27]. They mainly focused on the case of implicit rejection and show the ANO-CCA security of $\mathsf{FO}^{\not\perp}$ in the QROM from the weak anonymity, the one-wayness and the strong collision freeness (SCFR-CPA) of the underlying PKE. Compared with their work, our "wANO-to-ANO" lemma (cf. Lemma 1) is more general. In addition, they analyzed the anonymity of three specific NIST PQC Candidates, including Classic McEliece (CM) [1], proto-Saber [17] and FrodoKEM [32].

2   Preliminaries

For a (finite) set X, we write $x \xleftarrow{\$} X$ for sampling an element x uniformly at random from X. All sets are initialized to the empty set unless stated otherwise. We assume that all algorithms and adversaries in this paper are probabilistic; otherwise, we will state it. For an algorithm, we write $y \leftarrow \mathcal{A}(x_1, \ldots, x_n)$ when $\mathcal{A}$ outputs y on input $(x_1, \ldots, x_n)$. We may write the randomness r explicitly as $y := \mathcal{A}(x_1, \ldots, x_n; r)$. If an algorithm $\mathcal{A}$ has access to an oracle $\%_0$, we write $\mathcal{A}^{\%_0}$. We follow the notations of reduced complexity as in [21] to analyze the time and memory complexity of algorithms, namely, if $\mathcal{A}^{\%_0}$ is an adversary that calls another adversary $\hat{\mathcal{A}}$ and provides $\hat{\mathcal{A}}$ with oracle access to $\%_0$ and H (which is either a pseudo-random function or a random function), then $\mathbf{Time}^*(\mathcal{A}) := \mathbf{Time}(\hat{\mathcal{A}})$ and $\mathbf{Mem}^*(\mathcal{A}) := \mathbf{Mem}(\hat{\mathcal{A}})$. Essentially, the reduced complexity is reasonable, since it excludes the cost for simulating a hash function. Also, the oracle $\%_0$ is external to $\mathcal{A}$, and thus its complexity does not count towards $\mathcal{A}$. We use $\mathcal{O}$ to denote asymptotic upper bounds, indicating growth up to a constant factor.

2.1   Key Encapsulation Mechanism

Let par be system parameters. A key encapsulation mechanism KEM consists of three algorithms (KeyGen, Encap, Decap) defined as follows:

- The key generation algorithm KeyGen is an algorithm that on input par outputs a public and secret key pair (pk, sk).
- The encapsulation algorithm Encap is an algorithm that on input of a public key pk outputs a pair (k, c), where k is the encapsulated key and c is the encapsulation ciphertext.
- The decapsulation algorithm Decap is a deterministic algorithm that on input of a secret key sk and a ciphertext c outputs a key k or a special symbol $\perp \notin \mathcal{M}$ indicating that c is invalid.

Definition 1 (KEM Correctness). *Let* KEM $=$ (KeyGen, Encap, Decap) *be a key encapsulation mechanism. We say that* KEM *is δ-correct if*

$$\Pr\left[\mathsf{Decap}(sk, c) \neq k \;\middle|\; \begin{array}{l}(pk,sk)\leftarrow\mathsf{KeyGen}\\(k,c)\leftarrow\mathsf{Encap}(pk)\end{array}\right] \leq \delta.$$

Our security analysis also requires the ciphertext second preimage resistance [5] (C2PRI) of a KEM that is defined as follows.

Definition 2 (C2PRI). *The C2PRI advantage of an adversary $\mathcal{A}$ against* KEM $=$ (KeyGen, Encap, Decap) *is defined as*

$$\mathsf{Adv}_{\mathsf{KEM}}^{\mathsf{C2PRI}}(\mathcal{A}) = \Pr\left[\mathsf{Decap}(sk, c) = k^* \wedge c \neq c^* \;\middle|\; \begin{array}{l} (pk,sk) \leftarrow \mathsf{KeyGen}(par) \\ (k^*,c^*) \leftarrow \mathsf{Encap}(pk) \\ c \leftarrow \mathcal{A}(pk,sk,k^*,c^*) \end{array}\right].$$

Definition 3 (Collision of the public keys). *The collision advantage of the public keys of* KEM $=$ (KeyGen, Encap, Decap) *is defined as*

$$\mathsf{Adv}_{\mathsf{KEM}}^{\mathsf{COLL}} = \Pr\left[pk_0 = pk_1 \;\middle|\; \begin{array}{l} (pk_0,sk_0) \leftarrow \mathsf{KeyGen}(par) \\ (pk_1,sk_1) \leftarrow \mathsf{KeyGen}(par) \end{array}\right].$$

We define seven different security notions in Definition 4 that are needed here: ANO and wANO stand for (weak) anonymity respectively, WCPR for weak chosen-preimage resistance, IND for indistinguishability, OW for one-wayness, PCA for plaintext-checking attacks, and CCA for chosen-ciphertext attacks. CCA* is a stronger form of CCA, where an adversary $\mathcal{A}$ can query decapsulation on the challenge ciphertext c^*. WCPR-CCA, wANO-CCA*, and wANO-PCA are new notions defined in this paper as intermediate notions for our (later) security analysis. The remaining ones are taken from [23].

Definition 4 (Security notions for KEM). *For* KEM $=$ (KeyGen, Encap, Decap), *let $\mathcal{A}$ be an adversary against* KEM; *we define a set of security notions using the games in Fig. 1. For* X-Y $\in$ {ANO-CCA, wANO-PCA, wANO-CCA, wANO-CCA*, WCPR-CCA, IND-CCA}, *the advantage of $\mathcal{A}$ is defined as*

$$\mathsf{Adv}_{\mathsf{KEM}}^{\mathsf{X\text{-}Y}}(\mathcal{A}) = \left|\Pr[\mathsf{X\text{-}Y}_{\mathsf{KEM}}^{\mathcal{A}} \Rightarrow 1] - 1/2\right|. \tag{1}$$

For X-Y $\in$ {OW-PCA}, *we define the advantage of $\mathcal{A}$ as*

$$\mathsf{Adv}_{\mathsf{KEM}}^{\mathsf{X\text{-}Y}}(\mathcal{A}) = \Pr[\mathsf{X\text{-}Y}_{\mathsf{KEM}}^{\mathcal{A}} \Rightarrow 1]. \tag{2}$$

We say KEM *is* X-Y *secure if for any efficient adversary $\mathcal{A}$,* $\mathsf{Adv}_{\mathsf{KEM}}^{\mathsf{X\text{-}Y}}(\mathcal{A})$ *is negligible.*

2.2 Public-Key Encryption

A public-key encryption scheme PKE consists of three algorithms (Gen, Enc, Dec) defined as follows:

- The key generation algorithm Gen is an algorithm that on input par outputs a public and secret key pair (pk, sk).
- The encryption algorithm Enc is an algorithm that on input of a public key pk and a message m from the message space $\mathcal{M}$ outputs a ciphertext c.
- The decryption algorithm Dec is a deterministic algorithm that on input of a secret key sk and a ciphertext c outputs a message m or a special symbol $\perp \notin \mathcal{M}$ indicating that c is invalid.

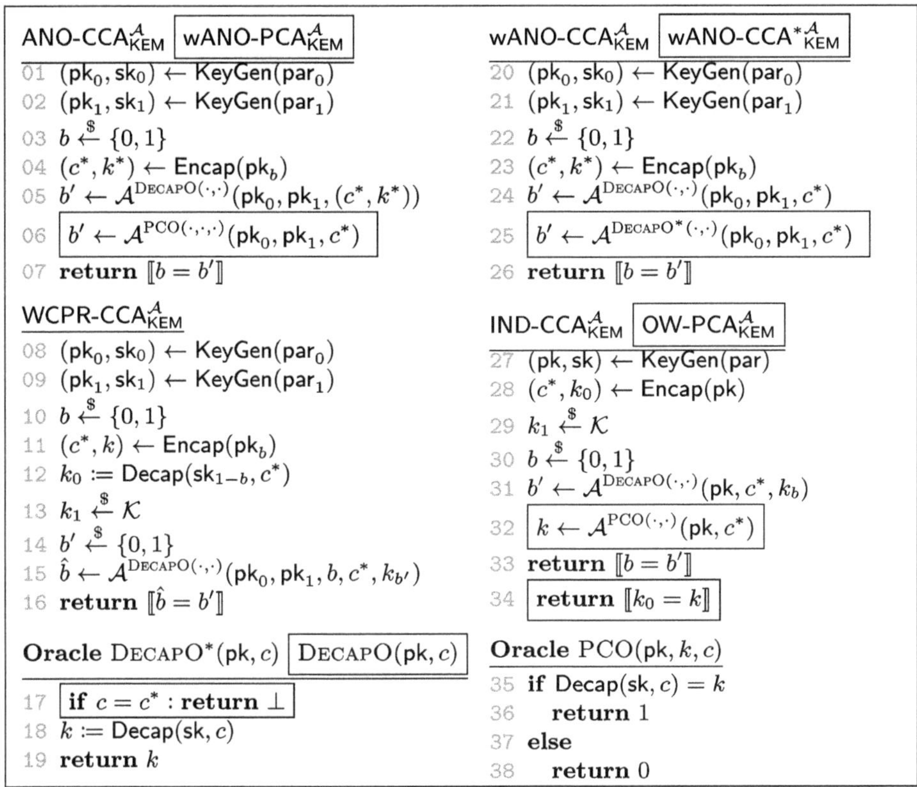

Fig. 1. Security games for KEM. Boxed codes are only executed in the corresponding games. Without loss of generality, here we assume that $\mathcal{A}$ is allowed to query the oracles only with the public key pk in games IND-CCA and OW-PCA, and with pk_0 or pk_1 in the other games. The sk in the oracles denotes the corresponding secret key generated together with the input public key pk.

Definition 5 (PKE Correctness [27]). *Let* $\mathsf{PKE} = (\mathsf{Gen}, \mathsf{Enc}, \mathsf{Dec})$ *be a public-key encryption scheme. We say that* PKE *is δ-correct if*

$$\mathbb{E}\left[\max_{m \in \mathcal{M}} \Pr[\mathsf{Dec}(sk, c) \neq m \mid c \leftarrow \mathsf{Enc}(pk, m)] \right] \leq \delta,$$

where the expectation is taken over the distribution over all the key pairs $(pk, sk) \leftarrow \mathsf{Gen}(par)$.

Definition 6 (PKE γ-spreadness [19]). *Let* $\mathsf{PKE} = (\mathsf{Gen}, \mathsf{Enc}, \mathsf{Dec})$ *be a public-key encryption scheme. We say that* PKE *is γ-spread if for any key pair* (pk, sk), *message* $m \in \mathcal{M}$, *and ciphertext* $c \in \mathcal{C}$,

$$\Pr[c = \mathsf{Enc}(pk, m; r) \mid r \xleftarrow{\$} \mathcal{R}] \leq 2^{-\gamma}.$$

We define seven different security notions in Definition 7 that are needed here: ANO and wANO stand for (weak) anonymity, WCFR weak collision freeness, OW one-wayness, PCA plaintext-checking attacks, CPA chosen-plaintext attacks, and CCA chosen-ciphertext attacks. All these notions are taken from [23].

Definition 7 (Security notions for PKE). *For* PKE $=$ (Gen, Enc, Dec), *let* $\mathcal{A}$ *be an adversary against* PKE; *we define a set of security notions using the games in Fig. 2. For* X-Y $\in$ {ANO-CCA, ANO-CPA, wANO-CCA, wANO-CPA}, *the advantage of* $\mathcal{A}$ *is defined as*

$$\mathsf{Adv}^{\mathsf{X\text{-}Y}}_{\mathsf{PKE}}(\mathcal{A}) = \left| \Pr[\mathsf{X\text{-}Y}^{\mathcal{A}}_{\mathsf{PKE}} \Rightarrow 1] - 1/2 \right|. \tag{3}$$

For X-Y $\in$ {WCFR-CCA, WCFR-CPA, OW-CPA}, *we define the advantage of* $\mathcal{A}$ *as*

$$\mathsf{Adv}^{\mathsf{X\text{-}Y}}_{\mathsf{PKE}}(\mathcal{A}) = \Pr[\mathsf{X\text{-}Y}^{\mathcal{A}}_{\mathsf{PKE}} \Rightarrow 1]. \tag{4}$$

We say PKE *is* X-Y *secure if for any efficient adversary* $\mathcal{A}$, $\mathsf{Adv}^{\mathsf{X\text{-}Y}}_{\mathsf{PKE}}(\mathcal{A})$ *is negligible.*

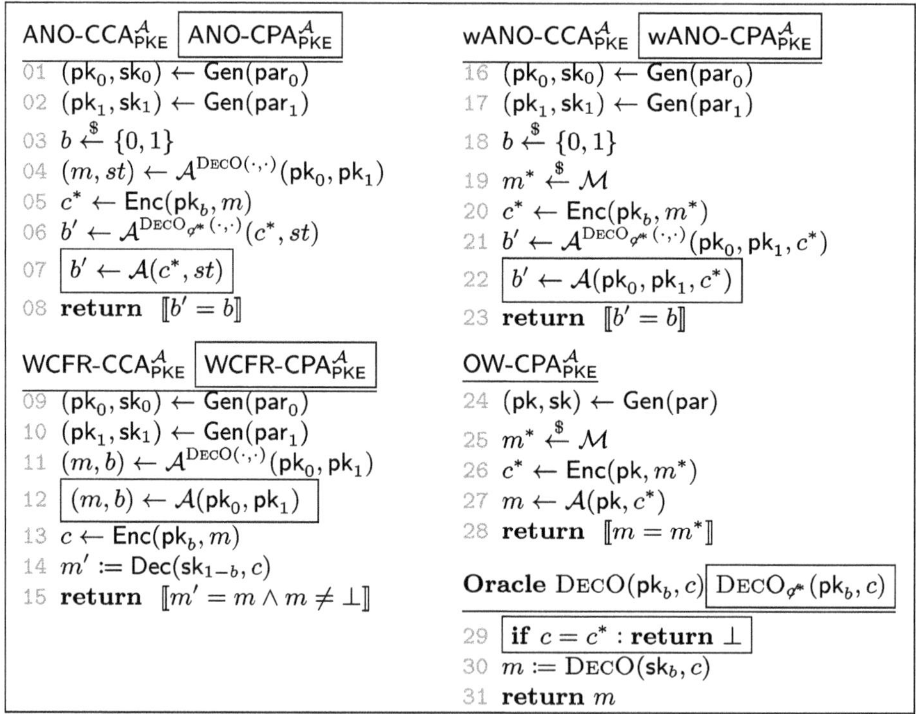

Fig. 2. Security games for PKE. Boxed codes are only executed in the corresponding games. Without loss of generality, here we assume that $\mathcal{A}$ can only query the oracles with the public keys pk_0 or pk_1.

3   From Weak to Standard Anonymity

The standard anonymity requirement is ANO-CCA. In some intermediate steps of our proofs in this paper, we often show that a KEM is weakly anonymous. The following Lemma 1 shows that if a KEM is IND-CCA secure, then its wANO-CCA security implies the ANO-CCA security. Hence, it is sufficient to prove the weaker anonymity (wANO-CCA) of a KEM. Our proof of Lemma 1 preserves the tightness of a KEM in terms of advantage, time, and memory.

Lemma 1 (wANO-CCA + IND-CCA $\Rightarrow$ ANO-CCA). *Let* KEM $=$ (KeyGen, Encap, Decap) *be a key encapsulation mechanism. Let* $\mathcal{A}$ *be an adversary against the* ANO-CCA *security of* KEM, *making at most* q_D *queries to the decapsulation oracles. Then there exists a* wANO-CCA *adversary* $\mathcal{A}_1$ *and an* IND-CCA *adversary* $\mathcal{A}_2$ *against* KEM *such that*

$$\mathsf{Adv}_{\mathsf{KEM}}^{\mathsf{ANO\text{-}CCA}}(\mathcal{A}) \leq \mathsf{Adv}_{\mathsf{KEM}}^{\mathsf{wANO\text{-}CCA}}(\mathcal{A}_2) + \mathsf{Adv}_{\mathsf{KEM}}^{\mathsf{IND\text{-}CCA}}(\mathcal{A}_1), \tag{5}$$

and

$$\mathbf{Time}^*(\mathcal{A}_1) \approx \mathbf{Time}(\mathcal{A}), \quad \mathbf{Mem}^*(\mathcal{A}_1) \approx \mathbf{Mem}(\mathcal{A}),$$
$$\mathbf{Time}^*(\mathcal{A}_2) \approx \mathbf{Time}(\mathcal{A}), \quad \mathbf{Mem}^*(\mathcal{A}_2) \approx \mathbf{Mem}(\mathcal{A}).$$

PROOF. Let $\mathcal{A}$ be an adversary against the ANO-CCA security of KEM. Consider the sequence of games $\mathbf{G}_0$-$\mathbf{G}_1$ shown in Fig. 3.

Game $\mathbf{G}_0$ - $\mathbf{G}_1$

01 $(\mathsf{sk}_0, \mathsf{pk}_0) \leftarrow \mathsf{KeyGen}(\mathsf{par})$
02 $(\mathsf{sk}_0, \mathsf{pk}_1) \leftarrow \mathsf{KeyGen}(\mathsf{par})$
03 $b \xleftarrow{\$} \{0, 1\}$
04 $(c^*, k^*) \leftarrow \mathsf{Encap}(\mathsf{pk}_b)$ $\| \mathbf{G}_0$
05 $k^* \xleftarrow{\$} \mathcal{K}$ $\| \mathbf{G}_1$
06 $b' \leftarrow \mathcal{A}^{\mathrm{DECAPO}(\cdot,\cdot)}(\mathsf{pk}_0, \mathsf{pk}_1, (k^*, c^*))$
07 **return** $[\![b = b']\!]$

Fig. 3. Games $\mathbf{G}_0$-$\mathbf{G}_1$ for the proof of Lemma 1.

Game $\mathbf{G}_0$: This is the ANO-CCA security game for KEM.

$$\left| \Pr[\mathbf{G}_0^{\mathcal{A}} \Rightarrow 1] - \frac{1}{2} \right| = \mathsf{Adv}_{\mathsf{KEM}}^{\mathsf{ANO\text{-}CCA}}(\mathcal{A}).$$

Game $\mathbf{G}_1$: In this game, instead of honestly computing k, we choose k uniformly at random. We can bound this change by reducing to the IND-CCA security of KEM. In the reduction, the simulator $\mathcal{A}_1^{\mathrm{DECAPO}(\mathsf{pk},\cdot)}$ chooses the random bit b, let pk_b be the public key used in the IND-CCA security game, and generates another key pair $(\mathsf{pk}_{1-b}, \mathsf{sk}_{1-b})$, as described in Fig. 4. When $\mathcal{A}$ queries the decapsulation oracle with (pk_b, c), $\mathcal{A}_1^{\mathrm{DECAPO}(\mathsf{pk},\cdot)}$ queries its own decapsulation oracle and

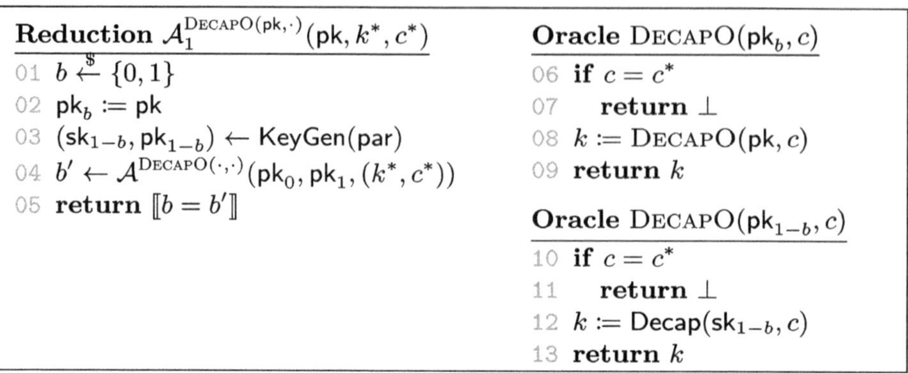

Reduction $\mathcal{A}_1^{\text{DECAPO}(\text{pk},\cdot)}(\text{pk}, k^*, c^*)$

01 $b \xleftarrow{\$} \{0,1\}$
02 $\text{pk}_b := \text{pk}$
03 $(\text{sk}_{1-b}, \text{pk}_{1-b}) \leftarrow \text{KeyGen}(\text{par})$
04 $b' \leftarrow \mathcal{A}^{\text{DECAPO}(\cdot,\cdot)}(\text{pk}_0, \text{pk}_1, (k^*, c^*))$
05 return $[\![b = b']\!]$

Oracle $\text{DECAPO}(\text{pk}_b, c)$

06 if $c = c^*$
07   return $\perp$
08 $k := \text{DECAPO}(\text{pk}, c)$
09 return k

Oracle $\text{DECAPO}(\text{pk}_{1-b}, c)$

10 if $c = c^*$
11   return $\perp$
12 $k := \text{Decap}(\text{sk}_{1-b}, c)$
13 return k

Fig. 4. The adversary $\mathcal{A}_1^{\text{DECAPO}(\text{pk},\cdot)}$ against the IND-CCA security of KEM for the proof of Lemma 1. In the reduction, $\mathcal{A}_1$ queries $\text{DECAPO}(\text{pk}, \cdot)$ at most q_D times.

returns the corresponding output. When $\mathcal{A}$ queries the decapsulation oracle with (pk_{1-b}, c), the simulator uses sk_{1-b} to decapsulate.

$$\left| \Pr[\mathbf{G}_1^{\mathcal{A}} \Rightarrow 1] - \Pr[\mathbf{G}_0^{\mathcal{A}} \Rightarrow 1] \right| \leq \text{Adv}_{\text{KEM}}^{\text{IND-CCA}}(\mathcal{A}_1).$$

Finally, as shown in Fig. 5, by choosing k uniformly random, we can reduce the success probability of $\mathcal{A}$ in $\mathbf{G}_1$ to the wANO-CCA security game for KEM, therefore

$$\Pr[\mathbf{G}_1^{\mathcal{A}} \Rightarrow 1] \leq \text{Adv}_{\text{KEM}}^{\text{wANO-CCA}}(\mathcal{A}_2) + \frac{1}{2}.$$

Reduction $\mathcal{A}_2^{\text{DECAPO}(\cdot)}(\text{pk}_0, \text{pk}_1, c^*)$

01 $k^* \xleftarrow{\$} \mathcal{K}$
02 $b' \leftarrow \mathcal{A}^{\text{DECAPO}(\cdot,\cdot)}(\text{pk}_0, \text{pk}_1, (k^*, c^*))$
03 return b'

Oracle $\text{DECAPO}(\text{pk}_0, c)$

04 if $c = c^*$
05   return $\perp$
06 $k := \text{DECAPO}(\text{pk}_0, c)$
07 return k

Oracle $\text{DECAPO}(\text{pk}_1, c)$

08 if $c = c^*$
09   return $\perp$
10 $k := \text{DECAPO}(\text{pk}_1, c)$
11 return k

Fig. 5. The adversary $\mathcal{A}_2^{\text{DECAPO}(\cdot,\cdot)}$ against the wANO-CCA security of KEM for the proof of Lemma 1. In the reduction, $\mathcal{A}_2$ queries DECAPO^* at most q_D times.

Combining all the bounds above, we have Eq. (5).   □

4 X-Wing and Its Anonymity

The hybrid KEM X-Wing is built by combining the (post-quantum) ML-KEM and the ElGamal KEM. For readability, we generically view the ML-KEM as KEM_1 and the ElGamal KEM as KEM_2, and we show the anonymity for this generic construction in Theorem 1. Since X-Wing is a standardized scheme in [5], we omit the concrete descriptions of X-Wing, ML-KEM, and ElGamal KEM in this paper and refer to the full version [4] for details.

4.1 Generic Construction Behind X-Wing

Essentially, X-Wing [5] follows the parallel KEM combiner proposed in [22]. As a hybrid KEM, it uses two KEMs $\mathsf{KEM}_1 = (\mathsf{KeyGen}_1, \mathsf{Encap}_1, \mathsf{Decap}_1)$ and $\mathsf{KEM}_2 = (\mathsf{KeyGen}_2, \mathsf{Encap}_2, \mathsf{Decap}_2)$ as black boxes, and combines them. We denote by HKEM the generic construction underlying X-Wing, and the description of HKEM is shown in Fig. 6. Let $\mathcal{K}_1$ and $\mathcal{K}_2$ denote the key space of KEM_1 and KEM_2 respectively, and let $\mathcal{C}_2$ and $\mathcal{PK}_2$ denote the ciphertext space and the public key space of KEM_2 respectively. Let $\mathcal{L}$ be the label space for label and $\mathcal{K}$ be the key space for HKEM.

Algorithm $\mathsf{KeyGen}(\mathsf{par})$	**Algorithm** $\mathsf{Encap}(\mathsf{pk})$	**Algorithm** $\mathsf{Decap}(\mathsf{sk}, c)$
01 $(\mathsf{sk}_1, \mathsf{pk}_1) \leftarrow \mathsf{KeyGen}_1(\mathsf{par}_1)$	06 parse pk as $(\mathsf{pk}_1, \mathsf{pk}_2)$	12 parse sk as $(\mathsf{sk}_1, \mathsf{sk}_2, \mathsf{pk}_2)$
02 $(\mathsf{sk}_2, \mathsf{pk}_2) \leftarrow \mathsf{KeyGen}_2(\mathsf{par}_2)$	07 $(k_1, c_1) \leftarrow \mathsf{Encap}_1(\mathsf{pk}_1)$	13 parse c as (c_1, c_2)
03 $\mathsf{pk} := (\mathsf{pk}_1, \mathsf{pk}_2)$	08 $(k_2, c_2) \leftarrow \mathsf{Encap}_2(\mathsf{pk}_2)$	14 $k_1 := \mathsf{Decap}_1(\mathsf{sk}_1, c_1)$
04 $\mathsf{sk} := (\mathsf{sk}_1, \mathsf{sk}_2, \mathsf{pk}_2)$	09 $k := H(\mathsf{label}\|k_1\|k_2\|c_2\|\mathsf{pk}_2)$	15 $k_2 := \mathsf{Decap}_2(\mathsf{sk}_2, c_2)$
05 **return** $(\mathsf{pk}, \mathsf{sk})$	10 $c := (c_1, c_2)$	16 $k := H(\mathsf{label}\|k_1\|k_2\|c_2\|\mathsf{pk}_2)$
	11 **return** (k, c)	17 **return** k

Fig. 6. Description of HKEM, as the generic construction behind X-Wing. According to the definition in [5], the label is encoded as 6-byte ASCII string `"\.//^\"`.

Remark 1 (Limitations of X-Wing and our variant in Sect. 5). As it was pointed out by Günther et al.[24], the anonymity of X-Wing requires both underlying KEMs to be anonymous simultaneously. This is because X-Wing runs both KEMs in parallel (cf. Line 09 in Fig. 6) and concatenates their ciphertexts. Hence, as long as one ciphertext leaks which public key it belongs to, the anonymity of X-Wing is broken. Although we relax the requirement of the underlying KEMs to weak anonymity, the problem remains. The same holds true for our variant in Sect. 5 as well.

Unlike X-Wing and our variant, the construction in [24] is "sequential", and it does not require both KEMs to be anonymous. More precisely, their construction requires the outer KEM to have statistically uniform ciphertexts (cf. Figures 1 and 4 in [24]). This property can be achieved by the ElGamal KEM[4], and we

---

[4] It is named as DHKEM in [24].

use such a property (cf. EG-KEM is unconditionally wANO-CCA*) as well. Hence, they claimed that their combiner is not fully generic. Their design uses several additional cryptographic primitives, including a pseudorandom generator (PRG) and a length-preserving symmetric encryption scheme (SE), and a split-key PRF. Besides the anonymity of one KEM and the PRF security, the anonymity of their hybrid KEM requires either the security of the PRG together with the one-time pseudorandomness of the SE ciphertext, or the strong uniformity (where the adversary has the secret key) of the ciphertext of the other KEM.

4.2 Anonymity of HKEM

The anonymity of HKEM requires KEM_2 to be wANO-PCA secure and in the case of X-Wing, KEM_2 is the ElGamal KEM that is unconditionally wANO-CCA* secure, which is stronger than wANO-PCA. Hence, it trivially satisfies this requirement.

After that, we distinguish if KEM_1 is further IND-CCA. If it is the case, the anonymity of HKEM requires wANO-CCA and WCPR-CCA of KEM_1 (cf. Theorem 1). Our security proof for this is memory-tight [3], and we adapt some techniques from [13,21]. If KEM_1 is not IND-CCA, the anonymity of HKEM requires KEM_1 to be wANO-PCA (cf. Lemma 2). Although Lemma 2 only proves weak anonymity of HKEM, by Lemma 1 we can show HKEM is (standard) anonymous, if HKEM is IND-CCA secure, which is concluded in Lemma 3. If HKEM is X-Wing, then it has been proven to be IND-CCA secure in [5]. However, the proof in [5, Theorem 1] is not memory-tight. We use some techniques in Theorem 1 to avoid the memory loss in the security proof for X-Wing.

CASE I: KEM_1 IS IND-CCA SECURE. The following Theorem 1 proves the ANO-CCA of HKEM under the case when KEM_1 is IND-CCA. In this case, the only requirement for KEM_2 is wANO-PCA, and all the reductions are tight in both time and memeory.

Theorem 1 (Anonymity of HKEM (Case I)). *Let* $\mathsf{KEM}_1 = (\mathsf{KeyGen}_1,$ $\mathsf{Encap}_1, \mathsf{Decap}_1)$ *be a* δ-*correct key encapsulation mechanism. Let* $\mathsf{KEM}_2 = (\mathsf{KeyGen}_2, \mathsf{Encap}_2, \mathsf{Decap}_2)$ *be a* wANO-PCA *secure key encapsulation mechanism. Let* $H : \mathcal{L} \times \mathcal{K}_1 \times \mathcal{K}_2 \times \mathcal{C}_2 \times \mathcal{PK}_2 \to \mathcal{K}$ *be a random oracle and let* $\mathcal{A}$ *be an adversary against the* ANO-CCA *security of the hybrid KEM* HKEM, *making at most* q_H *queries to the random oracle and* q_D *queries to the decapsulation oracles. Then there exists an* IND-CCA *adversary* $\mathcal{B}_1$, *a* WCPR-CCA *adversary* $\mathcal{B}_2$, *and a* wANO-CCA *adversary* $\mathcal{B}_3$ *against* KEM_1, *and a* wANO-PCA *adversary* $\mathcal{C}$ *against* KEM_2 *such that*

$$\mathsf{Adv}^{\mathsf{ANO\text{-}CCA}}_{\mathsf{HKEM}}(\mathcal{A}) \leq \mathsf{Adv}^{\mathsf{wANO\text{-}CCA}}_{\mathsf{KEM}_1}(\mathcal{B}_3) + \mathsf{Adv}^{\mathsf{IND\text{-}CCA}}_{\mathsf{KEM}_1}(\mathcal{B}_1) + \mathsf{Adv}^{\mathsf{WCPR\text{-}CCA}}_{\mathsf{KEM}_1}(\mathcal{B}_2)$$

$$+ \mathsf{Adv}^{\mathsf{wANO\text{-}PCA}}_{\mathsf{KEM}_2}(\mathcal{C}) + \delta + \frac{1 + 2q_H + 2q_D}{|\mathcal{K}_1|}, \tag{6}$$

and

$$\begin{aligned}
\mathbf{Time}(\mathcal{B}_1) &\approx \mathbf{Time}(\mathcal{A}), & \mathbf{Mem}^*(\mathcal{B}_1) &\approx \mathbf{Mem}(\mathcal{A}), \\
\mathbf{Time}(\mathcal{B}_2) &\approx \mathbf{Time}(\mathcal{A}), & \mathbf{Mem}^*(\mathcal{B}_2) &\approx \mathbf{Mem}(\mathcal{A}), \\
\mathbf{Time}(\mathcal{B}_3) &\approx \mathbf{Time}(\mathcal{A}), & \mathbf{Mem}^*(\mathcal{B}_3) &\approx \mathbf{Mem}(\mathcal{A}), \\
\mathbf{Time}(\mathcal{C}) &\approx \mathbf{Time}(\mathcal{A}), & \mathbf{Mem}^*(\mathcal{C}) &\approx \mathbf{Mem}(\mathcal{A}).
\end{aligned}$$

PROOF. Let $\mathcal{A}$ be an adversary against the ANO-CCA security of HKEM. Consider the sequence of games $\mathbf{G}_0$-$\mathbf{G}_7$ shown in Fig. 7.

Game $\mathbf{G}_0$ - $\mathbf{G}_7$

01 $(\mathsf{sk}_{1,0}, \mathsf{pk}_{1,0}) \leftarrow \mathsf{KeyGen}_1(\mathsf{par}_1)$
02 $(\mathsf{sk}_{1,1}, \mathsf{pk}_{1,1}) \leftarrow \mathsf{KeyGen}_1(\mathsf{par}_1)$
03 $(\mathsf{sk}_{2,0}, \mathsf{pk}_{2,0}) \leftarrow \mathsf{KeyGen}_2(\mathsf{par}_2)$
04 $(\mathsf{sk}_{2,1}, \mathsf{pk}_{2,1}) \leftarrow \mathsf{KeyGen}_2(\mathsf{par}_2)$
05 $\mathsf{pk}_0 := (\mathsf{pk}_{1,0}, \mathsf{pk}_{2,0})$
06 $\mathsf{pk}_1 := (\mathsf{pk}_{1,1}, \mathsf{pk}_{2,1})$
07 $\mathsf{sk}_0 := (\mathsf{sk}_{1,0}, \mathsf{sk}_{2,0})$
08 $\mathsf{sk}_1 := (\mathsf{sk}_{1,1}, \mathsf{sk}_{2,1})$
09 $H_b, H_{1-b} \xleftarrow{\$} \Omega_H$ $\qquad\qquad$ $\| \mathbf{G}_5\text{-}\mathbf{G}_7$
10 $H' \xleftarrow{\$} \Omega_H$ $\qquad\qquad$ $\| \mathbf{G}_6\text{-}\mathbf{G}_7$
11 $b \xleftarrow{\$} \{0, 1\}$
12 $(k_1^*, c_1^*) \leftarrow \mathsf{Encap}_1(\mathsf{pk}_{1,b})$
13 $k_1^* \xleftarrow{\$} \mathcal{K}_1$ $\qquad\qquad$ $\| \mathbf{G}_2\text{-}\mathbf{G}_7$
14 $k_1' \xleftarrow{\$} \mathcal{K}_1$ $\qquad\qquad$ $\| \mathbf{G}_3\text{-}\mathbf{G}_7$
15 **if** $k_1^* = k_1'$ $\qquad\qquad$ $\| \mathbf{G}_5\text{-}\mathbf{G}_7$
16 $\quad$ $\mathrm{BAD}_2 := \mathbf{true};\ \mathbf{abort}$ $\qquad$ $\| \mathbf{G}_5\text{-}\mathbf{G}_7$
17 $(k_2^*, c_2^*) \leftarrow \mathsf{Encap}_2(\mathsf{pk}_{2,b})$ $\qquad$ $\| \mathbf{G}_0\text{-}\mathbf{G}_6$
18 $(k_2^*, c_2^*) \leftarrow \mathsf{Encap}_2(\mathsf{pk}_{2,0})$ $\qquad$ $\| \mathbf{G}_7$
19 $k^* := H(\mathsf{label}\|k_1^*\|k_2^*\|c_2^*\|\mathsf{pk}_{2,b})$ $\qquad$ $\| \mathbf{G}_0\text{-}\mathbf{G}_4$
20 $k^* \xleftarrow{\$} \mathcal{K}$ $\qquad\qquad$ $\| \mathbf{G}_5\text{-}\mathbf{G}_7$
21 $c^* := (c_1^*, c_2^*)$
22 $b' \leftarrow \mathcal{A}^{\mathrm{DECAPO}(\cdot,\cdot),H(\cdot)}(\mathsf{pk}_0, \mathsf{pk}_1, (c^*, k^*))$
23 **return** $[\![b = b']\!]$

Oracle $H(\mathsf{label}\|k_1\|k_2\|c_2\|\mathsf{pk}_2)$

24 **if** $k_1 = k_1^* \vee k_1 = k_1'$ $\qquad\qquad$ $\| \mathbf{G}_5\text{-}\mathbf{G}_7$
25 $\quad$ $\mathrm{BAD}_3 := \mathbf{true};\ \mathbf{abort}$ $\qquad$ $\| \mathbf{G}_5\text{-}\mathbf{G}_7$
26 **if** $\mathsf{pk}_2 = \mathsf{pk}_{2,0} \wedge \mathsf{Decap}(\mathsf{sk}_{2,0}, c_2) = k_2$ $\quad$ $\| \mathbf{G}_6\text{-}\mathbf{G}_7$
27 $\quad$ **return** $H'(\mathsf{label}\|k_1\| \star \|c_2\|\mathsf{pk}_2)$ $\qquad$ $\| \mathbf{G}_6\text{-}\mathbf{G}_7$
28 **if** $\mathsf{pk}_2 = \mathsf{pk}_{2,1} \wedge \mathsf{Decap}(\mathsf{sk}_{2,1}, c_2) = k_2$ $\quad$ $\| \mathbf{G}_6\text{-}\mathbf{G}_7$
29 $\quad$ **return** $H'(\mathsf{label}\|k_1\| \star \|c_2\|\mathsf{pk}_2)$ $\qquad$ $\| \mathbf{G}_6\text{-}\mathbf{G}_7$
30 **return** $H(\mathsf{label}\|k_1\|k_2\|c_2\|\mathsf{pk}_2)$

Oracle $\mathrm{DECAPO}(\mathsf{pk}_b, c)$

31 **if** $c = c^*$
32 $\quad$ **return** $\perp$
33 parse sk_b as $(\mathsf{sk}_{1,b}, \mathsf{sk}_{2,b})$
34 parse c as (c_1, c_2)
35 **if** $c_1 = c_1^*$ $\qquad\qquad$ $\| \mathbf{G}_1\text{-}\mathbf{G}_7$
36 $\quad$ $k_2 := \mathsf{Decap}_2(\mathsf{sk}_{2,b}, c_2)$ $\qquad$ $\| \mathbf{G}_1\text{-}\mathbf{G}_4$
37 $\quad$ **return** $H(\mathsf{label}\|k_1^*\|k_2\|c_2\|\mathsf{pk}_{2,b})$ $\qquad$ $\| \mathbf{G}_1\text{-}\mathbf{G}_4$
38 $\quad$ **return** $H_b(\mathsf{label}\|c_1^*\|c_2\|\mathsf{pk}_{2,b})$ $\qquad$ $\| \mathbf{G}_5\text{-}\mathbf{G}_7$
39 $k_1 := \mathsf{Decap}_1(\mathsf{sk}_{1,b}, c_1)$
40 **if** $k_1 = k_1^* \vee k_1 = k_1'$ $\qquad\qquad$ $\| \mathbf{G}_4\text{-}\mathbf{G}_7$
41 $\quad$ $\mathrm{BAD}_1 := \mathbf{true};\ \mathbf{abort}$ $\qquad$ $\| \mathbf{G}_4\text{-}\mathbf{G}_7$
42 $k_2 := \mathsf{Decap}_2(\mathsf{sk}_{2,b}, c_2)$ $\qquad$ $\| \mathbf{G}_0\text{-}\mathbf{G}_5$
43 $k = H(\mathsf{label}\|k_1\|k_2\|c_2\|\mathsf{pk}_{2,b})$ $\qquad$ $\| \mathbf{G}_0\text{-}\mathbf{G}_5$
44 $k = H'(\mathsf{label}\|k_1\| \star \|c_2\|\mathsf{pk}_{2,b})$ $\qquad$ $\| \mathbf{G}_6\text{-}\mathbf{G}_7$
45 **return** k

Oracle $\mathrm{DECAPO}(\mathsf{pk}_{1-b}, c)$

46 **if** $c = c^*$
47 $\quad$ **return** $\perp$
48 parse sk_{1-b} as $(\mathsf{sk}_{1,1-b}, \mathsf{sk}_{2,1-b})$
49 parse c as (c_1, c_2)
50 **if** $c_1 = c_1^*$ $\qquad\qquad$ $\| \mathbf{G}_3\text{-}\mathbf{G}_7$
51 $\quad$ $k_2 := \mathsf{Decap}_2(\mathsf{sk}_{2,1-b}, c_2)$ $\qquad$ $\| \mathbf{G}_3\text{-}\mathbf{G}_4$
52 $\quad$ **return** $H(\mathsf{label}\|k_1'\|k_2\|c_2\|\mathsf{pk}_{2,1-b})$ $\quad$ $\| \mathbf{G}_3\text{-}\mathbf{G}_4$
53 $\quad$ **return** $H_{1-b}(\mathsf{label}\|c_1^*\|c_2\|\mathsf{pk}_{2,1-b})$ $\quad$ $\| \mathbf{G}_5\text{-}\mathbf{G}_7$
54 $k_1 := \mathsf{Decap}_1(\mathsf{sk}_{1,1-b}, c_1)$
55 **if** $k_1 = k_1^* \vee k_1 = k_1'$ $\qquad\qquad$ $\| \mathbf{G}_4\text{-}\mathbf{G}_7$
56 $\quad$ $\mathrm{BAD}_1 := \mathbf{true};\ \mathbf{abort}$ $\qquad$ $\| \mathbf{G}_4\text{-}\mathbf{G}_7$
57 $k_2 := \mathsf{Decap}_2(\mathsf{sk}_{2,1-b}, c_2)$ $\qquad$ $\| \mathbf{G}_0\text{-}\mathbf{G}_5$
58 $k = H(\mathsf{label}\|k_1\|k_2\|c_2\|\mathsf{pk}_{2,1-b})$ $\qquad$ $\| \mathbf{G}_0\text{-}\mathbf{G}_5$
59 $k = H'(\mathsf{label}\|k_1\| \star \|c_2\|\mathsf{pk}_{2,1-b})$ $\qquad$ $\| \mathbf{G}_6\text{-}\mathbf{G}_7$
60 **return** k

Fig. 7. Games $\mathbf{G}_0$-$\mathbf{G}_7$ for the proof of Theorem 1.

Game $\mathbf{G}_0$: This is the ANO-CCA security game for HKEM.

$$\Pr[\mathbf{G}_0^{\mathcal{A}} \Rightarrow 1] = \mathsf{Adv}_{\mathsf{HKEM}}^{\mathsf{ANO\text{-}CCA}}(\mathcal{A}) + \frac{1}{2}.$$

Game $\mathbf{G}_1$: In the decapsulation oracle $\mathrm{DECAPO}(\mathsf{pk}_b, \cdot)$ of this game, if $c = (c_1^*, c_2)$, then we use k_1^* instead of $\mathsf{Decap}(\mathsf{sk}_{1,b}, c_1^*)$ to decapsulate the ciphertext, where $(k_1^*, c_1^*) \leftarrow \mathsf{Encap}_1(\mathsf{pk}_b)$.

Since KEM_1 is δ-correct, we can bound the difference of $\mathbf{G}_1$ and $\mathbf{G}_0$ by

$$\left| \Pr[\mathbf{G}_1^{\mathcal{A}} \Rightarrow 1] - \Pr[\mathbf{G}_0^{\mathcal{A}} \Rightarrow 1] \right| \leq \delta.$$

<table>
<tr><td>

Reduction $\mathcal{B}_1^{\text{DecapO}(\mathsf{pk},\cdot)}(\mathsf{pk}, k_1^*, c_1^*)$

01 $b \xleftarrow{\$} \{0,1\}$
02 $\mathsf{pk}_{1,b} := \mathsf{pk}$
03 $(\mathsf{sk}_{1,1-b}, \mathsf{pk}_{1,1-b}) \leftarrow \mathsf{KeyGen}_1(\mathsf{par}_1)$
04 $(\mathsf{sk}_{1,0}, \mathsf{pk}_{1,0}) \leftarrow \mathsf{KeyGen}_2(\mathsf{par}_2)$
05 $(\mathsf{sk}_{2,1}, \mathsf{pk}_{2,1}) \leftarrow \mathsf{KeyGen}_2(\mathsf{par}_2)$
06 $\mathsf{pk}_0 := (\mathsf{pk}_{1,0}, \mathsf{pk}_{2,0})$
07 $\mathsf{pk}_1 := (\mathsf{pk}_{1,1}, \mathsf{pk}_{2,1})$
08 $(k_2^*, c_2^*) \leftarrow \mathsf{Encap}_2(\mathsf{pk}_{2,b})$
09 $k^* := H(\mathsf{label}\|k_1^*\|k_2^*\|c_2^*\|\mathsf{pk}_{2,b})$
10 $c^* := (c_1^*, c_2^*)$
11 $b' \leftarrow \mathcal{A}^{\text{DecapO}(\cdot,\cdot),H(\cdot)}(\mathsf{pk}_0, \mathsf{pk}_1, (c^*, k^*))$
12 **return** $[\![b = b']\!]$

Oracle $H(\mathsf{label}\|k_1\|k_2\|c_2\|\mathsf{pk}_2)$
13 **return** $H(\mathsf{label}\|k_1\|k_2\|c_2\|\mathsf{pk}_2)$

</td><td>

Oracle $\text{DecapO}(\mathsf{pk}_b, c)$

14 **if** $c = c^*$
15   **return** $\perp$
16 parse c as (c_1, c_2)
17 **if** $c_1 = c_1^*$
18    $k_2 := \mathsf{Decap}_2(\mathsf{sk}_{2,b}, c_2)$
19   **return** $H(\mathsf{label}\|k_1^*\|k_2\|c_2\|\mathsf{pk}_{2,b})$
20 $k_1 := \text{DecapO}(\mathsf{pk}, c_1)$
21 $k_2 := \mathsf{Decap}_2(\mathsf{sk}_{2,b}, c_2)$
22 $k = H(\mathsf{label}\|k_1\|k_2\|c_2\|\mathsf{pk}_{2,b})$
23 **return** k

Oracle $\text{DecapO}(\mathsf{pk}_{1-b}, c)$

24 **if** $c = c^*$
25   **return** $\perp$
26 parse c as (c_1, c_2)
27 $k_1 := \mathsf{Decap}_1(\mathsf{sk}_{1,1-b}, c_1)$
28 $k_1 := \mathsf{Decap}_2(\mathsf{sk}_{2,1-b}, c_2)$
29 $k = H(\mathsf{label}\|k_1\|k_2\|c_2\|\mathsf{pk}_{2,1-b})$
30 **return** k

</td></tr>
</table>

Fig. 8. The adversary $\mathcal{B}_1^{\text{DecapO}(\mathsf{pk},\cdot)}$ against the IND-CCA security of KEM_1 for the proof of Theorem 1. In the reduction, $\mathcal{B}_1$ queries DecapO at most q_D times.

<u>**Game $\mathbf{G}_2$**</u>: In this game, instead of getting k_1^* by computing $(k_1^*, c_1^*) \leftarrow \mathsf{Encap}_1(\mathsf{pk}_b)$, we choose a uniformly random $k_1^* \xleftarrow{\$} \mathcal{K}_1$. As shown in Fig. 8, we can bound this change by the IND-CCA advantage of KEM_1.

After receiving the challenge $(\mathsf{pk}, k_1^*, c_1^*)$, the simulator $\mathcal{B}_1$ chooses a random bit b and lets pk be the challenge public key of KEM_1 (i.e. $\mathsf{pk}_{1,b}$). Then $\mathcal{B}_1$ generates another key pair $(\mathsf{pk}_{1,1-b}, \mathsf{sk}_{1,1-b})$ for KEM_1 and two different key pairs for KEM_2. Therefore, $\mathcal{B}_1$ has all the secret keys except $\mathsf{sk}_{1,b}$ for KEM_1. Thus in the decapsulation oracles, $\mathcal{B}_1$ can use these secret keys and its oracle DecapO to answer the queries from $\mathcal{A}$, except for the case when $\mathcal{A}$ issues a query (c_1^*, c_2) to $\text{DecapO}(\mathsf{pk}_b, \cdot)$. In the latter case, $\mathcal{B}_1$ first uses $\mathsf{sk}_{2,b}$ to get $k_2 := \mathsf{Decap}(\mathsf{sk}_{2,b}, c_2)$, and then outputs $H(\mathsf{label}\|k_1^*\|k_2\|c_2\|\mathsf{pk}_{2,b})$ as the corresponding session key. Therefore,

$$\left| \Pr[\mathbf{G}_2^{\mathcal{A}} \Rightarrow 1] - \Pr[\mathbf{G}_1^{\mathcal{A}} \Rightarrow 1] \right| \leq 2 \cdot \mathsf{Adv}_{\mathsf{KEM}_1}^{\mathsf{IND\text{-}CCA}}(\mathcal{B}_1).$$

Game $\mathbf{G_3}$: In this game, if the adversary $\mathcal{A}$ queries the decapsulation oracle $\textsc{DecapO}(\mathsf{pk}_{1-b}, \cdot)$ with $c = (c_1^*, c_2)$, where c_1^* is the encapsulation ciphertext of $\mathsf{Encap}_1(\mathsf{pk}_{1,b})$, then we use a uniformly random $k_1' \stackrel{\$}{\leftarrow} \mathcal{K}_1$ instead of $\mathsf{Decap}(\mathsf{sk}_{1,1-b}, c_1^*)$ to decapsulate the ciphertext.

If $\mathsf{Decap}_1(\mathsf{sk}_{1,1-b}, c_1^*)$ is indistinguishable from a random session key k_1', then $\mathcal{A}$'s view in $\mathbf{G_2}$ and $\mathbf{G_3}$ are the same. Thus by using the reduction shown in Fig. 9, we can bound the difference of $\mathbf{G_2}$ and $\mathbf{G_3}$ by the WCPR-CCA advantage of KEM_1 and obtain

$$\left| \Pr[\mathbf{G}_3^{\mathcal{A}} \Rightarrow 1] - \Pr[\mathbf{G}_2^{\mathcal{A}} \Rightarrow 1] \right| \leq \mathsf{Adv}_{\mathsf{KEM}_1}^{\mathsf{WCPR\text{-}CCA}}(\mathcal{B}_2).$$

Reduction $\mathcal{B}_2^{\textsc{DecapO}(\cdot,\cdot)}(\mathsf{pk}_{1,0}, \mathsf{pk}_{1,1}, b, c_1^*, k_1')$

01 $(\mathsf{sk}_{2,0}, \mathsf{pk}_{2,0}) \leftarrow \mathsf{KeyGen}_2(\mathsf{par}_2)$
02 $(\mathsf{sk}_{2,1}, \mathsf{pk}_{2,1}) \leftarrow \mathsf{KeyGen}_2(\mathsf{par}_2)$
03 $\mathsf{pk}_0 := (\mathsf{pk}_{1,0}, \mathsf{pk}_{2,0})$
04 $\mathsf{pk}_1 := (\mathsf{pk}_{1,1}, \mathsf{pk}_{2,1})$
05 $(k_2^*, c_2^*) \leftarrow \mathsf{Encap}_2(\mathsf{pk}_{2,b})$
06 $k_1^* \stackrel{\$}{\leftarrow} \mathcal{K}_1$
07 $k^* := H(\mathsf{label}\|k_1^*\|k_2^*\|c_2^*\|\mathsf{pk}_{2,b})$
08 $c^* := (c_1^*, c_2^*)$
09 $b' \leftarrow \mathcal{A}^{\textsc{DecapO}(\cdot,\cdot), H(\cdot)}(\mathsf{pk}_0, \mathsf{pk}_1, (c^*, k^*))$
10 **return** $[\![b = b']\!]$

Oracle $H(\mathsf{label}\|k_1\|k_2\|c_2\|\mathsf{pk}_2)$

11 **return** $H(\mathsf{label}\|k_1\|k_2\|c_2\|\mathsf{pk}_2)$

Oracle $\textsc{DecapO}(\mathsf{pk}_b, c)$

12 **if** $c = c^*$
13   **return** $\perp$
14 parse c as (c_1, c_2)
15 **if** $c_1 = c_1^*$
16      $k_2 := \mathsf{Decap}_2(\mathsf{sk}_{2,b}, c_2)$
17   **return** $H(\mathsf{label}\|k_1^*\|k_2\|c_2\|\mathsf{pk}_{2,b})$
18 $k_1 := \textsc{DecapO}(\mathsf{pk}_{1,b}, c_1)$
19 $k_2 := \mathsf{Decap}_2(\mathsf{sk}_{2,b}, c_2)$
20 $k = H(\mathsf{label}\|k_1\|k_2\|c_2\|\mathsf{pk}_{2,b})$
21 **return** k

Oracle $\textsc{DecapO}(\mathsf{pk}_{1-b}, c)$

22 **if** $c = c^*$
23   **return** $\perp$
24 parse c as (c_1, c_2)
25 **if** $c_1 = c_1^*$
26      $k_2 := \mathsf{Decap}_2(\mathsf{sk}_{2,b}, c_2)$
27   **return** $H(\mathsf{label}\|k_1'\|k_2\|c_2\|\mathsf{pk}_{2,1-b})$
28 $k_1 := \textsc{DecapO}(\mathsf{pk}_{1,1-b}, c_1)$
29 $k_2 := \mathsf{Decap}_2(\mathsf{sk}_{2,b}, c_2)$
30 $k = H(\mathsf{label}\|k_1\|k_2\|c_2\|\mathsf{pk}_{2,1-b})$
31 **return** k

Fig. 9. The adversary $\mathcal{B}_2^{\textsc{DecapO}(\cdot,\cdot)}$ against the WCPR-CCA security of KEM_1 for the proof of Theorem 1. In the reduction, $\mathcal{B}_2$ queries $\textsc{DecapO}$ at most q_D times.

Game $\mathbf{G_4}$: In this game, if $\mathcal{A}$ queries the decapsulation oracles with $(c_1 \neq c_1^*, c_2)$ such that $\mathsf{Decap}_1(\cdot, c_1)$ equals to k_1^* or k_1', then we abort the game. We define this event as BAD_1, and when BAD_1 never happens, the distribution remains the same. Since both k_1^* or k_1' are chosen uniformly random and hidden from the adversary $\mathcal{A}$, we have

$$\left| \Pr[\mathbf{G}_4^{\mathcal{A}} \Rightarrow 1] - \Pr[\mathbf{G}_3^{\mathcal{A}} \Rightarrow 1] \right| \leq \Pr[\mathsf{BAD}_1] \leq 2 \cdot \frac{q_D}{|\mathcal{K}_1|}.$$

Game $\mathbf{G}_5$: In this game, we choose k^* uniformly random and modify the decapsulation value of $\textsc{DecapO}(\cdot, (c_1^*, c_2))$ by reprogramming the random oracle. Specifically speaking, in the decapsulation oracles $\textsc{DecapO}(\cdot, \cdot)$, for the random session keys k_1^* and k_1', we replace the hash values $H(\mathsf{label}\|k_1^*\|k_2\|c_2\|\mathsf{pk}_{2,b})$ and $H(\mathsf{label}\|k_1'\|k_2\|c_2\|\mathsf{pk}_{2,1-b})$ with $H_b(\mathsf{label}\|c_1^*\|c_2\|\mathsf{pk}_{2,b})$ and $H_{1-b}(\mathsf{label}\|c_1^*\|c_2 \|\mathsf{pk}_{2,1-b})$ respectively, where H_b and H_{1-b} are random functions. If $k_1^* \neq k_1'$ and $\mathcal{A}$ never queries the random oracle H with an input containing k_1^* or k_1', then $\mathcal{A}$'s view in $\mathbf{G}_4$ and $\mathbf{G}_5$ are the same because $\mathcal{A}$ is not allowed to query (c_1^*, c_2^*) to the decapsulation oracles.

We define the event BAD_2 to denote $k_1^* = k_1'$, and define the event BAD_3 occurs when $\mathcal{A}$ queries H with $(\mathsf{label}\|k_1\|k_2\|c_2\|\mathsf{pk}_2)$ where $k_1 = k_1^* \vee k_1'$. Since both k_1^* and k_1' are chosen uniformly random and hidden from the adversary $\mathcal{A}$, we have

$$\left| \Pr[\mathbf{G}_5^{\mathcal{A}} \Rightarrow 1] - \Pr[\mathbf{G}_4^{\mathcal{A}} \Rightarrow 1] \right| \leq \Pr[\mathsf{BAD}_2] + \Pr[\mathsf{BAD}_3] \leq \frac{1}{|\mathcal{K}_1|} + 2 \cdot \frac{q_H}{|\mathcal{K}_1|}.$$

Game $\mathbf{G}_6$: In this game, instead of using the secret keys of KEM_2 to recover k_2 from c_2 in the decapsulation oracles $\textsc{DecapO}(\cdot, \cdot)$, we simply return $H'(\mathsf{label}\|k_1\| \star \|c_2\|\mathsf{pk}_2)$ as the decapsulation value of (c_1, c_2), where H' is a random function. By doing this, we no longer need the secret key of KEM_2 in the decapsulation oracles.

In order to keep the consistency, for each query $(\mathsf{label}\|k_1\|k_2\|c_2\|\mathsf{pk}_2)$ to the random oracle H, if $(k_2, c_2, \mathsf{pk}_2)$ is a valid pair (i.e. there exists a bit $\hat{b}$ such that $\mathsf{Decap}_2(\mathsf{sk}_{2,\hat{b}}, c_2) = k_2$ and $\mathsf{pk}_{2,\hat{b}} = \mathsf{pk}_2$), then we reprogram the corresponding hash value as $H'(\mathsf{label}\|k_1\| \star \|c_2\|\mathsf{pk}_2)$. Since there is a bijection between (c_2, pk_2) and $(k_2, c_2, \mathsf{pk}_2)$, this modification does not change the distribution, thus we have

$$\Pr[\mathbf{G}_6^{\mathcal{A}} \Rightarrow 1] = \Pr[\mathbf{G}_5^{\mathcal{A}} \Rightarrow 1].$$

Game $\mathbf{G}_7$: In this game, instead of using the random bit b to get c_2^*, we compute it by fixing the bit to be 0, that is $(k_2^*, c_2^*) \leftarrow \mathsf{Encap}_2(\mathsf{pk}_{2,0})$. Games $\mathbf{G}_7$ and $\mathbf{G}_6$ will only have a difference when $b \xleftarrow{\$} \{0,1\}$ is chosen to be 1. By using the reduction shown in Fig. 10, we can bound this difference by the wANO-PCA advantage of KEM_2:

$$\left| \Pr[\mathbf{G}_7^{\mathcal{A}} \Rightarrow 1] - \Pr[\mathbf{G}_6^{\mathcal{A}} \Rightarrow 1] \right| = \frac{1}{2} \cdot \left| \Pr[\mathbf{G}_7^{\mathcal{A}} \Rightarrow 1 | b = 1] - \Pr[\mathbf{G}_6^{\mathcal{A}} \Rightarrow 1 | b = 1] \right|$$

$$\leq \mathsf{Adv}_{\mathsf{KEM}_2}^{\mathsf{wANO\text{-}PCA}}(\mathcal{C}).$$

Finally, as shown in Fig. 11, we can bound the success probability of $\mathcal{A}$ in $\mathbf{G}_7$ by the wANO-CCA advantage of KEM_1. In the reduction, after receiving the challenge $(\mathsf{pk}_{1,0}, \mathsf{pk}_{1,1}, c_1^*)$, $\mathcal{B}_3$ chooses a random $k^* \xleftarrow{\$} \mathcal{K}$ and generates two key pairs of KEM_2. Then $\mathcal{B}_3$ computes c_2^* by $\mathsf{Encap}_2(\mathsf{pk}_{2,0})$, and sends $((\mathsf{pk}_{1,0}, \mathsf{pk}_{2,0},)(\mathsf{pk}_{1,1}, \mathsf{pk}_{2,1}), (c_1^*, c_2^*), k^*)$ to $\mathcal{A}$ as the challenge input. For any bit $\hat{b} \in \{0,1\}$, if $\mathcal{A}$ queries the decapsulation oracle $\textsc{DecapO}(\mathsf{pk}_{\hat{b}}, \cdot)$ with $c = (c_1^*, c_2)$, then $\mathcal{B}_3$ returns $k = H_{\hat{b}}(\mathsf{label}\|c_1^*\|c_2\|\mathsf{pk}_{2,\hat{b}})$ as the decapsulation value of c,

Reduction $\mathcal{C}^{\text{PCO}_2(\cdot,\cdot,\cdot)}(\mathsf{pk}_{2,0}, \mathsf{pk}_{2,1}, c_2^*)$

01 $(\mathsf{sk}_{1,0}, \mathsf{pk}_{1,0}) \leftarrow \mathsf{KeyGen}_1(\mathsf{par}_1)$
02 $(\mathsf{sk}_{1,1}, \mathsf{pk}_{1,1}) \leftarrow \mathsf{KeyGen}_1(\mathsf{par}_1)$
03 $\mathsf{pk}_0 := (\mathsf{pk}_{1,0}, \mathsf{pk}_{2,0})$
04 $\mathsf{pk}_1 := (\mathsf{pk}_{1,1}, \mathsf{pk}_{2,1})$
05 $H_b, H_{1-b} \xleftarrow{\$} \Omega_H$
06 $H' \xleftarrow{\$} \Omega_H$
07 $(k_1^*, c_1^*) \leftarrow \mathsf{Encap}_1(\mathsf{pk}_{1,1})$
08 $k_1' \xleftarrow{\$} \mathcal{K}_1$
09 $k_1^* \xleftarrow{\$} \mathcal{K}_1$
10 **if** $k_1^* = k_1'$
11    $\mathrm{BAD}_2 := \mathbf{true};$ **abort**
12 $k^* \xleftarrow{\$} \mathcal{K}$
13 $c^* := (c_1^*, c_2^*)$
14 $b' \leftarrow \mathcal{A}^{\text{DECAPO}(\cdot,\cdot), H(\cdot)}(\mathsf{pk}_0, \mathsf{pk}_1, (c^*, k^*))$
15 **return** b'

Oracle $H(\mathsf{label}\|k_1\|k_2\|c_2\|\mathsf{pk}_2)$

16 **if** $k_1 = k_1^* \vee k_1 = k_1'$
17    $\mathrm{BAD}_3 := \mathbf{true};$ **abort**
18 **if** $\mathsf{pk}_2 = \mathsf{pk}_{2,0} \wedge \mathsf{PCA}_2(\mathsf{pk}_{2,0}, k_2, c_2) = 1$
19   **return** $H'(\mathsf{label}\|k_1\| \star \|c_2\|\mathsf{pk}_2)$
20 **if** $\mathsf{pk}_2 = \mathsf{pk}_{2,1} \wedge \mathsf{PCA}_2(\mathsf{pk}_{2,1}, k_2, c_2) = 1$
21   **return** $H'(\mathsf{label}\|k_1\| \star \|c_2\|\mathsf{pk}_2)$
22 **return** $H(\mathsf{label}\|k_1\|k_2\|c_2\|\mathsf{pk}_2)$

Oracle $\text{DECAPO}(\mathsf{pk}_0, c)$

23 **if** $c = c^*$
24   **return** $\perp$
25 parse c as (c_1, c_2)
26 **if** $c_1 = c_1^*$
27   **return** $H_0(\mathsf{label}\|c_1^*\|c_2\|\mathsf{pk}_{2,0})$
28 $k_1 := \mathsf{Decap}_1(\mathsf{sk}_{1,0}, c_1)$
29 **if** $k_1 = k_1^* \vee k_1 = k_1'$
30    $\mathrm{BAD}_1 := \mathbf{true};$ **abort**
31 $k = H'(\mathsf{label}\|k_1\| \star \|c_2\|\mathsf{pk}_{2,0})$
32 **return** k

Oracle $\text{DECAPO}(\mathsf{pk}_1, c)$

33 **if** $c = c^*$
34   **return** $\perp$
35 parse c as (c_1, c_2)
36 **if** $c_1 = c_1^*$
37   **return** $H_1(\mathsf{label}\|c_1^*\|c_2\|\mathsf{pk}_{2,1})$
38 $k_1 := \mathsf{Decap}_1(\mathsf{sk}_{1,1}, c_1)$
39 **if** $k_1 = k_1^* \vee k_1 = k_1'$
40    $\mathrm{BAD}_1 := \mathbf{true};$ **abort**
41 $k = H'(\mathsf{label}\|k_1\| \star \|c_2\|\mathsf{pk}_{2,1})$
42 **return** k

Fig. 10. The adversary $\mathcal{C}^{\text{PCO}_2(\cdot,\cdot,\cdot)}(\mathsf{pk}_{2,0}, \mathsf{pk}_{2,1}, c_2^*)$ against the wANO-PCA security of KEM_2 for the proof of Theorem 1. In the reduction, $\mathcal{C}$ queries PCO_2 at most $2q_H$ times.

where $H_{\hat{b}}$ are random functions chosen by $\mathcal{B}_3$. For any other $\mathcal{A}$'s queries to the decapsulation oracle $\text{DECAPO}(\mathsf{pk}_{\hat{b}}, \cdot)$, $\mathcal{B}_3$ can use his own decapsulation oracle $\text{DECAPO}(\mathsf{pk}_{2,\hat{b}}, \cdot)$ to recover k_1, and then returns $k = H'(\mathsf{label}\|k_1\| \star \|c_2\|\mathsf{pk}_{2,\hat{b}})$. In the meantime, for each query $(\mathsf{label}\|k_1\|k_2\|c_2\|\mathsf{pk}_2)$ to the random oracle H, $\mathcal{B}_3$ uses the corresponding secret keys of KEM_2 (which are generated by himself) to justify whether $k_2 = \mathsf{Decap}_2(\mathsf{sk}_{2,\hat{b}}, c_2)$ and to keep the consistency with the decapsulation oracles. This perfectly simulates $\mathcal{A}$'s view in game $\mathbf{G}_7$ and we have

$$\Pr[\mathbf{G}_7^{\mathcal{A}} \Rightarrow 1] \leq \mathsf{Adv}_{\mathsf{KEM}_1}^{\mathsf{wANO\text{-}CCA}}(\mathcal{B}_3) + \frac{1}{2}.$$

We have Eq. (6) by combining all the bounds above. $\qquad\square$

CASE II: KEM_1 IS NOT IND-CCA SECURE. Now we consider the case that KEM_1 may not be IND-CCA secure. We first use the following Lemma 2 to show the weak anonymity of HKEM, which requires the wANO-PCA of both KEM_1 and KEM_2. Since the ciphertext of HKEM simply concatenates the ciphertexts of

---

Reduction $\mathcal{B}_3^{\textsc{DecapO}(\cdot,\cdot)}(\mathsf{pk}_{1,0}, \mathsf{pk}_{1,1}, c_1^*)$

01 $(\mathsf{sk}_{2,0}, \mathsf{pk}_{2,0}) \leftarrow \mathsf{KeyGen}_2(\mathsf{par}_2)$
02 $(\mathsf{sk}_{2,1}, \mathsf{pk}_{2,1}) \leftarrow \mathsf{KeyGen}_2(\mathsf{par}_2)$
03 $\mathsf{pk}_0 := (\mathsf{pk}_{1,0}, \mathsf{pk}_{2,0})$
04 $\mathsf{pk}_1 := (\mathsf{pk}_{1,1}, \mathsf{pk}_{2,1})$
05 $H_b, H_{1-b} \xleftarrow{\$} \Omega_H$
06 $H' \xleftarrow{\$} \Omega_H$
07 $k_1' \xleftarrow{\$} \mathcal{K}_1$
08 $k_1^* \xleftarrow{\$} \mathcal{K}_1$
09 **if** $k_1^* = k_1'$
10    $\mathrm{BAD}_2 := \mathbf{true}$; **abort**
11 $(k_2^*, c_2^*) \leftarrow \mathsf{Encap}_2(\mathsf{pk}_{2,0})$
12 $k^* \xleftarrow{\$} \mathcal{K}$
13 $c^* := (c_1^*, c_2^*)$
14 $b' \leftarrow \mathcal{A}^{\textsc{DecapO}(\cdot,\cdot), H(\cdot)}(\mathsf{pk}_0, \mathsf{pk}_1, (c^*, k^*))$
15 **return** b'

Oracle $H(\mathsf{label}\|k_1\|k_2\|c_2\|\mathsf{pk}_2)$

16 **if** $k_1 = k_1^* \vee k_1 = k_1'$
17    $\mathrm{BAD}_3 := \mathbf{true}$; **abort**
18 **if** $\mathsf{pk}_2 = \mathsf{pk}_{2,0} \wedge \mathsf{Decap}(\mathsf{sk}_{2,0}, c_2) = k_2$
19   **return** $H'(\mathsf{label}\|k_1\| \star \|c_2\|\mathsf{pk}_2)$
20 **if** $\mathsf{pk}_2 = \mathsf{pk}_{2,1} \wedge \mathsf{Decap}(\mathsf{sk}_{2,1}, c_2) = k_2$
21   **return** $H'(\mathsf{label}\|k_1\| \star \|c_2\|\mathsf{pk}_2)$
22 **return** $H(\mathsf{label}\|k_1\|k_2\|c_2\|\mathsf{pk}_2)$

Oracle $\textsc{DecapO}(\mathsf{pk}_0, c)$

23 **if** $c = c^*$
24   **return** $\perp$
25 parse c as (c_1, c_2)
26 **if** $c_1 = c_1^*$
27   **return** $H_0(\mathsf{label}\|c_1^*\|c_2\|\mathsf{pk}_{2,0})$
28 $k_1 := \textsc{DecapO}(\mathsf{pk}_{1,0}, c_1)$
29 **if** $k_1 = k_1^* \vee k_1 = k_1'$
30    $\mathrm{BAD}_1 := \mathbf{true}$; **abort**
31 $k = H'(\mathsf{label}\|k_1\| \star \|c_2\|\mathsf{pk}_{2,0})$
32 **return** k

Oracle $\textsc{DecapO}(\mathsf{pk}_1, c)$

33 **if** $c = c^*$
34   **return** $\perp$
35 parse c as (c_1, c_2)
36 **if** $c_1 = c_1^*$
37   **return** $H_1(\mathsf{label}\|c_1^*\|c_2\|\mathsf{pk}_{2,1})$
38 $k_1 := \textsc{DecapO}(\mathsf{pk}_{1,1}, c_1)$
39 **if** $k_1 = k_1^* \vee k_1 = k_1'$
40    $\mathrm{BAD}_1 := \mathbf{true}$; **abort**
41 $k = H'(\mathsf{label}\|k_1\| \star \|c_2\|\mathsf{pk}_{2,1})$
42 **return** k

Fig. 11. The adversary $\mathcal{B}_3^{\textsc{DecapO}(\cdot,\cdot)}$ against the wANO-CCA security of KEM_1 for the proof of Theorem 1. In the reduction, $\mathcal{B}_3$ queries $\textsc{DecapO}$ at most q_D times.

KEM_1 and KEM_2, it is impossible to achieve the weak anonymity of the hybrid KEM if any ciphertext of these two underlying KEMs reveals the challenge bit in the anonymity game, which has been observed in [24] as well. Therefore, requiring both KEMs to be wANO-PCA is inherent. However, we need some memory to record the decapsulation values and hash queries in order to keep the consistency, and thus the reductions are not memory-tight. We note that adding the ciphertext of KEM_1 into the hash can avoid this memory loss, and we give formal treatments of this in Sect. 5.

Lemma 2 (wANO-CCA* of HKEM). *Let* $\mathsf{KEM}_1 = (\mathsf{KeyGen}_1, \mathsf{Encap}_1, \mathsf{Decap}_1)$ *and* $\mathsf{KEM}_2 = (\mathsf{KeyGen}_2, \mathsf{Encap}_2, \mathsf{Decap}_2)$ *be two* wANO-PCA *secure key encapsulation mechanisms. Let* $H : \mathcal{L} \times \mathcal{K}_1 \times \mathcal{K}_2 \times \mathcal{C}_2 \times \mathcal{PK}_2 \to \mathcal{K}$ *be a random oracle and let* $\mathcal{A}$ *be an adversary against the* wANO-CCA* *security of HKEM, making at most* q_H *queries to the random oracle and* q_D *queries to the decapsulation oracles. Then there exists a* wANO-PCA *adversary* $\mathcal{C}$ *against* KEM_1 *and a* wANO-PCA *adversary* $\mathcal{B}$ *against* KEM_2 *such that*

$$\mathsf{Adv}^{\mathsf{wANO\text{-}CCA}^*}_{\mathsf{HKEM}}(\mathcal{A}) \leq \mathsf{Adv}^{\mathsf{wANO\text{-}PCA}}_{\mathsf{KEM}_1}(\mathcal{C}) + \mathsf{Adv}^{\mathsf{wANO\text{-}PCA}}_{\mathsf{KEM}_2}(\mathcal{B}), \tag{7}$$

and

$$\mathbf{Time}(\mathcal{B}) \approx \mathbf{Time}(\mathcal{A}), \quad \mathbf{Mem}^*(\mathcal{B}) = \mathbf{Mem}(\mathcal{A}) + \log|\mathcal{L}_H|,$$
$$\mathbf{Time}(\mathcal{C}) \approx \mathbf{Time}(\mathcal{A}), \quad \mathbf{Mem}^*(\mathcal{C}) = \mathbf{Mem}(\mathcal{A}) + \log|\mathcal{L}_H| + \log|D|,$$

where $\mathcal{L}_H$ *and* D *denote the lists used to simulate the random oracle and the decapsulation oracle respectively, and* $|\mathcal{L}_H| = \mathcal{O}(q_H)$, $|D| = \mathcal{O}(q_D)$.

PROOF. Let $\mathcal{A}$ be an adversary against the wANO-CCA* security of HKEM.

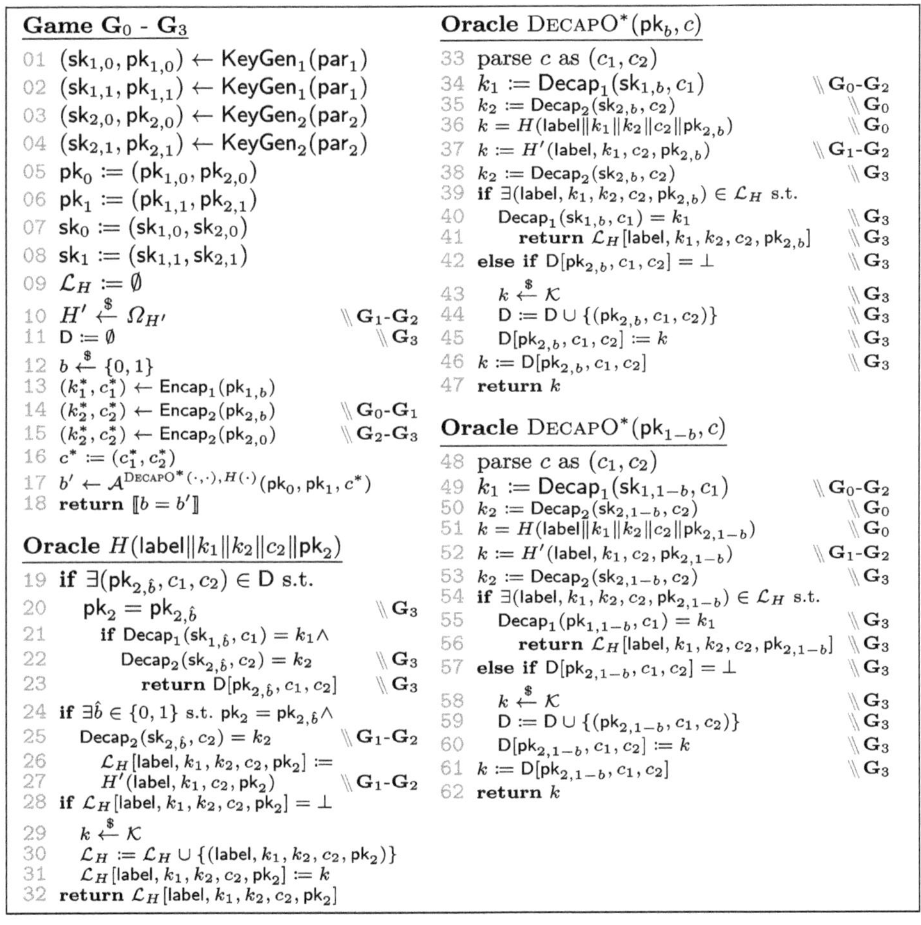

Fig. 12. Games $\mathbf{G}_0$-$\mathbf{G}_3$ for the proof of Lemma 2.

Consider the sequence of games $\mathbf{G}_0$-$\mathbf{G}_3$ shown in Fig. 12:

Game $\mathbf{G}_0$: This is the wANO-CCA* security game for HKEM.

$$\Pr[\mathbf{G}_0^{\mathcal{A}} \Rightarrow 1] = \mathsf{Adv}_{\mathsf{HKEM}}^{\mathsf{wANO\text{-}CCA^*}}(\mathcal{A}) + \frac{1}{2}.$$

Game $\mathbf{G}_1$: In this game, for all the hash values $H(\mathsf{label}\|k_1\|k_2\|c_2\|\mathsf{pk}_2)$ which satisfy $\mathsf{Decap}_2(\mathsf{sk}_{2,0}, c_2) = k_2$ (or $\mathsf{Decap}_2(\mathsf{sk}_{2,1}, c_2) = k_2$, resp.), we reprogram them by the corresponding random function value $H'(\mathsf{label}\|k_1\|c_2\|\mathsf{pk}_{2,0})$ (or $H'(\mathsf{label}\|k_1\|c_2\|\mathsf{pk}_{2,1})$, resp.). By doing this, we do not need the secret key of KEM_2 in the decapsulation oracles. Since there is a bijection between $(k_2, c_2, \mathsf{pk}_2)$ and (c_2, pk_2), this reprogramming does not change the distribution. Therefore,

$$\Pr[\mathbf{G}_1^{\mathcal{A}} \Rightarrow 1] = \Pr[\mathbf{G}_0^{\mathcal{A}} \Rightarrow 1].$$

Reduction $\mathcal{B}^{\mathrm{PCO}_2(\cdot,\cdot,\cdot)}(\mathsf{pk}_{2,0}, \mathsf{pk}_{2,1}, c_2^*)$

01 $(\mathsf{sk}_{1,0}, \mathsf{pk}_{1,0}) \leftarrow \mathsf{KeyGen}_1(\mathsf{par}_1)$
02 $(\mathsf{sk}_{1,1}, \mathsf{pk}_{1,1}) \leftarrow \mathsf{KeyGen}_1(\mathsf{par}_1)$
03 $\mathsf{pk}_0 := (\mathsf{pk}_{1,0}, \mathsf{pk}_{2,0})$
04 $\mathsf{pk}_1 := (\mathsf{pk}_{1,1}, \mathsf{pk}_{2,1})$
05 $\mathcal{L}_H := \emptyset$
06 $H' \overset{\$}{\leftarrow} \Omega_{H'}$
07 $(k_1^*, c_1^*) \leftarrow \mathsf{Encap}_1(\mathsf{pk}_{1,1})$
08 $c^* := (c_1^*, c_2^*)$
09 $b' \leftarrow \mathcal{A}^{\mathrm{DECAPO}^*(\cdot,\cdot), H(\cdot)}(\mathsf{pk}_0, \mathsf{pk}_1, c^*)$
10 **return** b'

Oracle $H(\mathsf{label}\|k_1\|k_2\|c_2\|\mathsf{pk}_2)$

11 **if** $\exists \hat{b} \in \{0, 1\}$ s.t.
12 $\quad \mathsf{pk}_2 = \mathsf{pk}_{2,\hat{b}} \wedge \mathrm{PCO}_2(\mathsf{pk}_2, k_2, c_2) = 1$
13 $\quad\quad \mathcal{L}_H[\mathsf{label}, k_1, k_2, c_2, \mathsf{pk}_2] :=$
14 $\quad\quad H'(\mathsf{label}, k_1, c_2, \mathsf{pk}_2)$
15 **if** $\mathcal{L}_H[\mathsf{label}, k_1, k_2, c_2, \mathsf{pk}_2] = \bot$
16 $\quad k \overset{\$}{\leftarrow} \mathcal{K}$
17 $\quad \mathcal{L}_H := \mathcal{L}_H \cup \{(\mathsf{label}, k_1, k_2, c_2, \mathsf{pk}_2)\}$
18 $\quad \mathcal{L}_H[\mathsf{label}, k_1, k_2, c_2, \mathsf{pk}_2] := k$
19 **return** $\mathcal{L}_H[\mathsf{label}, k_1, k_2, c_2, \mathsf{pk}_2]$

Oracle $\mathrm{DECAPO}^*(\mathsf{pk}_0, c)$

20 parse c as (c_1, c_2)
21 $k_1 := \mathsf{Decap}_1(\mathsf{sk}_{1,0}, c_1)$
22 $k := H'(\mathsf{label}, k_1, c_2, \mathsf{pk}_{2,0})$
23 **return** k

Oracle $\mathrm{DECAPO}^*(\mathsf{pk}_1, c)$

24 parse c as (c_1, c_2)
25 $k_1 := \mathsf{Decap}_1(\mathsf{sk}_{1,1}, c_1)$
26 $k := H'(\mathsf{label}, k_1, c_2, \mathsf{pk}_{2,1})$
27 **return** k

Fig. 13. The adversary $\mathcal{B}^{\mathrm{PCO}_2(\cdot,\cdot,\cdot)}$ against the wANO-PCA security of KEM_2 for the proof of Lemma 2. In the reduction, $\mathcal{B}$ queries PCO_2 at most q_H times.

Game $\mathbf{G}_2$: In this game, instead of using the random bit b to get c_2^*, we compute it by fixing the bit to be 0, that is $(k_2^*, c_2^*) \leftarrow \mathsf{Encap}_2(\mathsf{pk}_{2,0})$. Games $\mathbf{G}_2$ and $\mathbf{G}_1$ will only have a difference when $b \overset{\$}{\leftarrow} \{0, 1\}$ is chosen to be 1. By using the reduction shown in Fig. 13, we can bound this difference by the wANO-PCA advantage of KEM_2:

$$\left| \Pr[\mathbf{G}_2^{\mathcal{A}} \Rightarrow 1] - \Pr[\mathbf{G}_1^{\mathcal{A}} \Rightarrow 1] \right| = \frac{1}{2} \cdot \left| \Pr[\mathbf{G}_2^{\mathcal{A}} \Rightarrow 1 | b = 1] - \Pr[\mathbf{G}_1^{\mathcal{A}} \Rightarrow 1 | b = 1] \right|$$

$$\leq \mathsf{Adv}_{\mathsf{KEM}_2}^{\mathsf{wANO\text{-}PCA}}(\mathcal{B}).$$

Game $\mathbf{G}_3$: In this game, we use a different way to reprogram the random oracle such that the decapsulation oracles no longer need the secret key of KEM_1. This can be viewed as a "symmetric" way of the change from $\mathbf{G}_0$ to $\mathbf{G}_1$, but because the input of H does not involve c_1, we have to record all the queries to the decapsulation oracles and the random oracle in order to keep the consistency. Since $\mathcal{A}$'s view is the same as before, we have

$$\Pr[\mathbf{G}_3^{\mathcal{A}} \Rightarrow 1] = \Pr[\mathbf{G}_2^{\mathcal{A}} \Rightarrow 1].$$

Reduction $\mathcal{C}^{\mathrm{PCO}_1(\cdot,\cdot,\cdot)}(\mathsf{pk}_{1,0}, \mathsf{pk}_{1,1}, c_1^*)$

01 $(\mathsf{sk}_{2,0}, \mathsf{pk}_{2,0}) \leftarrow \mathsf{KeyGen}_2(\mathsf{par}_2)$
02 $(\mathsf{sk}_{2,1}, \mathsf{pk}_{2,1}) \leftarrow \mathsf{KeyGen}_2(\mathsf{par}_2)$
03 $\mathsf{pk}_0 := (\mathsf{pk}_{1,0}, \mathsf{pk}_{2,0})$
04 $\mathsf{pk}_1 := (\mathsf{pk}_{1,1}, \mathsf{pk}_{2,1})$
05 $\mathcal{L}_H := \emptyset$
06 $\mathsf{D} := \emptyset$
07 $(k_2^*, c_2^*) \leftarrow \mathsf{Encap}_2(\mathsf{pk}_{2,0})$
08 $c^* := (c_1^*, c_2^*)$
09 $b' \leftarrow \mathcal{A}^{\mathrm{DECAPO}^*(\cdot,\cdot), H(\cdot)}(\mathsf{pk}_0, \mathsf{pk}_1, c^*)$
10 **return** b'

Oracle $H(\mathsf{label}\|k_1\|k_2\|c_2\|\mathsf{pk}_2)$

11 **if** $\exists (\mathsf{pk}_{2,\hat{b}}, c_1, c_2) \in \mathsf{D}$ s.t. $\mathsf{pk}_2 = \mathsf{pk}_{2,\hat{b}}$
12 $\quad$ **if** $\mathrm{PCO}_1(\mathsf{pk}_{1,\hat{b}}, k_1, c_1) = 1 \wedge$
13 $\quad\quad$ $\mathsf{Decap}_2(\mathsf{sk}_{2,\hat{b}}, c_2) = k_2$
14 $\quad\quad\quad$ **return** $\mathsf{D}[\mathsf{pk}_{2,\hat{b}}, c_1, c_2]$
15 **if** $\mathcal{L}_H[\mathsf{label}, k_1, k_2, c_2, \mathsf{pk}_2] = \bot$
16 $\quad$ $k \overset{\$}{\leftarrow} \mathcal{K}$
17 $\quad$ $\mathcal{L}_H := \mathcal{L}_H \cup \{(\mathsf{label}, k_1, k_2, c_2, \mathsf{pk}_2)\}$
18 $\quad$ $\mathcal{L}_H[\mathsf{label}, k_1, k_2, c_2, \mathsf{pk}_2] := k$
19 **return** $\mathcal{L}_H[\mathsf{label}, k_1, k_2, c_2, \mathsf{pk}_2]$

Oracle $\mathrm{DECAPO}^*(\mathsf{pk}_0, c)$

20 parse c as (c_1, c_2)
21 $k_2 := \mathsf{Decap}_2(\mathsf{sk}_{2,0}, c_2)$
22 **if** $\exists (\mathsf{label}, k_1, k_2, c_2, \mathsf{pk}_{2,0}) \in \mathcal{L}_H$ s.t.
23 $\quad$ $\mathrm{PCO}_1(\mathsf{pk}_{1,0}, k_1, c_1) = 1$
24 $\quad\quad$ **return** $\mathcal{L}_H[\mathsf{label}, k_1, k_2, c_2, \mathsf{pk}_{2,0}]$
25 **else if** $\mathsf{D}[\mathsf{pk}_{2,0}, c_1, c_2] = \bot$
26 $\quad$ $k \overset{\$}{\leftarrow} \mathcal{K}$
27 $\quad$ $\mathsf{D} := \mathsf{D} \cup \{(\mathsf{pk}_{2,0}, c_1, c_2)\}$
28 $\quad$ $\mathsf{D}[\mathsf{pk}_{2,0}, c_1, c_2] := k$
29 $k := \mathsf{D}[\mathsf{pk}_{2,0}, c_1, c_2]$
30 **return** k

Oracle $\mathrm{DECAPO}^*(\mathsf{pk}_1, c)$

31 parse c as (c_1, c_2)
32 $k_2 := \mathsf{Decap}_2(\mathsf{sk}_{2,1}, c_2)$
33 **if** $\exists (\mathsf{label}, k_1, k_2, c_2, \mathsf{pk}_{2,1}) \in \mathcal{L}_H$ s.t.
34 $\quad$ $\mathrm{PCO}_1(\mathsf{pk}_{1,1}, k_1, c_1) = 1$
35 $\quad\quad$ **return** $\mathcal{L}_H[\mathsf{label}, k_1, k_2, c_2, \mathsf{pk}_{2,1}]$
36 **else if** $\mathsf{D}[\mathsf{pk}_{2,1}, c_1, c_2] = \bot$
37 $\quad$ $k \overset{\$}{\leftarrow} \mathcal{K}$
38 $\quad$ $\mathsf{D} := \mathsf{D} \cup \{(\mathsf{pk}_{2,1}, c_1, c_2)\}$
39 $\quad$ $\mathsf{D}[\mathsf{pk}_{2,1}, c_1, c_2] := k$
40 $k := \mathsf{D}[\mathsf{pk}_{2,1}, c_1, c_2]$
41 **return** k

Fig. 14. The adversary $\mathcal{C}^{\mathrm{PCO}_1(\cdot,\cdot,\cdot)}$ against the wANO-PCA security of KEM_1 for the proof of Lemma 2. In the reduction, $\mathcal{C}$ queries PCO_1 at most $O(q_H \cdot q_D)$ times.

Finally, as shown in Fig. 14, we can bound the success probability of $\mathcal{A}$ in $\mathbf{G}_3$ by the wANO-PCA advantage of KEM_1. In the reduction, $\mathcal{C}$ can justify whether

$\mathsf{Decap}_1(\mathsf{sk}_{1,0}, c_1) = k_1$ (or $\mathsf{Decap}_1(\mathsf{sk}_{1,1}, c_1) = k_1$, resp.) by querying the oracle PCO_1 with $(\mathsf{pk}_{1,0}, k_1, c_1)$ (or $(\mathsf{pk}_{1,1}, k_1, c_1)$, resp.), and we have

$$\Pr[\mathbf{G}_3^{\mathcal{A}} \Rightarrow 1] \leq \mathsf{Adv}_{\mathsf{KEM}_1}^{\mathsf{wANO\text{-}PCA}}(\mathcal{C}) + \frac{1}{2}.$$

We have Eq. (7) by combining all the bounds above.   □

We have shown the wANO-CCA* security of HKEM in Lemma 2. Since the wANO-CCA* security is stronger than the wANO-CCA security[5], we get the ANO-CCA of HKEM by Theorem 1, and we describe it in the following corollary:

Lemma 3 (Anonymity of HKEM (Case II)). *Let* $\mathsf{KEM}_1 = (\mathsf{KeyGen}_1, \mathsf{Encap}_1, \mathsf{Decap}_1)$ *and* $\mathsf{KEM}_2 = (\mathsf{KeyGen}_2, \mathsf{Encap}_2, \mathsf{Decap}_2)$ *be two* wANO-PCA *secure key encapsulation mechanisms. Let* $H : \mathcal{L} \times \mathcal{K}_1 \times \mathcal{K}_2 \times \mathcal{C}_2 \times \mathcal{PK}_2 \to \mathcal{K}$ *be a random oracle and let* $\mathcal{A}$ *be an adversary against the* ANO-CCA *security of* HKEM, *making at most* q_H *queries to the random oracle and* q_D *queries to the decapsulation oracles. Then there exists an* IND-CCA *adversary* $\mathcal{A}_1$, *a* wANO-PCA *adversary* $\mathcal{C}$ *against* KEM_1 *and a* wANO-PCA *adversary* $\mathcal{B}$ *against* KEM_2 *such that*

$$\mathsf{Adv}_{\mathsf{HKEM}}^{\mathsf{ANO\text{-}CCA}}(\mathcal{A}) \leq \mathsf{Adv}_{\mathsf{HKEM}}^{\mathsf{IND\text{-}CCA}}(\mathcal{A}_1) + \mathsf{Adv}_{\mathsf{KEM}_1}^{\mathsf{wANO\text{-}PCA}}(\mathcal{C}) + \mathsf{Adv}_{\mathsf{KEM}_2}^{\mathsf{wANO\text{-}PCA}}(\mathcal{B}). \quad (8)$$

and

$$\mathbf{Time}(\mathcal{A}_1) \approx \mathbf{Time}(\mathcal{A}), \quad \mathbf{Mem}^*(\mathcal{A}_1) \approx \mathbf{Mem}(\mathcal{A}),$$
$$\mathbf{Time}(\mathcal{B}) \approx \mathbf{Time}(\mathcal{A}), \quad \mathbf{Mem}^*(\mathcal{B}) = \mathbf{Mem}(\mathcal{A}) + \mathcal{O}(q_H),$$
$$\mathbf{Time}(\mathcal{C}) \approx \mathbf{Time}(\mathcal{A}), \quad \mathbf{Mem}^*(\mathcal{C}) = \mathbf{Mem}(\mathcal{A}) + \mathcal{O}(q_H) + \mathcal{O}(q_D).$$

5   Our Variant of **X-Wing**

In this section, we consider a variant of X-Wing with one change, where our hybrid KEM outputs $K := H(\mathsf{label}\|k_1\|c_1\|k_2\|c_2\|\mathsf{pk}_2)$ with the additional ciphertext c_1 from KEM_1. According to the definition in [5], here the label is encoded as 6-byte ASCII string "`"\.//^\""`. We denote this variant as HKEM$'$ and prove its ANO-CCA and IND-CCA security in the random oracle model. These changes allow us to give memory-tight reductions. We highlight the changes in Line 09 and Line 16. Let $\mathsf{KEM}_1 = (\mathsf{KeyGen}_1, \mathsf{Encap}_1, \mathsf{Decap}_1)$ and $\mathsf{KEM}_2 = (\mathsf{KeyGen}_2, \mathsf{Encap}_2, \mathsf{Decap}_2)$. The definition of HKEM$'$ is given in Fig. 15. Let $\mathcal{K}_1$ and $\mathcal{K}_2$ denote the key space of KEM_1 and KEM_2 respectively, and let $\mathcal{C}_1$ and $\mathcal{C}_2$ denote the ciphertext space of KEM_1 and KEM_2 respectively. Let $\mathcal{PK}_2$ be the public key space of KEM_2, $\mathcal{L}$ be the label space for label and $\mathcal{K}$ be the key space for HKEM$'$.

Theorem 2 shows the wANO-CCA* security of HKEM$'$ in the ROM, based on the wANO-PCA security of KEM_1 and KEM_2. By instantiating KEM_1 with

---

[5] Because in wANO-CCA* an adversary can ask decapsulation on a challenge ciphertext.

Algorithm KeyGen(par)	**Algorithm** Encap(pk)	**Algorithm** Decap(sk, c)
01 $(\mathsf{sk}_1, \mathsf{pk}_1) \leftarrow \mathsf{KeyGen}_1(\mathsf{par}_1)$	06 parse pk as $(\mathsf{pk}_1, \mathsf{pk}_2)$	12 parse sk as $(\mathsf{sk}_1, \mathsf{sk}_2, \mathsf{pk}_2)$
02 $(\mathsf{sk}_2, \mathsf{pk}_2) \leftarrow \mathsf{KeyGen}_2(\mathsf{par}_2)$	07 $(k_1, c_1) \leftarrow \mathsf{Encap}_1(\mathsf{pk}_1)$	13 parse c as (c_1, c_2)
03 $\mathsf{pk} := (\mathsf{pk}_1, \mathsf{pk}_2)$	08 $(k_2, c_2) \leftarrow \mathsf{Encap}_2(\mathsf{pk}_2)$	14 $k_1 := \mathsf{Decap}_1(\mathsf{sk}_1, c_1)$
04 $\mathsf{sk} := (\mathsf{sk}_1, \mathsf{sk}_2)$	09 $k := H(\mathsf{label}\|k_1\|c_1\|k_2\|c_2\|\mathsf{pk}_2)$	15 $k_2 := \mathsf{Decap}_2(\mathsf{sk}_2, c_2)$
05 **return** (pk, sk)	10 $c := (c_1, c_2)$	16 $k := H(\mathsf{label}\|k_1\|c_1\|k_2\|c_2\|\mathsf{pk}_2)$
	11 **return** (k, c)	17 **return** k

Fig. 15. Definition of the variant HKEM$'$.

ML-KEM-768 and KEM$_2$ with EG-KEM, EG-KEM satisfies wANO-PCA without any assumption. Thus we can conclude that HKEM$'$ is wANO-CCA* (and also wANO-CCA) if ML-KEM-768 is wANO-PCA secure. The wANO-CCA* security proofs of EG-KEM and ML-KEM-768 are given in the full version [4], and wANO-CCA* directly implies wANO-PCA security.

Then, we analyze the IND-CCA security of HKEM$'$, as shown in Theorem 3. The IND-CCA security of HKEM$'$ only requires the OW-PCA security of either KEM$_1$ or KEM$_2$ in the ROM. By combining Lemma 1 and Theorem 2, we obtain the ANO-CCA security of HKEM$'$, with the tightness of advantage, time, and memory.

To summarize, if we instantiate KEM$_1$ and KEM$_2$ with ML-KEM-768 and EG-KEM respectively, then we can obtain the ANO-CCA security of HKEM$'$ under the wANO-PCA and OW-PCA security of ML-KEM-768, without any other assumption. Or, we could also reduce it to the wANO-PCA security of ML-KEM-768 and the StCDH assumption, where the latter implies the OW-PCA security of EG-KEM.

The following Theorem 2 gives a memory-tight reduction from wANO-CCA* of HKEM$'$ to wANO-PCA of both KEM$_1$ and KEM$_2$. Comparing to Lemma 2, this reduction can achieve the memory tightness because c_1 is included in the hash query. As pointed out in [5], when implementing H with SHA3-256, omitting c_1 (which is the ciphertext of ML-KEM-768) from the input of H provides about a 9% performance improvement. Hence, we trade this 9% efficiency for memory-tightness, subsequently, stronger security guarantees. We mainly view our HKEM$'$ as a theoretical contribution, rather than a drop-in practical replacement.

Theorem 2 (wANO-CCA* of HKEM$'$). *Let* $\mathsf{KEM}_1 = (\mathsf{KeyGen}_1, \mathsf{Encap}_1, \mathsf{Decap}_1)$ *and* $\mathsf{KEM}_2 = (\mathsf{KeyGen}_2, \mathsf{Encap}_2, \mathsf{Decap}_2)$ *be two* wANO-PCA *secure key encapsulation mechanisms. Let* $H : \mathcal{L} \times \mathcal{K}_1 \times \mathcal{C}_1 \times \mathcal{K}_2 \times \mathcal{C}_2 \times \mathcal{PK}_2 \to \mathcal{K}$ *be a random oracle and let* $\mathcal{A}$ *be an adversary against the* wANO-CCA* *security of the hybrid KEM* HKEM$'$*, making at most* q_H *queries to the random oracle and* q_D *queries to the decryption oracle. Then there exists a* wANO-PCA *adversary* $\mathcal{B}$ *against* KEM$_2$ *and a* wANO-PCA *adversary* $\mathcal{C}$ *against* KEM$_1$ *such that*

$$\mathsf{Adv}^{\mathsf{wANO\text{-}CCA}^*}_{\mathsf{HKEM}'}(\mathcal{A}) \leq \mathsf{Adv}^{\mathsf{wANO\text{-}PCA}}_{\mathsf{KEM}_1}(\mathcal{C}) + \mathsf{Adv}^{\mathsf{wANO\text{-}PCA}}_{\mathsf{KEM}_2}(\mathcal{B}) + \mathsf{Adv}^{\mathsf{COLL}}_{\mathsf{KEM}_2}. \tag{9}$$

and

$$\mathbf{Time}(\mathcal{B}) \approx \mathbf{Time}(\mathcal{A}), \quad \mathbf{Mem}^*(\mathcal{B}) \approx \mathbf{Mem}(\mathcal{A}),$$
$$\mathbf{Time}(\mathcal{C}) \approx \mathbf{Time}(\mathcal{A}), \quad \mathbf{Mem}^*(\mathcal{C}) \approx \mathbf{Mem}(\mathcal{A}).$$

PROOF. Let $\mathcal{A}$ be an adversary against the wANO-CCA* security of HKEM$'$. Consider the sequence of games $\mathbf{G}_0$-$\mathbf{G}_2$ shown in Fig. 16.

Game $\mathbf{G}_0$ - $\mathbf{G}_2$	**Oracle $\mathrm{DECAPO}^*(\mathsf{pk}_0, c)$**
01 $(\mathsf{sk}_{1,0}, \mathsf{pk}_{1,0}) \leftarrow \mathsf{KeyGen}_1(\mathsf{par}_1)$	21 parse c as (c_1, c_2)
02 $(\mathsf{sk}_{1,0}, \mathsf{pk}_{1,1}) \leftarrow \mathsf{KeyGen}_1(\mathsf{par}_1)$	22 $k_1 := \mathsf{Decap}_1(\mathsf{sk}_{1,0}, c_1)$
03 $(\mathsf{sk}_{2,0}, \mathsf{pk}_{2,0}) \leftarrow \mathsf{KeyGen}_2(\mathsf{par}_2)$	23 $k_2 := \mathsf{Decap}_2(\mathsf{sk}_{2,0}, c_2)$
04 $(\mathsf{sk}_{2,1}, \mathsf{pk}_{2,1}) \leftarrow \mathsf{KeyGen}_2(\mathsf{par}_2)$	24 $k = H(\mathsf{label}\|k_1\|c_1\|k_2\|c_2\|\mathsf{pk}_{2,0})$ $\backslash\!\backslash \mathbf{G}_0$
05 **if** $\mathsf{pk}_{2,0} = \mathsf{pk}_{2,1}$ $\backslash\!\backslash \mathbf{G}_1$-$\mathbf{G}_2$	25 $k = H_0(\mathsf{label}\| \star \|c_1\| \star \|c_2\|\mathsf{pk}_{2,0})$ $\backslash\!\backslash \mathbf{G}_1$-$\mathbf{G}_2$
06 BAD $:=$ **true**; **abort** $\backslash\!\backslash \mathbf{G}_1$-$\mathbf{G}_2$	26 **return** k
07 $\mathsf{pk}_0 := (\mathsf{pk}_{1,0}, \mathsf{pk}_{2,0})$	
08 $\mathsf{pk}_1 := (\mathsf{pk}_{1,1}, \mathsf{pk}_{2,1})$	**Oracle $\mathrm{DECAPO}^*(\mathsf{pk}_1, c)$**
09 $\mathsf{sk}_0 := (\mathsf{sk}_{1,0}, \mathsf{sk}_{2,0})$	27 parse c as (c_1, c_2)
10 $\mathsf{sk}_1 := (\mathsf{sk}_{2,1}, \mathsf{sk}_{2,1})$	28 $k_1 := \mathsf{Decap}_1(\mathsf{sk}_{1,1}, c_1)$
11 $b \xleftarrow{\$} \{0, 1\}$	29 $k_2 := \mathsf{Decap}_2(\mathsf{sk}_{2,1}, c_2)$
12 $H_0, H_1 \xleftarrow{\$} \Omega_H$ $\backslash\!\backslash \mathbf{G}_1$-$\mathbf{G}_2$	30 $k = H(\mathsf{label}\|k_1\|c_1\|k_2\|c_2\|\mathsf{pk}_{2,1})$ $\backslash\!\backslash \mathbf{G}_0$
13 $(c_1^*, k_1^*) \leftarrow \mathsf{Encap}_1(\mathsf{pk}_{1,b})$	31 $k = H_1(\mathsf{label}\| \star \|c_1\| \star \|c_2\|\mathsf{pk}_{2,1})$ $\backslash\!\backslash \mathbf{G}_1$-$\mathbf{G}_2$
14 $(c_2^*, k_2^*) \leftarrow \mathsf{Encap}_2(\mathsf{pk}_{2,b})$ $\backslash\!\backslash \mathbf{G}_0$-$\mathbf{G}_1$	32 **return** k
15 $(c_2^*, k_2^*) \leftarrow \mathsf{Encap}_2(\mathsf{pk}_{2,0})$ $\backslash\!\backslash \mathbf{G}_2$	
16 $K^* := H(\mathsf{label}\|k_1^*\|c_1^*\|k_2^*\|c_2^*\|\mathsf{pk}_{2,b})$ $\backslash\!\backslash \mathbf{G}_0$	**Oracle $H(\mathsf{label}\|k_1\|c_1\|k_2\|c_2\|\mathsf{pk}_2)$**
17 $K^* := H_b(\mathsf{label}\| \star \|c_1^*\| \star \|c_2^*\|\mathsf{pk}_{2,b})$ $\backslash\!\backslash \mathbf{G}_1$-$\mathbf{G}_2$	33 **if** $\exists \hat{b}$ s.t. $\mathsf{pk}_{2,\hat{b}} = \mathsf{pk}_2$ $\backslash\!\backslash \mathbf{G}_1$-$\mathbf{G}_2$
18 $c^* := (c_1^*, c_2^*)$	34 **if** $\mathsf{Decap}_1(\mathsf{sk}_{1,\hat{b}}, c_1) = k_1 \wedge$
19 $b' \leftarrow \mathcal{A}^{\mathrm{DECAPO}^*(\cdot, \cdot), H(\cdot)}(\mathsf{pk}_0, \mathsf{pk}_1, c^*)$	35 $\mathsf{Decap}_2(\mathsf{sk}_{2,\hat{b}}, c_2) = k_2$ $\backslash\!\backslash \mathbf{G}_1$-$\mathbf{G}_2$
20 **return** $[\![b = b']\!]$	36 **return** $H_{\hat{b}}(\mathsf{label}\| \star \|c_1\| \star \|c_2\|\mathsf{pk}_2)$ $\backslash\!\backslash \mathbf{G}_1$-$\mathbf{G}_2$
	37 **return** $H(\mathsf{label}\|k_1\|c_1\|k_2\|c_2\|\mathsf{pk}_2)$

Fig. 16. Games $\mathbf{G}_0$-$\mathbf{G}_2$ for the proof of Theorem 2.

__Game $\mathbf{G}_0$__: This is the wANO-CCA* security game for HKEM$'$.

$$\Pr[\mathbf{G}_0^{\mathcal{A}} \Rightarrow 1] = \mathsf{Adv}_{\mathsf{HKEM}'}^{\mathsf{wANO\text{-}CCA}^*}(\mathcal{A}) + \frac{1}{2}.$$

__Game $\mathbf{G}_1$__: In this game, we change all the possible decapsulation values of HKEM$'$ by reprogramming the random oracle H (i.e. including all the hash values that might be used in the decapsulation oracles and the value of $K^* = H(\mathsf{label}\|k_1^*\|c_1^*\|k_2^*\|c_2^*\|\mathsf{pk}_{2,b}))$. Specifically speaking, for all the tuples $(\mathsf{label}\|k_1\|c_1 \|k_2\|c_2\|\mathsf{pk}_2)$ satisfying $\mathsf{pk}_{2,\hat{b}} = \mathsf{pk}_2$ (here $\hat{b} \in \{0,1\}$ denotes which public key of KEM$_2$ corresponds to pk_2), if $k_1 = \mathsf{Decap}_1(\mathsf{sk}_{1,\hat{b}}, c_1) \wedge k_2 = \mathsf{Decap}_2(\mathsf{sk}_{2,\hat{b}}, c_2)$, we change the corresponding hash value into $H_{\hat{b}}(\mathsf{label}\| \star \|c_1\| \star \|c_2\|\mathsf{pk}_2)$.

Define a event BAD : $\mathsf{pk}_{2,0} = \mathsf{pk}_{2,1}$, then $\mathcal{A}$'s view in $\mathbf{G}_0$ and $\mathbf{G}_1$ are the same when BAD never occurs. Since the probability of BAD happening can be bounded by the collision advantage of public keys of KEM$_2$, we have

$$\left| \Pr[\mathbf{G}_1^{\mathcal{A}} \Rightarrow 1] - \Pr[\mathbf{G}_0^{\mathcal{A}} \Rightarrow 1] \right| \leq \Pr[\mathrm{BAD}] \leq \mathsf{Adv}_{\mathsf{KEM}_2}^{\mathsf{COLL}}.$$

Reduction $\mathcal{B}_2^{\mathrm{PCO2}(\cdot,\cdot,\cdot)}(\mathsf{pk}_{2,0},\mathsf{pk}_{2,1},c_2^*)$	**Oracle** $H(\mathsf{label}\|k_1\|c_1\|k_2\|c_2\|\mathsf{pk}_2)$
01 $(\mathsf{sk}_{1,0},\mathsf{pk}_{1,0})\leftarrow \mathsf{KeyGen}_1(\mathsf{par}_1)$	13 **if** $\exists\hat{b}$ s.t. $\mathsf{pk}_{2,\hat{b}}=\mathsf{pk}_2$
02 $(\mathsf{sk}_{1,0},\mathsf{pk}_{1,1})\leftarrow \mathsf{KeyGen}_1(\mathsf{par}_1)$	14 **if** $\mathsf{Decap}_1(\mathsf{sk}_{1,\hat{b}},c_1)=k_1\wedge$
03 $\mathsf{pk}_0:=(\mathsf{pk}_{1,0},\mathsf{pk}_{2,0})$	15 $\mathrm{PCO}_2(\mathsf{pk}_{2,\hat{b}},k_2,c_2)=1$
04 $\mathsf{pk}_1:=(\mathsf{pk}_{1,1},\mathsf{pk}_{2,1})$	16 **return** $H_{\hat{b}}(\mathsf{label}\|\star\|c_1\|\star\|c_2\|\mathsf{pk}_2)$
05 $(c_1^*,k_1^*)\leftarrow \mathsf{Encap}_1(\mathsf{pk}_{1,1})$	17 **return** $H(\mathsf{label}\|k_1\|c_1\|k_2\|c_2\|\mathsf{pk}_2)$
06 $c^*:=(c_1^*,c_2^*)$	
07 $H_0,H_1\xleftarrow{\$}\Omega_H$	**Oracle** $\mathrm{DecapO}^*(\mathsf{pk}_1,c)$
08 $b'\leftarrow \mathcal{A}^{\mathrm{DecapO}^*(\cdot,\cdot),H(\cdot)}(\mathsf{pk}_0,\mathsf{pk}_1,c^*)$	18 parse c as (c_1,c_2)
09 **return** b'	19 $k=H_1(\mathsf{label}\|\star\|c_1\|\star\|c_2\|\mathsf{pk}_{2,1})$
	20 **return** k
Oracle $\mathrm{DecapO}^*(\mathsf{pk}_0,c)$	
10 parse c as (c_1,c_2)	
11 $k=H_0(\mathsf{label}\|\star\|c_1\|\star\|c_2\|\mathsf{pk}_{2,0})$	
12 **return** k	

Fig. 17. The adversary $\mathcal{B}_2^{\mathrm{PCO2}(\cdot,\cdot,\cdot)}$ against the wANO-PCA security of KEM_2 for the proof of Theorem 2. In the reduction, $\mathcal{B}_2$ queries the PCO_2 oracle at most $2q_H$ times.

<u>**Game $\mathbf{G}_2$**</u>: In this game, instead of using the random bit b to get c_2^*, we compute it by fixing the bit to be 0, that is $(c_2^*,k_2^*)\leftarrow \mathsf{Encap}_2(\mathsf{pk}_{2,0})$. Games $\mathbf{G}_2$ and $\mathbf{G}_1$ will only have a difference when $b\xleftarrow{\$}\{0,1\}$ is chosen to be 1. By using the reduction shown in Fig. 17, we can bound this difference by the wANO-PCA advantage of KEM_2:

$$\left|\Pr[\mathbf{G}_2^{\mathcal{A}}\Rightarrow 1]-\Pr[\mathbf{G}_1^{\mathcal{A}}\Rightarrow 1]\right|=\frac{1}{2}\cdot\left|\Pr[\mathbf{G}_2^{\mathcal{A}}\Rightarrow 1|b=1]-\Pr[\mathbf{G}_1^{\mathcal{A}}\Rightarrow 1|b=1]\right|$$

$$\leq \mathsf{Adv}_{\mathsf{KEM}_2}^{\mathsf{wANO\text{-}PCA}}(\mathcal{B}_2).$$

Reduction $\mathcal{C}^{\mathrm{PCO1}(\cdot,\cdot,\cdot)}(\mathsf{pk}_{1,0},\mathsf{pk}_{1,1},c_1^*)$	**Oracle** $H(\mathsf{label}\|k_1\|c_1\|k_2\|c_2\|\mathsf{pk}_2)$
01 $(\mathsf{sk}_{2,0},\mathsf{pk}_{2,0})\leftarrow \mathsf{KeyGen}_2(\mathsf{par}_2)$	13 **if** $\exists\hat{b}$ s.t. $\mathsf{pk}_{2,\hat{b}}=\mathsf{pk}_2$
02 $(\mathsf{sk}_{2,0},\mathsf{pk}_{2,1})\leftarrow \mathsf{KeyGen}_2(\mathsf{par}_2)$	14 **if** $\mathrm{PCO}_1(\mathsf{pk}_{1,\hat{b}},k_1,c_1)=1\wedge$
03 $\mathsf{pk}_0:=(\mathsf{pk}_{1,0},\mathsf{pk}_{2,0})$	15 $\mathsf{Decap}_2(\mathsf{sk}_{2,\hat{b}},c_2)=k_2$
04 $\mathsf{pk}_1:=(\mathsf{pk}_{1,1},\mathsf{pk}_{2,1})$	16 **return** $H_{\hat{b}}(\mathsf{label}\|\star\|c_1\|\star\|c_2\|\mathsf{pk}_2)$
05 $(c_2^*,k_2^*)\leftarrow \mathsf{Encap}_2(\mathsf{pk}_{2,0})$	17 **return** $H(\mathsf{label}\|k_1\|c_1\|k_2\|c_2\|\mathsf{pk}_2)$
06 $c^*:=(c_1^*,c_2^*)$	
07 $H_0,H_1\xleftarrow{\$}\Omega_H$	**Oracle** $\mathrm{DecapO}^*(\mathsf{pk}_1,c)$
08 $b'\leftarrow \mathcal{A}^{\mathrm{DecapO}^*(\cdot,\cdot),H(\cdot)}(\mathsf{pk}_0,\mathsf{pk}_1,c^*)$	18 parse c as (c_1,c_2)
09 **return** b'	19 $k=H_1(\mathsf{label}\|\star\|c_1\|\star\|c_2\|\mathsf{pk}_{2,1})$
	20 **return** k
Oracle $\mathrm{DecapO}^*(\mathsf{pk}_0,c)$	
10 parse c as (c_1,c_2)	
11 $k=H_0(\mathsf{label}\|\star\|c_1\|\star\|c_2\|\mathsf{pk}_{2,0})$	
12 **return** k	

Fig. 18. The adversary $\mathcal{C}^{\mathrm{PCO1}(\cdot,\cdot,\cdot)}$ against the wANO-PCA security of KEM_1 for the proof of Theorem 2. In the reduction, $\mathcal{C}$ queries the PCO_1 oracle at most $2q_H$ times.

Finally, as shown in Fig. 18, we can bound the success probability of $\mathcal{A}$ in $\mathbf{G}_2$ by the wANO-PCA advantage of KEM_1, therefore

$$\Pr[\mathbf{G}_2^{\mathcal{A}} \Rightarrow 1] \le \mathsf{Adv}_{\mathsf{KEM}_1}^{\mathsf{wANO\text{-}PCA}}(\mathcal{C}) + \frac{1}{2}.$$

We have Eq. (9) by combining all the bounds above.   □

As shown in Lemma 1, wANO-CCA and IND-CCA together impiles ANO-CCA, so we prove the IND-CCA security of HKEM' in the following Theorem 3. Our proof shows that IND-CCA of HKEM' only requires one of the underlying KEM is OW-PCA, and the reduction is memory-tight.

Theorem 3 (OW-PCA$_1$/OW-PCA$_2$ $\Rightarrow$ IND-CCA). *Let* $\mathsf{KEM}_1 = (\mathsf{KeyGen}_1,$ $\mathsf{Encap}_1, \mathsf{Decap}_1)$ *and* $\mathsf{KEM}_2 = (\mathsf{KeyGen}_2, \mathsf{Encap}_2, \mathsf{Decap}_2)$ *be two key encapsulation mechanisms. Let* $H : \mathcal{L} \times \mathcal{K}_1 \times \mathcal{C}_1 \times \mathcal{K}_2 \times \mathcal{C}_2 \times \mathcal{PK}_2 \to \mathcal{K}$ *be a random oracle and let* $\mathcal{A}$ *be an adversary against the* IND-CCA *security of the hybrid KEM* HKEM', *making at most* q_H *queries to the random oracle and* q_D *queries to the decryption oracle. Then there exists an* OW-PCA *adversary* $\mathcal{B}$ *against* KEM_1 *or* KEM_2 *such that*

$$\mathsf{Adv}_{\mathsf{HKEM}'}^{\mathsf{IND\text{-}CCA}}(\mathcal{A}) \le \min(\mathsf{Adv}_{\mathsf{KEM}_1}^{\mathsf{OW\text{-}PCA}}(\mathcal{B}), \mathsf{Adv}_{\mathsf{KEM}_2}^{\mathsf{OW\text{-}PCA}}(\mathcal{B})), \tag{10}$$

and

$$\mathbf{Time}(\mathcal{B}) \approx \mathbf{Time}(\mathcal{A}), \quad \mathbf{Mem}^*(\mathcal{B}) \approx \mathbf{Mem}(\mathcal{A}).$$

PROOF. Let $\mathcal{A}$ be an adversary against the IND-CCA security of HKEM'. Consider the sequence of games $\mathbf{G}_0$-$\mathbf{G}_2$ shown in Fig. 19.

Game $\mathbf{G}_0$ - $\mathbf{G}_2$	**Oracle $H(\mathsf{label}\|k_1\|c_1\|k_2\|c_2\|\mathsf{pk}_2)$**
01 $(\mathsf{sk}_1, \mathsf{pk}_1) \leftarrow \mathsf{KeyGen}_1(\mathsf{par}_1)$	16 **if** $\mathsf{Decap}_1(\mathsf{sk}_1, c_1) = k_1 \wedge$
02 $(\mathsf{sk}_2, \mathsf{pk}_2) \leftarrow \mathsf{KeyGen}_2(\mathsf{par}_2)$	17 $\quad \mathsf{Decap}_2(\mathsf{sk}_2, c_2) = k_2$ $\quad\quad\quad \backslash\backslash \mathbf{G}_1\text{-}\mathbf{G}_2$
03 $\mathsf{pk} := (\mathsf{pk}_1, \mathsf{pk}_2)$	18 $\quad\quad$ **if** $c_1 = c_1^* \wedge c_2 = c_2^*$ $\quad\quad\quad \backslash\backslash \mathbf{G}_2$
04 $\mathsf{sk} := (\mathsf{sk}_1, \mathsf{sk}_2)$	19 $\quad\quad\quad$ **BAD := true; abort** $\quad\quad \backslash\backslash \mathbf{G}_2$
05 $(c_1^*, k_1^*) \leftarrow \mathsf{Encap}_1(\mathsf{pk}_1)$	20 $\quad\quad$ **return** $H'(\mathsf{label}\| \star \|c_1\| \star \|c_2\|\mathsf{pk}_2)$ $\backslash\backslash \mathbf{G}_1\text{-}\mathbf{G}_2$
06 $(c_2^*, k_2^*) \leftarrow \mathsf{Encap}_2(\mathsf{pk}_2)$	21 **return** $H(\mathsf{label}\|k_1\|c_1\|k_2\|c_2\|\mathsf{pk}_2)$
07 $c^* := (c_1^*, c_2^*)$	
	Oracle DECAPO(pk, c)
08 $K_0 \xleftarrow{\$} \mathcal{K}$	22 **if** $c = c^*$
09 $K_1 := H(\mathsf{label}\|k_1^*\|c_1^*\|k_2^*\|c_2^*\|\mathsf{pk}_2)$ $\backslash\backslash \mathbf{G}_0$	23 $\quad$ **return** $\perp$
10 $H' \xleftarrow{\$} \Omega_H$ $\quad\quad\quad\quad\quad\quad\quad\quad \backslash\backslash \mathbf{G}_1\text{-}\mathbf{G}_2$	24 parse c as (c_1, c_2)
11 $K_1 := H'(\mathsf{label}\| \star \|c_1^*\| \star \|c_2^*\|\mathsf{pk}_2)$ $\backslash\backslash \mathbf{G}_1$	25 $k_1 := \mathsf{Decap}_1(\mathsf{sk}_1, c_1)$ $\quad\quad\quad\quad \backslash\backslash \mathbf{G}_0$
12 $K_1 \xleftarrow{\$} \mathcal{K}$ $\quad\quad\quad\quad\quad\quad\quad\quad\quad \backslash\backslash \mathbf{G}_2$	26 $k_2 := \mathsf{Decap}_2(\mathsf{sk}_2, c_2)$ $\quad\quad\quad\quad \backslash\backslash \mathbf{G}_0$
13 $b \xleftarrow{\$} \{0, 1\}$	27 $k = H(\mathsf{label}\|k_1\|c_1\|k_2\|c_2\|\mathsf{pk}_2)$ $\quad \backslash\backslash \mathbf{G}_0$
14 $b' \leftarrow \mathcal{A}^{\mathrm{DECAPO}(\mathsf{pk}, \cdot), H(\cdot)}(\mathsf{pk}, (c^*, K_b^*))$	28 $k = H'(\mathsf{label}\| \star \|c_1\| \star \|c_2\|\mathsf{pk}_2)$ $\backslash\backslash \mathbf{G}_1\text{-}\mathbf{G}_2$
15 **return** $[\![b = b']\!]$	29 **return** k

Fig. 19. Games $\mathbf{G}_0$-$\mathbf{G}_2$ for the proof of Theorem 3.

Game $\mathbf{G}_0$: This is the IND-CCA security game for HKEM'.

$$\Pr[\mathbf{G}_0^{\mathcal{A}} \Rightarrow 1] = \mathsf{Adv}_{\mathsf{HKEM}'}^{\mathsf{IND\text{-}CCA}}(\mathcal{A}).$$

Game G_1: In this game, we reprogram the hash values of all the tuples $(\mathsf{label}\|k_1\|c_1\|k_2\|c_2\|\mathsf{pk}_2)$ which satisfy $k_1 = \mathsf{Decap}(\mathsf{sk}_1, c_1) \wedge k_2 = \mathsf{Decap}(\mathsf{sk}_2, c_2)$. Specifically, if $k_1 = \mathsf{Decap}(\mathsf{sk}_1, c_1) \wedge k_2 = \mathsf{Decap}(\mathsf{sk}_2, c_2)$, then we replace the corresponding hash value of $(\mathsf{label}\|k_1\|c_1\|k_2\|c_2\|\mathsf{pk}_2)$ with the value of $H'(\mathsf{label}\|\star\|c_1\|\star\|c_2\|\mathsf{pk}_2)$, where H' is a random function. By doing this, we no longer need the secret key in the decapsulation oracle.

Since there is a bijection between $(\mathsf{Decap}(\mathsf{sk}_1, c_1), c_1, \mathsf{Decap}(\mathsf{sk}_2, c_2), c_2)$ and $(\star, c_1, \star, c_2)$, this change preserves the distribution, we have

$$\Pr[\mathbf{G}_1^{\mathcal{A}} \Rightarrow 1] = \Pr[\mathbf{G}_0^{\mathcal{A}} \Rightarrow 1].$$

Game G_2: The only difference between $\mathbf{G}_2$ and $\mathbf{G}_1$ is that we choose k uniformly random here. If the adversary $\mathcal{A}$ never queries the random oracle H with $(\mathsf{label}\|k_1^*\|c_1^*\|k_2^*\|c_2^*\|\mathsf{pk}_2)$, then the environment of these two games are exactly the same. We denote this event as $\mathtt{BAD}$ and can bound the difference of $\mathbf{G}_1$ and $\mathbf{G}_2$ by it.

Without loss of generality, here we reduce the probability of $\mathtt{BAD}$ to the OW-PCA security of KEM_1. As described in Fig. 20, if $\mathtt{BAD}$ occurs, then $\mathcal{B}$ can win the OW-PCA game of KEM_1 by returning the corresponding k_1. Thus we have

$$\left| \Pr[\mathbf{G}_2^{\mathcal{A}} \Rightarrow 1] - \Pr[\mathbf{G}_1^{\mathcal{A}} \Rightarrow 1] \right| \leq \Pr[\mathtt{BAD}] \leq \mathsf{Adv}_{\mathsf{KEM}_1}^{\mathsf{OW\text{-}PCA}}(\mathcal{B}).$$

Reduction $\mathcal{B}^{\mathrm{PCO}_1(\mathsf{pk}_1, \cdot, \cdot)}(\mathsf{pk}_1, c_1^*)$

01 $(\mathsf{sk}_2, \mathsf{pk}_2) \leftarrow \mathsf{KeyGen}_2(\mathsf{par}_2)$
02 $\mathsf{pk} := (\mathsf{pk}_1, \mathsf{pk}_2)$
03 $(c_2^*, k_2^*) \leftarrow \mathsf{Encap}_2(\mathsf{pk}_2)$
04 $c^* := (c_1^*, c_2^*)$
05 $K^* \xleftarrow{\$} \mathcal{K}$
06 $H' \xleftarrow{\$} \Omega_H$
07 $b' \leftarrow \mathcal{A}^{\mathrm{DECAPO}(\mathsf{pk}, \cdot), H(\cdot)}(\mathsf{pk}, (c^*, K^*))$
08 **abort**

Oracle $H(\mathsf{label}\|k_1\|c_1\|k_2\|c_2\|\mathsf{pk}_2)$

09 **if** $\mathrm{PCO}_1(\mathsf{pk}_1, k_1, c_1) = 1$
10   **if** $c_1 = c_1^*$
11      $\mathtt{BAD} := \mathbf{true}$; **abort**
12   **else if** $\mathsf{Decap}_2(\mathsf{sk}_2, c_2) = k_2$
13   **return** $H'(\mathsf{label}\|\star\|c_1\|\star\|c_2\|\mathsf{pk}_2)$
14 **return** $H(\mathsf{label}\|k_1\|c_1\|k_2\|c_2\|\mathsf{pk}_2)$

Oracle $\mathrm{DECAPO}(\mathsf{pk}, c)$

15 **if** $c = c^*$
16   **return** $\perp$
17 parse c as (c_1, c_2)
18 $k = H'(\mathsf{label}\|\star\|c_1\|\star\|c_2\|\mathsf{pk}_2)$
19 **return** k

Fig. 20. The adversary $\mathcal{B}^{\mathrm{PCO}_1(\mathsf{pk}_1, \cdot, \cdot)}$ against the OW-PCA security of HKEM' for the proof of Theorem 3. In the reduction, $\mathcal{B}$ queries the PCO_1 oracle at most q_H times.

If KEM_1 is not OW-PCA secure, we can also reduce the probability of $\mathtt{BAD}$ to the OW-PCA security of KEM_2 by using a similar reduction, where we only need to substitute KEM_1 and KEM_2. Therefore,

$$\left| \Pr[\mathbf{G}_2^{\mathcal{A}} \Rightarrow 1] - \Pr[\mathbf{G}_1^{\mathcal{A}} \Rightarrow 1] \right| \leq \Pr[\mathtt{BAD}] \leq \min(\mathsf{Adv}_{\mathsf{KEM}_1}^{\mathsf{OW\text{-}PCA}}(\mathcal{B}), \mathsf{Adv}_{\mathsf{KEM}_2}^{\mathsf{OW\text{-}PCA}}(\mathcal{B})).$$

Since in this game, both K_0 and K_1 are chosen uniformly random, we have

$$\Pr[\mathbf{G}_2^{\mathcal{A}} \Rightarrow 1] = \frac{1}{2}.$$

We have Eq. (10) by combining all the bounds above. $\qquad\square$

Acknowledgments. We thank the anonymous reviewers from PKC 2026 and Taehun Kang for their careful reading of our paper and valuable suggestions for a better comparison with the work of Günther et al.[24] and a more detailed efficiency comparison between our HKEM′ and the original X-Wing scheme.

References

1. Albrecht, M.R., et al.: Classic McEliece. Tech. rep., National Institute of Standards and Technology (2020). https://csrc.nist.gov/projects/post-quantum-cryptography/post-quantum-cryptography-standardization/round-3-submissions
2. Albrecht, M.R., Player, R., Scott, S.: On the concrete hardness of learning with errors. J. Math. Cryptol. **9**(3), 169–203 (2015). https://doi.org/10.1515/jmc-2015-0016
3. Auerbach, B., Cash, D., Fersch, M., Kiltz, E.: Memory-tight reductions. In: Katz, J., Shacham, H. (eds.) CRYPTO 2017. LNCS, vol. 10401, pp. 101–132. Springer, Cham (2017). https://doi.org/10.1007/978-3-319-63688-7_4
4. Bao, J., Pan, J.: Anonymity of x-wing and its variants. Cryptology ePrint Archive, Paper 2026/396 (2026). https://eprint.iacr.org/2026/396
5. Barbosa, M., et al.: X-Wing. CiC **1**(1), 21 (2024)
6. Becker, A., Ducas, L., Gama, N., Laarhoven, T.: New directions in nearest neighbor searching with applications to lattice sieving. In: Krauthgamer, R. (ed.) 27th SODA, pp. 10–24. ACM-SIAM (2016)
7. Beguinet, H., Chevalier, C., Pointcheval, D., Ricosset, T., Rossi, M.: GeT a CAKE: generic transformations from key encapsulation mechanisms to password authenticated key exchanges. In: Tibouchi, M., Wang, X. (eds.) ACNS 2023, Part II. LNCS, vol. 13906, pp. 516–538. Springer, Cham (2023). https://doi.org/10.1007/978-3-031-33491-7_19
8. Bellare, M., Boldyreva, A., Micali, S.: Public-key encryption in a multi-user setting: security proofs and improvements. In: Preneel, B. (ed.) EUROCRYPT 2000. LNCS, vol. 1807, pp. 259–274. Springer, Heidelberg (2000). https://doi.org/10.1007/3-540-45539-6_18
9. Bellare, M., Ristenpart, T.: Simulation without the artificial abort: Simplified proof and improved concrete security for Waters' IBE scheme. In: Joux, A. (ed.) EUROCRYPT 2009. LNCS, vol. 5479, pp. 407–424. Springer, Berlin, Heidelberg (2009). https://doi.org/10.1007/978-3-642-01001-9_24
10. Bellare, M., Rogaway, P.: The exact security of digital signatures: how to sign with RSA and Rabin. In: Maurer, U.M. (ed.) EUROCRYPT'96. LNCS, vol. 1070, pp. 399–416. Springer, Berlin, Heidelberg (1996). https://doi.org/10.1007/3-540-68339-9_34
11. Ben-Sasson, E., et al.: Zerocash: decentralized anonymous payments from bitcoin. In: 2014 IEEE Symposium on Security and Privacy, pp. 459–474. IEEE Computer Society Press (2014)

12. Bernstein, D.J., et al.: KyberSlash: exploiting secret-dependent division timings in kyber implementations. TCHES 2025 (2025). https://eprint.iacr.org/2024/1049
13. Bhattacharyya, R.: Memory-tight reductions for practical key encapsulation mechanisms. In: Kiayias, A., Kohlweiss, M., Wallden, P., Zikas, V. (eds.) PKC 2020. LNCS, vol. 12110, pp. 249–278. Springer, Cham (2020). https://doi.org/10.1007/978-3-030-45374-9_9
14. Camenisch, J., Lysyanskaya, A.: An efficient system for non-transferable anonymous credentials with optional anonymity revocation. In: Pfitzmann, B. (ed.) EUROCRYPT 2001. LNCS, vol. 2045, pp. 93–118. Springer, Heidelberg (2001). https://doi.org/10.1007/3-540-44987-6_7
15. Chen, Y., Nguyen, P.Q.: BKZ 2.0: better lattice security estimates. In: Lee, D.H., Wang, X. (eds.) ASIACRYPT 2011. LNCS, vol. 7073, pp. 1–20. Springer, Heidelberg (2011). https://doi.org/10.1007/978-3-642-25385-0_1
16. Connolly, C., Wood, C.A., Ounsworth, M., van der Merwe, T., Fluhrer, S., McGrew, D.: X-wing: general-purpose hybrid post-quantum kem. Internet-Draft draft-connolly-cfrg-xwing-kem-09, Internet Engineering Task Force (2025). https://datatracker.ietf.org/doc/draft-connolly-cfrg-xwing-kem/, work in Progress
17. D'Anvers, J.-P., Karmakar, A., Sinha Roy, S., Vercauteren, F.: Saber: module-LWR based key exchange, CPA-secure encryption and CCA-secure KEM. In: Joux, A., Nitaj, A., Rachidi, T. (eds.) AFRICACRYPT 2018. LNCS, vol. 10831, pp. 282–305. Springer, Cham (2018). https://doi.org/10.1007/978-3-319-89339-6_16
18. Fujisaki, E., Okamoto, T.: How to enhance the security of public-key encryption at minimum cost. In: Imai, H., Zheng, Y. (eds.) PKC 1999. LNCS, vol. 1560, pp. 53–68. Springer, Heidelberg (1999). https://doi.org/10.1007/3-540-49162-7_5
19. Fujisaki, E., Okamoto, T.: Secure integration of asymmetric and symmetric encryption schemes. In: Wiener, M. (ed.) CRYPTO 1999. LNCS, vol. 1666, pp. 537–554. Springer, Heidelberg (1999). https://doi.org/10.1007/3-540-48405-1_34
20. Fujisaki, E., Okamoto, T.: Secure integration of asymmetric and symmetric encryption schemes. J. Cryptol. **26**(1), 80–101 (2013)
21. Ghoshal, A., Ghosal, R., Jaeger, J., Tessaro, S.: Hiding in plain sight: memory-tight proofs via randomness programming. In: Dunkelman, O., Dziembowski, S. (eds.) EUROCRYPT 2022, Part II. LNCS, vol. 13276, pp. 706–735. Springer, Cham (2022). https://doi.org/10.1007/978-3-031-07085-3_24
22. Giacon, F., Heuer, F., Poettering, B.: KEM combiners. In: Abdalla, M., Dahab, R. (eds.) PKC 2018, Part I. LNCS, vol. 10769, pp. 190–218. Springer, Cham (2018). https://doi.org/10.1007/978-3-319-76578-5_7
23. Grubbs, P., Maram, V., Paterson, K.G.: Anonymous, robust post-quantum public key encryption. In: Dunkelman, O., Dziembowski, S. (eds.) EUROCRYPT 2022, Part III. LNCS, vol. 13277, pp. 402–432. Springer, Cham (2022). https://doi.org/10.1007/978-3-031-07082-2_15
24. Günther, F., Rosenberg, M., Stebila, D., Veitch, S.: Hybrid obfuscated key exchange and KEMs. In: Kalai, Y.T., Kamara, S.F. (eds.) CRYPTO 2025, Part III. LNCS, vol. 16002, pp. 575–609. Springer, Cham (2025). https://doi.org/10.1007/978-3-032-01881-6_18
25. Herold, G., Kirshanova, E.: Improved algorithms for the approximate k-list problem in euclidean norm. In: Fehr, S. (ed.) PKC 2017, Part I. LNCS, vol. 10174, pp. 16–40. Springer, Berlin, Heidelberg (2017). https://doi.org/10.1007/978-3-662-54365-8_2
26. Herold, G., Kirshanova, E., May, A.: On the asymptotic complexity of solving LWE. DCC **86**(1), 55–83 (2018)

27. Hofheinz, D., Hövelmanns, K., Kiltz, E.: A modular analysis of the Fujisaki-Okamoto transformation. In: Kalai, Y., Reyzin, L. (eds.) TCC 2017. LNCS, vol. 10677, pp. 341–371. Springer, Cham (2017). https://doi.org/10.1007/978-3-319-70500-2_12

28. Hövelmanns, K., Kiltz, E., Schäge, S., Unruh, D.: Generic authenticated key exchange in the quantum random oracle model. In: Kiayias, A., Kohlweiss, M., Wallden, P., Zikas, V. (eds.) PKC 2020, Part II. LNCS, vol. 12111, pp. 389–422. Springer, Cham (2020). https://doi.org/10.1007/978-3-030-45388-6_14

29. Katz, J., Lindell, Y.: Introduction to Modern Cryptography. CRC Press, Boca Raton, FL, 3rd edn. (2021). see Section 12.3, Hybrid Encryption: The KEM/DEM Framework

30. Langley, A., Hamburg, M., Turner, S.: Elliptic Curves for Security. RFC 7748 (2016). https://www.rfc-editor.org/info/rfc7748

31. Lyubashevsky, V., et al.: CRYSTALS-DILITHIUM. Tech. rep., National Institute of Standards and Technology (2020). available at https://csrc.nist.gov/projects/post-quantum-cryptography/post-quantum-cryptography-standardization/round-3-submissions

32. Naehrig, M., et al.: FrodoKEM. Tech. rep., National Institute of Standards and Technology (2020). available at https://csrc.nist.gov/projects/post-quantum-cryptography/post-quantum-cryptography-standardization/round-3-submissions

33. Ni, Z., Khalid, A., Liu, W., O'Neill, M.: Bitstream fault injection attacks on crystals kyber implementations on fpgas. In: 2024 Design, Automation & Test in Europe Conference & Exhibition (DATE), pp. 1–6 (2024)

34. NIST: Module-lattice-based key-encapsulation mechanism standard (2024). https://doi.org/10.6028/NIST.FIPS.203

35. Pablos, J.I.E., González Vasco, M.I., Pérez del Pozo, A.L., Soriente, C.: Anonymous authenticated key exchange. In: Fischlin, M., Moonsamy, V. (eds.) ACNS 2025, Part I. LNCS, vol. 15825, pp. 516–546. Springer, Cham (2025). https://doi.org/10.1007/978-3-031-95761-1_18

36. Pan, J., Wagner, B., Zeng, R.: Tighter security for generic authenticated key exchange in the QROM. In: Guo, J., Steinfeld, R. (eds.) ASIACRYPT 2023, Part IV. LNCS, vol. 14441, pp. 401–433. Springer, Singapore (2023). https://doi.org/10.1007/978-981-99-8730-6_13

37. Pan, J., Zeng, R.: A generic construction of tightly secure password-based authenticated key exchange. In: Guo, J., Steinfeld, R. (eds.) ASIACRYPT 2023, Part VIII. LNCS, vol. 14445, pp. 143–175. Springer, Singapore (2023). https://doi.org/10.1007/978-981-99-8742-9_5

38. Sako, K.: An auction protocol which hides bids of losers. In: Imai, H., Zheng, Y. (eds.) PKC 2000. LNCS, vol. 1751, pp. 422–432. Springer, Heidelberg (2000). https://doi.org/10.1007/978-3-540-46588-1_28

39. Schwabe, P., et al.: CRYSTALS-KYBER. Tech. rep., National Institute of Standards and Technology (2020). https://csrc.nist.gov/projects/post-quantum-cryptography/post-quantum-cryptography-standardization/round-3-submissions

40. Unruh, D.: Revocable quantum timed-release encryption. In: Nguyen, P.Q., Oswald, E. (eds.) EUROCRYPT 2014. LNCS, vol. 8441, pp. 129–146. Springer, Heidelberg (2014). https://doi.org/10.1007/978-3-642-55220-5_8

41. Xagawa, K.: Anonymity of NIST PQC round 3 KEMs. In: Dunkelman, O., Dziembowski, S. (eds.) EUROCRYPT 2022, Part III. LNCS, vol. 13277, pp. 551–581. Springer, Cham (2022). https://doi.org/10.1007/978-3-031-07082-2_20

A Novel Leakage Model in OpenSSL's Miller-Rabin Primality Test

Xiaolin Duan[1], Fan Huang[1], Yaqi Wang[1], and Honggang Hu[1,2(✉)]

[1] School of Cyber Science and Technology,
University of Science and Technology of China, Hefei, China
{duanxl,lanplush,yaqi127}@mail.ustc.edu.cn
[2] Hefei National Laboratory, Hefei, China
hghu2005@ustc.edu.cn

Abstract. At CRYPTO 2009, Heninger and Shacham presented a branch-and-prune algorithm for reconstructing an RSA private key given a random fraction of its private components. This method has been widely adopted in side-channel attacks, and its complexity is closely related to the specific leakage pattern encountered. In this work, we propose a new leakage model that enables efficient key reconstruction by exploiting a vulnerability in the modular exponentiation invoked by OpenSSL's implementation of Miller-Rabin primality test. This vulnerability reveals the least significant b bits of each window. Through our proposed model, these bits form new leakage patterns, which we term aligned and misaligned. In particular, the misaligned case includes previously undocumented scenarios where full key recovery is achievable without branching. Then we analyze the global and local behavior of key reconstruction under these patterns. Our evaluation demonstrates that they yield more efficient key reconstruction and maintain this advantage even in the presence of additional erasures. Moreover, in specific scenarios, successful reconstruction remains practical even if the bits obtained are less than 50%. Finally, we conducted a series of experiments to confirm the practicality of our work, successfully recovering the lower 4 bits from each 6-bit window and demonstrating efficient key reconstruction under our model.

Keywords: Partial key exposure attacks · Primality test · Modular exponentiation · Power analysis

1 Introduction

RSA is a mainstream public key cryptosystem that has provided various cryptographic services for decades. Its security relies on the practical difficulty of integer factorization and has been intensively discussed by the community. One research direction pursued by cryptanalysis is to examine this assumption when side information is available, known as partial key exposure attacks, which seek efficient key reconstruction given a fraction of the secrets. To carry out real-world

S. Bai and E. Persichetti (Eds.): PKC 2026, LNCS 16554, pp. 461–493, 2026.
https://doi.org/10.1007/978-3-032-26740-5_15

attacks, a growing field of research has emerged known as side-channel attacks (SCAs), drawing inspiration from Kocher's seminal works [31,32]. This area leverages physical information from running cryptosystems, including power, electromagnetics, time, sound, cache footprints, etc., to extract sufficient secret bits. Some of these attacks have considerable strength, allowing them to derive the full key based solely on the physical information obtained [29,35,36,40]. In practice, noise and countermeasures usually result in incomplete key acquisition, and partial key exposure attacks are required to finish the analysis [7,8,50,51].

1.1 Partial Key Exposure Attacks From Non-consecutive Bits

Ideally, cryptosystems are expected to offer a certain security strength even if partial key bits are compromised, but it is well known that RSA does not enjoy this property. For security purposes, it is critical to know how many partial bits of the secret components suffice to break the system.

Let the public key be (N, e) and the private key be (p, q, d), with $N = pq$ and $d \equiv e^{-1} \mod (p-1)(q-1)$. n denotes the length of p and q. In 1985, Rivest and Shamir [44] indicated that given 2/3 least significant bits (LSBs) of p or q is sufficient to break RSA in polynomial-time. In Coppersmith's pioneered work [19], this result was improved to 1/2 of the most significant bits (MSBs) or LSBs of a factor by utilizing the lattice reduction technique. Later, Howgrave-Graham [27] presented an alternative method to settle this problem by introducing the dual lattice. In 1998, Boneh et al. [10] presented a polynomial-time attack when a quarter of the LSBs of d are given. As the Chinese Remainder Theorem (CRT) is often used to speed up RSA implementation, in 2003, Blömer and May [9] investigated partial key exposure attacks on CRT-RSA and stated that known half of the bits of $d_p = d \mod (p-1)$ or $d_q = d \mod (q-1)$ could efficiently factorize N.

In 2008, Herrmann and May [26] demonstrated that the problem of factorizing N could be solved in polynomial-time when given at most $\mathcal{O}(\log\log N)$ blocks of bits. Concurrently, Halderman et al. [23] proposed cold boot attacks and introduced a new leakage pattern that reveals a random fraction of secret bits. According to the bound presented in [26], lattice-based techniques are not directly applicable to this case. In 2009, Heninger and Shacham [25] explored substantial redundancy in RSA key storage. Based on cold boot attacks, they developed a branch-and-prune algorithm that could efficiently recover the private key given a random fraction of p, q, d, d_p, d_q.

Heninger and Shacham considered an idealized scenario in which all given information is error-free, later termed the erasure model. Under this assumption, their algorithm reconstructs the key deterministically. However, when the given bits contain errors, this algorithm fails as the correct solution is inevitably pruned during the process. In 2010, Henecka et al. [24] proposed a probabilistic algorithm capable of correcting a secret key corrupted by random bit-flip errors. This work was subsequently refined by Paterson et al. [42] with their asymmetric bit-flip model. Later, Kunihiro et al. [33] analyzed the key reconstruction in the presence of both errors and erasures. Saito et al. [45] adapted Henecka's algorithm to efficiently handle leakage in windowed exponentiation.

1.2   Side-Channel Attacks on RSA Modular Exponentiation

Numerous attacks have been proposed to exploit vulnerabilities in RSA implementations, including but not limited to modular exponentiation [1,3–5,8,11,14, 15,21,22,28,29,34–37,39,43,45–47,50–52], binary GCD computation [7], modular inversion [2,6,40], key validation [49] and pseudorandom number generators [17,18].

Modular exponentiation is a core operation in the entire life cycle of RSA, spanning key generation, encryption, and decryption. Its implementation in cryptographic libraries has undergone rigorous scrutiny and several significant iterations to enhance security and reliability. The square-and-multiply method, which exploits the binary representation of the exponent, is less efficient and has been proven to be insecure in Kocher's timing attack [31]. To improve performance, modern open-source cryptographic libraries employ window exponentiation techniques, including fixed-window exponentiation (as in OpenSSL) and sliding-window exponentiation (as in Libgcrypt).

However, windowed exponentiation alone cannot guarantee constant-time execution, as loading precomputed multipliers remains vulnerable to cache-based attacks [8,43,51]. To mitigate this issue, a dummy load technique has become a widely adopted countermeasure. This method works by loading all precomputed operands and then selecting the desired value through bitwise masking operations, thereby eliminating observable timing differences. In [5,28,45], single-trace attacks are presented against this countermeasure. Specifically, Alam et al. [5] circumvented this countermeasure by targeting the exponent extraction in OpenSSL's modular exponentiation. Saito et al. [45] focused on the GNU Multiple Precision Library, developing a deep learning based classifier that uses power analysis to reliably distinguish secret-dependent memory accesses from dummy operations. Hu et al. [28] demonstrated that the dummy load technique introduces measurable power differences during mask computation, allowing efficient key extraction in the sliding-window exponentiation implemented within Libgcrypt.

1.3   Motivation

Lattice-based RSA key reconstruction methods typically require consecutive known bits of the private key [9,10,19,26,27,44]. In comparison, the branch-and-prune algorithm introduced by Heninger and Shacham effectively handles randomly distributed known bits, rendering it suitable for SCAs [25]. While originally proposed in the context of cold-boot attacks, this algorithm has been applied to a variety of side-channel leakage settings [8,16,40,51]. Heninger and Shacham [25] demonstrate that under a random leakage model, key reconstruction is achievable in polynomial time once a certain fraction of private key bits is available. The complexity of this process decreases as more bits are revealed.

However, it should be noted that the efficiency of the branch-and-prune algorithm depends not only on the number of known bits but also by their distribution, that is, the specific leakage pattern.

Given the same amount of known bits, the complexity of key reconstruction via the branch-and-prune algorithm differs significantly across different leakage patterns. Consider an adversary who obtains 50% of the bits of p and q. If these bits form a block of consecutive least significant bits, the branch-and-prune algorithm faces significant computational challenges. Under the constraint $N = pq$, knowledge of either $p[i]$ (the i-th bit of p) or $q[i]$ is sufficient to uniquely determine the other. In this scenario, the redundant information concentrated in the lower bits offers nothing for determining the higher bits during the branch-and-prune process. As a result, the algorithm need to examine up to $2^{n/2}$ candidates to recover the remaining bits, making the reconstruction process computationally infeasible in practice. However, if the known bits follow a distribution, where at each index i, exactly one of $p[i]$ and $q[i]$ is known, the branch-and-prune algorithm can reconstruct the key without generating false candidates. Consequently, its execution becomes highly efficient, with negligible computational cost.

The behavior of Heninger and Shacham's algorithm described above motivates further investigation of new leakage in real-world implementations. OpenSSL, a widely deployed cryptographic library, prevents timing leakage by employing multiple mechanisms to achieve constant-time modular exponentiation, including: (1) a fixed-window method to prevent leakage through square-and-multiply chain; (2) padding the most significant bits of the exponent with zeros to avoid leaking its higher bits; (3) a constant-time look-up table using dummy load operations. The combination of these countermeasures increases the difficulty of attacking modular exponentiation in OpenSSL. Nevertheless, OpenSSL's implementation of modular exponentiation remains vulnerable to other forms of leakage, such as power consumption. When examining the modular exponentiation invoked during primality testing in key generation, an interesting form of leakage emerges. Through our proposed leakage model, we identified new leakage scenarios, including cases where the branch-and-prune algorithm recovers the key without generating any false candidates, which is observed for the first time in a real-world setting.

1.4 Our Contributions

The main contributions of this work are summarized as follows:

- We propose a novel leakage model that enables RSA key reconstruction with the branch-and-prune algorithm by exploiting a previously unnoticed leakage in OpenSSL's Miller-Rabin primality test. First, we reveal a vulnerability in OpenSSL's constant-time modular exponentiation that allows an adversary to extract b bits from each w-bit window during execution. When this operation is invoked by the Miller-Rabin test, it leaks partial information about p and q. Our model maps these leaked bits to an exploitable form. The partial information of p and q is then partitioned into three blocks, among which the leakage pattern of **Block 3** governs the complexity of the key reconstruction process. It comprises two patterns: aligned and misaligned, with the latter including a notable scenario in which the key can be rebuilt without generating any false candidates.

– We characterize the complexity of key reconstruction in aligned and misaligned cases by evaluating the number of candidate solutions examined. To this end, the branching behavior of the branch-and-prune algorithm within a single window (local) and across the entire process (global) is analyzed. We derive the mean and variance of the total number of candidates examined during the reconstruction process and establish an estimated upper bound. Further discussion is instantiated with specific OpenSSL-based parameters: $b = 4$, $w = 6$ for RSA-2048/4096; and $b = 2$, $w = 4$ for RSA-1024. The efficiency observed in misaligned cases, particularly when reconstructing the key without branching, suggests potential tolerance for additional erasures. Our analysis confirms that the speed advantage in misaligned cases persists even with the introduction of additional erasures.

– We conducted practical simple power analysis (SPA) attacks targeting the fixed-window modular exponentiation in OpenSSL's Miller-Rabin primality test, running on an ARM Cortex-M4 processor. The targeted implementation uses dummy load operations to access a pre-computed table in constant time. For a 6-bit window, the first two bits determine the row of the target element in this table, and the remaining four bits determine its column. Table lookup performs 16 iterations. In 15 of these, an all-0 mask is applied, and only the iteration corresponding to the target element uses an all-1 mask. This creates a detectable difference in power consumption between the target iteration and the others. By exploiting this leakage, we successfully recovered the least significant 4 bits from each 6-bit window during a single execution of the modular exponentiation. These recovered bits were then used in our proposed model to perform RSA key reconstruction. Furthermore, we analyzed the occurrence likelihood of the proposed scenarios by repeatedly invoking OpenSSL's key generation, confirming that misaligned scenarios exhibit non-negligible occurrence probabilities.

OpenSSL Long-Term Support Version. Notably, OpenSSL currently maintains two long-term support (LTS) versions: OpenSSL 3.0 and OpenSSL 3.5, both of which generate probable primes with conditions based on auxiliary probable primes [41]. The only difference lies in the number of MillerRabin tests (or modular exponentiation calls) performed. Taking RSA-2048 as an example, OpenSSL 3.0 [48] executes 64 tests on each auxiliary probable prime, as well as on the resulting primes p and q. In contrast, OpenSSL 3.5, updated from NIST FIPS 186-5 standard [41], performs 38 tests on auxiliary primes and only 5 tests on p and q. Nevertheless, these differences do not affect the applicability of our method, since our SPA attack relies solely on a single execution of the modular exponentiation to extract the bits required for key reconstruction. For demonstration purposes, all OpenSSL source code presented in the following sections is taken from the latest version of the 3.0 series.

Conclusion. The vulnerability in modular exponentiation exploited in this work is also applicable to attacks on RSA decryption. In practice, the widespread use of the Chinese Remainder Theorem in RSA implementations indicates that such attacks often result in partial leakage of d_p and d_q. As demonstrated in CacheBleed [51], reconstructing the private key based on partial bits of d_p and d_q requires guessing both k_p and k_q, where $ed_p = 1+k_p(p-1)$ and $ed_q = 1+k_q(q-1)$. In the common case where $e = 65537$, this involves searching through 65,537 possible pairs of k_p and k_q [51], significantly increasing attack complexity.

In conclusion, attacking the modular exponentiation in the Miller-Rabin primality test within OpenSSL's RSA implementation (as opposed to other stages) provides the following advantages: (1) Key reconstruction benefits from our new leakage model, with improved efficiency and additional erasure tolerance. (2) Adversaries recover p and q directly, bypassing the complexities associated with implementations of the Chinese Remainder Theorem.

1.5   Paper Organization

The remainder of the paper is organized as follows. Section 2 gives the preliminaries of the leakage model and describes Heninger and Shacham's work. Section 3 details the vulnerability in the Miller-Rabin primality test implemented in OpenSSL and introduces our proposed leakage model. In Sect. 4, we conducted a comprehensive evaluation of the global and local behavior of the key reconstruction based on the new model, including analysis of scenarios with additional erasures. Section 5 demonstrates our practical attack and experimental results. Section 6 offers conclusion and implications.

2   Background

In this paper, we denote variables by uppercase italic letters (e.g., X) or lowercase italic letters (e.g., x). Upright uppercase letters, such as $\mathrm{G}(\cdot)$ denote the probability generating function (PGF), while $\mathrm{Pr}(\cdot)$, $\mathrm{E}(\cdot)$, and $\mathrm{Var}(\cdot)$ represent probability mass function, expectation, and variance, respectively. $p[i]$ represents the i-th bit of variable p, and $p[i:j]$ denotes the bits from the j-th bit (lower) to the i-th bit (higher) of p, inclusive of both $p[i]$ and $p[j]$.

2.1   Fixed-Window Modular Exponentiation in OpenSSL

Several algorithms have been suggested for RSA modular exponentiation, including the square-and-multiply, the sliding-window, and the fixed-window approach. The latter has gained widespread adoption in cryptographic libraries due to its inherent feature against leaking the square and multiplication sequence.

Given a fixed window of size ω, a base a, a modular N, and an n-bit exponent p denoted as a sequence of digits in base 2^ω, fixed-window exponentiation outputs $r = a^p \mod N$ using two steps. It first computes a set of multipliers $a_j = a^j \mod N$ for $0 \le j \le 2^\omega - 1$. Then from the most significant to the least significant digit of p, r is accumulated by squaring ω times and multiplying a_{p_i} in each iteration.

A naive implementation of fixed-window exponentiation suffers from severe lookup table leaks, especially from cache-based channels. OpenSSL mitigated this vulnerability by integrating dummy load operations with a scatter-gather memory layout, following Intel's recommendation [12,13]. This technique partitions each precomputed multiplier into blocks and interleaves blocks from different multipliers within the same cache line, thereby making cache-line access patterns independent of the specific multiplier being processed. Under this memory layout, identifying specific cache line accesses could leak partial bits of the window exponent, necessitating dummy loads to obscure cache access patterns. Building on this implementation, Yarom et al. [51] devised CacheBleed, a subcache-line attack capable of exposing the least significant three bits of each window through cache bank conflicts. In response, OpenSSL 1.0.2 g implemented a patch that iterates over all chunks of each multiplier and applies a masking operation for selection. This countermeasure remains active by default in current OpenSSL releases.

2.2   Miller-Rabin Primality Test

Cryptographic libraries typically call a random number generator followed by a primality test to obtain secret components p and q. Miller-Rabin test, a probabilistic algorithm that returns whether a given number is likely to be prime, is frequently employed to check for prime numbers.

Given a prime $p = 2^s \cdot p' + 1$ and an integer base a such that $0 < a < p$, then one of the following congruence relations holds: $a^{p'} \equiv 1 \mod p$ and $a^{2^r \cdot p'} \equiv -1 \mod p$ for some $0 \le r < s$. This can be proved based on two facts:

- Fermat's little theorem: $a^{p-1} \equiv 1 \mod p$;
- The only square roots of 1 modulo p are 1 and -1.

However, the inverse of the above property is incorrect. One of the above congruence relations holding does not guarantee p is prime. It only promises such p is a strong probable prime to base a. A small fraction of composites, known as strong pseudoprimes, also pass this test. Miller-Rabin algorithm assesses the primality of a given number with different bases. If enough tests are passed, the number is said to be prime with high probability. The number of tests is determined according to the size of p and the desired probability.

2.3   Probability Generating Functions [30]

The probability generating function refers to the power series expression of the probability mass function of random variables. It is often used to describe the probability distribution of a discrete random variable.

Algorithm 1 Miller-Rabin Primality Test

Require: prime candidate $p = 2^s \cdot p' + 1$, number of rounds j,
Ensure: statement "p is composite" or "p is likely prime".
 1: **for** $i = 1$ to j **do**
 2:     choose a random $a \in \{2, 3, ..., p - 2\}$;
 3:     $u = a^{p'} \bmod p$;
 4:     **if** $u \neq 1$ and $u \neq p - 1$ **then**
 5:         **for** $j = 1$ to $s - 1$ **do**
 6:             $u = u^2 \bmod p$;
 7:             **if** $u = 1$ **then**
 8:                 **return** ("p is composite")
 9:             **end if**
10:         **end for**
11:         **if** $u \neq p - 1$ **then**
12:             **return** ("p is composite")
13:         **end if**
14:     **end if**
15: **end for**
16: **return** ("p is likely prime")

Definition 1 (Probability Generating Functions). *Let X be a discrete random variable taking values in the non-negative integers. The PGF of X is defined as*

$$G_X(s) = E(s^X) = \sum_{x=0}^{\infty} s^x \Pr(X = x).$$

The following properties can be obtained according to the definition of PGF, expectation, and variance: (1) $G_X(1) = \sum_{x=0}^{\infty} \Pr(X = x) = 1$, (2) $E(X) = G_X'(1)$ and (3) $\mathrm{Var}(X) = G_X''(1) + G_X'(1) - G_X'(1)^2$.

Theorem 1. *Assume that $X_1,...,X_n$ are independent random variables, and $Y = X_1 + ... + X_n$. Then*

$$G_Y(s) = \prod_{i=1}^{n} G_{X_i}(s).$$

Theorem 2. *Assume that $\{X_i\}$ is a sequence of independent and identically distributed random variables with the common PGF G_X. Let $Y = X_1 + ... + X_M$, where M is a random variable independent of X_i. Denoting the PGF of M as G_M, the PGF of Y is*

$$G_Y(s) = G_M(G_X(s)).$$

2.4   The Heninger-Shacham Algorithm [25]

At CRYPTO 2009, Heninger and Shacham utilized the algebraic relationship between the private components to develop a branch-and-prune technique for key reconstruction with known bits. They discussed this algorithm in the context of cold boot attacks and demonstrated a lower bound on the number of known bits required for the algorithm to succeed within polynomial-time.

Let (N, e) be an RSA public key, where N is $2n$-bit and $e = 65,537$. The corresponding CRT private key set is $(p, q, d, d_p, d_q, q_{inv} = q^{-1} \mod p)$, which simultaneously satisfies the following equations: (1) $N = pq$, (2) $ed = 1 + k(p - 1)(q - 1)$, (3) $ed_p = 1 + k_p(p - 1)$ and (4) $ed_q = 1 + k_q(q - 1)$, where k, k_p and k_q can be enumerated if e is small. The key exhibits high levels of redundancy, as knowledge of any of its components can lead to the factorization of N. Heninger-Shacham's algorithm leverages these constraints to progressively determine the parameters. It starts from the least significant bit, and at each iteration, partial solutions are branched or pruned depending on the knowledge of bits for that position. Specifically, given the knowledge of bits 0 to $i - 1$, the i-th bit of each argument can be solved by lifting the solution from the constraint equations mod 2^i to the solution mod 2^{i+1}.

Cold boot attacks could result in partial information of $(p, q, d, d_p, d_q, q_{inv})$ being obtained at random. However, in other side-channel models, only some of them may be obtained, such as $\{p, q\}$, $\{d\}$, or $\{d_p, d_q\}$. This study focuses on the first case in which partial knowledge of p and q is revealed. The following part reviews the behavior of the algorithm in this case.

According to Hensel's lifting lemma, the dependency between the i-th bit and known bits is expressed as

$$p[i] + q[i] \equiv (N - \bar{p}\bar{q})[i] \quad \mod 2, \tag{1}$$

where $\bar{p}$ and $\bar{q}$ denote the partial solution of p and q up to i of the bits. Given $\bar{p}$ and $\bar{q}$, the algorithm's branching behavior at bit i can be summarized as follows.

- When both $p[i]$ and $q[i]$ are unknown, the algorithm branches;
- When one of $p[i]$ and $q[i]$ is unknown, there is a unique solution;
- When the i-th bit of p and q are known, the wrong solution is pruned with approximate 50% probability (empirically).

Understanding these cases is straightforward, as the right side of Eq. (1) is given.

Heninger and Shacham conducted a complexity analysis of the reconstruction by examining the algorithm's local and global branching behavior. They evaluated the number of erroneous solutions generated during the process. Specifically, at bit i, the algorithm generates one correct solution and some incorrect solutions. As the number of unknown bits increases, the expansion of branches tends to be exponential; conversely, it converges swiftly when the number of unknown bits decreases.

In their random model, it is assumed that the knowledge of $p[i]$ and $q[i]$ is mutually independent, each occurring with a probability of δ. To establish the relation between the number of branches examined during the reconstruction and δ, the authors calculated the expected number of wrong solutions generated from a correct and incorrect one, denoted as $\mathrm{E}(Z_g)$ and $\mathrm{E}(W_b)$, respectively. Subsequently, using PGF and the sequence, they derived the expected total number of branches produced at step i, represented as $\mathrm{E}(X_i) = \frac{\mathrm{E}(Z_g)}{1 - \mathrm{E}(W_b)}(1 -$

$E(W_b)^i)$. Given that the expressions for the expected values of $E(Z_g)$ and $E(W_b)$ are dependent solely on δ, it follows that when $E(W_b) < 1$, $E(X_i)$ can be bounded by a constant that only depends on δ.

Adding up the incorrect solutions generated at each bit, one can calculate the expected total number of branches examined for an n-bit key. Heninger and Shacham also provided the variance of X_i as a measure of how far $\sum_{i=0}^{n-1} X_i$ is spread from its average value. The following lemma plays an important role in this computation.

Lemma 1.

$$\mathrm{Var}(\sum_{i=1}^{n} X_i) \leq n^2 \max_i \mathrm{Var}(X_i)$$

In sum, if the algorithm has partial knowledge of p and q, it checks no more than $29n^2 + 29n$ keys with a probability higher than $\frac{n^2-1}{n^2}$ when $\delta = 0.59$.

3   A Novel Leakage Model

This section presents a leakage model derived from OpenSSL's implementation of the MillerRabin primality test. We begin by identifying the source of this leakage, followed by a formal characterization of the model and its corresponding leakage scenarios. Finally, we compare these scenarios and analyze the reduction in computational complexity observed in specific cases.

3.1   Root Cause of the Leakage Model

Assuming that an adversary is capable of extracting b bits from each window in a fixed-window modular exponentiation. The proposed leakage model, which emerges when an adversary targets the modular exponentiation invoked during the Miller-Rabin primality testing, arises for two reasons:

- The input to the modular exponentiation in the Miller-Rabin primality test is $\frac{p-1}{T(p-1)}$, as shown in line 3 of Algorithm 1, where $T(p-1)$ denotes the largest power of 2 that divides by $p-1$;
- At the beginning of the modular exponentiation, OpenSSL pads the exponent to the public size of p, which is n, as shown in Listing 1.

The most significant 0 bits of the exponent could be disclosed by analyzing the number of iterations performed in the modular exponentiation. To avoid such a leakage, OpenSSL uses all bits stored in the exponent variable. Listing 1 is a code snippet of constant-time modular exponentiation used in OpenSSL. It computes **rr** $= \mathbf{a^P}$ mod **m**. **BIGNUM** is a structure that holds a single large integer. The member variable **top** represents the number of words used. **BN_BITS2** indicates the word size specified in the *bn.h* file. **bits** corresponds to the public size of the exponent, which ensures that the number of iterations in fixed-window modular exponentiation is independent of the actual size of the exponent.

```
1 int bn_mod_exp_mont_fixed_top(BIGNUM *rr, const BIGNUM *a
      , const BIGNUM *p, const BIGNUM *m, BN_CTX *ctx,
      BN_MONT_CTX *in_mont)
2 {
3       ...
4       /* Use all bits stored in stored in variable p to
      prevent leakage of leading zero bits. */
5       bits = p->top * BN_BITS2;
6       ...
7 }
```

Listing 1. OpenSSL pads the exponent to its public size.

Therefore, the operands for the modular exponentiation in OpenSSL's Miller-Rabin primality test are $p' = \frac{p-1}{\mathrm{T}(p-1)}$ or $q' = \frac{q-1}{\mathrm{T}(q-1)}$, padded to a length of n, as shown in Fig. 1. In our assumption, an adversary can extract b bits from each window of these operands. Given that Heninger and Shacham's branch-and-prune algorithm works by exploiting dependencies between the i-th bits of p and q, the partial bits obtained here are not directly usable as input. A new model is required to characterize the mapping from p' and q' back to p and q, as illustrated in Fig. 1.

3.2 The Proposed Leakage Model

OpenSSL implements the fixed-window exponentiation from left to right, starting from the most significant bit. Since n may not be a multiple of w, the first window can be partial, with a length of $n \bmod w$. All remaining windows are of the full w-bit size. Given this, the bits recovered under our assumption can be expressed as: $p'[xw + y]$ and $q'[xw + y]$, where $0 \leq x \leq \lfloor \frac{n}{w} \rfloor$, $0 \leq y \leq b - 1$, and $0 \leq xw + y \leq n - 1$. p' and q' are recovered in the same manner; thus, the i-th bits of p' and q' are known, or neither is known.

Our model describes the leaked bits as following:

$$\begin{cases} p[(xw + y + \mathrm{T}(p - 1)) \bmod n], \\ q[(xw + y + \mathrm{T}(q - 1)) \bmod n], \end{cases}$$

where $0 \leq x \leq \lfloor \frac{n}{w} \rfloor, 0 \leq y \leq b-1, 0 \leq xw+y \leq n-1$, and $1 \leq \mathrm{T}(p-1), \mathrm{T}(q-1) \leq n$. Since $\mathrm{T}(p - 1)$ is not necessarily equal to $\mathrm{T}(q - 1)$, the i-th bits of p and q exhibit three possible states:

- $p[i]$ and $q[i]$ are known;
- $p[i]$ and $q[i]$ are unknown;
- One of $p[i]$ and $q[i]$ is known.

Suppose $\mathrm{T}(p - 1) > \mathrm{T}(q - 1)$, both p and q can be partitioned into three blocks, as shown in Fig. 2. Specifically,

- **Block 1** $(\mathrm{T}(q - 1) > i \geq 0)$: $p[i] = q[i] = 0$, except $p[0] = q[0] = 1$;
- **Block 2** $(\mathrm{T}(p - 1) > i \geq \mathrm{T}(q - 1))$: $p[i] = 0$ and $q[i]$ may be revealed;

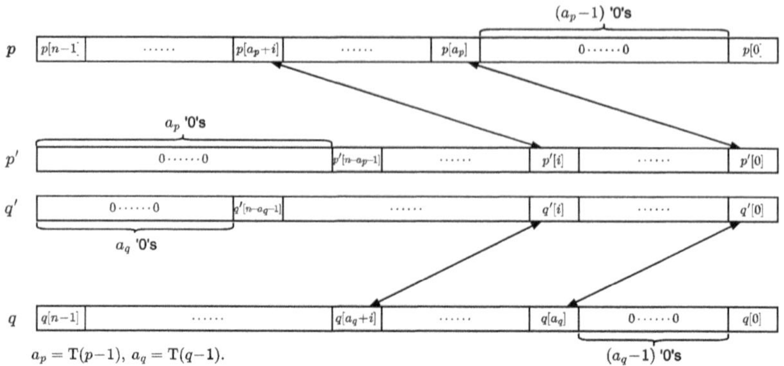

Fig. 1. Map the recovered $p'[i]$ and $q'[i]$ to p and q.

		Block 3		Block 2	Block 1	
p	$p[n-1]$	......	$p[a_p]$	$0 \cdots 0$	$0 \cdots 0$	$p[0]$
q	$q[n-1]$	......	$\cdots$	$q[a_q]$	$0 \cdots 0$	$q[0]$

$a_p = \mathrm{T}(p-1),\ a_q = \mathrm{T}(q-1).$

Fig. 2. p and q recovered from the side-channel oracle.

- **Block 3** $(n - 1 \geq i \geq \mathrm{T}(p - 1))$: each window of p (or q) is revealed in a fixed pattern.

When $\mathrm{T}(p - 1) < \mathrm{T}(q - 1)$, the situation is analogous. **Block 2** is absent when $\mathrm{T}(p - 1) = \mathrm{T}(q - 1)$.

Given $\mathrm{T}(p-1)$ and $\mathrm{T}(q-1)$, **Block 1** is fully determined, and either p or q in **Block 2** can be uniquely computed, yielding exactly one valid partial solution for **Block 3**. Consequently, the efficiency of key reconstruction depends on its performance in **Block 3**, subject to the knowledge of $p[i]$ and $q[i]$ within each window. Notably, the bits recovered in **Block 3** exhibit a periodic pattern within each window. This periodic structure allows τ to be interpreted as defining a ring over the integer w, where τ is defined as the absolute difference between $\mathrm{T}(p-1)$ and $\mathrm{T}(q - 1)$.

In our leakage model, **Block 3** falls into one of following scenarios based on the value of τ.

- The aligned, where $\tau \equiv 0 \bmod w$: $p[i]$ and $q[i]$ are either recovered or unknown;
- The misaligned, where $\tau \not\equiv 0 \bmod w$: $p[i]$ and $q[i]$ could be one of the following: both recovered, one recovered, or both unknown.

For simplicity, the modulus in the above equivalence will be omitted in subsequent discussions.

Table 1 demonstrates both scenarios for a window size of 6, with 4 bits successfully recovered in each window, where $*$ denotes the unknown bit. The remainder of this paper will utilize this assumption as a case study and present corresponding experimental validations. Our model is not constrained by this specific assumption. In Sect. 4, we develop a generalized analysis that extends our results to various assumptions, including 3-bit recovery from 5-bit windows[1] and 2-bit recovery from 4-bit windows[2].

Table 1. Left: an aligned case,   Right: a misaligned case.

$i+2$	$i+1$	i	$i-1$	$i-2$	$i-3$	$i+2$	$i+1$	i	$i-1$	$i-2$	$i-3$
*	*	1	0	1	0	*	*	1	0	1	0
*	*	1	0	1	1	1	0	1	1	*	*

3.3 Reduced Complexity

The occurrence of either scenario during an attack depends on the value of τ, or more precisely, on the randomly generated primes p and q. Before analyzing the probability of these two cases, we discuss their differences.

Due to the branching behavior of the branch-and-prune algorithm at the i-th bit, under the constraint $N = pq$, knowing either $p[i]$ or $q[i]$ is sufficient to uniquely determine the other. This explains why: when $p[i]$ and $q[i]$ are unknown, only two branches are generated, not four; when $p[i]$ and $q[i]$ are known, the redundant information helps to identify and prune incorrect branches.

In the aligned scenario, $p[i]$ and $q[i]$ are unknown or known, indicating that the algorithm branches or performs pruning with a certain probability[3]. In misaligned scenarios, the frequency of such fully known or fully unknown bit-pairs decreases, and cases where only one of them is known become more common. As a result, the reconstruction involves fewer branching operations, which reduces the number of false candidates and thus lowers computational complexity. In the specific scenario studied in this paper, where at least one $p[i]$ or $q[i]$ is available at each bit, the key is reconstructed without generating false candidates.

4 Algorithm Runtime Analysis

This section explores the complexity of key reconstruction under different leakage scenarios by evaluating the number of partial solutions.

4.1 Global Branching Behavior

Given that the proposed leakage scenarios differ only in their window-level recovery patterns, we first establish a general equation characterizing the algorithm's global behavior, then investigate the local branching process in the window.

---

[1] This leakage pattern has been demonstrated in [51].

[2] This leakage pattern represents the specific case we analyzed for 1024-bit RSA.

[3] This probability is estimated by generating multiple pairs of p and q for complexity analysis; however, for fixed p, q, and given bits, the execution of the branch-and-prune algorithm is deterministic.

Let Y_i denote the number of partial solutions checked at window i in **Block 3**, and a sum of Y_i yields the total number of partial keys examined in the third block, where $1 \leq i \leq \lceil (n - max(\mathrm{T}(p-1), \mathrm{T}(q-1)))/w \rceil$.

$$Y_i = \sum_{j=1}^{X_{i-1}} Z_j + Z_c, \tag{2}$$

where Z and Z_c are random variables that count, within a window, the number of key validation attempts triggered by a wrong and a correct solution, respectively. There is only one correct partial key in the whole process. Since the number of incorrect solutions is not constant, it is imperative to estimate how many incorrect solutions are likely to remain after lifting the window i, denoted as X_i.

Let C and W be two random variables representing the number of incorrect candidates remaining after a correct and a wrong solution passes a window in **Block 3**, respectively. Then

$$X_i = \sum_{j=1}^{X_{i-1}} W_j + C. \tag{3}$$

To explore the characteristics of the distribution of Y_i, we have the following expressions.

Theorem 3.

$$\mathrm{E}(Y_i) = \frac{\mathrm{E}(C)\mathrm{E}(Z)}{1 - \mathrm{E}(W)}(1 - \mathrm{E}(W)^{i-1}) + \mathrm{E}(Z_c). \tag{4}$$

Proof. See Appendix A in the full version [20].

$\square$

Theorem 4.

$$\mathrm{Var}(Y_i) = c_3 \mathrm{E}(W)^{2(i-1)} - c_2 \mathrm{E}(W)^{i-1} + c_1, \tag{5}$$

with

$$c_1 = \frac{\mathrm{E}(C)\mathrm{Var}(W) + (1 - \mathrm{E}(W))\mathrm{Var}(C)}{(1 - \mathrm{E}(W)^2)(1 - \mathrm{E}(W))} \mathrm{E}(Z)^2$$

$$+ \frac{\mathrm{E}(C)}{1 - \mathrm{E}(W)}\mathrm{Var}(Z) + \mathrm{Var}(Z_c),$$

$$c_2 = \frac{\mathrm{E}(C)\,\mathrm{Var}(W)}{(1 - \mathrm{E}(W))^2\mathrm{E}(W)}\mathrm{E}(Z)^2 + \frac{\mathrm{E}(C)}{1 - \mathrm{E}(W)}\mathrm{Var}(Z),$$

$$c_3 = \left(\frac{\mathrm{E}(C)\,\mathrm{Var}(W)}{(1 - \mathrm{E}(W)^2)(1 - \mathrm{E}(W))\mathrm{E}(W)} - \frac{\mathrm{Var}(C)}{1 - \mathrm{E}(W)^2}\right)\mathrm{E}(Z)^2.$$

The expression presented above is derived under the assumption that $\mathrm{E}(W) \neq 1$. For the sake of generality, when $\mathrm{E}(W) = 1$,

$$\mathrm{E}(Y_i) = (i - 1)\,\mathrm{E}(C)\mathrm{E}(Z) + \mathrm{E}(Z_c). \tag{6}$$

Similarly,

$$\mathrm{Var}(Y_i) = (\frac{(i - 1)(i - 2)}{2}\mathrm{E}(C)\,\mathrm{Var}(W) + (i - 1)\mathrm{Var}(C))\mathrm{E}(Z)^2$$
$$+ (i - 1)\,\mathrm{E}(C)\,\mathrm{Var}(Z) + \mathrm{Var}(Z_c). \tag{7}$$

Proof. See Appendix A in the full version [20].

$\square$

4.2   Local Branching Behavior at Each Window

Recall that the program's local behavior at each bit depends on the knowledge of $p[i]$ and $q[i]$. Within a window, the leakage pattern is fixed by providing w, b, and τ, where w is given by the implementation of modular exponentiation, b is subject to the attacker's capabilities, and τ is determined by randomly generated p and q. In the reconstruction process, the only variable is the probability of a wrong branch that will be pruned when $p[i]$ and $q[i]$ are known, denoted as φ.

We consider the scenario where the least significant b bits of each window are recovered. When $\tau \equiv 0$, a correct partial solution passes the window and generates $2^{w-b} - 1$ wrong candidates. An incorrect partial solution produces 2^{w-b} erroneous candidates after passing the evaluation with probability $(1-\varphi)^b$. This is the case of alignment.

Depending on the degree of misalignment, the number of situations where $p[i]$ and $q[i]$ are unknown within a window, denoted as Δ, could be reduced at most to

$$\begin{cases} 0 & \text{if } w - b \leq b, \\ w - 2b & \text{if } w - b > b. \end{cases}$$

Considering the attack on fixed-window modular exponentiation, $w - b > b$ implies that less than half of the bits of p and q are obtained. This situation produces a large number of incorrect candidates, rendering key reconstruction infeasible within a reasonable time.[4] Hence, only the case of $w - b \leq b$ is discussed in this study.

Assuming $\mathrm{T}(p - 1) \geq \mathrm{T}(q - 1)$, $\overbrace{*...*}^{w-b} \overbrace{\diamond...\diamond}^{b}$ denotes the least window of p in **Block 3**, where $*$ and $\diamond$ represent unknown and known bits, respectively.[5] As

---

[4] According to [42], the branch-and-prune algorithm works if more than 50% of the secret bits are acquired. Although known bits could be slightly lower than 50%, such as $p[i]$ and $q[i]$ are recovered alternatively, $w - b > b$ indicates two many erasures.

[5] $\mathrm{T}(p - 1) < \mathrm{T}(q - 1)$ is analogous since p and q are equivalent here.

τ increases from 0 to w, the leakage pattern in the corresponding window of q constructs a cycle, while Δ initially decreases from $w - b$ to 0 and then increases back to $w - b$, as shown in Fig. 3.

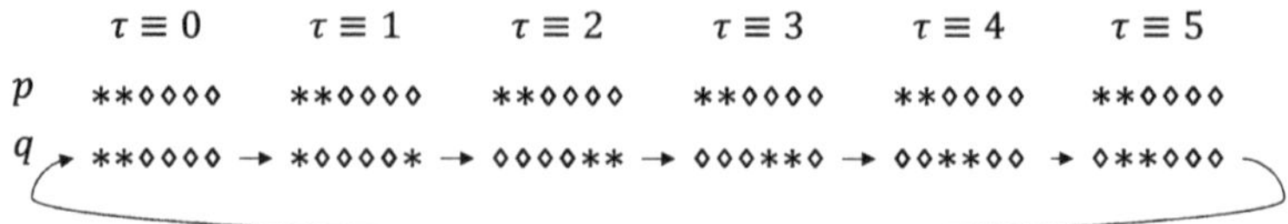

Fig. 3. Take $w = 6$ and $b = 4$ as an example to illustrate the leakage pattern of the window in **Block 3**.

Based on the branching behavior exhibited by the algorithm, it can be observed that C, the number of incorrect candidates remaining after a correct solution passes a window in **Block 3**, is directly related to Δ.

$$\mathrm{E}(C) = 2^{\Delta} - 1, \qquad\qquad \mathrm{E}(C^2) = (2^{\Delta} - 1)^2.$$

Let Λ denote the number of bits where $p[i]$ and $q[i]$ are known in the window. Λ determines the probability of retaining an incorrect input solution, Δ specifies how this solution forks.

$$\mathrm{E}(W) = 2^{\Delta}(1 - \varphi)^{\Lambda}, \qquad\qquad \mathrm{E}(W^2) = 2^{2\Delta}(1 - \varphi)^{\Lambda}.$$

When discussing the number of partial keys verified within a given window, it should be noted that Z and Z_c are determined by Δ, Λ, and the position of known bits. Consider $\tau \equiv 1$ and $\tau \equiv 5$ depicted in Fig. 3. When $\tau \equiv 1$, a correct partial key passes through five bits and branches at the last bit. However, the latter case produces a false branch at the 5-th bit, requiring an additional calculation at the 6-th bit.

The general expressions for the expected values and variances of Z and Z_c require knowledge of the position of known bits, leading to complex expressions. To simplify the computation, we provide $\mathrm{E}(Z_c)$, $\mathrm{E}(Z_c^2)$, $\mathrm{E}(Z)$, and $\mathrm{E}(Z^2)$ under specific w and b, as shown in Table 2. These results can be directly extended to other scenarios.

To demonstrate the results in Table 2, we use the alignment case as an example. After the first 4 evaluations, a correct solution passes the lower 4 bits of the window. Two branches are generated after evaluating the next bit. Then, two candidates are evaluated at the last bit. Thus, a correct solution involves a total of 7 evaluations. In contrast, an incorrect solution may be discarded after each of the first 4 evaluations with a probability of φ. Once an incorrect solution is retained with probability $(1 - \varphi)^4$, it behaves identically to a correct solution in the last two bits. Consequently, $\mathrm{E}(Z) = \sum_{i=1}^{4} i(1 - \varphi)^{i-1}\varphi + 7(1 - \varphi)^4$.

Under the random model, [25] empirically demonstrates that the probability of independently pruning an incorrect candidate approaches $1/2$ for known $p[i]$ and $q[i]$. Since our scenarios can be viewed as special cases of this random model, $\varphi = 1/2$ is expected to hold here. Our simulations confirm this expectation.

Table 2. The expected values and variances for Z and Z_c when $w = 6$ and $b = 4$.

	$\tau \equiv 0$	$\tau \equiv 1$	$\tau \equiv 2$	$\tau \equiv 3$	$\tau \equiv 4$	$\tau \equiv 5$
$E(Z_c)$	7	6	6	6	6	7
$E(Z_c^2)$	49	36	36	36	36	49
$E(Z)$	$\frac{33}{16}$	3	4	3	$\frac{5}{2}$	$\frac{9}{4}$
$E(Z^2)$	$\frac{107}{16}$	$\frac{43}{4}$	$\frac{35}{2}$	$\frac{27}{2}$	$\frac{21}{2}$	$\frac{35}{4}$

4.3 Bounding the Total Number of Keys Examined

The total number of keys examined over an entire program can be represented
as

$$Y = |\mathrm{T}(p-1) - \mathrm{T}(q-1)| + \sum_{i=1}^{l} Y_i + \varepsilon,$$

where $l = \lfloor (n - max(\mathrm{T}(p-1), \mathrm{T}(q-1)))/w \rfloor$ is the number of complete windows in **Block 3**. Specifically, the first term counts the evaluations executed in blocks 2. The second term plus ε represents the total number of keys examined in **Block 3**, where ε denotes the number of keys evaluated in the last window. If $n - max(\mathrm{T}(p-1), \mathrm{T}(q-1))$ is divisible by w, $\varepsilon = 0$. For $E(W) \leq 1$, the program either converges continuously or alternates between divergence and convergence in each window. Thus, the tree does not spread exponentially, which implies that ε will not be too large. In addition, empirical investigations demonstrate that $\mathrm{T}(p-1)$ and $\mathrm{T}(q-1)$ are usually small, as shown in Fig. 4. Therefore, the primary contribution to $E(Y)$ arises from the accumulation of $E(Y_i)$.

Given w, b, τ, and estimation of φ, $E(C)$, $E(W)$, $E(Z_c)$, and $E(Z)$ are constants. According to Theorem 3, we give a bound on $E(Y)$ to facilitate estimation.

$$E(Y) < E\left(\sum_{i=1}^{\left\lceil \frac{n}{w} \right\rceil} Y_i \right) \tag{8}$$

$$\begin{cases} \leq \left\lceil \dfrac{n}{w} \right\rceil \left(\dfrac{E(C)E(Z)}{1 - E(W)} + E(Z_c) \right) & \text{if } E(W) < 1, \\[2ex] = \dfrac{\left\lceil \frac{n}{w} \right\rceil^2 - \left\lceil \frac{n}{w} \right\rceil}{2} E(C)\, E(Z) + \left\lceil \dfrac{n}{w} \right\rceil E(Z_c) & \text{if } E(W) = 1. \end{cases}$$

Next, Lemma 1 gives a bound for the variance of $\sum_i Y_i$, where $1 \leq i \leq \left\lceil \frac{n}{w} \right\rceil$.

$$\mathrm{Var}\left(\sum_i Y_i \right) \leq \left\lceil \frac{n}{w} \right\rceil^2 \max_i \mathrm{Var}(Y_i).$$

From Eq. 5, we observe that it converges to c_1 as i increases. When $i = 1$, $c_3 - c_2 \leq 0$. As i grows, the expression $c_3 E(W)^{2(i-1)} - c_2 E(W)^{i-1}$ remains negative but increases monotonically. Consequently, $\max \mathrm{Var}(Y_i) = c_1$ at $i = \left\lceil \frac{n}{w} \right\rceil$, where c_1 is a constant determined by w, b, τ, and the estimate of φ. The result holds when $E(W) = 1$, where the maximum variance occurs at $\imath = \lceil \frac{n}{w} \rceil$.

Table 3 gives $E(Y)$ and $\mathrm{Var}(Y)$ when $w = 6$, $b = 4$, and $\varphi = 1/2$. Our analysis reveals that both: (i) the expected number of keys examined during reconstruction, and (ii) their degree of dispersion are lower in misaligned cases compared to aligned cases. Despite the fact that the number of recovered bits remains constant, the system exhibits significantly reduced complexity in misalignment scenarios. Furthermore, the cases in which $\tau \equiv 2, 3,$ and 4 yield identical estimates for $E(Y)$ and $\mathrm{Var}(Y)$. These cases can be treated as equivalent in subsequent analyses. Although cases where $\tau \equiv 2$ and $\tau \equiv 3$ show minor differences in $\mathrm{Var}(Y)$, we classify them into the same category. This grouping is justified because both have exactly one bit where $p[i]$ and $q[i]$ are recovered. The observed difference in variance arises from the position of this bit.

Table 3. $E(Y)$ and $\mathrm{Var}(Y)$ when $w = 6$, $b = 4$, and $\varphi = 1/2$.

	$\tau \equiv 0$	$\tau \equiv 1$	$\tau \equiv 2$	$\tau \equiv 3$	$\tau \equiv 4$	$\tau \equiv 5$
$E(C)$	3	1	0	0	0	1
$E(W)$	$\frac{1}{4}$	$\frac{1}{4}$	$\frac{1}{4}$	$\frac{1}{4}$	$\frac{1}{4}$	$\frac{1}{4}$
$E(Z_c)$	7	6	6	6	6	7
$E(Z)$	$\frac{33}{16}$	3	4	3	$\frac{5}{2}$	$\frac{9}{4}$
$E(Y) <$	$\frac{61}{4} \lceil \frac{n}{6} \rceil$	$10 \lceil \frac{n}{6} \rceil$	$6 \lceil \frac{n}{6} \rceil$	$6 \lceil \frac{n}{6} \rceil$	$6 \lceil \frac{n}{6} \rceil$	$10 \lceil \frac{n}{6} \rceil$
$\mathrm{Var}(C)$	0	0	0	0	0	0
$\mathrm{Var}(W)$	$\frac{15}{16}$	$\frac{7}{16}$	$\frac{3}{16}$	$\frac{3}{16}$	$\frac{3}{16}$	$\frac{7}{16}$
$\mathrm{Var}(Z_c)$	0	0	0	0	0	0
$\mathrm{Var}(Z)$	$\frac{623}{256}$	$\frac{7}{4}$	$\frac{3}{2}$	$\frac{9}{2}$	$\frac{17}{4}$	$\frac{59}{16}$
$\mathrm{Var}(Y) \leq$	$\frac{107}{4} \lceil \frac{n}{6} \rceil^2$	$\frac{119}{15} \lceil \frac{n}{6} \rceil^2$	0	0	0	$\frac{121}{15} \lceil \frac{n}{6} \rceil^2$

4.4 Discussion on Additional Erasures

Results in Table 3 suggest that the algorithm could be reconstructed in a reasonable time, even if the recovered partial key contains additional erasures. In this subsection, we examine scenarios in which some windows are totally erased. This happens in some SCAs. For example, in cache-timing attacks, system interruptions may lead to information loss [7,50]. In [38], system noise in power or EM traces may cause some windows to be recovered with a low probability.

Let ρ be the probability that a given window fails to be recovered in either p or q. In this context, the recovery of a window does not imply obtaining all bits, but rather refers specifically to the recovery corresponding to our assumption. For each window, there exist three possible cases:

- Both of p and q are recovered with probability $(1 - \rho)^2$;
- One of p and q is recovered with probability $2\rho(1 - \rho)$;
- Both of p and q fail to be recovered with probability ρ^2.

As additional erasures do not impact the algorithm's global behavior, we only need to re-estimate C, W, Z_c and Z.

$$\begin{aligned}
\mathrm{E}(C) &= (2^\Delta - 1)(1 - \rho)^2 + (2^{w-b} - 1)(2\rho - 2\rho^2) \\
&\quad + (2^w - 1)\rho^2, \\
\mathrm{E}(W) &= 2^\Delta(1 - \varphi)^\Lambda(1 - \rho)^2 + 2^{w-b}(2\rho - 2\rho^2) + 2^w\rho^2.
\end{aligned} \tag{9}$$

According to Eq. (8), $\mathrm{E}(W)$ should be ≤ 1 to avoid an exponential increase in the complexity of the key reconstruction. Given w, b, φ, the expression for $\mathrm{E}(W)$ in (9) depends solely on ρ[6].

Case1: $w = 6$, $b = 4$, *and* $\varphi = 1/2$.

$$\mathrm{E}(W) = \frac{225}{4}\rho^2 + \frac{15}{2}\rho + \frac{1}{4}.$$

Solving the inequality $\mathrm{E}(W) \leq 1$ yields $-\frac{1}{5} \leq \rho \leq \frac{1}{15}$. Since ρ is a probability that should be in $[0, 1]$, we have $\rho \leq \frac{1}{15}$.

Table 4. E(Y) and Var(Y) when $w = 6$, $b = 4$, $\varphi = 1/2$ and $\rho = \frac{1}{15}$.

	$\tau \equiv 0$	$\tau \equiv 1$	$\tau \equiv 2$	$\tau \equiv 3$	$\tau \equiv 4$	$\tau \equiv 5$
$\mathrm{E}(C)$	$\frac{49}{15}$	$\frac{343}{225}$	$\frac{49}{75}$	$\frac{49}{75}$	$\frac{49}{75}$	$\frac{343}{225}$
$\mathrm{E}(W)$	1	1	1	1	1	1
$\mathrm{E}(Z_c)$	$\frac{1{,}631}{225}$	$\frac{497}{75}$	$\frac{1{,}603}{225}$	$\frac{1{,}561}{225}$	$\frac{1{,}519}{225}$	$\frac{1{,}673}{225}$
$\mathrm{E}(Z)$	$\frac{2{,}653}{900}$	$\frac{301}{75}$	$\frac{1{,}211}{225}$	$\frac{973}{225}$	$\frac{833}{225}$	$\frac{742}{225}$
$\mathrm{E}(Y) \approx$	$4.8\left\lceil\frac{n}{6}\right\rceil^2$	$3.1\left\lceil\frac{n}{6}\right\rceil^2$	$1.8\left\lceil\frac{n}{6}\right\rceil^2$	$1.4\left\lceil\frac{n}{6}\right\rceil^2$	$1.2\left\lceil\frac{n}{6}\right\rceil^2$	$2.5\left\lceil\frac{n}{6}\right\rceil^2$
$\mathrm{Var}(C)$	$\frac{3{,}584}{225}$	$\frac{876{,}176}{50{,}625}$	$\frac{103{,}124}{5{,}625}$	$\frac{103{,}124}{5{,}625}$	$\frac{103{,}124}{5{,}625}$	$\frac{876{,}176}{50{,}625}$
$\mathrm{Var}(W)$	$\frac{301}{15}$	$\frac{4{,}417}{225}$	$\frac{1{,}456}{75}$	$\frac{1{,}456}{75}$	$\frac{1{,}456}{75}$	$\frac{4{,}417}{225}$
$\mathrm{Var}(Z_c)$	$\frac{702{,}464}{50{,}625}$	$\frac{29{,}372}{1{,}875}$	$\frac{1{,}202{,}616}{50{,}625}$	$\frac{1{,}004{,}654}{50{,}625}$	$\frac{57{,}736}{3{,}375}$	$\frac{724{,}346}{50{,}625}$
$\mathrm{Var}(Z)$	$\frac{16{,}907{,}891}{8{,}100{,}000}$	$\frac{120{,}799}{5{,}625}$	$\frac{1{,}489{,}754}{50{,}625}$	$\frac{1{,}502{,}396}{50{,}625}$	$\frac{1{,}348{,}886}{50{,}625}$	$\frac{1{,}197{,}686}{50{,}625}$
$\mathrm{Var}(Y) \approx$	$47.5\left\lceil\frac{n}{5}\right\rceil^3$	$40\left\lceil\frac{n}{5}\right\rceil^3$	$30.6\left\lceil\frac{n}{5}\right\rceil^3$	$19.8\left\lceil\frac{n}{5}\right\rceil^3$	$14.5\left\lceil\frac{n}{5}\right\rceil^3$	$11.5\left\lceil\frac{n}{5}\right\rceil^3$

Table 4 presents the estimation of $\mathrm{E}(Y)$ and $\mathrm{Var}(Y)$ computed from equations (6) and (7), accounting for $\frac{1}{15}\%$ unrecovered windows (equivalent to additional erasures). Here, $\approx$ is used instead of $<$ and $\leq$, as we discard lower-order polynomial terms that have a negligible impact on overall expression. Comparing Table 4 with Table 3, the expected number of partial keys verified in the reconstruction scales quadratically with n (as opposed to linearly), due to the introduced erasures. It is observed that the speed advantage in misaligned cases persists even when the introduced erasures approach the algorithm's maximum tolerance. Moreover, the variance of Y indicates that the aligned case is more prone to generating candidates with larger search spaces, which leads to a longer time for key reconstruction in practice.

---

[6] $\mathrm{E}(W)$ is independent of Δ and Λ if $\varphi = \frac{1}{2}$.

Case2: $w = 4$, $b = 2$, *and* $\varphi = 1/2$.

$$E(W) = 9\rho^2 + 6\rho + 1.$$

Solving the inequality $E(W) \leq 1$ yields $\rho = 0$. This is consistent with the results of [25] and [42], which show that revealing 50% of the bits of p and q is necessary to prevent the algorithm's complexity from growing exponentially.

In this case, $\frac{b}{w} = 50\%$ indicates that the key reconstruction cannot tolerate additional erasures. However, $\tau = 2$ in Table 5 suggests that allowing some additional erasures may be feasible in practice. When $\tau = 2$, the reconstruction process verifies at most n correct partial keys. In practical scenarios, although an additional 25-bit erasure would expand the candidate solution space up to 2^{25}, the computational cost remains well within the means of modestly resourced adversaries [16]. For 1024-bit RSA($w = 4$), an additional 25-bit erasure corresponds to approximately 10% windows remaining unrecovered.

Table 5. E(Y) when $w = 4$, $b = 2$, and $\varphi = 1/2$

	$\tau \equiv 0$	$\tau \equiv 1$	$\tau \equiv 2$	$\tau \equiv 3$
$E(C)$	3	1	0	1
$E(W)$	1	1	1	1
$E(Z_c)$	5	4	4	5
$E(Z)$	$\frac{9}{4}$	3	4	3
$E(Y) <$	$\frac{27}{8}\left\lceil\frac{n}{4}\right\rceil^2 + \frac{27}{8}\left\lceil\frac{n}{4}\right\rceil$	$\frac{3}{2}\left\lceil\frac{n}{4}\right\rceil^2 + \frac{5}{2}\left\lceil\frac{n}{4}\right\rceil$	$4\left\lceil\frac{n}{4}\right\rceil$	$\frac{3}{2}\left\lceil\frac{n}{4}\right\rceil^2 + \frac{7}{2}\left\lceil\frac{n}{4}\right\rceil$

In sum, misaligned cases outperform the aligned case in both efficiency and tolerance to additional erasures. Although it is possible in SCAs that the recovered partial key contains errors, we omit this discussion in this work. According to the result presented in [33], the success rate is as low as 4% when p and q contain 1% errors and 25% erasures. In the absence of more efficient error-correction algorithms, the conventional approach treats potential errors as erasures in subsequent processing.

5   Experiment Evaluation

This section illustrates the practical implications of our proposed model from the following perspectives.

- Statistical analysis of the distribution of aligned and misaligned scenarios confirms that they exhibit non-negligible occurrence probabilities.
- SPA attacks are conducted on the target implementation, successfully recovering $T(x - 1)$ and the lower 4 bits within each 6-bit window, empirically validating the practical implications of our leakage assumption.
- An evaluation of key reconstruction is performed between theoretical predictions and practical outcomes.

5.1   Experimental Setup

The experiments in Sects. 5.2 and 5.4 were performed on an AMAX server equipped with 64 CPU cores and 503 GB of RAM. A Python module `pyOpenSSL` is used to generate the key pairs of RSA. Leveraging multiprocess parallel computing, each experiment was completed in minutes to tens of minutes.

The experiments in Sect. 5.3 were carried out on the ChipWhisperer CW308 platform with an STM32F303 target board. The STM32F303 features an ARM Cortex-M4 core operating at 7.38 MHz. Power traces were recorded using CW-Lite at a sampling rate of 4×7.38 MS/s (4 samples per clock cycle) with 10-bit resolution. The trace processing was performed on a ThinkPad X1 laptop running Ubuntu 20.04, equipped with an Intel i7-8550U CPU (1.80 GHz) and 8 GB of RAM. We targeted the RSA implementation in the current version of OpenSSL, using an additional trigger signal to facilitate trace recording. Our analysis focuses on two functions:

- `BN_is_bit_set()`, invoked by `ossl_bn_Miller_rabin_is_prime()` in the source file `bn_prime.c`.
- `MOD_EXP_CTIME_COPY_FROM_PREBUF()`, called by `bn_mod_exp_mont_fixed_top()` in the source file `bn_exp.c`.

5.2   The Distribution of Aligned and Misaligned Cases

To demonstrate that the misaligned cases occur with non-negligible probability, we conducted the statistical analysis by repeatedly invoking OpenSSL to generate the private key set, from which we extracted p and q.

This test was performed 100,000 times for 1024-, 2048-, and 4096-bit RSA, respectively. We recorded the value of $T(p-1)$ and $T(q-1)$. Due to the symmetric roles of p and q in this context, the distributions of $T(p-1)$ and $T(q-1)$ are identical. Figure 4(a) presents the distributions of $T(x-1)$ for 2048-bit RSA, where x represents either prime. Notably, $T(x-1)$ consistently takes relatively small values. Figure 4(b) shows the distributions for the proposed scenarios. As noted previously, these scenarios can be classified by the value of Δ due to the similarity of the computational complexity. Specifically:

- Class 1 ($\tau \equiv 0$): 34,422;
- Class 2 ($\tau \equiv 1, 5$): 35,927;
- Class 3 ($\tau \equiv 2, 3, 4$): 29,651.

Each class occurs with non-negligible probability. Similar behavior is observed for both RSA-1024 and RSA-4096.

5.3   Recovering $T(x-1)$ and `idx[3:0]` via SPA Attacks

Recovering $T(x-1)$. To map the information recovered by SCAs back to p and q, the values of $T(p-1)$ and $T(q-1)$ need to be known. In OpenSSL,

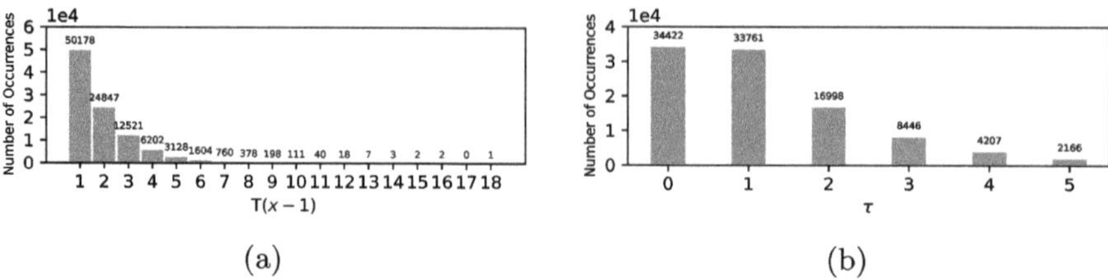

(a)   (b)

Fig. 4. (a) and (b) represent the distributions of $\mathrm{T}(x-1)$ and τ, respectively, for RSA-2048 over 100,000 trials.

the Miller-Rabin primality test calculates $\mathrm{T}(x-1)$ and reduces x to x' before invoking the modular exponentiation.

Listing 2 is a code snippet illustrating the process of calculating $\mathrm{T}(x-1)$ in OpenSSL. The implementation repeatedly calls `BN_is_bit_set()`, which tests whether the a-th bit in `w1` is set to 1. Since this operation is not constant-time, the exact number of function calls, which is $\mathrm{T}(x-1)$, can be leaked through the power channel.

```
1 int ossl_bn_Miller_rabin_is_prime(const BIGNUM *w, int
      iterations, BN_CTX *ctx, BN_GENCB *cb, int enhanced,
      int *status)
2 {
3     ...
4     /* (Step 1) Calculate largest integer 'a' such that
      2^a divides w-1 */
5     a = 1;
6     while (!BN_is_bit_set(w1, a))
7         a++;
8     /* (Step 2) m = (w-1) / 2^a */
9     if (!BN_rshift(m, w1, a))
10         goto err;
11     ...
12 }
```

Listing 2. Computing $\mathrm{T}(x-1)$ in OpenSSL.

In function `ossl_bn_Miller_rabin_is_prime()`, the variable w holds the candidate prime to be tested. line 67 in Listing 2 sequentially check each bit of `w-1`, starting from the second least significant bit, to count the number of trailing zeros. This operation exhibits two properties that introduce a distinct timing channel exploitable via SPA: (1) The execution time of this operation depends on the value of $\mathrm{T}(x-1)$; (2) The execution time for each iteration is nearly constant.

Our experimental analysis successfully identified the power trace corresponding to a single iteration, enabling a precise determination of the iteration count through visual inspection of the power traces. Figure 5(a) displays the power trace when $\mathrm{T}(x-1) = 15$. Each iteration is distinguishable, separated by alternating gray and white intervals. Although all subsequent intervals contain the

168 samples, the first interval initially contains a reduced count due to missing control instructions in the initial loop. To ensure consistent analysis, we padded the first iteration's samples to 168 by borrowing preceding data points. This preprocessing explains the visible deviation in the blue trace (Bottom of Fig. 5(a)) compared to the others. To enhance visibility, we deliberately offset the traces vertically along the y-axis, as well as in Fig. 5(b). Notably, the power trace of all subsequent iterations exhibits highly consistent patterns, enabling a reliable identification of the iteration count through visual inspection.

Figure 5(b) presents a comparison of power traces for $\mathrm{T}(x-1) \equiv 1$ to 6. The colored traces represent the execution of the loop body, whereas the gray traces correspond to unrelated operations. These colored traces overlap at the execution of each iteration. A straightforward method to determine the number of iterations involves cross-correlating a reference single-loop trace (or a reference trace that contains 30 loops) with the target trace, and the number of overlapping segments directly yields the value of $\mathrm{T}(x-1)$.

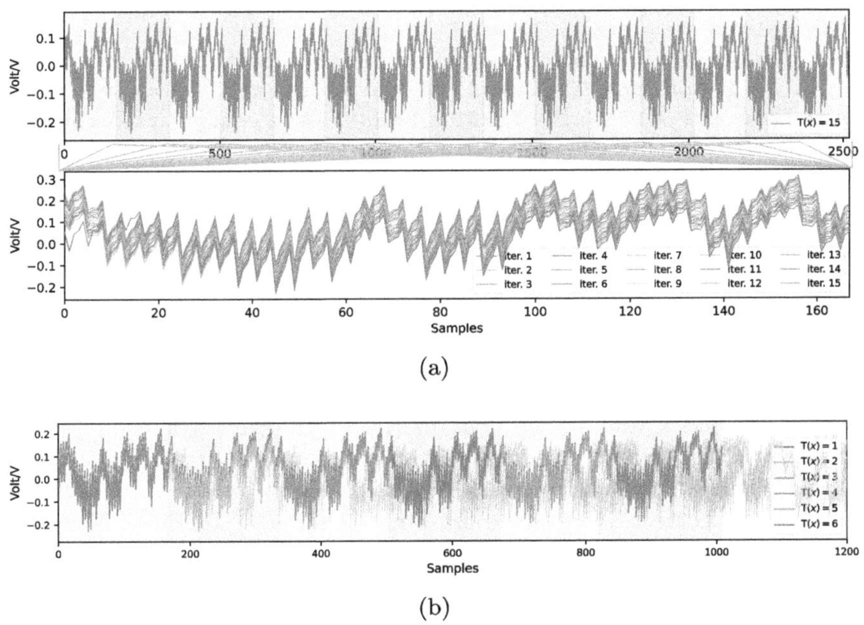

(a)

(b)

Fig. 5. Determining the value of $\mathrm{T}(x-1)$ via SPA.

Moreover, Fig. 4 indicates $\mathrm{T}(p-1)$ and $\mathrm{T}(q-1)$ are typically small. Hence, an exhaustive search for possible values of these two parameters may also lead to successful key reconstruction.

Recovering Partial Bits of p and q. In this subsection, we conducted an SPA attack on the fixed-window modular exponentiation implemented in OpenSSL to validate the practical implications of our leakage assumption.

Target Function: Listing 3 presents the core implementation of fixed-window modular exponentiation in OpenSSL. The computation proceeds in each window as follows:

- Line 4–5 perform the squaring.
- Line 6–7 extract the current window of bits from the exponent.
- Line 9 retrieves the precomputed multiplier corresponding to the bits extracted in line 7.
- Line 10 multiplies the intermediate result by the retrieved multiplier.

```
 1 int bn_mod_exp_mont_fixed_top(BIGNUM *rr, const BIGNUM *a
       , const BIGNUM *p, const BIGNUM *m, BN_CTX *ctx,
       BN_MONT_CTX *in_mont)
 2 {
 3     ...
 4     for (i = 0; i < window; i++)
 5         bn_mul_mont_fixed_top(&tmp, &tmp, &tmp, mont,ctx)
 6     bits -= window;
 7     wvalue = bn_get_bits(p, bits) & wmask;
 8     /* Fetch the appropriate  precomputed value */
 9     MOD_EXP_CTIME_COPY_FROM_PREBUF(&am, top, powerbuf,
       wvalue,window)
10     bn_mul_mont_fixed_top(&tmp, &tmp, &am, mont, ctx)
11     ...
12 }
```

Listing 3. fixed-window modular exponentiation in the current version of OpenSSL.

Listing 4 defines the target function MOD_EXP_CTIME_COPY_FROM_PREBUF(). For a window size of 6, buf holds 64 precomputed multipliers, and their arrangement can be visualized as a 4×16 table. The variable idx (or wvalue in Listing 3) acts as the index for selecting the multiplier to read, where its value represents the partial secret. To protect idx from potential attacks, this function employs a dummy load that sequentially reads all 64 precomputed multipliers and selects the correct one via the masking technique. The mask is computed as: (0 - constant_time_eq_int()&1). This expression yields **0** (all zeros) or -1 (all ones, in two's complement).

```
 1 int MOD_EXP_CTIME_COPY_FROM_PREBUF(BIGNUM *b, int top,
       unsigned char *buf, int idx, int window)
 2 {
 3     ...
 4     int width = 1 << window;
 5     int xstride = 1 << (window - 2);
 6     BN_ULONG y0, y1, y2, y3;
 7     i = idx >> (window - 2);
 8     idx &= xstride - 1;
 9
10     y0 = (BN_ULONG)0 - (constant_time_eq_int(i,0)&1);
11     y1 = (BN_ULONG)0 - (constant_time_eq_int(i,1)&1);
```

```
12        y2 = (BN_ULONG)0 - (constant_time_eq_int(i,2)&1);
13        y3 = (BN_ULONG)0 - (constant_time_eq_int(i,3)&1);
14
15        for (i = 0; i < top; i++, table += width) {
16            BN_ULONG acc = 0;
17            for (j = 0; j < xstride; j++) {
18                   acc |= ( (table[j + 0 * xstride] & y0) |
19                            (table[j + 1 * xstride] & y1) |
20                            (table[j + 2 * xstride] & y2) |
21                            (table[j + 3 * xstride] & y3) )
22                   & ((BN_ULONG)0 - (
        constant_time_eq_int(j,idx)&1));}
23            b->d[i] = acc;}
24        ...
25 }
```

Listing 4. Implementation of fetching the precomputed multiplier.

In line 7–8, `idx` is decomposed into: (1) the upper 2 bits (stored in `i`) as the row index; (2) the lower 4 bits (stored in `idx`) as the column index. Then line 1013 make the selection of the row, where the mask equals to all ones only when the row index matches the upper 2 bits of `idx`. Similarly, in line 15–22, the mask outputs all ones only when the loop counter matches the lower 4 bits of `idx` and **0** otherwise. By distinguishing whether the mask is **0** or all ones, we can recover secret bits in each window. Our experiments focus on line 15–22 in Listing 4, which handle the extraction of 4 bits per window(`idx[3:0]`), rather than retrieving all bits in each 6-bit window. This is because the computation in line 10–13 is too brief to reveal detectable leaks through SPA.

The top of Fig. 6 shows a trace fragment for MOD_EXP_CTIME_COPY_FROM_PREBUF(), extracted from the complete power trace, where `idx[3:0]`= 0. The target function performs 16 iterations, line 22 in Listing 4 compares `idx[3:0]` with j, where j is range from 0 to 15. (0 − `constant_time_eq_int`()&1) outputs all ones when `idx[3:0]`=j. We highlighted the 16 iterations in the target function using alternating gray and white backgrounds, and a distinct downward dip can be observed in the first block, indicating `idx[3:0]`= 0. The middle plot of Fig. 6 overlays the traces of all 16 iterations, where the red line represents `idx[3:0]`= 0, while the remaining 15 lines are shown in gray. Zooming in (bottom plot), the red line is visually distinct from the gray lines. Similar results are observed when `idx[3:0]` takes values from 1 to 15.

Figure 7 shows the trace fragments extracted from the power trace, with each subplot representing the sensitive operations in MOD_EXP_CTIME_COPY_FROM_PREBUF(). The subplots are sorted by `idx[3:0]`, ranging from 0 to 15. Red arrows in the subplots mark leakage locations. It can be observed that the values of `idx[3:0]` corresponding to different traces can be directly distinguished through visual inspection. In sum, we could recover the lower 4 bits of each window by launching SPA attack on an ARM Cortex-M4 device, demonstrating power-based leakage.

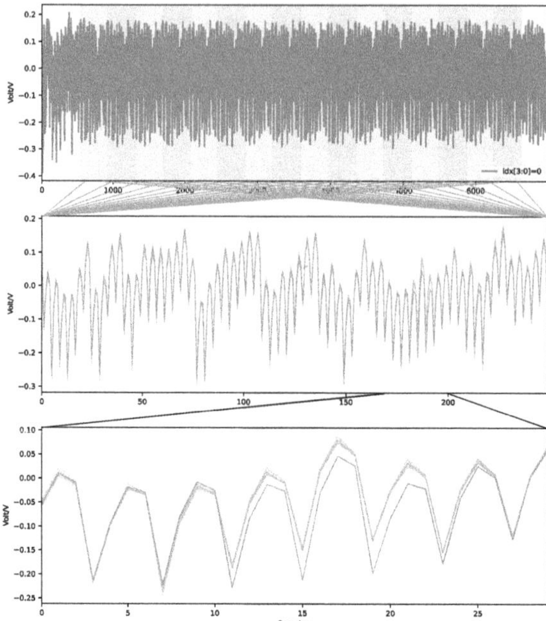

Fig. 6. The power traces of the sensitive operations in MOD_EXP_CTIME_COPY_FROM_
PREBUF().

5.4   An Evaluation of Key Reconstruction

Figure 8 displays the distributions of incorrect partial solutions observed in
100,000 trials for RSA-2048 and RSA-4096. The green line represents cases where
$\tau \equiv 2$, 3 and 4, none of which produced incorrect solutions. These scenarios
occur 29,651 times for RSA-2048 and 29,545 times for RSA-4096, respectively.
We adopted non-uniform intervals in this figure since the number of incorrect
solutions in the remaining two classes varied significantly, ranging from hundreds to hundreds of thousands. For example, when $\tau \equiv 0$, the false solutions
in Fig. 8.(b) varied between $1,849$ to $111,723$. As the interval width increases,
the probability that the number of incorrect solutions falls within a given range
drops rapidly.[7] The blue and orange lines demonstrate that most the results
cluster around the expected value, with only a few trails significantly exceeding
it. This observed distribution aligns well with our theoretical predictions.

Table 6 compares the average number of incorrect partial solutions examined
in theoretical estimates and experimental results. For both RSA-2048 and RSA-
4096, the first row corresponds to the values derived from Table 3, representing
our estimated count of false branches generated during key reconstruction when

---

[7] Interestingly, both of the figures have an unexplained increase in the interval $[5,000-$
$6,000]$. We skip it here because of its minimal influence on the overall analysis. The
increase in $[10,000-20,000]$ is reasonable since the interval is enlarged by a factor
of 10.

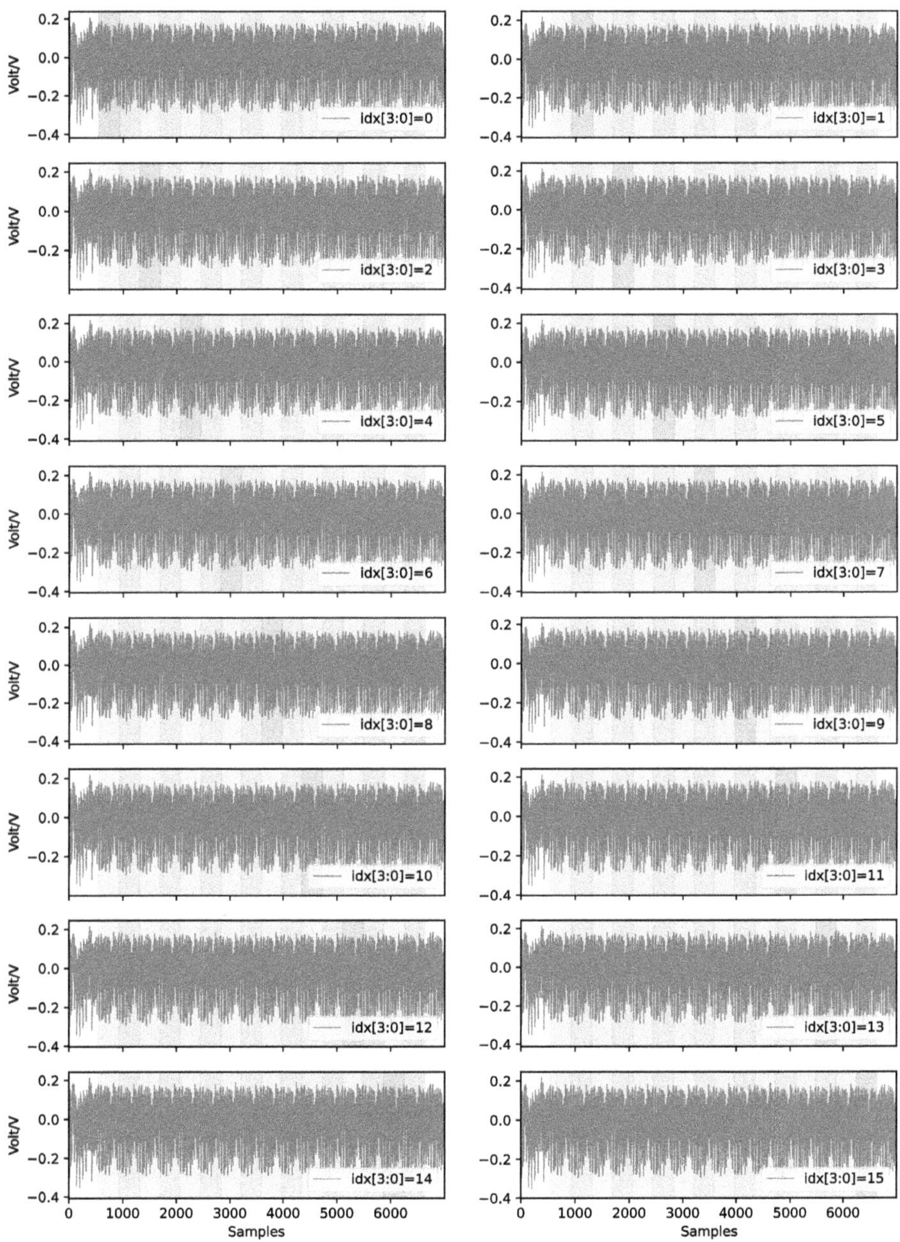

Fig. 7. The power traces of the sensitive operations in MOD_EXP_CTIME_COPY_FROM_ PREBUF(), where idx[3:0] takes values from 1 to 15.

$\varphi = 1/2$. The second row demonstrates the average number of false branches counted in our experiments. The observed discrepancies between theoretical predictions and empirical results may arise from inaccuracies in estimating φ, which implies a potential relationship between φ and the uncertainty in the key reconstruction. Furthermore, the third row presents the observed proportions of the three scenarios among 100,000 trials. In summary, the estimated complexity of the key reconstruction is consistent with results observed in practical attacks.

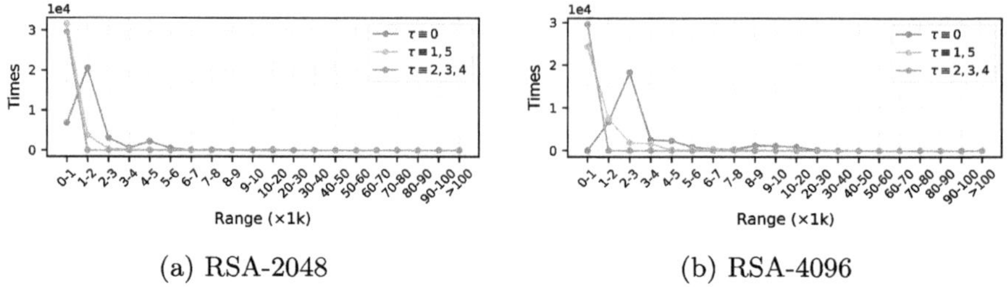

(a) RSA-2048   (b) RSA-4096

Fig. 8. The distributions of incorrect partial solutions examined in 100,000 experiments for RSA-2048 and RSA-4096.

As shown in Table 6, the difference in average complexity between the alignment and misalignment cases seems trivial, since hundreds of false candidates can be examined in seconds on a modern computer. However, in scenarios that generate extensive candidates, especially in RSA-4096, key reconstruction may take several hours. This occurs even as $\frac{4}{6} \approx 66.7\%$ bits are recovered. With additional erasure bits being introduced, the reconstruction time increases significantly, demonstrating the efficiency advantages of our misaligned scenarios.

Table 6. Comparison of the average number of incorrect partial solutions examined in theoretical estimates and experimental results.

		$\tau \equiv 0$	$\tau \equiv 1, 5$	$\tau \equiv 2, 3, 4$
RSA-2048	Theoretical	1,579	683	0
	Practical	1,739	640	0
	Occurrence	34.4%	35.9%	29.7%
RSA-4096	Theoretical	3,158	1,366	0
	Practical	3,484	1,278	0
	Occurrence	34.5%	36%	29.5%

6   Conclusion and Implications

In this work, we have demonstrated that the complexity of the branch-and-prune algorithm is closely tied to observed leakage patterns, and identified a new vulnerability in OpenSSL's implementation of Miller-Rabin primality test. Our proposed leakage model transforms the extracted bits into an exploitable form. Complexity analysis shows that these leakage patterns not only enable highly efficient key recovery in certain scenarios but also suggest a tolerance for additional erasure bits.

We emphasize that targeting the modular exponentiation invoked in the MillerRabin test offers several advantages:

- It benefits from our novel leakage patterns;
- It enables direct recovery of partial bits of p and q, bypassing complications associated with CRT-based implementations.

Moreover, repeated exponentiation calls improve the reliability of recovered information. Although not utilized in this work since our SPA attack requires only a single execution of modular exponentiation, this redundancy may serve as a valuable asset for attacking noisier environments.

Finally, this work operates under an erasure model, assuming the correctness of extracted secret bits, and has been validated on an ARM Cortex-M4 platform. Lattice-based methods are not employed due to the low complexity of the proposed attacks. Future work may extend this approach to an error model, potentially combining lattice-based techniques with the recovery of the lower 50% of bits to enhance attack efficiency.

Acknowledge. The authors thank anonymous reviewers for their insightful suggestions and comments that improved this work. This work was supported by National Cryptographic Science Foundation of China (Grant No. 2025NCSF01001), National Natural Science Foundation of China (Grant No. 62472397), and Quantum Science and Technology-National Science and Technology Major Project (Grant No. 2021ZD0302902).

References

1. Acıiçmez, O.: Yet another microarchitectural attack: exploiting i-cache. In: Ning, P., Atluri, V. (eds.) CSAW 2007, pp. 11–18. ACM, New York (2007). https://doi.org/10.1145/1314466.1314469
2. Acıiçmez, O., Gueron, S., Seifert, J.-P.: New branch prediction vulnerabilities in OpenSSL and necessary software countermeasures. In: Galbraith, S.D. (ed.) Cryptography and Coding 2007. LNCS, vol. 4887, pp. 185–203. Springer, Heidelberg (2007). https://doi.org/10.1007/978-3-540-77272-9_12
3. Acıiçmez, O., Koç, Ç.K., Seifert, J.: On the power of simple branch prediction analysis. Cryptology ePrint Archive, Paper 2006/351 (2006). http://eprint.iacr.org/2006/351
4. Acıiçmez, O., Schindler, W.: A vulnerability in RSA implementations due to instruction cache analysis and its demonstration on OpenSSL. In: Malkin, T. (ed.) CT-RSA 2008. LNCS, vol. 4964, pp. 256–273. Springer, Heidelberg (2008). https://doi.org/10.1007/978-3-540-79263-5_16

5. Alam, M., et al.: One& done: a single-decryption EM-based attack on OpenSSL's constant-time blinded RSA. In: Enck, W., Felt, A.P. (eds.) USENIX Security 2018, pp. 585–602. USENIX Association (2018). https://www.usenix.org/conference/usenixsecurity18/presentation/alam
6. Aldaya, A.C., Brumley, B.B.: Novel single-trace attacks on ECDSA and RSA. IACR TCHES **2020**(2), 196–221 (2020). https://doi.org/10.13154/tches.v2020.i2.196-221
7. Aldaya, A.C., García, C.P., Tapia, L.M.A., Brumley, B.B.: Cache-timing attacks on RSA key generation. IACR TCHES **2019**(4), 213–242 (2019). https://doi.org/10.13154/tches.v2019.i4.213-242
8. Bernstein, D.J., et al.: Sliding right into disaster: left-to-right sliding windows leak. In: Fischer, W., Homma, N. (eds.) CHES 2017. LNCS, vol. 10529, pp. 555–576. Springer, Cham (2017). https://doi.org/10.1007/978-3-319-66787-4_27
9. Blömer, J., May, A.: New partial key exposure attacks on RSA. In: Boneh, D. (ed.) CRYPTO 2003. LNCS, vol. 2729, pp. 27–43. Springer, Heidelberg (2003). https://doi.org/10.1007/978-3-540-45146-4_2
10. Boneh, D., Durfee, G., Frankel, Y.: An attack on RSA given a small fraction of the private key bits. In: Ohta, K., Pei, D. (eds.) ASIACRYPT 1998. LNCS, vol. 1514, pp. 25–34. Springer, Heidelberg (1998). https://doi.org/10.1007/3-540-49649-1_3
11. Brasser, F., Müller, U., Dmitrienko, A., Kostiainen, K., Capkun, S., Sadeghi, A.: Software grand exposure: SGX cache attacks are practical. In: Enck, W., Mulliner, C. (eds.) WOOT 2017, p. 11. USENIX Association (2017). https://www.usenix.org/conference/woot17/workshop-program/presentation/brasser
12. Brickell, E.: A vision for platform security. In: Oswald, E., Rohatgi, P. (eds.) CHES 2008. LNCS, vol. 5154, pp. 444–444. Springer, Heidelberg (2008). https://doi.org/10.1007/978-3-540-85053-3_29
13. Brickell, E., Graunke, G., Neve, M., Seifert, J.P.: Software mitigations to hedge AES against cache-based software side channel vulnerabilities. Cryptology ePrint Archive, Paper 2006/052 (2006). https://eprint.iacr.org/2006/052
14. Briongos, S., Malagón, P., Moya, J.M., Eisenbarth, T.: RELOAD+REFRESH: abusing cache replacement policies to perform stealthy cache attacks. In: Capkun, S., Roesner, F. (eds.) USENIX Security 2020, pp. 1967–1984. USENIX Association (2020). https://www.usenix.org/conference/usenixsecurity20/presentation/briongos
15. Brumley, D., Boneh, D.: Remote timing attacks are practical. In: Boneh, D. (ed.) USENIX Security 2003. USENIX Association (2003). https://www.usenix.org/conference/12th-usenix-security-symposium/remote-timing-attacks-are-practical
16. Chuengsatiansup, C., Feutrill, A., Sim, R.Q., Yarom, Y.: RSA key recovery from digit equivalence information. In: Ateniese, G., Venturi, D. (eds.) ACNS 2022. LNCS, vol. 13269, pp. 193–211. Springer, Cham (2022). https://doi.org/10.1007/978-3-031-09234-3_10
17. Cohney, S., et al.: Pseudorandom black swans: cache attacks on CTR_DRBG. In: Shacham, H., Oprea, A. (eds.) SP 2020, pp. 1241–1258. IEEE, San Francisco (2020). https://doi.org/10.1109/SP40000.2020.00046
18. Cohney, S.N., Green, M.D., Heninger, N.: Practical state recovery attacks against legacy RNG implementations. In: Lie, D., Mannan, M., Backes, M., Wang, X. (eds.) ACM CCS 2018, pp. 265–280. ACM, New York (2018). https://doi.org/10.1145/3243734.3243756
19. Coppersmith, D.: Small solutions to polynomial equations, and low exponent RSA vulnerabilities. J. Cryptol. **10**(4), 233–260 (1997). https://doi.org/10.1007/s001459900030

20. Duan, X., Huang, F., Wang, Y., Hu, H.: A novel leakage model in OpenSSL's miller-Rabin primality test. Cryptology ePrint Archive, Paper 2025/977 (2025). https://eprint.iacr.org/2025/977
21. Gras, B., Razavi, K., Bos, H., Giuffrida, C.: Translation leak-aside buffer: defeating cache side-channel protections with TLB attacks. In: Enck, W., Felt, A.P. (eds.) USENIX Security 2018. pp. 955–972. USENIX Association (2018). https://www.usenix.org/conference/usenixsecurity18/presentation/gras
22. Guo, Y., Zigerelli, A., Zhang, Y., Yang, J.: Adversarial prefetch: new cross-core cache side channel attacks. In: Holz, T., Ristenpart, T. (eds.) SP 2022, pp. 1458–1473. IEEE, San Francisco (2022).https://doi.org/10.1109/SP46214.2022.9833692
23. Halderman, J.A., et al.: Lest we remember: cold-boot attacks on encryption keys. Commun. ACM **52**(5), 91–98 (2009). https://doi.org/10.1145/1506409.1506429
24. Henecka, W., May, A., Meurer, A.: Correcting errors in RSA private keys. In: Rabin, T. (ed.) CRYPTO 2010. LNCS, vol. 6223, pp. 351–369. Springer, Heidelberg (2010). https://doi.org/10.1007/978-3-642-14623-7_19
25. Heninger, N., Shacham, H.: Reconstructing RSA private keys from random key bits. In: Halevi, S. (ed.) CRYPTO 2009. LNCS, vol. 5677, pp. 1–17. Springer, Heidelberg (2009). https://doi.org/10.1007/978-3-642-03356-8_1
26. Herrmann, M., May, A.: Solving linear equations modulo divisors: on factoring given any bits. In: Pieprzyk, J. (ed.) ASIACRYPT 2008. LNCS, vol. 5350, pp. 406–424. Springer, Heidelberg (2008). https://doi.org/10.1007/978-3-540-89255-7_25
27. Howgrave-Graham, N.: Finding small roots of univariate modular equations revisited. In: Darnell, M. (ed.) Cryptography and Coding 1997. LNCS, vol. 1355, pp. 131–142. Springer, Heidelberg (1997). https://doi.org/10.1007/BFb0024458
28. Hu, X., Meunier, Q.L., Encrenaz, E.: Blind-folded: simple power analysis attacks using data with a single trace and no training. IACR TCHES **2025**(1), 475–496 (2025). https://doi.org/10.46586/TCHES.V2025.I1.475-496
29. Huo, T., et al.: Bluethunder: a 2-level directional predictor based side-channel attack against SGX. IACR TCHES **2020**(1), 321–347 (2020). https://doi.org/10.13154/TCHES.V2020.I1.321-347
30. Karlin, S., Taylor, H.M.: A First Course in Stochastic Processes. Gulf Professional Publishing (1975)
31. Kocher, P.C.: Timing attacks on implementations of Diffie-Hellman, RSA, DSS, and other systems. In: Koblitz, N. (ed.) CRYPTO 1996. LNCS, vol. 1109, pp. 104–113. Springer, Heidelberg (1996).https://doi.org/10.1007/3-540-68697-5_9
32. Kocher, P., Jaffe, J., Jun, B.: Differential power analysis. In: Wiener, M. (ed.) CRYPTO 1999. LNCS, vol. 1666, pp. 388–397. Springer, Heidelberg (1999). https://doi.org/10.1007/3-540-48405-1_25
33. Kunihiro, N., Shinohara, N., Izu, T.: Recovering RSA secret keys from noisy key bits with erasures and errors. In: Kurosawa, K., Hanaoka, G. (eds.) PKC 2013. LNCS, vol. 7778, pp. 180–197. Springer, Heidelberg (2013). https://doi.org/10.1007/978-3-642-36362-7_12
34. Lee, S., Shih, M.W., Gera, P., Kim, T., Kim, H., Peinado, M.: Inferring fine-grained control flow inside SGX enclaves with branch shadowing. In: Kirda, E., Ristenpart, T. (eds.) USENIX Security 2017, pp. 557–574. USENIX Association (2017). https://www.usenix.org/conference/usenixsecurity17/technical-sessions/presentation/lee-sangho
35. Li, M., Zhang, Y., Wang, H., Li, K., Cheng, Y.: CIPHERLEAKS: breaking constant-time cryptography on AMD SEV via the ciphertext side

channel. In: Bailey, M., Greenstadt, R. (eds.) USENIX Security 2021, pp. 717–732. USENIX Association (2021). https://www.usenix.org/conference/usenixsecurity21/presentation/li-mengyuan

36. Lipp, M., et al.: PLATYPUS: software-based power side-channel attacks on x86. In: Oprea, A., Holz, T. (eds.) SP 2021, pp. 355–371. IEEE, San Francisco (2021). https://doi.org/10.1109/SP40001.2021.00063

37. Liu, F., Yarom, Y., Ge, Q., Heiser, G., Lee, R.B.: Last-level cache side-channel attacks are practical. In: Bauer, L., Shmatikov, V. (eds.) SP 2015, pp. 605–622. IEEE, San Francisco (2015).https://doi.org/10.1109/SP.2015.43

38. Mangard, S., Oswald, E., Popp, T.: Power Analysis Attacks - Revealing the Secrets of Smart Cards. Springer (2007)

39. Mantel, H., Schickel, J., Weber, A., Weber, F.: How secure is green IT? The case of software-based energy side channels. In: Lopez, J., Zhou, J., Soriano, M. (eds.) ESORICS 2018. LNCS, vol. 11098, pp. 218–239. Springer, Cham (2018). https://doi.org/10.1007/978-3-319-99073-6_11

40. Moghimi, D., Van Bulck, J., Heninger, N., Piessens, F., Sunar, B.: CopyCat: controlled instruction-level attacks on enclaves. In: Capkun, S., Roesner, F. (eds.) USENIX Security 2020, pp. 469–486. USENIX Association (2020). https://www.usenix.org/conference/usenixsecurity20/presentation/moghimi-copycat

41. NIST: FIPS 186-5. digital signature standard (DSS) (2023)

42. Paterson, K.G., Polychroniadou, A., Sibborn, D.L.: A coding-theoretic approach to recovering noisy RSA keys. In: Wang, X., Sako, K. (eds.) ASIACRYPT 2012. LNCS, vol. 7658, pp. 386–403. Springer, Heidelberg (2012). https://doi.org/10.1007/978-3-642-34961-4_24

43. Percival, C.: Cache missing for fun and profit (2005)

44. Rivest, R.L., Shamir, A.: Efficient factoring based on partial information. In: Pichler, F. (ed.) EUROCRYPT 1985. LNCS, vol. 219, pp. 31–34. Springer, Berlin, Heidelberg (1985). https://doi.org/10.1007/3-540-39805-8_3

45. Saito, K., Ito, A., Ueno, R., Homma, N.: One truth prevails: a deep-learning based single-trace power analysis on RSA-CRT with windowed exponentiation. IACR TCHES **2022**(4), 490–526 (2022). https://doi.org/10.46586/TCHES.V2022.I4.490-526

46. Schwarz, M., Weiser, S., Gruss, D., Maurice, C., Mangard, S.: Malware guard extension: using SGX to conceal cache attacks. In: Polychronakis, M., Meier, M. (eds.) DIMVA 2017. LNCS, vol. 10327, pp. 3–24. Springer, Cham (2017). https://doi.org/10.1007/978-3-319-60876-1_1

47. Shinde, S., Chua, Z.L., Narayanan, V., Saxena, P.: Preventing page faults from telling your secrets. In: Chen, X., Wang, X., Huang, X. (eds.) ASIACCS 2016, pp. 317–328. ACM, New York (2016). https://doi.org/10.1145/2897845.2897885

48. The OpenSSL Project: OpenSSL: Cryptography and SSL/TLS toolkit (2025). https://www.openssl.org/. Accessed 23 Oct 2025

49. Weiser, S., Spreitzer, R., Bodner, L.: Single trace attack against RSA key generation in intel SGX SSL. In: Kim, J., Ahn, G.J., Kim, S., Kim, Y., López, J., Kim, T. (eds.) ASIACCS 2018, pp. 575–586. ACM, New York (2018). https://doi.org/10.1145/3196494.3196524

50. Yarom, Y., Falkner, K.: FLUSH+RELOAD: a high resolution, low noise, L3 cache side-channel attack. In: Fu, K., Jung, J. (eds.) USENIX Security 2014, pp. 719–732. USENIX Association (2014). https://www.usenix.org/conference/usenixsecurity14/technical-sessions/presentation/yarom

51. Yarom, Y., Genkin, D., Heninger, N.: CacheBleed: a timing attack on OpenSSL constant time RSA. In: Gierlichs, B., Poschmann, A.Y. (eds.) CHES 2016. LNCS, vol. 9813, pp. 346–367. Springer, Heidelberg (2016). https://doi.org/10.1007/978-3-662-53140-2_17
52. Zhang, Y., Juels, A., Reiter, M.K., Ristenpart, T.: Cross-VM side channels and their use to extract private keys. In: Yu, T., Danezis, G., Gligor, V.D. (eds.) ACM CCS 2012, pp. 305–316. ACM, New York (2012). https://doi.org/10.1145/2382196.2382230

On Verifiable Delay Functions
from Time-Lock Puzzles

Hamza Abusalah[1], Karen Azari[2], Dario Fiore[1], Chethan Kamath[3],
and Erkan Tairi[4(✉)]

[1] IMDEA Software Institute, Madrid, Spain
{hamza.abusalah,dario.fiore}@imdea.org
[2] Faculty of Computer Science, University of Vienna, Vienna, Austria
karen.azari@univie.ac.at
[3] IIT Bombay, Mumbai, India
ckamath@cse.iitb.ac.in
[4] University of California, Berkeley, Berkeley, USA
erkan.tairi@berkeley.edu

Abstract. A verifiable delay function (VDF) [Boneh et al., CRYPTO 2018] is a function f that is slow-to-compute, but is quickly verifiable given a short proof. This is formalised using two security requirements: i) sequentiality, which requires that a parallel adversary is unable to compute f faster; and ii) soundness, which requires that an adversary is unable to generate a proof that verifies wrong outputs. A time-lock puzzle (TLP), on the other hand, is a puzzle that can be quickly generated, but is slow-to-solve. The security requirement here is sequentiality, which requires that a parallel adversary is unable to solve puzzles faster.

In this paper, we study the relationship between these two timed primitives. Our main result is a construction of "one-time" VDF from TLP using indistinguishability obfuscation (iO) and one-way functions (OWFs), where by "one-time" we mean that sequentiality of the VDF holds only against parallel adversaries that do not preprocess public parameters. Our VDF satisfies several desirable properties. For instance, we achieve perfectly sound and short proofs of $O(\lambda)$ bits, where λ is the security parameter. Moreover, our construction is a *trapdoor* (one-time) VDF that can be easily extended to achieve extra properties (defined in our paper) such as trapdoor-homomorphic and trapdoor-constrained evaluation.

Finally, when combined with the results of Bitansky et al., [ITCS 2016], this yields one-time VDFs from any worst-case non-parallelizing language, iO and OWF. To the best of our knowledge, this is the first such construction that only relies on polynomial security.

1 Introduction

Verifiable delay functions (VDFs) are functions that are slow to compute but efficient to verify. Introduced by Boneh et al. [15], it consist of three algorithms:

K. Azari—Part of the work was done while the author was affiliated with ETH Zurich.
E. Tairi—Work done while the author was affiliated with ENS Paris.

S. Bai and E. Persichetti (Eds.): PKC 2026, LNCS 16554, pp. 494–526, 2026.
https://doi.org/10.1007/978-3-032-26740-5_16

Setup(t) takes a time parameter t and outputs public parameters pp;[1] Eval(pp, x) takes an input x and returns an output y and a short proof π; and Ver(pp, x, y, π) accepts or rejects a proof π that vouches for y being the output corresponding to x. The "slow to compute but efficient to verify" concept is characterized via three main properties: *efficiency* requires Eval to be computable in sequential time t and Ver in time $\mathrm{polylog}(t)$; *t-sequentiality* ensures that no parallel machine can compute the function in significantly less than t steps; *soundness* means that no efficient adversary can find a proof for an input x that is deemed valid for an output y' different from the correct output y produced by Eval.

An important efficiency measure of VDFs is its tightness. A VDF is $\delta(t)$-*tight* if (y, π) can be computed in (sequential) time $\delta(t)$. Related to tightness is *space efficiency* of Eval. It is desired that $\delta(t)$ is as close to t as possible, say $t + O(1)$ or $t + \mathrm{polylog}(t)$, and that the space complexity be constant or poly-logarithmic.

VDFs essentially allow proving that a certain amount of time has elapsed, a property which has been shown useful in a variety of applications like random-ness beacons [15,29,30,45], computational timestamping [44], resource-efficient blockchains [24], proofs of replication [5], and even complexity theory [10,22,29]. For instance, when generating random beacons from blockchains or through the commit-and-reveal approach, a common problem is that parties may actively manipulate the random source to obtain a desired bias in the resulting beacon. Passing the beacon through a VDF enables introducing a long delay so that the attacker learns too late the impact of its manipulation on the final beacon.

Motivated by these timely applications, a sequence of works has proposed var-ious VDF constructions [3,10,14,15,21,26,27,29,30,32,36–38,40,46,51,54,57]. These VDFs rely on sequentiality assumptions (e.g., that a certain function is computable only sequentially) and cryptographic assumptions (e.g., the sound-ness of SNARGs). These two classes of assumptions are somewhat incomparable and play two distinct roles in VDF constructions: the former are used to argue sequentiality, and the latter are typically needed to prove soundness.

Constructions of Delay/Sequential Functions. A function $f : \mathcal{X} \to \mathcal{X}$ is called *t-iterated sequential function* (t-ISF) [15] if it is t-sequential and is of the form

$$f(x) := \tau^t(x) := \underbrace{\tau(\cdots \tau(\tau(x)) \cdots)}_{t \text{ times}} \quad \text{where} \quad \tau : \mathcal{X} \to \mathcal{X}. \tag{1}$$

Sequential functions that do not necessarily have this iterated structure are simply called *sequential functions*.

A number of ISFs are known from ideal and number-theoretic assumptions. Below we assume for simplicity that evaluating $\tau(x)$ takes a single time unit. For example, for a random oracle $\tau(\cdot)$, the function $f(\cdot)$ from (1) is provably t-sequential in the ROM [47], i.e., it can't be computed in $t - 1$ RO *rounds* except with negligible probability. Also repeated squarings in groups of unknown order give rise to ISFs. That is, for a group of unknown order $(\mathbb{G}, \cdot)$ and $\tau : \mathbb{G} \to \mathbb{G}$

---

[1] For simplicity of exposition, we will omit the security parameter in this section and keep explicit only the time parameter.

defined as $\tau(x) = x \cdot x$ for $x \in \mathbb{G}$, the function $f(\cdot)$ is assumed to be a t-ISF [39,51,57]. Lattice-based ISFs are based on the iterated application of the binary decomposition operation, followed by a collision-resistant hashing based on the short integer solution (SIS) problem. In particular, let $\tau : \mathbb{Z}_q \to \mathbb{Z}_q$ be such that $\tau(x) = -AG^{-1}(x) \mod q$ where $A \leftarrow \mathbb{Z}_q^{n \times m}$ and $G^{-1} : \mathbb{Z}_q^n \to \mathbb{Z}_2^m$ is the binary decomposition operator. Then, $f(\cdot)$ is assumed to be an $o(t)$-ISF [42].[2]

Besides ideal and number-theoretic candidates, ISFs can be constructed *generically* assuming FHE and the (mere) *existence* of ISFs [38], where the latter in turn reduces to the existence of *average-case non-parallelizing languages*.[3]

Constructions of VDFs. All known VDF constructions [3,10,14,15,21,26, 27,29,30,32,36–38,40,46,51,54,57] follow the same design principle: evaluate an (I)SF and generate a proof of correctness based on an appropriate succinct proof system. One can further classify these VDFs based on the generality of the underlying (I)SF and the overlying succinct proof system.

The first category of VDFs is based on *concrete* ISFs and *concrete interactive* succinct proof systems. The VDFs of Pietrzak [51] and Wesolowski [57] are both based on the ISF from repeated squarings in groups of unknown order, and furthermore, both VDFs come with concrete *interactive* succinct proofs of exponentiation, which are then made non-interactive in the ROM by relying on the Fiat-Shamir heuristic [31]. Neither VDF [51,57] achieves $t + O(1)$ tightness while maintaining a polylog(t) space complexity. However, [51,57] can be made $(t + O(1))$-tight by applying the result of [27], which, given any $(t + O(t))$-tight VDF *built from any ISF* $f(\cdot)$, transforms it into a $(t + O(1))$-tight VDF. However, this transformation comes at the cost of a multiplicative log(t) factor on the proof size, verification time and parallelism of Eval.

A lattice-based VDF is obtained by combining the lattice-based interactive succinct proof system [23][4] for SIS relations with the lattice-based ISF [42]. This is made non-interactive in the ROM by relying on the Fiat-Shamir heuristic [31].

Relying on the statistical soundness of Pietrzak's VDF, [10] constructed a variant of Pietrzak's VDF, and then made it non-interactive by instantiating Fiat-Shamir in the standard model by assuming the hardness of LWE.

The second category of VDFs is based on *any* (I)SF and *generic* succinct non-interactive arguments (SNARGs) for P. The first line in this category constructs VDFs [15] from any t-ISF with a succinct description[5] and any SNARG for P with quasi-linear time provers. The resulting VDFs are $(t + O(1))$-tight and require $O(\log(t))$ space and $O(\log(t))$ parallelism to compute.[6] The second line in this category constructs $(t + \text{polylog}(t))$-tight VDFs [32] from any t-SF

---

[2] Known attacks [50] break bounded-norm variants of $f(\cdot)$, but do not apply to this exact form of $f(\cdot)$.

[3] Due to reliance on universal circuits, this generic construction, however, suffers from an undesirable gap between the honest and adversarial computations of the ISF.

[4] [23] constructs a lattice-based SNARK for NP in the ROM that in particular is efficient for proving SIS relations.

[5] Therefore, the ROM-based ISF does not fall into this category either.

[6] The constants hidden in the O notation can be as large as 10^5 (see [15, Sect. 5.1]).

(not necessarily an ISF) and a non-interactive succinct parallelizable argument (SPARG) for P with quasi-linear time provers. The resulting VDF, however, requires polylog(t) parallelism to compute.

In Sect. 1.3, we discuss more related work on isogeny-based VDFs and VDFs based on computing roots in finite fields.

Our approach: Time-lock puzzles. As seen so far, all known VDFs are constructed from generic/concrete (iterated) sequential functions and succinct proof systems. In this work we propose a novel design paradigm that breaks free from this blueprint. Concretely, we relate VDFs to time-lock puzzles (TLPs) by showing how to construct VDFs from any TLP (by additionally relying on indistinguishability obfuscation, puncturable PRFs and injective one-way functions).

A TLP [12,52] for a message space $\mathcal{S}$ is a tuple (PGen, Sol), such that PGen, on input a solution $s \in \mathcal{S}$ and a hardness parameter t, outputs a puzzle z in polylog(t) (sequential) time, and the puzzle solver, Sol, on input a puzzle z, outputs a solution s in t (sequential) time. The first TLP construction dates back to Rivest, Shamir and Wagner (RSW) [52], who constructed a TLP based on the sequentiality assumption of repeated squaring in groups of unknown order. Bitansky et al. [12] constructed TLPs from (succinct) randomized encodings [4] by additionally assuming the *existence of worst-case non-parallelizing languages* (wcNPL). Informally speaking, for a parameter t, a t-non-parallelizing language is decidable in time t but hard for circuits of depth significantly lower than t. This is arguably a rather minimal complexity-theoretic assumption related to sequentiality. Recently, Bitansky and Garg [11] constructed succinct randomized encodings suitable for TLP constructions assuming circular LWE, and hence, reducing the complexity of constructing TLPs to circular LWE and wcNPL.

Let us, at least informally, highlight the main differences between these two seemingly (un)related timed primitives, namely, VDFs and TLPs. Informally, VDFs and TLPs are located at the extreme ends of the sequential computation asymmetry: a VDF takes time t to compute and time polylog(t) to verify, while a TLP takes polylog(t) time to generate a puzzle and t time to retrieve the solution contained in the puzzle. Moreover, while TLPs can be viewed as one-time primitives, VDFs are not. Furthermore, while TLPs do not come with a setup algorithm and their security is not required to hold against pre-processing adversaries, VDFs come with a setup algorithm that outputs public parameters that are used to evaluate the function on all inputs and security must hold with respect to polynomial-time pre-processing of the public parameters.

Therefore, it is not surprising that these differences translate into different VDF and TLP constructions both in terms of techniques and assumptions.[7] To illustrate, on the one hand, while TLPs can be constructed from wcNPL and suc-

---

[7] For completeness, we mention that TLPs based on repeated squarings that achieve advanced features such as homomorphism [48] and batchability [28] are defined with a setup algorithm and are assumed to be secure against pre-processing attacks. However, standard TLPs [12,52] without advanced features are defined and constructed without setup and their security does not readily extend to the pre-processing setting. In this work, we rely on standard TLPs.

cinct randomized encodings [12], no VDF construction is known from the same assumptions/techniques. On the other hand, while we have VDF constructions from general assumptions such as iterated sequential functions and SNARGs with quasi-linear time provers [15], or from sequential functions and SPARGs [32], no TLP constructions are known from these assumptions/techniques. However, despite these differences, some of the early VDF constructions [51,57] resemble those of the original RSW TLP construction [52], but this is the exception rather than the rule. In fact, these VDFs can be seen as adding public verifiability to the otherwise designated-verifier RSW construction.

It is also worth pointing that given a *trapdoor* VDF (TVDF) it is possible to trivially construct a TLP. A TVDF is a keyed function family $\{\mathsf{F} \colon \mathcal{K} \times \mathcal{X} \to \mathcal{Y}\}$ with a trapdoor-key space $\mathcal{K}$. In a TVDF, there is an additional evaluation algorithm TEval. The Setup algorithm, in addition to outputting pp, samples a uniformly random trapdoor key $k \in \mathcal{K}$ such that $\mathsf{TEval}(k, x)$ running in $\mathrm{polylog}(t)$ sequential time outputs a valid pair (y, π), i.e., y coincides with the output of $\mathsf{Eval}(\mathsf{pp}, x)$ and $\mathsf{Ver}(\mathsf{pp}, x, y, \pi) = 1$. Given a TVDF[8] with output space $\{0,1\}^\lambda$, we can construct a TLP $(\mathsf{PGen}, \mathsf{Sol})$ with solution space $\{0,1\}^\lambda$ as follows: $\mathsf{PGen}(\lambda, t, s)$ runs $(\mathsf{pp}, k) \leftarrow \mathsf{Setup}(\lambda, t)$, samples a random $x \leftarrow \mathcal{X}$, computes $(y, \pi) \leftarrow \mathsf{TEval}(k, x)$ and outputs $(\mathsf{pp}, x, s \oplus y)$; $\mathsf{Sol}(z := (z_0, z_1, z_2))$ computes $(y', \pi') \leftarrow \mathsf{Eval}(z_0, z_1)$ and outputs $y' \oplus z_2$. (Note that the VDF verifiability is not necessary for the implication.)

Given this state of affairs, formally relating TLPs and (plain) VDFs is both challenging and interesting as it advances our understanding of these two central timed primitives and opens a new avenue for their design.

1.1   Our Contributions

Our main result is a VDF construction from any TLP, together with indistinguishability obfuscation, puncturable PRFs and injective OWFs. This in turn constitutes a first step towards understanding how TLPs and VDFs are related.

Our VDF inherits its sequentiality guarantees from those of the TLP and it relies on the cryptographic assumptions to obtain soundness. Our VDF (a) is the first construction that relates VDFs to TLPs, (b) is *perfectly* sound, (c) achieves $t + \mathrm{polylog}(t)$ tightness, (d) inherits the parallel and space complexities of the underlying TLP, (e) has pseudorandom outputs, (f) can be extended to a trapdoor VDF and (g) allows for *homomorphic* and *constrained* trapdoor keys.

However, the downside of our VDF is that it only achieves a weaker security notion: its sequential security does not hold against pre-processing attacks, i.e., this can be viewed as a *one-time* VDF where time starts kicking once Setup is finished running, that is, the VDF is not re-usable. While for TLPs it is standard to consider a model without preprocessing, in the setting of VDFs this is non-standard and results in a definition of less broad applicability. Generalising our

---

[8] For simplicity, we assume, as we achieve in our construction, that the TVDF has pseudorandom outputs, otherwise, one can rely on the unpredictability of the TVDF output to extract pseudorandom bits.

results to a model with preprocessing is a very exciting open question and will most likely require novel ideas (if possible at all).

Nevertheless, compared to the state of the art, our VDF offers the following advantages:

- *New approach:* Our construction departs from known methodologies of building VDFs, which seemed to inherently require sequential functions. We believe that diversifying construction techniques for VDFs could bring new insights towards a better understanding of this relatively novel cryptographic primitive. Additionally, our approach unveils a new connection between two timed-release cryptographic primitives, VDFs and TLPs, which despite their (dis)similarity were not known to be connected.
- *Assumptions:* Combined with the previously mentioned result of Bitansky et al. [12], we obtain the feasibility of VDFs from the existence of iO and OWFs (on the cryptographic side), and wcNPL (on the sequentiality side). Prior to our work, (non-tight) VDFs were known, via adaptively-sound SNARGs for **NP**, from any sequential function, *sub-exponentially* secure iO and *structured* variants of OWF [55,56]. In contrast, we relax the complexity-theoretic requirement to the bare minimum of wcNPL, and weaken the cryptographic assumptions to polynomially-secure iO and standard OWFs.
- *Perfect soundness:* Our construction provides the only VDF from general assumptions that achieves perfect soundness. Before our work, the strongest notion of soundness for any VDF was statistical soundness, which was achieved by VDFs over (certain) groups of unknown order [14,51].
- *Tightness:* Our VDF achieves $t + \mathrm{polylog}(t)$ tightness and produces constant-size proofs without any additional parallelsim. Prior tight VDFs [15,27,32] require $\log(t)$ parallelism and their proofs are at least of $\log(t)$ size.
- *Pseudorandom outputs:* Our VDF directly achieves pseudorandom outputs (i.e., they cannot be distinguished from random in time significantly less than t), and this property comes for free, without the help of randomness extractors.
- *Trapdoor VDFs:* Our VDF can be extended to a trapdoor VDF (TVDF) [57]. The only known TVDFs are the constructions of VDFs in groups of unknown order [51,57], and hence, ours is the only *generic* TVDF.
  We note that TVDFs can be used to construct *short-lived signatures* [6]. These are signatures that are only valid up to a specified future point in time, after which signatures are forgeable. Using our TVDFs from general assumptions gives rise to the first construction of such signatures from general assumptions.
- *Extensions: trapdoor homomorphic and constrained VDFs:* Our VDFs easily lend themselves to two novel extensions that we introduce: trapdoor-homomorphic and trapdoor-constrained VDFs. We can easily achieve these extensions because the trapdoor evaluation algorithm of our trapdoor VDF constructions is simply identical to the evaluation of a pseudorandom function (PRF). Therefore, instantiating the underlying PRF with a PRF that has extra features, such as key-homomorphic or constrained PRFs, directly gives us these novel trapdoor VDFs. We note that we do not know how to

achieve these extensions for existing VDF constructions, such as those based on repeated squaring, due to the lack of homomorphism and constraining capability. Hence, we see this as another benefit of having a novel construction approach for VDFs. In more detail:

- *Trapdoor-constrained VDFs.* There is an additional constraining algorithm Constr such that on input a trapdoor key k and a subset S from a set of subsets $\mathcal{S}$, Constr outputs a constrained key k_S that allows evaluating the VDF on inputs $x \in S$ fast, i.e., in $\mathrm{polylog}(t)$ time. By plugging in our trapdoor-constrained VDF in the short-lived signatures construction [6], we directly get *constrained short-lived signatures* where signing keys can be constrained to sign a subset of messages. The concept of constrained short-lived signatures was not defined/constructed before.

- *Trapdoor-homomorphic VDFs.* There is a homomorphism from the trapdoor key space to the output space. Let $(\mathcal{K}, \oplus)$ and $(\mathcal{Y}, \otimes)$ be groups, $i \in \{0,1\}$, then for trapdoor keys k_i and evaluations $(y_i, \pi_i) \leftarrow \mathsf{TEval}(k_i, x)$ and $(y, \pi) \leftarrow \mathsf{TEval}(k_0 \oplus k_1, x)$, it holds that $y_0 \otimes y_1 = y$. To the best of our knowledge no other TVDF is trapdoor-key homomorphic.

As an additional technical contribution, we construct prefix-constrained signatures, which we need for the security proof of our main construction, using one-time signatures and constrained PRFs. Our construction of prefix-constrained signatures is in fact the same as the puncturable signature scheme of [20], but we need to rely on constrained PRFs for the constraint class of "dual" prefixes and arbitrary-length inputs, which can be obtained by minor modification of the PRF construction of Goldreich, Goldwasser and Micali (GGM) [34] based on OWFs. We believe that the construction of constrained signatures for larger constraint sets can be of independent interest.

1.2   Technical Overview

For this overview, we focus on constructing VDF from TLP, iO and injective one-way function (IOWF). Our main result follows thanks to prior works which showed how to construct (1) TLP from non-parallelizing languages and iO [12] and (2) IOWF from (polynomially-secure) iO and OWF [13].

VDF from TLP: seems straightforward? Let's first recall the definition of TLPs. It consists of two algorithms: a randomised puzzle generator algorithm PGen that, on input a solution s and a hardness parameter t, outputs a puzzle z; and a puzzle solver Sol that, on input a puzzle z, outputs a solution s. Sequentiality requires it to be hard for parallel adversaries of depth "much less than t" to solve z and obtain s (even for worst-case solutions).

Let us first focus on constructing a plain VDF for some fixed hardness parameter t. The construction proceeds in two stages: we first describe how to use a TLP and iO to obtain just a delay function (DF), and then add verifiability to this construction using a one-way permutation. A first attempt would be to mimic the already-discussed blueprint of combining a sequential function, which a TLP implies, with a succinct non-interactive argument (SNARG). However, note that a TLP only allows sampling a puzzle by first sampling the solution – it is not clear how to publicly sample just a puzzle as required for a VDF.[9] To resolve this issue, we rely on indistinguishability obfuscation (iO): the public puzzle sampler consists of an obfuscation of the TLP puzzle sampler. However, since TLP puzzle generation is a randomised procedure, we need to somehow *derandomise* it.[10] To this end, we employ a puncturable pseudorandom function (PPRF) [53]. Recall that a PPRF F is a PRF that additionally supports *puncturing* of any key k at any input x^*, such that: 1) the punctured key k^* preserves functionality on non-punctured inputs $x \neq x^*$; and 2) the evaluation of the PRF at x^* is pseudorandom even given k^*. We use PPRF twice, first to generate an unpredictable solution s from the DF input x, and then to sample pseudorandom coins for the TLP puzzle sampler. Thus, the public parameters of the DF consist of an obfuscation of the following Sample circuit, where k_1 and k_2 are two hardwired PPRF keys.

$z := \mathsf{Sample}_{[k_1, k_2]}(x)$

1. Generate a pseudorandom TLP solution $s := F_{k_1}(x)$
2. Use s and pseudorandom coins to generate a TLP puzzle $z := \mathsf{PGen}(s, t; F_{k_2}(x))$
3. Output z

Thus, to evaluate the DF on an input x, first use the obfuscated Sample circuit (available as part of the public parameter) to generate a puzzle z, and then run the TLP solver to compute the solution s, which is defined to be the output of the VDF. Note that thanks to perfect TLP correctness, a unique solution s is guaranteed.

Arguing sequentiality via punctured programming. Recall that sequentiality of a (V)DF requires it to be hard for parallel adversaries of depth "much less than t" to compute the output on random inputs. The sequentiality of the DF described above can be reduced to sequentiality of the underlying TLP using two applications of the punctured programming [53], as explained below.

– First, we *undo* the derandomisation in Step 1 by switching the solution corresponding to x^* from $F_{k_1}(x^*)$ to a (truly) random s^*. To this end, we puncture k_1 at a randomly *pre-sampled* VDF challenge x^* and program Sample to output s^* when the input is x^*.[11] This switch is computationally indistinguishable due to iO security, preservation of PPRF functionality at non-punctured

---

[9] In fact, a TLP can be thought of as a "designated verifier" VDF, where the verifier is given the TLP solution.

[10] One could use instead *probabilistic* iO, but presently we only know how to construct it from sub-exponentially secure iO [19].

[11] Note that the derandomisation is undone *only* for the "$x = x^*$ branch". This is crucial since the corresponding solution s^* needs to be hardwired into (modified) Sample, and thus we cannot afford to derandomise solution generation for all inputs.

points and pseudorandomness of PPRF at x^*. Crucially, the pseudorandomness of PPRF holds even given the punctured key k_1^*, which is required to generate the obfuscated Sample circuit.

- Then, we undo the derandomisation in Step 2 by switching the coins used to generate the challenge puzzle z^* from pseudorandom $F_{k_2}(x^*)$ to a random r^*. To this end, we puncture k_2, also at x^*, and program Sample to use r^* when computing the challenge puzzle z^*. This switch is computationally indistinguishable for the same reasons as above.
- At this point, the distribution of z^* is identical to the distribution of TLP puzzle generator and, and hence, the only use of s^* is to generate z^*. Thus, it is possible to invoke TLP sequentiality to argue sequentiality of the DF.

Note that for the whole approach to work it is crucial to be able to pre-sample the (V)DF challenge x^*, which is required to generate the punctured keys hardwired in the obfuscation of Sample in the public parameter. However, this is possible in the VDF sequentiality game.

To see this, let's recall the VDF sequentiality game in a bit more detail. The game works in two phases: First, the adversary receives the public parameters and might do some polynomial-time preprocessing on them. In the second phase, the adversary receives a uniformly random challenge input x^* and is then restricted to depth "much less than t". When simulating the security game, a reduction can clearly sample the challenge x^* already with the public parameters, however must not release it to the adversary before the second phase.

The reason why we only achieve sequentiality *without preprocessing* is that we also hardwire the puzzle z^* in the obfuscation of Sample. A preprocessing adversary, as in standard VDF definitions, would receive the public parameters (i.e., the obfuscated circuit containing the TLP puzzle) and could now do polynomial but otherwise sequentially unrestricted computations on it. Since sequentiality of the TLP only holds against adversaries of restricted sequential computation, it is unclear how to prove security in that adversarial model. We refer to the end of this section for further discussion.

Adding verifiability, with perfect soundness. To add verifiability to the DF described above, an obvious solution is to rely on SNARGs, which are implied by iO and OWF, e.g., as constructed in [53]. However, this approach runs into several problems. First, the soundness requirement of VDF is *adaptive* in nature: given the public parameters, the adversary needs to come up with a proof that attests to a wrong evaluation for a domain point of *its choice*. Most constructions of SNARGs from iO only satisfy *selective* soundness, and the recent works that achieve adaptive soundness [55,56], do it at the cost of relying on sub-exponentially secure iO (and other additional assumptions). Moreover, the soundness will be inherited from the SNARGs, and therefore, will only be computational. On the other hand, our VDF achieves perfect soundness.

To resolve this, we delegate the proof generation from Eval to the obfuscated circuit in the public parameter. In more details, instead of the standard approach where the VDF evaluation algorithm generates a (succinct) proof while evaluating the VDF, our proof generation is delegated to the obfuscated Sample circuit. (Thus, the VDF evaluation algorithm outputs empty proofs.) To this end, Sample is altered to additionally output a "proof" $f(s)$ of the solution s, where f is an injective one-way function. Hence, the public parameter now consists of an obfuscation of the following Sample$'$ circuit (with differences from Sample highlighted in red).

$(z, \pi) := \mathsf{Sample}'_{[k_1, k_2]}(x)$

---

1. Generate a pseudorandom TLP solution $s := F_{k_1}(x)$
2. Use s and pseudorandom coins to generate a TLP puzzle $z :=$ $\mathsf{PGen}(s, t; F_{k_2}(x))$
3. Output $(z, \pi := f(s))$

Consequently, to verify that the value s generated by the evaluation algorithm on input x is indeed the correct output, it suffices to:

- re-run the obfuscated Sample circuit on x to obtain the proof π; and
- check if $f(s) = \pi$ holds.

Assuming perfect correctness of iO and TLP, for an adversary's output (x, s^*), such that $s^* \neq s := F_{k_1}(x)$, to be accepted, it must be that $f(s^*) = \pi = f(s)$. However, this contradicts f's injectivity.

Finally, note that although the proof leaks information about the solution s, we show that it does not affect sequentiality thanks to f's one-wayness. We refer the reader to Sect. 3 for the technical details.

Achieving advanced features. Building up on the basic construction described above, we obtain VDFs with additional features:

- Obtaining a *trapdoor* VDF (TVDF) is straightforward: the PPRF key k_1 can be used to directly compute the output using PPRF evaluation algorithm.
- Due to the fact that the trapdoor evaluation algorithm of our basic trapdoor VDF construction is just a PRF evaluation function, we can easily obtain trapdoor VDFs with more advanced features, by replacing the underlying puncturable PRF with a PRF with additional features. More precisely, we obtain trapdoor-homomorphic VDFs by using a key-homomorphic puncturable PRF [7,18] and trapdoor-constrained VDFs by using a constrained PRF [16,17,41]. We refer to Sect. 5 for the definitions and instantiations of these advanced VDFs.
- The basic construction requires the verifier to re-run the obfuscated Sample circuit to obtain a "proof". Evaluating obfuscated circuits can be costly for resource-constrained verifiers, and to remedy this we provide an alternative construction where the verifier only needs to verify a digital signature. The construction is obtained by augmenting Sample to additionally output a digital signature σ as shown below, where sk denotes the signing key of the digital signature.

$(z, \pi, \sigma) := \mathsf{Sample}'_{[k_1, k_2, sk]}(x)$

1. Generate a pseudorandom TLP solution $s := F_{k_1}(x)$
2. Use s and pseudorandom coins to generate a TLP puzzle $z := \mathsf{PGen}(s, t; F_{k_2}(x))$
3. Generate signature $\sigma := \mathsf{Sign}(sk, x \| f(s) \| z)$
4. Output $(z, f(s), \sigma)$

For the proof of soundness to go through, we need to rely on digital signatures with extra structure, namely a *constrained signature scheme* (a.k.a. policy-based signatures) [8] for a particular class of prefix constraints. The soundness of the resulting scheme is only *selective* though. We refer the reader to Sect. 4 for more details.

– We view our construction of *prefix-constrained signatures* as a contribution of independent interest. Our construction relies on a previous construction of puncturable signatures [20], and is based on one-time signatures (OTS) [43] and constrained PRFs [16,17,41]. The construction of [20] is based on a binary tree structure, similar to the paradigm for constructing (many-time) signatures from OTS, where each node in the tree is associated with a pseudorandom seed (generated through a puncturable PRF) that is used to derive a OTS key pair. In order to sign a message m, given the secret seed associated to the root of the tree, one generates all signing keys associated with nodes on the path from the root to the leaf associated with string m and then uses these keys to compute signatures signing the public keys associated to the two children of a node under the secret key associated to that node.

To prove security of this construction, [20] rely on security of the underlying PPRF for *variable-length* inputs as well as the one-time security of the OTS. For our construction of *prefix-constrained* signatures, we similarly rely on *constrained* PRFs for the class of "dual" prefixes and OTS. We instantiate these underlying primitives from OWFs by using Lamport's OTS scheme, and a minor modification of the GGM PPRF [34]. This GGM PPRF modification supports variable-length inputs (note, the plain GGM construction is *insecure* for variable-length inputs) and (similar to the GGM PPRF) can be used as a constrained PRF for the required constraint class. This gives us prefix-constrained signatures from the minimal assumption of OWFs.

Open problem: Achieving VDFs with preprocessing. As mentioned above, our VDF construction achieves perfect soundness and can be instantiated to achieve advanced functionalities. On the downside, we only achieve sequentiality in a security model without preprocessing. This means, when applying our VDF construction one needs fresh parameters for each evaluation, opposed to reusing public parameters and only sampling the uniformly random input to the VDF freshly. The issue here is that in our proof, in order to reduce to the sequentiality of TLP, we embed a challenge puzzle in the public parameters, and hence, commit to this puzzle ahead of time. Also when considering a notion of

TLP with preprocessing, this issue remains. Even with equivocation techniques there does not seem to be an obvious solution and we believe it will require novel ideas to solve the problem (see Remark 3).

We view this somewhat unexpected difficulty to achieve full-fledged VDF from TLP as an interesting observation that points out that the two notions are probably more different than one might expect at first sight. We hope this will encourage further research on timed primitives from generic assumptions.

1.3   Additional Related Work

A number of isogeny-based VDFs are proposed in [3,21,26], however, these schemes fall short of satisfying the standard VDF definition. In particular, sampling a VDF instance [26] is as inefficient as the function evaluation itself, and furthermore, the function instance description is as large as the time parameter itself. For example, let $t = 2^{40}$, then it takes roughly 2^{40} sequential steps to generate a VDF instance for time parameter t, and the instance's size is in the order of 2^{40} bits. On the other hand, the VDFs of [3,21] suffer from inefficient sampling: sampling a domain element is as (in)efficient as evaluating the VDF.

The VDF constructions given in [40,54] and the "sloth++" VDF of [15] are built from ISFs $f(\cdot) = \tau^t(\cdot)$, where τ involves computing roots in prime-order finite fields, or extensions thereof. The root computation's sequentiality is put into scrutiny recently. In particular, [9] shows how to speed up root computation beyond their conjectured security. It is instructive to mention that [9] does not find shortcuts in the computation of $f(\cdot)$, i.e., their attacks still evaluate $\tau(\cdot)$ in t steps sequentially, but the individual evaluation of $\tau(\cdot)$ is sped up.

A Related Talk. We became aware of a talk [49] at MIT VDF Day 2019 that presents a VDF construction from (the existence of) NPL and iO. In comparison, our base construction and theirs rely on the same assumptions: while we directly rely on a TLP plus iO, they rely on NPL plus iO, which together imply a TLP (OWFs are implied by TLPs [12]). However, to the best of our knowledge, their work is neither published nor available online in a written form. Our work shows that, even with these strong tools, it is still open to actually construct a full fledged VDF from TLP and iO, and it is even non-trivial to prove one-time security. Moreover, we also define and construct VDFs with additional features, such as trapdoor-constrained and trapdoor-homomorphic VDFs, which were not considered prior to our work.

2   Preliminaries

In this section, we first set up our notation and then describe the computational model. Finally, we define the cryptographic primitives that we rely on, namely one-time signatures, indistinguishability obfuscation, constrained PRFs, prefix-constrained signatures, time-lock puzzles and verifiable delay functions.

Notation. For $n \in \mathbb{N}$, let $[n] := \{1, \ldots, n\}$, and let $\lambda \in \mathbb{N}$ be the security parameter. For a finite set $\mathcal{S}$, we denote by $s \leftarrow \mathcal{S}$ the process of sampling s uniformly from $\mathcal{S}$. Let $y \leftarrow \mathsf{A}(\lambda, x)$ be the process of running a *randomised* algorithm A on input (λ, x) with access to uniformly random coins and assigning the result to y (we may omit to mention the input λ explicitly and assume that all algorithms take λ as input). To make the random coins r explicit, we write $\mathsf{A}(\lambda, x; r)$. We use $y := \mathsf{A}(x)$ to denote a *deterministic* algorithm A outputting y on input x. We use $\perp$ to indicate that an algorithm terminates with an error and A^B when A has oracle access to B, where B may return $\top$ as a distinguished special symbol. We say an algorithm A is probabilistic polynomial time (PPT) if the running time of A is polynomial in λ. If an algorithm A runs in polynomial time, but it is deterministic, then we say that it is deterministic polynomial time (DPT). A function f is negligible if its absolute value is smaller than the inverse of any polynomial (i.e., if $\forall c \exists k_0 \forall \lambda \geq k_0 : |f(\lambda)| < 1/\lambda^c$). We denote the class of negligible functions by negl, and hence, we write $f \in \mathsf{negl}$ or $f(\lambda) \in \mathsf{negl}(\lambda)$ if f is a negligible function. We write $q = q(\lambda)$ if we mean q depends on λ.

Computational Model. We follow the convention from [12] of modelling honest algorithms as uniform machines, and adversaries as non-uniform machines. In particular, an efficient adversary A is modelled as a family of polynomial-sized circuits $\mathsf{A} = (\mathsf{A}_\lambda)_{\lambda \in \mathbb{N}}$. For timed cryptographic primitives, we need to consider parallel adversaries, which are modelled by a family of polynomial-sized, depth-bounded circuits. For a circuit C, we use $depth(\mathsf{C})$ to denote its depth and $|\mathsf{C}|$ to denote its size. Thus, the overall running time of a circuit is determined by $|\mathsf{C}|$, whereas its parallel time is determined by $depth(\mathsf{C})$.

2.1 Basic Cryptographic Primitives

One-Time Signatures. First, we define one-time signatures, which are signatures that allow to use a key pair to sign a single (arbitrary) message, and offer no security guarantees if the same key pair is used to sign a second message.

Definition 1 (One-Time Signatures). *A one-time signature (OTS) scheme* OTS *for a message space* $\mathcal{M} := (\{0,1\}^{\ell(\lambda)})_{\lambda \in \mathbb{N}}$, *where* $\ell(\cdot)$ *is a polynomial, is a tuple of algorithms* $(\mathsf{KGen}, \mathsf{Sign}, \mathsf{Ver})$ *with the following syntax:*

- $(\mathsf{msk}, \mathsf{pk}) \leftarrow \mathsf{KGen}(1^\lambda)$: *On input a (unary represented) security parameter* λ, *it outputs a master signing-verification key pair* $(\mathsf{msk}, \mathsf{pk})$.
- $\sigma := \mathsf{Sign}(\mathsf{msk}, m)$: *On input a (master) signing key* sk *and a message* $m \in \{0,1\}^{\ell(\lambda)}$, *it outputs a signature* σ.
- $b := \mathsf{Ver}(\mathsf{pk}, m, \sigma)$: *On input a verification key* pk, *a message* m *and a signature* σ, *it outputs a bit* b *indicating accept (1) and reject (0).*

We require OTS *to satisfy the following properties:*

- Correctness. *For all* $\lambda \in \mathbb{N}$ *and every* $m \in \{0,1\}^{\ell(\lambda)}$, *the following holds:*

$$\Pr\left[\mathsf{Ver}(\mathsf{pk}, m, \sigma) = 1 : \begin{array}{l} (\mathsf{sk}, \mathsf{pk}) \leftarrow \mathsf{KGen}(1^\lambda) \\ \sigma := \mathsf{Sign}(\mathsf{sk}, m) \end{array}\right] = 1.$$

– One-time existential unforgeability. *For every efficient two-stage adversary* $\mathsf{A} = (\mathsf{A}_{0,\lambda}, \mathsf{A}_{0,\lambda})_{\lambda \in \mathbb{N}}$, *we have that*

$$\Pr\left[\begin{array}{c} \mathsf{Ver}(\mathsf{pk}, m_\mathsf{A}, \sigma_\mathsf{A}) = 1 \\ m_\mathsf{A} \neq m \end{array} : \begin{array}{l} (\mathsf{sk}, \mathsf{pk}) \leftarrow \mathsf{KGen}(1^\lambda) \\ (m, \mathsf{st}) \leftarrow \mathsf{A}_{0,\lambda}(\mathsf{pk}) \\ (m_\mathsf{A}, \sigma_\mathsf{A}) \leftarrow \mathsf{A}_{0,\lambda}(\mathsf{st}, \mathsf{Sign}(\mathsf{sk}, m)) \end{array}\right] \in \mathsf{negl}(\lambda),$$

Indistinguishability Obfuscation. We recall what indistinguishability obfuscation (iO) is. Intuitively, iO requires that for any two circuits C_0 and C_1 of the same size that are functionally equivalent, i.e., $C_0(x) = C_1(x)$ for all inputs x, we have that obfuscations $\mathsf{iO}(C_0)$ and $\mathsf{iO}(C_1)$ are computationally indistinguishable.

Definition 2 (iO [33]). *A PPT algorithm* iO *is an indistinguishability obfuscator (iO) for a circuit class* $\{\mathcal{C}_\lambda\}_{\lambda \in \mathbb{N}}$ *if the following hold:*

– Functionality. *For every* $\lambda \in \mathbb{N}$, *every circuit* $C_\lambda : \{0,1\}^{n(\lambda)} \to \{0,1\}^{m(\lambda)} \in \mathcal{C}_\lambda$ *(where* $m(\cdot)$ *and* $n(\cdot)$ *are polynomials), and every input* $x \in \{0,1\}^{n(\lambda)}$,

$$\Pr\left[\tilde{C}_\lambda(x) = C_\lambda(x) : \tilde{C}_\lambda \leftarrow \mathsf{iO}(C_\lambda)\right] = 1.$$

– Indistinguishability (security). *For efficient distinguisher* $\mathsf{D} = (\mathsf{D}_\lambda)_{\lambda \in \mathbb{N}}$ *and for any pair of circuits* $C_{0,\lambda}, C_{1,\lambda} \in \mathcal{C}_\lambda$, *such that for all input* $x \in \{0,1\}^{n(\lambda)}$, $C_{0,\lambda}(x) = C_{1,\lambda}(x)$ *and* $|C_{0,\lambda}| = |C_{1,\lambda}|$, *it holds that*

$$\left|\Pr\left[\mathsf{D}_\lambda(\mathsf{iO}(C_{0,\lambda})) = 1\right] - \Pr\left[\mathsf{D}_\lambda(\mathsf{iO}(C_{1,\lambda})) = 1\right]\right| \in \mathsf{negl}(\lambda).$$

2.2   Constrained Cryptographic Primitives

Constrained PRFs. Constraint PRFs (CPRFs) [16] are PRFs for which a constraint key for some set S can be given out, that allow evaluation of the PRF on all inputs belonging to S and nowhere else.

Definition 3 (Constrained Functions). *A function family* $\mathcal{F}_\lambda = \{F \colon \mathcal{K} \times \mathcal{X} \to \mathcal{Y}\}$ *with key space* $\mathcal{K}$, *input space* $\mathcal{X}$ *and output space* $\mathcal{Y}$ *is constrained for a family of subsets* $\mathcal{S}_\lambda$ *over* $\mathcal{X}$ *with a constraint key space* $\mathcal{K}_\mathcal{S}$ *such that* $\mathcal{K}_\mathcal{S} \cap \mathcal{K} = \emptyset$ *if there exists a tuple of PPT algorithms* (Gen, Eval, Constr) *s.t.*

– $k \leftarrow \mathsf{Gen}(1^\lambda)$: *On input a security parameter* $\lambda \in \mathbb{N}$ *in unary,* Gen *outputs a key* $k \in \mathcal{K}$.
– $k_S \leftarrow \mathsf{Constr}(k, S)$: *On input a key* $k \in \mathcal{K}$ *and* $S \in \mathcal{S}_\lambda$, Constr *outputs a constraint key* $k_S \in \mathcal{K}_\mathcal{S}$.
– $y := \mathsf{Eval}(k, x)$: *On input a key* $k \in \mathcal{K} \cup \mathcal{K}_\mathcal{S}$ *and input* $x \in \mathcal{X}$, Eval *computes* $y = F(k, x)$ *if either* $k \in \mathcal{K}$ *or* $k \in \mathcal{K}_\mathcal{S}$ *and* $x \in S$. *(Otherwise* Eval *outputs* $y = \bot$.)

Definition 4 (Constrained PRFs [16,17,41]). *A constrained function family* $\mathcal{F}_\lambda = \{F\colon \mathcal{K} \times \mathcal{X} \to \mathcal{Y}\}$ *is a family of* selectively-secure constrained PRFs *if for every PPT stateful adversary* A *, there exists* $\delta \in$ negl *such that*

$$\Pr\left[\mathsf{Exp}_{\mathcal{F},\mathsf{A}}^{\mathsf{CPRF}}(\lambda) = 1\right] \le \frac{1}{2} + \delta(\lambda),$$

where the experiment $\mathsf{Exp}_{\mathcal{F},\mathsf{A}}^{\mathsf{CPRF}}(\lambda)$ *is defined below.*

$\mathsf{Exp}_{\mathcal{F},\mathsf{A}}^{\mathsf{CPRF}}(\lambda)$	$\mathcal{O}_{\mathsf{Eval}}(x)$
$1: b \leftarrow \{0,1\}$	$1:$ **if** $x \notin \mathcal{X} \vee x = x^*$ **then**
$2: k \leftarrow \mathsf{Gen}(1^\lambda)$	$2:$ **return** $\bot$
$3: x^* \leftarrow \mathsf{A}(1^\lambda)$	$3:$ **return** $\mathsf{Eval}(k,x)$
$4:$ **if** $b = 0$ **then**	$\mathcal{O}_{\mathsf{Constr}}(S)$
$5:$ $y := \mathsf{Eval}(k,x^*)$	
$6:$ **else**	$1:$ **if** $S \notin \mathcal{S}_\lambda \vee x^* \in S$ **then**
$7:$ $y \leftarrow \mathcal{Y}$	$2:$ **return** $\bot$
$8: b' \leftarrow \mathsf{A}^{\mathcal{O}_{\mathsf{Eval}},\mathcal{O}_{\mathsf{Constr}}}(y)$	$3:$ **return** $\mathsf{Constr}(k,S)$
$9:$ **return** $b = b'$	

Puncturable Pseudorandom Functions. Puncturable PRFs (PPRFs), introduced by Sahai and Waters [53], are PRFs for which a key can be given out, such that it allows evaluation of the PRF on all inputs, except for a designated polynomial-size set of inputs.

Definition 5 (Puncturable PRFs [53]). *A constrained PRF family* $\mathcal{F}_\lambda = \{\mathsf{F}\colon \mathcal{K} \times \{0,1\}^n \to \mathcal{Y}\}$ *where* $n = n(\lambda)$ *is a* puncturable PRF *family if it is constrained for sets* $\{0,1\}^n \setminus T$ *for* $\mathrm{poly}(n)$*-sized* $T \subseteq \{0,1\}^n$.

Prefix-Constrained Digital Signatures. Next, we describe prefix-constrained digital signatures, which are constrained digital signatures (a.k.a. policy-based signatures) [8] where the constraint function is restricted to a particular "dual" prefix relation. Our definition is adapted from [35], and is modified to suit our purpose. In the following definition we denote the prefix relation by "$\preceq$", i.e., for two strings m, m' we write $m \preceq m'$ if m is a prefix of m', and $m \prec m'$ if m is a *strict* prefix of m'.

Definition 6 (Prefix-Constrained Signatures). *A prefix-constrained signature (PCS) scheme* PCS *for a message space* $\mathcal{M} := (\{0,1\}^{\ell(\lambda)})_{\lambda \in \mathbb{N}}$, *where* $\ell(\cdot)$ *is a polynomial, is a tuple of algorithms* (KGen, CGen, Sign, CSign, Ver) *such that*

- (msk, pk) $\leftarrow$ KGen(1^λ): *On input a (unary represented) security parameter* λ, *it outputs a master signing-verification key pair* (msk, pk).
- sk* $\leftarrow$ CGen(msk, m^*): *On input a master secret key* msk *and a prefix* $m^* \in \{0,1\}^{<\ell(\lambda)}$, *it outputs a constrained signing key* sk*.

- $\sigma := \mathsf{Sign}(\mathsf{msk}, m)$: *On input a (master) signing key* sk *and a message* $m \in \{0,1\}^{\ell(\lambda)}$, *it outputs a signature* σ.
- $\sigma := \mathsf{CSign}(\mathsf{sk}^*, m)$: *On input a secret key* sk^* *constrained on* $m^* \in \{0,1\}^{<\ell(\lambda)}$ *and a message* $m \in \{0,1\}^{\ell(\lambda)}$, *it outputs a signature* σ *for* m.
- $b := \mathsf{Ver}(\mathsf{pk}, m, \sigma)$: *On input a verification key* pk, *a message* m *and a signature* σ, *it outputs a bit* b *indicating accept (1) and reject (0).*

We require PCS *to satisfy the following properties:*

- Correctness of signing using master signing key. *For all* $\lambda \in \mathbb{N}$ *and every* $m \in \{0,1\}^{\ell(\lambda)}$, *the following holds:*

$$\Pr\left[\mathsf{Ver}(\mathsf{pk}, m, \sigma) = 1 : \begin{array}{c} (\mathsf{msk}, \mathsf{pk}) \leftarrow \mathsf{KGen}(1^\lambda) \\ \sigma := \mathsf{Sign}(\mathsf{msk}, m) \end{array}\right] = 1.$$

- Consistency of signing using constrained signing key. *For all* $\lambda \in \mathbb{N}$, $m^* \in \{0,1\}^{<\ell(\lambda)}$ *and* $m \in \{0,1\}^{\ell(\lambda)}$ *such that* m^* *is* not *a prefix of* m,

$$\Pr\left[\sigma^* = \sigma : \begin{array}{c} (\mathsf{msk}, \mathsf{pk}) \leftarrow \mathsf{KGen}(1^\lambda) \\ \mathsf{sk}^* \leftarrow \mathsf{CGen}(\mathsf{msk}, m^*) \\ \sigma^* := \mathsf{CSign}(\mathsf{sk}^*, m) \\ \sigma := \mathsf{Sign}(\mathsf{msk}, m) \end{array}\right] = 1.$$

- Selective one-time constrained unforgeability under chosen-message attack. *For every efficient two-stage adversary* $\mathsf{A} = (\mathsf{A}_{0,\lambda}, \mathsf{A}_{1,\lambda})_{\lambda \in \mathbb{N}}$, *we have that*

$$\Pr\left[\begin{array}{c} \mathsf{Ver}(\mathsf{pk}, m_\mathsf{A}, \sigma_\mathsf{A}) = 1 \\ m^* \in \{0,1\}^{<\ell(\lambda)}, m_\mathsf{A} \in \{0,1\}^{\ell(\lambda)} \\ m^* \prec m_\mathsf{A} \\ m_\mathsf{A} \text{ not queried to } \mathsf{Sign}(\mathsf{msk}, \cdot) \end{array} : \begin{array}{c} (m^*, \mathsf{st}) \leftarrow \mathsf{A}_{0,\lambda} \\ (\mathsf{msk}, \mathsf{pk}) \leftarrow \mathsf{KGen}(1^\lambda) \\ \mathsf{sk}^* \leftarrow \mathsf{CGen}(\mathsf{msk}, m^*) \\ (m_\mathsf{A}, \sigma_\mathsf{A}) \leftarrow \mathsf{A}_{1,\lambda}^{\mathsf{Sign}(\mathsf{msk}, \cdot)}(\mathsf{st}, \mathsf{pk}, \mathsf{sk}^*) \end{array}\right] \in \mathsf{negl}(\lambda).$$

2.3 Timed Cryptographic Primitives

Time-Lock Puzzles. We define the syntax and requirements of time-lock puzzles, which are cryptographic puzzles where the solution s remains hidden from adversaries that run in time significantly less than t, including parallel adversaries with polynomially many processors.

Definition 7 (Time-Lock Puzzles [12]). *A time-lock puzzle* TLP *is a pair of algorithms* $(\mathsf{PGen}, \mathsf{Sol})$ *with the following syntax:*

- $z \leftarrow \mathsf{PGen}(t, s)$: *On input a time parameter* t *and a solution* $s \in \{0,1\}^\lambda$, *it outputs a puzzle* $z \in \{0,1\}^{w(\lambda)}$, *for a polynomial* $w(\cdot)$.
- $s := \mathsf{Sol}(z)$: *On input a puzzle* z, *it outputs a solution* s.

We require TLP *to satisfy the following properties:*

- Completeness. *For every security parameter* $\lambda \in \mathbb{N}$, *time parameter* t *and solution* $s \in \{0,1\}^\lambda$, *we have that* $\Pr\left[\mathsf{Sol}(\mathsf{PGen}(t, s)) = s\right] = 1$.
- Efficiency. *We require the following efficiency guarantees:*

- $\bullet$ $\mathsf{PGen}(t, s)$ *can be computed in time* $\mathrm{poly}(\log t, \lambda)$.
- $\bullet$ $\mathsf{Sol}(z)$ *can be computed in time* $t \cdot \mathrm{poly}(\lambda)$.
- Sequentiality (security). *A time-lock puzzle* TLP *is sequential with gap* $\varepsilon < 1$ *if there exists a polynomial* $\underline{t}(\cdot)$, *such that for every polynomial* $t(\cdot) \geq \underline{t}(\cdot)$ *and every efficient parallel adversary* $\mathsf{A} = (\mathsf{A}_\lambda)_{\lambda \in \mathbb{N}}$ *with* $depth(\mathsf{A}_\lambda) \leq (t(\lambda))^\varepsilon$, *there exists a negligible function* $\delta \in \mathsf{negl}$, *such that for every* $\lambda \in \mathbb{N}$, *and every pair of solutions* $s_0, s_1 \in \{0, 1\}^\lambda$, *we have that*

$$\Pr[\mathsf{A}(z) = b : b \leftarrow \{0, 1\}, z \leftarrow \mathsf{PGen}(t(\lambda), s_b)] \leq \frac{1}{2} + \delta(\lambda).$$

Trapdoor Verifiable Delay Functions. We define the syntax and requirements of trapdoor verifiable delay function (TVDF) [57]. Recall that they are a more general notion than the (plain) VDFs from [15] (see Remark 1). A VDF is a function that requires specific number of (e.g., t) sequential steps to evaluate, yet produce a unique output that can be efficiently and publicly verified. Compared to plain VDFs, in TVDFs there is an additional trapdoor that allows to evaluate the function in strictly less time than performing t sequential steps.

Definition 8 (TVDF [57]). *A trapdoor verifiable delay function* TVDF *is a tuple of algorithms* $(\mathsf{Setup}, \mathsf{Eval}, \mathsf{TEval}, \mathsf{Ver})$, *with the following syntax:*

- $(\mathsf{ek}, \mathsf{vk}, \mathsf{td}) \leftarrow \mathsf{Setup}(1^\lambda, t)$. *On input a statistical security parameter* $\lambda \in \mathbb{N}$ *(in unary) and a time parameter* $t \in \mathbb{N}$, *it outputs an evaluation key* ek, *a verification key* vk *and a trapdoor* td. *The keys* ek, vk *determine the domain* $\mathcal{X}$ *and range* $\mathcal{Y}$ *of the VDF function* $V : \mathcal{X} \to \mathcal{Y}$.
- $(y, \pi) \leftarrow \mathsf{Eval}(\mathsf{ek}, x)$. *On input* $x \in \mathcal{X}$, *it outputs* (y, π), *where* π *is a proof that the output* $y \in \mathcal{Y}$ *has been correctly computed.*
- $(y, \pi) \leftarrow \mathsf{TEval}(\mathsf{td}, x)$. *On input a trapdoor* td *and input* $x \in \mathcal{X}$, *it outputs* (y, π) *as in the (plain) evaluation algorithm*
- $b := \mathsf{Ver}(\mathsf{vk}, x, y, \pi)$. *Given as input a tuple* (x, y, π) *consisting of an input, an output and a proof, it outputs a bit* b *indicating accept (1) or reject (0).*

A TVDF must satisfy the following properties:

- Completeness. *Honestly-generated proofs must always accept, i.e., for any* $\lambda, t \in \mathbb{N}$ *and* $x \in \mathcal{X}$

$$\Pr[\mathsf{Ver}(\mathsf{vk}, x, \mathsf{Eval}(\mathsf{ek}, x)) = 1 : (\mathsf{ek}, \mathsf{vk}, \mathsf{td}) \leftarrow \mathsf{Setup}(1^\lambda, t)] = 1 \ .$$

- Consistency of trapdoor evaluations. *Honestly-generated trapdoor proofs must always accept, and honestly-generated trapdoor evaluations must always agree with honestly-generated evaluations, i.e., for any* $\lambda, t \in \mathbb{N}$ *and* $x \in \mathcal{X}$

$$\Pr\left[\begin{array}{l} y = y' \wedge \\ \mathsf{Ver}(\mathsf{vk}, x, y, \pi) = 1 \wedge \\ \mathsf{Ver}(\mathsf{vk}, x, y', \pi') = 1 \end{array} : \begin{array}{l} (\mathsf{ek}, \mathsf{vk}, \mathsf{td}) \leftarrow \mathsf{Setup}(1^\lambda, t) \\ (y, \pi) \leftarrow \mathsf{Eval}(\mathsf{ek}, x) \\ (y', \pi') \leftarrow \mathsf{TEval}(\mathsf{td}, x) \end{array}\right] = 1 \ .$$

- Efficiency. $\mathsf{Setup}, \mathsf{TEval}$ *and* Ver *run in time* $\mathrm{poly}(\log(t), \lambda)$. Eval *computes the output* y *and its proof* π *in time* $(t + o(t)) \cdot \mathrm{poly}(\lambda)$.

- Soundness. *We define three notions of soundness, in order of decreasing strength: perfect, adaptive computational and selective computational.*
  - Perfect *soundness requires accepting proofs for wrong evaluation* to not exist. *Formally, a TVDF is perfectly sound if*

$$\Pr\left[\begin{array}{c}\exists (x, y^*, \pi^*)\ s.t. \\ \mathsf{Ver}(\mathsf{vk}, x, y^*, \pi^*) = 1 \land \\ y^* \neq y\end{array} : \begin{array}{l}(\mathsf{ek}, \mathsf{vk}, \mathsf{td}) \leftarrow \mathsf{Setup}(1^\lambda, t) \\ (y, \pi) \leftarrow \mathsf{Eval}(\mathsf{ek}, x)\end{array}\right] = 0.$$

  - Adaptive computational *soundness requires it to be hard for an efficient adversary to come up with an accepting proof for a wrong evaluation. Formally, a TVDF is adaptively computationally sound if for all* $t \in \mathbb{N}$ *and efficient adversaries* $\mathsf{A} = (\mathsf{A}_\lambda)_{\lambda \in \mathbb{N}}$

$$\Pr\left[\begin{array}{c}\mathsf{Ver}(\mathsf{vk}, x^*, y_\mathsf{A}^*, \pi_\mathsf{A}^*) = 1 \land \\ y_\mathsf{A}^* \neq y^*\end{array} : \begin{array}{l}(\mathsf{ek}, \mathsf{vk}, \mathsf{td}) \leftarrow \mathsf{Setup}(1^\lambda, t) \\ (x^*, y_\mathsf{A}^*, \pi_\mathsf{A}^*) \leftarrow \mathsf{A}_\lambda(\mathsf{ek}, \mathsf{vk}) \\ (y^*, \pi^*) \leftarrow \mathsf{Eval}(\mathsf{ek}, x^*)\end{array}\right] \in \mathsf{negl}(\lambda).$$

  - Selective computational *soundness weakens the above requirement to the case where the adversary submits the challenge input* in advance. *Formally, a TVDF is selectively computationally sound if for all* $t \in \mathbb{N}$ *and efficient two-stage adversaries* $\mathsf{A} = (\mathsf{A}_{0,\lambda}, \mathsf{A}_{1,\lambda})_{\lambda \in \mathbb{N}}$

$$\Pr\left[\begin{array}{c}\mathsf{Ver}(\mathsf{vk}, x^*, y_\mathsf{A}^*, \pi_\mathsf{A}^*) = 1 \land \\ y_\mathsf{A}^* \neq y^*\end{array} : \begin{array}{l}(\mathsf{st}, x^*) \leftarrow \mathsf{A}_{0,\lambda} \\ (\mathsf{ek}, \mathsf{vk}, \mathsf{td}) \leftarrow \mathsf{Setup}(1^\lambda, t) \\ (y_\mathsf{A}^*, \pi_\mathsf{A}^*) \leftarrow \mathsf{A}_{1,\lambda}(\mathsf{st}, \mathsf{ek}, \mathsf{vk}) \\ (y^*, \pi^*) \leftarrow \mathsf{Eval}(\mathsf{ek}, x^*)\end{array}\right] \in \mathsf{negl}(\lambda).$$

- Sequentiality (security). *We consider two different notions of sequentiality: with and without preprocessing, with the former being the standard notion.*
  - *A TVDF is* sequential with gap $\varepsilon < 1$ *if there exists a polynomial* $\underline{t}(\cdot)$, *such that for every polynomial* $t(\cdot) \geq \underline{t}(\cdot)$ *and every efficient two-stage adversary* $\mathsf{A} = (\mathsf{A}_{0,\lambda}, \mathsf{A}_{1,\lambda})_{\lambda \in \mathbb{N}}$, *where* $\mathsf{A}_{1,\lambda}$ *is parallel with* $depth(\mathsf{A}_{1,\lambda}) \leq (t(\lambda))^\varepsilon$, *it holds that*

$$\Pr\left[y_\mathsf{A}^* = y^* : \begin{array}{l}(\mathsf{ek}, \mathsf{vk}, \mathsf{td}) \leftarrow \mathsf{Setup}(1^\lambda, t) \\ \mathsf{st} \leftarrow \mathsf{A}_{0,\lambda}(\mathsf{ek}, \mathsf{vk}) \\ x^* \leftarrow \mathcal{X} \\ y_\mathsf{A}^* \leftarrow \mathsf{A}_{1,\lambda}(\mathsf{st}, x^*) \\ (y^*, \pi^*) \leftarrow \mathsf{Eval}(\mathsf{ek}, x^*)\end{array}\right] \in \mathsf{negl}(\lambda).$$

  - *A TVDF is* one-time sequential with gap $\varepsilon < 1$ *if there exists a polynomial* $\underline{t}(\cdot)$, *such that for every polynomial* $t(\cdot) \geq \underline{t}(\cdot)$ *and every efficient adversary* $\mathsf{A} = (\mathsf{A}_\lambda)_{\lambda \in \mathbb{N}}$, *where* A_λ *is parallel with* $depth(\mathsf{A}_\lambda) \leq (t(\lambda))^\varepsilon$:

$$\Pr\left[y_\mathsf{A}^* = y^* : \begin{array}{l}(\mathsf{ek}, \mathsf{vk}, \mathsf{td}) \leftarrow \mathsf{Setup}(1^\lambda, t) \\ x^* \leftarrow \mathcal{X} \\ y_\mathsf{A}^* \leftarrow \mathsf{A}_\lambda(\mathsf{ek}, \mathsf{vk}, x^*) \\ (y^*, \pi^*) \leftarrow \mathsf{Eval}(\mathsf{ek}, x^*)\end{array}\right] \in \mathsf{negl}(\lambda).$$

Remark 1 (Standard VDFs). Note that the standard "trapdoorless" definition of VDFs can be recovered from Definition 8 by ignoring td and TEval.

Additionally, we require pseudorandomness from [15], which requires the output of the VDF to appear pseudorandom to sequentiality adversaries.

Definition 9 (TVDFs with pseudorandom outputs). *Analogous to sequentiality, we consider two notions: with and without preprocessing.*

- *A TVDF* (Setup, Eval, TEval, Ver) *is* pseudorandom *with* gap $\varepsilon < 1$ *if there exists a polynomial $\underline{t}(\cdot)$, such that for every polynomial $t(\cdot) \geq \underline{t}(\cdot)$ and every efficient two-stage distinguisher* $\mathsf{A} = (\mathsf{A}_{0,\lambda}, \mathsf{A}_{1,\lambda})_{\lambda \in \mathbb{N}}$*, where $\mathsf{A}_{1,\lambda}$ is parallel with $depth(\mathsf{A}_{1,\lambda}) \leq (t(\lambda))^{\varepsilon}$, it holds that*

$$\left| \Pr\left[\mathsf{A}_{1,\lambda}(\mathsf{st}, x^*, y^*) = 0 : \begin{array}{l} (\mathsf{ek}, \mathsf{vk}, \mathsf{td}) \leftarrow \mathsf{Setup}(1^\lambda, t) \\ \mathsf{st} \leftarrow \mathsf{A}_{0,\lambda}(\mathsf{ek}, \mathsf{vk}) \\ x^* \leftarrow \mathcal{X} \\ (y^*, \pi^*) \leftarrow \mathsf{Eval}(\mathsf{ek}, x^*) \end{array} \right] - \Pr\left[\mathsf{A}_{1,\lambda}(\mathsf{st}, x^*, y^*) = 0 : \begin{array}{l} (\mathsf{ek}, \mathsf{vk}, \mathsf{td}) \leftarrow \mathsf{Setup}(1^\lambda, t) \\ \mathsf{st} \leftarrow \mathsf{A}_{0,\lambda}(\mathsf{ek}, \mathsf{vk}) \\ x^* \leftarrow \mathcal{X} \\ y^* \leftarrow \mathcal{Y} \end{array} \right] \right| \in \mathsf{negl}(\lambda) \quad (2)$$

- *A TVDF* (Setup, Eval, TEval, Ver) *is* one-time pseudorandom *with* gap $\varepsilon < 1$ *if there exists a polynomial $\underline{t}(\cdot)$, such that for every polynomial $t(\cdot) \geq \underline{t}(\cdot)$ and every efficient distinguisher* $\mathsf{A} = (\mathsf{A}_\lambda)_{\lambda \in \mathbb{N}}$*, where A_λ is parallel with $depth(\mathsf{A}_\lambda) \leq (t(\lambda))^{\varepsilon}$, it holds that*

$$\left| \Pr\left[\mathsf{A}_\lambda(\mathsf{ek}, \mathsf{vk}, x^*, y^*) = 0 : \begin{array}{l} (\mathsf{ek}, \mathsf{vk}, \mathsf{td}) \leftarrow \mathsf{Setup}(1^\lambda, t) \\ x^* \leftarrow \mathcal{X} \\ (y^*, \pi^*) \leftarrow \mathsf{Eval}(\mathsf{ek}, x^*) \end{array} \right] - \Pr\left[\mathsf{A}_\lambda(\mathsf{ek}, \mathsf{vk}, x^*, y^*) = 0 : \begin{array}{l} (\mathsf{ek}, \mathsf{vk}, \mathsf{td}) \leftarrow \mathsf{Setup}(1^\lambda, t) \\ x^* \leftarrow \mathcal{X} \\ y^* \leftarrow \mathcal{Y} \end{array} \right] \right| \in \mathsf{negl}(\lambda) \quad (3)$$

3   Trapdoor VDF from TLP

In this section we present VDF_1, our basic construction of TVDF from TLP. The construction is formally described in Fig. 1. Note that the domain of VDF_1 for parameters (λ, t) is $\mathcal{X}_\lambda := \{0,1\}^\lambda$, while the range is $\mathcal{Y}_\lambda := \{0,1\}^{m(\lambda)}$, the range of the PPRF.[12] The function (assuming iO is perfectly correct) itself is defined as $V(x) := \mathsf{FEval}(k_1, x \| t)$. A formal proof that VDF_1 is a TVDF follows in Theorem 1.

---

[12] Here we assume that t is at most 2^λ and thus $|t| \leq \lambda$. Thus, whenever the input to PPRF is shorter than 2λ bits, we assume that it is appropriately padded.

Given an ensemble of IOWF f, a PPRF family $\mathsf{PPRF} = (\mathsf{KGen}, \mathsf{FEval}, \mathsf{Puncture})$, a TLP $\mathsf{TLP} = (\mathsf{PGen}, \mathsf{Sol})$ and an IO iO, all defined as in Theorem 1, the construction of our TVDF $\mathsf{VDF}_1 = (\mathsf{Setup}, \mathsf{Eval}, \mathsf{TEval}, \mathsf{Ver})$ is described below.

$\underline{(\mathsf{ek}, \mathsf{vk}, \mathsf{td}) \leftarrow \mathsf{Setup}(1^\lambda, t)}$
1. Sample two PPRF keys $k_1, k_2 \leftarrow \mathsf{KGen}(1^\lambda)$
2. Sample $\mathsf{ek} \leftarrow \mathsf{iO}(\mathsf{Sample}_{[t, k_1, k_2]}(\cdot))$ where

> $\underline{(z, \pi) := \mathsf{Sample}_{[t, k_1, k_2]}(x)}$
>
> (a) Generate a pseudorandom TLP solution $s := \mathsf{FEval}(k_1, t\|x)$
> (b) Use s and *pseudorandom* coins to generate a TLP puzzle $z := \mathsf{PGen}(s, t; \mathsf{FEval}(k_2, t\|x))$
> (c) Compute the "proof" $\pi := f_\lambda(s)$
> (d) Output (z, π)

   3. Set $\mathsf{vk} := \mathsf{ek}$, $\mathsf{td} := k_1$ and output $(\mathsf{ek}, \mathsf{vk}, \mathsf{td})$

$\underline{(s, \perp) := \mathsf{Eval}(\mathsf{ek}, x)}$
1. Use ek to generate a puzzle: $(z, \pi) := \mathsf{ek}(x)$
2. Solve the TLP to compute the output of the VDF: $s := \mathsf{Sol}(z)$
3. Output $(s, \perp)$, where $\perp$ denotes an empty proof

$\underline{(s, \perp) := \mathsf{TEval}(\mathsf{td}, x)}$
1. Output $(s, \perp)$, where $s := \mathsf{FEval}(\mathsf{td}, t\|x)$

$\underline{b := \mathsf{Ver}(\mathsf{vk}, x, s, \perp)}$
1. Use vk to re-generate the puzzle: $(z, \pi) := \mathsf{vk}(x)$
2. Accept (i.e., $b := 1$) if and only if the "proof" verifies, i.e., $f_\lambda(s) = \pi$.

Fig. 1. VDF_1: Basic construction of TVDF from TLP.

Theorem 1. *For a polynomial $m(\cdot)$, let $\mathcal{F} := (F_\lambda : \mathcal{K}_\lambda \times \{0,1\}^{2\lambda} \to \{0,1\}^{m(\lambda)})_{\lambda \in \mathbb{N}}$ be a PPRF family defined using $\mathsf{PPRF} = (\mathsf{KGen}, \mathsf{FEval}, \mathsf{Puncture})$ (Definition 5). Let $f = \{f_\lambda : \{0,1\}^{m(\lambda)} \to \{0,1\}^{2m(\lambda)}\}_{\lambda \in \mathbb{N}}$ be a family of injective one-way functions. Moreover, let $\mathsf{TLP} = (\mathsf{PGen}, \mathsf{Sol})$ be any time-lock puzzle (Definition 7) and iO be any indistinguishability obfuscator (Definition 2). Then the construction $\mathsf{VDF}_1 = (\mathsf{Setup}, \mathsf{Eval}, \mathsf{TEval}, \mathsf{Ver})$ described in Fig. 1 is a TVDF. In particular,*

- *VDF_1 is perfectly* sound,
- *if Sol runs in time $t \cdot p_1(\lambda)$, Sample runs in time $p_2(\lambda)$, and IO has an efficiency overhead $p_3(\lambda)$ for some polynomials $p_1(\cdot)$ $p_2(\cdot)$ and $p_3(\cdot)$ then Eval runs in time $(t + \log^{O(1)}(t)) \cdot p(\lambda)$, where the polynomial $p(\cdot)$ is determined by $p_i(\cdot)s$.*
- *if TLP is sequential with a gap ϵ, iO and PPRF are secure, and f is one-way then VDF_1 is one-time sequential with gap $O(\epsilon)$,*
- *if TLP is sequential with a gap ϵ, iO and PPRF are secure, and f is one-way then VDF_1 is one-time pseudorandom with gap $O(\epsilon)$.*

Remark 2. While in Theorem 1 we consider iO that is secure against PPT adversaries, we note that we can relax this requirement and consider only fine-grained iO. Concretely, since in the model without preprocessing the VDF adversary is purely of bounded depth, it suffices to also consider iO that is secure against the same bounded depth adversaries.

Proof. The completeness of the construction follows from the correctness of the underlying primitives (i.e., IO and TLP). The efficiency of the construction is straightforward to establish. In the rest of the proof, we focus on soundness, sequentiality and pseudorandomness, which we prove in the following claims.

Claim. VDF_1 is *perfectly* sound.

Proof. Note that in our construction the VDF proof output by the evaluation is empty, and that the verifier simply checks whether $f_\lambda(s) = \pi$, where π is generated using (honestly-generated) ek. By perfect correctness of iO and TLP, for an adversary's output $(x, s^*, \perp)$, such that $s^* \neq s := \mathsf{FEval}(k_1, t\|x)$, to be accepted it must be that $f_\lambda(s^*) = \pi = f_\lambda(s)$. However, this contradicts f's injectivity. $\qquad\square$

Claim. If TLP is sequential with gap ϵ, iO is perfectly correct, iO and PPRF are secure, and f is one-way then VDF_1 is one-time sequential with gap $O(\epsilon)$.

Proof. We proceed by a hybrid argument consisting of $\mathbf{Hybrid}_0, \cdots, \mathbf{Hybrid}_5$, which we describe below. Each hybrid is parametrised by the VDF adversary A against one-time sequentiality (see Definition 8), i.e., without preprocessing, which we drop to avoid clutter. The difference from the previous hybrid is highlighted in red.

- $\mathbf{Hybrid}_0$ is the distribution of the "real" sequentiality experiment. Hence it is generated according to the protocol description in Fig. 1 and the experiment outputs 1 if and only if the adversary breaks sequentiality of VDF_1. Note that assuming perfect correctness of iO and PPRF, the winning condition simplifies to "$s_\mathsf{A}^* = \mathsf{FEval}(k_1, t\|x^*)$".

$\mathbf{Hybrid}_0(1^\lambda, t)$
1. Sample two PPRF keys $k_1, k_2 \leftarrow \mathsf{KGen}(1^\lambda)$
2. Sample $\mathsf{ek} \leftarrow \mathsf{iO}(\mathsf{Sample}_{[t,k_1,k_2]}(\cdot))$ and set $\mathsf{vk} := \mathsf{ek}$, where

> $(z, \pi) := \mathsf{Sample}_{[t,k_1,k_2]}(x)$
> ---
> (a) Generate a pseudorandom TLP solution $s := \mathsf{FEval}(k_1, t\|x)$
> (b) Use s and *pseudorandom* coins to generate a TLP puzzle
> $z := \mathsf{PGen}(s, t; \mathsf{FEval}(k_2, t\|x))$
> (c) Compute the "proof" $\pi := f_\lambda(s)$
> (d) Output (z, π)

3. Sample a random challenge $x^* \leftarrow \mathcal{X}_\lambda$
4. Run A on $(\mathsf{ek}, \mathsf{vk}, x^*)$ to obtain s_A^*
5. Output 1 if and only if $s_\mathsf{A}^* = \mathsf{FEval}(k_1, t\|x^*)$

– In $\mathbf{Hybrid}_1$, we puncture the key k_1 at the challenge $\{t\|x^*\}$. The resulting distribution is indistinguishable from $\mathbf{Hybrid}_0$ thanks to preservation of PPRF functionality under puncturing and IO security.

$\mathbf{Hybrid}_1(1^\lambda, t)$

1. Sample two PPRF keys $k_1, k_2 \leftarrow \mathsf{KGen}(1^\lambda)$
2. Sample a random challenge $x^* \leftarrow \mathcal{X}_\lambda$, and a punctured key $k_1^* \leftarrow \mathsf{Puncture}(k_1, \{t\|x^*\})$
3. Pre-compute the *challenge* solution-puzzle pair with a proof:
   (a) Generate a pseudorandom TLP solution $s^* := \mathsf{FEval}(k_1, t\|x^*)$
   (b) Use s^* and *pseudorandom* coins to generate a TLP puzzle $z^* := \mathsf{PGen}(s^*, t; \mathsf{FEval}(k_2, t\|x^*))$
   (c) Compute the challenge "proof" $\pi^* := f_\lambda(s^*)$
4. Sample $\mathsf{ek} \leftarrow \mathsf{iO}(\mathsf{Sample}_{[t, k_1^*, k_2, x^*, z^*, \pi^*]}(\cdot))$ and set $\mathsf{vk} := \mathsf{ek}$, where

> $(z, \pi) := \mathsf{Sample}_{[t, k_1^*, k_2, x^*, z^*, \pi^*]}(x)$
> ---
> • If $x = x^*$ then output (z^*, π^*)
> • Else
>   (a) Generate a pseudorandom TLP solution $s := \mathsf{FEval}(k_1^*, t\|x)$
>   (b) Use s and *pseudorandom* coins to generate a TLP puzzle $z := \mathsf{PGen}(s, t; \mathsf{FEval}(k_2, t\|x))$
>   (c) Compute the "proof" $\pi := f_\lambda(s)$
>   (d) Output (z, π)

5. Run A on $(\mathsf{ek}, \mathsf{vk}, x^*)$ to obtain s_A^*
6. Output 1 if and only if $s_\mathsf{A}^* = s^*$

– $\mathbf{Hybrid}_2$ is similar to $\mathbf{Hybrid}_1$ except that the challenge solution s^* is sampled at random. The resulting distribution is indistinguishable from $\mathbf{Hybrid}_0$ thanks to pseudorandomness of PPRF at punctured points.

$\mathbf{Hybrid}_2(1^\lambda, t)$
$\vdots$

3. Pre-compute the *challenge* solution-puzzle pair with a proof:
   (a) Sample a *random* TLP solution $s^* \leftarrow \{0, 1\}^{m(\lambda)}$
   (b) Generate the TLP puzzle $z^* := \mathsf{PGen}(s^*, t; \mathsf{FEval}(k_2, t\|x^*))$ from s^* using *pseudorandom* coins
   (c) Compute the "proof" $\pi^* := f_\lambda(s^*)$

$\vdots$

6. Output 1 if and only if $s_\mathsf{A}^* = s^*$

– In $\mathbf{Hybrid}_3$, we puncture the key k_2 at $\{t\|x^*\}$. Looking ahead, the purpose of this step is to undo the "derandomisation" carried out in Setup for generating the TLP puzzle. As for $\mathbf{Hybrid}_1$, this change is indistinguishable thanks to preservation of PPRF functionality under puncturing and IO security.

Hybrid$_3(1^\lambda, t)$
1. Sample two PPRF keys $k_1, k_2 \leftarrow \mathsf{KGen}(1^\lambda)$
2. Sample a random challenge $x^* \leftarrow \mathcal{X}_\lambda$, and a punctured key $k_1^* \leftarrow \mathsf{Puncture}(k_1, \{t\|x^*\})$
3. Pre-compute the *challenge* solution-puzzle pair with a proof:
   (a) Sample a *random* TLP solution $s^* \leftarrow \{0,1\}^{m(\lambda)}$
   (b) Sample a punctured key $k_2^* \leftarrow \mathsf{Puncture}(k_2, \{t\|x^*\})$
   (c) Use s^* and *pseudorandom* coins to generate the TLP puzzle $z^* := \mathsf{PGen}(s^*, t; \mathsf{FEval}(k_2, t\|x^*))$
   (d) Compute the "proof" $\pi^* := f_\lambda(s^*)$
4. Sample $\mathsf{ek} \leftarrow \mathsf{iO}(\mathsf{Sample}_{[t, k_1^*, k_2^*, x^*, z^*, \pi^*]}(\cdot))$ and set $\mathsf{vk} := \mathsf{ek}$, where

   > $(z, \pi) := \mathsf{Sample}_{[t, k_1^*, k_2^*, x^*, z^*, \pi^*]}(x)$
   > ___
   > - If $x = x^*$ then output (z^*, π^*)
   > - Else
   >   (a) Generate a pseudorandom TLP solution $s := \mathsf{FEval}(k_1^*, t\|x)$
   >   (b) Use s and *pseudorandom* coins to generate the TLP puzzle $z := \mathsf{PGen}(s, t; \mathsf{FEval}(k_2^*, t\|x))$
   >   (c) Compute the "proof" $\pi := f_\lambda(s)$
   >   (d) Output (z, π)

5. Run A on $(\mathsf{ek}, \mathsf{vk}, x^*)$ to obtain s_A^*
6. Output 1 if and only if $s_\mathsf{A}^* = s^*$

- In **Hybrid**$_4$, we switch the random coins used for generating the challenge TLP puzzle from pseudorandom to truly random. This is necessary to invoke sequentiality of TLP in the next step. As for **Hybrid**$_2$, this change is indistinguishable thanks to pseudorandomness of PPRF at punctured points.

Hybrid$_4(1^\lambda, t)$
  ⋮
3. Pre-compute the *challenge* solution-puzzle pair with a proof:
   (a) Sample a *random* TLP solution $s^* \leftarrow \{0,1\}^{m(\lambda)}$
   (b) Sample a punctured key $k_2^* \leftarrow \mathsf{Puncture}(k_2, \{t\|x^*\})$
   (c) Sample random coins $r^* \leftarrow \{0,1\}^{\mathrm{poly}(\lambda)}$
   (d) Use s^* and *random* coins to generate the TLP puzzle $z^* := \mathsf{PGen}(s^*, t; r^*)$
   (e) Compute the "proof" $\pi^* := f_\lambda(s^*)$
     ⋮
6. Output 1 if and only if $s_\mathsf{A}^* = s^*$

- Finally, in **Hybrid**$_5$, we decouple the proof from the puzzle: a *second* solution s_2^* is used to generate the challenge puzzle (but the adversary wins if it still outputs s_1^*). However, this change is indistinguishable to *bounded-depth* adversaries thanks to TLP sequentiality, and thus the probabilities that a bounded-depth adversary outputs s_1^* in $\mathbf{Hybrid}_4$ and $\mathbf{Hybrid}_5$ are negligibly close.

$\mathbf{Hybrid}_5(1^\lambda, t)$
$\vdots$

3. Pre-compute the *challenge* solution-puzzle pair with a proof:
   (a) Sample a *random* TLP solution $s_1^*, s_2^* \leftarrow \{0,1\}^{m(\lambda)}$
   (b) Sample a punctured key $k_2^* \leftarrow \mathsf{Puncture}(k_2, \{t\|x^*\})$
   (c) Sample random coins $r^* \leftarrow \{0,1\}^{\mathrm{poly}(\lambda)}$
   (d) Use s_2^* and *random* coins to generate the TLP puzzle
       $z_2^* := \mathsf{PGen}(s_2^*, t; r^*)$
   (e) Compute the "proof" $\pi^* := f_\lambda(s_1^*)$

   $\vdots$

6. Output 1 if and only if $s_{\mathsf{A}}^* = s_1^*$

The probability that experiment $\mathbf{Hybrid}_5(1^\lambda, t)$ outputs 1 can be bounded by the one-wayness of f since the only the proof π^* has any information about s_1^*. Since the depth of all the reductions depends on t only by a $\log(t)$ factor, the gap of VDF is sequential with $O(\epsilon)$ gap.

$\square$

Claim. If TLP is sequential with a gap ϵ, iO and PPRF are secure, and f is one-way then VDF_1 is one-time pseudorandom with gap $O(\epsilon)$.

Proof. This follows from the proof of sequentiality above by observing that the distribution of s_2^* in $\mathbf{Hybrid}_5$ is random.

$\square$ This completes the proof of Theorem 1. $\square$

Remark 3. We can potentially consider advanced equivocation techniques to allow to embed the TLP into the input x^* instead of the public parameters, and hence, only embed the TLP challenge at a later point during the security game. However, unfortunately, we do not see how to instantiate this idea, and we believe it will require new ideas. The main difficulty here seems to be that puncturing techniques only allow to change the output of the obfuscated circuit at certain *predetermined* input points. Concretely, we would require some input x^*, that to some extent is set already in the public parameters, to later be mapped to some z^* which is unknown at the time of public parameter generation but can be extracted from x^*. Hence, we should only fix some partial information on x^* in the public parameters, such that later we can embed the TLP z^*. On the other hand, if the obfuscated circuit maps all inputs x with the same partial information as x^* to a new TLP derived from x in a different way than the original circuit, this would mean that we need to reprogram the circuit on many inputs at the same time.

Corollary 1 (VDF$_1$ from any non-parallelizing language, iO and OWF).
Assuming the existence of non-parallelizing languages with worst-case hardness, polynomially-secure iO for circuits and polynomially-hard one-way functions, then there exist TVDFs that are one-time sequential and one-time pseudorandom.

Proof. This is a consequence of Theorem 1, taking into account [12,13]:

1. [12] established that TLPs exist assuming worst-case hardness of non-parallelizing languages and polynomially-secure iO for circuits.
2. [13] showed that it is possible to construct IOWF from polynomially-secure iO and polynomially-hard OWF. □

4   Efficient-Verifier Trapdoor VDF from TLP

In this section we present VDF$_2$, our second construction of TVDF from TLP. The main advantage of VDF$_2$ over VDF$_1$ from Fig. 1 is that the verifier – since it doesn't have to invoke an obfuscated program – is more efficient. To this end, we additionally rely on prefix-constrained signatures (PCS, see Definition 6). The assumptions relied upon are the same as in the basic construction since prefix-constrained signatures can be constructed based on OWF (see Sect. 4.1). However, soundness achieved by the construction is only selective. The construction is formally described in Fig. 2. We prove its security in Theorem 2. Note that the VDF function is exactly as in the basic construction.

Theorem 2. *For a polynomial $m(\cdot)$, let $\mathcal{F} := (F_\lambda : \mathcal{K}_\lambda \times \{0,1\}^{2\lambda} \to \{0,1\}^{m(\lambda)})_{\lambda \in \mathbb{N}}$ be a PPRF family defined using $\mathsf{PPRF} = (\mathsf{KGen}, \mathsf{FEval}, \mathsf{Puncture})$ (Definition 5). Let $f = \{f_\lambda : \{0,1\}^{m(\lambda)} \to \{0,1\}^{2m(\lambda)}\}_{\lambda \in \mathbb{N}}$ be an ensemble of injective one-way functions. Let $\mathsf{TLP} = (\mathsf{Gen}, \mathsf{Sol})$ be any time-lock puzzle with puzzles of length $w(\cdot)$ (Definition 7). Moreover, let $\mathsf{PCS} := (\mathsf{KGen}, \mathsf{CGen}, \mathsf{Sign}, \mathsf{CSign}, \mathsf{Ver})$ be any prefix-constrained signature with message-space defined by $\ell(\cdot) := \lambda + 2m(\cdot) + w(\cdot)$ (Definition 6) and iO be any indistinguishability obfuscator (Definition 2). Then the construction $\mathsf{VDF}_2 = (\mathsf{Setup}, \mathsf{Eval}, \mathsf{TEval}, \mathsf{Ver})$ described in Fig. 2 is a TVDF. In particular,*

- *if PCS is selectively one-time constrained unforgeable then VDF$_2$ is selectively computationally sound,*
- *if Sol runs in time $t \cdot p_1(\lambda)$, Sample runs in time $p_2(\lambda)$, and IO has an efficiency overhead $p_3(\lambda)$ for some polynomials $p_1(\cdot)$ $p_2(\cdot)$ and $p_3(\cdot)$ then Eval runs in time $(t + \log^{O(1)}(t)) \cdot p(\lambda)$, where the polynomial $p(\cdot)$ is determined by $p_i(\cdot)$'s.*
- *if TLP is sequential with a gap ϵ, iO and PPRF are secure, and f is one-way then VDF$_2$ is one -time sequential with gap $O(\epsilon)$,*
- *if TLP is sequential with a gap ϵ, iO and PPRF are secure, and f is one-way then VDF$_2$ is one-time pseudorandom with gap $O(\epsilon)$.*

Due to lack of space we defer the proof of Theorem 2 to the full version [1].

Given a family of OWP f, a PPRF $\mathsf{PPRF} = (\mathsf{KGen}, \mathsf{FEval}, \mathsf{Puncture})$, a PCS $\mathsf{PCS} :=$ $(\mathsf{Gen}, \mathsf{CGen}, \mathsf{Sign}, \mathsf{CSign}, \mathsf{Ver})$, a TLP $\mathsf{TLP} = (\mathsf{PGen}, \mathsf{Sol})$ and an IO iO, all defined as in Theorem 2, the construction of our TVDF $\mathsf{VDF}_2 = (\mathsf{Setup}, \mathsf{Eval}, \mathsf{TEval}, \mathsf{Ver})$ is described below.

$\underline{(\mathsf{ek}, \mathsf{vk}, \mathsf{td}) \leftarrow \mathsf{Setup}(1^\lambda, t)}$

    1. Sample two PPRF keys $k_1, k_2 \leftarrow \mathsf{KGen}(1^\lambda)$

    2. Sample a PCS key-pair $(\mathsf{pk}, \mathsf{msk}) \leftarrow \mathsf{Gen}(1^\lambda)$

    3. Sample $\mathsf{ek} \leftarrow \mathsf{iO}(\mathsf{Sample}_{[t,k_1,k_2,\mathsf{msk}]}(\cdot))$ where

> $(z, \pi, \sigma) := \mathsf{Sample}_{[t,k_1,k_2,\mathsf{msk}]}(x)$
>
>   (a) Generate a pseudorandom TLP solution $s := \mathsf{FEval}(k_1, t\|x)$
>
>   (b) Use s and *pseudorandom* coins to generate a TLP puzzle $z :=$ $\mathsf{PGen}(s, t; \mathsf{FEval}(k_2, t\|x))$
>
>   (c) Compute the proof $\pi := f_\lambda(s)$ and signature $\sigma :=$ $\mathsf{Sign}(\mathsf{msk}, x\|\pi\|z)$
>
>   (d) Output (z, π, σ)

    4. Set $\mathsf{vk} := (\mathsf{ek}, \mathsf{pk})$, $\mathsf{td} := (\mathsf{ek}, k_1)$ and output $(\mathsf{ek}, \mathsf{vk}, \mathsf{td})$

$\underline{(s, (z, \pi, \sigma)) := \mathsf{Eval}(\mathsf{ek}, x)}$

    1. Use ek to generate a puzzle: $(z, \pi, \sigma) := \mathsf{ek}(x)$

    2. Solve the TLP to compute the output of the VDF: $s := \mathsf{Sol}(z)$

    3. Output $(s, (z, \pi, \sigma))$

$\underline{(s, (z, \pi, \sigma)) := \mathsf{TEval}(\mathsf{td}, x)}$

    1. Use ek to generate a puzzle: $(z, \pi, \sigma) := \mathsf{ek}(x)$

    2. Use k_1 to generate the solution $s := \mathsf{FEval}(k_1, t\|x)$

    3. Output $(s, (z, \pi, \sigma))$

$\underline{b := \mathsf{Ver}(\mathsf{vk}, x, s, (z, \pi, \sigma))}$

    1. Accept (i.e., $b := 1$) if and only if both proof and signature verify, i.e.,

        (a) $f_\lambda(s) = \pi$ and

        (b) $\mathsf{Ver}(\mathsf{pk}, \sigma, x\|\pi\|z) = 1$

Fig. 2. VDF_2, an efficient-verifier TVDF from TLP.

4.1 Prefix-Constrained Signatures from OWF

We argue that the *puncturable* signature scheme from [20], built from PPRF and one-time signatures (OTS), already gives rise to a prefix-constrained signature scheme as per Definition 6. Their construction follows the paradigm of constructing (many-time) signatures from OTS using a tree of pseudorandomly generated one-time signatures. The seeds used to derive the one-time signature key pairs are derived using a PPRF. We note that OTS as well as PPRF can be constructed from OWF, namely by the one-time signature scheme of Lamport [43] and the PPRF construction of Goldreich, Goldwasser and Micali [34]. However, the construction of [20] cannot directly be instantiated with the GGM PPRF due to a mismatch of input domain as explained next.

In fact, for the security of the puncturable signature scheme one requires a PPRF with *variable-length* input domain $\mathcal{X} = \{0,1\}^{\leq \ell}$ opposed to fixed-length as in the GGM construction. Unfortunately, the basic GGM PPRF is *not* secure when punctured on a prefix. A generalisation of GGM, however, easily solves this issue: For each $i \leq \ell$ one can sample a separate key $k_i \leftarrow \mathsf{KGen}_{\mathsf{GGM}}(1^\lambda)$ according to the GGM construction and then define a PPRF with input space $\mathcal{X} = \{0,1\}^{\leq \ell}$ as $\mathsf{Eval}((k_i)_{i \leq \ell}, x) := \mathsf{Eval}_{\mathsf{GGM}}(k_{|m|}, m)$. It is easy to see that this construction can be proven secure based on OWF in the same way as the GGM construction itself.

Another useful property of the GGM construction is that it gives rise to a *constrained* PRF for the constraint classes of prefixes and "dual" prefixes, as required for our application. Using the above construction of a variable-length PPRF based on the GGM PPRF, one therefore obtains a constrained PRF based on OWF with input domain $\mathcal{X} = \{0,1\}^{\leq \ell}$ supporting constraints of the form

$$S_{x^*} := \{0,1\}^{\leq \ell} \setminus \left(\{x\}_{x \prec x^*} \cup x^* \| \{0,1\}^{\leq \ell - |x^*|} \right), \tag{4}$$

i.e., the set consisting of all input strings *except for* prefixes and extensions of some $x^* \in \{0,1\}^{\leq \ell}$.

Our construction of PCS is the same tree-based construction as the puncturable signature scheme [20], but based on constrained PRF for the above more general constraint class, see Fig. 3 for how to generate constrained keys and use them for signing. To prove that the construction is indeed a selectively one-time prefix-constrained signature scheme, one can generalise [20, Theorem 1] to the different constraint class. We refer to [1] for a formal statement and a proof.

5   Trapdoor VDFs with Advanced Features

In this section, we define more advanced trapdoor VDFs, such as trapdoor-homomorphic and trapdoor-constrained VDFs. Due to the generality of our VDF constructions, we achieve these advanced VDFs by simply replacing the underlying PRF from our constructions with a more advanced PRF, such as key-homomorphic or constrained PRF. Hence, one can also consider these advanced VDFs as adding both a notion of delay and verifiability to the underlying PRFs.

5.1   Trapdoor-Homomorphic VDFs

We define trapdoor-homomorphic VDFs. These are trapdoor VDFs in which there is a homomorphism from the trapdoor key space to the output space. We first define the notion of key-homomorphism.

Definition 10 (Key-Homomorphic Functions). *A function family* $\mathcal{F}_\lambda = \{\mathsf{F} \colon \mathcal{K} \times \mathcal{X} \to \mathcal{Y}\}$ *is* $(\oplus, \otimes)$*-key-homomorphic if* $(\mathcal{K}, \oplus)$ *and* $(\mathcal{Y}, \otimes)$ *are groups and for every* $k_1, k_2 \in \mathcal{K}$ *and* $x \in \mathcal{X}$, *it holds* $F(k_1, x) \otimes F(k_2, x) = F(k_1 \oplus k_2, x)$.

Definition 11 (Trapdoor-Homomorphic VDFs). *A trapdoor VDF* $\mathsf{TVDF} = (\mathsf{Setup}, \mathsf{TEval}, \mathsf{Eval}, \mathsf{Ver})$ *with input and outputs spaces*

Given a one-time signature scheme $\mathsf{OTS} = (\mathsf{Gen}_1, \mathsf{Sign}_1, \mathsf{Ver}_1)$ with public-key space $\{0,1\}^{\ell_1}$, message space $\{0,1\}^{2\ell_1 + \log \ell_1 + 1}$ and randomness space $\mathcal{R}_1$, and a constrained PRF $\mathsf{CPRF} = (\mathsf{KGen}, \mathsf{FEval}, \mathsf{Constr})$ with $\mathcal{X} := \{0,1\}^{\leq \ell}$ with $\ell = 2\ell_1$ and $\mathcal{Y} = \mathcal{R}_1$, a PCS $\mathsf{PCS} = (\mathsf{Gen}, \mathsf{CGen}, \mathsf{Sign}, \mathsf{CSign}, \mathsf{Ver})$ with message space $\{0,1\}^{\ell}$ is described below.

- $(\mathsf{sk}, \mathsf{pk}) \leftarrow \mathsf{Gen}(1^\lambda, 1^\ell)$
    1. Sample a CPRF key $k \leftarrow \mathsf{KGen}(1^\lambda)$
    2. Compute $r_\epsilon := \mathsf{FEval}(k, \epsilon)$ and $(\mathsf{sk}_\epsilon, \mathsf{pk}_\epsilon) := \mathsf{Gen}_1(1^\lambda; r_\epsilon)$
    3. Output the PCS key-pair $(\mathsf{msk} := (k, \ell), \mathsf{pk} := (\mathsf{pk}_\epsilon, \ell))$

- $\mathsf{sk}^* \leftarrow \mathsf{CGen}(\mathsf{msk}, m^*)$
    1. Sample a constrained key $k^* \leftarrow \mathsf{Constr}(k, S_{m^*})$ for S_{m^*} as in Eq.4
    2. For each $u \prec m^*$:
        (a) Let $r_u := \mathsf{FEval}(k, u)$ and $(\mathsf{sk}_u, \mathsf{pk}_u) := \mathsf{Gen}_1(1^\lambda; r_u)$
        (b) Compute $\sigma_u := \mathsf{Sign}_1(\mathsf{sk}_u, (pk_{u\|0}, \mathsf{pk}_{u\|1}, u))$
    3. Output $sk^* := (k^*, (\sigma_u, (pk_{u\|0}, \mathsf{pk}_{u\|1}, u))_{u \prec m^*})$

- $\sigma := \mathsf{Sign}(\mathsf{msk}, m)$
    1. For each $u \preceq m$, let $r_u := \mathsf{FEval}(k, u)$ and $(\mathsf{sk}_u, \mathsf{pk}_u) := \mathsf{Gen}_1(1^\lambda; r_u)$
    2. For each $u \prec m$, compute $\sigma_u := \mathsf{Sign}_1(\mathsf{sk}_u, (pk_{u\|0}, \mathsf{pk}_{u\|1}, u))$
    3. Output the tuple $\sigma := (\mathsf{Sign}_1(\mathsf{sk}_m, m), (\sigma_u, (pk_{u\|0}, \mathsf{pk}_{u\|1}, u))_{u \prec m})$

- $\sigma := \mathsf{CSign}(\mathsf{sk}^*, m)$
    1. Parse sk^* as $\mathsf{sk}^* := (k^*, (\sigma_u, (pk_{u\|0}, \mathsf{pk}_{u\|1}, u))_{u \prec m^*})$
    2. If $m^* \prec m$ output $\perp$
    3. Let v be the longest common prefix of m and m^*
    4. For each u with $v \prec u \preceq m$ compute $r_u := \mathsf{FEval}(k^*, u)$ and $(\mathsf{sk}_u, \mathsf{pk}_u) := \mathsf{Gen}_1(1^\lambda; r_u)$
    5. For each u with $v \prec u \prec m$ compute $\sigma_u := \mathsf{Sign}_1(\mathsf{sk}_u, (pk_{u\|0}, \mathsf{pk}_{u\|1}, u))$
    6. Output the tuple $\sigma := (\mathsf{Sign}_1(\mathsf{sk}_m, m), (\sigma_u, (pk_{u\|0}, \mathsf{pk}_{u\|1}, u))_{u \prec m})$

- $b := \mathsf{Ver}(\mathsf{pk}, m, \sigma)$
    1. Parse σ as $(\sigma_m, (\sigma_u, (pk_{u\|0}, \mathsf{pk}_{u\|1}, u))_{u \prec m})$
    2. Output 1 iff $\mathsf{Ver}_1(\mathsf{pk}_u, (pk_{u\|0}, \mathsf{pk}_{u\|1}, u), \sigma_u) = 1$ for all $u \prec m$ and $\mathsf{Ver}_1(\mathsf{pk}_m, m, \sigma_m) = 1$

Fig. 3. Construction of PCS from CPRF and OTS.

$\mathcal{X}, \mathcal{Y}$ and trapdoor key space $\mathcal{K}$, is a trapdoor-homomorphic VDF if $(\mathcal{K}, \oplus)$ and $(\mathcal{Y}, \otimes)$ are groups and for any $\lambda, t \in \mathbb{N}$ and $x \in \mathcal{X}$,

$$\Pr\left[y_1 \otimes y_2 = y : \begin{array}{l} (\mathsf{ek}_1, \mathsf{vk}_1, \mathsf{td}_1) \leftarrow \mathsf{Setup}(1^\lambda, t) \\ (\mathsf{ek}_2, \mathsf{vk}_2, \mathsf{td}_2) \leftarrow \mathsf{Setup}(1^\lambda, t) \\ (y_1, \pi_1) \leftarrow \mathsf{TEval}(\mathsf{td}_1, x) \\ (y_2, \pi_2) \leftarrow \mathsf{TEval}(\mathsf{td}_2, x) \\ (y, \pi) \leftarrow \mathsf{TEval}(\mathsf{td}_1 \oplus \mathsf{td}_2, x) \end{array} \right] = 1 \ .$$

Constructing Trapdoor-Homomorphic VDFs. Replacing the standard PPRF used to compute the VDF value in our basic VDF construction of Fig. 1 with a key-homomorphic PPRF results in a trapdoor-homomorphic VDF.

Corollary 2. *Let $\mathcal{F}_\lambda = \{\mathsf{F}\colon \mathcal{K} \times \mathcal{X} \to \mathcal{Y}\}$ be a $(\oplus, \otimes)$-key-homomorphic puncturable PRF family. If we use $\mathcal{F}_\lambda$ for the PRF defined by the key k_1 inside the trapdoor VDF construction given in Fig. 1, then we obtain a trapdoor-homomorphic VDF.*

Such key-homomorphic constrained PRFs $\mathcal{F}_\lambda$ in the standard model exists from (R)LWE assumption [7,18]. However, the (R)LWE based constructions achieve only approximate homomorphism, i.e., they are "almost" key-homomorphic PRFs, due to the underlying error term, and hence, they only allow for a bounded number of homomorphic operations. Therefore, instantiated with such key-homomorphic PRFs, our trapdoor-homomorphic VDF also inherits the same limitations, and becomes "almost" trapdoor-homomorphic VDF.

5.2   Trapdoor-Constrained VDFs

We define trapdoor-constrained VDFs. These are trapdoor VDFs in which keys can be constrained to allow the VDF evaluation on subsets of the domain.

Definition 12 (Trapdoor-Constrained VDFs). *A trapdoor VDF $\mathsf{TVDF} = (\mathsf{Setup}, \mathsf{TEval}, \mathsf{Eval}, \mathsf{Ver})$ with input and outputs spaces $\mathcal{X}, \mathcal{Y}$ and trapdoor key space $\mathcal{K}$ is a trapdoor-constrained VDF w.r.t. a family of subsets $\mathcal{S}_\lambda$ over $\mathcal{X}$ with a constrained trapdoor key space $\mathcal{K}_\mathcal{S}$, such that $\mathcal{K}_\mathcal{S} \cap \mathcal{K} = \emptyset$, if TEval accepts inputs from $(\mathcal{K} \cup \mathcal{K}_\mathcal{S}) \times \mathcal{X}$ and there exists a PPT algorithm Constr that, on input a key $\mathsf{td} \in \mathcal{K}$ and a set $S \in \mathcal{S}_\lambda$, outputs a constrained trapdoor td_S such that for any $\lambda, t \in \mathbb{N}$ and $x \in S$,*

$$\Pr\left[\begin{array}{l} y' = y \,\wedge \\ \mathsf{Ver}(\mathsf{vk}, x, y', \pi') = 1 \end{array} : \begin{array}{l} (\mathsf{ek}, \mathsf{vk}, \mathsf{td}) \leftarrow \mathsf{Setup}(1^\lambda, t) \\ \mathsf{td}_S \leftarrow \mathsf{Constr}(\mathsf{td}, S) \\ (y, \pi) \leftarrow \mathsf{TEval}(\mathsf{td}, x) \\ (y', \pi') \leftarrow \mathsf{TEval}(\mathsf{td}_S, x) \end{array}\right] = 1 \;,$$

and $\bot \leftarrow \mathsf{TEval}(\mathsf{td}_S, x')$, for any $x' \notin S$.

Constructing Trapdoor-Constrained VDFs. Replacing the standard PPRF used to compute the VDF value in our basic VDF construction of Fig. 1 with a constrained PRF results in a trapdoor-constrained VDF.

Corollary 3. *Let $\mathcal{F}_\lambda = \{\mathsf{F}\colon \mathcal{K} \times \mathcal{X} \to \mathcal{Y}\}$ be a constrained PRF family. If we use $\mathcal{F}_\lambda$ for the PRF defined by the key k_1 inside the trapdoor VDF construction from Fig. 1, then we obtain a trapdoor-constrained VDF.*

Depending on the constraining predicate, we can obtain constrained PRFs from different assumptions. We have prefix-constrained [16,34] and constrained PRFs for t-CNF predicates from OWFs [25], for inner-product predicates from LWE [25], for P/poly and sets recognizable by Turing machines from (differing-input) obfuscation [2,25].

5.3 Trapdoor-Homomorphic Trapdoor-Constrained VDFs

We define trapdoor-homomorphic trapdoor-constrained VDFs. These are trapdoor VDFs that combine the functionality of both trapdoor-homomorphic VDFs (see Sect. 5.1) and trapdoor-constrained VDFs (see Sect. 5.2).

Definition 13 (Trapdoor-Homomorphic Trapdoor-Constrained VDFs). *A trapdoor VDF is a* trapdoor-homomorphic trapdoor-constrained *VDF if it is trapdoor-homomorphic (Definition 11) and trapdoor-constrained (Definition 12).*

Constructing Trapdoor-Homomorphic Trapdoor-Constrained VDFs. This can be constructed by instantiating our trapdoor VDF construction from Fig. 1 with a key-homomorphic constrained PRF.

Corollary 4. *Let $\mathcal{F}_\lambda = \{\mathsf{F}\colon \mathcal{K} \times \mathcal{X} \to \mathcal{Y}\}$ be a key-homomorphic constrained PRF family. If we use $\mathcal{F}_\lambda$ for the PRF defined by the key k_1 inside the trapdoor VDF construction from Fig. 1, then we obtain a trapdoor-homomorphic trapdoor-constrained VDF.*

The proof of Corollary 4, which subsumes the proofs of Corollary 2 and Corollary 3, is simple and can be found in the full version [1]. As described in Sect. 5.1, we have key-homomorphic constrained PRFs from (R)LWE assumption [7,18], which we can use to instantiate our construction in order to obtain "almost" trapdoor-homomorphic trapdoor-constrained VDFs.

Acknowledgments. We would like to thank Gennaro Avitabile for pointing us to the utility of witness maps in our context, and an anonymous reviewer from TCC'24 for bringing to our attention the talk [49]. Hamza Abusalah and Dario Fiore are supported by the PICOCRYPT project that has received funding from the European Research Council (ERC) under the European Unions Horizon 2020 research and innovation programme (Grant agreement No. 101001283), partially supported by projects PRODIGY (TED2021-132464B- I00), ESPADA (PID2022-142290OB-I00) and CEX2024-001471-M funded by MCIN/AEI/10.13039/501100011033/. Erkan Tairi is supported in part by the France 2030 ANR-22-PECY-003 SecureCompute Project, by the Austrian Science Fund (FWF) Project J4879-N, by the Bakar Funds and Peder Sather Funds.

References

1. Abusalah, H., Azari, K., Fiore, D., Kamath, C., Tairi, E.: On verifiable delay functions from time-lock puzzles. Cryptology ePrint Archive, Report 2025/1782
2. Abusalah, H., Fuchsbauer, G., Pietrzak, K.: Constrained PRFs for unbounded inputs. In: CT-RSA 2016
3. Ahrens, K., Zumbrägel, J.: DEFEND: towards verifiable delay functions from endomorphism rings. IACR Cryptol. ePrint Arch
4. Applebaum, B., Ishai, Y., Kushilevitz, E.: Cryptography in NC^0. In: 45th FOCS

5. Armknecht, F., Barman, L., Bohli, J.M., Karame, G.O.: Mirror: enabling proofs of data replication and retrievability in the cloud. In: USENIX Security 2016

6. Arun, A., Bonneau, J., Clark, J.: Short-lived zero-knowledge proofs and signatures. In: ASIACRYPT 2022, Part III

7. Banerjee, A., Fuchsbauer, G., Peikert, C., Pietrzak, K., Stevens, S.: Key-homomorphic constrained pseudorandom functions. In: TCC 2015, Part II

8. Bellare, M., Fuchsbauer, G.: Policy-based signatures. In: PKC 2014

9. Biryukov, A., et al.: Cryptanalysis of algebraic verifiable delay functions. In: Advances in Cryptology - CRYPTO 2024 - 44th Annual International Cryptology Conference, Santa Barbara, CA, USA, 18–22 August 2024, Proceedings, Part III

10. Bitansky, N., et al.: PPAD is as hard as LWE and iterated squaring. In: TCC 2022, Part II

11. Bitansky, N., Garg, R.: Succinct randomized encodings from laconic function evaluation, faster and simpler. In: Advances in Cryptology - EUROCRYPT 2025 - 44th Annual International Conference on the Theory and Applications of Cryptographic Techniques, Madrid, Spain, 4–8 May 2025, Proceedings, Part VII

12. Bitansky, N., Goldwasser, S., Jain, A., Paneth, O., Vaikuntanathan, V., Waters, B.: Time-lock puzzles from randomized encodings. In: ITCS 2016

13. Bitansky, N., Paneth, O., Wichs, D.: Perfect structure on the edge of chaos - trapdoor permutations from indistinguishability obfuscation. In: TCC 2016-A, Part I

14. Block, A.R., Holmgren, J., Rosen, A., Rothblum, R.D., Soni, P.: Time- and space-efficient arguments from groups of unknown order. In: CRYPTO 2021, Part IV

15. Boneh, D., Bonneau, J., Bünz, B., Fisch, B.: Verifiable delay functions. In: CRYPTO 2018, Part I

16. Boneh, D., Waters, B.: Constrained pseudorandom functions and their applications. In: ASIACRYPT 2013, Part II

17. Boyle, E., Goldwasser, S., Ivan, I.: Functional signatures and pseudorandom functions. In: PKC 2014

18. Brakerski, Z., Vaikuntanathan, V.: Constrained key-homomorphic PRFs from standard lattice assumptions - or: how to secretly embed a circuit in your PRF. In: TCC 2015, Part II

19. Canetti, R., Lin, H., Tessaro, S., Vaikuntanathan, V.: Obfuscation of probabilistic circuits and applications. In: TCC 2015, Part II

20. Chakraborty, S., Prabhakaran, M., Wichs, D.: Witness maps and applications. In: PKC 2020, Part I

21. Chávez-Saab, J., Rodríguez-Henríquez, F., Tibouchi, M.: Verifiable isogeny walks: towards an isogeny-based postquantum VDF. In: Selected Areas in Cryptography - 28th International Conference, SAC 2021, Virtual Event, 29 September–1 October 2021, Revised Selected Papers

22. Choudhuri, A.R., Hubacek, P., Kamath, C., Pietrzak, K., Rosen, A., Rothblum, G.N.: PPAD-hardness via iterated squaring modulo a composite. Cryptology ePrint Archive, Report 2019/667

23. Cini, V., Lai, R.W.F., Malavolta, G.: Lattice-based succinct arguments from vanishing polynomials - (extended abstract). In: CRYPTO 2023, Part II

24. Cohen, B., Pietrzak, K.: The chia network blockchain. https://www.chia.net/wp-content/uploads/2022/07/ChiaGreenPaper.pdf. Accessed 29 Sept 2024

25. Davidson, A., Katsumata, S., Nishimaki, R., Yamada, S., Yamakawa, T.: Adaptively secure constrained pseudorandom functions in the standard model. In: CRYPTO 2020, Part I

26. De Feo, L., Masson, S., Petit, C., Sanso, A.: Verifiable delay functions from supersingular isogenies and pairings. In: ASIACRYPT 2019, Part I
27. Döttling, N., Garg, S., Malavolta, G., Vasudevan, P.N.: Tight verifiable delay functions. In: SCN 20
28. Dujmovic, J., Garg, R., Malavolta, G.: Time-lock puzzles with efficient batch solving. In: Advances in Cryptology - EUROCRYPT 2024 - 43rd Annual International Conference on the Theory and Applications of Cryptographic Techniques, Zurich, Switzerland, 26–30 May 2024, Proceedings, Part II
29. Ephraim, N., Freitag, C., Komargodski, I., Pass, R.: Continuous verifiable delay functions. In: EUROCRYPT 2020, Part III
30. Ephraim, N., Freitag, C., Komargodski, I., Pass, R.: SPARKs: succinct parallelizable arguments of knowledge. In: EUROCRYPT 2020, Part I
31. Fiat, A., Shamir, A.: How to prove yourself: practical solutions to identification and signature problems. In: CRYPTO 1986
32. Freitag, C., Pass, R., Sirkin, N.: Parallelizable delegation from LWE. In: TCC 2022, Part II
33. Garg, S., Gentry, C., Halevi, S., Raykova, M., Sahai, A., Waters, B.: Candidate indistinguishability obfuscation and functional encryption for all circuits. In: 54th FOCS
34. Goldreich, O., Goldwasser, S., Micali, S.: How to construct random functions (extended abstract). In: 25th FOCS
35. Goyal, R., Kim, S., Manohar, N., Waters, B., Wu, D.J.: Watermarking public-key cryptographic primitives. In: CRYPTO 2019, Part III
36. Hoffmann, C., Hubácek, P., Kamath, C., Klein, K., Pietrzak, K.: Practical statistically-sound proofs of exponentiation in any group. In: CRYPTO 2022, Part II
37. Hoffmann, C., Hubácek, P., Kamath, C., Krnák, T.: (Verifiable) delay functions from lucas sequences. In: TCC 2023, Part IV
38. Jaques, S., Montgomery, H., Rosie, R., Roy, A.: Time-release cryptography from minimal circuit assumptions. In: Progress in Cryptology – INDOCRYPT 2021
39. Katz, J., Loss, J., Xu, J.: On the security of time-lock puzzles and timed commitments. In: TCC 2020, Part III
40. Khovratovich, D., Maller, M., Tiwari, P.R.: Minroot: candidate sequential function for ethereum VDF. IACR Cryptol. ePrint Arch
41. Kiayias, A., Papadopoulos, S., Triandopoulos, N., Zacharias, T.: Delegatable pseudorandom functions and applications. In: ACM CCS 2013
42. Lai, R.W.F., Malavolta, G.: Lattice-based timed cryptography. In: CRYPTO 2023, Part V
43. Lamport, L.: Constructing digital signatures from a one-way function. Technical Report SRI-CSL-98, SRI International Computer Science Laboratory
44. Landerreche, E., Stevens, M., Schaffner, C.: Non-interactive cryptographic timestamping based on verifiable delay functions. In: FC 2020
45. Lenstra, A.K., Wesolowski, B.: Trustworthy public randomness with sloth, unicorn, and trx. Int. J. Appl. Cryptogr
46. Lombardi, A., Vaikuntanathan, V.: Fiat-Shamir for repeated squaring with applications to PPAD-hardness and VDFs. In: CRYPTO 2020, Part III
47. Mahmoody, M., Moran, T., Vadhan, S.P.: Publicly verifiable proofs of sequential work. In: ITCS 2013
48. Malavolta, G., Thyagarajan, S.A.K.: Homomorphic time-lock puzzles and applications. In: CRYPTO 2019, Part I

49. Paneth, O.: Alternate vdf constructions. MIT VDF Day. https://www.youtube.com/watch?v=ckIYmtY3KAw. Accessed 15 Feb 2026
50. Peikert, C., Tang, Y.: Cryptanalysis of lattice-based sequentiality assumptions and proofs of sequential work. In: CRYPTO 2024, Part V
51. Pietrzak, K.: Simple verifiable delay functions. In: ITCS 2019
52. Rivest, R.L., Shamir, A., Wagner, D.A.: Time-lock puzzles and timed-release crypto. Technical report, USA
53. Sahai, A., Waters, B.: How to use indistinguishability obfuscation: deniable encryption, and more. In: 46th ACM STOC
54. StarkWare: Veedo. https://medium.com/starkware/presenting-veedo-e4bbff77c7ae. Accessed 1 Oct 2024
55. Waters, B., Wu, D.J.: Adaptively-sound succinct arguments for NP from indistinguishability obfuscation. In: 56th ACM STOC
56. Waters, B., Zhandry, M.: Adaptive security in SNARGs via iO and lossy functions. In: CRYPTO 2024, Part X
57. Wesolowski, B.: Efficient verifiable delay functions. In: EUROCRYPT 2019, Part III

Author Index

© International Association for Cryptologic Research 2026
S. Bai and E. Persichetti (Eds.): PKC 2026, LNCS 16554, pp. 527–528, 2026.
https://doi.org/10.1007/978-3-032-26740-5